# Henri Peyre

# Henri Peyre

HIS LIFE IN LETTERS

John W. Kneller, GENERAL EDITOR

Collected and Transcribed by Mario Maurin

FOREWORD BY MARY ANN CAWS

Yale University Press   New Haven and London

Published with assistance from the Florence Gould
Foundation, the Henri Peyre French Institute, and the Yale
Department of French.

Copyright © 2004 by the Estate of Henri Peyre and
John W. Kneller.
All rights reserved.
This book may not be reproduced, in whole or in part,
including illustrations, in any form (beyond that copying
permitted by Sections 107 and 108 of the U.S. Copyright
Law and except by reviewers for the public press), without
written permission from the publishers.

Designed by Sonia Shannon.
Set in Galliard type by Binghamton Valley Composition.
Printed in the United States of America.

Library of Congress Cataloging-in-Publication Data

Peyre, Henri, 1901–1988
Henri Peyre : his life in letters / John W. Kneller, general
editor ; collected and transcribed by Mario Maurin.
Foreword by Mary Ann Caws.
p. cm.
ISBN 0-300-10443-X (alk. paper)
1. Peyre, Henri, 1901–Correspondence. 2. French teachers—
United States—Correspondence. 3. Critics—United States—
Correspondence. I. Kneller, John William, 1916–
II. Maurin, Mario. III. Title.

PQ67.P44A4 2004
843'.912—dc22          2004042041

A catalogue record for this book is available from the British Library.

The paper in this book meets the guidelines for permanence
and durability of the Committee on Production Guidelines
for Book Longevity of the Council on Library Resources.

10 9 8 7 6 5 4 3 2 1

*To the many friends of Henri Peyre*

# Contents

Foreword by Mary Ann Caws ix
Preface xiii
Introduction xvi

ONE
The 1920s 1

TWO
The 1930s 44

THREE
The 1940s 103

FOUR
The 1950s 294

FIVE
The 1960s 557

SIX
The 1970s 689

SEVEN
The 1980s 865

A Brief Biography of Henri Peyre 1083
Index 1085

# *Foreword*

We know that Herman Melville left only about 300 letters and that Henry James left about 12,000. Henri Peyre left a number somewhere in between. It is not, however, the number of letters that matters to the life of the writer, to the recipients, or to those who read them later. In the case of Henri Peyre, it is the extraordinary range of friends, colleagues, students, and well-known personalities with whom he corresponded, often at length. Henri Peyre was, along with all his other matchless qualities, a most beloved friend of an impressive number of impressive persons. He represented the very best of America to many French people, and the very best of France to many Americans. Along with the famous names included here, Henri Peyre welcomed ongoing conversations with many correspondents, always writing with the same wit, warmth, and style. You never feel in any of his letters the kind of distance so prevalent in the letters of those whose network of acquaintances and friends has an equivalent width. An ability to convey a strong sense of engagement was one of his great talents and makes the letters worth reading, even to those who did not know him. Once they read them, they will wish that they had.

The legendary but approachable Henri Peyre was my professor at Yale and director of the French program when I was there. René Girard at Bryn Mawr had thought I should work with Peyre: he was right about that, as about much else. At Yale we all noticed that when we went to see him about anything, we never felt pushed or rushed, but suddenly, easily, we once again found ourselves with him at the door of his office. The story ran that undergraduates would find themselves there in two minutes or less, M.A. students in three, and Ph.D. students in five. And yet he always did it all with a grace that the pagan gods in Provence must have given him.

From 1969 Henri Peyre was the executive officer of the Ph.D. program in French at the Graduate School of the City University of New York, and also the star member of the faculty of the comparative literature Ph.D. program while I was the latter's executive officer. Both at Yale and in New York, as his students and colleagues, we noticed his ability to do many things at once. In 1980, when I became director of the French Ph.D. program directly after Henri—the year we set up the Henri Peyre Institute—I saw at closer hand the unflappable charm and efficacy with which he ran everything. I never saw anyone else demonstrate this talent so successfully. Henri had an ease about him and a grace about everything that felt totally egoless, without a trace of arrogance.

Occasionally our amazement at his abilities was mixed with consternation. As the most valued faculty member of the Graduate Center's French and comparative literature programs, he was invited to sit on almost every interesting examination or thesis defense. While the rest of us were concentrating on one question or field, Henri would be simultaneously writing a letter, reading a book or term paper, and questioning the candidate, without losing even a filament of a complex threading of ideas. He showed no strain, forgot no detail, but rather added to our knowledge about whatever detail it was. We all learned from him and at the same time were entertained and made happier by his presence.

The many letters he wrote were like essays on topics close to his mind and heart. In them he carried on extraordinary conversations about what books we were reading, what we were writing, and how we were thinking. But perhaps what comes across most strongly and clearly in this vast correspondence is Peyre's immense curiosity about everything, a kind of radiant interest in the world, its art and literature, and its ways of knowing that irresistibly engaged anyone to whom he was writing. The effect of a correspondence conversant with so much is to intensify one's engagement with the world.

These letters come from many sources; Henri's life touched many during his teaching at Yale and in New York. For example, the founder of surrealism, André Breton, gave his vastly important lecture "The Situation of Surrealism between the Two Wars" at Yale on December 10, 1942, in response to Henri's invitation in October of that year. It was published in the second number of the still surviving journal *Yale French Studies*, founded, like so many things, by Henri Peyre. The great French poet René Char, who had gone to the same Avignon lycée as Peyre, remembered Henri's visit to him with fondness and delight. "Ah yes," he said to me one day, "and, by the way, do tell Henri Peyre I won't want the Nobel Prize." And that was because we all assumed (not entirely without some basis) that Henri was the one person in America who would be consulted by the Swedish authorities when a French writer was under consideration.

He was in fact consulted by more people in more fields than one could possibly imagine. It became well known that Henri knew more about more subjects in more countries and disciplines than almost anyone. Anyone who had had the exhausting and uplifting experience of asking him about some simple biographical detail or some abstruse fact or for some complex advice would never question the depth or extent of his learning. I well remember, after one of his breathtakingly rapid and informative talks somewhere in the Midwest, asking him some question about a writer who had engaged my interest, then following it up with him later somewhere in the East. Henri had not only remembered my having asked the question, but in the meantime had extended his own search on the subject. He treated person after person in place after place to an extensive summary of whatever subject was broached in whatever situation. Henri was never at a loss for an answer. But what was most remarkable about an exchange with him was that if you brought up something he had not read or fully examined (a rare situation), the very next time you saw him he would have read the book or piece and thought out its ramifications in a larger context.

Perhaps that is a good way to put it. Henri was a man of such wide context that it could encompass anything, from Julian the Apostate (one of his favorites) to a verse or *verset* in Paul Claudel (another of his favorites). You never felt any topic was too small to be of interest or too large to overwhelm him. The bibliography compiled by John Kneller and published in the *André Malraux Review* 24, nos. 1–2 (1992–93), reflects the breadth of his interest and knowledge. Whatever the topic, he not only knew it, but how to explain it. This is the way I and so many others learned exactly what symbolism was, what romanticism was, and the rest. His moral system also seemed to encompass a range as large as the human mind. During the Vietnam War, when he was a commencement speaker somewhere, he wore a black armband over his gown; it was perhaps not widely noticed, but since I too was wearing one, I was moved. It happened often that one was moved by Henri's outspoken positions, which often had about them a sense of moral rectitude without self-righteousness.

But what remains clearest in my mind is something else, and I will put it as best I can: we learned what we were and what our minds could be. That is why so many wanted to share so much with Henri, not just in our professional lives, but also in our personal ones. Many of us did share much, and received much in return. Because of him, we went some way toward finding ourselves. We found ourselves writing our articles for him, as well as our letters to him. We found ourselves dedicating our books to him. But above all the qualities his correspondents prized in him, I think, above his vast knowledge and compassion, was his apparently limitless responsiveness.

Henri's boundless curiosity never let him or anyone else down. On board a ship, he would ask for the passenger list and would arrange to meet whoever sounded interesting. Sometimes I think of his correspondence as a long passenger list—as if we were all invited to travel along with him and his multitude of friends and acquaintances on a great trip of the mind and, often, the heart.

Mary Ann Caws

# *Preface*

During a December 9, 1988, memorial service for Henri Peyre, A. Bartlett Giamatti (1938–1989), former president of Yale (1978–1986), of baseball's National League (1986–1989), and, just before his death, commissioner of major league baseball, said this:

> We all saw him read, and write, letters — in meetings large and small, between appointments as chairman, in faculty meetings . . . during oral examinations . . . on trains, on planes — always reading stacks of mail, and answering them, all of them, in that distinguished, looping, bold hand that used every bit of the letter paper — brush strokes filling all the canvas, if you will, as he filled the canvas of his life; letters that were tireless, passionate, precise, radically decent, ever caring for what the recipient cared for, capable of immense tenderness and a steely eloquence — letters impatient with cant, unafraid of sentiment — letters that in every way reflected the man.

And now here are the letters of Henri Peyre. We owe them to Mario Maurin, who tells us in his introduction how and why he collected them — how he began seeking them shortly after Peyre's death and finished transcribing them some ten years later. No student, colleague, or friend has ever given a greater measure of devotion to a revered teacher, mentor, and friend.

Mary Ann Caws, whose foreword traces her cordial, affectionate, and fruitful relationship with Henri Peyre, was his student, colleague, and friend. She replaced him as executive officer (chair) of the Ph.D. Program in French at the Graduate School of the City University of New York and conceived the idea of the Henri Peyre French Institute, which she and I codirected for twenty years.

Henri Peyre, by his own account, "stubbornly refused" to write his memoirs. In a letter to Wallace Fowlie on November 12, 1983, he ridiculed professors who in writing their memoirs yielded to the temptation of inflating their egos, taking themselves too seriously, and indulging in petty remarks about university politics, colleagues, and the powers that be. Although he exonerated Fowlie of succumbing to this temptation, he also avoided memorializing himself in any autobiographical work.

But if we do not have his memoirs, we have his letters. As Giamatti said, they show concern for the concerns of the intended recipients. Their tenor is dialogical, without self-justification or self-aggrandizement.

Henri had a certain *pudeur*, or sense of propriety, when it came to writing about personal matters. His letters concerning his second wife's mental and emotional problems and their eventual divorce, as well his concerns for the future of his son, Brice, are restrained by this sense of propriety. With regard to public figures and social issues, however, he is unrestrained: he lashes out against President Reagan, the state of American education, and the practices of some contemporary critics; he denounces anti-Semitism and any failure to speak out against it.

In preparing Mario Maurin's typescript for publication I have had access to the original letters (for the most part, photocopied), but I have not attempted to proofread the typescript against the letters. I have corrected a few misspellings and grammatical slips and broken some long sentences into two or three smaller ones. Peyre had a habit of using dashes within sentences, whenever commas might do, and dashes instead of periods at the end of sentences; I have taken the liberty of reducing the number of these interior dashes and of substituting periods for many sentence-ending dashes. Where the owner of the letter has cut out, struck out, or erased a passage, I have indicated the omission by an ellipsis. In doing this editing, I have tried to avoid making changes that would detract from the quintessential spontaneity of the letters.

Aside from these detailed matters of style there are two broader issues that had to be resolved. First, whether to translate into English the letters that are written in French. I have decided not to do so myself, or to have it done by someone else, because this exercise would prolong an already lengthy document, delay its publication and perhaps offend the book's likely readers.

The second issue concerns the inclusion of letters that Henri Peyre received from well-known authors and donated to the Yale's Beinecke Library. The Beinecke stored these letters in twenty-five boxes and had them microfilmed for research purposes. But, as it explicitly reminds potential researchers, "literary rights, including copyright, belong to these authors or their legal heirs and assigns." Publishing the letters that Henri Peyre received from these distinguished authors may well form a significant future project; but it will require negotiations with the authors or heirs and their permission to publish.

Henri Peyre liked to quote, in French or in English, an observation by Goethe to the effect that "literature is but a fragment of fragments; of all that was done and was said, only the smallest part was ever written; of what was written only the smallest portion has survived." This thought may console us for not being able to print all his letters. Those that we offer here, however, constitute a unique document on the era during which he taught, wrote, spoke, and lived. They impart his characteristic warmth, his generous availability, and his steadfast devotion to French culture.

I thank the Florence Gould Foundation, the Henri Peyre French Institute, and the Yale University French Department for their financial assistance in making this book possible. I also wish to thank John G. Kulka, senior editor at Yale University Press, and Nicholas Pappas, computer scientist, neighbor, and friend, for their patient, sympathetic, and expert guidance throughout the redaction process.

John W. Kneller

# *Introduction*

At Yale during the late 1940s, I didn't think it behooved me, a French speaker, to take courses in French. But Henri Peyre's reputation had spread through the college, and so I decided to take an undergraduate course with him on the modern French novel. At that time I already felt the stirrings of an urge to do some writing. Going on to graduate school and eventually to a teaching career would keep me involved with literary texts. Peyre encouraged me to follow that path, and so I enrolled in the French doctoral program. Like all his other students, I benefited from his advice and active benevolence. He directed my M.A. thesis and Ph.D. dissertation and found me a position at Bryn Mawr College, where he himself had started out and where I stayed for the whole of my career.

During those early para-Nietzschean years of mine (I was nineteen when I received my B.A., twenty-two when I received my Ph.D.) I felt that only superior beings deserved my attention. Peyre qualified. He seemed to have read everything and to be able to speak compellingly about anything literary, historical, or political. He was ready at the drop of a hat to draw a map, as it were, of the topic at hand and to structure it exactly with the problems, the works, the people involved. His range of knowledge never ceased to amaze us. A prodigious memory enabled him not only to quote multilingual texts at will but to tell a student in search of bibliographical information to look in chapter 4 of this book or in that 1936 article.

What we all admired most of all were his boundless energy, generosity, and availability. He dispensed knowledge and encouragement with unfailing good humor. While he was with you, he gave you the impression you had his undivided attention. The letters he wrote to me while I was still a student and just beginning my career offered invaluable encouragement and cordiality. I realized, nevertheless, that what he did for me he had done and would continue doing for many others. Wouldn't it be instructive someday, I wondered, to collect the correspondence that we saw him pursue while listening to a student's oral report—a report that he would then proceed to critique minutely and accurately?

I idealized him, yes. I didn't idolize him. There were traits in him that were amusing and sometimes just short of annoying. He liked now and then to say something outrageous or even irresponsible, just for the fun of it, and to watch his listeners recoil in dismay. He once started a public lecture on existentialism by saying: "Existentialism is the introduction of tragedy in everyday life. I've only been married once, so my exposure to tragedy has been limited." Mme. Marguerite Peyre was sitting in the first row. I don't know whether she was amused.

Henri's legacy resides in his published works and in his students' and his students' students' capacities to assess literary values and to analyze texts. But for those of us who knew him, in addition to the elegant clarity of his discourse, there remain memories of Henri's warmth, the very tone of his voice. Some of these traces persist in his daily correspondence.

I have never been jealous of the many talents of my good friends Georges May, Victor Brombert, Jack Kneller, and Mary Ann Caws. I have sometimes envied them, however, the good fortune that allowed them to be Henri's colleagues. I would have loved to see him regularly instead of once every five or seven years—to know him better, to let experience supplant conjecture. Collecting his correspondence has been a compensation. Over the years, as I received so many Peyre letters, usually sent with great enthusiasm by their original recipients, I was able to imagine that I was coming to know more about him than anybody else.

I should also admit to an obscure penitential urge: for Henri, publishing was the be-all and end-all of academic life. Though I enjoyed writing and publishing in my early years, the enjoyment gradually paled. I was sure he was disappointed, but he never let me know it.

My project changed shape as I went along. At first, my thought was to ask a small number of correspondents for half a dozen letters each, to provide a representative sampling of his epistolary relationships. But for many years, Peyre sometimes wrote twenty letters a day. As the letters came in, it became evident that their number was far greater than could have been imagined. The fidelity with which he kept up this correspondence until he turned eighty, in the midst of a life freighted with professional responsibilities, can be ascribed to his *disponibilité*. He immediately answered all his letters—almost always by hand in a violet ink that definitively turned blue only after his retirement.

The scope of the project was further enlarged when I gained access to Henri's intramural correspondence with the various university administrators to whom he directed his requests or whom he kept informed of his activities. They document almost week by week the problems he faced, the initiatives he took, the way he understood and discharged his responsibilities. They reveal a man attending to important daily tasks while keeping in touch with faraway colleagues and students.

This correspondence, like all published correspondences, is incomplete. Some recipients have censored passages from the letters they sent. And there are other letters that remain inaccessible for various reasons. Some are buried deep in boxes or files, too difficult for their owners to extract. Many (such as all but one letter to his publishers) have disappeared.

In some cases, there are problems of identification. Except for those of famous writers, Peyre did not keep the letters he received; as soon as he had answered them, he threw them away. That tidy habit has made it difficult to identify Henri's most likely correspondents: former students, colleagues, and friends.

Other lacunae reflect deference to Henri's private life. Over the years, he had three wives. He married the first, Marguerite Vanuxem, who was a French student at Bryn Mawr, in 1927. They were not often apart, and no letters to her remain. A few months after Marguerite's death in 1962, Henri married a young American woman, Lois Haegert, who worked for him at Yale. This union seemed happy at first and rapidly issued in a son. But Lois' psychological balance was precarious, and the couple's relations became difficult. After a divorce, Henri had the good fortune to meet Diana, whose intelligent and tender care nurtured the luminous old age his friends admired and envied. The delicate circumstances of Henri's separation from Lois, with whom he faithfully kept in touch, dissuaded me from asking her for any correspondence. Diana Peyre, on the other hand, trusted me with a few letters Henri sent her. After some hesitation, I decided not to use them. Although Henri was reserved about his private life, this is not my main reason for holding back. Had letters to his three wives been equally available, I would have had no compunction in introducing them. They would have added an important dimension to the self-portrait that emerges from this collection, whereas an isolated sample would not be representative. For the same reason I didn't even ask for Henri's letters to his son, Brice.

The few early letters in this collection are almost all to family. We all know we don't write home as we would to friends. We show our familiar, domestic face. We supply or request details on everyday occurrences. We mention what could be of interest to family members, not necessarily what is of interest to us. In short, these few letters are invaluable in allowing us to form an idea of the life that young Henri Peyre led, first in Cambridge, then in the States; but they are fragmentary, and their scope is limited. They have also been obviously culled, since none of them mention his courtship of and marriage to Marguerite.

I would have loved to find letters to friends of Peyre's youth — the friends with whom he was probably most relaxed, most expansive. In a couple of letters Henri alludes to a close friendship with a Jewish fellow student at l'École Normale who was killed during the war. During those student years, he sometimes visited other friends. He mentions them without naming them. Have such Peyre letters been kept? Possibly, but by whom? An inquiry published in *La Quinzaine Littéraire* drew a response from an Italian scholar; not a word from France. Of all his later colleagues, Georges May is the one to whom Henri's letters best show, in their mixture of trust, regard, and warmth, what we miss in not having any early correspondence addressed to close acquaintances.

It would also have been fascinating to discover in his letters how Henri "managed" his career during his American beginnings. Was he one of these ambitious and clever young men from the provinces who traveled up to Paris and whom nineteenth-century novelists like Balzac or Zola used to portray? There are a couple of episodes in the correspondence that show him quite capable of playing politics and maneuvering deftly.

As soon as he settled again in New Haven, the war elicited from him an unceasing effort of propaganda for the cause of French culture—an effort that he assumed with great energy and perhaps with secret backing from the French government. He appears from then on in his correspondence exactly as we all knew him: affable, contagiously dynamic, amusing without striving to be funny, concerned with everyone's interests, quick to decide and quick to simulate retreat if others' opinions didn't coincide with his, belittling himself gracefully in order to reinforce his authority.

Despite these gaps, one can only be amazed that so many colleagues, former students, and friends kept so many letters over so many years. And that they were willing to share them with others.

In the end, this correspondence, abundant as it is, has not dispelled the mystery that fifty years ago exerted such a powerful spell on me. I don't know whether I should fear or hope that for those who read these letters Henri will remain what he has always been in my eyes: irresistible and elusive; sovereign and droll; delicate and impudent; marvelously benevolent and profoundly indifferent; exquisitely tactful and deliberately clumsy. Will he be for the readers of these letters a solar being—one of those gods whom Giraudoux set on the stage and who may well go about disguised as a pharmacist in a small Normandy town?

Let us rather say that he gallops right through his correspondence, leaving his shadow behind—a fleeting shadow speckled with light, a hologram we strive to grasp as we too walk through it. Already it has resumed its capacity to thwart and delight us as before.

It is a pleasure to express my heartfelt thanks to all those who readily contributed to this collection: the former students or colleagues of Henri Peyre and the archivists and librarians at Yale, Harvard, and other institutions of higher learning. The gathering of these letters could never have been undertaken without the authorization and cordial encouragement of Diana Festa-Peyre.

Mario Maurin

# the 1920s

## CHAPTER ONE

### À son frère:

[Sans date]

. . . Je viens de terminer mon devoir sur les rapports de la définition et de la classification. J'ai fouillé tous les bouquins que j'ai pu trouver, et je me suis creusé la cervelle là-dessus; car je t'assure que le sujet ne m'inspirait guère et que j'ai eu de la peine à écrire 8 ou 10 pages là-dessus. A propos, es-tu content de tes bachotages? J'ai aussi composé en français hier le sujet n'était pas épatant et ce n'est guère du genre de ceux que l'on donne généralement au concours. C'était de commenter ces quelques lignes d'A. France [*La Vie littéraire*].

"Tous les livres en général, et même les plus admirables, me paraissent infiniment moins précieux par ce qu'ils contiennent que par ce qu'y met celui qui les lit. Les meilleurs, à mon sens, sont ceux qui donnent le plus à penser, et les choses les plus diverses. . . . Il faut que la critique se pénètre bien de cette idée que tout livre a autant d'exemplaires que de lecteurs, et qu'un poème, comme un paysage, se transforme dans tous les yeux qui le voient et dans toutes les âmes qui le conçoivent." Que dis-tu d'un pareil sujet? Je ne l'ai pas trouvé très commode.

En composition de Version Latine, avec le même prof. (Canat), je suis 7e avec 14 ¼ — (1er Chauvelon avec 16. Jacques — tu peux te reporter à loisir à *ta* photographie pour voir leurs têtes).

Hier, je suis sorti l'après-midi — je suis allé faire une manille au café, (que j'ai d'ailleurs triomphalement gagnée), puis je suis allé faire une visite aux Coste. Le mari, d'ailleurs, était à son bureau: ils vont bien, et m'ont chargé de vous donner le bonjour. Je suis rentré vers les 3 heures pour faire un peu d'histoire, car nous composerons la semaine prochaine en cette matière.

Je ne vois plus grand'chose à ajouter. Il fait assez beau temps ici, aujourd'hui.

Bonnes caresses à tous,<br>HPeyre

Je te fais remarquer que j'ai maintenant une nouvelle signature, moins embrouillée que l'ancienne: HPeyre

### À sa sœur et à son beau-frère:

Londres. Ce mardi 29 mars 21

. . . Je ne sais si vous jouissez là-bas d'un temps agréable, mais cela est fort probable puisque le nom d'Italie ne suggère que soleil et ciel bleu. Ici, depuis que je suis arrivé, ou presque, il ne fait que pleuvoir et c'est une pluie aussi forte que les pires de chez nous. Ça n'est pas précisément très réjouissant, d'autant plus qu'ici, les jours de fête, théâtres, concerts — tout étant fermé, si l'on n'a plus la ressource de se promener, il ne reste plus qu'à mourir d'ennui chez soi, ou en écoutant les innombrables sermons dans les non moins innombrables églises de toutes confessions, ce qui est encore pire, je crois. . . .

### À ses parents:

Paris, ce 18 mai — 22

Chers parents,

Je vous remercie de ta lettre reçue avant-hier, ainsi que de ma carte d'électeur. Je ne pensais pas en effet que je pouvais déjà jouir de ce privilège (de voter), mais je dois dire d'ailleurs que je ne m'en enorgueillis pas beaucoup, car, pour le moment du moins, je serais bien embarrassé s'il me fallait voter pour quelqu'un et la politique m'intéresse assez peu.

...Pour moi, mon examen s'approche aussi: je ne m'en fais pas beaucoup pour ça, car j'espère réussir, à moins d'accident. La licence d'anglais est cependant plus difficile que la licence de lettres pures, alors que c'est le contraire pour l'agrégation; et il faut savoir déjà pas mal d'anglais, car les épreuves écrites (thème et version) se font absolument sans dictionnaire. Surtout c'est un examen ennuyeux, qui est presque uniquement une question de langue, de prononciation et de philologie.

Ce soir, M. Lanson doit nous réunir pour nous communiquer les notes de nos professeurs. C'est une innovation qu'il a instituée depuis l'an dernier: vers la fin de l'année, il fait appeler les élèves par promotions ou par spécialités, et leur communique les appréciations des professeurs avec qui ils ont fait une leçon, une explication, un devoir—Pour moi, je n'ai pas fait beaucoup de devoirs cette année, mais j'ai fait plusieurs fois des exposés ou des explications à la Sorbonne.

...Dimanche dernier je suis allé dans l'après-midi au Bois de Boulogne. Il y avait très longtemps, presque 2 ans, que je n'y étais plus allé. Il y faisait bon, mais il y avait vraiment trop de monde. J'irai peut-être y faire quelquefois du canot sur le lac, le matin. Ici, à part un peu de tennis, et encore assez rarement. Je ne fais pas beaucoup de sports. Peut-être papa commencera-t-il bientôt à prendre qqs bains du Rhône. Ici, nous n'avons pas cet avantage, et les piscines sont sales et pleines de populo.

Bonnes caresses,<br>Henri Peyre

## Aux mêmes:

(Cambridge, Sept. 1922)

[*Pages 1 et 2 manquent*]

... quitté Calais depuis 10 minutes que je sentais les premiers effets du mal de mer. J'ai donc passé 1 heure ½ environ de traversée de Calais à Douvres dans un assez mauvais état, et j'ai même dû rendre aux poissons une partie de mon dîner de la veille. Je n'étais d'ailleurs pas le seul sur le bateau. La mer était vraiment exceptionnellement agitée. Enfin, fort heureusement ce malaise m'a passé à peu près aussitôt que je suis remonté dans le train. . . . J'ai donc revu Londres rapidement puis j'ai pris le train pour Cambridge à 2 heures ½ et j'y suis arrivé à 4 h. ½. M. De Glehn, le professeur de la Perse School que je connais était venu m'attendre à la gare avec une automobile: et je serai logé ici dans 1 famille mais comme il n'est rentré de vacances que hier, il n'a pas encore eu le temps d'en choisir une. Il m'avait proposé d'aller chez lui, seulement, comme sa femme est Française & qu'ils parlent tout le temps Français je lui ai fait comprendre que je désirais 1 famille où je puisse parler et entendre de l'anglais. . . .

**Aux mêmes:**

Cambridge, 2 oct—22

. . . Ce sont donc des élèves assez âgés, mais ils sont en retard sur nos élèves correspondants de France sur plus d'un point, et ils sont en particulier absolument incapables de composer une dissertation. Ils n'ont pour ainsi dire pas le sens de la logique. Ils écrivent des phrases incohérentes, sans suite, sans que cela les choque le moins du monde. . . .

**Aux mêmes:**

65 Chesterton Rd.
Cambridge
29 oct. (1922)

. . . Je suis allé cette semaine voir plusieurs personnes que Mad. Frazer m'avait fait connaître, et je suis allé à qqs conférences: une de Cazamian, mon prof. de Paris, qui est venu ici faire 1 conférence en Anglais, et celles de Frazer qui va finir la semaine prochaine. Le nouveau livre de Frazer, qui est un gros résumé des 12 ou 14 volumes du Rameau d'or, a paru ces jours-ci à Londres. Sa femme va s'occuper tout de suite de le traduire en Anglais, et elle m'a embarqué dans sa traduction. Pour le moment, je vais commencer par faire l'index que je n'ai entrepris qu'à condition d'être payé directement par A. Colin (qui publiera la traduction française), et en argent anglais. Pour le reste, Lady Frazer va le traduire elle-même chapitre par chapitre, et j'aurai seulement à lui corriger sa traduction qu'elle m'enverra chapitre par chapitre, et à revoir ensuite les épreuves—Seulement, comme c'est un gros bouquin de près de 800 pages, je suis certain d'avance qu'elle en aura vite assez et me demandera aussi de faire la traduction proprement dite. Ça m'est d'ailleurs égal si je suis payé, mais c'est ce dont on n'est jamais sûr avec elle, car elle est assez brouillonne, et on ne peut jamais savoir au juste ce qu'elle veut, ni fixer rien de clair avec elle.

Je vais maintenant assez souvent à la bibliothèque de l'Université. C'est encore un vieux bâtiment du XIIIe siècle, mais très commode. Cette bibliothèque a ceci de particulier qu'on s'y sert soi-même. Il n'y a pas ou presque pas d'employés—On cherche soi-même la cote des livres dans le catalogue, on prend les livres sur les rayons, puis on les remet soi-même quand on a terminé. Et au lieu d'y avoir une salle réservée pour y lire et y travailler, il y a des tables avec des fauteuils placés çà et là dans les diverses salles, près d'une fenêtre, et au milieu des rayons. L'atmosphère y est agréable et il y a quelque chose de pittoresque à travailler à côté d'une vieille fenêtre du moyen âge, et en ayant devant soi une cour carrée, avec des arcades et une pelouse et des fleurs au milieu, qui ressemble tout à fait à un vieux cloître.

On est toujours ici dans l'incertitude politique et l'attente des nouvelles élections. Tout cela ne m'intéresse pas beaucoup, mais je pense pourtant aller assister à quelques réunions politiques par curiosité. C'est toujours intéressant pour un étranger. . . .

Henri Peyre

## Aux mêmes:

Ce 5 nov. 1922

Chers parents,

C'est aujourd'hui l'anniversaire d'Émile et peut-être êtes-vous allés à Mérindol, du moins maman, si tu es allée toi-même pour la Toussaint. Le temps est toujours assez gris ici, et plutôt froid; dans l'ensemble je crois que c'est à peu près le même temps qu'à Paris, légèrement plus froid.

Je vous remercie beaucoup pour le Temps que vous m'envoyez de temps en temps. Cela me fait bien plaisir, car j'ai ainsi qqs nouvelles de

Paris, de ce qui s'y joue, etc. — Merci aussi pour le Télémaque que j'avais oublié à Avignon. J'essaye de faire un peu d'italien ici et j'en fais un peu de temps en temps. Mais je suis sorti pas mal ces jours-ci et je n'ai pas le temps de travailler beaucoup. Je vais de temps en temps au théâtre ici. Les pièces qu'on y joue ne sont pas très intéressantes, car le théâtre anglais contemporain est assez pauvre. Les seules pièces intéressantes sont des pièces à tendance philosophique injouables le plus souvent et qu'on ne joue jamais, parce qu'elles ne plairaient pas au public. Quoi qu'il en soit, il est toujours utile pour moi d'entendre de l'anglais. . . .

Ici je suis comme je vous l'ai dit chez cette dame Mrs. Armstrong. Elle est très gentille et, je crois, la veuve d'un clergyman. Elle vit seule avec sa fille. Heureusement ce ne sont pas des gens trop puritains. Il est certain d'ailleurs qu'il y en a beaucoup moins en Angleterre. On se met depuis la guerre à jouer au tennis et au golf le dimanche, ce qui semble monstrueux aux défenseurs de la tradition. Je prends donc tous mes repas là. Je me lève en général à 8 heures du matin (car on se lève plutôt tard en Angleterre) et après le breakfast je vais à l'École. Mes classes sont en général de 10 à 12 le matin, ou de 11 heures à 1 heure. — Après le déjeuner de 1 heure, je vais lire à la bibliothèque. Puis je rentre pour le thé, ou bien je vais faire des visites, (car l'heure du thé est surtout l'heure des visites). Puis je rentre dîner vers 8 heures. Le soir je travaille en général, car ici il n'y a absolument rien d'ouvert après 7 heures. Les maisons de thé ferment à 7 heures, les magasins aussi, et comme il n'y a pas de café, on n'a plus qu'à rester chez soi ou bien à aller voir des amis. Ma vie ne me déplaît pas dans l'ensemble. Quant à la nourriture, elle est très suffisante. C'est, il est vrai, de la cuisine anglaise, mais je m'habitue assez facilement et ça m'est égal.

Je ne suis pas mal non plus à l'école, bien que je l'avoue, je ne conçoive pas une grande admiration pour le système d'enseignement anglais. L'école où je suis est très connue et passe pour l'une des meilleures d'Angleterre: mais pour moi qui suis habitué à l'organisation des lycées français, je ne puis m'empêcher de trouver que c'est la pagaïe. Le directeur choisit lui-même les professeurs comme il lui plaît, qu'ils aient des titres ou non. Et comme ici le directeur est un vieux monsieur plongé dans le grec (c'est d'ailleurs un helléniste assez connu), chaque professeur fait à peu près ce qu'il veut. On peut facilement arriver $1/4$ d'heure en retard, manquer sa classe et se faire remplacer, etc. Quant aux professeurs, je crois qu'ils ne valent pas les professeurs de lycée en France. On est d'ailleurs beaucoup moins considéré ici; c'est un métier assez dur, ils ont 22 heures de classe par semaine, et ne sont relativement pas mieux payés qu'en France: quant aux élèves, ils sont comme partout: je crois qu'ils sont incontestablement plus forts en grec et en latin que nos élèves français; il est vrai que les langues anciennes tiennent une plus grande place dans l'enseignement que chez nous, et à cette école en particulier, elles constituent avec le Français l'essentiel. . . .

## À son frère:

*Cambridge 8 nov.* (1922)

Cher frère,

Te voilà donc retourné à Montpellier depuis bientôt 1 semaine et j'espère que tu t'y plairas mieux que l'an dernier, bien que ta première impression n'ait pas l'air excellente. Je te remercie beaucoup de ta lettre et des détails que tu m'y donnes. J'espère que tu n'y auras pas ta compagnie de punaises, ni de tous les animaux, imaginaires ou réels, qui t'infestaient l'an dernier. As-tu beaucoup de cours et plus de travail que l'an dernier. Bon courage en tous cas pour ton travail, et bon succès. Quand sera ton 1r examen?

Pour moi je ne suis pas du tout de cours ici, seulement de temps en temps 1 conférence extraordinaire, mais rien de régulier. Ça ne me serait pas très utile je crois, et puis j'ai beaucoup de difficulté à pouvoir écouter un bonhomme parler pendant 1 heure, que ce soit en anglais ou en français. Pour le moment je vais chaque matin à l'École qui est à environ 20 ou 25 minutes de chez moi. J'y ai à peu près 2 heures de classe par jour. Ça n'est pas très pénible, car mes classes sont peu nombreuses et tranquilles. Je ne dirai pas cependant que ça m'amuse et j'ai plus souvent envie de bailler. L'après-midi je vais à la bibliothèque, puis je rentre à 4 heures pour le thé ou bien je vais faire des visites—et le soir en général je reste chez moi à lire parce qu'il n'y a rien à faire ici le soir personne dans les rues après 8 heures; pas de café, ni rien d'ouvert.

La famille chez qui je suis est composée d'1 dame, d'une cinquantaine d'années qui vit avec sa fille qui en a environ 25. Ce sont des gens aimables et je me trouve en somme bien chez eux. J'y parle anglais pendant les repas ou après, et cela m'est évidemment utile. J'y prends aussi tous mes repas: la nourriture suffisante, la cuisine n'a rien d'épatant, mais je m'y habitue facilement.

Les Frazer m'ont présenté à pas mal de gens quand ils étaient ici et je connais ainsi un certain nombre de personnes chez qui je vais de temps en temps. Aussi n'ai-je pas beaucoup le temps pour travailler véritablement. Je me contente de lire un peu ça et là et je m'aperçois que depuis plus d'un mois et demi que je suis ici, je n'ai pas fait grand'chose.

Dans l'ensemble je ne me déplais pas ici. J'ai, il est vrai, moins de camarades qu'à l'École Normale, où j'avais plusieurs bons copains pour blaguer ou rigoler de temps en temps. Ici je n'ai pas de camarades proprement dits. Je connais surtout des gens assez âgés. Je pourrais évidemment connaître qqs étudiants anglais; mais ça ne me dit rien, car ce sont des types qui pensent surtout aux sports et à tout ça, et pas très intéressants ni très amusants. Pour moi, d'ailleurs, ça m'est égal et, en un sens, je me sens plus libre, n'ayant pas de types venant vous déranger au moment où on veut travailler, et tout ça.

As-tu choisi ton restaurant? Et te coûte-t-il plus cher que l'an dernier? Je ne donne pas du tout de leçons ici; à vrai dire je n'en ai pas encore cherché. J'aimerais pourtant en avoir 3 ou 4. J'ai assez de pognon n'ayant pas beaucoup à dépenser en somme, mais le change a monté beaucoup ces jours-ci et c'est dégueulasse d'avoir à changer 70 francs pour avoir 25 francs anglais.

Bonnes caresses,<br>Henri

## À ses parents:

Le dimanche 19 Nov. (1922)

. . . Je suis toujours assez satisfait de ma vie ici; je dois dire cependant que je n'y travaille pas beaucoup. L'atmosphère générale n'est peut-être pas très favorable au travail. Par contre, il me semble que je mène ici une vie plus extérieure, ou plus extériorisée, ce qui est peut-être un avantage d'un certain côté. Les années qu'on passe à l'étranger quand on étudie les langues ne sont certes pas aussi utiles au point de vue du travail que celles que l'on passe à Paris, dans une atmosphère intellectuelle plus intense. Mais elles sont peut-être plus utiles au point de vue général de la formation de l'esprit; car on sort beaucoup plus, on voit beaucoup plus de gens, et des gens très différents de soi—Quant à mon enseignement, il est toujours le même, et je ne puis vraiment pas m'en plaindre, car il est aussi peu pénible que je pouvais le souhaiter, puisque je n'ai qu'un élève pour les ¾ de mes classes, et un élève déjà avancé. J'avoue cependant que le métier ne m'enchante pas; et la perspective d'avoir à passer toute ma vie à enseigner l'anglais à des gamins ne me sourit pas follement. Enfin, on doit s'habituer à la longue. . . .

## À son frère:

Cambridge, ce 19 mars 1923

Cher Jacques,

Tu as probablement appris par Papa que, définitivement, je pensais aller à Avignon pour une partie de mes vacances de Noël; j'espère ainsi que j'aurai le plaisir de passer 1 semaine avec toi. Je pense que vous ne rentrez pas à la faculté avant le lundi de Quasimodo, et je pense quand même être à Avignon vers le 30 mars et en repartir vers le 10 avril. En plus du plaisir de vous voir, j'aurai d'ailleurs celui de faire qqs économies, puisque je ne dépense en somme rien à Avignon, et qu'au contraire, maman m'y paie toujours quelques petites choses en fait de vêtements qui me reviennent en tous cas meilleur marché qu'ici où les prix sont notablement plus élevés. Après cette date je passerai 2 jours sans doute à Paris, une dizaine de jours à Londres et une semaine environ à voyager en Angleterre. En outre, je suis assez en retard pour mon travail de diplôme, et j'espère l'avancer notablement pendant ces quelques jours à Avignon.

Je sais que tu ne te foules pas depuis ton dernier examen. Cependant il serait sot de te laisser décourager, parce que tu n'as pas été noté aussi bien que tu aurais dû l'être. A ta place je ne m'en ferais pas pour ça et continuerais tout de même à travailler sans m'en faire: d'autant plus que je n'aimerais guère passer 11 heures par jour, ni même par semaine, à jouer aux cartes.

Tu n'as décidément pas encore abandonné l'idée de ta moto. A vrai dire, je ne vois pas trop ce que tu en ferais; d'autant plus, qu'une fois la moto payée, il te faut casquer pour l'essence, l'entretien, le garage, les réparations, les vêtements que tu esquintes quand tu t'en sers, et même je crois un impôt. Tu ferais mieux de placer tes 600 balles qui à 5% te feraient déjà 30 francs par an d'intérêt. Quant à mes 3000 frs dont tu parles encore, il y a longtemps qu'ils ont été convertis en livres sterling et dépensés comme telles, surtout pendant les vacances de Janvier. Mes richesses se montent en ce moment à environ 2.000 autres francs que j'ai touchés de l'École et pour quelques leçons que j'ai données ici: et cela même, comme tu le sais, est si peu en argent anglais que je suis obligé d'aller passer en France une partie de mes vacances pour les épargner, malgré les quelques 400 francs que me coûte le voyage.

Quant au reste, rien de bien neuf en ce qui me concerne—si ce n'est cependant que le temps s'est—enfin—remis au beau ici depuis 2 jours. C'est tout de même un peu plus gai de voir le soleil et un ciel relativement bleu.

Ça va toujours bien avec ton anglais à ton restaurant?

J'enseigne toujours chaque matin 1 h ½ (sauf 2 heures ¼ le lundi) à mon école. Ça n'est pas très rigolo, mais je ne m'en fais pas. Je fais ça à la coule: nous lisons simplement Hernani, ce trimestre, ce qui les amuse et me laisse tranquille comme il n'y a pas beaucoup de commentaires à faire. Et mes autres classes, avec 2 élèves seulement, sont de tout repos.

J'espère donc que je te trouverai en bonne santé bientôt, moins de quinze jours maintenant. Toi, tu dois sans doute être libre dès le dimanche des rameaux. Vas-tu te ramener à la maison avec les Testuts? Comment va aussi ce mal à l'oreille? Est-il complètement disparu?

Bons baisers en attendant,
Henri

## Au même:

Cambridge, le dimanche 6 mai [1923]

... Ce dernier trimestre à Cambridge est celui, en général, où l'on ne fait pas grand'chose, et la distraction principale est d'aller en barque sur la rivière. Cette rivière, qui s'appelle la Cam, est très agréable, très étroite (peut-être 30 mètres de large) mais avec des rives vertes et agréables. Je pense y aller aussi quelquefois, bien que mon temps soit fort limité. On joue beaucoup aussi au tennis et au cricket, un jeu anglais. Pour moi, j'ai plus à faire que jamais maintenant: d'abord mon diplôme, qui est fort en retard—puis en plus de mes dix ou onze heures de classe, des devoirs à corriger, et les allées et venues (j'habite à peu près à 2 kilomètres de l'école, c'est-à-dire 20 minutes), j'ai qqs leçons, 9 heures par semaine en ce moment. Ça ne sera que pendant un mois, jusqu'au moment des examens, et ça me procure en attendant quelque argent, comme j'ai grandement ébréché mes revenus pendant les vacances—en outre, l'assommante traduction pour Lady Frazer, et une révision de l'autre traduction que j'ai acceptée de faire pour un autre type qui est quelque chose dans le Temps à Paris—tout cela, avec les "parties de thé," comme on dit ici, c'est-à-dire les invitations qu'on reçoit et qu'on rend, et je suis bien obligé de voir de temps en temps les gens que je connais, remplit largement mes journées de 7 heures ½ à minuit—car j'ai décidé maintenant de me lever tous les jours à 7 h½ et jusqu'ici j'ai chaque jour tenu exactement ma promesse. . . .

## Au même:

16/6/23

Cher frère,

C'est de Paris, cette fois, que ma lettre te parviendra. J'y suis venu, comme tu le sais, pour mon examen. J'ai quitté Cambridge jeudi soir vers 5 heures. Je n'ai fait que traverser Londres pour me rendre d'1 gare à l'autre, et j'ai traversé pendant la nuit de jeudi à vendredi par Douvres-Boulogne. Il faisait d'ailleurs beau temps, bien qu'un peu frais, et mer très calme. Je suis arrivé à la gare du Nord vers 5 heures du matin. Ce n'est pas une heure très commode: il est à la fois trop tard pour aller dormir quelque part & trop tôt pour sortir dans Paris. La seule alternative est donc de se raser pendant 2 heures dans 1 salle d'attente.

Je n'ai pas trouvé ici 1 temps bien préférable à celui de l'Angleterre. Il a plu & hier & aujourd'hui, et il est loin de faire chaud. Tout le monde sort encore en pardessus. J'ai retrouvé ici tous, ou presque tous mes anciens camarades, un peu inquiets à cause de l'approche de l'agrégation qui va commencer la semaine prochaine. Je suis, bien entendu, logé à l'école, bien que j'aie pris la + grande partie de mes repas dehors.

J'ai employé ma journée d'hier à faire quelques courses: j'ai surtout touché de l'argent. Ça ne va pas très bien, étant de l'argent français que j'aurai à convertir en livres, mais ça me permet en tous cas de remonter un peu une situation financière qui était tombée assez bas, si bas même que j'avais dû contracter des dettes la semaine dernière.

J'ai donc passé aujourd'hui mon oral: cela n'a pas été une grande affaire, car ce n'est pas un examen redoutable. J'étais cependant assez mal préparé, et je suis tombé pour 1 de mes textes sur un passage que je n'avais pas eu le temps de lire, ce qui m'a valu un 14. J'ai eu 16 partout ailleurs. J'ai donc mention Bien dans l'ensemble, mais j'arrive cependant premier des étudiants d'anglais. Ce qui importe, c'est surtout la connaissance de la langue, et j'ai fait quelques progrès cette année à ce point de vue. J'ai eu aussi 16 à l'écrit et mon correcteur m'a fait pas mal d'éloges.

En tous cas, me voilà débarrassé des examens pour un certain temps, et je vais pouvoir rigoler un peu pendant quelque temps à Cambridge et faire un peu ce que je veux—bien qu'à vrai dire j'aie fait cette année toute autre chose que préparer un examen. Bonne chance pour le tien & bonne santé?

Je trouve encore quelques timbres. Te servent-ils vraiment à quelque chose?

Bonnes caresses,<br>H

## À ses parents:

Ce vendredi 5 heures

Chers parents,

Nouvelles!!! La liste d'admissibilité a, paraît-il, été affichée aujourd'hui, au lieu de demain; une étudiante vient de me l'annoncer. Je me trouve donc sur la liste, avec 29 autres. C'est toujours autant de mis derrière soi. L'oral commencera mardi matin. On ne connaît pas encore l'ordre de passage. Je vais me dépêcher de voir quelques sujets et quelques textes d'ici là. Car, comme j'étais assez franchement mécontent de mon écrit, j'ai des raisons de craindre de n'être pas dans les premiers. Je vais donc essayer de me rattraper à l'oral, ce qui je l'espère n'est pas impossible, si je tombe sur des sujets traitables. Sur 30 admissibles, il y a environ 15 femmes. Comme il n'y aura pas plus de 15 agrégés ou agrégées au maximum, il faut donc qu'il en tombe une moitié à l'oral. Tout n'est donc pas fini.

Marcousel a dû être collé à Normale. Il n'est pas sur la liste d'admissibilité. Excusez ce mot à la hâte &

> Bonnes caresses,
> Henri

## Aux mêmes:

> 31/7/23

Chers parents,

J'ai terminé mon oral lundi dernier & depuis je ne fais qu'attendre le résultat. Je trouve même cette attente un peu longue. Dans l'ensemble je ne suis pas mécontent de l'oral, à parler franchement. J'aurais pu faire mieux, mais aussi plus mal. Je suis en somme tombé sur des sujets & des textes de moyenne difficulté. J'espère donc être reçu, mais ça ne prouve absolument rien. J'ai trop vu de mes camarades qui espéraient et ont été déçus. Mon explication n'a pas mal marché lundi; quant à ma version orale, j'avais 60 vers de W. Scott, assez durs: il y s'agissait de hache d'armes, de hallebardes, de bisons, de loutres, de phoques — tout ça sans dictionnaire. Mais enfin il est naturel que les textes soient difficiles à l'agrégation. Surtout, ce qui m'a ennuyé, c'est que mon texte était pondéré bizarrement, ce qui rendait 5 ou 6 vers absolument incompréhensibles. J'ai timidement deviné qu'il devait y avoir une faute d'impression et je l'ai dit au jury, mais sans trop d'assurance, car j'avais peur de me tromper.

La liste définitive ne sera connue que samedi très tard (7 heures 1/2 ou 8 h) ou dimanche matin. Je vous l'annoncerai aussitôt. Si je peux, je télégraphierai, mais ça ne doit pas être possible le dimanche.

En attendant, on se trouve tout désemparé, les premiers jours, de n'avoir plus rien à faire. On trouve sur sa table des notes et des bouquins qui ne serviront plus à rien, on a l'impression qu'on peut perdre son temps sans avoir ensuite des remords de conscience. A vrai dire je n'aime pas avoir absolument rien à faire. Je n'ai cependant pas beaucoup travaillé cette année. Mais j'aime du moins avoir à l'avance la perspective de quelque chose, soit des gens à voir, soit une distraction quelconque prévue à l'avance, soit un livre à lire. Il faut d'ailleurs que je traduise une nouvelle tranche de mon Frazer pour la remettre avant de quitter Paris. Je ne partirai pas sans doute avant la fin de la semaine prochaine, que je sois reçu ou que j'échoue. . . .

Henri

**To Lady Frazer:**

13/1/25

Dear Lady Frazer:

I want to enclose a few words to my letter of yesterday. I hadn't realized how wonderful was the new distinction which has been conferred on Sir James. It is really magnificent! I feel very proud to be one of his admirers & to try & help, to the best of my ability, the French public to know him as he deserves to be known. Let me also congratulate yourself, for it is greatly owing to your efforts that Sir James could achieve all that he has done. I will begin Taboo as you tell me to do. I will write later at length. Excuse hasty note, just to express all my warmest congratulations for Sir James's success.

Yrs gratefully,<br>Henri Peyre

**To the same:**

121. Bould Saint-Michel (V)<br>January 20th/1925

Dear Lady Frazer:

I can at last find a few minutes to write a few words about all those subjects. I am then going on with "Taboo." I suppose the conditions will be the same as for Attis; that is five francs a page (everything, notes, etc., included), & 200 francs for the index. I will do it with the greatest care & get it revised as I did for Attis. The number of pages of the English text is 440 (425 + XV) that is 2.200 francs, & 200 frs for the index = 2.400 frs. Whom shall I give the MS. to? At what date? & whom shall I be paid by? Excuse my insisting on such financial details:

the financial question is getting more & more important in my life & everything is determined by it.

I do not know Geuthner. I never had the opportunity to meet him. I might go & call on him one of these days or write to him first to have an appointment. I should like to know when the Attis-Osiris will be ready & when I shall have to correct the proofs. What is his address? I suppose a letter sent to the Musée Guimet would reach him.

I do not decidedly think it really worth while for me to go the Perse school next year. The work there was interesting for a year, & made me acquainted with modern methods of teaching; besides, it enabled me to live in Cambridge & know something about life in an English University. But the work is rather tedious (even more, I think, than in a French lycée), takes up much time & is poorly paid. Moreover, England does not appeal to me as much as it used to: I had so much rather stay in France & try to find a job here.

Of course, "The dying God" is "le dieu qui meurt" and not "le dieu mourant," which is not at all the meaning.

I hope you are well. I wish this damp, foggy winter would be over; it is most unhealthy. My work is not too strenuous, but little intellectual, which is perhaps a good thing. Yet I find time enough to read & write or translate at home in the evening.

Yours ever gratefully,
Henri Peyre

## To the same:

121. Boul*d*. S*t* Michel
Paris (Ve)
March 5/1925

Dear Lady Frazer:

I am sincerely sorry to hear you are unwell again & to find you don't seem to be pleased with what I have been doing, or not doing, about Geuthner. Yet I can assure you I am considering this affair as very important *for you* & *for me* & I am doing my best to urge the man to print my MS. without any further delay. I called again as soon as I got back from the Camp of Mailly, that is last Tuesday, before I received your cards. There were several people in the shop, but I went straight to him & insisted on his fulfilling his promises & beginning to print the Isis *at once*. Soyn's Ms is just over now & the printer is going to begin with mine. I told him definitely I did not want to have vague, evasive answers & I should not be able to correct the proofs after beginning of September. He then promised first proofs by end of May, & I will call again now & then to remind him of his promises. I did not allude to your financial affairs with him (payments & accounts to be settled) as I didn't feel I was qualified to do so, but I discussed the question of printing & publishing as soon as possible, for my own sake, as a grateful friend of yours & as an admirer of Sir James. I do not see what else I could do—the best would have been to have another editor for Sir James' works in France.

As for Taboo, I am working on it as regularly as I can. We had agreed about my having the 150 first pages of it ready by the end of April & your paying me 800 *frs* for them. I expect to have them ready in a week or two. I am going home (to Avignon, 2 rue Dorée) for a week to-night & I shall have them carefully re-read by my father from the point of view of handwriting & French. So you have only to tell me definitely to whom I must give my MS (150 pages of English text, with notes) &, if I am to send it to you, *how* & *when?*

I have not yet made up my mind about next year. But it is ten to one I shall not stay in Paris. I find life is much too expensive there & one's time is so taken up by a thousand & one things that one can't work & earn money as much as would be needed.

In the meanwhile, we seem to be now plunged into inextricable financial troubles—I suppose our exchange is going to fall down again! Spring has come at last, with a wild weather. I hope I shall have a few days real rest with my people at home as I feel tired now & thin & sick of that wearying life.

Yrs ever gratefully,
Henri Peyre

## To Marion Park:

> 121.Boulevard St. Michel
> Paris (Ve)
> March 15/1925

Dear Miss Park:

It is now a week since I received your letter offering me to go to Bryn Mawr next year as a substitute of Miss Pardé; I have not been able to reply before as I wanted first to get all the necessary information about Bryn Mawr College. My intention is indeed to go to America next year & to spend a year or more in a university of the States. I applied for a post a few weeks ago through Mme Petit-Dutaillis & Champenois, & I feel very much honored at receiving an offer from such a college as Bryn Mawr. I have called, as you advised me to do, on M. L. Foulet & on Miss Dillingham. They were both extremely kind to me & gave me all particulars about the college, the way French is taught there & life at Bryn Mawr. They spoke so warmly of the college, of the Faculty, and of the quality of the work that is done there that I feel very much tempted to accept your offer. Miss Dillingham also lent me the calendar, so that I might get acquainted with the full & exact program of the French studies, both for undergraduate & graduate work. I hope that, if I go, I may prove useful & I am sure it will be interesting for me to teach in such a college as the one you are President of.

I am not in a position to give you a definite & final answer just now; for, since I applied for a post in U.S., I have received letters from other universities: M. Champenois offered me the Chapman scholarship at Harvard, which I do not intend to accept. But I have been negotiating for some time with Ann Arbor University & with the Rice Institute in Texas. On the whole, all that I hear about Bryn Mawr & the situation of the college, near Philadelphia & New York, in the East, will certainly make it preferable for me, unless the financial conditions offered by other colleges would be considerably better. I should only ask you to give me some information about one or two points that are not mentioned in your letter. First, as to the traveling expenses, which, as you know, are very heavy on account of the rate of exchange, are they to be paid entirely by me, & would it not be possible for the college to grant me an indemnity for them? — Secondly, is it quite definitely fixed that, if I go to Bryn Mawr, it will be only for *one* year, during Miss Pardé's absence? Of course, I may succeed or I may not succeed there, & I do not know myself how long I shall stay in America, as I have a possible situation in French teaching. This is a mere question I am asking you in order to be as fully informed as possible, & I do not object to going to Bryn Mawr only for one year & as Miss Pardé's substitute.

So, on the whole, I should very much like to go to Bryn Mawr next year—Only I had rather wait, before I pledge my word, until I can write to, & receive an answer from, those other colleges I have been in correspondence with. The best thing would probably be for me to meet Professor Schenck when she comes over to Paris next June & to take a final decision then—unless you should think it absolutely necessary to have the affair settled before, in which case I shall make up my mind sooner.

Yours v. sincerely,<br>Henri Peyre

P.S. I am not sending you my testimonials, lists of references & of degrees or diplomas I have got, as you did not mention any. I will do so in a future letter if you ask me to.

## To Lady Frazer:

121. Bould. St Michel (V.)<br>April 16, 1925

Dear Lady Frazer:

I have come back from Avignon yesterday & I hasten to reply to your long & most welcome letter. I am sorry to hear your health still worries you. Don't you think the Cambridge climate may be partly responsible for it? I hope Sir James's health is quite good, since he can work so hard & bring out another work. I cannot help admiring his amazing power of work & his wonderful regularity!

I will briefly take up all the very interesting points you mentioned in your letter.

1) as to (?) I wrote to him at once as you advised me to do, but I

suppose he is not in Paris this week, for I had no reply. I suppose he will answer & give me the interview I asked him [for] next week. I will let you know the results. I want to see him first, before I call on Geuthner again—& to ask him to urge G. himself, so that everything may be ready before he sails for Argentine.

2) I will see *Geuthner* again soon after. I am determined to call on him now & then as soon as I get a chance. I have noted down all I have got to say to him (that he must hurry & publish, according to the contract with the Musée G., 2 vol. a year—that he must let me deal direct with the printer, who will send proofs directly to me—that generally speaking, he is not serving your & Sir James's interests as he ought to do—etc.)

3) I thank you very much for what you mention about the *50 frs* I cheated myself of. The mistake was mine. We had agreed about 250 frs & I wrote to Moret 200. Thank you for your calling my attention to it. Of course 50 frs are not a huge sum, but I am not a very rich man either (not yet at any rate!)

4) *Taboo*. I have done the first "tranche" with all possible care. I daresay the hand is clear enough & will cause no mistakes. I had it read over again last week & the whole is now finished.

Thank you very much for your kindly allowing me to leave *blanks*. I think it is better for me to do so when ever I have doubts about the real meaning of the F. thought. As it happens, I have not left any in this first "tranche" I am sending today. So you will have *nothing at all* to fill.

I am sending here the 150 first pages, + the preface—as we had agreed. You will find enclosed two slips of paper—one repeating this—the other being a copy of our agreement, as you proposed it to me in a previous letter.

Will you please tell me when you have received it as one always entertains some fears, when MS. are traveling?

As for payments, as I have little time in the daytime to go to Barclay's or anywhere, I had rather you would pay me (if possible) by an ordinary cheque, which would be paid to me at *my* bank, without having to go there myself.

5) In my last letter, I asked you *where* I was to send the MS. because in a previous letter, & in the agreement you had written on a separate leaf, you had stated I was to send it to the publisher 13, rue Jacob & to

send my receipt to you. So now things are quite clear. I will *always* send it all to Sir James Frazer.

> Yrs ever gratefully,
> Henri Peyre
> Trinity College
> Cambridge

## À ses parents:

> B. Mawr, ce 13 mai — (soir) (1926)

Chers parents,

...Il continue à faire beau et assez chaud — sans excès, pourtant. On peut vivre, en bras de chemise à la rigueur. Les gens se promènent même dans les rues comme cela — Mais nous autres, malheureux professeurs, il nous faut faire nos cours avec cols, cravates & vestes.

J'ai eu une semaine calme & semblable à peu près à toutes les autres — travail le matin. Le soir quelque promenade ou visite. Je profite de ce mois, le plus agréable de beaucoup ici, & je ne reste plus guère enfermé. Je n'aurais (sic) pas beaucoup travaillé cette année, mais j'ai fait pas mal de lectures, & la 1re année d'enseignement demande toujours plus de soins. Cela n'aura pas été trop long après tout & j'arriverai à Paris pour trouver mes anciens, ou jeunes, camarades encore anxieux dans l'attente de leur agrégation. C'est presque triste de penser à la peine que l'on prend chez nous à côté de la "légèreté d'âme" avec laquelle les étudiants vont à leurs examens. S'ils sont collés, ils font autre chose, deviennent ouvriers, chauffeurs. C'est un pays ici où les gens changent aisément & vite de métier.

...Je suis allé écouter hier 1 conférence par un député travailliste anglais qui faisait de la propagande en faveur de la grève générale. C'est ici le pays idéal pour les conférences — Cela vient de la paresse des gens, qui ne lisent pas beaucoup & aussi de leur curiosité de nouveaux riches. Ils aiment à voir la tête des gens fameux en Europe — et les européens viennent volontiers. Ils savent qu'on paye bien. Aussi n'y a-t-il guère de semaine où il ne vienne au Collège un conférencier, américain ou autre. Mais je ne me dérange pas toujours pour les écouter. Celui qui a laissé le plus éclatant souvenir était Maeterlinck qui, ne sachant pas un mot d'anglais, avait appris tout son discours en transcription phonétique. Il s'imaginait ainsi se faire comprendre. Mais le résultat & le chahut furent tels qu'il dut s'interrompre & faire rembourser leur argent aux spectateurs. Ceci était d'ailleurs avant la guerre. . . .

### Aux mêmes:

Ce 10 octobre 1927

. . . Enfin le mercredi matin vers 7 heures, nous sommes arrivés en vue de New York. On entre dans le port lentement & nous avons pu jouir une nouvelle fois du spectacle, qui est vraiment beau, même après Constantinople & la Corne d'or ou la baie de Naples. New York a une très belle rade, semée d'îles, & quand on approche tout à fait de la ville, on pénètre le long de quais où sont amarrés d'immenses paquebots, dans le quartier de la ville qui est celui des affaires & aussi des gratte-ciels. Ce jour-là, il faisait très beau & nous avons été d'autant plus heureux de revoir la terre. L'air était pur & vif & le soleil même très chaud. Le débarquement s'est effectué assez vite pour nous. L'entrée en Amérique est compliquée, car on doit subir plusieurs examens & présenter rigoureusement toute sorte de papiers; mais il faut ajouter qu'on est frappé par ce que les Américains appellent leur "efficiency," et que tout est bien organisé pourvu qu'on se plie aux règles. . . . Bien entendu, nous n'avions déclaré que quelques affaires, pour 3000 frs environ, et caché le reste avec toute sorte de précautions dans les malles. Nous avons passé 10 mauvaises minutes, car justement cette fois-ci l'inspecteur a fait ouvrir toutes les malles & valises, a regardé dans chacune, dans chaque tiroir & chaque coin. Par bonheur, il n'a rien vu de ce que nous avions caché. Nous avions mis en évidence & déclaré les 2 grands écrins d'argenterie & le plateau du service à café. Enfin après un temps qui nous a paru long, il nous a donné les tickets de sortie et nous n'avons pas eu à payer un sou de droits—Après quoi, il n'y avait plus qu'à nous précipiter en taxi à la gare. Nous n'avons que jeté un coup d'œil sur New York par un beau soleil et le train de 11 heures nous emmenait à Philadelphie—et après un déjeuner rapide, nous sommes arrivés à Bryn Mawr mercredi à 3 heures.

Marguerite s'est aussitôt occupée de chercher provisoirement une chambre & en a loué une pour 1 semaine pour nous donner le temps de regarder des appartements — Je suis moi-même allé au collège directement: les cours avaient déjà commencé, mais je n'en avais pas encore eu & je n'arrivais en somme pas en retard. La plupart des figures sont les mêmes que l'an dernier, parmi les professeurs veux-je dire, & j'en ai revu plusieurs avec plaisir. Il faut bien leur répondre à tous la même chose, sur la façon dont on a passé l'été, le temps qu'il a fait en Europe, etc. Mais ils ont l'air ainsi de s'intéresser à vous. Quant à mes cours, je les ai commencés jeudi matin: je les travaille un peu ces jours-ci, car le début exige toujours pas mal de lectures & il faut quelques jours pour se remettre & reprendre l'habitude de parler.

. . . Enfin, après 2 jours seulement, nous avons trouvé un appartement agréable: 1 2e étage d'une maison assez grande, bien située, pas en plein dans le village, mais à part, comme une villa, entourée d'arbres & d'herbe — à 10 minutes du collège, 5 de la gare. La dame qui possède la maison a justement beaucoup de meubles & nous le laisse meublé pour le même prix, ce qui est une chance inespérée. Et enfin nous avons pu (ceci, je dois dire, est dû à la diplomatie de Marguerite, et non à moi) obtenir un arrangement par lequel nous n'aurons pas à payer les 4 mois d'été. Le prix est de 85 dollars par mois (pour 8 mois donc. . . . Dans l'ensemble, tout le monde nous dit que nous avons eu beaucoup de chance & je crois que c'est vrai. . . .

## Aux mêmes:

Jeudi 24 nov./27

. . . Hier soir donc nous avons vu au cinéma un film assez bon: des paysages de la jongle malaise, avec des animaux de toute espèce. C'était un peu comme à un cirque ou à un jardin zoologique, avec des paysages en couleurs en plus. A part cela nous ne sortons presque jamais le soir: je reste en général à travailler à mon bureau, pendant que Marguerite s'occupe de cuisine ou d'autre chose. Nous sommes ainsi assez occupés pour n'avoir pas besoin de distractions. Nous allons cependant quelquefois chez des amis. Dimanche dernier après-midi, nous avons été à un thé intéressant — & lundi soir, Miss Schenck, professeur de Français (mais dame américaine, qui est mon "chef de département") donnait un dîner en l'honneur de Marguerite; il y avait les autres prof de Français, et ceux d'Italien & d'Espagnol. Ça été intéressant et agréable: il y a ici bien des gens d'esprit très large & de connaissances vastes & approfondies qu'il est plaisant de fréquenter. Beaucoup de nos collègues ont une connaissance de l'Europe vraiment étendue & sont de conversation brillante. Il y a dans ce pays plus encore qu'ailleurs une différence frappante entre l'élite intellectuelle & la foule, si vulgaire & si étroite d'idées, si uniquement américaine & si préoccupée de confort matériel. Et à côté de la plèbe des touristes (souvent d'ailleurs très riches) qui parcourent l'Europe dans les tours de Cook ou autres agences, il y a des connaisseurs d'art comme j'en ai rarement rencontrés en France.

. . . Je vais aussi en profiter [des fêtes de Thanksgiving] pour travailler un peu. Je recommence à me mettre à un sujet que je défriche un peu en vue d'une thèse d'anglais, sur le romancier américain Henry James. Mais c'est un auteur difficile & qui a beaucoup écrit, si bien que je n'avance pas vite. Je veux cependant profiter de le lire tant que je suis en Amérique, car les livres me manqueraient là-dessus une fois en France. . . .

## Aux mêmes:

Mercredi soir
21 décembre 1927

. . . Marguerite est aussi en vacances depuis ce matin, & ce matin je l'ai vue revenir avec une valise & plusieurs autres paquets sous le bras. C'étaient les cadeaux de ses élèves; au moins une vingtaine de boîtes, soigneusement empaquetées de papier de soie et enrubannées, renfermant des petits mouchoirs, ou une paire de bas, un pompon de poudre — Mes élèves à moi ne m'en font pas autant; ce n'est pas, je crois, la coutume au collège, & je crois d'ailleurs qu'elles n'oseraient pas avec moi, car je passe pour froid & intimidant, & peut-être même sévère. Nous allons donc rester tranquilles pendant ces vacances, & nous n'aurons même pas de visites, puisque la plupart des gens s'en vont. On finit d'ailleurs par perdre trop de temps à sortir. Dimanche dernier nous avons encore passé toute la journée dehors. Nous avons dîné chez les Leuba, ce professeur de psychologie avec qui nous avons fait notre dernière traversée. Lui est gentil, quoiqu'un peu raide d'ailleurs & très pointu & dogmatique (dans le sens anticlérical). Il est l'auteur de plusieurs livres de psychologie du mysticisme, traduits en plusieurs langues

& jusqu'en Japonais, mais un peu partiaux & pleins d'une ironie cruelle pour les mystiques & tous les gens religieux en général. Il est d'ailleurs ancien protestant & même fils d'un pasteur suisse! C'est souvent ainsi.

. . . Je vais profiter de ces quelques jours pour travailler, & tout d'abord, rédiger la communication que je dois faire la semaine prochaine à la réunion de l'"Association des Langues modernes." J'y ai pris (je vous l'ai peut-être déjà écrit) comme sujet "Le conflit entre l'orient et l'occident dans la littérature française contemporaine." C'est un sujet un peu bateau, mais général, & susceptible d'intéresser la majorité des gens. Je dois lire ceci, en effet, à une assemblée générale, où il y a plusieurs centaines de membres & dans une grande salle. . . .

## Aux mêmes:

40, Rosemont Avenue, Rosemont (Pa)
Ce 29 février 1928

Chers parents,

Vous ne vous plaindrez dorénavant de ma mauvaise écriture, si du moins j'ai le courage d'écrire cette lettre à la machine jusqu'au bout. Nous venons, comme vous le voyez, de faire l'achat d'une machine à écrire; c'est même une machine épatante, sur laquelle, avec un tout petit changement de clé, nous pouvons taper à volonté du français, de l'anglais, de l'allemand, du grec, et même de l'arabe ou du chinois. Il semble d'ailleurs qu'on s'habitue très vite à écrire à la machine & aussi à penser et à composer en même temps. Mais nous avons résolu de faire cet achat pour des raisons plus pratiques; ici pour beaucoup de lettres d'affaire, pour donner nos sujets d'examen, et surtout dès que l'on a un article ou quoi que ce soit à faire imprimer, on n'accepte que les manuscrits ainsi tapés, et il est encore plus commode et moins coûteux de le faire soi-même que de le faire faire.

Nous avons reçu de vos nouvelles vers le milieu de la semaine dernière deux lettres nous sont même parvenues le même jour (jeudi). Mais votre santé parait continuer à être bonne, ainsi que celle de Grand'mère, et nous sommes donc tranquilles sur ce point quels que puissent être les retards fortuits de la poste. Les journaux nous arrivent aussi régulièrement; cependant je voulais te dire que parfois la bande portant l'adresse a complètement disparu dans le voyage, et pour éviter qu'ils ne s'égarent, il vaudrait peut-être mieux mettre une bande encore plus forte ou les entourer d'une ficelle par exemple, et écrire l'adresse sur le journal même. J'ai lu avec intérêt ces grands discours politiques à la chambre; Poincaré est certainement un homme d'une très grande honnêteté et modération de jugement—mais il est dommage qu'il reste si avocat, avec sa logique impeccable et un peu empesée. Sans faire de la démagogie, il pourrait chercher à avoir un peu plus de magnétisme (pour employer le mot à la mode ici). En attendant, je ne crois pas que ce soit la peine d'essayer de spéculer sur une hausse possible du franc pour après les élections. Ce qui pourrait monter encore, en mettant les choses au mieux, ce seraient les rentes françaises; et encore sait-on jamais?

Il nous est venu un retour d'hiver, avec 12 degrés au-dessous, succédant à des jours presque printaniers où les arbres commençaient presque à avoir des bourgeons, ce qu'ils font sans doute depuis longtemps chez vous. Mais enfin ces retours de froid finiront bien par disparaître aussi et cela fera encore un hiver de passé.

C'est toujours amusant de lire des nouvelles de France ici de temps à autre; d'autant que nous sommes privés du plaisir français de discuter politique, puisque je ne vois jamais d'autre homme de ma nationalité. Il est vrai que les nouvelles autres que littéraires (et même celles-ci bien souvent) paraissent assez vaines. C'est ainsi qu'on s'amuse toujours à Paris à discuter sur le problème de la circulation et de l'encombrement des rues. Ce n'est rien cependant à côté de New York, mais il est vrai que les Américains sont plus disciplinés. Les rues sont divisées tous les 100 mètres environ en blocs, à peu près carrés et personne ne traverse quand il ne faut pas: la circulation est gouvernée par des lumières tournantes successivement vertes et rouges, et l'on ne peut passer, à pied ou en auto que s'il y a la lumière verte. Il y a peut-être ainsi plus de sécurité, mais pour les gens comme moi qui n'aiment pas à perdre leur temps, il n'est rien de plus énervant. C'est sans doute la raison pour laquelle je me suis si facilement habitué ici à vivre à la campagne, ce que je n'aurais jamais cru possible auparavant. Les villes vous font connaître ici toutes les horreurs de la civilisation: on prend le métro, et on y est serré comme un anchois, avec une odeur qui ne doit pas être très différente de celle qui s'exhale des boîtes d'anchois. Mais les anchois dans cette situation ont sur nous l'avantage d'être morts et de ne rien sentir. Quant aux autos, on est arrivé au point où il y en a tant que c'est de l'avis général, le mode de locomotion le plus lent dans les villes. Il fallait s'y attendre, puisque les rues ne sont pas plus larges qu'il y a 20 ans, alors que les maisons géantes sont 10, 20, ou 30 fois plus hautes et contiennent donc 10, 20, et 30 fois plus de monde qu'auparavant.

Mais j'ai l'air de me lancer dans de grands topos généraux; cela est tout au plus de mise les premiers mois de séjour dans un pays étranger, lorsqu'on est surtout sensible aux différences. Au point où j'en suis maintenant, j'ai pu acquérir plus de sagesse, et je commence à me ranger dans la catégorie des gens mariés, assagis et philosophes depuis l'Ecclésiaste jusqu'à Anatole France, et à croire que, Nouveau Monde ou Ancien Monde, Anglo-Saxons, Latins ou Chinois, nous ne différons guère sous ce soleil.

Pour vous tenir en attendant au courant de la question qui nous préoccupe surtout cette semaine, (ce que nous ferons l'an prochain), nous sommes toujours dans l'incertitude, mais cette incertitude est un mol oreiller, car elle ne vient que du grand nombre de possibilités, tu m'avais comparé, je crois, il y a deux ans, à ce brave Homère qu'on se disputait, mais, après sa mort; ma vanité ne se hausse pas encore jusqu'à prétendre me comparer à de tels génies, mais il est vrai qu'elle est assez flattée ces jours-ci. Ce serait trop compliqué d'entrer dans le détail des lettres, télégrammes et voyages qui ne sont pas épargnés. En tous cas, j'ai eu deux entrevues déjà avec les autorités de l'université de Princeton, et ils ne m'ont pas caché qu'ils désiraient beaucoup m'avoir. C'est évidemment beaucoup d'honneur, car c'est une université importante et où l'on fait du bon travail. Ils ne me donneraient que des cours avancés et à peu près ceux que je voudrais. En même temps, ils ont amélioré leur première offre, en me proposant 200 dollars de plus pour l'an prochain et une augmentation aussitôt après, si, comme ils l'espèrent, disent-ils, je réussis.

D'autre part, je pense avoir une offre nette de l'université d'Yale d'ici deux jours et je choisirais alors entre l'une et l'autre. En ce cas, je quitterais donc Bryn Mawr, à moins que Bryn Mawr au dernier moment décide de m'offrir une augmentation suffisante pour me retenir. L'avantage le plus sérieux ici est que les vacances y sont sensiblement plus longues qu'ailleurs l'été (deux semaines de plus au moins). En outre Marguerite étant connue et sur les lieux, aurait son poste plus facilement; en fait, on lui en a déjà offert un qu'elle acceptera, si nous nous décidons à rester ici. Mais comme c'est évidemment mon poste ici qui a le plus d'importance, Marguerite sera obligée de sacrifier les possibilités peut-être meilleures qu'elle pourrait trouver autrement.

Pendant que je tapais cette partie de ma lettre, je viens encore de recevoir un télégramme de Yale, où l'on pense m'offrir 3.500 dollars. Nous allons donc considérer toute la question et prendre une décision définitive vendredi matin, de toute façon, j'espère que nous n'aurons pas lieu de regretter ce que nous aurons fait; et d'ailleurs je ne m'engage nulle part pour plus d'un an. Tout cela me flatte en tout puisque ça montre qu'on m'apprécie ici—je dois même le dire—beaucoup plus que je ne le mérite; mais ici, bien entendu, je me prends très au sérieux, et feins de croire tous les compliments qu'on m'adresse. Mais quelle habileté et quelle diplomatie il faut dans ce pays! Je crois qu'après ces quelques semaine, j'aurais acquis assez d'expérience pour être ambassadeur!

J'ai dû abandonner ma machine pour me précipiter à la cuisine, où Marguerite venait de pousser un grand cri. Ce n'était qu'une souris sur laquelle elle avait mis la main en croyant toucher des pommes de terre. Cela m'a du moins appris que je vais me régaler de pommes de terre frites à mon dîner! Je vais donc m'arrêter là dans ma lettre.

Vous excuserez l'irrégularité de mes lignes & mes fautes pour un premier essai. J'ai été aussi si occupé ces jours-ci que je n'ai pas eu le temps d'écrire à Jacques. Vous l'aurez sans doute avec vous bientôt, s'il n'est même pas déjà reparti. Bonnes caresses à vous tous & vœux de bonne santé.

Henri

## To Marion Park:

40, Rosemont Avenue, Rosemont (Pa)<br>March 6—1928

President Park
Bryn Mawr College (Pa)
Dear President Park,

I am sorry to have to confirm to you the news that I have accepted a post at Yale University for the year 1928–1929.

At the same time, I want to tell you again how much my wife and myself have appreciated the very favorable conditions that you offered us, and I beg you to believe that, although other considerations prevailed on the whole and caused our present decision, I am very thankful to you and to Bryn Mawr for the very pleasant conditions I have enjoyed here for three years. I have always found the greatest pleasure in working under Miss [E. M.] Schenck and with my colleagues of the French Department, and a sympathetic interest from the part of the students. I am sure I shall always look back with regret upon the years spent here, and miss the many friends who have welcomed me in this community and contributed to make our stay in Bryn Mawr a very happy one.
I am,

> Very gratefully and sincerely yours,
> Henri Peyre

## À ses parents:

[Sans date]

Je suis tout de mauvaise humeur; je viens de chercher pendant une heure des notes sur Verhaeren que j'avais prêtes pour mon cours de demain sans pouvoir les trouver. Il n'y a rien de plus vexant, d'autant plus que ça commence à m'arriver souvent. Notre appartement nous laisse cependant bien au large, mais je me mets à avoir tellement de notes et de fiches depuis que j'enseigne ici que cela m'en fera près d'une malle au moment où nous déménagerons. Mais il ne m'a fallu (sic) longtemps pour trouver que c'est au fond beaucoup plus embêtant d'enseigner la littérature contemporaine que les bons vieux classiques. Il est rarement possible de trouver à parler toute une heure sur plusieurs de ces bouquins modernes, et on en est réduit pour tous renseignements à quelques articles de revues ou à ces notices, pourtant bien maigres et bien vides, des Nouvelles Littéraires, que je découpe consciencieusement. Je vais finir ce cours par Claudel et Valéry. Claudel ne m'est guère sympathique avec son mysticisme échevelé. On a donné à quelque temps (sic) un dîner en son honneur à Philadelphie, où nous avons négligé d'aller. (J'ajoute que le dîner coûtait 5 dollars par personne, ce qui est considérable, même en Amérique). Sa prétendue philosophie et critique est bien faible, mais il a évidemment du génie, par éclairs, dans sa poésie et ses drames. Mais il est bigrement difficile—et ici, depuis qu'il est ambassadeur à Washington, tous les gens qui veulent se dire renseignés se sont mis à le lire et à demander des conférences sur lui, bien entendu sans rien y comprendre.

Il est naturel que je commence par parler de lectures, car nous venons de subir 2 ou 3 jours de pluie continue, où on ne pouvait guère faire autre chose. Pour moi, cela a même été renforcé par une fluxion à la joue, dont j'ai pris prétexte pour manquer 2 jours mes cours. Cette fluxion n'avait d'ailleurs rien de douloureux, et j'en ai eu assez autrefois, comme vous vous souvenez, pour savoir ce que c'est. J'espère seulement que ce n'est pas le présage d'une autre dent sur le point de se gâter— car ce n'était pas du même côté que celle qu'on m'a arrachée récemment. J'ai déjà plus de 16 dents fausses ou couronnées d'or, mais il me faudra sans doute les remplacer toutes avant mes trente ans.

. . . Tout ça est sans doute beaucoup plus cher que chez nous, mais tout est à l'avenant, et cet allemand dont tu parles qui plaint les traitements misérables des professeurs ici a sans doute commis la faute de généraliser, comme tant d'observateurs étrangers. En réalité, il n'y a ici nulle uniformité et le traitement, à poste et valeur égale des professeurs, dépend de la richesse de l'université. Par exemple l'université de Philadelphie (d'ailleurs énorme, avec plus de 12.000 étudiants) paye moins bien que Bryn Mawr. Yale, où je serai l'an prochain, paye mieux que Bryn Mawr à grade égal. Ici, les traitements sont de 1800 dollars par an à 5200, maximum. J'ai eu moi-même 2.800 et 3.000. A Yale, on a, je crois, jusqu'à 6.000, et même 8 ou 10.0000, comme professeur titulaire plus âgé. En fait, je ne vois pas que nos collègues soient bien malheureux. Ce qui est vrai, c'est que la plupart des banquiers, hommes d'affaires, docteurs, peut-être même épiciers, gagnent en Amérique bien davantage que les professeurs. Mais c'est ainsi partout, et après tout c'est juste. . . .

## Aux mêmes:

Ce 18 avril 1928

. . . Quant au nationalisme exagéré de beaucoup de gens de chez nous et ailleurs, tu as bien raison de dire que ce n'est pas un progrès. Je m'amuse souvent à dire aux Américains que si les Français sont mieux reçus et en général plus estimés ici que les autres étrangers, c'est parce qu'il y en a relativement si peu qu'ils ne les connaissent pas assez pour les détester—et que plus les peuples se connaissent, moins ils s'aiment. Ils me traitent alors de cynique, parce qu'avec leur sentimentalité anglo-saxonne, il y a toujours des choses qu'on n'aime pas dire ou reconnaître ici. Mais il est certain que quand nous avons aimé les Anglais au 18e siècle, ou les Allemands au début du 19e, c'était parce qu'on les connaissait très mal. Et depuis 1918, comme on a eu l'occasion de mieux observer les Américains avec leurs soldats d'abord et leurs touristes ensuite, on a adopté envers eux une attitude moins sentimentale et peut-être moins sotte. . . .

## À sa sœur Louise et à sa famille:

40, Rosemont Avenue Rosemont (Pa)
Ce 2 mai 1928

Chers beau-frère et sœur et chère petite Lélène,

Nous sommes aujourd'hui à notre première journée de printemps. C'est un peu tard, devez-vous vous dire, vous qui souffrez déjà sans doute des chaleurs de l'été. Et il est vrai que nous n'avons pas été favorisés cette année. Il a beaucoup plu ces derniers temps, il a fait très froid, nous avons eu à subir des ouragans, de tardives chutes de neige, et voilà enfin les premières feuilles qui percent. Le printemps, d'ailleurs, n'existe vraiment pas dans ce climat et nous nous attendons à passer d'un jour à l'autre à des 30 degrés. Cela n'a pas été fait pour nous faire paraître le temps plus court et nous avons plusieurs fois regretté la Barthelasse à l'époque de ses premiers moustiques et plus encore Paris, qui est si agréable en cette saison, avec les marronniers en fleurs et les premières soirées à la terrasse des cafés. Hélas! le temps nous paraît d'autant plus long cette année, que nous verrons partir les autres au début de juin et devrons rester nous-mêmes, puisque nous avons héroïquement retardé de deux mois l'arrivée de nos vacances. Enfin! nous nous consolerons en pensant que cela en vaut la peine, si nous nous décidons, comme c'est probable, à nous meubler cette année. Nous resterons donc à Bryn Mawr jusqu'à la fin de juin; nous pourrons toujours employer ces 3 semaines après la fermeture du collège à choisir des meubles, à nous promener un peu, ou même à préparer nos cours. Le premier juillet, nous commencerons à enseigner à Penn State College: deux heures chacun tous les matins, sauf le samedi. Ce ne sera pas très pénible. La plus grosse obligation sera d'avoir à parler français constamment, car ce cours d'été est fait pour des professeurs d'enseignement secondaire qui viennent rafraîchir leur français pendant les vacances et ne peuvent pas se payer le voyage en France. Ils promettent donc de ne pas dire un seul mot d'anglais de 6 semaines, et même de ne pas lire un seul livre ou journal anglais. Par ailleurs, il y aura bien quelques compensations: le pays est joli, quoique perdu dans la campagne, à quelques 400 mètres de hauteur et dans une région accidentée, arrosée de nombreuses sources. Je ne sais pas si cela nous fera complètement oublier l'été précédent, avec vous tous à Avignon, non plus que l'Égypte, Constantinople et le Lotus—et encore moins le gai zézaiement de Lélène, le bruit de son cheval de bois, et ses belles salutations du soir.

Notre temps à Bryn Mawr approche de sa fin. J'ai encore 2 semaines de cours en tout et pour tout. Mais pour être resté 3 ans ici, je dois dire que je ne me sens pas très triste de le quitter. J'y ai quelques bons amis, mais très peu en somme. Les autres sont, ou bien assez froids et peu liants, ou bien des Américains sans conversation et assommants. Ce dernier cas est surtout celui des professeurs de sciences, je dois dire. Ce sont souvent des hommes très savants et même réputés dans leur partie, ayant fait l'habituel voyage d'Europe, mais incapables d'exprimer aucune idée en public ou de se dérider. Décidément, les hommes ne brillent pas dans ce pays. Ils passent pour être toujours aux pieds des femmes et d'une galanterie qui nous paraît ridicule à nous. Mais si j'étais une Américaine, ils m'ennuieraient bien. C'est très joli de gagner de l'argent, mais ils ne savent pas le dépenser après. Leur seul intérêt est de payer de belles robes à leur femme, de belles autos, de grandes maisons, et de continuer à gagner de l'argent ensuite, puisque leur véritable passion est pour les affaires. Rien ici n'est organisé pour flâner. Il faut toujours "faire quelque chose," comme ils disent, et être en mouvement.

Nous pensons l'an prochain être plus occupés. J'essaierai pour ma part de profiter de ce que nous habiterons dans une ville et serons dans une plus grande université pour travailler davantage en dehors. Quant à Marguerite, elle n'aura plus le déplacement fatigant tous les matins et sera ainsi moins fatiguée l'après-midi. Cette année, nous aurons eu naturellement pas mal à faire. D'abord, toutes les recettes de cuisine à essayer et, l'appartement étant grand, quelques nettoyages à faire, sans domestiques bien entendu, c'est là une chose à laquelle on est résigné ici, et pour cause. Tout cela sera sans doute plus facile à mesure que nous avançons en âge et en expérience.

Mon successeur ici vient d'être choisi. C'est un nommé Canut, agrégé d'histoire qui doit avoir un peu plus de 30 ans. Il a été professeur à Alger l'année avant vous, car il était, m'a-t-il dit, grand ami de Maublanc. Il a l'air très gentil et j'espère qu'il se plaira ici. Il est déjà en Amérique depuis un an ou deux.

Vous allez sans doute faire bientôt votre apparition à Avignon, heureux que vous êtes! Peut-être dès la fin juin et en hydravion, puisque votre traversée l'an dernier vous avait mis en goût. Jacques a dû être très occupé encore par ses leçons. Sa thèse est-elle terminée et va-t-il la soutenir avant les vacances? Je regretterai dans ce cas de ne pouvoir être là pour l'applaudir. Quels sont vos projets pour cet été, ceux de Jacques surtout, car pour Louise, elle ne bougera guère sans doute de son cher Avignon. Ce ne sera pas trop sans doute de toutes les vacances pour trouver une bonne qui vous serve au moins jusqu'à Noël. Notre arrivée à Avignon nous parait encore bien lointaine! Nous essaierons de jouir d'autant plus de nos vacances qu'elles seront plus courtes. Nous devrons sans doute nous rembarquer le 19 septembre. Mais nous vous écrirons encore d'ici là pour vous souhaiter bon voyage.

Notre vie est toujours bien calme. Nous n'avons guère le temps de sortir beaucoup. Avec le beau temps cependant, Marguerite commence à jouer au tennis sur les terrains du collège. Nous n'aurons jamais dansé cette année et n'aurons pas de nouveautés à montrer à la dame qui jouait si bien du piano (la maman de Cloclo). Ces jours-ci cependant il va y avoir à Bryn Mawr de grandes fêtes pour célébrer le mois de mai. Ce sont des fêtes en plein air données tous les 4 ans et reconstituant les fêtes de mai données en Angleterre autrefois du temps de la reine Elisabeth. Les étudiantes vont y jouer des pièces dans les décors de verdure du parc du collège, comme le songe d'une nuit d'été (d'un nommé Shakespeare) et d'autres pièces du 16e siècle. On y vient de tous les coins du pays: cela vaudra donc bien la peine que nous nous dérangions aussi. Je finis à la main, car je viens de taper mes sujets d'examen de fin d'année et je commence à en avoir assez. Je réussis à cet exercice avec une rapidité assez grande, mais non sans faire des fautes. C'est mon éternel défaut, comme lorsque je jouais la méthode Czerny avec M. Armand. Le piano est une des choses qui me manquent ici: j'aimerais, en guise de récréation, aller de temps en temps tapoter Raymonde & le Pélices; Lélène viendrait m'admirer bouche bée ou danser. J'espère que cette petite coquine ne nous aura pas trop oubliés après si longtemps.

Nous n'avons pas eu directement de vos nouvelles de quelque temps: mais vous dites peut-être la même chose de nous et les excuses réciproques sont inutiles. Nous attendons que Lélène soit en mesure d'écrire, et alors les lettres se feront plus fréquentes. En attendant, grosses caresses pour elle—et pour vous.

Henri

## À ses parents:

Ce jeudi 3 mai 1928

... Nous n'avons cependant guère entrepris de promenade—peut-être parce que habitant à la campagne même, cela a moins d'attrait, pour moi au moins. Je crois qu'au fond j'aime mieux la nature de loin ou par intermédiaire, dans les livres ou chez les poètes. Quand j'ai comme ici des oiseaux et des branches à la fenêtre, et que, pour aller faire mes cours, je marche sur du gazon vert, et même littéralement parmi des violettes, j'y suis moins sensible. En fait c'est en cette saison que je regrette le plus Paris, avec les marronniers en fleurs, les pelouses de tulipes aux Tuileries, des flâneries le soir avec des gens gais & bavards prenant le frais à leur porte et les terrasses des cafés toutes peuplées. Ici one ne sait pas flâner. Dès qu'il fait beau, les gens grimpent dans leur auto et circulent sur les routes jusqu'à ce qu'ils en aient assez. Aussi regrettons-nous plus vivement le retard apporté à l'arrivée de nos vacances, et jusqu'aux moustiques de la Barthelasse & aux concerts de la Rich Tavern. Le piano surtout me manque pour y tapoter mes airs harmonieux. J'exerce mes doigts sur la machine à écrire par compensation, mais la musique en est moins suave.

Ici tout sent déjà la fin de l'année. Je n'ai plus que deux semaines de cours & je prépare déjà mes sujets d'examens. Mais cela ne change rien à ma vie, puisque je passe toujours régulièrement le même nombre d'heures à lire à ma table. Je dois dire cependant que, à mesure que j'ai plus d'expérience de l'enseignement, je passe moins de temps à préparer mes cours. Je ne me suis pas trop foulé cette année, pour la bonne raison que je commence à avoir fait à peu près toutes les époques & que je n'ai qu'à regarder mes anciennes notes—L'an prochain, après le premier travail d'adaptation à un nouveau milieu, je crois que je n'aurai pas trop à faire non plus—et surtout, dans les cours avancés que j'aurai, pas de devoirs à corriger.

Ce soir nous allons au théâtre. C'est presque un événement, car ça ne nous est pas arrivé souvent cette année. Lundi dernier, nous avons déjà fait une expédition en ville; nous étions invités à dîner par un musicien de l'orchestre de Philadelphie et sa femme, que nous connaissons depuis longtemps. Ce sont des gens heureux et, étant français, très portés sur la nourriture. Le dîner, au restaurant, était certainement bon; il était cher aussi—Mais le dit musicien gagne 10.000 dollars pour sa saison de 7 mois à Philadelphie, et se fait encore pas mal d'argent en dehors. Il est vrai qu'il passe pour un homme de grand talent, et avec raison. Ils ont fait bâtir dans le midi, près de Bandol, et espèrent s'y retirer après encore 2 ou 3 ans d'Amérique. Le même soir, Roland Manuel, directeur de la Bibliothèque Nationale, faisait une conférence à l'Alliance française. Mais il faisait chaud, nous avions bien mangé (et même pour une fois bu un ou deux cocktails) et, après 5 minutes, nous avons décampé. Le conférencier n'en était encore qu'à Colbert dans son historique de la bibliothèque. Écouter les conférences est d'ailleurs de moins en moins mon fait. . . .

## Aux mêmes:

Jeudi 24 mai 1928

Chers parents:

Le jeudi est ici un jour tellement comme les autres, où les écoles n'ont jamais congé, que j'ai de la peine à repenser aux jeudis français d'autrefois que marquait surtout la leçon de piano redoutée, suivie quelquefois de la leçon d'instruction religieuse, pendant que papa passait sa matinée à couper du bois ou à tirer du vin. Ma foi! malgré tout mon vif regret de la maison et d'Avignon, il y a bien des choses que je ne regrette pas dans cette période tant vantée de la jeunesse, et surtout toutes ces leçons à ingurgiter sans cesse de physique, d'histoire et du reste. Du moins, après cette période des études, on ne fait plus que du travail qui vous intéresse à peu près, et avec beaucoup plus de liberté. . . .

## À sa famille:

Ce 6 juin 1928

Chers Parents,

Chère Louise, Chère Petite Lélène,

. . . Je viens de taper à la machine une lettre d'affaires et je continue ainsi pour la lettre familiale. On m'a demandé à l'université d'Yale de faire commander tous les livres dont je crois pouvoir avoir besoin l'an prochain et j'en profite largement pour leur faire acheter tout ce que je veux lire. C'est l'avantage d'être dans une université riche et cela m'évite d'acheter des livres pour mon compte tant que je suis ici. Je viens donc de leur taper une longue liste d'ouvrages plus ou moins savants.

Pendant ce temps, Marguerite est en train de jouer, ou plutôt de faire jouer, le phonographe, et un morceau de qualité, s'il vous plaît: L'Après-midi d'un Faune de Debussy que nous avons parmi nos disques. C'est pour célébrer la fin de son année scolaire et de ses voyages à Philadelphie. Elle a en effet terminé ce matin même ses classes avec un soupir de satisfaction. Nous voilà donc enfin en vacances complètes. Ici, au collège, la cérémonie finale de graduation a lieu demain matin. Ça consiste pour moi à prendre part à la procession des professeurs et à essuyer ensuite un discours et la lecture de la liste des docteurs, maîtres-ès-arts, et bacheliers-ès-arts du collège cette année. J'arborerai à cette occasion ma robe toute neuve et mon ermine. Après quoi, on prend part à un déjeuner en plein air offert par les autorités du collège et nous en profiterons pour dire au revoir à tous les amis et connaissances que nous allons quitter. Ces jours-ci, d'ailleurs, ce ne sont que thés et fêtes, jeunes filles se promenant en belles robes blanches ou d'autre couleur dans les jardins. Il y a notamment un jardin japonais qui n'est ouvert qu'en cette époque de l'année pour quelques jours et qui, le soir, avec ses jets d'eau, ses statues, et ses lanternes chinoises, rappelle tout à fait un jardin de conte de fées, ou, pour des âmes plus raffinées, un de ces jardins avec jets d'eau, bassins et allées cachées chers à H. de Régnier.

. . . Nous avons aussi aux dernières nouvelles changé de bateaux.

Non que nous puissions partir plus tôt, puisque cela ne dépend pas de nous. Mais, pour faire une légère économie, nous allons voyager cette fois-ci sur une ligne anglaise en troisième ou plus exactement dans une classe spéciale appelée "troisième touristes." C'est moins cher que les secondes et on y mange sans doute moins bien. Mais c'est distinct des troisièmes ordinaires fréquentés par les immigrants et c'est très couru par les professeurs et étudiants impécunieux. Nous partirons donc le 11 août sur l'"Olympic" et repartirons, hélas! le 19 septembre sur l'"Homeric." . . .

## À ses parents:

Ce jeudi 14 juin/28

. . . Lundi dernier, nous sommes partis en expédition. Nous nous sommes arrêtés d'abord à Princeton, entre Philadelphie & New York, où j'ai un camarade Foulet avec qui nous avons fait un peu de canotage sur le lac. Comme c'est un petit endroit, nous avons en l'espace d'une heure, rencontré tous les gens que nous y connaissons, notamment le professeur qui m'avait offert d'y aller enseigner l'an prochain. Il est très gentil & cordial, et ne s'est pas fâché de mon refus, ce qui arrive quelquefois. Ici même, la dame qui est chef du département semble s'être assez vexée de notre décision de partir & s'est montrée très froide depuis.

. . . Après avoir couché à New Haven, nous nous sommes mis à une journée d'affaires, notre but étant de visiter des appartements. Tout est allé d'ailleurs très vite et nous avons pu rentrer chez nous le soir même. . . . C'est moins grand, certes, que notre appartement actuel, mais d'autant plus facile à entretenir, et cela fera aussi d'autant moins de meubles à acheter. . . . Nous paierons 60 dollars par mois, ce qui, pour ici, bien entendu, n'est pas trop. La raison en est que New Haven n'a pas l'air d'une ville très chère & qu'on y a beaucoup bâti ces dernières années. Enfin nous espérons nous y plaire et nous sommes très contents du changement. La ville est en outre agréable, du moins dans certains quartiers, car la moitié de la population est italienne et ouvrière. Elle ressemble à Oxford ou Cambridge, avec le cachet de vieux temps en moins, c'est à dire une ville où l'Université est tout et où les professeurs sont fort respectés. C'est peu de chose, quoique cela flatte la vanité des membres de cette respectable profession; surtout, pour nous, nous espérons y trouver un milieu agréable, et en tous cas, beaucoup plus de variété qu'ici, car c'est incomparablement plus grand. . . .

## Aux mêmes:

Institute of French Education<br>
Penn State College, Pa<br>
Ce 3 juillet 1928

Chers parents,

Nous voici en villégiature en pleine montagne, et dans un pays dont vous aurez sans doute de la peine à vous imaginer l'aspect. C'est sur un plateau, entouré de montagnes de tous les côtés, et à 1200 pieds de hauteur, c'est à dire 400 mètres. L'air y est frais, même au milieu de la journée, mais surtout le soir et la nuit, il fait sec & l'on sent une énorme différence avec le climat humide de Philadelphie. En somme, c'est tout à fait comme si nous étions venus passer 6 semaines à la montagne et à la campagne—et quelle campagne! Il n'y aurait rien ici sans le collège ou université: c'était sans doute un désert quand on l'a fondé là et il n'y a maintenant que le village, plus petit encore que Bryn Mawr, avec quelques restaurants, marchands de légumes & de fruits, librairies & papeteries. Le collège est d'ailleurs très grand. Il y a, paraît-il, environ 2.500 étudiants pendant la session d'été: étudiants venus compléter leurs études, professeurs d'enseignement primaire ou secondaire, plus toutes sortes d'autres types bizarres—Mais ce qu'on appelle "l'Institut français" où nous sommes est tout à fait à part et nous ne voyons rien du tout des autres.

. . . Nous sommes logés dans une maison qui ressemble à un chalet suisse, toute en bois, et murs en papier mâché, avec quelque 8 autres professeurs ou étudiants. Nous tâcherons de vous en envoyer plus tard des photographies. Le grand avantage de cette maison est sa proximité du bâtiment principal où nous prenons les repas et sa proximité, encore plus immédiate (10 mètres) des terrains de tennis. Son inconvénient est le petit nombre des salles de bains, ce nombre étant même réduit à l'unité. Or, comme dans ce pays il n'y a pas de lavabos dans les chambres, il faut se succéder dans la dite salle de bains avec une habileté rusée dont nous avons déjà saisi les procédés. Notre chambre est tout près de cette salle de bains, et nous pouvons nous en rendre maîtres avant tous les autres — C'est d'autant plus important que les règles de vie dans notre Thélème ne sont strictes qu'en un seul point, celui des repas. Petit déjeuner pour tous à 7 h — déjeuner à midi 15 — dîner à 6 heures — Pour être à 7 h au petit déjeuner, il faut, suivant l'expression que je viens d'enseigner à mes élèves, "se manier le train" — Il faudrait voir avec quelle tête ensommeillée on arrive à la salle à manger, pour un petit déjeuner bien fait pour vous rendormir: orange, céréale, œufs au lard, toast, lait & café à volonté. Marguerite commence ses cours à 8 h — je ne fonctionne que de 10 à midi; mais l'enseignement est relativement peu de chose; ce qui compte, c'est surtout la présence de Français et leur conversation. Aussi à table sommes-nous obligés de parler et, ce qui est moins facile, de faire parler des Américains et quelques-uns en sont vraiment comiques. Il y a ici toute sorte de numéros bizarres. Il y a environ 35 ou 40 étudiants en tout, dont 5 à 6 hommes et le reste femmes. La plupart enseignent le français dans des écoles secondaires ou supérieures (qu'est-ce que ce doit être?). Le niveau, même pour l'Amérique, est des plus bas. Mais ils ont au moins tous la bonhomie et le désir d'apprendre et sont de braves gens sans grande finesse. Mes disciples les plus fervents jusqu'ici sont une dame de 55 ans, qui parle très bien le français et l'enseigne depuis longtemps à New York, et un pasteur protestant de 58 ans, qui quitte sa famille pendant 6 semaines pour venir ici rafraîchir son français. Marguerite a un disciple plus comique encore, plus jeune, mais tellement ignorant du français qu'il en est réduit à ne dire que des "oui" et des "non" de ses 24 heures, la règle étant de ne pas prononcer un seul mot d'anglais.

Rosenthal est ici, curieux de tout comme un jeune homme, acceptant tout, même la cuisine, la cuisine ordinaire américaine dont nous nous étions déshabitués et qui nous fait quelque peu maugréer, nous autres. Elle est abondante, mais monotone & peu digestible avec ses salades à la mayonnaise, ses gâteaux spongieux et ses légumes bouillis à l'eau et souvent sortis de boîtes en conserve. Il est même tout à fait "à la page" ici et j'ai été surpris de retrouver l'ancien Cœur à Vache de Louis le Grand si dégourdi. Il est vrai qu'il rencontre ici plus de respect qu'auprès de ses auditeurs de lycée français. Il est arrivé en Amérique 8 jours à l'avance pour visiter New York, Boston & Philadelphie; mais, en bon Sémite, il utilise tout ça pour des articles sur l'architecture américaine et autres sujets. Il a l'air d'avoir roulé à pied autant que le Juif errant lui-même, auquel il se compare — et, ici, il trouve tout charmant, bon et reposant. La faiblesse des étudiants & de la plupart de ses collègues, et l'aspect perdu du pays ne l'ont même pas trop déçu, et il se dit comme nous qu'il va se reposer tout en gagnant quelques dollars. Nous sommes, pour notre part, très contents qu'il soit là, car il est le seul Français intéressant. . . .

## Aux mêmes:

ce 8 juillet

. . . Le plus souvent nous sommes avec Rosenthal qui aime beaucoup parler et trouve en nous de complaisants auditeurs, car il est intéressant. Quelquefois nous assistons même à ses conférences sur les cathédrales gothiques ou sur Ingres ou Corot. C'est un moyen d'apprendre de l'histoire de l'art sans fatigue. Heureusement il ne pontifie pas et nous le traitons avec beaucoup de liberté. Il est amusant avec sa curiosité toute fraîche pour l'Amérique & tout ce qui est américain. Il ne manque pas d'esprit critique, cette qualité dont tous les Français sont si fiers. Mais il l'exerce sans excès et il ne maugrée pas sans cesse. . . . Ici, nous avons découvert une terrasse d'hôtel qui sert de café, c'est à dire qui est quelque chose de tout à fait unique en Amérique, où les cafés ne sont jamais en plein air. Inutile de dire que nous en profitons abondamment les soirs après le dîner, & que je ne fais pas autant de travail que je pensais. Du moins ce n'est pas la préparation de mes cours qui m'occupe. Mon cours d'histoire se fait à coups de Malet: il n'est d'ailleurs pas très couru—et l'autre, où j'explique des textes, n'exige de moi qu'un seul effort, celui de parler lentement. . . .

## To Henry Allen Moe:

121, High Street<br>
Yale University<br>
New Haven, Conn.<br>
November 9—1929

Dear Sir:

I should be very grateful to you if you could send me some information on the Guggenheim fellowships, the conditions one must fulfill in order to apply for them, and the date for sending in all applications.

Could you also tell me if, although not being yet an American citizen, I could apply for a Guggenheim fellowship with any chance of success? I have done up to now, and I am going to do, all my teaching career in American universities. I was for three years assistant-professor of French at Bryn Mawr College, and this is my second year as assistant-professor of French in the Graduate School of Yale University. I have written several articles in the scholarly reviews of America and I should now very much want, if I could afford it with the help of some fellowship, to spend a year in Europe collecting material for a book of some length which I intend to publish soon. That book is a study in the field of French literary history, at which I have been working for the past three or four years.

Yours very sincerely,<br>
Henri Peyre<br>
Prof. H. Peyre

## To Henry Allen Moe:

216, Bishop St.<br>
New Haven, Conn.<br>
November 14 — 1929

Mr. H. A. Moe
Secretary of Guggenheim Memorial Foundation.
551, Fifth Avenue.
Dear Sir:

I am sending at once my application for a Guggenheim fellowship for the year 1930–31. If further information were necessary I shall be at your disposal to give it, to write for other references, etc.

I hope the Committee may consider my application favorably, although I have lived for years in France myself and may not need the foreign experience, the contact with foreign scholarship, in the same sense as native-born Americans may. I feel that foreign professors resident in this country are seriously handicapped, in their advanced work of research, by the lack of first-hand material on foreign literatures (Manuscripts, original documents, etc.), with the result that they become discouraged and often give up all original research which may partly explain why the level of scholarship in French literary history, for instance, is not, in this country, what it should be.

Very sincerely yours,<br>
Henri Peyre<br>
Prof. H. Peyre

## To the John Simon Guggenheim Memorial Foundation

(Statement of application for a fellowship)

a) I was born in France and am not yet, though I intend to be, an American citizen. But I am a permanent resident of this country, to which I came in Sept.1925, to fill a teaching position which I had been previously offered. I have done up to now, and I intend to do all my teaching career in America.

b) Before I came to this country, I published a few articles in France and translated several volumes, both from French into English and from English into French. As a student at the École Normale Supérieure, I wrote my dissertation for the Diplôme d'études Supérieures on "some aspects of pessimism in French and English poetry, 1850–80." Part of that dissertation was published in the *Revue Anglo-Américaine,* Dec.1924 and febr.1925. My work was conducted under Professors Lanson and Cazamian, both of the Sorbonne.

In this country, I have taken as a subject for my research Louis Ménard and have worked at it for four years. In the meantime, I did also some other research in French literary history and published a dozen articles on several topics. I have not studied under any American professor, as I had already all my degrees when I came here.

In my proposed field of study, I have part of my book already fairly advanced, but I have now to wait until I can devote several months to the study of Manuscripts and private papers recently given to the *Bibliothèque Nationale* in Paris.

c) List of Publications.

1) Translations.
   J. G. Frazer. *Atys et Osiris,* traduit par H. Peyre.
   Geuthner (Paris), 1928, 306p.

J. G. Frazer. *Tabou ou les périls de l'âme,* traduit par H. Peyre
Geuthner (Paris), 1927, 446p.

J. Poux. *The City of Carcassonne,* translated into English by H. Peyre.
Privat (Toulouse), 1928, 262p.

2) Articles in American publications.
In *Modern Language Notes,* Johns Hopkins Press, Baltimore
1927 Febr. p. 135 sq.
1927 Nov. p. 486 sq.
1928 Jan. p. 71.
1929 Febr. p. 124 sq.
—March. p. 196 sq.
—Nov. p. 447 sq.
in *The Dial,* New York.
May 1928, p. 377–384
in *University of California Chronicle,* Berkeley, Cal.
July 1928, p. 326–336
in *Publications of Modern Language Association of America.*
March 1929, p. 288–308
in *Romanic Review,* Columbia University.
March 1929, p. 131–136

To appear shortly, an article on "Racine et la critique contemporaine."

In *Publications of Modern Language Association,* and an article on G. Duhamel, in *The French Review* (New York).

I read scholarly papers at the meetings of the *Modern Language Association of America* in 1927, at Cambridge, Mass.—in 1928 at Louisville, Ky.—and in 1929 at Toronto, Ont.—

## PLANS FOR STUDY

If granted a fellowship, I should spend about twelve months gathering material on my subject.

1) The subject I am studying, Louis Ménard, although until recently still neglected, is an important topic in XIX*th* century literature. The man was a poet, a prose-writer and a philosopher of rare value and originality. Nothing of much importance has ever been published on him, for all the manuscripts, unpublished papers, letters, etc., of Ménard had disappeared.

I succeeded in discovering the owners of those papers last summer (1929) and after much negotiation they agreed to give everything to the manuscript department of the Bibliothèque Nationale, Paris, with the clause that I alone could utilize them until January 1, 1931. Unfortunately I had to be back to my position at Yale and could not avail myself of that opportunity. As I cannot afford to go back to Europe for some time, or to take a year off at my own expense, I am afraid that the facilities thus granted me will be wasted, and that somebody else may, in 1931, utilize those manuscripts. There are, among these papers, letters of Renan, Michelet, Fustel de Coulanges, L. Blanc, M. Barrès; a subject, if secondary [to my project], touches almost every aspect of French literary history of the XIXth century.

The book I intend to complete, when I can make further use of the material in Paris, will be a volume of about 400 or 500 pages. I believe it will throw much light on several aspects of the XIXth century in France, and will be a precise contribution to our knowledge of that important and complex period.

I am including several letters: two (nos. 1 and 2) from the person who gave the papers in question to the Bibliothèque Nationale, with the clause in my favor; a third (no. 3) from the publisher Éd. Champion, who wrote a book on the subject of L. Ménard and is said to possess documents on the topic; two others (nos. 4 and 5) from well-known French professors who approve of my working on that subject and would give me valuable advice.

2) I have now gathered all the material and done all the reading that can be gathered or done in this country. I have written part of my proposed work and I shall be glad to send that part for examination, to the members of the Committee. However, I have now to wait until I can complete my documentation in the French libraries.

3) I should not follow courses in any foreign university, but do my research in the libraries. I expect to have the advice of Professors Lanson, Mornet and Cohen of the Sorbonne.

4) I expect to publish the results of my research as early as I can after my year of study abroad, almost certainly at the end of 1931.

5) My ultimate purpose is to continue my teaching career in this country, to interpret French literature to American students, and to pursue research in the field of literary history.

# the 1930s

## CHAPTER TWO

**To Henry Allan Moe:**

216, Bishop St.
New Haven, Conn.
April 15, 1930

Dear Mr. Moe:

I am very much obliged for your letter and the information about the cable address of the Foundation. I am sending here the information for the annual report.

PEYRE, Henri, Maurice. Appointed for the continuation of researches in France on Louis Ménard, a Frenchman of letters of the XIXth century, and the completing of a work on that subject.

Born Feb. 21, 1901 at Paris, France. Education: Lycée Louis le Grand, Paris, Sorbonne and École Normale Supérieure, University of Cambridge. Degrees: Baccalauréat ès Lettres—Philosophie, 1917–8, Licence ès Lettres, 1922, Diplôme d'Études Supérieures, 1923, and Agrégation, 1924, Sorbonne.

Lecturer and associate in French, Bryn Mawr College, 1925–28; Assistant-Professor of French, Yale University, 1928—Visiting Professor, Summer 1930, University of Chicago.

PUBLICATIONS: Translated, into French J.G. Frazer's *Attis and Osiris,* 1926, and *Taboo,* 1927; into English, J. Poux's *The City of Caracassonne,* 1926. Published articles in *Revue Anglo-Américaine, Modern Language Notes, Publications of Modern Language Association of America, The Dial, University of California Chronicle, The Romanic Review, The French Review.*

Yours very sincerely,<br>Henri Peyre

## To the same:

Paris, Sept. 25—1930

My dear Mr. Moe:

I have got settled in Paris and I have started working satisfactorily. My address will be as follows: 8, rue du Val de Grâce, Paris (v).

Yours very sincerely,<br>Henri Peyre<br>Prof. Henri Peyre<br>C/o American Express Co.<br>1 rue Scribe—Paris

## To the same:

August 15—1931

Dear Mr. Moe:

I am replying at once to your letter of July 27th, and taking the opportunity to express again my deep gratitude to the Trustees of the Guggenheim Foundation. I have been able to accomplish my work very satisfactorily, & I am taking some rest for the last three weeks of my fellowship—I shall sail for the U.S. early in September & resume my academic work at Yale University. The work I was able to prepare & to write this year is now at the printer's. It will include two volumes in 8vo, of 550 & 200 pages respectively. Yale has granted me the necessary funds for publication: those two books will be printed by Didot in France & be published by the Yale Press. They are to come out next

June—I shall send you a copy of each as soon as I have them; in a prefatory note, I acknowledge the help given me by the Guggenheim Foundation.

I have nothing to mention for the Report under the item "Appointments, promotions, honors." I have published several articles in learned American journals, which are not directly the result of the work I undertook for my fellowship. However, I suppose you may mention them if you think advisable to do so: e.g. H. *Peyre*. "Racine et la critique contemporaine," P.M.L.A. (Publications of the Modern Language Association), sept. 1930, vol. LXV, no. 3, p. 848–856; "Pascal et la critique contemporaine," *Romanic Review*, vol. XXI, Oct. dec. 1930, p. 325–340; "Baudelaire devant la critique actuelle," *Modern Philology*, vol. 28, no. 2, november 1930, p. 221–229; and several book reviews in the *Yale Review*, *Modern Philology*, etc.

I am sorry I cannot just now send you reprints of these articles. I am traveling, for rest, far from my notes & from my typewriter. I shall be glad to send you more details as to the work I did this year when I reach the States, if you wish me to do so.

Yours very sincerely,
Henri Peyre

## À Pierre Bédard:

Yale University
New Haven, Conn.
Ce 7 nov. 1932

Cher Monsieur:

Je vous remercie infiniment de votre lettre. Je crois bien en effet que la lettre en question, par laquelle vous m'avisiez que vous me recommandiez au Ministère, a dû s'égarer. Je recevais mon courrier, cet été, par les soins de l'American Express, et il y avait un désordre indescriptible dans cette maison, si bien que j'ai perdu ainsi plusieurs lettres. Je m'excuse donc de n'avoir pu vous remercier de votre si aimable démarche. Je sais qu'une lettre de votre part aurait grand poids auprès des bureaux compétents à Paris, et c'est pourquoi je m'étais permis de vous demander ce service. Je ne doute pas qu'on n'attache l'importance voulue à cette recommandation de l'Institut, quand on examinera mon dossier.

Veuillez donc accepter, cher Monsieur, l'expression de mes remerciements très vifs, et croire à mon bon souvenir.

Hri Peyre

## À Charles Du Bos:

Graduate School<br>
Yale University—New Haven (Conn.)<br>
Ce 26 novembre 1932

Monsieur & cher Maître,

Puis-je me permettre de m'adresser à vous comme à celui de nos contemporains qui a parlé avec le plus de pénétration et d'amour de la poésie anglaise, à celui que beaucoup d'entre nous, vos jeunes admirateurs inconnus, saluons comme notre plus profond critique?

Je suis professeur détaché à l'Université de Yale (U.S.A.) & je prépare un ouvrage sur *Shelley et la France,* dans lequel je me propose de suivre de près les lents progrès de la fortune de Shelley en France, son influence à l'époque symboliste, et de déterminer enfin quelle place ce "poète des poètes" anglais occupe aujourd'hui, dans l'affection des connaisseurs français de poésie anglaise. Je ne manquerai pas, bien entendu, d'attacher la plus grande valeur aux pages que vous avez consacrées à Shelley, çà & là, dans les *Approximations,* et récemment dans *Vigile,* et le *Roseau d'Or*—Il me serait fort précieux d'obtenir de vous quelques autres précisions, et, si vous ne jugez pas mes questions trop indiscrètes, pourrais-je me permettre de vous demander par exemple: Comment vous avez découvert la poésie shelleyenne? si c'est par Shelley que vous avez abordé la poésie anglaise, ou si vous n'êtes venu à lui qu'après Byron, ou Keats, par exemple?—Si votre goût pour Shelley a quelque peu évolué et si vous vous êtes détaché, dans une certaine mesure, de ce lyrisme trop éthéré & trop immatériel, pour lui préférer la poésie plus humaine d'un Goethe, les odes plus artistes de Keats ou les vers plus profondément douloureux de Baudelaire.—Avez-vous constaté aussi, parmi d'autres écrivains ou penseurs contemporains, ou même parmi des "amis inconnus" du poète, qui n'ont rien écrit, une influence réelle du lyrisme shelleyen, et croyez-vous que cette influence ait été vraiment importante en France depuis le symbolisme?—Enfin, si je puis ajouter une question plus délicate encore, mais que je dois poser sans cesse dans mon livre, et essayer de résoudre, quels sont les éléments de la poésie shelleyenne qui vous paraissent les plus différents du génie français, qui manquaient justement à notre poésie jusqu'à ce que, tandis que se développait parallèlement chez nous la connaissance de Shelley, nos poètes de la fin du XIXe siècle nous aient enfin donné comme un équivalent du lyrisme anglais?

Je m'excuse encore une fois d'avoir aussi indiscrètement recours à votre obligeance. Peut-être croirez-vous pouvoir répondre à mes questions sans inconvénient et sans trop grande perte de temps. Je vous remercie d'avance, cher Maître, en vous assurant de ma reconnaissance la plus profonde et de ma vive admiration.

> Henri Peyre
> (Prof. Henri Peyre
> Professeur à Yale University
> Ancien Élève de l'École Normale
> Agrégé & Docteur ès Lettres)

## À son frère:

> 216 Bishop St.
> New Haven (Conn.)
> Ce 3 jan. 33

Mon Cher Jacques,

... Notre plus récent ennui, dans cet ordre d'idées, a consisté dans des troubles dentaires, qui ont nécessité de longues & fréquentes visites — Cela sans gravité pour notre santé, et seulement pour notre bourse.

À part ça, ce dont nous nous plaignons le plus est l'ennui, la monotonie de la vie, & l'imbécillité incurable de la plupart des gens que le sort nous fait rencontrer. Il semble difficile pour nous de nous faire des relations agréables dans cette ville, que nous avons fini par prendre en grippe. La seule ressource est de travailler — mais encore faut-il travailler avec 1 but. Autrefois, c'était pour ma thèse, & l'avancement que j'espérais en récolter. Mais les avancements sont arrêtés par la crise, & par la jalousie ou l'incompréhension de mesquins collègues; et l'avenir ne s'annonce pas souriant. Les choses continuent à aller assez mal, & ne promettent pas d'aller mieux. La vie a baissé sensiblement, mais les gens n'achètent guère et se restreignent. Les chômeurs sont légion, même dans les professions comme la nôtre; et ils sont encore patients en ce moment, mais il faut bien tôt ou tard arriver à leur donner des secours officiels, & ce sera alors un nouveau trou dans le budget! En attendant, les réductions de traitement s'annoncent. Mais c'est la même histoire dans tous les pays. La vérité est que ces misères matérielles ne nous seraient pas autrement graves, (car il y a des gens à famille nombreuse autrement malheureux que nous) si le marasme, la mauvaise humeur générale, ne rendaient la vie si déplaisante—L'affaire des dettes est déjà à demi-oubliée; elle n'a pas accru notre popularité, mais cela ne nous nuit guère, car on respecte davantage ici les gens à culot que les moules toujours prêtes à accabler les Américains de compliments & de flatteries. Il n'est guère possible que les Américains (à part une petite élite) ne nous aiment beaucoup; leurs qualités sont trop différentes des nôtres, et même leur mentalité; mais qu'importe?

Notre hiver a été froid jusqu'ici. Mais, n'étant guère friands de promenades, nous le passons le plus souvent chez nous, à lire, discuter ou flâner. Nous n'avons pas bougé d'ici pendant nos vacances; seul le cinéma (d'ailleurs de plus en plus médiocre & vulgaire) nous a fait [*quelques mots illisibles*]. Un Congrès de Professeurs de langues modernes a amené à New Haven une foule de gens de toutes les parties de l'Amérique, parmi lesquels quelques amis. J'ai lu au cours des débats deux communications sur des sujets d'histoire littéraire, et je me prépare maintenant à faire 1 série de conférences publiques sur la litt. contemporaine. Tout cela ne rapporte rien ou presque; mais ça m'exerce à la parole publique. Nous commençons donc l'année, non sans lassitude devant la monotonie et la demie (sic) solitude de notre vie ici, mais en parfaite santé & avec l'espoir impatient de voir bientôt survenir les vacances d'été, & la traversée de l'océan vers les rives françaises.

Et toi? Comment va la pratique en ces temps de crise? Et la conduite de la maison qui t'incombe seul désormais? Et ton auto? Merci toujours pour les journaux que tu continues à nous envoyer. Merci aussi pour m'avoir indiqué ce prix de thèses de *Candide;* mais, tant que tu y étais, que ne l'as-tu fait avec plus de hâte?!?!? Ces choses là demandent à ce que l'on cuisine un peu les membres du jury & je suis pas mal handicapé à avoir à le faire par lettre. Je ne nourris donc pas d'espoir, d'autant que mon livre, ayant paru en Amérique, intéresse forcément beaucoup moins éditeurs & libraires de France; et il y a toujours des cuisines d'éditeurs derrière ces prix littéraires. Ça a dû d'ailleurs être décerné depuis longtemps maintenant. . . .

**Au même:**
New Haven, ce 6 février 1933

Mon cher Jacques,

. . . Ce qui nous pèse le plus est la monotonie de toutes choses ici: par ex. de la nourriture, sans rien, ni liqueurs, ni gâteaux; peu de choix de légumes; un régime dont on finit par se dégoûter, surtout quand il faut faire soi-même ses 2 repas par jour pour 2 personnes seulement. Dehors, les restaurants sont infects; la ville est sale & triste—et nous n'avons que très peu de bonnes connaissances, que nous ayons plaisir à voir souvent. Après plusieurs années ici, nous ne nous plaisons pas davantage—au contraire—en partie, parce que les inconvénients s'accentuent, l'ennui, la demi-solitude font boule de neige & pèsent davantage—en partie, parce que l'esprit & les conditions ont changé: un peu contre les Français, mais cela nous touche peu; plutôt avec le marasme & le découragement général qu'a causés cette crise—L'égoïsme, la mesquinerie de chacun ressortent beaucoup mieux—surtout chez les Américains qui, peu habitués à souffrir, ont besoin d'un optimisme un peu naïf et se sentent désemparés dès que ça ne va plus.

Enfin, pour toutes ces raisons, nous nous décidons en ce moment à re-tenter de l'Europe. Après bien des réflexions, vu le peu d'intérêt de notre vie ici, l'ennui qui nous pèse beaucoup, (surtout pour Marguerite, qui n'a guère de distraction après son travail, tandis que mon travail à moi m'occupe même aux heures de loisir, à lire, etc.—), & aussi, comme je n'ai pas réussi ici à faire apprécier mon doctorat & à me faire augmenter, j'ai demandé pour l'an prochain une année de congé—nous essaierons ainsi de la France—Je demanderai une position de Faculté, (si j'en puis obtenir une, ce que j'espère, sans pouvoir en être sûr) & nous verrons comment nous nous réhabituerons. Evidemment, au point de vue argent seul, nous y perdrons. Mais si le milieu nous paraît plus sympathique, la vie plus variée & un peu plus gaie (tant qu'on est encore jeune), les gens moins étroits, cela vaudrait la peine. Enfin, c'est à voir. Ici, après 5 ans de Yale & 8 ans d'Amérique, ayant beaucoup travaillé & beaucoup écrit, il faudrait que j'avance considérablement & vite, pour que cela vaille la peine de s'expatrier. Or il y a la crise—et il y a surtout les jalousies de collègues: des abrutis qui ont peur que je les dépasse & que je leur enlève leurs chances d'avancement, qui sont un peu jaloux parce que je brille plus facilement qu'eux, qui sont incapables de dire dix mots en public sans bafouiller. Enfin, cela se rencontre dans tous les métiers—mais surtout ici, envers les étrangers, et en ce moment où chacun a tellement peur de perdre sa place qu'il en fait dans ses culottes!

Dans tous les cas, si je ne reviens pas à Yale, je me suis fait assez connaître en Amérique pour avoir plus tard quelques chances d'arriver à une bonne position ailleurs, dans une autre université américaine, quand je serai un peu plus âgé, & que cette crise sera atténuée, ou sera devenue l'état de choses normal. . . .

## À Paul Claudel:

> Yale University
> New Haven, Conn.
> le 27 février 1933

Son Excellence Monsieur l'Ambassadeur de France
French Embassy
Washington, D.C.
Monsieur l'Ambassadeur—et Cher Maître,

Je me suis empressé de répondre, affirmativement, à votre télégramme me demandant, aujourd'hui même, si j'étais disposé à accepter la succession de M. Carré, comme professeur de littérature française à l'Institut français du Caire. Ma candidature avait en effet été proposée au Ministère des Affaires Étrangères pour ce poste, et j'avais été en correspondance avec M. Carré à ce sujet. Puis-je me permettre de vous demander si le Ministère a voulu dire, par la question qu'il vous a prié de me poser, que ma candidature avait été acceptée, ou s'il ne s'agit que de renseignements généraux et préliminaires. Mon impatience vient de la nécessité où je vais me trouver d'annoncer à Yale ma démission, si je dois m'engager pour trois ans à assurer au Caire la succession de M. Carré.

Puis-je me permettre, Monsieur l'Ambassadeur, de saisir cette occasion pour vous poser, dans un ordre d'idées tout différent, une question à laquelle vous voudrez peut-être bien répondre lorsque les pressants soucis de votre charge laisseront quelque loisir au poète et au critique? Je compose en ce moment un ouvrage sur SHELLEY ET LA FRANCE, ou plutôt, en prenant Shelley comme type du lyrisme anglais le plus pur, j'essaie de suivre en France l'évolution même de la notion de poésie, d'expliquer pourquoi les lecteurs de Lamartine, de Victor Hugo, de Vigny, n'étaient pas prêts, en France, à sentir ou à comprendre le lyrisme shelleyen; pourquoi, au contraire, grâce à cet immense élargissement et approfondissement de la notion de lyrisme, que nous devons à Baudelaire, à Rimbaud, et aux poètes de la fin du XIXe siècle et du début du XXe, la compréhension de Shelley nous est aujourd'hui si grandement facilitée.

Vous savez quelle admiration je professe pour votre œuvre de critique et de poète. Je ne manque pas d'utiliser dans mon ouvrage les pénétrantes suggestions de vos *Positions et Propositions,* et j'emprunte à plusieurs reprises à l'*Arbre,* au *Cantique du Rhône,* et à d'autres encore de vos ouvrages, des exemples de ce lyrisme "élémental," cosmique qui n'existait point, ou presque point, en français, avant Rimbaud, quelques tentatives de Verhaeren (malheureusement terriblement diffuses et gâchées), et votre œuvre poétique et dramatique. Il n'est nullement de mon intention, bien entendu, de rechercher là une influence de Shelley. Mais il me serait très précieux de savoir par vous-même si vous pensez que l'exemple de la poésie anglaise a servi, à un moment donné, de stimulant ou de modèle à votre inspiration. Peut-être voudrez-vous bien me dire à quel moment et par quels poètes, vous avez fait la connaissance du lyrisme anglais? si votre curiosité a été attirée vers l'œuvre de Shelley, lors de vos brefs séjours à Paris, par Mallarmé, par Marcel Schwob, par exemple, ou tel autre des poètes qui semblent alors l'avoir connu? si ce lyrisme anglais vous a séduit, de préférence à la poésie romantique française, et si vous croyez devoir quelque chose à ses modèles — et dans ce cas, serait-ce à Blake, à Fr. Thompson, (sans parler de Shakespeare) que serait allée votre admiration plus qu'à Shelley par exemple, ou à Coleridge ou Keats?

Veuillez me pardonner ces questions, sans doute indiscrètes et importunes. Cela doit saisir d'un frisson de dégoût, que de songer aux thèses futures où sera péremptoirement démontrée l'influence biblique, l'influence chinoise, l'influence japonaise, l'influence américaine, sur votre œuvre! Je voudrais, du moins, s'il y a quelque rapport véritable entre votre lyrisme et le lyrisme anglais, le préciser en connaissance de cause —

c'est-à-dire avec l'approbation du principal intéressé. Il est certains vers de TETE D'OR QUE je sais par cœur depuis mon adolescence, et que je n'ai jamais pu me réciter sans songer à certains passages de Shelley (surtout dans *Alastor*).

> Le froid matin violet
> Glisse sur les plaines éloignées, teignant
> Chaque ornière de sa magie. . . .
> Le jour blafard éclaire la boue des chemins
> Et, sous les haies, les feuilles de choux et les fleurs
> Versent sur la terre jaune leur charge de pluie.

Non certes que je croie déceler là une influence inexistante—mais, ce qui est d'ailleurs bien plus curieux, une affinité cachée. Sans doute jugerez-vous que je me trompe. . . .

En vous priant de me pardonner ces questions importunes, je vous prie d'agréer, Monsieur l'Ambassadeur, mes remerciements les plus profonds, et l'expression de mes hommages respectueux, et de mon admiration toujours fervente.

Henri Peyre

## Aux siens:

Mailly—ce samedi soir 12 août (1933)

Cher Papa chère Louise & chère Lélène,

Je pense que ce mot vous trouvera encore à votre adresse précédente. Avec la chaleur persistante, il ne doit pas être très tentant de reprendre le chemin de fer & mieux vaut rester auprès de la mer "battue par les orages." Je vous envie sans cesse—autant pour la fraîcheur des bains que pour la purification qu'ils apportent. Mon unique uniforme est si souvent trempé de sueur qu'il en garde des odeurs persistantes—et je n'ai pas encore eu la joie de me laver à l'eau chaude de 15 jours. Vous avez dû continuer à voir de belles choses: Tréguier, Perros-Guirec, etc. Quelles sont vos impressions sur ces paysages, sur les habitants, les hôtels & la nourriture? La dernière carte de Papa était sobre de détails. C'est encore la faute de cette Action Française qui lui prend les loisirs laissés par le nettoyage des pipes—Et vos bains? Lélène nage-t-elle, ou pêche-t-elle crevettes & crabes?

De mon côté, la santé va—le moral aussi, une fois les habitudes prises. Cette semaine aura été la plus dure. La prochaine sera raccourcie par les vacances du 14 & 15 août—et après ce sera presque fini. Je pousserai un soupir de soulagement—& j'irai à mon tour me plonger dans la Méditerranée. Pourvu que le temps, qui s'obstine à rester au beau & au sec, ne change pas alors trop complètement! Le fait est, de l'avis de tous, qu'on nous a fait barder pas mal—en partie, à cause des bruits de guerre de l'hiver dernier, pour assurer une préparation efficace à la campagne—en partie, me dit-on, parce que nous sommes ici la division de Paris—et qu'on veut faire rattraper à cette division, dans le séjour au camp, les manœuvres qu'elle ne fait pas l'année, étant prise par défilés, revues, etc. À deux reprises, nous avons fait cette semaine des marches de nuit, de minuit à 10h du matin. Ce n'était pas laid, par pleine lune—avec la fraîcheur de l'aube, les oiseaux chantant vers 4 heures, tous les cris des chats-huants. Mais on a peu de temps pour la contemplation esthétique de la nature: on est obligé de penser au paysage en militaire, c'est-à-dire d'"utiliser le terrain," de placer les mitrailleuses, de faire creuser les abris, camoufler les hommes, etc. Le métier de lieutenant est le plus dur, parce qu'au lieu de se reposer une fois arrivé, comme les soldats, il faut courir des uns aux autres, les stimuler, les presser, les diriger. On ne s'assied guère du matin jusqu'à midi.

Ce matin, nous avons fait une manœuvre de grand style, devant le Gal Gouraud & quelques grands chefs. J'étais en avant-garde avec ma section, et j'ai filé à l'assaut avec tellement d'entrain, m'a-t-on dit, que je me suis égaré en plein dans la zone ennemie. C'est à la fois drôle, & tragique si l'on pense que dans la réalité il y aurait blessés et morts. Pour le moment, on se contente de suer, de se couvrir de poussière, & de pester contre la soif & la chaleur.

Demain, dimanche, je suis obligé de rester comme officier de jour de ma compagnie—mais je partirai en permission lundi & mardi. J'irai tout bonnement à Paris, pour changer d'air, me reposer, me laver et reprendre le contact avec la vie civilisée.

Si l'on n'était pas si occupé, il y aurait de bons moments. J'ai quelques bons camarades—et même les relations avec les hommes sont agréables. Ils rouspètent un peu, mais ils marchent très bien—et, mieux avec nous, les officiers de réserve, qui savons mieux les prendre—Les officiers d'active sont vraiment trop raides et distants avec eux—et il y a, parmi ces officiers, une forte proportion d'imbéciles ou de froussards, qui tremblent devant leurs supérieurs.

Quant au reste, tout va—mes pieds sont guéris. J'ai pris le parti de mettre 2 paires de chaussettes l'une sur l'autre, & encore, très épaisses. Ça protège mieux contre les chocs. Car on marche, non sur route, mais sur des pistes, ou sous des bois, à la boussole. La nourriture continue à être abondante, quoique médiocre. Mais on boit avidement—et on rattrape ainsi, et au delà, ce que l'on perd en sueur.

J'ai des nouvelles de Jacques & de Marguerite, qui était repartie chez sa sœur et va retourner ces jours-ci sur la Côte d'Azur. À part quelques lettres, je m'assieds rarement à ma table pour écrire—et encore moins pour lire. Comme on est 15 ou 20 lieutenants dans le bâtiment, on est d'ailleurs sans cesse dérangé par les visites des camarades qui veulent blaguer ou boire un coup. La solitude & l'intimité sont ce qui manque le plus à la vie militaire. Ça a d'ailleurs du bon, & ça fait mieux apprécier les avantages d'une profession indépendante & libre comme la nôtre—et plus encore, la position enviable d'un professeur en retraite, voyageant avec sa fille & sa petite-fille.

Grosses caresses à vous tous—et encore vœux de bon voyage,

Henri

## À son frère:

6 rue Walda Pacha
Garden City
Le Caire
Ce 10 jan./34

Mon cher Jacques,

. . . Quant à nous, il y aurait tant à dire sur notre nouveau pays & notre nouveau milieu, & l'on devient ici si peu énergique en matière épistolaire, qu'on réserve paresseusement le plus gros pour les vacances d'été.

Nous sommes déjà très bien habitués à notre vie—malgré la rigueur du climat—car, quelque peine qu'on ait à le croire, on a froid ici. On n'a aucun moyen de chauffage: ni cheminée ni poêle dans les maisons,

&, certains jours, on le sent! — Certes, nous n'avons pas connu les rigueurs de votre vague de froid. Mais, vers Noël, la température est tombée à 2º un jour, &, sans feu, cela fait frissonner. En général, nous allons de 20 à 12º, 10º comme minimum ordinaire, ce qui est en somme supportable. Et, sauf rares exceptions, le soleil, au milieu du jour, procure une douce chaleur réchauffante. Surtout, on n'a, par ailleurs, nullement l'impression de l'hiver. Les arbres sont toujours couverts de feuillage, toute la campagne reverdit en ce moment, à la suite des inondations fertilisatrices du Nil. On joue aux sports, on sort en veston, au milieu du jour. Cela rajeunit, car on se croit toujours à une douce fin d'automne. Et les moindres promenades contribuent encore à vous faire sentir votre jeunesse, en vous mettant en présence de monuments plusieurs fois millénaires, de coutumes & de mœurs non moins antiques. Nous allons souvent aux Pyramides, qui sont à 15 kils du Caire, & d'où l'on contemple des couchers de soleil splendides sur le désert. Il faut te dire que nous avons acquis une auto — une jolie Ford, à deux places & un siège arrière confortable, d'occasion, mais état de neuf, modèle 1933, vieille seulement de 5.000 kilomètres. Nous avons pris quelques leçons, & conduisons maintenant en maîtres, avec prudence cependant, car le Caire, avec ses quartiers fourmillant de petits Arabes, ses rues étroites, sa circulation mal réglée, est, nous disent nos amis, plus difficile que Paris. Nous jouissons aussi plus de la campagne, de la lumière & de la vie en général qu'en Amérique, où le travail absorbait toutes nos énergies. Il faut dire que le travail ici s'en ressent, au moins pour moi qui n'ai pas le temps de rien faire pour moi. Mais il vaut mieux faire provisions de sensations nouvelles que de connaissances livresques.

Ces jours-ci, du 12 au 15, après la fin de Ramadan, nous allons avoir nos vacances & nous entreprendrons sans doute 1 voyage en Haute-Egypte, jusqu'à Louksor & Assouan, à 1.000 kilomètres du Caire. Il y a là, paraît-il, de très belles ruines de l'Egypte ancienne, & de magnifiques paysages, tout le long du Nil & du désert. Malheureusement, ces voyages, qu'entreprennent en général les riches touristes anglais & américains, sont fort coûteux — tandis que la vie, ici-même, n'est pas trop chère. À part cela, nous ne sommes sortis du Caire, jusqu'ici, que pour quelques excursions aux environs, et pour aller à Alexandrie & Port-Saïd, villes où j'ai donné des conférences.

Ma carrière de conférencier se poursuit en effet. J'épuise même mon stock, car les gens sont très friands ici de conférences, & j'ai dû en donner beaucoup pour répondre à diverses demandes — sur divers sujets de littérature contemporaine, en particulier. Le public accourt en foule: français, italien, juif, et quelques égyptiens proprement dits, ceux-ci toujours les moins nombreux, car ces grandes villes (Alexandrie, le Caire) sont au moins autant européennes qu'égyptiennes.

Nous connaissons aussi déjà beaucoup de monde, & les invitations à déjeuner, dîner, ou thé, pleuvent. On y gaspille même trop d'heures précieuses, sans compter qu'ici il faut se mettre en smoking, & même en habit, pour un rien. D'où toilettes, etc. L'année prochaine, quand nous serons mieux connus ici, et que nous connaîtrons mieux, nous espérons conserver un peu plus de temps libre, Marguerite pour les sports, moi pour la lecture & la réflexion. En attendant, le temps passe vite. La plupart des gens de la société sont d'ailleurs gentils & distingués, et sont dans la banque, le Suez, etc., donc en dehors de l'Université. Cela nous change aussi de l'Amérique, où l'on ne fréquentait guère que des professeurs. Quant à l'Université, elle est imposante par ses bâtiments et par ses règlements. Mais les professeurs européens ne la prennent guère au sérieux. Ils voient là un excellent moyen, avec quelques heures par semaine d'enseignement facile, de tirer de. . . .

L'autre jour, j'ai été présenté au Roi, avec tout un cérémonial et en costume de rigueur: longue redingote et tarbouche. Le Roi n'est pas, semble-t-il, très aimé de son peuple; mais il est soutenu par une forte police, une administration servile, et appuyé par les Anglais. Au reste, il paraît intelligent, et il a l'habileté de se faire accorder la plus haute liste civile d'aucun souverain d'Europe — Ici, chacun doit le flatter quelque peu, tous les livres lui sont dédiés avec compliments flatteurs. Pour un français, cela paraît amusant: on se croirait reporté au temps de Louis XIV. . . .

## Au même:

Ce 6 mars 1934

. . . Le climat a beaucoup de charme — cependant nous n'y sommes pas encore accoutumés au point d'oublier les plaisirs d'une bonne averse de temps en temps, ou de ce printemps qui, chez nous, doit, ces jours-ci, faire tout fleurir, reverdir & embaumer. La plupart des Français que nous voyons sont très habitués à l'Egypte, & éprouvent par exemple un délice à faire des randonnées en auto dans le désert—sur des pistes innombrables—car les routes vraies sont rares en Egypte. Nous sommes encore un peu réfractaires. Une immense étendue de sable & de rochers est belle—mais des arbres, de la verdure, des sources, cela serait bien beau aussi. Je ne dirais pas non plus que nous soyons emballés par l'art arabe ou la couleur locale. La nouveauté s'émousse vite—et on voit alors tout ce qui se cache de routine, de saleté, de superstition, d'inertie mentale, chez les Arabes—tout ce que les relations avec eux exigent de précaution, de diplomatie, de méfiance—Mais tout ceci ne nous empêche pas de nous y plaire—pour quelque temps. J'ai relativement peu à faire—et je travaille d'ailleurs beaucoup moins qu'en Amérique. Nous voyons beaucoup de gens agréables—nous nous promenons—Marguerite améliore encore (si c'est possible) sa compétence au tennis—et notre santé se maintient florissante.

Nous avons enfin roulé 3 ou 4.000 kms sans avoir un seul accident et nous sommes des automobilistes prudents, mais satisfaits et même rapides. Nous conduisons l'un ou l'autre suivant les moments et les humeurs. Si, comme probable, nous emmenons notre Ford en France, tu nous verras sillonner les campagnes provençales avec dextérité. Il n'y a qu'un inconvénient: c'est que ces Ford coûtent cher d'essence, & sont bigrement dures à démarrer par les temps froids. Nous y avons usé une batterie le mois dernier.

Ma lettre n'est pas entièrement désintéressée—Elle vise d'abord à susciter de ta part une réponse prompte, détaillée, sur ta vie et tes œuvres—Elle t'adresse aussi une demande d'envoi. Veux-tu bien chercher dans mes livres les 3 suivants, & me les faire parvenir par les soins dévoués de Cécile: tu me rendras service, car je manque ici d'instruments de travail, & ces 3 volumes me seront utiles:

1. Chevrillon. *Études anglaises*. livre relié en marron, un peu plus gros que le format ordinaire Hachette—doit être dans la *bibliothèque de ton cabinet*—sinon, dans ma chambre, lettre C.

2. Rabbe. *Shelley, vie et œuvres*. broché, jaune, vieilli—dans la bibliothèque de *ma chambre*, près de la lettre S. (les livres y sont plus ou moins en ordre alphabétique).

3. Ch. Du Bos. *Approximations*.

1 volume broché blanc, doit être dans ton cabinet—mais je n'en suis pas très sûr—

Mille mercis d'avance—et mille caresses et affections de nous deux.

Henri

## À Charles Du Bos:

Combloux (Hte Savoie)
Ce 4 sept. 1934

Monsieur,

M. Sencourt, dont je suis le collègue à l'Université Egyptienne, m'avait parlé l'an dernier déjà de son projet de vous inviter à venir faire au Caire quelques conférences. Je suis, de longue date, un admirateur inconnu de vos livres, & je l'avais, au nom de la section de français, vivement engagé à insister auprès de vous. Je sais quel stimulant & quel enrichissement mes collègues & moi, nos étudiants, & la partie la meilleure de notre public "mondain," trouverons dans vos causeries. C'est donc avec un grand plaisir que j'apprends que vous avez accepté de venir, & je me permets de vous écrire pour vous souhaiter, d'avance, la bienvenue & vous dire avec quelle impatience j'attendrai pour ma part cette occasion de faire votre connaissance—J'aurais voulu me permettre d'aller vous rendre visite le mois dernier, comme M. Sencourt, que je venais de voir à Oxford, me l'avait conseillé. Je n'ai pu malheureusement m'arrêter à Paris assez longtemps, ma femme étant alors fatiguée. Mais M. Sencourt m'a transmis la liste des conférences françaises que vous projetiez de donner, & je m'empresse de vous écrire qu'elles me paraissent tout à fait convenir à notre public.

Ce public est cosmopolite & curieux—composé de Français & Françaises, d'une partie de la société cosmopolite du Caire sachant très bien le français (Italiens, Grecs, etc.), de quelques Egyptiens musulmans (en minorité) & d'un grand nombre d'Israélites. Ils ont en général l'esprit ouvert; ils répugnent peut-être un peu à l'effort & préfèrent être instruits tout en étant distraits ou amusés à la sévérité de ton. Mais ils savent toujours apprécier un conférencier qui sait être au-dessus d'eux & leur donner quelque chose de personnel & de substantiel. D'ailleurs nous

nous efforcerons, M. Sencourt & moi, de les préparer comme il convient à votre visite et, sans battage vulgaire, mais avec un peu de réclame qu'il faut bien faire en Orient — & ailleurs — de préparer vos auditoires à votre venue.

Claudel & la Comtesse de Noailles sont certainement d'excellents sujets; le public du Caire connaît déjà ces deux auteurs & saura, je crois, apprécier tout ce que vous apporterez de personnel & de profond. Vos articles de la Revue Hebdomadaire sur la Comtesse de Noailles m'ont personnellement déjà fort intéressé & j'attendrai avec impatience votre conférence sur ce sujet. Barrès, en général, intéresse toujours moins les étrangers qu'on ne croirait; mais l'aspect particulier que vous proposez de traiter (l'Orient, & l'Egypte, chez Barrès) ne manquera pas là-bas d'être d'actualité. Mon prédécesseur, M. J.-M. Carré, avait déjà parlé au public du Caire de Th. Gautier en Egypte. Vous connaissez sans doute, & en tous cas vous trouverez au Caire ses chapitres sur ce sujet dans ses *Voyageurs & Écrivains français en Egypte* parus l'an dernier. Mais, là encore, votre méthode originale renouvellera le sujet pour ceux même qui le connaissent déjà — Vous verrez sans doute que le public des conférences en anglais est en général moins averti & moins varié que celui de nos cours publics en français. Les sujets un peu généraux, & sans doute contemporains ou modernes, sont, je crois, ceux qui porteraient le mieux auprès de lui. En français, à côté des conférences de l'Université pour lesquelles vous serez invité, il est probable que plusieurs petits groupements vous demanderont de parler chez eux: les Essayistes (groupe de jeunes Israélites, d'esprit très curieux, un peu lassants peut-être par leurs manies & leurs insistances à s'emparer des visiteurs éminents venus d'Europe) — les Amis de la Culture française (association respectable, qui organise des conférences payantes) — le Cercle Catholique de la Jeunesse Syrienne, etc. — À Alexandrie, M. Fort, proviseur du Lycée, dirige une société des conférences distinguée où vous parlerez certainement, si cela vous convient — à Port Saïd & à Ismaïlia, il y a des cercles français, un peu isolés & provinciaux, mais qui sont heureux & reconnaissants de recevoir la "bonne parole."

Excusez, Monsieur, une lettre un peu hâtive; je repars pour le Caire le 23 sept. et je vous serais très reconnaissant de vous adresser sans réserve à moi pour tout ce que je pourrais faire, (comme renseignements complémentaires, etc. — ), en dehors de ce que M. Sencourt pourra, bien entendu, vous conseiller — Mon adresse fixe de vacances sera, pour fin septembre, M. Henri Peyre, 2 rue Chauffard, Avignon—et ensuite, M. H. Peyre, Prof. à la Fac. des Lettres, Guizeh—(Egypte).

Croyez, Monsieur, à mes sentiments très profonds d'admiration & de dévouement.

Henri Peyre

## À son frère:

18 Shari El Gezira
Gezira
*Le Caire*
Le 6 déc. 34

Cher Jacques,

. . . Par contre, me voici victime—depuis quelques jours, des mêmes amibes. J'entreprends donc le traitement d'émétine: cela est fatigant et un peu décourageant au moral. J'espère cependant que mon tempérament résistant triomphera vite. . . .

Et toi? Comment maintiens-tu ta santé, avec le froid que tu redoutes tant, & les soins de Cécile? Voilà que viennent bientôt les fêtes. On ne s'en aperçoit guère ici, où le climat en est encore à l'automne, où l'on se sent loin, des familles, des souvenirs d'enfance, & même des fêtes de Noël en général et de la religion des chrétiens. Demain commence ici le Ramadan, avec ses scènes de rues pittoresques—Mais nous vivons dans un quartier si européen & même si anglais, entouré de jardins & de verdure, que nous assistons bien rarement à des scènes pittoresques. À vrai dire, nous ne sommes pas très curieux des Arabes: ils sont ici trop peu artistes, trop sales & trop paresseux—et on devient un peu colonial d'esprit, c'est-à-dire uniquement disposé à les engueuler ou à marchander avec eux.

Par contre, l'isolement même, la vie un peu factice ici des colonies étrangères, nous laissent plus à l'écart des mille soucis de l'Europe—soucis de guerre, d'assassinats, de désordres politiques, d'impôts excessifs. On ne participe pas trop à la mauvaise humeur de la crise et aux convulsions de classes de notre pauvre pays. L'époque d'aujourd'hui n'est pas gaie—Même le Midi doit se ressentir maintenant du marasme général. Je ne crois pas que le départ de Doumergue doive inspirer trop de regrets: il n'avait pas su saisir le moment pour imposer ses réformes, & il était devenu le jouet de quelques Tardieu et Cie, le poussant pour prendre ensuite sa place. Il faudrait une refonte beaucoup plus générale que cela, & je ne vois pas qui osera la tenter. . . .

## To Henry Allan Moe:

> Faculty of Arts
> Egyptian University
> *Cairo*
> May 23, 1935

Dear Sir:

I have just received the reports of the Secretary & Treasurer for 1933–34. May I ask you to mention, in the next report, under *Publications of fellows,* the two following books which I have published in 1934–35.

PEYRE, HENRI. *Qu'est-ce que le classicisme?* Droz, Paris, 232 p.

PEYRE, HENRI. *Shelley et la France. Lyrisme anglais et Lyrisme français au XIXe siècle.* Barbey, Cairo and Droz, Paris, 510 p.

> Sincerely yours,
> Henri Peyre

## Au Ministre de l'Instruction:

> Le 30 juin 1935

Monsieur le Ministre:

J'ai l'honneur de vous adresser une demande de renouvellement de mon détachement comme professeur à l'étranger.

J'ai été détaché comme professeur à l'étranger (États-Unis) une première fois à dater du 1 octobre 1925 (par arrêté No.5645 du 13 avril 1928). Ce détachement a été renouvelé à dater du 1 octobre 1930 (No.2589 du 22 septembre 1931). J'occupe depuis 1933 les fonctions de professeur de Littérature française à la Faculté des Lettres de l'Université Egyptienne, Le Caire.

Veuillez agréer, Monsieur le Ministre, l'expression de mes plus respectueux hommages.

> Henri Peyre
> Agrégé de l'Université
> Docteur ès Lettres

## To Henry Allan Moe:

> Cairo—
> May 24, 1936

Dear Mr. Moe:

I am glad to hear of the new donation made by Senator & Mrs. Guggenheim to the Foundation & to hear of its continued progress. I consider it one of the finest & most gratifying opportunities of my career, to have been selected as a fellow some years ago.

May I ask you to record my new address? I have been appointed Professor of Comparative Literature at the University of Lyons, France, & I will take up my new post this fall. My address will then be:

> Professor Henri Peyre
> Faculté des Lettres
> 66, rue Pasteur, *LYON* France

> Yours very sincerely,
> Henri Peyre

## À son père et son frère:

> Ce 4 août 36

Cher Papa, cher Jacques,

J'attendais, pour écrire avec quelques détails, que nous eussions une adresse un peu précise. Nous voici enfin "installés" une fois de plus—autant qu'on peut l'être dans notre vie de pérégrination. Après avoir quitté Vienne, nous avons été à Salzbourg (à la frontière de la Bavière) pour assister pendant qqs jours au célèbre festival—Nous ne l'avons pas regretté. Salzbourg est une ville pittoresque & originale, très vieillotte, avec de petites rues contournées, à la fois germanique & fortement marquée d'influence italienne dans son architecture. Les environs en sont ravissants: des montagnes qui commencent la chaîne du Tyrol. Malheureusement le climat est très pluvieux, & le 30–31 août, ce n'était que de la pluie, de la pluie. Aussi, après avoir assisté à quelques beaux concerts de Mozart & à une grandiose représentation de Faust, nous avons gagné le sud—le sud de l'Autriche n'est pas très lointain, à vrai dire—mais c'est un versant des Alpes tout de même un peu plus chaud—et, étrange à dire, cet été, nous cherchons plutôt la chaleur. Marguerite se plaint d'avoir sans cesse eu froid en Autriche, à part une dizaine de belles journées. Il faut croire que l'Egypte nous avait plus profondément marqués & gâtés que nous ne pensions!

Nous sommes donc en Carinthie (Kärnten en alld.), province qui touche à la Yougoslavie, au bord d'un lac, le Wörther See. À l'une des extrémités de ce lac est la ville de Klagenfurt, à l'autre Velden, où nous sommes. Nous avons passé 3 jours à Velden même, au bord du lac [*1 ligne illisible*] atmosphère de vacances, un grand nombre d'étrangers—pas mal de Français, et surtout beaucoup de Tchèques—qui nous ont déçus—ou plutôt, ce n'était pas ce que nous cherchions en Autriche. Lac pour lac, le lac d'Annecy est beaucoup plus beau et surtout on mange mieux en France! Aussi avons-nous fui, après examen, ces hôtels & pensions, où nous n'aurions eu de conversation que celle des aubergistes; et nous venons de prendre pension dans un château, à 4 kilomètres du lac, au village de Rosegg. La famille chez qui nous logeons est illustre: nous sommes les hôtes (payants) de Prince & de Princesse de Lichtenstein, l'une des grandes familles autrichiennes. Ils possèdent encore, autour d'ici-même, & ailleurs, d'immenses domaines. Mais ils n'en sont pas moins ruinés, depuis l'inflation. Les bois de leurs forêts & les produits de leurs champs ne rapportent strictement rien, une fois payés les impôts & la main d'œuvre, et personne ne se porte acquéreur si on cherche à vendre. Cette pauvre Autriche est vraiment dans une triste condition. Les gens ont conservé l'orgueil d'autrefois, le souvenir de leur empire & de leur prospérité; mais ils sont réduits à la demi-misère—Pas de débouchés pour leur industrie, car aucun des pays environnants ne veut rien acheter. Une capitale trop grande pour leur pays—une jeunesse sans emploi. Ils supportent cela avec encore pas mal de bonne grâce, &

à Vienne même, on a toujours l'impression d'un peuple gai & plaisant. Mais la situation politique profonde reste incertaine. [*1 ligne illisible*], des élections régulières, il y aurait une forte majorité de Nazis. Non qu'ils aiment l'Allemagne. Ils s'en sentent très différents & tiennent beaucoup à leur culture autonome, à leurs traits autrichiens, à leur réputation de grâce, de finesse. Mais il leur semble que ce serait le seul moyen de sortir de leur crise, d'avoir accès à la mer, une flotte, des débouchés, des frontières douanières moins resserrées. Les gens de l'ancienne génération s'intéressent beaucoup à la France—mais ils sont très anxieux sur notre compte. Notre cabinet Blum n'a pas ici bonne presse. Ils nous voient engagés sur la voie de perdition, & ils le regrettent pour eux. Le récent accord italo-austro-allemand ne les a pas remplis d'enthousiasme: mais ils y voient le résultat de notre politique socialiste & de notre faiblesse en Europe—Nous avions voulu organiser l'Europe centrale pour nos alliances, mais sans tenir compte des facteurs économiques. Mais pour compter sur l'alliance des Serbes ou des Tchèques, il faut d'abord que ces gens-là puissent vendre leurs produits et au moins entretenir considérablement une armée et acheter des munitions. Or, nous ne pouvons rien pour eux économiquement. L'Allemagne va maintenant essayer d'organiser l'Europe centrale contre nous, en vendant chez ces peuples les produits de son industrie & en leur achetant en échange du blé. Notre prestige est bien bas. Nous ne donnons plus l'impression d'un peuple solide socialement et fort militairement. Partout on se détourne de la démocratie telle que nos socialistes la rêvent encore. On nous juge fous de nous obstiner à augmenter nos salaires, alors que dans ces pays-ci, les ouvriers sont 4 fois moins payés que les nôtres. Individuellement, les Français sont très bien reçus en Autriche. Mais, dès qu'on parle un peu à fond avec les gens, ils hochent la tête & nous jugent d'une obstination téméraire & aveugle.

C'est encore en français que nous faisons ces conversations-là. Les gens un peu âgés, surtout dans l'aristocratie, parlent très bien le français. À la vérité, nous savons encore trop mal & trop peu l'allemand pour imposer cette langue. Nous comprenons à peu près couramment & le fait de lire les journaux, les revues, les enseignes, etc. peu à peu vous forme à la lecture courante & rapide. Mais parler couramment & correctement est une autre affaire! Que de fautes de genre, de construction! Cette langue est vraiment rebutante & il faut un effort assidu pour s'y mettre. Du moins, après ce séjour, nous aurons le goût de continuer, &,

avec de l'étude, j'espère que plus tard nous serons enfin des germanistes compétents. . . .

## À son père et à sa sœur:

Ce 20 de janvier/37
12 Boul. J. Favre *Lyon*

Cher Papa, Chère Louise,

. . . Le temps de France nous gâte: il fait sec presque sans interruption, beau soleil—et si Lyon pouvait être beau, il le serait quelquefois avec ces nuages dans un ciel bleu, plus méridional tout de même que parisien. Par contre, toutes les lettres d'Egypte nous annoncent, là-bas, un temps exceptionnellement froid, de la neige ou presque, chose incroyable! & du soleil toujours voilé.

Cependant j'avais eu la stupide pensée d'attraper, dans ces plaines lyonnaises, des douleurs genre lumbago ou sciatique, qui m'ont bien tourmenté 3 semaines—assez gênantes, et vexantes plus encore, car cela semble vous rapprocher déjà des rhumatismes, du retour d'âge, et injustes quand elles accablent un homme sérieux & rangé comme moi. Comme disent les joueurs à la roulette, il n'y a décidément pas de justice.

Nous sommes enfin lyonnais, c'est-à-dire confortablement installés chez nous. Deux grandes pièces, larges, ensoleillées quand elles peuvent l'être, meublées de façon claire & gaie—où nous nous tenons. Une vaste cuisine, propre & pratique—chambre, salle de bains, force placards, enfin un appartement complet, suffisant, & finalement meublés dans tous ses détails concertés. C'est beaucoup, car ici, chacune des personnes à qui j'ai rendu visite à mon arrivée me l'a signalé—la vie de famille chez soi est le plus grand charme. Nous nous tenons donc beaucoup chez nous, autour de nos livres, nombreux depuis que j'en ai rapporté d'Avignon, de tableaux, càd. gravures & reproductions acquis au cours de nos voyages. À dire le vrai, c'est tout de même un peu solitaire. Mais j'ai idée que nous resterons, dans cette ville, assez longtemps étrangers. Nous n'arrivons pas à nous y plaire. La rue, ses spectacles, tout y est triste, à côté de Paris, surtout. Des usines partout, entremêlées aux quartiers d'habitation eux-mêmes. Un caractère méfiant du nouveau chez les habitants. Nous avons déployé tous nos efforts & fait beaucoup de visites, à des collègues. Mais il n'y a pas grand'chose à en tirer. Leurs femmes sont trop préoccupées par les soucis d'intérieur, de famille—les hommes, refroidis & desséchés, déformés par le métier. Les jeunes professeurs, à la Faculté, se prennent au sérieux, pour qu'on les y prenne aussi: leur grand sujet de conversation, c'est les élections probables de nouveaux collègues, les cuisines "ejusdem farinae" de cooptation intérieure, etc., & leur ambition à travailler, à arriver; les vieux sont "service." Mon collègue de français, Delaforge, est un brave homme, dévoué, appliqué, mais qui n'a qu'un seul sujet: les étudiants, les dissertations qu'il leur donne, qu'il corrige, etc. Je fais bien mon travail, mais je n'aime pas en parler dehors à ce point. J'aime encore mieux, à ce tarif-là, rester chez moi & ne voir personne. Marguerite a la même expérience avec les épouses—d'où solitude relative—tant pis. Quant aux autres groupes, docteurs, industriels, il semble qu'il faille beaucoup de temps, & des occasions, avant de faire connaissance.

D'ailleurs, le travail ne manque pas. Nous n'avons jamais eu tant à faire! À la maison, nous avions une bonne à la journée, une Allemande. Voilà qu'une maladie l'a forcée de repartir pour l'Allemagne. Il faut rechercher quelque autre, la mettre au courant. C'est un travail lassant. En attendant, nous nous en passons. Mais comme il n'y a pas autant de commodités qu'en Amérique, c'est beaucoup de temps pris. Achats au marché, etc. Aussi le temps pour des promenades éventuelles est rare: quelquefois, un tour au parc. Mais plus de tennis, que Marguerite pratiquait l'an dernier assidûment.

Pour moi, travail très lourd. Jamais je n'en ai autant eu & et jamais je n'avais été aussi mal payé—avec des prix qui montent partout. Vraiment, la façon dont est rémunéré le travail intellectuel est indigne de notre pays—et menace de l'être de plus en plus. Un ouvrier spécialisé est certainement plus favorisé: et mes semaines ont plus de 40 heures— Je suis forcé à des lectures, préparations, du matin au soir—& ne puis rien faire pour moi. Le surmenage des élèves, dont parlent tant les journaux, n'épargne pas les professeurs. Cela sera évidemment moindre les années suivantes. Mais la 1ère année, il faut d'abord se faire connaître— puis on a des programmes tout nouveaux, qu'il faut préparer à fond— enfin il se trouve que j'ai assumé du travail supplémentaire encore. Je fais, en français, un cours public, auquel succède, le cours public fini, un cours de littérature comparée—un cours de licence, sur les *Contemplations,* texte joliment difficile à expliquer—deux cours d'agrégation de lettres, où j'explique en ce moment Jocelyn—Xe époque. J'ai repris les notes que, jadis, tu m'avais préparées & adressées sur ce texte et qui me sont fort précieuses: j'y ai retrouvé ta subtilité, la précision de tes connaissances de style & de grammaire, & la sûreté de ton goût, ce qui a facilité ma tâche de préparation. Mais il y a des tas de choses récentes à lire sur Lamartine, & le texte même demande à être vu de près—enfin, pour remplacer un collègue qui s'absente jusqu'à la fin de l'année scolaire, j'ai accepté de faire ses 2 heures de cours d'agrégation d'anglais: il faut que je m'appuie là 3 ou 4 auteurs difficiles, dans un domaine où je n'ai aucune habitude de l'enseignement, ce qui ajoute beaucoup à ma charge & cela pour une misérable rémunération de 2.000 francs peut-être. Il est vrai que je l'aurais fait pour rien, puisque c'était pour rendre service— et avec la vague idée que, si je réussis plus tard à obtenir quelques fugues à l'étranger, loin de Lyon, je serais heureux qu'on me rendît la pareille. Enfin, avec tout ça, je regrette, tu le vois, nos douces heures du Caire, où j'allais à mes cours les mains dans mes poches, sans rien préparer— et où les gens, dans la colonie française, étaient tellement plus hospitaliers & cordiaux qu'ici. Ici, pour les dérider, il faudrait une patience ou un talent comique que je n'ai pas. La vie matérielle est dure dans nos métiers, c'est entendu, pour ceux qui ont plusieurs enfants, surtout. Mais pourquoi l'attrister encore? Comme dit Montherlant dans un livre récent, il faut croire que le bonheur & la jouissance de la vie ne commencent qu'avec le 25º ou le 30º degré de température extérieure, là où les thermomètres portent: "température des vers à soie." Vous en êtes juges, là-bas, en Tunisie. Nous rêvons plus que jamais d'exotisme. Palerme! Athènes! Ce doit être plus gai à habiter, et plus divertissant, & plus chaleureux!

Pendant ce temps, la politique nous tient en haleine. Peur de la guerre! Inquiétude du côté italien, maintenant! Tu vois tout ça dans les journaux. En France même, les prix montent, les gens achètent beaucoup; les affaires reprennent; la spéculation pousse à la hausse & à la reprise en France; si le gouvernement réussit à ramener quelque confiance, cela pourra aller quelques mois. Pour le moment, la trésorerie paraît être à sec & les gens préfèrent dépenser leur argent plutôt que de le confier à l'État. Je ferais comme eux si j'en avais. J'avoue que je lis les journaux un peu en observateur détaché. La bêtise est trop accablante, & la folie, & la médiocrité égoïste de nos compatriotes. Je ne me sens guère comme faisant partie d'eux, de leur groupe & de leur sottise aveugle. Assez grogné cependant! Nous sommes aussi fous, je suppose, que ces gens dont tu étudies les guerres dans les vieilles chroniques. Et dire que, plus tard, quelque historien à toi comparable (en moins bien) s'attachera aussi à étudier nos querelles plus ou moins religieuses (idéologiques, comme on dit) et frémira de relire, après 3 siècles, nos journaux et notre stupide littérature politique! C'est à vous décourager de ces recherches! . . .

## À son frère:

ce 28—ii—38

Mon cher Jacques,

Voilà en effet une éternité que je veux t'écrire—& je te remercie d'avoir pensé à me souhaiter un anniversaire qui, à mon âge, commence à être plutôt une addition à un fardeau déjà lourd. Que deviens-tu? Tu sembles las de trop de besogne, & Papa nous écrivait en effet que ce travail excessif t'énervait & te fatiguait. Je ne sais pas comment tu tiens le coup, moi qui trouve le mien déjà lourd. Tu es apparemment plus solide, & plus patient aussi que je ne le serais, s'il me fallait écouter tant de monotones doléances de malades. Tu as des compensations aussi plus réelles, plus sonnantes, ce qui n'est pas à dédaigner par ces années de vie toujours plus chère.

Ici, nous nous plaisons toujours aussi peu, et de moins en moins. L'hiver est interminable, gris & brumeux souvent: nous aspirons après des vacances ensoleillées & calmes et, si nous le pouvons, nous tâcherons de faire, à Pâques, une escapade. La ville, reste, pour nous, aussi dénuée de charme. Les gens sont froids, pas du tout hospitaliers, ne sachant pas se rendre aimables, accueillants. Nous nous sentons toujours à l'étranger. Nos collègues, braves gens, sont des raseurs, gauches, sans aucun vernis social, sans nulle aisance—tout à fait le type traditionnel & caricatural du professeur. Aussi absence totale de stimulant extérieur dans ce genre de vie. D'autre part, l'exiguïté de nos traitements ne permet guère de vie sociale: on est contraint d'éviter les moindres dépenses, et aujourd'hui on ne peut guère avoir d'amis & de divertissements sans une automobile. Enfin, tu vois, nous nous morfondrions—si ce n'était que la besogne abonde. Une domestique, que nous avions, est partie; depuis, soucis d'intérieur aggravés pour Marguerite—Pour moi, cours, préparation, routine de lectures, jamais ou presque de vrai loisir. Professionnellement, mes cours ont eu beaucoup de succès, et on ne nous témoigne que d'excellentes intentions. Mais nous avons du mal à nous faire à ce genre de vie solitaire & étriqué. Nous nous réfugions dans notre intérieur, qui est, à notre avis, l'endroit le plus propre & le plus clair de Lyon, & le temps s'écoule ainsi. D'ailleurs, les Français semblent tous être devenus si stupidement égoïstes, si fermés à toute grandeur, qu'on est peu désireux de frayer avec eux. Si tu lis les journaux, tu vois combien nous brillons peu dans le monde.

Donne-nous un peu plus substantiellement de tes nouvelles—et viens nous voir quelque fin de semaine. Le printemps finira bien par venir tout de même! Et tu te percheras attendri sur Fourvière, sur le lieu de tes exploits équestres, sur la Saône & ses brouillards. Que se passe-t-il à Avignon? Ta bonne est-elle toujours aussi diligente?

Nous t'embrassons tous deux—avec surtout la recommandation de ne pas trop t'esquinter la santé pour soigner celle des autres. Tu as bien droit aussi à un peu de loisir, et à plus de sommeil!

Caresses,
Henri

## To Joseph Seronde:

[No date]

[fragment of letter included by Prof. Seronde, of the Yale French Department, in a letter to President Charles Seymour of March 10, 1938, urging action on a Peyre appointment]

. . . It is very kind of you to think of me after all these years, for an eventual professorship at Yale. The memories of our colleagues, of the students, of the facilities for work there, have remained very dear to us, as you know, and I should be especially glad to work with you again, under the presidency of Mr. Seymour, who must be a very broad-minded and efficient President. As I wrote to Mr. [Albert] Feuillerat last fall, I would consider going back, under certain circumstances. It would mean such a complete change of career, that, of course, it would take some careful meditation. I mean, as a question of courtesy to my own country, where they have been very kind to us; they have appointed me to a full professorship here, after an exceptionally short stay, and the people in

Paris are very kindly telling me that they will be glad to have me come to the Sorbonne when an opportunity arises. I mean also, from other points of view. I would not like to be at Yale, or anywhere else, if there were to be the slightest ill-feeling from the part of my American colleagues. And then, of course, the financial side. I hate, you know, all that might look like bargaining; but the decision to make a career in America, instead of Europe, is a momentous one, in its way, for us, and would require some careful consideration of the probable expenses and of the question of salary.

However, there is plenty of time, and, when you think it advisable to press the question further, you might let me know some more precise details about the possibilities. I have been asked to go to Columbia this summer, and have accepted. I shall be there for six weeks from the 5th of July, I believe.

## To Charles Seymour:

12, Boulevard Jules Favre. LYON
April 29th — 1938

President Charles Seymour
Yale University
New Haven, Conn.
Dear President Seymour:

I have found, on our return from a trip to Sicily during our Easter vacations, your letter of April 12th, and I want to express at once my very warm gratitude, both for the very flattering offer it contains, and for the manner, so direct and so kindly obliging, in which it is presented. I had been approached once or twice by American institutions since I left the United States and I must confess that I had not contemplated going back, at least not so soon. I seemed to have settled down to a French career, more limited in its possibilities, but enjoyable in its way. Even when Professor Feuillerat and Professor Seronde wrote to me some months ago, I thought it meant only a vague and distant proposal.

I am all the more grateful to you for the prompt and flattering offer which you have made very attractive. The pleasant memories we have retained from our brief association with Yale, the cordial spirit of the department, the vast possibilities for work and for research offered by

Yale, the keen personal interest I should take in the new "College plan" and, if I may mention it with full sincerity, the stimulating prospect of working at Yale under your leadership, have carried my decision. I am very glad to accept the offer made in your letter, and would like to ask you to thank, on my behalf, the Yale Corporation as well as the members of the French Department.

I am replying very soon after having found your letter and have not had time, as yet, to consult anyone in Paris. This is such a momentous decision for me, involving a complete change in my career, that I would like to mention it to the French Ministry of Public Education, and, as a matter of courtesy, to some professors at the Sorbonne who kindly and repeatedly assured me that they wanted to call me to Paris as soon as there would be a possibility. I have no doubt, however, that the authorities will feel, as I do, that I shall serve the cause of French culture and civilization even better by my presence at Yale. A few questions about my personal status will have to be settled. But those are only minor points.

While I want to accept without delay an offer so obligingly presented, I am afraid, however, I shall have to ask you to allow me to defer my going to Yale for another academic year. The reason is not a personal one and, personally, if I could make myself free, I would much prefer starting my new career in New Haven without delay. But here is what happened in February–March. Egypt where I spent three years as a professor of French Literature, wanted me to go back there. I declined, as I felt little inclined, then, to give up or to interrupt more serious work at Lyon, and for other motives. But the Egyptians appealed to the French Minister of National Education, M. Jean Zay, when he visited there some time ago: they told him that they were especially insistent on having me back, and wanted no other French professor for the present; they definitely threatened to suppress the French professorship in Cairo if I did not accept. In such circumstances, the French Ministry appealed to me on patriotic grounds, urged me to serve, for one more year, the cause of French culture in the Near East, which they have at heart, and I finally accepted to go back to Cairo, for one year only, 1938–39.

It thus seems to be an engagement of honour, which I only agreed to on the first day of April. I regret it now all the more, as we would prefer settling in New Haven at once and not having so many moving difficulties accumulated within the next eighteen months. But, since the Egyptians refused all the other candidates which were proposed to them, I feel there is no other course now, but for me to teach another year in the very oldest of the old worlds, before settling more decisively in the New. I beg to apologize, and can only express the hope that such a delay would not prove too detrimental to the schemes of the French Department at Yale.

There would be ample time to discuss the details of my future work. May I repeat, however, that I shall be glad indeed to remain in contact with the Yale undergraduates, while doing also work in the Graduate School? And, if that fits with Professor Seronde's plan, it seems to me that I could be most useful to them in a modern course, e.g. "modern tendencies in French Literature," or some such title; or "French poetry of the XIXth and XXth centuries," etc.

May I also ask if the Professorship offered would carry an eventual sabbatical leave or twohalf-sabbaticals? I am especially curious of that point, because I would like to remain in a position to do extensive work in the French field and in the French libraries, as I have several schemes for research in which I am already engaged.

While thanking you once more for your very kind and flattering offer, and the pleasant and hopeful prospect of working at Yale with such possibilities, I beg to remain with respectful regards,

Very sincerely yours,
Henri Peyre

## To the same:

June 16 — 1938

Dear President Seymour:

I apologize for not having thanked you for your very kind letter of May 16th, appointing me officially as a member of the Yale Faculty, the appointment to be made effective as of July 1st, 1939. I am deeply grateful to you for the very cordial and flattering way in which the offer and the appointment have been made. I would like to thank you personally without delay, and to express my appreciation and gratitude. I am sailing for New York on June 29th, on the Queen Mary, for I am to give a series of lectures at the Columbia Summer School. You may be in Europe yourself at the same time or absent from New Haven. If, however, there was a chance of meeting you in New Haven, in July or early in August, I should be very glad to run up from New York for an interview. My very sincere desire will be to cooperate with the Yale Faculty and the French Department to the best of my ability and I should be happy to hear more exactly what your wishes may be in that respect. Professor Seronde has written to me already, and I am to meet Professor Feuillerat in Paris within a week.

I am, with warm regards,

Sincerely yours,<br>Henri Peyre

My New York address will be, from July 5th, Maison Française, 411, 117th St., Columbia University. New York.

### To the same:

Columbia Univ. Maison Française<br>Thursday, July 7th (1938)

Dear President Seymour:

I saw Professor Feuillerat in Paris, before sailing, and he spoke to me of some of the questions concerning the French Department at Yale and its future. I should be very glad if I could have an opportunity to meet you while in this country. I would like to thank you again personally and orally for the honour you made me, and to hear what your wishes may be in connection with some of the delicate problems which will have to be solved, in order that Yale may build a French Department worthy of the highest expectations of the University. If you have not yet left New Haven, could I come up one afternoon for a brief interview? All my mornings are taken up here by lectures and conferences. It would be a great pleasure for me to meet you before I leave again for Europe and for Egypt.

Yours very sincerely,<br>Henri Peyre

## To the same:

Faculty of Arts
Egyptian University
Guizeh (Egypt)
January 29—1939

Dear President Seymour:

The present year is about half completed, and I am sincerely looking forward to the time when I shall be able to take up my new duties at Yale. It does seem more and more as if America were to provide a safer refuge for studies and culture than our war-ridden Europe!

May I ask you if you would kindly inform me, through the Dean or the French Department, of all the new developments or new plans for study which have been put forward recently, so that I may feel better equipped for my new task when the time comes.

We expect to sail for America early next September, so as to have ample time to get settled before the opening of the academic year. In that connection, I should be much obliged if you could request the Secretary's office to forward to me the following documents: 1) A copy of the decision of Yale Corporation, appointing me as Professor at the University, which I shall have to hand to the consular authorities establishing my visa; 2) if possible, a letter from your office asking the American consular or Immigration authorities to facilitate the granting of my visa (perhaps mentioning the fact that I was already a member of the Yale Faculty from 1928 to 1933); 3) could I get some information from the University Service Bureau as to the formalities for shipping our furniture to America, and direct to New Haven if possible, and about the possibility of passing it free through the Customs, which I believe we are entitled to as foreign persons settling in the United States. In case our furniture should reach New Haven before us next summer, would it be possible to have someone help us in seeing it through the Customs. There must have been cases similar to ours of foreign professors appointed to Yale and taking their furniture there, and I suppose the Service Bureau would be in a position to give us information and help us in that respect.

Thanking you deeply for whatever help the University may give me in these practical matters, and looking forward to meeting you and my colleagues at the end of the coming Summer, I am,

> Very sincerely yours,
> Henri Peyre

## À André Gide:

> 15 rue Emir Husein
> Zamalek, le Caire
> Le 6 février 1939

Monsieur,

Pardonnez à un inconnu de s'adresser à vous, avec bien des hésitations. Il y a longtemps déjà—dix-huit ans, je crois—que, jeune normalien, j'ai découvert les *Nourritures Terrestres,* puis *Paludes;* puis le *Retour de l'Enfant Prodigue,* et contracté envers vous une immense dette de reconnaissance. Depuis, professeur dans plusieurs universités étrangères, j'ai, à bien des reprises, parlé de votre œuvre et, je crois, toujours avec admiration et respect, jusque dans la "critique." J'ai récemment écrit quelques pages sur vous dans un modeste ouvrage paru chez Corréa, Hommes et Œuvres du XXe siècle, que j'aimerais vous envoyer si j'osais vous accabler de telles lectures, au cours d'un voyage que vous souhaitez reposant. Je suis actuellement professeur de littérature comparée à l'Université de Lyon, et détaché pour cette année à la faculté de lettres du Caire. Je me permets, vous sachant en Egypte et craignant un peu moins de vous déranger ici qu'à Paris, de vous écrire pour vous demander l'autorisation d'entreprendre un travail sur votre œuvre et solliciter de vous lors de votre passage au Caire quelques moments d'entretien.

J'ai l'intention, dont vous sourirez peut-être, d'écrire une série d'articles, ou même un livre, sur "André Gide et les littératures étrangères." J'espère y éviter toutes les sottises que nos étudiants et nousmêmes, "comparatistes," débitons souvent sur les influences. En lisant et relisant vos livres, et récemment encore vos *Œuvres Complètes,* j'ai été pris d'une vive admiration pour les pénétrantes suggestions que vous prodiguez (à propos de Verhaeren, de Nietzsche, de Dostoïevski, etc.—)

sur ces questions d'influences littéraires, du nationalisme en littérature, de l'élargissement que vous ont apporté, non des influences, mais des rencontres d'écrivains étrangers. Je voudrais m'efforcer, en rassemblant vos nombreux jugements sur les écrivains d'Allemagne, d'Italie, d'Angleterre, de Russie, de Perse, etc., en les étudiant, de vous présenter comme l'esprit le plus ouvert et le plus généreux, le critique le plus pénétrant et le plus sûr qu'ait compté notre littérature moderne (ne voyez en ceci aucune flatterie). Il me semble que, de l'examen attentif de vos découvertes successives de Goethe, de Dante, des philosophes allemands, de Nietzsche, des Russes, des poètes et des romanciers anglais, devrait apparaître l'une des courbes de votre évolution, et l'admirable spectacle d'un esprit toujours plus vaste, toujours plus sincère et plus courageux, toujours plus jeune.

Si vous croyez que je puis entreprendre un travail de ce genre, si vous voulez bien me le permettre, j'aimerais vous poser quelques questions auxquelles votre œuvre publiée répond mal: sur la date de vos premières lectures allemandes et italiennes, sur votre étude de l'anglais et du russe, sur la place que vous accorderiez à quelques écrivains étrangers dont vous n'avez parlé qu'occasionnellement, sur quelques uns de vos voyages à l'étranger, le rôle qu'ont pu jouer, comme intermédiaires, dans vos découvertes d'auteurs étrangers, Wilde, Arnold Bennett, Raverat (dont il est question dans l'un des passages de votre Journal), Ch. du Bos, etc. C'est avec le plus profond respect et l'admiration la plus sincère pour le grand écrivain que vous êtes; le modèle que vous êtes resté pour tous ceux de ma génération, que je voudrais entreprendre ce travail. Je ne sais si vous consentiriez à avoir quelque estime par avance pour une critique de ce genre, "universitaire" et saisissant en apparence le côté livresque de votre œuvre: la lecture de la plupart des livres qui vous ont été consacrés par d'autres critiques m'a si souvent empli d'impatience ou d'indignation que j'ai toujours souhaité m'acquitter envers vos livres d'une vieille et précieuse dette, en parlant d'eux et de leur auteur avec "bonne foi."

Je serais heureux de pouvoir vous être utile à quelque chose pendant votre séjour en Egypte. Veuillez croire que je l'écris avec la plus franche sincérité, en vous assurant par avance de mon dévouement entier. Si je puis, sans vous importuner, solliciter de vous quelques moments d'entretien lorsque vous repasserez par le Caire, je me permets de vous assurer de ma vive gratitude.

Veuillez croire en attendant, Monsieur, à l'expression de mes sentiments d'admiration la plus sincère.

Henri Peyre<br>
(Henri Peyre<br>
Adresse ci-dessus)

## Au même:

15 rue Emir Husein<br>
Zamalek, le Caire<br>
le 6 février 1939

Monsieur,

À peine venais-je de vous écrire sur un sujet tout autre, que le Doyen de la Faculté de Lettres du Caire m'a prié de le faire en son nom. Peut-être connaissez-vous, de nom ou de réputation, le Doyen Taha Husein, homme remarquable, aveugle de naissance ou presque, éminent arabisant, formé à notre culture, grand ami de nos lettres, et de l'avis général, le plus remarquable des écrivains égyptiens d'aujourd'hui, représentant régulier de son pays aux Entretiens de la Coopération Intellectuelle et Président du P.E.N. Club égyptien.

Il sait que vous tenez fort peu à parler en public durant votre séjour en Egypte et que vous fuyez volontiers les corvées mondaines ou autres que des admirateurs trop chaleureux voudraient peut-être vous infliger. Mais il me prie de vous demander en son nom si — sans aucun apprêt, sans aucun discours de vous ni de personne — vous ne voudriez pas accepter qu'il organisât, avec les quelques membres égyptiens du P.E.N. club, un dîner auquel vous vous contenteriez d'assister — dans la plus grande simplicité et à la date que vous voudriez bien indiquer par avance. Je vous transmets sa requête qui vient chez lui, je le sais, du désir très sincère et fervent d'honorer, le plus simplement possible, l'écrivain français d'aujourd'hui qu'il admire le plus.

Si, en outre, vous vouliez bien accepter de parler à la Faculté de Lettres à nos étudiants seuls (en l'absence de tout public mondain, de tout tapage) et pour ainsi dire dans l'intimité, à cette jeunesse étrangère qui, vous le verriez, révère votre nom et votre œuvre, Taha Husein me charge de vous dire que l'Egypte et lui-même vous en seraient reconnaissants. Il ne s'agirait que d'une causerie fort "informal," comme disent les Anglais, sur le sujet que vous voudriez et pendant le temps qu'il vous plairait.

Je me permets de vous transmettre les deux souhaits d'un Egyptien qui est non seulement un de nos amis les plus fidèles mais un grand savant et l'auteur d'un récit très émouvant et humain de son enfance (traduit en français sous le titre "Le Livre des jours" et en anglais "An Egyptian Childhood"), l'un des livres les plus révélateurs qu'ait écrits un Egyptien sur son pays. Veuillez me pardonner ce que vous jugerez peut-être comme une indiscrétion importune—et croyez, Monsieur, à mon très profond et entier dévouement.

> Henri Peyre
> (Professeur à la Faculté de Lettres de Lyon et du Caire)

## Au même:

> 15 Sh. Emir Husein
> Zamalek. Le Caire
> Le 19 mars 1939

Monsieur,

Je vous suis plus reconnaissant que je ne saurais vous le dire de votre accueil si cordial, si inlassablement aimable, de cette magnifique jeunesse que votre regard, votre parole, votre abord ont conservés et qui mettent aussitôt à l'aise quelqu'un qui eût dû être intimidé de se trouver devant un des plus grands écrivains de ce temps, celui dont les moindres livres lui ont toujours parlé comme s'ils avaient été écrits pour lui—ces moments d'entretien passés avec vous m'ont empli d'une grande et pure joie, d'une vive exaltation intellectuelle ou spirituelle, après l'abattement où les derniers événements politiques m'avaient plongé. Permettez-moi, sans phrases, de vous remercier.

Je vous envoie mon pédant ouvrage sur Shelley & un certain lyrisme anglais que j'ai beaucoup aimé, auquel, peut-être, j'ai confronté le vôtre avec un peu d'injustice. Il me tarde beaucoup de lire l'anthologie que vous préparez. Comme j'aurais aimé me trouver en même temps que vous à Louxor et vous en entendre parler plus longuement! Pardonnez les erreurs dont je suis responsable, et qui sont malheureusement nombreuses dans ce livre, & celles de mon imprimeur, que ma vie trop errante ne m'avait jamais permis de corriger.

Excusez la couverture jaunie—je ne trouve en libraire que cet exemplaire d'un livre à peu près invendu.

Les pages de Renan sur l'Egypte & l'art égyptien sont (ainsi que les curieux "vingt jours en Sicile") dans les *Mélanges d'histoire et de voyage.* Je me rappelle que les *Études d'Histoire Religieuse* renferment un article curieux sur Mohamed & les origines de l'Islam. Mais il y a encore ailleurs des pages très dures et très justes, de Renan sur, ou contre, l'Islam (L'Islam & la Science, je crois). C'est peut-être dans les "Nouvelles études d'histoire religieuse," ou dans les très beaux *Discours & Conférences,* je ne sais plus.

Le poète américain que je me permettais de vous signaler comme l'un de ceux qui donnent le plus sûrement l'impression de génie est Robinson Jeffers. Il vit en Californie et a écrit, entre autres, *Tamar, Roan Stallion, The Women at Point Sur,* etc.

Je vais reprendre Simenon et regretterai votre conférence sur cet original sujet.

Je n'ose espérer que vous viendrez un jour aux États-Unis et cependant bien des aspects de ce pays vous séduiraient, je crois. . . .

Veuillez croire, du moins, que vous y compteriez un fidèle admirateur de plus et, si j'ose dire, un "ami" tout dévoué. Mon adresse, dès octobre prochain, sera: French Department, Yale University, New Haven, Conn.

Encore merci bien profondément et avec tous mes vœux pour votre voyage en Grèce.

Henri Peyre

## To Charles Seymour:

Hotel Taft, New Haven, Conn.<br>Sept. 2—1939

Dear President Seymour:

The worst seems to have come—& it was to be expected. I am sorry that my new connection with Yale begins in such oppressing and anxious circumstances. I had been looking forward to our arrival here with keen impatience.

I am awaiting instructions from Washington or New York as to my personal status & hoping your kind letter may help solve this problem favorably. If not, my chief concern will be the inconvenience I will involuntarily cause the French Department & the University.

Meanwhile, following your advice, we have reserved an apartment at 309, St Ronan's St. Tel. 7-4705. Through some delay in the shipment of our furniture, we shall not be able to move there before Sept. 5—

I am very grateful to you for your help & kind encouragement in these matters & remain,

                                        Very sincerely yours,
                                        Henri Peyre

## À son père:

                                        Yale University
                                        New Haven, Conn.
                                        U.S.A.
                                        Ce 4 sept. 1939

Mon cher Papa,

Depuis hier, ça y est donc—la troisième guerre franco-allemande à laquelle il t'aura été donné d'assister. Il y a quinze jours seulement, nous étions dans le calme & ne nous doutions de rien encore, tant on s'était accoutumé à vivre dans ces alarmes répétées. Maintenant encore, on s'éveille la nuit en se demandant si ce n'est pas un cauchemar, si vraiment ce Paris que nous avons encore connu gai, riant, artiste, malicieux, cet été peut-être en partie démoli, si les obus devront creuser les champs & déraciner les arbres, & les hommes mourir. Nous en sommes tous deux encore accablés. Notre journée, dans ces premiers temps d'inaction forcée pour nous, se passe à lire les journaux, à sonder les nouvelles & les cartes, à nous demander où passera notre armée, si elle doit passer quelque part, & comment on pourrait, pour se rassurer un peu, envisager au moins une guerre plus courte que l'autre. Tout ceci est terrible—parce que, après les Anglais, nous sommes les plus durement coupables. Nos hommes politiques ont tout laissé faire, alors qu'il y a 3 ans, 2 ans même, il était encore facile de tout écraser dans l'œuf. Briand a été dupé, les autres ont été des faibles & des hésitants, les derniers des maladroits. Nous payons cher notre erreur de n'avoir pas su vaincre après la victoire, et de n'avoir pas suscité chez nous, au moment voulu, les gens à vision large et hardie. Maintenant, tout est à recommencer. Et après une saignée affreuse, ce sera le déséquilibre économique, l'inflation, la misère, la ruine pour quarante ans. Les neutres, les poltrons, & les heureux du nouveau continent hériteront de nos dépouilles.

Dans ce malheur, nous n'avons pas cessé de penser d'abord à nos parents, à nos amis. Tu as dû retourner à Paris à temps, puisqu'Hitler a bien voulu nous accorder un répit. Je suppose que Louise & Hélène ont rejoint aussi Avignon. Et s'il se confirme que l'Italie doive rester neutre pour de bon, même en marchandant, la route de Tunis demeurera ouverte — je l'espère du moins. C'est déjà beaucoup de gagné si nous disposons de la Méditerranée, et pour les civils, et pour organiser plus tard une expédition vers la Roumanie, si le front occidental ne devient qu'une tuerie sur place. Il nous tarde d'être rassurés sur vous. Dans tout cela, que devient Jacques? lui qui travaillait si dur pour se reposer ensuite, qui se souciait tant de conserver sa clientèle et ses succès si rapides, le voilà aussi en uniforme. Quel est au juste son rang? & son affectation? dans un corps de troupe, ou dans un hôpital — & où? Rassure-nous là-dessus bientôt, & dis-lui de nous écrire lui-même. Il a beaucoup d'amis, & il est débrouillard — cela lui évitera-t-il les dangers les plus pressants?

Pour nous, nous souffrons d'être isolés ici, sans nouvelles, harassés seulement par les crieurs de journaux, leurs gros titres alarmants, & vexés parfois par le bonheur insouciant de ces gens. Nous déplorons cette catastrophe qui arrête tous nos nouveaux espoirs, au seuil d'une nouvelle phase de notre existence. Mais enfin nous sommes partis à temps & je suis heureux pour Marguerite, sensible & encore obsédée des souvenirs de l'autre guerre, qu'elle soit ici. Quoi qu'il arrive, j'espère qu'elle recevrait de l'Université au moins une aide modeste, et elle s'emploierait de son côté à travailler. Du moins, les alarmes d'avion, les bombardements, la vue de tant de misères & de blessés, lui sera épargnée. Et, si on ose se réjouir en de telles circonstances, elle a eu l'heureuse idée de faire expédier, le 18 août, le jour même de notre départ, tous nos meubles & possessions. C'est une chance inouïe, due à ses pressentiments inquiets, alors que, de mon côté, je me refusais à croire pour sitôt à une telle solution brutale.

Pour moi, je ne sais rien. J'ai signalé à l'Ambassade & au Consulat ma présence ici. Je suis lieutenant d'infanterie, en résidence à l'étranger, attendant donc un ordre spécial. Nous devons être plusieurs milliers dans ce cas en Amérique. On rapatriera la plupart d'entre nous, aussitôt sans doute que les conditions de la navigation paraîtront plus sûres. Me gardera-t-on, vu mon âge, & ma position, qui peut-être ici très importante, comme une sorte de "propagandiste" ici? C'est possible, & je l'espère encore. Mais le contraire aussi est possible. Quoi qu'il arrive, j'aurai évité le désordre des premiers jours & les affectations dues au hasard. Si l'on peut parler raisonnablement de choses qui sont souvent réglées par le caprice & le hasard, je crois fermement qu'une fois en France (si l'on m'y renvoie bientôt) je serai utilisé selon mes capacités: interprète, censure, services d'information, etc. Je rendrais évidemment beaucoup plus de services là que comme officier d'infanterie, & nous ne manquons pas d'officiers de réserve pour le moment. Il me paraît même probable que, si je suis renvoyé en France, je sois plus tard ramené en Amérique. Mais c'est un grand peut-être. Il n'y a qu'à attendre les ordres.

Nous avons retenu un appartement, agréable & gai, tout neuf—& ce serait, en temps normal, une joie d'y disposer nos meubles, livres & souvenirs de France. Mais trop d'angoisse nous étreint. Un retard d'expédition nous a d'ailleurs empêchés de nous installer encore: peut-être demain (5 sept.) pourrons-nous enfin le faire. Et les occupations, les travaux même, seront salutaires, au lieu de cette attente de nouvelles décevantes & de ces méditations sur ce que fera notre pays ou ce qu'il adviendra de lui.

Ici, l'Amérique nous réserve toute sa sympathie. Mais elle ne veut pas entrer dans ces querelles, en tous cas pas à la légère. Elle abomine Hitler & son régime—mais, dans l'ensemble, ce sera dur, (si c'est possible) de l'amener à verser son sang pour une cause européenne, où beaucoup de pays d'Europe se réfugient dans une neutralité prudente, où les Anglais eux-mêmes ne fournissent encore que de maigres contingents. Pourtant, beaucoup de forces sont pour nous: l'élite cultivée, la jeunesse; ici, dans cette grande université, il y aurait beaucoup à faire, & qui rendrait, pour orienter la jeunesse, et la faire intervenir plus activement. Mais pour un tel résultat, il faudra du temps, des maladresses de l'Allemagne, et à la fois un idéal sentimental et généreux à proposer à l'Amérique & des raisons d'intérêt. Si nous étions menacés de perdre, je crois que l'Amérique se déciderait vite, et j'espère pas trop tard. En attendant, si elle fournit des armes, sinon des hommes, ce sera déjà beaucoup. Et l'avenir, d'ici quelques mois, peut annoncer mieux encore. . . .

## To Edgar Furniss:

September 29, 1939

Edgar S. Furniss, Provost
Yale University
Dear Mr. Furniss:

I have asked Professor H. B. Richardson to be our Head of Instruction for the Freshman Year, with the approval of the freshman office. The details and routine of the work will naturally require a great deal of telephoning on his part, or to him—and it seems reasonable and fair, under these circumstances, that this telephone in his office in the Hall of Graduate Studies should be charged to the University (the Freshman Year having no budget or no provision for that). Do you think that it is possible and can be done in all fairness to Professor Richardson and to the University?

Yours very sincerely,
Henri Peyre

## À son père:

Le 1er oct. 1939

... Du moins j'ai assez bon espoir. À la précédente guerre, on avait mobilisé sur-le-champ tous les Français de l'étranger, souvent pour garder des voies ou des chevaux; et le résultat a été la perte pour nous de beaucoup de situations d'importance, industrielles, intellectuelles, etc.; alors que les Allemands, non mobilisés par suite du blocus, ont pris notre place. Pour mon cas particulier, l'Université a prié l'ambassade française de me laisser ici si possible, & elle a demandé aussi à l'ambassadeur américain à Paris, Bullitt, ancien étudiant de Yale, d'intervenir à Paris dans ce sens. Cela aura-t-il quelque effet? Je n'en sais rien, & n'ai pas la moindre réponse encore. Mais c'est encourageant. Or l'Université n'a nullement fait cela sur ma demande, mais par désir très sincère de me garder & conviction que je servirais mieux mon pays ici qu'en combattant.

J'ai donc commencé à travailler, & à enseigner, comme si tout était normal. J'ai pas mal de cours, pas mal de travail administratif aussi, beaucoup de points délicats, de susceptibilités personnelles, dont il faut tenir compte. On attend beaucoup de moi; &, si je reste ici, j'espère en effet redonner au Département français, qui compte une vingtaine de professeurs de divers grades, une vigueur & une valeur nouvelles. La tâche est belle et en vaut la peine. L'Université m'a offert d'emblée ce qu'elle avait de mieux, en termes flatteurs, & je ferai de mon mieux pour la servir. La jeunesse des étudiants a ici beaucoup de qualités: courage, franchise, curiosité vive, ardeur au travail. Et, avec les circonstances présentes et songeant à ce que je ferais en ce moment si j'étais en France, je trouve évidemment qu'une bonne fortune nous a guidés ici. Sans parler de la ruine qui risque de suivre cette guerre en Europe, & de l'avantage qu'il y aura alors—si tout va bien ou est bien allé—à être payé en monnaie moins dépréciée, à avoir des moyens de travail amples & riches.

Sans cela, et cette égoïste, & peut-être provisoire, satisfaction, notre inquiétude est grande de vous sentir loin, angoissés peut-être. Nous dévorons les journaux, pleins d'informations, mais jusqu'ici, avec cette défaite brusque de la Pologne, cette trahison russe, ce désordre balkanique en perspective, peu encourageants. Je persiste à être partisan d'une lutte obstinée, mais n'ai pas le droit de parler tant que mon sort m'évite d'y prendre part—Tout peut sortir de cette alliance russe avec les Allemands, y compris une lutte entre les deux partenaires, ou une contamination de leur armée. En attendant, force nous est de prévoir le pire, & une guerre longue, qui sera peut-être plus courte qu'on ne le croit quand même. . . .

## To Edgar Furniss:

October 11, 1939

Dean Edgar S. Furniss
Yale Graduate School
Dear Dean Furniss:

I called on Mr. Feuillerat just after I met you on the street yesterday. He mentioned the same subject that we had been discussing and raised several objections and advised patience and prudence. He is probably right and is more familiar with the routine of the Graduate School than I am, and with the difficulties which some of our colleagues might raise. I would not like to differ from him, except if very strong objective reasons urged me to do so; nor would I like to antagonize our colleagues in the other Romance Languages, unless the sincere interest of our students makes it necessary.

Mr. Feuillerat's point, about the Philology requirement, is, I believe, as follows: that requirement (two courses out of ten) is not excessive. The trouble is rather that these two courses are given by Professor Hill, who puts the emphasis on the Old French Language exclusively and gives little attention to the Old French literature. There again, I suppose more flexibility is what we need. If a course, dealing entirely or partly with Old French literature, could be substituted for a course in pure Old French Philology, or chosen by the students instead, when that is the interest of the student, the problem might be solved. (This suggestion is my own.)

As to the Spanish and Italian requirement, Mr. Feuillerat feels reluctant to propose any drastic changes. He will discuss it with you, of course. He thinks that the Ph.D. students that Yale has turned out are highly valued outside because they are in a position to teach, not only French, but Spanish and Italian if need be. Moreover, when he first came here, he talked the matter over with Professor Luquiens, and they agreed, in a sort of gentlemen's agreement, to send students from French to Spanish and from Spanish to French for courses. He feels that he is bound by his pledged word in that respect.

I would like to think a little more about this subject and consult with our colleagues, and examine what is the practice, in this respect, in other leading universities. It seems to me that, if Mr. Feuillerat agrees and feels it can be done without hurting anyone's feelings, we might aim at more flexibility—retain, in every case, one other Romance language for candidates whose major field is modern French; insist upon a good knowledge of that language (Spanish or Italian) and of its literature, then leave the choice of the second "minor" to the student and his advisers. It might be (and would very often be) the second other Romance language. In some cases, it might be another field more closely connected with the special interest of the candidate—English, German, History, Philosophy. Such a move would be very moderate and might succeed better in some cases.

As you know, all this is more a question of manner than an essential problem. Both Mr. Hill and Mr. Lipari, out of genuine enthusiasm for their own subject, have perhaps over-burdened our students in some cases; and too little time is thus left for their studies in their primary field. A slight adjustment, and less rigid formulae, might be all that is needed.

All this tentatively, and with the sincere and anxious desire not to suggest anything which might antagonize Mr. Feuillerat or place him in a false or delicate position with his colleagues in Romance Languages. Sometime later, when it is convenient for you, I shall be glad to talk with you again on these points.

Yours very sincerely,<br>Henri Peyre

## À Pierre Bédard:

Le 1 novembre, 1939

Cher Monsieur,

Votre aimable lettre du 26 octobre ne me parvient qu'aujourd'hui, et ici. Elle avait été mêlée au courrier du Directeur de la Maison française et a été retardée là-bas. Je regrette infiniment ce contretemps qui m'a privé du plaisir de vous voir à New York. J'ai aussi entendu beaucoup parler de vous et de vos plans par M. Marx et j'aimerais beaucoup vous rencontrer et causer avec vous, en ce moment où il devrait y avoir tant à faire en ce pays pour nous faire mieux comprendre et mieux aimer.

Je serai sans doute de passage à New York demain jeudi 2 novembre et je vous téléphonerai à l'Institut vers le milieu de l'après-midi pour essayer de vous voir ce même jour ou plus tard.

Veuillez agréer, cher Monsieur, l'assurance de mes sentiments les meilleurs et de mon plus fidèle souvenir.

## À son père:

Ce 7 nov. 1939

. . . Voici ma situation. Ici, on ne mobilise pour le moment (et encore qu'avec un délai de 3 mois) que les lieutenants de 30 ans et au-dessous. Apparemment, on n'a pas besoin d'hommes encore, et bien des surprises (diplomatiques & économiques) peuvent avoir lieu avant le printemps. De plus, je suis personnellement l'objet de la sollicitude de ceux qui m'ont employé au Ministère des Aff. Étrangères. On m'avait recommandé à l'Ambassadeur. Et on me considère comme l'un des Français les plus utiles ici et les plus aptes à la propagande — Après quelque correspondance avec Paris, l'Ambassadeur (que je suis allé voir avant-hier à Washington) m'a confirmé que j'étais l'objet d'une affectation spéciale me maintenant ici indéfiniment. Bien entendu, cela m'imposera des tâches. On me demandera des conférences, de participer à des comités où l'on ébauche (assez mal pour le moment) notre œuvre de propagande ici. Ce sera double travail, ajouté à une lourde tâche de professeur & de chef du département français — Mais j'aurais mauvaise grâce à me plaindre: sécurité, traitement américain, bel appartement plein de charme & d'élégance, bon souper & bon gîte, et le tout sans forfaire à l'honneur — Le sort nous a favorisés. Nos inquiétudes sont pour Jacques, pour toi, pour Louise & Hélène, pour les parents de Marguerite. Jusqu'ici, les dangers sont peu réels. Mais les conditions de vie ne vont-elles pas devenir plus dures? Dites-nous bien & si nous pouvons vous être de quelque secours.

En attendant, la besogne nous accable. Marguerite a peu de service domestique & notre position nous oblige à recevoir pas mal. Cela fait des heures à la cuisine, à nettoyer, à mettre de l'ordre & de la propreté. Et cette angoisse de la guerre nous fait sentir davantage à l'étranger, & nous partageons mal l'insouciance de beaucoup d'Américains. Marguerite est beaucoup seule — car je suis parti presque toute la journée. Je dois donner de nombreux cours — puis l'organisation de toute la section de français (qui compte de 15 à 20 professeurs de divers grades) me prend énormément de temps. Il s'agit de remonter cet enseignement, de donner au français plus de place. Je compte y réussir. Mais ça exige beaucoup d'énergie & de lutte. En sus de cela recruter de nouveaux professeurs, congédier quelques autres, organiser de nouveaux cours pour l'avenir, plus vivants, faire des conférences de demi propagande politique sous un voile littéraire, cela prend le plus clair de mes heures. Je ne risque pas d'entreprendre, comme toi, une œuvre de longue haleine et un dictionnaire! Mais, encore une fois, ce sont là des besognes peu héroïques. Elles empêchent de penser à bien d'autres choses et sans doute est-ce mieux ainsi. Mais je n'ai jamais encore été aussi [*illisible*].

. . . Si l'on arrive même à obtenir des promesses fermes & des garanties de l'Italie, on tentera sans doute quelque expédition vers les Balkans. Là doit se concentrer le jeu diplomatique. Pour le moment, notre péril le plus sérieux serait l'invasion allemande en Hollande: cela ferait pour l'Allemagne une base d'opérations contre l'Angleterre, et, s'ils épargnaient la Belgique comme c'est probable, nous serions gênés pour intervenir là-bas. Si au moins ces neutres s'entendaient et se promettaient aide mutuelle au lieu de se laisser bouffer l'un après l'autre! Pour le reste, il semble bien qu'au printemps nous commencerons à avoir une supériorité aérienne qui ira en s'accentuant. Les Anglais auront des soldats plus nombreux à côté des nôtres pour recevoir les coups. Et, si la famine est encore loin en Allemagne, la pénurie de pétrole & de fer sera tout de même sensible. Espérons. Pour ma part, je suis sans crainte. Et, dans mes discours, je parle déjà de "l'au-delà," de l'organisation de l'Europe après la paix. Il n'est pas adroit de trop parler du démembrement de l'Allemagne, pour le moment. L'opinion américaine, toujours protestante, idéaliste, en serait indisposée; les Anglais ne voudront qu'une chose après la guerre: refaire du commerce avec une Allemagne modérément prospère & démunie de bateaux. Et, de notre côté, le maintien d'une telle Allemagne exigerait une constance dans la vigilance dont notre démocratie n'est guère capable. Au moins pourra-t-on occuper la rive gauche du Rhin & ne plus en déloger! Mais pour le moment, le public américain ne veut pas être entraîné dans la guerre—et surtout pas malgré lui. Il a horreur de la "propagande," et il faut en faire ici avec tact & adresse pour la lui faire avaler. Il y a quelques point sur lesquels il faut faire porter notre effort, & je m'emploie à les signaler à Paris: montrer que la critique du traité de Versailles, si chère aux Allemands, est en grande partie fausse & inspirée par la propagande adverse; que ce traité, même en ce qui concerne les Tchèques, les Sudètes, l'Autriche Hongrie démolie par son propre aveuglement & non par nous, était modéré & assez juste; que ce n'est pas nous qui avons aidé Hitler en n'aidant point la république allemande; Hitler c'est l'Allemagne éternelle & on ne démolira l'un qu'en abattant durement l'autre. Surtout, faire bien voir que nous ne combattons ni pour notre empire ni pour nos anciennes conquêtes devenues légitimes par l'effet du temps, mais pour une [*illisible*] pour laquelle nous nous sacrifions. . . .

## To Edgar Furniss:

November 13, 1939

Dear Mr. Furniss,

As your time must be taken up by many matters similar to the present one at this season of the year and you will probably be able to see me only for a short while on Tuesday at 9.30, I am taking the liberty to mention the most important points on which I want to consult you then. I shall be discussing some of these points again with our Department on Tuesday afternoon, and would be glad to have your precise advice before then.

A. We are contemplating a general reorganization of all our elementary courses for next year (five-hour courses, 10–20, 20–30 substituted for French 10, French 20, French 30—the proposal to that effect is being submitted to the different committees on Course of Study. I am enclosing a copy of that proposal for information. We do not expect the proposed reform to cause any increase in our budget, except that I would like, if possible, to be granted $2400 instead of our present $1800 from the President's Fund. (The sum of $2400 was the sum granted our Department from that fund in 1938–39, and was subsequently reduced to $1800, on our own proposal for 1939–40). Such a moderate increase would appear to be justified, considering the experimental and educational value of the reform we are trying to put through.

B. For the present year, the Department having suffered the loss of one associate professor (Jackson) and one assistant professor (Berthold), a sum of $8500 remained unused by us. Out of those $8500, $2100 went to a new instructor, Cornell; $2000 went to two new assistants; $500 to provide for Mr. Morehouse's promotion. A sum of $3900 thus remained on our credit balance. In your letter to Mr. Seronde of May 18, 1939, you explained that a saving equivalent to that sum (or to Professor Barthold's salary, $3500) had been appropriated to give relief to certain overburdened departments, but that such an action would have no injurious effect on our request for an appropriation this year.

I am thus, if you agree, in proposing our new budget, taking into account that credit balance as added to the total of our budget. However, taking into consideration the Corporation's request for reductions in educational expenditures, I would suggest that we use only part of that credit balance, and our budget for 1940–41 would be about $2000 less than the total we might have been entitled to for 1939–40, and only $1900 more than the total actually spent in 1939–40.

C. May I ask if, with the approval of the Administration, we may assure our present Associate professors (and our new ones, if any promotions to that rank are made) of permanent tenure?

D. Are we to understand that the new scale of salaries now being discussed ($4000 for first year of an associate professor, $3000 for first two years of an assistant professor,) are to be put into effect with our new appointments, if any?

E. We have, at present, four instructors serving their third year in that rank. Three of those I will propose to reappoint for another year, which will be their last one: Messrs. Favreau, Gilmore and Sturm. For Mr. Edsall, who has proved very useful in his teaching and as a supervisor of the freshman work, I would, if you agree, suggest an increase from $2100 to $2500 for 1940–41, and a promotion to Assistant-Professor for 1941–42. Mr. Cornell, who is now serving his first year as a regular full-time instructor, is also a man from whom we hope a great deal; and he might be promoted to an assistant-professorship in 1942–43.

F. Among our three assistant-professors, I will, if you agree, propose that Mr. Bates be reappointed for two, or three, years, according to what is preferable—, that Mr. [Jean] Boorsch be promoted to Associate-Professor. The case of Mr. [E. B.] Ham is an especially difficult one. He has been serving here six years as assistant-professor. The rigid application of the new rules of tenure leaves three eventualities in his case:

1) A promotion to associate-professor, which is not judged desirable.

2) A notification that he should try and leave Yale University after his present term expires.

3) An exception to the new rules, which would grant him an extra term of one, or three, years as assistant-professor.

I will be glad to have the clear advice of the Administration before choosing or proposing one of the last two decisions. The situation is naturally an embarrassing one for me, since I am new-comer here and hardly know Mr. Ham. He has been arguing very strongly that he is a highly productive scholar; that he was given a vague assurance, in 1934, when he first came here, of a permanent future for him at Yale; that he fills a definite need in the Department; and that he is being discriminated against, through some jealousy and conspiracy of some other, or former, members of the Department.

My reply has been that: the wish of the Administration was to apply the new rules of tenure in his case as well as in many others, without delay; that he was rather a Graduate-School man, and that there was, consequently, not much room for him here where the Old French and philological field was already crowded; that, while moderately useful here in Yale College, he had not been so conspicuously successful as to be indispensable. In that case, and there being no hope for promotion to a higher rank, the Administration preferred him to look for a new position while he is only 37 or 38 years old, and that such an application of the rules was not caused by any ill-will or grave dissatisfaction, but was a consequence of the general policy of the University.

G. If Mr. Ham is formally asked to go after the present year, and in order to replace both Mr. Barthold and Mr. Jackson, I would suggest appointing two new assistant professors, with the definite understanding that such appointments, for five years, will not imply any promotion or renewal. The French Department has at present too many younger men, assistants and instructors. In order to raise our level and to make our courses more attractive to the students, we need a fair number of more mature men, able to give a more cultural turn to their teaching of language.

However, I will have to ask the permission to apply for two assistant-professor salaries (i.e. $6000) in blank (or for one only if Mr. Ham stays here). I cannot expect to find any suitable candidates before early in January. If I did not find them this year, I would ask for the corresponding balance to be credited our Department until another year.

H. On two more minor points, I would like to have some information: — the precise date when Professor Feuillerat will retire (in order to plan in advance for the future of the Department), and if, in the case of a chairman of a department going, practically on business and duty, as I shall have to, to the annual convention of Modern Language Professors, which happens to be this year at New Orleans, Louisiana, some indemnity can be reasonably applied for, under the general funds or research funds of the University. (I have been asked, moreover, to deliver two papers at that convention, which I have promised to do so that our Department would be represented.)

If you will kindly give me the information and helpful advice on these points when I see you on Tuesday morning, I shall be extremely grateful, and

Very sincerely,
Hri Peyre

## To the same:

November 15, 1939

Dear Mr. Furniss,

Our department met yesterday and approved the measures which I suggested, following our conversation in the same morning.

1) After long, frank and impartial discussion, the following proposal was unanimously voted, as concerns the case of Mr. Ham: "That Mr. E. B. Ham be nominated assistant-professor for one year, at his present salary, with the understanding that his appointment shall thus be terminated."

I told my colleagues that the university would not act ruthlessly towards Mr. Ham and that, if he were not reappointed after the present year, you had agreed to retain him for an extra year. They preferred to vote for the above motion, which may help Mr. Ham in securing a new position, since he will not feel cramped by the prospect of an imminent departure. Moreover, we thought this might be more fair, since the new rules of tenure demand that the merits of an assistant professor be scrutinized carefully "in the spring of the fourth year of his term," and that could only be done, in the present case, in the fall of the sixth year of Mr. Ham's appointment.

If you agree to this proposal of the department, I will thus provide for the full salary of Mr. Ham in next year's budget. There is, of course, a strong possibility of Mr. Ham securing a new position in the course of the present year, and the above motion, while having helped him somewhat, would remain without effect.

2) Mr. Seronde suggested that an increase of $500 be proposed for him, as he has not received any for a long time, and he could not very well apply for one, as long as he was chairman of the department and prepared the budget himself. President Angell, he says, had told him, when he refused an offer from Swarthmore some years ago, that he would eventually receive a salary as high as any at Yale. The full professors in the Department, i.e. Mr. Seronde, Mr. Feuillerat and myself, agreed unanimously to present the proposal to the Administration.

May I request the favor of a reply on these two points, so that I may present my final budget as soon as possible — or, if you would prefer to discuss them with me again, would you grant me an appointment at your convenience?

Yours sincerely,
Hri Peyre

(PS) I am enclosing a copy of the Harvard requirements, for which I had to wait until I received a precise reply from the Department there — to be added to the similar list I left with you already.

## To Charles Seymour:

November 16, 1939

Dear President Seymour,

I am enclosing a copy of the results of an informal inquiry I made, early this year, concerning the Graduate School requirements in other leading universities. As you will see, our request that our rather rigid requirements in Philology and in our minors (Spanish and Italian) be made somewhat more flexible is not unduly revolutionary. We would be rather falling in line with what has already been done in other universities.

A little more flexibility, added to a better training in written and spoken French (given in a very advanced and difficult course called, for instance, *Explications de textes et Études de style*), and supplemented by a little more discreet "propagande" in colleges and universities that could send us qualified students would, I feel, help our prospects in the Department of Romance Languages in the Graduate School.

It may prove desirable, in the future, in order to develop our French studies in the Graduate School, to suggest the addition of a new, and really eminent member to our staff, or the appointment of visiting-professors from France. As the other list enclosed will show, the upper ranks of our Department, as compared with other leading universities, are not overstaffed. There is, however, no urgency in this matter, and, in some respects, it may be best to wait for the coming of more peaceful conditions in Europe, and for the date (1943) when the retirement of Mr. Feuillerat will make it imperative that we should plan for the future.

For next year and the coming years, we expect to be able to present a stabilized budget, not exceeding the total credit which was allowed us for the present year, and part of which had to remain unused. . . . Out of the credit balance which we did not use this year (made possible by the departure of Mr. Jackson and of Mr. Barthold), we are asking to reserve $3000 for the possible appointment of a new assistant-professor, whom we urgently need. I shall do my best to find a suitable candidate in the future months, and the balance may remain unused if I do not succeed.

With grateful thanks again for your kind suggestions and approval, I am,

Very sincerely,
Henri Peyre

## To Edgar Furniss:

November 16, 1939

Dear Dean Furniss,

On November 14, the professors and associate-professors in the French department voted unanimously to recommend the promotion to the rank of Associate Professor, at the proposed new salary for that rank ($4000 for the first year), Mr. J. Boorsch, now completing his sixth year as assistant-professor.

Mr. Boorsch has proved a very competent and successful teacher in the Graduate School and in Yale College. His personal qualities and his scholarly abilities are great. It is expected that he will soon produce an important work in the scholarly field. It seems to the Department that Yale should make a keen effort to retain him here, the more so as circumstances are pointing to a scarcity of competent and successful native Frenchmen teaching in this country.

The above recommendation is thus submitted to the Dean and to the faculty of the Graduate School, to which Mr. Boorsch is assigned.

Yours sincerely,
Henri Peyre

## To the same:

November 21, 1939

Dear Dean Furniss,

   Now that we seem to have reached, thanks to your very kind understanding and help, a solution of some of the problems connected with the future of our Department in the undergraduate section, may I again mention the question of our Graduate School requirements? As you know, I had only tried to give a few discreet hints in that matter, which is more Professor Feuillerat's concern than my own, and I merely transmitted the results of an inquiry made as to the practice of other leading universities. I had the opportunity to mention some of my views to Professor Luquiens and to Professor Rose, and, more recently, to Professor Lipari. I feel sure that it will be very easy to agree with them and they are convinced, as well as myself, of the desirability of cooperating in a spirit of mutual trust and help, of the necessity of making some of our requirements more flexible and of wording our announcements differently, of the advisability of increasing somewhat the number of our graduate students and of thus choosing better students out of larger numbers. If you agree (after some consultation with other members of our Department who are connected with graduate teaching, such as Professors Hill, Richardson, Boorsch and Morehouse), I would take the liberty to suggest that you might take up the matter directly with our colleagues and especially with Professor Feuillerat; and I feel confident that it will be easy to reach an agreement and to carry out some of our modest proposals in the very near future. It might be desirable to have such an agreement reached before Christmas, so that some of us might discreetly mention it to our colleagues from other colleges and universities, when we meet them at our December annual convention.

   After some talk with Professors Luquiens, Rose and Lipari, I would modify my views slightly and present them, very briefly, as follows:

   1) It is highly desirable for our department, for the morale of the professors giving graduate courses and for our reputation, to have a larger number of graduate students in Romance languages (50 to 60 eventually, instead of our present 30). From a larger number we might choose better ones, notifying some students (after 1 year of graduate studies, for instance) that they do not seem to come up to our expec-

tations, or even advising some not to pursue their studies beyond an M.A. degree.

2) I feel that, even if we were to fail in our attempt or to be disappointed in our hopes, we are now in the presence of certain conditions which make our effort worth trying: several other universities, which had recently been attracting more graduate students than Yale, have allowed their Romance Languages Departments to deteriorate. Many prospective good graduate students might be less drawn towards Harvard, Johns Hopkins, Princeton and would probably come here where we have library facilities, opportunities for research and publication as good as in any institution, and a staff which can already compare very favorably with that of other institutions of high standing.

3) A little discreet propaganda (in the form of talks with our colleagues from other institutions, letters to colleges in the eastern and north-eastern part of the country) might be useful in that respect. A small pamphlet of 5 or 6 pages (extract from our catalogue) might be sent around. That pamphlet might mention more precisely which courses will be given in the next two years, and omit part of the long and confusing series of titles which we now seem to be offering.

4) Since graduate students are to be teachers of languages as well as prospective scholars, I would be inclined to insist on some training (difficult and of really advanced standing) in the language—for instance, in French, a competent and difficult course in "stylistics" or "Études de Style." Later on, advanced phonetics should be included. The absence of any teaching and training in phonetics is, at present, a regrettable gap in both our undergraduate and graduate schools. Such a practical course in the study of language and style might partly offset some of the obvious drawbacks of the geographical situation of Yale: the scarcity, in New Haven, of opportunities for speaking, and hearing French, or for receiving competent private instruction, in that field, from independent native French teachers.

5) I would not favor any change in our practice as to: a) not requiring the publication of the dissertation; b) giving the Latin and German examinations as they are being given now; c) not distinguishing between a Ph.D. in Romance Philology and Romance literatures, although, in practice, we might advise those of our candidates primarily interested in Philology to take courses accordingly. In every case, each Director of Graduate Studies would, in cooperation with the other Di-

rectors and according to the present "Gentlemen's agreement," feel free to plan the program of each student according to his own interests and curiosity. Some exceptions to our requirements might thus be suggested, in individual and exceptional cases.

6) This would lead to our most needed reform: more flexibility in our requirements, and a different wording of our Bulletins accordingly. I would favor, (as Professor Luquiens, Professor Lipari and Professor Feuillerat would too, I believe) requiring one course of *Introduction to Romance Philology* from all our students. A second philological course would also be taken by all of them: — that second course might be Old Spanish or Portuguese for students of Spanish; Provençal for students of Italian; Old French phonology and morphology (and perhaps also, eventually, Provençal or Portuguese) for candidates wishing to specialize in Romance Philology in the Old French field; a course in Old French literature (read in the texts) for candidates whose major field of interest would be modern French literature; History of the Modern French Language, for the same group of students.

7) In the same spirit, we would continue our present practice of requiring knowledge of the three Romance languages and literatures for all our graduate students. I would not be in favor, after more careful consideration of the possible objections, of distinguishing between a first and second minor. I would suppress the paragraphs (b) and (c) page 228 of our Graduate School Catalogue, and say merely that we "require normally a satisfactory knowledge of the three Romance Languages and Literatures," without mentioning any number of years of courses. It would be understood that we would be willing to consider the case of each particular student and plan his program accordingly, and not expect from him, if his major field is, for instance, French, an ability to speak and write Italian and Spanish perfectly, but an ability to follow one advanced course in each of these two languages and literatures and to develop some feeling for the literary texts read in the language. Whenever the dissertation of some of our students demanded extraneous knowledge (in philosophy, Art, German literature, English literature), the Directors of Graduate studies would easily agree not to be too exacting in their requirements in, for instance, one of the other Romance literature courses taken by the student, so as to consider each particular case in a spirit of flexibility and collaboration.

In making these very moderate suggestions, I believe I am interpreting in a fair and objective way the wishes of our most serious students and stating the best interests of our Romance Languages department in the Graduate School. As I said previously, however, I do not wish to interfere (or even to seem to be interfering) with what is Professor Feuillerat's field. His own competence and long experience should prevail, and any decisions or action in reference to these matters should, I believe, be left to him and to you.

Very sincerely yours,<br>Henri Peyre

## À son frère:

Yale University<br>New Haven, Conn.<br>Le 22 novembre 1939

Mon cher Jacques,

Ta dernière lettre, qui date déjà de cinq semaines, nous a fait le plus grand plaisir. Qu'es-tu devenu depuis lors? Parfois je me flatte de l'espoir que tu as pu être démobilisé, car on doit se plaindre aussi à l'armée du manque de médecins, et en avoir un trop grand nombre aux armées, où, Dieu merci, les blessés pour le moment n'abondent pas. Il semble qu'on ait fait chez nous, cette fois-ci, une mobilisation fort rationnelle et excellemment organisée. On a essayé au moins d'adapter chacun à spécialité. Indirectement, j'en profite.

Comme tu vois, je suis toujours ici. On n'a pas encore mobilisé beaucoup de Français d'Amérique & les officiers de réserve de moins de 30 ans qu'on a rappelés ne seront pas rapatriés avant les mois du début du printemps. On semble vouloir laisser les autres pour ne pas recommencer l'erreur de 1914, où on a, par la méthode contraire, perdu un bon nombre de places que les Allemands ont occupées aussitôt—Dans mon cas particulier, j'ai reçu l'assurance qu'on me garderait ici en "affectation spéciale," en raison des fonctions assez importantes que j'occupe—Je ne suis pas poltron à l'excès et j'aurais fait la guerre avec un courage résigné, s'il avait fallu, après l'avoir, un des premiers, proclamée inévitable et nécessaire. Mais je reconnais que l'avantage est considérable, pour Marguerite & moi, de rester ici à l'abri, loin de tout péril, chauffé, nourri, payé comme d'habitude. Parfois, nous éprouvons même quelque honte de notre confort—Notre appartement est agréable et même luxueux. Nous avons retrouvé le décor de notre intérieur lyonnais, sous un ciel plus froid mais aussi plus bleu—Mais la pensée de ces événements, des malheurs possibles ou menaçants, de votre dispersion à vous autres ou de vos épreuves, nous saisit souvent & nous tourmente. Te voilà parmi les camions, à rouler de ville en ville—Que transportent tes gens? ravitaillement, munitions? Cela peut-être dangereux si les bombardements de l'arrière commençaient. Que dit-on parmi vous? À quoi s'attend-on? D'après les journaux français que papa m'a fait parvenir, on se plaint surtout de l'ennui & de l'inactivité. Est-ce ton cas aussi? Tu vas voir que l'idéal du retraité oisif, que tu prônais parfois, n'est pas si rose que cela! Il est vrai que tu insistais sur un certain climat et un certain pays. Je suis passé une fois dans ma vie à Langres, & ce pays de Diderot ne m'a guère impressionné. Encore était-ce en plein été—Il doit faire froid & boueux l'hiver. Es-tu d'ailleurs resté là?

Papa nous écrit quelquefois—Il semble supporter calmement son sort—mais, à son âge, pareille solitude n'est guère gaie, & la compagnie de Pipo lui est, moins qu'à toi, une aide. Il est vrai qu'il a ses lectures & son insatiable curiosité historique et philosophique. Est-il bien soigné? Quelles nouvelles reçois-tu de tes amis d'Avignon? Pour peu que cette aventure se prolonge, ne faudra-t-il pas tout recommencer avec vos clientèles? Tout cela doit souvent t'inspirer quelque nostalgie et peut-être même quelque cafard—Dis-nous bien si nous pouvons faire quelque chose pour toi, & quoi? De quoi as-tu besoin, ou envie? Peut-être vas-tu te mettre à étudier l'anglais, par distraction.

Dans ce malheur, il est encore heureux que l'Italie soit restée tranquille. Sans cela et à Avignon et à Tunis vous risquez de courir de plus grands dangers, & un ennemi supplémentaire sur mer et en Méditerranée n'aurait pas été une drôle d'affaire—Pour le moment, je suppose que Louise et Hélène se trouvent à peu près en sécurité & à l'aise—On semble, chez nous, vouloir ramener pas mal de choses à un état aussi normal que possible—C'est pourquoi je ne désespère pas qu'on te démobilise.

D'ici, ces jours-ci, on a l'impression assez encourageante que les choses vont bien pour nous, justement parce que nous n'avons pas encaissé, & que les Allemands sont bien embarrassés. Ils semblent intérieurement divisés sur les décisions à prendre. S'ils se risquent à travers la Hollande, nous avons de fortes chances de les attendre dans les Flandres & de les y battre. Sinon, nous patienterons aussi & espérerons peut-être un nouveau front, avec l'Italie ou dans les Balkans. Bien entendu, c'est l'imprévu qui surviendra & il est encore possible que tout ceci soit plus rapide que nous ne soupçonnons. Le plus dangereux pour nous était le début, dans les airs & sur terre, & nous l'avons franchi. La lutte économique & diplomatique va de plus en plus tourner en notre faveur. Mais il faudra pour les Allemands, tôt ou tard, une défaite militaire — ce n'est que là-dessus qu'on pourra tâcher de fonder la réorganisation d'une Europe désarmée.

Comment cela va-t-il autour de toi? Quel est l'emploi de tes journées? Comment est le moral de tes gens? Quel confort a-t-on? Tu dois surtout souffrir de l'isolement, et d'avoir à te coucher si tôt & te lever si tôt. Je le comprends d'ailleurs. Tu avais raison de professer (& de pratiquer avec mesure) une philosophie épicurienne!

Nous devrions au moins t'écrire plus souvent. Marguerite n'y est pas très assidue, elle a fort à faire avec le soin de notre logis. Je suis moi-même surchargé de besogne: lourd enseignement, tâches de direction & d'orientation de toute l'importante section de français, nombreuses petites reformes auxquelles je m'applique — et tâches diverses en dehors: conférences etc. Je m'occupe & vais m'occuper plus encore de la propagande. J'ai vu à Washington l'Ambassadeur de France à qui j'en ai parlé. Jusqu'ici la France, contente de jouir ici de nombreuses sympathies, ne fait pas grand'chose — pas assez à mon avis. Pour le moment, nous aurons ici la possibilité d'acheter armes & munitions. C'est beaucoup, & ce sera plus encore pour l'avenir. Mais on ne peut pas compter sur une intervention *armée* de l'Amérique. Il faudrait, pour que cela survienne, un grand événement, une vague soudaine d'indignation, une énorme maladresse de l'Allemagne. C'est tout à fait possible, mais pour le moment peu prévisible. L'opinion est au fond déroutée par l'étrange caractère qu'a pris cette guerre, alors qu'on s'attendait dès le début aux cataclysmes les plus mélodramatiques.

Envoie-nous cartes ou lettres quand tu as un instant. La tienne (& toutes vos lettres jusqu'ici) sont arrivées intactes, sans aucun examen de censure. Je ne sais si je souhaiterais très vivement la Syrie à ta place. Il y a du soleil, mais l'hiver y est plus froid que tu penses. Et de là, il est fort possible qu'on forme quelque jour un corps expéditionnaire vers les Balkans. Là, fièvres & maladies s'ajouteraient au danger — et, en camion dans ces pays-la, vous ne rouleriez pas sur un billard. Mais qui peut prévoir? L'an dernier, nous nous croyions dangereusement exposés en Egypte & c'est un des pays les plus heureux. Nous le regrettons parfois, nos amis là-bas, notre vie plus agrémentée. Ici, tout est pour le travail.

Porte-toi bien (nous allons fort bien, nous-mêmes) et renseignez-nous sur toi & sur [*illisible*].

Henri

# the 1940s

## CHAPTER THREE

## To Charles Seymour:

January 12, 1940

Dear President Seymour,

I have taken the liberty to telephone in order to ask for an appointment with you. As we are approaching the middle of the academic year, we can perceive and formulate more clearly some of the problems of our department, and I should like both to mention to you some of the results already obtained and to ask your advice and approval about our plans or our desiderata for the future. May I state them briefly in this letter, before I have an opportunity to discuss them with you orally?

As you may have heard, our department has recently proposed and put through, thanks to the very obliging collaboration of Dean Furniss, of Dean DeVane and of Dean Buck, a number of minor reforms, from which we expect tangible improvements very soon.

The rule voted some years ago, allowing students entering Yale with a satisfactory grade on French CP 4 for admission to be considered as having satisfied the modern language requirement of Yale College, has been abolished. Exceptions or compromise rulings will of course be granted whenever advisable.

The language courses have been thoroughly reorganized and two five-hour courses, called French 12 and French 22, will, in the future, enable students to meet the language requirement in two years, when they enter the college without any French, or in the traditional French 30 course, which will also be reorganized and renovated. They will thus be free of language drill in their junior and senior years, and able to use the language while doing personal work in the department in which they major.

The French 39 course is being reorganized under my own direction and given, as a cultural course in French civilization, for advanced freshmen.

The work of our majors in French is being also reorganized, on lines parallel to those already prevailing in the departments of History and English, with a departmental essay, and an oral part added to the final examination.

A new course, French 58, will be offered next year, in which, in order both to fill a gap in our list of courses and to satisfy the present trend in the curiosity of our students, French criticism, history and political thought will be treated. I am calling it:

French Criticism, Historians and Political Thinkers: (Literary Criticism, history, the essay and political thought from Montesquieu and Rousseau to Sainte-Beuve, Michelet, Taine, Renan, Gobineau, Péguy, Maurras and to political writers of the present day).

Finally, thanks to the kind and effective cooperation of Dean Furniss and of our colleagues in the other Romance languages, the requirements for our studies in the Graduate School have been made much more flexible. It is to be hoped that they will cease keeping away prospective students and that our wish of getting more and better graduate students in the Romance languages may be fulfilled.

I have, at the December meeting of the Modern Language Association at New Orleans, tried to "advertise" those changes discreetly with some of our colleagues from all over the country, and interviewed several young men with the hope of finding suitable new colleagues when we need some. The problem of eminent or promising new colleagues in French remains a difficult one. Men of real distinction are not very numerous, in America, in the field of Romance languages; in Europe on the contrary, and particularly in France, foreign languages have recently been attracting many of the brilliant men, who have preferred that field to specializing in their own literature, i.e. French. It is not in our power to change these general conditions, at least for a number of years. Moreover, the necessity of not increasing our expenses which has been pressed upon us may prevent us from contemplating the addition of eminent men to our staff.

I cannot help feeling that our most delicate—yet our most urgent and most important problem will lie with our graduate school work. That is probably the field, too, where, if successful, we can render the most valuable service to the country as a whole, by sending better teachers of Romance languages and of Romance civilizations in schools, colleges and other universities. Unfortunately, our field does not as a rule attract as promising students as the professional schools do; we do not get many students of fairly independent means and with some cultural background, as do other subjects like English, which tempt literary-minded young men who hope to write. Moreover, we are not in a position through an ample supply of scholarships to attract many young men; the level and quality of our undergraduate teaching forbid us from appointing many assistants, giving the elementary courses in French and studying in our graduate school at the same time, as is the practice in large state universities.

In spite of those difficulties, it seems to me a vigorous effort should be made without delay, since circumstances seem to open an opportunity for us at this moment: many students who might have gone to France for their advanced studies are temporarily prevented from doing so; others who in recent years went to Harvard or Johns Hopkins may feel that, with the loss of several eminent professors and the consequent lowering of morale in Romance Departments in those universities, Yale may be in a better position, with excellent library facilities, less rigid requirements and a competent staff, to give them the instruction they need.

Some minor reforms, which Dean Furniss has very kindly suggested or approved of, will, I feel confident, help our prospects in that field. There is another one, however, which I would like to suggest as an urgently advisable step: *the appointment of a visiting-professor in French*. Harvard, Columbia, and at a certain time Princeton, have enjoyed or still enjoy the facility of inviting an eminent French professor, staying a whole year, more frequently half a year with them (or in the case of Professor Hazard at Columbia, three months every other year). Such an arrangement does much to stimulate the research of the younger men in the Department; it attracts graduate students and may prove a great help to us, both for teaching and for "publicity" purposes; at Yale, it would also prove beneficial to our advanced undergraduates, if, as I hope, the visiting professor could devote half or one third of his time to them, be interested in their extra-curricular activities in French, etc. I would suggest that such a visiting-professor might be called here for four months every other year, for instance. He would be, usually and to begin with, a specialist of French literature or Philology or of Comparative literature. Eventually, if the difficulty of the language might be solved easily, he might also be an eminent professor of French History, Philosophy, Geography even or English, as has, I believe, been the case at Harvard. I imagine that the financial provision should be, approximately and with possible variations, about $5000 every other year.

The second point where I would advocate concentrating our efforts and eventually our expenses, if and when the corresponding grant could be found, would concern more particularly (though not exclusively) our undergraduate students: it would be the establishing of a *French center* at Yale. Not necessarily a Maison Française, as exists in some other American universities, but a meeting-place, which might be modest at first, where our students interested in French would get together. French tables have been organized successfully in several colleges; we have started some, this year, in the Freshman Dining Halls, and we are trying to give a new impetus to our students' interest in extra-curricular activities in French. But many of them still complain of not having a chance to talk and converse in French while at Yale. The quality of their spoken French is, indeed, not always equal to their good will.

I believe much could be done for them (graduates and undergraduates, prospective teachers, diplomats, economists, students in drama or in fine arts, etc.), if a center could be founded, in some conveniently central location, where they might come and meet members of the French Department and eventually other professors or French visitors to the University. There would be, not merely informal conversation or more regular conversation-groups, but some lectures or talks in French occasionally, phonetic (and other) records, and some practical training in phonetics (which is, at present, the greatest gap in our offerings in French), a room with reviews, magazines in French, and where the books purchased in the last few years from the French Government's fund might be placed; a few pictures or engravings or photographs concerning French art, occasionally a small exhibition. If the plan were encouraged and made more precise, it would be possible to estimate the cost of such a *Centre Français* which, I trust, would not be very high. I could easily undertake a discreet inquiry at other universities where such a Maison Française exists, and profit by the experience and results obtained elsewhere.

Such are the two suggestions which I would like to present, with the sincere conviction that they would meet two urgent needs of our Department and soon prove highly beneficial to the University as a whole. I realize that the time is not considered favorable for any increase in our expenses, however comparatively modest these might be considering the necessary task to be accomplished. But I thought I would formulate these proposals by writing without delay and ask your opinion about them when you may have a few moments free.

Yours very sincerely,
Henri Peyre

## À Pierre Bédard:

January 17, 1940

Cher Monsieur,

Je vous remercie de votre aimable lettre et je serai très heureux de faire devant vos auditoires les deux conférences dont vous me parlez, de vous revoir à cette occasion et de m'entretenir avec vous des questions qui nous préoccupent.

La date du mardi 20 février me convient, ou à défaut celle du mardi 27 février qui me serait même plus commode encore—et je vous remercie de vouloir bien mettre à ma disposition l'appartement de l'Institut à cette occasion.

Voici quelques sujets entre lesquels je vous prierai de choisir, selon la connaissance que vous avez de votre public et le sens que vous désirez, donner à ces conférences dans les circonstances présentes. Les numéros 1, 2, 3 et 4 sont plus purement littéraires; le n° 6 toucherait (mais avec discrétion et surtout dans le domaine moral) aux questions actuelles; le n° 5 insisterait, sans phrases ni esprit de creuse propagande, sur la force de rénovation, la fécondité, la robuste vigueur de notre littérature, de notre art, de nos techniques dans ces dernières dizaines d'année, par opposition à la préciosité, à la joliesse, au raffinement décadent que l'on associe trop souvent ou trop uniquement à notre nom.

Veuillez agréer, cher Monsieur, l'assurance de mes sentiments les plus cordialement dévoués.

Hri Peyre

1. Alain Fournier
2. Le plus jeune des grands écrivains d'aujourd'hui: Paul Claudel.
3. Les aspirations nouvelles de la littérature française: Montherlant, Malraux, Giono.
4. La nouvelle poésie française contemporaine.
5. Jeunesse de la France.
6. Le problème français d'aujourd'hui: les responsabilités, les données, les solutions.

## To Edgar Furniss:

January 19, 1940

Dear Dean Furniss,

I am very grateful to you for your kind acceptance of my suggestions and your helpful advice.

I am going ahead with the different schemes which you kindly approved of.

1) The possible appointment of a visiting-professor, invited by our Department every other year, to start probably in 1941–42. I will submit a more definite memorandum later.

2) The prospective creation of a French center, on which I will also submit more precise information later.

3) I am encouraging our younger men to prepare for publication whatever work we shall judge worthy of it and of our standards, with the hope that the publication will be undertaken whenever possible without too much difficulty.

4) I am consulting with Professor Feuillerat on our little "publicity"

pamphlet concerning our work in the Graduate School, and we shall hope to present it to you fairly soon.

5) I shall consult Mr. Lohmann about some provision for lectures in French or talks on French subjects before our Romance Club and shall be grateful if you can support our proposal when you have an opportunity.

As to the question of assistantships and scholarships, I shall examine the question very carefully with our colleagues and we shall make an effort to use the facility which you are granting us in a spirit of economy. I shall take it for granted that: a) the traveling-fellowship in French given to a Yale College student who wants to continue his studies in the Graduate School will, when unused for travel abroad or when no suitable candidate is found, be reserved for our Department in the Graduate School and utilized in the most suitable manner.

b) Exceptionally, for 1940–41, the sum of $3000 provided for in our budget (new assistant-professor replacing Professor Barthold) may be used, whole or in part, for assistantships or scholarships. We shall be very careful in our choice not to impair the quality of our teaching in Yale College; we shall be equally careful to select, for assistants or fellows, very promising candidates who will do credit to our Department and to our Graduate School. It is understood that this use of part of our instruction budget for assistantships or fellowships is exceptional for this year. The young men thus called to Yale will, if they prove to be up to our expectations, have some possibility of remaining here after 1940–41, since the appointment of Messrs. Favreau, Gilmore, Sturm, Kurth and perhaps others will then be terminated.

With my sincere thanks for your very kind help,

Very sincerely yours,
Henri Peyre

## To the same:

January 23, 1940

Dear Dean Furniss,

May I ask your opinion and approval on a minor point connected with our Department for next year, before you leave on your speech-making tour?

Mr. Gilmore, who has been an instructor with us for two years and a half, would like to be teaching only part time next year, so as to start his new studies at the Law School, which he thinks more in line with his real interests. We shall regret him when he decides to leave the teaching of French altogether, for he was one of our most promising young men in the field.

For next year, 1940–41, I shall ask him to teach half-time as he desires, which may be six to seven hours according to our needs. Theoretically, according to our new rules, his salary should not be more than half the basic instructor's salary, i.e. $1000. Since Mr. Gilmore has experience and is distinctly more useful than a new untrained assistant, and since he has been getting $2100 this year and might have had $2500 now, according to our rules, would you agree if I suggested for him a slightly higher salary, $1200 or $1100 at least? This of course would not increase our total budget, since the new assistant whom we would engage to teach the hours left vacant by Mr. Gilmore's decision would probably receive $800 or $900 at the utmost. Mr. Gilmore's present salary of $2100 might thus be divided into two assistants, himself and another man, at $1200 and $800 respectively.

Yours very sincerely,<br>
Hri Peyre

## À Pierre Bédard:

Le 23 janvier, 1940

Cher Monsieur,

Je vous remercie de votre prompte réponse et cela est bien entendu pour les deux sujets que vous avez choisis. Je serai très heureux de cette occasion de parler à l'Institut Français que vous avez si heureusement développé et rénové.

Cette semaine du 20 février sera justement pour moi très bousculée, en raison d'engagements antérieurs. Je pense que nous tâcherons d'arriver à New York, ma femme et moi, le lundi après-midi, et repartirons le mercredi, où je dois parler à New London.

Je ne pense pas que vous désiriez d'autres renseignements. Je suis personnellement professeur à la fois à l'Université de Lyon et à Yale, mais en présence réelle en Amérique pour le moment comme vous savez.

Je me réjouis de cette perspective de pouvoir causer avec vous plus longuement le mois prochain et vous prie de croire à mes sentiments les plus dévoués.

Hri Peyre

## To Charles Seymour:

February 12, 1940

Dear President Seymour,

You were kind enough to welcome and encourage my proposal for the establishment of a visiting-professor in French in our Department. May I outline briefly the considerable advantages that we expect from such a proposal, and mention the approximate and limited burden it would represent for the budget of the Department and for the University?

1) Other leading universities in the country have, regularly or at varied intervals, adopted such a scheme of inviting a professor from abroad. Columbia has on the staff of its French Department Professor Paul Hazard, of the College de France and has had several others in the past. Harvard has called regularly a French visiting-professor every year. Princeton, Chicago, Johns Hopkins, California have had a similar arrangement in the past. Yale has adopted the principle of a regular visiting-professor, with conspicuous success and marked benefit, in the School of Fine Arts. The French Department feels it would profit greatly from a similar arrangement. The system would work even more smoothly and more quickly, if properly applied, as the difficulty of language would not exist. The visiting-professor in French would naturally be understood readily by the graduate and undergraduate students whom we would have.

2) The benefits to be expected would be: primarily to the students, of Yale College and of the Graduate School. An eminent professor from France would every other year, give a full graduate course concentrated in one semester. His reputation, the assistance he would give to the research of our Ph.D. candidates would be a great help in attracting good students to our Department in the Graduate School. We would, moreover, ask the visiting professor to take one of our advanced courses for the undergraduates, and to talk with some of our French majors or

with students of other Departments who might be interested in French History, French Philosophy, etc. The younger members of our Faculty in the French Department would also derive great benefit from the presence and advice of an eminent French scholar.

3) Such valuable advantages to be gained by the students of French, the faculty and the University as a whole would be obtained with a limited expense. Our suggestion is that the visiting-professor in French might be appointed every other year, for four months (October to January or February to May), beginning with 1941–42. It might be possible, in the years when such a visitor would come to Yale, to alternate his visit with that of the French professors in the School of Fine Arts. The same apartment in a college or (if one were available in the future and if the visiting professor is married) outside a college might be used, in succession, by the visitor in the Art School and the visitor to our Department. Our intention would be, after very careful survey of the field by our colleagues and myself, to choose a very eminent scholar or critic. The salary which I would suggest would be, at the maximum, $5000 every other year, and might be less in some cases, especially if living arrangements were provided.

The French Department might probably arrange to provide part of that expense ($5000 every other year, i.e. $2500 a year) out of its budget. Although the total budget of the French Department is reasonably limited, I would suggest that it might provide $1500 or $2000 every other year out of its allowance; $3500 or $3000 only would thus be asked, as a special grant, from the University, or an average of $1750 or $1500 a year. This total is lower than an instructor's salary; and the total expense of $5000 a year (in alternate years) would not be more than the salary of an associate-professor. The profits, from every point of view, would be much greater than those we might expect from the appointment of a regular associate-professor.

4) I would mention also the real benefit that such a plan of an eminent professor or critic visiting Yale every other year would bring to the reputation of Yale abroad. Many friends of Yale traveling in France or in Europe have noticed the lesser fame enjoyed by our University, as compared to institutions like Harvard which have regularly called visitors over here and thus made lasting friends in many European universities or among literary critics abroad (Princeton had A. Maurois as a visiting-professor some years ago). Our Department (and by way of consequence

Yale College and our Graduate School) would thus both gain greatly by the plan we are suggesting and it would serve the reputation of our University, as the appointment of visiting-professors in the Art School has done already.

My colleagues and I shall be very happy, if the Corporation and the officers of the University consent to approve of our plan, and I shall, if you wish me to proceed with our plans for 1941–42, submit precise suggestions of names of prospective visiting-professors in French to be considered.

Sincerely yours,
Henri Peyre

## To the same:

February 19, 1940

Dear President Seymour,

I have just received the copy of Mr. Ham's letter that was forwarded to me by the Provost. I would like to comment briefly upon some of its points, so that you will have full information on the point of view of the French Department.

Many, if not all, of the arguments advanced by Mr. Ham seem to me both weak and presented in a way which cannot help his cause greatly, either at Yale or in other universities where we are recommending him. I am sorry he chose to act this way, without consulting me. Some of the points mentioned in his memorandum (such as points 2, 4, 8, 9) played no part whatever in our deliberation and decision.

As I see them, Mr. Ham's main contentions are:

a) That the Chairman of the French Department (Mr. Seronde) implied in 1934 that a permanent future was open for him at Yale, and as late as 1939 encouraged his hopes for an associate-professorship.

I will merely say that Mr. Seronde never said so to me in so many words, and that (even before the present rules of tenure were voted) it was impossible to promise an associate-professorship many years in advance. When the question officially came up for discussion at the meeting of professors and associate-professors of our Department held early in November, not one of the six professors present proposed a promotion to an associate-professorship for Mr. Ham.

b) That the prospective "dismissal" of Mr. Ham was contemplated as early as the first months of 1939.

That may be, and if so, the administration thought nothing could or should be done until the new chairman of the Department had taken up his duties and his responsibilities.

In any case, since, under our new rules of tenure, it would have been necessary to warn Mr. Ham in the spring of the fourth year if his appointment were to be terminated after five years, we unanimously decided to let him know in November 1939 that his appointment would be extended only until June 1941.

c) That the Administration's wish to "discuss" Mr. Ham was "mandatory" to the Department. That is not the fact. The chairman of the Department in October and November duly consulted on the matter the President and the Provost, the Deans of the different Schools, the Master of Mr. Ham's college, and the other professors in the Department. He found a widespread and general feeling that Mr. Ham's promotion to a higher and permanent grade was not justified or desirable from their point of view, *if such was the opinion of the French Department.*

Each member of the French Department may, in private conversation, have showed sympathy for Mr. Ham's case. I did so more than anyone else. The situation was not a very pleasant one for me as a newcomer. I conscientiously tried to ascertain all the facts, to banish all rumors and all mention of past quarrels. When the six professors and associate-professors met as a body to discuss the possible promotions and the future of the Department, the agreement was complete, the discussion full and impartial, and the vote unanimous to propose Mr. Ham for reappointment as assistant-professor for one more year only.

d) This was or is not exactly a "dismissal." The application of our rules makes promotion to an associate-professorship the reward for exceptional services and exceptional promise. If such a promotion is not granted, it is advisable for the assistant-professor to leave while still young and while it is comparatively easy for him to secure another position elsewhere.

I examined the case very attentively. Mr. Ham's scholarship is indeed very productive, and should, it seems, secure for him a place in a graduate-school of high standing. However, when I consulted the Director of Graduate Studies, he told me that such scholarship (accurate and minute text-editing) was not what he wanted for our Graduate School; that Professor Hill's courses filled the needs of our students perfectly in that field; that the *quality* of scholarship counted, for him, more than quantity, and that he thought there was more thought and promise in Mr. Boorsch's little book on Descartes than in all Mr. Ham's productions.

In the undergraduate Department, we found that Mr. Ham's work, while useful and of a good average, was not so *exceptionally* good as to justify a promotion to an associate-professorship; that his courses could easily be given by a new assistant-professor; that, such being the case, it was better for the College and for Mr. Ham himself to suggest his replacement, after another year, which would be a mere application of the rules of tenure adopted by Yale.

e) The point raised in Mr. Ham's fifth reason is more delicate to discuss (charge of playing politics). The fact is that, in my very impartial efforts to find out all about the case, I inquired diligently as to the motives, and found a feeling that Mr. Ham's personality, in spite of many achievements, had not filled the students or his colleagues with enthusiasm. His constant references to Mr. Boorsch (even in the present memorandum) or, elsewhere, to Mr. Bates, even if excusable in a man trying hard to defend his own position, are not very skillful and would seem to justify the contention that Mr. Ham brings too many "political" considerations into our academic discussions. These imponderable elements are delicate to put in words, but I grant that they may have played a part in not securing many friends for Mr. Ham among the Administration. Mr. Ham's present memorandum seems to me an equally ill-advised move.

All the other reasons (such as 2, 4, 6, 7, 8, 9) never entered into our minds when we merely decided that Mr. Ham was not so *exceptionally* brilliant as to justify a promotion here; was not indispensable so as to justify an exception to our rules of tenure and be retained here indefinitely as assistant-professor; that such a move would, in any case, be contrary to the policy of the University, to the wishes of the Administration, and to Mr. Ham's own interests.

It was unanimously decided by Messrs. Feuillerat, Seronde, Hill, Richardson, Morehouse and myself that a request for retaining Mr. Ham as assistant-professor for one more year (1940–41) was the just solution of the problem raised by our application of the new rules of tenure, and would fulfill the wishes and the interests of the Department. That request was granted by the Provost and the Administration.

Yours sincerely,<br>Henri Peyre

**To the same:**

February 28, 1940

Dear President Seymour,

I am sorry about the delay in answering your letter of February 20 about Mr. Ham's visit. Several engagements for lectures out of town prevented my doing so promptly last week. Since then, I have written to my colleagues, asking them whether they felt that they had voted under some form of pressure, last November, when a decision was taken as to Mr. Ham's status. I am forwarding their answers to you.

I can only add, once more, my own testimony. I voted freely, of course, as every one of us did. But I did my best to ascertain all the facts about Mr. Ham before discussing the case with my colleagues. It was my duty to find out whether the Administration was favorably disposed to the promotions we were contemplating, or to other modifications as to the status of some of our colleagues. It was obvious that a promotion to an associate-professorship for Mr. Ham was not deemed highly desirable, for budgetary reasons and considering the interest of the Department, which received more valuable service from Mr. Boorsch. None of us suggested such a promotion. That being so, we thought we should both be fair to Mr. Ham, in difficult circumstances, and show our effort to apply the new rules of tenure of the University in a cooperative spirit, by asking that he be reappointed for one year in that capacity. This "year of grace" might have been refused by the Administration, since it was an exception to the new rules just voted. It was however immediately accepted by the Provost, who said he would abide by the decision of the Department.

Our action was taken in a spirit of cooperation with the Administration and, primarily, in the interests of the Department. I gather that all our colleagues who voted for it still agree that it was the best solution.

I am transmitting their letters to you and shall be grateful if, on his return, you will kindly show them to the Provost. I have no further need for them myself.

I am sincerely sorry (and, as I told Mr. Ham, a little hurt) if my actions in connection with this unpleasant question have been misunderstood or misinterpreted. I sincerely think that I did my best to act as fairly and frankly as I could in this case.

Mr. Ham has since written to me that he was considering the whole affair as closed; and Mr. Seronde handed me a memorandum in which he stated the precise circumstances in which Mr. Ham was appointed here. I will add that it never occurred to me or to anyone in our Department meeting to criticize Mr. Seronde for bringing Mr. Ham here. Mr. Ham looked like a very good candidate for an assistant-professorship and was a good one. But the Department and the University reserve the right not to promote to an associate-professorship, or not to retain indefinitely as assistant professor, a colleague who does not come up at (sic) all their expectations.

May I add that I shall be very glad, when you have a little time, to have an appointment with you and submit any more information that you may desire on this case and on the affairs of the Department.

Yours very sincerely,<br>
Hri Peyre

## À son père:

Ce 26 mars 1940

... Nous avons vécu tranquillement cette fin d'hiver, nous portant fort bien, travaillant dur. Marguerite a fondé dans notre ville (& s'en occupe activement depuis) un groupe d'aide aux réfugiés & soldats français. Il y a de nombreux groupes similaires ailleurs en Amérique. Les dames récoltent de l'argent, tricotent pour la France chandails, chaussettes, etc., envoient des paquets à nos soldats. Même si l'utilité pratique de tout cela est modeste, ce sont des sympathies profrançaises qui se réunissent, se rendent actives. Un jour peut-être, seront-elles plus actives encore — Nous persistons à souhaiter l'intervention américaine qui donnerait un coup dur au moral allemand; mais, malgré nos efforts, cela ne viendra que de façon imprévue, probablement lente, si cela vient. Nous y travaillons en général, avec ardeur, sans illusions excessives.

De mon côté, je t'ai déjà dit en quoi consistait mon travail: mille détails infimes qui me prennent du temps. Ici, les universités sont d'énormes machines (18 profs dans notre seul département français), & cependant très individuelles. On choisit soi-même (le chef du département) ses nouveaux collègues, on propose pour l'un ou l'autre des promotions, on encourage l'un ou l'autre à écrire, à publier, à enseigner différemment ou mieux. On choisit aussi ses étudiants avancés, on les dirige: il faut les attirer de son mieux, pour les enlever aux autres langues étrangères, aux sujets à la mode (sociologie, économie politique, histoire diplomatique, etc.). On ne s'endort pas dans une douce sérénité. D'une façon générale, tout ce qui reste français a besoin ici d'être rajeuni, rénové. Notre influence culturelle (longtemps la seule à s'exercer) est la plus ancienne: le résultat est que nos groupements ou institutions (Alliance Française, etc.) sont un peu vieillis, n'attirent pas assez la jeunesse, les forces vives du pays. Les méthodes de propagande & de publicité allemandes, plus grossières, sont aussi plus vigoureuses. Il nous faut leur emprunter quelque chose, de même que nous ne gagnerons cette guerre qu'en empruntant pas mal aux méthodes allemandes d'autarcie, de production en série, de système de [*illisible*], & de bousculade des neutres. Les sympathies sont pour nous en Amérique (plus encore que pour les Anglais, à cause de la haine invétérée des Irlandais envers l'Angleterre, & de la jalousie américaine pour la marine & l'empire britanniques). Encore faut-il les raviver, les stimuler. Il n'est nullement question d'un choix entre France & Allemagne. C'est une vieille illusion de chez nous de croire que le monde entier se [*illisible*] par sa francophilie ou sa francophobie. Ce n'est pas la germanophilie que nous avons à combattre ici, à part quelques exceptions: c'est l'indifférence. C'est le sentiment commun que tout cela est loin, un peu comme pour nous la guerre entre Chine & Japon; que les intérêts américains n'en sont guère affectés. La sympathie est pour notre cause: mais pour que ce potentiel devienne actuel, il faudra: 1) l'impression que les intérêts américains auraient trop à souffrir d'une victoire allemande, de l'autarcie généralisée, fermeture de débouchés au commerce américain, rivalité industrielle allemande, disparition de cette police somme toute raisonnable qu'a faite depuis cent ans l'empire britannique sur les mers du globe — 2) un grand choc émotif, qui remue la masse du pays, soit par la peur, soit par la sympathie avivée pour notre cause.

En attendant, nous travaillons d'une façon générale; et ce que nous conservons ou développons pour la culture française sera utile un jour. J'ai été en plusieurs endroits faire des conférences: New York, Boston; nous revenons en ce moment d'un voyage à Washington. Nous avons fait ce voyage en auto, dans notre grosse & solide voiture, sans accroc. Mais que nous regrettions les routes, les champs, les villages pittoresques de France, les restaurants & cafés de nos villes. Ce pays n'a guère de charme pour le voyage. Et ce nous est une grande peine de songer que cet été nous devrons y rester, dans la chaleur & l'isolement. Nous aurions tant aimé revoir la France & te revoir, Jacques, les parents ou beaux parents à Annecy, etc. — peut-être Hélène grandie & Louise. Il est probable que l'on me chargera d'abord des bachots à New York, puis d'une mission d'enseignement à Columbia University, New York, puis qu'en septembre le ministère français me demandera d'aller à Mexico pour les bachots de là-bas & quelques conférences. Je ne chômerai pas! — Mais notre santé est solide, et d'autres sont bien plus à plaindre.

À Washington, nous avons été reçus très aimablement par l'Ambassadeur, M. de St Quentin, & son personnel — à dîner, puis pour des entretiens touchant nos questions de propagande. Je trouve qu'on n'agit pas tout à fait autant qu'on devrait le faire ici, ni toujours dans un sens assez énergique. Daladier manquait un peu d'éloquence, de don de la formule, de vibrant. Certes, il faut des actes plus que des paroles. Mais de solides menaces aux neutres hésitants, des mots d'ordre frappants & susceptibles de rallier les autres, seraient d'un heureux effet. Reynaud, malgré les attaques de l'A. F[rance] & son peu de scrupules, a davantage ce don. Il a eu de réelles qualités aux finances & a vite compris le caractère économique de cette guerre. Nous n'avons pas encore le très grand homme. Les autres l'ont-ils?

L'affaire de la Finlande a produit mauvais effet, & on l'a trop présentée comme une défaite morale pour nous. À mon avis, il fallait, ou intervenir tôt en décembre & et entraîner du coup & par surprise Norvège & Suède dans la guerre, ou s'abstenir nettement. La vérité est que l'expédition là-bas avait de fortes chances de tourner à l'échec, & que rien n'est perdu si nous savons agir plus vite, sur un terrain plus favorable — D'après les excellents renseignements que l'on a ici (journaux, revues, radio ne traitent que de la guerre), le blocus n'agira avec une réelle efficacité en Allemagne qu'au bout de 2 ans environ, et surtout sur le pétrole, le fer, les matières grasses, & si l'Allemagne est obligée de dépenser pas mal de produits dans une guerre active. Il faudra alors, encore, une vraie guerre & une défaite militaire allemande; mais elle sera obtenue moins coûteusement. Le curieux est que, si les Allemands sentent qu'ils ont quelque supériorité aérienne ou militaire en ce moment, ils tardent tant à en profiter & à agir. Ils sont, au fond, plus hésitants que les démocraties. D'ici là d'ailleurs, comme tu l'écrivais, c'est l'imprévu qui surviendra, bien entendu.

Tu as parfaitement raison sur la psychologie allemande & la vraie manière de la traiter. C'est nous, Français, qui nous sommes toujours le moins trompés sur l'Allemagne, moins que les Anglo-Saxons certes. Il n'empêche que l'on ne peut revenir en arrière: deux données sont fondamentales aujourd'hui: 1) notre population est la moitié de celle de l'Allemagne; 2) l'on ne peut qu'aller vers plus, et non moins, d'industrialisation. Il nous faut & il nous faudra faire des avions, des bateaux, exporter, vendre, en un mot gagner la paix après la guerre. Si nous devons nous saigner pour gagner cette guerre, puis nous retirer à nouveau de l'Europe centrale & laisser l'Allemagne seule vendre et acheter à ces pays danubiens & balkaniques, notre sacrifice aura été vain. Nous devons présenter au moins un plan positif d'organisation de ces pays-là, et un plan qui ne soit pas seulement politique.... Diviser l'Allemagne, fort bien; mais cela ne servira que si ces gens-là ont quelque prospérité matérielle & de quoi vivre, et tant que nous serons les plus forts pour imposer notre ordre par la force. Certes, les Allemands iront vite au désespoir & à la platitude lâche quand ils seront vaincus. Mais c'est leur relèvement qu'il faudra empêcher.

Assez de haute politique.

[Sans signature]

## To Edgar Furniss:

March 28, 1940

Dear Dean Furniss,

I hope your trip has been pleasant, not too tiring and fruitful in every way. After you had left, I wrote to President Seymour very fully concerning the difficulties raised by Mr. Ham and his ill-advised (as I saw it) plea that his case be reconsidered. I asked President Seymour to communicate the documents and my view of the case to you on your return. If you would like to have more information, I shall be glad to call on you any time that you find convenient.

Professor Feuillerat has probably reported to you and the Associate Dean our proposals as to scholarships and fellowships for next year. May I add my own plea that our Department may be treated as favorably as possible in the granting of scholarships for our graduate students? We are making a very vigorous effort to develop our graduate Department, as you know, and have been gratified in receiving many promising applications from prospective graduate students. We shall be grateful if the Administration and the committee on fellowships can help us develop our Department during the few years in which we shall have to be encouraged and to pursue our efforts steadily.

While you were away, Professor Morehouse received a very flattering offer of a full professorship at the University of Pennsylvania (to succeed Professor Schinz, who is retiring), with mostly graduate work and direction of theses, a salary $1000 higher than his present one and prospects of increase. He has decided to stay here, and has refused any appearance of bargaining, or even to let it be known to any but a few friends and colleagues. He is very helpful to both our graduate and undergraduate work, and we feel very happy that he chose to stay here and thus showed his faith in the future of our Department. Both Professor Feuillerat and I expect a good deal and substantial and eminent contributions to scholarship from Mr. Morehouse in the future. In order to make things a little easier for him, I hope we shall be able to relieve him from a little teaching in the future.

I would like, however, in this connection, to ask you if the question of permanent tenure for our present associate professors could be cleared up. Mr. Boorsch, who has just been promoted this year, is now, theoretically, the only one assured of permanent tenure. Could not the same official guarantee be given to Messrs. Morehouse, Hill and Richardson? Or should they consider a mere oral reassurance as sufficient until their name comes up for reappointment? I suppose the Administration has decided upon some general policy in respect to the present associate professors, and shall be glad if you will inform me of it more precisely when the occasion arises.

Yours sincerely,
Henri Peyre

## To the same:

May 13, 1940

Dear Dean Furniss,

The Corporation, on April 13, 1940, had approved of our recommendation to appoint Mr. P. Baudet as assistant in instruction, at a salary of $700 a year, for the coming year.

Mr. Baudet has since been called elsewhere and has asked to resign the appointment he had accepted at Yale. I have accepted his request, and have at once offered the assistantship to Mr. L. Wayne Adams. Mr. Adams has accepted.

He is a Yale graduate (B.A. 1929), has taken all his graduate work with us, taught in our department for some years (1931–34) and was quite successful as a teacher. He has since been teaching in Dallas, Texas. The present appointment of Mr. Adams as assistant in instruction in our department will greatly help the organization of our language courses, and it will enable him to complete his thesis within two years.

I am sending the appointment form concerning Mr. Adams, in the hope you will approve of it, and asking the Administration to accept the resignation of Mr. P. Baudet.

Sincerely yours,
Hri Peyre

## To Charles Seymour:

[No date]

Dear President Seymour,

I have asked Miss Chatfield for an appointment with you on Wednesday morning. I realize how busy you must be towards the end of the year, and how harassing must be all the problems connected with the budget situation and the threatening possibilities of the future.

I would like, however, to keep you informed, as the year draws near its close, of the task we have tried to accomplish this year in our Department, of our prospects and of our difficulties. The trend among undergraduates is decidedly not towards modern languages or foreign culture just now, and however much one may regret it, in the interests of America herself, I suppose we must accept it for the present. However, several conversations I have had here and there and other signs show that our Department at Yale is being held in increasingly high esteem, and I hope we may continue and even take the leadership in our field in the country.

You probably remember the two questions on which I had consulted you earlier in the year, and on which you were kind enough to give provisionally favorable advice: the possibility of appointing, at some regular intervals, a visiting-professor in French, and the advisability and possibility of creating a "French Center" at Yale. Both entail financial problems, I suppose, and both may have to wait for the clarifying of the present general situation both in Europe and America. As the first question may be linked with the replacement of Professor Feuillerat, after 1942 or 1943, I should like to be able to plan a solution in advance in the best interests of our studies.

On the second point, I had asked the assistance of the French Embassy and the French Ministry of Foreign Affairs. Both have replied very favorably. My suggestion was that France, even in the present difficult circumstances, grant a sum of $10,000, once for all, to help the creation of that center, and then give us in the future books, periodicals, pictures, etc. The Ambassador has received the news that my suggestion, which he recommended warmly, had been approved. I have thanked him already, and I am transmitting his letter to you, as it concerns the University and not only our Department.

Very sincerely yours,<br>Henri Peyre

## FRENCH CENTER

### Tentative Plan

1. *Expenses to be incurred at the outset and once for all.*
Building, provided by the university.
Furniture, rugs, chairs for lecture room, etc.      $2000
Decoration, pictures, engraving, etc.      400

| | |
|---|---:|
| Set for tea, glasses, plates, etc. | 100 |
| If necessary, electric stove and Frigidaire provided by the univ. Phonetic apparatus, records, etc. | <u>1000</u> |
| | $3500 |

2. *Expenses to be incurred every year.*

| | |
|---|---:|
| Upkeep | 250 |
| Service (part time) | 600 |
| Typewriter (rented) | 40 |
| Supplies (paper, ink, etc.) | 100 |
| Allowance for lectures. | <u>250</u> |
| | $1240 |

A bursary student would be necessary, and 3 to 6 hours from the time of one of our instructors would be used for tuition, phonetics, conversation classes. $1240 for annual expenses for upkeep would represent (at 3% interest) a capital of $41300 at the outset, plus $3500 necessary for initial expenses, = $44,800.

## À son père:

Ce dimanche 19 mai 1940
Yale University
New Haven, Conn.

Mon cher Papa,

J'ai reçu hier, en bon état & au complet, l'envoi de livres (Taine, Renan, Rousseau, Montesquieu) que tu m'as fait si vite & aimablement il y a 5 semaines & t'en remercie. Je l'ai défait & ouvert avec émotion, pensant à ton bureau, à ces rayons où j'ai souvent feuilleté ces ouvrages, à l'odeur de tabac, à tes papiers étalés devant toi & ton travail, jadis de professeur, maintenant d'historien—à nos conversations là—À quand reverrons-nous tout cela ? Quel doit être ton état d'esprit devant ces récents événements, & le sort de Jacques ? Mille souvenirs pacifiques reviennent en ce moment à l'esprit : nos promenades autour de la ville, dans cette sereine campagne ; notre tournée errante à Merindol & Bicoux( ?) l'an dernier, et la nostalgie devant ces guerres, cruelles mais humaines, du passé, ces ruines, ces paysages, ces souvenirs. Même les persécutions des Vaudois paraissent poétiques, indulgentes, au regard des événements d'aujourd'hui ! Étant de conversations avec Jacques où il disait son goût de la vie, du repos entrevu, son horreur du péril, de la discipline, sa passion pour sa villa ensoleillée, nos repas quelquefois au Mont Ventoux ou ailleurs, alors que lui, ses amis, toi parfois, nous jouissions de la vie tranquillement, plaisantions. Qu'est-il advenu de lui dans ces affreuses luttes qui n'épargnent rien, dans ce régiment dangereusement exposé de transport où le sort l'a placé ? L'a-t-on précipité en Belgique ? A-t-il reflué vers le Nord ? As-tu toi-même des nouvelles?

Nous sommes dans une angoisse très grave. En neuf jours de cette nouvelle offensive, les mauvaises nouvelles se sont accumulées. Ce matin prise de St Quentin. Marguerite voit déjà ses parents d'Amiens tristement évacués, revit les heures de l'autre guerre ; la même déception, la même rage impuissante nous remplit tous d'amertume. Encore une fois envahis ! Encore une fois chez nous, avec des ruines, des morts, des destructions. On avait pourtant espéré autre chose. Et on aurait dû prévoir : des fortifications seules, une défensive perpétuelle ne pouvaient gagner indéfiniment. S'il fallait plus de tanks & d'avions, que n'en a ton fait, commandé en Amérique depuis 2 ans ? Tout n'est pas perdu — mais il faut bien désormais tout voir en face. Ces quelques jours à venir peuvent apporter l'arrêt, le redressement. Mais après ?

D'ici j'ai souffert de mon inaction relative. Mais qu'aurais-je fait, simple fantassin peu instruit dans cet enfer ? Serais-je encore en vie, seulement ? Dans ma vaine colère, j'aimerais me précipiter en avant, aider, combattre. Partout nous avons manqué de *vision* de l'avenir, de sens du nouveau, de goût du risque. Nous avons préparé la dernière guerre, non celle qui se livre. Ici même, nos représentants n'ont pas bien compris l'opinion, ne sont pas allés de l'avant. Il fallait placer aussitôt d'énormes commandes. Les crédits auraient été accordés ensuite.

L'Amérique est très secouée, ébranlée — mais elle n'a pas d'hommes pour entrer en guerre aujourd'hui, n'en aura guère avant un an. Et l'opinion n'est pas encore prête aujourd'hui à suivre le Président. Il faut d'abord leur faire comprendre le danger que pour eux, à brève échéance, comporterait une victoire allemande. Je m'y emploie de mon mieux. Mais ils sont encore comme étaient les Anglais avant Munich, comme nous entre 1933 et 38, lors de nos luttes vaines, de notre aise de paresse discutailleuse. Si seulement nous pouvions gagner & que ceci nous serve de leçon !

Écris-nous régulièrement, malgré le retard avec lequel les lettres ordinaires apportent les nouvelles (3 semaines). Tout arrive d'habitude sans encombre & sans nulle censure—Sur Jacques, surtout—Où est-il ? Ne le mettra-t-on pas dans un hôpital à l'arrière, où sa compétence serait mieux utilisée ? Quel dommage qu'il n'ait point, jadis, préparé les concours et acquis une spécialité, une chaire, qui le désigneraient pour un service plus spécialisé & plus protégé sans doute. N'as-tu besoin absolument de rien ? Comment vis-tu, comment vois-tu la situation ? Nous sommes loin, favorisés, mais notre angoisse est vive. Et si l'Italie se mettait de la partie, à Avignon, nos parents à Annecy, Louise en Tunisie seraient exposés encore davantage!

Caresses inquiètes & affectueuses,<br>Henri

Ne te prive de rien, soigne-toi. Dis-nous si ta situation matérielle n'est pas satisfaisante (argent, confort, etc.) et Jacques.

## To Charles Seymour:

309, St.Ronan St.<br>New Haven<br>June 29, 1940

Dear President Seymour:

I suppose business messages will pursue you, even in your summer retreat! I apologize for sending one.

You doubtless know M. Jacques Maritain, the great Catholic philosopher, the chief exponent of Neo-Thomism, who is, to my mind (and I may say so objectively, since I am neither a catholic nor a neo-Thomist) a great philosopher even more than a great Catholic, and a remarkable personality. His influence is wide and profound all over the world to-day, and not merely among Catholics, but in England, at the University of Chicago, etc. He has written, not only about metaphysics, Bergson, etc., but about art, modern poetry: but above all about the Middle Ages.

Maritain was in this country this year, and has lectured (mostly in English) at several universities (Chicago, Princeton, Columbia, etc.). He was to spend the summer here, preparing a book for publication by a

New York publisher. With the recent events and the uncertainty about everything in France, his friends are advising him to stay in America for at least one more year. Many universities will probably try and attract him: catholic ones, where I don't suppose he would care to go particularly, and others and more important ones. My timid suggestion is: do you think that Yale would be interested in inviting him as a "visiting-professor," for the year or part of the year, and could do it? I have mentioned it to Mr. Hendel, the new chairman of the Philosophy Department, and I know John Allison would be interested. Maritain has been remarkably successful, not only in arousing enthusiasm for philosophy and a broad-minded spiritual attitude among young men, but in encouraging mediaeval studies. He is undoubtedly one of the finest personalities in Europe today. The spiritual and moral rebirth which we hope will occur in France in not too distant a future will undoubtedly need him. In the meanwhile, American institutions may be glad to welcome him.

Please excuse this suggestion. I am not making it to help a compatriot, but in the sincere belief that Yale might like, and gain, to have such a visiting-professor who would contribute greatly to our philosophical, mediaeval and literary studies. I will add that M. Maritain's address in New York is: 30, Fifth Avenue.

Will you and Mrs. Seymour accept our best regards and wishes for quiet vacations, and believe me,

Very sincerely,
Henri Peyre

## À Pierre Bédard:

Le 4 octobre 1940

Mr. Pierre Bédard
The French Institute
22 East 60th Street
New York, New York
Cher Monsieur,

J'avais l'intention—je l'ai toujours—d'aller vous rendre visite à New York à la première occasion. Mais je ne sais quand sera cette occasion. Le début d'une nouvelle année est toujours fort affairé.

Je voulais vous parler de bien des choses. On m'a déjà prié à deux ou trois endroits de parler devant des alliances. La nôtre, ici, toujours un peu pâle, semble vaciller. À mon avis, il faudrait que nous (les conférenciers et professeurs d'Amérique) adoptions quelques règles strictes: ne pas faire de polémique et toucher le moins possible aux sujets qui aujourd'hui nous divisent ; ne salir en aucun cas notre pays, même si nous n'aimons pas le visage qu'il peut revêtir momentanément ; maintenir les positions de notre langue et de notre culture ici, en rappelant à l'occasion que jamais notre influence culturelle et artistique n'a été plus forte qu'après la défaite de 1870–71 ; et montrer par l'exemple que notre bonne volonté et peut-être nos qualités n'ont pas baissé. N'êtes-vous pas d'accord ?

Oui, j'ai préparé quelques nouvelles conférences et je vous en enverrai la liste si vous désirez. Je ne tiens pas très fortement à faire ma réclame d'avance et à me proposer ; mais je n'ai jamais refusé de parler là où il est vraiment utile de le faire.

Voici les quelques détails "égoïstes" que vous me demandez : Né à Paris en 1901, ancien élève de l'École Normale Supérieure, Agrégé de l'Université, Docteur ès lettres ; ai enseigné à Bryn Mawr College, à l'Université du Caire ; puis professeur de littérature comparée à l'Université de Lyon, actuellement Sterling Professor of French et chef du Département français à Yale University ; ai donné des conférences en Amérique du Sud, Egypte et dans divers pays d'Europe ; auteur de nombreux articles et de plusieurs ouvrages d'histoire et de critique littéraire : *Qu'est-ce que le Classicisme ?*, — *Louis Ménard*, — *L'Hellénisme en France au milieu du 19e siècle*, — *Shelley et la France*, — *Hommes et Œuvres du XXe siècle*.

Merci encore de votre lettre et, en attendant le plaisir de vous revoir, je vous prie de croire à mon souvenir fidèle.

Henri Peyre

## To Edgar Furniss:

October 18, 1940

Dear Dean Furniss,

As you probably remember, I asked you, a few weeks ago, if it could be possible to use the sum of $100, which was provided in our budget for a reader in my French courses, for different purposes, as follows:

$50 for our miscellaneous expenses (our budget of $100 for that item having proved too small), as Mr. Farnam suggested.

$50 for one or possibly two talks before our Romance Language Research Club, to be offered to a lecturer from outside, that would stimulate the interest of our colleagues and graduate students and might prove useful to them.

If I have your consent on these two proposals, I will at once ask Professor Paul Hazard, of the French Academy, to give us a talk in the coming months, at the same time as the University invites him for one of the Woodward lectures.

Would you also kindly send me an official note repeating what you mentioned orally about the $500 increase which I suggested for Professor Seronde, and the prospect of including that proposal or not including it in our budget?

With many thanks, and very sincerely yours,

Hri Peyre

## To the same:

October 28, 1940

Dear Dean Furniss,

I had not omitted to consider the aspect of the question that you mention, concerning Mr. La France's replacement. I know how anxious the University is to effect any saving in its educational expenses, and we are very anxious, too, not to make any unreasonable proposals.

We examined the question in our department, and we thought we could not dispense with some new assistant, *this year,* to fill Mr. La France's place. The course to be given (French 22, five hours a week) is a new undertaking in our department, enabling students to meet the modern language requirement after intensive study. We are giving a good deal of care to it, and could not cut it up among two men or make the division any larger. As you know, the situation is going to be more difficult for the French language in the coming years, and we are trying to maintain all we can through raising the quality of our courses, devoting much care and personal attention to the students.

Besides, after I saw you on October 23rd, I immediately proceeded on the assumption that Mr. [Louis] Hudon would replace Mr. La France on November 1st and Mr. Hudon has already been initiated into the work, attended the classes, and seems to understand the students well. I feel somewhat bound towards him now.

I shall bear in mind your suggestion of possible reductions in our project for the 1941–42 budget, which our Department will soon prepare, and I think and hope we shall not contribute to the University deficit.

Sincerely yours,
Hri Peyre

## À Pierre Bédard:

Le 28 octobre, 1940

Cher Monsieur,

Je crois que je n'ai pas encore répondu à votre demande d'une liste de sujets. Excusez-moi, et la voici enfin, le gros affairement du début d'année un peu calmé !

Pour répondre à des craintes possibles, je me permets d'ajouter que même ceux de ces sujets qui semblent toucher à la politique traitent en réalité d'idées et du "background" de la politique, mais que, dans aucun cas, je ne me lance dans la polémique partisane, qui me paraît, plus que jamais aujourd'hui, déplacée.

Croyez à mon souvenir le meilleur,
Henri Peyre

1. La situation française éclairée par la littérature française récente.
2. Les directions du roman français contemporain.
3. Le roman poétique et le message de Jean Giono.
4. Renaissance et grandeur de la jeune poésie française.
5. La France a-t-elle perdu le sens de la grandeur?
6. La démocratie en France a-t-elle échoué?

## To Edgar Furniss:

November 4, 1940

Dear Dean Furniss,

I have talked the situation over with Hudon. I apologize again for not having known about his scholarship before asking you to appoint him, and Mr. Feuillerat had failed to remind me of it. I only thought of choosing the best possible men, and if we had chosen either of the other two advanced graduate students whom I considered, the same embarrassing situation would not have occurred, but no economy would have been possible for the University.

Here are the facts: Mr. Hudon is a very needy student who without this assistantship, was supposed to get this year:

$415 on a University fellowship.
$300 on National Youth Administration (working on bibliography with Mr. Ham).
A total of $715.

The second item (N.Y.A.) takes him 37 hours and a half a month, and it would be difficult to combine that with his new five hours of teaching. That would be distinctly detrimental to his work as a student taking three courses this year.

If he relinquished that, would that N.Y.A. money constitute a saving for the University, through being used somewhere else, or would it just be lost?

Otherwise, if Hudon has to lose both his N.Y.A. $300 and his $415 fellowship, he would be the loser by $155 from teaching five hours with us. He will only receive a total of $560. Considering his real need and the fact that he was appointed at the last minute, after five weeks of college work, it would be unfair to him.

If that N.Y.A. money is not a saving for the University, could he, through a very exceptional favor which, I can assure you, we would never consider as a dangerous precedent to embarrass the University, be granted at least his $300 tuition (he is only taking 3 courses, equivalent to $225 this year, but, I believe, is supposed to receive or to pay $300 all the same). That amount was going to be paid for him on November 1st and he will not receive his first check as an assistant until Nov. 30th.

The saving, in that case, if you granted us that exceptional favor, would be: $100 on his fellowship (only his tuition being paid), plus $300 on N.Y.A. (being sick in October, he could not do his work on that item, and the total that he would get this year would thus be $270).

Does that seem fair to you? I sincerely believe Hudon's exceptional situation and lack of private means justify it.

Sincerely yours,<br>
Hri Peyre

This letter was ready to be sent to you, when we learned (Monday morning) that Mr. Booth, (who is an assistant in our department and a graduate student who already had had two years of graduate study at Brown and one year in France) is being called for military service, as a lieutenant of the reserve, on Nov. 10. He has to leave his courses and those he gives in the College on November 8.

If you agree, we shall tell him that we shall hope to keep his assistantship open for him next year, when he is to be released on November 7. He will also take up his three graduate courses where he left them.

He has received two monthly checks of $70 each for his salary. I do not know whether anything will remain due him for the first week in November. In any case, we shall divide his course between Professor Richardson and Professor Bates, and thus save the balance unpaid on his total salary of $700. Perhaps this will make it easier to arrange for Mr. Hudon's scholarship or to settle his financial problem.

## To Charles Seymour:

November 7, 1940

Dear President Seymour,

As you probably have been informed, one of the Woodward lectures (next Wednesday, November 13th at 4.15) is going to be given this year by a distinguished Frenchman, M. Paul Hazard, professor at the Collège de France and a member of the French Academy. He comes over regularly to America to give courses at Columbia University.

If it were convenient and if you wished me to, I should be glad to take him to your office, next Wednesday before his lecture, for a very brief visit. You may already have met him, perhaps at the Harvard celebration of some years ago where I think he received an honorary degree. If ever we could afford to have an eminent visiting-professor in French at Yale, he would be one of the best choices we could make.

Sincerely yours,
Henri Peyre

## To Edgar Furniss:

November 8, 1940

Dear Dean Furniss,

The sum of $50 (which is half of the sum provided in our budget for 1940–41 for a reader in my courses) has been, exceptionally, as stated in your letter of October 21, 1940, reserved for two lectures to be given to our Romance Languages Research Club.

The first lecture will be given on November 13 by Professor Paul Hazard; a compensation of $25 has been offered him.

The second will be given on December 9 by Professor André Morize. The same sum, $25 remains available.

Will you kindly ask the Comptroller's office if the two checks of $25 each can be made ready for those lecturers, on the dates mentioned?

With many thanks,

Very sincerely yours,<br>Hri Peyre

## To the same:

November 8, 1940

Dear Dean Furniss,

Before I consult you on Monday morning about preparing our proposals for the budget of the French Department, may I leave you a written statement which will explain the few questions on which I would particularly like your advice?

The enclosed sheets (a copy of which I am keeping for my own use) will explain themselves, and show that our Department expects to propose no increase but a slight reduction (which may well prove to be larger) of the total budget of the French Department. Of course, it is understood that circumstances may decrease the number of students in our classes, and we would adapt ourselves to them reasonably.

The two main points which I believe our Department must keep in mind are:

1) Both for the graduate and undergraduate studies, our department needs more men of distinct brilliance or eminence, well known as scholars and lecturers, in order to attract more students, or better ones. Some ranks (instructor and assistant-professor) are, at present, not sufficiently represented. If the study of French literature and culture is to resist the unfavorable circumstances which it may have to face in the near future, it must be given by men who are not merely able teachers of language, but of fine quality and promise. The budget for 1941–42 should then include two new assistant-professors (posts left vacant in 1939 through the resignation of Professors Jackson and Barthold), and, if this is made possible by the departure of Mr. Ham, a visiting-professor or a similar position. As will appear from the column b) of enclosed sheets, these promotions or appointments mean no increase for the total budget.

2) The present composition of the department includes too large a

number of assistants in instruction (eight), on a one-year appointment. Those appointments proved necessary and useful, as a temporary replacement of Jackson and Barthold in 1939 and as a means of attracting promising scholars to our graduate department. They will be supplemented gradually (two in next year's budget, and the others the year after, once those men have obtained their degree with us and have been sufficiently trained in our teaching methods to help spread them elsewhere). One of those assistants will, in 1941–42, do the work previously required from our reader or readers, whose position is consequently eliminated.

The total figure for 1941–42 would thus be $72,300 (including $2400 from the F.E.S. and our miscellaneous expenses of $850), or $69,150 without these two items. This represents a saving of $660 on the budget granted us in 1940–41, which, in its turn, had saved $1400 on the sum granted us (but not actually spent) in 1939–40.

The practical questions of detail on which I would also be glad to have your approval are:

1) The appointment of an extremely brilliant candidate, Wallace Fowlie, as assistant-professor. If provisional or preliminary approval can be given to the unanimous proposal of the Department to appoint Mr. Fowlie, I would like to be able to negotiate with him without delay so as to secure his collaboration for our department.

2) The promotion of Mr. Edsall to an assistant-professorship, also unanimously recommended by the Department.

3) The policy to be adopted in the case of Mr. Ham who, having been an assistant-professor for six years, was reappointed for a seventh year (1940–41), with the understanding that he would have to leave the University after that period.

4) The advisability of considering the appointment of a visiting-professor whose salary would be provided by the corresponding sum paid Mr. Ham this year. The principle of such a visiting-professorship was presented to the President last year, and approved by him provided it did not, for the present, increase our total expenditure.

5) The position of Mr. Sturm who, according to our rules of tenure, cannot be appointed as an instructor for a fifth year and whom several members of our department would like to propose for an assistant-professorship now if possible.

6) The exact position of Mr. Cornell who, having been "part-time

instructor" in 1938–39, should (according to our interpretation) be considered as having been a "real" instructor for only two years (1939–40 and 1940–41), and who might be retained for two more successive years according to our rules of tenure.

I hope these tentative proposals, which I have tried to make in accordance with the budgetary situation of the University and with a view to the future, will meet with your approval, and that your advice will help us frame the final budget proposals for 1941–42 in a satisfactory way.

Very sincerely yours,
Hri Peyre

## To William C. DeVane:

November 13, 1940

Dean William C. DeVane
Connecticut Hall

Dear Dean DeVane:

As I told you in our conversation, our plans about a possible enlargement of the scope of our Major-work in French are very vague, as I have not yet discussed them fully with my colleagues or with the other Departments concerned. Roughly speaking, however, my impressions would be as follows:

1) It is clear that the present choice of Majors among Yale students is often illogical, and not done according to the best interests either of the students concerned or of the educational policy of the University. Sudden changes in the "fashion" which sometimes drive the students to a certain field and then to another, might endanger the stability of some Departments, force the appointment of new instructors and then no longer justify those additions to our staff, etc.

It seems, moreover, regrettable to me that in a large university like ours, so few students should elect majoring in the field of classics or of modern foreign languages. I do not think that we should fully admit the choice (often an almost irrational choice) of the students in their freshman or sophomore year, without trying to enlighten it a little more. To resist a fashion should be the task of educators, who are supposed not merely to follow, but to guide. It would not be for the good of the country if its "élite" of future leaders remains complacently ignorant of foreign cultures and concentrates on the present and often ephemeral problems of international relations among nations whose present often depends upon a rich and long past.

Finally, there should remain in the country at least a few universities in which the immediate and practical interest of a certain field (languages, economics, etc.) should not be the only criterion of a student's choice, but where broad, permanent and disinterested cultural values should be emphasized. In our department for instance (French), some students want to specialize with us because they have some intention of teaching French later on; those will and should always remain a small minority. But the larger part of our Majors in French should be composed of young men who find in French, not merely a language but a literature and a civilization. As the influence of a classical education and the knowledge of the Greco-Roman tradition are likely to decrease in America, for better or for worse, many educators (outside of France) feel that a study of the language, of the thought and of the art of France, can be the best substitutes for a humanistic tradition which emphasized clear thinking, orderly reasoning, stable moral and psychological values, artistic workmanship, etc.

A French Department in a large university should not only help students satisfy an elementary requirement in modern languages and prepare a few prospective teachers; it should also, it seems to me, serve as a rallying-point to students desiring to know more about the history, the thought, the art and literature of a foreign country which has something to teach them. In the present effort to break down some of the barriers which keep departments apart, it seems advisable to consider the creation of an enlarged and freer Major in French. It might be called: *Major in French Civilization* and include two divisions: in the first, the stress should be laid on the language (spoken and written) and the literature (our present courses in French amply provide for that); in the second, the students taking French as a focus, might concentrate either on the thought and philosophy (in collaboration with the Department of Philosophy), or on History (with the department of History), or on relations between French culture and literature and another literature directly accessible to the student (English, or in some cases Spanish, Italian, German), or on relations between French literature and French art.

The present offerings of Yale would make such a program easily feasible. A prerequisite for such a Major in French Civilization might be either French 39 or a section of French 30, modified and enlarged so as to be an introductory course to French Civilization.

Then instead of taking four courses in the field of their Major, the students might take only three (perhaps two) and organize the rest of their schedule with the collaboration of another department under a coherent and coordinated plan which might include four divisions:

a) Philosophy.
b) History.
c) English or Spanish, Italian, German.
d) History of Art.

Many courses already given in Yale College would find a place in such a program, e.g.:

a) Philosophy 12, 15, 22, 23, 28.
b) History 32, 33, 39, etc.
c) English 31, 32, 33, 34, 35, 37, 38, etc.
d) Art 30, 35, 38.

It seems likely that, if circumstances allowed, and if such a plan proved promising, the French Department would offer two new courses which would be especially designed for such a Major in French Civilization: *Great* French Thinkers (Thomas Aquinas, Calvin, Montaigne, Descartes, Pascal, Rousseau, A. Comte, Renan, Bergson, and Contemporary Thought).

2) *Anglo-French Literary relations,* or some such subject, covering, in different years, different aspects of French Literature (Age of Enlightenment, Romanticism, Realism and the Novel, Symbolism and Contemporary Literature).

It is clear that such a program (here only tentatively outlined) would require the cooperation of several Departments, — which is probably desirable and seems to present no insuperable obstacle. Besides, every precaution would be taken (as is done in H.A.L.) not to make such a major in French civilization too easy or too lax for the students electing it. While the language used by the instructors in the French Department would continue to be French, the students would be allowed to write and answer in English whenever they would choose to do so.

Such are some of the suggestions which I would like to present. They would be modified and improved after very careful examination by all the departments concerned and the Administration of Yale College. I cannot help feeling that a plan of this kind, if successful and well carried out, might serve the University as a whole and utilize more fully the services of many members of the faculty who, while belonging to some Language Department, are willing and able to give more cultural teaching than the mere practice in language.

I shall be most grateful for your advice and suggestions on my tentative suggestions.

Yours very sincerely,<br>
Henri Peyre

## To James Osborn:

Nov. 27, 1940

Dear Mr. Osborn:

It was most like your sweet & gracious ways to send me those complimentary copies of your erudite & formidable compilation. I am most grateful to you for thus enlightening my way. I do feel, however, that, at least as a humble contribution to England's war for modern humanity, I should pay the dues in arrear that these volumes represent. Won't you let me, & enter me as a member of that learned group, & believe me (with best regards from both of us to Mrs. Osborn),

Very sincerely,<br>
Henri Peyre

## To the same:

[December 1940]

Dear Mr. Osborn:

May I just mention one or two slips in Work in Progress 1939 — only to show that I am a conscientious reader?

Nº 3902 should be placed under seventeenth century (Gomberville) & not nineteenth.

Nº 4070 should follow Nº 4009, as it really refers to H. Monnier's work entitled *Joseph Prudhomme* & not to the poet Sully-Prudhomme.

I would add a few notes which I made in glancing at the French section of 1939 Work in Progress:

Nº 2967. The book has been published since (Winifred Newton) 1939

3310 — same remark (Frame) 1940

3326 same remark (Bishop) 1940

3260 same remark (Hulubai) 1939

3318. The name of the author should be BAILLOU (not final N, but U).

3365 (Lancaster) is being published (or has just been), I believe.

3405 (Schwartz & Olsen) has been published.

3425 (Wickelgren) has been published, & is very bad.

Subjects like 3404 & 3427 (by Scherer) are so universally wide that they do not enlighten much, & each would be a life-work. The same young scholar is voracious, for he also announces two huge works (2979 & 3991).

Nº 3459 has been published (Clark) 1939.

Nº 3507 should be spelt (sic) GUILHOU (not a final N, but U)

Nº 3683 is same as 3310 & has been published this year (1940)

Nº 3959 (by George) has just been published, at the Columbia Press, under the title "Lamartine's romantic Unanimism"

Nº 4147 will not be treated, Mr. Michaud having died last year.

Mlle E.M. Rodrigue is also down for four very different & huge subjects (2210, 1974, 4208, 5242). As some young people *do* imagine that subjects thus mentioned in W. in P. are "reserved" or will be treated soon, would it not be advisable to ask the person to choose & announce, in some future edition, only one or two subjects, on which she is *actually* engaged?

The same applies to Mr. J. Treche(?), who is down for three very different topics on Proust (4247, 4248, 4249). Couldn't he do one first?

- Nº 4234 (Alden) has appeared this year (1940).
- Nº 4273 (Storer?) has been published by Harper in 1939.
- The same remark (excessive number of projects announced by a young colleague who is, actually, looking for a position & was hoping to help his prospects that way) applies in W. in Progress 1940, for M. Brun, Nº 3249a, 3345a, 3345b, 3345c, 3493a.
- Ibid. (W. in P. 1940) Nos. 3523 & 3708a are the same subject announced twice. Besides, the same young man (who is also known to be looking for a position) has announced a huge title on Chateaubriand in W. in P. 1939, Nº 3848, & a wide one on Gide in W. in P. 1940, Nº 4206a.

The same remark applies to another dissatisfied colleague, M. Denkinger, who announced five titles in Work in P., 1940.

It seems to me the accuracy & reliability of W. in P. should be increased if some "restraint" were delicately proposed for voracious scholars who announce as a project every work which they dream of undertaking before their old age, or before they obtain a full professorship, or before they choose the less glorious path of a wife & a few children-

Although W. in P. says so, & we say so, many young people are deterred from working on a subject which appeals to them, because so & so of De Pauw or Loyola or Tufts College (whose thesis will *never* be published, probably) has announced his intention of treating it. If the list of titles announced were a little less large, it would fill its purpose all the same & perhaps all the better.

This is my "constructive" criticism (from a grumbling Frenchman) & evidence of my genuine admiration for your splendid, Joycean labor— with New Year wishes for both of you.

Sincerely,
Henri Peyre

## To Charles Seymour:

December 10, 1940

Dear President Seymour,

The Vicomte d'Aumale, Ministre de France, who is now acting Consul-General in New York, has expressed the desire to visit Yale next Friday, December 13th. He is a career diplomat and (I am adding this since everything concerning the French is so easily misinterpreted now) was appointed to New York before the French defeat and the change of cabinet. He was then Minister in Colombia, and some years ago in Palestine, where I knew him.

He is, of course, not doing any politics or propaganda over here, and merely trying to do his best to help Frenchmen of every party, while waiting and hoping for better times and, like most of us, for a British victory.

Being a newcomer to America, he is anxious to visit some of the large universities, of which he has heard much, and he is particularly interested in oriental textiles, of which, it appears, we have a fine collection at Yale. Dean Meeks is very glad to arrange for his visit of those treasures.

The purpose of my letter is to let you know of his unofficial visit, and to ask you if you would wish to receive M. d'Aumale for a few minutes if, as I suppose he will, he asks to call on you or to leave his card and greetings. As he will drive to New York, I suppose the best time would be late in the morning, between 12 and 1.

I apologize for this long explanation, and for seeming to impose on your time—as I realize such a visit must be a frequent and too welcome ordeal for a University President.

Sincerely yours,
Henri Peyre

## À Pierre Bédard:

Le 13 décembre, 1940

Cher Monsieur,

Je n'ai pas encore répondu à votre aimable lettre du 9 décembre, parce qu'elle posait pour moi quelques petits problèmes de dates que je n'ai pas encore pu résoudre.

Je serai bien entendu très heureux de me rendre à votre aimable invitation de parler à l'Institut. Je conserve un excellent souvenir de ma visite de l'année dernière, et de plusieurs auditeurs et auditrices qui ont bien voulu, depuis, me parler en termes aimables de mes conférences.

Il se trouve seulement que j'avais proposé cette même date (le 21 janvier) à Vassar College, qui désirait m'entendre un mardi en janvier. J'ai essayé depuis de transporter à un autre jour cet "engagement" à Vassar, mais j'ignore encore si cela est possible.

Pour le cas où ce ne le serait pas, pouvez-vous me dire si un autre mardi (postérieur au 21 janvier) peut se trouver libre à l'Institut? Aussitôt que j'aurai la réponse précise de Vassar, je vous avertirai par télégramme ou téléphone.

J'ai été si pris en effet par ces premiers mois que je n'ai passé que quelques heures, pour affaires, à New York, et n'ai pu même faire un bond à votre bureau. Mais il me tarde beaucoup de vous voir, en cette année où les efforts et les bonnes volontés doivent se concerter plus que jamais pour sauver ce qui nous reste de plus précieux, et peut-être de le développer encore.

Croyez, cher Monsieur, à mes sentiments les plus dévoués.

Hri Peyre

## Au même:

Ce vendredi 13 décembre

Cher Monsieur,

Aussitôt après vous avoir écrit ce matin pour expliquer le retard apporté à ma réponse, je reçois un télégramme de Vassar qui libère pour moi la date du mardi 21 janvier. Je serai donc très heureux de parler à l'Institut ce jour-là—Nous *passerons sans doute la nuit du 21 au 22 à l'Institut & peut-être celle du 20 au 21,* puisque vous nous en offrez l'hospitalité.

À bientôt, cher Monsieur, & veuillez croire à mes sentiments bien sincèrement dévoués.

Hri Peyre

### Au même:

Ce 10 janvier 1941

Cher Monsieur,

Si vous voulez bien, j'arriverai à l'Institut lundi 20 janvier, vers 6 ou 7 heures du soir, & nous occuperons l'appartement que vous mettez obligeamment à notre disposition, ma femme & moi, jusqu'au mercredi — Je serai heureux enfin de vous voir un peu à loisir. Des tâches menues et lourdes en fin de compte, pas mal de conférences en Nouvelle Angleterre m'ont tenu très bousculé — À dire le vrai, je n'ai pas non plus beaucoup recherché New York & ces querelles partisanes auxquelles nos compatriotes ne veulent pas cesser de se livrer — Je trouve vain d'épiloguer sur ce qui aurait pu ou dû être fait; et j'avoue que je trouve les Américains (d'abord un peu durs envers Pétain & ses gens) pleins de délicatesse envers nous & de cordiale hospitalité. L'essentiel que nous puissions faire est que le français & la culture française ne perdent pas trop. Avez-vous été satisfait de la réponse des groupes d'Alliance au début de cette année? Le nôtre n'est pas très actif, mais il survit, & cela est déjà quelque chose.

Excusez ce mot hâtif & négligé — Croyez à mes sentiments dévoués.

Henri Peyre

### To Edgar Furniss:

February 27, 1941

Dear Dean Furniss,

Here are the volumes (not including articles in periodicals) by Gustave Cohen that we have in our library. I have no doubt that Professor

Karl Young must know about him as a scholar, and Professor Focillon, who was his colleague at the Sorbonne.

[*List of 15 titles*]

For his scholarship, eminence in publication, lively interest in his students, and general distinction, I sincerely think Professor Cohen is one of the most eminent scholars in France to-day. I shall try to get more information on his personality from colleagues who know him better than I do.

Sincerely yours,<br>Hri Peyre

(PS.) Since I wrote this, I have been in New York & have started a discreet inquiry on Prof. Cohen's merits, personality, human qualities, etc. I hear that he has been for many years a Roman Catholic, but that conversion (and the fact that, born a Belgian, he adopted French nationality in 1914 in order to fight for France, which he did) apparently have not helped to have him retained in French Universities. He is from a distinguished family, married a Belgian "society lady" some years ago, has no children, I think. Every one agrees on his eminence as a productive scholar, as a writer. His interests include mediaeval history, art, as well as literature, & modern periods also. Prof. Grégoire, of Brussels, now in New York, imagines that he knows English well; at any rate, he is supposed to have facility for languages & lectures in German & Dutch. His career has been brilliant: he taught at the Universities of Amsterdam or Hague (I forget), Strasbourg & Paris.

The more I think of it (& Feuillerat seems to agree), the more I feel this might be a happy solution, & a clear gain for Yale. If Alvin Johnson or Mr. Duggan could provide Prof. Cohen with $2,500 a year for 1942–3 (or more), if we could add $1,000 still provided in our French Dep*t* budget, & the University a sum almost equivalent to what we saved this year, we could try Prof Cohen for two years & then keep him until 1948 if we chose to, & if conditions in France urged him to stay. We would then have time to look for a younger scholar, which might not be possible in these next years, or not feasible if the younger scholar could not leave Europe.

Will you some time give me your impressions on this—I shall, in the meanwhile, ask for Focillon's opinion, & perhaps that of one or two mediaeval scholars.

Sincerely,<br>Hri Peyre

### To the same:

March 3, 1941

Dean Edgar S. Furniss
Yale Graduate School
Dear Dean Furniss,

Thank you for your prompt and encouraging answer concerning the possibility of calling Professor Cohen here. I am still trying to get the opinion of competent persons here and there, without spreading the rumor of our vague projects too much, because other universities might take advantage of this opportunity and forestall us. I have not yet discussed it with our colleagues, and plan to do so very soon, in order to examine clearly what sort of courses Mr. Cohen might give, in the next two years, if he were attached to Yale. After Professor Feuillerat's retirement, things would be made much easier.

I am afraid I did not express myself clearly in my letter. Before any financial arrangements are contemplated, I would like to call upon Mr. Johnson and Mr. Duggan and see what their contribution might amount to. A Harvard colleague has just written me that Alvin Johnson seems reluctant to invite Mr. Cohen on account of his age, because it might be difficult for a university to appoint him at 61 or 63. I believe this is quite a mistaken view. Professor Baldensperger, who was appointed at Harvard at 63 and retired last year, was at once called (at 69) by the University of California.

My first impressions were as follows: if we can secure for Professor Cohen from Mr. Alvin Johnson or from Mr. Duggan a sum of at least $2500, it seems to me that we could not very well (in order to be sure to attach Professor Cohen to us) offer him a total salary inferior to $6000 until 1943. Now, in the budget of the French Department, there remains a sum of $1000 for an assistant, not yet attributed, which we might allocate to Professor Cohen if his schedule helped solve our teaching problems. More may happen to be freed if some of our younger colleagues are drafted next year, but that is still uncertain.

In that case, and considering the reduction of over $3000 made in our budget this year, and the advantages we should derive from Professor Cohen's services, do you think the University could provide an extra sum of $2500 and appeal to the Corporation for it? Naturally, if I could obtain more from Mr. Johnson or Mr. Duggan, so much the better; but that seems most uncertain, unless they know that Yale is substantially contributing to Professor Cohen's salary.

In the meanwhile, I shall try to have the advice of some of our colleagues, like Professor Nicoll and Professor Karl Young here.

Sincerely yours,<br>Henri Peyre

## À son frère:

Ce 15 mai 1941

Mon cher Jacques,

Nos correspondances se font rares. Peut-être certaines d'entre elles se sont-elles égarées dans ce parcours désormais difficile, demain peut-être tout à fait infranchissable—Sans doute aussi as-tu moins de loisir que lors de la guerre, des malades et nul moyen de les atteindre commodément. Et puis la vie matérielle doit être devenue si difficile qu'elle absorbe sans doute tout le loisir. Il doit falloir des calculs de sauvage pour arriver à se procurer l'essentiel pour subsister & ne pas trop souffrir du froid. Avignon était normalement dans une région bien située; mais cela signifie sans doute peu de chose aujourd'hui et tous les produits fabriqués & importés doivent manquer tout à fait: y compris pour toi le savon, le linge, les produits pharmaceutiques. Qu'il faut peu de chose pour démolir tout l'édifice compliqué de la civilisation matérielle & des échanges aujourd'hui!

Papa, dont les lettres sont rares aussi, nous disait que tu étais revenu de ta campagne avec de vives & persistantes douleurs. Pourras-tu aller un peu au soleil de la Méditerranée cet été? Les radieux souvenirs de la Riviera & de Rayol semblent une dérision aujourd'hui dans la misère matérielle & morale de la France. La vie a-t-elle repris une allure normale? Clients, paiements, vie économique? La misère matérielle se traduit-elle en mauvaise humeur & désespoir?

Ici il nous parvient bien des nouvelles; mais elles concernent souvent ce que font les ministres ou amiraux, ou citent abondamment les journaux français, qui ou vénèrent le chef du gouvernement ou prônent la soumission [*adj. illus.*] aux Allemands. Quelques nouvelles officielles, de Vichy, transmises par Havas, nous sont régulièrement envoyées par l'ambassade française. Elles sont très inspirées & formulées avec grande prudence. Les problèmes semblent toujours se ramener à une réforme intérieure & à un redressement moral, que nous croyons réel d'ici; & à une politique extérieure très difficile, qui voudrait être d'expectative, pour le cas d'une victoire alliée & doit cependant donner force gages à l'occupant.

Ici les gens continuent à espérer en une victoire, sans pouvoir deviner où ou comment elle serait assurée. Pour le moment, cela est difficile à concevoir; mais tout ce qui est arrivé jusqu'ici n'était pas ce que chacun avait conçu. D'autre part, il restera toujours la nécessité pour la France de faire partie de l'Europe continentale, & ni l'Angleterre ni l'Amérique n'ont encore proposé de solution, c.à.d. de moyen d'établir une paix durable, une coexistence pacifique et économiquement viable de la France & de l'Allemagne—L'Amérique réarme très fortement & vite; elle s'engage de plus en plus, et certes il y a des résistances, surtout dans la jeunesse. Mais quand on y songe, c'est déjà admirable qu'elle s'engage à ce point, quand elle a peu à craindre, directement. Si l'Allemagne devait réussir à dominer & à organiser l'Europe, je crois pour ma part que se livrerait tôt ou tard une guerre économique & morale germano-américaine. Mais il faut de la vision pour le prévoir dix ans d'avance—

Nous sommes évidemment heureux d'être ici, quoique incapables de faire grand'chose. Les colis pour la France (sauf lait & habits pour enfants & colis pour prisonniers) sont interdits par le blocus anglais. Marguerite essaie, malgré les circonstances qui rendent l'opinion peu favorable à notre pays & à son acceptation de la collaboration, de fonder un centre d'aide à la France non occupée. Nous parlons, discourons, parfois agissons. Mon travail, surtout professionnel, est très lourd. Mais nous sommes favorisés & ne regrettons même pas l'Egypte jadis plus clémente & gaie, aujourd'hui menacée....

## To Edgar Furniss:

111, Low Memorial Library
Columbia University
July 9—1941

Dear Dean Furniss,

I have answered the letter from Professor Cohen, which Miss Feinemann forwarded to me. The latest news I had from the New School is that he reached Lisbon several days ago & is awaiting the departure of the boat. I hope no more obstacles will prevent his sailing.

As you may have heard, we have succeeded in "placing" Favreau quite well, at Georgetown University. I should now like to consult you on a question concerning Mr. Wadsworth, our instructor.

Mr. Wadsworth has just passed the physical examination for military service & has been placed by his Local Board in class I.A. This means he will probably be called in September or October. He asks me whether, after that year (if it is only one year) of service, he could find his position at Yale.

I replied that the University's policy was, not to bind itself to any promise in the case of their staff on a one year contract. So that, after a year of service, Mr. Wadsworth, being out of contact with us, might have great difficulty to find a new position.

He would prefer, & I would too, the following solution. If you approved of it (& Dean Buck), I would communicate it to him as likely to be adopted:

Mr. Wadsworth would enlist now for a year; he might thus get a type of work where his knowledge of French, Spanish, Italian, would be utilized; he might also (if the war or the emergency does not keep him in service over a year) be freed next summer, before the academic year 1942–43.

We would agree to reappoint him for 1942–43 instead of his appointment for 1941–42, which was approved in the budget, for one year only (his third year in the rank of instructor).

To replace him in 1941–42, we might use his salary to solve (for a year, & as an *exceptional* violation of our rules of tenure) the problem of Mr. Sturm, & appoint Mr. Sturm as a substitute for 1941–42. (It does not seem possible to do without a substitute for Mr. Wadsworth, if he is drafted, in 1941–42 & save the money altogether, since the Department will be faced with an increased amount of teaching next year, as previously reported.)

I shall be grateful to have your advice on this & to transmit it to Mr. Wadsworth, so that he may enlist now, if it is, as I believe, both to his benefit & to that of the department, which will not have to upset his work in the course of the next academic year.

Yours very sincerely,<br>Hri Peyre

## À Pierre Bédard:

Ce 7 août 1941

Cher Monsieur:

J'ai enfin trouvé le temps pour lire et goûter en paix le rapport que vous avez bien voulu me communiquer. Inutile de vous dire que j'en approuve l'esprit et en admire le courage, ainsi que la fermeté d'expression. Je crois que vous ne pouviez plus nettement mettre les choses au point. Et ceux qui ne vous comprennent pas sont vraiment aveuglés & amèneraient un jour la ruine de toute indépendance pour nos sociétés. Il y aura encore, comme vous le dites, bien des changements politiques, et peut-être une France coupée en deux par la guerre civile plus cruellement encore qu'aujourd'hui par l'ennemi. Mais nous survivrons, et l'Amérique aura toujours besoin de notre culture & l'aimera toujours. Les Anglais eux-mêmes le proclament en ce moment avec générosité (Ch. Morgan dans le dernier *Atlantic,* d'autres dans les numéros de juillet de la *Contemporary Review,* du *Nineteenth Century*). Mais le grand problème en attendant est de gagner ou de garder à notre langue, à nos études, à nos groupes d'Alliance, les jeunes, les moins de quarante ans. Il y faut du travail, de la foi, et aussi un peu de cette nette franchise que vous maintenez comme le principal article de votre politique.

J'ai eu grand plaisir à vous revoir l'autre jour parmi nos étudiants

& collègues—Dans quelques jours je pars pour de tranquilles vacances, & espère vous revoir—par temps plus frais—

Bien sincèrement & merci,<br>Henri Peyre

Gustave Cohen arrive cette fin de semaine. Je lui conseillerai d'aller vous rendre visite prochainement.

## Au même:

Ce 28 septembre 1941

Cher Monsieur Bédard,

J'espère que vous avez pris quelque repos et avez consenti à vous éloigner quelque temps de la chaleur New Yorkaise et de ce que les gens simples appellent les émanations malsaines des villes. Mais vous supportez tout avec le sourire stoïque d'un vrai épicurien!

Merci encore d'avoir aidé Cohen à son arrivée. Tout s'est-il bien passé lors de son séjour. Il doit gagner Yale demain, & semble vaillant & très actif, moins sceptique que les "vieux" comme nous, peut-être pas assez sceptique sur tout ce que l'on peut, ou devrait, faire en Amérique pour le français.

Je crois me rappeler que vous aviez un jour suggéré, pour vos lecteurs, que la Bibliothèque de l'Institut voudrait avoir mon petit livre épuisé sur le Classicisme: et je crois me rappeler que je n'en avais plus trouvé d'exemplaire—Il vient de m'en tomber un sur la tête, littéralement, pendant que nous faisions repeindre notre logis & déménagions tout. Je me permets de vous l'envoyer—

Avec mon souvenir fidèle,<br>Henri Peyre

Si Gustave Cohen désire parler à quelques publics de vos Alliances, voudrez-vous mentionner son nom—Il ne se déplace pas très facilement, du moins tant qu'il n'a pas d'automobile—mais il l'a fait en Europe. Merci.

## To Charles Seymour:

October 21, 1941

Dear President Seymour,

I believe you have been informed, through Focillon, of the project of a French Institute or Center of higher studies, which several eminent refugee scholars hope to found in New York, with the help of the New School for Social Research. The plan is developing and seems to be meeting with fine success, in a preliminary way, and to have met a favorable reception. Some objections have been presented, and I may say that I am among those who have pointed out the objections and the difficulties most strongly. The contemplated Institute is likely to be only a temporary undertaking; it may prevent French and foreign students, French and Belgian scholars from becoming integrated into American universities, as they might be otherwise.

However, since the project seems to be developing, and since it brings a convincing sign of the fine courage of refugee scholars who refuse to be mere "émigrés" and a burden to the country that welcomed them but want to go forward and be useful, I thought objections should be limited to details of policy and counsels of prudence; the constructive work should go ahead without any further obstacles.

The organizers of the future Institute have kindly urged me to assist them in their branch of French literary studies. My answer has been, informally, that I would be glad to give them whatever competent guidance I may offer and to sit on their committees which will examine the candidates and, perhaps, give French degrees, or degrees similar to French ones. I have made two reservations: 1) that I considered that my loyalty to Yale University should come first in every case; 2) that my time was limited, and belonged first to the university to which I am attached and to my department at Yale, and that I would be glad to help only for a few public lectures or irregular courses or guidance of students.

Before I reply to them formally, I am taking the liberty to submit the question and my own position to you. I would have thought it a lack of courage and of solidarity, from French scholars already in America and permanently established there, not to help their compatriots now trying to carry on, under difficult circumstances, in a strange country.

At the same time, I would not like to promise to devote any of my time or activity which belong primarily to Yale, to any outside group without first letting you know and requesting the informal approval and authorization of Yale. If there any objections, I should be sincerely grateful if you would present them to me very clearly.

> Very sincerely yours,
> Hri Peyre

## To Edgar Furniss:

> November 10, 1941

Dear Dean Furniss,

I find it extremely difficult to propose a budget for the French Department for 1942–43 which would include a full 5 % reduction on the sum approved for us for 1941–42 and yet meet our minimum requirement of necessary hours of teaching. It may be fair to state the reasons for which, with the most earnest desire on our part to meet the wishes of the Administration and to do our share in the present emergency, we think we cannot propose a full 5 % reduction on our budget of 1941–42. . . .

## To the same:

> Dec. 12, 1941

Dear Dean Furniss,

With your encouragement, & that of President Seymour which followed yours, I am going ahead with plans for a "memorial" volume to Professor Feuillerat to be ready for June 1943, & starting on a basis of a book of 300 pages approximately, similar to the other volumes in the Romanic Series. I believe President Seymour would be glad to write a few introductory pages, & you would perhaps contribute too. And I shall try to have a varied group of collaborators, more or less as follows:

1) From other departments of Yale: perhaps Tucker Brooke or Karl Young; or Allison or some one from Berkeley College—Focillon, Jackson; 2) From other leading universities where Feuillerat lectured: Columbia (Torrey); Johns Hopkins (Lancaster); Harvard (?); California

(?); 3) From our Department & our former students: Boorsch, Cohen, Morehouse, Bates, Fowlie, Cornell, Edsall, etc., & some of our best graduates who might have a good brief article ready; 4) A bibliography of Feuillerat's publications, which Mme Feuillerat would compile for us.

All this is very tentative. I have mentioned it to Feuillerat, who is too modest to say so, but is deeply touched &, I believe, will feel proud & honored by this token of gratitude of Yale. To convince him I have added (which is a true & good point) that such a volume would serve our Department greatly & those whose publication or contribution would appear there, under such auspices & for such an eminent occasion.

Unless you have any objection to this very vague & tentative plan, I shall go ahead with it at the earliest opportunity.

With many thanks again for your very sincere & cordial help, & very sincerely

Hri Peyre

## To the same:

Febr. 6—1942

Dear Dean Furniss,

I am much obliged to you for your kind note & for suggesting that beautiful room in 119 College St. We shall be very pleased to make use of it & it will help our new-born & fast growing ATELIER.

I have sent to Mr. Lehmann a draft for a circular letter which (if the officers of the University do not object) will be sent to prospective members of our French group. We hope Mrs. Furniss & you will kindly accept to be among our "sponsors" & thus help our list to be even more imposing.

I would like to explain in two words my position as to Mr. Bates. I do not think he is unfairly treated, & I do not consider it worthy of a chairman of a department to reopen the case & bargain for a promotion, & leave the final refusal to the executive Committee.

But it did seem to me yesterday that the question had not been well presented. If exceptions are made on the ground of previous commitments, we understand & might perhaps be assured that the exceptions will remain exceptions i.e. a minority. If other exceptions are made on the ground of need to the Departments, flattering letters of recommendation, etc., the doors open to endless discussions. I do think the case in question (Mr. Mansfield) is, or appears to be, a stronger one than that of Mr. Bates. But I also thought it might have been made clearer.

I am enclosing a copy of the statement I am sending to Mr. Lehmann & of my letter to him.

With thanks & sincerely,<br>Henri Peyre

## To Marion E. Park:

March 9, 1942

President Marion E. Park
Bryn Mawr College
Bryn Mawr, Pennsylvania
Dear President Park,

Miss Schenck had spoken to me of the very flattering and intimidating honor which Bryn Mawr thought of bestowing upon me. I am very grateful indeed to the Committee on the Flexner lectures which has, in these trying times, selected the field of French culture among other subjects in the humanities, and which has suggested my name in preference to that of many more eminent scholars. I am very much touched by the kind esteem which my colleagues in an institution where I spent some very happy years, are thus expressing towards me. I am very happy and proud to accept, and hope I shall prove worthy of their confidence, and of yours.

The six weeks beginning early in February 1944 and the subject you mention seem the best suited to Bryn Mawr College and, as far as I can foresee in these times of uncertainty, they are equally suitable to me. I shall write again to Miss Schenck when the time appointed for the lectures draws nearer and shall fix the other details with her and the committee on the Flexner lectures. In the meanwhile, I shall be looking forward to the time when I shall spend those six weeks among the faculty and students of Bryn Mawr College. It is a source of keen regret to me that you will no longer be there yourself.

Very sincerely yours,<br>Henri Peyre

## À Pierre Bédard:

Ce 7 avril 1942

Cher Monsieur:

Merci de votre bonne lettre. Mon année a été très chargée: déplacements de conférences, travail ici même, un livre à écrire, & voilà que nous devrons enseigner ici l'été prochain. Aussi suis-je peu allé à New York. Je vais aller faire quatre "leçons" à l'École libre à partir du jeudi 9 avril sur "Directions du roman français contemporain." Je saisirai une de ces occasions pour sauter vous rendre visite. Mais je dois malheureusement faire défaut ce samedi 11. Nous avons organisé ici un groupe littéraire & dramatique, l'Atelier de Yale University, qui a assemblé beaucoup de bonnes volontés & revivifié l'intérêt aux choses françaises. Nous avons justement une réunion le 11.

Votre programme est beau: méfiez-vous de l'éloquence parfois intarissable & brouillonne de Grégoire. Il vous faudrait le coup du crochet.

Bien sûr que c'est à nous, les "locaux," à nous effacer devant ces messieurs qui ont beaucoup plus besoin que nous d'être encouragés, aidés et ont beaucoup plus de choses à dire!

Bien sûr que je suis aussi, comme de coutume, d'accord avec vous. C'est maintenant le moment pour les Français de s'entendre: plus rien, ou presque, ne doit nous diviser, lorsque nous sommes hôtes d'un pays en guerre. Mais plusieurs Français ne se rendent pas compte que, à persister à polémiquer & à blâmer la pauvre France de là-bas qui n'en peut mais, ils perdent ici la sympathie du Département d'État & même de toute l'opinion, à part quelques journalistes virulents & vains!

L'idée d'un jury littéraire et d'un prix est excellente & neuve ici. Je crains seulement, à première vue, que votre comité ne soit (terriblement!) universitaire. Lancaster est un érudit que j'admire dans son domaine: mais il est très étroitement cantonné dans l'étude du théâtre du 17e siècle; très peu au courant de la littérature moderne; et je crois que ce lui serait un honneur, mais une corvée, de lire des manuscrits de romans; et qu'il sera très piètre juge.

H. Mumford Jones est bien. Horatio Smith aussi, sage, réticent, diplomate sachant ménager chacun, et excellent administrateur de comité.

Mais tout cela risque de ne guère représenter la littérature vivante & de vous donner un jury d'historiens littéraires un peu desséchés.

J'insisterais vivement pour deux ou trois noms d'auteurs qui peuvent ne pas parler le français à merveille, mais sentent la littérature vivante et s'y connaissent en roman: peut-être Thornton Wilder; peut-être Waldo Frank, homme très fin & très subtil juge de notre littérature. Willa Cather a bien pratiqué Mérimée et quelques-uns de nos conteurs: mais elle sait peut-être assez mal le français. Le traducteur de St Ex., Lewis Galantière (je ne le connais pas personnellement) devrait être un bon choix, éventuellement. Et, si vous preniez un Anglais, Somerset Maugham connaît bien nos auteurs & notre technique. Un jury de professeurs, quelque estimable qu'il soit, serait exposé à faire des choix ridicules & académiques.

Mais je devine qu'il y a d'autres aspects à la question & parfois ces messieurs illustres dans la littérature demandent forte compensation de leurs services, & même de leur nom.

Excusez-moi de vous griffonner ceci chez moi & à la main, en hâte.

Bien sincèrement,
Henri Peyre

Si je puis vous être d'autre utilité, dites-le moi, bien entendu.

## To Edgar Furniss:

July 7, 1942

Dear Dean Furniss,

As you know, one reason why the Department was anxious to invite Professor G. Cohen to Yale was the hope that his eminence and great productivity as a scholar would contribute much to the success and reputation of the French Department.

Professor Cohen has published several articles and a little book in the last year. He has now a volume of considerable value and of more permanent interest ready: a collection of unpublished French medieval farces which will add much to our knowledge of the medieval drama.

I did not encourage Professor Cohen to propose his MS to the Yale Press or to the Romanic Series, since he could not very well, for obvious financial reasons, meet our new rule which asks for an author's contribution of 2/5 of the cost. He sent it to the Medieval Academy of America. The reply which he received (copy enclosed) is very encouraging. The Medieval Academy, however, could only contemplate publishing it with some outside financial help. I am taking the liberty of asking you the question very directly: Could Yale consider contributing to the publication of that important work by a scholar now attached to our University and in difficult circumstances? Perhaps the fact that Professor Cohen is not receiving a grant from Yale this year, as he did last year, might be a motive inciting the University to find some fund to that effect.

I realize that many more urgent problems must press the Administration in these times. It may, however, be considered wise and worth while to have scholarship continue and publications appear, whenever those activities do not take any energy or money away from the war effort.

Very sincerely yours,
Hri Peyre

## To the same:

July 13, 1942

Dear Dean Furniss,

I am much obliged to you for your prompt reply concerning Professor Cohen's MS. I am forwarding it to him.

I am very glad the Committee is favorably disposed to Cornell's candidacy to the Billings Award. I take it that the donor had no objection to the fund being used for the spring term, instead of the summer, of 1942–43.

I always understood that, if Cornell were granted that fellowship while receiving his regular salary that should entail no additional expense to the University. Our work is mostly with freshmen, and our heavy terms are, in the present system, summer, and, especially, fall. Our spring term work will be lighter, since there will not be many new freshmen entering in February. We can very well distribute Cornell's work among other members of the department in the spring. We should all be very glad to facilitate for him this opportunity of doing some research in other libraries, and we know the award would go to a colleague fully worthy of it.

If you agree, I shall mention that possibility to Cornell and shall ask him to go and see you and, if this is the time to do it, to propose his candidacy to the fellowship.

Sincerely yours,<br>Hri Peyre

## À Pierre Bédard:

Ce 9 août 1942

Cher Monsieur,

J'étais de passage à New York hier matin (samedi) & ai, à tout hasard, téléphoné pour demander à vous voir. Je voulais vous remettre en hommage très modeste un exemplaire de mon livre sur le classicisme, auquel vous aviez eu la bonté de vous intéresser. Je l'ai récrit & repensé quelque peu au courant de l'année dernière. Et je voulais vous poser quelques questions, vagues d'ailleurs & de pure information, sur les Alliances & la conduite éventuelle à observer. Ce sera pour quelque autre visite.

Comme je vous le disais d'un mot le jour où je vous ai rencontré au restaurant, notre petite Alliance de New Haven avait montré quelques velléités (inspirées, je suppose, par Waterbury) de se rallier au groupe travaillé par Londres. J'ai prononcé la conférence finale de l'année sur ce sujet, & la nécessité de maintenir ce qui existait déjà, *dans l'union,* de préserver nos institutions culturelles au-dessus de la politique. Les braves gens qui composent ces groupes veulent absolument qu'il n'y ait que deux sortes de Français, les uns loyaux aux Alliés, les autres traîtres. Mes sympathies vont à bien des égards à ce qu'on appelle France Libre; mais la cause est, là, plus belle que ceux qui, souvent, la défendent. Et je m'évertue à dire qu'il y a mieux à faire aussi qu'à fonder des groupements pompeux où chacun veut être président, membre d'un Comité directeur ou d'une académie lilliputienne. Notre brave Cohen a donné libre cours à certaine vanité pompeuse d'une manière qui, ici, m'embarrasse bien des fois!

Aurez-vous l'an prochain un conférencier officiel, & des plans ou propositions pour les Alliances? On sent un retour au français, aux choses de culture & d'intellectualité française: nous devrions l'encourager. Ici, à Yale, la situation s'est assez bien maintenue. Espérons.

Excusez ce mot très hâtif & croyez à mon bien cordial souvenir.

Henri Peyre

**Au même:**

Le 4 septembre, 1942

Cher Monsieur,

Merci encore de votre lettre. Je ne vois pas encore clairement mon programme de cet hiver; mais il me paraît, à première vue, difficile d'y insérer un voyage au Canada pendant que l'université ici est ouverte, et je crains que l'époque de Noël convienne mal pour des conférences là-bas.

Peut-être au cours de la saison suivante 1943–44 serai-je plus libre.

J'ai été hier, pour un seul jour, aux "Entretiens" de Mount Holyoke, et mon impression a été bonne. Malgré des défauts d'organisation et de direction, la chose marche bien. Un bon nombre de Français intéressants se sont réunis là. Avec des précautions à observer (élargir l'entreprise, ne pas paraître la limiter à des réfugiés surtout extra-racistes; ne pas rivaliser, mais collaborer avec Middlebury; organiser un peu plus de publicité de bon aloi), je crois qu'il y a là de belles possibilités pour une entreprise française de premier ordre.

J'ai rencontré là Jean Wahl, philosophe de la Sorbonne, l'un des meilleurs esprits de l'université française, poète également et critique littéraire, très lié avec la plupart de nos hommes de lettres de premier plan et l'ancien groupe de la Nouvelle Revue Française. Il a la mine chétive et a souffert durement, ayant été emprisonné et maltraité par les Allemands; mais j'ai pensé que vous auriez plaisir à rencontrer un esprit de sa qualité, et je me suis permis de lui conseiller d'aller vous voir.

À bientôt et avec mon souvenir le plus fidèle,

Hri Peyre

## À Georges May:

10 sept. 1942

Cher Monsieur,

Monsieur Focillon est, comme vous le savez peut-être, gravement malade depuis plusieurs mois, mais toujours héroïque de cœur et magnifique d'esprit, et admiré de nous tous comme le chef de notre École Libre et le chef spirituel des Français libres d'Amérique. Madame Focillon vous répondra, je crois en son nom, pour vous dire combien elle est touchée par ces souvenirs et ces nouvelles concernant Georges Dumas et Louis Gillet. Elle m'a confié votre lettre, à laquelle je réponds de mon côté....

## Au même:

18 septembre 1942

Cher Monsieur,

Je reçois aujourd'hui votre seconde lettre. Je suis heureux que vous alliez à Illinois. Le pays passe pour un peu triste et plat; mais vous aurez là une bonne bibliothèque, d'excellents collègues, quelques bons étudiants. C'est modeste pour commencer, mais il y a un an vous auriez eu de la peine à trouver même cela. On n'engageait plus personne pour le français nulle part. Maintenant le pendule a oscillé quelque peu.

Surtout avec la mobilisation progressive de beaucoup de célibataires, il va y avoir bien des postes vacants, au moins temporairement; et le Français qui se fera estimer comme collègue et comme professeur a des chances de voir devant lui s'ouvrir bien des possibilités. Le 17$^e$ siècle est une époque ici où peu d'Américains (excepté Lancaster et ses disciples de Johns Hopkins) ont beaucoup travaillé. Les Américains préfèrent en général nous laisser l'enseigner. C'est un champ vaste et riche....

## Au même:

5 oct. 1942

Cher Monsieur May,

Je suis heureux de vos bonnes nouvelles, et que votre première impression à Illinois soit favorable. Vous pouviez certes tomber plus mal, et les espoirs ou facilités pour l'avenir sont probablement plus grands là-bas qu'autour de New York, où il y a tant de nos compatriotes.

Je serais content de prendre connaissance du Giraudoux, *Littérature*, et du Brisson, *Molière;* et comme ces livres de France sont rares, (et aussi parce que je crois pouvoir vous dire que telle est mon habitude), je vous promets d'en prendre grand soin. Je crois que l'André Rousseaux est parvenu ici de Suisse et je possédais déjà le *Tableau* de la NRF. J'aurais beaucoup aimé voir les poésies qui se sont publiées récemment en France (Cahiers du Rhône, les deux volumes de Louis Aragon, etc.), mais vous ne pouviez vous douter de cette conséquence paradoxale de la guerre qui nous prive ici des livres français, même les plus innocents. . . .

## To Charles Seymour:

October 16, 1942

Dear President Seymour,

You may remember that I spoke to you last spring of our plan to offer a volume of scholarly Essays and Studies to Professor Feuillerat when he retires at the end of the present academic year. The volume would be published in the Romanic Series, which Professor Feuillerat has ably and devotedly created and directed. I am receiving the last articles just now, and I hope to give the MS to the Yale Press very early in November. The book will not, I believe, be a mere collection of brief and often insignificant articles, but will contain substantial and solid studies in the field of Romance, English or comparative literary history. The contributors include (if, as I hope, they are all ready on time): Profs. Baldensperger, now in California; Lancaster, Johns Hopkins; Chinard, Princeton; Morize, Harvard; Torrey, Columbia; Tucker Brooke; J. Allison; K. Young; S. Rose; Lipari. And, from the French Department of

Yale: Profs. Bates, Boorsch, Cohen, Cornell, Ezban, Fowlie, Hill, Morehouse and Peyre. Professor Focillon to his great regret has not been well enough to write or dictate lately.

We should all be very happy and proud if you would agree to write a brief introduction to the volume, probably mentioning a few details about Professor Feuillerat's personality and his association with Yale, and the meaning of the volume, appearing as the twenty second in the Yale Romanic series, started by Professor Feuillerat twelve years ago. I know how busy you must be in times like these; but if you could do us the honor of a few lines for an introduction, all the contributors to the volume and Professor Feuillerat himself would, I am sure, feel highly gratified. I should be glad personally to provide you with any data or any information that you may wish to that effect.

Very sincerely yours,<br>Henri Peyre

**To the same:**

1560, Timothy Dwight College<br>November 2, 1942

Dear President Seymour:

I apologize for taking a little of your time and attention for a small personal question in this letter, when you have so many grave and urgent problems to solve. I thought I might feel free to do it out of a sincere desire to serve the American and Allied war effort in the way in which I may perhaps best do so.

I am, as you know, a citizen of France; I repudiated the Vichy Government soon after the Armistice and became affiliated with the Free French. My loyalty to America and to Yale is, as you know, unreserved and profound.

Under the Selective Service plan, I have been classified as 3 A, as married and having only one direct dependent in this country (my wife). My age is 41 and 8 months. My local draft board is Board 8 A, 185 Church St.

This Board has just asked its 3A men for a new affidavit on their families and occupational status. I understand that men engaged in necessary work and in key positions will be deferred temporarily, others reclassified and to be drafted soon.

I am not, of course, trying to evade my duties to this country or to the allied cause. But I am very anxious to serve as fully and as competently as possible where I may best do so. My foreign citizenship (I cannot yet be an American citizen, having only lived here three years since 1939) makes it impossible for me or men in my position to apply for a commission in the U.S. Army, particularly in an intelligence service where I could probably be useful. I do not sincerely believe I could serve the war effort efficiently as a private in the American army. Even the French Government in 1939–40 chose not to recall me for military service (although I hold a commission in the French army) and felt that my teaching at Yale and my research were more valuable than the services I could have rendered as an officer in the army.

I am taking the liberty, since you personally and very kindly invited me to return to America and to join the Yale faculty in 1938, to ask you a few personal questions concerning my own case (which, I believe, as that of a foreign professor under 44, married and with no other dependents than his wife, is only paralleled, among the Yale faculty, by that of Mr. Driver):

Would the University feel that my position at Yale and my research activities warrant asking my local Draft Board to consider my work as essential and justifying a deferment or reclassification?

If so, and if later the University feels that my services could be dispensed with or would be more useful elsewhere, would it consider recommending to the proper authorities to utilize my competence, eventually, in fields where it might prove really useful (intelligence work, propaganda, lecturing, work in liaison with the Free French or the French), I cannot help feeling that I could do more valuable work in those fields than as a private in the army, where I fear I would be worse than useless.

I am putting this delicate personal question to you, since this seems to be the proper time for men in my age-group to try and see as clearly as possible into the future. The plans for the French Department and for the continuance of part at least of our work through the war and after the war require some continuity of purpose. I have also been asked, as a French scholar, but also as a representative of my profession and of Yale, to give important series of lectures elsewhere (the Messenger Lectures at Cornell in 1943, the Flexner lectures at Bryn Mawr in 1944), and I must plan for those in advance. Finally, I would presume to say that the whole problem of utilizing foreign scholars in the war effort, and particularly French professors loyal to their Universities and to this country, has not yet been approached by Washington. I suppose it would be, and might be solved constructively and in the best interests of the war effort, if you and some College presidents brought the attention of the authorities to it.

I shall be happy if I may see you for a few minutes this week, so as to give you more information about this, and about the Feuillerat volume of essays, if you have a little time and I am,

Very sincerely yours,
Henri Peyre

## To the same:

November 6, 1942

Dear President Seymour,

My colleagues and I are very grateful to you for agreeing so promptly and gracefully to write a foreword for our projected volume of essays in honor of Professor Feuillerat. It is a great encouragement to all of us.

May I add to the table of contents that I left with you, the titles of the two essays by Professor Lipari and Professor R. T. Hill: "The Structure and Real Significance of the *Decameron*," by A. Lipari, and "The Influence of the Noie on the Poetry of Joachim du Bellay" by R. T. Hill.

Contrary to what I thought, Madame Focillon told me yesterday, she would send me promptly an article, recently written by her husband, for our volume where he is very anxious to appear among the colleagues and friends of Professor Feuillerat.

I believe you have the few data on Professor Feuillerat's association with Yale. He came here first after the First World War as visiting-professor of English in the Graduate School, again in that capacity in 1928–29 when he became Director of Graduate Studies in French.

Our graduate department has trained, under his direction and supervision, excellent students whose dissertations have often reached a very high level, the highest in the country, I believe. The characteristics of Professor Feuillerat as a scholar have been, I think, the extreme minuteness of his method and the truly scientific search for accuracy, objectivity and truth on the one hand; on the other, a refined literary sense combined with the most precise method, taste added to knowledge, and a constant and successful effort to write with beauty of works which are beautiful and to leave or to restore life to writings which, while belonging to the past, are not dead but alive.

His example has proved influential and beneficial, not only at Yale, but in America and in Europe. At a time when American scholarship had been fascinated and perhaps sterilized by a narrow factual method imported from Germany, he fought for reconciliation between scholarship and criticism, accumulation of knowledge and interpretation of life. His ideas on that subject have been best expressed in a striking article in the *Yale Review,* Jan. 1925, vol. 14, pp. 309–324, in which he foresees a bright future for intelligent and solid criticism, "the guide and arbiter of good thinking," and, when the world was just emerging from a crisis similar to the present one, he voiced his hope in the ultimate triumph of man, and of what the humanities stand for: "The world will grope its way out of the present chaos, and the enormity of the task will precisely be the cause of its redemption" (p. 324).

The characteristic feature of his own publications is their equal eminence in the field of English and in that of French literature. He published a big volume on *John Lyly* in 1910, a standard critical edition of Sir Philip Sidney at Cambridge (England) in 1912–1920, an edition of Shakespeare's Poems at the Yale Press in 1927 and a partial translation of Shakespeare into French (1921–25).

He also brought out, at the Yale Press, *French Life and Ideals* (1925), a very important study of Marcel Proust in 1924, a volume on Paul Bourget, 1937, and two recent studies of Baudelaire.

In the Romanic Series which he founded when he came to Yale, there have already appeared twenty-one volumes by members of our department. The present volume will be the 22nd.

Very sincerely yours,
Henri Peyre

## À Pierre Bédard:

Le 15 novembre 1942

Cher Monsieur,

Excusez cette réponse rapide griffonnée dans la paix du dimanche.

Certes, je serai flatté de donner à l'Institut une conférence. Je suis si pris ce trimestre (qui va pour nous jusqu'à fin janvier) que février serait pour moi préférable; ou avril, à défaut, & si l'on ose encore voir l'avenir si lointain.

Si vous choisissez un mardi de février, voulez-vous me l'annoncer d'un mot, pour que je réserve le jour en conséquence.

Comme sujet, il ne manquera pas de temps pour choisir. Je crois que vous tenez (avec raison) à des sujets qui touchent à la politique ou aux événements actuels, même de loin, de haut & avec impartialité. En ce cas, dans la littérature contemporaine, "Charles Péguy, symbole de la France héroïque" pourrait vous convenir, si l'on a peu parlé de Péguy chez vous—Ou bien: "Le sens de l'œuvre de Saint Exupéry: besoin de grandeur." Ou encore "L'âme de la France actuelle: la poésie contemporaine." Je crois qu'il ne serait pas déplacé de parler de quelques-uns de ces nouveaux poètes, qu'on lit beaucoup en France aujourd'hui, & moins difficiles qu'il ne paraît. Vous me direz là-dessus votre avis.

Avec mes sentiments les plus sincèrement dévoués,

Henri Peyre

## To Edgar Furniss:

November 25 — 1942

Dear Dean Furniss:

There is a great probability that Mr. Kenneth Cornell, instructor in French in his fourth year in that capacity & one of our most promising scholars & most successful teachers, will be drafted soon. He has only secondary dependents (his father) & has just been reclassified as 1A. We shall greatly miss him, & regret that the research fellowship which he was promised last summer for the spring term may thus not be utilized by him. I shall notify you when (& if) he is actually called by the Army.

In the meanwhile, I would like to ask your advice on the following question: it was (& is) the desire & intention of the Department to propose Mr. Cornell for promotion to an assistant-professorship this fall. I believe such a proposal would have met with the full approval of Dean Buck (& of Dean DeVane, too). Mr. Cornell has already produced a good & important book, several articles; he is an excellent scholar, & successful as a teacher.

Partly because we appreciate his services, & want to keep a few possibilities for the rebuilding of the Department after the war (which may be sooner than we expect), we would like to propose him for promotion when the time comes to make arrangements for next year; & either to have him leave as assistant professor on leave of absence, or at any rate to present the vote of the department to the Administration, for the record & for the future. May I ask you how you would be disposed to such a proposal on our part? I hope it is not indiscreet to ask such a question now.

Sincerely,
Hri Peyre

## À Georges May:

30 nov. 1942

Cher Monsieur,

J'admire, par vos remarques, votre sagesse cultivée et déjà si nuancée. Vous possédez un sens critique et une méthode sûre rares à votre âge, car je vous suppose jeune. Cela tranche avec nos étudiants de ce pays, d'ailleurs charmants.

Je conserve quelques jours encore votre Giraudoux. Le *Molière* m'a vivement intéressé et est agréablement écrit. Il est surtout touchant de se dire qu'on peut lire ce que lisaient nos compatriotes il y a un an.

Voilà la France bien fermée et souffrant dans le plus noir silence! . . .

## To Norman Donaldson:

December 7, 1942

Mr. Norman V. Donaldson, Secretary
Yale University Press
Dear Mr. Donaldson,

    I am sorry to have been obliged to put off the date on which I expected to bring to the Press the complete MS of the volume of "Essays and Studies in Honor of Albert Feuillerat." It is always difficult, and just now more difficult than ever, to secure fifteen or twenty different contributions by so very many busy men. One has not yet arrived, from a colleague at Princeton University. But I thought I could already consult you on several points which should probably be settled before the printing begins.

    As you remember, the principle of the volume was approved last year by the Administration. A sum of approximately $1500 is set aside for that purpose, from the Romanic Series Fund. The volume would be in the Romanic Series and similar in appearance to the recent "Studies by Members of the Department" published in that series. The length would be approximately 300 printed pages.

    There was some discussion as to the best title for such a volume. Many objections can be offered, and rightly so, to volumes offered as "Festschrift" or "Mélanges" to some eminent scholar. They often consist of small and insignificant articles which their authors have not thought worthy of publication before. A glance at the present volume will show that this is not the case. All the articles were written expressly for this volume and all of them have solid merit; some are, I believe, of outstanding value as scholarly contributions. No other title but "Essays and Studies in Honor of Albert Feuillerat" could be fitting; to omit the second part of the title would suppress the open purpose of the volume, would certainly make no difference whatever to its sale, and would make it unworthy of the scholar who served Yale for many years and founded and directed the Romanic Series.

    The number of copies to be printed and the selling price will, of course, be determined by the Yale Press. My own suggestion would be the same as I have offered for the other volumes in the series: since the money is as a rule provided by the University or from some fund, it would be worthwhile lowering the price and thus probably selling a larger number of copies (especially, in normal times, in France). The rate of exchange will certainly make it almost impossible for Europeans to buy American scholarly works after the present war; and it might be not merely a generous part of the program of relief to war-ridden countries but a useful move for the reputation of Yale and of American scholarship, to send a few copies free to important foreign libraries. Our specialized volumes often remain unsold and have to be given away after a few years or to be sold at a discount. A somewhat smaller price at the time of publication might be just as profitable and give the volume a wider sale.

In fixing the number of copies to be printed, it might be well to keep in mind that each author (there are eighteen collaborators), should probably receive two copies of the volume to which he has generously contributed an article, as a homage to a Yale professor and to Yale, and Professor Feuillerat himself should probably be offered four or five copies.

In order to avoid that the different essays which constitute the present volume remain unnoticed and unknown, it is important, as Professor Notestein pointed out, that a large number of reprints of each essay (at least fifty) be sent to important libraries and catalogues, or be reviewed in the suitable learned journals.

As a compensation (at least partial) for that expense, I would like to suggest that no royalties whatever be given to any of the authors of the present volume; the authors will feel that they are amply rewarded for their contribution by appearing under the auspices of the Yale Press and, as I hope may be possible, by a reasonable number of reprints of their particular essay.

One at least of the contributors has expressed the wish to be allowed to reprint his article, later on, in some volume which he is preparing. I hope the Press could grant that permission.

[No signature]

## To Edgar Furniss:

Dec. 7—1942

Dear Dean Furniss:

I am enclosing a copy of my letter to Professor Tinker. Of course, there is nothing there that you are not familiar with already.

Also a copy of my letter to the Press on the Feuillerat volume. I shall take that letter to Mr. Donaldson with the MS in a day or so.

Historians of literature contend we do not write any letters in the present century, as our great-grandmothers did. But letter-writing still seems to prosper at Yale!

With all due apologies for these pedantic enclosures,

Hri Peyre

## To the same:

December 7, 1942

Dear Dean Furniss,

May I submit in writing the few questions which I would like to put to you this afternoon, in connection with the budget of our Department for 1942–43?

As you realize, the prospect of parting with all our instructors is a very grim one. While we are aware of the very hard financial conditions in which the University will find itself through probable big losses in tuition, we all regret that the burden should be borne almost exclusively by the younger men. This is regrettable because we are thus gravely jeopardizing the future of research and of education in this country. Some of those younger teachers may go into another field and be lost for ever for our studies. The training of new teachers, especially in French, is in the meanwhile being interrupted in our graduate schools. It will be very hard to rebuild our department when the time comes for such a reconstruction (and that time may come sooner than we think). Circumstances connected with the war and the post war conditions may determine a wide movement back to the study of French, both as a practical language in Europe, Africa, Indo China, etc., and as a literature which may well become more in demand when there is as there often is after a war, a return to the arts and refinements of life and of culture.

You are, of course, aware of our fears, which are shared by other departments in the humanities. The solution which consists in not reappointing the instructors is probably the easiest and the best one; but it will make our departments top heavy and composed mostly of older men who will in many cases be psychologically very remote from young students, with the middle aged group (from 28 to 48) almost entirely absent. In some cases, the University might find it more profitable in the long run to retain a few promising younger men (if their military status allows it) and to encourage men in the middle ranks to accept positions where they would serve in the war effort. These men would be readier to look for such positions if the University were disposed to supplement the salary received in a military or civilian position so that the total would reach their present salary, up to $5000 for instance.

It is especially regrettable to be faced with the non-reappointment of all instructors in a department like ours, where much of the teaching is elementary or not very advanced and is often done better and with newer methods by the younger men. Moreover, in recent years, we have already moved swiftly in the same direction. We had fourteen instructors and assistants in instruction in 1940–41; we dropped to eight in 1941–42; to four in 1942–43. We have also just lost Mr. Bates, who taught mostly freshmen. In terms of money, our budget has dropped consistently from $71,160 (as approved, plus $1800 FES) in 1939–40 to $64,850 (plus $2400 FES) in 1942–43 and, as suggested now, to $44,250 (no FES grant). The reduction would be equivalent to 38 % over five years.

We are of course willing to do our utmost to accept these severe conditions, so as to assist the University in the present circumstances. It may be that a very marked drop in the number of our students will enable us to carry on without instructors. I would like to point out, however: that our work is mostly with the freshmen, and we may have a large share of our work left next year; that signs of a renewed interest in French are already evident; we have just had, among the present sophomore class, more applications for majors than we have had for a long time; that more students than we expect (either deferred for physical reasons, or in the Naval or other reserves) may be here, even after next June; that, through some sudden and not improbable demand for French by the Army or by the Foreign Area study or Relief groups, we may be faced with the prospect of looking for new instructors after having dismissed ours. The supply of teachers of French seems to be very low just now in the country. We cannot even find persons willing or able to do outside tutoring, for which students who are not taking our classes often apply.

Among our four present instructors, one case of non-reappointment would be especially disappointing: that of Mr. Cornell. Our intention, as I told you, was and is, if at all possible, to propose him for an assistant-professorship. He is an excellent teacher and already a productive scholar. There is a strong possibility that he may be drafted soon, as having only a secondary dependent (his father), in which case the saving would be effected automatically. If he were not, it would be rather ungrateful to dismiss him at this time, when he has taught with us for five years.

Mr. Ezban, who is our second oldest man in the rank of instructor, might prove very useful as a teacher of Arabic, Moslem customs, and of French and Italian as well, to the Foreign Area study group or to the Army if they wish such teaching. I would suggest that he be kept under another budget if possible. He has proved a very able and efficient teacher of French conversation and composition.

If Messrs Tenney and Douglas, who are both married and respectively 30 and 32 years old, are not taken by the draft, and if both Mr. Cornell (if drafted) and Mr. Ezban (used elsewhere) are taken from our department, it is hard for me to see just now how we can do without at least one of them. Mr. Douglas, who has an excellent knowledge both of French and of German, has traveled and lived in several parts of the world and done relief work with the Quakers in Austria after the other war, might be utilized by the Foreign Area study group or by the Army.

A slight adjustment might be made in our budget and in our favor if part of the salary of Mr. Hill were theoretically charged to another fund. His teaching, lately, has been in Portuguese even more than in French. It may be that Portuguese will be needed in the Foreign Area group, in any case. Portuguese, if it is to be taught permanently at Yale, might logically be tucked with Spanish, or with South American studies, rather than with French.

I shall add two more questions. 1) Messrs Hill and Richardson were reappointed as associate-professors for five years in 1938. The rules of tenure were subsequently modified and it was understood Messrs Hill and Richardson would be made permanent automatically when their present term expired. This, of course, means no extra financial burden. If you approve, I shall forward proposals to that effect to the Deans concerned. 2) If Mr. Cornell were called by the Army this month, would it be possible to apply for a deferment of a few weeks until the end of the term and of the month of January? This fall term is a very heavy one for all of us, and the death of Mr. Bates has just imposed an extra burden on his colleagues. We would be put to great difficulty if we had to take Mr. Cornell's 12 or 14 hours of teaching, even for a few weeks.

Sincerely yours,<br>
Hri Peyre

**To the same:**

December 15 — 1942

Dear Dean Furniss:

It may be that you are a little less busy during the vacations & may have a few moments to glance at this. These letters or reports were written, at my request, by some of our young Ph.D.'s & assistants in instruction who have recently left us. I had asked to state freely, not compliments but objective criticisms which they thought our methods deserved. We are trying to do our best with the means & the staff at our disposal & there is, no doubt, room for improvement in our Department. Much of what they find fault with, is what we also consider faulty; but their point of view is interesting.

I had told them their remarks would remain confidential, especially if they happened to touch upon "personalities." Will you also consider them as such?

In our teaching of language courses, we are already trying strenuously to remedy some of the points which our young men found open to criticism. Recent events (the prospect of having to teach on an accelerated plan, of having to teach "Foreign Area" people & army officers in a very few weeks) are encouraging us to reform our language teaching. We are busy studying the methods used by the linguistics people & advertised as new. Much may be borrowed from them, although we are not certain as yet how far the method applied in Japanese will be valid for French or German: the very purpose is different, since even "accelerated" Army officers cannot entirely separate spoken French from French as a language easily read & even easily written. The method followed at Yale in the teaching of Japanese has by common consent proved very fruitful & has been excellently well practiced. The comments one involuntarily hears on the way Russian is taught are, I must confess, much less flattering.

 The remarks here presented on our graduate school Department seem to me justified to a large extent, & you are already, no doubt, familiar with them. To take them up in order, some may be easily remedied (among our faults) & others will be more difficult. 1) Our oral comprehensive exam. I believe we shall reform that in one or two years. 2) The course in methods, and an earlier choice of a thesis subject and a more intensive practice in written essays, as a preparation for the dissertation. 3) New courses in criticism & in stylistics have been introduced & offered by me since 1940. 4) A course in the syntax (scientifically & historically studied) of modern French could be given; but it is difficult for our students to be able to take it, as long as our requirement in philology remains as rigid & exacting as it is. This is regrettable, as such a course should help attract teachers & future teachers of language. Our Graduate School Department has put the emphasis nobly, but too exclusively, on research & very advanced scholarship. We should also do some training of teachers in the field of language, & help bridge the excessive gulf between our Graduate School & teachers in high or secondary schools. 5) Our philology (Vulgar Latin, Old French) is relatively too difficult & too excessive. Some improvement was effected, two years ago, after I had already raised the question. But it is difficult to change the habits of an old & devoted teacher. On the other side, Old French *literature,* if we lose Mr. Cohen for good & since we lost Mr. Bates, is not taught at all. This is a very grave gap. 5) The problem of Italian is also a delicate one. The Dean of the Graduate School, an energetic move by the chairman of the Spanish-Italian Department & by the future Director of Graduate Studies in French may, one day, solve it. 6) The most serious & most fundamental difficulty lies in our requirements—the heaviest, I daresay, of any department. As one of the enclosed letters points out, to be accepted at the Graduate School (and, normally, to be considered favorably for a scholarship) and to be able to get a Ph.D. degree in three, even in four years, an entering graduate student must have had before his BA degree: at least three years of Latin, German (or two at least), Italian, Spanish. He must be: a specialist of French. And, of course, he must have filled the usual college requirements in Mathematics & Science, Classical Civilization, History, American History, English. To do well in our studies, he *must* have had a good grounding in English Literature and in Philosophy.

Our requirements are thus hard and extremely varied. Our graduate studies here force the candidate to study at the same time at least four different subjects: his major subject, e.g. French literature; Philology & Vulgar Latin; Spanish; Italian. As a consequence, too little time remains for French literature proper, which in itself is as rich as English literature & covers more centuries.

Many good students (as I have had occasion to find out again recently), gifted for the study of literature & attracted by French, are kept away by our requirements & often go over to English, where the level of studies is very high & justly admired, but where they concentrate on *two* fields instead of *four:* Philology and Old English, English Literature.

The evil is not limited to Yale. It is worse in some other places, somewhat less grave in others. But our profession, all over the country, is waiting for a new lead & a reform. The number of good men & first-rate scholars in the field of romance literatures is woefully small. A bold step in the right direction taken here would serve our profession as a whole & be an example.

It may seem strange to think of the future & submit these remarks to you at a time when all our studies are interrupted & our graduate department practically non existent. When circumstances again allow it, & before anything can be done, we should of course need a strong appointment in the place of Mr. Feuillerat & another one in the field of Old French literature. But it may be well to be ready for the moment when we have to rebuild, & in the meanwhile to face frankly the points where we have not been perfect.

Sincerely yours,<br>Hri Peyre

Would you kindly, without any haste, return the enclosed letters to me later?

## À Pierre Bédard:

Ce 15 décembre 1942

Cher Monsieur,

Merci de votre lettre qui m'arrive à l'instant. Je crois que le texte qui devrait y être inclus a dû être omis par mégarde. Mais je vous confirme ce qu'il mentionnait sans doute: que je suis bien d'accord pour la date (mardi 16 fév-, à 4 heures) & le titre: "Le sens de l'œuvre de Saint-Exupéry: Besoin de Grandeur."

Si vous voulez bien m'envoyer deux ou trois exemplaires du Bulletin correspondant, je le ferai parvenir à quelques amis ou groupes auxquels je songerai; et peut-être vous suggérerai-je plus tard un ou deux noms d'invités.

Je serai enfin heureux à cette occasion (sinon auparavant) de pouvoir causer un moment à loisir avec vous. J'ai été bien peu à New York ce trimestre, mais déplore d'y voir, toujours & malgré tout, nos compatriotes divisés. *Pour la Victoire* devient une vulgaire feuille de chou.

Mes sentiments les plus cordiaux et—déjà—mes vœux.

Hri Peyre

## Au même:

Ce 8 février 1943

Cher Monsieur,

J'attends avec impatience le plaisir de vous revoir & de causer quelques moments avec vous le 16 de ce mois, avant ma conférence sur Saint-Exupéry.

Peut-être vous demanderai-je asile pour la nuit du 15 au 16—en tous cas pas plus longtemps, car je dois rentrer à New Haven le mardi soir pour mes cours du lendemain, & je ne suis pas encore sûr de pouvoir m'échapper le lundi soir.

J'aurais beaucoup voulu aller écouter Saint Ex le 5 janvier—mais j'avais malencontreusement accepté une conférence ailleurs ce jour-là, moi-même. Vous me redirez peut-être ce qu'il a dit alors.

Parmi les personnes à qui j'avais pensé vous prier d'envoyer une annonce de ma conférence, ou des autres que vous avez données ou allez donner (votre programme de janvier février est magnifique), je voulais vous indiquer: Mr. Alexander Makinsky. Rockefeller Foundation. 49 West 49th St., N.Y. City; Mrs. Willis Lyman, 28 Holmes Ave., Glenbrook, Conn.; Miss Berthie Zilkha, 300 Central Park West. NYC; Prof. Norman Torrey 411 West 114th St., NYC; Mrs. E. A. Dennisson, 1075 Park Avenue.

Croyez à mon souvenir bien fidèlement dévoué & à bientôt,

Henri Peyre

## To Edgar Furniss:

April 12, 1943

Dear Dean Furniss,

I expressed surprise at your reply on the telephone last week that the decision of the Executive Committee was left where it stood (only one instructor provided for the French Department).

My anxiety, which is shared by all our colleagues, is not a selfish one (a desire on the part of the permanent members of the Department not to teach elementary courses and to retain young men to give them). In fact, we have gradually lost our assistants in instruction and our reader in French, and we are all going to teach elementary courses next term. But we felt that, having lost so many teachers of our Department this year (Mr. Bates, Mr. Cornell, Mr. Feuillerat, Mr. Cohen), we were being treated more rigorously, as far as our instructors were concerned, than the Department of German for instance, in which the three instructors asked for by the Department, Messrs White, Nordmeyer and Moulton, are I understand being retained, the latter through a promotion.

My reasons for hoping for a more favorable decision from the Executive Committee are as follows:

1) We may lose to the draft Messrs Fowlie and Tenney. We shall know the results of their physical examination by April 21st. Others among us may go into some other service, while we are certain that no addition will be made to our number.

2) The new calendar of the University coming after the summer work of 1942 and 1943 is going to be a severe one. Some of us may need

a little relief (a lighter schedule one term if not a term off). That will only be possible if we are not out to a sub-minimum.

3) We shall have to give three or four graduate courses, even for a very few students. If the Foreign Area work goes on and develops, however little, it will take the full time of Mr. Boorsch plus at least half the time of another instructor. If the University decides to admit 400 or 500 freshmen, we cannot possibly cope with the probable work without the help of our present instructors.

4) If things developed contrary to our expectations and we had more free time than we imagine, some of us would be available for other tasks, as was indicated in our replies to the University questionnaires—German, European History, American History, and in two cases (Messrs Richardson and Edsall) Mathematics.

5) I understand from Dean DeVane that the course in Arabic having been approved by the Yale Faculty, that approval implies that Mr. Ezban will be available at Yale for part-time instruction in Arabic next fall.

For all these reasons, I believe it would be wiser to reappoint for one year our present instructors: Messrs Douglas and Ezban, and Mr. Tenney if (we shall know on April 21st) he is rejected by the army. The sum in excess of that granted by the Executive Committee would be either $2750 or (if Mr. Tenney stays with us) $5500. If Mr. Fowlie is taken by the army (which I doubt, since he was already rejected once for physical reasons), our budget would be cut by another $3250. The total extra expense is certainly not considerable. It guards us against the future, and avoids the unpleasantness (for Yale) of having to dismiss our present instructors late in the year, when one (Mr. Douglas) has to support a wife and a child, when the other (Mr. Ezban) is a potentially very useful man.

I shall look forward to talking this matter over with you on Wednesday morning and am,

Very sincerely yours,
Hri Peyre

## À Georges May:

9 mai 1943

Mon cher ami,

Votre lettre m'a vivement intéressé. C'est en effet une expérience originale que la vôtre: après avoir servi dans l'armée française, vous voilà soldat américain. De Corneille et Racine, de la technique dramatique et de Théagène et Chariclée, vous passez à un langage que je suppose moins noble et moins délicat. Comme vous dites, c'est une manière énergique de faire connaissance avec l'Amérique.

Je ne sais que vous dire sur l'avenir qui vous est réservé. Vous auriez évidemment pu être admis avec un grade parmi les groupes d'officiers de liaison que l'on forme en Géorgie pour l'armée Giraud. Si vous êtes venu en Amérique pour y faire votre carrière et adopter la nationalité américaine, vous avez bien fait de choisir la voie la plus dure. Cela sera même utile pour votre avenir en ce pays.

J'ai eu souvent des nouvelles d'étudiants américains mobilisés (je ne connais pas de cas semblable au vôtre d'un Français entré dans l'armée; mais il y en a!). Après les deux ou trois premières semaines, parfois les trois premiers mois de désordre et de confusion, ils trouvent en général leur voie et une utilisation logique et intelligente de leurs capacités. Faites-vous connaître à vos chefs le plus possible pour les intéresser à votre cas, et ils vous aiguilleront peut-être. . . .

## To Charles Seymour:

July 30, 1943

Dear President Seymour:

May I express the gratitude of all my colleagues and collaborators and my own for the fine Preface you kindly wrote for the volume of *Essays in Honor of Albert Feuillerat*. It has added greatly to the value of the book and has expressed very fully the meaning of such a volume, appearing in the present circumstances. We are deeply grateful to you.

Professor Feuillerat asked me not to arrange any gathering at which the volume would have been formally presented to him, as I had planned to do. He prefers to retire as modestly as he has taught and worked. All his colleagues and former students are none the less deeply grateful to him and have expressed their satisfaction that a volume of essays prefaced by you and sponsored by the University could appear at the time of Professor Feuillerat's retirement.

With thanks and very sincerely yours,<br>Henri Peyre

## To Edgar Furniss:

August 4, 1943

Dear Dean Furniss:

May I submit to you a few questions which occur to me on reviewing the memorandum on extra-stipends for continuous teaching?

1) Contrary to what I had originally understood, the memorandum seems to encourage members of the faculty to be relieved of teaching duties one term (or rather three-fourths of one term, 12 weeks out of 16) every year, and not every two years.

This is certainly fair, and approximates the practice already observed in other large institutions. It happens, however, that this year 1943–1944, the news of such possibility of relief having reached our colleagues very late, they will not find it possible to take a term off for practical reasons (lease or rent for those who would wish to be away, children's schooling, etc.). Since they will be present in New Haven and at Yale, they will prefer teaching a full schedule for three continuous terms, and in most cases it will be easy to give them such a full schedule, for our staff has been sharply reduced. Would they be entitled to the extra stipend, even though this might mean revising the budget and increasing it to some extent?

2) In order that the costs to the university be kept to a minimum, I would suggest that in our Department I might tell our colleagues above the rank of instructor that anyone who receives the extra stipend for 1943–44 would not normally be entitled to it in 1944–45 and would be expected to take a term of "relief" that second year.

3) The "normal" load of 36 weeks will make difficulties. Should we interpret it as two of our present (Navy) terms, plus one-fourth of another term? This will lead to awkward changes of teachers. I suppose

we might eventually calculate the equivalent load in hours spread over two terms. 36 weeks at 12 hours = 432 hours. 432 hours spread over two terms of 16 weeks, i.e. over 32 weeks would give an average of 13 hours and a half a week, 13 hours one term and 14 the next for instance.

4) If for some unforeseen reason it becomes absolutely impossible for a teacher to be dispensed with, both in 1943–44 and in 1944–45, would he be entitled to the extra stipend for two successive years? We shall try and hope to avoid this, both as a measure of economy and in the interest of the teacher's health and scholarship; but it may prove unavoidable with the scarcity of teachers of French to be hired as substitutes and the eventual increase in Foreign Areas work.

5) It is obvious that the practical difficulties in working out a relief term every year will come mostly from the far greater desirability of the summer term as a term of relief. Since this summer's work is already under way and all the teachers present are needed, next summer (1944) will be in great demand. When the time comes, and if such an arrangement were not to prove detrimental to the quality or the efficiency of the teaching, I shall try to persuade our colleagues to be satisfied with only half of a summer term. In the future and when the war is over, it might prove more economical to the University and more beneficial both to the health and to the scholarship of faculty and students to substitute a brief summer session, with intensive courses in not more than three subjects (at 5 hours a week each) for our present summer term. Such a transition measure would take care of students and ex-soldiers in need of acceleration in their studies. The members of the faculty teaching it would be comparatively few and receive an extra stipend for it.

6) The practical plans for relief or extra stipend in our Department will be formulated later, when the needs of teaching are clearer. Our Department has two full professors, who, I think, should not be considered for extra stipend whether they are obliged to stay here or not. It has two instructors, in their second year, already paid on the basis of $2,500, who will be expected to teach three full terms in 1943–44. It has four associate professors and two assistant professors. Out of these, Morehouse could be away in Fall 1943; Fowlie in Spring 1944. Hill would probably not teach a full load. But three members of the Department remain (Richardson, Boorsch, Edsall). It may prove impossible to do without them in any of the three terms of 1943–44 (Boorsch on account of Foreign Areas and perhaps a graduate course; Edsall to re-

place Morehouse or Fowlie, while they are on leave; Richardson because he would be needed both by our Department and Mathematics. He gives 6 hours of Math this term and they would like him to give 12 if we could dispense with him).

In such circumstances, could we foresee the possibility of an extra stipend ($600 in the case of Richardson and Boorsch; $500 in Edsall's) this year 1943–44, with the understanding that this would not be renewed for them in 1944–45 and that we would then hope to provide them with one term of relief?

This is merely a tentative and preliminary inquiry. More precise information and work sheets would be sent later.

Sincerely yours,<br>Hri Peyre

## À Fernand-Laurent:

October 11, 1943

Monsieur Fernand-Laurent
Député de Paris
200 Central Park South
New York City
Monsieur:

Je vous remercie vivement de votre lettre et de votre prompte acceptation. Ce nous sera un grand plaisir de vous accueillir ici le 21 octobre. Je vous reconnaîtrai certainement sans difficulté à la gare; et je souhaite que votre journée ne vous paraisse pas trop chargée ou trop pénible.

Pour la conférence du soir, devant notre groupe d'Alliance française, j'annoncerai donc un titre assez général pour vous laisser toute liberté: "Paris sous l'occupation allemande: Notes d'un témoin oculaire." Ces conférences durent environ une heure.

Pour l'exposé discussion de l'après-midi à notre groupe d'officiers, en anglais, nul titre précis n'est nécessaire, puisque vous voulez bien accepter les exigences de notre programme et parler des Conséquences de l'affaire Dreyfus sur la vie politique française, des partis à ce moment là et depuis.

Mon collègue M. Allison et moi vous sommes très obligés de votre bienveillante réponse; et je vous prie d'agréer. Monsieur le Député, l'expression de mes sentiments les plus dévoués.

[Sans signature]

## To Edgar Furniss:

November 5, 1943

Dear Dean Furniss:

May I take the liberty to offer one or two remarks, which have probably occurred to other chairmen of departments and which the Executive Committee and the Administration may think worthy of being taken in consideration?

Members of our Department, like all members of the Yale faculty, are very happy at having been fully occupied in the last two years and of having thus contributed, in a humble and indirect way, to the war effort of the country. They have also appreciated the vote of the Corporation which promised extra stipends for members of the faculty who had been unable to take any relief this year. Some embarrassing comparisons with other institutions (where the extra stipend granted for the extra term of teaching was substantially higher) have been made in some cases; but the advantages offered by Yale and the loyalty of our faculty are such that I hope there is little danger of losing to other universities even our assistant professors, whose tenure is not assured.

There is a group of young men, however, for whom it may be reasonably thought that the University is not proving very generous: the instructors in their second year of tenure. Their total salary of $2,500 for three full terms of work at an average of 12 hours a week is modest; for those of them who have a family, living has become extremely difficult lately; they are obliged to look for extra work outside, which is demoralizing, and prevents them from taking advantage of the fine library and research facilities of Yale. With the suppression of vacations, and often their few leisure hours taken up by outside work, poorly paid, they cannot prepare any substantial plan of research, as young Ph.D.'s should. Moreover, other universities (like Harvard, if I am not mistaken) are now offering $3,000 even to first year instructors, and may tempt ours away from us before long.

My tentative suggestion would be that the Administration consider whether a total salary of $2,750 (instead of $2,500) for second year instructors should not be justified. We have recently discovered that we cannot afford to let any more of our young men go, and that it seems absolutely impossible to attract new ones with the present advantages that we offer. I believe it would be fair, and perhaps wise, to grant an extra stipend of $750 (instead of $500) to instructors in their second year in that rank at Yale, and that such an increase, if it were possible, should apply in the present academic year.

In the Department of French, we have two instructors in their second year (the only two instructors left to us): Messrs Douglas and Tenney. They are aware of the fact that new colleagues, often younger and less experienced, are being appointed at $3,000 in their first year at other institutions. They have both had a heavy burden last year, and have again a full schedule this year. The total extra expense of $500 which I am taking the liberty of suggesting, might be judged amply justified by the fact that our Department has requested no part-time or temporary appointment to replace those of our colleagues taking a term off, and that we have contributed several hours to other departments (last term six to Mathematics, three to American History, three to English Composition), thus making a corresponding saving possible to the University.

Yours very sincerely,
Hri Peyre

## À Pierre Bédard:

January 7, 1944

Monsieur Pierre Bédard
Mission militaire française
1759 R Street, N.W.
Washington, D. C.
Cher Monsieur,

Je vous remercie de votre lettre et de ce que vous me dites d'aimable sur ma brochure. Votre approbation m'est très précieuse, car votre jugement m'a toujours frappé par sa justesse et son impartialité. J'aimerais beaucoup parler avec vous plus à loisir de ces problèmes, que j'ai abordés en quelques pages.

Ma brochure se vend, me dit Brentanos, à Washington. J'en ai bien entendu, aussitôt reçue votre lettre, envoyé un exemplaire au Général Beynet. Si vous voyez des personnes, à la Mission militaire ou autour de vous, à qui je devrais la faire connaître, ne manquez pas de me le dire.

Le mardi 15 février me convient pour les deux conférences à New York. À 4 heures, "Foi en la France. Que doit être la France de demain?" À 8h 30, "La Littérature française dans la France captive, 1940–1943." Je vous admire d'organiser ainsi le travail de l'Institut tout en accomplissant une lourde besogne à New York.

À partir du 6 février, pour environ 5 semaines, je serai à Bryn Mawr College, Pennsylvania, où je dois donner une série de conférences littéraires. Si vous aviez quelque détail à modifier ou à préciser au dernier moment, voulez-vous m'écrire là?

Avec mes remerciements et mes sentiments les plus dévoués, ainsi que mes vœux pour l'année qui s'ouvre, qui sera enfin la bonne.

Henri Peyre

## To Edgar Furniss:

January 10, 1944

Dear Dean Furniss:

The Office of War Information has insisted urgently with Mr. Fowlie, who has accepted to enter that service and leave for England—probably next month, after the preliminary ordeal of vaccination imposed upon all persons going abroad.

He will be interrupting his courses here on Monday, January 17 and be put on the O.W.I. payroll that day. The only way we can take care of his work is to interrupt Morehouse's leave of absence and have him take charge of part at least of Fowlie's work as of January 17th. We will not need any one in the spring term and I hope I can find an instructor for the Summer.

Could you therefore leave in our budget the sum provided for Mr. Fowlie? His leave of absence will be from January 17th to June 30th. If he does not come back then, it will be extended. In that case, I should try to find someone to replace him temporarily.

I believe it would be fair to grant Mr. Morehouse a compensation for the work he will do from January 17th to February 15th. This seems to be equivalent to one-third of the work of the term and you may think he deserves compensation equal to one third of the extra-stipend he would have received if he had not received a term of "relief."

The hope of the Department is that Mr. Fowlie's rights to promotion will be retained or reserved while he is absent on government service—if he is by 1945–46, when the question of his promotion will occur.

Excuse this hurried note and very sincerely,

Henri Peyre

## À Georges May:

15 janv. 1944

Cher Monsieur,

... Mes vœux vous accompagnent dans la besogne, utile j'en suis sûr, et héroïque peut-être, que vous allez accomplir cette année.

Peu de changements pour moi—sinon la continuité lassante dans le même travail: enseignement, organisation, comités, étudiants d'armée et de marine à instruire en sus des nôtres. En février–mars je dois faire un séjour à Bryn Mawr College (Penna) pour y donner des conférences—en mars aussi, le 20 je crois, je ferai une visite rapide à Washington. À part cela, la guerre se passe pour nous sans incident, mais dans l'attente anxieuse et fervente de ce que cette année doit nous apporter—enfin! ...

## To Edgar Furniss:

February 19—1944

Dear Dean Furniss:

I am temporarily, as you know, at Bryn Mawr College, Pa (The Deanery). Mr. Wallace Fowlie has been keeping in contact with me here. Things have not gone in the way he had expected at the O.W.I.; the kind of work which had been promised him and which seemed to justify his immediate departure from Yale has turned out to be routine work in which he was little interested. The position which he was supposed to fill in London has been unexpectedly suppressed. Mr. Fowlie, rightly or wrongly, felt that he was not being useful at the O.W.I. and resigned.

I am thus asking you to ask for a cancellation of the leave of absence granted him at the February 12 meeting of the Prudential Committee (starting from January 15). His resignation from the O.W.I. is dated February 18. This would entitle him, if the Administration and Corporation approves, to his regular salary until the end of the present financial year.

I would also like to withdraw my previous suggestion that Mr. Morehouse receive, with the approval of the Special Committee in charge, a compensation for the extra month of teaching he did in January-February 1944, replacing Mr. Fowlie. Mr. Morehouse was on leave on a "relief" term last fall. Mr. Fowlie, who was to enjoy a "relief" term this Spring, will compensate, through taking one of his courses for instance, Mr. Morehouse for the extra time given by the latter last month. I would no longer feel justified in suggesting an expense for a member of our staff, in the present circumstances, since Mr. Fowlie's salary will not be saved to an appreciable extent.

I trust all has gone well during the first week of my absence & am,

Very sincerely yours,
Hri Peyre

## To Archibald MacLeish:

May 9, 1944

Mr. Archibald MacLeish
Librarian, The Library of Congress
Washington, D.C.
Dear Mr. MacLeish:

I am planning to publish a scholarly work on criticism at the Cornell University Press in a few months. I would like to quote a few lines from your very fine address *A Time to Speak,* from your book entitled *The Irresponsibles,* in my final chapter entitled "For a Reconciliation of Scholarship, Criticism and Literature." I am also writing to Messrs Fuell, Sloane and Pearce to secure the permission from the publishers. I have repeatedly quoted in oral lectures from that address, which many men in my profession should meditate, and I would like to quote it in writing to support my thesis that scholars have erred in dehumanizing their theories.

The quotation reads as follows:

"He was a man of learning whose learning was employed, not for its own sake in a kind of academic narcissism, but for the sake of decent living in his time. He was a writer whose writing was used, not to mirror an abstract and unrelated present, but to illuminate that present by placing it in just relation to its past. . . .

"The irresponsibility of the scholar is the irresponsibility of the scientist upon whose laboratory insulation he has patterned all his work. The scholar has made himself as indifferent to values, as careless of significance, as bored with meanings as the chemist. . . . The Ph.D. thesis is the perfect image of his world. It is work done for the sake of doing work—perfectly conscientious, perfectly laborious, perfectly irresponsible."

I should be grateful for permission to quote these lines, for which due acknowledgment would be made in the Preface.

Yours very truly,
Henri Peyre
Professor of French
Yale University

## To the editor of the *Atlantic Monthly:*

[published in the July 1944 issue]

Sir:

Your issue of May, 1944, is a very good one. It is interesting to see Herr Thomas Mann expressing his faith in democracy and championing "the liberal tradition"—that is, "the claim of reason to dominate the dynamics of nature, of instinct, of blood, of the unconscious." Twenty-five years ago, however, in a big volume entitled *Betrachtungen eines Unpolitischen* (1918), Herr Mann violently attacked all the Western and liberal ideas, scornfully denounced humanitarianism and democracy; it would be most enlightening to his readers to have Herr Mann explain how and why he was converted from his former Pan-Germanist and pro-Nazi views to his present attitude.

An earlier volume of his, *Friedrich und die grosse Koalition* (1915), which has never been translated in this country, provides horrifying but instructive reading. A few typical quotations, already made in the *Times Literary Supplement* (London) of August 21, 1943, may be in order:

"War! It is purification, liberation, an enormous hope. . . . The victory of Germany will be a paradox, nay, a wonder: a victory of the soul over numbers. . . . The German soul is opposed to the pacifist ideal of civilization, for is not peace the element of civil corruption? . . . The greatest and most important contribution to the moral apology of war has been done by German minds. . . ."

Commenting upon the bombing of Rheims cathedral, Herr Mann exclaimed: "Civilization! But first of all, Rheims cathedral has absolutely nothing to do with civilization. It is a monument of Christian culture, a flower of fanaticism and superstition. . . ."

The Allies were then already talking of re-educating the Germans. Herr Thomas Mann derided their naive claims: "They want to make us happy. They want to bring on us the blessings of demilitarization and democratization, and as we resist, they want to make human beings of us by force."

The great novelist held out slim hopes of seeing a democratic Germany arise out of a military defeat. "Only the victory of Germany will guarantee the peace of Europe. . . . If Germany fails in her fight, the Germans could and would not rest till they stood again where they are today, and in this unfortunate case the miseries and sufferings of Europe will not have an end for a long time."

No one suspects the sincerity of Herr Mann's conversion. But it is well to bear in mind that he wrote those pages, not in a youthful outburst, but in his forties, when he was already the respected author of *Buddenbrooks, Tristan, Death in Venice, Tonio Kröger.* If a man of his eminence and of his wide culture could think and speak thus in 1915–1918, can he now expect his readers readily to dissociate the German people from the Nazis?

Professor Henri Peyre<br>
Yale University

## To Barbara Howes:

West Chop
Martha's Vineyard, *Mass.*
June 18–1944

Dear Miss Howes:

Thank you for your letter of June 13, suggesting I write or give to *The Chimera* an article on Claudel. I suppose Mr. Fowlie was alluding to a study on Claudel which appeared, in French, in 1938, in my book *Hommes & Œuvres du Vingtième siècle*. That study had had the good fortune to be commented favorably by many admirers of the poet, including Gide. If you would care to have any portion of that essay translated and reprinted in *The Chimera,* I should be very glad to have you do so. As to rewriting part of it myself in English, I am afraid it would not be possible for me to do so for a long time. I am now away on vacation, until August 10 & shall be taken up by several promised articles or works on my return for many months.

I would not include Bernanos among the really important writers who should be better known in this country; but Mauriac, Giono, Cocteau certainly deserve to be more widely read over here.

May I take this opportunity to congratulate you on the fine level of the articles recently published in *The Chimera,* and also (although, inevitably, more unequally) of the poetry? The review will soon be one of the liveliest & of the best in this country—

Sincerely yours,
Henri Peyre
(Yale University)

## To the same:

Henri Peyre
The Cedars—West Chop
June 29–1944

Dear Miss Howes:

It is very kind of you to suggest translating my chapter on Claudel, or part of it, for *The Chimera,* & to suggest having it done by so able a stylist as Wallace Fowlie. He would write a better article on Claudel himself, & he would certainly be the best man to write on Cocteau. Breton is too dogmatic in his Surrealist creed to write on other writers, & I am not sure Yvan Goll, as a poet-critic or interpreter of other writers, would do as well as he occasionally does as a poet. Wallace Fowlie has a friend, Frank Jones (now in the Army), who could probably do an interesting reevaluation of Gide, & doubtless also of Cocteau. Such articles (the English review *Horizon* had a series of them recently on Nerval, Rimbaud, etc. & the *Scrutiny* another series on R. de Gourmont, Molière, etc.) can be very valuable & may help American literary opinion to be less obsessed by ambitious & pedantic disquisitions on the nature, terminology & methods of criticism & to be more interested in actually writing good critical articles.

With thanks & very sincerely yours,
Henri Peyre

**To the same:**

Sept. 11 — 1944

Dear Miss Howes:

Thank you for your kind note. I am glad you liked the article. I wish I could have found the time to rewrite it completely & therefore to rethink it & reframe it. I have just gone through (alas, it is not over) a very busy period, with many requests for talks on French affairs which I could not refuse.

I think it would be well to send notices to colleagues in colleges where students might take an interest in the review & in what it represents today among American periodicals. Here are a few such names: Prof. Jean Seznec, Harvard University, French Depart.; André Morize, Harvard French Depart.: Prof. E. K. Brown, Univ. of Chicago, Depart. of English; Prof. Joseph Jackson, Univ. of Illinois, Urbana, Dept. of French; Prof. Ruth Clark, Wellesley College, Dept. of French; Miss B. R. Lang, Wells College, Aurora, N.Y.; Miss D'Arlin, Vassar, Poughkeepsie, N.Y.; Miss E. M. Schenck, Bryn Mawr College, Bryn Mawr, Pa.; Miss Margaret Gilman, Bryn Mawr College; Miss K. M. Scruggs, Randolph Macon College, Lynchburg, Va.; Prof. Horatio Smith, Columbia Univ.; Prof. N. L. Torrey, Columbia; Prof. Maynard Mack, Yale Univ. Depart. of English; Prof. Vincent Guilloton, Smith College Depart. of French.

Thank you again for your kind words. I have asked my publishers, (this time the Cornell University Press) to send you a copy of a new book, *Writers and Critics,* which may lend itself to a book review — & perhaps to a challenging one.

Henri Peyre

## To the editor of the *Atlantic:*
[published in the December 1944 issue]

Sir:

Mr. Thomas Mann's brief article, "In My Defense," is highly welcome and will rank among his most moving pronouncements. I am very happy to have been instrumental in eliciting from Mr. Mann this full statement of his present position to the problem of Germany and such a clear repudiation of the views he had entertained during the First World War.

I regret, however, that Mr. Mann should have answered with bitter and at times ponderous irony the humble questions which I had asked, as one among other readers of his political articles. Many indeed are the admirers of Mr. Mann, as I can testify from many letters received, who had heard of his earlier and rabid *Gedanken im Kriege.* They were deeply disturbed, especially after quotations from that essay had been made in the *Supplement* of the London *Times* and Mr. Mann had not thought fit to disown them publicly.

Those readers will now be relieved. For it was disquieting to admit that the great German writer was guilty of a discreet sin of omission when he consistently neglected to allude to his earlier "errors," either in his *Three Essays* (in which the reader was not told that the article on Frederick II, translated there, had originally appeared with two other articles deeply tinged with pan-Germanist and anti-democratic views) or his *Order of the Day* (1942), in which a long "Foreword" and a substantial list of "Thomas Mann's Principal Works" carefully left out the essays in question.

I, for one (I may be permitted the use of the first person, since Mr. Mann condescended to personal remarks), had long been familiar with Mr. Mann's bellicose essays of 1914 as well as with his *Betrachtungen* of 1918—the latter an indispensable key to the understanding of Mr. Mann's works. I was fully aware of the heavy sacrifices which Mr. Mann had made subsequently to the cause of anti-Nazism and of freedom, the heaviest of all being probably the sharp decline in the quality of his purely literary works written since he left Germany. I was above all grieved, as were many admirers of the better aspects of German culture, to find that Mr. Thomas Mann, like many other and lesser German writers, artists and scholars, had remained so long "politically immature," and had been carried away in his early days by those irrational and evil forces which he has since passionately and eloquently condemned.

Henri Peyre<br>
New Haven, Conn.

## À Pierre Bédard:

Ce 23 novembre 1944

Cher Monsieur:

Je vous remercie de votre aimable mot sur mon article anglais sur la situation française. Ces modestes pages m'ont valu des commentaires qui m'ont touché, car ils venaient de lecteurs sérieux & compétents, souvent parmi des personnes d'influence dans les bureaux de Londres et de Washington. Le vôtre, si éclairé, me touche également.

Mais ne croyez pas que je devienne homme politique—ou me louange moi-même, comme votre ami Cohen (aujourd'hui à la Sorbonne, je pense) ! Le hasard & les événements ont fait que j'ai dû parler beaucoup de politique, de "la France de demain," de "Que faire de l'Allemagne ?" ces derniers temps. Aussi suis-je plus bousculé que jamais. Et je profite d'une minute le jour de Thanksgiving (qui ne nous vaut même pas de vacances ici) pour vous répondre.

Je vais très, très peu à New York, ou ne fais que traverser pour quelque déplacement à Philadelphie ou ailleurs : aussi suis-je embarrassé pour vous dire quand je pourrai avoir le plaisir de passer à votre bureau—Après Noël (le 27 ou 28) je sais que je dois présider quelque groupe à la réunion de la Modern Language Association—Mais c'est encore bien loin.

Je suppose qu'également occupé vous ne vous arrêtez jamais par ici?

Je serai heureux bien entendu de paraître à nouveau dans vos belles séries de conférences—mais il faut aussi de la variété, surtout aux publics féminins ! et des nouveaux venus de France (s'il en est) devraient passer d'abord.

        Croyez à mes sentiments les plus fidèlement dévoués,
        Henri Peyre

## To Barbara Howes:

        Yale University
        New Haven, Conn.
        Nov. 27—1944

Dear Miss Howes:

Thanks for the *Chimera* issue in which the article on Claudel appeared. It was a very interesting number (I mean, in *other* respects) & the article by Koestler on Hillary was exceptionally welcome, I thought. I was very happy to appear in it.

Please enter my subscription for a year.

        Sincerely,
        Henri Peyre

## À Pierre Bédard:

        Ce 18 décembre (lundi soir) 1944

Cher monsieur,

Je trouve seulement votre lettre cet après-midi. Les lettres "special delivery" sont victimes d'un mauvais sort: elles me courent après d'un bureau à l'autre. Je vous réponds aussitôt, et à la main pour ne pas réveiller les voisins, car il est déjà fort tard.

Le mardi 27 ou le mardi 20 février me conviendrait le mieux comme date. Je suppose qu'il s'agit de l'après-midi, bien entendu.

Comme sujets, je n'ai aucune objection à m'en tenir aux sujets littéraires, au contraire. Sur les autres, je préfère parler en anglais; on atteint ainsi des auditoires moins gagnés d'avance.

Je viens de publier un livre sur un gros sujet, qui semble intéresser assez vivement quelques auditoires. Je pourrais en parler sous ce titre:

1. "Peut-on comprendre la littérature de son époque? La critique et les contemporains."
2. "Les Directions du roman contemporain."
3. "La leçon et l'héritage de Marcel Proust. Vingt ans après."
4. "Un Centenaire: Paul Verlaine."
5. "Charles Péguy, poète et prophète de la France héroïque."

Je réserve pour une autre année les beaux sujets que seraient Mauriac ou Malraux, étudiés à la lumière de leurs livres de ces années de guerre & de leur action dans la résistance. J'espère que leurs ouvrages parus ces dernières années me parviendront bientôt.

Vous me direz si l'un de ces titres vous convient, & lequel. Ce me sera un grand plaisir de vous revoir à cette occasion. Veuillez croire, en attendant, à mes sentiments les plus cordialement dévoués,

Henri Peyre

## À Jorge Guillén:

Ce 24—XII—1944

Merci, cher Ami, de cette jolie & savante brochure sur Ticknor. Elle est admirablement faite, par un poète qui sait être précis, grave, savant comme un érudit ennuyeux (mais non pas ennuyeux lui-même!), et qui reste modeste tout en étant inspiré! Je ne crains qu'une chose après cela: c'est qu'Harvard ne vous invite à occuper là-bas la chaire d'espagnol & je voudrais tant (par quelque miraculeux bouleversement du département d'espagnol ici) que ce soit à Yale que vous veniez échouer!

Avez-vous eu des précisions sur Cassou? Je crois qu'il faut espérer encore—La France se conduit magnifiquement; et ce dernier coup, qui m'a fait bien peur, va peut-être décider vraiment les Américains à prendre de gros risques, eux aussi, & à affaiblir l'Allemagne pour de bon.

J'espère que vous avez de bonnes nouvelles des vôtres, des parents de Mme Guillén et de votre fils. Quant à l'Espagne, l'heure de la liberté va bientôt sonner pour elle. Les changements d'ambassadeurs sont un signe précurseur. Écrasons l'Infâme!

Votre Cantique (des Cantiques) a-t-il jamais reparu au Mexique? Ne négligez pas de m'en donner la référence.

Mille bons vœux pour tous deux—et amitiés bien cordiales,

Henri Peyre

## To Christopher Morley:

January 1, 1945

Mr. Christopher Morley
Green Escape
Roslyn Heights, New York
Dear Mr. Morley:

Of course I was not teased, although I enjoy being; but I was greatly amused and flattered by your delightful letter to Mr. Scherman. I have long admired your wit and humor, and that leisurely way of taking your literary pleasures with discriminating and voluptuous refinement, which endeared your name to a Frenchman. I even almost went up to talk to you, several years ago, when I taught in Bryn Mawr and found the Pennsylvania atmosphere somewhat stifling. You had just published, I believe, *Thunder on the Left* and were pointed out to me by friends. But it takes more courage than I could muster for a professor to go and approach a creator.

I am very glad that you read my book, and were not too much annoyed by it, as some professors and scholars, incapable of receiving unrequested advice, seem to be. I suppose I have not been quite fair to the Book of the Month Club. There must be some selective agencies, and the men who select the books for the Book of the Month Club all have my esteem and do a very good job. But the complacent conviction of your subscribers, who imagine they read *all* the important books, just because they belong to the Club, and who have lost all taste for adventure among other books, or all desire for acquiring that taste, is a sad calamity. I know of no remedy. But I hope that some of the gentlemen who have acquired such an authority over the public through choosing books for them will one day boldly found a critical and literary review worthy of this country.

I do like e. e. cummings, although he too has failed to give all we expected from him twenty years ago. And I still think scholars and teachers could and should do more than they do to arouse their students and friends to good literature. As to O. W. Firkins, I confess my almost complete ignorance. I am going to read him at once.

With my sincere thanks for your entertaining and kind letter, and my best wishes for a happy new year and for an unusually good crop of monthly books.

Very sincerely,<br>Henri Peyre

## To William DeVane:

January 3, 1945

Dear Dean DeVane:

I am sending you a proposal to promote Mr. Kenneth Douglas as assistant-professor of French for one year at the salary of $3,000. Reasons for this proposal, which was strongly urged by the Department, are given below. I would like to add a few remarks on the set up of our Department as I see it at this time, I believe in full agreement with my colleagues.

As you well know, the French Department is now composed of nine members, as compared to 16–20 in pre-war years and our proposed budget for 1945–46 amounts to $48,000 (exclusive of salaries to be paid the women assistants in our intensive beginners' course, and of extra stipends promised members who may have to teach three full terms). This figure of $48,000 for the coming year is approximately $24,000 short of our budget for 1940–41, the last normal one and the first which I personally prepared as chairman.

It is clear that our Department is now understaffed, first because we have great difficulty in carrying on from term to term if we grant relief to our senior members, second because we need more brilliance and more scholarly production in some of our ranks. I am having considerable difficulty at this time in planning for our courses for the spring and the summer of 1945, as we do not have enough men to give all the courses required from us. The replacement of V-12 students by Navy ROTC will give us more work, since more ROTC students will probably be free to elect our classes. Conditions should be a little easier after the fall of 1945 since all the members of our department will teach at the same time for two terms, with the prospect of being free during the summer of 1946. Even then, however, language departments like ours may have to provide for intensive language courses in the summer for veterans.

Our department is at present composed of: 2 full professors, 4 associate professors, 2 assistant professors, 1 instructor. Our need is clearly for:

1) one full professor as soon as we can make an important appointment. That appointment should probably be in the Graduate School, to fill the place of Professor Feuillerat: but the appointee would give at least one course in Yale College.

2) another full professor in a few years, roughly around 1951 when Professor Seronde will be 68 years of age and will retire. One of these two important appointments should be, if possible, in the field of the Middle Ages where we are extremely weak at present. Professor Hill, who takes care of the philological study of French medieval texts, is also due to retire in 1951.

3) one at least of our present assistant professors, Mr. Fowlie, seems to be fully deserving of an associate professorship, and proposals to that effect will be made by the Department next year. His success with our students has been conspicuous and his publications, while falling in the field of criticism more than of literary history, and of semi-creative writing more than of traditional scholarship, have won for him recognition in this country and abroad.

4) The Department is at present understaffed in assistant professors and in instructors. Our normal need would be for 3 or 4 assistant professors at least and for 4 or 5 instructors. We have now two assistant professors, one of whom, Mr. Fowlie, should in our opinion be promoted to an associate professorship in 1946, while the other one, Mr.

Edsall, would normally find a suitable position in another institution (perhaps after one supplementary and terminal year). We would like to appoint Mr. Douglas as an assistant professor, at least for a few years, and Mr. Cornell (assigned to Freshman Year) when he returns from war service.

5) We had several very competent instructors who are now serving in the armed forces. We could easily utilize two or three of them for one or two years as instructors when they come back, as the growing number of our students will then make it imperative to add younger members to our staff. Our policy, however, will be to encourage those promising young men, trained at Yale, to find positions and to gain experience and recognition elsewhere as soon as possible.

The set-up of our Department in the years to come could thus be represented as follows:

|  | as on our staff in 1945 | normal need | approx. cost |
|---|---|---|---|
| Full professors | Seronde (age in 1945: 62) | three | $25,000 |
|  | Peyre (" " " 44) |  |  |
| Associate professors | Hill (" " " 62) | four | $25,000 |
|  | Richardson (" " "56) | five |  |
|  | Morehouse (" " "50) | Fowlie | (after 1946) |
|  | Boorsch (" " "39) |  |  |
| Assistant professors | Edsall ( " " "40) | three or four | $10,000 |
|  | Fowlie (" " "37) |  |  |
|  | Douglas (" " "35) |  |  |
|  | Cornell (" " " 38) |  |  |
| One or two others after promotion of Fowlie and departure of Edsall and Douglas |  |  |  |
| Instructors |  | 4 or 5 | $11,000 |

Assistants to be appointed when conditions require it and when circumstances allow it

Total approximate cost $71,000

The total budget, approximately reached, of $71,000 would thus be near our instruction budget for the last year before the war. The composition of our department would be well balanced. The number of men in the upper ranks would certainly not be excessive, as compared either with other similar departments at Yale or with French Departments in other large universities. One point, remaining not fully satisfactory, will be the relatively large number of our associate professors and their relatively small scholarly output. This seems an inevitable consequence of the legacy of the past in our Department and of our rules of tenure. The Chairman will do his best, when the abnormally high teaching load of recent years is lightened, to stimulate our associate professors to produce more and gain more recognition outside.

I am sending a copy of this letter to the Provost, and adding here, on another sheet, our reasons for the proposal to promote Mr. Kenneth Douglas to an assistant professorship for one year (renewable).

Sincerely yours,
Hri Peyre

## To the same:

January 3, 1945

Dear Dean DeVane:

The French Department, at its meeting of January 1, 1945, voted to recommend Mr. Kenneth Douglas for a promotion to an assistant professorship and asked the Chairman to explain to the Dean and the Committee concerned the strong reasons which seemed to make this promotion desirable, even in the face of the financial difficulties mentioned in the Provost's letter to the Chairmen of Departments.

Mr. Douglas, born in Dublin in 1906, studied at Trinity College, Dublin, in 1933–37; he received First Class Honors in French, and German, several prizes in French, Provençal, Spanish, a special gold medal for distinction in modern languages, and was Chairman of the Modern Language Society.

He was sent as Exchange Lecturer to the École Normale Supérieure, in Paris, and received flattering testimonials from the then Director of that famous French institution, Professor Bouglé.

He studied in Vienna, Austria; came to this continent and studied and taught at Toronto, where he received his M.A. degree in 1940. In

1940, he was appointed assistant in instruction at Yale, reappointed at that rank for 1941–42. Since 1942, he has been for three successive years instructor in French. He received his Ph.D. from Yale in 1943, with a dissertation on *The Vocabulary of Jacques de Henricourt.*

The dissertation written by Mr. Douglas did not come up to what we expected from him. After some discussion, the members of the Department felt that this had been due in part to an unfortunate subject and a faulty method which had been urged upon Mr. Douglas by a Swiss professor then in Chicago, Professor von Wartburg. The senior members of our Department (with the exception of Mr. Hill) agree that Mr. Douglas is capable of much better work than his dissertation demonstrated. They consider him as a promising scholar, who has accumulated a vast store of knowledge, whose culture and personality are far above those of an average instructor. I myself am convinced that he is a true scholar, who will in time give an excellent account of himself.

He has not produced very much. We do not think this should prevent his promotion at the present time, for Mr. Douglas has had to teach 12 hours a week continuously for ten terms without any respite (that is, since the Fall of 1941), and promotion is not easy for a young man under these circumstances. He has, however, contributed half of the French section (Middle Ages, 19th and 20th centuries) to the *Guide to World Literature,* to be published this year under the auspices of Columbia University: a critical bibliography which he did intelligently and skillfully under my direction. He also read at the 1945 Modern Language Convention a brilliant article on "Paul Valéry and Pascal," which will be published soon in the P.M.L.A. He is working on two other articles on Paul Valéry. His interests are varied; but his most promising work will, in our opinion, be done in the field of modern literature and especially in psychological study of literature, for which he is well equipped through his previous philological and semantic studies.

As a teacher, Mr. Douglas has proved very able. He has had to give a large variety of classes (French 22, 25, 30, 32, 39, & 42) and has handled them well. His standards are exacting, and he is sometimes severe; he never tries to flatter the students. But he succeeds in teaching them how to speak and write French, and how to think with rigor and express themselves with accuracy.

Recently we have assigned Mr. Douglas as an assistant to Professor Boorsch in the new intensive beginners' course, French 25. Mr. Douglas, through his training as a linguist and as a philologist, is especially well equipped to handle this course. He is taking a keen interest in it. One of the reasons why the department is suggesting that he be promoted to an assistant professor (and not merely retained as an instructor, even at a higher salary than the normal one for that rank) is that we hope he will handle more and more of that course next year and the year after. Since he will have to direct "informants" who may be instructors or assistants in instruction, he would be in a much better position to supervise his collaborators if his rank is that of an assistant professor.

The French Department also agreed that Mr. Douglas was certainly the equal of our good assistant professors in the past or of present assistant professors in departments similar to ours (for instance of Mssrs Nordmeyer and White, who are directing the same work in German as Mr. Douglas will more and more in French).

For all these reasons, intellectual qualities, skill as a teacher, promise as a scholar, and usefulness to the Department, I am transmitting to you and the committee concerned our proposal to promote Mr. Douglas to an assistant professorship. I may add that Mr. Douglas speaks French (and German) excellently, in fact better than any other non-French teacher in our Department except Mr. Fowlie; and that the Department is confident that Mr. Douglas can get a position in another institution in a fairly near future, on the strength of his merits and of the experience he has gained here. We shall be glad to let him go to a better position where he can spread our methods and exercise a valuable influence. But we should be most embarrassed, considering the present dearth of competent teachers, if we lost him now.

Very sincerely yours,
Hri Peyre

## To Edgar Furniss:

Jan. 5, 1945

Dear Dean Furniss:

I asked Mr. Richardson to answer the question on the comparative cost of the new intensive course in language & of the old one—I am forwarding his statement to you: it is beyond my mathematical comprehension, but should of course be easy reading for an economist. My layman's impression is that the new course, as practiced now (starting every term, with small classes, for French, of 18–25 men) is a good deal more expensive than the old one. It might be less costly, and only a little more costly than the regular course, in normal times, if there are many beginners in French (50 at least).

Could you kindly send me a sheet stating what the recent policy on extra stipends for members of the faculty teaching three full terms is, and what those stipends are? I seem to be unable to find the one you sent me some months ago in our files.

Sincerely yours,<br>Hri Peyre

## À Jacques Maritain:

Ce 17 février 1945

Cher Maître,

Je ne puis malheureusement me rendre à New York le 20 février pour assister à la séance d'adieux qu'organise Alvin Johnson. Puis-je du moins vous dire tous mes vœux d'heureux voyage, de longue & fructueuse mission, et la très grande joie que j'ai eue à vous rencontrer parfois en Amérique, à être attaché à l'École que vous dirigiez? Votre exemple d'espoir & de foi inflexibles en la France, de dévouement qui sacrifiait tout au service de notre pays à reconstruire a, ainsi que celui de Focillon, fait beaucoup pour nous—exilés volontaires en Amérique. Je ne l'oublierai jamais—et je voudrais vous en dire ma profonde reconnaissance.

Veuillez transmettre à Madame Maritain mes hommages bien respectueux & me croire,

Votre très sincèrement dévoué,<br>Henri Peyre

## To Edgar Furniss:

April 4, 1945

Dear Dean Furniss:

After our conversation the other day, I discussed the question of the Secretary of the French Department with Miss Reese, of the Personnel Bureau; and she promptly agreed with me that our Secretary is underpaid at present and that we could not replace her adequately, or at all, if we had the misfortune of losing her now. Miss Reese said she was familiar with Mrs. Andersson's superlative qualities and agreed that her salary should be raised to $1400 a year. This will cover her work of four and a half days, which is for us the most efficient and useful way of distributing her hours.

The salary provided in the budget for 1945–46 for our secretary is $960 ($760 for half time secretary plus one extra afternoon a week during the normal academic year, plus $200 for the summer). The new total for our secretary would now be $1400, covering her employment all year round from July 1st, 1945, with one month vacation, for four days and a half weekly. The difference would thus be an extra $440 which I am asking the Corporation to grant us.

As I told you, our work has been unusually heavy, or rather has become permanently heavy in the last two years: this is due to more activity and letter-writing on the part of some of us and chiefly to the dearth of French texts for our classes. We have to type or mimeograph most of our texts and to distribute them to our students. This has imposed a heavy extra burden on our secretary who often had to work outside her regular hours.

I hope you may successfully explain to the Corporation that we regret not having presented this proposal earlier, as we were not yet sure of our plans at that time. I also hope it will make no difficulty, as our total secretarial expenses, as you know, remain modest.

Sincerely yours,
Hri Peyre

## To William C. DeVane:

April 20, 1945

Dear Dean DeVane:

I spoke with some bluntness the other day at the Faculty Meeting which considered the Experimental Program, partly because I thought some one at least should present the other case and some of the possible objections to it.

I am of course happy at the vote of the Faculty which confirmed the program, although secretly proud to be in the minority, and I do not mean to reopen a closed debate or to obstruct the working out of the details of the program. But it seems to me I might add a few words to explain in writing what the position of my colleagues in French (for I was expressing their unanimous feeling) is on the language part of the Experimental Program.

1) Educationally, it is totally unadvisable to give up one language studied already for three or four years, and to take up a new one while practically forgetting the first one. It may be desirable in principle to have good students know two languages instead of one; but with the suggested program, they will know very little of the two. Their knowledge will only be sufficient as reading knowledge for prospective graduate students. It will not be the spoken knowledge which we consider today as inseparable from any training in languages. As a rule, it would seem to us far better to have students know one language very well, to really live with it, read it with ease (and not just pass a reading knowledge test and never touch it again) and speak it, instead of having a superficial acquaintance with two.

2) I would add that I am presenting this remark on very general and objective grounds, and not out of any fear that French would lose by not being the second language chosen. In fact, all statistics at the present time point to Spanish as having been the chief language studied in the schools in the last five years, then German and French. And most of the students choosing a second language in the five or ten years to come would probably interrupt Spanish or German and begin French and Russian. Regardless, however, of any gains and losses, the program seems open to grave objections.

3) The course suggested on page 38 of the program aims at "reading facility." This is moving the clock back in a way which I feel bound to

call reactionary. Recent experiments at Yale and elsewhere have proved clearly enough that the approach to language must first be *oral*. As a point of fact, it is not possible to give a course aiming at developing "literary appreciation" of a foreign literature (which includes poetry and artistic prose) without an oral approach to the sound-values of the language.

4) A course enabling students to read literary works after one term of five hours is impossibility. Even with *ten* hours a week and an oral approach in the present intensive course, students can only begin competent reading of "literary" texts after *two* terms, i.e., a whole year.

5) Our department does *not* offer such a course now. A new one would have to be created, completely opposed to our present oral intensive course and directly contrary to the theories of linguists. Such a course will cost us five hours a year for, perhaps, 8 or 10 students. In point of fact, in a department like ours and probably in several others, the courses given to four classes of 160 students under the experimental program will be costly, as they will save no money whatever from our regular courses, except perhaps one division in a few divisional courses. In all of our semi-advanced or advanced courses, numbering from 10 to 20 students, the loss of four or five students absorbed in the experimental program would mean no saving whatever of hours of teaching.

May I add, as a Frenchman, that the aims formulated in the introduction to the Experimental Program (emphasize "the value of a completely required system of distribution" and provide "a common intellectual basis" for students) are closely related to the characteristic features of French education as it has been developed, somewhat rigidly, since Napoleon! It has undeniable advantages, especially in the training of thinkers, scholars, writers, men of general culture. It has also showed conspicuous faults, and will probably be corrected after the experience of the last thirty or forty years. The lack of a common basis to young men who come from different "classes" and different geographical parts of the country, the absence of "integration" or of a similar concern with similar issues have, in my humble opinion, been greatly offset in this country by a richer variety, a keener independence, a more imaginative approach to problems of the present.

I am not adding anything here concerning the Field Major in Literature and the Arts, although I confess not being won to either its content or its present formulation.

I hope this clarifies the point my colleagues and I feel should be presented in connection with the details of the Experimental Program.

> Very sincerely yours,
> Henri Peyre

## To Edgar Furniss:

Monday May 28—1945

Dear Dean Furniss:

I am advising Mr. Boorsch to go & explain to you a tentative proposal just made to him on which he has to decide, at least provisionally, this morning. It is being offered to him that he go over, with Professor Freeman of Middlebury College, to organize courses in the French language & in French literature for American soldiers & officers abroad (Great Britain & France, probably).

I have considered the question at once with Mr. Boorsch & find that it is possible for us to let him go: we take this to be a flattering offer both to him personally & to the manner in which he has handled the language courses for officers & for civilians at Yale.

Our plans for 1945–46 were to have Mr. Boorsch be free from teaching this summer; in any case (he has had no "relief" at all since 1941). If the assignment abroad happens to be for the summer alone, it is thus easy for him to go. If it should come through only later & cover the fall term as well, we shall ask for a leave of absence for Mr. Boorsch for the Fall term. As you know, Mr. Boorsch's assignment is to the Graduate School Faculty. We shall manage to take care of his graduate course then. Mr. Douglas was to take over Mr. Boorsch's intensive course (French 25) during the Summer term in any case.

Mr. Boorsch has to give an affirmative answer this morning: Mr. DeVane is away today. I am asking him to explain the question to you & to get your consent, provisionally, so that he can make arrangements with Mr. Freeman accordingly.

Excuse this hurried note, as I could not get you on the phone.

> Sincerely,
> Hri Peyre

# To Charles Seymour:

May 29, 1945

Dear President Seymour:

The French Department finds it very difficult to find competent and trained teachers to give some of its courses this summer and next fall. The increase in the number of students taking French is already very sharp with the incoming freshman class and will probably remain so for some years. We are faced with a total of twenty hours of instruction, at least, for which we have to find instructors outside, and such instructors do not seem to be readily available.

We are of course going to do our best to find them. But our Department was unanimous in expressing the wish that one of our teachers, Mr. William Kenneth Cornell, now in the Armed Forces, might be released from military service to come back to us during the summer term, if at all possible. After a conversation with the Provost, I am taking the liberty to suggest that you might perhaps be willing to take the matter up with the War Department. The facts of the case are as follows:

Mr. Cornell, now serving in Italy when we last heard of him, is now 37 and a half years old. He will not, obviously, be useful in the war against Japan. He is only a Corporal and has no special qualifications from the military point of view (except his knowledge of French and Italian). He will probably be discharged in the course of the coming year in any case, like most men of 38. He would render more valuable services to the country if he were discharged now and were allowed to resume his teaching with us—part of which would be to take care of returning soldiers taking our courses. We thought the Secretary of War or his Department might accede easily to such a reasonable request.

Here is the necessary information on Mr. Cornell.

Corporal William Kenneth Cornell, 31273683
3rd P.T.S., 3rd P.G.R.
APO 650
Care Postmaster, New York

Mr. Cornell has been serving in Italy for a year and a half, approximately, but on account of his age, not on combat duty! He is not married, but was supporting his mother in part when he left for the Army. He would thus not have the points necessary for discharge.

He was born on December 14, 1907, in Eagle City, Oklahoma, and will thus be 38 this year.

He taught for ten years at the University of Kansas (1927–37) and has been teaching at Yale from 1938 until he was drafted early in 1943.

He has been, to our knowledge, of no special service to the Army and would be much needed here by the French Department. He is to be made Assistant-Professor of French on his return to Yale.

We would very much like to have the services of Mr. Cornell if possible for the opening of the Summer Term, if not during the Summer Term, so that he can take up his work with us again by the Fall Term if not earlier.

I hope you may consider our request reasonable and justified. Our Department would be very grateful if you could act favorably upon it.

Yours very sincerely,<br>Hri Peyre

## À Keith Botsford:

Ce 6 juin (1945)

Cher Poète,

Si vous êtes ici ce dimanche (10 mai) après midi & avez un moment, voulez-vous venir prendre le thé avec nous et quelques jeunes Français, vers 4 h ½—Nous habitons à 309, St Ronan St., maison d'appartement à droite en montant, au 2e étage. La rue est entre Prospect St. & Whitney Ave., à 20 minutes environ de Yale à pied, à la hauteur de Lawrence St., un peu plus haut.

Bien cordialement,<br>Henri Peyre

## To Helen McAfee:

> West Chop
> Martha's Vineyard, *Mass*.
> July 9—1945

Dear Miss McAfee:

    I am much obliged for your kind note. The summer is comparatively cool here & we are enjoying it fully. Hotels are crowded this year, & food has its problems, & provides too monotonous a topic for conversation—but otherwise the Island is as pleasant as ever. We wish you could spend part of it at Nantucket.

    It is very kind of you to suggest my writing the article in question. Dean DeVane had transmitted to me your thoughts & suggestions (on the desirability of concentrating, in a comparatively brief article, on the few writers most likely to survive among the French resistance authors). The difficulty is that the books by these writers have, with only a few exceptions, not reached us here. I tried at once to obtain a few volumes from Paris, but they have not yet arrived & the difficulty of getting books is very great: they are sold out almost at once, partly because people think they are stable values for investment, partly because genuine interest in literature & art seems indeed to be very ardent in France.

    I have, however, read enough, though fragmentarily, of what has appeared in France to write an article on the trends indicated by recent works of poetry & prose. I could concentrate on three of the poets (Aragon, Éluard, Reverdy) and discuss Malraux, St Exupéry & Sartre from their recent works. While I would not pose as a revealer of unknown geniuses or of new talent, I could, in such an article, comment on the meaning, scope & probable lasting value of the best of this recent French literature. I shall try, if this is agreeable, to complete the article by the date you mention & to submit it to you in any case.

    With our wishes for a pleasant summer &

> Very sincerely yours,
> Henri Peyre

## To Robert Penn Warren:

October 28 — 1945

Dear Mr. Warren:

I do not believe I have the honor to be known to you. I listened to you last year with great interest & pleasure when you lectured at Yale, but missed meeting you. I know you are familiar with the personality and the writings of Wallace Fowlie, & I am asking you if you would be willing to express an opinion on him & on them. He has now been with us for several years as Assistant-Professor of French. As Chairman of his Department, I am now going to propose that he be made Associate-Professor. It is customary in such cases to present a few letters from well-known authorities in other institutions, not necessarily to eulogize the man and compliment the department on their proposal, but stating a frank opinion on the candidate, his published work, his promises, his ranking among other men of the same age in the field. I would be very glad if you would consent to write me such a letter.

We have liked Wallace Fowlie very much as a colleague and as a teacher: and he has been a very productive writer, as you know. All that he writes may not be to our taste, & one is free to disagree with him. But his outstanding qualities far outweigh, I think, what some may call his faults. Of course, we are not proposing his promotion on the grounds of traditional scholarship or of achievement as a "scientific" literary historian. But we think departments of modern literature should also include one or two men informed of recent literature as well as trained in the past, retaining or establishing links with the world of contemporary letters.

If you will kindly send me a few lines, as frank and as precise as you care to make them, I am sure it will be a real help for me and will impress my colleagues as it should. I apologize for thus making a request on your time early in a new academic year & I am,

Very sincerely yours,
Henri Peyre

## À Jorge Guillén:

Ce 24 décembre 1945

Cher Monsieur Guillén:

Merci de votre récente lettre, qui m'a touché: je suis heureux de savoir prochaine la publication de votre chef-d'œuvre, que beaucoup de curieux ont dû désirer comme moi en ces dernières années. Du moins je vous ai lu récemment dans l'anthologie de la poésie espagnole, avec les amusants et aimables commentaires de M. [Pedro] Salinas.

Puis-je vous demander de me renvoyer les petits livres de poésie française de Cassou, Mougin? J'ai promis à l'éditeur de Voices de préparer une anthologie très brève, avec traduction, de poésie française récente: je voulais remplir ma promesse pendant ces vacances, et inclure dans ce choix un sonnet de Cassou et peut-être un ou deux des autres poèmes dont je vous ai passé le texte. Je serais curieux d'avoir votre avis sur ces vers, et sur ceux de Cassou que vous préférez.

Il m'arrive quelques autres livres de France, mais surtout de la prose, et des débats sur l'existentialisme. Les livres semblent coûter des prix fous; Mallarmé (éd. de la Pléiade) fait prime au marché noir. Pauvre cher Stéphane! S'il savait qu'on offre 5000 francs & plus pour l'acquérir!

Allez-vous bien, et Mme Guillén? Votre fils est-il de retour, & civil? J'espère toujours qu'un jour, à Yale, vous ferez un arrêt et une visite — Claude de Messières devrait vous dire les charmes de notre université.

Avec mes vœux les plus cordiaux & fervents de Noël,

Henri Peyre

## To the editor of the *New York Times*:

Dec. 31, 1945

It is disheartening to read in The Times of Dec. 31 the results of the Army survey conducted by the Research branch of the European Theatre Service Forces' Information and Education Division, according to which the opinion of American soldiers shows a growing preference for the Germans over other continental nations of Europe.

Have the American soldiers not realized, and not been told by their indoctrinating officers, that those very German men and women who prove affable fraternizers, who seem clean, well-dressed, sanitary, obliging and even obsequious to the occupation forces, are precisely the same Germans who organized, with the same sanitary efficiency, the mass murders of Dachau and Buchenwald?

There were also trim flower gardens, tiled shower rooms and gas chambers there to adorn the neat homes of those who presided over the most shameful crimes committed in Europe for five centuries. If the GI's, and presumably the officers as well, fail to realize that the material paraphernalia of civilization can co-exist with the most barbaric behavior; if they fail to discriminate between those who, inflicting the suffering on others, thrived on it for three years, and those whom suffering reduced to shabbiness and to an over-sensitive pride taken in their purer conscience, is there not something basically wrong with spiritual and moral education in America?

Henri Peyre
New Haven, Conn.

## À Georges May:

26 janvier 1946

Cher Monsieur,

Je m'étonne que l'Univ. d'Illinois n'ait pas besoin de vos services immédiatement, car on prévoit de partout un assez grand afflux d'étudiants pour le 1er mars. Dans combien de temps encore penseriez-vous finir là-bas votre Ph.D.? Si l'on ne vous renomme pas pour septembre, je pense qu'il sera aisé de trouver un poste alors.

Il est très possible que nous ayons ici besoin d'un collègue temporairement du 1er mars au 20 juin. Il s'agit de remplacer un professeur qui s'absente ce trimestre. Si vous désiriez avoir l'expérience de ces quelque 15 semaines avec nous, je verrai de plus près la situation et tâcherai de vous l'offrir comme position d'attente. L'enseignement est environ de 12 heures par semaine, et surtout de langue, car le grand accroissement est chez les étudiants de 1re, 2e années. Mais nos étudiants sont intéressants et je crois que notre département passe pour avoir un bon esprit de corps et des méthodes intéressantes à observer. La chose est encore vague dans ma pensée, mais si en principe elle vous séduisait, je la pousserai davantage. Je suppose qu'une "compensation" de 1000 (mille) dollars pour un trimestre (de près de 4 mois) serait ce que m'accorderait l'Administration, pour un instructeur non encore muni du Ph.D. (en principe, chez nous, tout instructeur doit l'être). Si vous préfériez moins d'heures que 8, être payé en proportion et travailler mieux à votre thèse (notre bibliothèque est très bonne), vous me le diriez bien entendu. Le plus tôt pour votre réponse à ce projet serait le mieux. . . .

## Au même:

10 fév. 1946

Mon cher Ami,

Un mot encore, et encore à la hâte: je dois être demain à New York pour une conférence et serai à nouveau à mon bureau mardi. Nous aviserons alors, le 13 ou le 14, pour le cas où vous ne pourriez venir ici. . . .

## Au même:

17 février 1946

Cher Monsieur,

Je suis heureux de votre acceptation, confirmée par votre lettre du 11 février. . . .

Par malheur, me voici malade et c'est de mon lit que je vous envoie ce mot: le docteur me dit atteint de jaunisse et retenu en chambre pour quelques semaines. . . .

Je demande à l'Université qu'on vous alloue 1200 dollars pour un service complet (12 ou 13 heures) pendant ce trimestre (1er mars — 18 juin). J'espère que cela sera accordé. . . .

## À Keith Botsford:

Febr. 20 — 1946

My dear Botsford,

Je n'ai pu vous voir ces jours-ci, étant malade & condamné à la chambre, apparemment pour quelques jours. Mais on m'a transmis votre mot.

Pour ma part, rien ne me serait plus divertissant que d'apercevoir souvent dans le couloir de notre sombre étage votre visage illuminé de flamme intérieure & de poésie—Mais le poste en question est en réalité celui de "bursary-student" de M. Richardson, et c'est à lui à choisir. Or il est en ce moment à l'hôpital St Raphaël, où il vient de subir une légère opération. Mais il sera rentré chez lui prochainement (probablement vers le 25 février): (Henry B. Richardson.). Je sais qu'un autre étudiant, Keniston, était venu se proposer à lui pour ce même poste il y a quelques semaines & ne pourrais vous dire ce qu'il avait décidé.

Le travail en question, je dois vous avertir, est ennuyeux: il consiste en détails monotones, et surtout à taper des emplois du temps, des listes d'étudiants & de notes. M. Richardson est un homme aimable & fin, mais qui vous demandera une précision constante. Pour votre intérêt, j'aurais mieux aimé vous savoir "bursary student" à l'école de musique, ou dans le Beaux Arts, ou adjoint à un poète non académique, s'il s'en trouve parmi les professeurs de Yale—

Dites donc à Mrs. Rowe qu'en l'absence de M. Richardson, vous lui demandez de remettre la décision jusqu'au début du trimestre prochain, quand M. Richardson aura pu être consulté.

Bien cordialement à vous,
Henri Peyre

Les notes finales ont-elles été bonnes?

## À Jorge Guillén:

Ce 25 mars 1946

Mon cher Poète,

J'ai fait lire récemment Cantico à mon collègue d'espagnol, Selden Rose, & lui ai redit quel intérêt Yale aurait à attirer un homme comme vous. Je sais qu'il a été frappé d'admiration pour vos vers. Ai-je été indiscret en parlant ainsi?

Je me demande si, bien qu'en apparence peu voyageur, vous ne consentiriez pas à vous arrêter à New Haven un soir et à faire une lecture de vos vers, dans l'original, avec quelques mots de causerie? Nous avons un petit groupe relativement informé, et "informal," qui s'appelle Romance Languages Journal Club. Il se réunit le second jeudi, ou le troisième jeudi, d'avril (le 18 par exemple, nous serait un grand honneur—et une joie pour vos amis). Vous rencontreriez ainsi quelques uns de nos collègues et passeriez la nuit comme l'hôte d'un de nos collèges ou "houses." Je ne mentionne pas d'honoraires parce que notre riche Université semble incapable de trouver des fonds pour ces visites d'hôtes distingués! Mais j'examinerai mieux la question si je sais que vous pourriez venir. Vous serait-il possible de me répondre très bientôt?

Avec mon souvenir bien respectueux à Madame Guillén, et nos vives amitiés,

Henri Peyre

## To Norman S. Buck:

April 17, 1946

Dear Dean Buck:

Following our previous conversation and your preliminary approval as well as that of the Provost, I am sending to you the proposal of the French Department to appoint Mr. Theodore Andersson as Associate Professor of French, with indefinite tenure and with assignment to the Freshman Year. The understanding is that Mr. Andersson would take charge of a large number of details of an administrative character and be active in planning and reorganizing our language work. He would do approximately eight hours of teaching a week and would devote the rest of his time to assisting the Chairman in the running of the Department. This proposal comes to you with the unanimous and enthusiastic approval of the Professors and Associate-Professors in the Department.

With the heavy increase in the number of students at Yale and the marked increase in those who take French (the number is likely to run in the seven hundreds next year, exclusive of a sizable enrollment in the Graduate School), it has become clear that the burden of administrative and organizing work falling upon the Chairman is too heavy for him to bear. Professor Richardson is a very valuable colleague and takes care of several aspects of the freshman work; but much remains to be done or remains undone. The selection and supervision of the young teachers for the language classes, the improvement of our methods, the development of the intensive courses in language and of the use of mechanical equipment, the relations to be maintained with professional associations and other institutions, the ever-increasing amount of correspondence connected with scholarships, recommendations, applications, etc., are some of the fields in which the Department needs an active member, with administrative ability and authority, who could assist and often replace the Chairman.

We have given much thought to this evident need in the past months and, after several suggestions were examined, we decided that the most desirable man should be a mature person, exercising authority upon our instructors, but still young enough to be active and imaginative in formulating new plans and proposing reforms; a person familiar with our habits and traditions at Yale, and agreeable to our colleagues so as to work smoothly with them; a good teacher and a man having given full proof of his competence as a scholar, respected in other institutions; yet an administrator as much as a scholar, since a very productive scholar could not be expected to devote to administrative details a time needed by his research and might not do it, in any case, with the desirable efficiency. Our choice fell unanimously upon Mr. Theodore Andersson, and we consider ourselves fortunate in having convinced him to accept our tentative offer and to forsake a higher salary and tempting prospects at the State Department, where he is now working. . . .

In all his positions, Mr. Andersson has proved a very competent and inspiring teacher; he has won the esteem and respect of students and colleagues alike, as I was personally able to ascertain in the course of visits to Wells College and to his senior officials in the State Department. He has published a book and some brief articles, not a bulky amount, but what he has done has been of solid and fine quality. His knowledge of languages is exceptionally wide, extending as it does to French, Spanish, Portuguese, Italian, German, Swedish, and even Russian. His chief interest, ever since he left Yale in 1937, has been in organization and administration, where he has been conspicuously successful. He was considered as one of the desirable candidates for the Presidency of Wells College last year, and it is not unlikely that, in some years, he may be offered a Deanship or a Presidency of a college. We hope that, meanwhile, he could give us very useful service at a time when we need such a man most, while planning a vigorous post-war reorganization. . . .

## To Charles Seymour:

April 26, 1946

Dear President Seymour:

I am sending you, in two copies, the booklet which our Department has just prepared on our Graduate work, and which was printed thanks to the help of Nr. Lohmann.

This booklet includes a thorough reorganization of our courses, an enrichment of our offerings, and what we consider as an altogether new spirit in graduate work in Romance languages: the direction in which we have moved, and in which we expect to be followed by several other Departments in the country, is one of greater flexibility, of relative independence between the different Romance literatures, of emphasis upon literature as distinct from philology (though connected with it), and it should envisage combining the study of any of the Romance literatures with the Literatures of England, Germany, Russia, etc.

We believe that these reforms, while lowering in no way our level or our requirements, will attract to us some of the better students in the country and will enable us, when we have enlarged our faculty in its upper ranks, to train these students better.

Very sincerely yours,
Henri Peyre

## À Keith Botsford:

Yale Univ.
Aug. 26/46

Mon cher ami,

Oui, je peste souvent contre les lettres—mais elles me font plaisir quand elles m'apportent des nouvelles de jeunes gens originaux, rebelles, obstinés, irrévérencieux . . . Je vous imaginais près de votre tour, sur les bords de l'Adriatique—ou convertissant à la poésie impétueuse & à la scolastique rebutante sur la poésie (Y P Review!!) les obtus esprits du Canada français, vivant de racines & de pain bis comme un ermite.

Et vous voilà soldat. Je suis convaincu que vous n'étiez pas à votre place à Yale: il vous faut, ou beaucoup plus de discipline (l'armée ou le monastère), ou pas du tout. Mais l'armée (& peut-être le cloître) ont du moins l'avantage qu'ils ne tâchent en rien d'influencer votre vie intérieure & de refréner vos projets indépendants de quadrilatère métaphysico lyrique. Je ne vous envie pas, & je ne dirai pas avec tous les aînés que cette discipline militaire était justement ce qu'il vous fallait. Je crois que vous êtes assez intelligent pour vous y plier, sans y perdre votre personnalité. "Leopards even grow tame, yes, but change not their spots" dit Shakespeare. Conservez votre fraîcheur et votre rébellion en profondeur, jusqu'à la cinquantaine. En attendant, plongez-vous dans la vie extérieure: voyez des gens, touchez des objets, contemplez des paysages réels, exprimez-vous avec clarté, force, simplicité, rédigez même des lettres administratives en style fonctionnel—Vous resterez, ou plutôt deviendrez de plus en plus, vous-même dans le fond.

J'ai été un jour à San Antonio: le caractère factice de ces maisons espagnoles m'a agacé. C'était un samedi soir: et je me rappelle surtout le nombre de gens saouls vers minuit dans les rues & dans l'hôtel, la splendeur un peu grossière des femmes. Un soldat doit apercevoir une plus belle face aux choses.

Je me repose à Martha's Vineyard pendant quelques jours, après avoir enseigné vigoureusement cet été à Columbia, & préparé notre année prochaine qui s'annonce lourde de besogne. Bientôt ce sera une fois de plus les téléphones, les visites, les lettres. Jouissez de votre intégrité de jeune homme qui vous permet de méditer des heures sur quelques auteurs préférés.

Ainsi Kafka, Rilke & Hölderlin vont vous amener à faire du contre-espionnage (funny, that equivalence, intelligence: espionnage), je suppose en Allemagne? Ironie de la vie—Mais je crois sincèrement (& je suis de ceux qui ont foi en vous) que vous avez quelque besoin d'un grand bain de concret.

Bonne chance & mes bons vœux,
Henri Peyre

## To Robert Greer Cohn:

October 19—1946

Dear Mr. Cohn:

I am very grateful to you for the remarks & suggestions made in the collective letter which I received yesterday. I am answering you because your name seems to come first on the list & I cannot write a note of acknowledgment to all the signers.

Some of the criticisms you make are probably justified; I confess I am not convinced, however. As to interest in modern, living literature, I do not believe any other French Department shows more than we do; as to whether it should receive more emphasis than it does at present, in a graduate training which is bound to be, to a great extent, professional (like Law or medicine), I am not quite sure. But I am certain that my colleagues & I are fully open to suggestions & can gain by criticism.

The best would be for us, teachers, to meet with you more often & more informally & talk these problems & desiderata over with you. Perhaps our Romance Club is not the most suitable place for that; but why don't you ask, say, six or seven of the graduate students to talk this over with me next Wednesday at 3 P.M. (Oct. 23), in my office in 1560 Timothy Dwight College. (I have not more than 6 or 7 chairs!)—& the others the following Wednesday if they like. I would like some of you to take up more in detail & informally & cordially some of the points made in your letter—

Very sincerely,
Henri Peyre

Will you kindly communicate my letter to the others & ask them to excuse me for not answering them individually.

## To Charles Seymour:

November 25, 1946

Dear President Seymour:

It seems clear to most thoughtful persons that the best means of promoting both American culture abroad and world understanding and world peace will be, in the immediate future, through the intelligent and efficient exchange of students between American universities and universities abroad. The task is of such primary importance that it should recommend itself to educational foundations and far-sighted alumni as well as to governmental agencies in Washington and in foreign capitals.

After consultation with the French Cultural Counselor in New York and in the confident belief that French universities would welcome any initiative taken by Yale and would try to grant American students the same privileges and facilities as would be granted here to French students, I am taking the liberty of suggesting the following tentative plan of exchange.

Yale University would invite five advanced French students to spend a year (renewable in some cases) at Yale. Those students would be carefully selected, through the existing cultural agencies, *by Yale University* on the basis of their previous training, their character and intelligence, their knowledge of English, and their promise. They would be preferably graduate students anxious to study here in fields where they would have most to learn: American literature, history and government, international relations, anthropology, sociology, metallurgy, chemistry, physics, engineering, medicine, law, etc. They would be granted a stipend covering their tuition and expenses for a year: probably $1200 or $1500 a year. The total expense might thus be $6000 a year (for either four or five fellowships).

Five French universities or institutions of higher learning would in exchange grant fellowships to five American students. These would be selected with the same care as the corresponding French students, probably through the French Cultural Office in New York. They would go to the universities where they would have most to learn: Lyon, Strasbourg, Montpellier, as the case might be, and probably two out of five to Paris. The arrangements could be made directly between the universities in France and Yale. A sum approximately equivalent to that proposed for the French scholars at Yale would be given by the French universities, enabling the students to live in France for a year. (The tuition in French universities is only nominal: five or ten dollars a year.) It would be hoped that two or three of the American students thus sent to France would be graduate students in French, preferably in their second year of graduate work. It is indeed imperative that future teachers of French should have studied in the country whose language and culture they will teach; the level of the teaching of modern languages in this country would be greatly raised if such an essential requirement were more frequently filled.

The minor difficulties which such a scheme would raise could easily be ironed out. The main question to be solved is obviously that of the funds to be found; for such a project would soon be followed by others in connection with other foreign countries. The need to develop mutual good will among nations and to found such good will upon the informed and intelligent understanding fostered in cultured persons by study abroad is so evident today that I need hardly point out the urgency of putting into practice a project of this kind. May I hope that Yale University can soon lead in establishing scholarly exchanges of the kind here outlined with French universities, and that the funds necessary for that purpose may soon be made available to the University? The comparatively modest expense would be a rich investment in terms of scholarly gain, of better appreciation between the two countries, and of deeper mutual understanding and respect.

Yours very sincerely,
Henri Peyre

## To the same:

December 3—1946

Dear President Seymour:

I am much touched by your kind words on my modest talk to the Taft School. I meant to offer you this copy, of course, & hope you will not bother to return it.

As to M. Léger, I thought & still think this may be a unique opportunity to have a lecture by him here, because he has showed some inclination to respond favorably to a suggestion made to him by Mrs. W.S. Coffin, & has repeatedly expressed a favorable opinion of some writings of mine that he had seen. I know that there would be a good, & qualitatively a fine, student body to hear him here, for he is held in high esteem by many English students & readers of poetry. I believe a visit by him would eventually bring us honor & distinction, for M. Léger has not lectured elsewhere in America yet. A similar lecture, by a very different man (André Breton, the head of the Surrealist group) given at Yale four years ago, in French, has thrown the name of Yale in the front page of many a French periodical & newspaper; for it was published, & warmly praised, last year in France as "Discours aux Étudiants de Yale" & is now studied in many books of criticism & seminars as the second great Surrealist manifesto—I hope the University does not regret this association of Yale with Surrealism.

I am writing this letter, in this informal fashion, for which I apologize, to mention another detail to you, as you probably would wish me to: Columbia University has offered me a few days ago to join their ranks, as the unanimous choice of the French Department & of a special Presidential Committee *ad hoc*, to succeed the late Horatio Smith. They would like me to be the "Executive officer" of their Department, although they would not force those administrative duties upon me if I declined them, the Editor in Chief of the *Romanic Review*, & to supervise eventually a French Institute, for Area studies on the graduate level. They know that I am deeply attached to Yale, but request me not to answer negatively now, & to discuss the possibility & the prospect with them. Financially, they offer me terms similar to the salary I am enjoying at Yale & add that this is only a minimum offer which may be modified later.

I have answered with a cordial expression of my grateful appreciation &, without being flatly negative, I added that I felt a deep loyalty to Yale and legitimate pride in what had been accomplished here recently in our Department, with the cordial & understanding cooperation of the Administration; & that I would have to be sure that I would be more useful professionally, & happier, in New York than in New Haven in order to make such a change. I am not, of course, going to do any bargaining, either with Columbia, or with Yale which has, from the beginning, treated me most generously. My preference, thus far, is for remaining here. I shall go to New York next week to thank my Columbia friends orally & talk it over with them before finally reaching a decision.

Very frankly, however, I would like to ask you one or two questions. If Columbia shows some insistence in their offer & attempt to lure me away definitely, could I feel that two requests which are dearest to my heart could be considered favorably here: the first would be my desire (motivated chiefly by the necessities of my work) to be granted a semester's sabbatical leave every three years & a half, with full salary, instead of every seven years. The second would be a hope that (also in the advantages of my research & productive activity, which I am finding hard to maintain in the face of heavy demands upon my time) my research grant as Sterling professor could be increased so as to pay for a half time secretary working solely for me.

I hope you will not find it indiscreet of me thus to mention frankly the two points which might make my association with Yale (I shall not say, more pleasant; it has been fully & unreservedly pleasant) more satisfying and more productive. I shall naturally keep you informed of any hesitations I might feel after I have personally examined the situation at Columbia.

Very sincerely yours,<br>Henri Peyre

## To Harry Levin:

December 9, 1946

Dear Professor Levin:

I was at Harvard last Friday and inquired of our colleagues in Romance Languages about the organization of your work in Comparative Literature there. I am very anxious to establish regular work in Comparative Literature at Yale, where some of our colleagues, especially in English, have been very timid about it. I heard that you were now going to be in charge of it and I rejoice; for ever since your first essay on The Broken Column down to your recent and very remarkable articles on Taine, Stendhal, Balzac, I have felt convinced that you are one of the most promising academic critics (in the best sense of the word) in America.

The points on which I would like some information are more specifically the following:

1. Do you have at Harvard or are you going to have a Department of Comparative Literature with an autonomous budget?

2. Which are the Departments of Modern Literatures taking part in the study of Comparative Literature?

3. What are your prerequisites, especially in the matter of Romance Languages, for enrollment in Comparative Literature?

4. Do you accept M.A. students in Comparative Literature or only Ph.D. students?

5. Have you met with any serious objections from other departments (English, German) springing from the fear that the establishment of a Comparative Literature Department might mean lowering of scholarly standards and might prove detrimental to good students in the sense that they could not be placed as well as graduates from the regular departments?

I shall be very grateful if some time at your convenience you could enlighten me a little on these points and any others that may come to your mind.

Sincerely yours,
Henri Peyre, Chairman

## À Jorge Guillén:

Décembre 16, 1946

Mi querido amigo:

Nous nous sommes mis en campagne pour chercher quelque logis convenable pour le poète et sa famille. Ma femme vous dira le résultat, jusqu'ici médiocre, de son annonce dans le journal. Il est clair que ce n'est pas facile. Vous trouverez toujours quelque chose, avec l'usage d'une cuisine, probablement partagée; mais cela risquera d'être relativement coûteux, loin du centre (avec peut-être 30, 40 minutes de tramway), fatigant et peu confortable. Si c'est loin de l'Université, vous perdriez l'avantage de la Bibliothèque, de la compagnie commode d'étudiants ou de collègues.

Aussi me permettrai-je d'attirer à nouveau votre attention sur l'avantage qu'il y aurait pour vous sans doute, même pour votre santé et votre repos, à envisager encore la solution de venir pour trois jours par semaine et de séjourner au collège. Il n'est absolument pas possible d'admettre les femmes (même et surtout épouses et mères) dans nos collèges de jeunes athlètes vertueux et naïfs. Mais je crois pouvoir assurer Madame Guillén que nous prendrions tous ici excellent soin de vous. Vous mangeriez, soit au Collège, soit au Faculty Club, où la chère est saine et bonne, extrêmement simple. Vous auriez un calme parfait. Vous trouveriez le voyage hebdomadaire moins fatigant que des parcours quotidiens en tramway; et vous pourriez vous reposer totalement de mercredi soir à dimanche soir parmi vos vieilles filles, vos jeunes disciples et les arbres de Wellesley. M. Rose me dit que vos cours pourraient vous permettre d'arriver le lundi vers midi et de repartir le mercredi soir. Enfin il y aurait à cette combinaison un avantage d'économie considérable.

J'ajoute que cette solution (si elle n'est pas absolument impossible pour des raisons personnelles) aurait l'avantage de vous permettre de mieux vous familiariser avec Yale, avec vos étudiants, avec des collègues d'ici. Si, comme je l'ai toujours souhaité, votre séjour ici doit mener à une installation permanente à Yale, il vous sera plus commode de vous faire connaître des collègues qui désireraient votre présence continue ici si vous pouvez les rencontrer à des déjeuners d'hommes (coutume répandue ici), être non loin d'eux les soirs du lundi ou du mardi où l'on vous saura ici. Mme Guillén aurait bien entendu tout le loisir de venir vous retrouver parfois et nous lui réserverions alors, pour elle et vous, un logement temporaire à l'hôtel. Et elle ferait ainsi la connaissance des lieux et de quelques amis. Je me permets d'insister ainsi, peut-être avec indélicatesse, parce que je crois vraiment que vous seriez moins fatigué, plus confortablement installé, et plus délivré de menus soucis et de contacts peut-être difficiles, en conservant votre maison à Wellesley et ne passant ici que trois jours par semaine, tous problèmes matériels résolus.

Il nous tarde beaucoup de vous avoir, en tous cas. Ce sera comme un afflux de poésie et de gentillesse d'âme dans ma vie d'homme bousculé. Excusez le mot indiscret et croyez à nos bonnes amitiés et à mes hommages pour votre femme.

Henri Peyre

## To Norman Torrey:

December 17, 1946

My dear Norman:

It is exactly a week ago I had lunch with you, Professor Fackenthal, the Dean, and your eminent colleagues, and it has taken me all of that time to reach a decision about your very kind proposal. I have not even acknowledged your telegram and letter and Dean Pegram's letter, which came before the week-end. Let me tell you once more, and more deeply and sincerely than words can say, how touched I have been by this evidence of the friendly esteem in which I am held by you and your colleagues. I have considered this suggestion of your Department and of the Columbia Administration as carefully as I could and I confess quite frankly that I was tempted both by your kindness and by the challenging opportunities that such an important position in New York offers. It takes my profound attachment to Yale, which I have realized more fully upon envisaging for a while the possibility of leaving it, and the imperious duty I feel I have towards my colleagues here and my graduate students to bring me finally to a decision which I regret to say must be negative.

I believe I can say that I have tried above all to think of the professional interests involved in a contemplated change and of the greater usefulness I would have in New York or New Haven. I suppose I am still young enough to make a change if necessary and to adapt myself to new conditions, especially when the new conditions promise to be as flattering and as cordially pleasant as you depicted them at Columbia. However, my colleagues at Yale and several of my graduate students, as soon as they heard indirectly that I was hesitating between staying here and accepting your offer, made such a pressing plea to me that I feel a little like a captain who would be abandoning his ship—not in stormy seas, to be sure, or in a sinking condition—while there is still a great deal to accomplish. I was greatly touched by some of their arguments, and decided that I could probably accomplish as much at Yale as I could anywhere at present.

I was also impressed by the argument that Columbia has already a fully equipped department, with men of real eminence in practically every field, and an already large number of good graduate students. It was pointed out to me that it is probably more important for me to remain here where our graduate department, while giving us full reward at present, is still capable of development and where other scholars both American and French may and should be attracted.

I am fully aware of all the devoted and earnest efforts you made in this matter, and especially in kindly securing from the Administration, which naturally must have many graver problems to solve and many opportunities to spend its funds, a salary substantially larger than the one which I enjoy here. It is to me a touching sign of the generosity of you and your colleagues that you do not hesitate in suggesting an important part of your budget for a colleague who, however full of good will, would not add very great distinction to a department already so distinguished. The cordial welcome extended to me by Professor E.H. Wright, by Professor Ernest Simmons, by Frohock in the name of Columbia College, and by your colleagues in the Graduate School was the greatest of all temptations, as I prize a warm and stimulating atmosphere for teaching and research even more highly than the material advantages. But after seriously weighing every aspect of the case, I have come to the decision that, if I am of real use in our profession, I am in truth more needed in a center like Yale than in a university like yours, which already has several French scholars and several men in the upper ranks.

The friendly rivalry that departments like yours, like ours at Yale, like Harvard's and Princeton's can develop among each other is an incentive for all of us; and perhaps some distribution of scholars and of students among several outstanding institutions is preferable to a concentration in one large center. Will you convey to your colleagues the expression of my very sincere regrets that I feel that my decision should after all be negative? I shall write a note to the Dean and to the President and, as soon as I have a few minutes, to [Jean-Albert] Bédé and [Justin] O'Brien. With them at your side, and of course Peckham, [Mario] Pei, and Mme [Jeanne M.] Varney, your Department certainly suffers no lack of brilliance or of efficiency. I deeply respect O'Brien's qualities of intellect and of character; he showed them again with fine results during the war. If you hand over to him the executive duties, I know that the succession of Horatio Smith will be most competently assured, and along the lines that Horatio himself would have wished.

I hope that I have not inconvenienced you too much by this week of delay and hesitation. Please accept my apologies and my renewed thanks. You know that whether in New York or at Yale, whether with you or away, I hope to remain a devoted friend of your Department. Do not fail to resort to me for any help and advice I can give.

Very sincerely yours,<br>Henri Peyre

## To George B. Pegram:

December 18, 1946

Dear Dean Pegram:

It was a great honor for me to have that interesting conversation with you after our lunch last Tuesday. I greatly appreciated the honor that you and your colleagues at Columbia bestowed upon me by asking me to become executive officer of the French Department. I was even more touched by your subsequent letter which readily offered me a higher figure for the salary connected with the position and thus added to the very strong temptation already presented.

I hesitated for a few days, as you see, and weighed the strong personal attractions of a brilliant department in a university which has the reputation among all American universities of being broadly liberal and forward-looking and of New York City against my own duty here to my colleagues and to my graduate students. After mature reflection, it seemed to me that it was wiser to decline the flattering offer made by Columbia and to continue trying to develop our own French Department at Yale. Whatever my own wishes might be (and my visit to Columbia where everyone was so cordial made me wish sincerely to be working there under you and President Fackenthal), I believe that my professional duty lies here in New Haven for at least a few more years. Please accept my very sincere thanks for your kindness and that of Columbia University in this matter and my regrets that I can not join a group of colleagues whom I already consider excellent friends.

May I ask you to convey my regrets and the expression of my gratitude to President Fackenthal, whom it was a pleasure to meet?

Very sincerely yours,
Henri Peyre

## To Charles Seymour:

Dec. 19—1946

Dear President Seymour:

May I enclose copies of my letters of "refusal" for your information—& of the magazine where your picture & a small article of mine came out? I am supposed to have one or two other articles on Yale ready there at some future time.

If I may, I shall drop in for a brief visit tomorrow at 11 A.M., as Miss Chatfield suggested, and explain to you my regrets at having seemed to balance the very real advantages & the cordial charms of Yale against the temptations of another university & of another city. I was honestly trying to think of the interests of our profession, & not primarily of personal advantages.

Very sincerely yours,<br>Henri Peyre

## À Keith Botsford:

Ce Jan. 1, 47

Mon cher ami,

Il y a un si grand nombre d'écrivains de talent aujourd'hui que je ne sais lesquels vous désigner—lesquels se trouvent à Paris. Le mieux est pour vous de vous procurer en arrivant quelques revues (leurs titres suivent) & d'aller voir les auteurs qui vous paraissent les meilleurs parmi ceux qui y sont représentés ou critiqués:

Poésie 46
Fontaine
L'Arche
La Nef
les Temps modernes
Critique
Confluences
Europe

Les meilleurs poètes sont aujourd'hui: (1) Paul Eluard; (2) Pierre Reverdy; (3) Jules Supervielle; (4) Pierre Jean Jouve (tous fort connus déjà); puis (5) Francis Ponge; (6) Jacques Prévert; (7) René Char.

Les meilleurs critiques de poésie sont: (1) Aragon (*Europe*); (2) Armand Hoog (*La Nef*) (3); Maurice Blanchot (*L'Arche*); (4) Henri Hell (Fontaine); (5) Roger Caillois; (6) Étiemble (*Temps modernes*). L'Amérique doit avoir à Paris un attaché culturel qui peut vous donner des adresses & vous aider: je crois qu'il me connaît.

Je pense que vous avez bien fait. Votre avenir littéraire a besoin encore de l'expérience du concret & de la vie la plus variée, & même d'obstacles.

Oui—écrivez-moi de Paris ou d'Europe. Wallace Fowlie est passé—semblait bien au physique—un peu triste peut-être.

Mes bons vœux & amitiés,<br>Henri Peyre

## To Charles Seymour:

Febr. 7—1947

Dear President Seymour:

I have just received the Provost's letter approving our Departmental budget and announcing that my own salary has been raised to $12,000. I am deeply touched by the generosity of the University in doing this, and very grateful to you for the special kindness and the sympathetic understanding which you gave me when I seemed to hesitate between staying at Yale or accepting another offer.

Some features of the position at Columbia, as it was glowingly depicted to me, had seemed tempting. But I felt deeply how attached I was to Yale & how much I should lose if I left: I felt it also when I was approached by Paris some two years ago. I have always met with the most cordial cooperation on your part & that of the Provost & the Dean. The little administration which I have to do here has been a pleasure in most circumstances, as it could be conducted smoothly and efficiently thanks to the fine spirit of cordial confidence which prevails. I have an especial debt of gratitude to you for calling me to Yale when you did almost as soon as you were elected President of the University and before the difficult times that I would probably otherwise have lived in Europe.

Will you accept my very sincere thanks and believe me

Very gratefully yours,<br>Henri Peyre

## À Pierre Bédard:

Ce 7 février 1947

Entendu, cher Ami, & ce sera un grand plaisir de vous rencontrer, avec ces deux messieurs que je connais assez bien, le mardi 25 au Century Club—je suppose à une heure, sauf avis contraire.

Ce sera une grande joie de vous revoir après assez longtemps.

Outre Amadou, nous venons de faire venir un nouveau collègue, Michel MOHRT, Breton, très distingué & littéraire, auteur d'un livre sur Montherlant, d'un autre sur les moralistes du 17e siècle, d'un roman sur ses expériences de guerre en 1939–40, et éditeur de la Gazette des Spectacles. Il est en Amérique pour quelques mois seulement et était récemment en France conseiller d'une maison d'éditions—trente ans environ.

À bientôt, merci encore & bien à vous,
Henri Peyre

## À Keith Botsford:

Yale University
New Haven, Conn.
Ce 10 mai 1947

Mon cher Ami,

J'ai été heureux de vos bonnes nouvelles. Je sais que cette expérience de l'Europe, d'une vie autre dans un décor neuf, sera excellente pour vous, & pour votre œuvre future. Certains spectacles seront peu édifiants: on dit que l'attitude des troupes d'occupation n'est pas belle! & cela est dommage, même pour la paix future & le prestige dont nous aurions eu besoin d'être revêtus—Mais un romancier doit avoir quelque expérience de la vie & même de ses laideurs: il ne doit pas, comme dit Stendhal, tendre ses filets trop haut & trop vite planer dans les hauteurs du symbolisme. Vous aurez certainement eu le loisir de contempler "un monde cassé." Gabriel Marcel avait fait jadis une pièce assez bonne de ce titre. Faites-vous des vers aussi? Lisez-vous beaucoup d'allemand?

Ici, l'année s'achève. Beaucoup d'étudiants, & les cours sont intéressants à faire—Mais c'est toujours la même complainte: trop de travail, trop de corvées trop diverses. J'ai désappris le loisir. Il me faudra m'accoutumer à nouveau à m'asseoir pour flâner à une table de café. J'espère aller en France cet été, voir parents, amis, des paysages neufs, des amis anciens. M. Fowlie, vous le savez sans doute, a obtenu une Guggenheim Fellowship pour écrire son livre sur Mallarmé, mais ne la prendra que l'année suivante (1948–49). Vous serez rentré en Amérique d'ici là, officier pour le moins, riche, romancier illustre.... Qui sait? Peut-être reviendrez-vous à Yale écrire une thèse sur les quatre R?

Amitiés & bons vœux,<br>Henri Peyre

Je garde votre adresse & vous écrirai de France.

## À Claude Vigée:

Ce 17 mai 47

Cher Monsieur,

Merci vivement de l'envoi de la revue *Cronos*. Elle est magnifiquement présentée, illustrée avec talent, et pleine de choses intéressantes, pensées avec talent & bien écrites. Je m'emploierai à la faire connaître autour de moi, car elle est l'une des meilleures publications que j'ai encore vu surgir de nos centres universitaires. On devine qu'elle a été faite avec amour & dévouement autant qu'avec talent, avec de la foi autant qu'avec de l'argent. Je vous en félicite.

Bien sincèrement à vous,<br>Hri Peyre

## À Jorge Guillén:

Ce 30 mai /47

Très cher poète,

Voulez-vous vraiment avoir la bonté de lire ceci avant mon départ? Vous avez un immense dévouement, car la personne qui a tapé ceci me dit qu'elle n'a jamais rien lu d'aussi ennuyeux!

J'aimerais vos critiques de tous genres & votre vérification de l'orthographe & de l'accent de mes noms Espagnols. Car j'y parle de ce que je ne connais pas—vice français!

C'est de votre part une grande marque d'amitié.

Que es amistad? Lo que es.

H. P.

## À Marcel Gutwirth:

Ce 22 juillet, 1947

Cher Monsieur Gutwirth:

Certes je ne vous ai pas oublié. Vous êtes, j'en suis convaincu, un jeune homme fort doué et qui fera un jour un professeur de français hautement qualifié. Je ne doute pas que vos résultats à Columbia ne soient excellents.

Il n'est pas facile en effet d'obtenir de poste au milieu de l'année scolaire, mais il n'est pas impossible que quelque "assistantship" se présente alors, à Yale ou ailleurs. Mais ce ne pourrait être qu'une position provisoire et aléatoire, à moins que vous ne poursuiviez en même temps vos études graduées en vue de doctorat. D'ici un, deux, ou trois ans, il y aura à nouveau beaucoup de Ph.D.s préparés, et eux seuls vraisemblablement seront conservés par les "départements," alors obligés de diminuer leur personnel. Je vous conseillerais nettement de poursuivre vos études avancées après le M.A., et de viser à passer le plus tôt possible les conditions requises (allemand, vieux français et philologie, etc.), soit à Columbia soit ailleurs si vous remplissez les formalités d'admission, qui varient quelque peu selon les écoles graduées.

En principe, il me paraît possible en tous cas que vous puissiez être employé, soit en 1948–49, soit même en février, 1948. Récrivez-moi au cours de l'automne.

Croyez à mon souvenir le meilleur et transmettez mes vœux à votre frère.

Henri Peyre

## À Jorge Guillén:

Ce 30 août 1947

Cher Ami,

Votre bonne & affectueuse lettre m'a fait grand plaisir. J'aime à lire votre espagnol, même prosaïque. Il y a dans cette langue quelque chose de plus chaleureux, de plus confiant qu'en français & qu'en anglais. Le génie espagnol est entre autres, celui de l'amitié—la ferme, noble amitié masculine, qui ne redoute pas de se confier, de se livrer. Après une trop longue habitude de l'"understatement" anglo-américain, de la fausse pudeur qui ne fait parler que de travail & de détails extérieurs, ç'a été une joie de trouver des personnes comme vous & votre femme—spontanées & cordiales, et aussi . . . supérieures.

Je suis heureux que vous vous plaisiez à Paris & à Provins—et surtout que votre femme se sente mieux. La nouvelle qu'elle était sérieusement malade & avait dû être opérée, ce printemps dernier, nous avait littéralement bouleversés. Elle incarne le goût de la vie, la joie spontanée et toute discrète; et elle a la riche variété d'intérêts, musicaux, littéraires, & simplement humains, qui lui permet de comprendre & de sentir beaucoup de choses. Puisse-t-elle se rétablir complètement pour jouir pleinement de cette année de libre inspiration que sera, je l'espère, pour vous cette année française.

Et parfois, donnez-nous de vos nouvelles—Vous allez nous manquer beaucoup à New Haven—Harkness Hall sera une prison plus grise & sombre sans son poète; et les abords de East Rock Park nous paraîtront plus déserts. Cet été en France nous a fait beaucoup de bien. La réadaptation a pris quelques jours: les difficultés de la vie sont réelles, hélas, quoique fort supportables, & impatientent d'abord. Puis on est pris par la beauté des paysages & des bâtiments, la gentillesse des contacts humains. Nous avons trouvé les gens très généreux & accueillants—très peu poussés à l'amertume malgré leurs difficultés. Le Midi était beau: très sec, aride, rocheux, mais d'une splendeur sévère, à l'espagnole, à laquelle je suis sensible. Nous avons ensuite passé deux semaines à Baden Baden, où nous avons des parents dans l'occupation française en Allemagne. C'était fort intéressant, & la Forêt Noire est splendide—Les Allemands eux-mêmes ne sont pas si malheureux qu'ils le disent: ils vivent, & mangent, grossièrement mais assez. Ils ne sont pas profondément transformés: un peuple l'est-il jamais? Mais pour le moment sont apathiques & amers. Le spectacle de leurs villes est désolant. Ces destructions sont tout de même une honte pour notre civilisation. Moi qui prêche, pour la France & l'Europe, plus de machines, plus d'industrie, me sens pris de doutes.

    Oui. Boivin imprime mes *Générations* & j'ai déjà corrigé les épreuves. Le livre devrait paraître cet hiver. Il vous devra beaucoup. Votre affectueux encouragement m'a beaucoup aidé à continuer & à terminer, & m'a épargné bien des erreurs. — Nous repartons d'ici le 2 septembre, & de Paris le 10 sur le De Grasse. J'essaierai de vous téléphoner si vous êtes à Paris pendant cette semaine, la dernière pour nous. J'aimerais vous apercevoir avant ce départ pour une autre longue année — mais j'ai peur que des détails matériels de tous genres n'accaparent le plus gros de ces 7 ou 8 jours. En principe nous séjournerons à nouveau à l'Allée Borghèse. Neuilly s/Seine. Maillot 13–52.

    Nos vœux les plus sincères de prompt & total rétablissement pour votre femme — nos hommages à Madame Cahen & à votre belle sœur — & nos amitiés les plus vives.

Henri Peyre

## To Keith Botsford:

On S.S. De Grasse<br>Sept. 18 — 1947

My dear Botsford,

    I am on the SS taking us back from Europe — tomorrow we land in N.Y.; & going over in my mind what I have done this Summer & what I have failed to do & missed, I am carried back in thought to you. I did hope very earnestly to see you some time somewhere in France — but my time just was too short, & was cut even shorter by some unpredictable accidents: I was taken sick in the south of France (stomach or liver ailment, now gone, which wasted part of my free time). Some relatives whom I had to see in France called us way off from where I had planned to stay, which was near or in Paris. Finally I had trouble trying to get into Germany, where I hoped I might perhaps look you up. My passports, which I had left in Paris where a visa was to be put on them, were lost for several weeks, & I was stranded in Strasbourg. My trip into Germany was thus greatly shortened—And now it's Yale again, & America for at least a steady 12 or 18 months—

Well. I'll hope to see you again over here before long, & to read you someday soon in print, & to hear about your whereabouts & spiritual progress—"Pilgrim's, Saint's, or Daemonic Author's" progress. I greatly enjoyed France, & seeing friends & relatives & the scenery, & breathing a different intellectual atmosphere. I was amazed at the degree of material recovery, which I had not expected, & favorably impressed by the deeper prospects underlying real but superficial political & financial turmoil. The literature, I found interesting—with much, to be sure, that is second-rate, & an excess of critical analysis, & many over-intellectual novels—but it's refreshing to live again in an atmosphere permeated by discussion of books & art & philosophy, & not to have those things artificially reserved for secluded university seminars. Many of the reviews are fun to read, even when the fun is preceded with hard effort at unraveling metaphysical riddles and translating scholastic terminology. After all, certain articles in the Y P R trained us for Existentialist criticism & Heidegger's definitions of *Dasein* & nothingness!

Are you in Europe for a long stretch of time still or is the Army sending you back to the States soon? and if so what will you do while securing the fame & money which publishers will, some day, enable you to enjoy? I am glad that your work is going so well, & that warring in Germany has for you—as it once did for Descartes—been such a source of inspiration. The metaphysical novel is a very different genre, & I admire your ambitions, & your titles (very striking & apt) & your summary of what you plan to treat in your tetralogy. After all, except for a few novels in which the originality of the psychology satisfies me fully (Stendhal's for instance, Tolstoy's), the only novel to which one goes back is the novel which involves the greatest problems of philosophy. I was afraid that you would put too much dogmatic exposition & abstract terminology in your early books: your criticism was contemptuous of simplicity—But your experience in Germany must have helped you come back to concrete problems & take an interest in political & social issues. The best I could wish to you would be, after you leave the army, a stay in France or Italy. They say Italy is pleasant again to live in, cheap (for any one who has dollars), & literature & the movies are very much alive there.

Our year at Yale should be somewhat easier. We now have a more numerous staff, with many able young men teaching—many students, too, but they are now reaching the more advanced literary courses & study with seriousness. Fowlie will only take his Guggenheim in 1948–9, in France, to do a book on Mallarmé. He is now at work on Surrealism. I believe he feels happier in Chicago, where he has been markedly successful (as I knew he would be). T[imothy] D[wight] is the same as ever, cordial, a bit boyish—getting a new master, the new Dean of Fine Arts.

I am sorry you lost your father. I understand that your life in your family did not spoil you with that complacent happiness which some children are blessed (or cursed) with. You seem to have been strengthened by solitude, & perhaps internally torn by it. Art will be the way to the true synthesis, or reconciliation of contradictory shreds.

With all good wishes & my regrets to have missed you,

Henri Peyre

## To Charles Seymour:

October 6, 1947

Dear President Seymour:

I hope your summer was pleasant and that your trips this fall have proved very fruitful and interesting to you.

I was very pleased to hear during the summer of the appointment of Mr. Holden, and I shall make a point when I go out of town, as I occasionally do during the year, to inform him and the Alumni organization at Yale so that my services, if at all useful, may be put at the disposal of those valuable groups of friends of Yale.

I believe you know something about the Franco-American organization called France-Amérique. As you may remember, I wrote an article on Yale and its President last year. The group is composed of many eminent Americans who live in Paris and of a number of French personalities or dignitaries who make serious efforts to develop a better understanding between the two countries. Several academicians, former ambassadors, and other important men are among them. That group has always tried to entertain close relations with the most important

American universities, Yale among them. Dean Meeks was until last year their delegate at Yale. With him and with Professor Focillon and Professor Feuillerat, we have organized a few times in the past debates in French among our undergraduates, the winner of which received a medal sent by France-Amérique, or other prizes. I have been associated with this group for several years, at least nominally. They maintained their activities very courageously during the war, went underground, published several clandestine booklets on America to encourage French hopes when the situation was darkest. As soon as France was liberated, they settled again in Paris in their building, 9 avenue Président-Roosevelt, Paris 8.

This summer I saw in Paris the President, M. Gabriel Louis Jaray, who succeeded a long time ago M. Hanotaux, former Minister of Foreign Affairs, who founded and inspired France-Amérique and guided it for several decades. M. Jaray, who is among other things "membre du Conseil d'État," which is as you know a kind of supreme court of France, asked me to be his "délégué adjoint" at Yale, which means I would take care of any correspondence and any details in connection with French debates here or any other activities that we may organize under the sponsorship of France-Amérique. The letter officially asking me thus to be their representative at Yale is herewith enclosed; perhaps you will return it at your convenience.

M. Jaray and the whole Committee of France-Amérique are very anxious to have you accept the title of Official Delegate of France-Amérique. Obviously, the titular delegate should be an American and a very important personality. Nothing would flatter the Committee more than to have you accept this official title, which will, I believe, entail no extra burden for you. The letter asking you to accept, which M. Jaray left with me, is herewith enclosed. I am adding a few printed items which may show you, if you are not already informed on this group, what kind of activities France-Amérique wishes to foster. I hope you will find it possible to accept and thus to make Yale the first university in the United States to have resumed active relations with France-Amérique.

Very sincerely yours,
Henri Peyre
Chairman

## To Harry Levin:

November 17, 1947

Dear Professor Levin:

February 19th seems an excellent date thus far, and we shall put it down as the impatiently awaited day of your visit to us. I believe you agree on 4:30 in the afternoon as a convenient time. Unless you write otherwise, shall I take it for granted that the title would be "Joyce and France and Italy," or is that too clumsy a formulation which you might want to improve upon?

A group of young men of our Department here are now forming the project of starting a review, of a scholarly character, publishing some of the best essays written by our graduate students and perhaps some of the faculty of the French Department. It is probably to be called *Yale French Studies*. It is a modest venture for which we have no money, so that the students are paying for it themselves, but it will be, I believe, serious and very much worthwhile. They are already at work on the first number, to come out late next spring. In the second issue, which will probably be presented next fall, they would very much like to have the honor of publishing the substance of your lecture, if you would agree to have them do so and would provide them with a manuscript. I apologize for transmitting such a suggestion, which you must feel free to reject if you believe it inopportune, since we cannot unfortunately offer anything more substantial than our gratitude for having your cooperation with a sister university. Those students' publications represent, however, a fine and courageous undertaking, and we want to help them in every way. One of the most effective would be to count among the contributors a man whose critical essays are already among the most esteemed and sought after in this country. I have just written to Jean-Paul Sartre to ask him for an article for the first number, which will probably be devoted to Existentialism, a subject that we have been bold enough to treat here in a graduate course, following your boldness in *Finnegans Wake* in a Harvard seminar.

Looking forward to seeing you in February and at your disposal for any information until then, I am,

Very sincerely yours,
Henri Peyre
Chairman

## À Jorge Guillén:

(le 29 nov. 47)

Mon très cher et pauvre ami,

J'étais hier à New York, libéré pour un jour par le Thanksgiving, et Mme [René] de Messières nous apprend, presque par hasard, la terrible nouvelle. Nous marchions sur quelque avenue, et nous en avons été, ma femme & moi, saisis et comme effondrés. Nous ne pensions pas que la maladie de votre chère épouse fût tout à fait aussi grave, et votre coup de téléphone en septembre, à la veille de notre départ, était plutôt rassurant. Souvent son nom & le vôtre étaient revenus dans notre conversation : New Haven nous semblait plus triste, moins artiste, moins stimulant de beaucoup, sans vous—J'espérais vous y revoir & accueillir bientôt—et vous voilà veuf, mon cher Guillén—veuf d'une femme admirable de courage et d'intelligence, comprenant tout si vite, sentant en même temps qu'elle comprenait, juge extraordinairement lucide de poésie et de musique, avec un sens si droit pour deviner le présent aussi et savoir quelle voie suivre même en politique : la voie de la générosité et du courage libéral. Elle était beaucoup pour vous, et pour vos enfants, dont il était aisé de voir qu'elle était adorée. Plus que toute autre, elle va vous manquer et toute la beauté des souvenirs en commun dont vous allez vous repaître ne pourra consoler une douleur aussi immense. Elle écartait de votre sentier les épines, vous libérait avec sollicitude de beaucoup de soucis. On aurait dit qu'elle voulait tout faire ici avec avidité, pressentant un jour combien elle manquerait un jour, tôt.

Les mots sont vains—mais nous voulons vous dire, ma femme & moi, et pour Madame Cahen, et pour Madame La Jeunesse, toute notre sympathie, tout notre chagrin. En quelques brèves semaines, nous avions senti en elle une amie comme la vie en fait bien rarement rencontrer : esprit supérieur, belle âme, bonté mariée à l'esprit et à l'humour, grande capacité d'aimer. Vos deux enfants sont tout pénétrés d'elle & de l'influence qu'elle a été sur eux, pour leur bien. Et cela peut-être est une consolation moins illusoire que d'autres.

Revenez-vous ? Quand ? Nous voudrions savoir comment est venu le malheur—nous avions tant pensé que la joie de revoir la France redonnerait la santé à cette femme si Française entre les Français—Hélas!

Partagez avec les nôtres votre souvenir affectueux et notre très vive & profonde sympathie.

Henri Peyre

## To Charles Seymour:

December 4 — 1947

Dear President Seymour:

As I told you last night, if you had a brief moment & wished to see Norman Torrey when he comes next Wednesday (December 10th), I believe 4 p.m. that day or 5 p.m. or 5.30 p.m. would be a good time if you could spare the few minutes then, or even 3.30 at your own convenience. Your secretary might just let me know.

Torrey has kindly consented to come down & give us a talk at our Romance Club Wednesday evening, & will leave the next morning.

He feels, after some hesitation for he has remained a close friend of our Department, that he must stay at Columbia for the rest of his career. We regret it, but will bow to his motives. Since he knows us well & is familiar with the situation in Romance Languages in the country at large, I thought you might wish to hear from him any criticism or "outside opinion" on our Department that he might have to offer. We want to avoid being complacent, & to be judged according to national, & even international, standards.

Very sincerely yours,<br>Henri Peyre

## À Pierre Bédard:

Le 7 décembre, 1947

Monsieur Pierre Bédard
Director, French Institute
22 East 60th Street
New York, New York
Cher Monsieur:

Je compte bien avoir le plaisir de vous voir aussitôt que j'irai à New

York. Mais je suis obligé de laisser cela incertain jusqu'à ce que je sache avec quelque précision quand je puis m'absenter.

En attendant, c'est entendu pour le titre et je me contente de vous dire deux mots sur la question posée. Franchement (et pas seulement parce qu'il est mon collègue), je crois que de ces deux personnes Monsieur Mohrt vous fera la conférence la plus brillante et la plus vivante. Il est écrivain et mêlé aux milieux littéraires, ce que (sic) donne toujours une note originale. Enfin, il va retourner en France après cette année et c'est une occasion pour votre public de l'entendre.

Je connais Monsieur Pamplume, que Harvard va sans doute examiner, en l'écoutant, avec l'idée de l'attirer là-bas. Il est extrêmement intelligent et un professeur de grand avenir qui restera sans doute pas mal d'années dans ce pays. Mais il est plus universitaire et peut-être pour un public comme le vôtre, un peu plus pondéré, un peu plus froid. Mais j'espère que vous l'aurez tôt ou tard, car il est bon que votre Maison lance ainsi quelques nouveaux de belle qualité, alors que les plus vieux commencent à se faire rares ou fatigués.

Bien à vous et à bientôt,<br>
Henri Peyre<br>
Chairman

## To Charles Seymour:

December 12, 1947

Dear President Seymour:

I was reluctant to press the question which I put yesterday at the professors' meeting; making a motion on the lowering of the retirement age would have been indiscreet on my part, taking the group by surprise. But I believe the point is a vital one. The most embarrassing and yet the most essential difficulty that we face does not lie, indeed, in the accumulation of associate professors but in the stagnation that is occasionally to be met in full professors. The difficulty may be insoluble; but the Deans might well want to consider it. Some gentle pressure on chairmen or on professors, with the prospect of salary increases within the same rank, might incite to more active scholarship or more publication of high quality.

Meanwhile, it might be advisable to move gradually toward a uniform retiring age of 65. Professors (and associate or assistant professors) who would be 65 by July 1, 1948, would retain the option to retire at 68. Those who would be 62 on that date might choose to retire at an age not higher than 67. Those who would be 60, at an age not higher than 66. Those who would be under 60 on July 1, 1948, would have to retire at 65. Some such arrangement might well prove practical.

It would certainly do much to relieve in part our present difficulty, and the difficulty of several more years to come. We shall, between 1948 and 1951, be turning out from our graduate schools an unusual number of fine Ph.D.'s, who were detained from completing their studies earlier by the war. They will deserve promotion and will have to be encouraged by the prospect of such promotion if they are to be kept in our profession. A lower retiring age will help in part to make the turnover more rapid and will create more positions for a promising generation of scholars.

The Administration might, of course, retain the right to continue until 67 a few professors for whom an exception would be desirable in the interests of the University.

I hope this suggestion will not seem indiscreet from a man soon nearing his forty-seventh birthday.

Sincerely yours,
Henri Peyre

## To Keith Botsford:

Dec. 27—1947

My dear Botsford,

I am pleased to hear you are back, & deeply engaged in your literary work. The novel, which I only study from the outside, & hesitantly at that, always appears to me as the most difficult of genres. It requires a vast technique, & yet one which must never intrude, & never give the impression that the authors were, like Henry James, proposing all sorts of problems to his self-conscious virtuosity. I have faith in what you will do with it, some day, perhaps soon. If I were you, I would try to get one of my fictional attempts into print now—you are much more mature than your years, since you have been writing for quite a while already—

And the exteriorization of publication, even the criticism of readers are a help to one who has faith in himself & ability to learn & grow.

I agree with you on the possibility of films: they are certainly not well exploited these days. The few movies I have seen are miserable, & the foreign ones (French especially) are now often overpraised here. Can a writer produce scripts, live on it (as you should until you win fame in other *genres*), & not sell his soul & subject his talent to mechanization? I wonder—& hope.

I am going to look around for opportunities for translation. Few, however, come to us. Publishers seem to get their own translators, & the best might be to go & see them (Random House, Knopf, etc.) & suggest some French, Italian or German book which should be translated in your opinion. They probably will ask you for a sample of a few pages. It is a poorly paid business, as a rule. I shall keep your name in mind & suggest it whenever an opportunity to do some decently rewarded work occurs.

I do not often go to N.Y. Work of some kind or other seems to detain me here. But why don't you come up here one day—say the first Friday after our vacations (Jan—9th). You probably would enjoy seeing a few friends again, & might have lunch with me, I hope. You might come for me in the office in W L Harkness around 12.30—It would be a pleasure to see you again.

Sincerely,<br>
Henri Peyre

## To Charles Seymour:

Febr. 17—1948

Dear President Seymour:

Will you accept these few recent articles from one of your professors who, complaining occasionally of stagnation in his profession foolishly thinks he escapes it by taking a superficial interest in too many things, & probably by talking & writing too much?

Very sincerely yours,<br>
Henri Peyre

## To Joseph Barker:

February 19, 1948

Professor Joseph E. Barker
Sweet Briar College
Sweet Briar, Virginia
Dear Professor Barker:

My congratulations on your fine junior-year project and on your courage in taking it over. I am very pleased that of all colleges it should be Sweet Briar which is undertaking such a thorny job. But I know that you, with the help of your wife, will do it splendidly. I offer you my personal wishes, and I hope to be in France on a half-sabbatical next spring and shall be looking forward to seeing you and to seeing how it works out.

At Yale, since Dean DeVane took things over, we are much more internationally minded and readier to cooperate with such a junior-year plan than we were in the past. Our Dean goes so far as to say that eventually, if Sweet Briar preferred to retain the feminine part of the program, we would be the logical people to organize the men students over there. I am not quite so optimistic or so open to the suggestion of more delicate work, but meanwhile we shall make a beginning, I hope, by sending three or four French majors to Paris next year, and I hope to persuade them that joining your group is the only way in which they can do well-organized work and receive credit for it. I suppose that, like Smith College, you will allow quite a little flexibility in the programs and that you will permit some, for instance, to take courses at the École du Louvre, others at the French School of Political Science, etc. I suppose also that you will get lycée teachers from outside to check the work of the boys, help them with their essays, direct them in a general way, and thus supplement the rather vague and loose Sorbonne courses. Smith, I believe, asks of the student a total sum roughly equivalent to what the girls pay in the College ($1400), their traveling expenses not included.

Could you, at your earliest convenience, let me know what the total sum required would probably be, if some of the students we have in mind who already have some living accommodations over there could make use of them, and what program of courses they would take. Also whether they would attend some courses at a provincial university before going to the Sorbonne and, finally, when they would have to leave the United States. The three or four boys we have in mind are good in French and reliable and we believe they would be a very good addition to your group. If the work could include, later on, more government, economics, and such subjects, I am sure there would be even more students eager to go from our University.

Meanwhile, I should be very pleased to establish this cooperation between our two colleges and happy at the prospect of seeing you again some time in connection with it. My regards to your wife and,

Very sincerely yours,<br>
Hri Peyre<br>
Chairman

## À Keith Botsford:

Ce 20/2/48

Mon cher Ami,

Vous êtes bien aimable & rien ne me ferait plus de plaisir. Mais le doyen de Teachers College, Russell, pour qui & chez qui nous devons parler ce soir-là, a déjà organisé un dîner pour les 4 ou 5 conférenciers, & je m'échapperai aussitôt après la séance, vers 10 heures. Je ne pourrai donc être libre.

Je le regrette vivement.

Ç'a été un grand plaisir de vous voir, mûri, sage, mais toujours ardent & jeune, et plein de splendides projets.

Amitiés,<br>
Henri Peyre

## To Joseph Barker:

February 22, 1948

My dear Barker:

My letter crossed with yours of Febr. 18, most interesting, which I am answering personally. As I had said, I am much interested in your project as is our Dean, who is very forward and liberal. I believe that it could become a much larger experiment than before 1939, & one that would & should eventually send abroad some of the very best undergraduate minds in the country, among *men* too. The Fulbright bill, the new spirit in international Cultural relations, the interest in UNESCO, bid fair for the success of the project.

Your suggestion about my colleague is an excellent one. It raises many problems which I would like to look into for 2 or 3 days before answering you more clearly: whether we could dispense with him next year, whether you would not have him another year, whether he could manage such an absence (having a wife & two children of school age), what the extra expenses involved would be (traveling to France & back), & the living expenses over there.

But Theodore Andersson is obviously as good a man as you could get: he is Director of Undergraduate Studies in French here, a fine executive, clear-headed, patient, efficient & constructive; he is very familiar with all these problems, having directed the Romance Department at Wells College, having taught in Washington before, being a very understanding student of foreign countries. He knows French very well, & Spanish, & other European languages too. For at least four years, he was in the State Department, Assistant Director of one of the Cultural Relations Divisions, & is therefore well known to Leslie Brady & others, & at home in administration & Cultural Relations problems. He is 43 or 44, a fine personality, firm with students, generous of his time with them, & would be very good at organizing the courses by the French professors over there, seeing people, etc. Norman Torrey & Andrew Morehouse are good friends of his. His salary here is, next year, $6500.

I'll examine the matter with him, see what his wife thinks of it all & discuss the possibility with our Dean. I hope to have four or five students enrolled in your group for the coming year & to work at it with a view for the future.

Would the probable expenses for living over there be very heavy, to your mind? & does the work start early? (Dr. Andersson is due to teach at Harvard next Summer, for the Summer Term there.)

Best regards to your wife & most sincerely,<br>Henri Peyre

## À Marcel Gutwirth:

Ce 23—ii—48

Cher Monsieur,

Merci de votre bon souvenir—Je crois que vous avez bien fait de poursuivre vos études & de prendre un degré plus avancé—& le voilà vite obtenu. Mes compliments. Votre titre de thèse est joli & séduisant—mais suggère un travail malaisé. Il vaudrait la peine, certes, de le reprendre.

Si vous le pouviez, vous devriez demander l'an prochain quelque bourse qui vous permettrait de vivre une année & d'écrire votre thèse avec tout le loisir désirable. Vous avez intérêt à faire un ouvrage soigné & assez vite publiable—Columbia doit offrir de ces bourses. Mais si vous préférez enseigner aussitôt, ce sera possible aussi (quoique plus facile, & mieux rémunéré, avec le grade de docteur déjà obtenu). Je ne suis pas sûr que nous ayons quelque vacance l'an prochain. Notre pratique est ici de nommer, ou des Ph.D.'s ou agrégés pour les cours déjà avancés, ou des "assistants" qui préparent en même temps leur doctorat chez nous. Un peu plus tard peut-être, cela sera possible. En attendant, écrivez à diverses universités comme Wayne (Detroit), d'où un Français s'en va; comme Illinois, Ohio, Indiana—Il y a là des changements fréquents qui ouvrent souvent des possibilités : insistez bien sur votre qualité de bilingue & sur le fait que vous êtes prêt à enseigner la langue (pour commencer) en Français—je ne doute que vous obteniez un poste sans peine.

Croyez, cher Monsieur Gutwirth, à mon souvenir le meilleur,

Henri Peyre

Vos amis connaissent-ils cette dernière (?) revue, lancée par nos étudiants gradués ?

## To Joseph Barker:

March 23, 1948

Professor Joseph E. Barker
Department of Romance Languages
Sweet Briar College
Sweet Briar, Virginia

Dear Mr. Barker:

Your letter is most cordial and gives me great pleasure indeed. We consider it an honor at Yale to be associated through Theodore Andersson and through a few of our students with the new junior year organization that you and your courageous and imaginative president have started under excellent auspices. We shall miss Andersson, but we know he will be an ideal man to deal competently, patiently, and tactfully with all problems that may arise. I hope the year will be a restful one for him in the sense that his normal activity will not be disturbed by unhappy events. I am really confident it will not be, although times are threatening again. I can not believe it will be anything more than a threat which wise policy will avert.

I hope we shall have the pleasure of seeing you and your wife some time here in what we call the East. De Messières told me about the excellent impressions he received on his trip to Sweet Briar, which revived my own fine memories of some years ago.

I have just received in the mail the very kind letter written to me by Miss Martha Lucas. I am very much touched by it. Will you extend my thanks to her for her very thoughtful attention? It was a great fortune for the College to have Miss Glass, whom I met with great pleasure some years ago, and I know from having heard it said on many sides that this fortune has been happily duplicated in the fine president that has succeeded her.

Again, my congratulations and best regards,

Very sincerely yours,
Hri Peyre
Chairman

## À Claude Vigée:

Ce 20 avril/48

Mon cher Ami,

J'ai eu grand plaisir à vous voir à New York, entre mes deux trains. Votre femme & vous formez le plus aimable, le plus fervent des couples, courageusement dévoué à la beauté & à l'art, plein de foi dans ce que vous avez à dire & à donner au monde—qui est réel & précieux. Vous avez, à votre âge, non seulement un talent rare, mais une flamme chaude & brillante, une vie spirituelle qui anime une immense, presque déconcertante, érudition.

Je vous renvoie, par paquet MS, votre 1er volume. On s'y plonge avec joie, on s'y perd un peu (les divisions des chapitres dans chaque partie sont difficiles à suivre), on y est ébloui de tant de science & de réflexion, parfois déconcerté par la difficulté à saisir la suite des idées et la richesse du verbe, des allusions. Je ne discuterai pas la thèse centrale: elle est trop personnelle, trop l'expression de votre talent. J'ajouterai que je ne me sens pas compétent. L'esthétique est une discipline qui m'attire peu, je l'avoue, à moins qu'elle ne se fasse concrète & ne permette de sentir davantage & de comprendre plus lucidement la beauté. C'est dire que je me perds un peu dans votre 1re partie.

Vous y touchez à énormément de choses, et forcément passez vite, affirmez beaucoup : le ton n'est guère celui d'une thèse ; parfois celui d'un inspiré, plutôt, ou d'un révélateur de mystères. Les parties précises, d'application, m'ont séduit et éclairé davantage : sur le rythme de la phrase, sur Flaubert, sur le démonique, sur la musique & la poésie. Certaines de ces parties, reprises, précisées, séparées un peu de votre thèse générale, pourraient faire de bons articles de revues "learned" qui attireraient sur votre talent une attention méritée. La publication du volume en entier effraiera un peu. Si on vous la paie, tant mieux. Sinon, vous pourriez vous demander (un peu comme fit Renan avec ce gros "Pourana" qu'était son *Avenir de la Science*) s'il ne vaudrait pas mieux débiter des parties de cela en articles, mais ne pas entrer dans la vie littéraire avec cette énorme masse d'idées & de pages, que peu, forcément, liront avec attention. Vous posez là tous les problèmes de l'esthétique, dans une sorte de prolégomènes à une esthétique future—

et parfois le ton est un peu juvénile de ferveur apocalyptique. Votre seconde partie sera sans doute plus précise : ne peut-elle se détacher de la 1ère ? Se comprendre isolément ? S'illustrer d'exemples concrets nombreux ?

Je crois aussi (je suis très professoral & critique) que vous abusez des citations. Parfois votre pensée semble sévir de lien à des citations, presque toujours ingénieuses et rares, mais trop hétéroclites et quelquefois gratuites, un tantinet pédantes. Vous en avez du Nord & du Midi, de l'Inde & de la Chine, en espagnol et en allemand—On est un peu dérouté. Puisque c'est au fonds un traité personnel, pourquoi si souvent vous appuyer sur Goethe, Nietzsche & Novalis—ou même Alexander, Bergson, etc.—ou même tant citer les *Four Quartets* au lieu d'exprimer directement votre pensée ? Je crois que vous gagneriez, en ceci, à élaguer beaucoup.

Vous pourriez aussi, pour la publication, les traduire toutes—au moins toutes les citations en prose. Parfois vous traduisez Nietzsche, parfois pas (pp. 22, 40, 44)—parfois vous les répétez (Eliot p. 62 & 74)—Quelquefois les références sont vagues : quelle page de tel livre ? Baudelaire, *Œuvres Complètes,* tome III : mais quelle édition de quelle année des *Œuvres Complètes*. Ce sont de menus détails, mais que l'éditeur vous priera de corriger.

J'ai l'air d'insister sur les réserves, ce qui fausse ma pensée, car j'ai été surtout séduit et, littéralement, c'est le mot—ébloui. Mais je crois que mes menues réserves seront partagées & exprimées par d'autres à la publication, & c'est pourquoi je crois plus loyal de vous les dire. Vous avez une pensée originale, nourrie à la source, étayée sur des connaissances énormes, et assimilées : car ce n'est pas le 1er venu qui connaît en profondeur Hegel, Schiller, Nietzsche, Bergson, Claudel, Valéry, etc., comme vous—Vous avez ici la substance de plusieurs volumes à venir, ou de quoi nourrir maint article. Et tout cela n'a nui en rien à votre inspiration de poète—Mais la présentation de cet ensemble est touffue; elle déroutera. Votre pente est de mettre beaucoup, sinon tout, dans tout, sans faciliter les choses pour le lecteur moyen ; une grande richesse d'associations vous fait lier un thème à un autre, une citation à une autre. Je me demande si vous ne gagneriez pas à élaguer, à conserver beaucoup de ceci, mais à l'acheminer progressivement au public. Paru ici, en français, ce sera presque perdu. Découpé en deux ou trois petits volumes plus concrets, plus limités d'objet, en France, vous attirerez davantage l'attention &, ce qui est plus, vous atteindrez plus sûrement ceux que vous voulez toucher.

Pensez-y sérieusement ; & dites-moi ce que vous décidez de faire. J'ai eu vraiment plaisir à vous voir & à causer un peu. Cela se renouvellera.

Bien des choses à votre femme, & bien à vous.

Hri Peyre

## À Jorge Guillén:

Avril 28 — 1948

Cher ami,

Acceptez nos vœux amicaux de retour point trop triste en ce pays & de bienvenue. Cela va être bien dur pour vous de vous retrouver seul ici ; pour vous plus que pour tout homme que je connaisse, parce que vous vivez par le cœur autant que par l'esprit, cette absence va être totale & constante — "Busca el mundo una blanca, / total, perenne ausencia." Mais si l'amitié & l'admiration de vos collègues & amis peut être de quelque réconfort, acceptez-la.

Passerez-vous par ici ? Si vous vouliez vous arrêter à New Haven, Damaso Alonso certainement, d'autres amis & nous aimerions vous revoir, parler de vous, de votre chère disparue, de votre vie, de votre poésie. Nous sommes ici jusqu'au 3 ou 4 juin.

Rappelez-nous au souvenir de votre gendre, de votre fille, & de votre fils plus tard.

Bien à vous,
Henri Peyre

## To Allen Tate:

[letterhead: Princeton University Library]
Yale University,
New Haven,
May 2, 1948

Dear Mr. Tate:

Ever since my hurried & somewhat brutal "intervention" in the Baltimore Symposium, I have been wanting to explain to you how rushed I was that week, with several engagements previously accepted elsewhere, & how sorry I had been to miss your speech — & to lose the opportunity to become better acquainted with you. I have had a long admiration for your poetry & for a great deal of your criticism; I often quote from it to my students or refer them to it; & it would have been pleasant & profitable for me to listen to you a little more & to talk with you a bit more leisurely. I am sorry it was not possible — but perhaps it will be some day. I would greatly appreciate your coming to Yale some time for a visit or for a lecture if that is not impossible. I was happy, at least, to have met you — however briefly.

Very sincerely,
Hri Peyre

## À Claude Vigée:

Ce 10 mai 48

Mon cher Ami,

Je vous ai renvoyé ce matin votre 2nd vol. (manuscrit). Quelques mots seulement (car le lundi est un gros jour pour moi, sans cesse interrompu) pour vous dire, à nouveau, mon estime pour ce travail. Vous savez énormément, vous avez beaucoup réfléchi à ces problèmes terriblement complexes, vous apportez du neuf & une sensibilité de poète à leur solution; et vous évitez les "dadas" qui ont séduit trop souvent les poètes parlant de ces sujets de prosodie, [André] Spire lui-même, Aragon, & Claudel parfois.

Cependant, comme conseil pratique, je vous redirais: avez-vous intérêt à publier ceci tel quel? C'est touffu, un peu trop morcelé & éparpillé en citations trop diverses, difficiles à suivre. Vous touchez à tellement de choses à la fois. Si j'étais vous, je reprendrais du temps pour repenser à tout cela, & le débiterais graduellement en morceaux, en effaçant un reste de caractère de thèse universitaire. Par exemple pourquoi ne pas publier, avec vos poèmes, un long appendice sur la prosodie & votre prosodie, car après tout vous faites aussi un plaidoyer "pro domo," convaincant d'ailleurs? En même temps, en présentant d'abord vos idées par morceaux, vous donnerez moins l'impression d'avoir tout un ambitieux système d'esthétique dans lequel il faut entrer & qu'il faut accepter *in toto*. Vous paraîtrez plus insinuant, gagnerez plus de lecteurs—et un jour vous exposerez le corps de doctrine qui unit ou soustend vos différentes vues. Vous devriez écrire sur "l'art & le démonique" certes; sur Flaubert dans le détail, sur le rythme de Claudel &, pourquoi pas, sur celui de St John Perse, etc.

Je ne m'inquiète pas pour vous! Vous avez immensément à dire, & le direz. Je craindrais plutôt que l'on ne vous accuse de "manque de clarté & de maturité" si vous disiez tant trop vite & trop tôt. Publiez un volume de vers en France d'abord, selon les conseils de Léger. Je suis content qu'il vous ait reçu avec amabilité ainsi. S'il voulait vous présenter dans une préface!! Il ne l'a jamais fait pour personne—mais qui sait.

Excusez ces phrases disjointes—Mes vœux encore, & mes compliments.

Bien à vous & bon souvenir à votre femme,

Hri Peyre

Oui, je dois aller à Columbus les 4 & 5 nov, je crois.

## To Keith Botsford:

Berkeley, Cal. French Dept.<br>U of California (until July 29)<br>July 13 [1948]

My dear Botsford,

Thank you for the good news from you, which reached me in this beautiful & remote land. I congratulate you on completing your *Job*, &

on the change of title: the new one is probably just as apt, & more attractive. You are modest in your confession that some of it does not satisfy you; yet I am sure it has much of your very real gifts. And often the freshness of a first major achievement like this offsets the lack of smoothness in the technique. All the important novels from Proust to Kafka, Malraux & even [*Sartre crossed out*] Faulkner have been failures (or innovations) in technique, but important just for that.

I am not the man to give you much practical advice, from being too preoccupied in part, chiefly from being imperfectly familiar with English, & too old already to feel with the attempts of your generation. Some one like Harvey Shapiro, or Ted Morris who is very shrewd, could reread it & give you some advice. But it may be best now not to do any more rewriting & get it published: how? I don't know the literary world well, & agents inspire me with distrust. Why not type it in several copies & write to several publishers, Random House, Hayers, Little Brown, etc. Explain in your letter who you are & that you believe you represent something fairly typical of a new generation of young writers.

I shall be traveling about during most of August & back by September 15 or so. I shall hope to see you some time then. Warn me a few days ahead when you can.

Yours,<br>Henri Peyre

## À Pierre Bédard:

Ce 13 septembre 1948

Cher Monsieur — ou me permettez-vous de dire, cher ami?

Vous êtes bien aimable de songer aux "vétérans" qui commencent à vieillir sous le harnais. C'est toujours un plaisir pour moi de vous revoir & de retrouver votre public. L'habileté avec laquelle vous avez su le conserver & l'accroître à travers toutes ces années est admirable.

Je serai heureux de venir un mardi. Mais je pars cette année en congé sabbatique pour la France le 8 ou 9 février: ce devrait donc être avant, si cela s'arrange avec votre programme. Pas le 9 novembre où je suis pris ailleurs, mais quelque autre mardi, et peut-être le plus tôt sera le mieux.

Voici quelques sujets.

Si ma conférence venait avant la fin de cette année, il y a deux sujets d'actualité qui ont fait beaucoup parler & écrire en France cette année;

    1. La signification de 1848 — À propos d'un centenaire;
    2. Le Jubilé de Paul Claudel;
    (On a célébré ses 80 ans cette année, republié ses œuvres et publié *Partage de Midi,* son chef d'œuvre, jusqu'à ces derniers mois non livré à la circulation — admirable drame d'amour & de religion sur lequel la conférence serait centrée.)
    3. Le roman américain récent en France;
    (Succès de ces œuvres: pourquoi? ce que l'on demande en France aux ouvrages américains & ce qu'on trouve en eux.)
    4. Marcel Proust — Vingt-cinq ans après;
    (Où en sommes-nous avec Proust 25 ans après sa mort — Quelle est aujourd'hui notre perspective sur son œuvre?)
    5. Signification du Surréalisme;
    6. Baudelaire et nous.

Parmi les jeunes, vous aviez songé à Pamplume, aujourd'hui à Harvard — solide, fin, un peu universitaire. Il y aura cette année à Chicago Canu, âgé de 50 ans environ, spirituel, disert: est-ce trop loin? — Pierre Emmanuel, comme vous savez, doit venir, et Jules Romains peut-être — J'ai à Yale un collègue de talent, Georges May (Français), qui pourrait parler sur Diderot, Giraudoux, Alphonse Daudet avec charme, et sur bien d'autres sujets: il est licencié, diplômé de France, docteur de chez nous. 30 ans environ — Bruneau sera à Columbia — Hytier semble se tenir à l'écart.

J'aimerais fort avoir le plaisir de déjeuner avec vous et j'espère un jour que nous rencontrerons Madame Bédard. Puis-je vous récrire quand je saurai un peu mieux mes projets.

Avez-vous reçu, pour votre belle Bibliothèque, l'annonce ci-incluse?

                                      Merci encore & bien à vous,
                                      Henri Peyre

## To Charles Seymour:

Sept. 24 — 1948

Dear President Seymour:

A distinguished French visitor, M. Jean Marx, is flying from France early next month and will visit Yale around October 7–10. He is the former Director of the important Division of the Foreign Affairs Ministry called "Division of Cultural Relations" & now (since he reached the age at which such persons normally retire, 60 or 65) Technical Counselor of that Division. He has had the rank of Minister Plenipotentiary for years. He was an old friend of Focillon.

He is coming over to visit some American Universities which have especially close relations with France & with suggestions to develop still further exchanges of professors & of students — the former especially. He offered us last year to establish a regular exchange of professors between Yale & the Sorbonne. It would be helpful to have him talk with the Provost & the Dean while here. And I am writing to ask if you would receive M. Marx when he visits Yale. I would call up your office when I know his definite plans to ask for an appointment.

May I enclose a little book which I published early this summer & which I beg you to accept (though not to read) with my respectful regards?

Sincerely yours,
Henri Peyre

## To Joseph Barker:

Oct. 17/1948

Dear Mr. Barker:

Excuse this informal Sunday reply to your kind letter. I am very glad that the Junior Year is going so well & that Tug [Theodore Andersson] is happy over the job, & efficient about it: I had no doubt of the latter. He is a good administrator, & cordial & gentle as well as firm. But a great deal was due to you & your wife, & your strenuous efforts through the Summer.

I shall be in France myself this spring or summer, but [Jean] Collignon will take charge of supervising & checking applications here, & we hope again to have a fair number of Yale men going over. It would be a good thing if Harvard, Princeton followed suit, & established the Junior Year as for *men* as well as women, & for the very best juniors in the supposedly better universities.

We shall do our best here, & post your announcements at once. Will you be in charge in France yourself next year? That would be the best possible arrangement, &, I imagine, a pleasant one for you.

Things are busy here, with 3 of our professors away in France & an inordinately large number of excellent graduate students at the thesis stage—but we are well & active. You must have seen the enclosed announcements already, but I'll add them for library or colleagues. I shall see you at the December NY meeting, probably. I am due to speak somewhere in Virginia in November, coming back from North Carolina, but not anywhere near enough your college to stop by & say "hello!," I fear.

Many regards to your wife & very sincerely,
Hri Peyre

## To the same:

Nov. 26—1948

My dear Barker:

I was glad to have your letter, with the detailed comments on our students. This is a real help at a time when Collignon & I shall soon be thinking of recruiting a new, & if possible better, group for 1949–50. Some of our men do not seem to be first-rate material &we should be even stricter in accepting candidates next year: we naturally would like to see Yale men among those obtaining the finest results. But it is still very early in the year & there is much room for improvement still. I shall keep in touch with Tug, of course, & discuss the question with him next Spring.

I really think it would have been grand for the group to have you & Mrs. Barker over in Paris next year. Rogers would be the ideal choice. I shall go over the whole problem of juniors (& try to encourage Harvard at it, when he comes here next Wednesday to confer with us). I doubt, however, he will be able to escape as long as he is Chairman. That sort of work is an implacable "engrenage," & one finds one can't be missed for a whole year easily

At Harvard I see no one else right now. The Department counts but few outstanding people at present. Mac Allister, of Princeton, is a fine administrator, better at home in Italian than in French, not really brilliant, but a good & solid head, competent for details—It may [be] that [E. B. O.] Borgerhoff, of Princeton, would be an even better choice: [Ira] Wade would tell you. I don't know Borgerhoff personally.

Columbia might have good men, like Donald Frame or Edelman (Nathan)—fine in every way, human & cordial, & excellent scholars. You certainly know them. Some time, you might have a woman, like Miss Clark from Wellesley or Miss De Schweinitz from Vassar, or someone younger.—If you would just as well have a French professor of an American university, fully familiar with American ways, grading, discipline, curricula, etc., Salvan of Brown Univ., Beyer of Buffalo, & some day Collignon, now with us, would be excellent.

I wouldn't be surprised if some day soon your numbers would reach 100 or 150—The thing will be quite a job, then!

Hoping to see you at the MLA, crowded as that meeting is likely to be!—

Best regards to your wife.

Sincerely,
Hri Peyre

Financially, I suppose the organization is making both ends meet. Will the tuition remain the same next year?

## À John Kneller:

Dec. 12/48

Cher M. Kneller:

Je crois que vous êtes sur la bonne voie dans votre étude. Le sujet est difficile, mais il est grand & beau. Bien entendu, étant vaste, il aura besoin d'être limité. Vous verrez cela quand vous en aurez d'abord fait le tour. Par ex. il est possible que vous deviez le limiter aux "grands" poètes romantiques (dont Nerval, Gautier peut-être), bien que cela fût dommage. Je crois aussi que vous aurez intérêt à vous fixer une date limite, quitte à la dépasser en vous servant d'œuvres de Lam., Hugo, Vigny parues après cette date — Lam. n'a guère évolué, surtout après les *Recueillements*. Hugo après 1852 est bien loin de Rousseau. L'intérêt est quand même de voir ce que les poètes dits romantiques, à l'époque dite romantique, ont dû à R.

Bien sûr, il sortira de vos lectures des groupes d'idées, que vous pouvez reprendre peut-être en conclusion — L'action de R. sur 1) la nature, la solitude, — la rêverie;

2) le thème du souvenir (déjà si marqué dans les Confessions, III), du regret du passé — de l'enfance;

3) le sentiment & sa primauté — les droits de la passion — la sensibilité opposée à la raison;

4) l'amour, l'amour de l'amour — le désir d'être aimé — l'impuissance au bonheur (Confessions VII);

5) la religiosité — la prière — ("que d'hommes entre Dieu & moi": le Vicaire savoyard;

6) le moi — la révolte.

Comme vous le dites, il faudra, à côté de cela, marquer des différences — il y en a beaucoup aussi — De l'artificialité & de la rhétorique dans la reprise de thèmes rousseauistes, aussi.

Le sujet sera donc un sujet d'idées, d'histoire de la sensibilité, etc. Vous pouvez accentuer cet aspect, & ne pas vous perdre dans les petits détails. D'autre part, c'est aussi un sujet d'histoire littéraire: il vous faudra, sans vous y noyer, avoir pas mal de références précises à R. chez ces poètes, appuyer vos dires sur des preuves — mais dépasser parfois ces preuves. Même quand tel poète n'a guère cité Rousseau, vous avez le droit d'identifier le rousseauisme chez lui.

Bien sûr aussi, méfiez-vous parfois. Certains sentiments romantiques existaient avant Rousseau ou en dehors de lui, & ne viennent pas forcément de lui — la poésie de la nuit & des tombeaux (voir livre de Van Tieghem):

"Et le dernier bien qui me reste
Est-il la douceur de pleurer"

de Léonard, cité dans H. Potez, L'Élégie en France avant le rom.

Bien sûr, jetez également un coup d'œil à Chateaubriand, Mme de Staël & George Sand (Hist. de ma vie, II, 313-4) intermédiaires entre Rousseau & les poètes romantiques.

Sur Lamartine, vous semblez avoir lu l'essentiel. Vous pourriez tenter déjà une synthèse sur Lam & R. Tant pis pour la correspondance non encore parue. Il y avait autrefois à Yale l'édition en 4 vols de la Correspondance: elle a dû être volée.

> Voyez aussi Lettres d'Elvire (R. deux Mondes — 1er février 1905) —
> Lettres de Lam à sa fiancée, Ibid. 15 août. 15 sept 1905–1907
> "Lam & le catholicisme" Guillemin, Revue de France, 1er mai 1934
> Jean des Cognets La vie intérieure de Lam. 1913
> Lacretelle. Jeunesse de Lam.
> Zyromski "Le rom. de Lam.," dans le Romantisme & les lettres 1927
> R. Waltz, "La tristesse de Lam," revue de l'Université de Lyon, jan 1928
> Viatte Le Cathol des romantiques 1922
> Claire El Engel La littérature alpestre en France. 1930
> Barrière La musique de la poésie de Lam, Revue d'Hist. Litt. 1929, vol. 36
> aussi Bisson "Rousseau & the Romantic Experience" Modern Lang. Review, Jan 1942

Dans Vigny, regardez si nous avons le récent Lauvrière, en 2 vols, Vigny, sa vie & son œuvre —

> le Georges Bonnefoy, La pensée religieuse & morale de Vigny
> le gros & touffu Citoleux
> l'Estève comme point de départ
> Boerbach, Le rationalisme mystique de Vigny. 1929

&  le vieux Ernest Dupuy. S/Vigny & ses amitiés.
Dans Musset, Emile Henriot,
Montégut (bon encore)
Gastinel — Le romantisme de Musset.

You should do as much of that reading as possible here, with our convenient library & attempt a general outline — may be start writing some parts, then complete next year in France.

I hope we can get one of those French fellowships for you next year & there is no reason why we should not. It will help only little financially but some — & I think your year there will be worth while, in any case. I am glad you have decided for *one* year. I congratulate your wife on the decision.

Sincerely, H. P.

## To Joseph Barker:

December 15, 1948

Professor Joseph E. Barker
Department of French
Sweet Briar College
Sweet Briar, Virginia

Dear Professor Barker:

Excuse this hasty answer to your letter. I want to tell you at once that Blanchard Rideout, whom I had not thought of, seems to me by far the best man you could wish for. He knows French very well, is very efficient and obliging, has been an administrator for years, has a charming wife, and I believe he would do the best job of anyone as Director of the Junior Year. I suppose Cornell is participating.

I am sorry that Princeton has been discouraging. Rogers was here the other day and hopes sometime to reverse the trend at Harvard and persuade the faculty to send a few juniors. Meanwhile we hope at Yale to make an even stricter and therefore better choice next year, sending ten or twelve students. Collignon is in charge of that and is doing very well, aware of all the elements to be weighed in every case. As soon as the program becomes better known, I believe it will not be difficult to persuade people to grant fellowships.

I hope to see you at the MLA meeting, although there will not be time to say much there in the big crowd. I hope you will not allow lecturers favoring German reconstruction to have it all their own way in preaching to American colleges the necessity of strengthening Germany at the expense of the rest of Europe. I hope I can be considered as one who is not anti-German, but merely a good European. I have sent you an article on the topic which I wrote this last week. I believe it would be proper for you and Randolph Macon to have a change in your visitors and to think of some other Frenchmen first. There is safety in variety. Otherwise and after we have spoken in New York, I could run down sometime during the early part of February. My boat fails to sail when she was scheduled to, and though my semi-sabbatical leave will begin February 1st I am afraid I may not leave until the end of the month.

My best regards to your wife.

Sincerely yours,
Hri Peyre

## À Vera Lee:

Ce 6 février 1949

Dear Mrs. Lee:

Puis-je vous demander quelles sont exactement vos intentions pour l'année prochaine? Voulez-vous trouver un poste dans l'enseignement quelque part, avec (ou — God forbid! — sans) votre mari? Songeriez-vous à poursuivre ici, ce qui veut dire examens de langue & latin dit vulgaire, et, corvées pénibles pour vous qui avez toujours l'air si joyeuse & sans souci! En ce cas, demandez-vous une bourse? Je vais peu au bureau ces jours-ci, mais vous pouvez toujours me dire d'un mot vos projets, & mes collègues & moi vous aiderons de notre mieux.

Bien à vous & mon bon souvenir à votre mari,
Henri Peyre

## À Pierre Bédard:

Ce 12 — ii — 49

Cher Ami,

Tous mes regrets pour Ste. Fare Garneau. Il a dû retarder quelque peu son départ.

Je sais peu de précis sur Maurice Merleau-Ponty. Il doit être né en 1906, entra à l'École Normale Supérieure en 1926, est agrégé de philosophie & professeur à la Faculté des Lettres de Lyon.

Il s'est placé tout de suite au premier rang des philosophes français de sa génération. Il est le psychologue et, en un sens, le vrai philosophe de l'Existentialisme. Ses livres sont: un volume technique, *la Structure du Comportement,* 1942, Presses Universitaires; *Phénoménologie de la Perception,* 1945, Gallimard très importante thèse, analysant la perception du point de vue de la phénoménologie. Il publiait en même temps de nombreux articles dans lesquels il appliquait la phénoménologie & la psychologie existentialiste à la littérature, à l'art & à la politique. Un remarquable article sur Cézanne dans la revue *Fontaine* a été très remarqué & a ouvert sur Cézanne des perspectives neuves.

Il a fait partie dès le début de l'équipe des Temps Modernes, où il a publié une série d'articles qui firent du bruit, *le Yogi & le Prolétaire.* Il essayait, en gros, d'y proposer l'existentialisme, au lieu du marxisme, comme philosophie de la classe ouvrière & des mouvements révolutionnaires. Il a depuis repris d'autres articles dans un volume, *Humanisme et Terreur, essai sur le problème communiste,* 1947, Gallimard.

C'est un esprit de premier ordre, &, je crois, avec le sens du concret. Simone de Beauvoir a défini le mouvement existentialiste comme un effort pour "comprendre concrètement l'abstrait": cela s'applique bien, je crois, à Merleau-Ponty.

En hâte & bien fidèlement,
Henri Peyre

## To Joseph Barker:

Feb. 13—1949

Dear Barker:

I am imposing too much on you, with your visit to N. York & all the tiring business of the details connected with the Junior Year abroad, & still making you write letters & arrange plans for my visit. I am ashamed of putting you to such inconvenience!

Just one word to say that, if possible, I shall try to reserve space on the early morning train of Thursday from Monroe to N. York; & the only favor I would thus ask would be to have a taxi ordered to take me to the station on Thursday morning.

If you wish me to appear at an 18th century class, I shall be glad to do so, though I claim no especial competence in the field. I could give a general exposé of the Idea of Progress in the 18th century, if you like, a subject important for both French & English majors; and sum up an article I have appearing soon in the Journal of the History of Ideas on "The Influence of 18th century Philosophy on the French Revolution," also a subject of general interest.

It will be ample time if you tell me on Wednesday morning.

Most cordially,
Hri Peyre

## To the same:

Feb. 18—1949

My dear Barker,

Again, my very heartfelt thanks. You & your wife are magnificent examples of cordiality, of devotion—& of efficient achievement. What you have put through with the Junior Year is truly splendid: it has won respect at once, & high standing. Sweet Briar has conquered Yale & Harvard at one stroke—It is due, in very large measure, to you & your wife.

I enjoyed my visit very much. Your girls are among the finest anywhere in America: their questions were very shrewd. You train them well.

I found a letter from Miss X asking me to put in a word for her when I should see you. Well—I don't know her much directly—Y., who knew her at Wells, would speak of her, & most unfavorably. She is cultured, refined—but terribly bad tempered & notoriously hard to get along with. She seems to have brought trouble wherever she has been, & she has been in 3 or 4 places. I frankly would hesitate before calling her to a relatively small community like Sweetbriar.

This is uncharitable—but I want to serve you rather than this lady—with whom, personally, I got along well when I met her at Wells &, once, in New Haven.

Couldn't you find someone younger?

> Sincerely & with renewed thanks & regards to your wife,
> Hri Peyre

Thanks for the generous check, duly received.

## À Mario Maurin:

Ce 20—ii—1949

Mon cher ami,

Je ne sais si j'ai eu raison pour vous conseiller de travailler dans un siècle (le 17e) pour lequel il se peut que vous ayez peu de goût. Parlez un peu avec M. Boorsch là-dessus et à M. May, à qui cette période a bien réussi, car elle lui a valu (ainsi que ses dons) plusieurs offres ailleurs, assez flatteuses. Peu d'Américains se sentent qualifiés pour ce siècle dit classique.

Il y a à faire dans la poésie de cette époque. Cela vous dirait-il? Jean de Sponde, La Cépède, Tristan l'Hermite (on a écrit sur ce dernier). J'avais souvent songé à des thèmes plus vastes, qui ont fait hésiter, mais qui pourraient vous séduire: le thème de la mort dans la poésie du 17e siècle; ou la poésie pure au 17e siècle, envisagée selon un coup d'œil moderne, retrouvée chez divers poètes dont La Fontaine.

Si vous aimez l'histoire, il serait tentant de suivre par exemple la peinture du moi (& la sincérité envers soi-même) dans les mémoires du 17e siècle. Ou le portrait & la psychologie de la femme dans ces mêmes mémoires.

Gilles Boileau, le père Bouhours, Furetière surtout sont des gens très curieux. Mad. Dacier & l'hellénisme & la traduction du grec au 17e siècle mériteraient une monographie; Mazon a une petite brochure sur elle. Les idées sur l'art antique au 17e siècle seraient aussi curieuses à explorer.

La Motte le Vayer devrait tenter quelqu'un, après Pintard. Et Retz (si Kosciusko n'achève pas sur lui sa thèse commencée), ou St Evremont, sur qui Ternois ne terminera sans doute jamais.

Sur St Simon, il n'y a presque rien.

À une autre époque, Lautréamont serait-il de votre gibier?

Au fond il est bien peu de sujets communs à la France & à l'Espagne (à part Cervantès en France, fait; Ruben Dario, fait; l'Espagne et les romantiques français, fait). Il y aurait une énorme enquête à entreprendre sur la connaissance de la langue & de la littérature espagnoles en France au 17e siècle—du genre de celle d'Ascoli pour l'Angleterre. Une autre (peu suivie & toute brisée) sur l'Espagne chez les écrivains français depuis 1870 ou 80; Barrès, Montherlant, Lacretelle & d'autres. Mais je vous les conseille peu.

Je vois que je vous connais trop peu pour vous aider en connaissance de cause. Vous êtes très mystérieux, en partie timidité sans doute, en partie défi juvénile à la vie qui intimide à son tour vos aînés, en partie aussi originalité qui vous a fait "puissant & solitaire"? Avez-vous quelque goût très marqué pour Racine, Pascal, St Simon, Fénelon (pourquoi pas? il est très curieux & peu connu).

Justement je reçois & dois renvoyer cet article en épreuves. Voulez-vous le regarder, y signaler à Katie des erreurs car il doit en rester, & le rendre à Katie pour qu'elle le renvoie avant le 23 ou 24? Peut-être vous aidera-t-il à voir ce qui se fait dans le 17e siècle?

Bien à vous,
Henri P.

## To Robert G. Cohn:

February 24, 1949

Mr. Robert G. Cohn
258 Augur Street
Hamden, Connecticut

Dear Mr. Cohn:

I could not wait to read your work on *Un Coup de Dés*. I read it almost as soon as you brought it. It is, in its present somewhat sketchy form of a rough draft, an extremely impressive piece of work. You certainly know Mallarmé as well as any man alive and, I believe, more deeply than any, and you utilize with the best academic method all the hints and sometimes remote assistance provided by any allusions of contemporaries of the poet. What is more, of course, you have gone very deep into the structure of his mind, and I sincerely believe you have revealed him to be a greater metaphysical genius than I and most others suspected. Your thesis is packed with far-reaching remarks and with original thought. It contains all the elements, not only of a substantial contribution to knowledge, but of an outstanding work of exegetic interpretation of the most difficult poem of any literature.

Naturally, your success is due to the fact that there happened to be an almost preordained correspondence between the poem and all your own philosophical views on dual polarity, the masculine and feminine principles, the vertical, horizontal meanings, etc. Such pre-established harmony should almost lead you into believing in providence, perhaps even in a non-Marxist God. The promises you hold out repeatedly of more commentaries on Mallarmé are extremely alluring. I honestly believe you have enough here to work on for four or five years. I do not feel competent to discuss most of the detailed points which you bring up and I agree that your explanation must be accepted in toto. However, I hope you will understand if I make a few remarks which may help improve this draft and turn it into a somewhat more artistic thesis. Most of my notes are of a purely practical character, but they are the points to which readers of a dissertation often attach much importance.

1. Your footnotes are often too long and detract one's attention from the text. What you say in them is most valuable. Could you not integrate more of them into the text (e.g. pp. 36–7, 39, 44, etc.)?

2. The style is, and is bound to be, philosophical and even math-

ematical. I wish all the same that you would avoid some of the difficulty (e.g. p. 15) which makes the reading of your masterpiece truly a little painful. I believe it is possible to pull down some of the hurdles that deep minds like yours like to place before themselves and the readers.

3. The conventions require that one add a bibliography to a thesis, and you might make this bibliography only a list of all the passages in Mallarmé which are directly relevant to the *Coup de Dés*.

4. And this is my only really important criticism. Could you not divide your work into chapters and thus make one feel the progression to your fine conclusion? You would thus lead your readers to share your opinions more gradually and more convincingly. Could you not, for instance, separate an important introductory chapter from the bulk of the work and explain and define your method in it and also present *Un Coup de Dés* as the aim and climax of all Mallarmé's efforts and of most 19th-century poetry? You would thus enhance the significance of your subject for the lay readers, who should not be scorned, for they may thus be attracted to Mallarmé. In the same way, a chapter of conclusions summing up your points and reassessing the *Coup de Dés* both as a great philosophical poem and as a work of art would be very useful. Generally speaking, if I were you, I would stress far more than you have the importance of the *Coup de Dés* as a work of art. Your approach is rather more scientific than esthetic. Could not the two be fused into one, at least to some extent? In other words, and you recognize my old criticism, why not temper and sweeten your *ostinato rigore* with a little more of the suave grace of what you call the feminine principle?

I am dictating this letter so that your readers, when the time comes, may see both what an extremely high opinion I have of your very original thesis and the few criticisms which I am presenting in order to help you improve upon it. As you remember, I have asked Messrs. Boorsch, Douglas, and May to be your readers.

Will you remind your wife of the date of her examination, Tuesday afternoon, March 1st, probably at two o'clock, and give her our best wishes? By the way, [Charles] Mauron committed a "Psychanalyse d'Hérodiade" in Cahiers du Sud, no. 291, 1948, pp. 288–297.

My congratulations.

Sincerely yours,<br>Henri Peyre

## À Saint-John Perse:

Ce 3 mars 1949

Mon cher Maître,

J'ai reçu votre magnifique don, amicalement dédicacé et je suis infiniment touché de votre aimable et généreuse pensée. Je désirais beaucoup lire ce livre, le seul de vos ouvrages, je crois, que je n'avais pas réussi à me procurer. Il est plus beau encore que les autres très beaux poèmes que vous aviez fait paraître depuis la guerre, et je le goûterai plus profondément encore quand je l'aurai relu plusieurs fois. Ce très précieux don a ravivé en moi les souvenirs de ces moments de conversation d'une richesse éblouissante que nous avons eu la joie d'avoir chez les La Grange. Je m'étais souvent dit depuis que quelqu'un aurait dû noter vos propos et pensées ainsi prodiguées à vos interlocuteurs. Et puis, relisant récemment quelques-uns de ces volumes de pensées et de pointes où Valéry s'est trop imprudemment répété et vidé, je me suis dit que, de tous nos grands contemporains, c'est vous qui aviez choisi la meilleure part et aviez les plus sûres chances de durer.

Merci très profondément et avec mes très sincères et respectueux sentiments,

Henri Peyre

## À Claude Vigée:

Ce 5 mars 49

Mon cher Ami,

C'est au moment de m'échapper vers l'Europe sur le De Grasse que je vous remercie enfin de votre papier, utile & précis, sur vous. J'espère, dans les années qui vont venir, en faire bon usage. J'ai conservé le souvenir, à Columbus, d'un milieu agréable à bien des égards pour vous, & qui vous estime fort. Mais tôt ou tard vous voudrez bien sûr une atmosphère plus propice encore, et je ne dis pas plus stimulante, mais mieux apte à être par vous stimulée.

Si votre article est en français, il gagnerait à paraître dans une bonne revue française — Cela est estimé ici, & vous maintient en France dans l'esprit d'un public qui, un jour, doit être le "juge" de vos poèmes. Pour de l'érudition pure, ce serait mieux en Amérique. Mais vous dépasserez toujours la pure, c'est à dire stricte, érudition.

J'espère me reposer un peu en France, flâner, & écrire aussi. Et vous? À quand le voyage de retour pour vous retremper un peu? Le bébé va-t-il bien? Mes amitiés à votre femme & aux Pradal. Quel couple charmant de ferveur intérieure & de générosité spirituelle!

Bien à vous,
Hri Peyre

## À sœur Marie-Louise Hubert:

Ce 7 mars 1949

Ma chère sœur Marie Louise,

Je suis littéralement à quelques minutes de m'embarquer, mais je veux vous rendre ce chapitre que j'ai pu lire hier, pour ne pas vous le garder au delà des mers! Qui sait quel serait son sort?

Et aussi je tenais à vous dire quel excellent chapitre ceci est: vous montrez une belle vigueur d'esprit; vous possédez & dominez à fond le sujet; vous avez mûri longuement vos réflexions sur le plan de Pascal, ingénieusement utilisé les plus récents travaux, & tissé tout cela en un ensemble harmonieux, personnel & vraiment fort.

Je n'ai que de l'approbation & des compliments à offrir, vous le voyez, & c'est pourquoi j'étais dans l'impatience de vous les communiquer. Je ne vois pas de grosses objections, ou même d'objections à présenter, ni qu'on puisse vous en présenter à un chapitre aussi achevé.

Simplement pp. 12–13 le passage sur le dialogue est original, mais un peu gauchement présenté ici, un peu abrupt, & pas tout à fait assez développé pour être convaincant. Vous pourriez en faire une digression un peu plus considérable.

p. 18 note 36. La Bruyère surprend un peu parmi les apologistes ou auteurs chrétiens qui ont fait usage du pari. Il est chrétien, mais assez peu.

Sur le pari, les ancêtres de l'argument étudiés par Blanchet, et dans un article de ces dernières années de la Revue Philosophique (était-ce par Le Roy?) méritaient une mention.

p. 37, je ne suis pas très convaincu de la force de l'argument sur les prophéties, malgré le P. Lagrange. Mais elles méritent peut-être, ces prophéties, une réhabilitation. Ce sera une grosse affaire

sur Mahomet, l'affirmation de Pascal est un peu faible, & dogmatique.

sur le Dialogue chez Pascal et l'utilisation probable qu'il en aurait faite, ce que vous dites est original. Ce dialogue, comme procédé, est-il vraiment plus "fair," plus loyal pour le libertin que la démonstration ordinaire? ne fait-on pas un peu dire au libertin ce qu'on veut qu'il dise?

Je me demande encore si vous ne devriez pas dire un mot de l'évolution possible, de la chronologie de ces pensées, de l'état différent de la pensée pascalienne & du plan de l'apologie entre 1654 & 1661? Pascal a-t-il d'abord pensé à des dialogues, puis à une démonstration plus théorique? Probablement on ne peut rien dire là-dessus—mais dites au passage que la question doit être résolue par la négative, ou par votre confession d'ignorance. La conférence rapportée par Filleau de la Chaise mentionne-t-elle dialogues & lettres?

Busson a un autre volume récent, qui touche curieusement à l'accueil fait à Pascal. J'en ai dit quelques mots dans un article à paraître dans la prochaine *Romanic Review*.

Mes compliments encore, mes vœux & mes amitiés, chère sœur Marie Louise.

Bien à vous,<br>Henri Peyre

Pardonnez-moi de plier ce beau manuscrit.

## To Joseph Barker:

C/o American Express<br>Rue Scribe<br>Paris (9e)<br>March 31—1949

My dear Barker,

It's a joy to be back here, for a long & leisurely stay. Leisure, I haven't yet had, but it will come. There are so many people to see, so many old friends and colleagues, and such a variety of shows, of art galleries. Things are plentiful; people seem to enjoy life & not to worry about war or politics: the situation is stabilized. But prices are high. How people manage is a mystery to me.

You will, I am sure, Mrs. Barker & you, have a very happy summer if you come again—refreshing & heart-warming at once. We may be gone in the country by then—if not, I shall count on seeing you. Thus far, I have tried to resist all engagements except visits, but I may go to Italy to give some lectures in May.

I have been to Reid Hall twice already, to attend a reception given by Miss Leet for the Ambassador, & to see the Anderssons & the group. My impression of the juniors is *excellent:* the boys in particular have matured, reason very ably on America, France, education, art. The gain is imponderable, but enormous in them—Their French is fine, fluent, uninhibited—but their general development & their intelligence of life have gained more than anything. It's a fine organization, this Junior Year, & it must go on. It does more than whole groups of diplomats, than propaganda, tourists, & all the rest.

Tug has done a good job, so has Miss Monaco. They have been deans, teachers, organizers, parents, advisers at once. They have been extraordinarily devoted. I hope you will have a similar success with all their successors.

I thought I would take the liberty to mention two points which struck me in particular, & I am doing so, of course, as an objective observer and a well-wisher to your very happy & successful Junior plan. The first is this: the cost of living is now very high in Paris, practically as high as in America. Both Andersson & Miss Monaco have to spend much more than they get—just to live, go about & "represent," see the French professors. It has been ruinous on them. In all honesty, I believe the professor in charge should get 9 or 10,000 dollars, his assistant 4,500 or 5,000. It seems high in terms of American college salaries, seems very high in French francs, but really represents the actual expenses they have to incur, without any luxury or lavishness. I believe you would readily agree if you took charge for a year—Maybe such a desirable adjustment can be effected in the future. Could not any compensation for the heavy extra expenses incurred by the present Director & his assistant be found *this* year? It would only be just. Andersson has not told me (he is too much of a gentleman), but I gather he had to borrow heavily in order to see this year through. True, he had his two children. But they would have cost him just as much at school in America.

The second point, connected with the first, is: obviously Sweetbriar cannot by itself fund the increase in funds which you will, I believe, find indispensable for the staff in charge in Paris plus scholarships for American students. What about Fulbright funds—the help of some foundation—or maybe a campaign to get a contribution from the participating colleges? The first & second possibilities must be feasible, & preferable to the third. Are they in the realm of the truly feasible? Would not your President approach a Foundation to help the Junior Year be started on a very solid basis, & become all it must be as an instrument for cultural cooperation among nations? What is your feeling on all this? I hope I am not indiscreet in thus meddling?

Are you & your wife well? Many very good wishes & renewed thanks again for your fine & cordial welcome to Sweetbriar last month.

Will you offer my thanks to Mrs. Levi d'Ancona for her kind letter & my congratulations on Vivaldo's marriage? He is a very fine young man, keen, sensitive, courageous with sweetness, and deserving all the happiness I hope he will get.

Very sincerely yours,<br>
Hri Peyre

## To Charles Seymour:

April 1—1949<br>
C/o American Express<br>
Rue Scribe, Paris (9)

Dear President Seymour:

I was much touched by your kind note wishing me a pleasant trip to France. I have enjoyed the change greatly, although it has provided little real rest thus far: there were a number of things I had to do in Paris in connection with our exchanges of scholars & professors (Paris-Yale), with the Fulbright committees to prepare the way for colleagues & graduate students planning to come over next year, etc.—I am afraid, in spite of very firm resolutions to devote most of my time to rest & research, I shall have to accept a few lectures in London & Oxford, in

Rome & Florence, & a few talks on America & American education which the American cultural attaché feels I can do in France without laying myself open to suspicions of being a "Marshall Plan cultural imperialist." There is some misunderstanding in Europe of American motives & policy, partly, I believe, on account of inadequate presentation of the true spirit of America by Washington, & by the French press. But on the whole the great majority of sensible people are behind the "Third" or middle Force, & sympathetic to America unreservedly. The economic recovery is very real: France is now a land of plenty. Prices are high; a deflation is beginning and the problem will be for the French to export. But one can be hopeful — & life here is enjoyable.

The Comité France-Amérique wrote you a letter, or two letters, on March 10 & 25, on their "Congrès" of June–July. I do not suppose you will be in France then, or will care to spend much time on those official festivities and lectures. I could represent Yale if you wished me to, since I shall be present at least for one day at the "Congrès" & am due to give a talk on American University life at one of the sessions. But if an American professor from Yale were to be in France then, & willing to spend a few hours on this representation, I believe it would be even better — preferably a member of your Faculty able to speak French with some ease.

I hope you & Mrs. Seymour are well & will enjoy a little rest in April. The spring is already far advanced here & the weather mild.

With best regards & very sincerely,
Henri Peyre

## To John W. Kneller:

c/o American Express
Rue Scribe
Paris (IX)
April 14 — 1949

My dear Kneller:

Many thanks for your kind & interesting letter, just received. I am very glad, of course, to hear from you, & anyone else, & much pleased with the news of your success in negotiating a new issue of the *Yale*

*French Studies*, no 1. You are not only a thorough & penetrating scholar, & one whose achievement at Yale has gratified me highly, but a very shrewd & efficient man of affairs. Your career will lead you straight to a University Presidency, in time, & you will be a good money-getter (in the best sense) as well as a respected administrator. This is a success. I believe you will not only help the prestige of the magazine & of our Department, but score a financial success also. It will take some advertising to sell the new 2000 copies, but it is worth the effort & I am pretty sure they will be disposed of, over the years.

I should be glad if you would accept my order for 10 copies (ten) now anyway—& if you find that reprints with covers are possible, I should also like fifty (50) such reprints of my own Existentialist contribution—all at my own cost, of course.

I believe you are right to have selected the Theatre as a topic for another issue. The topic will interest, & will sell the issue easily—& one cannot altogether neglect this aspect, as you know—And a great deal can be done on the French theatre which has not lately been attempted in America—Collignon, Boorsch, others among our younger men would be excellent contributors, & several men from outside. I suppose you could not envisage illustrations, as the Theatre Arts Magazine has? If you plan to approach French writers (Claudel? Salacrou? Gabriel Marcel? Simone de Beauvoir?), the time might be now.

If Katie will send me my number of the third issue, I shall enjoy reading it here—I hope I shall have a little time for reading this summer. It doesn't look as if I shall have much before then—

As to your own plans, as you may have heard from Mr. Boorsch, with your GI bill & 20.000 frs. a month next year, things should look fair for you & your wife—If, of course, the Fulbright bill would be available for you, it would be even better, & real luxury. I don't believe they allow continuing Fulbright assistance & another fellowship, such as the French Govt. would give you. But the Government Fellowship is assured, anyway—& you'll choose when & if. . . .

I suppose it's true that there is little influence of Rousseau on V[ictor] H[ugo] the poet—he praised Voltaire (& Rabelais) more warmly. Are you reading his *William Shakespeare*, too, & his *Litt. & philosophie mêlées*, etc. The man is exasperating, but he is undeniably big.

Your crop might be richer with Nerval—& Sainte-Beuve the poet, certainly—& the smaller ones. If your subject proved not rich enough, you might take in the prose-poetry too (Maurice de Guérin, Lamennais), but a thesis need not be big in size—& I know yours will be thorough, & good.

Our regards to your wife & our best wishes for the spring—& then for your trip.

Sincerely,<br>Henri Peyre

A. Vigny (2 vols. Ed. de la Pléiade) came out & I ordered it for Yale—I forget whether Chadbourne told me he had found a Renan (2 vols. Calmann Lévy, each including 4 volumes of Renan) or had not & looked for it. I heard of one set of 2 vols. at 2500 francs the two. Hasn't the Library received it? The *Revue de Métaphysique* had a good article on Rousseau's religion.

## À Georges May:

14 avril 1949

Mon cher ami,

J'aurais dû plus tôt vous complimenter de cette nouvelle tentative qu'on fait pour vous arracher à Yale. Le monde américain tout entier conspire contre nous, et peut-être pour vous. Quelle chance que vous nous aimiez d'abord, et soyez resté avec nous, et aussi que vous soyez resté modeste et parfois même défiant de vous-même! Il n'y a rien de tel, d'ailleurs, que le mariage (laver la vaisselle, se couper les doigts en ouvrant les pamplemousses, se les noircir en cirant les souliers de sa femme, se les brûler en faisant griller des toasts, se voir critiqué par l'épouse quand on veut acheter soi-même ses cravates) pour vous rappeler à la modestie. Mais votre succès auprès des Américains est littéralement exceptionnel et témoigne en votre faveur en tous les sens, car, quoi qu'on en dise, ce sont gens difficiles. . . .

Malheureusement beaucoup de "demandes" m'ont rogné mes loisirs ici, et je ne vais que peu à la Nationale. Conférences çà et là, visites, contacts à établir ou à rétablir, commissions d'histoire littéraire, etc., etc. Je me sens plus pris qu'à Yale, mais pris aussi par les plaisirs de Paris, le théâtre, les plantureux repas, la joie de la rue, les discussions vaines et charmantes. Les gens sont calmes, parlent peu de politique et peu de l'avenir, jouissent intensément du présent. Vous faites de même sans doute, dans le bonheur de vie partagée, donc décuplée. . . .

**Au même:**

De Viareggio<br>Du 2 juin 1949

Mon cher Georges May,

Vos dernières lettres me sont arrivées à Rome—par un curieux hasard le jour même où je rencontrais dans une très belle villa de la Campagne romaine, chez une dame exquise, un des fils de Gillet dont la jeune femme me parlait de vous. . . .

Notre voyage en Italie s'achève heureusement. C'est une tâche parfois lourde que de conduire une voiture trop grosse pour ces routes, à travers des tournants qui montrent le dégoût de ce peuple, et de sa géographie, pour la ligne droite. Mais nous prendrons 2 ou 3 jours de repos pour la Pentecôte (on oubliait en Amérique combien cette fête compte en Europe), puis regagnerons lentement Paris. Après n'avoir accepté que de mauvaise grâce des conférences, j'en ai été satisfait car les auditoires m'ont paru très fins et très au courant, et j'ai rencontré par ce moyen beaucoup d'Italiens intéressants qu'on n'aperçoit pas en touriste. . . .

Sur la partie critique, je dirais seulement ceci: nos étudiants ne se rendent pas toujours compte de ce qui leur faut ou leur convient le mieux, ou de ce que nous voulons faire, progressivement, de notre Département. 1) les cours de "survey" ou traitant de tout un genre, toute une période, appartiennent plutôt à l'"undergraduate college" et les étudiants venus d'ailleurs, parfois insuffisamment préparés à cet égard, devraient les prendre là. 2) Il est très difficile et peut-être nuisible de tracer une ligne tranchée séparant les chefs-d'œuvre des œuvres dites secondaires. Où mettra-t-on D'Aubigné, Scève, les libertins, Marivaux, Laclos (ô Mohrt!), Nerval, Renan, etc.? 3) Surtout, plus encore qu'à l'"orals," où nos jeunes gens peuvent se préparer seuls à la rigueur, les cours doivent conduire à du travail personnel qui amènera à un sujet de thèse, souvent sur un auteur secondaire: c'est là la grosse pierre d'achoppement pour nos étudiants. C'est dans des cours un peu spécialisés qu'ils acquièrent la méthode de travail, vont en profondeur. Des trous! Ils en ont, en auront longtemps, comme nous en avions et en avons encore. Et quand nous donnons des cours sur "un" auteur, nous ne manquons pas d'élargir le sujet en touchant à d'autres qui l'avoisinent, à de plus vastes problèmes. . . .

## Au même:

Du 6 août 1949

Mon cher ami,

Votre aimable lettre du 28 juillet m'atteint à Bormes (Var) où je suis pour 7 ou 8 jours encore. Je suis heureux que votre session se soit bien passée, bien que vous sembliez sans enthousiasme excessif sur les résultats. Il est doublement difficile de faire réussir quelque chose de neuf dans le Sud, et peut-être nos vacances sont-elles trop précieuses? Personnellement j'ai souvent travaillé l'été et ne le déteste pas — mais un nouveau marié! . . .

J'ai travaillé un peu ici, mais toujours des tas de petites bribes d'articles déjà promis — et je ne fais rien de bien longue haleine. Le pays est très beau; et écrire devant la mer et les montagnes, parmi les eucalyptus, mimosas, pins capricieux, est un fréquent sujet de distraction! Mais je me sens baigné de nature et reposé. Cela est beaucoup.

La France était en effet splendide cette année. Il y a certes encore bien des difficultés à l'horizon, mais cela va remarquablement bien dans l'ensemble; et la gaieté des gens est frappante. Chants, danses, rires . . . mais aussi on redevient obèse (j'ai grossi moi-même), on se gorge d'apéritifs, on procrée des enfants sans compter.

## To John W. Kneller:

Aug. 16 — 1949

Dear Mr. Kneller:

Thank you for your last letter & detailed statement on the *Y[ale] Fr[ench] Studies*. It is beautifully clear & on the whole comforting. We hope, next year, to draw from outside sources & to secure extra help — for we cannot count on any substantial increase in the number of subscribers. As it is Y. F. St. have been a splendid achievement, & much credit is due to you this year for our success, the reprinting of no. 1, &

the fine condition in which your successor will receive the business managership. We shall have a meeting in late Sept., with you if you are still there, & the editors & discuss plans & prospects. Thank you, meanwhile.

The Fulbright help is the most confused bureaucratic mess I have ever heard of! If you &/or others get help through it, so much the better, & accept it by all means, since it will pay better than the French Government scholarship. But one should know some time soon! On what basis & who makes the selection is a mystery to me.

Meanwhile, concentrate on some rest & your work now. If you could possibly complete your thesis for May 1950 & get your degree then for sure, it is a help in securing a position, or is likely to be in the future—not that I am a pessimist on the subject. Yours should & will be a good thesis, & there will always be room for good men.

You are free to limit your subject as you think fit, when you have enough substance, & when you have made an organic outline. My own feeling was still that the subject might be a bit slim if limited to the so-called four "big" poets, but I may be wrong. I should think that, on the one hand, the actual imitations & mentions of Rousseau must not be very many by 1830–1840—on the other hand, Rousseau's influence had then acted powerfully through several decades & through more immediate transmitters (G. Sand, Chateaubriand, Obermann, etc.), so that poets needed little recourse to Rousseau himself. But this very fact is interesting, & your work should obviously go beyond mere mentions of Rousseau, to Rousseauistic themes in 1830–1840: solitude, misanthropy, praise of wild or primitive life, suicide, memory of happiness previously enjoyed by lovers, etc. Important points, deriving in some manner from Rousseau, must be: religiosity, natural religion, God in nature, etc. (Vicaire savoyard)—goodness of the child, praise of "education of nature" in the Wordsworthian sense—Hugo, "Ce qui se passait aux Feuillantines" in Rayons & Ombres, etc.—love & sin, nature, etc. as depicted in La Nouvelle Héloïse—a general feeling of bitter rebellion against the State, all social laws & conventions—; perhaps some influence of Rousseau's sensuous scenes in les *Confessions*.

Of course, it is difficult not to take into account what may have passed from Rousseau to Byron, to Lamennais, Lamartine, & influenced other Romantics that way, indirectly.

I recently went through the 2 vol. edition of Vigny in the Pléiade edition. No index, alas. But Vigny (besides La Sauvage) mentions Rousseau in *Stello,* thinks of him as a persecuted writer, & alludes to him often in *Journal d'un poète* (vol. ii, pp. 1076, 8, 1088, 1170, 1183, 1288, 1298. The volumes must be at Yale.

Maxime Leroy has some mentions of Rousseau in Quinet, Ballanche, etc. in his Histoire des Idées sociales en France (Gallimard 1947, I believe), a confused book, & not much in your line—I mean, more of political thought—

Maurice de Guérin might be worth your while, as well as Nerval & Sainte Beuve?

Excuse these hasty notes. I shall look forward to seeing you in late September. Any progress on Proust & la musique?

Yours,<br>
Henri Peyre

## To James F. Mathias:

[letterhead: Yale University]<br>
October 5, 1949

Mr. James Mathias
John Simon Guggenheim Memorial Foundation
551 Fifth Avenue
New York, New York
Dear Mr. Mathias:

Thank you for your autobiographical note. It was a pleasure to deal with you here when you were one of our important administrators, and it will now be a pleasure again to deal with you in your capacity as Associate Secretary. I always had, for very good reasons, an extremely high respect for Mr. Moe's judgment, and this will be strengthened by the decision he has made to associate you with him.

I shall be pleased of course to continue pointing out to you the eventual candidates who in my opinion would do most credit to the highly coveted Guggenheim fellowships and who are considered by most of us as most promising in our field. As you may know, one of the points I made repeatedly in the last few years in the correspondence with Mr. Moe was the necessity to go back to rather younger scholars of promise and already of positive achievement. It seems to me that only very exceptionally should men over 45 and already well known and probably well paid in their profession be appointed. However, a slight embarrassment due to the fact that although I am familiar with quite a number of men in the country at large among the scholars in romance languages, I often feel obliged to mention Yale men among the top ones. The reason is obvious: If I know of any men who are first rate I naturally do my best to bring them here to our department. . . .

## To Joseph Barker:

October 10, 1949

Professor Joseph E. Barker
Department of Romance Languages
Sweet Briar College
Sweet Briar, Virginia
My dear Barker:

I too have retained excellent memories of our brief but pleasant meeting in Paris. I hope you and your wife are well, and I wish you a happy year for the Junior Year program.

In reply to your inquiries, I should say without much hesitation that C. F. is not one of the very best men for the position of professor-in-charge. He is one of our own Ph.D.'s and certainly not one of the best. He teaches well I hear, although on the scholarly side he was just passable, and he has been in France and I think courageous and efficient during the war. Even so, I doubt he would be the man most likely to make a success of the year over there and to become readily persona grata with the French.

The second candidate, Wylie, is unknown to me, but I know that Miss Monaco had a high opinion of him. There is another Wiley at the university of North Carolina at Chapel Hill who would be a splendid man, and he is happy enough to have a very nice wife. You might look into his case. I do not believe I have met him.

I cannot think of anyone at Harvard but MacAllister, and Douglas Alden at Princeton as well as Frohock and Frame of Columbia are probably known to you. Borglum of Wayne and Samuel Will of Indiana might also be excellent directors. Since the expense of the director-in-charge, it might perhaps be better to appoint someone who would be getting less than the sum allowed over there in his present position. This obviously mean a younger man, while Will and Borglum are both chairmen of their departments. On the Pacific Coast there is a very capable and charming gentleman at Stanford University whose name unfortunately escapes me right now. He speaks perfect French, has lived in France long although he is a specialist in Spanish. He and his wife are extremely intelligent and would I think appeal to the French people very much. He was acting chairman of the department when I visited over there in 1948, and he is of English birth. There is also a young gentleman called Eustis at Berkeley who speaks admirable French (his wife too), and has most of the qualifications for the position. He used to do a good deal of work as the right-hand man of the chairman of the department.

Other names may occur to me in the next few weeks, and I shall let you know of them. Meanwhile I shall of course be glad to write to Dean Brooks about Mr. Damon, Junior.

Many regards to your wife.

Very sincerely yours,<br>
Hri Peyre<br>
Chairman

**To James Mathias:**

October 13, 1949

. . . We should, however, continue getting the very best men for the Guggenheim fellowships and I suppose a good way might be to offer marked encouragement as to the prospects of publication for the book which a Guggenheim fellowship should normally produce. The difficulty of getting scholarly books published has become so great that it is hampering the efforts of the promising young men. Unless the foundations step in and give us some help, the whole condition of American intellectual activities in the scholarly field will soon become tragic.

I shall send you, as soon as I have a little more time, a selective bibliographical notice of some of the things I have published in the last few years, since you include those in your yearly reports.

Sincerely yours,<br>
Henri Peyre<br>
Chairman

## To Joseph Barker:

Oct. 20 — 1949

Dear Mr. Barker:

This is the answer — not too hopeful.

Frohock, I hear, is not interested in going to Paris with the Juniors — Have you thought of others?

Enclosed for your library — if it has any funds for such library purchases. The book [Robert Greer Cohn, *Mallarmé's Un Coup de Dés*] is by a young colleague & original, though difficult.

## À Pedro Salinas:

Ce 28 octobre 1949

Cher Collègue — & cher Ami,

J'ai passé sept mois en France (et en Italie) et ne suis rentré que fin septembre. Parmi la masse de revues & de papiers qui m'attendait, j'ai trouvé votre volume. J'ai attendu d'avoir un peu de loisir pour le savourer. Quel (sic) admirable série d'essais, discontinus et ondoyants en apparence, mais en vérité graves, acharnés même et animés par la belle unité d'un professeur, d'un poète & d'un savant qui est un *homme* & lutte pour le meilleur de notre héritage humaniste. Comme vous avez raison de défendre, avec chaleur & humour, avec d'ingénieuses digressions et une culture de gentilhomme qui jouit de ce qu'il a lu, la lettre, la lecture, les droits de la minorité littéraire ("c'est toujours dans la majorité qu'il y a le plus d'imbéciles," disait A. France) & la langue! Et vous écrivez une prose si spirituelle, si fine, si gracieusement exempte de toute rhétorique, & qui sait couler avec aisance même pour dire un message grave! Un tel livre, l'un des plus charmants depuis les essais de Virginia Woolf que je connaisse, devrait être classique dans les cours d'espagnol.

Que je vous envie, vivant en Amérique, d'avoir pu échapper à la mécanisation, au trop lourd labeur, au dessèchement, au pédantisme etc., ... c'est mon plus grand malheur — à l'administration & à l'efficience. Vous, Guillén, quelques autres Espagnols, savez garder votre âme et jouir en hommes de goût & de loisir des lettres & de la vie—Je vous imagine heureux—et un homme vraiment libre!

Merci de m'avoir envoyé ce charmant ouvrage, & très cordialement à vous,

Henri Peyre

## To Harry Levin:

October 31, 49

Dear Mr. Levin:

I found your article on Proust, among a great mass of accumulated mail, on my desk after returning from six or seven months abroad. I finally came around to read it & want to tell you how grateful I am to you for allowing me not to miss it—It enlightens one on a very curious point—And it is impeccably documented. How can you thus keep informed on four or five literatures & the most precise scholarly publications in them?

I believe we have both been asked to take part in a Balzac series of lectures. It is always hard to know what aspect of such an immense subject to elect—& my mind being somewhat open on this, I shall wait for your decision, & Hytier's. Maybe a rather general lecture taking up Balzac's strength & weakness as we see them *today* would be, for me, the easiest & for the audience the most useful. I believe Hytier is more interested in the technique of the novelist. Of course Balzac & his influence on the English and/or American novel would be a magnificent topic—but, I fear, beyond my competence—not beyond yours, however.

With cordial regards,
Henri Peyre

## To Kathryn McBride:

November 11, 1949

Miss Kathryn McBride, President
Bryn Mawr College
Bryn Mawr, Pennsylvania

Dear President McBride:

I am so terribly sorry that I left you so long without any news of my work in progress for the Flexner volume. The truth is that I was full of remorse and of shame for not having moved ahead as quickly as I had hoped to on this project. My excuses are many and the demands upon my time extraordinarily numerous, and while this volume should have come first, I wanted to devote the most serious part of my time to it and therefore kept doing smaller assignments in the meanwhile. But I have never lost my interest in it, and it was uppermost in my thoughts last spring when I spent some months in France. The trouble with a book on the modern novel is that the modern novel keeps on being born every year and there seems to be no end of trying to catch up with it. Perhaps also I was too rash in refusing to write the lectures as they had been given and in rethinking the book altogether. I believe this would eventually make a better book, but it has meant a considerable delay, for which I again apologize.

May I say that I confidently hope to have the manuscript completed by next fall, 1950, which might enable the Oxford Press to bring the book out by the following spring? I shall keep you informed, and I do hope that you will not think me ungrateful for having caused the Flexner series such a long delay. I have never forgotten your very warm and kind welcome and the great pleasure I had in accepting this honor. Indeed, I felt a little intimidated by it, and that is perhaps why, hoping to make the book better through thinking a little more about it, I kept on deferring it.

Please remember me to my Bryn Mawr colleagues and believe me

Very sincerely yours,
Henri Peyre
Chairman

## To Sister Marie-Louise Hubert:

Nov. 15/1949

Dear Sister Marie Louise:

I only heard that you had had the misfortune to lose your father. May I express my very sincere sympathy? I know that the blow was not unexpected, & he had been sick a long time. But it is none the less cruel; & even the spiritual comforts which you can find in faith & the intellectual comforts which your work & an unusual wisdom & generous devotion to others bring you are of little avail in presence of such bereavement. The sympathy of your friends is, however, real & deep—

I am, very sincerely yours,
Henri Peyre

## To Harry Levin:

Nov. 21—1949

Dear Mr. Levin,

Your subject is a splendid one, & one of which I had often thought—Abraham & Feuillerat had perceived some of its possibilities, but there is much more to be said: on the respective technique of the two novelists, on the "retour des personnages," the "roman d'une société." The theme of sexual inversion, the "grossissement" of some vices, the parallel Hulot-Charlus, etc. I am glad you will be the man to treat it in a definitive way & hope you will publish it soon.

It is kind of you to express your appreciation of Cohn's book. It is ambitious, at times abstruse, but it has depth.

I saw Seznec the other day. His departure will be a loss to all of us. I hope Harvard will make the two or three appointments which should now be necessary, in French. But none will replace him adequately—I was pleased, incidentally, that he had made on his own side the same suggestion that I had: that you be made a Knight of the Legion of Honor à propos of the Balzac centenary—not only as a Balzac scholar, but as one of the men in this country most familiar with, & most original critics of French literature. I hope this will be acted upon with no excessive delay.

With my very best wishes &<br>
Sincerely,<br>
Henri Peyre

### To John W. Kneller:

November 23, 1949<br>
Pension Domecq<br>
70, rue d'Assas<br>
Paris 6<sup>e</sup> France

Dear Mr. Kneller:

I hope your trip went well. Indeed I heard from Tug that it was pleasant. And I hope even more that you are not being discouraged by some of the early difficulties of getting settled in the Ville Lumière which lacks warmth right now. Thanksgiving is that time for expatriates to feel nostalgia.

After you left I took the liberty of writing to Oberlin saying that they could not find a better man than you, and that taking into account your qualifications and the fact that you are practically certain to have your degree by next June, I hoped they would be able to offer you something like $3400 or 3500. I since heard from Mr. Grubbs that they were making you an offer of somewhat less than that, but that if you consulted me before accepting it, I would tell you that it would not be quite final and they would try to raise it somewhat. I hope you will not take this as bargaining on their part but merely as one of those annoying necessities of departmental budgets. In any case you might feel free to let them know that you are interested but that you would not make up your mind right away, if you have strong hopes of getting $3400 or $3500 elsewhere.

Take Paris very patiently and you'll soon like it immensely.

Very sincerely to both of you,<br>
Henri Peyre<br>
Chairman

P.S. Had your letter this morning. Their offer is not quite so bad as you think. Morris was placed at 2600 or 2700. Chadbourne 3000, others at 3200, 3400, just a bit more in one or two places. Yet I believe they should give him 3400 or 3500 and they will, I believe. The relief is to know that you will have a place where to go when you get back is worth $100 less or so.

Sincerely,<br>HP

## À sœur Marie-Louise Hubert:

Nov. 27/49

Chère sœur Marie Louise:

C'est encore un excellent chapitre — très solide & nourri de lectures difficiles, rarement faites dans les textes — bien raisonné & bien conduit — neuf à bien des égards.

Votre position centrale me paraît très juste: qu'il ne faut pas se dépêcher d'appeler janséniste orthodoxe, hérétique telle ou telle position de Pascal, mais que Pascal rentre au fond beaucoup plus dans la position orthodoxe qu'on ne l'a dit, & qu'il a surtout *mis l'accent* de manière autre — Dans la conception centrale, l'originalité des Pensées comme apologie n'était pas tellement grande: & il y a sans doute quelque chose à dire pour l'opinion que, si P. avait achevé son apologie, elle y aurait beaucoup perdu pour la postérité.

N'allez-vous pas un peu loin, page 5, en définissant le but de Pascal de manière aussi nette & en insistant tellement sur la rationalité de la foi? Ne négligez-vous pas le *besoin* psychologique de croire qu'il veut éveiller, la terreur devant l'univers & l'homme?

Je crois que Pascal reste tout de même très original (re pp. 13–14) dans son emploi du pari, par le *ton* passionné de ce développement, par l'*argumentation* serrée qui est la sienne & qui veut emprisonner l'incrédule, par la *place centrale* qu'il semble avoir voulu accorder à cet argument. C'est un des cas où le ton & la place, la passion d'un ancien joueur chez Pascal, font d'une vieillerie une nouveauté surprenante.

Votre passage sur Grotius est intéressant et convaincant. Les emprunts à Martin semblent moins évidents, moins littéraux: et certains de ceux à St Augustin (p. 44) restent un peu lointains aussi. Le mécanisme de transformation par Pascal de certains emprunts possibles à St Augustin est très révélateur. On voit vite poindre chez P. l'amour du dilemme, & presque le goût du sophisme (p. 48 note 81). D'autres passages (p. 54) sur le combat & la victoire, la chasse & la prise que vous voyez en germe chez St Augustin pourraient bien venir aussi de Sénèque & de Cicéron, et devaient être assez banals.

Votre conclusion p. 65, est un peu banale & semble maintenir l'originalité de P. avec respect, mais un peu pour la forme. Il faudrait, je suppose, mieux faire ressortir cette originalité dans une autre partie de votre thèse.

Un chapitre aussi long ne gagnerait-il pas à être divisé en sous-titres, avec un petit sommaire de quelques lignes au début? Le lecteur devrait savoir aussi qu'il y s'agira de Grotius, St Augustin, R. Sebonde, etc.— L'ordre du développement sauterait mieux aux yeux.

J'aimerais revoir le plan complet de votre thèse, pour me rendre compte de la place qu'occuperont les chapitres que je lis détachés.

C'est un travail remarquable & de grande valeur—fortement repensé & réfléchi, bien écrit. . . .

## To Keith Botsford:

December 15, 1949

Mr. Botsford Keith
726 1/2 East Market Street
Iowa City
Iowa
My dear Botsford:

I was surprised to receive a letter from you from such a remote part of the world, but very happy you were well and have decided for a while to return to more conventional studies. Although it shows that you have disciplined yourself and have learned how to submit to pedantic teachers and dry critics, I am convinced you have the strength of character and the originality of inspiration never to become really desiccated. I hope even after some years in the Army, a B.A. at Iowa, and the decision to embark on the ship of married life, you will always retain some element of rebellion in your heart.

I congratulate you on getting married and offer you my very warmest wishes. Of course it is very good news, because it can be both a stabilizing influence and an inspiration for a young man like you who, beneath his occasional fits of unconventionality, conceals a warm heart and a great need for affection. Naturally it will mean also that for a while you will have to live on little money and to feel responsibilities hanging over you. But you are a fighter and obstacles will not daunt you.

It was good news also to hear that the magazine is going on steadily, and I suppose you continue with your own writing. You don't mention your novel, but I hope we may see it in print soon. As to the question of your further study, truth would compel me to say that in comparative literature Harvard has the edge on us. Poggioli, Levin, and two or three others make a more active and a richer than ours (sic) where Wellek is practically single-handed. But either place is very good, and Yale has the advantage of being nearer to New York. You know of course that comparative literature does not lead to positions in teaching quite so easily as a standard subject like English or one modern language and that it is good to combine it with another subject in which a young teacher can find a position. It still seems to me however that your own bent would be towards writing and maybe review or magazine work, and you should perhaps try to combine the two while pursuing your studies.

I am well myself and busy as you always knew me, and hope to go back to Europe next summer in order to enjoy a change. I am sorry I missed you when you came last spring. Please give my best to your wife and to your mother, and believe me,

Very cordially yours,
Henri Peyre
Chairman

# the 1950s
## CHAPTER FOUR

### À Malcolm McIntosh:

Ce 6 janvier 1950

Mon cher Mackintosh:

Il y a de fort bonnes choses dans votre essai de M.A. & je crois que vous pourriez le reprendre pour une thèse. Vous avez fait preuve ici d'une bonne connaissance de Baudelaire, d'une habile utilisation de tous les textes relatifs à votre sujet, d'une familiarité réelle avec l'époque, l'œuvre de Balzac & de Flaubert. Il y a de la méthode, de la précision, de la pénétration & du goût littéraire.

Bien sûr, il y a aussi des gaucheries: le sujet est mal présenté au début, les conclusions sont décevantes; dans le corps des chapitres, l'ordre est un peu flottant, pas assez imposé de haut. Certains points ne sont qu'indiqués. Mais d'un sujet un peu dispersé & morcelé par nature, vous avez tiré quelque chose de bon et d'intéressant.

Il faudrait refaire ces deux chapitres avec plus de méthode, enrichir parfois votre documentation chez les modernes—sur Balzac, que vous sentez avec beaucoup de finesse, il y aurait à fouiller un peu la critique de Balzac par ses contemporains (Sainte Beuve, Revue des 2 Mondes vers 1840–50) & après sa mort, le grand discours d'Hugo à ses funérailles, l'article de Taine, pour faire ressortir l'originalité de Baudel, voyant en lui un visionnaire—à suivre cette notion chez Focillon, "Balzac & Daumier," *Essays in Honor of A. Feuillerat,* Yale Press; Albert Béguin, Balzac visionnaire. J'ai cité aussi Baud. dans un article sur le roman français dans Esquisse de la France par plusieurs auteurs—il faudrait pousser le parallèle entre Balzac & Poe, créateurs du roman détective littéraire, du fantastique intégré dans le roman, maîtres d'un art volontaire & calculé séduisant Baudel—insister sur le rôle de la volonté chez Balzac & la fascination de cela pour Baudel—voir un article sur Baudel & Lavater de Hughes (je crois)—répondre aux reproches de Baudel. puriste sur le style de Balzac (voir Alain, En lisant Balzac—Bardèche, Balzac)—insister aussi sur la vision de Paris chez tous deux—et même sur les lesbiennes & l'amour interdit chez B & Baud (La Fille aux yeux d'or—cf. Proust, Chroniques, article sur Baudel & allusions à l'homosexualité chez Balzac).

Sur Flaubert, où votre chapitre est bon, insister sur l'analogie de leur jeunesse, tous deux dans la même génération: le pessimisme de leur jeunesse, hantise du suicide. Mémoires d'un fou. Voir aussi alors, 1840–48, Alfred le Poittevin, Maxime du Camp—et en général tracer un parallèle entre leur pessimisme (cf. P. Bourget, Essais de Psychologie)—aussi les rapprocher dans la génération de l'art pour l'art—voir le livre d'A. Cassagne & le bon compte rendu de ce livre, à l'époque, par Lanson, dans Rev. Histoire littéraire, et un peu aussi par leur brutalité de surface & leur adoration de la femme, & besoin d'idéalisation (cf. L'Education sentimentale). Il est curieux que Sartre se soit attaqué à tous deux.

Vous pourriez en outre traiter de

Champfleury
Léon Cladel
Nerval
Monnier
Stendhal
Les romans de V Hugo (Misérables)
Peut-être même Chateaubriand
& Laclos & Diderot romancier—

Même ainsi la thèse n'aura jamais beaucoup d'unité, mais elle vaut la peine d'être entreprise: l'unité proviendra de la personnalité (contradictoire) de Baudelaire.

Parlez-en à M. Cornell. Vous pourriez travailler avec lui si vous voulez—

Bien sûr, si une monographie sur Balzac vous attirait davantage, songez-y encore. Mais ici vous avez déjà une bonne partie du travail.

Bien à vous,<br>HP

## To Charles Seymour:

January 16, 1950

Dear President Seymour:

I am sending you a little more information concerning the project that Miss Dorothy Leet, Director of Reid Hall in Paris, discussed with you the other day.

She has had the idea for several years of organizing a summer course in Paris for well-qualified American students. She felt that there was a keen and urgent need for that and also that on the French side it was a very desirable thing to organize such a course in Paris instead of letting American students go to Germany or Switzerland where they often had less to learn, or to commercial travel groups which have set themselves up lately. The project went into actual effect last summer, 1949, when it was sponsored by Bryn Mawr College and directed by Miss Germaine Brée from Bryn Mawr. Although it was started late in the spring and had received only scant notice in the American colleges, it was an immediate success and paid its way financially, even left a slight profit for Bryn Mawr College. Many members of our profession now feel that it would be better all around if an important men's university sponsored it, since there would thus be greater hope that serious students, who want to engage in diplomatic, economic, or business work, could participate in the project. Dean DeVane responded very favorably and advised us to go ahead with the plan: he felt that its cultural importance was great and that Yale should be proud to sponsor this undertaking in closer cultural relations with Europe.

A certain number of students, probably from thirty to fifty, about evenly divided between young men and young women, from good colleges, would make up the group. The total cost for each of them including travel from New York to New York would be $750.00. The prequisites are four years of French or the equivalent, a good general scholastic average, and recommendations on their character and responsibility. Reid Hall, which is located in the Montparnasse quarter of Paris, would provide residence and board for the students. Reid Hall would also provide for the director-in-charge and give scholarships to students. The session in France would last from approximately July 5 to August 16. It would be preceded by a week to ten days' trip along the Normandy Coast, Mont St Michel, Loire Châteaux, and Chartres. It would also include one weekend trip to Vezelay, Fontainebleau and two theatres. The essential part would of course be three hours of regular courses every morning in the language, literature, and civilization of France (including history and cultural history), and other courses which would be according to the choice of the students, either history of art at the Ecole du Louvre or international relations at the Institut d'Études Politiques. The students successful in their work would receive six credits.

A committee from several American universities would be entrusted with the supervision and sponsorship of this summer course. We hope to have on hand representatives from Bryn Mawr and Wellesley, Harvard, Yale, and probably one western or mid-western university. For the first year Professor Andersson of Yale would be the Director-in-Charge, in 1950, and he would receive and sift the applications this spring. The part played by Yale in all this would entail no financial guarantee of any kind and no risk. The authority of Yale would merely guarantee academic standards, efficient organization, and help attract the best students to it. We believe that there is much in this plan to commend itself, and that it will satisfy the high standards we hope to set for it.

We hope that, as you intimated, the approval of the Corporation will be given to this plan, endorsed by the French Department and by Dean DeVane, and that we can start making it known to American students without delay.

Very sincerely yours,
Henri Peyre
Chairman

## À Mario Maurin:

Ce 2—ii—50

Mon cher ami,

Votre lettre m'a fait plaisir. D'abord parce qu'elle est pleine de vous, spirituelle, ironique, tendre à sa manière, vivement tournée; et puis parce que vous y apparaissez vaillant et jeune, converti même à quelque naturisme, sportif, plein d'espoir et vous étant refait dans la neige et la propreté helvétique une fraîche virginité. J'avais vaguement entendu dire que vous aviez été malade, nul ne savait de quoi; et je m'inquiétais. Vos ennuis d'oreille n'auguraient rien de bon—et je redoutais pour vous l'excès de travail, la vie trop recluse et livresque que vous aviez menée, l'effarante précocité de votre développement.

Ce changement d'air & de pays vous aura été salutaire. De là-bas, peut-être aurez-vous vu l'Amérique autrement, réfléchi à l'avenir, à votre carrière, à ce que vous aimeriez franchement faire: professeur en Amérique? Écrivain? Il ne serait pas mauvais pour vous, si vous êtes tout à fait solide, de frayer un peu avec les milieux littéraires de Paris & de découvrir vraiment si cette vie souvent envieuse, aigrie, cynique, privée de foi, mais avec une si prodigue dépense d'intelligence vous agréerait.

En attendant, bien sûr, achevez votre thèse. Votre sujet sur La Fontaine & la satire politico sociale chez lui est très possible: il faudra, bien sûr, le rénover. Il m'embarrasserait pour ma part, parce que je ne vois pas trop comment je le renouvellerais; mais je crois en effet qu'il y a là un sujet & que, sous votre plume, il deviendrait convaincant & passionnant. Evitez un ton peut-être cavalier, une virtuosité éblouissante, et freinez votre facilité, "cette grâce du génie." Sur Suarès, je n'avais pas goûté autant votre essai (toujours en panne, avec notre volume entier) que d'autres choses de vous. J'étais d'accord avec vous sur l'Homme (avec des réserves, car il est souvent imitateur & quelquefois creux). Mais vous affirmiez plus que vous ne convainquiez. Mais Suarès est quelqu'un—Je crois que La Fontaine est un sujet plus "raisonnable." Vos vues originales sur la poésie pourraient aussi vous amener à un sujet là dessus, dans le passé. Mais cela vaudra mieux pour un livre, un jour. Votre retour à quelque sorte de classicisme m'effraie un peu: ce terme a couvert tant de médiocrités, jusqu'au récent *Babel* de Caillois. Je confesse un faible même pour le déchaînement de Pichette, mais une paresse alanguie devant ce que je parcours de la poésie d'aujourd'hui. J'espère lire la vôtre.

Reposez-vous bien encore. Je me suis vite rétabli moi-même, mais travaille trop—Ici chacun va bien, l'activité est grande, beaucoup d'élèves—Avez-vous organisé votre vie l'an prochain? Séjournerez-vous à N. Haven ou à N. York? Cherchez-vous à enseigner?

Mes très fidèles & amicales pensées,<br>Henri Peyre

## To Henry Allen Moe:

[No date]

Henry Allen Moe, Secretary General
The John Guggenheim Foundation
551 Fifth Avenue
New York, New York
Dear Mr. Moe:

You have an uncanny insight into men, indeed, and your rating is admirable in its fairness and in its discrimination. Such expert judgment of men is rare, and duly impressed by it, I joined my wishes to those of many who thought you should be among the first to be considered for our Presidency at Yale. Whether one should wish such a position on a man one likes is, of course, another story. If those things were determined by the votes of connoisseurs, I know many who would elect you, and quite a few of them to keep away Mr. Frank Ashburn, your coworker on our Humanities Committee, whose report disappointed us as too fond of platitudinous truths and venerable and conventional quotations and ideas. . . .

## À Mario Maurin:

Yale, ce 2 mars 1950

Mon cher Ami,

Vous avez de la chance d'être comme Séraphita parmi les neiges, pur, serein, virginal, alors que nous pataugeons ici dans la vile neige fondue, dans les innombrables besognes de détail qui fondent sur nous à ce moment de l'année, où il faut voir dans le présent des cours & conférences & dans l'avenir de l'an prochain à préparer dans le plus grand détail!

Sur La Fontaine, très franchement, je crois que vous pouvez faire quelque chose du sujet, parce que "c'est vous." Mais, pour ma propre part, je ne vois pas très bien, a priori, ce que je mettrais d'original ou de fort dans ce sujet: mais cela est ma propre faiblesse. Mais si la besogne est bien faite, elle doit en effet en valoir la peine: c a d relations avec des événements contemporains, rapports de La F. avec le goût de son époque, habile mélange de hardiesse & d'adaptation, etc. Elle peut aussi apporter quelque chose de frais sur la satire dans les Fables & au XVIIe siècle, et sur la structure des Fables, leur esthétique, etc.

Avec l'Allemagne vue par les Français, il y a un petit livre rapide, récent, de J. M. Carré (chez Boivin), "Les écrivains français & le mirage allemand." Si vous étudiez le pays plutôt que les penseurs & écrivains, cela devient étude de récits de voyage souvent très médiocres (le *Rhin* même est en grande partie pillé aux sources allemandes). Je crains que ce ne soit décevant. Et ceux que l'Allemagne a le plus touchés en profondeur ne l'ont pratiquement jamais vue (Taine, Renan). Ceux qui l'ont vue se sont mépris sur elle—Et le sujet serait vaste. Vous devriez finir votre thèse, sinon vite, du moins sans travail excessif.

Pour Suarès, ceux qui l'ont connu se sont souvent plaints de sa manie de piller leurs idées & leurs conversations pour se parer de ces plumes (Gide, Journal, entre autres). R. Rolland dans ses lettres à Frau von Meysenbug, Claudel & Gide dans le volume de lettres récemment publiées, parlent de lui. Il n'en reste pas moins qu'on pourrait faire une monographie utile sur Suarès, mais en gardant son sang-froid et sans imiter ses hyperboles & ses haines & amours passionnés—La vérité d'ailleurs est que tout notre volume collectif est resté en souffrance, faute d'argent & d'éditeur entreprenant.

J'en ai fini avec les *Générations,* je crois. Cela m'avait amusé—Non, *Babel* ne vaut rien. Pichette a de grands dons, verbaux surtout. Voir ses *Apoèmes*. Pour l'an prochain, nous ne saurons qu'à la rentrée de septembre—Mais il me semble certain que soit en espagnol (M. Bergin s'occupe de cela & je lui ai parlé) soit en français nous aurions pour vous quelques heures d'enseignement. 5 h. sans doute si c'est chez nous—Pas de poste complet, si à l'avenir nous devons pour cela exiger le Ph.D. Mais vous-même ne devriez pas trop travailler—Je vois qu'en fait vous êtes à Neuilly. Heureux plus encore!

Bien sincèrement à vous,<br>Henri Peyre

## À Franco Simone:

March 6, 1950

Professor Franco Simone
Via Amaretti 4
Poirino Torino
Italia
Cher monsieur:

J'ai eu un très grand plaisir à trouver les publications que vous m'avez si aimablement envoyées. J'avais gardé le meilleur souvenir de notre rencontre l'été dernier, et j'étais très anxieux de lire votre étude sur les grands rhétoriqueurs. Je viens en effet de la lire. Elle est très originale et m'a beaucoup appris. Vous modernisez ce que l'on croyais (sic) le plus mort dans la pré Renaissance. Vos articles sur la *Pléiade et ses prédécesseurs* et sur la *Reductio artium* sont également savants, et vous avez une manière très originale de prendre ces sujets lointains et de les remplir de vie. C'est également un plaisir pour moi d'avoir votre édition des *Amours de Ronsard* avec votre substantielle préface et la série de vos études sur la *Conscience de la Renaissance chez les humanistes* que j'avais appréciée et déjà signalée à mes collègues. Je vous enverrai de mon côté quelques menues publications, et je serais très heureux de rester informé de vos travaux. Vous vous êtes placé d'emblée au premier rang des seiziémistes de l'avenir.

Croyez, cher monsieur à mes sentiments les plus dévoués.

Hri Peyre<br>Chairman

## To Harry Levin:

March 10—1950

Dear Professor Levin:

I greatly appreciated my visit to Harvard & the very stimulating evening with the Junior Fellows. I envy you the institution, the cordiality & the fine & healthy intellectuality of such gatherings. And the Committee on the next morning was a very impressive affair, in which you helped tremendously.

I wonder if you would be willing to write me a letter giving your opinion on Auerbach. I am trying to decide Yale to appoint him as Professor of Old French & Romance Philology; he might naturally also help with our Comparative Literature setup. But anything you say, with your authority, on the man, his books, his eminence, may help me.

I may fail in the attempt, on account of age, excessive prudence on the part of Yale. But I want to make quite an attempt all the same, & enlist your support, that of Amado Alonso & some others.

Many thanks in advance & very cordially yours,
Henri Peyre

## To John W. Kneller:

Ce 11 mars 1950

My dear Kneller,

I received your chapter on Nerval a few days ago (the envelope torn, I suppose by the customs, but the MS intact). I forget what you said in an earlier letter & suppose you want it back, but I'll check with Tug on Monday that you are not going to be on the water soon. I know that your stay in Paris was made difficult by lack of adequate funds, & I regretted that you had not known about a Fulbright in time. For a married man, those French scholarships are inadequate—I hope you kept up a good morale, however, & enjoyed yourself—& that your wife had a good rest & some entertainment after her ordeal of last fall.

Your chapter is very good, like the others. It is solid, very well informed, prudent in its conclusions, well developed, brings out several points which appeared new to me: I had never known of the project of a play on Rousseau. Amazing how bad Nerval could be, & then how great & moving, with a note all his own, at times! All that you assert is founded on texts & firm & subtle reasoning. You purposely avoid all the easy & general development (on Nerval & Rousseau compared as delineators of man's inner life, on Nerval as an intermediary between Rousseau &, say, Proust). I believe you are right. It makes your thesis a bit dry & negative, or over-prudent in its treatment of Rousseau's influence on the romantic poets, & makes that influence appear small — But it is much safer this way, & more honest.

I believe you may complete it confidently & send it or bring it (May 1st is the date, as you remember). It is a good piece of work. In the conclusion, you will pose, perhaps, some larger problems on Rousseau in the 19th century & on the question of his influence — Next year, if you have a little leisure, you may rework on this — & perhaps publish some parts from it.

My very best wishes once more — & very sincerely,
Henri Peyre

Cook is also going to Oberlin next year, as you may know. He is doing a thesis on J. Rivière. Few of the others are placed as yet. I think you did well to guarantee your future.

## À Mario Maurin:

Ce 2 avril 50

Mon cher ami,

Avec votre admirable prose classique, vous êtes, pour parler comme Suarès, un romantique tout de flamme & de nerfs. Votre lettre récente était écrite d'un splendide élan & elle constituait un plaidoyer pour Suarès auquel nul ne saurait résister.

Je voyais mal en effet ce que vous pourriez faire sur Lafontaine qui fût très neuf; et, oserai-je l'avouer, je redoute légèrement votre facilité, votre tour de main qui peut vous faire écrire joliment sur n'importe quel sujet, d'une main rapide, en disant mille choses fines au passage, en distribuant quelques coups de lance à droite & à gauche, mais sans creuser à fond le sujet & convaincre que vous avez réalisé ce "définitif" comme on appelait autrefois en France les thèses de diplôme.

Or je crois que vous devez, par amour-propre, parce que cela vous sera facile, et par calcul d'avenir, faire une *très bonne* thèse, qui, en livre, vous imposera; et, sans rien perdre de votre élan, de votre impatience de nos trop pédestres méthodes, de votre génie, vous devez la faire solide & durable, n'embrassant pas un champ trop vaste & creusant à fond quelque thème. Vous devez la faire avec amour, & c'est pourquoi je vous dis aussitôt: allez pour Suarès. Mais essayez aussi de trouver en lui quelque angle de vision qui soit le vôtre, & qui vous permette d'éviter les "périls du sujet" car votre modèle a touché à tout, s'est répété, a peu évolué me semble-t-il, et risque de disperser l'énergie de qui l'étudie.

Essayez d'éviter ce qui demanderait trop de précisions sur sa vie, mal connue & trop proche—et ses relations littéraires, influences sur lui, etc., sujet extérieur et qui risquerait de le faire voir sous un jour peu louangeur—Le style serait un splendide sujet, & dans le style rentrerait beaucoup de la substance de l'œuvre: c'est peut-être ce qu'il y a de plus beau chez Suarès, qui a en effet une belle prose—Le mécanisme de l'aphorisme est curieux chez lui, & peut-être dangereusement aisé à démontrer. La tension de la phrase, sa nervosité, son art de la pointe, ses images: tout cela serait un riche terrain.

Ou préférez-vous saisir en lui le moraliste, et sa constante méditation sur le héros—ou son nietzschéisme, qui l'a entraîné à beaucoup rabâcher sur (et contre) la femme (qu'il doit l'avoir aimée!) et sur la force? Le sujet le plus facile serait ses opinions littéraires (et musicales), mais trop facile pour vous. Avec le style, c'est la sensibilité de Suarès qui importe le plus, & sa structure mentale—Le sujet est beau mais en vérité difficile. Je l'ai plusieurs fois suggéré en Amérique & personne, que je sache, ne l'a jamais pris, ou mené à bien.

J'ai beaucoup admiré Suarès, et Elie Faure, & ai jadis converti à cette admiration bien des gens. Je l'ai loué souvent (pour ce qu'il a dit sur le classicisme, sur le "siècle de Louis XIII," sur Baudelaire, pour son triptyque sur l'Italie). J'aimais moins ses efforts vers le dramatique & ses dialogues semi mythologiques, décharnés, tendus, mais si peu dramatiques & dénués de la fantaisie ironique qui sauve Giraudoux. C'est dire que votre enthousiasme ne me choque nullement: il me rappelle que je l'ai éprouvé moi-même. Et qu'il ait pris à Gide & autres (& beaucoup à Nietzsche, & souvent le pire, & au pire Nietzsche, celui de Zarathoustra) ne me gêne pas. Mais je ne vous suivrais pas quand vous lui trouvez la pensée la plus brûlante depuis Pascal. L'homme se sent trop en lui, comme dans Barrès, & dans Chateaubriand, & me gêne: il manquait par trop d'humour, & son impuissance à composer de vrais livres organiques, où il aurait échappé à son perpétuel "je" a dû le gêner. Et puis, il a mélangé le bon & le pire. Je m'occupe ces jours-ci de Baudelaire & suis agacé quand je lis, dans mes notes sur quelque article de Suarès sur Baudelaire, "Verlaine excepté, Baud. est le plus vivant de nos poètes—Tout portait Baudelaire à être classique. En art, c'est le destin des aristocrates et dans le récent 'Musiciens' Baud est notre Dante (on l'a dit depuis 1858); mais à la française. . . . Tous les poètes sont issus de Baudelaire, Walt Whitman seul excepté." C'est vraiment un peu péremptoire! Et sur Gœthe, sur Wagner, sur Racine, que de jugements de ce genre, d'ailleurs fréquemment contradictoires d'un livre à l'autre! Et la pose de ce cher homme: "Voici l'homme est une œuvre qui doit offenser tout le monde. . . . Étant sans préjugés, elle est dangereusement libre. . . ."

J'avoue que parfois il amènerait (presque) le contradicteur que je suis volontiers à détester Nietzsche, & la force, et la misogynie, & les Grecs, & tout ce que je sens de Suarès au fond de moi. (C'est des Baux qu'est issue ma famille, & c'est en dînant là, à un exquis restaurant avec un docteur qui me parlait de Suarès, que j'eus l'été dernier quelque accident à une dent, qui eut quelques suites fâcheuses.)

Lancez vous donc dans Suarès. Lisez tout. Vous délimiterez après—et obtenez le plus de documents possible. Ici nous avons pas mal de ses livres & sans doute quelque thèse allemande sur lui. C'est tout.

Tout va bien. Wadsworth s'en va l'an prochain (à Northwestern), plusieurs jeunes aussi, dont Cohn dont le livre sur le Coup de Dés vous est peut-être connu: beau & profond livre. Boorsch va en France cet été & j'y vais aussi. Etes-vous tout à fait remis? Décidé à vivre modestement l'an prochain? (Le "modestement" n'est pas de rigueur, mais je veux dire du peu que vous rapporterait un enseignement "part time" ici.) Quand rentrerez-vous?

Vous devriez absolument nous donner un article (10 pges au maximum) pour le no. sur Gide des Yale French Studies, pour octobre—peut-être sur Suarès & Gide, ou Gide & Dostoïevski.

Bien cordialement à vous,<br>Henri Peyre

## To Sister Marie-Louise Hubert:

April 1950

Dear Sister Marie Louise:

This is a nice piece of work & I have nothing to suggest which would be of importance. The last chapter is a bit hasty & surveys many editions & plans: a more detailed criticism would have been worth while (say of Brunschvicg, etc.), with precise suggestions on how their plan could be remodeled & improved, how you would do yours if you had to. It reads a little like a superfluous adjunct to the rest—But your judgment is wise throughout & extremely impartial. In many ways I found you so tolerant, so just, so fair to Catholics & non-Catholics alike that I trembled for your orthodoxy!

On Filleau de la Chaise (for whose Discours I have a "faible"), Étienne Périer, etc. I believe you are also admirably fair & balanced. You are hardest on Madame Périer & on poor M. de Saci, whose "pietistic narrowness" you treat more harshly than I would! But all that you say is perspicacious, relevant, well-documented & well-reasoned, & finely written. You might have "stuck your neck out" & added an appendix on your own "Plan ideal," & where you would fit the pari & the Mystère de Jésus, & how you would bring out man's greatness more than others have done, etc., & combine all the indications from Périer & Filleau & others. But maybe that would be another book!

Congratulations!
HP

You heard that Sister Amelia is getting a Guggenheim fellowship. She is overjoyed. It will be announced in the papers on April 17th

## To the same:

April 21, 1950

My dear Sister Marie Louise:

I heard from Mr. Morehouse the dreadful news of the blow that fell upon you. Following so soon upon the death of your father, this new affliction must be doubly cruel on you. With all your courage & cheerfulness in facing the ordeals of life, you must need all your faith and all your reason to bear such a conjunction of catastrophes. Your friends are full of sympathy & share your sorrow with you, affectionately.

If this were to delay the completion of your work by a few days, do not worry: we should attend to that, of course.

>With deep sympathy & most sincerely,
>Henri Peyre

## À Jorge Guillén:

>Ce 8 mai 1950

Cher Ami,

J'étais à Baltimore cette semaine & Salinas m'a appris que vous veniez de perdre votre père. Je sais combien grande doit être pour vous cette nouvelle perte, alors que vous vous apprêtiez à revoir celui dont vous parliez si bien, que vous aviez tout fait pour revoir il y a deux ou trois ans. Sans doute n'était-il plus jeune; mais le déchirement que doit être la brisure de ce dernier lien pour ainsi dire charnel avec l'Espagne est un cruel chagrin pour l'exilé, déjà privé du sol de sa patrie, de sa langue pourtant autour de lui conversée, de ses amis.

Nous partageons votre peine. Je vous sais courageux.

Salinas était merveilleux de verve comme toujours. Quel homme admirable. Par contraste avec tant de professeurs en ce pays, il *vit,* il *sent,* & il prodigue les idées les plus neuves—et il parle bien de vous.

>Croyez à notre sympathie & amitié,
>Henri Peyre

## À Pedro Salinas:

>Ce 9 mai [1950]

Cher ami,

Nous avons été si contents de faire la connaissance de votre femme, & de mieux faire la vôtre. J'ai bien compris que vous aviez de sérieux soucis avec la santé de Mme Salinas, mais vous étiez courageux, plein de verve, d'ardeur. Vous êtes non seulement un vrai & grand poète & un critique admirable, mais le plus merveilleux des causeurs; et vous êtes tout cela avec une belle sincérité, en mettant tout l'homme dans tout ce que vous faites. Pour un latin, c'est un plaisir de vous rencontrer & de reprendre orgueil de ce genre d'homme complet qui vit sa pensée & ses sentiments, avec une verve spontanée & fraîche.

Je me suis permis, en remerciement pour votre amitié, de vous envoyer un petit livre de Camus qui rappellera à votre femme l'Algérie, & un, hélas! en anglais de Claudel qui dit de belles choses sur l'art espagnol.

Amitiés,<br>Henri Peyre

## To Harry Levin:

May 15, 1950

Dear Mr. Levin:

I should have been more prompt in expressing my gratitude for the very fine & very rich volume that you kindly sent me. May has been, however, an extremely busy month & continues to be, with theses in dangerous quantities & other tasks. And, alas! our reading periods have been a war casualty, while I understand you have been wise enough to retain them at Harvard.

I have at last spent several hours with the volume on Sunday, yesterday. I am much impressed by it. It may seem like a vain compliment to say that I found your article the most far-reaching & the most perspicacious of all. It is an important essay. I enjoyed Seznec's greatly; he has written a very finished & ingenious demonstration. Poggioli taught me much, as usual. The other articles are all of a fine level & the book as a whole does great credit to your Department. They are unusually clearly & cogently written & splendidly edited.

I was touched by your too kind mention of my name in your introduction. I am not sure I wish to reduce critics to reviewers. I would rather have them not only have theories on literature & ideas on criticism, but also the taste, the insight, the boldness of discrimination which would enable them to discern what is great in what is new. I am less serene than the Hegelian optimists who accept the grossest mistakes &

the stupidest cruelties of some critics as part of a developing process which ultimately will assign its place, if any is ever fixed, to a work of art. And I do wish that reviewing might more often be criticism—as it was with some reviewers in the past—& as you know how to make it yourself—But let me not appear to be fighting querulously for my thesis! I was not fully convinced by your paragraph, but sincerely grateful that you should deem some of my impatient paradoxes worthy of a mention.

I hope you will have a good & restful Summer. I earnestly hope to have some rest myself, after too busy a year. I shall be in France for three months or so. Shall I have the pleasure to meet you over there?

Very sincerely & with many thanks,
Henri Peyre

## To Keith Botsford:

June 1—(1950)

My dear Botsford,

I had just left this for you. I shall not be in New Haven on the 6th, & on the 5th I shall be on a Committee meeting all day. I fear therefore I may not meet you when you come, if you do—But you should normally be accepted here, if the Dean & his committee admit my suggestion. It's always "on trial" the first year anyway.

Yours,
HP

## To the same:

June 2/1950

My dear Botsford,

It is too late to answer your letter in Iowa & this is in case I miss you when you call on or after the 4th. I am leaving for France on the 7th, am busy all day the 5th with a committee & the 4th away giving a commencement speech or some address in Pennsylvania.

As far as I am concerned, I am very happy to welcome you here &

am passing upon your application at once: it just reached me. I suppose Dean Simpson will agree. It is not easy to get an MA in French in a year, even with your fluency. You will find the level of our graduate students quite high (& over serious): your MA essay (70 to 100 pages) should be a solid & methodical (as well as inspired) piece of work. But nothing is difficult for an epic poet & a married man who has already accomplished several of the labors of Hercules!

If I am not here, you may have a talk with Mr. Cornell (in WL Harkness) & with Mr. Morehouse (in Pierson) about your future work. I was hoping to meet your wife—but these last days are hectic. Have a good summer & my very cordial wishes,

Henri Peyre

**To the same:**

C/o American Express<br>Rue Scribe<br>Paris (IX)<br>June 18/1950

My dear Botsford,

I was sorry indeed to miss you in New Haven. I had several engagements, rashly accepted, just before sailing—& my regret was keen—& all the keener when we discovered in our cabin the very lovely flowers that you sent us. They adorned our table for every day of the crossing—We are now in Paris, a bit hectic & bewildered as always after such a change, but very happy. Life is gay & the food is or might be an inspiration to any creator—if not to dull & over-prudent critics.

I hope you will enjoy a quiet summer, before coming back as a conqueror to the place which you once scorned to conquer. It will be fine to have you again—even if you scare your teachers as you like to do, & if we try to scare you with the "scholarly" character of Graduate study. I believe it should not be too difficult for your wife to find some work in N. Haven. We had, in the Department, engaged a secretary one or two months ago; but Mrs. Botsford should register with the Personnel Bureau (Mr. Carter Nyman), somewhere on Wall St.—& we may find at least some part time work for her, but I believe she should try first for the best job available & the most decently paid one—through Carl Nyman's office.

Excuse this hurried note, scratched on my arrival here—I hope the address to which I am sending it is the right one—I seem to have lost the other. Many thanks for your very thoughtful & kind present & sincerely

Henri Peyre

## À Georges May:

Du 28 juillet 1950
De St-Jean de Luz

Mon cher ami (sur mes genoux, d'un café),

. . . Nous voyageons. C'est délicieux! Que les provinces sont belles. On parle peu ou pas de la guerre, de l'avenir: on compte sur l'Amérique, non sans se railler un peu d'elle, sottement. Il n'y a nulle panique. On mange, on boit: le matérialisme a bien envahi le Français, au moins le voyageur; mais il y a du bon après tout. Nous avons fait le tour de la Bretagne nord et sud, puis la Vendée (médiocre), La Rochelle (très jolie), Bordeaux, Arcachon, le pays basque. J'ai été rassuré de constater que somme toute ce midi-ci ne vaut pas l'autre. Il fait beau, pas trop chaud—et l'auto se comporte à merveille. . . .

## To James Osborn (Marguerite Peyre's handwriting):

[postcard: view of L'Hôtel Riviera]
Aix-en-Provence
August 13 1950

Stopping at Aix on our way back from the coast we are thinking of you & hoping you had a nice summer Aix is as beautiful as ever. We are on our way to Ste. Victoria.

Yours v. cordially
H. & M. PEYRE

## To Keith Botsford:

Le 29 août 1950<br>(Baden Baden)

Mon cher ami,

 Je vous remercie, avec retard, de votre bonne lettre du 15 juillet. J'ai passé un été tout de repos & de voyage, presque sans lectures. J'ai vu bien des paysages & des vieux monuments de France que je ne connaissais pas, et quelques écrivains ou lu quelques livres—mais les hommes de lettres (en ce pays) sont d'une affreuse vanité & leur vantardise de leurs prouesses sexuelles est bien ennuyeuse. Leurs romans, ces temps-ci, ne sont pas fameux. Je m'apprête maintenant à repartir—mais mon bateau, l'*Ile de France,* vient de subir un accident & un retard; & si je ne réussis pas à trouver place sur un départ antérieur, il se peut que je sois retardé jusqu'au 28 septembre. Voyez, au début de l'année, MM Boorsch & Morehouse pour les conseils dont vous pourriez avoir besoin, & dites à votre femme de chercher aussitôt quelque position, au Personnel Bureau. M. Morehouse pourra l'y aider.

 J'espère que l'été, malgré la chaleur de l'Iowa, se sera montré propice à votre imagination créatrice & que votre roman sera presque achevé à la rentrée. Votre idée de récit ou de conte sur un vieillard est très ingénieuse. La vieillesse, à part quelques caricatures de Bromfield, de Victoria Sackville-West (All passion spent) n'a jamais été sentie par les écrivains.

 Vous êtes sévère sur le livre de Harold March. J'ai fait bien des réserves sur le livre, dès le début, et surtout sur sa manière & son esprit, si peu proustiens. Mais l'auteur visait un certain public: d'étudiants non informés, de lecteurs ne sachant rien de Proust. Avec ses moyens, qui sont d'un professeur clair plus que d'un écrivain très sensitif, il a fait un livre honnête. Pour ma part, je n'y ai point appris, & et je préfère Green en effet, qui a plus d'antennes, & bien du dogmatisme. Mais à le juger pour le public auquel il s'adressait, il avait de réels mérites.

 Oui—il y a à faire sur les œuvres en prose de Valéry. Nous n'acceptons pas d'habitude des traductions pour une thèse, même de M.A. Mais vous pourriez étudier, dans cet énorme fouillis, souvent décevant, de l'œuvre en prose de Valéry soit l'art de la prose, soit le moraliste, soit le critique, soit le théoricien de la poétique, soit la critique de la philosophie, l'art de l'épigramme, etc. Il faudra, je crois, choisir un angle particulier. Voyez, dès sa rentrée, M. Douglas à ce sujet: il est très fort sur Valéry.

Il me tarde de rencontrer votre femme, & de vous revoir. Croyez en attendant, à mes sentiments bien dévoués.

Henri Peyre

## To Vera Lee:

Sept. 12 — 1950

My dear Vera,

Your letter, received on the eve of our sailing, amused me & — saddened me, since it was a farewell from a faithful, ever smiling, ever alert, ever witty collaborator who will be sadly missed next year. She was a Secretary, but also a friend, a critic, an adviser & . . . . a woman first & last. 1949–50 remains like a pleasant year in my memories. I didn't do half of what I should have, but who does?

The summer was lovely — a bit rainy — but we drove about France, fleeing the rain most successfully. The food was gorgeous, if expensive. The people seem jolly & free from care — almost to an excess. We had to take an earlier ship, the one we planned to sail on having been delayed — And I am really quite impatient to see the new office & settle in it. With your artistic taste, I know you will have made a splendid room of it.

We hope to see you back occasionally. This moving to Baltimore may be the beginning of a happy "vita nuova" for you — cooking (cookies, of course, & steaks, & cabbages: they are supposed to fertilize candidates to motherhood), teaching perhaps, filling the would be artistic dreams of Baltimore doctors, etc. — Of course, if I can help at all in recommending you, do resort to me — or if I can help in any other way with wise, old man's advice. I sincerely wish much happiness to you: you deserve it fully, all the more so as you know how to avoid self-pity, ponderousness, & excessive reasoning. You'll always be unpredictable — like a Frenchman. And you may not carry your conscience on a sling & nurse it with radiant pride, but you have one — & a charming one.

Do remember me to your husband & give him once more my congratulations for being your husband & for this fine Baltimore appointment. And believe me,

Sincerely & faithfully,<br>Henri Peyre

## To Edgar Furniss:

Sept. 18 — 1950

Dear Mr. Furniss:

We find, on organizing our work for the year, that the number of students taking our French courses, especially the language courses, is larger than we could reasonably expect. We had prepared estimates not too conservative, but keeping in mind the need for economy. But it turns out that we have to create an extra section of Fr. 22, an extra one of Fr. 42, & that, even so, we shall have more than the number of students considered as a safe maximum in the other divisions (i.e. over 12 in French 15, an intensive course; over 20 in Fr. 22, over 18 in French 41. My own course will run over 120 students, French 56). We thus shall need more money as follows. I suppose when some departments must increase their expenses because they have more students, others correspondingly decrease theirs & everything falls out harmoniously for the executives in charge of the overall budget; but I am an incurable optimist.

Our budget as approved in your letter of May 16, 1950, was (for salaries): $110,916. 67. I had hoped we would save one or two thousands on that. But apparently we shall need a total of $111,716. 67, even keeping down our requirements as much as possible. The extra sum requested amounts to: $800.00. The detail would be:

A) 94,416.67 (for professors, associate, assistant professors, instructors, all already appointed or on permanent tenure), and for reader ($700) & visiting lectures ($400), & for course for grad. students ($250).

B) 17,300 for assistants in instruction, where the increase will lie. The names are here listed, so that your office may check when all appointment blanks are ready. . . . The salaries for these assistants are, as you know, being kept to a minimum, in fact lower than we are supposed to give: $1,000 being for 5 hrs a week & a year, $1200 for 6 hours, $300 for 3 hrs a term.

I trust we can proceed on this basis. Excuse this dry note & accept my best wishes & warm greetings.

Hri Peyre

## To Harry Levin:

September 21, 1950

Dear Harry Levin:

I found on my return from a long summer abroad your very acute and illuminating reprint. As usual, you have managed to say something original on a subject which one might have thought trite. Your name, or rather your book on Joyce, was all over the place in the windows of French booksellers. It should attract more writers to Joyce and no name could be more alluring than yours which to many Frenchmen means le vin. That is how they pronounce it.

I meant to thank you as soon as I read your article and to thank you for your kind help in getting Roger Shattuck as one of the Fellows. His work with me in the past has been sometimes a little immature as was natural at his age, but I have nothing but warm praise for his recent volume, Apollinaire. The introduction is especially good. I have corresponded with Seznec repeatedly on the question of French candidates for Harvard. It's not easy to think of the ideal man, but I am glad that Bénichou had not accepted when I saw him again in Paris. With all his intellectual qualities he would not have been cooperative enough with things American.

I offer you my very best wishes for the present year, and I am,

Very sincerely yours,
Henri M. Peyre

## To Edgar Furniss:

September 25, 1950

Dear Mr. Furniss:

M. Jean Marx whom we have appointed as visiting lecturer?

[No signature]

## To Whitney Griswold:

September 26—1950

Dear President Griswold:

These first weeks, or days, must be very busy for you. When there is more leisure, I shall be glad some day, if you wish me to do so, to explain or present to you the state of our department & to submit some projects for the future.

Meanwhile I wonder if you would have a few minutes (I *mean* a few) to receive our new and eminent colleague, Erich Auerbach, and M. Jean Marx, of Paris, who will be here next week. That is the week of your "coronation," unfortunately. If however some morning (the 4th, 5th, or 6th) I could briefly introduce at least the latter to you, I should be pleased to do so. M. Marx is an elderly gentleman who was for many years head of the French Cultural Relations & a man of some importance in the French Foreign Office; he is a scholar also. It was through him that we arranged exchange of professors & of students with France, decorations to some members of our Faculty, etc—He will be giving some lectures for us as "visiting lecturer" the week of October 4–11.

I do not intend to inflict my publications upon you; but I thought I should let you see some French articles I wrote in the most influential French newspaper, "Le Monde," this Summer, because they touch on politics or America as she appears abroad. The language should offer no difficulty to a former reader of the Physiocrats.

Sincerely yours,
Hri Peyre

## À Franco Simone:

Ce 28 septembre 1950

Cher Monsieur:

J'ai trouvé ici en rentrant votre brochure sur la fortune de Pétrarque poète latin en France. Je vous en suis très reconnaissant. J'y ai beaucoup appris. C'était un sujet tout neuf, et vous avez le don de faire des découvertes de première main & d'aller aux textes, & ainsi de renouveler les sujets. Je m'étonne de tout ce que vous avez lu déjà, à votre âge qui paraît fort jeune. J'ai passé votre écrit, qui m'a fort intéressé & beaucoup appris, à M. Erich Auerbach, qui vient de devenir notre collègue à Yale.

J'ai été heureux de vous apercevoir, trop vite, à Paris. J'étais fort pressé, car je devais partir le lendemain pour l'Amérique. J'ai regretté que ce congrès ne permît pas davantage de contact entre les membres, de libre discussion. Si le temps m'avait été donné, cela m'aurait fait plaisir d'avoir un repas ou une heure tranquille en votre compagnie.

Croyez à mon souvenir fidèle & dévoué,
Hri Peyre

## À Pierre Bédard:

Ce 3 octobre 1950

Mon cher Ami,

J'ai été bien heureux d'entendre votre voix, toujours chaude et accueillante, aussitôt après mon retour ici. Vous voilà à nouveau devant une saison d'activité culturelle qui devrait être fructueuse. On s'intéresse beaucoup à la France partout, mais les œuvres littéraires qui sont sorties récemment sont décevantes. Elles semblent marquer le pas.

Outre Marc Chadourne (New London), il y a donc ici, à Yale, Jacques GUICHARNAUD, jeune agrégé normalien fort distingué, Jean COLLIGNON, que vous connaissez peut-être déjà: Georges MAY va être en France cette année avec une bourse Guggenheim. Princeton est un peu vidé, a fait une offre assez belle à Michel MOHRT, qui a préféré cependant rester en France et écrire un nouveau roman. Je ne vois personne de très "éminent" à part cela près d'ici. Jules ROMAINS doit venir, & BAZIN, conservateur au Louvre, qui a de fort bons sujets.

J'ai pensé à quelques titres pour le mardi 21 novembre, que voici:

1. Peut-on être sincère en littérature?
2. Pourquoi la littérature moderne est-elle difficile?
3. L'Amérique vue de France en 1950 (J'ai écrit dans le *Monde* cet été quelques articles sur ce sujet, qui semblent avoir été remarqués & disaient peut être des choses utiles).
4. La France au seuil du nouveau demi-siècle.
5. L'éducation française et l'éducation américaine (traité avec un peu d'humour et sans gravité excessive—ramené au problème de la jeunesse telle qu'elle est formée aujourd'hui dans les deux pays).

L'un de ces sujets vous conviendrait-il? Sinon il m'est facile de parler sur un auteur en particulier, Rimbaud, Malraux, Sartre, etc., mais vous avez sans doute eu bien des sujets là-dessus déjà ces dernières années— ou Guillaume Apollinaire—ou Baudelaire sur qui je viens de terminer un livre. Vous me direz.

Bien amicalement à vous & à bientôt,<br>
Henri Peyre

## To Harry Levin:

October 6, 1950

Dear Harry Levin:

Thank you for your letter. I am sorry that your book on Joyce was thus maltreated in the French version. You are such a careful and even fastidious writer that it must hurt bitterly to be thus misrepresented. I had meant to say in my earlier letter that the publishers of the ITALIAN DICTIONARY OF LITERATURE in Milan (Bompiani) are very anxious to have us do something to attract some American attention to the completion of that huge and magnificent work. They would welcome articles in the NEW YORK TIMES or NEW YORK HERALD or THE NATION. I shall see here with Bergin what we can try and do, though

I am skeptical of getting articles there in a foreign language. Perhaps you and Poggioli might also think about something to be done on your own side.

I am very fond of Pierre Emmanuel. He is eloquent as a speaker and as a poet, and has an extremely warm and winning personality. With all his gifts, I think it should be added that he is likely to be more successful and happier hence in a comparatively brief stay in America (a year at most) than if he ever were called here permanently or semi-permanently. For one thing, like many creators, he will teach best what interests him vividly and prove unfair to the rest. He owes a great deal, of course, to D'Aubigné. He can be also a little "léger"and perhaps over conscious of the charm he has for young ladies. When all is said, I believe an academic man will eventually be the real solution for Harvard, and a visitor, Emmanuel or Bergin, for an occasional stay.

I hate also to be or to seem rather negative, but I would be a little careful also of Georges Poulet, and of anyone suggested by Jean Wahl. Jean Wahl can be erratic or over generous in his recommendations, and lured some people here into some rather regrettable mistakes. I don't know anything about the personality of Poulet and, therefore, can say nothing competent. The obvious thing would be for Seznec to meet him in Edinburgh. His book is supposed to be an excellent book on time and the novel. I ordered it for Yale a year ago and, mysteriously, it hasn't yet arrived.

I don't know what the academic career of Poulet was before he went to Scotland. He may be the same man who some years ago wrote a novel on the theme of night or darkness, but I don't know for sure.

There are some men in America whom we left out of our consideration list here and whom it might be far easier to transplant than some French scholars straight from France. They are not absolutely first rate, but may become so with time. One of them is André Delattre of Pennsylvania, just now in Paris. Two or three books by him will come out this year. Another possibility might be Bonno, full professor at Berkeley and a man of fifty-five or so. He lacks boldness and certainly modernity, but he is a good traditional scholar in his field.

Again, with my best wishes and

Very sincerely yours,<br>
Henri M. Peyre

I just heard from Seznec who seems to see no better choice in France than Barrère, faculté des lettres, Lyon, author of a book on "La fantaisie de Victor Hugo" & of one or two able articles in recent numbers of French studies (Oxford). He is good—if not superlatively so. But he has four children. What a transplantation!

## À Jeanne Maurin:

Ce 18 octobre 1950

Chère Madame:

J'espère que vous êtes tout à fait remise de votre accident & à nouveau pleine de vaillance. J'avais bien reçu, & j'ai communiqué à la Bibliothèque, le manuscrit de Suarès. Je ne pense pas qu'ils veuillent offrir plus de cinquante dollars pour un manuscrit en ce moment. Nous en reparlerons avec Mario à son retour.

Bien sûr, je serai heureux de répondre au Selective Service. Nous avons ici un Office of Selective Service, Sheffield Hall, dirigé par Alan D. Ferguson, qui s'occupe des étudiants, des exemptions ou délais possibles. Votre fils devra y expliquer son cas à son retour. Je pense qu'un délai au moins serait possible & qu'il pourrait terminer sa thèse cette année. Jusqu'ici, je ne connais personne dans son cas qui ait été appelé aussitôt. Mais je crois en outre qu'étant donné ses migraines récentes & ses ennuis de santé, votre fils aurait toutes chances de ne pas être pris pour le service.

Nous avons tous ici grande estime pour ses extraordinaires qualités intellectuelles, vous le savez; et j'ai constaté avec joie qu'il a aussi beaucoup "mûri" dans le sens d'une plus grande tolérance de ceux qui sont moins doués que lui, d'un sens plus aigu des valeurs concrètes. Il a très bon cœur d'ailleurs & le sentiment profond & délicat qui l'attache à vous lui fait le plus grand honneur. Il devrait travailler moins, compléter sa vie de l'esprit par une vie physique et "réaliste" plus intense—et son avenir est des plus splendides.

Croyez, chère Madame, à mes sentiments les plus dévoués,
Henri Peyre

## To Edgar Furniss:

October 26, 1950

Dear Mr. Furniss:

This is the correct list as we recently made it in our office of the students taking courses in our Department. As you see, the total comes up to 950. Added to this should be our graduate students the number of whom seems to come up to 63 according to the list enclosed plus 7 from other departments. Perhaps, once you have glanced at it, you might pass on the enclosed list to Dean Simpson for him to utilize if he needs it.

I realize, of course, that my visit this morning was a little premature since we can not make definite plans about next year, but I greatly enjoyed talking with you, as always, and meeting with such encouragement as one may expect these days. To repeat what I said, the saving to be effected next year will certainly amount to $6,500 (Hill), $500 (actually $400 spent on Visiting Professor), $250 (Special Assistant for graduate students in other Departments). I hope, moreover, as the number of students decreases, to save at least on one Instructor and on several Assistants in Instruction, but that should wait until we know more definitely about the prospects. In other words, the clear saving would be at least $7,250, and a good deal more if needed.

The increases which are requested, even if generously granted, would not come up to that. Meanwhile, as you well know, neither Professor Feuillerat nor Professor Seronde was replaced until we appointed Auerbach, and our staff among the Full and Associate Professors is certainly less numerous and less costly than that of departments like German, Philosophy, English, and, of course, the Queen or the Empress of departments at Yale, History. In fact, much as I may be flattered to hear that many students want to study in our Graduate School on my account, I believe we owe it to them to have a fuller slate of Full Professors.

I am returning a letter which has somehow stayed in my files through the summer and I am enclosing the articles which I mentioned to you, published in a most influential French newspaper this summer, as well as a magazine which the E.C.A. publishes in France. I wonder if I could have my article from the newspaper back as I have no copy left.

Very sincerely yours,<br>Henri M. Peyre

As you know, our Department also (generously) lends its services to Italian (Dante course given by Prof. Auerbach, 3 hrs a week or one third of his time) & to Comparative Literature (Cornell's comparative 107, one third of his time also).

## To Sister Marie-Louise Hubert:

Oct. 29/50

Dear Sister Marie Louise,

I am sorry this has taken me so long—not in itself, of course, since I was already familiar with it, but because I have had a huge amount of work lately. It is always growing, in fact, & I have less freedom than a monk or than a nun, & also alas! less time for meditation.

I have the same good impression as I had last year. It is a *very able* work: well documented with much thought behind it, personal meditation, enthusiasm but duly restrained, & an extraordinary fairness of interpretation. You have avoided the usual faults of theses: excess of references & quotations in foreign languages, excess of summaries of other works & petty caviling at other scholars. It is clear, readable throughout, informing. It will take only little work to turn it into a very creditable book.

You might look at Pt ii, ch ii again & if you think it deserves it, strengthen the part on other apologists in the 17th century, if you are convinced the similarities with Pascal are striking.

Also stress Pascal's appeal to reason, his "rationalism," as against the fideist interpretations of some 50 years ago—see Jeanne Russier's book on Pascal, just now in the New Book Room.

Maybe strengthen in last chapter the part on dialogue, as essential to P's mind & an original way of looking at his dramatic, antithetic mental structures. Stress the artistic advantages of the dialogue, also (cf. Plato, Berkeley, Renan).

The last chapter is the least satisfying—for it would deserve a book in itself. You might explain gracefully that you are not doing a thorough job there & that you are suggesting, rather, what is to be done—I am not sure you are not too favorable to Giraud, or am I unfair to him? Havet's edition & plan would deserve closer attention: it molded people's knowledge of P. for generations, as Brunschvicg did later. Important conclusions should be reached in this last chapter: how the plan of Pascal reflects & molds the Pascalian views, & the more general philosophical views of a whole generation; the intricate questions unsolved, namely be fair to P's probable intentions in 1658 or 1660, but also be fair to Pascal today & keep in mind his present public ("art d'agréer") & not rebuke it by plunging the reader into miracles & figuratifs for the first 100 pages.

Your conclusion is a bit dry. It should be rethought & rewritten. You are very brief indeed on le Pari (p 278) & on le Mystère de Jésus, & don't develop your arguments enough.

Stewart's edition & translation of Pascal just came out (Pantheon Press). I gave it to Mr. Morehouse: look at it.

Also Lafuma's Recherches pascaliennes, with good preface (disagreeing) by Albert Béguin, in New Book Room.

Whenever you can save (eliminating French text of quotations, some references, abridging,) you will gain, in terms of money too—although the Church should not worry about such petty considerations.

If we do start a series here at Yale Press, your book might well appear there—It might come up to 200 printed pages, i.e. very near to $2.00. It would be worth while—& the crowning of several years of steady & fruitful work. We should be proud of it.

You must also, or may, try, for the MLA prize. The thing to consider there is whether it has enough appeal to a fairly general public, which it thus keeps interested in the results of scholarship. Any such judgment is relative, to the reader's own interest, & to the quality of other MSS competing.

Do go ahead with this, & promptly, before you lose your fervor.

Very sincerely yours,
Henri Peyre

## To Edgar Furniss:

November 17, 1950

Dear Mr. Furniss:

I have spoken with Professor Raymond Hill about the subject that we discussed, and I believe the arrangement on which we tentatively agreed will also prove agreeable to him and will not prevent the Department from going ahead with the plans it had to reform the philological part of its studies. I presented the arrangement as a fair and generous gesture from the University. In other words, he would be getting for another year, July 1, 1951 to June 30, 1952, the required stipend of $300 a month, or $3,600 a year. I added that the work required from him would be light and in some ways nominal; he would be given one undergraduate course, French 50, for which the enrollment is always small and one small graduate course, probably Provençal. Although he would be employed full time as far as social security goes, his work with your agreement would only amount to half of what it was in the last few years, which I think would be better for everyone concerned. I hope this satisfies you, and you might in conversation confirm it to him subsequently.

With your approval, I am going ahead with some of the plans that I discussed with you earlier, and while I am preparing my budget I shall ask the Dean of the College to take up the question of promotions in the French Department as I outlined them to you even before the final approval of the figures by the administration.

I should like to mention a third item which I am sorry to say also has to deal with money. The French Department, which has a room on the top floor of W. L. Harkness used as an experimental room with soundscriber and phonograph, finds that it needs to add to the machines in that room another machine the cost of which is $191.35. I am enclosing the memorandum given to me by the colleague who is in charge of that aspect of our work, Howard Garey. He has gone over the problem very carefully and has tried the machine here with his colleagues. The machine can be obtained easily from a firm in the city all complete at the price of $191.35 mentioned above. The advantages of such a machine are very great. The student may study a text recorded by a teacher, then record in imitation any portion of the tape in the reverse direction; he can listen to the teacher's voice and then to his own and this saves our time considerably since the teacher does not have to be present while the student is working in our experimental room upstairs outside of the regular class hours.

Could we get a special grant of $191.35 in order to buy the machine? Although money cannot be transferred from an educational budget to a miscellaneous budget, I should like to point out that we have saved this year $250 from the sum allotted in our budget to the reader and $100 on the sum allotted for the special course for graduate students. If money can be transferred from one to the other, it would therefore be available. We could also make a purchase from our regular miscellaneous expense fund, but that fund, as you know, amounts to only $700 plus $500 for the Yale French Studies. If we paid for this new machine from our regular fund which usually goes to stamps, letters, and miscellaneous expenses, we would almost certainly have to overspend a sum approximately equivalent. We might do that with your permission if you prefer it, not finding the extra fund desirable at present. I shall be glad to receive a word of advice from you as to what you think is best.

Very sincerely yours,
HM Peyre

## To the same:

Nov. 27—1950

Dear Mr. Furniss:

I seriously think it is high time you should consult the members of the French Department, down to the rank of instructor, included or not, on the way their department has been run, how satisfied they are with it, what changes they might desire in its administration, whether they think it wise to have the same chairman continue or if they would prefer another member of the Department to hold that office.

I believe I have done tolerably well in the job & I believe I enjoy the confidence of my colleagues; but I also feel that it would be healthier to have a frank expression of opinion, anonymous or not shown specifically to me, from my colleagues. I am glad to continue working at the job if desired, as you know, for somehow there seems to be no one quite ideal for it (assuming that I was!), & more particularly, I have drawn so much business to the position here (editorial consultative committees outside, chairmanship of societies or groups, reading of manuscripts, etc.) that in all likelihood I would have to continue assuming those outside burdens, whether I would be chairman of the Department at Yale or not—or else, I would be passing too heavy a load to my successor & I would pity him. But people now seem to take it for granted that I was made to be a department Chairman, just as you obviously were made to be an executive & an organizing brain. I was indignant last spring when my Harvard colleagues, who are looking for a chairman & haven't yet found one, suggested I desert Yale for Cambridge & assumed as a matter of course that I would have to be a chairman for life! I would sincerely feel better if you provoked an expression of opinion from all my colleagues, & maybe persons from other departments—& I would not at all mind any criticism of me thus expressed—on the contrary.

Will you bestow two more titles—at no cost to the University?

1) It would be a good thing, if Mr. Babb concurred, to make R. T. Hill "Curator of the Romance Seminar Library." That library, gradually accumulated by him, has 3.200 volumes or so & is in the Romance Seminar in [the] H[all of] G[raduate] S[tudies]. He could go on cataloguing the books given him after he retires & retain a link with the University.

2) We decided, at our Romance Languages Graduate Faculty meeting last Nov. 17, on my motion, that we appoint Prof. Auerbach "Director of Graduate Studies in Romance Philology." If you agree, we'll submit it to Dean Simmett & put it in the Graduate School Catalogue. We have 2 or 3 students every year who work for a Ph.D. in Romance Philology (overlapping Old French, Spanish, Old Italian, Provençal, etc.), & it would be good to receive especial advice & attention, & Mr. Auerbach is the competent person to do it. He is proving, by the way, very adaptable & very successful with the students.

Sorry to be always bombarding you with letters.

Sincerely,
Hri Peyre

I told Hill about his Graduate School office. It's a fair decision & should be all right.

## To William DeVane:

November 27, 1950

Dear Dean DeVane:

I am sending you (and a copy to Provost Furniss) the proposals of the French department for 1951–52. Some information on the plans here submitted and on the background behind them may not be out of order.

The French Department has made great progress in the last decade. Boastful as it may seem of its chairman to state it thus bluntly, it has won a position of acknowledged leadership in the country. It attracts the best graduate students in the nation, and good undergraduates at Yale to its courses, though too few majors as yet. Its methods of language teaching have drawn visitors and imitators by the dozens; its staff is envied by many and indeed has been drawn upon already and largely; every one of its graduate students having completed his work here last year was easily placed in the profession, exactly twelve out of twelve; our journal, *Yale French Studies,* is said by many to be the best in our field in the country. The chairman sits on many, too many committees of professional organizations, learned journals, as the representative for French studies in the country at large.

The policy has been all these years to rebuild a staff of very high quality through encouraging younger men, urging them to publish, insisting upon good teaching and upon an atmosphere of harmony and cordiality. It seems to have been successful. The French Department, however, unlike other departments at Yale which are top heavy, has lacked men at the top, in the full professor rank. There were three such professors ten years ago, when I took over; there was only one last year, when a second one, Professor Auerbach was appointed. Meanwhile the number of students has increased. Unlike the majority of universities where Spanish became the language most widely elected, French at Yale attracts twice as many students as either Spanish or German (950 undergraduates this year). It has increased relatively and even absolutely last year. Graduate students in French are, including some fifteen now in France on a scholarship, 65 in number, practically all Ph.D. candidates, or over four or five times the number in German or Spanish. The load weighs heavily upon a few members of the Department who have to organize the work, direct the theses, and generally provide information and guidance to other French Departments in the country.

I have tried repeatedly to get scholars and teachers of eminence to join our staff as professors or associate professors. It has not proved easy, for the upper ranks in our profession or in our special fields are not very brilliantly provided. Our lack, especially at the associate professor rank, was in substantial publication. Professor Hill, who has long served the University, will soon retire. Professor Richardson will retire in 1957 and, though very valuable in his courses, is not likely to publish very much. Professor Andersson is very busy with the organization of the undergraduate work, the supervision of classes, the representation of our Department outside at conventions and international gatherings. Professor Cornell was made associate professor last year and further production can confidently be expected from him. Two names remain: those of Professors Morehouse and Boorsch, who have served in that rank for respectively eleven and ten years. Although in quantitative terms they have not published big books, they are excellent scholars, with fine qualitative output behind them, respected in the profession, with very alert minds, fine intellects, great teaching ability and unstinted devotion. They are both at work on books which will constitute substantial additions to their published work. But it seemed advisable and indeed imperative not to delay further their accession to a higher rank, amply deserved in each case. Accompanying letters and promotion blanks are proposing that Morehouse, aged 55, and Boorsch, aged 45, be made full professors of French, at a salary of $8,000. This would bring the number of our full professors up to four, which is modest enough as compared to other French Departments elsewhere, and as compared to the Department of German, or of Philosophy, or of Geology, or of Classics at Yale.

At the same time, it is proposed that Georges May, at present assistant professor of French, an excellent teacher, the author of three books and ten articles, who has received flattering invitations from five or six rival institutions, be made associate professor without delay. This was promised him when he rejected other offers to stay with us. He is a very promising man.

Another assistant professor, Kenneth Douglas, who has a very sharp mind, a powerful intellectual grasp, a wide scholarship, but has had to delay writing a book though he is the author of many articles and essays, will, we hope, be made associate professor in another year (1952–53).

Our ambition would be to enable him to complete the volume on which he has been at work through a research assistant professorship as provided by a recent and generous grant.

Finally, Imbrie Buffum, now completing his first term as an assistant professor, is being proposed for a second term at the higher bracket in the same rank ($4,500). . . .

It is hoped that these proposals will meet with the approval of the Administration, with whom they were previously discussed, and of the competent committees.

Sincerely yours,<br>HM Peyre

## À Mario Maurin:

Ce mercredi 30 nov. (1950)

Mon cher ami,

Vos deux articles sont précieux & je compte bien que nous les utilisions tous les deux: je n'ai encore pu les montrer à Cornell, mais j'en suis emballé. Les pages sur Gide sont fort curieuses & joliment bien venues: elles affirment, insultent, vitupèrent. Elles abaissent Gide, & cela ne me gêne point. Je ne suis pas sûr qu'elles élèvent Suarès, mais l'homme est à prendre tel qu'il était — & quel styliste!

Votre article sur leurs relations est excellent aussi — et juste quoique penchant un peu du côté de Suarès — Bien sûr, j'avais aussitôt ajouté les pages du Journal qui manquaient: page 5, p. 293–7 (Pléiade) & p. 7, date 1921, & je fais p. 6 l'addition que vous dites.

Vous sembliez un peu fatigué lundi, & je l'étais un peu ce jour-là. Mais j'ai eu une vraie & profonde joie à vous revoir & à parler avec vous. Vous avez l'un des cerveaux les mieux organisés & les plus prodigieusement précoces qui soient — et vous avez, en plus, une âme, un grand fond de sensibilité, une noblesse dans la recherche de ce qu'il y a de plus grave & de plus frémissant en vous, qu'à vous connaître d'abord quand vous étiez plus jeune étudiant, je ne soupçonnais pas toujours. Votre recherche présente, votre évolution doivent être vôtres, et je ne vous souhaite pas de trouver vite ou aisément. Mais jamais ce que vous deviendrez ne me sera indifférent.

Vous m'écrivez des choses imméritées. Je n'ai pas de fausse modestie

& je ne sais même pas assez m'humilier pour espérer un jour être élevé. Mais je ne me crois que fort médiocre, désespérément embourbé dans la facilité, & me faisant pardonner ce que plus jeune j'avais rêvé de faire & n'ai pas accompli par des services menus que je rends à d'autres. Du moins, je crois être resté assez jeune pour découvrir & encourager les vocations de plus ardents & juvéniles esprits, assez généreux pour les envier mais les aider et non les étouffer. Vous avez beaucoup à donner, Maurin—aux vôtres, à votre famille un jour, mais aussi dans le domaine littéraire, critique, philosophique. Comme on le dit un jour à Du Bos qui le rapporte & plus que lui aussi, vous êtes responsable de tout ce que vous portez en vous. Donnez-le un jour—mais pour cela ménagez-vous—ne vous accablez pas de besognes qui usent, je ne le sais que trop.

Je n'ai pu encore lire vos poèmes—mais vais y venir. Pour l'article en français (pages de Suarès lui-même), notre règle étant de publier en anglais, selon notre prospectus même, nous devrions sans doute ajouter à votre page liminaire un résumé en anglais de ces mots bien peu résumables. Voulez-vous préparer ces 15 ou 20 lignes vous-même pour qu'elles ne trahissent pas Suarès ou son grand prêtre, et me les envoyer quand vous aurez fini votre pièce—d'ici le 8 déc. par exemple?

Merci & mes amitiés,<br>
Henri Peyre

## À Georges May:

Du 3 déc. 1950

Mon cher ami,

Nous avons eu un ouragan féroce qui a privé presque tous les quartiers de lumière et de feu, a battu impitoyablement les plus hauts arbres sur notre rue et Whitney Ave., a tué 60 à 70 personnes. Puis voilà la débâcle en Corée et le pays n'est pas content ni rassuré. Il semble en effet (quoique les Français soient beaucoup trop sévères là-dessus) que MacArthur n'ait pas été très habile et n'ait pas su s'arrêter et négocier, mais cela est raisonner après coup. Le fait est que l'Amérique ne veut pas trop s'empêtrer en Asie et sait qu'elle n'y peut rien gagner à la longue; et le fait est aussi qu'après avoir aidé le monde entier elle n'est pas aimée. Je crois encore qu'il n'arrivera rien de grave, et que le pire danger est celui des exaltés dans ce pays même qui veulent guerroyer contre les Communistes partout où il y en a.

Merci de vos bonnes nouvelles et de vouloir bien consacrer un peu de votre temps à nos brebis errantes dans Paris, mais ne vous dévouez pas plus que de raison à cet office pastoral. Vous avez à faire l'initiation de votre femme à la cuisine de France, aux robes des couturiers, aux musées, à la conduite experte dans Paris: ne négligez pas la province, Langres! Nancy, Honfleur . . . Avignon bien sûr, et même quelques pèlerinages à Port Royal, ou à Meaux, pour expier auprès de ces nids ecclésiastiques les ors gagnés avec votre livre [*D'Ovide à Racine*] sur l'auteur de l'art des caresses. . . .

Nous avons une lourde besogne. J'avais des doutes très sincères, si je devais continuer comme chairman, non par paresse ou dérobade, mais par scrupule. J'ai demandé au Provost de vous consulter à ce sujet à mon insu. Si vraiment un autre de nos collègues devait faire neuf, être peut-être moins accaparant ou moins dominateur que moi, je n'ai cure des honneurs et ai assez de quoi m'occuper par ailleurs. Votre avis serait précieux, car vous jugez avec lucidité vos collègues. Ce n'est pas des compliments que je veux, vous le savez. D'ailleurs j'ai prié qu'on consulte les collègues en secret.

[Sans signature]

## To Robert Greer Cohn:

December 20, 1950

Mr. Robert G. Cohn
c/o M. Goguel
7, Avenue Foch
St. Cloud (Seine-et-Oise)
France

My dear Cohn:

Your book continues to be talked about, and therefore, I hope, to be read and bought. Just yesterday a friend of Hermann Brock was urgently asking for a copy to offer as a Christmas present. A week earlier, a French lady, the ablest, I think, who teaches in this country, was stimulated by it to undertake a new explanation of the Coup de Dés. She expects her own interpretation to be more interior than yours and deeper. I told her to go ahead and the public will judge. You probably saw Rhodes' long and thoughtful review in the last number of the Romanic Review. If you have not, I could lend you my copy. Obviously you cannot expect people merely to agree with your views without dissent, but a healthy exchange of interpretations serves both your own volume and Mallarmé and seems to me all for the best.

Things have deteriorated on the political front, as you know, and there is some feeling of panic over here and I suppose some deep anxiety in France also. We may well have lost the whole of Asia to communism. I am not sure it is better for Asia, and I do not believe we should despair. Americans are very determined and I am confident myself we may thus avoid the war, at least for several years, and the terror that a Russian occupation would mean for Western Europe. It is not communism so much that is feared as the Asiatic soldiers who would make up most of Russia's armies and whose reign of terror would be far worse than anything the Germans ever did. But there is too little time for me, alas, to write on politics. I shall wait for your return to have longer discussions with you and to hear about your impressions which strike me as extremely interesting. Sometime you should write me also a little more on your life and that of your wife, on how you may enjoy yourself over there, and, above all, about the progress of your work and the trends you are now following. You always suffered from excessive solitude which came partly from pride, partly from shyness, and I believe you should go out of your way to meet as many French intellectuals and scholars as possible. What are your plans for next year? Do tell your wife that I consider her raising your child at least as worthy as writing a thesis, but I still nourish the hope that she may somehow do both, if you can be trained to take care of the child for half of the day.

Our best regards to both of you and

Very sincerely.
HM Peyre

## To Harry Levin:

Jan. 1—1951

My dear Harry Levin:

I had to cut myself into pieces at that crowded meeting, & to fight my way along lobbies & against old & new acquaintances refusing to be forgotten—& one of the papers I was most curious & anxious to hear, yours, I had to miss. If & when you publish "The tradition of tradition" will you let me know or let me have a reprint? The title & the topic puzzled me & I should very much want to read you on the subject.

I am sorry I failed to even see you. But I was not my own master. In fact, I seldom feel I am a free man any longer. Still, courage for the New Year & my very cordial & sincere wishes.

Henri Peyre

Your article in our last number was brilliant & suggestive—& many of us envy your style! Thank you for it.

## To Edgar Furniss:

Jan. 8/1951

Dear Mr. Furniss,

If I understand you right, I should get Mr. Douglas reappointed for one year as Assistant-Professor for 1951–52, so that he is on the faculty while enjoying a Research Assistant-Professorship. That would be an appointment without stipend, since the stipend is provided from other sources.

Do I take it for granted that we may have, in 1951–52, three exchange students from France, paid as in the past from Sterling funds ($1500 each), in exchange for which I'll send three of our graduate students to Paris on French government fellowships? The system has been beneficial to the two sides & is more than ever necessary, now, it seems to me, when a better understanding between Americans & Europeans, starting on the student level, is imperative. If I have your OK & that of the President, I shall start examining the French candidates & shall later submit our proposals to Hartley [Simpson, dean of Graduate Studies] as usual. Our three men this year (from France) study in Physics, International Relations & American literature & are all able & serious young men.

Sincerely,<br>
Hri Peyre

## À Georges May:

Du 18 janv. 1951<br>
De New Haven à Paris

Mon cher ami,

... C'est du train [à Boston] que je vous écris. ...

Vous avez eu raison de me croire quand je m'époumonais à répéter "Faites des livres!" comme le professeur de gymnastique disait "Mesdemoiselles, faites-vous des cuisses!" L'année prochaine ne sera pas si mauvaise qu'on le craint: il y aura peut-être des jeunes gens que nous renverra l'armée ou la marine—et je crois toujours qu'il n'y aura pas de guerre. Pour le point délicat sur lequel je sollicitais votre avis, à cause de l'affection que j'ai pour vous et de ma confiance en votre jugement et votre dévouement, je suppose que vous avez raison. Je crois vraiment que, sans le vouloir, j'encombre un peu parce que je fais beaucoup de choses et que beaucoup de gens s'adressent à moi—et envers Tug dont la femme traverse une crise de marasme, je sens que les décisions importantes lui échappent, puisque je les prends. Mais souvent, sans doute, elles ne seraient pas prises du tout si je ne les prenais, et ma présence dans bien des comités, qui a depuis longtemps cessé de chatouiller ma vanité, me permet, parce que je suis craint, d'obtenir bien des choses. Mais je ne veux surtout pas me montrer accaparant, et trop respecté par les amis et les jeunes, vous, Douglas, Boorsch, etc. Toute critique m'est utile et me fait plaisir. J'espère ne jamais tourner au "patron" ossifié. Et, confession bête, j'aime lire les livres (même érudits), et j'aime même en écrire, et voudrais en écrire encore, si le temps m'en est laissé!

Pour le moment, j'ai 5 ou 600 demandes de bourses Guggenheim à examiner de près, dans les domaines les plus divers, et la routine habituelle mais toujours hérissée de besognes imprévues. Je rêve souvent de

Paris que j'adore, et l'achat d'une auto, les impôts accrus, un livre à faire m'empêcheront peut-être d'y retourner cet été. Cela nous attriste. . . .

## À Mario Maurin:

Ce 24—i—51

Mon cher ami,

Voici votre chapitre. Il a de l'éclat, de la flamme, il campe bien le personnage; il est bien écrit—un peu vite, toujours. Vous gagneriez parfois à écrire & récrire, à composer avec plus de science voulue. Mais il est fort bon, bien entendu.

Je vois mal encore comment il va s'insérer dans l'ensemble; reviendrez-vous plus tard sur la biographie ou non? À quels aspects de son portrait psychologique vous attacherez-vous plutôt? Ce 1er chapitre est-il comme le cadre général dans lequel vous insérerez plus tard d'autres analyses de Suarès?

Quelques points ici sont obscurs que les lecteurs de votre thèse voudront peut-être savoir. Sans doute les indiquerez-vous quelque part: 1) Sur quoi fondez-vous tout cela? Quelles sont vos sources documentaires? Qu'y a-t-il d'imprimé, d'inédit, dont vous tiriez votre savoir? 2) ne serait-il pas utile de poser au moins quelques-unes des questions conventionnelles auxquelles on répond d'ordinaire dans une thèse, mais aussi dans un livre? Par exemple à quoi dans son hérédité, dans sa formation Suarès doit-il son caractère, en partie? Juif & marseillais (le 2e point n'est pas rendu très clair dans votre chapitre, ni pourquoi il en était accablé. J'ai connu à Paris bien des Marseillais qui ne l'étaient pas intimidés, pas plus que Valéry d'être Cettois ou Sétois, Giono d'être de Manosque, Cézanne ou Brémond d'être d'Aix). Au physique par exemple il a dû être nerveux, susceptible, vite irrité? Était-il maladif? Redoutait-il la maladie qui emporta son père? Au moral, quelles influences subit-il? Religieuses, philosophiques, littéraires, artistiques? Fut-il fort impressionné par ses études classiques, Grecs, Latins etc.? Apprit-il les langues? Pourquoi se spécialisa-t-il dans l'histoire? Parmi les grands hommes de l'époque, fut-il très tôt impressionné par Baudelaire? Par Mallarmé quand? Par l'atmosphère symboliste? Par Taine, Renan? Villiers de l'Isle Adam peut-être, autre grand isolé? etc. Votre chapitre adopte l'optique de Suarès: mais *quid* d'autres alors avec qui il eut quelque chose en commun, mêmes études, même atmosphère littéraire & musicale, etc. Gide dont les mémoires nous instruisent; Benda, autre Juif; Valéry; Pierre Louys; etc. De Rolland, vous parlez surtout avec sarcasme & il mérite mieux que cela.

Enfin ne devriez-vous pas vérifier ce que vous savez de l'intérieur sur Suarès par quelques témoignages autres ou datés. Par ex. p. 4, Marsan: quelle référence exacte dans les *Nouvelles litt.*? On le voudra dans votre thèse, & même dans votre livre? et Marsan n'erre-t-il pas? Je vois dans un catalogue ici que Suarès (& Rolland) sont à l'ENS de la promotion 1886, non 84. Est-il possible que Suarès soit entré à l'Ecole normale étant en philosophie—? Je ne crois pas. Les deux bachots sont exigés avant le concours. Une petite vérification auprès du Secrétariat de l'Ecole serait de mise.

Plus tard encore, sur le groupe de la NRF (1909–14) vous passez bien vite; ou sur ce qu'était cette Grande Revue, son atmosphère, ses collaborateurs, sa tendance—et pp. 15–16, n'escamotez-vous pas le reste de sa vie? Il y aurait un peu plus que votre lecteur voudrait savoir sur Suarès pendant l'occupation, son attitude, ses malheurs. L'espèce de gloire qu'il eut tout de même entre 1930 & 39, avec plusieurs de ses livres lus par l'élite, un succès d'estime réel. . . .

Je crains que vous n'alliez un peu vite et vous libériez un peu facilement de quelques précisions tout de même utiles dans une thèse. Réfléchissez-y vous-même.

Avec mes amitiés,<br>Henri Peyre

## À Claude Vigée:

Ce 4 février/51

Mon cher Ami,

Je ne vous ai jamais encore remercié de votre très gentil don de cette belle traduction. Je l'ai pourtant lue peu après et je l'ai trouvée très *belle,* réussie à tous égards, traduction d'un érudit & d'un poète. Vous avez certainement une vocation pour rendre Rilke en français comme il aurait voulu l'être, par votre bilinguisme mais plus encore par votre ferveur et votre don poétique, & cette pénétration si aiguë, presque sensuelle, dans les secrets d'un texte.

J'ai malheureusement & plus que jamais tant de besogne que je ne puis consacrer aux lettres qui devraient être sincères & longues le temps qu'il faudrait! Mais vous pensez bien que j'ai soutenu, & soutiendrai encore, votre candidature à une bourse Guggenheim. Le choix en est fait avec beau coup de loyauté & de soin; mais on pèse tant d'éléments (valeur du projet, s'il peut être accompli aisément sans bourse & pendant les vacances d'un professeur, son intérêt général, les promesses du candidat, etc.) que le choix entre un nombre énorme de candidats reste incertain & n'est connu que tard. Mais je crois que vous devriez avoir de l'espoir.

De tous côtés vous travaillez, produisez, créez. Profitez de ces années où la vie ne vous a pas encore submergé d'obligations! Hélas! Je ne puis songer à collaborer à votre beau projet sur Rilke & l'Europe. Steiner, oui, bien qu'il soit surtout l'homme de petits détails; Mrs. Renée Lang, de Wells College, Aurora (NY) aurait là-dessus beaucoup à dire; il vous faudrait qqc. sur R & Cézanne, R & Valéry, R & Jacobsen, R & la Russie. Mon ancien collègue Warren Ramsey (auj. à Berkeley, Cal, French Depart.) connaît bien Rilke aussi, & Laforgue, & la poésie moderne.

Je n'ai jamais vu Malaquais. Ses livres ne m'emballent pas, mais ont eu du succès. On l'a dit, de plusieurs côtés, pas commode de caractère & il serait bon d'enquêter d'abord là-dessus. Les "créateurs" n'ont pas à être adaptables, évidemment . . . mais je ne sais rien de première main.

Amitiés à votre femme.

> Bien à vous & merci encore de votre livre,
> Hri Peyre

## À Mario Maurin:

> Fevr. 7/51

Mon cher ami,

Merci de votre lettre et d'avoir bien pris mes très menues critiques. Tous n'ont point cette grâce—et croyez bien que les éloges que je vous fais, et qu'à d'autres je fais de vous, sont d'une totale sincérité. Ces critiques sont une égale marque d'intérêt.

Les pages, que je vous renvoie, expliquent en effet beaucoup & me rappellent à l'esprit, de façon qui sera plus durable, le peu que vous m'aviez dit de votre projet: où il ira (1914), ce qu'il embrassera. Cela s'annonce excellent. Continuez.

Non, sur R. Rolland, vous n'êtes pas injuste. Votre nature est passionnée derrière sa sérénité en apparence nuancée d'ironie. Et vous ne pourrez pas vous empêcher d'aimer Suarès comme il faut aimer—contre. Mais vous restez juste. Et même si vous exagériez parfois la grandeur de votre homme, ce ne serait que juste, & nécessaire pour que le balancier retombe ou retourne après vous où il doit être.

Vous êtes le seul à qui j'aie jamais reproché d'écrire vite. D'ordinaire, je blâme tous nos faiseurs de thèse pour donner l'impression qu'ils ont enfanté dans la douleur & que leurs chapitres se suivent mal, que leur travail manque d'élan. Le mal est bien léger dans votre cas—vous avez l'art de faire croire que vous écrivez la bride sur le cou et vous ne laissez pas de bavure ni de tache dans votre style. Vous courez, mais sans tomber.

Encore mes vœux & amitiés,<br>Henri Peyre

## To Edgar Furniss:

Febr. 8—1951

Dear Mr. Furniss:

With full appreciation of the present uncertainty & difficulties due to outside causes, I am wondering if it would not be wise to give some assurance to the "full" instructors who will very probably be needed next year that their reappointment will be acted upon soon.

One of our men, Guicharnaud, the one we rate highest & whom we shall certainly need (instructor, with $3800 proposed for him in next year's budget), is being approached by the University of Oregon. I have told him to answer them courteously but to say that, as far as he knows, he will be needed here & I believe he prefers to stay here; but it would be embarrassing if later we had to disappoint him, or men in a similar case. I believe it would be wise for us to go ahead with some of the most desirable appointments.

In our case, we have many assistants in instruction whom we shall only reappoint at the last minute anyway—with the prospect of Mr.

Andersson being engaged on other activities, we shall not be overstaffed next year, even if we lose one fifth of our students or more.

Sincerely,<br>Hri Peyre

## À Georges May:

[Sans date; timbre d'oblitération 16 fév. 1951]

Mon cher ami,

...Vous avez aimé Londres. Je m'y suis déplu moi-même en 1949, mais peut-être parce que je n'y retrouvais pas mes étonnements et joies de jeune homme. J'avais vivement aimé la ville à 20 ans. La ville a une adorable poésie. Dommage que vous n'ayez pas été à Cambridge que je préfère peut-être à Oxford.

[À propos de divers jeunes collègues qui ne "produisaient" pas]. Pour ma part, peu importe. Mon père était prof. de lycée et n'a fait de livres qu'après sa retraite; je le considérais néanmoins comme un des hommes les plus fins et les plus intelligents que j'aie jamais rencontrés. Mais un lycée permet cela—ou en Amérique une université reculée....

## To Harry Levin:

Febr. 18/51

My dear Levin:

May I merely transmit the enclosed letter? Wade seems to fear you, & to overrate my influence—The young man, Rudich, is blind, or "à peu près." He seems to be very gifted & to have worked with extraordinary courage & with good results. He is now ready to teach, after two years in France: I have never met him, but corresponded with him & I have much sympathy for him, & sincerely believe he could do well. Would there be any chance for him, at Harvard, of doing some French civilization & some Comparative Lit?

Of course, it's a bad year for jobs & your university will probably put off decisions, like ours, until the last minute. You may hear of other possibilities for Rudich, however. I had the feeling that a smaller college, in the country, might be the best.

I have lately corresponded with Poulet & read his book & some articles with more care: he is a profound mind, has range, originality, &, doubtless, is superior to Hoog in several respects. Hoog is probably the better choice, when all is considered (lecturing, influence on undergraduates, liveliness), but Poulet should be brought over to this country, either if a second opening were created at Harvard or in some other University. Your instinct, or rather your considered judgment about him (I distrusted Wahl's a little) was right.

Are you well & not too busy, as I fear I am? Is Shattuck proving a success, as a Fellow? I had some slight hesitations, for there are big & grave shortcomings in his translation of Apollinaire & I did not feel he was quite up to the originality of Cohn, who had been turned down; but he has will, steadiness of purpose & good judgment.

Most cordially yours,<br>Henri Peyre

## To Edgar Furniss:

February 21, 1951

Dear Mr. Furniss:

Would you kindly appoint Professor H. B. Richardson as Director of Undergraduate Studies to replace Professor Andersson starting July 1st? Mr. Richardson, of course, is by far the most competent person to fill the post which Mr. Andersson's new job will leave vacant.

I suppose you will make some kind of arrangement so that Mr. Andersson's salary starting July 1st will either be modified according to the terms proposed to him and remain in our budget or be provided for in a separate budget, as you see fit. I should like to point out that it would be very just to take advantage of the funds made available by Mr. Andersson's new functions to increase Mr. Richardson's salary by $500. Mr. Richardson is a man of approximately sixty-two who has done excellent service to the University for very many years as an associate professor. For a while, during the war and just after, he took some extra work outside, as you remember, which never brought him more than a few hundred dollars. But his connection with that accounting business was completely broken off a long time ago, and he has had lately to assume a far larger share of our graduate work, giving the graduate course in medieval literature. I believe he should be receiving $7,000 as an associate professor of great competence, usefulness, and devotion, who will have to assume the burden of directing most of our undergraduate work.

Sincerely yours,<br>
Hri Peyre

## To the same:

February 21, 1951

Dear Mr. Furniss:

I do not mean to press the vexing question of instructors' appointments for next year in an undue and embarrassing way. But since conditions must vary from one department to another, I believe I should keep you informed of prospects in the French Department.

This year (1950–51), if I am correct, and counting every graduate course as the equivalent of three hours a week (they meet for at least two hours and often for a third hour of discussion, or more), our Department gave 264 hours of instruction, divided as follows:

| | |
|---|---|
| 2 full professors: | 15 hours |
| 9 associate and assistant Prof.: | 80 hours |
| 6 instructors: | 66 hours |
| assistants in instruction: | <u>103 hours</u> |
| | 264 hours |

Next year, Mr. Andersson, being called to other duties, will only give three hours (one graduate course). Mr. Douglas will be on leave on a fellowship, but Mr. May will be back with us. One assistant professor, Mr. Collignon, is being lured by Cornell and will leave us. One at least of our instructors, Mr. Galand, is also invited elsewhere. Others may also be tempted, but I believe it would be a mistake to let more than one other instructor, at most, go.

We shall thus have as "regular" members of our staff:

| | |
|---|---|
| 2 full professors: | 15 hours |
| 5 associate professors, plus Mr. Hill on half time and Mr. Andersson for one course: | 53 hours, plus thesis direction, etc. |
| 1 assistant professor | 9 hours, plus majors |
| 5 instructors, at the most: | <u>55 hours</u> |
| | 132 hours |

The total thus forecast happens (by mere chance) to be 50 percent of the total of hours taught this year, which is 264 hours. Thus, even if the cut in student registration reaches 50 percent, we should not cause the University any serious problem if we gave some assurance to our instructors that there will be room for them next year.

The large number of assistants in instruction, usually appointed at the last minute (in September) and if need be for one term, gives our Department much leeway. But the plight of several of those assistants, who are married men and often veterans having exhausted their G.I. Bill entitlement, is a difficult one, and discouragement is spreading among the young and promising members of our profession. What can be done about it, I of course do not know.

Sincerely yours,
HM Peyre

## À Georges May:

Du 3 mars 1951

Mon cher ami,

Diverses absences (comités, conférences, etc.) m'ont empêché de vous répondre—et quelquefois, devant l'amas de lettres sur ma table, un certain désespoir me saisit et je me plonge, au lieu d'y répondre, dans quelque lecture ardue. Je sors du *Contrat social*. C'est fort, mais c'est dur. . . .

## À Mario Maurin:

Le 9 mars/51

Mon cher ami,

Vos chapitres sont excellents & votre thèse s'annonce ferme, forte, profonde. Vous enrichissez cette analyse de Suarès de votre curiosité, qui est vaste, de votre culture, sans pédantisme & avec profit: vous élargissez ses débats en problèmes philosophiques, & ils le furent en effet. Dans le 1er de vos chapitres, votre portrait juxtapose beaucoup de traits & évite de construire en force la figure spirituelle de Suarès—mais tout compte fait je crois que c'est avec raison. Et ce qui fut évidemment chez lui hypersensitivité nerveuse, "allergies" diverses, et culture un peu obstinée de ces "vapeurs" est par vous respecté—encore avec raison. Vous évitez tout jargon psychanalytique, même toute indiscrétion sur sa vie sexuelle, cette curieuse conviction de S., qu'il n'était pas beau, pas homme à succès. En vérité, n'y avait-il pas chez lui un fond de misogynie, fréquent d'ailleurs dans notre sexe & parmi les intellectuels?

Je crois que vous devriez poursuivre & faire de votre 1ère rédaction votre version définitive, sans avoir nul besoin de me la soumettre. Bien sûr, j'apprends à vous lire & tiens à vous lire, pour le profit & la joie—mais en ami, & non en "maître." Je n'ai pas un mot à changer.

Je serai absent de dimanche 18 au 25 environ. Si vous veniez alors reprendre cela, je le laisserai pour vous sous enveloppe—ou peux vous l'envoyer—Allez-vous bien? Mes bons vœux.

H. P.

Ai-je jamais dignement remercié votre mère de ce cadeau qui a été fort apprécié. La qualité de ce parfum & de cette exquise eau de cologne était très haute!

## À Jorge Guillén:

Ce 31—3—1951

Mon cher poète,

Ce livre que vous avez eu la gentille pensée de m'envoyer du Mexique m'a beaucoup touché. Il est d'ailleurs très bien écrit & fort intéressant. Merci. Votre gendre m'avait donné le sien, d'un vrai & sûr savant.

C'est un hispanisant d'avenir! Je l'ai prêté aussitôt à Damaso Alonso, qui est ici ce trimestre. Il trouve Yale un peu étrange (vous vous rappelez l'atmosphère de ce département d'espagnol, timoré et parent pauvre) — mais il se repose & se plaît — & économise pour le retour à son siège académique. En français, par contre, nous regorgeons d'élèves & moi de travail. J'écris surtout des lettres & des corrections sur des devoirs & des plans de thèses — mais des articles cependant, et parfois quelque livre. Je vous enverrai un tout modeste hommage à Baudelaire un de ces jours.

Vous êtes donc le poète errant. Vos vers, dans *Asomante,* m'ont ébloui: splendeur! Mais vous ne voulez conserver votre inspiration qu'à condition de fuir Wellesley & ses fruits mûrs — et vous êtes en conséquence loin de nous, perdu dans les brouillards. Voyez-vous Ramsey, mon collègue, ici fort regretté? Êtes-vous inspiré?

Notre très affectueux & fidèle souvenir,
Henri Peyre

## À Claude Vigée:

Ce 25 avril/51

Mon cher ami,

Je vous félicite de la bourse, & vous envie. J'ai été content de pouvoir persuader mes collègues du Comité de votre incontestable talent. Le sujet paraissait peu orthodoxe et soulevait quelques objections, mais j'ai bien insisté pour que l'on fît attention à l'*homme* & à ses promesses, surtout.

Je ne crois pas qu'il y ait de guerre & l'ai toujours dit — et vous devriez profiter de votre congé. Après, enfants, profession, avenir vous dévoreront. Si j'en juge par moi-même, on cesse vite, après 40 ans, d'être un homme libre.

Mes félicitations aussi pour vos poèmes & publications. Vous êtes magnifique d'énergie et de foi. Je ferai acheter, & connaître, l'anthologie allemande. L'anthologie de la poésie allemande sera aussi précieuse. S. Astre en a publié une assez bonne de la jeune poésie anglaise.

Pour vos idées théoriques sur la chose poétique, le rêve, etc., je crois que vous devriez les mûrir, les alléger, les filtrer, & les publier en volume en France. Ici, cela passe difficilement. Après le 1er lecteur, j'ai dû rejeter votre article pour PMLA. Ce n'est pas le genre & vous n'auriez pas eu d'intérêt professionnel à paraître là avec cet article. Si vous devez aspirer à une chaire enviée dans une plus grande université, il faut que vous jouiez le jeu et écriviez des articles plus clairs, plus objectifs, moins chargés de citations & d'allusions, plus aisément convainquants. Il y avait des tas d'idées dans celui-là, sur Breton, le rêve, etc., mais, franchement, mal mises en œuvre. Nous sommes, à PMLA, obligés de n'accepter à peu près qu'un article sur 4 ou 5, et de préférer donc les articles qu'apprécie la majorité des lecteurs et qui sont inattaquables. J'espère que vous ne m'en aurez pas voulu les tâches qu'on m'impose de tous côtés, là, au Guggenheim, et me contraignent à paraître dur envers bien des amis et à dire non plus souvent que je ne le souhaiterais. Mais vous savez de reste combien je vous estime.

Pour notre revue, Yale French Studies, voudriez-vous songer à présenter un article (10–15 pges) en anglais, convenant à notre public d'environ 2.000 lecteurs ou exemplaires, donc pas trop spécial ni abstrus? Le n° (MSS dûs 15 nov. 1951) auquel je pense sera sur "Symbole Symbolisme," mais pourrait étudier le symbole de Claudel, de Reverdy, etc.—ou Rilke & le Symbolisme.

Voulez-vous afficher ceci, dans l'espoir que cela suscitera autour de vous quelques abonnés?

> Bon souvenir à votre femme & bien à vous,
> H. P.

## À Mario Maurin:

> Ce 28/IV/51

Mon cher ami,

Votre thèse est fort bonne—très bien écrite & agréable—pénétrante souvent et élevant le sujet (déjà assez haut par lui-même) à une belle généralité philosophique. Elle mérite de devenir un livre—et je ne vois pas pourquoi, si vous ne voulez pas en ce moment reprendre le sujet et écrire sur Suarès un livre complet & général, vous ne la publieriez pas telle qu'elle est. On pourrait essayer Emile Paul ou Grasset—ou la publier dans la série de travaux que nous avons à Paris en français, aux Presses Universitaires. Les frais sont à la charge de l'auteur, mais je crois que vous feriez là un bon placement pour votre carrière. Si vous devez vraiment enseigner en Amérique il faudra que vous ayez un livre derrière vous assez tôt—et celui-ci vous fait honneur. Il sert la mémoire de Suarès & la cause du bon goût—et le fait avec talent.

J'en parlerai, quand ils l'auront lue, à vos lecteurs & je pense que ce sera aussi leur avis.

Il y a (comme il se trouve, c'est le 2e exemplaire qu'on m'a donné) de petites tâches—d'impression surtout. Quelquefois des incorrections (qu'attirent p. 32)—une affirmation erronée qui fait (p. 19) passer Claudel par la Rue d'Ulm. (Tout de même!)—des jugements légèrement discutables (le renouveau pascalien avait commencé dès Lachelier, Boutroux, 1885 sq.) p. 33—Rousseau, Discours sur l'Inégalité avait dit aussi que l'espèce humaine est la seule qui sache qu'elle doit mourir—p. 65. Mais ce sont des détails. L'ensemble est fort beau—très peu thèse orthodoxe et conventionnelle & tant mieux.

Mes compliments encore & amitiés,<br>H. P.

## To Keith Botsford:

May 8—1951

My dear Botsford,

No, in all conscience I should blame myself for too much, & deservedly so, if, at the end of a year which was very strenuous for you & three times too heavy already, I accepted your suggestion to redo your essay in a week. You cannot & must not do that.

Let me say this instead.

1) As to the M.A., you deserve it; & if the essay is not all that it could have been, it is in part our fault. I should have *forced* you more energetically to submit an outline to Mr. Douglas, to talk it over with him, to have your French reread by him. I believe we are to blame, too, in this case. But I know, & my colleagues must know, that you deserve an M.A. & it is no charity or no special act of friendship to let you have it. We have an oral exam on which we'll talk on the Faust more particularly & that's all. You must *rest* now & finish your year without becoming exhausted. Be obedient on this for once.

2) Now, during the Summer, rewrite an essay on *Faust*. In fact, I believe you could do it in English, in the form of one or two articles that you might try to publish. In any case, a precise essay, with your culture & your insight, & also with more method & more "rigor" on the subject, is a much needed thing. You might explain in it how the Faust is the aboutissement of a current Léonard-Teste in Valéry, & study the "drama" itself.

For the rest, you really embraced too much. One quality which academic work must have & that very few of the things we do in life later have, after our university study is over, is thoroughness. Even an essay like Léonard & les philosophes, not the hardest by far of the Leonard essays, deserved a more thorough & methodical discussion than you gave & could give. You are at bottom modest, and a very fine & kind young man, but you sometimes give the impression of lacking humility, of being a bit condescending to scholarship & academic work. I don't mind, but you will often meet others who will. Yet what we do in training not writers but teachers, in extracting from the backwoods of America some young men of good will & of some gifts & in preparing them for an academic career, is worthwhile, & justified.

3) Now for the Ph.D. I still don't feel it's your true vocation, & it would be more courageous to recognize it & determine to make a living some other way & write. If you go in for this Ph.D. training, you should play the game fairly & do the work, attend the courses, strengthen your written French strenuously among other things. Will not such training sterilize you, discourage your career as a writer? The question is yours, also.

But I would not stand in your way. I'll talk with each of your professors & we'll have a chat on it once more.

Meanwhile, *rest,* do us your Genet article, & leave off the Valéry thing for further & later reworking. Your nervous resistance cannot be strained overmuch & you have done enough this year. Please give your essay to M. Guicharnaud, so that he may read it for May 25th or so & forget my reproaches if they were too hard. I was truly provoked by many of its faults & mistakes, but I am severe & perhaps more severe than I should be to those whom I like & to my countrymen & friends.

Sincerely yours,<br>
Henri Peyre

## To Edgar Furniss:

May 18, 1951

Dear Mr. Furniss:

May I once more take the liberty to remind you of our strong desire to see Mr. Auerbach have a telephone placed in the new office (H.G.S. 124, at present occupied by Professor Hill)? I am arranging for him to move there for July 1st so as to vacate Professor Kökeritz's office, which was assigned temporarily this year. Professor Hill has been very cooperative. Dean Sinnott expresses his approval of this telephone, charged to the University, i.e. to our department budget, since Professor Auerbach will have to take a much more active part in our departmental business next year: He will direct our students and studies in the doctorate in Romance Philology, although, as you remember, we have avoided creating a new title for the purpose.

I may add that the French Department has been charged, without knowing it until lately, for the telephone in professor Goetz's office ever since Mr. Boorsch was asked to vacate that office almost two years ago; so that the cost of the telephone to be transferred from Professor Goetz's office to H.G.S. on or before July 1st is already included and approved in our budget.

Before Professor Hill retires next June, I believe it would be fine to have a photograph of him made and framed and placed in the Romance Seminar, 307 H.G.S. We have a few large photographs of three or four Romance Philology specialists in that room, and it would be only fair to add that of one of our professors who have served the field, and the University with long devotion and competence. I wonder if the photographing service in the Yale News Bureau could be asked to do such a photograph at the University's expense and if there is or could be a small fund for the purpose? If not, we shall collect a little money to pay for the expense.

Very sincerely yours,
HM Peyre

## À Keith Botsford:

June 18/51

My dear Botsford,

J'ai bien trouvé votre article—mais à un moment où je suis chargé de manuscrits à lire pour le prix de la Modern Language Association & j'ai dû le passer à Cornell. Voyez avec lui dans quelques jours ce qu'il en pense.

Je n'ai pu que le parcourir, & le début m'a un peu déçu, peut-être parce que la présentation manquait de clarté & introduisait mal le sujet. Ce début pourra évidemment être récrit, et rendu plus frappant. J'éprouve toujours quelque pudeur quand un auteur dit "je," "I," mais je suis d'une vieille mode. Je dois m'absenter pour jusqu'à la fin juin. Après j'aurai le temps de relire votre article & de faire des suggestions peut-être plus utiles.

Vous avez beaucoup trop fait cette année. Vous ne tiendrez pas à cette vie. Plusieurs—dont Bob Cohn (en France) à qui j'avais donné le même conseil de ne pas tant travailler & tendre leurs nerfs—ont eu un véritable "collapse" & je le craindrais pour vous, si vous ne vivez pas plus sagement. Vous feriez aussi un travail bien plus achevé si vous aviez plus de repos. (Bien entendu, je ne pratique pas ces avis moi-même—mais j'ai tort.)

Je ne sais plus ce que Wellek avait décidé—mais je crois que son conseil à Simpson était que vous preniez un cours dans le département de français, ou deux, mais que vous ne changiez pas de département pour peut-être une seule année. Wellek sera d'ailleurs absent l'an prochain.

Amitiés à votre femme & à vous,
Henri Peyre

## À Jorge Guillén:

Ce 22 juin 1951

Cher Ami,

Je suis en retard pour vous dire merci. Vous savez les mille raisons: thèses, manuscrits à lire pour d'autres, dispersion d'une vie amenuisée à cent petitesses — Mais je voulais aussi lire, sinon tout votre *Cantico* définitif, au moins relire ça & là — Là-dessus sont arrivées vos traductions et variations sur les sonnets de Cassou. Que puis-je vous dire? Vous êtes un grand, un très grand poète, l'un des plus purs de notre temps, l'un de ceux chez qui il y aura le moins de déchet. Je serai fier de vous avoir approché — je le dis sans phrases. Vos vers sont splendides, neufs après plusieurs lectures, et d'une grande profondeur de pensée vécue et sentie — Et qu'un tel poète n'ait rien des vanités, des petitesses de l'homme de lettres, parle à peine de lui — mette si peu de prose dans sa vie, et si peu de fierté. Vous êtes adorablement humain.

Que faites-vous? Je suppose que j'ai laissé passer la date de votre séjour en Californie & vais, à tout hasard, envoyer ce mot d'excuses aux soins de votre gendre. Nous n'allons pas en France cet été — à regret. Et je serai en partie ici à lire un peu & à écrire, en partie à l'île de Martha's Vineyard où sera ma femme.

Damaso Alonso a passé ici quelques semaines — mais peu heureuses, je crains. L'isolement où l'a laissé ici votre étrange & inerte département d'espagnol, la médiocrité des étudiants l'ont attristé. Il a parlé de vous avec haute admiration. Son dernier livre de critique est admirable. C'est un pénétrant critique, tellement au-dessus de tout ce qu'on écrit en ce pays sur la stylistique, le baroque, Gongora & le reste.

Nos bons vœux à votre fille, à votre gendre. Lui, & votre fils, marchent vers de belles destinées — et votre petit fils suivra. Beau destin.

Merci, du fond du cœur. Où êtes-vous?
Henri Peyre

## À Robert Greer Cohn:

Ce 24 juin/51

Mon cher ami,

Je regrette bien de ne pouvoir aller cette année en France. J'ai eu tant à faire que le surplus de besogne non encore accomplie va déborder sur mon été & me priver de vraies vacances, au moins jusqu'en août. Je me suis sauvé pourtant quelques jours à Martha's Vineyard.

Je suis désolé d'apprendre que vous avez traversé une crise de fatigue. Vous vous donnez trop à ce que vous faites, dans de grands élans d'inspiration, vous privant alors de sommeil & de repos: cela n'est pas sain et vous jouera de mauvais tours. Croyez-en quelqu'un qui travaille trop lui-même, mais avec régularité & en laissant le temps pour un peu de marche ou de répit. Et votre fièvre mallarméenne est trop intense. Mallarmé et Joyce, et Kafka, et Freud sont des génies qui fascinent et détraquent. Si j'osais ironiser avec vos dieux, je vous conseillerais, votre présent travail achevé, de vous mettre à quelque antidote. Mais même si vous deviez étudier les romans de Victor Hugo ou le théâtre de Molière, vous le feriez toujours avec passion et de toute votre âme! Rançon du génie!

Vous devriez songer sérieusement à une position possible à l'Unesco, ou dans le journalisme américain à Paris; la prosaïque carrière universitaire américaine vous tente peu, & elle se fait bien difficile, cette année, avec la rareté des postes. Au fond, vous êtes l'homme de tous les hommes qui aurait dû naître capitaliste et vivre de ses rentes, étouffant quelques remords de conscience, et sans avoir à accepter les bas compromis de la vie.

Je crois comme vous que les choses vont de moins en moins bien en France. Le grand espoir d'après la Libération est étouffé. Les socialistes sont devenus des petits-bourgeois. La droite ne comprendra jamais rien. La 4e force n'a aucune politique sociale, et la résolution nécessaire ne viendra pas. Mais les Français semblent peu se soucier de tout cela et vivre en égoïstes, en redoutant les Russes, et les Américains plus encore. Ceux là mêmes qui, dans la bourgeoisie, ne doivent qu'à l'aide américaine de conserver leurs privilèges s'acharnent à dire pour eux leur mépris. C'en est pitoyable, et incurable.

Ici, comme vous savez, il y a bien des ridicules odieux. La chasse anticommuniste, le réactionnarisme sont bêtes et malfaisants; mais il y a tout de même une réaction de jeunesse, une productivité qui marche et, même dans le domaine intellectuel, de très grands dons, avec plus d'acceptation du neuf qu'en France. Avez-vous approché quelques écrivains?

Les lettres à Lefébure sont curieuses. Quand donc Mondor publiera-t-il toute la correspondance de Mallarmé en un volume?

À propos, pouvez-vous me dire qui est l'héritier littéraire de Mallarmé aujourd'hui? Nous avons quelques lettres inédites pour le futur no. de Y. Fr. St. & je suppose qu'il vaudrait mieux avoir l'autorisation de l'héritier.

Cet H. Charpentier est un bien médiocre poète, & si peu mallarméen—plus proche de Maurras ou de Valéry "at his worst."

Ne travaillez pas trop—et pas trop la nuit. Gardez la nuit pour votre femme et la vie du cœur—"ce cœur qui dans la nuit parfois cherche à s'entendre." Donnez lui (à votre femme) nos amitiés, & bien à vous,

Henri Peyre

## À Franco Simone:

Ce 27 juin 1951

Cher Monsieur,

Merci de cette seconde partie de votre belle étude pétrarquiste. Elle complète très richement la première & m'a beaucoup appris. Vous ajoutez tellement à l'histoire du pétrarquisme en France que vous la renouvelez en fait: un jour, vous devez reprendre ceci, & la fortune des successeurs de Pétrarque en France & leur influence, en une grande œuvre. Car il y a beaucoup à redire au Vianey, qui fut utile en son temps, & rien n'est si mal fait dans les manuels d'histoire littéraire que ces chapitres, cependant indispensables, sur ce que fut le pétrarquisme français—

Vos travaux sont des plus utiles qui soient, pour ceux comme moi qui aiment à apprendre & à lire du neuf; vous ne vous tenez jamais aux chemins battus. Grâce à vous, à Saulnier & quelques autres en France, à Weinberg, Lapp, Silver & quelques américains, les seiziémistes sont ceux aujourd'hui qui apportent le plus de fraîcheur à l'histoire littéraire de la France.

Croyez, cher Monsieur, à mes remerciements & à mes sentiments les plus fidèles,

Hri Peyre

## To Whitney Griswold:

July 19/51

My dear Whit,

It was a pleasure to see you quietly on the island, & to see that Mary & you not only have carried your burdens triumphantly this hard first year, but have remained charmingly simple & humorous & — yourselves.

I sent you the book by that student of America, Guérin, who quotes you lavishly, & my latest productions. One, *Pensées* from Baudelaire, of which I believe I have made an original choice, is less dull, not being mine own altogether, & may interest the feminine scholars in your household.

I am trying hard to concentrate on more writing. You gave us a lofty ideal to live for, with your fine talk on the creative mind, which Marguerite cut out & posted for me in my study, so that I try to be worthy of it — but how many things must one fight against, just to enjoy a few undisturbed hours of solitude!

> With my best to Mary & you & best wishes
> for your family & your summer,
> Hri

## À Judd Hubert:

> [carte postale: vue de Parsonage Pond, Martha's Vineyard]
> Ce 4 août/51

Cher Monsieur,

J'ai été vraiment attristé d'apprendre qu'il semble être si difficile de trouver un poste pour un homme de vos mérites. Je sais bien qu'on veut surtout des professeurs de langue en ce moment, mais tout de même! J'ai écrit en un ou deux endroits à votre sujet, mais bien loin d'ici, & l'on a dû redouter mes chaleureux éloges & craindre que, si fort érudit, vous ne vous plaisiez qu'à demi aux enseignements plus humbles requis. J'essaierai encore si vous n'êtes pas déjà pourvu. Je n'ai pas eu trop de mal à placer mes "produits" de Yale, mais plus que d'habitude, la vraie difficulté doit être celle d'un double poste — ou la proximité de N.Y., à laquelle vous devez ardemment tenir. Vous me direz ce qui vous arrive.

> Bien à vous,
> Hri Peyre

## À Mario Maurin:

> The Cedars, West Chop, Martha's Vineyard, Mass.
> Ce 4—VIII—[1951]

Mon cher Ami,

Au fond vous voulez jouer au condottiere. Il y a toutes chances pour qu'on vous envoie en Europe (c'est le courant en ce moment) et pour que vous y deveniez interprète important, conseiller de quelque état-major, organisateur des menus plaisirs de quelque général. Eh bien! Suarès vous aura appris à mépriser bien des choses. C'est une formation excellente.

Mais ne faites pas de zèle—tirez au flanc puissamment, pour vous préserver pour votre mère, pour vos maîtres qui vous aiment, & pour votre avenir immense.

Il me paraît difficile de faire quoi que ce soit avec votre MS à moins de l'avoir à ma disposition—c.à.d. avant de savoir pour sûr que Gallimard ne le prend pas—ce qui serait l'idéal & le souhaitable. Si vous savez qu'il ne s'y décide pas, vous le feriez essayer, dans Paris, en m'avertissant pour que je vous donne d'abord une lettre pour l'accompagner aux Presses Universitaires (Boulevard St Germain, 186 je crois). J'essaierai de le convaincre de le prendre à ses frais, mais l'édition en France est dans le marasme & je doute de mon succès.

Au pis, mettons qu'une édition de 1500 exemplaires, ou de 2000, revienne à 800 dollars. Je tâcherai de vous en donner 250. Sur le reste, si vous en vendiez en 2 ou 3 ans 1500 à 400 frs,= 600.000 frs, vous en retireriez 40%= 240.000 frs, c.à.d. en étant un peu optimiste, votre débours. Et vous entreriez dans la carrière avec éclat. Un livre derrière vous, cela veut souvent dire $500. de plus de traitement.

Voilà une lettre bien mercenaire.

J'ai fui la chaleur. J'essayais de commencer un livre sur le roman moderne, en anglais &, j'avoue, pour un éditeur qui me l'a dès longtemps demandé. Cela oblige à faire des livres plus généraux, pour un public défini. Mais j'ai payé en partie mon dernier livre sur Baudelaire & compensé à l'éditeur, qui y avait perdu, partie de mon élucubration générationniste. Je m'en lasse.

Mes vœux à votre mère & à vous,
Henri Peyre

## À Pedro Salinas:

Ce 2 septembre 1951

Très cher ami,

Je termine demain mes vacances et je songe que, paresseux, je ne vous ai pas bien dit la tristesse que m'avait causée la nouvelle de votre maladie. Vous avez une inspiration plus féconde et plus authentique que jamais, une magnifique force d'âme et une vie spirituelle intense: il faut que tout cela l'emporte sur ces atteintes à votre corps. L'exil, la tristesse qu'inspire le sort de l'Espagne, la stupide politique américaine & le monde actuel en général a accablé votre très grande sensibilité. J'espère que cet été aura restauré votre résistance & que Madame Salinas va, de son côté, assez bien.

Vous avez trop gentiment apprécié mes modestes essais baudelairiens. Ce genre de critique est bien peu de chose à côté d'écrits comme les vôtres, devant lesquels je m'incline avec une sincère admiration, parce qu'ils rayonnent de vie & de personnalité.

Croyez à mes vœux de total et rapide rétablissement.

Henri Peyre

## À Franco Simone:

Ce 8 septembre 1951

Cher Monsieur—cher Collègue,

J'avais bien reçu votre envoi de cette riche, précise & intéressante étude sur la culture avignonnaise tirée de *Convivium*—doublement intéressante pour moi car c'est de cette ville en France que viennent mes ancêtres, que je viens moi-même, bien que né à Paris. Vous montrez votre même don, dans cet écrit, d'apporter du neuf avec science mais sans pédantisme & de l'intégrer à l'ancien. Merci mille fois.

J'ai fait lire à Damaso Alonso, de Madrid, qui était ici au printemps dernier, & à Erich Auerbach, l'auteur de Mimesis, qui est à Yale, votre livre sur la Renaissance chez les humanistes. Ils l'ont apprécié—et je ne manque pas de me faire le laudateur de vos écrits toutes les fois que je le puis.

Je suis sûr que l'érudition & l'université américaine gagneraient beaucoup à vous avoir ici—si vous vouliez vraiment songer à abandonner tant de belles choses, & si précieuses, à Gênes, en Italie, en Europe! La vie ici est terne, monotone, un peu dure—et très laborieuse. Mais elle est plus large, et matériellement, et pour les facilités de travail, & sereine d'atmosphère.

Je vais parler de vous à divers collègues. Les questions préalables seraient: savez-vous l'anglais, assez bien? Envisageriez-vous (je n'en doute pas) d'enseigner l'italien & la littérature italienne, donc probablement Dante, la Renaissance italienne, etc., car il est probable qu'il paraîtrait plus normal à une université de vous employer d'abord dans ce domaine, puis, éventuellement, pour enseigner la Renaissance française.

Envoyez-moi un petit curriculum vitae—spécifiant age, éducation, charges & conditions de famille, postes occupés et poste actuel, publications (avec précision), projets, sujets que vous enseigneriez (mentionnez y libéralement votre compétence en littérature italienne, votre habitude des étudiants étrangers). J'essaierai ici de répandre ce petit papier.

Peut-être pourriez-vous d'ailleurs l'envoyer vous-même, en disant que je vous ai donné ce conseil, à diverses personnes ici, en indiquant votre désir de venir éventuellement occuper une chaire dans ce pays: notamment à

    Professor Thomas Bergin,
       Dept. of Italian,
       Yale University.
    Prof. Charles Singleton
       Harvard Univ.
       Cambridge, Mass.
    Prof. Robert Vigneron
       Chm. Dept of French,
       Univ. of Chicago
       Chicago 37, Ill.
    Prof. Arnold Rowbotham
       Chm, Dept of French,
       Univ. of California,
       Berkeley, Cal.
    Prof. Clinton Humiston
       Chm, Dept of French
       Univ of California at Los Angeles, Cal

Prof. Joseph Jackson
  Chm, Dept of French
  Univ. of Illinois,
  Urbana, Ill
Prof. Samuel Will
  Chm, Dept of French & Italian
  Indiana University
  Bloomington, Ind.

Essayez de voir M. Bernard Weinberg, qui travaille sur la Renaissance française & italienne & doit être à Rome cette année avec un "Fulbright Fellowship"—c/o the American Cultural attaché, je suppose. Il est prof. à Northwestern University, Evanston, Ill. & un vrai savant.

Vous pourriez aussi écrire au Chairman of the Depart. of Italian, Columbia University, New York 27, NY—et à l'occasion envoyer un court article, d'intérêt assez général, mais érudit à la Romanic Review de la même université (Editor: Prof. Norman L. Torrey).

Tout cela peut aider et je pousserai à la chose moi-même. Merci vivement de votre bonne lettre, trop gentille pour mon livre, dans lequel j'ai malheureusement laissé beaucoup de mauvaises fautes d'impression.

Croyez à mes sentiments dévoués,
Hri Peyre

## À Judd Hubert:

Le 12—IX/51

Cher M. Hubert:

Merci de votre article. Il présente très bien quelques-uns des points les plus précieux de votre thèse & nous sera une excellente illustration et "preview" de vos recherches, résultats & livre à venir. Vous attendrez encore plusieurs mois la publication (avril ou mai) & nous n'envoyons pas d'épreuves. Mais ne vous inquiétez pas.

Avez-vous quelque résultat? Il me semble vraiment que, en attendant peut-être quelque chose de plus stable, Columbia ou quelque université à New York devrait avoir recours à vous. Vous devriez maintenant et publier votre livre si possible, & vous imposer par quelques articles, communications, conférences si possible — ne pas apparaître trop timide ou subtil. Votre place, un jour ou l'autre, doit être dans une des très bonnes universités américaines. Mais au début d'une carrière qui sera littéraire, il n'est pas inutile de convaincre les gens que vous avez des idées sur les problèmes de l'enseignement des langues, de la civilisation, etc. Pardonnez ces conseils & à l'occasion envoyez-moi un curriculum sur vous, age, enseignement, titres, publications, etc. Cela peut servir de l'avoir sous la main.

En hâte car je suis déjà en pleine rentrée, merci & amitiés,

Hri Peyre

## À Jorge Guillén:

Ce 19 – IX – 51

Cher Ami,

Quel heureux homme vous êtes d'aller en France — et en Espagne! Je voudrais bien retourner dans votre pays & revoir Tolède & l'Andalousie. Mais les voyages sont devenus chers.

Je suis désolé que votre belle mère soit malade. C'est une femme admirable de courage & de bonté, dont nous avons gardé le meilleur souvenir, ainsi que de votre belle-sœur, elle aussi femme remarquable — Vous avez eu le rare bonheur d'être entouré de femmes de goût, d'esprit, de beauté & d'*âme* — et votre fille poursuit la tradition.

Je ne savais pas Salinas si malade. Il m'a écrit une fois ou deux, mais je croyais qu'il s'agissait d'arthrite. Quelle tristesse! et il est en pleine veine créatrice. Votre dédicace finale, si affectueuse, est fort belle — au "parfait ami."

Auerbach est un excellent collègue et grand professeur, et en général exempt de dogmatisme. Il n'a sans doute pas *senti* le D. Quijote — mais sa position est, je crois, de vouloir se tenir en dehors de la tradition Unamuno, chère aux Espagnols, qui accentue le côté tragique de Cervantes et de son roman, & peut-être l'exagère. Ce titre sur le sentiment tragique de la vie a trop marqué tous les commentateurs de l'Espagne! J'aime que vous chantiez aussi l'allégresse, et les nuits de lune, et l'acceptation de la vie —

Wellesley n'est pas si mal — et savez-vous que vous y vivez dans la pensée, dans les rêves, peut-être dans les désirs & les nostalgies de plusieurs belles jeunes filles?

À quelque jour ici, quand vous redeviendrez Américain.

Bien à vous, en vraie amitié & fidèle souvenir à votre fils (est-il rentré?),

Henri Peyre

## To Edgar Furniss:

September 28, 1951

Dear Mr. Furniss:

I wonder if it would not be possible for the University to grant some research help to Professor Auerbach. He is at present engaged upon a big and very important work which will be at least as considerable as his *Mimesis* which, as you probably know, has been translated into English and Spanish, and has won much scholarly praise. Since his years previous to his coming here were difficult to the point that he hasn't yet finished paying some of his debts, it is not possible for him to get any research help in his present work, and it seems that he could not complete the manuscript without some further verification in the European libraries. He doesn't know I am suggesting this and he is very happy at Yale where all his colleagues and students have been very much impressed by him. But it would be generous and certainly justified to find a few hundred dollars, if not as an annual grant tying up future funds, at least for the coming two years. I hope this is not impossible.

Very sincerely yours,
HM Peyre

## To the Yale French Department:

(October 1951)

To Professors of all grades in the French Department:

It is the conviction of your chairman that we should devote a special meeting of the assistant professors and above in our Department to proceed to a frank and thorough examination of what has been done in the last twelve years or so, of what might be done further, and of views, criticisms and suggestions which may lead us to some improvements. While an oral discussion may prove fruitful, it may also tend to be too cordial and to show an excessive deference to the Chairman. He would therefore be sincerely happy if members of the Department would send to one of them, say Professor H. B. Richardson, an anonymous and typed letter embodying some of their fuller criticisms, or if the Department would elect a committee of three of its members to present definite, critical and constructive suggestions to the Chairman.

Some of the questions which should be reviewed, after a long period of "guidance" by one chairman, might well be of a personal character. They might include some of the sample questions in group I. Matters of policy and of reform, and any other matters not listed in this incomplete enumeration, should also come under discussion.

I. Are you satisfied with?

The opinion in which the French Department is held at Yale—and outside?
The treatment by the Administration? The Chairman's relations and dealings with the Administration?
The general rate of promotions, the basis on which they are made?
The policy which seems to prevail on appointments?
The general proportion of American and French members?
The use made of the services of each one?
Is due attention granted to research and publications? Are they encouraged? Do teaching qualities receive their full due?
Should the Department try to cooperate more actively with others (Spanish, English, History, etc.)?
Are there enough committees to assist and advise the Chairman?
Does the Chairman appear to you as just? flexible? tyrannical? impatient? tolerant? humorous?
Does he devote an excessive amount of his time to outside pursuits or activities?
Does he make contacts between members of his Department and Deans, etc., easy?
Does he delegate some of his duties enough?

Does he accept new ideas or tend to be set or ossified in his views?

II. Undergraduate Schools

Does the Chairman show enough interest in them?
Is the language instruction adequately supervised?
Is the turnover of teachers too fast?
Is the placement well done?
Is there any excessive routine, complacency in our courses?
Is the oral French stressed sufficiently?
Is the proportion between English and French a happy one?
Could elementary courses be made more attractive?
Is our grading uniform, fair? Is cheating a problem?
Do we stress the social aspects of language and literature adequately?
Are we too traditional and therefore lose students to newer subjects?
How can we develop our advanced courses better?
Should we rotate them or some of them?
Do we take adequate care of our majors in French?
Is our French Center effective?

III. Graduate School

How do you look upon the reforms made in the last eight years? Lightening of philological requirement, of other Romance literatures' requirement? Reorganization of Philology and Old French courses? of M.A. degree?
Are graduate students well selected? Could other methods be used?
Do we guide them enough? Too much?
Are you satisfied with the level of our theses? of our M.A. essays? of our language examinations? with our grading?
Are the Ph.D. orals satisfactory? fair? revealing? Would you like a different emphasis in the subjects treated?
Is our Romance Club attended satisfactorily? interesting? useful?
Are you satisfied with the placement of our Ph.D.'s?

Is our atmosphere too liberal? too literary?

Do our Ph.D.'s appear to you as a rule to be well-trained as teachers? well-rounded men and not only specialists?

Is our choice of courses varied enough? Should we vary them even more and stress other topics or periods?

Should we attempt to reach more unity (of methods if not of views and tastes) among our Graduate School teachers?

Is it wise to entrust young teachers (assistant professors, occasionally instructors) with graduate courses?

Are there any features of other Graduate Schools in French (Princeton, Harvard, etc.) which we might envy or borrow? etc., etc.

I hope we can have a meeting in October and I should be grateful if you would offer your views and criticisms then, if not before in writing, on those and other questions.

Very cordially yours,<br>Henri M. Peyre

## To Norman S. Buck:

October 4, 1951

Dear Dean Buck:

I have received the reports of the freshmen on their instructors. I have discussed them with Mr. Richardson and several of our colleagues. Mr. Richardson, who has taken over the direction of our undergraduate teaching and has undertaken to reform it where it needs reforming with great energy and devotion, is answering you in a detailed way and will be glad to take up any of the points which you may want to raise. He is determined to help us remedy some of the defects which have been pointed out by several of the freshmen in their reports. I am convinced that our department will not again incur some of the sharp but deserved criticism which assailed French 12 and French 22 last year. In any case, we are very glad that some of that criticism was so frank and we shall gain by it.

A few general remarks might be in order:

1) There are naturally divergences among the freshmen and some of their remarks flatly contradict other remarks made by other men in the same class. But on the whole, as last year, I have found their criticisms fair, clear-sighted and just. My most earnest wish would be to see those critiques extended to the students in Yale College. I shall again plead with Dean DeVane so that he may find the means to do so. A criticism extended to the upper classmen, as well, would be even more revealing and more helpful to us.

2) As happened last year, several of the young teachers who came in for rather sharp criticism were, as it happens, allowed to go, and I am glad to see that our judgment corresponded with that of the boys taking their courses. Some of the instructors like Lecuyer, Cronmiller and two or three others, who had been sharply criticized last year, obviously improved and were judged much more favorably this year. This is a gratifying proof of the usefulness of those critiques, which will all be communicated to the instructors themselves.

3) Our Department suffered last year from some change in the personnel and from insufficient direction of the elementary French courses, French 12 and 22, in particular. There was a lack of coordination among the sections of each course and not enough firmness in the organization of the courses, synchronization of the tests, etc. We were aware of that while unable to remedy it during the year, and we have now taken drastic steps to do better and thus fulfill our task to Yale College and to the Freshman Year more efficiently. Professor Richardson will explain to you those steps in detail and we shall be pleased to keep you informed of our results, perhaps at some of the Freshman Faculty meetings.

4) The fundamental evil is partly economic. Due to the uncertainty which prevailed last year, we were not allowed to appoint or reappoint instructors until late in the year. Good instructors were then unavailable at the mediocre rates that we offer. On the other hand, the number of students taking French increased and this year we have to have nineteen assistants out of thirty-four members of the Department. This is far too many. We must next year ask for more money so as to replace several of those assistants by full-time instructors. We should also be allowed to replace expert instructors or assistant professors whom we lost to other universities: Collignon, Galand. As conditions stand, it is almost impossible to find good instructors in French for $3,000. We place our men at $3,400 or $3,500 easily when they leave our Graduate School.

We should replace about ten of our assistants, who receive $1,000 a year as an average, by four or five full-time instructors receiving $3,500. In other words, we should spend at least $15,000 instead of $10,000 and acquire a new assistant-professor to supervise the courses. I believe a definite improvement can only be achieved through your request to the University that more funds be expended on better teaching of freshmen.

Very sincerely yours,<br>Hri Peyre

## To Edgar Furniss:

October 12, 1951

Dear Mr. Furniss:

As you remember, you enabled our Department, a few years ago, to buy two soundscriber machines to place in the modest French Center we have organized in the attic floor of William L. Harkness Hall, with Dean DeVane's approval. Students have utilized the refitted room and the machines for listening to records of French model-texts, of phonetic exercises and of their own voices, correcting defects in their accents and intonation, improving their French. Compared to language laboratories in other universities where the equipment is lavish, we have only a shabby and poorly provided center. For the present however it is proving helpful and we should be glad if some day you would let us show it to you.

To continue making good use of it however we shall need two additions or improvements, which as always involve an extra cost: the first one, if approved, immediate; the second, for next year. I believe you will find that as usual our requests are modest and indeed thrifty.

Our two machines have not proved sufficient to accommodate the students who want to use our French "Laboratory" Center. We have this year over 850 undergraduates, 450 of them freshmen, in our classes. The Soundscriber Company, in this city, has for sale a pair of machines, not new, but just reconditioned and guaranteed for six months, at about $400 for the two, i.e. two thirds of the price for new ones. That seems to be a good bargain. Would you have the funds which would make it possible to reserve those machines at once and to buy them, through the Service Bureau? Since our expense budget is itself very economical, we cannot of course subtract $400 from the $700 allowed us as "miscellaneous" (correspondence, typewriting expenses, etc.).

Next year, it seems necessary to ask in our budget for two "laboratory assistants" (graduate students receiving a fee as in the scientific departments) to take care of our "French Laboratory" upstairs; their task would be to work and keep the machines we have, supervise and direct the students doing their recording there or explain to them how to use the records and playbacks and how to gain a better phonetic training thereby. We have had thus far to do that ourselves and this imposes an extra and unfair burden on our already overworked instructors and assistants in instruction. We have no phonetician at Yale and no phonetics laboratory, an expensive affair. But a couple of young men *well trained in phonetics* and pursuing their studies here, if we could thus attract them, would do much helpful work. I understand that the payment in the scientific departments for such men is $800 plus tuition. If you approve, we should propose such an addition to our budget.

Sincerely yours,
HM Peyre

## To the same:

October 17, 1951

Dear Dean Furniss:

The role of a Chairman, even when he thinks he is a thrifty one, is humiliating, for he always goes begging for one thing or another. One of our men, Pierre Didier, an instructor & a graduate student, finds himself in very difficult financial circumstances. He has two children aged two and a half and 10 months, & he is going to have a third one in December. He is to blame, of course, but he is a good Catholic & so is his wife. But the poor wife's health is collapsing under the impact, & he himself is being afflicted with remorse & fear of the future.

Last year he had $3000 (of which $450 had to be paid back as tuition); this year he has $3250. He is terribly hard up.

My question is: is there any fund, any possible help from any source or friend of the University which could help a worthy & good teacher & graduate student meet his bills & get over a very difficult moment?

I am asking you, because your heart is as kind and merciful as your intelligence is broad & lucid.

Sincerely,
Hri Peyre

## À Judd Hubert:

Ce 11 nov./51

Mon cher ami,

Je ne sais pas très bien si M. Corti veut que je vous transmette ceci, ou s'il vous a de son côté écrit. Sa décision est négative. Étant donné les frais, je le comprends—mais ses arguments (bien que très fins et en partie justes) n'empêchent que votre livre mérite de paraître. Certes, il est trop subtil, & trop systématique; certes, il sera attaqué; vous ramenez en effet trop à l'ambiguïté, de ce qui s'appelait autrefois ironie, suggestion, vague, etc. & vous lisez un peu trop de choses dans quelques poèmes assez simples. Mais Corti se rend mal compte que vous êtes dans un courant très remarquable, plus visible en Amérique qu'en France, où la critique est en retard & très routinisée, & ignore tout ou presque de Richards & d'Empson, du paradoxe & de l'ambiguïté.

Ne vous découragez pas, & si vous en avez les moyens, faites paraître votre livre à vos frais à Paris—ou alors abrégez-le, refaites-le, rendez-le moins systématique. Mais il frappera aussi moins, alors.

Bien à vous,
Hri Peyre

## To Edgar Furniss:

Nov. 26—1951

Dear Dean Furniss:

I am arranging already for three Yale graduate students from our Department to go over to Paris next year with three exchange fellowships given by the French Government. I have to proceed early in order to have those students receive their passage through the Fulbright. Those fellowships have been very successful, & the French Government has lately raised the amount paid in francs, to take into account the increased cost of living.

I suppose I shall be able to count on the three Sterling fellowships given in exchange to three French students, & perhaps the stipend, which is, I believe, $1500 a year, will be slightly increased? The three French fellows have been, thus far, well chosen, & preferably in science, economics, social sciences. They have returned to France with a precise & rich knowledge of America, in fact have turned into excellent agents for disinterested American cultural propaganda, & have also helped Yale be better known over in France.

As soon as I have your O.K., I shall, in agreement with Dean Simpson, start the complicated machinery to appoint those Sterling exchange fellows. The funds are supposed to be at the President's discretion.

Sincerely,
HM Peyre

## To Harry Levin:

November 26, 1951

Professor Harry Levin
Holyoke House
Harvard University
Cambridge, Massachusetts

My dear Harry Levin:

Thank you for your kind thought in sending me the reprint of your article on realism. I like the issue very much and it was remarkably well directed and homogeneous. The inequality among the articles was much less striking than in similar attempts, and there was more variety of points of view. It is one of the most thoughtful contributions to realism we have.

I believe you are going over to France this year and, if the rumor is true, I wish to congratulate you, to wish you good luck, and, if there is any help I can provide with introductions, which you hardly need, or with the French version of your lectures, I shall be glad to offer it.

I have seen Dean Rogers and corresponded with one or two of your colleagues about the situation in French there. The humble opinion of an outsider is that you should promote Dieckmann to a full professorship without delay and that your next appointment might be made at the assistant professor rank with promise of a promotion to follow soon if the man is successful. One of the best Frenchmen in the country, still very young and very dogmatic but extremely gifted, is Champigny at Indiana. And one of the best Americans is Warren Ramsey, now at Berkeley, California, whom Poggioli well knew at Brown and whose training we completed at Yale. He would be excellent, especially with a view to participating in your comparative literature group. He has a very sure literary sense, but does not speak French as fluently and charmingly as some Americans. The news is still confidential, but he came out the winner among thirty-six contestants for the MLA Oxford Prize to be announced in December in Detroit.

I suppose you know Wallace Fowlie, a Harvard Ph.D. and a prolific writer. As a teacher, he is absolutely first-rate. What he writes is certainly open to question and as we say politely challenging, but he has matured greatly over the years and he is now reaching a wider public. In a large Department like Harvard's, his sometimes special ideas or shall we say his faults would be easily compensated by the colleagues around, and I dare say he would be found, as he was found here at Yale, a very welcome addition. But this would be potentially an important appointment and the matter should be gone into very carefully.

I hope you're very well, and perhaps I shall have the pleasure of seeing you here this year or in France in the summer.

Most cordially,
Henri M. Peyre

## To Edgar Furniss:

Dec. 2, 1951

Dear Mr. Furniss:

Thank you for your prompt answer in the exchange Sterling fellowships & the authorization to go ahead, at least for the present.

The suggestion that the stipends be granted these exchange fellows from France had come from Dean Simpson. I usually have succeeded in getting the passage of those men paid by France, or by Fulbright money, at least one way. But the strict ruling that foreign students with a student visa must not do any paid work over here makes it impossible for them to earn anything through coaching, occasional teaching, etc. On the other hand, the laws about foreign exchange prevent them from acquiring dollars abroad, even if they could afford to do so. Hence some difficulty encountered in the last few years. We had to advise these exchange students to take only a minimum of courses here, so as to spare their funds (full tuition, not needed in their cases, would leave them only $1,050 a year), & because courses are only part of the benefit they reap from their year at Yale. But I agree that, while there is some hardship, the grants are generous.

In the future, it might be well to take up the question of exchange of foreign students with the Ford Foundation or some such group. It should be encouraged and if possible financed from outside.

With thanks & sincerely yours,<br>HM Peyre

## À Judd Hubert:

Yale, 16 dec. [1951]

Cher Monsieur,

Je suis heureux de cette nouvelle pour Harvard—mais votre femme, à moins qu'elle ne trouve aisément qqc à Wellesley ou Brandeis ou Boston U., devrait peut-être garder son poste une autre année au moins pour voir venir. Si vous allez ensuite une année à l'étranger, etc., il y aurait le temps de voir venir. Votre plan sur Racine est très ingénieux & m'a beaucoup frappé. Inutile de m'envoyer maintenant votre MS là-dessus: c'est un projet subtil & difficile qui fera impression une fois réalisé & écrit. J'ai écrit chaudement en votre faveur—mais je sais qu'ils accordent rarement de bourse Guggenheim en l'absence de publication antérieure substantielle. Bédé se l'était vu refuser 2 ou 3 fois pour cette raison. Vous prendrez rang tout au moins.

Amitiés,<br>H Peyre

## À Mario Maurin:

Ce 26 déc. 1951

Mon cher ami,

Mes vœux vous accompagnent, à ce tournant de l'année. C'est une crête pour vous. Vous avez fini vos études & toute l'ère "scolaire" de votre vie. Vous avez résisté avec beaucoup de courage moral à ce que la vie militaire pouvait susciter en vous d'amertume, de révolte secrète, de désespoir, de culture d'une sensibilité fine & froissée. Vous vous êtes prouvé à vous-même que vous étiez robuste de corps & de courage, capable de sourire au sein d'un monde qui n'aurait pas dû être le vôtre, à même d'apprendre par cette solitude dénuée du meilleur de la solitude: l'intimité—et en tout cela vous savez rester vous-même. Vos lettres sont fines & acérées. Savez-vous que, si le temps vous en était donné, vous pourriez esquisser quelques plaisantes nouvelles avec le spectacle de la vie militaire qui est la vôtre? On connaît bien mal cela par la littérature, en dehors de ces gros livres dramatisés, pleins de venin & de verbe exubérant, de James Jones & autres. Ces contacts entre Portoricains et bureaucratie américaine, initiation de ces petits bonshommes aux gloires du Marine Corps, doivent être riches en épisodes tragi-comiques, & le spectacle de M. Maurin, Ph.D., poète, explicateur du Coup de Dés et des proses de Suarès, enseignant à ces gens les rudiments de l'orthographe ou des maladies vénériennes doit avoir ses moments drôles.

Quand venez-vous en permission? Avez-vous pu faire un saut jusqu'ici pour Noël? Avez-vous passé ces journées avec vos parents? Votre mère a eu la bonté de m'offrir un généreux cadeau de parfums qui m'a beaucoup touché, & touche ma femme tout autant. Mais cela est trop gentil d'elle et la confiance amicale d'un esprit tel que le vôtre, qui a toutes raisons d'être sévère pour ses maîtres, & d'une sensibilité telle que la vôtre, que l'étude & la culture n'ont pas rendu moins vive, sont la meilleure récompense qu'un "maître" & ami puisse souhaiter. Je m'absenterai quelques jours du 14 au 19 janvier, & quelques fois en février & mars, mais espère bien vous revoir à quelque autre voyage que vous ferez par ici.

Je crois encore que vous devriez vous ressaisir de votre thèse, la revoir à moments perdus si elle en a besoin—& sans tarder songer à la publication. Cela prend encore toute une année aisément, même les difficultés, monétaires & autres, résolues. Et il serait beau de la voir sortir juste au moment où, renaissant à une vie plus civile, vous songerez à une carrière universitaire. En même temps, un recueil de vos poèmes devrait paraître bientôt. Ne pouvez-vous parfois reprendre ceux que vous aviez, les compléter, les classer—peut-être en récrire d'autres? Est-ce Émile Paul, ou Gallimard qui a, en ce moment, votre MS?

J'essaie, vous le voyez, de pousser mes jeunes amis à écrire & à imprimer, pour me venger d'un destin, librement choisi à vrai dire mais souvent aussi maudit, qui m'empêche de le faire. Ma vie reste, même en vacances, dispersion, épuisement en trop de voies divergentes. Je ne sais résister aux demandes d'amis & dois rédiger 3 ou 4 articles, tous hâtifs, en ces quelques jours de répit. Nous allons bien du moins—et avons, à Yale, un groupe assez gai: Brombert enseigne, avec talent: Mendelson est revenu, guéri. Guggenheim, à Washington, va divorcer et, nature droite & sensible, en est malheureux. De Messières, toujours M.P, est en Allemagne—Richie quelque part en Californie—Quelle "diaspora"!

     Avec mes amitiés et mes vœux les plus cordiaux & fervents,
     Henri Peyre

## To Harry Levin:

Dec. 28—1951

My dear Levin,

It was kind of you, amid so many important tasks & impressive series of lectures, to answer me at length & with your usual kindness. Harvard's problem is indeed a difficult one to solve, but it can be, if energetic & productive young men are soon appointed who can rise to higher ranks. Hoog is fine & pleasant, a little on the light side, perhaps, & occasionally rash or naively immature in some of his judgments. But he may learn much from some discreet advice from you as to what he should concentrate on in America & what he might profitably neglect. He is very eager to do well.

I should be glad to help in any way with the form of your French lectures, if you did not have the desirable or available help (you need little) at hand. I don't see why you should not lecture on English literature there as well as on American—& the Renaissance (Marlowe, etc.)

is not well represented in Paris. In fact, English studies at present lack brilliance. My own suggestion (I'll be glad to interpret any wishes of yours when I go there next summer) would be that you see if any of the books placed on the "program" for the agrégation (announced in August) or for the licence suit you. Lecturing on them always proved more profitable to practically-minded French students. Then a few lectures outside on American culture or letters could be added. Do not neglect having the French settle your living conditions to your satisfaction. The Hôtel Montalembert is a quiet & discreet one — close to the Existentialist headquarters & they might put you up there at their expense, as they have done occasionally. If there again I can do anything, I'll be glad to.

Would you be willing to write me a few lines on Kenneth Douglas & what you know of him — & of his articles (he is now writing a book on Sartre). I am hoping to have him promoted to an Associate professorship next month & a letter from you would carry much weight with our committees. He is especially well versed in Comparative Literature & in languages, as you know, was born in Dublin & is about 40.

With cordial wishes & very sincerely yours,
Henri Peyre

## To William DeVane:

Jan. 8 — 1952

Dear Dean DeVane:

It seems clear, after a new & very close examination of our prospects for next year, that if the last new Instructor suggested in my budget is crossed out, as you intimated, a more or less similar amount will have to be provided for at the last minute, in September. It might then be 12 hours of assistants in instruction at $250.00 a year, i.e., $3,000.00 & a meager saving, instead of the $3,000 proposed, & would again leave us with too large a number of assistants in instruction. I thought I'd take the liberty to let you know in case you wish to communicate this to the Provost's office.

Sincerely yours,
HM Peyre

## To Edgar Furniss:

January 11—1952

Dear Mr. Furniss:

If I may say so, in another one of my innumerable letters, I believe it would be a timely move to explain to Chairmen that Associate professors appointed to that rank in the last five years are normally not brought up for promotion after five years in their rank, but reappointed as associate professors with indefinite tenure; and that promotion to a full professorship cannot be promised in any case and is not automatic.

Otherwise chairmen, being on friendly terms with associate professors who are of fine merits (such as Arrom in Spanish, Cornell in French & others), may be embarrassed if they do not push them promptly to a full professorial rank while other departments consider the associate professorship as a mere temporary Purgatory—The time is opportune, with the raising of salaries for associate professors to what is full professorial salary elsewhere, & before five years have elapsed since the Corporation ruling on the first term of associate professorships.

Excuse my perpetual indiscretion.

Sincerely,
HM Peyre

## À Judd Hubert:

Ce 1er février 1952

Mon cher Ami,

Je suis sincèrement content que votre position à Harvard ait été assurée (je crois du moins que cela est définitif, & sais que cela doit l'être). Vous y devriez être, à mon avis, assistant professor—mais si vous pouviez hâter votre publication, cela pourrait être vite. Le département là-bas n'est pas riche en hommes de votre qualité.

Avez-vous recouvré votre MS et essayez-vous ailleurs?

Pour la Guggenheim, le Comité ne se réunira que plus tard—mais comme je vous l'ai dit, à moins de quelque ouvrage déjà paru & tangible, vos chances seront faibles cette année—et le fait que vos recommandations, pour la plupart, viennent, forcément, de Columbia, vous nuit, puisque Frame & Fellows sont déjà candidats & loués hautement comme de juste par leurs collègues, revenez à la charge dans deux ou trois ans; et vous serez alors recommandé, outre par moi-même, par un ou deux de Harvard—Et ne prenez pas mal un refus, si cela doit être le cas. Il sera, dans l'esprit du comité, accompagné d'une réelle marque d'estime.

Votre femme va-t-elle essayer de trouver un poste à Wellesley? Ou à Brandeis? Ou à Simmons? Le 1er de ces collèges serait le mieux. Je ne sais si elles y auront une vacance, mais cela se pourrait. Miss Edith Melcher, chef du département, est de mes amies & je serais toujours heureux de lui écrire.

Si votre femme abandonne Sarah Lawrence, je serais heureux d'y recommander quelqu'un, par son entremise, mais lorsqu'elle saura elle-même. Mad. Yourcenar m'a envoyé ses Mémoires d'Hadrien, mais je n'ai pas le courage de les dévorer. Est-elle en France ou ici?

En hâte & amitiés,
Hri Peyre

## To e e Cummings:

Febr. 5, 1952

Dear Mr. Cummings:

You may have had occasion to glance at our review *Yale French Studies,* which, published by our Department without any financial backing, has proved successful enough to be printed 1800 copies per issue & to reach a number of cultivated persons in this country. The public we aim at is a "general" public interested in modern letters & in French writers.

We intend to devote our n° 10 (we appear twice a year) to French and American literatures in their mutual relations. We hope to have, among other articles which will touch upon the American novel in France, the influence of French writers over here, four or five brief articles, of a more personal character, stating what four or five eminent American writers feel they have owed to the example or to the stimulus of French writers.

I wonder if you could consent to give us a few pages on some French poet, or some French poetical movement since Rimbaud & Mallarmé, to whom or to which you feel you have owed something; or, on the contrary, on your reaction against some aspects of French poetry or on anything else which would refer to your position concerning French literature. I have great admiration for your poetry, & have repeatedly expressed it in writing & otherwise. And any statement, however brief, which you would be willing to make, would, I am sure, be very valuable for future students of your work: there will be many. Our review would be grateful & proud to publish them. We are gathering the articles for that issue (n° 10) for May 1st.

Very sincerely yours,<br>
Henri Peyre<br>
Chairman, French Department

**To the same:**

Febr. 25 — 1952

Dear Mr. Cummings:

 Thank you for your very kind & most delightful letter. I had expressed myself very clumsily, for I did not wish you to consider writing, for our Yale French Studies, anything so dull as a creative artist's reaction to France in general. I was hoping (may I continue hoping?) that you might feel willing to dash off a few lines, perhaps a brief poem, on your memories of Paris, on your reading of some French novel, poem or fairy tale, on your meeting of some entertaining (even if non literary) Frenchman. As to influences & even literary relationships, as conceived & usually peremptorily assigned by critics to writers, I do not believe much in them.

 If you do not find my insistence indiscreet & feel like sending us a few lines, I shall be immensely grateful. I have long admired your work immensely, & pleased Mrs. S. P. Baker here very much when I praised your poems very warmly once in some article. I was so happy when the admiration I expressed was, last year, shared by my colleagues on the Guggenheim Committee & meant to congratulate you. Let me do so, belatedly.

Very sincerely yours,<br>
Henri Peyre

## To Ms. Feinemann:

April 30/52

Dear Miss Feineman:

I apologize for making a mistake on the phone.

Mr. Holdheim should be down for only $1,000 & appointed for the first term only. Our total for assistants is thus down again to $12,000 — but we shall in all likelihood reappoint him for 8 hours again in the second term or perhaps for 5 hours & someone else for 3 hours. Anyway we shall need then another $1000, covered in the budget by the $750 left for assistants & $250 saved on Didier.

Sorry!

Very sincerely yours,
HM Peyre

## To Edgar Furniss:

May 20, 1952

Dear Mr. Furniss:

I spoke to Mr. Hill, as you suggested, on the question of the expenses for binding the books in our Romance Seminar library. Those books are of real value, and used daily by our graduate students. We have there a good collection, which we keep on adding to, through gifts (as we have no funds for purchase otherwise). Many of the books are in bad shape & need binding urgently.

Next year, 1952–53, Mr. Hill worked out, with the help of Harry Ginter, Head of the Binding Depart. in our library, an estimate for $100.00. The sum will be used for binding 40 French books in the Romance Seminar and 6 volumes of Larousse (A1 031/ 1–6): $70.00 for the 40 books and $30.00 for the Larousse.

The Sterling Library is reluctant, I fear, to spend money on what is not taken over by it, catalogued in its catalogue, etc. Could their budget provide for this sum of $100.00. Or is there another way in which it can be provided? Or would it be fair to ask that, another year, such a sum be charged to our Departmental miscellaneous budget? The books to be bound are often Italian or Spanish as well as French.

I'll wait for your advice in the matter.

Very sincerely yours,<br>HM Peyre

## À Mario Maurin:

21 Mai—1952

Mon cher Maurin,

Votre lettre était fort gentille, & trop aimable pour moi malgré l'air sévère que vous adoptiez, tout jeune, dans nos cours: une figure de Minos, mais nullement infaillible ou impudent, simplement stimulant ses maîtres à ne pas sombrer dans la facilité.

Hélas! Non—je ne serai plus ici après le 1er juin. Nous nous embarquons le 3. Je reviendrai de France au début de septembre. J'aurais aimé vous revoir avec vos galons, le ton mâle avec lequel vous réglez le destin de ces Portoricains et, pour leur avoir trop bien enseigné l'espagnol & l'anglais et l'hygiène médicale, vous les expédiez en Corée. L'idée que vous puissiez y aller m'effraie—& cette guerre coréenne est vraiment par trop bête, & inutile.

Alors ne voulez-vous, guerrier qui devez idéaliser les femmes et rêver au délassement de la gent militaire, point nous donner un article sur Eros chez Suarès? Chez Claudel? Chez quelque autre moderne? Pourquoi ne pas faire de force quelque place aux lettres, & à votre inspiration, dans votre vie présente?

Je griffonne ceci au cours d'un examen oral de doctorat, pour vous dire mon regret de vous manquer ici. Mais d'ici Noël peut-être—& avertissez-moi un peu d'avance—et rappelez-moi au souvenir de votre mère.

Fidèles pensées,<br>Henri Peyre

## À Pierre Bédard:

> Ce 19 juin 1952
> C/o American Express
> rue Scribe
> Paris

Cher ami,

Votre lettre m'a rejoint à Paris — Nous étions partis le 4 sur *l'Ile de France*. Paris n'a jamais été aussi beau que cette année: le temps est idéal, les gens semblent miraculeusement gais et amusés malgré les difficultés qui doivent être grandes. Nous passons ici quelques semaines: j'ai beaucoup de gens à revoir, puis voyagerons un peu vers la Belgique, la Hollande, l'Allemagne, etc.

J'ai une fois encore dû renoncer à une calme conversation avec vous. Je n'ai été à New York que pour le bachot, puis l'embarquement. À part ces étés où je m'échappe, je passe le reste de ma vie à m'affairer.

Bien sûr je serai heureux de parler chez vous. C'est un honneur, toujours, mes scrupules viennent plutôt de ce que je me demande si vous ne devriez pas avoir plutôt des voix neuves et mes sujets sont parfois chatouilleux, venant d'un quinquagénaire!

Puis-je réfléchir un peu à quelques sujets au cours de l'été & selon les courants d'actualité, & vous récrire dès mon retour sur le *Flandre* qui quitte Le Havre le 2 septembre.

Je parlerai bien entendu à Guicharnaud dont le charme comme conférencier est très goûté. Il a parfois, envers les nécessités de la correspondance, la nonchalance des jeunes. Il était sur le bateau avec nous & habite à Paris 20, rue Lacépède, Ve.

Rappelez-nous au souvenir de Madame Bédard et croyez-moi très fidèlement et cordialement vôtre,

Henri Peyre

## À Jorge Guillén:

> Yale ce 6 sept. (1952)

Mon cher Ami,

Je reviens d'Europe, débarqué d'hier: l'Europe était bien belle cet été, & semblait heureuse. Mais je n'ai pas vu l'Espagne, qu'on dit envahie de touristes peu distingués. J'espère y retourner une fois au printemps.

Je trouve parmi une masse de courrier le *numéro* sur Salinas. Je l'ai lu aussitôt, avec émotion. J'aimais beaucoup Salinas et sa mort a été un chagrin profond. Ce numéro est digne de lui et votre hommage, ou plutôt votre article est admirable. Vous y parlez si bien de lui, et de vous car il était vous aussi, et du "métier" de poète, et du poète professeur, et du critique "scientifique."

Je sais que votre fille va bien et est heureuse, que votre gendre travaille & réussit. J'ai peu de nouvelles de votre fils—a-t-il terminé Harvard? Avez-vous regagné le bercail féminin de Wellesley? J'ai conseillé à une dame très fine et, puisqu'elle est fine, admiratrice de vos vers, fort au courant de l'espagnol, Mme Alexandre, de vous rendre visite. Elle sera cette année à Pine Manor College, près de chez vous. Elle est française, veuve de guerre et a une vie difficile—et elle a besoin de quelques amitiés pour lui faire supporter cet exil.

Croyez à mes plus fidèles et amicales pensées.
Henri Peyre

## À Claude Vigée:

Yale
Ce 29—IX [1952]

Mon cher Ami,

Mes compliments! C'est un splendide bulletin de victoire que votre rapport à Mathias—et le témoignage d'une activité qui éblouit. Je suis très heureux de vos succès avec les éditeurs: en ce moment, où la profession est dans le marasme, c'est énorme—et bien peu ont eu autant de bonheur que vous, et de talent aussi, j'ajoute, car il paraît bien des médiocrités à Paris—et je suis très sincèrement heureux aussi de votre succès & promotion à Brandeis. J'avais craint un peu, quand vous êtes allé là, que vous ne soyez "enterré," loin du soi-disant stimulant de collègues nombreux dans votre domaine; et je souhaitais toujours pour vous Harvard, & l'ai dit à Hoog & à Dieckmann. Mais je me trompais peut-être. Vous avez à Brandeis un peu plus de loisirs & de paix, la nature plus présente, et vous n'y rencontrez pas ces petites jalousies & ces menues vanités que l'on trouve ailleurs.

Certes, j'aurais plaisir à aller une fois à Brandeis. J'entends très grand bien de la faculté; et les étudiants doivent y être fervents & ouverts. J'essaie de m'absenter peu, car je suis accablé de tâches: requêtes d'articles que je n'aime pas rédiger si vite et sur commande; visites aux fondations, avec lesquelles nous entreprenons une grande enquête sur les langues en Amérique, pour leur redonner prestige & étudiants; Guggenheim, qui signifie l'étude de 1500 dossiers, etc. Mais de toute manière (hélas!) je serai à la MLA & Boston à Noël & vous verrai là.

J'ai été en France et aussi un peu dans 3 ou 4 pays cet été & cela a été un agréable repos. À Paris même, j'étais trop pris par des Français à revoir & quelques affaires & n'ai pas essayé, malgré votre gentille lettre au printemps, de "toucher" des collègues d'Amérique.

Merci pour *Aurore souterraine*. Je l'avais vu et acheté, et lu, et donné à une amie curieuse de poésie—Je serai heureux de conserver cet exemplaire. J'ai aimé beaucoup vos vers dans ce petit livre et la transfiguration de votre forme. Vous n'avez rien perdu de votre chaleur, de votre réelle puissance de souffle, de votre hantise des mythes anciens—mais vos vers sont plus resserrés, plus purs, plus éloignés de certaine ampleur trop rhétorique qui me rebute souvent chez Emmanuel par exemple. J'avais vu plusieurs comptes rendus de votre recueil, tous très élogieux. Merci aussi pour l'article très sage & fin du Mercure. Comme vous avez raison! Faire de Rilke un philosophe systématique est puéril. N'est-il pas assez grand comme cela?

Votre femme va-t-elle bien? et votre si gracieux bébé—aujourd'hui vrai enfant ou davantage? Je fais commander ici aussitôt ce Rilke, qui promet beaucoup, et j'espère que Gallimard ne vous fera pas trop attendre sa réponse. Sinon, pourquoi pas les Editions de Minuit? La poésie chez eux est estimée, & on l'y va chercher.

Il y a cette année à Pine Manor, à la Maison Française, une Française très distinguée & fine (veuve de guerre), fort amie de poésie, Mme Alexandre. J'espère que vous la verrez, car elle doit trouver, comme vous, l'atmosphère de Wellesley même un peu étouffante et scolaire. Vous connaissez, bien sûr, Guillén et le jeune Galand?

Amitiés à votre femme & à vous,
Hri Peyre

## À Alex Szogyi:

Ce 14—X—52

Mon cher Szogyi,

J'ai été très touché de votre gentillesse & de votre geste. Vous n'auriez pas dû m'offrir ce livre, que je voulais seulement vous emprunter & parcourir. Mais je suis heureux de l'avoir—et, comme il touche à la "sincérité," et que j'espère toujours—quelque jour—revenir à ce sujet, je suis sûr que j'y aurai recours. Il est beau de ton, de naturel, de simplicité, d'aisance narrative. Ça et là, il apporte quelques révélations. Certes, ce n'est pas un livre très riche. Cette fin de Gide est un peu attristante, avec trop peu de surgissement de neuf ou de fort en lui; mais vous avez raison. Sa mort émeut et c'est une grande voix qui s'est tue, un cri de la conscience intellectuelle & de la sincérité littéraire.

Ce que vous me dites & ce que je lis de Decreux m'intéresse. J'aurais dû le connaître & l'avoue à ma honte. Gardez cette brochure & je vous la réemprunterai à l'occasion s'il nous le faut. J'espère que ce sera possible de l'avoir ici. Quand? Comment? Je ne sais encore.

Il me semble que votre traduction devrait paraître sans que la presse en question ait des droits d'auteur exorbitants. Le livre ne se vendra pas énormément ici. La Presse a-t-elle entamé des négociations avec Gallimard? Vous me tiendrez au courant.

Merci encore & amitiés,
Henri Peyre

## À Jorge Guillén:

Ce 30 oct./52
Yale

Cher Ami,

Merci de votre bonne lettre. Vous revoilà au bercail! parmi toutes dames en mal d'affection frustrée. Oui, Jean Santeuil a de bien jolies choses, d'autres agaçantes. Berl est un tourmenté, un demi malade de l'analyse comme il y en a tant chez nous. *Adolphe* a une riche postérité! Avez-vous vu Valéry, *Lettres à quelques-uns*? J'espère bientôt vous lire encore, en vers ou prose & la thèse de votre fils aussi un jour. Pauvre Amado Alonso! et mais en un sens moins final, pauvre Berrien!

Voudriez-vous aider la cause de la poésie? Il s'agirait que vous écriviez, très bientôt, une lettre à M. le Secrétaire de l'Académie Suédoise des Lettres, Stockholm, pour suggérer le nom de St J. Perse pour le prochain prix Nobel. J'ai touché Poggioli, Fowlie, je vais écrire à Ungaretti, Marcel Raymond, E.R. Curtius, Supervielle. On préviendra par ailleurs Archibald Mac Leish et T. S. Eliot. Votre nom serait bien précieux et d'un grand poids, & je me souviens de votre bel "hommage" à Perse dans le no. des *Cahiers de la Pléiade*. Il serait paraît-il à craindre que, si ce n'est Perse, Duhamel soit le candidat de quelques Français — & ce serait dommage.

Mes amitiés à votre fils — et à Mad. Alexandre à l'occasion, et à l'ardent et doué Claude Vigée.

Bien à vous,
Henri Peyre

Excusez l'enveloppe.
Je reviens de Washington.

## To Edgar Furniss:

November 3, 1952

Dear Mr. Furniss:

You may remember that I had asked in our budget for 1952–53 for two laboratory or language assistants, but that only one was granted. We have divided the sum provided ($800.00 plus $500.00 tuition) between two such assistants, Mlle Geoffroy and M. Chartier. Both are very successful, so much so that undergraduates are coming in great numbers to the modest language laboratory we have in W.L.H. and they are both giving more than 8 or 10 hours a week for a very modest stipend.

My proposal is that I save some money on another item in our budget, the one marked "reader," with a total sum of $700.00 for the year. Through correcting more papers myself, I can pay the reader, Mrs. Katherine Harper Mead, only $400.00 for the year. I should want to spend, out of that sum, $200.00 more, to be shared by the two readers ($50.00 each per term) as a just compensation for their long hours. The remainder, $100.00, I hope to save for the University. This is therefore not a request for funds, but for your permission to save on one item and spend part of the saving on another.

If you agree, will you kindly send the enclosed letter to the treasurer's office, with your O.K. if necessary?

Very sincerely yours,<br>HM Peyre

## À Marcel Gutwirth:

Yale<br>Nov. 5 [1952]

Cher Monsieur:

Je serai, bien sûr, heureux d'écrire & de vous recommander. L'idée est bonne. Malgré Moore, le récent Jasinski, il y a encore fort à faire sur le sujet.

Evidemment la compétition pour les Guggenheim est sévère; vous serez confronté avec des professeurs déjà arrivés et ayant beaucoup de publications (peut-être M. March, Miss Gilman, etc.); mais il est bon d'essayer, & on tient compte de l'âge.

Heureuse chance, bien à vous & amitiés à Wylie.

Henri Peyre

## To Marcus Robbins:

November 21, 1952

Mr. Marcus Robbins, Comptroller
Alumni Hall
Yale University
Dear Mr. Robbins:

I am sending you a personal check for $400 out of some money earned in the form of royalties by a member of the French Department and asking you to add that sum to the miscellaneous account of the French Department for the current year 1952/53. The account is Ca 41-

25-16. We have overdrawn our miscellaneous budget account in order to acquire some equipment essential to our language laboratory in William Harkness Hall and since no money had been provided by the University to that effect, we have decided to pay it ourselves. Next year we are asking for a small supplementary sum in our miscellaneous budget in order to pay for the machines which modern methods of teaching force us to use more and more extensively.

Very sincerely yours,<br>
HM Peyre<br>
Henri M. Peyre<br>
Chairman, Department of French

## À René de Messières:

[letterhead: Yale University]<br>
Ce samedi 22 nov. 1952

Mon cher ami,

J'aurais dû mieux m'excuser de m'être laissé, après l'exquise soirée lundi dernier, venant après une journée trop pleine pour moi, aller à un sommeil trop prolongé. À onze heures, m'éveillant enfin, je n'ai pu que sauter dans un train, étant ici attendu.

Cela me ferait plaisir, certes, si tu venais le jeudi 4, au train qui part de NY (Grand Central) à 10 heures. Mais en revoyant mes engagements je vois que le vendredi 5 décembre matin, mon train part de Penn Station pour le collège où je vais en Pennsylvanie à 11h30 A.M. Si tu préférais ce jour-là me rencontrer à Grand Central, upper level, à l'Information Desk à 10h25 (heure où arrive mon train de N. Haven), nous pourrions causer là ou près de là pendant près d'une heure & je t'épargnerais le dérangement. Si cela allait, dis-le moi d'un mot sur la carte ci-jointe.

Mais si de venir ici ne t'ennuyait pas le jeudi 4 déc. ce serait excellent.

J'ai, d'accord avec notre théâtre, proposé à J. L. Barrault la date du jeudi 8 janvier à 3 heures pour sa causerie illustrée ici.

S'il devait repartir avant, et à condition que je le sache avec précision très vite, je pourrais arranger quelque chose un jour de décembre, le 11, le 12, le 17 mercredi s'il n'y avait pas ce jour-là de matinée. Mais il y aurait grand intérêt à ce que Madeleine Renaud & lui pussent rester jusqu'en janvier, pour voir quelques universités. Leur action, là, serait féconde & durable.

Je n'ose pas te parler de ton départ prochain, tant j'en suis éploré et enragé. Que de choses, que d'édifices lentement élevés on brise ainsi! Ce que tu as accompli avec l'Alliance, avec les associations de professeurs pour réorganiser le bachot, pour le théâtre à N.Y., les expositions, les rapports avec des amis influents que la culture française jamais auparavant n'avait ralliés, tes brochures, tes excellentes bibliographies — cent autres choses encore. Tu me donneras peut-être quelques directives pour qu'un peu au moins de cela ne soit pas perdu.

Je te reparlerai de la question Harvard quand nous nous verrons.

Amitiés & merci
Henri Peyre

## À son père et à son frère:

Ce 26 déc. 52

Mon cher Papa, mon cher Jacques,

Noël s'est passé dans le calme pour nous. Nous avons passé une journée tranquille et solitaire et mangé le soir une dinde (au moins en partie) succulente en buvant un excellent Tavel. Comme il se trouve, nous avions comme invité Girard, le jeune homme d'Avignon, avec qui nous avons évoqué la vieille ville. Il enseigne dans le Sud, en Caroline du Nord; et comme la plupart des professeurs, il se rendait à Boston, où se tient du 27 au 30 décembre le congrès annuel des professeurs. Il y en aura 4000 cette année, professeurs de langues et littératures modernes. Je vais m'y rendre demain moi-même et je dois y faire quatre communications et y voir des vingtaines de jeunes professeurs qui veulent m'y rencontrer. Comme le dit Marguerite, je suis un peu le grand manitou ici dans l'enseignement du français! Et je paie ce prestige en écrivant à ma nombreuse clientèle d'incessantes lettres.

Le trimestre a été long & un peu lourd. Mais ces quelques jours de répit nous valent un peu de détente. Nous y avons eu le travail habituel, et à recevoir beaucoup de Français: les échanges avec la France sont maintenant très fréquents, et il est peu de maîtres français qui n'accourent pas ici à un moment ou un autre—En 8 jours il y a eu Massignon, arabisant du Collège de France; Ch. Picard, l'archéologue; 3 ou 4 autres Français; et le comédien Jean-Louis Barrault que j'avais invité à parler à Yale et qui a fait une très belle conférence. À chacun il faut consacrer du temps—et mes propres travaux en souffrent. Je ponds cependant de nombreux articles—mais le temps me manque pour les choses de plus longue haleine.

 La politique a fait beaucoup parler d'elle. Nous avons été déçus de l'élection d'Eisenhower, qui est un brutal et à bien des égards un réactionnaire. Mais peut-être est-ce la tendance du pays en ce moment. On pourchasse partout les Communistes, alors que les seuls dangereux sont à l'extérieur et que mieux vaudrait les comprendre! Enfin, après bien des événements, on est revenu à une attitude plus raisonnable sur la question de l'Afrique du Nord. L'Amérique se sait forte et aimerait bien refouler un peu les Russes en Europe; l'Allemagne, si elle est réarmée, la suivrait volontiers. Chez nous, on semble préférer la tranquillité relative de la situation internationale actuelle, assez peu tranquille d'ailleurs en Indochine & en Afrique.

 Allez-vous tous bien? Toi, Papa, malgré le grand froid qui a sévi? Jacques et sa femme? Le garçonnet? Hélène? Son fiancé est à nouveau en recul dans sa lutte contre ce maudit mal et ils doivent en être bien accablés. Louise va-t-elle bien là-bas et avez-vous de bonnes nouvelles? Donnez-lui des nôtres, et recevez tous nos plus tendres pensées & baisers.

Henri

À l'occasion, bien des choses à Grégoire, à Michel B.

## To Edgar Furniss:

Jan. 5—1953

Dear Mr. Furniss:

 You were very kind to show such sympathy & readiness to assist in the painful tragedy we had.

 I'll confirm it later but I am sure we shall assume a little extra work & only need an assistant in instruction for three hours a week (i.e.

$375.00) to replace Didier from February to June. We shall replace him fully ourselves in January.

The poor man had just paid his dissertation fee to the University: the receipt was found in his wallet. Could that be reimbursed the widow, since . . . there will be no thesis?

Some time at your convenience I'll be glad to come in & see what steps we may take for poor Mrs. Didier & her three babies. I believe they should go back to France soon. The man was not rich, of course; but not in penury. His work had been lightened considerably when we saw him worry. He just became mentally deranged.

Sincerely yours,<br>HM Peyre

## À Jean de Lagarde:

Le 5 janvier 1953

Monsieur Jean de Lagarde,
Ministre Plénipotentiaire
French Consulate
943 Fifth Avenue
New York 21, New York
Monsieur le Ministre:

Je vous remercie de vos vœux si aimables. J'espère que vous allez, enfin installé, pouvoir jouir d'une année relativement paisible et familiale, bien que votre activité soit déjà proverbiale parmi nous.

Vous vous rappelez que j'avais fait demander, avant votre venue dans l'est, la rosette de la Légion d'honneur pour notre Président, M. Griswold, et le ruban rouge pour Theodore Andersson, éducateur très actif qui fait énormément pour ramener l'Amérique aux langues et au français. Si, comme je l'espère, ces décorations sont accordées prochainement, cela pourrait être une belle occasion pour que vous nous rendiez ici une visite officielle et impatiemment attendue.

En attendant, je me permets d'avoir recours à vous pour aider à régler une situation extrêmement pénible, que j'ai déjà signalée il y a quatre jours à votre Vice-Consul. Un de nos collègues, instructor à Yale, Français de l'Est, Pierre Didier, né le 12 mai à Jarville-la-Malgrange

(Meurthe et Moselle), en Amérique depuis 1947 et à Yale depuis 1950, déprimé, sans doute malade, s'est suicidé l'autre jour (31 décembre 1952). Il laisse une veuve de 28 ans et trois tout petits enfants: l'aînée a cinq ans. Sa veuve, Eugénie Didier, née le 8 novembre 1924 Eugénie Henner à Schweyen, France, a 28 ans. Elle est démunie de ressources. Nous l'aidons un peu ici de nos maigres moyens. Mais il semble nécessaire qu'elle retourne en France, où sont ses parents et où une mère de trois enfants aura au moins quelque secours. Le malheureux n'avait même pas d'assurance suffisante.

Est-il possible pour vos services d'obtenir, pour la veuve de ce professeur licencié, qui allait être docteur et qui avait bien servi son pays, soit le passage gratuit pour elle et ses enfants, soit des facilités qui rendraient son retour prochain en France moins onéreux? Aussitôt qu'elle sera moins ébranlée, je m'informerai de l'état de son passeport. J'imagine que son mari, qui avait accompli en France son service militaire, était inscrit au consulat de New York.

Nous vous serons, mes collègues et moi, très reconnaissants de ce que pourront faire vos services, et je vous prie d'agréer, Monsieur le Ministre, l'assurance de mes sentiments les plus reconnaissants.

Henri M. Peyre
Chairman, Department of French

## To Whitney Griswold:

January 14, 1953

Mr. A. Whitney Griswold
Woodbridge Hall
Dear President Griswold:

You were very kind to mention yesterday the possibility of asking for some transportation to take Mme Pierre Didier and her three little children back to France. As soon as her husband died I wrote to the French Consul in New York and asked him to cable at once to Paris and present an urgent plea that she and the children be given free transportation by the French Government. This apparently is not easy to obtain, especially with the present French shortage of dollars, but I still hope I may secure it for them. If the other method which we thought of appears to you to offer any substantial hope, I am sure Mrs. Didier would be glad to be granted such a favor. I shall let you know at once in case the answer from the French Consul happens to be negative. I understand her intention would be to leave about the end of the present month.

Many thanks again for your kind words in this matter, and

Very sincerely yours,
Henri Peyre

## To Edgar Furniss:

Jan. 15, 1953

Dear Mr. Furniss:

I have not kept you informed of developments in connection with Mrs. P. Didier, because there were few or none thus far.

I believe I'll succeed in getting her passage back paid by the French. The Consul cabled very urgently & asked that the proper sum be allotted by the French Government. He cannot do anything without such an authorization. I believe it will be granted—perhaps only after the widow & the three babies have left. They would like to leave on Jan. 23 if possible.

President Griswold mentioned another possibility, of a plane occasionally returning empty which might take them home. But I was not too clear about what he meant.

The financial picture is not rosy, but not too dark. We & she are grateful to the University for the January check & the $500.00 payment for the funeral. We have collected, among the members of our Department & a few graduate students, some $600.00 which I have given her. They had no savings, for three children, on a $4,000 yearly salary, proved enough of a strain. If the University feels it can make another gift, it will be generous & we shall be grateful: but I am always asking for money & am embarrassed at doing so. Your judgment, as always, will be the wisest &, I know, the most humane.

I have felt nothing but approval for your recent directives to chairmen. I believe they are right & justified, & that few, very few associate professors should be up for promotion after fewer than 10 years at that rank, & I also believe our assistant-professor salaries, second term, are too high. But I am known to be thrifty.

In our own case, our need will be for native *French* instructors, as we have lost Didier, & two others, Bieber & Leblon, who have been taken by Connecticut College. And several other colleges are ready to snatch any whom we may have trained. Yet we absolutely need some French (native) instructors for some of our courses. I'll do my best to get them at the minimum salary ($3.500) or if not, to juggle around our allotted funds to attract them at a slightly better salary. But I trust I shall not make unreasonable or expensive requests.

Very thankfully yours,<br>Hri

## À Malcolm McIntosh:

Ce 31—i—53

Cher M. McIntosh:

J'ai lu avec intérêt vos chapitres. Ils ont bien des mérites et constituent (avec ce que je n'ai pas lu) une thèse très convenable.

Vous savez beaucoup de choses, vous vous êtes renseigné scrupuleusement, votre bibliographie est vaste & précise. Sur bien des points (notamment sur Claudel, Barbara, même Champfleury & Duranty), vous apprendrez bien des choses à vos lecteurs. Vous montrez les qualités que requiert, entre autres, une thèse: connaissances étendues & précises, méthode objective, bonne utilisation de votre documentation, sens des nuances & goût littéraire. Vous avez travaillé ferme, et avec de bons résultats. Vos chapitres sont dans l'ensemble bien composés. Vous avez bien tiré parti d'un sujet qui, parfois, pouvait paraître un peu maigre.

À mon goût, vous restez un peu pédestre, un peu trop près de vos notes & parfois encombré ou enchaîné par elles. Dans le chapitre sur Baudel. & Flaubert surtout, à côté des relations des deux hommes que vous précisez fort bien, des faits précis que nous avons & de quelques parallèles, il y avait peut-être lieu de tracer, en critique et presque en portraitiste, une esquisse de ce que les deux auteurs ont en commun & de ce par quoi ils diffèrent. Vous l'énoncez parfois, mais avec un peu de sécheresse. Il faudrait presque dépasser les faits, anecdotes et précisions et traiter une partie du sujet au dessus de tout cela—par ex., ce qu'ont de commun au départ trois ou quatre auteurs d'une même génération et en quoi ils vont ensuite différer: Flaubert, Champfleury, Baudelaire, Courbet.

Mais c'est peut-être là demander autre chose qu'une thèse & autre chose que ce que vous avez voulu faire, & est donc peu juste. Quelque chose dans votre manière et surtout dans votre style reste un peu craintive, un peu plat aussi, manque d'envolée.

Parfois aussi vous semblez vous étonner que Baudel. ait beaucoup goûté Champfleury tout en combattant le réalisme. Cela est fréquent en littérature. Il y avait chez Champfleury un apôtre du réalisme, mais aussi un critique d'art avisé, une espèce de révolté & de bohème, un homme de goût, etc. Baudel. pouvait fort bien ne pas aimer les romans de Champfleury mais s'entendre avec la partie négative du message de Champfleury, qui affirmait en attaquant ses prédécesseurs que la nouvelle génération avait quelque chose à dire. De même pour Courbet: Baudel. pouvait être attiré par ce que l'homme & le peintre avaient de solide, de robuste, de sain; aussi par l'érotisme de Courbet; par sa révolte anti-bourgeoise. Baudel. n'a jamais bien dit ce qu'il entendait par réalisme.

Je suppose que, quelque part, vous essaierez de dégager les idées de Baudel. sur l'art du roman, ses goûts en matière de roman, son envie d'être romancier, son impuissance à l'être, et ce qu'il y a de "roman" dans certains de ses poèmes.

Ne tardez pas trop à finir. Car ce sera long de revoir, de taper tout ceci et vous avez intérêt à être prêt pour le 1er mai sans faute. Ceci ne doit pas vous inquiéter. Ce pourrait être écrit avec plus de brillant, être un peu plus livre & moins thèse—mais je crois que ce sera très convenable ainsi.

Bien à vous,
HP

## To Edgar Furniss:

February 5, 1953

Dear Mr. Furniss:

Thank you for your kind telephone conversation. Here are the exact figures which I think you should have on the financial help thus far contributed for the widow and the three children of the late Pierre Didier. He died, as you remember, on December 31, 1952. The salary which would normally have been paid to him for the rest of the year, January to June 30, amounted to $2,000. The University generously repaid $500 for the cost of the funeral and the January salary which must have amounted to $333.33 (deductions not included) to the widow. Out of the remaining sum of $1,166.67 we asked the University to set aside $375 as a salary for one assistant in instruction taking over three hours which Didier was giving. If my calculation is right, the University therefore saved $791.67 and will save another sum next year since the new instructor replacing Didier is down for $750 less.

The French Department and a few friends collected among themselves a sum slightly in excess of $600 for Mrs. Didier. The French Government, after my insistent cabling to Paris, promised they would reimburse her for a substantial part of her traveling expenses back to France, probably some $500 (in French francs for they are short of dollars). The amount she had to pay was $647 on the passage for herself and three children, some $40 on taxes and incidentals and $160 for moving of books, furniture and some luggage.

We do not feel in any way that we have any claim on the University except for the general claim on the generosity of Yale to its professors for their families who have undergone tragic misfortunes. Any sum that the University felt it could set aside to help Mrs. Didier start her new life and place her children in France would, of course, be welcome. She has retained an account here in a local bank, and her address in France is: Mrs. Eugénie Didier, 23 rue Clemenceau, Jarville-la-Malgrabge (Meurthe et Moselle), France.

All the members of our Department have been very much touched by the sympathy of many in the University and by your prompt and very human and cordial reaction to the tragic event.

Very sincerely yours,<br>HM Peyre

# To the same:

February 17, 1953

Dear Mr. Furniss:

My colleagues and I are very deeply grateful to you and to President Griswold for arranging the payment of a generous sum of $750 to the widow of Pierre Didier. I have given Mr. Roberts the name of the bank (New Haven Savings Bank) at which she has an account. We all want to express our gratitude to the University for its generosity and its very touching and warmhearted response in this matter.

I have received news from Professor Renou in France. He has not yet recovered from his accident, but he assures me that will in no way affect the excellent memory he has retained of Yale. You may have heard that there was a good deal of difficulty with the New Haven Income Tax Bureau which had not understood from the Franco-American agreement in the tax laws whether a visiting professor here for teaching and scientific research should pay income tax in this country. Mr. Roberts, Assistant Comptroller, and I were convinced that the interpretation of the law should be that no American income tax was to be paid but that the income tax was to be paid in France and double taxation should thus be avoided. M. Renou finally was told by the New York office that the University's interpretation was correct, and he did not have to pay the American income tax which the University had refunded him after withholding it. I had on my own side written to the New York office which answered also that in cases like these the American income tax had not to be paid. I am sending you a copy of the answer which I received and which I believe should be, if you agree, communicated to the Comptroller's office for further reference.

I have made two payments of $500 and $250 respectively to Messrs. Brombert and May to help them publish their volumes in our series in France. Those were out of the funds which you allotted me for that purpose and I am sending you the letters of thanks and acknowledgment which I have received from those colleagues.

Very sincerely yours,
HM Peyre

## À Eléonore Zimmermann:

Febr. 22/53

Chère Mademoiselle,

Je regrette que l'on m'ait donné ceci par erreur & qu'on vous en ait privé. Mais j'y ai pris intérêt & plaisir. C'est un bon essai sur un sujet qui paraît banal mais est difficile. Certes, il y a encore en effet dans votre manière quelque chose d'un peu dur; la conclusion déçoit un peu; vous n'avez pas eu tout le temps pour mûrir le sujet; parfois vous touchez vite à des points complexes (Mall. & la nuit; Mall. & Tennyson, et le romantisme; Mall. & l'anglais; etc.)—mais votre vue des choses est juste, vos réflexions sur le vrai caractère de l'influence en général sont sages. Vous avez de la précision, de la décision aussi dans le jugement, du sens critique, de l'originalité. Ceci pourrait être repris, renforcé, et peut-être fournir un jour un bon article sur ce sujet. Votre style est plus littéraire déjà, quoique pas assez encore. Vous avez de belles promesses.

Puisque vous êtes maintenant sous l'autorité de M. Wellek (pour les bourses, les oraux, vos projets d'avenir, de thèse, de postes, etc.), voyez-le quelquefois & intéressez-le à vous, pour qu'il vous appuie efficacement, comme vous le méritez.

Pour un voyage d'été, je ne vois toujours rien—mais attendons encore.

Bien à vous,
HP

Ch. Chassé (Lueurs sur Mall) & dans un article curieux et aventuré & un peu fou de l'avant-dernière *Revue d'Histoire littéraire* a quelques pages curieuses sur Mall. & l'anglais.

## À son frère:

Ce 5 mars 53

Mon cher Jacques,

J'ai reçu ta lettre l'autre jour & j'avais bien reçu celle de janvier, où Pierre avait écrit quelques mots en anglais correct & élégant. C'est un excellent petit savant, extraordinairement mûr pour son âge, & avec une vie intérieure et une faculté de rêve qui promettent une fine sensibilité. Sa mère peut-être fière de lui ainsi que toi qui as su le comprendre et lui éviter tous les petits problèmes qui surviennent parfois entre enfants sensibles et parents remariés. Tu avais une admirable vocation de père. Je lui enverrai un mot sur une carte dès que je serai un peu moins bousculé.

Mon retard à te répondre a été comme de coutume dû à un amas de besogne, à des tiraillements causés par des voyages, des obligations de tous genres provenant de conférences, de comités ça & là. En ce moment même, je te griffonne quelques lignes de New York où j'ai dû venir pour deux jours et demi, comme membre d'un comité où l'on distribue de l'argent pour des recherches & des publications. Je suis assis autour d'une grande table, avec cinq graves messieurs qui m'empestent de leurs pipes et cigares. Au dehors, (nous sommes au 47e étage), des gratte-ciel éclairés (car ici on n'éteint jamais la lumière électrique de la journée, car il paraît qu'il est plus économique et de moins d'effort de laisser la lumière constamment que de la fermer & l'ouvrir). Sur la beauté de la ville, je suis un peu blasé, mais il y a quelquefois de merveilleuses couleurs dans le ciel, pur et bleu comme un ciel méridional. L'hiver a été très doux cette année, avec très peu de neige & de brume, et apparemment moins de tempêtes & de froid qu'en Europe: les journaux ont annoncé toutes sortes d'intempéries en France, & plus encore ailleurs. Nous avons nous-même—jusqu'ici—échappé à l'épidémie de grippe. Il y a eu plusieurs pneumonies autour de nous, vite enrayées grâce aux drogues modernes. Vous allez bien, semble-t-il, et Papa lui-même supporte l'hiver aisément. Le plus malheureux est ce pauvre Pierre, le fiancé d'Hélène, dont l'avenir est encore une fois interrompu ou assombri. Hélène supporte-t-elle cela sans trop d'amertume? J'admire son courage après ces années de jeunesse à ce point accablées. Elle aura vraiment été privée de la plupart des joies.

Nous allons donc bien tous les deux, et la vie continue à être un train assez monotone d'obligations et de tâches quotidiennes. Trois jours par semaine, j'ai des cours. Il est rare que je ne sois pas obligé d'aller à l'Université pour d'autres besognes, de caractère administratif, les autres jours. Et les fins de semaine se passent à rattraper les retards de courrier (lesquels ne sont d'ailleurs jamais rattrapés), à préparer les cours, à m'occuper de vingt autres choses. Il semble qu'on me mette de plus en plus à toutes les sauces, & je suis plus souvent politicien de choses universitaires qu'auteur de livres ou d'articles que je voudrais écrire. Mais j'ai eu l'autre jour 52 ans, comme tu as eu la gentillesse de te le rappeler; & bien que je me sente encore fort vert & assez énergique, & que je passe pour tel, je sens qu'il est difficile de sortir de quelque engrenage d'habitudes dans lequel je me débats. Il n'y a que l'été quand nous pouvons aller en France que je me sente un peu libéré—mais nous ne pourrons pas entreprendre le voyage, comme je vois, cet été prochain: cela entraîne trop de frais de tout genre, difficiles à concilier avec le coût de la vie & les impôts. Je crois qu'il faut nous contenter de la perspective d'un été sur deux seulement en Europe. Je resterai la plus grande partie de celui-ci à New Haven même où je ne manquerai pas de besogne, car j'ai beaucoup à écrire. Il y fait chaud & humide, mais je m'efforcerai de n'y pas trop penser.

La vie extérieure nous touche peu directement, en ce sens qu'elle ne transforme pas le calme de nos vies. Mais elle nous atteint par les journaux et les conversations. Voici Staline que l'on annonce aujourd'hui mourant. J'avais toujours pensé qu'il ne se lancerait jamais dans une guerre à 70 ou 73 ans: on verra ce que ses successeurs nous réservent. Mais je continue à n'avoir pas trop peur—pour l'avenir prochain. L'Amérique a des soucis de tous côtés et, comme son peuple est fait de braves gens dans le fond, elle s'inquiète beaucoup de ce qu'on lui rapporte sur la haine dont elle est l'objet dans le monde. On me demande souvent de parler en public sur l'antiaméricanisme en France aujourd'hui, & je ne manque pas de dire quelques vérités. On a une frayeur maladive des communistes, mais pour le reste le pays ne veut guère croire à la guerre: les affaires vont bien & on jouit de la prospérité & du plaisir de faire quelques sermons & de distribuer quelques avis, en même temps que des secours d'ailleurs, au reste du monde.

Dis nos bien fidèles & affectueuses pensées à Micheline & à Pierrot—et à Papa bien sûr, & à Louise & Hélène quand tu leur écris. Merci d'écrire parfois dans ta vie occupée.

Caresses,
Henri

## À Judd Hubert:

Yale, ce 16 — III 53

Cher Monsieur,

Vous avez été aimable, & m'avez fait plaisir, en m'envoyant cet article qu'une journée trop affairée m'avait empêché d'entendre à Boston. C'est un essai fort original — très subtil (un peu trop peut-être, c'est votre menu et mignon péché), comme ce que vous faites, mais en même temps très pénétrant & neuf. Bajazet lui même devient, pour vous, un héros au cœur inexpugnable, un personnage obsédé de son rôle cornélien & presque shakespearien. Vous n'avez pas tort, & cet aspect, éclairé par vous, apparaîtra en effet au lecteur un aspect vrai de ce personnage — un peu trop isolé, & accentué, peut-être, par votre ingénieuse insistance. Mais qu'importe? Publiez ceci, en le raccourcissant un peu peut-être, dans la *Romanic Review* par exemple et poursuivez votre Racine, avec un petit peu de méfiance de votre gentille inclination au paradoxe et au système. Vous êtes *quelqu'un*, je le sais depuis longtemps, & devez devenir l'un des premiers parmi nous en Amérique. Vous n'avez qu'à gagner en vous heurtant au public, à des contradicteurs possibles, sans jamais vous banaliser, mais en évitant peut-être de vous isoler dans des culs de sacs un tout petit peu égotistes.

Je serai heureux de lire le recueil de votre femme, & le volume sur les *Fleurs du Mal*. Je sais que le premier a du talent, dans sa fine discrétion, & que le second sera remarqué.

Je m'étonne que Wellesley ne soit pas *ravi* d'accueillir votre femme. C'est là qu'est sa place. Je connais bien Miss Melcher, & tout le monde là-bas; mais je crois que Miss Melcher souvent m'écoute. Dites à votre femme de se présenter à elle et de dire ses "sponsors," dont je suis. Elle y serait tout à fait à sa place. À Brandeis aussi, mais ils voudront peut-être là un homme. Vous devriez être réunis et il est vrai, à ce qu'on dit, que mieux vaut peut-être ne pas rester trop longtemps à Sarah Lawrence. Miss Fritsch à Wellesley, autrichienne d'origine, est une excellente érudite & y a quelque influence, je crois. Votre femme pourrait la voir aussi, de ma part si elle veut. Elle devrait aussi, du sujet de sa thèse ou d'un autre, extraire 2 ou 3 articles. Cela fera impression, car peu de femmes ici publient. Ayez foi en votre commun avenir.

Bien à vous,
Hri Peyre

## À Claude Vigée:

ce 26—III—53

Mon cher ami,

Je vous devais un mot pour vous remercier de ce n° des Cahiers du Sud. Votre article, que j'avais déjà lu, m'avait beaucoup intéressé & plu. De divers côtés, on a reçu vos poèmes avec compréhension. Après quelque marasme, il semble que l'activité littéraire reprenne en France: des revues se fondent en grand nombre, des livres de poésie paraissent. Seghers est vraiment héroïque. Je suis content que votre Rilke se poursuive. J'ai eu récemment à revoir divers poèmes, les derniers, posthumes, de votre livre & la traduction m'en a paru la plus heureuse & fidèle.

Je réponds à votre question. Des Français? On en cherche de tous côtés cette année. On m'a pris les miens (Conn. College) & j'en cherche en France. Bryn Mawr va prendre, sur mon conseil, M. un garçon de 1er ordre (poète d'ailleurs) & Girard, bon critique. Berkeley en veut un. Harvard aussi.

Je crois que je connais tous les Français de ce pays. On dit énormément de bien de Brandeis & ce que vous suggérez est fort enviable comme poste & traitement. Je crois que le meilleur est sans doute Collignon, (Jean) agrégé (d'anglais), excellent professeur, pas très productif, mais intelligent & fin. A-t-il intérêt à quitter Cornell où il est logé à "Telluride House," où il a un bel avenir? J'en doute.

Guicharnaud, normalien, agrégé, semble beaucoup se plaire ici. Il est très vivant, cordial, fantaisiste mais avec sérieux, écrit (théâtre, roman). Tôt ou tard, & bientôt, il faudra qu'il se mette à des travaux universitaires & "scholarly." Je ne lui ai rien dit de ceci, mais il a refusé d'autres offres d'ailleurs. Il aime la proximité de N. York. Il a ici $4750, est "fellow" d'un College.

Pamplume? Très bon érudit, excellent professeur, dit-on; mais moins de charme que les deux premiers, silencieux obstiné, pas très liant. Je le connais peu, mais on semble penser qu'il serait mieux en France, professeur de Première Supérieure, qu'ici.

Quelqu'un de très fort est Champigny, à Indiana. Normalien, agrégé, poète, philosophe, original, dogmatique aussi, un peu carré d'allures & de caractère, mais, me dit-on, fort apprécié là-bas. S'il vous intéressait, je vous montrerais de ses lettres pour que vous le jugiez mieux.

Carlut de votre ancienne université? Il sembler peu se prodiguer.

Il y a des Français qui viendraient volontiers de France, mais on ne sait jamais s'ils seront adaptables, séduits par ce pays, connaîtront assez la langue. Par ex, Georges Auclair, auteur d'*Un amour allemand,* désireux de venir pour un an ou deux. Un autre retraité, moins brillant qu'A. Guérard? Il y en a un, aux Nations Unies, Bouscharain, mais, évidemment, sorti de l'enseignement depuis pas mal d'années & susceptible en tous cas de ne rester que peu.

Je crois que j'avais indiqué à M. Guérard une ou deux dames. Je pense grand bien de la finesse, de la distinction d'esprit de Madame Alexandre, cette année à Pine Manor, tout près de chez vous. Elle comprend les Américains mais trouve ce collège trop mondain & trop école de jeunes filles.

Enfin, il y a quelques jeunes gens très forts, qui sont des Juifs allemands, mais très francisés, très cultivés & fins, parmi les gens du plus bel avenir en Amérique. J'en ai deux ou trois ici. Le mieux serait qu'une fois, avec préavis, vous vous arrêtiez ici. Leurs noms? Weinberg, Mendelson et Mark Temmer; je crois que celui-ci est suisse & je ne pense pas qu'il soit juif. Le 1er a 40 ans & passe sa thèse, le 3e. est déjà docteur (28 ans?), le second le sera dans un an. Mais Weinberg va peut-être être appelé à New York & les autres trouveront peut-être difficile de changer leurs plans aussi tard dans l'année. Est-ce vraiment pour la rentrée prochaine que vous cherchez quelqu'un?

Si je puis mieux vous aider, dites-le moi. Mes compliments & mon fidèle souvenir à votre femme, & bien à vous,

Hri Peyre

## To Harry Levin:

Yale, 29 mars 1953

My dear Harry Levin:

Your long & cordial letter gave me a very real pleasure. I am glad you have had a pleasant stay, if not a restful one. You are very discreet about your success, which, as I heard from many another source, has been great. Whom else could the French find who might have combined breadth & thoroughness, creative criticism & impeccable precision of knowledge, sensitiveness & depth? In all fairness, I hope my compatriots will at least have realized that there are not many men like you in America. Several times this year, once talking to Mr. Weeks of the Atlantic, once at the A[merican] Council of] L[earned] S[ocieties], then at other groups, & at Harvard, I heard, or I said: "What a pity there are not more men like Harry Levin."

Have you, at any rate & as a reward, enjoyed some leisure for travel, met colleagues & writers in Germany or Italy or the Netherlands & merely and prosaically, found some rest in just eating & idling occasionally, & sitting at a café instead of in a library cell—libraries over there offering few opportunities for work. Masochistically, I confess I rather enjoy working in some French libraries, for a while, & finding that a book is an important thing not to be had for the asking, & that getting its call number in mysterious hieroglyphics after imploring 3 or 4 catalogues is a piece of detective research *in se*. I must add that I am there only on vacation & that here my frustration is perpetual since I have an office next door to the library but can hardly ever enter there.

Your remarks on French teaching interested me very much, & although you make them courteous & very restrained, I know they are right. There is an air of "vétusté" about things & people. Criticism (acutely practiced in several magazines of literature) has remained, in French universities, complacently 30 or 50 years behind. It is conventional, heavy-handed, a little dull. Sorbonne courses are hopelessly "scolaires." Then there is a certain lack of energy about the academic life & everything else probably in the country. The great hopes aroused around the Resistance have been frustrated. Things & the minds of men have not been molded anew. There is a lack of boldness, of new ideas. The French system, in particular, is too heavily anchored to the desirability of turning out good lycée teachers. It is successful there, & of course we might well over here steal a number of pages from their books & reform our own secondary teaching. But Lucien Febvre, others, I myself once in *Le Monde,* have contended that the agrégation is the bane of French academic life & kills research. Anthropology, linguistics, economic history, history of religion, stylistics, oriental studies, etc. have a few first rate men, but very few, too few, and not enough research is being accomplished there, because those fields (& comparative lit. also) are not included in the regular agregation syllabus. I believe a thorough reform is overdue. In part because of the necessity of passing & of preparing for the agregation, the University professors are overwhelmed with work & have become sterile. Their quality, also, is lower than it used to be: several are selected (e.g. Laudié!) because they are plodding, conscientious, solid. But they are hopelessly heavy & don't even keep up with the information which might enrich or enliven their courses.

As to Comparative Lit., the Sorbonne professors are good friends whom I am deeply fond of. But (& Guyard's mediocre little book exemplified it), their conception of comparative lit. is a narrow, conventional & dry one. Their review (I wrote Munteano so a few months ago) is *not* alive; it lacks boldness, range, depth, ideas. They do not rethink, as we say in French, their objectives, their methods. Theses, even on "le mirage," have fallen into ruts of conventionality. In the best universities over here, I believe we now turn out better work. I hope your visit there proved beneficial to them & spurred them on to reexamine themselves & their methods & results.

Sorry things have happened over here, as you know. There are signs that McCarran, McCarthy & Co. are on the wane: for a while, one had a clear impression of being in a pre-fascist climate. But anti-intellectualism is not declining fast & it is doing much harm. A cloud of suspicion hangs over every one. I have spent much time this year on several committees which want to remain liberal (Guggenheim, among others) trying to limit the damage. But the Hiss case has done incalculable harm to Foundations here, in their attitudes & moods. Fear & suspicion have spread. The new administration could put an end to it, but will it?

At Harvard, the Romance Depart. is indeed torn. Jasinski, as you heard, wished to come. He has been the enforced choice of the committee. There was little if any enthusiasm: but he was the only choice, especially in the face of divisions inside the Depart. Certainly he will not bring any awareness of modern criticism, renewal of methods, sensitiveness to poetical values, philosophical insight. But another appointment may complete this one, later. Meanwhile Dieckmann, who is a very conscientious & devoted chairman, seems hypernervous. Singleton is equally tense. The spirit which prevails in that Department is one of suspicion & division. I wish (not upon you!), for their sake, that you might take it over & run it for some years.

But you should be spared stomach ulcers, especially after some solid months of French cuisine, & you must be allowed to write more books like your Marlowe, so beautifully finished & rich in lore and insight. Forget all about Harvard for some more months. I am still puzzled why a Harvard President should be ambitious enough & foolish enough to accept a position in Germany, in the present circumstances. But the humanities at Harvard will probably gain thereby. One thing this country refuses to learn: the sweetness & light of simply going into retirement, reading, dreaming, not feeling important. I cannot go over next, I mean *this*, summer, because I must have a little time to write & to save money for another summer—but I dream of "la douce retraite."

With very cordial wishes & very sincerely yours,
Henri Peyre

## To Keith Botsford:

Yale, April 7/1953

My dear Botsford,

I didn't know you were back. Hope nothing too unpleasant occurred.

Wed. 15th will be a busy day. I have a visitor, M. Laroque, a French jurist, to guide, entertain & direct from 12 noon until 10 P.M. or so. I'll leave for NY the next morning. I'll be away in Virginia on the 12th–13th & just back on Thursday 14th for our French play (*Le Bal des Voleurs*).

If a following Wednesday were more convenient, I'd have more time. On the 15th just a few moments between 11 & 12, when I have to meet the visitor at the station.

My best, & to your wife,
Henri Peyre

## À Mario Maurin:

Ce 9 avril 1953

Mon cher ami,

Ne vous fatiguez point & utilisez ces derniers mois de vie militaire à reposer votre esprit et à distraire votre corps.

Je crois que B. Mawr vous laisse plus de liberté & d'initiative et en un sens peut mieux se prêter à vos intentions d'écrire quelque chose de "personnel." Ce n'est pas que je craigne pour votre critique qui, personnelle, le sera toujours. Mais vous avez d'autres talents aussi & méritez de jouir de quelque loisir pour les mûrir. Je crois que Dieckmann vous aurait désiré pour Harvard: je lui avais parlé très chaudement. Il a été déçu quand il a appris, au moment d'aller vous voir, que vous aviez en fait accepté l'offre de Miss Gilman: mais je lui ai dit que vous n'étiez pas homme à jouer un jeu un peu double & qu'il n'avait qu'à vous parler ouvertement. C'est un esprit susceptible & un peu chagrin, mais, dans son tourment de perfection, qui l'honore, très droit & noble. Mais l'atmosphère à Harvard en ce moment a peu d'agrément.

Mes compliments donc—vous voilà, très jeune, bien lancé, avec études & carrière des armes derrière vous. Ménagez-vous surtout.

Merci pour l'article. Il se trouve hélas! que M. Morehouse, qui nous devait un article sur Simone Weil, vient d'être frappé à Chicago d'une grave attaque de cœur. Il n'est pas sûr qu'il s'en tire. En tous cas, il en aura pour des mois de repos. Je serais donc particulièrement heureux si vous pouvez toucher à Suarès & à S. Weil: arrangez le titre & l'article comme vous voulez—pourvu que ce ne soit pas trop long (12 à 18 pages tapées) et en anglais, & pas trop de notes.

Quelqu'un nous a déjà proposé un article sur "Sartre hanté par Dieu" ou à peu près: Champigny, d'Indiana. Je lui laisse donc ce sujet.

Mes bons vœux pour votre fin d'année de servitude & mon bon souvenir à votre mère.

Bien à vous,<br>Henri Peyre

L'article (au plus tard dû au 1er août) pourrait aller droit à Kenneth Cornell, si vous voulez—ou à moi, à votre guise.

## À Claude Vigée:

Ce 23—IV.53

Mon cher ami,

Vous m'avez fait plaisir en m'envoyant ce poème, beau & rare. Il paraîtra, j'imagine, en plaquette ou dans quelque volume à venir? Il renferme de grandes beautés. S'il est moins somptueux, moins chargé de comparaisons épiques, moins entraîné vers l'éloquence poétique (qui est la vraie) que certains de vos premiers vers, il m'émeut aussi davantage; il est plus naturel, il s'empare de la vie concrète, des enfants qui lugent, de votre fillette, de vos souvenirs de petit garçon au cimetière alsacien, de votre situation présente d'homme de deux continents et, sans artifices, il transforme tout cela en magie — Le monde que vous évoquez est moins un univers de rêve et de visionnaire, davantage un monde réel transfiguré par le don du poète. Vous n'êtes pas le poète qui risquerait de mourir jeune pour laisser place au critique ou au professeur; vous mûrissez, en *restant* poète.

J'ai l'impression que, et Collignon et Guicharnaud sont paresseux devant l'éventualité d'un changement, contents où ils sont, sans trop de responsabilités. On disait que Pamplume aurait aimé aller chez vous, mais passe pour étrange, réservé avec les étudiants, solitaire & peu désireux de s'adapter ici. Je ne sais & le connais peu. Il va, me dit-on, à Vassar.

J'ai placé, ou perdu, plusieurs de nos jeunes Français et vais en "importer" 2 ou 3 l'an prochain: mais ils sont, une fois ici, très demandés. Mon impression est qu'en ce moment quelques femmes, françaises comme Mad. Alexandre, américaines d'origine allemande (Mrs. Lang, Mrs. Edith Kern, en ce moment à Wellesley, Mrs. Riese Hubert dont le mari enseigne à Harvard) sont supérieures à la plupart des hommes dans la profession. Êtes-vous université mixte?

Bien des choses à votre femme — et merci à vous-même & amitiés,

Hri Peyre

## To Edgar Furniss:

April 25, 1953

Dear Mr. Furniss:

I am embarrassed at having to ask so many generous favors from the University this year, but we have been afflicted with every kind of calamity.

Some friends of Morehouse who came from out of town for the funeral expressed concern at the news (I don't know where they heard it, but Morehouse's son in law was probably told that at the Treasurer's office) that his salary from Yale would be cut off after April 30th. I called up the President who asked me to deny any rumors to that effect. I don't wish to suggest or dictate anything, of course, but I'll tell those well meaning but over testy friends of Andy that the University knows all he meant for us & all he did for Yale.

We hope to have a memorial fund collected in tribute to Andy, probably to provide for a friendship or prize in his memory.

I'll enclose our last *Yale French Studies* & a few insignificant papers, one on Feuillerat as a tribute, as a friendly & admiring homage to you.

Sincerely,<br>Henri

## To Whitney Griswold:

April 25, 1953

Dear Whit:

I am sorry if I caused you any embarrassment. I realized, when you first spoke to me on the phone on Friday, that your kind reply expressed the generosity of your feelings and a natural impatience with over hasty persons prompt to misinterpret. I did not take it as a promise, & left at once a note to the Provost, stating the question & submitting it to the generous decision of Yale. I was aware of the ruling that the salary of a deceased professor is normally only paid up to the month in which he died. I purposely said nothing to Mrs. Morehouse until your spontaneous reaction was confirmed. I only spoke to her after Mr. Holden spoke in your name on Saturday.

Personally, as in Didier's case, as in the case of last winter's freeze, and in others previously, I am convinced that the University has always taken a generous and wise course, and perhaps only failed in "publicizing" its generous wisdom — an honorable failure which assumes that we are among gentlemen and critical spirits able to discern rumors from the truth. I shall make every effort to let it be known that the University showed the most grateful appreciation of Mr. Morehouse's long services & went way beyond dues, rights and justice. A circular clarifying these points for the future & sent every four or five years to chairmen might be useful.

I am enclosing the essay I gave to the Benjamin Franklin lectures in

Philadelphia, when asked (along with Franz Neumann, Tillich, Panofsky & Wolfgang Kohler) to consider the phenomenon of the "cultural migration" to America. I believe some points are similar to those which you often make.

Very gratefully,<br>HM Peyre

We included the sailing specialist, whom you recommended in a colorful letter, among the Guggenheim fellows, & several eminent Yale professors, but I failed to persuade the Committee to retain Marshall Bartholomew's name & was sorry.

## À Franco Simone:

Ce 28—IV.53

Cher Monsieur,

L'envoi de vos "tirages" m'a honoré et fait grand plaisir. J'ai beaucoup goûté celui sur la poésie baroque & nous en parlerons ici, où ce sujet passionne beaucoup de gens—à l'excès sans doute. J'avais lu votre très bel article sur Croce: avec celui de Wellek dans la revue américaine, *Comparative Literature,* c'est le meilleur que j'aie lu sur Croce. Et j'ai bien regretté de ne pas être présent au Congrès des Études Françaises, mais il est difficile d'aller en Europe chaque été. Je devrai, hélas! m'abstenir cet été de 1953.

Je parle souvent de vous ici, et j'espère toujours qu'un jour on vous invitera ici: l'Amérique aurait beaucoup à gagner à attirer un érudit de votre classe. M. Herbert Dieckmann, qui dirige à Harvard le département de langues romanes & à qui j'ai parlé de vous, a conçu lui aussi une très haute opinion de votre livre sur "la conscience de l'humanisme." À l'occasion, communiquez-lui (ou à M. Singleton, aussi à Harvard) quelques-unes de vos publications. Si en quelque chose je puis d'ici vous être utile, pour vos travaux ou votre documentation, n'hésitez pas à me le dire.

Croyez à mes sentiments très dévoués,<br>Hri Peyre

## To the American Philosophical Society:

April 28, 1953

Dear Mr. Eisenhart:

I feel much honored & greatly flattered to have been elected to the American Philosophical Society. There is no other group of wise and learned men in this country to which I should be prouder to belong.

I shall hope to attend the next meeting on November 12–13, unless something unforeseen occurs. I shall be very happy to be formally inducted at that date.

Please accept my thanks & very sincere regards,
Hri Peyre

## To Keith Botsford:

May 4, 1953

Mr. Keith Botsford
300 East 56th Street
New York 22, N.Y.

Dear Mr. Botsford:

I am sorry it was not possible for me to see you on that particular Wednesday. It is difficult for me to reserve time except by doing it long in advance and I practically never go to New York unless to be there for a very precise engagement. But I hope you may call again sometime late in May when things will be easier.

Of course I shall be pleased to recommend you to Bard College. It usually is much better policy to write them in reply to a particular request for a recommendation originating from them. But if you tell me whom to write to and if you prefer for me to write of my own initiative, I shall be glad to do so.

Our very best regards to your wife and

Very sincerely yours,
Henri M. Peyre

Excusez l'anglais. Je suis si pressé que je ne puis même écrire une carte en paix.

## To Ted Weiss:

May 18, 1953

Professor Ted Weiss
Box 287
Bard College
Annandale-on-Hudson, N.Y.
Dear Ted Weiss:

I am so happy to hear that you are going away on a Ford Fellowship. I hope your magazine won't suffer in your absence if you are going to be in some remote part of this country and in Europe and I offer to you and your wife my very best wishes. Wallace Fowlie was here yesterday and we spoke about you. You have not been forgotten by us around here.

Keith Botsford is an extremely gifted, very intelligent, very energetic young man. He is not the orthodox academic type, and we were glad of it here as I believe you would be at Bard. As an undergraduate he went through some trying periods finding himself out, preserving his very real talent against the routine of academic life, and sometimes clashing with some of the professors around here. He matured greatly while in the Army and because he proved very open to criticism and married a very delightful young lady who has done very much for him. He has great creative talent and, while several of us objected to features which we thought were immature in some of his early writing, there are many among us who think he may well go far as a novelist. He knows the foreign languages well and speaks French perfectly. He does not write it quite so well which is usual with persons who first learn the language orally. But we found that he taught well for us, efficiently, energetically, liking his students and proposing interesting refinements to some of the standardized courses. In a word, while he is not perhaps of the meek and somewhat dull and plodding type, he's got remarkable qualities which I think would make him a good man on your faculty and one who would bring a good deal to other departments than French itself.

Very sincerely yours,
Henri Peyre
Henri M. Peyre
Chairman, Department of French

## To Edgar Furniss:

May 25 — 1953

Dear Mr. Furniss,

I am grateful to you for the possibility, left open by your letter of May 21, that some additional funds may be found to assist in the publication of the volumes we expect to have ready in our Romance series in 1953–54.

It is difficult to give very precise estimates, as I use the subvention in every case to bargain with the Press & persuade it to cover the sum remaining after the subvention and the author's contribution have been promised. But I expect we shall have four volumes (indeed, we have them now ready) deserving publication this coming year.

One, by Geoffrey Hartman, is an extraordinarily good work by a very young man of something like critical genius. It treats four XIXth century poets (Wordsworth, G.M. Hopkins, Paul Valéry, Rilke) and proposes an original critical approach. It is in English & publication will easily cost $2500 or so, out of which I believe half may be recovered. The MS is being presented to the Yale Press Committee this afternoon (May 25). If they cannot take it, we shall try the Princeton Press. I should like to be able to say that I could contribute $500 at least to the cost, to help the decision of the Press.

The other three are in French and would be done in France: each would probably cost $1200 to $1300 there, & a contribution of $500 in each case would be justified, the author putting in the rest or the French Presses Universitaires if they agree. The MSS are: Michel Guggenheim, Yale Ph.D., 1953, *Renan et l'Esprit Français;* Kurt Weinberg, on our faculty, *Heine et les courants intellectuels français de son époque;* Konrad Bieber, *La littérature française de la Seconde Guerre Mondiale et l'Allemagne.*

If each of these volumes received $500.00 from Yale, the amount would thus be: $2.000, of which I have already at my disposal $50 and $900 earmarked by you for our series, i.e. $950. The supplementary sum desired would then be $1050.00.

Very sincerely yours,
Hri Peyre

## À Jacques Maritain:

Ce 29 mai 1953

Cher Monsieur,

J'ai été pris, en cette fin d'année, dans un vertige de thèses & d'examens & de comités de tous genres, et je suis bien en retard pour vous remercier de votre si bonne lettre. Votre permission très généreuse de nous laisser reproduire quelques pages de votre livre m'a beaucoup touché; je ne pense pas que nous nous en servions, parce que notre "politique" a été constamment de ne rien reproduire en anglais de ce qui est accessible *en anglais* et a paru dans ce pays. Mais votre lettre m'a envoyé aussitôt à mon libraire & j'ai fait venir et dévoré votre livre. Les pages en question (325–333) sont particulièrement belles, mais auraient perdu beaucoup de leur beauté à être isolées ou détachées, séparées des textes qui les étaient.

Mais votre livre est extrêmement beau et l'un des plus riches que je connaisse sur l'art & la poésie. Votre érudition, en matière de poésie anglaise même, n'a rien à envier aux plus savants spécialistes de choses anglaises. Mais ce n'est jamais une érudition complaisante ou vaine. Vous donnez soudain un sens neuf à des tableaux, à des poèmes, à des pensées esthétiques en les chargeant de votre pensée, en les rapprochant d'autres peintures ou d'autres textes. Votre discours est à la fois gouverné par l'unité d'une pensée originale et forte et sinueux, nuancé, accueillant à tout ce qui l'illumine de beauté spirituelle. Et les textes poétiques que vous citez sont presque toujours admirables. J'aime depuis longtemps la poésie de Madame Maritain, que je crois parmi les plus belles poésies d'expérience spirituelle et mystique de notre époque, & j'ai été heureux que vous ayez eu le courage de la rapprocher de Blake ou des plus grands poètes d'aujourd'hui. C'est la vraie place de ces vers.

Nous ne partons pas pour la France cette année et je n'aurai donc pas l'espoir de vous rencontrer. Mais veuillez croire, cher Monsieur, à mes vœux d'heureuses vacances et à mes remerciements pour votre lettre & pour la joie très vraie que j'ai éprouvée à vous lire en ce splendide & profond ouvrage—joie que je fais en ce moment partager à d'autres.

Henri Peyre

## To the Provost's Office:

June 8—1953

Dear Miss Feinemann:

I have to be away until June 10, giving some commencement addresses elsewhere. Last June 6, the Corporation must have passed upon the appointment of one of my new French instructors, Barthélémy. I now understand the University has to fill out a complicated set of forms, as enclosed, to bring over with a preferential visa a foreigner.

Would you kindly, with the Provost's authorization, fill out—Mrs. Harrison or Miss McLennan might do it, if you call either of them up: I believe Mrs. Harrison works at Mr. Andersson's office in my absence— the enclosed two copies. I have written out the answers in long hand, under the number concerned. Since I don't suppose there is any provision for such expenses, I shall pay the $10.00 fee required—If the Hartford office absolutely demands them, I shall have to write for a copy of Mr. Barthélémy's degrees. The University can, I suppose, get the thing notarized easily.

If this is not too much trouble & if you will send it back to me by June 10 or 11, I shall then forward it.

I fear I may have to do the same thing for our other appointee from France, Choquet. I shall warn him.

My apologies for inflicting a new burden upon you,

Very sincerely yours
HM Peyre

## To the Assistant to the Provost:

June 15, 1953

Dear Hartley [Simpson],

Excuse my bothering you with details, when your year should be over.

William Roberts (1911 Yale Station) gave the graduate reading course in French this year with the understanding that he would be paid what the students taking the course (at $25.00 each) would pay if the total was less than $250.00 a term—which it was.

He tells me that one of the persons taking the course was Capt. Adrian C. Mandell. He took the reading course this spring. U.S. Army must be billed for the $25.00 fee, but before that, his army contract with Yale has to be amended.

Roberts writes me: "M. George Williams, at the Bursar's Office, said he could pay me around July 1st, but that it would be easier if the French Department paid me. The $25.00 credit has already been turned over to the French Department account."

Now we don't receive such money at the Depart. The payment of the fees for such courses & the payment of the instructor were done, I believe, through your office & the Provost's. Will you kindly check on this $25.00 & have it paid directly to William Roberts, if that is the correct procedure?

Many thanks &

Sincerely,
HM Peyre

## À son père:

Ce 21—juillet—53

Mon cher Papa,

Jacques récemment nous a gentiment donné de vos nouvelles à tous, en répondant à quelques questions médicales que lui avait posées Marguerite: c'est preuve de la confiance qu'il inspire—sans doute aussi de la défiance, en grande partie irrationnelle, que l'on éprouve, même après 20 ans de séjour dans un pays, envers ses médecins et ses remèdes. Chez moi, cela se manifeste par la négative, car je ne vais à peu près jamais voir les docteurs. La grande rage étant en ce moment de conseiller à tout le monde de maigrir, je remplis les gens d'étonnement en déclarant que je ne me suis pas pesé depuis des années. Ils sont d'ailleurs aussi abasourdis quand je leur déclare que je ne bois jamais ni whisky ni jus d'orange; le jus d'orange est absorbé ici rituellement tous les matins par tous les Américains et le whisky tous les soirs avant le dîner. L'autre jour, une dame est tombée à la renverse, a cassé son verre et a failli briser son fauteuil parce que je lui avais répondu, comme elle m'offrait un verre, que je n'avais jamais encore goûté au whisky de ma vie. Les gens d'ailleurs sont tout aussi effarés de nous voir aller à pied. Cela est mal vu en Amérique et considéré comme antisocial à double titre, parce qu'on gêne les automobilistes sur les routes, et parce qu'on est coupable de résistance à la consommation. Or on produit trop ici et quiconque ne renouvelle pas son auto ou ses machines tous le deux ou trois ans est considéré comme un traître à l'évangile américain de la production et de la consommation. Dans certaines villes de l'ouest, le piéton est souvent arrêté et questionné par la police: on le soupçonne d'être un rôdeur dangereux. Dans le petit endroit où nous sommes, sur cette île, sur deux ou trois cents personnes, je suis le seul à ne pas assister au service du dimanche, service d'ailleurs qui n'a rien de religieux et se contente de dispenser des conseils éthiques très vagues. Aux premiers temps, on était choqué quand je disais que j'étais athée, et comme ce mot est maintenant en mauvaise odeur et synonyme de communiste, je dis maintenant que je suis polythéiste. Ça fait grande impression, et mes meilleurs amis sont un évêque anglican et un pasteur unitarien, pleins de respect pour mon polythéisme.

Il fait chaud & humide ici. Je vais néanmoins dès demain repartir pour New Haven. Je profiterai de cet été passé ici, par la force des choses, pour tâcher d'achever un livre en anglais sur le roman moderne. Cela ne m'inspire pas trop, mais je l'ai promis il y a longtemps & l'éditeur l'attend. Je dois ensuite faire une anthologie de la littérature contemporaine en France, après quoi, si l'énergie & le temps me sont laissés, je passerai à des travaux plus solides. J'aurai chaud dans notre appartement à New Haven, où l'aération, en été, est médiocre—mais je ne puis guère travailler sérieusement ailleurs que près d'une bibliothèque et de mes notes. Ici j'ai passé une quinzaine de jours en plein air et me sens tout à fait reposé.

Jacques nous a donné de bonnes nouvelles, de lui & de toi. Pierre réussit magnifiquement aux études et sera bientôt plus savant que son beau-père! Mais les nouvelles de Louise & d'Hélène continuent à être peu encourageantes et c'est un triste exemple de l'impuissance de la médecine! Je suppose que cet accroc survenu au fiancé d'Hélène a bouleversé leurs plans d'avenir & de mariage: qu'en advient-il? Il ne servirait de rien de donner de loin des conseils & je n'ai d'ailleurs nulle solution. Passer d'une vie de fermentation intellectuelle & d'espoir d'une profession libérale à une vie toute physique, à la campagne, dans quelque humble carrière serait peut-être à conseiller médicalement—mais je reconnais que je serais le premier à refuser cette éventualité s'il s'agissait de moi. Il faut avoir grandi entièrement à la campagne pour l'aimer au point d'y vivre—et la discussion intellectuelle et politique est un poison pire que le whisky.

Donne-nous parfois de vos nouvelles, pendant la dispersion qu'apportera cet été—et surtout sache, cher Papa, que mes pensées te suivent fidèlement malgré l'absence & que le souvenir des rares, mais pour moi très riches, journées passées avec toi depuis 1947 m'est très présent et a renforcé tant d'autres souvenirs des années d'autrefois que je conserve, enfouis en moi, avec reconnaissance & profonde affection.

Henri

## À Kurt Weinberg:

Ce 2 août 1953

Mon cher Ami,

Vous me comblez de gentillesses qui me touchent mais que je dois vous gronder de faire. Cette "gravure fantastique" est très belle—mais je ne la mérite en rien et ai des scrupules à l'accepter. Si un sentiment m'anime lorsque je pense à vos années ici, c'est le remords de vous avoir trop peu vu, trop rarement aidé. Sans doute, est-ce en partie que, esprit si riche déjà et si mûr, vous aviez moins besoin d'aide que certains autres de nos "étudiants"—vous conserviez sur vous-même bien des doutes, qui vous honorent, vous laissiez parfois aller aux doux supplices de l'héautontimorouménos, mais en vérité vous étiez un maître déjà, & nous n'avons fait ici que vous procurer l'atmosphère où vous pouviez retrouver quelque quiétude et relier en une gerbe d'éclat rare & riche tous les épis que vous aviez moissonnés au cours de bien des années douloureuses. Merci encore, et aussi d'avoir si généreusement donné votre temps & votre talent pour remplacer M. Morehouse ce dernier trimestre.

J'ai relu ceci; vous verrez mes remarques, de pure forme & de détail, sur des points aisés à corriger. Pour le reste, c'est un livre remarquable. Vous y montrez une culture énorme, une grande finesse littéraire, une pénétration dans le secret psychologique des êtres et dans les procédés d'art des poètes. Vous construisez autour & à propos de Heine une cathédrale riche en rosaces, et petits autels secrets et confessionnaux ornés pour quelque érotisme pimenté de religiosité. Car au fond, si vous n'étiez doué pour être professeur, vous aviez tout pour être un merveilleux sacristain. Votre don des rapprochements (ils sont presque toujours très sûrs, très éclairants) est presque excessif. Vous aviez tant acquis de savoir au cours de ces dernières années que vous le prodiguez ici. Mais cela fait un livre idéal pour ce genre de comparatisme. Peut-être, plus tard, quand vous vous mettrez à un autre livre, devriez-vous, pour vous prouver que vous avez plusieurs manières, écrire quelque chose de serré, de très limité, qui impressionne un autre genre de "scholars." Au fait, si vous aviez, du don de M. Koneff, de l'argent de reste pour publier votre petite monographie sur A. France, cela ne vous serait pas inutile dans votre carrière.

Très bon livre donc, encore amélioré par votre révision. Il n'a qu'à paraître tel quel. J'écris en ce sens une lettre aux Presses Universitaires, & si vous l'approuvez, mettez-la à la boîte.

Je n'aurai d'objection qu'à votre dédicace. Elle me flatte, mais à l'excès. Dans un livre imprimé, je la trouve un peu gênante pour ma modestie, & je n'ai pas fait pour vous plus que M. Jean Fabre ou M. Auerbach ou M. Guicharnaud. Je ne sais si vous ne devriez pas la supprimer ou tout au moins la simplifier. Vous verrez.

Mes amitiés encore & mes félicitations. Vous nous avez beaucoup apporté ici ces dernières années: talent, goût, musique, poésie, diabolisme dissimulant la bonté, érotisme recouvrant votre sentimentalité & votre recherche de Dieu dans l'éternel Féminin, camaraderie. Vous nous manquerez & nous songerons à vous parmi deux cents demi vierges séduisantes, médisantes et vampires.

H. P.

## To Edgar Furniss:

September 8, 1953

Dear Mr. Furniss:

Our department is going to give more extensive administrative functions to Associate Professor Georges May. We even hope that he may, within the reasonably near future, take over much of Professor Richardson's work as Director of Undergraduate Studies. He is already a very active collaborator for me, and it has become necessary for him to have a telephone in his office, Room 321, W.L. Harkness.

We should be very grateful if you would approve our request and ask the Service Bureau to provide his office with a telephone, if possible soon enough for the extension number to be given in the new directory now being prepared. The sum for the telephone rental put down in our budget amounts to $436.02, plus $48.98 for toll calls. The details are mysterious to me, but I doubt that the expenses for the telephone that we actually have amount to that much. In any case, I hope to make some saving in the educational budget as approved last spring, and to come and talk to you about it in the near future.

Very sincerely yours,<br>
Henri Peyre

## À Kurt Weinberg:

Ce 13 — IX — 53

Mon cher ami,

Merci de votre carte, & de votre si bonne lettre, qui m'a fort intéressé. Vous êtes gentil de tenir à nous & de nous regretter. Vous avez vous-même beaucoup apporté à ce que nous avions & étions, & vous laissez ici un grand trou. Rien n'est plus triste dans ce métier que de former de jeunes collègues, de les avoir quelques années auprès de soi, & de devoir ensuite s'en séparer, les savoir loin, peut-être seuls & d'être soi-même ravi par le flux de l'éternelle hâte.

Mais sursum corda! L'année s'ouvre à peine. C'est le moment des grands projets. Ne regardons vers le passé que fugitivement. Vous avez raison de penser (en sus de l'A. France, peut-être précisé, mûri, dégagé de quelque gaine scolaire) à un grand ouvrage: *Exil*. Ce serait, je crois, le grand livre de votre carrière, celui pour lequel vous seriez mûr, dans lequel vous mettriez beaucoup de vous, mais en évitant peut-être le léger arbitraire que comportent les rapprochements avec le moderne, Gide(?), etc. Votre premier livre prêtant le flanc aux réserves de quelques chicaniers & esprits à œillères, l'autre devrait prouver avec éclat que vous ne manquez pas de sens historique & savez aussi caractériser l'originalité propre de chaque moment: votre premier livre étant tout vibrant d'enthousiasme pour Heine & ce que vous lisez en lui & lui prêtez, le suivant devrait vous trouver un peu plus sur vos gardes pour être objectif, un peu plus humoriste peut-être aussi—souriant parfois du foisonnement ingénieux de vos rapprochements.

Merci pour votre idée sur les livres rares, et sur les zetas. Je vais voir ce qu'on peut en faire—vous avez raison. Merci aussi de ce que vous me dites sur Tafoya: je ne savais pas très exactement tout cela, qui me touche, & et je vais essayer de le voir davantage. Mais pour les retards dans les cours, il est impossible, je le crains, de violer cette règle. Elle est absolue, pour compenser la liberté assez grande qui est laissée par ailleurs aux étudiants gradués. Ses oraux peuvent attendre: ce n'est pas si pressé.

Je pense que j'aurai bientôt votre devis & que, d'ici un an, vous sortirez, triomphalement. Attendons. Bonne chance en attendant & peut-être à bientôt.

Henri Peyre

## To Harry Levin:

Oct. 8—1953

My dear Harry (may I call you simply by your first name, & beg you to do likewise?)

Many thanks for your kind answer. I shall hope for a visit from you as it would be interesting & informing to hear some of your impressions. I shall not plan to go to Chicago, for if I go to these conventions I get saddled with too many papers & meetings, & it is high time I should make way for younger men! Perhaps you won't either. But New Haven, however unattractive, does lie astride the New York road, do not forget!

I agree with you that much, in the literary, even in the political atmosphere, of France is comforting as well as stimulating. But the teaching staff at the Sorbonne is mediocre; there is no formulation of new methods, no deep or vigorous thinking about them, no broad vision of literary problems. Comparative literature is in an especially pitiful state.

Yes, Jasinski will prove a serious & helpful teacher. I have a very true affection for Dieckmann, & he should be persuaded to worry less, & thus to make others less uncomfortable, to round off some thorny angles. Suspicion breeds diffidence. Perhaps you can advise & help him.

I was very incensed when I learned that, through some negligence, you had not been "décoré" as you should have been two or three years ago, & I took the liberty to demand the corrective gesture from the Embassy & fill the papers customarily required on your achievement. I hope that this little arrow is now pointing to your heart, or will be when you next go through the French customs, which is the only time when I display mine!

Your kindness in leaving a door ajar, or an ivory gate, is very great. I am at once writing to Douglas, who is taking our own review, to inform him of this possibility. I hope very much you will give us a few pages; & the romantic background of realism would fall within our scope; & I am also mentioning to him the lead on the word Howard Hugo. I want to read his book very much.

Most sincerely yours,
Henri Peyre

## À Eléonore Zimmermann

Ce 11—X—53

Chère Mademoiselle,

M. Wellek n'a pas l'air très heureux de votre sujet, & je le comprends (le Bildungsroman, roman d'adolescence etc. en deux pays). C'est énorme, vague, confus; en vérité, cela ne peut montrer que des oppositions connues d'avance entre deux mentalités—et pour un esprit précis & net comme le vôtre, ce ne peut être que l'imprécis même et le fragmentaire, car rien qu'en France il y a des dizaines de romans d'adolescence & de formation autres que Stendhal et Balzac. Surtout vous risquez de vous y perdre & de vous y décourager, seule, l'an prochain, en France.

Un sujet précis, délimité, serait plus heureux, et éventuellement pourrait faire un livre publiable (votre sujet proposé [pour une demande de bourse] n'attirerait guère le comité des University Women! Il n'y a rien de tel que les femmes-scholars pour se méfier du fumeux). Si j'avais votre âge & votre énergie, je préférerais un beau sujet classique, où l'on atteint un individu vivant & mouvant: Quinet & l'Allemagne; Benj. Constant & l'Allemagne; Taine etc., à la rigueur même Sainte Beuve & la littérature allemande. Si vous vouliez de l'histoire des idées, de l'histoire de l'histoire, les sujets composés y abondent.

Dans le domaine de la poésie, qui est celui pour lequel vous avez le plus d'affinités, c'est plus difficile d'être comparatiste & au fond assez vain. L'hégélianisme, par ex., de Villiers, Mallarmé, des symbolistes français, à la rigueur, sujet traitable. . . .

Il serait curieux d'étudier la critique de la poésie française par les Français, par ex. entre 1850 et 1950, souvent à l'aide d'exemples étrangers (Heine, Shelley, Novalis, etc.)-combien de poètes en ont voulu à la poésie & à la poétique de leur pays (& déjà Vigny, Sainte Beuve). J'y avais un peu touché dans mon livre sur Shelley — mais c'est à peine comparatiste.

En vérité, il est plus facile de faire de la littérature comparée sans être obligé d'en faire, sans être limité . . . à ce cadre par un programme d'études & un département. Mais tout ceci reste un peu négatif.

Bien à vous,
H. P.

## To Edgar Furniss:

November 20, 1953

Dear Mr. Furniss:

You may remember that, at my request, Professor Raymond T. Hill was on his retirement appointed Curator of the Collections in Romance Languages in the University Library. Mr. Hill has, ever since last June, been gravely ill. Arteriosclerosis has created such trouble in his brain that he is not thinking clearly any more; in fact, he will never again, in all likelihood, leave the nursing home in Bridgeport where he is now. Our collections in the Romance Seminar, 302 Hall of Graduate Studies, are in a sad state; valuable but dilapidated books are in urgent need of binding. A credit of $250 was set aside in our miscellaneous budget to that effect.

My proposal is now that, as discreetly as possible, the title of Curator of our collections be transferred from Professor Hill, no longer available, to Professor Henry B. Richardson, who is actually attending to the task of binding, supervising and reorganizing the books in our Romance Seminar library.

Would you just inform me when it is done? A copy of this is being sent to Mr. Babb.

Sincerely yours,
HM Peyre

## À Rosette Lamont:

Ce 23 — XI — 53

Chère Madame,

Votre visite nous a fait grand plaisir et vous nous avez gâtés de ces beaux, & délicats présents, mais je veux vous en gronder. Une "disciple" comme vous a déjà assez abondamment récompensé son professeur par ses immenses progrès, son acharnement à la recherche & à la découverte, et la manière dont vous poursuivez et approfondissez les très humbles suggestions que vous avez pu recevoir. Vous ne devez plus ainsi nous combler — Cette rare bouteille est d'ailleurs toute mallarméenne, d'exquise condensation, évocatrice de nonchaloir.

Mais la nouvelle de votre séparation d'avec votre mari nous a chagrinés — non que nous devions le regretter ou vous conseiller autrement — vous seule savez, & je pense dans le fond que vous avez raison, tous les deux, d'être d'accord dans le désaccord. Mais cela a dû être une pénible déception pour vous & une souffrance, que dissimule votre stoïque courage.

Je vous envoie ce chapitre — ou plutôt ces trois. Ils terminent en effet heureusement une lourde & belle tâche. Le *Villiers* me semble bon, solide, précis — un peu tiré par les cheveux, bien sûr, comme souvent c'est le cas lorsqu'on veut montrer des affinités, parfois presque à côté du sujet, mais y rentrant vite. La conclusion est aussi très acceptable. Elle sent un peu la lassitude, & n'apporte pas de vue très neuve, puisque tout a été dit. Mais elle clôt heureusement l'ouvrage.

L'introduction offrira peut-être plus de prise à la critique. Elle est longue, et erre & vagabonde, on part de haut. On croit parfois qu'on va lire un ouvrage sur Mme de Staël & d'autres voyageurs en Allemagne.

On arrive enfin au sujet un peu par surprise et si l'on devait avoir autant de pages sur Mme de Staël, etc., pour situer la fascination d'Hamlet avant 1850–60, pourquoi réduire si fort Delacroix, Hugo lui-même etc.? Je crois que la dame de Coppet vous a un peu trop fascinée et ce que vous dites d'elle est forcément de seconde main et bien connu. N'auriez-vous pu aller plus vite, à travers l'Hamlet du 18e siècle, vers une caractérisation de celui des romantiques; indiquer que, sauf Musset (peut-être Montégut ou des *minores*) les romantiques ne se sont pas sentis frères d'Hamlet au même degré que la génération de Baudelaire, Villiers, etc. — la différence entre ces années 1820–50 et 1850–1890.

Relisez à loisir votre introduction. Si vous la trouvez satisfaisante ainsi, gardez-la. Mais je crois que les plus précis & exigeants de vos juges y trouveront à redire, comme n'introduisant pas le sujet assez directement.

> pp. 5–6 sont un peu banales
> p. 8. "Le germanique Constant," dites-vous. Mais p 5 vous disiez que Constant ne savait pas d'allemand. Il l'a su d'ailleurs.
> p. 9. Pourquoi cet emploi du présent, un peu bizarre en anglais. Vérifiez si vous ne préférez pas tout mettre au passé.
> p. 10. Le Globe, "Goethe's paper!" expliquez en quel sens!
> Dans le chapitre sur Villiers, vous conjecturez beaucoup. He must have . . . "had to . . ." Quelque part dans vos premières pages, expliquez que vous avez, dans ce genre de travail, dû conjecturer beaucoup & qu'il était rarement question de *prouver*.
> Villiers p. 22. Quel est donc cet article sur Villiers et Eliphas Levi? De qui? citez-le ou donnez la référence en note.

Ma femme vous remercie encore de ce beau châle et je vous félicite encore d'avoir achevé cette thèse en dépit de tant d'obstacles.

Redites-moi d'un mot à qui exactement (nom, initiales, adresse) vous voulez que j'écrive pour dire que votre thèse est achevée & sera passée. Je le ferai sans retard.

Bien cordialement,<br>
Henri Peyre

## À Philip Kolb:

Ce 26 nov. 53

Cher Monsieur,

C'est à votre amabilité, je pense, que je dois l'envoi par Plon de la Correspondance de Proust & de sa mère & je vous en remercie vivement. Je vous en félicite non moins vivement. L'édition est admirablement faite—précise, méticuleuse, avec des notes sobres mais riches, jamais indiscrètes. Je me doute quel énorme labeur cela représente de lecture de la presse, d'archives etc.—le contraste est frappant avec le Jean Santeuil si pauvrement & insuffisamment préfacé par Maurois, si mal édité (autant qu'on en puisse juger). Je suppose que Bernard de Fallois a voulu conserver l'essentiel pour son ouvrage futur; mais c'était un peu se moquer du monde. Vos lettres apportent sur le livre quelque lumière, comme vous l'indiquez; et je suis assez de l'avis d'Antoine Adam que la "composition," si l'on peut dire, de J. Santeuil, a dû s'étendre sur pas mal d'années, & empiéter peut-être même sur le nouveau siècle. Je souhaite que vous ayez une part aux publications futures qui pourront se faire de manuscrits proustiens. Toute la correspondance est à reprendre par la base & à compléter & ce serait une belle tâche que de s'y dévouer!

Mes compliments sur votre patience & votre précision, & votre magnifique français (on vous a fait mettre, par erreur, reproches, au féminin, page 102, mais il n'y a presque nulle tache)—et je vous prie de croire à mes sentiments les plus dévoués.

Henri Peyre

## À Jorge Guillén:

21—XII—53

Bien cher Ami,

Vous êtes toujours gentil et vous, si nerveux et chargé de suggestion discrète dans votre poésie et adonné à l' "understatement" à l'espagnole (le plus efficace de tous), vous montrez si chaleureux et débordant dans l'amitié.

Non, je n'irai pas à Chicago: c'est trop loin, trop froid. Je sais que votre gendre y aura grand succès. Les yeux de beaucoup de "départements" sont fixés sur lui. Étrange gendre qui, si heureusement marié, père des plus beaux enfants du monde, respectueux envers son beau-père de génie, consacre ses veilles, sinon ses nuits, à ces histoires d'entremetteuse de la Célestine. Il est vrai que les entremetteuses ordinaires, celles de France au moins, ont peut-être du poids, mais n'ont pas la "STRUCTURE"!

Bien sûr, je serai heureux de jouer mon rôle (d'admirateur ardent de Guillén & d'ami) dans le comité Guggenheim. Je ne savais pas encore que vous aviez fait cette demande: les dossiers ne nous sont pas encore parvenus. Mais il me semble que votre autorité n'a besoin de nulle aide.

Croyez moi votre très profondément dévoué,
Henri Peyre

## À Kurt Weinberg:

Ce 21–XII–53

Mon cher Ami,

Je vais être beaucoup absent ces vacances, bien que je n'aille pas à Chicago—mais je voulais prendre une minute pour vous dire mes regrets de cette décision défavorable à Hunter. Je m'y attendais, après ces incidents des débuts. On juge si vite dans ce pays, & on n'y pardonne pas les critiques de ceux (surtout étrangers) qui semblent regretter un trop bas niveau intellectuel. Cela blesse. C'est une leçon, mais coûteuse pour vous & qui risque de froisser votre vive sensibilité.

Sans doute parlez-vous trop—peut-être un peu vite. Vous passez, même ici, pour un peu difficile, & pour avoir une langue pointue. Ce n'est pas ce que j'ai trouvé moi-même, qui ai toujours vu en vous un parfait gentleman, un homme du goût le plus raffiné & le plus sensible, & aussi quelqu'un qui a beaucoup souffert, qui a réalisé deux ou trois changements de vie et de pays avec un courage héroïque & que ces épreuves n'ont pas rendu amer.

Mais ceux qui vous connaissent moins bien & vous jugent vite ont pu se méprendre. C'est tant pis pour eux. Quant à vous, vous irez ailleurs & ferez un nouveau départ. Où? Je ne vois trop encore. Dès que vous aurez des précisions plus fermes encore sur votre avenir immédiat à Hunter, vous essaierez ailleurs. Cela peut vouloir dire aller assez loin:

Middle West? Far West? Je ne sais. L'origine allemande est un handicap, comme je m'en aperçois, puisque j'ai plusieurs jeunes gens d'origine allemande à placer. Mais il serait trop fort de vous faire souffrir à cause du pays qui vous a martyrisés! Je ferai de mon mieux; voyez de votre côté les possibilités. Je voulais en attendant vous dire toute ma sympathie & mes vœux.

Henri Peyre

## To Norman S. Buck:

January 27, 1954

Dear Dean Buck:

From February 1, 1954, Mr. Georges May, Associate Professor in French, will take over from Mr. Richardson the duties of Director of Undergraduate Studies in French and Head of Instruction in the Freshman Year. I trust this has the agreement of the Deans directly concerned.

Mr. Richardson has filled those duties with great devotion and competence for a number of years. He now has only three more years to go before retirement and it seemed to us that it would be good to have a new member of our department take over those administrative jobs. Mr. Georges May has displayed unusual gifts of efficiency and organization. He will still receive the advice of Professor Richardson whenever needed. We expect things should work out smoothly under his direction of the undergraduate work. His address is Room 321, William L. Harkness Hall, and his telephone extension 792.

Mr. Howard Garey will serve as Assistant Head of Instruction in the Freshman Year, as he has in the past. He is familiar with most of the details concerning freshmen in our department, and elementary courses. Since Mr. Garey will be on leave of absence in 1954–55 on a Morse Fellowship, I shall then ask Mr. James Stephens to take over Mr. Garey's duties during the nest academic year.

I shall always be pleased to hear from any of the Deans any remarks, especially critical, concerning the way in which our department is run and any suggestions for improvement.

Very sincerely yours,
Henri Peyre

## À son frère:

309 St Ronan St.<br>
Ce 4 février (1954)

Mon cher Jacques,

Je reçois ce matin, jeudi, ton câble. Le coup est dur, même si en quelque manière nous nous attendions un peu, depuis quelques mois ou années, à une nouvelle brutale. Depuis cet accident, la vigueur de Papa avait baissé, son moral était plus bas. Ton câble fait prévoir le pire, et probablement à brève échéance. Malheureusement, je suis forcé de te laisser, avec Micheline, peut-être avec Louise, supporter seul ce chagrin, ces soucis & de te confier, s'il en est temps encore, de dire à Papa mes pensées d'un fils qui l'aime du fond du cœur et a toujours souhaité d'être le plus possible digne de lui. Je ne puis tenter un voyage en France en ce moment, faute de papiers (nécessaires pour rentrer dans ce pays & que je ne me suis pas procurés, n'attendant pas ce malheur de quelque temps et reportant tous nos espoirs sur l'été). Je suis en outre affligé d'une bronchite & laryngite sans gravité mais qui m'ont abattu & empêché de sortir depuis 3 jours. Cette absence en de si pénibles moments me fend le cœur; j'aurais bien voulu revoir Papa, lui reparler. Elle est la rançon de cette vie d'exilé que j'ai choisie et qui m'inspire parfois bien des regrets & des plaintes. Tu me comprendras et tu diras à Louise mes sentiments de chagrin & d'affection, et à Hélène. Quand tu seras un peu remis de ces terribles coups, écris-moi un peu longuement quelques détails de cette maladie, du moral de Papa et de tes sentiments.

Caresses, & de Marguerite et d'Henri

## To Mrs. Malcolm McIntosh:

February 26, 1954

Mrs. M. E. McIntosh
P.O. Box 2427
University, Alabama

Dear Mrs. McIntosh:

Of course you are quite right to write me and very kind to do so. I often teased your husband about being such a perfect gentleman that he appeared too shy and too modest to most of us living in this vulgar world, which is too brutal for him.

I have not forgotten him and I have written here and there, mentioning his name. Just lately Renaud at Northwestern mentioned him for an instructorship there, for which Rossi had already mentioned the names of Weinberg and some other former colleagues of your husband here. What will come out of it I do not know, and no doubt we won't know about probable positions for next year until much later this year. Thus far nothing has turned up for any of our men looking for positions, or even for former instructors now placed already. I am not pessimistic and I believe there will be positions later in the spring, when departments know about their registration figures. All the same, since your husband has a family to think of and other duties, it might be best for him to accept the renewal which is now offered to him, placing security first and the advantage which accrues to one from working at one place for at least two years in succession. The second year often is less exacting in the way of preparation of courses and adaptation to the surroundings. I am not saying that your husband would like it very much better, as I doubt he would settle in the South permanently, but it is not bad professionally to have had a little continuity somewhere before moving on to some more desirable post. The chances are that there would be many positions open three or four years from now, when the population of college age will be much larger. The problem, therefore, is to be able to wait during the interim period and it would be too bad if your husband had to accept an instructorship after having had a more advanced title where he is now.

The business language is, as always, a little inhuman, for I well realize that you and he are probably not happy down in Alabama. All your friends here were well aware that your and his fine personality and sensitive and perceptive natures would have been much happier in more congenial surroundings. But we all know how courageous you are, and it might be best for a while to be patient until you find yourselves in a climate somewhat more in accordance with your affinities and aspirations.

Do give my best to your husband and accept the regards of my wife.

Very sincerely yours,<br>
Henri Peyre

# To Whitney Griswold:

April 9, 1954

President A. Whitney Griswold
President of the University
Woodbridge Hall
Yale University

Dear Whit:

I was very much interested by our conversation the other morning, and I regretted that it was necessarily hasty. I hope some time when neither of us is quite so busy we may have a chance to say a few more words about these problems.

As you rightly said, I am in full agreement with the aims that you pursue and I believe I have tried to pursue them on my own side, with my modest means and whatever energy I am endowed with. I am taking the liberty to enclose here (asking you to return them at your convenience) two documents, one a copy of a letter of mine on the Humanities and how to revivify them, the other the Princeton report, which, I think, makes some good points very cogently on the Humanities. I am adding an article explaining and, perhaps, justifying recent French policy to keep your French or your wife's in shape.

The real problem, however, is clearly to pass from the agreement on the aims to some kind of effective cooperation on the means with which to implement the ends. It is too bad that some of us were asked to comment publicly and in writing on a project which was only tentative and should not have been divulged as it was. Being human and being probably conceited and unable to resist cracking a few jokes or shining at the expense of some flaws, we, or I, failed to do due justice to the long-range virtues of the report and especially to the imaginative or constructive spirit which lay at the source of it. My own independent conviction is that some tactical mistakes were committed and that you might have rallied more of the faculty behind the plan or behind some of its views, if you had been less sincere and less ardent about it, but then you would not have been the president whom many of us admire and like. Still, I believe that a strong effort should be made to salvage the inspiration behind the plan while it is timely to do so and while the country expects from you a leadership in the development of the Humanities in this country. The Deans could probably be made to stand behind the general proposals that you would present along these lines with determination. The faculty would be grateful and much impressed if you yourself would explain the reasons for the report to them and steer the plan through their councils with fairness, but with the warmth that they appreciate in you. I am embarrassed to suggest the names of members of the faculty who might turn out to be more helpful if sincerely convinced of the advisability of taking strong measures to reach the ends defined by you. But I strongly feel there would be among such faculty members three or four of the older members of the faculty who were not supposed to share your views from the start or be influenced by you. It might also be well to have some members with more roots here and closer association with their colleagues than Professors Kirkwood and Fesler had (maybe Gabriel, Rudin, someone from English, etc.). It would also obviously be well if the rarer aves among scientists and the eloquent speaker among those practitioners of experiments and star-gazers, maybe Pollard among the physicists, some mathematician, Sinnott, of course, and some psychologist or anthropologist not inclined to redefine every word used and to question every assertion, and the logic implicit in, or absent from, proposals which have to be humane as well as logical.

Excuse these hasty notes done in the midst of a very busy week and without much previous thought. They stem from my sincere desire to see the procrastination of the faculty committees come to an end and the appearance of a rift between some members of the faculty and the President whom they sincerely admire be dispelled.

Very cordially yours,
Hri Peyre

## To Keith Botsford:

May 3—54

My dear Botsford,

I am glad you have had such a pleasant & fruitful year. I never doubted that you would become a good teacher whenever you set your heart on it, and I never had much doubt of your promises as an author, while I formulated reservations on the little I had seen of your work (scholastic & critical) in the past. In fact, I don't believe there is any one else about whom I used the word "possibly a genius" more often & convincedly. Mr. Crane Brinton of Harvard told me the other day they had chosen a mathematician instead of you as Junior Fellow. Too bad—but perhaps teaching is just as well for you at the present stage.

You are late in trying to get a job & it may not be easy to succeed. Both Berkeley & Riverside College (Cal.) have lately taken some of our men, but they wanted full Ph.D.'s. So may UCLA & the University of Southern Cal. The only thing is to write the chairmen of these two places & give your references, mine included. But they may very well have all their staff by now. Every one is already preparing for summer vacations. I am leaving for Europe on June *1st*. If I were you, I would think *twice* before refusing another year at Bard. There are still more candidates than jobs. If you did leave, a very good successor might be Kurt Weinberg, 429 E. 80th, N.Y. 21, now at Hunter College—a top man & very literary & artistic.

Did you know Francis Ritchie at Yale? He was teaching at UCLA & you might mention that I told you he was leaving for a year or two in Europe & you'd like his succession. Mention clearly that you are not a candidate for a degree & plan to write. You might also write to Pier Pasinetti, Depart. of Comparative Lit., UCLA: he is very good, a Yale Ph.D., & might, perhaps, have a course or two for you there. Make your application somewhat personal & interesting, & not just dry & factual.

We are both well, but overburdened with work, but carrying on. Do give our best to your wife & believe me as ever,

Most cordially,
Henri Peyre

## To Edgar Furniss:

May 5th, 1954

Dear Mr. Furniss:

I am afraid that I have to ask you for an increase in the sums allotted to us in the Budget. You and the Committee of Deans were kind enough not to effect any cuts in our proposals last January and we were confident that, if everything remained as it was in the last two years, we should get along with the eleven instructors, permitted by our Budget as approved, and a sum of $8,000 for assistants-in-instruction, paid at the yearly rate of $250 an hour. But the election figures which have just reached us and which we have carefully analyzed give us a total of 437 upperclassmen in our courses for next year, as compared to 324 in 1953–54, and to 333 in 1952–53. To this we should add a number of freshmen, which was this year, 1953–54, 422, and will at least remain the same next year, as far as we can foresee. The chances are it might increase, if anything. Our total number of undergraduates will thus amount to at least 850, which is considerably more than we have had over the last few years.

It all boils down to this: we need:

| | |
|---|---|
| one new section of French 15 | (5 hours/week) |
| one new section of French 12 | (5 hours/week) |
| one new section of French 22 | (5 hours/week) |
| one new section of French 30 | (3 hours/week) |
| one new section of French 32 | (3 hours/week) |
| | Total 21 hours/week |

We still have in the Budget as approved one instructor, not yet appointed because we have not found a man, who could cover approximately 13 hours. We have tentatively assigned the $8,000 for 32 hours to be given by assistants-in-instruction, but our need, as yet not provided in the Budget, will be for 8 more hours (thirteen + eight = twenty-one), for which we ask your permission to appoint assistants-in-instruction when the time comes, the sum needed being $2,000. Even this is clearly a minimum need.

I am always sorry to have to request more money than was granted, but the necessity in this case seems obvious.

Sincerely yours,
Hri Peyre

## To Katharine McBride:

May 8, 1954

Dear President McBride:

I am sorry that a ridiculous coincidence prevented me from meeting you both when you visited New Haven & when you kindly asked us to come down to Bryn Mawr to celebrate (sadly) the retirement of Professor Chew. I had to be out of town each time, keeping previous engagements.

Before I leave for Europe this summer, I thought I should let you know of the progress on the publication of my book. The Oxford Press, like most Presses, especially those with a British tradition, seems to feel that the future is theirs, & indeed Eternity. It proceeded leisurely. It also feared that the length of the MS would make the book very expensive, with the unceasing increase in manufacturing costs. After a good deal of resistance on my part, I decided to shorten the book by about one fourth or more—which meant, of course, rewriting several parts and not unbalancing the work by cutting off some chapters. The MS, revised, shortened, has now been with the press for one or two weeks & I believe they plan to start work on it.

I had taken it for granted that the book was going to be one of the Mary Flexner Lectures series &, as you remember, it is dedicated to Bryn Mawr College & has a foreword mentioning the Flexner Lectures, explaining the delay & the fact that the book is not like the original lectures but a new work. Mr. Grove of the Oxford Press raised a question which he wishes, I believe, to take up with you. He asked me what arrangements or contracts had been made with Bryn Mawr. He then suggested, of his own accord (I had never mentioned the point), that the Oxford Press would propose a royalty of 7 ½% of the list (retail) price of the first 3.000 copies & proposed an advance against royalties to help meet expenses of typing the revised MS, etc. I refused the advance & added that his proposal for the contract was agreeable (I have never considered a book as a money-making proposition for the author).

But my question is, & Mr. Grove will put it to you, I believe: am I supposed to negotiate these matters, or is Bryn Mawr College supposed to? Are the rights Bryn Mawr's, or the author's? Should this be considered as a regular Flexner Lectures volume or, since it no longer resembles lectures & is a totally different book, as a book, paying tribute to Bryn Mawr College & the Flexner lectureship? Mr. Grove asked me what arrangements had originally been made with Bryn Mawr. I know of none, except that the original letters inviting me to deliver the lectures (from Miss Park, March 5, 1942) stated: "The . . . lectures are published in the series of Flexner lectures of the Oxford University Press. The honorarium is $2500, half paid at the close of the series and half when the lectures are published."

Would you kindly let me know of your own views or wishes in these matters? I am not obviously trying to make any profit on this book & feel remorse enough for having long delayed it. And I wish to give Bryn Mawr College all the credit I can for having brought it about, if there is any good in it. And if it is customary or desirable for the College to make the proper arrangements, contracts, etc., with the Oxford Press, I am very glad to let it be that way.

I hope this is not adding to your burdens at a busy time of the year & I am,

Most sincerely yours,
Henri Peyre

## À Artine Artinian:

Le 24 mai 1954

Professor Artine Artinian
Junior Year in France
173 Boulevard St Germain
Paris, 6e
Cher Monsieur,

On ne devrait écrire que de ce qu'on aime, et j'avoue ne guère aimer Maupassant. Peut-être est-ce pour l'avoir lu jeune, à un âge où ce qu'il a de grossier et de direct impressionne un adolescent et sert assez heureusement de contrepoids à l'intoxication de la poésie et de sentiment qui est le danger de ces années un peu molles. Lui en voulais-je secrètement d'avoir alors goûté ses romans que j'ai toujours craint de relire depuis lors? Il me semble qu'ils sont minces, sans secrets replis, trop peu artistes et d'un homme, derrière l'auteur, trop satisfait de lui-même, brutal envers les femmes et l'amour, un peu fat.

Il m'est arrivé, professeur, d'analyser quelques-unes de ses nouvelles: elles restent sans doute admirables, mais me touchent peu—infiniment moins que *Un Cœur simple* et que huit ou dix nouvelles de Balzac, notre plus grand nouvelliste. Je sais bien que, de Galsworthy à Somerset Maugham, de bons juges étrangers placent Maupassant très haut. Mais l'étranger cherche dans une littérature autre que la sienne les leçons dont il a secrètement besoin; il est frappé par une vision froide et nette, une concision et même une dureté de métal chez Maupassant, qualités que la nouvelle anglaise peut en effet envier. Et d'ailleurs l'enthousiasme de l'étranger ne va pas toujours aux grandes œuvres: nous sourirons un jour d'avoir surfait Charles Morgan et Graham Greene, et naguère Aldous Huxley.

Le Symbolisme a vieilli pour nous Maupassant, à qui manquait le sens de la poésie. Lorsqu'avec Gide, Proust, Giraudoux, Larbaud, l'influence du Symbolisme a contribué à poétiser notre roman, Maupassant s'est mis à dater. Proust nous a ensuite, et Freud avec lui, fait découvrir de nouvelles dimensions dans la psychologie; Maupassant, en regard, a vite paru mince. Enfin est venu l'âge de la métaphysique, du roman existentialiste, de l'absurde et de l'angoisse, de la liberté et du projet. Maupassant avait connu, certes, et vécu l'angoisse; il avait écrit à Marie Bashkirtseff que "nul homme sous le soleil ne s'embêtait plus que lui," et laissé dans *Sur l'eau* le plus pessimiste des journaux intimes. Mais il lui manquait, au goût de quelques uns d'entre nous, une certaine puissance d'intellect, un sursaut tragique de révolte contre le monde, qu'il nous plaît de trouver chez Kafka, Malraux ou Joyce.

Pour ou contre Maupassant? Ni l'un ni l'autre. Il est loin de nous, tout simplement.

Peut-être aussi, professeurs, lui en voulons-nous d'être pris de court devant une œuvre qui ne permet point les développements philosophiques, psychologiques ou esthétiques. Jules Lemaître avait raison de remarquer que Maupassant "offre très peu de prise au bavardage de la critique."

Croyez, cher Monsieur, à mon souvenir le plus fidèle et à mes bons vœux pour votre seconde année de vie parisienne.

Henri Peyre

## À Franco Simone:

Ce 1er juin [1954]

Mon cher Collègue,

Je suis tellement en retard avec vous que j'en ai honte! Mon année a été chargée à un point extrême & ce n'est enfin qu'en triant les masses d'enveloppes accumulées sur mes tables que j'ai trouvé la notation où je m'étais promis de vous remercier. Pardonnez-moi! J'avais cependant lu vos articles, celui sur Croce & ces deux très forts, très sûrs, très justes essais sur l'histoire de la littérature française & son renouvellement. Vous êtes vous-même un rénovateur audacieux & précis, et on vous connaît en Amérique de plus en plus. On a l'œil sur tout ce que vous écrivez. M. Auerbach vous estime fort; M. Wellek aussi. D'autres ailleurs.

Je pars demain pour la France & peut-être vous verrai-je, par quelque hasard à Paris: je n'irai guère en Italie cet été—peut-être seulement pour aller à Venise m'embarquer pour la Grèce. Je n'aurai d'ailleurs d'autre adresse en Europe que c/o American Express, rue Scribe, Paris, 9. Un jour d'ailleurs, vous viendrez en Amérique où on vous attirera.

Merci de l'attention que vous avez de m'envoyer aussi aimablement vos écrits.

Croyez à mes sentiments les meilleurs,
Hri Peyre

## À Jacques Maritain:

Le 8 juin 1954
(À bord le) Flandre

Cher Monsieur,

J'ai appris avec beaucoup de chagrin, à bord de ce bateau où j'avais un peu espéré vous trouver, par John Neff et Mirkine, que vous aviez été sérieusement malade ces derniers mois et condamné pour quelque temps au repos. Puis-je vous dire mon sincère chagrin de cette nouvelle et vous offrir mes vœux de rétablissement total? Il était à craindre que vous ne subissiez quelque jour le contre coup de tant d'héroïques efforts, pendant la guerre, pour lutter contre la douleur du désastre et maintenir haut le courage & la foi d'amis innombrables, souvent inconnus. Et l'adaptation à un autre pays, à une autre langue n'est pas elle-même sans exiger une dure rançon. Mais nous sommes beaucoup à souhaiter que votre femme et vous connaissiez de longues années de repos; et donniez d'autres livres comme ce beau recueil de poésie bilingue et ce grand livre sur l'art. Vous avez su, je pense, qu'une exposition d'art moderne rapproché de la poésie d'aujourd'hui et envisagé dans ses qualités poétiques, à la nouvelle galerie d'art à Yale, a été placée sous vos auspices, ou du moins inspirée par votre ouvrage?

Veuillez croire, mon cher Maître, à nos sentiments les plus dévoués et à nos vœux de meilleure santé, et présenter à Madame Maritain & à sa sœur notre très fidèle souvenir.

Henri Peyre

## À Georges May:

[Paris]
Du 1er juillet 1954

Mon cher May,

. . . je vais bientôt quitter Paris et je perdrai alors le contact direct avec Yale.

C'est là d'ailleurs le charme des vacances. À la fin de l'année, toujours trop pressé, arrivant à grande peine à répondre à tout, je deviens comme obsédé de ce qu'il reste de MSS, articles, etc., ici, malgré tout, c'est la flânerie. Paris s'y prête si bien: je reprends goût aux longues heures des repas, aux terrasses des cafés, à regarder jouer les enfants aux Tuileries, même à suivre les lignes, le plus souvent immobiles, des pêcheurs et les péniches sur la Seine. Et, signe de vieillissement, je me plais à mes souvenirs du passé, à écouter, tel Sylvestre Bonnard, la sotte mais charmante jeunesse discutant au Luxembourg.

Tout est bien allé pour nous. Excellent voyage, quoique agité par la mer. Temps frais ici, mais ensoleillé. Paris est cher, les repas surtout, mais on arrive à y vivre mieux qu'ailleurs pour ce prix-là. . . . Ces jours-ci, la B. Nat. est pleine d'Américains et même d'Egyptiens et autres, qui m'interrompent sans cesse; aussi ai-je décidé de la fuir . . .

## To James and Mrs. Osborn:

(Lion's Gate at Mycenae)
6 — VIII — 54

Dear friends,

We thought of you, when we just had to miss Mistra & Sparta. But we saw Crete, Olympia, Santorin & several isles. It was hot but bearable; & the scenery is perhaps the greatest marvel of Greece. We are getting back to Venice, then to Edinburgh for a contrast. How is Edgehill Rd. — & your early morning walks & your cows? With our best wishes & most cordial Greek thoughts —

H. & M. Peyre

## À Keith Botsford:

15 — 8 — 54

Mon cher Ami,

Kurt Weinberg est placé en Iowa — Oxenhandler revient enseigner à Yale pour un an au moins. Il a bien réussi, il est artiste, fin & original. Il faut quelqu'un de vivant & original en effet pour Bard & je suis heureux que vous y ayez réussi & que ç'ait été vous. Vous avez dû entraîner les élèves loin du culte de Maupassant!

Il y a à Harvard un garçon (Ph.D. sur Proust, Strauss) dont Shattuck pourrait vous parler. Il a l'air de quelqu'un de bien & de littéraire, mais il pourrait bien être placé d'ici là. La demande pour des Ph.D.'s est assez vive en ce moment. Morris va sans doute à Harvard.

Si l'on voulait un monsieur déjà arrivé, 40 ans ou 42 environ, je connais un Allemand de 1er ordre, Hans Marchand, philologue intelligent, linguiste disert, littéraire aussi; il a été à Istanbul, professeur de français, 10 ou 15 ans — gentleman distingué. Il est arrivé en Amérique en octobre dernier, & nous l'avons pris à Yale pour un an. Il a bien réussi. Son adresse est donc ici: c/o French Department, Yale. On pourrait le voir.

J'espère que ça ira à L. Angeles — mais attention de ne pas finir en auteur de scripts pour le cinéma ou la T.V. Il faut que vous paraissiez bientôt en publication, avec quelque livre qui convaincra tous ceux qui n'ont pas cru assez en vous. Êtes-vous prêt?

Amitiés,<br>H. P.

## À Claude Vigée:

[carte postale: vue de St. Andrews]<br>Ce 25—VIII—54

Cher ami,

Il y a bien longtemps que je vous dois des remerciements pour le n° des Cahiers du Sud où je vous ai lu ou relu avec profit toujours sinon entièrement convaincu. Et cet été divers poèmes de vous, notamment ceux des Lettres nouvelles, d'un ton différent, très mûr & fini m'ont beaucoup plu. Nous achevons cet été par un tour en Ecosse, très agréable.

À bientôt peut-être & bien à vous,<br>Henri Peyre

## To Edgar Furniss:

September 20, 1954

Dear Mr. Furniss:

I have asked to see you on your return to offer my greetings and wishes and to check with you on a small adjustment to be made on our budget.

We are appointing to our last, as yet unfilled, post of instructor, in order to replace Frank Bowman whose resignation was accepted by the Corporation on May 15, 1954, W. H. Matheson. Mr. Matheson was appointed as instructor for 1953–54, but resigned soon after the year began, in November, I believe, when he was called by the Army. The Army is now discharging him for reasons of health. His salary, as provided in the budget, will be $3,500.00.

Our registration is higher than last year's by one hundred undergraduates or so. We shall try to keep our supplementary need at a minimum, through some shifting of courses. I mentioned, in my letter of May 5th, 1954 (which you answered in longhand), that we would very probably need some extra appointments. As we see things now, we may be satisfied with one more assistant in instruction, Mr. Alfred Proulx, now in our Graduate School, who will receive $1,250.00 for five hours a week. The appointment blank is being sent accordingly, and I take it that the sum of $1,250.00, not provided in the budget, will be granted.

You have heard me speak often, with high praise, of Georges May, now Associate Professor for the term of 1951–56. He is the author of four books and some twenty articles, a remarkable achievement for a young man of thirty-four. He is very successful as a teacher. He has been offered full professorships elsewhere, and lately at the University of Illinois, when we raised his salary here to $7,000; he chose to stay here, although losing financially by it, when we told him that a full professorship (Mr. Morehouse's) would be open for him when his term would be completed, in 1956–57. We hope such will indeed be the case.

Meanwhile he has been approached by the Junior Year in France, an organization run by Sweetbriar College to which Yale has long sent the largest (and, we are told, the finest) group of juniors from any American institution. They offer him to be their Director in residence in Paris for one year (1955–56). The position is a flattering one, and we believe it is an excellent thing for Yale to have one of our men (as Professor Andersson once was) occupy it. It is a way of enhancing Yale's prestige in Europe, to establish close relations with French universities, and to help our university assert its leadership in the field of French.

The salary provided by the Junior Year is only $7,000. The University from which the appointee is selected normally supplements this sum (now insufficient to live in Paris with a wife and a child) by another grant. Mr. May has not been very eager to accept the offer, especially because I shall be away on sabbatical leave, I hope, in the second half of the year 1955–56, and he feared he would seem to be deserting his functions as our new Director of Undergraduate Studies. I assured him that we would take all necessary steps to have the Department run efficiently, and that it was to his interest, and to ours even more, that he accept the position. I added that I would suggest to you that a supplementary grant of $1,500 be made to him by Yale, somewhat similar with the grants you make to Yale scholars accepting a fellowship which needs to be supplemented.

Obviously, we would replace Mr. May, in 1955–56, at a salary not exceeding $5,500, so that, if the grant of $1,500 is made to him, the total sum provided for him in the budget would remain the same and Yale would suffer no undue increase from his leave of absence ($5,500 plus $1,500 = $7,000).

Since Mr. May must give an answer to the Junior Year by September 30, I thought I would present my request to you in writing and see you, if necessary, for an answer when the academic year reopens.

Very sincerely yours,<br>Henri Peyre

## To James Osborn:

Oct. 3 — 54

My dear Mr. Osborn,

Your beautiful "dinner" article pleased me much. It is delightfully written, with a true Johnsonian flavor, & very entertaining, & full of curious documents, & the printing & presentation are worthy of the content.

Many thanks for including me among the readers, owners, of such a fine booklet. I appreciate it deeply.

I am still full of regret that we missed seeing Mistra, yet we had a wonderful Greek pilgrimage.

We hope to see you soon—first, probably, among nude, Picasso-esque Negroes of the African wilds.

Sincerely,<br>Henri

## To Whitney Griswold:

Oct. 13 — 1954

My dear Whit:

We have appointed, as assistant-in-instruction in the French Department, a negro, Alvis Tinnin, who has lived in France, studied French thoroughly, then been admitted to our Law School here, changed to

MAT in French, received his MAT, then started his studies for a Ph.D. in French.

He is a fine man & a gentleman, tactful, dynamic. The Provost approved & Dean DeVane, who saw him first, approved. Tinnin is a married man, from New Haven, I believe. We feel sure all will go well in his undergraduate class of French 12. I wanted, however, to say a word to you about this appointment, in case you are questioned on it. I also wanted to be sure there will be no embarrassment to anyone or to you & Mrs. Griswold if we bring Tinnin & his wife to your tea for the new members of the Faculty on October 24th. If you foresaw any embarrassment, just let me know & of course I'll be discreet on it & find a subtle way to leave that new colorful colleague out.

Most sincerely,
Hri Peyre

## À Claude Vigée:

Ce 1er nov. 54

Mon cher ami,

Merci de ces poèmes. Dois-je vous les renvoyer? Dites-le moi. Vous atteignez à une densité, et aussi à une variété de manières, en même temps qu'à un accent *à vous,* qui dénotent bien un vrai poète, & qui ne mourra pas en l'homme mûr—que le critique & le professeur ne tueront pas. J'aime que vous aimiez aussi puissamment la nature—avec ce frisson cosmique, cette fougue qui fuit cependant la monotonie & la facilité de l'éloquence. "Le Nid du Phénix" dans sa Iè*re* strophe, & même vers la fin ("m'a battu sous les doigts" ou l'avant-dernier vers) m'a semblé moins original—Mais vous dépassez de beaucoup, non seulement la moyenne des vers publiés chez Seghers, mais les "poulains" des Cahiers du Sud tels que Luc-André Marcel.

Je serais certes heureux de faire la connaissance de Brandeis. Vous y avez un président courageux et de tous côtés on loue vos étudiants & vos méthodes. Vous avez eu raison d'aller là & c'est une université bien partie—et j'aimerais vous revoir et Mme Alexandre, que j'estime fort. Réussit-elle bien? J'emploie le conditionnel, parce que je suis si pris et ne vois guère encore de date où m'échapper. Je vais ce samedi à Boston, en coup de vent. En décembre, je crains d'être bien pris. En janvier, sans doute le samedi vous convient mal, sans quoi j'aurais pu aller à Waltham le samedi 8—Puis-je vous répondre mieux plus tard?

Dites à votre femme mon souvenir et mes félicitations de vous inspirer ainsi—et croyez moi, bien fidèlement à vous

Hri Peyre

## To Leon Roudiez:

November 17, 1954

Professor Leon S. Roudiez
Pennsylvania State University
State College, Pennsylvania

Dear Mr. Roudiez:

I am forwarding to you these announcements, which are probably your concern more than mine, since by your very title you must be an efficient business man.

I hope all goes well with the work of the Review. I am active, on my side, in starting a number of reforms and changes, which I hope will give more variety to our issues in the future and answer some of the needs of our members better, giving them more information on France and on current literature, as well as on some of the past authors, with whom most of our articles deal at present.

It will be best to speak on all that and other matters when we meet in December. By the way, we shall probably have to change the hour of our reception at the French Cultural Office in New York from Wednesday afternoon to Thursday afternoon, so as to leave Wednesday afternoon entirely free for the Modern Language Association Foreign Language Program. I shall inform you later or at the convention.

Many thanks indeed, and,

Very sincerely yours,
Henri Peyre

## À Jorge Guillén:

Ce 26 – XI – 54

Cher Ami,

    Je suis bien ingrat envers vous, qui m'avez dit des choses si touchantes à la suite de ma désinvolte causerie amoureuse. J'attendais toujours d'apercevoir un grand trou de ciel bleu dans mon programme & de vous prier de venir y planer. "Sin cortes ni penumbras." Mais j'ai eu d'affreux comités & autres déplacements à Philadelphie, Washington. Et voilà Thanksgiving passé, fête horrible d'ailleurs dans mon esprit, alourdie de dinde bouillie & farcie et d'inodorante gelée de petits fruits en boules. Le jeudi prochain (2 déc.), j'ai une séance chez le dentiste & une conférence l'après-midi. Si le jeudi suivant, vous vouliez passer ici quelques moments, arrivant pour déjeuner, ce serait merveilleux; ce serait le 9 déc., ou bien le samedi 11, ou bien aux vacances de Noël si vous descendez alors vers des climats plus doux ou allez voir votre famille? Nous entrons en vacances nous-mêmes le 17 décembre, & ma semaine du 26–31 sera accaparée par les "conventions" annuelles que vous fuyez comme une Terreur—mais moi, hélas!

    Dites-moi quand vous pourriez venir?

    Vos poèmes de la Hudson Review sont beaux, très beaux, et assez bien traduits. Quel orgueil fut le mien quand l'an dernier, je pus dire à mes 4 collègues du Guggenheim Committee: "There is no question about him. He is one of the 3 or 4 greatest poets alive, & he must be ranked first wherever he is, bien au-dessus de tous les pauvres, très pauvres 'Spanish scholars.'"

Mille très chaudes amitiés,<br>Henri Peyre

## To Edgar Furniss:

Dec. 2, 1954

Dear Mr. Furniss:

    I am not presuming to give advice to the Executive Committee— but merely adding a note to the effect that Mr. Douglas's salary (as explained on accompanying sheets) should henceforth be charged to the

Department entire. We had a talk once or twice on the high merits of Prof. Auerbach, who should truly receive more than the minimum full professor's salary, & on Mr. Richardson, due to retire in 2 years (1957), but doing us full & very active service, not too generously rewarded: he will take on even more work next year to help replace Mr. May.

I trust you did not wish us to do the adding up of these fragmentary sums.

Sincerely yours,
Hri Peyre

## To Harry Levin:

Dec. 12, 1954

My dear Harry Levin:

Many thanks for your reprint. It was a very perceptive & keen review, & Brombert must have been proud of it. His book is good, & he'll do even better ones. We have great hopes for him.

I hope your year has gone well & fruitfully & for your admirable Department of Comparative Literature, the model for all others here & abroad—or it *should* be their model. I hear little from Harvard & the Romance Department there, which must be a sign of a "vie sans histoire." I had a fine summer in 5 or 6 countries, mostly Greece, which brought some relief from the perpetual angst of never being able to do justice to any job. But I am back at it & shall now long for a sabbatical—maybe the year after next or next one.

Incidentally I reasoned, through some very keen & helpful remarks in "your" report, that you must have been the reader of my MS on the novel. I am thankful; but I pity you, for that MS was in a bad shape & too unwieldy. I have since shortened it, as you had suggested, & have just gone over the proofs. Even if the book is somewhat improved thus, I am not too proud of it. I have not really done it "con amore."

Won't you stop here some day (with a few days' notice) when you are on your way to N.Y., for lunch or overnight? It would be a true pleasure to see you again—

Very cordially,
Henri Peyre

## À Claude Vigée:

Ce 12 — XII — 54

Mon cher ami,

Je vois que vous parlerez, & sur quelque chose d'assez fascinant, à la MLA. J'espère que, malgré des tas de corvées stupides qui m'accablent à ces réunions, je vous verrai et même vous entendrai. J'ai une très haute estime pour votre poésie, & je la cite souvent à ceux (ils sont plus nombreux qu'on ne croirait) qui me demandent ce qui compte dans la poésie française depuis Michaux & Char. Je parlais de vous avec Guillén avant hier encore. Quel homme admirable de gentillesse & de simplicité dans la grandeur.

Pour Brandeis, le 17 mars (au jeudi, St Patrick's Day) vous conviendrait-il? C'est bien loin encore, mais je suis obligé à des combinaisons de ce genre pour être sûr de mon temps. L'après-midi ou le soir, cela est indifférent — Vous me direz un de ces jours.

Mes vœux pour les vôtres, pour vous et mon amical souvenir.

Hri Peyre

Si vous avez des collègues membres de l'AATF, dites-leur, voulez-vous, que la réception pour M. Donzelot offerte à *tous* les membres est placée au jeudi 30 déc., à 3 heures, au French Institute; la veille au soir, l'Ambassadeur nous fera ses adieux à notre dîner.

## À Jorge Guillén:

Ce 18 — XII — 54

Bien cher ami,

Merci de votre si cordiale & réchauffante visite. Vous avez fait oublier la morose tristesse de ce jour de décembre. Quel poète est jamais resté aussi modeste que vous, aussi plein d'humour & débordant de verve, aussi lucide dans ses vues critiques, aussi modestes ou acharnées à refouler son orgueil dans le profond inconscient de son être? Ces vieilles filles de W. n'ont pas le moins du monde réussi à mordre sur vous. Les jeunes vous enserrent sans vous tenir captif dans "leur soie aux baumes de temps," sinon dans ce que le même Mallarmé appelle "leur considérable touffe" où expire le "diamant." Vous êtes resté humain, libre et splendidement espagnol!

J'espère que le fils imprudent & prodigue vous reviendra enfin au début de l'année nouvelle & que votre solitude en sera moins dure pour le mois que vous aurez à patienter ici. Et en ami, en prêtre de votre gloire, je voulais vous redire de considérer favorablement la si magnifique offre de Harvard. Vous y représenteriez l'Espagne libre & créatrice, la poésie et la sagesse critique aiguë et originale, contrastant avec tant de jargon pédantesque. Ce n'est pas vous vendre que de donner un an ou deux de votre vie à la prose pour vous retrouver ensuite inspiré. Et vous feriez vibrer d'envie tous les Hispanisants d'Amérique et frissonner d'orgueil toutes les dames à demi damnées de Wellesley!

Nos vœux les plus affectueux pour vous, votre fille, fils, gendre et amitiés chaleureuses,

Henri Peyre

Merci de l'adresse.

## To William DeVane:

Jan. 10, 1955

My dear Bill,

I am quite disappointed about your Committee's decision. Buffum has served 7 years as assistant professor, is now completing his third book and is doing very well with us. I felt so confident of his future here that I dissuaded other places (Johns Hopkins, in particular) seeking a 16th century man and trying to tempt him away. Compared to some other departments and considering the number of our students, we are certainly not overstaffed in the permanent ranks and our future depends upon some younger men whom we wish to retain. Among them, Buffum is almost the *one* American born. We would in the end create more harm than good if we systematically preferred foreign or foreign born scholars and spoil the excellent feeling which seems to prevail in our midst.

I hope this decision in no way reflects upon our plan to promote May (for 1956–57) to the full professorship left vacant by the death of

A. Morehouse. If you will let me, I'd like to present that to the Committee this spring (since I'd like to be away after February next year). We repeatedly gave him assurances of such a promotion and I have dissuaded him from accepting approaches made elsewhere, and again lately by Illinois; I should feel to have been unfair to him if a delay were subsequently imposed.

I know how hard your task is and I sympathize. But the envy with which colleagues elsewhere speak of our young men here shows that we are not being provincial or inbred and favoring people who are just "the nice Yale type."

Cordially yours,
Henri

**To Philip Kolb:**

Jan. 10/55

Dear Mr. Kolb:

I hold your publications in very high esteem & I shall be glad to suggest your name when an opportunity arises, or to provoke one if I can. But I should have thought that Illinois had much interest in encouraging & pushing to the top a productive member of the faculty, respected in France & here.

What is your rank, may I ask, & approximate salary? Just in order to know where or what sort of post to suggest you.

Perhaps (I have never heard it) some people may judge you to be specialized too exclusively on Proust? Have you written on other periods, or taught them? Just now the demand seems to be chiefly for the 16th & 17th centuries. Do you care for administrative work & consider yourself as gifted for it?

Excuse these hasty questionings & believe me,

Very sincerely yours,
Henri Peyre

## À Mario Maurin:

Ce 17—1—55

Merci, cher ami, de votre mot. Je vais fort bien, mais je n'ai jamais été aussi fatigué (& dégoûté aussi) qu'à cette réunion au Statler. Quel dommage de présenter aux jeunes, idéalistes dans le fond, cette face de notre profession. Mais las aussi et le jour de ce malheureux "discours" sur la sincérité j'avais siégé sans arrêt de midi à 9h1/2 du soir au Conseil de l'AATF. J'en sortais mal en point pour parler en public. De plusieurs côtés, on m'a dit que j'avais parlé trop vite, de trop de choses (je ne m'en corrige guère) & que l'on aurait dû m'avertir que le microphone n'était pas ajusté comme il m'aurait fallu. Je le regrette bien, car je n'ai aucun désir d'être désinvolte. Je suis si sérieux dans le fond, & parle vite par timidité, de peur d'ennuyer ou d'appuyer avec lourdeur.

Heureux homme qui avez 2 semaines de vacances. Je n'en entrevois plus jusqu'à l'été & l'heureux loisir d'un bateau. Du 18 au 21 je suis à Washington au Board de l'ACLS, si vous savez ce que c'est & sinon cela n'importe. Les lundis sont mauvais pour moi, mais si vous veniez, *pour d'autres raisons surtout,* un autre jour, j'aimerais bien vous voir—soit à l'Université, soit si vous téléphonez chez moi & y faites un saut. Je vois cependant que je dois aller le 27 (jeudi) à Philadelphie & les 29 & 30 à N.Y. à un comité de la Mod. Language Assoc, où j'aide à chercher un nouveau secrétaire exécutif—Tout cela fait bien serré—mais je m'arrangerai pour vous voir, si je ne suis pas loin. Votre vie (intérieure mais à extérioriser) m'intéresse beaucoup, vous le savez.

Merci de votre gentil mot & bien à vous,
H. P.

## To Philip Kolb:

Jan. 23—1955

Dear Mr. Kolb:

Thank you for those details. I trust I was not indiscreet. It is true that Illinois has not been too fortunate in its French Department leadership, or in building up for an expanding future. I have great confidence in Wadsworth's judgment: he is an able organizer & a very just & fair man. I hope his advice will be heeded.

It is of course not easy to receive or to provoke offers of a full professorship, but that is clearly what you should have. Yet it should not be impossible in the coming years if some long-delayed moves are made by Stanford, or Berkeley or large Southern universities. And if Illinois were thus to promote you without more ado, you would be probably just as happy staying there, provided personal relations are fairly smooth. I'll do my best.

Sincerely yours,<br>Henri Peyre

## À Claude Vigée:

Febr. 10—1955

Mon cher Ami,

Je vous ai bien peu vu, ou entraperçu, dans cette affreuse foire, mais écouté du moins avec plaisir. Je viens (il y a déjà 8 ou 10 jours) d'écrire avec chaleur pour votre demande de bourse Guggenheim, mais, par mon expérience antérieure, je crains que vous ne vous attiriez la réponse que cette seconde demande vient trop tôt après la première. C'est au moins ce que la Fondation semble dire en bien des cas; ils sont beaucoup plus difficiles pour les renewals.

Vous avez cependant le plan d'un beau livre là! J'espère que vous l'écrirez néanmoins, tôt ou tard. Vous le devez et vous avez vécu si longtemps déjà avec ces idées.

Voulez-vous me préciser vos intentions pour un éventuel voyage à Waltham et quelle sorte de sujet vous désiriez? Je vous avais indiqué, je crois, un jeudi de mars, le 17 où je suis libre. Je vois que c'est St Patrick's Day. Cela vous est égal—et à moi.

Mes amitiés à votre femme & à vous,<br>Hri Peyre

## À Leon Roudiez:

Ce 14—II.55

Cher Monsieur Roudiez:

Merci de la copie de votre lettre à Harris. J'ai correspondu avec lui depuis. Il serait bon en effet d'avoir des noms de jeunes (30–45 ans), avec assez d'autorité pour pouvoir refuser, corriger, faire récrire les articles soumis, et assez de vivacité pour n'être pas lassés et routiniers. Il faudrait surtout de *bons* articles littéraires, & ce n'est pas facile à obtenir. Ceux que je reçois ces jours-ci pour PMLA ont tous l'air de chapitres de thèse retapés. Quand je vois des "jeunes" de promesse, je leur suggèrerai d'écrire pour nous.

Vous avez bien chagriné ce brave P. avec votre c.r. qu'il m'a envoyé. Il n'écrit pas très bien, certes, & manque de discrimination; mais votre c.r. avait l'air d'une mise en accusation en règle, je crois, un peu injuste. Vous cachez en vous un brin de tigre!

Par contre je vous trouve trop clément pour les *Mandarins*. Il y a de belles pages, surtout dans les monologues de la femme mariée psychiatre qui s'éprend de l'Américain (le grand amour de S. de Beauvoir pour Nelson Algren, évidemment) — mais ces petites garces qui peuplent le livre, cette banalité de style, ces immenses remplissages. J'aimais beaucoup mieux l'*Invitée* & le *Sang des autres,* je l'avoue. Mais les livres récents ont ceci de bon que tout le monde a raison à la fois sur eux.

Pourquoi n'écrivez-vous pas vous-même pour le FR davantage, & des c rendus?

Bien cordialement & à votre femme mon fidèle souvenir,
Henri Peyre

## To Edgar Furniss:

Feb. 15, 1955

Dear Mr. Furniss:

I am very sorry about the indiscreet & premature article in the *Yale News* announcing that I'll take a half-sabbatical next year! I don't see why these boys are so interested in me! They heard I was omitting my course next year & telephoned my office & printed the information—before my request for a sabbatical leave had probably reached you, & the Corporation. I apologize.

Cordially yours,<br>Hri Peyre

By the way, I'll be giving two graduate courses in the first term & there will be no need of a replacement—as per enclosed.

## À Léon Pierre-Quint:

Le 15 février 1955

Cher Monsieur,

Je vous suis très reconnaissant de m'avoir offert & envoyé votre nouveau livre sur Proust. Cela m'a beaucoup touché et permis de lire votre ouvrage, aussitôt paru ou presque, en même temps que j'ouvrais la belle & utile édition de Proust en trois volumes de la Pléiade. Votre ouvrage est fort curieux & révèle chez Proust un stratège des lettres & un auteur très, trop humain. C'est une précieuse addition à vos anciens livres sur Proust; & j'espère pour ma part que vous ferez peut-être un jour sur lui un plus gros ouvrage, semblable à votre second Gide, qui serait, de toute la bibliographie proustienne, la pièce la plus pénétrante et la plus utile.

Veuillez croire, cher Monsieur, à mes sentiments les plus reconnaissants.

Henri Peyre

## À Claude Vigée:

Ce 22 fev. 1955

Mon cher ami,

Je voulais d'abord lire *L'été indien* avant de vous écrire: je vous remercie de me l'avoir envoyé dans cette forme & me fais un vrai plaisir de cette lecture; mais ces semaines sont affreusement chargées & je dois attendre. Je vous réponds donc en attendant & provisoirement.

Cela est entendu pour la date: 17 mars (dix sept), jeudi. J'arriverai dans l'après-midi, selon les trains de Boston à Waltham (que j'ignore). Vous me diriez où me rendre. Je préfère dîner en petit comité et le moins de cérémonie possible. Je passerai la nuit à Brandeis et repartirai de Boston au début de la matinée (9h–10h au plus tard).

Cela m'est indifférent de parler en anglais ou en français. Tant pis pour le public si c'est en anglais! Il convient surtout qu'il y ait quelque discussion de la part des élèves. Mais quel *genre* voulez-vous? Erudit, spécialisé, pour collègues? Ou bien pour étudiants surtout? et se prêtant mieux à la discussion qu'un sujet spécialisé sur Pascal, ou Racine, ou Rousseau, etc.? Dites-le-moi bien franchement.

Personnellement je me suis intéressé récemment au problème de la sincérité en littérature, qui est énorme & touche à tout: au roman contemporain (j'ai un livre qui sort sur ce sujet en avril); aux questions d'éducation. Il m'arrive aussi souvent d'être appelé à parler sur la France d'aujourd'hui et sa situation politique & économique, si vous vouliez un sujet non littéraire. La poésie est au fond ce que j'aime le mieux, mais je n'oserais pas en parler devant un auditoire enseigné par un poète!

D'un mot, dites-moi donc un peu ce que vous voudriez: je mets au hasard quelques titres en anglais (Ils peuvent toujours être traduits).

    The Prospects for France today
    Can we count on France?
    French & American education.
    Reflections of a French professor in America —
    Is Existentialism a humanism?
    Existentialism & French literature.
    Women-writers in contemporary France —
    Trends in the contemporary French novel —
    The problem of literary sincerity.
    ou bien un sujet sur un homme: Malraux
            Claudel (il est bien capable de mourir d'ici là)
            Baudelaire
    Ou, si vous y teniez, sur la poésie récente.

J'attends vos vues. D'avance je vous remercie & dis à votre femme mes amitiés.

                                                                Hri Peyre

## À Keith Botsford:

Ce 24/2 (1955)

Mon cher ami,

Je ne vous oublie pas. Mais il n'y a pas grand'chose encore cette année, il me semble; du moins je ne vois rien de précis. En mars ou avril, souvent, les choses s'éclaircissent. Je suis optimiste, d'ailleurs; ici ou là, quelque chose surviendra. (Je ne crois pas qu'un doctorat vous aide beaucoup: vous aurez publié des livres. C'est mieux—et un doctorat est une longue affaire.)

Amitiés toujours,
Henri Peyre
Yale

## À Claude Vigée:

Ce 28—II—55

Mon cher ami (ne m'appelez pas "Monsieur!"),

Rien de grave en tout ceci. Nous changerons les plans, voilà tout. Je m'incline avec humilité devant Aaron Copland & si le jeudi ne va pas, nous trouverons autre chose. Le jeudi ne s'impose pas tellement pour moi. Simplement, il m'est difficile de trouver des jours libres & j'avais marqué celui là d'un petit caillou blanc. Par hasard si le soir du vendredi 18 (le lendemain) vous convenait, j'aurais pu l'arranger. Mais il me semble que vous aviez dit que le vendredi n'était pas commode pour vous. Sinon, pourrais-je renvoyer cette visite au mois d'avril ou de mai. Un mercredi soir doit pouvoir s'arranger, si le jeudi vous agrée mal. Nous sommes en vacances du 1er au 12 avril, vous aussi sans doute. Mais après cela, selon vos convenances et mes jours libres.

Comme sujet, vous pourriez donc prendre

1. The present temper in France judged through French literature.
2. The recent French novel.
3. Paul Claudel.
4. The present trends in French Poetry

selon vos préférences.

Je m'arrêterai donc à Route 128, ce qui est en effet bien commode & vous remercie d'avance vivement.

Si vous décidiez pour le 18 au soir, dites-le-moi très vite, voulez-vous? Sinon, rien ne presse.

Amitiés & merci,<br>Hri Peyre

## To Malcolm McIntosh:

March 25, 1955

My dear McIntosh:

Many thanks for your long and interesting letter, very thoughtful as always and very sincere in its wise discrimination between the good and the less good in your present location. You are not the only one who finds a good deal "à redire" in the South, and I sympathize with you. Still, as you know, the times were not too good when you took that job and it sounded then like a promising one, at least for some years.

One of the gentlemen from Missoula, Montana, though not the chairman, visited me here once and I was very well impressed by him and by what he said about the University. If the offer is finally made to you, I should suggest that you accept. Nothing much seems to turn up at the present time elsewhere, and in most places it is the same old story about preferring someone young. I know how much the education of your boy matters to you and to your wife. You are as concerned as any French couple might be, and you are right. The moral and spiritual atmosphere in the Northwest would probably be better in any case than in the South.

There certainly are possibilities in a subject on Baudelaire and Champfleury, and I hope your article will go through the usual hurdles and reach me, although I imagine Miss Margaret Gilman, whom I was replacing this year, will probably be the one to get it, since she is now returning from Europe. Your other idea and "discovery" are all promising, and I believe *Modern Language Notes* is the best place for that. Champfleury himself deserves a good deal more study than the little he has received, and not so much as a novelist, but rather as an art critic and as a critic of literature. I am glad that the atmosphere in Alabama has not dried up your courage and your freshness.

Many thanks for your kind words on that essay of mine, and our best to you and to your wife, from both of us,

Very sincerely yours,<br>Henri Peyre

## To Harry Levin:

[letterhead: The Biltmore, New York]<br>March 26 — 1955

My dear Harry,

Thanks for the book review of Paul Goodman's book: one more book of aesthetics I won't read! Your reviews are always sharp & splendidly dense: you manage to suggest the essential in such a short space!

I am scribbling this word while on a Committee — the Guggenheim — in which it proved hard to make a case for many of our modern literature historians & for our specialists of criticism. Are we in a low tide period in our studies? Do we need greater leaders, more fervently convinced of the value of their method & of their studies, than we have at present?

I did not have time to write a line of "dedication" on the book I asked Oxford Press to send you. Do receive my thanks for all that you did to make an imperfect book a little less imperfect.

Sincerely yours,<br>Henri Peyre

## To Keith Botsford:

March 30, 1955

Mr. Keith Botsford:
Barrytown, New York
My dear Botsford,

Fiedler is a nice man, I am told, and a fine, though maybe too universal and too prolific, critic, certainly one who keeps a lively interest in creative literature. I should think he would be a fine man to work with. But, of course, I can't earnestly encourage anyone to go to Montana, since I would not myself, and you might be a little forlorn there. I do not know what to say, but if Bard College should offer you an assistant professorship, with some prospect of staying around this part of the country, I suppose you are better off where you are. The hope of everyone in the profession is that there will be and should be many free positions in the near future.

I have not seen the latest *Quarterly Review*. Somehow, I have given up reading that, but I shall glance at it. Leopardi has been one of my favorite poets since I was sixteen.

My best to your wife and to you,

Very sincerely yours,<br>Henri Peyre

## À Claude Lévi-Strauss:

[letterhead: Island Inn, Sanibel, Fla.]<br>Ce 10—IV.55

Mon cher ami,

Au hasard d'un voyage, non pas d'ethnographe mais de professeur fatigué, je vous écris ce mot de félicitation. J'avais lu avec beaucoup d'admiration votre brochure de l'Unesco; de beaucoup la plus forte de la série & posant un problème que j'avais souvent rencontré, en enseignant Gobineau & Renan comme il m'arrive de le faire: le problème de l'inégalité des "races" ou des races résultats ou des cultures, que les criminelles utilisations du racisme nous ont amenés à éluder ou à ignorer. Votre petit livre, que vous reprendrez un jour, j'espère, est le seul qui s'y attaque pour indiquer les voies d'une solution, & prodiguer en passant les vues les plus perçantes.

Dans le train, je viens de lire votre réplique à Caillois dans les Temps Modernes: Caillois est parfois un bon écrivain, aux phrases d'ailleurs ronflantes & creuses, un homme tourmenté par son passé & au fond souffrant d'un arrêt précoce de développement, qui ne s'attaque plus aux grands sujets que pour les écrémer. Une NRF qui se l'attache, avec Arland & Paulhan, deux autres survivants, alors qu'il y a chez nous d'admirables esprits critiques parmi les jeunes, dans *Critique,* même dans *Esprit* & les *Cahiers du Sud,* ne s'honore guère. Votre réplique est d'une verve & d'un brio splendides—du vrai Voltaire, mais pensé en profondeur. J'en ai eu tant de joie que je me permets de vous en féliciter.

Venez-vous parfois en Amérique? J'espère vous y revoir. On y parle beaucoup de vous; votre nom y rehausse notre prestige auprès des gens des sciences sociales.

Croyez à mon sentiment le plus dévoué,<br>Henri Peyre<br>Yale

## À Mario Maurin:

Ce 25 avril 1955

Mon cher ami,

C'est vrai que je me mêle de votre vie, mais vous savez que c'est par amitié—et parce que certain sens de justice serait en moi vexé si vous, qui avez des dons supérieurs peut-être à ceux de n'importe qui en ce pays, restez par excès de modestie "derrière" d'autres qui se soucient tant de se mettre en avant. On demande de bien des côtés des Français ces temps-ci: je pense que vous êtes heureux où vous êtes. Mais de belles perspectives s'offrent à Pennsylvania, J. Hopkins, Indiana, etc.; j'y suggère votre nom, mais on ne vous connaît pas encore assez, professionnellement ou par vos écrits. Peut-être serait-il sage de vous souiller quelque peu par des communications ou boniments à nos foires annuelles et de consentir à publier, à côté de vos poésies & de quelques essais très fins & que je trouve très riches, quelque volume. Votre *Suarès* aurait fait un très bon livre.

Mais cela doit venir de vous et doit être dans vos goûts. Bien sûr, ne faites pas une étude d'influence: ce genre est stérile, à moins qu'on ne veuille l'élargir en étude du mirage de vision imaginative d'un pays par un autre. Et au fond toute littérature comparée est entachée d'artifice. Mais n'est-il pas quelque auteur moderne, ou d'autrefois, qui vous séduise? Un jour qu'enfin nous nous verrons, nous parlerons de ce qui est faisable ou attrayant; je ne sais trop quand, harassé que je continue à être jusqu'à fin mai. Allez-vous en Europe cet été? Je resterai ici sagement, à lire & à jouir de quelque silence. Bercez-vous parfois le jeune Girard? Vous seriez un excellent oncle.

Champigny (Girard le sait sans doute) a obtenu une bourse Ford. Pourquoi n'en auriez-vous pas une vous-même un jour? Son livre sur A. Fournier n'est pas trop de mon goût, mais je commence sans doute, tel Sylvestre Bonnard, à sentir les jeunes très loin de moi.

Bien à vous en toute amitié,<br>Henri Peyre

## To Katharine McBride:

May 1, 1955

Dear President McBride,

My long delayed Flexner volume is at last officially out & I am happy that you, & Mr. Chew & other colleagues who wrote from Bryn Mawr, seem to have been pleased with it. The Oxford Press people seem confident that it will be well received—not uniformly well, I hope, for my sake, for I have much to learn from criticism.

I hope you found the negotiating with the Oxford Press satisfactory. They seemed very much in the dark about your Flexner series & I refrained from meddling, but felt that perhaps a clear formulation of your arrangement with them should be made, for future authors who might otherwise be confused by the vagueness of their well-meant but ill informed dealings.

The first half of the total stipend offered for my Flexner Lectures was paid me in 1944, at the conclusion of the lectures themselves. I am in no hurry whatever to receive the half which is supposed (wisely enough) to be paid on the publication of the book. Indeed I feel I hardly deserve it after such a long delay. If it is easier for your accounting to close this long-standing chapter, you may wish to tell them to do so. I hope that a moderate sale will bring some royalties to the College & soften my feeling of guilt for having been, not lazy, but too busy over too many years. I am proud, however, that my name is thus, in print, associated with a College to which I am very proud to have belonged.

Very sincerely yours,<br>Henri Peyre

## To William DeVane:

May 11, 1955

Dear Dean DeVane:

I am sending you the last instructor appointment to be made in the Department of French for the year 1955–56. The young man is a Ph.D. from Columbia University who is known to me and has published already and seems extremely promising. He is also experienced, since he has taught for several years. We are appointing him to the position left vacant by the departure of M. Choquet, at $4,250, which was the sum provided in the budget for Choquet. I hope this can go through promptly and I shall meanwhile give assurances to the young man, who is married and has a family, that he may count on joining our Faculty next year.

As usual, the assistants-in-instruction will only be appointed early in September, when we know the exact freshman registration. Both instructors and assistants-in-instruction in our field seem to be very scarce and the replacements in one or two years may prove quite difficult, but we shall solve those problems later.

Very sincerely yours,
Henri Peyre

## To Edgar Furniss:

June 11, 1955

Dear Mr. Furniss:

Excuse my pursuing you with a letter even while Commencement is going on — & with the usual request.

One of the younger men in our Department, Raymond Giraud (now in his third year as instructor & next year to be a Morse fellow) has done a very good book, *The Unheroic Bourgeois Hero*. It is a study of the new type of hero in the fiction of Stendhal, Balzac, Flaubert, & touches on social history as well as literature. It is ably written.

The Yale Press, as you may know, & as Eugene Davidson reported to me, likes the MS very much. But they have no money to put into it

& will gladly publish it if the money is forthcoming. Gene's estimate is $2780 for 1000 copies of the 192 printed pages book.

Naturally the young author does not have even one fourth of the sum; I have no fund for publications, & you had none this current year. Could money be found after July 1st? Or had I better, at once, drop the matter, or perhaps try another Press? Naturally this book should appear right here, if at all possible. It will do us credit.

I hope you will have enjoyable vacations. I am staying around for a good part of the summer.

Very sincerely yours,<br>Hri Peyre

## To the same:

July 7, 1955

Dear Mr. Furniss:

We have recently appointed (the appointment was approved at the June meeting of the Corporation) Mr. Robert Nelson (residing at 90 Morningside Drive, New York 27, a Columbia Ph.D. who has already taught several years at Columbia) as instructor in French at the salary of $4,250. The man has been married eight years and has a family (one child, I believe). He is moving to New haven to live. He wonders if it is at all possible to receive compensation from Yale for his moving expenses, amounting to $185.00. I am very sympathetic to his request, but had to tell him I could only transmit it to the proper, and higher, authorities, without leaving him too much hope of a totally favorable answer. I thus turn to you for an answer, which you may choose to give directly to Mr. Nelson, or through our Department office.

Sorry to add another request, and letters, to your summer work and,

Very sincerely yours,<br>Henri Peyre lg

## À Leon Roudiez:

[letterhead: AATF]
7 — IX — 55

Cher ami,

J'espère que vous jouissez d'un temps plus frais sur votre plateau montagneux parmi vos vaches et vos corbeaux.

Pour ma part, je n'ai pas de préférence sur la place à assigner à mon triomphant message. Cependant, comme cette année il renferme le programme préliminaire de notre réunion de décembre, je crois qu'il est préférable de le mettre en évidence ou d'indiquer à une place évidente où trouver ce programme. Faites à votre idée pour le reste. Julian Harris effectue diverses réformes qui me paraissent admirables.

Je suis très flatté de votre opinion indulgente sur mon livre, mais vous êtes beaucoup trop poli et de vous, à qui je donne la réputation d'être la sévérité même, j'attendais des critiques stimulantes. Sur la question Camus existentialiste, je reviendrai peut-être un jour. Il n'y a pas que l'existentialisme sartrien et je crois que par son obsession de l'absurde, par sa revendication de la liberté, par sa conception de l'histoire, par sa morale, Camus se rattache à ce mouvement d'idées et de sensibilité. Il ne serait pas d'accord lui-même et mieux vaut attendre sa mort pour le classer définitivement, malgré lui. Pour le reste, il est certain qu'il diffère de Sartre, autant que Vigny pouvait différer de Lamartine ou Michelet de Stendhal.

Une autre année, 1956 peut-être, ne voudriez-vous pas lire ou donner un "paper" à notre réunion annuelle? Vous avez tant à dire.

Mes amitiés à votre femme et à vous-même,
Henri Peyre

## To Robert Penn Warren:

Sept. 10, 1955

Dear Mr. Warren:

On returning from our vacation, we have found your book, generously offered & graciously dedicated. My wife is now reading it with interest & joy, & I have at once devoured it. I was looking forward to reading it, after glancing at some reviews which failed to satisfy me but enhanced my curiosity; & of course your very expressive reading of a chapter, last year, at our Romance Club, had whetted many appetites. I admire your book very much indeed—even more than your previous ones, if I may say so. It is splendidly written & contains some of the finest, restrained & poetically suggestive, American prose of our century. And I believe it is a superb novel, both technically & because it holds the reader's interest breathlessly & conveys a deeper significance without ever letting the "thought" intrude. I have gained more insight into the South & the middle of the last century & the tragedy of slavery through *Band of Angels* than from any other book I have read.

You were very kind to send it to us. We both are very grateful. Will you remember us to your wife? We hope your summer was pleasant, if not exactly cool—

Very sincerely yours,
Henri Peyre

## À Leon Roudiez:

Ce 15—Sept. 1955

Cher Ami,

Merci de ces nouvelles de la Revue. Nous avons en effet une belle équipe. Il s'agira de solliciter parfois des articles de 1er ordre, mais aussi de caractère synthétique, ou original, car notre public n'est pas tout à fait, dans l'ensemble, celui qui s'intéresse à de l'érudition spécialisée. À la réunion de déc. nous aurons du temps & tâcherons de discuter tout cela.

Ne vous plaignez pas de varier vos cours: cela est excellent dans une profession où l'on tend vite à se répéter. Mes collègues & moi ici, sauf en philologie, ne donnons pas deux fois le même cours dans un espace de 7 à 8 ans. On finit ainsi par tout connaître—Mais juste au moment de la rentrée (nous y sommes), on est pris de panique devant ces sujets neufs sur lesquels on se sent mal prêt. Puis on ouvre le cours, & on s'aperçoit qu'on a encore trop à dire.

Vous êtes un lecteur dangereux, plein de scrupules & de minutie:

vous devinez les faiblesses des livres, les manques, les préjugés de l'auteur. Vous auriez fait un admirable confesseur ou même un polémiste catholique ou un gardien des chemins du paradis. J'avais d'abord fait 2 chapitres dans mon livre, contenant une liste plus complète des plus de 50 ans, des moins de 50 ans. L'éditeur a voulu que je syncope les deux & diminue beaucoup des "vieux" ou des moins importants. J'ai alors balancé votre chère Zoé. Elle vaut mieux certes qu'Orieux, mais pas grand'chose quand même—à mon avis.

Peyrefitte—le succès fait à ses *Amitiés* m'a agacé, et je crois les éloges prodigués à ce livre immérités. Mais il est vrai que je suis, et peu séduit par l'atmosphère catholique, en ancien protestant pas tout à fait désaffecté; & enclin à croire les prêtres purs, propres, droits; et excédé de ces adolescents homosexuels. Nous en avons dans nos collèges & écoles graduées, & ils nous assassinent de leurs ennuis & de leurs problèmes. . . .

## To Edgar Furniss:

September 20, 1955

Dear Mr. Furniss:

Here is a somewhat more precise explanation of the one or two requests which I made either to you by phone or in conversation with Dean Simpson.

1) The number of students taking our beginners' course, French 15, which is given according to an accelerated method and in which, therefore, not more than fourteen students can be taken in per division, necessitates our shifting one of the instructors of French 22, who is a native speaker, to French 15 and replacing him in the five hours of French 22 with a new assistant in instruction, Bryant Freeman. The salary requested for him is, as usual, $1,500 a year for five hours a week of instruction. The appointment blank is being prepared. Will you see to it that the treasurer's office gets the proper information which they will need for his salary checks?

As I said over the phone, the sum of $1,500 is not altogether a new charge added to the university budget. There is, in our own budget, a sum of $300 left unused under the item "Assistants in instruction," for whom $9,600 were provided and for whom only $9,300 have thus far been assigned. At least half of the money requested for readers (the total being $700) would go back to the University, as we do not expect to use it this year. Finally, Mr. Freeman has a tuition scholarship of $600 which he is relinquishing since he will be teaching.

2) Exceptionally, we have asked Francis Tafoya, who is already teaching a full schedule with us and receiving a full salary, $4,000 as a third-year instructor, to take charge of the special course in reading French given to graduate students of other departments who are not proficient enough in that language. The salary provided extra to Mr. Tafoya will be $375, if, as seems likely, there are ten students enrolled in the course, paying $37.50 each for one term. If there were fewer than ten, he would get as many times $37.50 as there are students. If there are more than ten, his salary remains at $375 and the surplus goes to the University.

The reasons why, very exceptionally, we are asking a man receiving a full salary and teaching a full schedule to take on an extra course is that Mr. Tafoya has suffered from very grave financial difficulties due to the long hospitalization of his wife and the very delicate care which his two-year-old child requires. Dean Simpson agrees that we might and should, in this case, make the exception necessitated by the misfortunes incurred by that very deserving instructor.

Very sincerely yours,
Hri Peyre

## À Kurt Weinberg:

Ce 23 sept. 55

Mon cher ami,

Tout d'abord merci de votre article sur un sujet qui m'intéresse beaucoup. C'est un essai original, subtil, aigu, très pénétrant & qui décèle avec force de graves faiblesses chez Gide — Vous avez un don très vrai d'analyse, non pas seulement littéraire, mais psychologique. Vous êtes un amateur d'âmes en fait — un confesseur des esprits. Vous fouillez des recoins obscurs en moraliste aigu.

Le défaut de cet article est le revers de sa qualité. Il est très complexe, trop peut-être; très involué — il comprend trop de choses & la lecture en est ardue. Il faut s'y reprendre à plusieurs fois & vous suivre la plume à la main: vous êtes souvent tenté de suggérer plus que d'expliquer, de procéder par allusions, de vous engager dans des voies un tout petit peu transversales ou latérales, & je crois que, à l'avenir au moins, vous gagneriez à plus de simplicité. Ceci rappelle (ce n'est pas un mince éloge) les articles critiques de Blanchot, de Mauron, de Picon; vous ne trouverez guère de lecteurs pour ceci qu'en France.

En outre, vous tendez à être non seulement un commentateur objectif de Gide & de sa sincérité mais à devenir son accusateur. Votre ton devient très négatif, un peu acharné même, comme si vous vouliez brûler quelque ancienne adoration, vous délivrer de quelque emprise gidienne sur vous. Insensiblement, cela finit par fausser un peu la perspective, & moi même, qui ne chéris point Gide d'une tendresse excessive & crois aussi sa sincérité un peu truquée, suis tenté de le défendre contre vous.

Enfin dans le style aussi essayez d'être plus simple, plus direct, plus clair. Vous verrez quelques remarques çà & là.

Je crois que ceci est trop fin, trop subtil, un peu déroutant pour le lecteur de ce pays, & aussi & surtout trop long—& que vous ne pourrez guère le placer qu'en France; peut-être d'ailleurs en l'abrégeant. La *Table ronde* peut-être; *Les Lettres nouvelles;* le *Mercure*. Essayez là-bas. Pour ce pays ci, il vaudrait mieux délibérément écrire en anglais.

Votre photo est belle & votre femme y est splendide. Vous semblez rayonner de bonheur. Enfin vous voilà installé dans un beau cadre. Mais vos nouvelles du Département, de l'université sont peu encourageantes. Sans doute êtes-vous un peu sévère pour tout ce qui n'est pas aussi artiste, aussi raffiné, aussi connaisseur que vous. Il y a quelque bien aussi dans la simplicité fruste et dans la primitive fraîcheur—Mais je vous comprends aisément. Ce doit être un peu lointain pour qui apprécie la culture par dessus tout, et vit d'art, & pour le beau. Le malheur est que, de toutes parts, le littéraire cède la place au technique, & que nous faisons tous un peu figure d'inutiles, & d'aimables fossiles. Quelques centres de l'est nous donnent une illusion plus optimiste & nous rapprochent de l'Europe occidentale: mais ce sont de bien petits îlots.

Peut-être est-ce déjà beaucoup de ne pas avoir à enseigner la langue élémentaire et le b a ba de la littérature. Vous serez ainsi encouragé à écrire, et vous avez d'ailleurs un immense acquis où il n'y a qu'à puiser. Dans quelques mois, redonnez-nous vos impressions & dites quelles sont pour vous les perspectives là-bas. Penseriez-vous y rester?

Ma femme vous dit son très cordial souvenir. Tous vos amis ici sont heureux de votre bonheur. Je vous adresse moi-même mes bonnes amitiés.

Henri Peyre

En Amérique même, vous aurez grand peine à placer un article aussi subtil, de cette longueur, et en français. Là-dessus, je ne suis pas trop optimiste. À quoi pensiez-vous?

## To Edgar Furniss:

Sept. 26/1955

Dear Mr. Furniss:

Excuse the informality of this "official" note. I have one or two questions for you:

1) How strictly is the rule on sabbatical leaves enforced? I am thinking of Jean Boorsch. He had a leave, while an associate professor, in 1948–49, for a half a year, seven years ago. He was made full professor only two years & a half ago, on July 1, 1953, I believe. He would wish the favor of a new leave of absence for the first term of 1956–57: but he will have been full professor only 3 years by then, while on the faculty for twenty or so. The leave would be for research purposes, though I must confess the book he started on his earlier leave in 1948 is not yet out or completed. I would certainly wish he could be away & the department would manage. How would your office feel?

2) Of the sum marked for a reader ($700.00) in our budget, I would wish to spend only half ($350.00) during the first term, the other half remaining unspent. I am giving two graduate courses this term as well as one undergraduate, which is quite a burden; but I chose it. And if you have no objection I'd like to use the reader, to be appointed soon, to read, not only or mostly undergraduate essays, but graduate ones & to take over my course the few times in the term when I have to be away on some important committee or conference. The man I have in mind, M. Arnaud, an exchange scholar now at Yale, is a very capable scholar. Unless I hear from you that there is some objection, I'll go ahead with the plan.

Our budget would thus stand as it was approved, with the following changes:

Reader: provided $700; spent $350

Assistants: additional appointment of Mr. Bryant Freeman is provided for to the extent of 300, & will thus necessitate an additional sum of $1200, as an earlier letter explained. The $600 fellowship held by Mr. Freeman has gone back to the graduate School fellowship budget.

Laboratory assistants: provided: $1400 (in part tuition) will be appointed this week.

Very sincerely yours,<br>Hri Peyre

## To the same:

October 6, 1955

Dear Mr. Furniss:

I am extremely sorry that we have been guilty here of an oversight which, I fear, is going to cause you some embarrassment. We have listed, both on her appointment blank and in our budget, Mrs. Cecil Lang as teaching six hours a week in French 25 and receiving $1,800.00, that is, $300.00 per hour per year. During the summer, when we had our first indication of what probable registration we should have, we asked Mrs. Lang to take on another section, five hours per week per year, as she had done last year for us, for she proved to be an excellent language instructor, and the only woman for whom our virile department makes an exception, since we deem her worthy of teaching males. The extra course is French 15, which also requires a native, and where she is taking over Division 4. This means that she should receive another $1,500.00, and that I should have asked you for that extra sum, which was not provided for in our budget, but which the numbers in our French registration this year made absolutely necessary.

I have telephoned to Miss Feineman to express our embarrassment and apologies, and I am asking you to repair our mistake by allotting $1,500.00 more to our budget and to have Mrs. Lang's appointment blank modified accordingly. Her first salary should, of course, be supplemented.

In all due humility, and

Very sincerely yours,<br>Henri Peyre lg

## To Malcolm McIntosh:

Nov. 6/1955

My dear McIntosh:

Thank you for your kind letter & the copy of your letter to the Montana people. You may well overrate the charms of teaching & underrate the forces which sooner or later attract many of us to administration; I don't know. But I respect your judgment &, as always, your fine frankness & your standards. I was hoping that, if things materialized at Missoula, you would at least be much nearer home & able to combine teaching with some organizing & administering. The South, by all accounts, is not the most stimulating part of the country to live in. But you won't stay there for ever! We'll go on keeping an eye on openings & some day there may be something suitable for you in the Northwest or elsewhere.

I hope meanwhile your wife's health is good & your son does well in mind, soul & body. If you can find a limited topic (perhaps on Villiers) on which you can write, away from libraries, you certainly should display with less modesty your fine critical gifts. Can you at least get at your library some of the recent & interesting French works of criticism: Poulet, Jean Pierre Richard (Littérature & Sensation), Bachelard, Picon? I hope so.

All goes well here, but overwork is tiring me & I am looking forward to a term off in February or March 1956.

Our best wishes & faithful souvenir to both,<br>Henri Peyre

## To Edgar Furniss:

December 7, 1955

Dear Mr. Furniss:

Thank you for your recent communication on our budget. Unless I hear from you to the contrary, I shall take up with the Dean of Yale College in the near future the appointments and promotions which have to be made for next year, since I expect to be away after February and should like to leave things in as orderly a manner as possible.

Among other things and before I go to our Modern Languages convention in Chicago with the desire to interview some candidates for the teaching profession and look at possible new instructors for our Department, may I ask how literally we must take the stipulation that assistants in instruction are only appointed here for two years. We have several who will be at the end of their two years and we may find it safer and financially preferable to continue one or two of them for a third year rather than call upon outside persons.

You kindly mentioned the other night that there might be a possibility of finding some funds for exchange fellows with France for one more year. I do not mean to press you on this and I am working hard to secure outside help if possible. But if we could have the exchange continued for another year from Yale funds, it would give us much more time to plan for a new set of measures to be taken in the future.

Very sincerely yours,
Henri Peyre lg

## To Stanley Burnshaw:

Dec. 25, 1955

Dear Mr. Burnshaw:

I had been duly impressed by you, by your letters & your conversation & presence, but I have been even more impressed by your book of poems. It has extremely beautiful things: a comprehensive, imaginative structure, continuity of purpose & of effect which is rare these days, a great wealth of sensibility, a welcome avoidance of the more cerebral tricks of modern poetry. And I liked, I must confess, your musical songs as much as the Testament, because they are so very felicitous in their melody, concise & evocative in their phrasing: you rehabilitate love poetry among us. A technician of verse can be also a genuine romantic & an inspired singer. In this busy & at times sickening season, reading your book has been a source of joy. Thank you.

Very sincerely yours,<br>Henri Peyre

## To Edgar Furniss:

January 6, 1956

Dear Mr. Furniss:

I believe it is in order for the Department of French to send you the request that Professor Theodore Andersson, Associate Director of the Master of Arts in Teaching Program, Associate professor of French, be granted a leave of absence for the year 1956–57.

As you know, Professor Andersson is at present occupying the important position of Director of the Foreign Language Program of the Modern Language Association, in New York. He is proving extremely successful in this post and the request of the Modern Language Association, and of our Department, is that he be continued for one more year (a terminal year) in his present function and be accordingly granted a leave of absence without salary from Yale University.

The question in my opinion should be raised in the near future of the promotion of Mr. Andersson to the rank of Full Professor. Your answer, when I raised the point a year or two ago, could not yet be affirmative: some uncertainty still hanging over the future of the MAT program at Yale or over that of our Department of Education may have to be cleared. Meanwhile, however, Professor Andersson is occupying such an important position in the educational world in the nation and is fulfilling his functions so efficiently and competently that his being retained at the rank of Associate Professor is a paradox. The requirement of scholarly production properly speaking may not be met in his case and in the case of a few other men whose work is of a slightly different nature from that of the pure scholar. But the University cannot ignore the outstanding merits of such men and provisions should be made for their promotion to the highest rank, if need be, independently from Committees and Boards whose function is to stand as guardians over the scholarly quality of our professors.

Sincerely yours,<br>Hri Peyre

## To Harry Levin:

Jan. 12, 1956

My dear Harry,

Forgive this note scribbled on a train. I congratulate you on your new functions, which no one else certainly could assume. I do not envy your task, however.

I have heard lately from Jasinski that all was not for the best & even that some persons hinted that I, along with others, had, with unconscious perfidy, suggested for Harvard professors of French whom I had not wanted to call to Yale. Somewhat distressed & even more embarrassed, I wrote a letter to Dean Bundy which he might perhaps show you.

I shall be leaving for Georgia on Jan. 29 (Sunday). If the meeting that you mention is in New Haven on Jan. 28, won't you please arrive here at 12.45 or so & have lunch with me? I'd be delighted—I shall not be teaching next term (which for us begins this year on Jan. 16th) & shall sail for Europe on March 1 *st*.

I should like to count on you for the 28th & if you'd prefer to arrive the evening before, I'd have a room for you.

I'll drop this in the mail in Providence, regretting that I cannot go as far as Boston just now.

Very cordially yours,<br>Henri Peyre

## À Claude Vigée:

Ce 13 [janvier], 1956

Cher Ami,

J'aime beaucoup votre été indien—et non seulement les poèmes, qui se relisent avec une joie approfondie, leur forme témoignant d'une maîtrise musicale & évocatrice qui renouvelle votre manière, mais vos réflexions en prose. Le genre est périlleux. Valéry, Reverdy s'y sont parfois culbutés. Mais vous ne vous livrez pas, ou bien rarement, aux aphorismes impérieux à la René Char ou à l'Héraclite: vous avez là des scènes d'été indien, d'hiver, des esquisses de vos enfants, des pensées philosophiques riches de suc et d'une pénétration qui va loin. J'aime cette nostalgie de votre paysage natal d'Alsace, cette insistance à retrouver des racines françaises que je n'ai pas su avoir moi-même. Je comprends moins bien vos préoccupations de l'inceste—mais le sujet a toujours séduit les romantiques & les ethnologues.

Merci de m'avoir envoyé, si vite, votre dernier né. Je le goûte fort & le relirai souvent.

Bien à vous & à votre femme,
Hri Peyre

Trouvez-vous votre oiseau rare parmi ces jeunes professeurs? X est un grand esprit, ou peut le devenir—mais peut-être pas très flexible—

Encore cette feuille annonce, pour vos amis. Merci de votre essai sur Becker.

## To Allen Tate:

[letterhead: Princeton University Library]
January 19, 1956

Dear Mr. Tate:

Some time ago the Yale Press, at our suggestion, sent you two books, done by two very promising young critics of ours, Messrs. Melvin Friedman and Geoffrey Hartman, entitled, respectively, *The Stream of Consciousness* and *The Unmediated Vision*.

Several of us here thought that those books were likely to interest you. They do show a great deal of promise and much independent thought. But it is so difficult to persuade journals, even so-called learned ones, to review critical books by authors as yet unknown. I thought I would take the liberty to suggest that, if you found them worth your attention, you mention them occasionally to friends of yours and to potential readers. Your influence on criticism is very great, and it would be a service to those young men and to criticism in general.

Very sincerely yours,<br>Hri Peyre

## À Mario Maurin:

Ce 20 — i — 56

Cher Ami,

Vous allez croire que je vous fuis. Mais je pars pour un long comité à New York ce jour même. Le vendredi 27, je serai ici le matin, à 10h30 ou 11 heures, mais pris au déjeuner, & encore le soir; mais nous pourrions échanger quelques mots ce jour là & vous verriez d'autres amis. Le lendemain je pars pour la Géorgie & n'en reviendrai que le 3 février. Le 4, je parle à un groupe de l'AATF à New York & aurais pu, à la rigueur, vous voir là si vous y étiez & pour vous épargner le voyage. Le 6, lundi, je serai sans doute ici le matin, puis repartirai pour St Paul's School, NH, & Harvard. C'est une vie bien sotte, mais enfin encore un mois & je serai at home en congé.

Pouvez-vous venir un de ces jours là, si le peu de loisir qui m'est laissé vaut le dérangement?

Bien à vous,<br>Henri Peyre

## À Kurt Weinberg:

Ce 25 — I — 1956

Cher M. Weinberg,

Votre livre est en effet un mystère pour moi; je n'en vois pas de comptes rendus, comme ce devrait être le cas — Et cependant il était, et reste, excellent; il doit se vendre. Je m'en occuperai un peu quand je serai à Paris ou j'écrirai même auparavant, & je demanderai si vos comptes d'auteur ont été dressés.

En attendant, ne vous inquiétez pas. Surmontez ces crises de stérilité, ou plutôt de peur de la stérilité, qui vous affligent. Vous êtes un créateur, vous avez un énorme acquis, vous l'avez bien assimilé. Livrez davantage de vos richesses au public.

Mais je crois encore que de vous faire connaître en Allemagne vous sera de faible secours. En France, dans les revues, c'est difficile, mais non pas impossible. Et vous devriez travailler à vous faire un style anglais, à être connu en Amérique en anglais. Vous ne resterez pas en Colombie, mais il n'est pas mauvais d'y patienter, un an ou deux—le temps de dénouer ces nœuds de vipères ou de les désenvenimer! Avec le charme de votre jeune épouse, votre grâce musicale & poétique, vous devriez faire merveille!

Si j'étais vous, j'éviterais de me laisser croire l'homme de Heine avant tout, & je reviendrais à Baudelaire, ou à Constant et, pour l'usage américain, j'éviterais les complications psychologiques & les subtilités trop ténues.

M. Auerbach m'a parlé de votre suggestion de passer ici en mai et d'une demande qui pourrait vous faire obtenir une compensation de vos frais. J'avoue que la requête nous embarrasse un peu—d'abord parce que nos cours, cette année, finissent exceptionnellement tôt, (le 11 mai, je crois) & que les séances de notre Romance Club ne seront guère actives après le 1er mai; et puis il est un peu délicat d'arguer de ce modeste groupe, si peu officiel, où les invitations viennent des étudiants gradués eux-mêmes, le Romance Club, pour suggérer l'octroi d'une somme assez forte nécessairement pour frais de voyage. Votre administration risque de vous & de nous tenir en suspicion. Ne serait-il pas davantage de votre intérêt de demander un "grant" de recherche & de voyage pour venir à la Mod. Lang. Assoc. à Noël prochain, d'y lire un paper, & de donner en passant ou en revenant un paper ici à Yale? Professionnellement, vous auriez des chances d'en tirer plus grand profit. En décembre, la pénurie de gens de premier ordre pour de bons postes sera sans doute plus aiguë & il serait opportun alors de tenter une offensive.

Qu'en pensez-vous?

Croyez comme toujours à nos fidèles amitiés,
Henri Peyre

## To Edgar Furniss:

February 7, 1956

Dear Mr. Furniss:

I am not clear from your letter of February 1, 1956, what the details of the French Department budget stand at, as the budget will be recommended to the Corporation.

My original proposal for the salary budget amounted to a total of $151,200.00

Your letter of November 10 subtracted from that $250.00 each (Messrs. Duisit and Tafoya).

Your letter of December 6 subtracted another $500.00 (Cornell) and $5,250.00 (Stephens). The total to be subtracted from the original proposal thus stood at $6,250.00, which should have left our budget at $144,950.00, unless I am mistaken.

Your letter of February 1 mentions that $7,000.00 out of our total salaries budget is to come from the Mellon funds. The details of that sum are not clear to me. The funds to be provided from sources other than the regular budget were, I believe, to amount to:

| | |
|---|---|
| Directed Studies (Mr. Brombert, one third): | $1,750.00 |
| Sophomore Course in Saybrook College (Mr. Brombert, one third) | $1,750.00 |
| Sophomore Course in Silliman College (Mr. Buffum, one third) | $2,000.00 |
| HAL Course by Mr. Guicharnaud (as per Dean DeVane's letter of November 2) one third: | $2,000.00 |
| | $7,500.00 |

I thus seem to reach the total of $144,950.00 minus $7,500.00 = $137,450.00. To which the Miscellaneous budget of $5,146.00 should be added, reaching a total of $142,596.00.

But I am no financier and I submit this humbly to Miss Feineman's infallible reckoning.

Sincerely yours,
Henri Peyre lg

## To William DeVane:

February 15, 1956

Dear Dean DeVane:

I have kept the salary of the new appointee, Mr. Pierre Capretz, to the sum allotted in the budget. The young man, although he has a family of two children and the promise of a third one, proved willing to accept, as he considers it an honor to be in this university and to work in our Department; but I think I should mention to you that he was at the same time offered approximately $1,000 more elsewhere.

A similar offer, far more advantageous than what we give him here, was made to Robert Nelson, also instructor in French, who will be here in his second year next year and receiving $4,250. He also turned down the more attractive offer made elsewhere, although he has a family of two children.

I am not suggesting that anything be done for the present; but I believe it is fair to say that we cannot hope to get first rate instructors with a Ph.D. and already some publications in the future if other institutions keep on competing as they seem determined to.

Very sincerely yours,
Henri Peyre lg

C.c. for the Provost


## To Edgar Furniss:

February 20, 1956

Dear Mr. Furniss:

Thank you for being so cordial this morning and agreeing that, as an exceptional measure for the present at least, the two instructors whom I mentioned to you will receive $4,500 instead of $4,250. Their names, for your record, in case your infallible memory ever failed you, are Pierre Capretz and Robert Nelson.

Very cordially yours,
Henri Peyre lg

## To Kurt Weinberg:

February 28, 1956

Mr. Kurt Weinberg
5516 Corvette Crescent
University of British Columbia
Vancouver 8, Canada

My dear Weinberg:

This will be my last note before I sail, in which I should like to thank you for yours and congratulate you on your reappointment. It certainly is not all that it should have been, but some time soon I am sure you will beat the evil fate which has pursued you. I keep mentioning your name to several people looking for possible teachers in university posts, and this year or next I hope you may have the possibility of moving elsewhere.

I shall try and find out in Paris how your book is doing, but the PUF people are not especially easy to deal with. In any case, the important thing is that the book is out and that you can send copies to possible employers. If I were you, I should look ahead now and, as I hinted once, perhaps abandon both Heine and writing in German. There is, as you can well sense, a prejudice against German-born people; only showing even more adaptability than other foreigners and a greater willingness to abandon what is called "Teutonic jargon" in English style can dispel that prejudice in individual cases. I believe you could easily write as well in English as you do in French. It only takes a little effort to try at first.

As you know, I also quite agree with your criticism of American criticism, which is content with eternally attempting to define its metaphysical assumptions, but does not actually criticize the works. But there again, if I were you, I should not appear negative or engage in any polemics. I should go ahead and do the kind of critical articles which most of our philosophical or New Critics fail to do.

Will you give our best wishes to your wife and believe all of us here,

Most sincerely yours,
Henri Peyre

## À Malcolm McIntosh:

March 2, 1956

Cher Monsieur McIntosh:

Je pars pour la France dans quelques jours et je vous réponds donc rapidement, surtout pour vous remercier de votre intéressante lettre. J'espère que les choses iront bien à Hobart College. Vous y seriez mieux que dans l'extrême Sud.

Si je puis aider, ou Monsieur Boorsch en mon absence, dites-le nous. Il y a aussi des possibilités au Texas, à Rice Institute, mais je crois que le Sud vous a assez vu ou inversement.

Votre attitude dans la question qui déchire en ce moment l'Alabama est noble et courageuse. Je crois qu'il aurait pu être mieux de ne pas soulever la question aussi ouvertement et de chercher une solution graduelle, en admettant quelques étudiants, mais peu à peu. Mais peut-être un choc était-il nécessaire pour secouer certaines inerties. Le reste du pays, en tous cas, est fort ému par tout cela, comme vous le savez.

Mes félicitations pour vos travaux. Je suis certain que, dans un milieu plus sympathique et stimulant, vous diriez encore davantage par écrit de ce que vous avez à dire.

J'ai connu jadis et je crois bien nommé ce Monsieur Debien au Caire. Notre meilleur souvenir à votre femme et à vous.

Henri Peyre

## À Claude Lévi-Strauss:

Ce 9 avril 1956
Hôtel St James
211 rue St Honoré, 1r

Cher Ami,

Je crains d'avoir oublié, ou trop longtemps différé, de vous dire, merci, tout d'abord, pour l'envoi de votre livre, et ma très grande admiration pour *Tristes Tropiques*. J'admirais depuis longtemps le tranchant & la vigueur de votre intelligence, la puissance philosophique de vos généralisations fondées sur une vaste observation. Mais c'est l'artiste, avec toute sa sensibilité, & aussi un écrivain très remarquable que m'ont révélé vos pages. C'est un des très beaux livres de ces dix dernières années, sans nulle exagération. Je vous suis reconnaissant de m'avoir permis de le lire aussitôt. Il m'a donné plus de joie, & une joie plus durable, que bien des ouvrages dits littéraires que je dois feuilleter.

Nous sommes venus à Paris, interrompre une vie un peu trop absorbée de soucis minimes, cependant tous importants. Mais les premiers jours sont difficiles: froid, difficulté de logement, et politique timorée, duperie de soi-même chez beaucoup de Français. Mais déjà nous sommes repris par tout ce qu'a de fervent la vie artistique et la finesse d'esprit des Français, la douceur de leurs voix, leur courage aussi ont bien de l'attrait.

Allez-vous bien? J'aimerais un jour vous revoir. Nous resterons sans doute à l'adresse de cet hôtel, sauf en mai où nous voyagerons.

Merci encore & croyez à mes sentiments les plus dévoués,
Henri Peyre

## To Edgar Furniss:

C/o American Express
Rue Scribe, Paris
April 29 – 1956

Dear Mr. Furniss,

I am very grateful to you for your long & kind letter of April 18th concerning changes in the French department budget — & first of all for the generous increase made to my own salary as Sterling Professor & for the Sterling Professorship given to such a fine scholar as Professor Auerbach. His renown is great over here as well as in his adopted country & we shall all be proud of the great honor bestowed upon him. The other increases provided are equally generous & very gratifying, especially at a time when the appointment of very able men to instructorships & assistant professorships is going to meet with growing difficulties. I have been spending a little time over here trying to discover promising young scholars in our field, for Yale & other American institutions which often consult me on their plans, and it is not easy to lure the best away. Conditions in France are difficult, however, & it seems that logically, teachers, & others, should be leading very hard lives: but, paradoxically, they appear to live fairly well & to be satisfied with a minimum of grumbling & of cursing of the government.

The country is faced with very serious problems &, deep down, not too hopeful about a solution; yet there seems to a good deal of individual enjoyment of life & a good deal of creativeness & of inventiveness. After some inevitable trouble of readaptation (including a vain search for a suitable apartment &, for me, several attempts at locating ideal typists & secretaries), we are finding Paris very pleasant, though still chilly & rainy, & I am trying to achieve some work while I am freed from lecturing & some letter writing.

I hope you will enjoy some quiet rest this summer yourself, & Mrs. Furniss, too. We both ask to be remembered to both of you.

       Very thankfully & sincerely yours,
       Hri Peyre

## À Jorge Guillén:

  [letterhead: Le Prieuré, Villeneuve-les-Avignon]
  Le 9 mai 1956

Très cher ami,

Vous m'avez écrit avec cette gentillesse dans l'amitié que vous seul savez avoir et quelques autres Espagnols. Cela m'a fort touché, au cours d'un hiver très chargé d'occupations et de soucis. J'ai mis les bouchées doubles, car je partais en congé sabbatique en mars. Après un mois passé à Paris, à revoir des amis, à travailler, à lutter contre le froid, nous sommes venus chercher, et trouver, le soleil & la joie de vivre dans le Midi. Nous passons ici, en route vers St Paul de Vence, puis vers le Sud-Ouest. Plus tard, si tout va bien, y compris nos finances, nous voudrions aller revoir l'Espagne. Malgré toute la tristesse qui se dégage pour moi de la politique espagnole, ce pays reste le pays de la vérité humaine la plus noble, de la droiture et de l'audace de l'esprit.

On critique beaucoup la France & elle se critique elle-même. Cependant, la vie y reste délicieuse, variée, stimulante. La peinture y est extraordinairement vivante; la littérature moins. Mais la conscience morale du pays reste très belle et les réactions envers les malheurs d'Afrique du Nord font honneur aux intellectuels. Les jeunes érudits que je vois me paraissent extrêmement sérieux & doués. Il y a encore de l'espoir & de l'initiative dans cette vieille Europe.

Je suppose que votre grande période de clameur créatrice se poursuit et que vous donnerez bientôt le magnum opus. Je sais que votre gendre est de plus en plus respecté, & qu'on dit combien sa femme a de part à son succès. Nos amitiés à votre fils et nos très bonnes & affectueuses pensées.

Henri Peyre

## À Saint-John Perse:

C/o American Express<br>Rue Scribe<br>Paris IX<br>Le 8 août 1956

Cher Maître,

Vous n'aimez point, je pense, ce genre de lettre qui est un cri d'admiration suivi d'une requête intéressée. Mais vous m'avez témoigné à diverses reprises quelque indulgence, & cela m'enhardit. Vous savez, je crois, quelle ancienne et fervente admiration j'ai pour votre œuvre.

Je n'ai pu donc résister, vous lisant et vous relisant ("Étroits sont les vaisseaux") dans la dernière NRF, à vous dire combien ce poème est beau—l'un des plus merveilleux de ce siècle. Il a déjà saisi d'admiration et fait frémir plusieurs personnes de ma connaissance. J'en chante autour de moi les louanges.

À Washington, le 29 décembre prochain, doit se réunir l'American Association of Teachers of French. J'en suis le président cette année, ou ces années-ci. Ne voudriez-vous pas accepter, devant les 4 ou 500 membres qui seront là (sur 5000 que nous comptons dans tout le pays), beaucoup amateurs de poésie et serviteurs de notre culture, de lire pendant 20 à 25 minutes une partie de ces vers (ou d'autres). Il n'y aurait à cela ou autour de cela nulle publicité, sinon une annonce dans notre programme, à imprimer vers le 15 septembre, nulle charlatanerie, rien de laid, seulement des gens sérieux qui vous écouteraient avec joie et admiration. Et cela me ferait tellement plaisir!

Je me permets de solliciter une réponse. Je repars fin août pour Yale. Si vous ne pouvez ou ne voulez pas, je comprendrai. Veuillez croire à mes sentiments de très profond dévouement.

Henri Peyre

## To Mina Curtiss:

Sept. 14, 1956

Dear Mrs. Curtiss,

We did indeed have a very enjoyable & fruitful visit. I shall soon write Mr. Léger: I want to go over the Fowlie translation in the *Yale Review* with some care first: but will you tell him that nothing in my whole life has made me more proud than the generous esteem which he bestows upon us. I came back admiring him more than ever before as a person & as a poet: I have met a number of "gens" or "hommes de lettres," some eminent but none so unassuming & true as a human being.

The pleasure was great to get to know you. You have a frankness which went to my heart at once, a direct approach to everything, & at the same time a passionate & idealistic devotion to literature & to beauty. I was much interested by our all too brief entretiens & by your work in progress. I hope to meet you again. Meanwhile the memory of your exquisite house, of the trees & flowers outside, of the woods & brooks around is among the very few which I shall treasure. I have not seen any more attractive country anywhere.

Our best wishes for your trip & very gratefully yours,
Henri Peyre

## À Lester Crocker:

Ce 14—IX—56

Cher Ami,

Je suis rentré d'Europe il y a peu de jours & j'ai trouvé votre article. Il m'a beaucoup plu, car il exprime, fort bien, des réserves à l'égard de

M. Bell que j'aurais voulu formuler moi-même: et j'aime que vous protestiez contre une conception de la tragédie ridiculement étroite, mais à la mode. Vous avez avec vous le bons sens, la pénétration & la variété convaincante des exemples.

Vous devriez certainement enseigner au niveau le plus élevé en ce pays. À votre insu, j'ai plusieurs fois suggéré votre nom: il y a peu de temps, à Edelman, pour Hopkins (pourquoi pas?), & à Spagnoli pour Brooklyn College. On me répond que vous passez pour difficile. Je ne m'en suis pas aperçu. Mais qui de nous ne l'est pas, s'il veut être intègre et franc?

Il y a très, très peu de Français désireux de venir en Amérique: j'en ai consulté plusieurs cet été en France, & nul d'entre les *bons* n'est tenté. Je parlerai à Mlle Brée, que je connais bien, et ailleurs.

Je regrette que le français de Mrs. Bays ne soit pas parfait. Elle est venue un peu tard au français, et je pensais qu'elle se serait beaucoup perfectionnée en Europe. Mais elle intéresserait puissamment les élèves: elle a des idées, de la vie, de la flamme & une belle personnalité. Il y a à J. Hopkins cette année une autre de nos Ph.D.'s, Mrs. Gabrielle Friedman: Français de 1er ordre, intelligente & vive, quoiqu'un peu moins originale. Vous devriez la voir à l'occasion. Son mari enseigne à l'U of Maryland & elle habite à Washington.

[Sans signature]

## To Edgar Furniss:

September 17, 1956

Dear Mr. Furniss:

After a good deal of examination of the present numbers in our courses we are faced with a considerable increase in our courses French 22, 30 and even 42 and, through some shifting around of sections, we find that we do need, as I wrote you last week, an extra sum of probably $2100 for the year, representing seven more hours of assistantship, paid, as you remember, at $300 per hour per year. To keep the future open and perhaps effect a slight saving during the second term, when we may have a little more time from Mr. May and Mr. Douglas (in case we do not give French 50, which is only slightly elected), we are suggesting that some of these assistantship appointments be made for the first term only. The blanks will be ready very soon and I trust all may be in order for these young men to be gratified with their first salary check at the convenience of the Treasurer's office.

The extra young men to whom we are resorting are two experienced assistants who have already taught for us at that rank. We are thus suggesting that the rule limiting the term for assistants to two years be broken exceptionally and that Mr. Tinnin be allowed to serve as assistant with us for a third year, Mr. Desroches for a fourth year. Both should get their Ph.D.'s at the end of the present year. The rule is designed in part to protect them against our exploitation of them; in this case they are both ready and eager to accept the position and we need fear no grudging feeling on their part.

Incidentally, I am not quite clear, even after your letter of last April 18th, of three points. Probably you may answer them quickly:

1) I take it that the salary of assistant professors in their second term remains the same as in their first term, that is $5500.

2) What is the rate for instructors without a Ph.D., since we shall continue to have some in the future? Those with Ph.D.'s are taken away from us very promptly.

3) What would you consider in the future to be the fair salary to be paid to an assistant in instruction? I believe that varies according to departments. We have kept our young men at the rate of $300 per hour per year, that is to say, $1800 for half time. If other departments do differently, I believe we should propose an increase for ours too, so that they do not feel unequally treated. We usually pick young men with experience and we are quite satisfied with their work.

Very sincerely yours,<br>Hri Peyre

## À Saint-John Perse:

Le 24 septembre 1956

Monsieur Alexis Léger
Ambassadeur de France
c/o Mr. Francis Biddle
Wellfleet, Cape Cod
Massachusetts

Cher Monsieur (vous avez été si simple et si cordial avec nous que je me permets d'écarter les titres officiels),

Puis-je vous dire, enfin, combien nous avons été touchés de l'amabilité de votre accueil et quelle joie nous ont donnée ces entretiens, trop brefs, malheureusement? Je ne veux pas vous redire quelle admiration j'éprouve, de longue date, pour votre œuvre de poète, la première de ce temps à mes yeux, et pour votre œuvre, lucide et courageuse, de diplomate. Mais je n'ai jamais eu dans le passé de très grande tendresse pour les diplomates qu'il m'a été donné de rencontrer et que je trouvais ossifiés dans leur mondanité et leurs vues traditionalistes. Quant aux écrivains, leur mignon péché est l'obsession de leur œuvre et de leur moi, et leur moins agréable vice est la soif de publicité et de renommée. La grâce exquise de votre simplicité, l'amour si sincère de la nature et de la vie, le rayonnement de cette humanité que vous incarnez ne m'ont jamais auparavant apparu réunis chez un même personnage. Vous redonnez foi en l'espèce humaine.

J'ai enfin reçu votre très belle lettre, renvoyée de Paris. Je comprends vos raisons. Je vous remercie de les exposer aussi aimablement. Dans le fond, je partage votre avis sur la lecture des vers par un poète, peut-être même par quiconque. J'aime cependant me redire à haute voix, mais seul, les passages de votre œuvre que j'aime le mieux, à côté de quelques autres de poètes français, anglais ou latins, mais une distraction solitaire est autre chose.

Vos idées, exprimées dans la lettre aux jeunes rédacteurs de la revue de Berkeley, m'ont beaucoup frappé. Si, triomphant de votre pudeur, vous vouliez bien les mettre un jour par écrit, ainsi que quelques-unes de vos intentions en matière d'images et de versification, vous rendriez un immense service, non pas à votre œuvre, qui n'en a nul besoin, mais aux critiques à venir. Mais peut-être que la vie posthume d'une œuvre est faite de ces déformations entêtées et que ceux-là mêmes qui chérissent le mieux une œuvre la déforment aussi le plus.

J'ai revu la traduction de Fowlie dans la *Yale Review*. Elle ne saurait satisfaire pleinement celui qui sent l'original dans sa richesse et sa force. Elle n'a pas assez de couleur, de musique; elle fausse parfois un peu. Mais j'en dirais autant de la version de vos *Eloges* par Louise Varèse: elle est exacte en surface, mais combien elle rend pâle et dur ce que vous aviez exprimé avec des prolongements si évocateurs! Par comparaison cependant avec d'autres traducteurs d'ouvrages français en Amérique, je crois que et Louise Varèse et Fowlie, qui savent du moins à fond la langue et peuvent à la rigueur vous demander avis, sont parmi les meilleurs que l'on puisse trouver pour affronter une tâche redoutable.

J'espère que, lors de ce congrès à Washington, nous pourrons avoir la joie de vous rendre visite. Je me permettrai alors, ou quelque temps auparavant, de vous envoyer un mot. Encore merci du fond du cœur de votre gentillesse, et ce poème "Étroits sont les vaisseaux," l'un des plus vibrants et profonds de notre époque. Ma femme joint au mien son souvenir dévoué.

Henri Peyre<br>
Chairman<br>
French Department

## To Edgar Furniss:

September 28, 1956

Dear Mr. Furniss:

Here is the arrangement I am proposing to you for the spending of the sum of $1,400, $600 of which should be tuition (provided in the French department budget for Laboratory Assistants). The sum is used, as you remember, for native French persons to assist undergraduates and occasionally a few graduate students with their phonetics and pronunciation in French. They also are asked to make recordings for our audio-visual centre of French voices reading material studied in the classes. The sum may seem cut up into many small bits. The reason is that it seems advisable to have a variety of different voices and accents. These arrangements are being made for the first term and will, unless the persons concerned do not prove to be satisfactory or available, be continued through the second term.

> Mrs. Marie-Cécile Francis (525 George Street, New Haven) for 6 hours a week as Laboratory Assistant, $300 for the first term, to be paid to her as a stipend in cash.
> Mr. Marc Dupuis (173 Lawrence Street, New Haven), graduate student in Chemistry, graduate of the Ecole Polytechnique, 2 hours a week, $100 for the term.
> Mr. Jean Bataillard (82 York Street, New Haven), graduate student in economics, 3 hours a week, $150 for the term.
> Mr. Jean-Pierre Barret (2695 Yale Station), graduate student in Electrical Engineering, 3 hours a week, $150 for the term.

The total should be $700 for the first term and will be the same amount for the second.

The stipend here mentioned for Messrs. Bataillard and Barret, $150 per term each, will be paid in the form of tuition. The sum should therefore be charged by the Bursar to the French Department budget. The total sum thus paid in the form of tuition will amount to $600 at the end of the year. It is naturally understood that the part of their tuition thus taken over by the French Department should be paid to them out of the equivalent sum made available in their scholarship stipends.

Will you kindly, if you approve, send copies of this letter to the persons whose names are below?

Very sincerely yours,<br>
Henri Peyre

C.c: Deans Simpson and Ferguson
    The Bursar
    The Treasurer

## À Philip Kolb:

Ce 3—X—56

Cher Monsieur,

J'avais lu votre article. Il est un peu méchant, mais très malin, joliment acéré, et puis . . . vous avez raison. C'est une démonstration impeccable. Je n'aime pas tellement les polémiques: mais la "vôtre," déjà vieille, m'a toujours paru un peu vaine. Vous avez démontré le mouvement en marchant: une méthode ne vaut que lorsqu'on l'applique, et en montre aux yeux de tous les résultats, donc l'efficacité. Vous l'avez fait.

Je vais ouvrir avec impatience vos lettres à R Hahn: j'admire votre zèle, votre labeur, et aussi avec quelle ingéniosité vous avez conquis Mme Mante Proust et avez obtenu d'elle ce qu'elle n'accordait guère; elle a eu foi en vous—non sans raison.

Vous ai-je félicité pour votre promotion? Je suppose qu'Illinois vous gardera donc. On ne doit pas y être mal, puisqu'on y peut travailler—et rester si au cœur de tout ce qui est français!

Croyez-moi bien cordialement vôtre
Henri Peyre

## To Frederic Musser:

October 15, 1956

Pfc Frederic O. Musser, Jr.
APO 301
Sans Francisco, California

My dear Musser:

Thanks for your very nice letter. I am answering in English, which I hope will not deter you from writing again in French. Your French was very elegant and not at all affected by the Korean winter or the Chinese ideograms. I had no idea that you were that far, and it is indeed regrettable that, unlike some others of our warriors, you were not sent to France or to Germany. I met a few American GI's last spring traveling in Chinon and in La Rochelle and they appeared quite lost in that strange Rabelaisian country, and certainly most inexperienced in the language. But we cannot question those mysteries.

Since your return might well take place next April, you should have little worry about a position. It may be that one will be available before then; indeed, I shall write to Haverford, reminding them of your availability. But the best would be for you to fill out some forms with our Graduate Placement Office at once, or rather to write back to me or to our secretary, mentioning whom you would like among us to fill out letters concerning you; those letters, three or four in number, will be put into your file. A little later in the year you should send a brief curriculum vitae and a letter a little less dry and factual in character to a number of chairmen in colleges where you think you might wish to teach. I believe we have to trust providence after that, and that the future should take care of itself. Jobs have not been too scarce for your predecessors thus far.

Our very best wishes and those of your colleagues, and bon courage.

Very sincerely yours,
Henri Peyre

## To Edgar Furniss:

October 22, 1956

Dear Mr. Furniss:

I am grateful to you for your note and for having listened with your customary kindness to my suggestions or questions relative to Mr. Andersson's future position here. I am distressed, and a little puzzled, that the important post which a man like him could fill with eminence in connection with the MAT program or the training of educators, educationists and school administrators at Yale should apparently be hard to find. Tug has displayed remarkable qualities as an organizer and as an animator (if the word is English) in his present Modern Language Association position—one of great responsibility. I am convinced that Yale would lose much if it did not find a way to utilize his services where they can do most for us and bring us real prestige.

You might perhaps be kind enough to see if Mr. Griswold (and Mr. Mendenhall, who has known Mr. Andersson as a fellow of his college) would, along with you and Dean DeVane, be willing to mention his name to colleges seeking a president. He would be a good one in many respects. I shall explore possibilities outside myself. Tug would also be a fine person to be attached permanently to one of the Foundations interested in developing the teaching of languages and more generally in reforming American secondary education.

Meanwhile, I should welcome your frank advice on immediate steps to be taken. Mr. Andersson is due to return to Yale after the present academic year. Would his return be to the MAT organization primarily, in some capacity? Or should I provide both courses and his salary for him in our plans and budget for next year? The role he would fill in our own Department would be humble and unworthy of what he has achieved, and of what he has become, while on the MAT and while lent to the MLA. I feel strongly, and my colleagues, Messrs. Auerbach, Boorsch and May agree, that Tug should have the rank of full professor at Yale. Can I propose it; on the understanding that such a proposal fits in with the President's plans to integrate the MAT competent staff with that of Departments? A question of general policy is at stake there and it would be best to have whatever proposal I should make be in harmony with the general plans to assure a standing and a stable future to the MAT program.

I shall, as always, welcome your advice and that of Mr. Griswold. Similar questions are likely to arise concerning Mr. Noyes and several of the members of the present MAT staff.

Very sincerely yours,
Hri Peyre

## To Harry Levin:

October 23, 56

Dear Harry,

I forget whether I heard that you were going to be on leave, & perhaps away, this term, or the next. But I thought I'd write you a line to add my plea to others that, if possible, you convince Dieckmann to stay at Harvard. He is tempted by the prospect of a chair in Germany. I wrote him to dissuade him from accepting. I am convinced that he will find readaptation difficult & may soon be quite unhappy there; and I am convinced that he sees the situation at Harvard as worse than it is — for him. Surely, those two French colleagues of his cannot be so tactless as to persecute him for being a German, & if they do, surely, they can only harm themselves & win neither sympathy nor esteem in Cambridge! Dieckmann's *Voyage de Bougainville* is a very thoughtful & expert piece; he has more good books to give, & he brings a meticulousness of method joined to a philosophical culture & to a penetrating insight which French studies need badly in this country. I hope the atmosphere can be purified in the Romance Department thanks to your own efforts & skill so as to make it possible for poor Herbert to breathe happily there.

Incidentally, may I congratulate you on Geoffrey Bush's book: it clearly owes you a good deal, even to your manner of writing? But it is also an original & fresh piece of work, uncannily wise for such a young man, & written with polish, art & vigor — a remarkable little book in every way. I wrote him to tell him so. You may be proud to have inspired & trained in part such a critic & such a writer. Il ira loin!

Will you not kindly pay us a visit here — have lunch, say, on your way to New York once? With a few days' notice, so that I be sure not to be disappointed by having made other plans if you were to stop here. I should be very deeply happy if you would come [*or:* once].

My very cordial regards,
Henri

## À Philip Kolb:

Ce 28 — X — 56

Cher Monsieur,

Vous avez fait là un beau livre et Gallimard l'a scrupuleusement et bellement édité. Votre préface est très joliment écrite & dit tout avec concision. Vos notes sont riches sans jamais offusquer, et préviennent toutes les questions. Les lettres elles-mêmes sont du Proust qui, je l'avoue, me plaît le moins: mais elles révèlent l'autre, cette obsession qui m'a toujours intrigué chez lui du processus par lequel les œuvres nouvelles réussissent à s'imposer après avoir été mécomprises. Comme le tragique secret de la vie intime de Proust, que révèle son œuvre, apparaît peu & mal dans toutes ses lettres: son enfer privé, ses angoisses sentimentales et passionnelles! Peut-être est-ce mieux ainsi pour sa grandeur auprès de nous.

Votre travail d'archiviste, d'historien & d'exégète, et tout bonnement de lutteur pour préserver ces textes a dû être énorme. Mais vous êtes des très rares parmi nous qui êtes assuré de survivre, marié à jamais à votre connaissance de Proust.

Merci de votre grande amabilité envers moi & croyez-moi

Votre très fidèle,
Henri Peyre

## À Jean-Jacques Demorest:

Ce 28—X—1956

Cher Monsieur,

Je ne vous connaissais pas ce don de romancier. Je savais un peu très peu que vous êtes la modestie même, votre magnifique rôle dans cette guerre. Mais vous avez su rendre avec une vérité rare ces dialogues de militaires, peindre leur vie extérieure et, sans phrases, sans pompe, très simplement, leur courage silencieux, leur don de camaraderie & de loyauté, leur patriotisme. Votre livre m'a ému—et il est remarquablement bien écrit. Vos petites phrases, acérées, évocatrices, charnues, coupant court à toute éloquence, rendent admirablement l'atmosphère et l'état d'âme de ces passionnés à qui la France doit tout, et son honneur. Je vous remercie et d'avoir écrit ce livre, & de me l'avoir envoyé.

Comment vont les choses à Cornell? Y êtes-vous heureux? Il y a là d'immenses possibilités de développement pour le français et pour la littérature. J'espère qu'on vous accordera les moyens nécessaires. Croyez à mes bons vœux et à la très grande estime que m'inspire en vous l'homme en même temps que l'auteur—

Henri Peyre

## To Harry Levin:

November 26, 1956

Dear Harry,

I appreciate your confidence and your friendship immensely. I should indeed regret it, for Dieckmann personally (for he would not long be happy in Germany), but does he wish to be? Santayana must have ranked him among the unhappy few of whom he said that "if artists are unhappy, it is after all because happiness does not interest them," and for Harvard and all of us in the modern language field in America. He is a man who must feel that he has friends who do not eye him with suspicion and who even accept his occasional strictures or his own suspicion of them in good grace. Such men do exist. With you and Frohock and some of the young men in the Romance Department at Harvard, he could work in trust and harmony.

The suggestion to fill the eventual vacancy with Hytier has advantages—more apparent perhaps than real. Since you invite me to, I shall venture to express my views on it.

I do not set too much store by the nationalistic side of the issue, as you know. If the foreigner is a man of recognized and superior merits and works for others and not just for himself, he soon attracts students and in turn opens up more opportunities and even more positions for young American scholars. The technical nationality of the man counts much less, in my eyes, than his adaptability to the American system and his readiness to serve. Spitzer is admirable, probably the one genius among us; Poulet is admirable, within limits; but they have not trained disciples, attracted students, and thus served Johns Hopkins as they might have.

I am very fond of Hytier, who is the sweetest of men, in a way at the opposite pole from Dieckmann: paying such compliments to his colleagues and to the books of younger men that it spares him all polemics and all involvement. He is the acutest critic of modern literature of all of us Frenchmen in this country. The few graduate students in whom he takes an interest work fruitfully with him.

But he keeps aloof, devotes himself to his own research and writing almost exclusively, pretends not to be familiar enough with English to sit on committees, even on examination committees; he throws no radiation outside, if I may be permitted such a cliché, stays away from conventions and lectures at other institutions. The part he has thus played in American academic and cultural life is therefore not commensurate with his talent. If Harvard wants a name, a subtle critic who will do two or three more astute books like his *Gide* (or like his *Valéry*, though the latter was less remarkable) and direct a few graduate students of proved ability, Hytier is the man. Any *ad hoc* committee would have to recognize that unanimously, as they did in the case of Jasinski.

But is an *ad hoc* committee the best judge of the situation? Admirable as the institution is, I have doubts. Mr. A., professor of English at Harvard, Mr. B., professor of Comparative Literature at Yale, Mr. C., professor of French elsewhere, will necessarily agree as to Hytier's, Jasinski's eminence. But they will not, and cannot, "repenser" rethink the problems of the Department as those problems should be "rethought."

Personalities count. Two important Frenchmen at the top will have allies, will fight together—and it is regrettable that one should at once use that non-irenic word "fight" à propos of that department. They will be about the same age group, Hytier a few years younger than Jasinski, who was born in July 1898. They will retire within a few years of each other. Will there then be younger men, staggered in several age groups, able to take over with *éclat*?

But the more important question seems to me to be: it is all very well to give excellent graduate courses and to have time for one's own research. But someone must: 1) attract the very best graduate students from all over the country. That often requires visiting other colleges, having friends there, guiding the vocation of future graduate scholars, and a good deal of activity outside one's own study room; 2) place the graduate students once trained where they will be happy, but also useful to the Harvard Department which trained them, will recruit promising young men for it. This is best done by two or three professors, American or French (Morize did it splendidly), who are known and seen outside, consent to do the minimum of politics required; 3) in the humanities and in the sciences, we, professors in the large universities who naturally prefer to teach graduate students already developed (and, in French, supposedly masters of the language and of the elements of literature), have signally failed lately. We attract far too few able undergraduates to our profession. For, to attract them requires the giving of undergraduate courses, even of freshmen or sophomore courses, for that is the stage when vocations are decided. We prefer to leave such courses to untrained young men. The result has been ascertained and is to be deplored: the best scientists and science teachers, often too the best literary scholars come from the smaller undergraduate colleges where they have received more attention from teachers who, not being preoccupied primarily by their graduate classes and their research, took greater pains to arouse vocations in their field.

We must all reverse that trend. Harvard has a much bigger role to play in the training of teachers of French and of scholars in French and Spanish. Under your leadership, with the help of Frohock in whom my own faith is great, it can play such a role. But frankly the Hytier appointment would not promote such an end conspicuously. It will only put off the issue.

I believe a committee headed by you, with members delegated by the overseers, should reexamine all the problems, the structure and the prospects of your Romance department and present comprehensive plans. Piecemeal appointments, however brilliant, will not suffice. We, at Yale and elsewhere, would all gain from a clear formulation of some of the problems confronting us all, to a greater or lesser degree, which Harvard might offer.

Wadsworth, I hardly know, but clearly, where publications are concerned, he is not a strong case. Hubert is too subtle, at times erratic, but he has much to say that is penetrating and original. Is he the man to attract undergraduates to French studies? I doubt it. From Harvard and Radcliffe students who took French there and were attracted to it, one hears that the inspiring teachers, whose departure they lamented or would lament, were or are Shattuck, Morris. But I am falling into Yale nationalism, on the very morning (when I am scribbling this at home) of our annual football encounter! Have mercy upon me!

As usual, it is dangerous to suggest that I suggest anything. For I am all too explicit and as profuse a giver of advice as the Secretary of State himself.

Most cordially yours,
Henri Peyre

## To William DeVane:

December 5, 1956

Dear Dean DeVane:

I am sending herewith the appointment blanks for the three assistants in instruction who were appointed only for the first term, Messrs. Freeman, Kolakowski and Proulx. In the case of Freeman, we have reduced his number of hours from 8 to 5, and his salary will in consequence be only $750.00 for the second term.

We are rearranging our second term courses as follows:

Professor Auerbach (away on leave of absence for the Spring Term) will be replaced in French 50 by Mr. Douglas.
Professor Boorsch, back from leave of absence, will teach the second term of French 54.

We are making the following changes, necessitated by our desire to give Mr. Freeman only 5 hours and thus to save the University $450.00:

French 15:2 will be given by Mrs. Lang instead of Mr. Duisit;
French 15:3 will be taken over by Mr. Duisit, replacing Mrs. Lang;
French 32:3 will be taken over by Mr. Buffum replacing Mr. Freeman;
French 42:3 will be taken by Mr. May (whose graduate course does not continue into the second term) replacing Mr. Duisit;
French 42:4 will be given by Mr. Duisit replacing Mr. Capretz;
French 43 will be given by Mr. Boorsch replacing Mr. May.

Mr. Capretz is giving a great deal of time and attention to the audio-visual work in French, done in the Library quarters. The number of students utilizing that audio-visual laboratory is considerably greater than ever before, which is very gratifying to both Mr. Kone and us. That work is an essential adjunct of language teaching as we now conceive it, and we are releasing Mr. Capretz of the equivalent of three hours a week in compensation for the many hours which he devotes to the audio-visual side of our teaching. So important is the work that we should like to make an urgent plea that more funds be allotted next year to the laboratory assistants, for whom only $1,400 was provided in our budget and is again being requested in the budget for 1957–58. We could profitably use twice that amount, which we are now parsimoniously dividing among three laboratory assistants so as to have a variety of voice and accents.

I am taking the opportunity to ask another question which I hope will not appear as unduly hurrying the examination of our French Department budget by the Deans and the Executive Committee: it is proving extremely difficult, in view of competition from other universities, to find the right man for the replacement of Professor Richardson, retiring next July, in his graduate courses in Old French and Romance Philology. If I am going to act promptly and secure a scholar of more than adequate competence, probably from abroad, I would have to be assured that the sum requested in the budget will be available, so that I may start negotiations without delay. As you may have noticed, the sum was for $8,000 — $1,000 less than the salary received this year by Mr. Richardson. I should like to get some assurance that negotiations, which will take time, are in order at the present stage.

Very sincerely yours,<br>Henri Peyre

C.c. Mr. Furniss

Explanations on the Need for<br>an Appointment in Romance Philology<br>(to replace Professor H. B. Richardson)

Every graduate department in English, French, German, Spanish must devote one fourth or one third of its work to the history of the language, which future teachers will teach, the syntax and structure of that language, the earlier periods of the evolution of that language and the literary works produced before the so-called modern era, i.e. the Renaissance. Language will be what most Ph.D.'s will have to teach later in life, as a prerequisite to foreign literature and because of its usefulness and of the liberalizing value of such a study, and it would be sheer highbrow hypocrisy not to prepare them for such an important part of their future work.

For French in particular, the older literature extends through several centuries (the eleventh to the fifteenth): it was exceptionally rich and it exercised a profound influence on the rest of Europe. For many decades, the preparation of Ph.D.'s in French was almost exclusively centered on the philology and literature of the Middle Ages. The emphasis then shifted to the more recent centuries; but a solid knowledge of the French Middle Ages remains indispensable to a future teacher of French.

Such a student, if he is a candidate for the Ph.D., must take a general introductory course (Romance 100b with us), then Old French Language (103a), a general course on Old French Literature (103b), and a more advanced course in one aspect of French literature, such as 114b, 107b. He must take further work in Provençal and in Romance Linguistics if he is a candidate for the Ph.D. in Romance Philology. These requirements are not just traditional ones. They are essential to a true perspective on French culture and to an adequate mastery of the language.

The giving of such courses poses difficult problems. Scholars are required who have a solid grounding in the Classics, in Vulgar Latin and in Medieval Latin; they must also have competence in Old Provençal and in the field of Romania [which, geographically, extended from Portugal to Rumania]. One of the scholars offering these courses should be primarily a philologist and historian of the language; the other one a literary scholar, able to relate the literature of the French Middle Ages to the art, the theology, the philosophy, the history of that period.

At the present time in America, it is hardly possible to find a younger man already advanced enough in the Classics, in Linguistics and Philology, in three or four Romance languages, to offer those difficult courses to graduate students. Few men publish much in that field before they are thirty-five or forty. Yet it is desirable that those giving graduate courses be well enough known to attract students to us from several parts of the country. They should be men with substantial publications. We always had at least two men working in that field at Yale: Raymond T. Hill and Henry B. Richardson, more lately Erich Auerbach and Henry B. Richardson, and a younger man, Howard Garey. Such men, while on the French Department budget, have given part of their time to students from Spanish and Italian, often also from English. Since 1935 or 1938, the number of our graduate students has increased from an average figure of 15 or 20 to an average figure of 50 or 60 or more (approximately 15 or 20 are admitted, selectively, every year). We have moreover to teach a substantial number of MAT students, for whom a course on the structure of the French language is essential, since their task will consist in teaching language at the school level and only very exceptionally literature. We must, if anything, strengthen the philological and linguistic side of our offerings.

The competition for scholars in Romance Philology and in the Middle Ages has become very keen lately. This country and European countries have trained few qualified men in a field which presupposed a good mastery of Latin. Our inquiry at seven or eight other universities has yielded scant result. We must, however, continue to offer at least six (term) courses in the field: 100b, 103a, 103b, 111a, 107b, 108b, 101 (see list enclosed); plus one three-hour undergraduate course in Medieval Literature. We are to have Professor Auerbach with us until 1961; we hope to entrust Mr. Garey with at least two term courses. The post which Professor Richardson occupies at present must be filled by another man, at least at the Associate Professor level, for no younger man is adequately equipped.

For next year (1957–58), we may be able to manage with an appointment of a visiting professor for one term, at a salary of $5,500. But we should in all likelihood request a salary of $8,000 at least the following year if we are to retain an able man against probably stiff competition from other graduate schools. It would be short-sighted not to continue providing our graduate students in French (there are over fifty of them, and their quality is high) with a training meeting their expectations and their high intellectual quality.

Hri Peyre

## À Judd Hubert:

Ce 5—XII—56

Cher ami,

Merci de votre mot. Je serai heureux de vous lire sur Racine—et même un jour sur Campistron ou Lagrange Chancel! Mais ne vous laissez pas intimider à l'excès par quelques réserves, faites naguère par d'autres & par moi, sur votre subtilité raffinée. Ne devenez pas historien littéraire à la vieille mode! Et allez à quelque grand sujet que vous prendrez droitement, "bêtement" mais à pleins bras. Harvard aurait bien tort de se passer de vous & j'espère encore que tel ne sera pas le cas. J'ai écrit mon sentiment à Levin mais je crains de n'être pas trop persona grata auprès de Jasinski.

Mais si le pire survenait, vae Harvard! Vous iriez ailleurs. Il y aura des places cette année, je crois, même pour des hommes déjà avancés comme vous (avancés en maturité et en talent).

Vous auriez eu le Guggenheim de haute main & vous l'aurez quand vous voudrez avec un bon projet. Rien ne presse.

Mes amitiés à votre femme & bien à vous. Quelle sorte d'hiver allez-vous passer, dans le froid, sans essence, quand janvier va souffler son vent mélancolique à l'entour des marbres du Père Lachaise?

Hri Peyre

## À Jorge Guillén:

Ce 19—XII—56

Cher Ami,

Je suis heureux de cette nouvelle, & fier, une fois de plus, de vous connaître. Ce "challenge" d'une telle invitation n'est pas à dédaigner: il sera bon que vous soyez contraint de jeter par écrit quelques-unes de vos vues sur la poésie. Et votre production n'en souffrira pas: vous êtes à la grande période de second enfantement, la plus féconde de toutes. Votre récent "Dolor" était admirable & m'a beaucoup ému. J'avais espéré que, si ce n'était St John Perse (c'était lui mon candidat), le prix Nobel vous serait allé. Mais il est bien que ce soit l'Espagne en tous cas, dans ce qu'elle a de poétique (et aussi d'un peu vieille fille susceptible).

Je redoute Washington & ce qu'a de dégradant, de privé de tout idéalisme, ce genre de réunion. Mais je serai heureux de vous y apercevoir. Votre fille & sa famille vont bien, j'espère? Et votre brillant et séduisant & volage fils?

Croyez à nos amitiés de tous deux & à nos vœux fervents,
Henri Peyre

## To Malcolm McIntosh:

Jan. 5—57

My dear McIntosh:

It is good of you to keep me informed. I believe you might well write M. Moraud Jr., whom I know quite well, telling him you were pleased to meet him & would like to work with him. It is an excellent college. I shall write to several places, mentioning you: Franklin-Marshall for ex. in Pa, the Univ of New Hampshire &, if the occasion arises, institutions on or near the Pacific Coast. I imagine your file at our Graduate School has been kept up to date? If not, you should check by letter with Mrs. Margaret Armstrong, who is in charge of our Placement Bureau. If Lafayette does not make a move to increase your salary & better your rank, you should try & leave.

Your article is good & well written. You have a real instinct for scholarship & literary texts.

I was pleased to see your wife again, not too saddened by your Southern experience.

Very cordially,
Henri Peyre

## To Joseph Barker:

January 11, 1957

Professor Joseph Barker
Department of Romance Languages
Sweet Briar College
Sweet Briar, Virginia

Dear Professor Barker:

I had heard from your President that your health has given you quite some trouble during December, and I was very sorry indeed. You have been working very hard over all those years and ever since your admirable wife left you in great solitude. You have withstood everything with courage, and I only hope that the task of finding one or several successors for the many jobs you accomplished will not prove too arduous.

I mentioned to Mrs. Pannell a few of the questions which people in our profession sometimes ask about the future of the Junior Year. She answered very kindly, knowing my old and persistent interest in the Junior Year that Sweet Briar has magnificently recreated since the end of the War. My questions aim at one thing: since a number of other colleges want to emulate Sweet Briar's example, I thought it would be good of Sweet Briar to reaffirm the continuity of its Junior Year organization, and perhaps to bring a number of improvements to the outstanding work already accomplished, such as more backing from foundations, larger number of scholarships, and perhaps more of an effort to attract young men from disciplines other than French, and even other than the Humanities. I hope I didn't appear to be an intruder in all this. Whatever is done in the future, you know, and this is no idle compliment, that the debt of gratitude that American education owes you and your college will never be forgotten. We are all immensely grateful to the vision and to the devotion that you and your wife displayed in the dismal years following World War II.

You probably made the right decision about L, and I am glad that Bégué accepted. Another person who would, I think, do very well as director in charge for a year and who has made an excellent impression on me is Walter Secor, of Denison University. He, of course, knows French well, is practical and clear-headed, as well as a pleasant gentleman, and you might well wish to have a word with him some time in the near future and receive a personal impression of his qualifications. If I can help discovering the rare man whom you are searching, I shall be glad to.

As to Mlle Idoine, she is certainly excellently fitted for the position, as would Gabrielle Friedman be some other year, if she is still interested. Mlle Idoine is probably a little more mature, and she will have a fine authority over the young ladies of your group.

Many thanks for your letter and

Very sincerely yours,
Henri Peyre

## À Frederic Musser:

Le 21 janvier 1957

Sp3 Frederic O. Musser, Jr.
APO 301 Sans Francisco, California

Cher Monsieur Musser,

Vous êtes le plus précis et le plus ponctuel des guerriers et l'Asie ne fera que vous rendre plus occidental, si cela veut dire clair d'esprit et riche de plans d'avenir. Votre longue épreuve, que vous avez subie avec courage, va enfin se terminer. Vous serez heureux de revenir vers les climats plus doux et vers notre atmosphère plus molle mais plus reposante.

Vous nous faites beaucoup d'honneur à songer à Yale d'abord et à désirer surtout enseigner dans votre seconde alma mater. Il n'est pas impossible qu'une vacance se produise chez nous, mais je n'en serai assuré que plus tard et je crois que vous ne devriez pas perdre une occasion d'un poste qui pourrait se présenter auparavant et qui serait tentant. Ce n'est pas tant parce qu'une vacance chez nous pourrait n'être que pour deux ou trois années; tel est aussi le cas ailleurs et l'avenir ne doit pas vous inspirer de craintes. Mais la raison pour laquelle j'ai l'air de vous pousser d'abord vers d'autres endroits est que nous avons plutôt besoin d'un ou de deux futurs médiévistes, et qu'il est de votre intérêt d'acquérir ailleurs une expérience différente, d'observer d'autres méthodes.

Je vous récrirai bientôt si, ici, quelque chose pouvait s'offrir. En attendant, je donnerai aussi votre nom à des universités de premier ordre où vous pourriez trouver un poste (Harvard, Reed College, Brown). Ecrivez de votre côté très prochainement aux chairmen à Harvard, Brown, Princeton, Cornell, Northwestern, Amherst, Oberlin et aux Deans de Reed College, Wesleyan, Rochester. Je vois que vous n'avez pas trop de goût pour les Universités d'état du Middle West. À certains égards, elles offrent cependant le plus d'avantages. C'est souvent le hasard, selon les postes disponibles, qui décide de ces questions de placement.

Croyez à mon souvenir le meilleur,
Henri Peyre

## To Edgar Furniss:

February 4, 1957

Dear Mr. Furniss:

As you and Dean DeVane know, I have tried pretty hard, and I am still trying, to find a scholar of some eminence to come here as an associate professor and replace Professor H. B. Richardson, who is retiring at the end of the present academic year. The field, because it requires a competence in the classical languages as well as in three or four Romance languages and a long preliminary training, is one in which very few scholars have been trained in the last few years in this country. After writing a number of letters to colleagues in Romance philology and medieval French literature at other institutions and abroad, I have come to the tentative conclusion that it would be best to wait another year until we find a scholar who is really first-rate whom we can appoint. This would mean leaving the money requested in the budget unused for a year, with the assurance that it would be available for us the following year. Some of my colleagues fear that this may be a dangerous procedure and would almost favor appointing a second-rate, or at least a person less good, so as to be sure that the money will not be taken away from us for having been left unused for a year.

It is not my nature to be suspicious of the Administration, which has always understood our needs and helped us fill them when they were reasonable. I should myself much prefer searching extensively for another year and making the right appointment to a position which is so very important in a self-respecting Department of Romance Languages. I should feel stronger in explaining the case to my colleagues if you would kindly approve of the policy which I favor and write me a brief note accordingly. Of the need for such an appointment there is, I trust, little doubt in the minds of those who know our Department and our Graduate School here.

Very sincerely yours,
Hri Peyre

## To Frederic Musser:

February 15, 1957

Pvt. Frederic O. Musser, US 52 407 002
APO 301 San Francisco, California
Dear Mr. Musser:

One of the Universities where we have recommended you has shown great interest in you: Bucknell University in Lewisburg, Pennsylvania. There is clearly quite a future there for someone who would have the ambition to become chairman of a small department and who would like to live in beautiful surroundings and in what is becoming a better and better place among the not too famous universities. The scenery, if that matters to a young teacher, is as beautiful as anywhere in the country. Life appeared to me very quiet there and the atmosphere favorable to research. The faculty work in close cooperation among the several departments and the whole spirit is one of stress on philosophy and the humanities.

The lady with whom I corresponded wrote you twice, Mrs. Cook, is very anxious to have an answer from you. I told her on the phone that you probably were either being sent back to this country or hesitating between her approach and others. You are free to decide, of course, but having been at the place, I may say that, while you would not find there the intellectual atmosphere of Yale or Harvard, you would certainly find there many pleasant compensations.

We hope to see you back in civilian life some time this spring, and I send my very best wishes.

Very sincerely yours,
Henri Peyre

## Au même:

Ce 20.II.57

Cher M. Musser,

Vite je réponds à votre mot. Ne vous inquiétez pas pour les postes. Je crois qu'il y en aura, surtout vers l'ouest (Californie) & le Middle

West, et jusqu'au mois de juin encore. Bucknell n'est pas un endroit de tout premier ordre; ce n'est pas si mal que vous croyez d'ailleurs & vous pourriez y être heureux, avec de belles perspectives d'avancement & d'avenir. Mais vous pourriez aussi ne pas y rester; tout dépendra ou dépendrait de vous (publications, activité aux réunions professionnelles, réputation acquise par vos efforts).

Vous ne risquez pas grand'chose à dire "non" si tel est votre sentiment. Vous irez ailleurs, voilà tout; et de toute manière, vous devriez peut-être gagner plus de $4000, vous pourriez demander 4500, sans marchander indûment, et différer une réponse en disant que vous êtes pressenti ailleurs pour d'autres offres. Mrs. Cook est pressée, mais elle est aimable et comprendra ou elle choisira quelqu'un d'autre si elle préfère. Si vous voulez même ne vous décider qu'une fois rentré aux USA, vous pouvez le faire. Quand *exactement* rentrez-vous? Ne pouvez-vous obtenir un congé qui raccourcisse votre service? Avez-vous le temps, en attendant, de songer à quelque article, à quelque chose à méditer & à publier, sur le XVIIe siècle, ou sur je ne sais quoi, Loti & le Japon, Gobineau & l'Asie, Claudel & la Chine, etc.? Avez-vous quelques livres là bas?

Ne vous tracassez donc pas & décidez absolument selon ce que vous croyez bon *pour vous,* selon vos goûts. Les grandes universités, poussant à la publication, vous menaçant sans cesse de vous laisser partir, créent, pour certains, un état de tension déplaisant; pour d'autres, elles offrent un stimulant avec ce risque. À chacun à choisir.

Amitiés,
Henri Peyre

## To Whitney Griswold:

March 13, 1957

President A. Whitney Griswold
President of Yale University
Woodbridge Hall
Dear Whit:

As you have probably heard, some hesitation is being evinced by members of the Board of Permanent Officers of the Graduate School to the proposal to make Nelson Brooks an associate professor in the department of French and in the MAT program, through a joint appointment. The man himself is acknowledged to be very fine and no objection is raised to him or to the French Department's need for him and eagerness to have him as one of theirs. The hesitation stems from the feeling that "second-class" appointments may be thus palmed off on the high-minded Graduate School Faculty and that the MAT program teachers of teachers would more fittingly belong to another faculty so that the "Noli me tangere" attitude of the Graduate School may be preserved.

Obviously it will take more than my feeble eloquence to convince those lofty-minded gentlemen that we have to pay more attention to training scholars who can teach and that unless we do, we shall dry up the recruitment of good teacher-scholars. It seems clear to me that this is a test-case which should be explained in the persuasive voice of the President himself. My conviction is that we fail conspicuously at Yale to train teachers of science in particular and to foster and elicit scientific vocations from our freshmen and sophomores: hence our glaring lack of balance between science majors and majors in American Studies, International Relations, English and such subjects. The MAT program should help us right here, and not only the schools, provided more cooperation is shown from the Faculties. Our fervent hopes, rolled into a neat ball, are placed on your lap. A president is a Sisyphus, determinedly rolling boulders up the hills of our rocky university.

Sincerely yours,
Hri Peyre

## À Keith Botsford:

[carte postale]
Mars 27—(1957)

Cher M. Botsford,

Bien, sûr, j'écris avec plaisir à Porto Rico & j'espère que ce séjour vous conviendrait—bien qu'un milieu américain puisse être, à la longue, plus salubre & plus stimulant. Bien sûr, vous avez dû mûrir et grandir depuis, et je sais que vos livres sont admirés de ceux qui s'y connaissent.

Merci de vos bonnes nouvelles et notre souvenir à votre femme.

Henri Peyre

## To William DeVane:

April 9, 1957

Dean William C. DeVane
Dean of Yale College
109 Strathcona Hall
Dear Dean DeVane:

The professors and associate professors of the French Department are unanimously recommending that Nelson Brooks, at present lecturer in language and Research Associate in the Master of Arts in Teaching Program at Yale, be made, through a joint appointment with the MAT program, Associate Professor of French with indefinite tenure.

Our Department, and presumably other departments of language and still others in the sciences and other fields, has long, and not very successfully, tried to solve the following problem: a large part of its work in Yale College consists of divisional courses (some, like French 22, with as many as ten or twelve sections) taken mostly by Freshmen and Sophomores. Such courses are given by younger members of the French Department and can only prove adequate if they are supervised and directed by a more experienced and, if possible, a permanent older member of the Department. But most of our permanent members are already occupied with our majors, our seven advanced courses (50 to 56) and our large number of graduate students (fifty or more, plus thirty from the MAT program and from Comparative Literature). Our practice has been in the last few years to have those essential language courses of ours directed by assistant professors who left Yale after a few years because their scholarship and their promises brought them enviable offers elsewhere. These young men were not especially interested in techniques of teaching or in improving those language courses; for they knew that their own future depended on their scholarly production, which was usually in the field of philology or literature. We clearly need an experienced teacher, a man with authority and, of course, with a first-rate mind, whose main concern is with the improvement of methods and ways of teaching and the training of our graduate students in such techniques. For, more probably than in English, history or the social sciences, we encounter a difficulty in the training of our graduate students: their advanced work consists of subtle analysis of texts, of literary scholarship, of discussion of ideas underlying French literature or of very learned philological and linguistic courses; but for several years, once their Ph.D. is obtained, they have to teach chiefly language, composition, conversation, grammar, and we do not prepare them specifically for what they will be asked to do, but only for far more advanced work and research.

We welcomed the creation of the MAT program a few years ago because we hoped that we could thus make our graduate teaching more practical through the competence of Mr. Nelson Brooks, appointed with Mr. Theodore Andersson on that program. Both were eager to teach MAT students and our own graduate students how to teach. At the same time, however, Mr. Theodore Andersson, who had been appointed in 1946 to supervise our language courses in Yale College and the Freshman Year, was taken away from us and has since been engrossed by other tasks. We now propose to fill the gap in our department by entrusting the direction of French 22, and probably later the direction of all our work with Freshmen (we have about 450 of them) and of much of our undergraduate language work, to Mr. Nelson Brooks. Mr. Brooks would teach one section of French 22 (five hours a week), would direct that large divisional course and brief the younger men giving it, and would in time take over even more of our language work. He would at the same time carry on part of his very able work in teacher-training in the MAT program. We are convinced that, while Mr. Brooks may not have done quite so much of the traditional scholarly publication in literature that we require from our associate professors concerned more directly with literary work, he has done a great deal of other work (along the lines of teacher-training, of reform of language work in the schools, of improvement of tests and of techniques, and a not inconsiderable amount of writing also) which designates him for the appointment which we contemplate. The letters here collected testify to the wisdom of our prospective appointment; they all endorse it heartily and express the conviction that Mr. Brooks is a man of sharp intellect whose appointment in Yale College will strengthen our faculty and enable the French Department to discharge its duties or services to Yale College most efficiently through a more expert handling of the courses satisfying the language requirement.

Mr. Brooks, born in 1902 in Hartford, Connecticut, was trained at Yale (Ph.B. 1927, Ph.D. 1934). His doctoral thesis was in the field of literature and dealt very ably with a French poet and thinker of the second half of the nineteenth century, Jean Lahor. He taught at Yale as an instructor between 1927 and 1936. Circumstances, such as the Depression and the shrinking of modern language teaching then, forced him to accept a position in an excellent private school (Westover School). Mr. Brooks' heavy load of work there never stopped him from reflecting assiduously on how to improve teaching methods and how to devise new ones.

When, in 1950 or thereabout, the country evinced its determination to rebuild its foreign language teaching, Mr. Brooks was called to give summer courses at Columbia University and at Yale. He then joined our MAT program in 1954 and at once impressed us by the excellence of the course he gave in the MAT program on "Foreign Languages for Teachers," which proved to be a course of high intellectual and scientific quality as well as of practical usefulness. He won the admiration of those who consulted him on problems of language teaching through the great sharpness of his analytical faculty and the loftiness of his standards. He spared no time and no effort in devoting himself to usually unrewarding and unrewarded tasks, such as preparing language tests for college entrance, composing syllabi and organizing material for teaching younger children a foreign language, and, last but not least, training teachers. His teacher training has been both practical and theoretical; we consider that, of all the men on our regular staff and of most men outside Yale, Mr. Brooks is the most competent to define the relationship of language learning to the study of literature and culture, and to the neighboring fields of psychology, descriptive linguistics and cultural anthropology.

Mr. Brooks has been called outside, especially by the Foreign Language Program of the Modern Language Association (organized through a Rockefeller Foundation grant), to advise on teacher training, to devise and write the syllabi indispensable to teachers of French in the elementary schools, and to place at the disposal of the Association and of the profession as a whole the experience he had acquired and the thinking he had done on language teaching. As letters here adduced show, his standing is high among scholars in the country who recognize the importance of the revolution in language teaching which Mr. Brooks, among others, has helped develop.

The publications of Mr. Brooks are composed, for the main part, of brief but pregnant reports on tests and the use of tests in language teaching, of syllabi for the teaching of beginning French in schools, of book reviews. He is very active intellectually and we know that our graduate students, our teachers of French in Yale College will be impressed by the rigor and the sharpness of his mind. He is now at work on a book, *Learning Another Language*, of which close to a hundred pages, already written, are here included. Far from us to claim for Mr. Brooks the profundity and the originality to which eminent Yale linguists have accustomed us. His achievements are more modest, but we are convinced that they are nonetheless considerable and we are happy to propose that Mr. Brooks thus be the first man whom we may invite to serve jointly as a member of our Department as Associate Professor. The move is not a sudden one, or one proposed for purely opportunistic reasons. We have thought long about it and are convinced it will serve language teaching and the training of future teachers and professors in our field at Yale.

The salary of Mr. Brooks will be provided, for the main part, by the MAT program and only to the extent of $1,500 by the French department, which is the sum available in our budget for the coming year. While this is not necessarily a precedent for the desirable integration of other MAT teachers into the regular Yale Faculty, and every case will have to be judged by the Department concerned on its own merits, we are very happy to initiate a much closer, and mutually profitable, cooperation between the MAT program and our Department. We believe we are thus serving Yale and our profession at large.

[Names of writers of letters in support of Nelson Brooks follow.]

Very sincerely yours,
Henri Peyre

## To Joseph Barker:

April 16, 57

Dear Mr. Barker:

It is very thoughtful & kind of you to let me know of the decision happily taken. We know how delicate it was to select the right man for a post which requires judgment, tact, imagination, unusual human warmth, & a gift to inspire & to attract confidence. It was all the more difficult to pick the right person, as, for many years, all the qualities required had been encountered in you & Mrs. Barker. We congratulate you & offer our best wishes to the new incumbent, & we shall be pleased to collaborate with him to the best of our good will. He may perhaps, while he is not too far off as yet, come & pay us a visit here one day this spring.

My very cordial thanks & regards.
Hri Peyre

## À Judd Hubert:

Ce 25—IV—57

Mon cher Ami,

Merci de vos bonnes nouvelles. Vous voilà donc docteur ou presque!

Pour notre n° sur le roman, nous avons refusé tout ce qui a trait au roman déjà ancien (même Proust, Gide, etc.). Le but est de faire connaître les nouveaux romanciers, ceux d'après 1930–35. Je crois donc que nous allons refuser l'article sur Proust & l'Affaire. Mais nous aurons un n° sur Proust dans un an ou un an ½. Le sujet est joli & neuf. Gardez-le.

Pour le n° sur Symbole Symbolisme (dû novembre 1er), un article (10–12 pages imprimées maximum, en anglais) sur cet aspect de Baudelaire devrait aller. L'idée est ingénieuse. Ne soyez pas trop, trop subtil, notre public est un peu, ou veut être, le *grand* public!

[Sans signature]

## To Harry Levin:

June 12, 1957

Dear Harry,

I suppose you are soon to return from California, refreshed & happy at finding your own setting & the Widener, & a few of the headaches which keep an administering mind from lethargy. As our own term drew to an end & I shook off a few of my minor headaches, I experienced a great delight in reading your Contexts of Criticism. The book seemed severe at first to a tired mind; but it was soon carried away by your wit & your originality, such colossal learning so lightly carried, your awareness of all that is alive in the contemporary world, your expert manner of addressing philologists, graduate societies, fellow critics, Joyceans . . . & Frenchmen. Your two lectures to French students are exquisitely adapted to them, & never condescending or easy. And you preserve, almost alone among the critics of our age, a refined art of writing. You were most kind indeed to let me have a copy of your book as it appeared. I have learned much from it & after nine months of assiduous giving out or giving away, I feel inclined to store up knowledge this summer & to light again my faith in literature, & in criticism. I am staying here or near here this summer & shall resort to your book again in moments of doubt.

With many thanks & most sincerely,
Henri

## To John Gassner:

June 28, 1957

Dear Mr. Gassner:

I was very much touched by the very gracious gift of your book of foreign plays in American adaptation. It is a very ingeniously & wisely selected anthology, in which France is generously represented. The introductions are brilliantly penned, as is all that you write — and your incisive judgments have met with my own modest but full approval in every case. I would be a bit more severe to Giraudoux & certainly to Anouilh than most of my countrymen & occasionally more lenient on

Cocteau—But your volume is a very well proportioned one & it should be very useful to us in our courses given in English.

May I seize the opportunity to say how glad & proud we are, in the French Department, & my wife & I in particular, to have you here as highly respected & long admired colleague, at last bringing our drama school what it needed: a wide & profound knowledge of the theatre of today & an adventurous & fastidious sense of discrimination? Yale has gained immensely by your coming here.

   With our best regards to your wife & very sincerely yours,
   Henri Peyre

## À Jean-Jacques Demorest:

Yale—ce 31 août 1957

Cher Monsieur,

Je ne sais si vous rentrez à Ithaca ces jours-ci ou devez passer en France une année scolaire—Mais ce petit mot voudrait vous remercier, ici ou là bas, du très aimable envoi de votre livre—Je viens de le lire & je l'ai aimé. Vous êtes allé aussi loin qu'aucun de vos prédécesseurs dans la lecture attentive & méditée du texte, dans ses variantes, son orthographe (si souvent effarante—au moins celle de secrétaires illettrés & de jeunes neveux), sa ponctuation. Et de cet examen à la loupe vous tirez des conclusions souvent importantes sur le style de Pascal. Je regrettais même que vous n'ayez pas repris en conclusion vos vues sur ce style, précisées & renforcées par ce second ouvrage, pour définir l'originalité de Pascal écrivain, rarement saisie sur le fait jusqu'ici. Mais il y a beaucoup à prendre, pour nous professeurs toujours intrigués par ces mystères pascaliens dans votre livre. Et vous unissez l'étude littérale du texte, faite avec une minutie extrême & une grande objectivité, à un premier chapitre & à un avant-propos belliqueux et verts, écrits d'une plume vive et audacieuse, bousculant familièrement diverses idoles au passage—Vous rappelez quelque moine soldat ou ardent mousquetaire, défenseur de Pascal, & de la vérité. Ce ton vibrant et alerte plaît dans un sujet qui aurait pu être si sèchement traité. Votre imprimeur s'est fort bien tiré d'une tâche qui aurait pu être très difficile. Il a bien reproduit vos parenthèses, vos orthographes, vos arrangements typographiques. Le livre est ainsi d'une clarté utilisable, précis & aigu, digne de l'homme à qui vous le dédiez et qui l'aurait goûté. Car il avait beaucoup de chaleur & de vibration d'âme, lui aussi, derrière son extérieur détaché.

Merci de votre envoi, & du profit que j'ai trouvé à votre livre. Croyez-moi votre bien dévoué

Henri Peyre

## To Edgar Furniss, William DeVane, Norman Buck, and Hartley Simpson:

October 2, 1957

*Memorandum on the Preparation of the French Department Budget.*
Gentlemen:

I am sending this memorandum in advance in the hope that it may help clarify matters where our Department is concerned and save time in the necessarily brief moments which pressed executives can grant a professor. Lest I, or other chairmen, appear to be on the defensive as lawyers pleading a case, I should like at the outset to say that we are all very grateful for the prospects outlined a few days ago and anxious to cooperate to the full. When it comes to specific measures, however, and if the essential interests of the students taught must be kept uppermost in our minds, it is difficult to hold out a promise of very substantial cuts in the budget of the French Department. Here are some of the reasons why.

1) It has been our policy to keep down at a minimum the number of men on permanent tenure and, unlike other departments, to appoint even brilliant men with some publication to their credit as instructors, not as assistant professors. Indeed, for several years, the Chairman was the only full professor. Professors who retired or died since 1943 (Feuillerat, Seronde, Morehouse, Richardson) were never replaced at once on the top level, but by some younger men to whom promise of advancement was given. Only in the case of R. T. Hill (Old French), who taught in a field where competent men are extremely scarce, did it prove necessary to appoint a very eminent scholar, Professor Auerbach, at the full professorial level. Our plan, however, is, if at all possible, to replace Mr.

Auerbach, due to retire in 1961, by a younger man; indeed to try and replace both Richardson, retired in 1957, and Auerbach, one in philology, the other in medieval literature and culture, by two younger men, one of them already on our staff (Howard Garey), the other still to be looked for. This year, straining matters to the breaking point in order to effect a saving, we have not spent the sum available in our budget ($8,000) for Richardson's replacement, and the sickness of Mr. Auerbach is making things most difficult for us.

The result of our policy has been to keep our Department from being top-heavy, to leave room for promotion of promising men, and thus to leave hope for merit; but it is imperative that we promote those gifted and productive young men when the time comes—or they will be snatched away (the peril was averted several times in the last two years, very narrowly) and the ultimate expense to replace them will prove in fact much heavier.

2) There is no need to comment, I take it, on professors and associate professors on permanent tenure. They all teach a fuller load than in most comparable departments: 8 to 9 hours, plus direction of theses (very heavy), plus majors (a handful, probably 12 or 15), plus a good many activities which do credit to Yale (lectures open to students and to the public, French plays, direction of undergraduate French Club, supervision of audio-visual work for undergraduates, etc.). They are all engaged in writing and they do publish, some more actively than others. Those who have been less productive (Boorsch, Douglas) have volunteered for a heavier than normal load of courses or, in the case of Douglas, put in many hours on the *Yale French Studies*.

3) This coming year (1958–59) is the one in which Guicharnaud, now completing his second term of three years as assistant professor, should be made associate professor. There can hardly be any hesitation in his case. We could not find another Frenchman of his qualifications and of his talent, even if we offered a higher rank and pay. He is a superb teacher, a creative writer of parts, and he has just completed the first volume (manuscript) of a big scholarly work on Molière's Tartuffe.

It is also the year when Messrs. Brombert and Garey should be made assistant professors for a second term of three years. Again there can be no question. Garey is indispensable to us, almost to an embarrassing point, to give Old French courses (described on sheets here enclosed) in the Graduate School, and very useful in a heavy undergraduate teaching. Brombert is so talented, so envied by other universities that we should advance him to an associate professorship at Yale before he even completes his second term of three years as assistant professor. The professors of English who have watched him in Directed Studies, those who have heard him lecture last June to the Alumni Seminar were all of one mind: that man must be kept at Yale at any cost. Without waiting for an offer to entice him away or to force him to bargain with us (which he has always been reluctant to do), we should honor ourselves by giving him permanency here before 1961 or even before 1960. I am convinced that we shall have to.

4) Other cases on which we shall have to act this year are Capretz and Nelson. Both are very good men, who deserve a rank and a salary far above the instructor's level where we have kept them. The first, Capretz, has served as instructor here for two years, previously as instructor at the University of Florida for five years and as assistant professor there for two more years. We would like to make room for him further, but economies will probably prevent us from doing so. In any case, we would need his services for three more years. If we let him go, we shall probably have to pay more to get a man less good than he.

Nelson, who had served as instructor at Columbia before he came here, has published a dozen substantial articles; he has a book now being printed by the Yale Press; he is writing another one while on a Morse fellowship. He is too active, too ambitious (legitimately so) to stay here and mark time. He has had good offers. I believe we should give him the security of a three-year appointment as assistant professor, or at most one or two years at that rank and, if we must, let him go to higher destinies.

5) If we can at all do it, we shall replace our instructors now reaching their fourth year with new men, at some (temporary) saving. Much will depend upon "the market" (as it is called) and it was a very narrow market last year, with the candidates being bid for heavily. The men slated to go are: Duisit, Mankin, Matheson, Trembley.

We shall also let go Stephens, now assistant professor for the present year, and replace him, if we can, by a new instructor. These seem to be all the savings that can be effected without serious injury. There is very little leeway in our Department. Indeed, this year, we refrained from asking for more new funds for new assistants, in part because it was very hard to find the persons to teach the sections which the number of students made necessary. Our intensive course French 25 (nine hours a week) is much too large, but we did not divide it up into two as we used to. Our French 43 has two sections (Messrs. Boorsch and May), but twice more students than last year. The fifty courses vary and occasionally have as few as 7 or 8 students, often as many as 15–18. But we cannot renounce those 50 courses for they would be in danger of disappearing altogether and our majors at least need them. Anyway the saving would be very small and Professors Auerbach and Buffum, I am sure, would rather teach courses like French 50 and 51 on top of their regular load than imperil our efforts to maintain electives in the face of heavy competition from other subjects.

6) I fail to see, I confess, how we could save on our very modest miscellaneous budget of $1,500, out of which we assist a much respected periodical, *Yale French Studies,* in surviving, doing practically everything ourselves and often at our own expense; or on our Secretary's salary; or on the $700 allotted for "Readers." My course, the only one on which I use a reader, has over 170 students who write lengthy essays, and the services of the reader do not save me from disgracing myself and the honor of our faculty by reading blue books at Faculty meetings.

7) A decision should be made as to the future means through which the MAT program might share with the French Department the salary of Nelson Brooks. As it is now, we use Mr. Brooks for many more hours (probably one third or one half of his time) than we (the French department) pay him for.

I hope all this does not appear negative or stubborn. I have effected many savings already and I do not see, in all honesty, what more can be done at the present time. But I shall be happy to listen, in all humility, to the opinions of the four judges and to abide by their decrees.

Very sincerely yours,
Hri Peyre

## À Mario Maurin:

Ce 25 oct. 57

Cher ami,

Miss Gilman, qui chante vos louanges en termes baudelairiens, m'écrivait que vous feriez peut-être, pour les Yale French Studies, no. sur la poésie d'aujourd'hui, un court article sur quelque poète qui vous serait cher. La date limite est le 15 décembre, la longueur 1200–1500 mots—la langue, l'anglais. Nous parlerions surtout de la poésie depuis la libération: Bonnefoy, Grosjean (celui ci promis), Frénaud, Follain, Char (promis), le dernier Aragon (promis), le dernier St J. Perse (promis), les plus jeunes. Quel poète vous tente? Ou quel thème commun à plusieurs poètes? Plus que jamais—puisque rares sont les bons juges de poésie, je souhaite vous voir écrire: Emmanuel a-t-il votre admiration? Jouve? Le dernier Cocteau?

Toujours, bien sûr, en hâte. Je pars pour l'Indiana dans un moment—et fidèlement néanmoins,

Henri Peyre

## Au même:

Ce 26 X 1957

Cher ami,

J'ai écrit bien sûr à Vigée. Des offres éventuelles ne font jamais de mal et vous verrez. La proximité de Boston vaut bien celle de New York, du moins à mes yeux: j'exècre de plus en plus New York, je dois dire. Mais vous y avez vos parents. Brandeis a d'excellents élèves. On risque d'y être un peu catalogué comme appartenant à une institution israélite, comme d'autres passent pour être "vendus" aux jésuites ou aux Méthodistes, & de n'en plus sortir—mais en fait l'esprit qui y règne est libre et très laïque.

Pour le poète, Bonnefoy serait le mieux—ou Vigée—mais vous, moi étant les amis de Vigée, nous aurions l'air de faire cénacle. Cependant à votre gré. Mais il me semble que l'homme de Douve vous conviendrait. Un court article suffirait—

Et vos vers à vous? En publiez-vous? Très pris, je ne lis pas toujours la poésie récente & les revues—ou avec bien des retards.

Merci encore & à bientôt,
Henri Peyre

## To Edgar Furniss:

October 28, 1957

Dear Mr. Furniss:

After a good deal of study of all the angles of the problem of replacing Mr. Auerbach next term, we have come to the conclusion that the best, in the interests of our numerous and demanding graduate students, is to ask Mr. Richardson to give the important graduate course required of our students, French 101b, *Old French Language*. This course will meet on Tuesday afternoon, and Mr. Richardson should get a compensation of $2,000.00 for it (he will be losing his social security meanwhile, since he will at the same time be teaching on other days in New London). Mr. Richardson makes the point—which I trust does not embarrass the Treasurer's Office in any way—that that sum should be paid to him in four installments, on the last days of February, March, April and May. He would thus receive his social security from June 1st on.

The other graduate course that Mr. Auerbach was to give, French 115b, *The Prose of the 14th and 15th Centuries,* will be given by Mr. Douglas. In exchange we shall have to take three hours of undergraduate teaching from Mr. Douglas and appoint an assistant in instruction to give those three hours of French 32. The compensation for that should be (at the rate of $366.66 per hour per year) $549.99.

Owing to the most regrettable and grievous loss that the Department has sustained, two thirds of Mr. Auerbach's salary should thus be saved; but from those two thirds (November 1st to June 30th), the sum of $2,000.00, plus $549.99, will have to be deducted. As you know, we already have saved the $8,000 provided for the replacement of Mr. Richardson.

A third course that Mr. Auerbach gave, French 50, is being given by Mr. Cornell, most graciously and at no cost to the University.

Very sincerely yours,
Hri Peyre

## To Hartley Simpson:

November 4, 1957

Dear Hartley:

The Frenchman on whom I was counting, semi-hopefully, to take charge of our teaching of Old French literature and whose presence is all the more imperative after Erich Auerbach's death, has at last accepted to come on our terms (assistant professor, second grade, salary of $6,500 + $500 as a tax-exempt traveling allowance for his first year here). He hesitated for a long time, and without urging him unduly and assuring him that living here with his wife and two children would be a perfectly easy matter, I pressed him to answer me "yes" or "no" for November 1st—which he just did. His name is Daniel Poirion. He is very warmly recommended to me as the most promising young scholar in France in his field. He does not promise to stay here and we shall keep the matter open for three years, which should be his term of appointment here. He has published very little, practically nothing as yet; but that is usual with young French scholars who, after having passed the Diplôme d'Etudes Supérieures and the Agrégation, which are at least equivalent to a Ph.D. degree, work steadily on their two and very bulky doctorate theses and usually come out with them at the age of 35 or 38—especially in fields like medieval literature and philology, which require a vast and long training. He has his "secondary thesis" ready, and is completing his work on the main one, which, however, will hardly be ready before 1961 or so.

But M. Poirion is the best man we could find, after a very arduous search in this country and in Great Britain. We are glad, indeed relieved, at his acceptance. The question now is (and the point of this letter) to hurry matters up in his case (since the funds were promised in the future budgets and available already this current year, but not spent) so that he may get his leave of absence from the French University system and the proper visa, and take steps to get here next September. Since Berkeley had also made advances to this Frenchman, I'd like to settle the matter now for good, and get the proper university appointment and the Yale seal to forward to Mr. Poirion and to be displayed to the U. S. Consulate in Paris. I believe this appointment should be in the Graduate School and I should appreciate being allowed to proceed soon, first before the

Humanities and Divisional Committee if such is still the procedure, then with the Graduate School Dean and Appointment Committee. I apologize if this seems like rushing our staid and thoughtful Board of permanent Officers of the Graduate School unduly and our no less thoughtful but agile Dean.

Sincerely yours,
Hri Peyre

## To Edward S. Noyes:

November 13, 1957

Professor Edward S. Noyes
Director
Master of Arts in Teaching Program
Dear Mr. Noyes:

I imagine some decision should be reached on how the salary of Mr. Nelson Brooks is, in the future, going to be shared between the MAT program and the French Department. The present arrangement is very favorable to the French department and we have, therefore, no complaint to offer; but we do feel embarrassed at taking at least half of Mr. Brooks' time and energy (a course of five hours a week, plus the general direction of that same course, which has eleven sections; the supervision of six or seven other instructors, the effort to have a new or an improved method understood and applied in all the sections, etc.). We have been very satisfied with the achievement of Mr. Brooks these last two months; he has fulfilled all the hopes we had set on him. But we also know that he cannot possibly retain all the time he used to devote to the MAT program while he works so strenuously for us.

This current year, our French Department budget only spent a sum of $1,500 on Mr. Brooks. Our budget is not to increase next year; it is on the contrary to undergo a substantial reduction. If funds available to the MAT program make it possible for the MAT to subsidize our Department by continuing to pay the largest share of Mr. Brooks' salary, we shall be glad to take advantage of such an arrangement. If the University authorities, however, prefer a more equitable distribution of Mr. Brooks' salary between the MAT and our Department, and are willing to have the French Department budget have the needed amount, we shall be equally happy. I imagine a decision should be reached soon, before we prepare our budgets.

Cordially yours,<br>Hri Peyre

## To R. P. Blackmur:

[letterhead: Princeton University Library]
Dec. 8, 1957

Dear Mr. Blackmur:

I suppose it will always be in vain that I'll hope & wish to attend one of your seminars—in order to be enlightened & deepened, not to contribute. Those days (Thursdays in particular) happen to be difficult ones for me, &, ironically enough, I find it easier to go & evangelize remote & eager populations in Texas (where I'll have to fly next week) or Missouri, or the monks at this Benedictine abbey in Latrobe, Pa., from where I am sending this note than to affront awe-inspiring Princeton. I meant to try & meet Mme Magny this month or next, but I'll have to forbear & thank you all the same for a kind invitation.

Perhaps we may hope to have Mme Magny for a lecture at Yale, to our own *Romance Club*. Will you give her the enclosed note in that hope? & accept my thanks & my regrets.

I read your Library of Congress lecture with *immense* pleasure. At first, I thought something was wrong with either you or me, for I seemed to understand you painlessly. But I soon realized that you had not lost any of your depth & that I had not ceased to be impressed by your critical thinking—that what you said aroused prolonged echoes & occasional resistance, as it always did & should. I am grateful to you for that booklet, & was only shocked that it sold for such a paltry sum that it might attract too wide a "vulgum pecus."

Sincerely yours,<br>Hri Peyre

# To Marcus Robbins:

December 11, 1957

Mr. Marcus Robbins
Comptroller of the University
Dear Mr. Robbins:

For a number of years, we have had a modest account with you under the title "Contes Modernes," made up of the royalties from a volume which our colleagues did in collaboration a number of years ago. That account is small by your standards, although we have tried to husband the money carefully, as we knew we would need it some day for the preparation of new volumes which our Department contemplated then, and still contemplates. The amount outstanding, if I am not mistaken, is, at the present time, $2,827.35 (two thousand eight hundred and twenty seven dollars and thirty-five cents).

Our department, at its last meeting of the professors and associate professors in November 1957, decided to use that fund for the preparation of a new volume which we want to do collectively. That new volume will be an anthology of modern French literature, for which we shall have to pay assistants doing the typing and some research for us and also varied sums for copyrights for the authors whose texts we plan to borrow and utilize. These payments will probably have to consist of small checks, some in foreign currency, and the department thought it best for us to ask you to make me, as chairman of the department, a check for the amount outstanding. We shall pay it into a checking account so as to draw on it frequently in the near future, and we shall probably exhaust the balance within a few months. If, at some future time, more funds were to accrue to us from that collective volume, we might again ask you to open an account for us and keep the money for our future use.

We are very grateful to you for the extra trouble we have given you in asking you to keep that fund and the accounts for us. Since this letter entails a sum which to us is not inconsiderable, I am asking my colleagues Professors Jean Boorsch and Georges May, both full professors in the Department, to countersign it with me, and also Mr. Douglas, associate professor of French, whose advice we have requested on this, and the secretary, Mrs. Giraud. We shall take steps, of course, to have that little fund, which we have saved over the years, be spent carefully and with all due safeguards.

I am sending a copy of this letter, also duly signed by my colleagues, to the provost's Office, for the provost's information.

Very sincerely yours,<br>Hri Peyre et al.

## To Edgar Furniss:

November 18, 1957

Dear Mr. Furniss:

As we are now engaged in preparing the budget for next year, I believe it would be useful for us to have some clarification as to what is likely to be the salary of our instructors with and without the Ph.D.

I well realize, of course, that we are to put on the budget only the salaries of the present year and that the increases, if any, will be added later by your Office. However, while we talk informally with the young men whom we should like to have as instructors next year and while we have, in fact, to try and keep them here against enticing offers from elsewhere (Williams, Amherst and Dartmouth have already sent emissaries to my office to look up candidates for instructorships on whom we also have designs ourselves, and they are suggesting higher salaries than ours), it would be useful for us to know what we may mention as the probable amount for instructors with the Ph.D. and without it. The latter obviously are easier to keep here if they are pursuing the writing of the dissertation for our Graduate School. Yet the figure allotted last year was woefully low ($3,750, in cases of men here for their first and second year), and we should like to be able to give our young men some reassurance.

Secondly, some unambiguous clarification would also be desirable as to the following points:

a) Must the Ph.D. degree be secured by June 1958 for our instructors to qualify for the higher sum, or is the date of September 1958 equally acceptable to your Office, although the increased salaries would have to start with July 31st, and there is always a chance that the dissertation may not be completed at the last minute?

b) I fully realize that all our rules must allow some leeway for exceptions, and it is one of the charms of participating in the Administration at Yale that exceptions, whenever reasonable, are always provided for by the Deans and the Provost. Nevertheless, it is embarrassing when sometimes there is a glaring discrepancy among the stipends paid to the assistants in instruction of related and parallel language departments. When those assistants, as often is the case in German, are ladies who have taught here for a number of years, an adjustment should obviously be made. But one of our assistants this year has repeatedly remarked, somewhat acrimoniously, that young men hired at the same time as he in the Department of Spanish were paid substantially more than he was. We have always abided by the fixed sum of, for last year and the present year, $366.66 per hour per year. A sum providing a fixed basis should also, it seems to me, be mentioned to several departments of modern languages for next year, so that a minimum of uniformity be assured.

Very sincerely yours,
Hri Peyre

## À Franco Simone:

[Sans date]

Monsieur Franco Simone
Studi Francesi
Corso Stati Uniti, 39
Torino
Mon cher ami,

Vous êtes bien trop gentil de m'avoir envoyé ce mot si aimable, alors que ma générosité se bornait en vérité à un don bien modeste. Mais mon geste voulait surtout vous redire combien votre Revue mérite notre estime et en fait l'a conquis ici déjà. Elle est excellente et nous sommes plusieurs à chercher à la faire mieux connaître en Amérique.

Je suis, d'autre part, avec beaucoup d'intérêt, vos très actives publications sur la littérature française, et j'apprends toujours énormément en vous lisant. Je sais que vous devez venir au mois de septembre pour ce congrès de Chapel Hill. Je ne crois pas pouvoir m'y rendre moi-même, car c'est un moment de l'année où tout recommence pour nous et je dois être ici pour recevoir nos nouveaux étudiants. Mais peut-être vous verrai-je si, comme je l'espère, je vais à Paris cet été, à la Bibliothèque Nationale ou au gentil café Poccardi, ou même à Turin, que je n'ai jamais visité. Ma seule adresse, lorsque je suis en France, est c/o American Express, rue Scribe, Paris IX, pour le cas où je m'y trouve à partir de juin.

J'aimerais beaucoup écrire pour vous, mais je n'arrive même pas à tenir ici mes engagements. Un jour viendra peut-être. En tout cas, mille mercis et croyez-moi très cordialement vôtre

Henri Peyre

P.S. J'espère que vous recevez notre *Yale French Studies* que, je crois bien, nous vous envoyons. Je dois dire que nous ne paraissons pas aussi régulièrement que vous. L'Italie est plus ponctuelle que l'Amérique.

## To Gaston Hall:

Jan. 25/58

Dear Mr. Hall:

Thank you for your very full note on the progress of your work. If you drop in to see me Monday or Wed. early (10.45 or so), Jan 27 or 29, I'll explore ways of applying for a small assistance for your very strenuous & effective research. At least, I'll try.

Sincerely,
Henri Peyre

## À son frère:

[letterhead: Biltmore Hotel, N.Y.]
Ce 13 mars 1958

Mon cher Jacques. Je suis dans une salle d'attente de gare, exposée à tous les vents, mais je secoue enfin la léthargie et les remords qui m'ont fait si longtemps différer de t'écrire & je commence au moins cette lettre pour qu'elle t'arrive avec les premières bouffées du printemps. Ici, nous ne faisons, il se trouve, nulle attention à Pâques, si bien que je ne sais quand survient cette fête qui, jadis, nous amenait rituellement à Merindol et qui vous transportera sans doute à ce lieu béni du Rayol. Que les mimosas, les amandiers s'il en est, & les fleurs plus terrestres ou plus modestement proches du sol doivent être beaux à ce moment là. Pierre doit avoir besoin de quelque répit, puisqu'il affronte déjà le bachot— nouveau génie précoce, Rimbaud (moins diabolique), Einstein enfant. Ne le poussez pas trop. Une ou deux années d'avance sont bien peu de chose dans la vie ultérieure, & je vois souvent de mes camarades de Khâgne ou de l'Ecole Normale, & même de Polytechnique que j'avais connus au Lycée à Paris, qui, après avoir offert de grandes promesses, se sont arrêtés assez piteusement. Ce ne sera pas son cas. Il a trop de fond & de solidité pour cela, & il est aidé par la compréhension de parents remarquables. Mais je m'aperçois tous les jours que l'essentiel de la vie est ce qu'on apprend plus tard, après 25 ou 30 ans, si l'on garde la capacité d'apprendre alors, & de changer.

Les vacances universitaires ici sont du 18 au 30 mars, mais je n'en profite guère, car je pars dès le 1r jour en avion pour faire diverses conférences (surtout sur la situation internationale, algérienne, etc. et de caractère politique) dans l'extrême sud du pays, en Alabama. Au retour, divers comités me requièrent à New York. Cela laisse Marguerite beaucoup seule, et elle n'est pas sans s'en lamenter. Mais il est difficile de se dérober à nombre de demandes qui m'assaillent, peut-être à quelque vanité qui pousse un Français (et un Méridional) à aimer s'écouter parler. Je crois vrai de dire cependant que j'ai, avec les années, acquis un assez grand ascendant sur divers publics américains auxquels je m'adresse, bien entendu, en anglais & que je semble avoir leur confiance. Dans bien des cas, je suis le seul Français convié à participer à des comités assez confidentiels où se discute la diplomatie, ou même la politique militaire, du pays. Je ne cesse de défendre une compréhension plus large de la France; mais, bien entendu sans anti-américanisme, car les Américains intelligents, et il n'en manque pas, sont des gens fort distingués, très ouverts et pleins de sympathie pour la France & même pour ses erreurs (& nous en commettons). En ce moment, notre relèvement économique, qui est extraordinaire, éveille beaucoup d'intérêt. On est moins émerveillé de notre politique, mais elle n'est pas funeste—sauf en Algérie où je crois, pour ma part, que nous manquons le coche à ne pas offrir à temps, en termes clairs, une promesse d'indépendance ferme, qui n'empêchera pas, au contraire, interdépendance économique. Mais c'est une question embourbée à plaisir.

Dans tout cela, la littérature, qui est tout de même ma vocation, souffre un peu & je n'ai guère le temps en cours d'année d'ajouter même un chapitre à mon livre en cours, resté en plan. J'attendrai l'été. J'ai beaucoup d'élèves et beaucoup de travail & de correspondance pour placer mes "gradués" ou docteurs, car ici cela se fait de manière privée, le gouvernement n'intervenant pas en ces matières d'éducation. Et la crise économique, qui est réelle sinon grave, a soudain affecté l'optimisme américain. Les autos se vendent mal, les machines à laver & autres plus mal encore. Je ne pense pas que cela empire beaucoup après 1958, mais on en sent les contrecoups. Nous, professeurs, avons du moins la sécurité.

Nous pensons aller en France cet été—dès le 6 ou 8 juin. Mais je ne sais encore ce que nous ferons. Nous n'emporterons pas d'auto d'ici, ce qui est trop coûteux et, à Paris où je dois être assez longtemps, un encombrement. Peut-être en louerons-nous une en France. La Dauphine est-elle la meilleure? Nous avons parlé de la Corse (mais alors, en avion), de l'Italie, mais dans le fond l'été en Europe, avec routes encombrées, hôtels bruyants, foules, nous fait un peu peur. Et nous n'apercevons pas de solution.

Nous vieillissons, lentement mais sûrement. Bientôt j'imagine que je devrais porter des lunettes pour lire. Marguerite le fait déjà. Elle va assez bien et est active, donnant elle-même des cours à un groupe de dames "chic" à New York. Elle est cependant isolée, moralement, par la faute en partie de son caractère, & aussi parce que nous n'avons pas eu d'enfant. Je suis si rarement libre moi-même, ne serait-ce que pour réfléchir, que je n'ai pas le temps de m'ennuyer. Mais je cours sans cesse après mon emploi du temps, & après moi-même.

## À Jorge Guillén:

Ce 16—3—58

Cher Ami,

Quelle joie de vous avoir vu ainsi à Cambridge! J'ai énormément aimé ces conversations avec vous—& j'ai aimé cette jeunesse parce que, malgré votre grande modestie, l'ironie teintée de bonté que vous maniez si joliment, elle vous admirait et vous aimait comme vous méritez de l'être. Merci de ce bon moment avec vous, au petit déjeuner.

Voulez-vous, d'un mot confidentiel et, si possible, prompt, me dire ce que vous pensez d'Angel Valbuena Briones, qui entre autres choses, a écrit un essai sur vous & la poésie pure en 1954. Le connaissez-vous? est-il adaptable de caractère, actif, dévoué? et esprit de vrai avenir? Puisque Marichal va à Harvard, que votre fils reste à l'ombre (toujours auguste) de Castro, nous pensons à lui pour ici. Merci à l'avance & bien des amitiés — de nous deux.

Henri Peyre

## To Norman Buck:

April 4, 1958

Dear Mr. Buck:

I am sorry I had to take some time to think over the complex question raised by the President's suggestion that we marry the departments of French and of Spanish-Italian. The spring vacation intervened and it was not easy to consult the Deans, as I wanted to. I have had brief talks with them, and with Mr. Bergin, who has proved very understanding and generous. Without his continual cooperation and advice, little, indeed, could be achieved. It is regrettable that the other senior member of the Spanish-Italian department, Mr. Arrom, should be away in Europe at this time. But I hope that his cooperation, equally necessary to any future program, will be forthcoming likewise.

I have not concealed my hesitations and scruples about the contemplated move. They are real and deep. I should like to state the few points which should be understood deeply as we make this attempt to unite the two departments under one chairman. 1) Essential is, of course, the financial backing of the administration. Money is not everything in these matters; but if one or two rather important appointments in Spanish are to be made, so as to attract graduate students to Yale in the Spanish field, to place them well once they are trained, and to have some continuity and expert guidance in the direction of undergraduate courses, the chairman must be able to count on the good will and the generosity of the administration. Two major appointments may well have to be made soon, and promotion for the most brilliant of the instructors now at Yale or to come to Yale in the future must be made possible.

2) Provision for a good secretary in Spanish-Italian must be continued and secretarial and miscellaneous expenses are likely to be increased, if expansion is foreseen. There again, while no needless expense will be proposed, the administration should deeply admit that the merging of two departments will not necessarily result in economies. 3) There is much to be said against too close a relationship between the departments of Spanish-Italian and French, from a theoretical point of view. In the fields of philology, medieval literature and mutual relations and influences between the three chief "Latin" countries, the relation indeed is close, at least as late as the seventeenth century. After that date, the literature of France in particular has, most often, to be studied in its relations with the literatures of Britain, Germany, Russia.

There prevails also a slight suspicion made of envy, rivalry, family distrust, between the rational, would-be universal and often imperialistic spirit of the French and the more particular, more emotional tempers of the two "peninsulas of passion," Spain and Italy. The three representatives, and even the American students of those three nations, all have in common a marked individualism and a reluctance to agree to disagree. It may well be that the proposed marriage should be dissolved again, three or five years from now, for the mental welfare of all concerned. My colleagues of the French Department urge me to state clearly that, if such an amicable severance of too close ties were deemed desirable after some of the progress expected has been achieved, the administration should allow it to proceed to such a parting of the way.

It is not without serious misgivings that I, personally, resign myself to this move which, I confess, I found very burdensome and likely to cause misgivings and to ruffle feelings on several sides. Without wanting to play the hypocritical role of a devoted Eli sacrificing his scant leisure and his weakening energy to his imperious, if not always venerated, adopted mother, I have decided to accept the new role, devolved upon me for a while, with good will. I shall place whatever capacity I have at the service of the Romance Languages at Yale. But I must not conceal the fact that my competence in Spanish is certainly most unequal to my good will. I should hope, at best, to use the interregnum now opening in the interest of the Spanish Department and of Yale, realizing full well that the difficulties encountered by Mr. Bergin and his predecessors in finding the ideal colleagues in Spanish to attract here will face their successor also.

May I have the assurance of your office that we can count on your full and generous cooperation? I am sending a copy of this letter to the President, Deans DeVane and Simpson and to Prof. Hilles, chairman of the Committee which this should concern.

Sincerely yours,<br>Hri Peyre

## To Whitney Griswold:

April 4 — 1958

[With copy of the preceding letter]
Dear President Griswold:

Will you pardon the discourtesy of sending you a mere carbon? I happen to be without a secretary: she got measles or some such disease & is feverish, & contagious. And, with many qualms & twinges of conscience, & questionings of my tongue (which can't pronounce Spanish sounds adequately), I finally agreed to take over this job. I'll be like Sancho Panza amid Spanish mystics & Greco angels — but it may be good for my soul, if not ultimately for the French Department.

Very sincerely yours,<br>Hri Peyre

## À Mario Maurin:

Ce 30.V.58

Mon cher Maurin,

Cette nouvelle m'a surpris & chagriné — J'avoue que je croyais Margaret inébranlable de solidité, et impatiente de voir sortir son nouveau livre — et je dis toujours qu'on meurt parce qu'on le veut bien.

La remplacer cet été? Non. Le poste est trop important pour qu'on aille si vite. Veut-on une femme? Une érudite? À quel rang? Tous les gens "bien" sont placés, y compris Deguise, naguère à Wellesley qui va à Conn. College. Et on ne peut plus "ravir" quelqu'un si tard dans l'année, en toute décence. Voyez-vous quelqu'un vous-même? L'essentiel

& le difficile serait le cours gradué: pour le reste, avec tous ses mérites, comme professeur, M. G. n'est pas irremplaçable.

Je pars pour la France sur Liberté le 6 et d'ici le 4, pour arranger au passage quelques affaires à N.Y. Et le 3 j'ai le "Ph.D. Committee" tout le jour, demain le bachot à N.Y. Allez-vous en France vous-même? Si les généraux & les prétoriens ne m'en empêchent, je serai à Paris en juin — c/o American Express, rue Scribe, est ma meilleure adresse — Mais je ne sais guère que conseiller à Bryn Mawr, à moins de savoir quels sont vraiment les besoins.

Passez de calmes vacances & croyez moi, bien amicalement
Henri Peyre

## À son frère:

[letterhead: *Liberté*]
Ce 12.VI.58

Mon cher Jacques,

Ce mot te dira vite que nous sommes sur le bateau & près de débarquer au Havre. Une autre année s'est heureusement passée, chargée certes, & c'est à peine si à bord j'ai à peu près mis à jour mon courrier toujours différé — pour en retrouver d'autre sans doute à Paris. Examens, soutenances de thèse, session de bachot à New York & autres préparatifs de départ ou règlements de fin d'année ont occupé ces dernières semaines. Les événements de France & d'Algérie nous ont inquiétés un moment — pas sérieusement, pourtant. Sans avoir le culte du grand homme, & de la grandeur trop tournée vers le passé, j'avoue que je n'ai pas sans soulagement vu venir De Gaulle au pouvoir. L'usure du régime était trop grande, personne n'était plus obéi & il faut au moins le courage d'effectuer quelques réformes constitutionnelles pour que tout remarche. La politique & surtout les étiquettes & les mots d'ordre des partis sont trop en retard sur la vie économique & l'efficacité administrative du pays: cela en est devenu dérisoire. Mais la fausse logique de nos raisonnements dissimule les réalités. Sur l'Algérie, je ne pense pas que la solution soit aisée ou qu'on puisse éviter l'indépendance, corrigée par la solidarité avec la France. L'intégration ne se fera pas par quelque mystique — mais la loi cadre était au moins aussi fausse, et qui pis est, incompréhensible.

Quoi qu'il en soit, & malgré quelques craintes, moins de la situation politique que du coût élevé de la vie & de l'impossibilité de trouver quelque lieu tranquille pour les vacances, nous voici en France, ou presque. Nous allons bien & ce magnifique bateau, avec sa cuisine hors de pair, son luxe et le soleil qui nous a éclairés, nous ont déjà donné quelque repos. Nous nous arrêterons 3 ou 4 jours en Normandie, serons à Paris le 16 ou 17 juin, Hôtel St James, 24 rue St Honoré 1r ou c/o American Express, rue Scribe, Paris 9e. J'aurai là bien des courses, gens & amis à voir et vers le milieu de juillet nous descendrons sans doute, peut-être avec des amis d'Amérique vers la Suisse ou la Savoie, puis l'Italie. Nos projets sont encore des plus vagues. Nous repartons en tous cas sur le *Flandre* le 23 août. . . .

## À Leon Roudiez:

Ce 24—VI—58
(Paris. Hôtel St James. 211 rue St Honoré—
pour qqs jours—ensuite c/o American Express)

Cher ami,

J'ai donc concocté un message dictatorial à nos troupes. Cette corvée annuelle détournerait quiconque d'être longtemps Président. Est-elle vraiment utile, ou une survivance du passé? Je crois bien que j'aimerais encore mieux relire toute la préface de la Musique Intérieure, & même quelques uns des poèmes, que de rédiger ces appels aux armes—Mais voilà que les idées de Maurras vont triompher sous l'égide de votre présent chef. Étrange retour de fortune!

Paris est bien beau, & presque trop calme—mais nous en jouissons avant d'aller explorer la province. Allez-vous bien? Vous a-t-on comblé d'or?

Mes amitiés à votre femme & vous,
Henri Peyre

## À Malcolm McIntosh:

Paris, ce 29—VI—58

Mon cher ami,

Merci de ces nouvelles que Mrs. Giraud m'a transmises. Je ne connais pas grand'chose d'Alfred, je l'avoue, mais je comprends aisément que vous ne souhaitiez pas y rester très longtemps. L'ouest vous conviendrait mieux, & vous pourriez y trouver, et un traitement convenant mieux à vos mérites, & peut-être plus de ferveur pour les choses littéraires & humanistes. Cette année a été médiocre pour les postes, mais les choses peuvent changer & il y aura pas mal de vides d'ici un an ou deux, & un grand afflux d'élèves. Il est vrai que souvent on préfère nommer des jeunes, à moindre prix, et on les croit plus adaptables. Mais vous avez l'estime de tous ceux qui vous connaissent, & nous veillerons à vous signaler ce qui pourrait se présenter de bon, & à signaler votre personnalité & votre expérience à ceux qui pourraient désirer les utiliser.

Nous sommes en France pour les vacances, jusqu'ici très affairées, car j'ai, à Paris, bien des besognes à accomplir. Mais nous pensons voyager dans le Midi & peut-être en Italie ensuite. Nous avions été, il y a deux ans, à Bordeaux & dans le sud-ouest, & avions pensé à vous, qui aviez si bien compris la France. Ce que vous me dites de votre curiosité littéraire actuelle m'intéresse toujours. J'ai été en Alabama ce printemps mais, comme les visiteurs hâtifs à qui on ne montre que le côté le plus riant des choses, je n'ai vu de cet état que la surface, & peut-être l'éclat.

Dites notre très fidèle souvenir à votre femme & croyez à nos bons vœux & amitiés.

Henri Peyre

## To Harry Levin:

Sept.1, 1958

Dear Harry,

I heard with keen regret that I had just missed you in Bormes. I have known Mayoux, & liked him, since our days at Louis le Grand together; he is the most alive & the broadest of the English group at the Sorbonne, and although at first, when we see them again in their picturesque house, our "American" sense of comfort is a bit jolted, we are promptly won over by the charm & youthfulness of his wife. Alas! The Grand Hotel is a run down, dismal place. Marguerite cried for two evenings & we looked around as far as St Tropez & Antibes for better quarters; but the beauty of the scenery, the walks around the hotel up the hill & the fragrance of the exotic flowers soon turned us into dirty French people again. We spent two delightful weeks there, & managed to bring quite an improvement to the cuisine.

Too bad we missed you. I have long wished to know your wife better, after an all too brief meeting last Spring. And I have felt even longer that, if I weren't quite so intimidated by your vast knowledge, never "pris en défaut" & by your incisiveness, there is no man I could learn more from—As it is, I read your book over again: blackness seemed even more powerful in those luminous lands. And I reread your MLN piece on my two colleagues. I had heard they were irked by it. But your critique is admirable, keen, a trifle biting, but their dogmatism & their cult of structure & their complacent tone to critical ideas & movements outside England deserved the strictures. I would be a little more charitable to the authors myself, especially to Wimsatt: he believes so firmly in standards &, as you know, I have none, that I feel inferior to a man of his stature. And then one has to show a little kindness to people who are so convinced there is another life & that their souls will immortally endure: they deprive themselves of the good things of this world meanwhile (such as Armagnac, which I now associate with you) & jocular flirt with women & ideas, & they won't even discover that their "pari" was a mistaken one—poor dears.

This silly note had really a very precise, though tiny, purpose. We are just back from Europe & going over my list of engagements, a meet labor for this day, I note that I am to follow you on Burnshaw's Institute of Book Publishing. I wish I could hear you on Modernism, of course. But Stanley set my lecture on half a dozen novelists for Febr. 12, 1959, on the mimeographed sheet (yours being given on Febr. 5th). I presume a change must have occurred & I wished to be certain, as I may have to meet with the Guggenheim Committee on the week which includes Febr. 12th. Could you drop me a postcard?

This is too long a note as it is. I won't ask about the health of your language children but offer my wishes for your arduous tasks & for their growth in fraternal love. I saw Benichou briefly in Paris. Jasinski's enormous volumes on Racine failed to convince me but they instructed me richly. It was in a way reassuring to see that "pure" historical scholarship can pour so much madness into its method —

>With kind regards to your wife & very sincerely yours,
>Henri Peyre

Sorry I can't go to Chapel Hill. That week requires my presence here, with the shortage of assistants, new classes to set up & no secretary for the Department as yet.

## À Kurt Weinberg:

Ce 8 — IX — 58

Mon cher Weinberg,

C'est gentil à vous de m'avoir envoyé votre essai sur Renan, & de l'avoir dédié à un grand homme qui vous a compris & aimé — et il faut vous aimer beaucoup, parfois vous pardonner un peu, pour vous aimer assez. L'éloignement, l'affairement nous ont séparés; mais vous n'êtes certes pas oublié ici — et j'imagine que vous êtes heureux en tous les sens, domi & urbi, et apprécié professionnellement — Vous n'êtes plus un adolescent; mais vous avez encore bien des années d'activité devant vous, beaucoup de choses à dire, & le talent de les dire bien. Allez de l'avant.

Votre essai m'a beaucoup intéressé, parce qu'il était de vous, et traite d'un sujet dont je me suis parfois occupé, & d'un auteur, Renan, que j'ai pas mal pratiqué. Vous le connaissez à fond, le jugez sans charité, avec lucidité et, sans épuiser le sujet (il y aurait un joli petit livre à faire sur Renan & les "races" juives et sa conception de la race dans l'histoire, relativement à Thierry, Michelet, Taine, Fustel), vous n'omettez rien d'essentiel.

Cependant je résiste. Très renanien vous-même, subtil, contradictoire parfois, nuancé, homme de sensibilité vive, vous vous déchirez un peu vous-même en l'accablant. Je crois que, non dans les textes ou les faits, mais dans "l'art de les solliciter doucement" que tout critique doué & personnel forcément pratique, dans votre ton acerbe & prompt à condamner, vous cessez d'être tout à fait juste. La conférence "Judaïsme—race ou religion" était tout de même courageuse, lucide et elle a *beaucoup* fait en France pour combattre quelque racisme latent vers 1885–1900. Employer si souvent les adjectifs "pernicieux," "néfaste" pour traiter d'une pensée qui s'est voulue sereine n'est pas d'une parfaite objectivité. Justement parce qu'il a chéri l'art des repentirs & des contradictions, Renan n'a pas été utilisé par les antisémites, n'a pas pu l'être. Sa pensée, à la différence de celle de Gobineau, ou de Wagner (quand il pense), n'a pas contribué aux monstruosités du racisme—Tout votre essai est incliné vers quelque hostilité amère envers R., que je crois excessive. Pourquoi ne pas écrire sur quelqu'un que vous *aimez,* avec qui vous êtes pleinement en *sympathie,* pratiquant la "critique des beautés"? Cela en vaut la peine—et, si j'ose le dire, écrivez aussi en vous abstrayant du judaïsme, pour ou contre. Vous êtes américain, ou français de culture, bien plus que Juif—comme je suis moi-même de ces deux pays plus que Provençal, protestant, même que polythéiste!

Je sais que cela m'est aisé à dire. Je n'ai pas souffert comme vous—Je n'ai pas cette angoisse de réparer des crimes, de vouloir passionnément la justice, ces cauchemars dans mon subconscient—Mais vous avez refait votre vie—Vous êtes loin de tout cela. Vous êtes reparti—oubliez un peu.

Vous savez, je crois, que le racisme m'a toujours indigné & je n'ai jamais pactisé avec l'antisémitisme. Ceci dit, je vous avoue que les vues de Renan me paraissent justes. Il y a des races—la race n'est pas, certes, une vérité physiologique; elle est le plus souvent acquise, une race-résultat. Mais enfin il y a une psychologie nationale, si vous voulez, ce qui se confond souvent avec l'autre—Et, j'espère ne pas vous choquer, il y a une inégalité des races. Les Juifs polonais sont les mieux doués de tous les groupes ethniques ou culturels, & je suis plein d'envie pour eux. Les Irlandais ont certains dons & les Italiens en ont d'autres. Certains peuples (groupes ou races) produisent peu de poètes, ou de musiciens, ou de logiciens. Certaines "cultures" n'ont pas apporté grande contribution à l'humanité. J'avoue que la phrase de R ("Je ne vois pas de raison pour qu'un Papou soit immortel") ne m'a jamais choqué. Si j'avais la naïveté de me croire immortel, cela me vexerait de devoir rencontrer des Papous ou des dames de la Nouvelle Guinée au Paradis. J'ai souvent parlé de cela avec des anthropologues: ils sont d'accord qu'il y a en effet des cultures, & des inégalités de dons (acquis peut-être, transmis héréditairement, mais en pratique, innés) entre ces cultures. En fait l'Unesco a publié là-dessus trois brochures depuis la guerre, toutes remarquables: *Race et Civilisation,* par Michel Leiris 1951; *Race & Histoire,* par Claude Lévi-Strauss, 1952; *The Race Concept, Results of an Inquiry,* 1952. Ces auteurs jugent que nier totalement l'inégalité des "cultures" ou des races, et même le concept de race, parce que Hitler a fait de ce concept un monstrueux usage, est erroné, & prépare des surprises périlleuses pour l'avenir. Je crois que beaucoup de savants ethnographes, même juifs comme Lévi Strauss, seraient plus indulgents pour le "racisme" de Renan que vous.

Mais je m'égare — et d'autres lettres m'attendent. Faites une heureuse rentrée & ayez une fructueuse année. Croyez à mon souvenir le meilleur — Et aidez à l'occasion nos Yale French Studies.

Bien à vous,
Henri Peyre

## À Konrad Bieber:

Ce 14 — IX — 58

Cher Ami,

Je vous dois mille excuses. Dans l'immense désordre de mon bureau après 3 mois d'absence, & le départ, que je pleure toujours, de Mrs. Giraud, j'avais égaré votre message. Je le retrouve en terminant ce dimanche mon triage, préliminaire à la rentrée. Excusez-moi donc.

Votre Bosco est fin & joli. Vous y exprimez, indirectement, la poésie délicate & rêveuse que vous portez en vous. Je résiste un peu à Bosco, après l'avoir aimé: je crains qu'il n'y ait du faux chez lui, & de la répétition. Mais s'il n'est pas des géants, il a de la grâce.

Un paper & un titre? J'avais, je l'avoue, oublié tout à fait. Si vraiment, *très vraiment,* vous n'avez personne de mieux, je m'exécuterai. Mais je suis, dans le fond, assez peu comparatiste — ou si je le suis, c'est sans fanatisme — et ma méthode consiste souvent à me refuser à en avoir une. Qui avez-vous d'autre au programme? Est-ce très nécessaire? Si oui (et ne me flattez pas — on ne m'entend que trop), je songerai vite à un titre — peut-être sur la notion d'influence — ou peut-être plus général, tel que "Comp Lit today: a balance sheet" ou "The Prospects for Comp

Lit in America." Je craindrais d'insister trop sur la notion, trompeuse, de comparaison, si je soulignais trop l'adjectif "comparative." Voulez-vous d'une simple carte me dire quel jour & à quelle heure vient cette réunion, pour que je sois sûr d'éviter tout conflit avec mes obligations d'AATF.

Nous avons eu un séjour agréable en France seule. La politique & l'avenir me tourmentent bien un peu, mais les Français semblent s'en accommoder.

J'imagine que votre femme a des Rimbaud, Mallarmé, même Verlaine, que je traiterai en cours gradué. Nous répandons ses catalogues, si utiles toujours.

Nos amitiés à elle, & à vous,<br>Hri Peyre

## Au même:

Ce 20 sept. 58

Mon cher Bieber,

Vous êtes comme toujours le plus aimable des collègues & le plus courtois des anciens élèves qui continuent à faire croire à leurs vieux maîtres qu'ils ont encore quelque chose à dire. J'avais oublié en effet que cette section était le 1er jour; dès le second, je suis requis par les conseils de l'AATF, préliminaires à la réunion de l'AATF du dernier jour. Je n'ai donc pas de raison de revenir sur ma promesse. Entendu.

Seulement pour le sujet, en y réfléchissant un peu & parce que j'ai écrit à quelques reprises déjà sur ce sujet des "Influences," ou de l'influence, & peut-être récrirai un jour plus longuement là dessus, je préférerais, en ces 20 minutes, en anglais, tenter une esquisse plus générale, peut-être plus stimulante, des résultats acquis & des déficiences de la littérature comparée. Un titre comme celui-ci vous conviendrait-il? "Comparative Literature Today. Assets and Liabilities." Ou, si cela fait trop financier & si quelque chose d'un peu plus bref peut aller:

"Seventy Years of Comparative Literature. A Backward & a Forward Glance"

Est-il encore temps? Si non, conservez l'influence: tant pis!

Quelque jour, vous me direz un peu ce qu'il en est de votre département, si Deguise est arrivé & s'adapte & si sa venue vous paraît, de votre point de vue, une bonne chose — ou si vous préférez envisager d'autres perspectives? si vous êtes vraiment content de votre année & de l'immense projet qui était votre point de départ — J'ai bien peu causé avec vous à loisir ces dernières années, et vous nous manquez toujours.

Bien des amitiés à tous deux,<br>H. P.

À l'occasion, laissez-nous encore quelques ex. du catalogue de votre femme. Merci.

## À Kurt Weinberg:

Oct. 18 — 1958

My dear Weinberg,

On me dit que vous me croyez fâché de votre article, alors que je n'ai offert que quelques critiques, sur le contenu de votre article & sur le ton que je trouvais un peu trop indigné, un peu partial ou pas assez détaché pour un essai érudit; & j'insinuais, dans la meilleure des intentions, que vous devriez peut-être écrire davantage en anglais & sur des sujets vous tenant moins à cœur, donc avec plus d'éloignement esthétique — Mais j'aimais fort votre essai & la subtile intelligence, l'étendue des connaissances dont il témoignait — & je n'ai certes cessé d'entretenir pour vous estime & affectueuse sympathie. Ces différences de doctrine sont peu de chose, & je ne les prends jamais au sérieux pour interférer dans les amitiés, mais assez au sérieux, parce que ce sont des idées, pour en discuter & lire de très près ce qu'écrivent les gens que j'estime — Ne soyez pas trop susceptible: vous avez, bien longtemps déjà, percé à jour tous mes défauts! & me savez maladroit & un peu taquin.

Croyez-moi, bien sincèrement à vous,<br>Henri Peyre

## À Mario Maurin:

Le 14—XII—58

Mon cher ami,

Cette nomination à l'une des "chaires" les plus royales du pays est un bel hommage à la confiance que vous avez inspirée. Je vous aurais néanmoins souhaité que cela vînt plus tard—car ces responsabilités vont rendre difficiles vos absences, vont vous imposer des vacances sans doute écourtées, nuire à ces masses d'écrits que le monde attend de vous. Vous vous en tirerez avec élégance—mais beaucoup va dépendre de vos nominations. Si vous nommez une dame jeune & jolie, gare! si une plus âgée & aigrie, gare encore; si un homme plus âgé que vous et déjà chevronné de cartes que ses livres occuperaient dans les catalogues des bibliothèques, il voudra vous suggérer des réformes, des cours nouveaux, se libérer de votre joug d'ancien sergent des "marines." Si vous attirez un ou deux jeunes hommes (n'y a-t-il pas et Girard et Miss Gilman à remplacer?), on dira que vous les choisissez inférieurs à vous & que le département risque de manquer d'autorité vis-à-vis d'autres départements plus riches en personnel éminent. C'est le meunier, son fils & l'âne, et le mieux est de vous fier à votre sagesse & à votre justice.

X . . . est bien; un peu mou, un peu éclipsé par sa femme, vigoureuse ancienne de B Mawr & de Yale; mais il a le sens de l'art, un français remarquable, de la finesse, du sens critique, quelque talent créateur aussi (il est romancier). Il ferait bien, je crois—nettement mieux que Y . . . , dont le français est moins sûr, dont la thèse (faite plus vite, il est vrai) révélait moins de dons. Il serait à son aise dans le 18e siècle (ou le 19e) & même ailleurs. Il est discret, d'agréables manières. Si Smith veut le perdre, tant pis pour Smith.

Cohn (Vassar) mériterait mieux qu'un assistant prof. et, avec tous ses dons et sa réelle force d'esprit, pourrait être difficile. Secor (Vassar aussi) vous est-il connu? Il serait, à l'occasion, un bon spécialiste du Moyen Age & du XVIe siècle & un peu mou lui aussi, mais très sérieux & cultivé, bon helléniste & latiniste, parle fort bien le français. Il pourrait vous plaire & s'entendrait très bien avec vous deux.

Parmi les dames, je trouve Priscilla Washburn Shaw (Haverford) très intelligente & excellente comparatiste: elle va divorcer je crois (en confidence), & ce sera peut-être tant mieux. Elle est un peu timide, tourmentée, mais d'un esprit très distingué, & même original.

À qui songez-vous encore? Si je puis offrir un avis (pour ce qu'il vaut), dites-le moi. Bryn Mawr mérite, exige, quelqu'un de très bien, de manières agréables, de commerce intellectuel assez riche, avec assez de ressources en soi pour ne pas s'ennuyer, sombrer dans la boisson ou le mariage. Cela se trouve, mais enfin—Puisque vous êtes deux Français (ou trois avec Mme Gougenheim [*sic*]), sans doute préférerez-vous un Américain?

À Swarthmore, vous avec un Français Silhol, qui cherche pour un an un poste. Je ne le connais que par lettre. Ici nous en avons un, agrégé, normalien, Forgero(?), supérieur à Silhol, je crois, qui peut rester à Yale, mais essaierait à l'occasion d'une autre année ailleurs (1958–59) si cela en valait la peine pour lui. Mais une nomination d'un an ne serait qu'un pis aller, ou pour vous remplacer si vous vous absentez.

Bien amicalement,<br>Henri Peyre

## À Norman McIntosh:

Jan. 2, 1959

Cher M. McIntosh,

Je vous ai aperçu à New York, mais bien vite parmi ces couloirs affairés. C'est donc par lettre que je vous salue & souhaite une année un peu heureuse. Alfred n'est pas le paradis, mais je persiste à croire que quelque chose surviendra dans l'ouest qui vous conviendra mieux, homme des montagnes & des neiges que vous êtes, habitant des sommets. Il devrait bientôt se produire pas mal de changements dans la profession.

Sur le roman du XIXe siècle, à part le Martin Turnell, incomplet, souvent injuste, mais intelligent; il n'y a pas de livre couvrant tout le domaine, mais il y a d'excellents ouvrages critiques (plus récents que le Saintsbury), tels que Pierre Martino, le Roman français sous le Second Empire; du même, le Naturalisme français, Jean Hytier, les romans de l'individu (avec extraits). En vérité, le mieux est encore de recourir aux meilleurs livres sur Stendhal: Armand Caraccio, dans Connaissance des lettres; Léon Blum, Stendhal & le Beylisme;

sur Balzac: Bertault, Balzac, l'homme & l'œuvre; A. Béguin, Balzac visionnaire; G. Picon, Balzac par lui-même; H. T. Hunt, Balzac, en anglais;

sur Flaubert, le Thibaudet, et le très bon Philip Spencer, en anglais; et Giraud, The Unheroic Hero; sur Zola, un bon livre en anglais de Angus Wilson.

Le sujet du roman français en général est si vaste qu'il a peu tenté les auteurs de synthèse.

Merci de songer à diriger vers nous vos meilleurs élèves. Nous n'acceptons pas beaucoup de candidats au MA seul, car la place dans nos séminaires est réduite—mais pour les *très, très* bons, il y en a toujours. Et le MAT program vaut la peine que les étudiants, que n'attire pas spécialement la recherche, l'élisent. Je retiens les noms de vos deux candidats possibles.

Croyez à notre souvenir toujours fidèle; vous & votre femme gardez une place assurée parmi ceux qui sont passés ici et dont la finesse d'esprit & la gentillesse de manières nous sont restées chères—et passez une heureuse nouvelle année.

Henri Peyre

## To Harry Levin et al.:

January 26, 1959

Professors Robert Gorham Davis
Columbia University
Victor Lange
Princeton University
Harry Levin
Harvard University
Mark Schorer
University of California (Berkeley)
Gentlemen:

You have probably been informed, by the MLA office, of your appointment by the Executive Council to the new Committees on Honorary Fellows created last December. I have the undeserved honor to be chairman of that committee and the eminence of each of the members fills me with confusion. But I shall let myself be guided by your wisdom and I hope to play the role of an active letter box, transmitting your opinions and suggestions.

You know that we are supposed to select a few distinguished contemporary writers whose works have been studied or are likely to be the subject of scholarly research by our members. I imagine the number, at the present time, should not exceed a dozen or so. We should obviously select them with great care and make reasonably sure that they would accept the honor thus bestowed upon them by those dispensers of the laurels of fame, the scholars. Some probably would not be touched by our declaration of intention to evaluate their work critically, to assign sources to their finest ideas and to scrutinize their grammar. Not many will probably be won over to attending our meetings and to hearing themselves dissected. But I personally welcome the attempt at a rapprochement between writers and critics. Let us build a bridge.

I imagine we should attempt to establish a preliminary list, from which the names to be voted on subsequently by our committee (by letter) might be selected. May I ask you to propose some ten names each, and to send me your list with any remarks and suggestions you may wish to add, by February fifteenth. We then might correspond further and agree both on principles (total number of Fellows, relative proportion of Americans and British among them, stress to be laid on elder statesmen such as Robert Frost, H. Mann, T. S. Eliot, Hermann Hesse or even E. M Forster, Maurois, presumably soon to be replaced) or on less venerable writers (Auden, Spender, Amis, Cummings, Moravia, Emmanuel, Camus, Arthur Miller); preference to be given to those who have not shown much eagerness to haunt the MLA conventions and the college campuses (St. John Perse, Robinson Jeffers, Hemingway, Faulkner) or to the tamer ones among creators (Thornton Wilder, Jorge Guillén, or even Arthur Miller, who tamed the reincarnation of Helen of Troy among us and may have become tamed in the process).

May I hear from you at your very kind and early convenience, and will you believe me,

Most sincerely yours,
Henri Peyre

Dear Harry,

This is a very shabby letter, typed on an unusually busy day. May I add a word to say how much we'll count on your lucid judgment in this, & how grateful I am for the reprints which you occasionally send me? And my words of gratitude are not perfunctory ones: I treasure your articles preciously under a folder entitled: "Critics, American," with a neat, fat subdivision "Harry Levin."

## À Saint-John Perse:

Le 23 avril 1959

Cher Maître,

Vous allez croire que je veux académiser le plus libre des poètes et emprisonner dans nos murs tapissés de livres le plus indépendant des chantres du vent, des mers, des pluies. Il n'en est rien. Mais une postérité chaque année grandissante va vers vos livres, veut vous crier son admiration.

Le Modern Language Association of America m'a mis à la tête d'un comité chargé de choisir, parmi les hommes de lettres vivants du monde entier, huit grands noms sur lesquels nous serions tous d'accord. Nous l'avons vite été sur le vôtre, et sur ceux de T. S. Eliot, W. Faulkner, Hermann Hesse, Jorge Guillén, peut-être Camus, Sartre, E. M. Forster. Nous voudrions donc, au nom de cette énorme association de 10.000 professeurs de cinq ou six littératures, dont l'anglaise & l'américaine, vous prier d'accepter le titre de Membre Honoraire. Si vous le voulez bien, la chose deviendra officielle en décembre prochain, à notre Congrès annuel tenu en fin d'année à Chicago. Cela veut dire que davantage encore d'études critiques & laudatives vous seront sans doute, et pour longtemps, consacrées; peut-être qu'un jour, lorsque notre Congrès aura lieu à New York ou à Philadelphie (en 1960 peut-être), vous voudrez bien faire une apparition et apercevoir quelques-uns de ces collègues qui vous étudient avec passion. Vous avez eu bien d'autres honneurs dans votre vie, & de plus éclatants: mais celui-ci vient de professeurs modestes, dévoués, plus influents qu'ils ne le croient eux mêmes, et moins fermés qu'on ne le dit parfois à la vraie grandeur.

Voulez-vous accepter en principe que la proposition de notre comité soit ratifiée ainsi & que vous soyez parmi nos huit membres honoraires?

Et veuillez croire encore à mon très grand dévouement, et agréer, ainsi que Madame Léger, nos hommages.

Henri Peyre

## À Claude Vigée:

Le 4 mai 59

Cher ami,

Vous êtes gentil & généreux de m'avoir permis de voir ces poèmes. Vous avez, avec tant d'autres dons, celui de vous renouveler comme le phénix et de renaître avec une manière toujours diverse. J'aime fort vos poèmes si denses, aux vers courts & concis, tous en diamants, comme le "Château de la Soif," pur de toute éloquence. Comme Emmanuel & Jouve avant lui, vous êtes allé du feu radieux et ardent qui embrasait vos premiers poèmes, scintillant de toutes parts, vers une expression sobre, nue, où chaque mot évoque, des émotions toujours plus humaines. "Le Soleil de la Toussaint" est un des poèmes les plus émouvants que j'aie lus chez aucun moderne. Rien dans la forme ne cherche à briller ou à frapper. Et votre fils riant sous l'érable a quelque chose des mystérieuses chansons rimbaldiennes.

Je vous envie cette année libre, & d'avoir le courage de vous arracher à l'emprise de ces besognes administratives qui usent affreusement. Vous êtes cependant le chairman admiré d'une énorme conglomération de langues, menez tout de front, introduisant à l'Amérique des figures toujours nouvelles d'écrivains et accroissant votre personnel — avec cela, conservant le loisir & la fraîcheur dont a besoin le poète. Qu'est devenu Henri Thomas? Reste t-il dans ce pays? y est-il heureux? et quand vient Bonnefoy? Ne manquez pas de m'avertir.

Le *Rilke* est un grand projet que vous formez depuis longtemps — Comment rendrez-vous en vers français ces longs ébranlements des Duineser Elegien? La traduction de la poésie (j'en regarde beaucoup en ce moment, de français en anglais, pour une collaboration à un projet d'anthologie) m'apparaît de plus en plus comme ce qu'il y a au monde de plus difficile. Serez-vous en Alsace? À Paris? Je suivrai dans les revues de France, qui vous font maintenant la place qui est la vôtre, sans rancœur étroite contre l'absent, les comptes-rendus de vos œuvres ou la publication de vos poèmes —

        Mes bons vœux à votre femme & à vous.
        Hri Peyre

## À Saint-John Perse:

                Le 16 mai 1959

Cher Maître,

 Nous nous faisons une joie de vous voir lors de votre visite ici pour cet honneur que vous faites à Yale. Les formalités cérémonieuses sont réduites au minimum. Le dimanche soir (7 juin), le Président reçoit d'ordinaire chez lui les nouveaux docteurs "honoris causa" et leur femme; le Commencement lui-même a lieu le lundi matin et se termine à midi et demi par un déjeuner auquel ma femme et moi assisterons aussi.

 Pourriez-vous et voudriez-vous, Madame Léger et vous, nous faire le plaisir, en toute intimité et modestement, de déjeuner avec nous le dimanche sept juin, si vous pensez arriver ici à temps? J'irais bien entendu vous chercher à la gare si vous venez alors de New York — Ou si cela vous paraissait plus commode, voudriez-vous dîner avec nous le lundi soir huit juin, si vous pouviez rester un peu davantage ici, la cérémonie officielle terminée?

 Nous ne voulons point vous accaparer, mais souhaitons pouvoir vous écouter un peu, faire mieux la connaissance de Madame Léger, vous accueillir dans cette université où votre œuvre a séduit beaucoup de jeunes, et d'autres aussi.

 N'hésitez point à recourir à nous si nous pouvons, à cette occasion, vous être utiles en autre chose. Veuillez dire à Madame Léger nos hommages et me croire,

        Votre très profondément dévoué,
        Henri Peyre
        (Téléphone à New Haven — State 7-4705)

## To Whitney Griswold:

June 1, 1959

President A. Whitney Griswold
Woodbridge Hall
Dear Whit:

I have had the pleasure (it was a very real one) to take part in several TV programs organized by Yale Reports and Mrs. Edith Kerr, while you were away in Europe. I am not a TV fan myself, and I do not believe I have any histrionic talents; my gesticulating is only that of the "homme moyen sensuel" of France and my face the average facial mask which Picasso might have taken as a butt for his exercises in ugliness. I yielded to the blandishments of our irresistible Director of Publicity with the reluctance of a skeptic forcibly inducted into the temple of sound and fury (of words) in Hartford.

I am, however, taking the liberty to report to you on my experience, because I have been literally astonished by the number of persons, in or around New Haven, who have spoken or written to me since those appearances. They are people from varied groups and most of them not the kind that we, university teachers, normally reach through our writings or through our lectures. Their reactions, their questions, the determination of a number of them to read further on the subjects broached were encouraging. I believe the service thus organized by Mrs. Kerr is an extremely efficient one in making Yale better known outside and in winning friends for us. This experience, added to many grateful reports which I have heard, in several parts of the country, on our June Alumni Seminars, has convinced me that we should, and easily might, build up a great deal of good will by strengthening further our services to the public outside and beyond our campus and by paying a little more attention to adult education and to the so-called mass media.

Your heroic campaign of the last decade for the improvement of secondary education is bearing fruit in several ways: one of those ways has been to make people aware of the fact that their own education has been deficient and that, to reach a minimum of understanding of themselves and of the world around them, they should pursue their education after the adult age. Many more people than I ever suspected, from lawyers to grocers and dowagers to office girls, are eager not just to be entertained by the antics of professors on TV, but also to know what to read, how to be informed on science and art today, how to think by themselves a little better. I believe there are great potentialities and nothing which any of us, so-called scholars, should deem undignified or cheap, in programs such as the imaginative Eumenid enthroned in the nether floor of Woodbridge Hall and gently pursuing the Yale faculty from there, has devised. I hope you do not mind my taking a minute of your time to say it in writing.

May I add a line of appreciation for the quiet wisdom, the convincing moderation with which, in the current Atlantic, you make the case for the place of the arts in education, and for the benefit that higher education can bring to the creative artist. A gap, however, still remains to be bridged in our universities: we fail to take enough interest in creative artists among or around us, and to train critics who might prove to be interpreters of those living artists to the public and to the artists themselves. The attitude of our departments of arts and modern literature remains, too often, a reactionary one or one of aloofness from the art of the present. It will be hard to reverse this current, even for a President who has the noble zeal of a reformer. But the recent changes effected in our Music School, the appointment of a fine man like Mr. Rudolph in architecture, have caused us to applaud and to rejoice.

Sincerely yours,
Hri Peyre

## À Georges May:

[Martha's Vineyard]
10 juillet 1959

Mon cher Georges,

Je suis un peu paresseux à vous répondre, car je n'ai guère de nouvelles, de ce lieu éventé et ensoleillé, très frais cette année, où je flâne sous les pins, mais j'ai été bien heureux quand j'ai reçu votre lettre. J'avoue que je redoutais pour vous ce long voyage, avec deux enfants, le souvenir encore récent d'une opération pour l'un, la fatigue inévitable de la fin de l'année scolaire, et surtout les dangers de tant de kilomètres [pour faire en Berkeley un cours d'été]. Vous voilà bien arrivé, reçu comme un prince—que vous êtes—herborisant à la Rousseau ou du moins arrosant vos fleurs, savourant vos fruits, humant l'air de l'océan à requins, mais aussi, je crois me rappeler, à poissons et coquillages fort comestibles. Ce séjour va être reposant pour vous, et, si votre tour d'imagination est semblable au nôtre (influence de J. Jacques), vous jouirez encore plus par le souvenir de tant d'impressions accumulées: campus d'eucalyptus, théâtre grec, causeries au faculty club, restaurants du port de San Francisco et l'admirable Stanford. Je me suis parfois dit que, si j'avais eu plus d'esprit d'aventure lorsqu'après ma première année d'Amérique, on m'avait invité à Berkeley, je me serais sans doute établi là, marié là et j'aurais mieux tranché ces liens, fort doux d'ailleurs, qui me rattachent à la France et me déchirent toujours en deux ici. Qui sait? Peut-être l'activité est-elle moindre là-bas, la concentration plus facile.

Mais au fond j'aime mes vices. Je vois, par l'amas de livres hétéroclites que j'ai apportés ici pour un premier séjour de deux semaines, que mon démon me poussera toujours à lire ou à parcourir des bouquins, sinon en 7 ou 8 langues, du moins en autant de littératures—et à accepter à la légère à participer à plus de projets que je ne puis faire en toute conscience. Je vais repartir bientôt et essayer de m'enfermer seul et de rédiger diverses choses—ce repos m'a fait du bien et le calme de l'endroit, les bons amis que nous y avons, la beauté du site nous y charment: c'est un peu en dehors de la vie, dans le style "country club," mais avec simplicité, artificiellement loin de tout ce qui fait la vulgarité riche de vitalité de l'Amérique, un peu suffisante. Je me venge de m'y trouver si bien en tenant parfois des propos libéraux, athées et même libertins, parmi ces gens qui traitent surtout de leurs exploits au golf et discutent gravement de la direction du vent et de la qualité des bains. Je m'étais rêvé plus révolutionnaire que cela dans mes jeunes années. O tempora!

J'ai tenu ma promesse de lire tout Lucrèce—très beau et fort par endroits, bien plus grand esprit que Virgile, mais souvent aussi bien lourdement didactique; je finis maintenant l'*Enéide*, dont les derniers chants ont de rares beautés; divers romans américains, exaspérants mais parfois forts; quelques traductions du scandinave. . . .

## À Saint-John Perse:

Le 21 juillet 1959

Cher Monsieur,

Il n'est pas trop tard, je l'espère, pour vous remercier de la gentillesse avec laquelle vous vous êtes prêté à nos cérémonies, de l'immense plaisir que vous avez fait tous deux, à ma femme et moi, en acceptant de passer avec nous dans l'intimité ces quelques heures, et de la richesse avec laquelle vous prodiguez, dans la conversation, idées, souvenirs et images. Madame Léger nous a également ravis: elle comprend tout, poésie, peinture, politique... et son mari. Nous espérons que vos vacances se passent agréablement.

À ce mot de remerciements, je joins une requête. Un de mes amis, l'un des professeurs de lettres françaises les plus distingués d'Amérique, directeur des études de français à l'Université de Chicago & auteur de divers ouvrages, M. Bernard Weinberg, admire passionnément vos œuvres & les étudie avec ferveur. Il vient d'achever une étude d'Anabase, assez longue et va la faire paraître dans un volume d'études françaises en Italie, à Pise. Il est contraint, & désireux, de citer le texte du poème dont il tente l'exégèse, certes la plus fouillée qui en ait encore été proposée. Brentano's, à New York, lui a répondu que c'est à vous qu'il doit s'adresser pour obtenir cette autorisation. Puis-je le recommander à votre bienveillance et lui confier ce mot? Sans doute votre courrier vous suit-il?

Veuillez redire nos hommages respectueux à Madame Léger, et croire, cher Monsieur, à notre très vraie gratitude.

Henri Peyre

## À Georges May:

30 juillet 1959

Mon cher Georges,

J'oublie quel jour est votre départ de l'Eden occidental, et peut-être vous attarderez-vous un peu. Il fera autrement chaud dès que vous aurez quitté les rivages du Pacifique. Je me rappelle que nous avons longé la côte jusqu'à San Diego, avec effroi quelquefois devant tout ce que l'homme a gâché de beautés naturelles, mais avec curiosité, et Las Vegas nous avait divertis. Ne pressez pas les étapes et voyez les arbres si étranges de ces grandes forêts et même quelques canyons au retour. Vous retournerez par là-bas, mais peut-être plus avec le même loisir de voyageurs automobiles.

Oui, la Californie est tentante, mais il m'avait paru que peu de gens (du moins de ceux qui s'intéressent encore passionnément à l'Europe) y étaient pleinement heureux; ils se croyaient exilés, mis à l'écart, privés de quelques biens qui eussent donné du mordant à leur paradis. J'ai grande admiration pour l'Université, d'après ce que j'en vois surtout dans les dossiers Guggenheim; je suis convaincu que c'est, à beaucoup d'égards, la 1$^{re}$ du pays. Nous sommes un peu étriqués ici, un peu étroits dans notre propagande d'humanistes, un peu en dehors de la science très vivante. . . .

Rien ne vaut, tout compte fait, dans notre métier, comme de former des élèves parmi les étudiants avancés, de les guider sans s'imposer à eux—mais ils constituent ensuite un réseau de liens qui emprisonne un peu et pour les aider, on forme soi-même des liens avec bien des collègues, qu'il convient ensuite de revoir, de conseiller. Je me suis tenu un peu caché ici et n'ai vu qu'au minimum les visiteurs, fort sympathiques, qu'attire ici l'été notre bibliothèque; j'ai accompli pas mal à ce régime et vais retourner à Martha's Vineyard me détendre un peu, car il fait fort humide ici et les nuits sont pénibles. Mais que de chemins s'ouvrent à chaque pas, dès qu'on travaille sérieusement, où on voudrait deux ou trois vies encore pour s'engager! Que de choses je n'ai pas lues et il est trop tard.

C'est pour faire profiter d'autres de mes lacunes et du regret que j'en ai que je pousse tant nos jeunes à écrire aussitôt la thèse achevée. C'est à ces lectures guidées par l'idée d'un livre qu'on apprend le plus, car elles vous convient à fouiller ce qui est en dehors des grandes voies et qu'on n'ouvrirait pas autrement. . . . bien que j'approuve fort le courant que vous avez fait beaucoup pour lancer, d'étudier dans le 18$^e$ siècle le roman, le théâtre, l'art, il faut quand même voir l'époque dans sa vraie perspective, et elle en a remué des idées, sur le bien et le mal, sur le progrès, sur l'individu et la société, sur l'éducation (nous devrions avoir aussi des thèses sur Diderot et le Plan d'une Université en Russie, sur Condorcet, sur l'*Emile*, ce très, très grand livre), sur l'esthétique, il y a bien des choses à faire—et il faut s'y prendre tôt dans une vie.

Revenons à notre cuisine plus modeste: d'abord j'ai déniché une charmante secrétaire, graduée de Smith, parlant excellemment le français, dont vous tomberez tous amoureux: Miss Haegert. Elle commencera au début de septembre. À vrai dire le choix est limité. Cela est très *mal* payé, et l'Université rechigne à payer mieux: plusieurs, mariées, ont refusé d'abord. Espérons que celle-ci résistera au mariage et à la maternité et dira comme la Jeune Parque: Peuple altéré de moi suppliant que tu vives/, non, vous ne tiendrez pas de moi la vie! Je dois dire que j'ai lu beaucoup sur la surpopulation récemment et je suis effaré de l'avenir du monde que je vais quitter: du moins je n'y ai pas accru le nombre de mortels destinés à souffrir à l'étroit! Celle-ci a l'air intelligent et se mettra vite au courant. . . .

Prenez quelque repos au cours de ce voyage; le Colorado, un des rares états que je ne connais pas, doit être très beau. Guicharnaud l'a aimé—moins les gens et le milieu, mais vous êtes tous trop férus de Yale comme de l'ombilic de l'Amérique cultivée! . . .

## To John Gassner:

August 11, 1959

Dear Mr. Gassner:

I am full of remorse when I think how tardy I have been in thanking you for your extremely, *unusually* fine essay on the drama of last season, which you so kindly favored me with. Your appraisal of the two "J.B.'s" was tactful, sensitive, generous, but balanced also & very just, I thought. So were your remarks on the other plays of the season. And I have likewise used the summer respite to read carefully the number of the Tulane Drama Review on Giraudoux: a rich & varied number indeed, one of the best treatments of Giraudoux I have seen, & your article is excellent. I am one of the (not too numerous) Frenchmen who agree with you—not quite on the *Enchanted,* which I do not rate high, or on *Amphytrion,* which I still enjoy, perhaps as a lovely & subtle treatment of a theme which had seemed to me flat & unprofitable with every other writer: you are severe to it. But your tepid estimate of *Electre* is mine: it really amounts to little more than verbal pyrotechnics, & so does *La Guerre de Troie,* a ridiculously overrated display of wit. My conviction is that Giraudoux is but "un petit maître" and not even a profound dramatist for those who, like me, like to read plays even more than to see them. Your essay reinforces me in my views, for it comes from a wise & active practitioner of the theatre & from one who *sees* it as well as reads it.

We hope you & Mrs. Gassner are well & enjoying some summer rest. I spend a little time with my wife at Martha's Vineyard, then some time at New Haven, working intensely. Our very best to you both—

Sincerely & thankfully,
Henri Peyre

## À Georges May:

[West Chop, Martha's Vineyard]
22 août 1959

Mon cher Georges,

Je m'excuse de vous laisser une bonne partie de la besogne de remise en train de l'année en m'échappant pour la fin des vacances. Après plusieurs semaines de chaleur assez dure, je viens chercher ici quelque fraîcheur et faire provision de repos en attendant de reprendre le travail d'enseignement, et j'ai deux ou trois livres par jour que je voudrais absorber, avant d'avoir à donner plus qu'à recevoir et à sentir le vide se faire en soi à mesure qu'on enseigne.

J'espère que vous serez rentré de votre long voyage point trop fatigué, heureux de la vision de tant de paysages nouveaux, normalement impatient de vie familiale enserré dans la carapace d'une auto, impatient d'échapper vers le bureau, le gymnase funeste aux fils d'Achille comme vous, enviant subconsciemment celui qui eut le courage de mettre ses enfants aux Enfants Trouvés. . . .

## Au même:

[West Chop, Martha's Vineyard]
4 septembre 1959

Mon cher Georges,

Je suis heureux de vous savoir de retour, soulagé pour vous des craintes qu'éveille la pensée d'une telle route parcourue avec lassitude, et, si vous êtes comme moi, avec le constant désir de lire d'un œil en conduisant pour maintenir l'esprit en éveil. Cette fin d'été est pénible, affreusement humide; notre île est vraie île cimmérienne; les sirènes des phares beuglent; les moustiques s'affairent, et persécutent le pauvre St Sébastien que je suis, seul à rester immobile à lire mes classiques sous les arbres tandis que les autres s'affairent à tennis, golf, cocktails, potins féminins, ou écartent ces bestioles grâce aux émanations de leurs pipes. . . .

Vous m'avez redonné foi en la jeune génération (la vôtre) par votre jugement sévère sur ce Zazie! J'avais trouvé ce livre inane, artificiel, plein de trucs enfantins et exaspérant de bêtise. J'ai même dissuadé au moins deux éditeurs de le traduire. Mais les éloges qu'on a déversés sur ce bouquin (et d'ailleurs sur plusieurs autres "jeunes" romans) avaient ébranlé ma confiance dans la rectitude de mon jugement. Je sais que je manque du sens du comique, mais je préfère en manquer que de me complaire à ces histoires. . . .

## À Gita May:

Le 22 dec. 1959

Chère mademoiselle,

Vous avez dû croire à ma très mauvaise volonté, ou à ma mésestime pour votre travail. Je suis seulement très pris, quelquefois paralysé devant un trop grand amas de lettres à répondre. La vôtre, & votre ouvrage, étaient restés sur un rayon où je les ai négligés.

Mais j'avais lu, beaucoup goûté, votre Diderot & Baudelaire, & signalé à pas mal de gens que voilà une jeune collègue dont nous devions beaucoup attendre. Avec de la méthode, du savoir rigoureux & précis, vous faisiez preuve aussi d'originalité, d'indépendance de vues, & de sensibilité artistique. Votre article que j'avais lu dans PMLA & que je suis heureux d'avoir sous la forme où vous me l'envoyez, n'est pas moins estimable. Il est joliment écrit, joliment illustré, et il éclaire pas mal de choses sur la technicité remarquable des observations de Diderot sur la peinture en général—sur Rembrandt en particulier, ce qui ne manquait pas d'originalité alors. Curieux que la spiritualité de Rembrandt ne l'ait cependant pas frappé, et son sens si aigu du mystère.

Vous parlez avec trop d'amabilité de la tâche modeste que j'essaie d'accomplir: notre plus grande fierté, à nous anciens, trop tiraillés entre trop de besognes, est de voir des jeunes comme vous réaliser des projets auxquels nous avions vaguement songé, traiter certains de ces beaux sujets qui sont restés si tentants, de faire preuve de talent comme vous le faites.

Croyez, chère Mademoiselle, à mes très vifs remerciements.

Henri Peyre

# the 1960s
## CHAPTER FIVE

**To Harry Levin:**

Jan. 6, 1960

Dear Harry,

My very best wishes to you & to your wife as this New Year hopefully opens. I don't believe you came to Chicago & it was a very exhausting affair; yet there were several excellent papers. With all the horrible side of our profession which those conventions display, there is also reason for believing we have effected great improvement over the last twenty years. The number of bright former students, who have remained bright, is comforting.

I fear I had to pass on to you the chairmanship of the Committee on honorary Fellows of the MLA. I hope you will find it possible to have more Americans & more British writers put forward. I was embarrassed to have several French, outnumbering the English speaking ones.

Camus tragically dead! We are, in great haste, getting together a number of Yale French Studies on Camus & his work. We should wish MSS (2500 words) for Febr. 29, so as to appear in April or May. At once, Douglas & I thought of you as the most eminent American, not specialized narrowly in French, whom we should like to have collaborate in that number. We thought of an article on the theme of revolt, perhaps ("L'homme révolté"), or on some other aspect of his thought, or on the reasons for his appeal to Americans, or anything else which would strongly appeal to you. I know all you have to do & all you do achieve — but this is a case of a "tribute" (an impartial & critical one) where your own voice is needed. If you could do it, we'd be immensely grateful.

Mayoux was here & we spoke of you, admiringly as you must know. I am ever regretful that Cambridge is too far for a busy man. Do accept my best wishes.

Henri Peyre

## À Norman McIntosh:

Jan. 13 — 1960

Cher monsieur McIntosh:

Merci de votre livre & de votre lettre. Nous sommes restés fidèlement attachés aux souvenirs que vous avez laissés et à votre bonne grâce toujours patiente et modeste. J'aimerais vous savoir dans le pays plus libre & plus ouvert qui vous est cher, dans les immensités de l'ouest: cela finira bien par arriver. Il y a des postes cette année, mais c'est toujours la même histoire: on prend de préférence les débutants jeunes & malléables. Attendons cependant: qui sait?

Votre livre est joli, bien présenté, très intelligemment annoté, avec précision et discrétion. Les épistoliers y apparaissent avec un caractère très marqué, séduisant dans sa rigueur & sa morgue — Les lettres sont parfois touchantes. C'est une publication de vrai mérite, & faite avec méthode & pénétration. Vous nous faites honneur.

Votre fils doit être un grand & beau garçon déjà et j'imagine que, digne fils de ses parents, il réussit bien à l'école. On doit skier, chasser, pêcher à Alfred — comme je m'imagine votre région. Mon idée de cette partie de l'Amérique est un peu celle de Chateaubriand. J'ai vu les Giraud à Chicago, assez heureux dans leur paradis terrestre de Stanford; Cohn est là-bas aussi, Temmer à Santa Barbara. L'ouest est peuplé de nos anciens.

Dites bien des choses à votre femme de nous deux, croyez à mes remerciements & à mon très bon souvenir.

Henri Peyre

## To W. M. Frohock:

13—1—60

From a train, while catching up on reading—

I have a fine, cultured, scholarly young man, John Darzins, born in Latvia, who would do well at the best universities—is working on the picaresque novel (18th century), but will probably only finish his diss. in 1960 (late) or 1961.

Just in case.

Missed you in Chicago. Papers seemed rather good.

You cannot resign as chairman yet. Impossible. Please do not!

Cordially,
HP

## To Stanley Burnshaw:

Sat. Jan. 17—60

Dear Stanley,

Thanks for this. It must have been *quite* a task to compile it & to type it, & I do admire you. The French part is all right. Of course, it offers only approximations (for *u* for example), but that's the best that can be done—It will be useful to many readers.

For the *prosody,* did you intend for me to do anything, I mean, to prepare something? Or are you (you're a specialist of French prosody anyway) going ahead & I might see it later?

For the note on "me" as one of its contributors, make it very modest & brief.

I gather you wish me to go ahead & pay Gallimard what he has suggested, through a friend I have who works there as reader & adviser:

there will be no further difficulty & no need to write to each author (when he is alive).

> Thanks once again & very cordially,
> Henri Peyre

## To Whitney Griswold:

January 21, 1960

President Alfred Whitney Griswold
Woodbridge Hall
Dear Whit:

    We know you have many crosses to bear, many buildings to raise, many ambitious or cantankerous professors to tolerate with a smile, many fellowships to endow. But your patience is great and your good will inexhaustible. Heinz Bluhm and I presume to appeal to you for a cause which we believe to be important for Yale University as a whole and for the fame and influence of Yale abroad. We are an internationally respected university and it is essential that our reputation be kept up.

    Ever since the end of World War II, we have had regular exchanges of students with the University of Paris, then with Heidelberg and we are now establishing some with Madrid. It is unfortunate that nothing similar to Rhodes scholarships, Clare fellowships exists for the countries of continental Europe. At first, at least for Franco-American exchanges, our Graduate School provided three fellowships to bring French students here (who usually elected physics, chemistry, engineering, industrial administration, often also economics, American studies, English); we sent three, or more, of our own seniors or of our graduates to the Sorbonne. We still send Yale men to the Sorbonne, thanks to the generosity of the French Government, and our future Ph.D.'s in French absolutely need such a year in the country whose language and culture they will teach. But the Yale funds have dwindled to nothing. We made an effort to stimulate gifts from outside to resume bringing gifted French students here in exchange for the Yale men we sent abroad. Mr. Swords helped us much. But our success has been scant. I understand that the exchange with Heidelberg is likewise in jeopardy, due to the exhaustion of the funds on this side of the water.

We are thus in the humiliating position of a rich university, known and esteemed for its language departments, in the richest and most generous country in the world, unable to bring students from France, Germany, Spain to study here although such students are attracted by the quality of our professors and the advantages of a fine American culture. Meanwhile, our own students are still being admitted and invited abroad, almost out of charity, in the hope that two-way exchanges will be resumed in the near future.

Through these exchanges, Yale would be better known abroad, as Harvard and Columbia manage to be. We would give our own American students an opportunity to gain a maturing experience abroad and to train themselves, presumably for the teaching profession, occasionally for the diplomatic one, for politics, for international business. The young foreigners invited, at a receptive age, to spend one year here would gain respect for our University, for American culture and remain forever friends of this country. No expense is more wisely incurred and constitutes a more fruitful investment than those exchanges of gifted students from leading European countries.

The minimum number of such students would appear to be nine yearly: three from France, three from Germany, one from Italy, two from Spain (other foreign students may, of course, be admitted in our Graduate or professional schools, if they prove desirable to the departments concerned and receive scholarships from them: but such cases become more scarce, as our tuition grows more expensive and our total number of students cannot rise and take care of native American candidates to admission). Naturally such students would have to be accepted by the departments in which they plan to study and by our Dean. The minimum sum to be envisaged (exclusive of travel costs, which can be borne by the Fulbright funds) would be $2,800 per student ($1,000 going for tuition, more if the student is registered in the Law School). The yearly income to be found is thus close to $25,000.

An endowment of half a million dollars is thus needed, or a yearly sum of $25,000 to $28,000 should be provided, if Yale is to play its part in international exchanges of advanced students. Our request is thus: can the President use his authority and influence either with individual donors or with one of the Foundations so that exchanges of such import for the future may be resumed? India, the Arab world, Africa appear to be engrossing the attention of some of the large Foundations these days.

These continents are indeed important. But we also need allies and friends in Western Europe, which has, in the last decade, showed such power of recuperation and such hopeful vigor as to deserve the adjective of "miraculous." Are we going to miss a chance to make friends "for country and for Yale" in these critical years? Can you help us?

Sincerely yours,<br>Henri Peyre

## To the same:

Febr. 9, 1960

Dear Whit,

We (faculty) always labor under the delusion that our writings deserve the critical & sympathetic eye even of the busiest of men. To my reply (tentative) to the State Department question, I am adding these just in case you have any patience with a Frenchman's English and a non-educationist's views on education.

Most sincerely yours,<br>Hri Peyre

## To Maria Jolas:

Febr. 10/60

I had indeed written Mme Sarraute, asking, very tentatively, if she had plans to come over here for a series of lectures. It was too late, in a country like this where everything is arranged months in advance, to envisage the possibility of any such trip for the spring: Butor, Ollier I believe, Bonnefoy are here already. But it could be possible in the fall.

The best thing would be: 1) without delay, to prepare a sheet, briefly describing Mme Sarraute's career & work, enumerating a few subjects (in French, Russian, perhaps English novel, on aspects of the novel to day, etc.) and to send it to some 30 or 40 chairmen of departments of French: Harvard, Brown (Providence), Vassar (Poughkeepsie), Bryn Mawr, U. of Pennsylvania, Johns Hopkins, Chicago, Indiana at Bloomington, Ind., Wisconsin, California. I should be glad myself to forward some of these notices to colleagues elsewhere—You could get in touch with Edel, Ellmann—Mme Sarraute should write directly to M. Édouard Morot-Sir, the French Cultural Counselor at 972 Fifth Avenue, New York, 21, & ask whether her voyage here & back could not be paid by the French Cultural Relations—I believe it could be—The fees for the lectures, if the dates are well arranged, October–November, should take care of the expenses over here—

You are very kind to take such an active interest in this trip of Mme Sarraute. Many of us are eager to make it possible and admire her talent. Your name, of course, is meaningful, & dear to us. I hope the project can be successful & there is no reason why it should not be.

Very sincerely yours,
Henri Peyre

## To James M. Osborn:

April 17, 60

Dear Jim,

Mr. Witten's small, discreet & truly fascinating piece on your library, so elegantly presented, makes a welcome Easter present. It is very informing, not only on your tastes—and on what a scholar with flair & insight was able to hunt out in the course of a few decades. You are a collector, but, unlike many, one who reads the books, interprets them, lets himself be led from one discovery to another & one who has also that rare gift among collectors: generosity, & who shares his pleasures with others. To you & to Mr. Witten, thank you.

Cordially yours,
Henri Peyre

## To Stanley Burnshaw:

April 27, 60

Dear Stanley,

I could only glance at the volume—what with De Gaulle in NY, theses, travels, etc., I seem to have no leisure just now for reading—but the book, at first glance, looks superb! elegant, intelligently presented, & it should be praised & used. Let's hope.

I know Walters a little & just sent him a book review. Even though I am "involved" in the book, I'll write him to suggest with some urgency that the volume, important as it is, be reviewed in their columns. If I can write in a personal way to any one else I more or less know, I'll be glad to.

H. M. Jones would be the best man—or an Englishman perhaps, even Auden?

I know Masui, from Cellais, & he has written me & will be here shortly. I have not yet answered him but shall soon do so.

Do hope for the deserved success. Il y a une justice! & you may be proud of it.

Thanks for the 12 copies I ordered: I'll pay the bill at once.

Congratulations.

H. P.

**To the same:**

April 28/60

Dear Stanley,

After I wrote you hastily yesterday, I took the liberty to write this letter (copy enclosed) to Mr. Walters—pretending that I meant to write on other matters anyway. I hope this is not indiscreet & suits you.

On second thoughts, will you order for me *eight* more copies of *The Poem Itself*, & bill me the 20 altogether. I must have easily twelve lady friends to whom, at my age, I can offer but poetical satisfactions (o! the virtues of symbolism)—& easily ten key people abroad who might be inspired to follow your method & your model. April, the cruelest month as T. S. Eliot & the Income tax department have decreed, will soon be departed & I'll feel rich again.

Most cordially,
Henri

## To the same:

May 15—1960

Dear Stanley,

I shall marvel no longer at your success in business, Stanley-Millions, who has retained the soul of a poet, the sensitiveness of a fanatic of friendship, the gentle affection of a prolific father for his daughters & for the collaborators to the *Poem Itself,* each of whom now feels like your son. I have never yet read, or received, such detailed accounts & such superb financial reports as you send us, though the depth of it all drowns me. But I am very grateful for the generous check & only worry because I feel it may not be deserved. Why do I seem to receive more than any one else? Or why was I so voracious in, perhaps, taking over too much? I had sent Kneller a check for $125.00 last August for his assistance. Was that enough? Or have I been unfair to him? Do tell me very candidly.

I'll see you Wednesday between 5 & 6 or so—it will be a pleasure—From several sides, from those who have already bought, or seen, the book at the local book store, I hear warm praise—for the original idea—& for the result. You may well congratulate Holt & Co.

After a few more absences, speeches, & the inevitable string of exams, I'll be in Europe this summer after June 10th or so. I'll try & live quietly there, at least for a while.

I haven't received the eight other copies I had asked you to tell Holt to send me (the first twelve had arrived a while ago). I suppose they will follow. I'll send a few to Europe.

Again, cordially yours & à bientôt,
Henri

## To the same:

May 26/60

Dear Stanley,

Your party was a *great* success—very few snobs, very few conceited, self inflated authors, very, very few over-talkative & over-jabbering ladies in your group. Many extremely interesting people, exquisite food & the two poles met: Robert Frost in his unfading vigor & serene glory, & Valérie Burnshaw, a bright & darkly luminous planet, as fair & obviously as intelligent as her remarkable parents.

Donald Adams' piece is a great thing & I was flattered by his selection of my piece on Baudelaire. I hear excellent things about the book, even from difficult judges like Poggioli (enclosed) & from the 5 or 6 persons to whom I have offered the volume. Your efforts have been rewarded.

J. Kneller sent me, endorsed to me, his check from you, for $39.00 & some cents. He insists he has no right to royalties since I had paid him beforehand—& is adamant on it. I am embarrassed still further by your prodigality. Tell me what seems right to you.

I shall be sailing on June 10th on *Flandre* & seem to be submerged with exams, theses, speeches until then. I fear I won't see you before I leave & accept my very best compliments for you & your wife.

Most cordially yours,
Henri Peyre

## À Saint-John Perse:

Le 14 juin 1960

Cher Maître,

Le très aimable envoi de la brochure qui renfermait d'admirables textes poétiques de vous et quelques articles fort beaux eux-mêmes m'a beaucoup touché. Il m'est parvenu en fin d'année—moment lourdement prosaïque pour nous, où il nous incombe de lire dans les thèses et examens d'étranges déformations des idées que nous avions cru avoir. J'ai différé jusqu'au calme du bateau qui nous amenait en France de savourer à loisir ces textes: sur le pont, parfois, j'ai récité à haute voix des versets de "Chronique." L'évocation du "grand âge" et l'appel aux générations qui sont appelées à leur tour à marcher "sur les chemins de pierre brûlante éclairés de lavande" sont parmi les pages les plus heureuses de votre œuvre. Je vous remercie de nous les avoir ainsi offertes, comme survenait l'anniversaire de votre visite à Yale qui nous avait donné à tous deux tant de joie. Voulez-vous redire à Madame Léger quel souvenir radieux nous gardons de sa visite & de la vôtre, et croire à mes très fidèles remerciements.

Henri Peyre

## To James & Mrs. Osborn:

[postcard: view of Swedish country church]
July 14 /1960

Dear friends,

That evening with you, all illuminated & radiant with dancing ephebes & nymphs & the flow of beverages, left us with fine memories to bear the hardships of traveling. But the hardships are bearable. Even in these northern lands, we have found sun, warmth occasionally & very lovely & serene people—a bit stolid & monolithic at times but gentle & dispassionate. We shall leave for Helsinki & Leningrad, then hide somewhere in France. We hope you are well & duly cool in your air cooled house.

Our very cordial wishes.<br>Marguerite & H. Peyre

## À Georges May:

[letterhead: Hôtels St. James & d'Albany, Paris]
27 juillet 1960

Mon cher Georges,

... Mais ne finit-on pas par exagérer la grandeur de Diderot? Je l'ai toujours aimé, étant à ma manière touche à tout, matérialiste convaincu, et moraliste prêcheur. Mais Rousseau est beaucoup plus grand, même comme romancier! Et l'Émile, le Gouvernement de la Pologne sont de splendides œuvres.

Reposez-vous. Je pars avec toute une valise de notes et de livres, dont je ferai sans doute très peu. Je relis des romans russes. Cette étrange Russie m'a rebuté (et je reste trop petit bourgeois et bien peu Spartiate et ami du peuple surtout en théorie), mais troublé aussi. L'Amérique, de loin, me déçoit, je l'avoue, et le charme de la France me reprend. . . .

## À Franco Simone:

Le 28/VII/60

Cher Ami,

Juste après vous avoir vu au Congrès, j'ai trouvé votre mot, envoyé de Yale. Bien sûr, continuez à me faire envoyer *vos deux revues & je règlerai, aussitôt rentré à Yale en septembre, mes abonnements pour trois nouvelles années.* J'admire énormément votre revue & apprends beaucoup à ce que vous, en particulier, y écrivez. Vous avez la rigueur d'esprit (ostinato rigore) & la largeur en même temps; et la vie qui vous permet de stimuler d'autres chercheurs, & de former des disciples. Je suis heureux de vous avoir revu, même si vite.

Croyez, cher Ami, à mes sentiments très fidèles.
Henri Peyre
Yale University
New Haven, Conn.

## To Richard Aldington:

(Calvi, Corsica)
August 15, 1960

Dear Mr. Aldington:

You are most kind to write me thus on my modest review of your very warm *Mistral* book. I hope it can help it be known as it deserves. It is a book full of sunlight & of joy & of vigorous vituperation against all that is mediocre in the modern world. I am a Southern Frenchman myself, & just now, disgusted with the Riviera and even with much in the Vaucluse region where my ancestors came from, I have looked for a little calm beauty in Corsica. In a few days, I shall be sailing for the U.S.A. I have often wished you would come there to lecture. There is much that audiences should enjoy hearing from you. And of most of the writers who entered the literary world just before World War I & who have been hopping about fighting for a variety of baffling & contradictory causes, Middleton Murry, Herbert Read, T. S. Eliot himself & others, may I say that I have always esteemed you the highest, & wished you'd write your memoirs & an outspoken record of much that went on in literature since 1910. You may not realize how many "amis inconnus" you have among men of my generation (nearing old age) &, I hope, younger ones.

Yes, "Tourism" is spoiling the world—as it has Italy for me. If pilgrims visiting these Mediterranean shores only were passionate ones— & would feel more & talk less!

Many thanks indeed, Cher Maître, & believe me,

> Very sincerely yours,
> Henri Peyre
> Yale University
> New Haven, Conn.

## To Stanley Burnshaw:

Sept. 9, 1960

Dear Stanley,

I got back today on the Liberté & find your note among a pile of letters & I'll answer it at once. *Of course,* we (I am sure I can speak for the others) are glad to lecture for 150 dollars or for 100 or even for nothing! Your group is a very challenging & interesting one & it is a pleasure to appear before it, not to mention the extra pleasure of seeing you on this occasion. The lectures were overpaid before, in fact.

Our summer went very well & I have returned rested & full of energy—& ready to tackle the several projects on which I'd like to spend a little spare time, if I ever spare any! We had three very quiet weeks in Corsica.

I have, being absent, not seen reviews of the *Poem Itself.* Were they understanding?

If you would rather have me do Balzac, or Proust, or some one else than Flaubert, it's all right with me. Just decide according to your needs.

Are your wife & daughters well? & are you rested yourself?

> Most cordially,
> Henri

## To Harry Levin:

Sept. 18—1960

Dear Harry,

I know that you are above any thanks from those who know less & see less deep than you, & that you do not expect any for a reprint. But I want to receive more of your productions & to assure you I read them, with delay, but with delight. I enjoyed your very fine article on *Romeo & Juliet* & the condensed & penetrating comments on the "formality" of the lines you quote. Your article sent me back to the whole play, from which I had kept away for many years, distrusting any rereading of it after having liked it overmuch at the romantic age. That entertained me as we traveled in several parts of Europe, occasionally (as in Leningrad) in need of patience to bear with the despicable "cuisine." Back now, as you must be, & soon to undergo the rejuvenation of the fresh batch of scholars & gentlemen at our feet & round our necks. I trust you are well & Harvard flourishes & your colleagues in French have not yet reached the dullness of peace & unanimity.

Very cordially yours,
Henri Peyre

## To Whitney Griswold:

Sept. 20/1960

Dear Whit,

It was good to see you smiling, full of vigor like a preacher who has just delivered his first sermons of the New Year & welcomed 1090 spiritual sons—the most promising ever to enter Yale, every year! Mary & you seemed exceptionally well.

Pardon this personal note. The French Government is bestowing the decoration of Chevalier de la Légion d'Honneur on Eugene Rostow. He, too, is Napoleonic indeed, among our group of enlightened despots! Monsieur Morot-Sir, the French Cultural Counselor, will come on Friday October seventh to give him the red ribbon & the accolade. I realize that's an exceptionally busy day for you with the first Corporation meeting. If, however, you could attend the small & brief gathering & event, at 12.15, on October 7th, in the Law School, & thus congratulate Rostow & shake hands with M. Morot-Sir, then have lunch as my guest at 12:45 with a very few Deans or colleagues, before you plunge into "la haute finance," I'd be honored. This is just to ask you first informally, & I'd send a more precise note to you later.

Very sincerely yours,<br>Henri Peyre

## To the same:

Sept. 28/1960

Dear Whit,

Thank you for your cordial & kind note. I am sorry I seemed to hint (or did I bluntly & irreverently say it?) that we see too little of a great man? I write my year-end reports far too fast.

I still hope I might, for 3 minutes, bring M. Morot-Sir to see you in Woodbridge Hall, at 11.55 on Friday the Seventh of October. (There is a possibility of the Ambassador of France coming to Yale later on a visit; he was first invited by our Political Union, & I thought it better for him to visit Yale more officially.) He is a very remarkable Ambassador. If you could come to Gene Rostow's accolade & champagne (Law School, Faculty Lounge), you would walk with us there. The ceremony is at twelve. It should be over by 12.30.

I was hoping you might join us for a gentlemen's lunch (10 or 12 of us) at 12.45 in the Governor's Room in the Graduate Club, after Rostow's decoration, with M. Morot-Sir, the Provosts & the Deans or some of them. If you can find your way to do it, please do so & just give a call to my office to confirm it. If higher statesmanship prevents it, we shall all bow & miss your cheerful presence & your vivacious French.

Sincerely yours,<br>Hri Peyre

## À Jacques Maritain:

Yale University<br>Le 15 octobre 1960

Cher monsieur,

 J'apprends que Mme Maritain est malade—gravement malade. J'en suis profondément attristé & je me permets de vous dire quelle part je prends à votre angoisse, à votre douleur. Vous avez vous-même vécu ces dernières années des heures cruelles, avec un courage qui fait notre admiration. Votre *Philosophe dans la Cité,* d'autres pages de vous attestent votre indomptable résistance en face de tous les coups du sort; le succès prolongé, tous les jours attesté par les jeunes qu'atteint l'édition brochée du livre, de votre *Creative Intuition* montre assez ce que les générations qui montent trouvent en votre pensée de nourriture. La perte de sa sœur aînée a été pour Mme Maritain un irréparable deuil et un immense chagrin. Mes vœux, ceux de vos amis inconnus & de tous bords, est qu'elle puisse encore quelque temps vous apporter ce qu'elle vous a toujours donné de dons de l'esprit, du cœur, & de l'âme, et que vous-même ne vous sentiez point abattu à l'excès de ces anxiétés qui vous assaillent aujourd'hui.

 Voulez-vous croire à ma très profonde et affectueuse sympathie, pour Mme Maritain & pour vous, en cette heure d'épreuve.

Henri Peyre

## To James M. Osborn:

[postcard: drawing of Venice by R. Dufy]<br>Oct. 17 [1960?]

Dear Jim,

 We missed you sadly at the Eliz. Club & would have liked to explain our personal, & unusually warm, thanks for all that you did. To all your achievements as scholar & breeder of bulls & electrifier of trees & flowers, you have added that of decorator (& a superb one indeed) & of a polished diplomat smoothly replacing a stubborn housekeeper by a smiling & gentle one. We were all grateful, & touched. Hope you are well by now.

Sincerely,
Henri Peyre

## To Whitney Griswold:

Oct. 18/60

Dear Whit,

I have written airmail, very discreetly, to Mlle Jeanne Saleil, who (I believe) is in charge of the Smith group this year in Paris, & to two friends, young, understanding, who may soon call on your daughter & see about making her feel more at home or help her find a family. I believe that may be useful & will in no way appear to her as an intrusion upon her privacy.

I also phoned M. Morot-Sir. Would you not send him a line (M. Édouard Morot-Sir, Cultural Counselor of the French Embassy, 972 Fifth Ave, NY 21), stating a few facts: age, name of your daughter, what kind of home you might prefer if she wishes to be in a family. Just a few "coordonnées" as we say in French; or your wife may do that & he'll act at once.

It was a pleasure to see you. Enclosed: a slight touch of paganism for your stoic moments, offset by a touch of Christianity.

Sincerely yours,
H. P.

## To President Griswold, Provost Buck, and Dean DeVane:

October 31, 1960

Gentlemen:

You probably remember that, for the last twelve years, we have had a summer session in France, called *The Yale–Reid Hall Summer Session in Paris;* through an arrangement entered into by President Seymour, we had one of our Yale teachers take a group of young people (girls and boys, from several colleges, a few of the boys from Yale) to spend six weeks of study in Paris and two weeks of cultural travel in the French provinces and art centers. The arrangement was satisfactory to both parties, and cost nothing to Yale University.

In the last few years, however, it proved more and more difficult to recruit the minimum number of students required to have the summer session pay off; the deficit, if and where there was one, had to be supported by Reid Hall. It also became difficult to find a Yale professor willing to go over there to devote his time to the supervision of the session, in spite of the very fair stipend offered the director in charge. The young members of our faculty who had the maturity and the authority required, at the rank of assistant professor or higher, became more and more anxious to devote their summers to their own research. After some correspondence with Miss Dorothy F. Leet, the President of Reid Hall, who has always showed the kindest understanding of our difficulties and was most generous to that session in collaboration between Reid Hall and Yale, we have decided, as of November 1, 1960, to abandon this undertaking in the common interests of Reid Hall and of Yale. This letter is to let you know of our decision. We shall be glad to advise our Yale students desirous of spending a few weeks of study in France during the summer to join any other organization which Reid Hall may run or sponsor and our gratitude to Miss Dorothy F. Leet, as a friend of Yale and a very effective interpreter of America to France and of France to America, is very great.

Sincerely yours,
Hri Peyre

Cc: Miss Dorothy F. Leet

## To Whitney Griswold:

Nov. 23, 1960

Dear Whit,

Will you be so kind as to tell Mary how sorry (& a little shocked) I am that the wives of our two envoys find it impossible to accompany their husbands on their visit next Monday? Are they afraid of our university of "surmâles" who slaughter all their football competitors? It is most gracious of her to arrange for a dinner when she is so busy elsewhere.

I shall meet M. Alphand at the New Haven airport at 2 P.M. on Monday Nov. 28th. He can, I hope, see a little of the University before four P.M. Would you consent to introduce him at his lecture, if you plan to attend it? And could I, in this case, bring him & M. Morot-Sir to your office a quarter of an hour before four thirty? Just a word of answer through Mrs. Tilson would be fine.

Very sincerely yours,<br>Henri Peyre

## To Willard Thorp:

[letterhead: Princeton University Library]
Jan. 10, 61

Dear Mr. Thorp:

Many thanks for your help & your part in the MLA convention. I was sorry to see but so little of you — & may I now ask you for further assistance?

Although I do not sit on it, the Council has asked me to be chairman of a committee (consisting of Bronson, G. Brée, N. Frye, Otis Green, Moulton) to select a new Secretary, to serve with Stone in 1961–2 & replace him in 1963. Our activities have grown immensely, as you know: the Secretary has to be fairly young, active, energetic, able to negotiate with the Foundations, to be a good editor, to sympathize with the F[oreign] L[anguage] program, & much besides. He would probably be attached to NYU, & ideally be in the English field. Our committee might well reexamine the whole problem of the secretaryship & what it entails, what it might or should be; & it should consider a number of names to start with.

Could you, as one of those who know the MLA best & whose judgment is most respected, offer me any views you have on the subject in general — & suggest any names which we might first consider, then choose from? My colleagues & I would be extremely grateful.

Very sincerely yours,<br>Hri Peyre

## To Stanley Burnshaw:

March 2, 61

Dear Stanley,

Welcome back to you & the spring which you have brought us from the eastern Mediterranean & your ever fresh & renewed inspiration. You are an agnostic pilgrim but a passionate one. I hope to see you soon & hear all about your impressions. Have your lectures continued in your absence? You *are* irreplaceable, though.

I'll do the Mme Bovary piece—but I have had a lot published lately & a lot written which had been promised & have had to delay that. I'll be ready with it soon, as soon as I can set up my mind on it. Thanks for the reminder.

Yes, I am still on the Guggenheim committee this year, though I begin to feel that after ten years I must get stale & should be replaced. Do you mean that your application would be to you as a translator-poet? Why not? Of course the number of applicants for poetry is large: often 70 or more, & very few are retained—& preference seems to be granted to younger men—but you might very well apply, before October 15th, 1961—& if I can help, let me know (perhaps with a draft in writing) what the project would be. There will also be announced a sizable Bollingen prize for poetry translations published within the year: again, why not you?

Most cordially yours,
Henri Peyre

## To Harry Levin:

March 11, 61

My dear Harry,

What a beautiful inaugural lecture, so brilliantly written—and so judicious, so fair on the grand old man, very likeable in spite of all his mistakes. He missed about as many of the significant writers of the last century and a half as Sainte Beuve had done in his time; he warped the views of many neo-humanists for several decades; but when all is said, no American in the field of French studies ever was his equal in this country—not Gauss, certainly not Lancaster, & neither Baldensperger nor Spitzer who failed to be interested in the life of the country enough to influence disciples & the public. It is an honor to be appointed to his chair. I wish I had been there to applaud you on November 7th.

I regret so never to see or to meet you. I give much of my time to many committees: Guggenheim, 2 or 3 other foundations, just now a very time-consuming committee to select a new Secretary for the MLA. I still cherish the hope that you may stop here for lunch some day & I shall plot, with other of your admirers, to have you elected to a cordial, if venerable, & motley, Society in Philadelphia, where perhaps you would occasionally repair.

> Many thanks meanwhile & very cordially yours,
> Henri Peyre

## À Konrad Bieber:

> Le 25. IV. 61

Cher ami,

J'étais absent mercredi, à Philadelphie: je le suis souvent, hélas! et je n'aurais pu aller jusque chez vous écouter Lusseyran; mais je sais d'avance qu'il a dû avoir grand succès. Peu d'hommes ont cette qualité de vibrante ardeur & de lucidité réchauffante. Je suis si heureux qu'il soit parmi nous, en Amérique, & rapproché bientôt de vous.

Vous êtes trop gentil pour mon tout petit compte-rendu, où j'avais craint ensuite d'avoir été léger & indiscret. Mais vous montrez toujours envers moi trop d'indulgence. J'ai besoin aussi de votre sévérité.

Chadourne est rentrée, je crois, je lui écrirai bientôt. Je ne crois pas que sa publication de ce pseudo Mme de la Fayette lui ait rendu service: l'attribution est trop évidemment hasardeuse. Va-t-il continuer à enseigner chez vous? Ecrit-il autre chose? Dites-lui mes amitiés, & je lui écrirai bientôt.

Ce *Silva* de Vercors est assez joliment tourné et ingénieux. Il réussit mieux dans la fable ou l'allégorie que dans le roman qui se veut tragique ou morbide & c'est à son honneur. Si sa visite se précise, voulez-vous me le dire dès la rentrée, pour que nous lui fassions place? Il y aura beaucoup de Français au début de l'automne: Guichard, Francastel, Gabriel Marcel.

Oui, je resterai beaucoup ici (à New Haven) cet été: je l'espère du moins. Je dois pousser quelques écrits & me cacher pour cela. Je regrette de manquer Utrecht.

Les Giraud sont passés ici — tout heureux & sereins. Nous les aimons beaucoup & ils nous manqueront toujours.

Bien à vous,<br>Hri Peyre

## To Stanley Burnshaw:

June 9, 1961

Dear Stanley,

Pardon a hasty line from a plane; I am flying off to Cincinnati to get an honorary degree there — then to one or two other places, to receive a similar & most dubious honor, & to deliver a few Commencement speeches & try to avoid platitudes. These events in America have become an imposing & pompous ending of a strenuous year. I suppose I should get off to Europe in order to avoid them, but I need my time & my notes this summer to work a little quietly. I have several books "in progress," but none progresses enough.

You should not have rewarded me for my very scant help on the Bompiani. I was glad to have had this opportunity to reopen the fine Italian volumes. I feared my comments would appear negative, defeatist; but on second and third thought, I am even more convinced that the thing would be preposterous. Some things are better done in other countries; let them be done there! Why not start a purely American enterprise, "ex ovo," & a feasible one?

I am glad for you that you'll be enjoying the country. Where is your idyllic retreat? I suppose you will be at the Holt office occasionally & I am dropping this informal note there. Is your family all well?

Do let me hear of your projects. Your head is a Balzacian one, ever conceiving new audacious enterprises & your heart remains . . . that of a poet.

Cordially yours,<br>Henri

## À Claude Vigée:

[Sans date]

Mon cher ami,

J'ai été absent 10 jours, à recevoir divers "degrés" honoraires, donner des discours de Commencement & autres corvées & je trouve ce soir votre lettre. Ce matin même, mettant en ordre ma correspondance, j'avais écrit à M. Rotenstreich—avec chaleur & conviction.

Je crois avoir répondu, tôt cette année, au très aimable envoi de votre livre; mais j'avais dû adresser ma lettre à Paris, aux soins de votre éditeur. Je ne vous savais pas en Israël. Je vous disais grand bien de ce beau livre, ardent, pénétrant, séduisant même là où (comme sur *la Princesse de Clèves*) je faisais quelques réserves.

Votre nouvelle lettre m'étonne. Comment pouvez-vous croire que je manque de foi en vous? J'ai été le 1er peut-être à vous admirer comme poète, à vous louer, à vous recommander sans que vous le sachiez et à ceux-là même qui, à Harvard par exemple, faisaient quelques réserves sur votre manière, si différente de l'histoire littéraire traditionnelle & pédestre. Vous avez plus d'intelligence que 98% d'entre nous, de la flamme & de la pénétration, et vous êtes un vrai & grand poète; seul Grosjean à mes yeux & très rarement Emmanuel & Claudel, bien sûr, vous égalent. Je ne savais RIEN de ces machinations: je ne connais pas, ou à peine, M. Duff, dont je n'ai jamais rien lu. Mais je sais qu'il y a place en Israël pour un *grand* centre d'études françaises; que vingt Français d'Amérique & Américains (Brombert par ex., de Yale, ou G. May, ou Lapp de UCLA, ou Fowlie) devraient y être invités; que l'on devrait avoir là les étudiants les plus doués du monde, peut-être, & qu'on y devrait construire avec liberté & avec foi. Si ce M. Duff se conduit ainsi, c'est un triste sire.

Ceci dit, je regrette que vous quittiez l'Amérique. Il y a fort à faire ici, peu de gens de talent, bien peu qui vous vaillent. Brandeis est décapité sans vous. On cherche de tous côtés des professeurs & vous auriez pu aller où vous voudriez. Avez-vous bien réfléchi à la place que vous occupiez ici? À la perte d'influence que nous allons subir? Serez-vous heureux là bas? En tous cas si je puis récrire encore, ou à d'autres personnes de ma connaissance rassemblées par Duff dans ce comité, dites-le moi & je le ferai. Harry Levin? Bonnefoy? Merci du 2nd exemplaire de votre livre. Ne voulez-vous pas que je l'envoie à quelqu'un, puisque j'en avais déjà reçu un de Paris, lu aussitôt?

> Mille choses à votre femme & bien à vous,
> HP

## À Wallace Fowlie:

Le 23—VI—61

Mon cher Michel,

Merci pour votre lettre si affectueuse et si aimable. Cela a été une vraie joie pour nous de vous revoir. J'ai apprécié tout ce que vous aviez fait & dit pour me permettre de rendre ainsi visite à Bennington: vous avez un Président très distingué, & qui sait votre valeur. J'ai eu plaisir à le connaître, mais j'ai surtout aimé de me trouver à Bennington, parce que c'est un endroit dont vous m'avez souvent parlé jadis—où vous avez formé des générations d'élèves, écrit, rêvé, pensé. Votre talent, inférieur à nul autre en ce pays dans les domaines des littératures modernes, méritait certes un cadre plus vaste, mais je ne sais si l'administration, l'organisation de multiples divisions de cours de langue, de laboratoires audio-visuels, peut-être les jalousies ou cabales ne vous auraient pas privé ailleurs de temps & de liberté. Je me demande souvent moi-même si je n'ai pas eu tort de choisir la voie de l'activité, mais aussi de la turbulence un peu vaine, plutôt que celle de la paix relative que j'aurais pu avoir à Bryn Mawr, peut-être même en Europe. Vous pouvez être fier de ce que vous laissez des livres comme votre Mallarmé, vos Illuminations, votre Dionysos (vous en avez vu, bien sûr, le compte-rendu dans le TLS de Londres), vos traductions, & bien d'autres que nul d'entre nous n'a égalés. Vous avez beaucoup sacrifié à l'affection que vous portez à votre mère. Ces années finales, pour elle, pour vous, sont cruelles. Tout votre courage moral n'est pas de trop. Si mon amitié peut vous être de quelque soutien, croyez bien qu'elle vous est depuis longtemps acquise & jamais n'a fléchi.

J'ai oublié le nom de ce monsieur que vous aviez invité avec Montesinos & qui traduit, je crois, Pablo Neruda. Pourrai-je l'avoir? Le MLA me demande justement qui pourrait communiquer avec Neruda, qu'elle voudrait faire "honorary member" comme le sont St J. Perse, Malraux, Sartre, & je voudrais signaler son traducteur & sans doute ami.

Je serai absent de "West Chop, Martha's Vineyard" du 16 juillet au 8 août environ. Mais si à un autre moment vous vouliez sauter nous voir, nous en serions ravis.

Encore merci du fond du cœur, et nos vœux pour la santé de votre mère.

Henri

## À Jorge Guillén:

Le 30 juin 1961

Mon cher & grand poète,

Vous avez dû me croire d'une ingratitude inhumaine. Je me sens coupable envers vous, l'homme que j'aime peut-être le plus de tous les hommes de lettres que j'ai connus & le génie le plus modeste qui soit, l'espagnol le moins enivré de fierté & le moins pétri de mysticisme. Car vous m'avez offert le très précieux don de trois des plus beaux volumes de ma bibliothèque, & je ne vous en ai même pas encore remercié.

J'attendais le répit de quelques jours de libres pour vous lire à loisir, surtout votre poésie que, sachant imparfaitement l'espagnol, je dois déchiffrer gauchement. Mais j'en jouis peut-être mieux aussi. Vos deux volumes sont pour moi pleins d'une rare beauté: nul tarissement de l'inspiration depuis Cantico & Clamor, au contraire: la substance, la pulpe en est d'une saveur sensuelle & comme vous le dites ailleurs dans les conférences de Harvard, c'est en même temps une poésie sur quelque chose, & quelque chose d'humain. Véritablement, à travers tout ce que vous célébrez de la nature, de l'amour, de la créature, vous chantez et vous inspirez l'espérance. Votre ouvrage "critique" n'est pas moins créateur. J'y ai retrouvé cette justesse pénétrante, méfiante de toute sottise pédantesque, de tout jargon, de toute froide théorie que j'aime dans votre conversation. Sur Gongora & Bécquer, que je goûte aussi, et sur Berceo que je ne connaissais pas, et sur les poètes qui sont vos contemporains, vous écrivez des choses fines, pénétrantes & adorablement modestes. C'est un des plus beaux livres de la série Norton, de beaucoup.

Allez-vous bien? Revenez-vous ici parfois? Vous nous manquez. Devrons-nous aller jusqu'à Rome pour vous revoir?

Merci & croyez à notre fidèle amitié,<br>Henri Peyre

## To Stanley Burnshaw:

[postcard]<br>Aug. 10 (1961)

Dear Stanley,

Superb, your article in Sewanee, not only important historically, but sparkling in style, humorous, skillful in making the ego not a bit "haïssable," on the contrary—& the article does you credit—a lad in his twenties!

I am off this very morning to Martha's Vineyard, having caught up with work & affairs here, & written steadily. I need a rest—I'll see you in the fall—at the Publisher's Institute, if not earlier—I am sending you a very modest collection of a few essays meanwhile.

Cordial greetings to you & your family.<br>Henri Peyre

## À Claude Vigée:

Ce 22 août 1961

Cher ami,

Je vous avais envoyé un mot pour vous féliciter à Brandeis, en spécifiant qu'on le garde pour votre retour—mais M. Gordon (ou Mlle?) me l'a renvoyé en m'indiquant votre adresse. Recevez donc ces lignes pour vous redire ma joie que tout se soit bien passé & que, tout de même, la justice l'ait emporté sur une sotte cabale. Vous allez nous manquer ici—mais vous pourrez enfin fonder en Israël un groupe d'études françaises, de critique créatrice et vivante, de ferveur poétique dont le pays a besoin. Quelques étudiants avancés, malheureusement peu au courant du français, sont venus d'Israël étudier à Yale en littérature comparée & je dois dire qu'ils étaient supérieurs—infiniment supérieurs en sérieux, ferveur, diligence & maturité aux meilleurs Américains. Un pays qui a de tels hommes, s'il sait les guider comme vous le ferez, peut compter sur l'avenir.

Pourrez-vous là-bas écrire, créer, vous sentir enraciné (comme vous tenez à l'être) suffisamment pour vous sentir inspiré? Votre talent poétique est chaque année plus divers, plus nuancé—et vous avez devant vous un avenir "créateur" fort beau—alors que bien des poètes se dessèchent trop vite.

Mon souvenir amical à votre femme & mes bons vœux,
Hri Peyre

## To Harry Levin:

Nov. 29/61

Dear Harry,

Many thanks for your kind letter on Brombert. It will be most useful. I am very glad that your *Power of Blackness* may reach the French in their own idiom. I hope the translator will do you justice, however! The French should know more about American literature before Sinclair Lewis. But they are doing a good job, at the Lettres Modernes & elsewhere, publishing critical essays on Faulkner & others.

We'll see you in April, if not before then. We'd love to have you & your wife, who charmed us, stop here for a meal once. And at the Philos. Society, let's at least have a drink together before affronting the archaeologists, Nobel prizes & other tenants of Franklinian "useful knowledge."

I had never been jealous of Harvard—but on that committee, I discover that Harvard men are so excellent, & (outside Cambridge, or outside the Depart. of Romance Languages!) they admire each other so much that they always co-opt more Harvard men. The poor Midwest is squeezed out. But Yale, which Santayana called a healthy Sparta in the face of the decadent Athens of the Charles River, can no longer boast of its muscles, or of its feet, to resist the Harvard athletes. It must be all due to the enforced chastity which the frightening proximity of Radcliffe imposes upon the Harvard men—hence their vigor at kicking balls.

À bientôt j'espère & bien des choses à votre femme.

HP

## To James M. Osborn:

[postcard: Joseph Hirsch, *The Senator*]
Dec. 5/61

Dear Jim,

I am, this time, *truly* sorry I cannot go to Chicago—since I shall miss that very mysterious & unique reception. I thought I'd be modest & invisible, for once, & keep away from those events & think & write at home for a few days. I shall miss your party & I thank you for thinking of me, or of us.

My very best wishes to both of you,
Henri Peyre

(It's really the smoke of senatorial cigars emitted by the Old Guard which I am fleeing from.)

## À Kurt Weinberg:

Dec. 21/61

Mon cher ami,

J'ai écrit, à sa demande, à M. Kaufmann, qui semble en effet très sérieusement vouloir vous appeler là-bas. Je crois que vous seriez heureux dans un tel poste de direction & d'indépendance, où vous seriez enfin reconnu. Réfrénez certaines susceptibilités, peut-être même certaines vivacités de tempérament qui ont, dans le passé, dérouté certains de vos collègues; soyez parfaitement maître de vous et acceptez certaines médiocrités de l'enseignement américain. Il y a assez de traits admirables ici pour compenser ces ombres du tableau. L'Amérique vous a influencé beaucoup plus que vous ne croyez & je crois que vous seriez à jamais inadapté en Allemagne si vous y retourniez. Il y a bien des choses là-bas, qui vous froisseraient & vite vous ulcèreraient. Un poste de caractère administratif ici vous insèrerait davantage dans le pays &, je crois, serait par là même pour vous une expérience salutaire: vous y verriez vite le meilleur côté de l'Amérique, qui est de regarder l'avenir, de faire confiance aux autres, d'accepter leurs faiblesses & de savoir travailler en commun. Et vous *créeriez,* réaliseriez quelque chose.

Quant à B[ritish] Col[umbia], si j'étais vous, je me tiendrais tout à fait à l'écart de ce qu'on peut y dire de moi, les uns pour, les autres contre. Je chercherais, discrètement, à partir; je partirais enfin, distribuant les sourires & sans rancune envers quiconque. C'est eux, non vous, qui y perdront & ils le verront un jour. Oubliez dans cette vie tout ce qui est horizontal, & les petitesses des petites gens autour de vous: allez verticalement, "excelsior," et écrivez votre œuvre de critique, qui devrait être belle & riche.

Si ça devait ne pas marcher à Rochester, nous verrions ailleurs. Ne vous découragez pas: il y a beaucoup de postes cette année.

Bien à vous,
Henri Peyre

## To Stanley Burnshaw:

Dec. 31, 1961

My dear Stanley,

Of course I *never* found you slow with the reading of my MS & no other man but you, the kindliest of friends & the most devoted to literature, would ever dream of apologizing. Why! many a reader (I know, for I often read MS of friends & colleagues) would have taken weeks to read 400 very dull pages. And you caught a cold in the sincerest part of you (your chest) reading me! & you did your juror's duty too.

I did not go to the MLA myself. I spent every day of the vacations reading & correcting essays, doing 3 or 4 book reviews. I had had to delay, catching up with letters (at my daily rate of 20 letters a day, all badly scribbled). I would have written you earlier, to clarify my ambiguous & embarrassed position on this MS, but I was afraid I would seem to fear your verdict on it if I wrote before I had heard from you.

Here is what appears to me I should do on this MS: originally, the

Oxford Press editor had asked me for it, soon after they had published my *Contemporary Novel* at their Press & I had vaguely said I'd bear it in mind & might give them my next book if it was fair to keep it from the Yale Press. At that time, the Yale Press was very conservatively run, by Eugene Davidson, & I did not much care to appear there.

Then the Yale Press changed altogether, got a new Director & a new Board. Someone having told the Director, Chester Kerr, that I had completed the MS I was working on, he has insistently asked me for it, ever since late November, has sent me three members of his Committee who are good friends of mine on the Yale Faculty to urge me to publish my book there. I have been for 15 years or more director of our Romanic Series where we publish about two books a year (the latest was Guicharnaud's, on the Contemporary French Theater) & it was hinted to me that it was my duty to be loyal to my own series & to appear there. I have not said "yes" yet, on account of a Puritan scruple I have against doing the easier thing in being published at the Press of my own University, instead of being judged on the merits of my case elsewhere, where my local reputation does not reach. But I confess I'd feel disloyal to my University & to my younger colleagues whose books appear at the Yale Press under my own sponsorship if I now told them I have preferred a sop called commercial Press outside. I have been bothered by this for several weeks & felt rather regretful for imposing upon you the burden of my MS on December 7th. I knew I needed, valued your advice & criticism, but should not perhaps utilize your friendship for my own ends. In a word, I believe, on second thoughts, I should submit my MS to the Yale Press first, in an official way. The Press will not make money on it, as it is a big, serious & somewhat scholarly work, so that it probably is not an honor I am doing them.

I got your letter in my box today (Sunday Dec. 31). I am profoundly grateful & most touched by the minute & devoted care with which you read me. None of your criticisms vexes my author's conceit: I have not got too much of that. My deep embarrassment is at having to tell you that I should give my MS to another Press *after* having read some of your strictures or suggestions with which I may disagree. But there is no cause-&-effect relationship there.

You *are* the Ideal Reader, in my eyes. All your remarks are thoughtful, precise, constructive. I am at once taking advantage of many of those you jotted down on the supplementary, white pages & making corrections on p. 43, 5th line; p. 44, line 12; p. 47 (I do not know March well enough to bring him in & shall take him up some day, but shall leave him out here); I shall also leave out the Troubadours, for their "insincere" art poses many special questions; altering, according to your suggestions, p. 68; p. 79; p. 113 (Emerson); p. 116 (*far*, of course); p. 126 (clea*n*sing); p. 130. I am very impressed by your very acute & *original* remarks on p. 163 & p. 169. On Keats & the difference between "negative capability" & the "chameleon." you are quite right; on Coleridge's overrated & rather sterile distinction between imagination & fancy, I agree with you & have often said so, even written so: you are far more independent from conventional clichés of criticism than 99% of teacher-scholars.—p. 183, *a*bjection, of course—p. 189, a good point, which I shall steal & insert in my conclusion on "revision." Maybe I should read James Russell Lowell some day. p. 190, Clough; yes, of course—p. 191, unfit (inapte in French); p. 159, on Kafka, I maintain my point, that he was cheerful in daily life, but phrase it differently; p. 279, characterology, of course; p. 289, no, that is Rivière's—p. 339, Proust's praise was disgusting, "fulsome." I'll put "obsequious" instead—p. 347 "pontificated." p. 347, I rather like "psittacine." Why not?

Now, to the more fundamental suggestions:

A) True, my emphasis is on *French* lit—perhaps I should have a subtitle. "The French example." but if I sign "Prof of French" & declare at the outset in the Introduction that the literature mainly considered is that of France, is not that enough? My point of view is still comparative, or not exclusively limited to one literature

B) Emphasis is on the modern & I do not rush, or go straight, to the moderns soon enough: true. Yet I confess that, unless forced to, I would not give up my first two chapters. Not out of "paternal" obstinacy—but I believe that the whole book rests on the examination of *how* & *why* the problem hardly arose before Montaigne & Rousseau, how the question slowly came to take on significance as it has. The few times I have spoken in public on the general subject of sincerity, people (scholars) were most keenly interested in my early remarks on the Latin poets, on Sidney, Donne, etc. I believe that I would remove the essential props of my structure if I curtailed those first chapters too much. With the romantics & the moderns, all is clearer & easier. It is with the earlier lineament of the notion that one is puzzled, *why* it took so long to invade literature.

C) on Freud, I confess to a personal grudge, or conviction, that we have greatly exaggerated his role, & that the obsession with his concepts has perverted much of modern criticism. Ever since Schopenhauer, & before, we have known about the immense "interior Africa within us." Nerval, Balzac, *et al.* among the French. But Freud's paneroticism has distorted everything. But, whatever my own allergies are, it is true that Freudianism acted upon our view of guilt, especially in English speaking countries, & I should add something on that somewhere.

D) I am not sure I quite follow your argument on "autobiography" (Chapter VII) being granted too much space there, since I deal elsewhere chiefly with works of the imagination, & there with the writer as citizen (your p. 2–3). If I give that impression, I must have erred somewhere. My intention was definitely to stress how autobiography invaded fiction, *became* modern fiction in many a case, & how private diaries made such inroads on the writer's creativeness that most of literature tended to be bogged down there: that many readers, certainly in France, will buy the Journals of Gide, J. Green, Kafka, *et al.* any time rather than their novels, be more fascinated by that than by their imaginative attempts, under the pretext that the authors are sincerely themselves there, I still believe that chapter (perhaps overlong, & cut) must have its essential function in my book.

Now, do, Stanley, tell me if I appear to you very stubborn in my answer to your very thoughtful remarks & if I am, in your view, gravely hurting my work by maintaining some of the chapters which you deem to be too long. I'll reconsider everything if you insist I am wrong, for no one else will ever read me with the care that you have lavished over this work.

And also if you do not find me rude, unappreciative of your kindness & efforts, if I yield to my scruples & offer my MS to the Yale Press first. I should have reached such a decision earlier & not imposed that labor upon you, or asked it from you as a friend's favor, & a very considerable one. But you are my literary & moral conscience, far more than you think & I would be disturbed if I incurred your disapproval, quite honestly & candidly, because of my connection with Yale & Yale's Press, & because the MS is rather scholarly in character & will bring no profit, & probably a financial loss, to whoever publishes it, would you not agree that the University Press is a better repository for it?

Would you then ship the MS back to me, as educational material, to my Yale Station address (box 2066)? I do not know how to show my gratitude for the immense & painstaking labor you have expended over it — won't you freely draw upon the big debt of gratitude I have toward you?

With my best wishes for you, your wife & your daughters & most thankfully,

Henri

## À Ruth Thomas:

Jan. 2/62

Merci, chère Miss Thomas, de ces fort bonnes nouvelles. J'aime le peu que je connais de Simmons College & je pensais que vous vous y plairiez. C'est tout de même près d'une grande ville, riche en ressources, assez corrompue pour que vous puissiez y observer la matière première des romans libertins du siècle léger! Avancez la maudite thèse, que M. May attend de lire, et passez une heureuse année.

Bien des vœux
Henri Peyre

## To Stanley Burnshaw:

(Chicago) Jan. 18/62

My dear Stanley,

I have delayed answering your second long, very thoughtul, very kindly letter, which accompanied the return of my MS. Exams & other duties took over, & I had to take a trip to Chicago, from where, in the cold & snow, I'll drop a line.

My gratitude to you is immense & words seem banal & empty which convey it. You are one of the truly generous men alive, with a gift of your time, of your patience, attention & energy which is rare — & probably seldom found in our own profession, the academic. Publishers & their advisers like you are real saints — even if they must also have a business-like concern in some of their actions, & who can blame them? You have helped me much with those remarks of yours, every one of them very apposite & very just. I lack the patience & the endurance to accept some of your views, but that is my own weakness. I am not a seeker after perfection & I am convinced that the little I have to say in life does not deserve such meticulous striving for perfection as you & a few fastidious minds desire. It is too ephemeral & light. I enjoy literature profoundly, still learn a few lines of poetry by heart every day as an antidote against the rest of my work, I like to write & to lecture, but what I say does not deserve to go down to posterity—barely to be printed—and a demon lurking in me always drives me on to further pursuits.

But I am going to take you up, especially on Cervantes, whom I need to reread anyway, & I have profited from your remarks & given my MS to the Yale Press meanwhile. I really owed a MS to them, in order to smooth out some ill feeling which stemmed from my having criticized our Press, & their behavior, when they dismissed Eugene Davidson in a rough handed way, a few years ago.

I have copied the embossed dedication, which you said would amuse you. What a poor play, too!

"Trobar clus" is the traditional phrase used by the Troubadours to designate their closed, hermetic art: "invention, to invent (trobar, trouver)" being "closed, chiuso, open only to those who were initiated."

I copied a French quotation from Valéry you wanted, but left it at home. I'll send it later.

Many thanks in advance for the books you have sent me. I am very eager to discover Hebrew poetry, on which I am so ignorant. You have played quite a part in my modest, half-ossified intellectual development, these last few years.

Most cordially yours,
Henri Peyre

## À Kurt Weinberg:

Le 19—1—62

Cher Monsieur Weinberg,

Ce résultat est magnifique. J'en suis vraiment heureux. Je savais que vous aviez fait là-bas la meilleure impression, mais n'osais espérer des conditions aussi belles. Vous voyez que l'Amérique mérite votre confiance.

Ne craignez rien dorénavant. Votre avenir est assuré. Vous êtes l'un des plus fins, des plus sensibles, des plus cultivés des hommes dans notre métier. Vous aurez là de magnifiques possibilités, de bons élèves, des collègues de quelque valeur: vous n'aurez nulle raison d'avoir de rancœur contre quiconque, car on vous a aussitôt compris, & votre charme a opéré. C'est une revanche contre les esprits étroits que vous avez rencontrés à New York, en Iowa & à Vancouver. J'en suis moi-même un peu réconforté sur la nature humaine!

Faites maintenant de grands livres, vous les portez en vous — et nous vous verrons parfois. Vous serez plus proches. Nos compliments, & à votre femme & nos vœux.

Je dirai vite cette nouvelle à M. May qui a beaucoup fait pour vous aider & s'est beaucoup chagriné de vos ennuis & de vos angoisses.

Bien à vous,<br>Henri Peyre

## À Franco Simone:

Le 16 — ii — 62

Cher Monsieur,

J'ai mis bien longtemps, bien trop longtemps, à vous remercier de ce très beau, de ce grand livre sur *La Renaissance*. J'avais beaucoup à faire au début de l'année scolaire et ne me suis enfin mis à le lire en détail que ce mois dernier. J'y ai énormément appris, et toujours avec allégresse: car vous écrivez joliment et portez avec grâce un énorme fardeau de connaissances. Même là où j'avais déjà lu certains de ces essais, je leur ai trouvé une signification nouvelle, ainsi réunis en volume et constituant une synthèse noblement audacieuse. Vous connaissez l'époque à fond, dans tous ses replis; et vous en renouvelez le visage. Très sincèrement, je n'ai pas encore lu un ouvrage réussissant à ce point à enrichir notre savoir de mille détails neufs, et évitant avec autant d'habileté de s'égarer dans l'excès de détails. L'originalité de la Renaissance française apparaît pleinement dans vos pages. Mes très vives félicitations. D'Italie nous vient la lumière — limpide & réchauffante.

Croyez à mes sentiments très dévoués et profondément amicaux.

Hri Peyre

## To Henry Allen Moe:

April 21/62

Dear Henry,

I am sure we are all grateful to you for an immensely fascinating financial report & for letting us know of your final success in securing the needed funds. We shared your concern this year & felt that a positive & liberal decision should be made, this year of all years, by your board, if the Guggenheim Fellowships are to remain the most coveted & the most honorable of all. Thanks to you, that will continue to be the case.

I occasionally feel, as you know, that you should feel absolutely free to drop members of your Committee of Selection as you think fit, so as to bring variety, freshness, open-mindedness to it, perhaps representatives of other disciplines. May I again say it, where I am concerned? I enjoy working with you, as you well know, but wonder also whether, I, & others, are not getting too set in our ways, too sure of our own rightness, of our righteousness. Next year, I shall take a sabbatical leave for the second term. I shall not probably leave before the end of March—but if you had to set the second meeting of the committee later, my plans (as yet vague) might inconvenience you—Much depends upon when one or two books I am completing are out—probably by February–March 1963. What planning life requires!

A few titles for Mrs. Moe's French readings.

Julien Green. Chaque homme dans sa nuit. Plon, 1961
Simone de Beauvoir. Mémoires d'une jeune fille rangée
                La Force de l'Age. 1961
François Ponthier. L'Homme à la cuirasse. Robert Laffont, 1962
Àndré Chamson. Le Crime des Justes (not recent)
Philippe Sollers. Une curieuse Solitude
Claude Simon. La Route des Flandres 1960.
Robbe-Grillet. Le Voyeur
              La Jalousie
Pierre Henri Simon. Le Somnambule.

As ever, with cordial & devoted regards,
Henri Peyre

## À Leon Roudiez:

Le 4—VI—(62)

Cher Ami,

Je suis fâché de vous savoir éprouvé, ou diminué de quelque organe mineur. Mais on dit qu'on se trouve mieux de ces ablations. Espérons.

Très intéressant, votre article sur le roman du dernier n° de FR.

Je reste aux USA cet été, mais serai assez mobile. Si je puis toutefois suppléer Mlle Brée & lire pour vous quelques MSS de ma compétence, je veux bien. Mon adresse la meilleure est "Yale Station." Mais vous êtes compétent vous-même, et juge sévère & juste, partout où je puis l'être.

Fin d'année, temps splendide. Enfin on peut se remettre à quelque travail suivi!

La revue est de mieux en mieux. Excellents articles littéraires.

Compliments & bien à vous,
H. P.

## Au même:

16—VI—62

Cher ami,

Votre topo est admirable—précis, concis, direct, sans rien de ce remplissage éloquent que les méridionaux comme moi (et Napoléon . . . et Maurras!) affectionnent. Il appelle les critiques des mécontents, mais il les désarme par avance. Vous avez raison: on publie trop! Et cependant il y a 2 ou 3 fois plus de professeurs de français, & d'élèves, qu'en 1920 ou 1940—et la qualité s'élève sans cesse. Nous le voyons par les meilleures de nos thèses. Le difficile est pour les jeunes de résister à la tentation de donner des chapitres de thèse, à la tentation du pédantisme & de la sécheresse. Nous devrions écrire davantage pour le "general reader" et davantage aussi sur l'histoire, la politique récente, la transformation sociale et économique de la France. J'espère que vous pourrez persuader Wylie d'être plus actif, ou de s'adjoindre des collaborateurs qui couvriraient ces aspects-là.

Bon courage pour cette œuvre. Elle en vaut la peine. Et vous avez le respect & l'estime de tous. Vos articles de la R. Review ou du N Y Times sont remarqués & loués.

Bien cordialement,<br>Henri Peyre

J'ai entendu *beaucoup* de mécontentement des récentes North East conférences. Il serait bon, certes, de les aérer dans votre revue. Notre succès, dans les langues & leur diffusion, doit s'accompagner d'auto critique.

## To Harry Levin:

July 1, 1962

Dear Harry,

"Tu quoque." When I first taught that book, in Bryn Mawr—in 1926!—everyone was shocked at my audacity & the flappers of that age were bored, as I am still, by Sade. Now, it is more than a classic & the same girls who, in the 20's, voted (at Smith) *Paul et Virginie* to be the greatest French novel, or their granddaughters, all elect *Les Liaisons*. I still refuse to wax enthusiastic over it, but I feel like a decrepit survival of an age when seduction was supposed to be so easy as to entail no geometric calculation & when Cecile would have been almost as boring as a love-companion as a Lolita &, worse still, a Zazie.

But you have done a very fine preface—it says a great deal, almost everything, in a few pages, with not a single banality. And of course you're right about the ridiculous inadequacy of "acquaintances" as a rendering. Aldington's version does seem to read well, from the hasty skipping I did of it.

Here we are back at our West Chop. I'll only stay two other weeks, accumulating reading, & then must return to some writing. We are truly sad you are not here & have chosen the Presidential cape instead. But would you be willing to come one day for a dip & for lunch & a few hours' respite from housekeeping. We'd meet you at the ferry landing of course. It would be a pleasure for Marguerite & me. We shall never see enough of your wife.

I forget your Cape residence & am sending this in a roundabout way—with my most cordial greetings & wishes.

Hri

## To James M. Osborn:

[postcard: view of Menemsha Pond, Martha's Vineyard]
July 23/62

Dear Jim,

Your memory is infallible & your devotion to your friends, marvelous. It is reciprocated—and that last evening with you & your wife & our Homeric-Swinburnian friends, in the quietude of the stars above us, the lights around & the delicious wine, charms our memories as we vacation among Philistines & the unenlightened. Our best to both.

Henri Peyre

## To Harry Levin:

Aug. 13/62

Dear Harry,

What a stoic you are, to have a house all your own, within reach of the President's ears for you to instill a few useful suggestions into them (it is said that Stendhal is his favorite novelist) & spend the Summer working! I shall be awaiting your *Gates of Horn* with impatience: what an apt title. You have a genius for titles indeed.

I had come home to read some proofs of my volume on Literature & sincerity, at last finished, & do a few other things, but our summer has been disturbed. Marguerite was taken ill with some gynecological trouble which baffles doctors but is most painful. She is very upset nervously & will need an operation later, when surgeons return from their vacations. All will be well in the end, I trust. Next year, we expect to spend the second half of the year abroad, or what I can preserve of it after I have attended to my duties on the Guggenheim Committee. It will be a sad year if we do not see you & your wife at all.

Many good wishes meanwhile to both.
Henri Peyre

## To Gordon Ray:

Aug. 13—1962

Dear Ray,

I am sure you must find this summer weather especially kindly this year. I am taking advantage of it to accomplish a good deal of reading & writing.

We have had to interrupt our vacation; my wife has been quite ill. She is now at home, but will have to return to the hospital for an operation in a week or so. It may well be at the time when you plan to pass through New Haven, & my nursing duties may then make it difficult for me to get any free time. But surely things should go better in the fall & we shall meet then.

With my best wishes,
Henri

## To Stanley Burnshaw:

Aug. 29/62

Dear Stanley,

Please thank your wife warmly for her very kind note to my wife. Marguerite will be touched by it when she picks up enough to read her mail & escape that concentration on recovering which is necessary just now. The operation went well & she will be recuperating, slowly, while needing more treatment. Let us now hope for the best. This has increased my admiration for surgeons & really good doctors: they know that they can only do that much, & that they know so little, really. Still, compared to us talkers, what a noble career!

I have received, read & liked the Gassner book on *Form & Idea in Modern Theatre*. You were shrewd to publish that in 1956. Somehow it had escaped me. It is a brilliant, well thought out book, full of ideas, of tremendous range. It is hard to pin down John Gassner: he embraces so much, passes so fast. He is *not* a name dropper. He knows & *feels* all the works he mentions. But the central focus, somehow, disappears under so many fulgurating, divergent rays.

At times, comparative literature frightens me!

An awful, sultry, rainy day today, I hope you don't get a hurricane to devastate your beautiful garden!

Many kind thoughts to both of you.

Cordially,
Henri Peyre

## To James M. Osborn:

[postcard: Manessier painting in Stockholm]
Aug. 29 [1962]

Dear friends,

Marguerite was deeply touched by your kindness & the exceptionally elegant flowers. All you do is always original—even your apparent pleasure in walking leisurely & keeping dogs at bay! She is recovering, slowly, & I hope we have seen the worst of this: some people, better Christians than I, laud suffering & say it makes us better. I still stand for cheerful living!

Most gratefully & cordially yours,
Henri Peyre

## To Henry Allen Moe:

Oct. 13/62

Dear Henry,

I had meant for a long time to write to you about several matters, & hoped even more to see you, as I detected some melancholy in some of your notes this year & wanted to tell you, with as little show of feelings as possible but with deep sincerity, that I, we, admire you *all the more* as you are nearing the age of retirement from some of your activities; if any great man ever failed to become spoilt by power, to become dogmatic as he was so often right, to refuse to listen to others, that exceptional man was, is, you.

I am on a plane to Los Angeles to give a series of lectures on modern art there; just left Houston, where there was a great celebration of Rice, the inauguration of a new President, several Nobel prizes, A. Toynbee & other celebrities, & my own modest self giving a speech & receiving a medal. I hesitated before making this trip, as (you may have heard it from Gordon Ray) my wife has been very seriously ill [since] last July: a very bad tumor, a long operation, exhausting treatment following it, etc. She is not fully well yet, but, I hope, on the way to a recovery. But it was a very painful summer. If things do get well, we would still plan to spend part of the second semester in Europe, leaving April first when, I believe you said, my share of the work on the Guggenheim Committee would be done. I have a book, or more than one, due to be out by then &, while nursing my poor wife, cooking, sweeping, etc., I found some comfort in working hard.

Among other things, I meant to express some of my scruples about the Philosophical Society, since I must miss the Committee on nominations this year, concerning the preponderance we seem to grant to scholars & scientists from Philadelphia, Princeton, Harvard naturally, &, except for California, our relatively too small number of members from other points of the country. Are we not a little provincial there? I was impressed by the caliber of several people whom Rice had gathered, & by the earnestness & future of Rice itself. Within the next few years, could we get more suggestions from the membership as to scholars from California (Bronson, for ex. in English, Schorer), Wisconsin (Germaine Brée), Chicago (R. S. Crane, when he was younger, should have been considered), Indiana, Texas (Ransom, at Austin, is a very good chancellor, if not a productive scholar). I did not arouse many echoes when I faintly mentioned A. W. Griswold as a possible Council nominee & would await your advice before suggesting him in one of the classes. Are we quite as "national" as we might be?

All this in great humility & with deep devotion to you & your wife,
Henri Peyre

## À Leon Roudiez:

Le 28—X—62

Cher ami,

Est-ce à vous que doivent aller ces épreuves, reçues de Heffernan sans autre indication? Je suppose que oui—mais sinon, voulez-vous avoir la bonté de les transmettre? Elles sont d'ailleurs excellentes.

Cet article de M. Hall me paraît, à dire le vrai, peu significatif, assez vide, mal écrit et médiocrement instructif pour nos lecteurs. Je doute, en outre, de la convenance du procédé qui consiste à citer des fragments de lettres, écrites poliment à un auteur étranger de thèse, alors que Roger M. du Gard a toujours été si pudique sur son œuvre. M. Hall vous cite beaucoup, & avec éloges, ce qui rend la publication de ses pages encore plus délicate. À mon avis, il gagnerait à récrire sur M. du Gard un article substantiel, où il pourrait à la rigueur citer en note l'autorité de l'écrivain sur laquelle il s'appuie. Mais cet essai, vu la place limitée dont vous disposez, me paraît de médiocre importance. Nous devrions préférer des articles mieux construits, plus substantiels, mieux écrits aussi. Le haut de la page 5 est affreux et le bas de la page 1 bien peu clair.

Cordialement,
Henri Peyre

## To Wayne Andrews:

[letterhead: Princeton University Library]
Tel. ST 7-3131
ext. 2368
Nov. 3, 1962

Dear Mr. Andrews:

Thank you for your rather mysterious letter of Oct. 26th, relative to some project you have in which I might assist & be interested, & on your words on my book on the novel. I am soon to bring out a volume on *Literature & Sincerity* in which I discuss, as illustrations, a number of authors & center on "le Culte du Moi"—not necessarily to approve of the passion for sincerity toward oneself so dear to the French.

I do go to New York, normally, a few times a year—but it happens that my wife is very sick & my plans are to be uncertain until she recovers, if she does. If I cannot make a date some day this month, or dash for a visit, I should be happy to have you & any colleagues of yours to pay me a visit here one day for lunch—or else you might write more at length, in a general way, on what you have in mind.

Thank you for your letter & very sincerely yours,
Henri Peyre

## À Jean Boorsch:

Mardi, 6 nov. (62)

Mon cher Jean,

Vous êtes certes, de nous tous, le plus photogénique, et souriant après vos infortunes grecques et le martyre d'une année de maladie. Je comprends mieux encore aujourd'hui tout ce que cela a dû signifier pour vous, pour Louise, de déceptions, d'impatience, de crainte.

Votre sympathie me touche. Nous ne prodiguons pas les mots de sentiments ou les paroles d'émotion d'ordinaire, vous du Septentrion & moi du Sud—mais je crois que tous deux, nous n'avons jamais mis le cerveau calculateur et l'efficacité au-dessus du cœur. En "vieillissant," vous avez rejoint, à travers Rousseau, Chateaubriand, Balzac & Hugo, mon romantisme éternel.

Vendredi, en allant au thé, je suis passé chez notre docteur & j'ai compris du coup que le rayon d'espoir luisait bien faiblement. . . .

## Au même:

Vendredi 9 nov. [62]

Mon cher Jean,

Merci encore. Nous communiquons par lettres, comme les amants d'il y a deux siècles! Mais je dois courir beaucoup et souvent.

Merci de vos paroles. C'est vrai, je hais la maladie, me révolte contre elle & voudrais la mépriser et l'abolir de mon mépris. Certains jours, les docteurs disent qu'on n'est sûr de rien et que le miracle peut arriver. On essaie maintenant une drogue toute nouvelle. L'autre jour, l'un d'eux m'avait démonté en me disant de me préparer au pire sans hésiter. Nous verrons. Bien sûr, j'ai assez de ressort ensuite pour réagir & l'exemple de ma malade, qui tient à la vie & [2 mots illisibles] m'encouragera. Je me rappelle mon père, à qui je ressemble: effondré après la mort de ma mère (il avait aussi 62 ans), il s'est repris ensuite. . . .

## To Stanley Burnshaw:

Nov. 10/62

Dear Stanley,

How you manage to make money for us—out of thin air—is beyond me! I appreciate your statement, although I fail to understand it, & the all-too-generous check.

I get the Sewanee & shall make a point of reading the story by Koch—especially since you esteem him. He seems like an interesting case.

On Frost? No. The Europeans have never written much on him; somehow they miss his greatness & see him as another Wordsworth, in New England. Perse never writes any criticism. I'll look if Maurice Lebreton has done one: he'd be the best man—but I doubt he has.

Marguerite is worse—much worse. Just 2 hours ago, after I fought hard, day & night, to relieve her, help her, soothe her pain, the Doctor ordered her back to the hospital, in an ambulance. She fights hard, wants to live for my sake—but I doubt she will live beyond December.

My distress is even greater than I ever thought possible. I'll try & work to half forget it.

My best to you both,
H. P.

## To Henry Allen Moe:

Nov. 18/62

Dear Henry,

You are one of the men I feel most affection for, & I admire & love your wife no less. This is the first note I feel able to write to day, and it is to say that after weeks & weeks of courageous struggle, of very painful radiation treatment, of all the loving care I could pour out to her, Marguerite died last night. The doctors had ordered her back to the hospital, as I no longer could cope with the disease. 35 years of married life ended! She was brave & generous to the end, bidding me eat, live on, work, travel. There will be no religious service & no funeral; only a very discreet & strictly private cremation. She hated all the "fuss" about death.

As usual, also, having to make long-range plans, may I bother you to inquire about dates of the Febr. & March meetings? I imagine February would fall around the 8–10 if you follow the usual pattern? My more precise question is about the one in March & whether it is possible to have it just a little earlier than the last week end (Friday 29, Sat. 30, Sunday 31 March), for example 26 to 28? Of course this is a mere tentative question, since the other members must be accommodated first & are more essential than I am — & the staff is even more important than puny personalities like mine.

Kindly convey my sad news to Gordon & to Jim, & of course to your wife. Otherwise I want as much discreet silence on this as possible. I'll take a few days away after Thanksgiving & shall try to work as usual otherwise.

Yours ever,<br>Henri

## À Leon Roudiez:

Le 19 – XI – 62

Cher Ami,

Un mot seulement. Ma femme, que les médecins ont soudain trouvée malade en août, est morte hier, après une longue lutte contre un cancer. Aussi ne suis-je pas sûr d'affronter les réunions de Washington.

Dites-le à O'Brien, Hytier, Bédé & professeurs de Columbia & croyez-moi, tristement, certes, mais fidèlement,

Vôtre<br>H. P.

## To Wayne Andrews:

[letterhead: Princeton University Library]
Nov. 19, 1962

Dear Mr. Andrews,

It was a pleasure to have your visit here & your conversation has such range & liveliness that I was amazed to find a writer & an editor far more learned than any professor & less fallible or timid as a critic.

Your audacity is equal to your intellectual grasp & I confess the sole idea of a book on the literature of the Western World, nothing less, set me dreaming & baffled. It also confounded me with the sense of my own inadequacy for such a challenging program. I would need a little more time & quietude of mind* to ponder over it. But with all the honor your suggestion bestowed on me, I fear I do not feel I am the man to do the book you envision.

I have several commitments & I am a very busy person with teaching & administration—I am probably too old at 61, and not fresh enough, to muster all the boldness required to cut into literature & make arbitrary choices, as one would have to. To be honest, the author of such a book should read & reread & I might lack the time. I still believe that Alfred Kazin, or George Steiner (who wrote on Tragedy, on Tolstoi & Dostoevsky), or some bold young talent would be more fit than I to attempt a book of that kind.

I shall reflect a little more but I believe I should not delay the accomplishment of a project you have at heart by dilatoriness. I am half, or more than half, convinced that my answer should be negative.

And the persistent question recurs: why not you?

Most sincerely yours,
Hri Peyre

* My wife, alas! died yesterday & it will take me a while to regain my balance.

## À Jean Boorsch:

Ce mardi 20 (nov. 62)

Mon cher Jean,

Votre mot, trouvé hier soir tard, m'a touché. Oui, je me sens bien proche de vous, bien que je vous voie si peu, faute de loisir—car cela fait 24 ans que nous travaillons ensemble, et sans un seul vrai nuage. Je vous en ai grande reconnaissance, à vous et à Louise; car Marguerite était souvent nerveuse, ombrageuse, parfois un peu épineuse, mais elle vous aimait beaucoup & avait grand cœur, avec de la maladresse à le témoigner. Nous avons somme toute vécu heureux ensemble, peut-être trop l'un sur l'autre; elle surtout avait tout concentré en moi, n'ayant pas d'enfant et plus guère de famille: je le lui reprochais, avec l'égoïsme masculin qui redoute qu'on s'attache trop à lui et l'emprisonne ainsi. Mais je lui répétais souvent que je devais beaucoup à son dévouement, à son goût, à tout ce dont elle me déchargeait. Quand je rentre le soir après mes cours ces jours-ci, je la revois, m'ayant préparé un daiquiri, mettant un des disques que j'aimais, préparant un repas délicat. Je n'avais jamais senti combien il y a de vérité dans le "Proustisme," les souvenirs attachés au concret, à des détails matériels tels que rideaux, tapis, étoffes, livres qu'elle préférait.

Mais il serait vain de se complaire à ces souvenirs et à quelque douleur, même douce. Nous avons après tout eu beaucoup d'années ensemble et pas mal de joies; et elle me disait, ces dernières semaines, que je devais regarder en avant, faire mon travail; elle sentait bien qu'elle n'en avait plus pour longtemps et ne comptait pas tellement survivre. Ces semaines de radiation l'avaient épuisée—et c'est certes une épreuve. . . .

## À Judd Hubert:

Le 20—XI—62

Cher M. Hubert:

Votre livre est d'une fine élégance—de présentation et aussi de style. Vous écrivez l'anglais mieux qu'aucun de nous, avec brio & légèreté, et vous avez du neuf, & du pénétrant à dire—sur Don Garcie, les Fâcheux, les Femmes Savantes, D. Juan, vous êtes le meilleur moliériste que j'aie jamais lu. Vous êtes dur pour ce pauvre Alceste, mais du moins vous n'écrivez jamais rien de banal. C'est un beau livre, qui vous fait honneur & devrait atteindre un vaste public. Il m'a donné de la joie, ces dernières nuits, où je dormais peu & tâchais d'oublier.

Ma femme allait mieux quand j'étais à Los Angeles & j'étais alors plein d'espoir. Mais le cancer est revenu ailleurs. Depuis le 1er nov. on m'avait ôté tout espoir. Elle avait un admirable courage, résistait, s'occupait encore de mon bien-être, mais je ne pouvais que pleurer à la voir. Elle est morte il y a deux jours. Sunt lacrymae rerum.

   Bien à vous & à votre femme & merci de ce beau don.
   H. P.

## To Stanley Burnshaw:

Nov. 21 — [1962]

Dear Stanley,

Of course you realized, from my unpolite behavior & concern when you came, that I had no expectation of averting the end long. Marguerite died on Saturday early. All is now over. But your sympathy meant much to her & means much to me. No other man, busy & important, would have taken a train to come & shake the hand of an absent-minded man.

   With gratitude,
   H.

## À Alexis et Mme Léger:

Henri Peyre
309 St Ronan St.
New Haven, Conn.
Le 25 nov. 1962

Chère Madame, Cher Monsieur,

J'ai le profond chagrin de vous annoncer, comme elle aurait, je sais, voulu que je le fisse, la mort de ma femme, il y a une semaine. Elle avait pour vous une très grande admiration et elle vous était reconnaissante de la sympathie que vous lui aviez souvent témoignée. Cet été, elle a dû être opérée d'une tumeur qui malheureusement fut vite déclarée cancéreuse. Elle souffrit beaucoup des traitements qu'elle dut subir ensuite, mais semblait aller mieux quand le mal a repris à l'intestin, puis au foie. Elle se sentait perdue mais luttait vaillamment et aurait tant voulu revoir la France.

Ma peine est grande mais je vais m'efforcer de regarder en avant. Je vous remercie par avance de la sympathie que votre amitié m'accordera et vous prie de croire à mes sentiments les plus dévoués.

Henri Peyre

## To Ruth Thomas:

Dec. 25/62

Dear Miss Thomas:

I am sorry you cannot stay at Simmons, but that is no catastrophe. There will be many jobs opening up this year—& why should you not try at Wheaton College? Wellesley? Or elsewhere (Sweetbriar?) or in a large & coeducational university? If I were you, I would prefer to work hard on the thesis now & this summer & try to finish it for September 15, 1963. Until you complete it, employers will be a little suspicious, however well you do.

If you *must* take a year off & finish it then, it will obviously be at a loss. Next year Mr. May will be so busy on other tasks that he will have to let you have another director: you will choose among us, preferably our younger men. We may have a few hours for you, but shall only know that in the fall, & it is far from certain. If you try elsewhere in New Haven (school, small college, etc.), it is likely to cut up all your time: so would Conn. College in New London, with the commuting.

If you still have a *large* part of the thesis to do, I would advise you to work very hard this Summer in our library, then in September to take a few hours if we have any available or to take the risk of having to borrow money & just live on while you write the thesis—surviving, composing, hoping. But you *must* leave it behind.

Sincerely yours,<br>Henri Peyre

## To John & Mollie Gassner:

[card bearing the imprint "Mrs. Henri M. Peyre." The *s* of Mrs. has been struck out by pen.]
Jan. 6/63

Dear Mr. & Mrs. Gassner:

You were so very kind to express sympathy with warmth & evident sincerity & I was touched. So was my dear wife always by your cordiality & the generous gift of your books which she read (& utilized) eagerly. I have been sadly broken up but I am now putting all the pieces of myself together again. I hope to pay you a quiet visit before I go off next term, probably not before late March.

Most sincerely yours,
Henri Peyre

## To Jean Law:

Jan. 14/63

Dear Mrs. Law:

Of course you do not bother me! I have always had much sympathy for you & this misfortune now strikes me as so unjust, so absurd & avoidable! A thinking & thoughtful man like him should have known better than that! Do not blame yourself in any way: men undergo these crises, they say, at middle age, especially when they have not been foolish enough in their youth. Time helps, of course—but you should, & I hope will, remarry. You have much to offer & men should soon know it.

I shall myself attempt to reconstruct my life somehow. Just now, I confess, I have been a prey to gloom & felt oppressed by the futility of everything in life; but I must triumph over that mood.

Do not take the trouble to see or hear me when I go to those Finger Lakes Colleges! You have enough worries as it is! But believe in my sympathy & cordial souvenir.

Henri Peyre

## To Henry Allen Moe:

[letterhead: Yale University]
Febr. 19/63

Dear Henry,

How cordially you always manage to write, & to feel, & what a marvelous model of a *great* man who has always shunned pride, pompousness, desiccation & makes us feel as if we could ever be your equals!

It was a very pleasant meeting once again—a bit rushed, but you will repair our omissions or failings.

May I add a few lines on my personal "situation" & projects, since you & your wife have always been so kind & sympathetic to me—to us?

I have gone through hard days while Marguerite was sick & since her death. It rocked me to my very foundations, left me all broken down, my stoicism (of which I used to be proud) vanished, all demoralized. I won't describe to you my moods & my utter despondency, & take pity upon myself. But I considered giving up all activity & retiring, accepting an offer from the Sorbonne to move there, even one from Austin, Texas. The solitude here was too much for me to bear, & the heaviness of my too numerous burdens. I have friends, but I live at home a good deal, & for my work; I prefer it that way. But I had to cook, clean, wash, see to many household details with which I cannot really cope, to receive dozens of graduate students & colleagues & visitors—& to be obsessed with solitude & many painful memories.

Finally, just last week, I have decided I cannot go on this way, & to remarry. And I'll rush into it, foolishly perhaps, but psychologically I knew I must, or crack up. A very young lady, ridiculously young for me (26 or so), who had worked with me on my books in the past after she graduated from Smith & was my secretary, is extremely fond of me. I told her all she should face: my old age, the prospect of prompt widowhood, the ridicule of a difference of 35 years or so, my dullness & my harassment with work & writing, & much besides. She is normal, lovely, very pure, very straightforward (& a pastor's daughter, to boot!). She insists that no young man attracts her & that her idea of happiness is to be with me & cook for me & take care of my old age & type for me. I am fond of her & touched by her foolish devotion & I'll nurture the hope of rejuvenating myself thus, or at least of hanging on to whatever vigor I have left—& to continue a few more years in my present job.

I don't wish for you, or anyone, to approve of me—for I realize that I am, in some ways, deciding upon a rash & probably selfish move. But I *must* emerge out of that despond which the loss of my companion of 35 years had plunged me into. I am not publicizing this—but I wanted you & your wife (& if you wish to say a word to them, Gordon & Jim) to be the first to know.

Most sincerely yours,<br>Henri

## To Sally Cornell:

[letterhead: Hotel Grosvenor, Fifth Ave. at Tenth St.]
Feb. 22/1963

Dear Sally,

Men can be fine creatures, but a whole day, meals included, spent with them discussing the state of research in America & what to do about it would turn anyone, or me, into a misanthrope—such ponderous seriousness. They do revive a little at the cocktail hour, but that's just when slumber tries to seal my spirit. Instead I went up to my room, to preserve my virginity from gin, & I'll briefly try to answer your lovely letter in red ink—most clearly legible & truly inspired.

You were foolishly stubborn to come out again on that snowy, slushy, slippery Tuesday, but I am sure Brother Antoninus was worth it. I'll always remember how you discovered his poetry, during those gloomy, anxious days of vigil in my room at home. Their memory still obsesses me. I have remained afflicted. I have remained afflicted with the horror of death & disease since then, humiliated by that defeat, inwardly mutilated. You alone, then discovered or understood, restored my faith in the worth of life. I lose that recaptured faith now & then: I do here, alone in the huge city & feeling little interested in all that I have to discuss & plan with those gentlemen & scholars brandishing their pipes. I wonder if I do not just play a comedy & pretend to take seriously all our committees & scholarly disquisitions & giving of fellowships & the warp & woof of American life when I really think all that is so insignificant. Some evenings, I feel like declaiming all the gloomy poetry of Leopardi & Robinson Jeffers & Leconte de Lisle asserting that the world is wrong & life stupid. That Thursday evening driving back in the snow behind rows of immobilized cars, I kept on envying Marguerite reduced to ashes & felt like giving up that senseless fight. Why live over sixty, after all?

But I am still alive, & have not even caught a cold & I shall pin my foolish hopes upon rejuvenation from an "amazing marriage" & upon getting away for a rest. I shall miss our few talks & our close spiritual affinity, but I need the change desperately. My work has piled up incredibly, to the extent that I could not find even half a minute, on Thursday morning, to attempt telephoning to Brother Antoninus; then I gave May's course & ran, out of breath, to catch a train for N. York & be at my first committee. A second one is meeting tomorrow. Kenneth is a wise man to have kept away from all this feverish nonsense & to have known how to stay at home & enjoy your company! My father was like him, serene, meditative, smoking pipe after pipe, reading Greek & Italian & the rest, & never bothering about the turmoil of the world, & being kind & patient. I must have inherited the impatient restlessness of my mother instead.

Your blue scarf, so delicate, so refined & caressing, & splendidly blue, pleased me much & I took it with me in this cold weather. But, Sally, you are *too* kind & generous & embarrass me. It is not just that there should exist persons like you, giving away so much & so thoughtfully, & receiving so little in return. It makes me wish to be a God, distributing happiness & joys, & to shower all my bounty upon you & it makes me resent my lack of freedom & of time, since I cannot even dispose of my own presence to lend it to the few for whom I care. I'll be back for a moment Sunday, then again have to be absent Monday, & then to face another crowded week. But I'll find one day, I hope, to go & see you & share a meal or a drink. I'll reserve March 4th & the best would be for me to come for lunch or to invite you to lunch that day. The rest of that week will be taken up for me by trips away & then I'll put an end to my bachelor's life.

No, I never did receive a letter of yours in Washington. I stayed at a small, isolated hotel there, as quiet & lonely as I could. The meeting was all confusion & I looked very gloomy & dejected, I fear.

You write so beautifully that I believe you should confide your feelings & thoughts to a diary, or transmute your sensibility into poetry, like Emily Dickinson, but with more inner joy. Your existence is replete with hidden treasures which shine only for the few knowing ones.

I must go back to my colleagues for dinner & they will tease me about my withdrawing from the social hour when they relax & flirt with the secretaries—Good bye, dear Sally. Have you noticed the splendor of some of the sunsets these wintry days? Thursday, it was so glorious I could have cried, in the train on which I rode to N.Y.

With love,
H.

## To Harry Levin:

March 6, 1963

Dear Harry,

Belated but truthful thanks for your review on Irony; it was more than a review & made me think. I had often wanted to elucidate the subject & its diverse meanings & connotations in Greek, German, French; but you are the man to do it. I have not enough irony myself, & too much on my hands anyway.

I have at last unburdened myself of my cogitations on "Sincerity," solving nothing naturally, but perhaps clarifying a little. You will see what you think. There's no judgment I respect (or fear?) more than yours.

I have lived very hard months since I lost my wife. I won't attempt to describe them, for self-pity, sorrow, regret get the better of me. I was all broken down, frustrated in my very incompetent efforts to cook & wash & clean & run a home & entertain colleagues & students; horribly alone spiritually & otherwise. I envisaged many a drastic solution: retiring to France, moving to California, etc.

I finally am choosing the most rash of all solutions: to remarry & try to shake off my despair—& to marry a very, very young person, 26 or so, a Smith graduate of a few years ago, Lois Haegert, who helped me in my work in the past & is extraordinarily devoted to me & fond of me. I am fond of her too, while full of the memories & regrets of Marguerite. I shall attempt a sort of rejuvenation—a perilous one—thus, for the few years of active life on which I still may count. I wished you & your wife to be among the first to be informed. I'll need wishes & prayers.

I'll be off to Europe on April first for six months. My wishes for a good summer & most cordially,

Henri

## To John & Mollie Gassner:

March 29/63

Dear Mr. & Mrs. Gassner:

You must have found me very rude all these days as I failed to call up or to pay you a last visit, as I hoped to. But I have this winter gone through many a difficult moment, grieving for the past, conjuring up memories & regrets, fighting despondency, finally rushing headlong into a remarriage which is paradoxical & somewhat ridiculous, but brings me some comfort & a new lease of hope just now. We are sailing on Monday April 1st on "France" & I have to travel very fast to Urbana on Friday (March 29) until Sunday. I fear there is thus no more time for trying to meet you & introduce Lois, who trembles at the idea of meeting such important people as the celebrated Gassners, but we shall get together next Fall, I hope. I may, if all goes well, return from France & Britain refreshed & cheerful. I still hope to write more books if—.

My very cordial best to you & Mrs. Gassner & most sincerely yours
[No signature]

## To Henry Allen Moe:

[letterhead: The May Fair Hotel<br>Berkeley Square, London]<br>April 29/63

Your letter to Mrs. Guggenheim which you communicated to me is not only a beautiful document—a memorable one in its sobriety & the elegant cogency of its style; it is also, for your friends & associates, a moving one. I confess that it filled me with sadness. The thought of your leaving the Foundation, while you are still in full vigor & could serve it long & splendidly, is a distressing one. Intellectually, I know that your decision is generous & right: the new commission which you will head can accomplish much, & can only do that under a man of imagination & of devotion like you. Still, I cannot help, as a fellow, as one of your collaborators, as one who has the welfare of American scholarship at heart, being melancholy. Things will never be the same when you are gone & to sit at the long table at the meetings of the Selection Committee without you would be for me like the first solitary meals I tried to prepare & take, at home, without my departed wife.

I shall see you again, however, at the Philosophical Society, if not before. I am paying a leisurely visit to London & England, with a few lectures here, at Oxford & in Scotland. I have always loved London & its charm, this spring, is even more winning than I remember it to have been in my youth. After a brief stay in Scotland, I expect we shall settle for a little time & work in Paris.

My very best to your wife & my affectionate gratitude to you.

Henri

## To Gordon Ray:

[letterhead: The May Fair Hotel]
April 30 — 1963

Dear Gordon:

Henry wrote me that he had decided to retire & take up other duties as of July next. The news is melancholy, for one of his old & faithful collaborators, but he is clearly right in undertaking new tasks *now*. And he knows that the ship is in capable hands, as all of us who served on the Committee know. The task for you will be an immense, challenging one. Henry's succession would intimidate almost any one else, but you will bring to it so many qualities of intellect, of imagination, of justice & of heart that the new era will in no way be unworthy of the past achievement.

I believe you should wish a renovation of many things, including your staff & your committee; the emphasis may be different in the future, some reorganization & realignment may seem to you to be in order. I would like to suggest that you feel altogether free to do so without the least indispensable of us, & I am the least. You are well versed in literature, English, ancient & foreign, in the arts, & in the fields where I could be credited with a little competence. I, on my side, am often too busy, too active on too many things to be thorough in any, perhaps impatient, & I sincerely believe I should be dispensed with. I often told Henry that I had scruples about serving too long & perhaps judging candidates, unwittingly, according to biases or prejudices or preferences which might detract from my wished-for objectivity. I am glad & proud to have served the Foundation for a number of years.

I am enjoying London vividly & eagerly & discovering new aspects of a city with which I always was in love. We are leaving for Scotland in a few days & we'll be back in Paris after May 10<sup>th</sup> (1 bis, rue Vaneau, VIIe). In spite of occasional moments of impatience, I enjoy working in European libraries; there are compensations.

Most cordially yours,<br>Henri Peyre

## À Jean Boorsch:

Le 16 juin 1963

Mon cher Jean,

Votre lettre, qui est la gentillesse même et pleine des plus utiles renseignements autant que de votre amitié, m'a rejoint en ce petit coin de la Côte des Maures: le Rayol (Var). Mon frère y a une villa, entourée de mimosas, d'eucalyptus et d'acanthes, à deux pas de la mer—négligée mais en cette saison très confortable. Nous nous y plaisons beaucoup. J'écris ou je griffonne dans le jardin, visité par les lézards—bientôt ce devrait être cigales & sauterelles, mais il n'a pas encore fait très chaud. Lois est pleine de gentillesse & vraiment affectueuse & dévouée: je lui impose une vie dure pour quelqu'un d'aussi jeune. Ni bal ni café ni même de connaissances ici. Cuisine à tous les repas (elle y devient experte), car les restaurants ne sont pas ouverts et nous en avons eu trop déjà à Londres, Paris & ailleurs. Mais elle rit et chante. J'ai moi-même beaucoup de souvenirs ici. J'avais si souvent séjourné avec Marguerite en face de ces îles d'or, à Bormes ou ici; je goûtais beaucoup son sens de l'art & des beautés de la nature, sa compagnie un peu ombrageuse, ses dédains de fausses valeurs. Vous avez deviné quel étrange désarroi fut le mien lorsque ma vie fut ainsi coupée par sa maladie et ce sentiment de défaite, de stupide absurdité de tout alors. Ma crise intérieure était profonde & je me sentais rongé par cette solitude soudaine. Peut-être ai-je besoin que quelqu'un s'occupe de moi, m'obéisse sans me priver de la liberté intellectuelle dont j'ai besoin? Peut-être suis-je de ces tempéraments romantiques & qui eussent dû être religieux, mais ne veulent & ne peuvent pas l'être et s'acharnent contre la religion pour être si décevante & puérile. Enfin, un peu grâce à ces vacances, à quelque flânerie (j'ai pourtant entrepris un nouveau travail dont je passe à Lois les pages à taper), je me sens changé & plus serein. Vous m'avez rendu un immense service, par votre amitié, votre discrétion d'abord. . . .

## Au même:

Le 21 juin 1963

Mon cher Jean,

Quel beau jour que ce 1*er* de l'été! Enfin sec, chaud, calme, après des semaines moins sereines que celles auxquelles on s'attend ici. Des oiseaux, des parfums d'eucalyptus partout. La mer est splendide. Il n'y a guère que des Allemands sur la Côte d'Azur en ce moment; quelques Anglais aussi, promenant leur mauvaise conscience: je ne les ai jamais vus aussi gênés (affaire Profumo, cas d'homosexualité, de trahison, perte de leur foi en les méthodes des conservateurs, au fond gêne à se sentir à la remorque des États-Unis). Par contre, Kennedy croît dans l'estime générale: il est en train (envers la question nègre, les accords possibles avec la Russie) de se montrer vrai homme d'état. Mais dommage qu'il n'ait pas encore envoyé une femme dans la lune, de préférence une femme de couleur. J'ai offert à Lois, quand elle pâlit à taper mes mss (je me suis remis à écrire avec fièvre) de se faire aviatrice & exploratrice lunaire au lieu de cette besogne trop terrestre; mais elle n'a pas de goût pour l'héroïsme. Elle parle plutôt de gigots, de courgettes & de pâté de foie, ce qu'elle trouve de meilleur en France, avec les fruits du Midi & le vin rosé de Provence.

Nous allons cependant partir d'ici le 25: passer 3 ou 4 jours à Avignon (2 rue Chauffard), faire un tour vers l'Italie (j'ai conçu une grande ferveur pour les églises & j'en visite tant et plus), puis nous reviendrons vers le Paris désert d'après le 15 juillet & j'y travaillerai un peu jusqu'au départ (16 août). Ne vous fatiguez pas trop à cette 1ère année directoriale; prenez quelques vacances ensuite et en septembre si vous êtes là, nous accueillerons les nouveaux élèves, expédierons les anciens avec leurs oraux, etc.

    Merci de tout—direction des étudiants, votre. . . .

Henri Peyre

## À Arnaldo Pizzorusso:

2 rue Chauffard<br>
Avignon<br>
(Vaucluse)<br>
Le 24 juin 1963

Monsieur & cher Collègue,

    Peut-être mon nom vous est-il connu? J'ai pas mal écrit sur les sujets de littérature dans ma vie (surtout en anglais ces dernières années!) & je suis depuis plus de vingt ans chef de la section de langues romanes à l'Université Yale, à New Haven, Conn. U.S.A. J'admire beaucoup les "produits," comme nous disons commercialement de votre Scuola Normale et les études italiennes dans le domaine français en particulier, comme je l'écris fréquemment à Franco Simone. Je ne suis pas sans connaître vos travaux et je sais en quelle estime & admiration vous êtes tenu.

    Je me trouve cette année en congé pour quelques semaines et je vais peut-être passer à Pise, en me rendant avec ma femme en auto à Florence, au début du mois de juillet, le 1er ou le 2 peut-être. À tout hasard, j'aimerais vous téléphoner alors pour essayer de vous rencontrer, ou sinon de vous rencontrer si vous deviez, plus tard dans l'été, vous trouver à Paris (où je serai en fin juillet à 1 bis, rue Vaneau, VIIe—SOLférino 52-60). Outre le plaisir de vous rencontrer, j'aurais profit à vous demander si, dans un avenir prochain, vous pourriez me conseiller pour trouver un Italianisant susceptible de venir aux États-Unis enseigner sa langue & sa culture, adaptable, ouvert & que tenterait cette expérience. Il y a beaucoup trop peu de jeunes érudits italiens de talent en Amérique & nous avons cependant besoin d'eux.

Ne répondez pas à ce mot, puisque je vous écris si tard & mes dates sont incertaines. Je tenterai de vous atteindre & sinon peut-être nous verrions-nous plus tard.

Veuillez agréer, mon cher Collègue, l'assurance de mes sentiments les meilleurs.

Henri Peyre

## To Harry Levin:

Yale Sept. 6/63

Dear Harry,

I could not quite believe it when I vaguely heard of Poggioli's death. I was, & am, profoundly grieved & only now did I find his theory of the avant-garde, among the books I am reading on my return. He had just reached the summit of his vast power, wrote abundantly, & never superficially, & every one of his notes was so kind & generous & jovial. If you have an opportunity, will you convey my sympathy & sense of personal loss to his widow who, I hope, will recover fully.

My own months in Europe have gone well. I encountered many memories there & it is indeed surprising to rediscover after & with Proust, how much of one's profound life is bound up with, enclosed in, objects, details of housekeeping, flowers which Marguerite especially cherished, music she played. Her part in my life had been large. My young wife is very understanding & courageous & helps me preserve the best of my past into the new existence which I am attempting to rebuild. It would be a very *real* pleasure to have you stop here once on your way to New York. Won't you?

You are much too kind to the few lines or pages I wrote about your book. To be sure, you put so much into it, such a wealth of ideas & of insights that a reviewer finds few statements to which he may take objection. And it would take a superhuman & saintly generosity for any of your colleagues not to feel at times humiliated by your vast knowledge & the brilliance of your writing. More than any critic in the English language today, you make me feel, whenever I read or reread you, my inadequacy in attempting to write in English. Your book is the most important on the literature of France which I have read over the last five years.

I was annoyed & not a little disgusted with the TLS lately, their review of your book & of several others, & the rather poor job it did, in editorials, of the comments which should have emerged from the articles on Criticism & Literary History. Yours was brilliant & far-reaching. But there is indeed in England today a corrosive jealousy of America, among scholars, and also among novelists & poets. I enjoyed lecturing there, but I resented the tone of some people which seemed to take pity upon poor me, condemning myself to live in the States. Oxford in particular is singularly lacking in humility. I admire your activity in writing on so many varied subjects, & always bringing new points of view on them. 1964 should be *your* year indeed. I wrote, of all things, on art history, this last summer & now, two articles for collective volumes & *Mélanges,* which are so hard to refuse.

I did not go to F[édération] I[nternationale des Langues et] L[ittératures] M[odernes]. I confess I am tired of talks on the relationship between literary history & criticism. Let each of us to what he is best fit for, or most inclined to do!

Have a good year, in spite of the bad & huge gap left by Renato's disappearance & do give our regards & wishes to your wife.

Most faithfully,
Hri

## To Stanley Burnshaw:

Yale—Sept. 7, 1963

Dear Stanley,

I am just back from Europe & one of my first joys was to read your volume of poetry—which was awaiting me here among a pile of books & magazines. It was a genuine & deep joy & I thank you for it. I knew some of the poems, & always remembered your talking to me on "listen," a very moving, tragic dialogue. I admired the skill of the translations & adaptations—Your rendering of Alberti, of Éluard, is extraordinarily deft & faithful, & makes a superb English poetry. Your apostrophe of Whitman, your "Time of Brightness" show a rare mastery of the long poem, with "longueur de souffle," but no filling of rhetoric whatever. And your mastery over words, your musical power, condensation of emotion into sparse, suggestive stanzas are perhaps nowhere more visible than in the poems placed first in your book, & the one which gives its title to the volume. There is no trickiness, no display of acrobatics or showmanship about any of the pieces. They will reward a third–fourth reading, I know; and I am grateful to have offered me the book so generously & cordially, as a present of welcome & an encouragement as I return with many sad memories, but also with hope for the future. You are a very fine artist and an imaginative one; but also a kind friend with a rare wealth of sentiment & affection—"un homme complet"—and one whose poetical vein will not dry up in spite of the passing of years.

I am slowly getting reaccustomed to things after my prolonged absence, but all seems to go well & sometime soon we shall meet, I trust.

> Very devoted greetings to Leda & very cordially yours,
> Hri

## To Vera Lee:

> Sept. 16/63

Dear Mrs. Lee:

Let me first say that I admire your courage & determination. Few women in your position, alone & with a child, would have gone on studying, writing & looking ahead. You always had fortitude, & humor, & the gift to spread some joyfulness around you on all the friends & admirers you "hypnotized."

I had read your article in the F. *Review* & cut it out to keep it. There were good things in it. And you should go on trying out your ideas in other articles. The *Partage de Midi* one (I adored the play when I was very young, & could have what Wordsworth calls "strange fits of passion") will especially interest me.

A book? Yes. The subject is difficult, because vague, immense. It poses indeed many questions. I take it you know the work by Ginestier, the essays by Vilar, Barrault, Guicharnaud's volume, etc. Sartre's lecture on the bourgeois public at the French theatre. (I am just back from Europe, remarried after my first wife's death last year, not yet clear where my notes are.) Interviews will be valuable, but also study of *Arts* & other periodicals, statistical data, detailed exploration of cases (Vilar's T[héâtre] N[ational] P[opulaire] & Avignon, other festivals). A book on the subject would, or could, eventually sell, attract Drama Schools over here, be discussed.

But how complete the work & your documentation? You will need 6 months at least over there. I would try in your place for an ACLS. I doubt you'd have a strong chance on the Guggenheim competition where they have about 35 people applying in French every year & 3 or 4 "élus" & those are persons with substantial achievement (a book or several articles), so that the Committee can judge their solid promises. But you would lose nothing to try both sources. Your chances may not be of the strongest, but it will force you to formulate your project precisely & perhaps to get started on it. Would your University give you a small grant? Has Boston Univ. any possibilities? Success or not, go on with it—get together a few articles & it will help if you try again, 2 or 3 years from now, with more bulky achievement to show.

Sincerely yours,
Henri Peyre

## To James Lawler:

Sept. 16, 1963

Dear Mr. Lawler:

Your articles, read this week after I had returned from Europe & sorted out some of the abundant mail which awaited me, have given me much pleasure. I appreciate & admire the close texture of your reasoning, the rigorous precision of your study of "le vierge, le vivace" (less paradoxical, more logical & convincing than any I have read), the constructive use of the early versions of poems like *le Platane* (which you made me like more warmly than I ever had before), the taste with which you dissect poetry and never are heavy-handed, dry or superior to the poet. I was so glad you praised, & elucidated, *le Rameur*, for which I have long nourished a special fondness. You are in a position to write what may be the finest book yet done on Valéry's poetry as poetry. It would be fitting indeed if it were done by an Australian, the cradle of several keen critics of modern French verse.

Your letter was also awaiting me here — I am so involved in projects here, behind in keeping promises to publishers, that I do not believe I could undertake a "voyage à la terre australe" in the relatively near future. Besides, since I am a French citizen, I doubt I could be eligible for a Fulbright grant. Germaine Brée has the advantage not to have any regular teaching, in her Institute at Wisconsin, & no administration. The headship of the Department here is time-consuming. I have held it long enough now and hope to free myself from it by 1965 or so & enjoy my last years of teaching with more leisure for writing. But before then I hope we shall have had another visit from you here. I wish you would let us know in advance next time & let our students & colleagues enjoy the benefit of a lecture by you. I have not yet had a chance to meet Mr. Lloyd Austin but I hope I shall this year. Last year was a difficult one for me.

Let me know if there are books or articles which I might send you from here, if any are hard to obtain on Australia. And accept my thanks again & my very cordial wishes.

Sincerely yours,
Henri Peyre

## To James Osborn:

Sept. 30/63

Dear Jim,

I do not always read immediately, but I always do read & enjoy what you so generously send me. After a long absence, & amid a mass of accumulated mail, I was glad to extract your charming Pope's "Umbra" & your detective work on the several Careys. The other essay on Travel Literature found me on more familiar ground, as I worked much on Hellenism & neo-Hellenism in my youth. Indeed I have remained the same sort of "mystical Pagan" on whom I published my first book at the Yale Press, over 30 years ago. I was delighted to recognize old friends, & to discover new ones: Wheler & Spon, Liotard, The travels of Anacharsis & others. You are remarkably well informed on the French side of that travel literature which prepared & preceded romantic neo-Hellenism & I admired the diligent use you made of your yearly honeymoon vernal trips to Europe: I always meant to work at the Gennadios Library in Athens myself & never yet did succeed in getting the time.

I stayed mostly in France this Summer, wrote a good deal, rested & tried to find some sweetness in memories which were at first hard to bear. A young wife requires some of my attentive care & forces me not to stay within myself & books overmuch. I hope you are both well & offer my very cordial & warm wishes for another active year. How lovely is our street just now!

Sincerely,
Hri

## À Lester Crocker:

Le 6 octobre 63

Mon cher Lester,

Votre livre est de premier ordre — remarquable au plus haut point — certes l'un des meilleurs que l'on ait écrits sur la pensée morale du XVIIIe siècle et le meilleur de notre génération en Amérique dans ce domaine. Votre documentation est riche, et nullement limitée à la France; elle est renforcée de tout ce que vous connaissez dans le domaine contemporain de sociologie, philosophie, anthropologie. Vous tenez tout cela sous votre regard avec une réelle puissance de synthèse. Tout se range harmonieusement sous vos chapitres, & sans artifice. Vous êtes des rares parmi nous à posséder le tour d'esprit philosophique que ce livre demandait. Vos sections sur l'utilitarisme & sur le nihilisme m'ont frappé comme apportant sur le siècle un jour nouveau pour moi. Vous ne faites au lecteur pressé ou superficiel aucune concession; d'où mon retard à vous lire. Je crains que les journaux & grandes revues ne prennent pas la peine ou ne fassent pas l'effort de vous rendre justice, & cela n'est pas à l'honneur de notre culture. Mais votre livre fera marque.

Enfin ce premier mois, le plus dur, s'achève. J'espère me débarrasser bientôt de ces fonctions administratives qui consomment trop du peu de temps qui me reste, & je ne vous envie pas les vôtres. Mais après un "Magnum opus" comme le vôtre, vous pouvez aimer un changement, et on doit pouvoir réaliser beaucoup dans un tel poste. Votre femme va-t-elle bien? A-t-elle un surcroît de travail comme Dean's wife? Elle semblait si détendue, si heureuse à Londres—et si belle.

Ces journées, radieuses et colorées, me ramènent en pensée à ces tristes moments de l'an dernier où ma femme se mourait & où je me sentais si impuissant, si amer contre la science & moi-même. Il se trouve que le voyage rapide que, grâce à votre toujours obligeante & généreuse entremise, je vais faire à Cleveland pour Mr. Pflejer, tombera exactement au même moment où je me trouvais chez vous, l'an dernier, l'esprit soucieux & le cœur gros. Mon remariage m'a apporté de vraies consolations & Lois se montre très compréhensive & dévouée & gaie. La rencontre avec des hommes profonds comme vous l'intimide—ce qui est naturel—mais après tout on n'en rencontre pas tous les jours. Je me remets au travail & à écrire—et espère me libérer bientôt de l'excès de mes tâches.

Vos enfants vont-ils bien? La dédicace est ingénieuse, & belle. Les livres vivent, mais causent moins de soucis que ces autres "œuvres" vivantes et souvent rebelles. Mais que de dons concentrés dans une famille de quatre! Et vos beaux-frères acteurs à Londres n'étaient pas moins riches de dons. J'aimerais avoir fait votre livre!

Croyez encore à mes très vives & affectueuses amitiés, Lois y joint les siennes—à vous deux.

Henri

## À Franco Simone:

Le 21 octobre 1963

Cher Monsieur,

Je reçois votre mot du 10 septembre, et m'excuse de ne pas avoir renouvelé mon abonnement aux Studi francesi pour 1963. J'ai dû égarer votre précédent avis. Mais je voudrais beaucoup recevoir le n° 19, le n° 20 et être à nouveau sur vos listes d'abonnés. Voici quinze dollars pour couvrir mon abonnement pour 1963-64-65.

Avec mes excuses, et mes remerciements pour l'excellence continue de votre revue,

Hri Peyre

## To Frederic Musser:

Oct. 22/63

Dear Mr. Musser:

Many thanks for writing at such length & such a well-written letter. I am sorry if Wesleyan loses you (& sorry for Wesleyan). It is one of the finest places in the country where to teach; but if they decide that their department needs more publishing members, & glamorous names, we shall understand & meanwhile the wisest would be for you to get good offers from elsewhere & then bring the decision, one way or the other, to a clear point. Luckily, this should be a good time to receive offers, & tempting ones. And perhaps a less cordial atmosphere, a more hectic or more challenging place than Wesleyan would prove a good one, too. You have a great deal of depth & penetration & originality in you; it might take only a little incitement from outside to invite you to write more, & you would probably derive great satisfaction from it. I felt, in the "old days" when you were with us, that you had more depth, more personal reflection in you & more literary sensitiveness, than most of our students, but perhaps also more reserve, more shyness, less of that slightly vulgar confidence in ourselves which leads some of us to believe that we have something new to offer to the world. But there is a sort of relief, & eventually a genuine satisfaction, in achieving a book, even not very original, & in offering it to others for public judgment or indictment.

It is unfortunate that poetry is less in demand than drama, or novels, & tempts publishers much less. If one does a textbook or an anthology, it is wiser to adapt oneself to the public or to write with an eye on the school & college potential audiences, and respond to its probable needs while staying just a little above them. For promotion purposes & the judgment of Presidents, Deans & colleagues, a critical or biographical work, even if dull & in part second hand, is a more practical undertaking. If I were you, I'd do a real book of some kind: on Rotrou, or Baudelaire, or St Pol Roux, or Germain Nouveau, or on French moralists or historians. Why not? If it serves no useful purpose at Wesleyan, it might help elsewhere, later. Some day come down here & talk to some of us about it.

I'll suggest your name for positions here & there, even this fall—there's no point waiting until you might perhaps feel that you *have* to go—and we'll see what comes of it. I imagine you would rather stay in the East, but a good offer from elsewhere might prove tempting, or helpful.

> Most cordially yours,
> Henri Peyre

## To the same:

> Nov. 3/63

Dear Mr. Musser:

Kenyon *is* isolated, but pleasant, with a fine level of students & teaching. The French Department has not been too happy or very forward looking there, & often teaches in English; hence some dissatisfaction. But you could do worse!

Meanwhile, do not hurry. There will be many good positions—& better paid ones in larger & more active cities. I have written about you to four or five places: Wayne, Iowa, California, Indiana. We'll see the results. You might find it more stimulating at those places than in a "secluded" college.

Sorry I could not be there last Tuesday. My life is still too full & hurried, but I hope to be able to reach some serenity some day!

> Cordially yours,
> Henri Peyre

## To Lester Crocker:

> Dec. 4, 1963

Dear Lester,

Much has happened since my pleasant & enriching visit with you, & I was deeply disturbed at first—we all were—but somehow that absurd event brought back, in my old man's memory, ominous fears which

I had experienced in Europe after Dollfuss was murdered, when absurd forces of evil began being unleashed in Europe in the middle thirties. Fortunately, things are now different in Europe, & this country has too much common sense & ingrained wisdom to have much to fear.

Now I can tell you again how I enjoyed my visit & appreciated all you did for me: every one of your very thoughtful attentions, the very cheerful meetings with your friends & with Dean Hurley & his wife, & your efficient assembling of a large & well disposed audience for my humble words.

Your two reviews—they are much more than that; they are articles full of reflections & a new thought—impressed me. You are one of the very, very few scholars alive today who brush aside all superficialities & discern the fundamental plans, or contradictions, in the work of their colleagues, while praising the good generously. Your review of Proust may be judged to be severe, but it strikes penetratingly at some of the contradictions in his thesis. There are so many contradictions in Diderot himself, &, I must own, hasty & inadequate views on natural law & on ethics! Have we not deified him too much? On Mauzi, you are severe, but superb: I had enjoyed his book because I learned much from it, on secondary figures; but, as I closed the book, I was confused by its queer composition, its wealth of hardly relevant matter & the lack of a central core of strict reasoning & in defining of happiness. You explain why superbly.

I hope your new functions will not prevent you from carrying on your independent & profound thinking on those subjects; we should otherwise all be the losers. I myself grow very impatient with my own job of placing people, recruiting others & scribbling letters. I shall try hard to be relieved of it soon. Meanwhile, I have to search for a medievalist, as ours is in danger of being lost. How few really first-rate men we have produced in that field & the Renaissance in the last quarter of a century.

I am enclosing the text of a statement which came up before our own board at Yale, on the M.A. & B.A. degrees being eventually combined for very gifted students. This is not official yet, but I am convinced it is the goal toward which we are evolving. Some time you'll probably travel around here & meet with our Deans & discuss such matters. It is no flattery to you to say that you have the best mind of any Graduate School Dean I know. We'll be looking up to you.

Our very best to Billie. She looked wonderful, I thought, & full of life & liveliness as always. Lois missed not seeing her & I reported to her all about my trip, one of the pleasantest I ever had.

Most cordially yours,<br>
Henri Peyre

## À Jorge Guillén:

Le 17 dec. 1963

Cher ami,

    Vous êtes toujours la gentillesse &, vous si grand poète, la modestie même. Je vous savais remarié & heureux: vous avez tant à donner, vous comprenez si bien les femmes (et pas mal d'hommes!) que vivre auprès de vous doit être une merveille quotidienne. Je me suis en effet, très vite, remarié moi-même. J'avais vécu très uni avec ma femme et le vide, soudain, m'était insupportable—je suis si peu pratique pour les détails de la vie. Ma jeune femme est très, très jeune pour moi—mais semble heureuse et m'est très dévouée. Elle n'a même pas eu peur de devenir enceinte et dans quelques mois encore, elle aura, si tout va bien, un enfant.

    Je ne vais guère à Cambridge—mais, après ces vacances (je m'absente pour dix jours, du 19 au 31 décembre), si vous vouliez venir en janvier un jour, ce serait une grande joie pour moi. Durán est en Italie, mais nous pourrions réunir quelques amis. Le lundi & le mardi sont pour moi peu commodes, mais presque tout autre jour—sauf les 27–28 janvier. Votre femme viendrait-elle avec vous?

    Mille cordiales pensées & mes très fidèles amitiés; et bien des choses à M. & Mrs Gilman.

Henri Peyre

## To Norman & Mrs. McIntosh:

110 Deepwood Drive, Hamden, Conn 06517
Jan. 4, 64

Dear Mr. & Mrs. McIntosh:

Many thanks for your message. I was very sincerely & deeply pleased to see you again in Alfred, saddened by Malcolm's recent bout with fatigue; but what a wonderful thing to have your son so successful at Harvard. I have indeed been rash enough to accept the risks of marrying a very young woman—risks of all kinds (see *l'Ecole des Femmes*), but most of all of paternity! But I do feel more hopeful & serene than when I last saw you.

Most cordially yours,
Henri Peyre

## To James M. Osborn (with text of article "An Appeal to Anglo-Saxon Fairness," Feb. 1963):

Jan. 4/64

Dear Jim,

Very warm wishes for you & your wife. With long delay, accept my thanks for the extremely fine reproduction of the *Pope* (he is so much more mysterious thus than in his poetry!) & for your earlier clippings on Britain & the prospects of the Common Market. Here was what I wrote on the subject last winter, for what it is worth—I hope it does not meet with too strong a disapproval from the Anglophile that you are—(that I am too, after a fashion).

Cordially,
Henri Peyre

## À Kurt Weinberg:

Le 5 jan./64

Cher ami,

Non, je n'ai pas voulu aller à Chicago; c'est si las, si vain, & j'aspire à quelque repos et à lire, à lire. J'ai affronté & débrouillé votre grand *Kafka* et, dans la mesure où mon allemand est à la hauteur & où j'ai quelque compétence (je suis un peu loin, par adoration de la Grèce, de tout ce qui est judaïque, & loin aussi des gens à complexes), j'ai beaucoup admiré votre livre. C'est le plus convaincant & le plus fouillé, de beaucoup, de tous ceux qui ont tâché d'expliquer Kafka. Vous raisonnez avec grande richesse d'arguments, une pénétration sensitive presque magique dans les arcanes des textes et beaucoup de finesse psychologique. Il faut que le livre soit traduit en anglais. Y songe-t-on?

Ce sera une joie de vous voir et de revoir votre femme dont la beauté, l'intelligence, le tact m'ont ébloui; mais je viendrai seul. Je me trouve alors très pressé par la réunion le 6 mars, vendredi, du comité Guggenheim. Je devrai partir le matin à une heure impossible, pour attraper un avion à 9h35 (#424, American Airlines). Je m'en excuse par avance. Et Lois, ma jeune femme—qui m'a redonné foi à l'avenir & à mon travail—attend pour le début de mai une progéniture. Mieux vaut qu'elle reste sage & immobile! Mais nous aurons le temps de parler la veille (le jour de la conférence) & le soir.

Avec mes amitiés et remerciements pour le livre, pour votre hospitalité future & mes vœux amicaux,

Henri

## À Franco Simone:

Le 17 janvier 1964

Cher collègue,

Je sais que vous êtes à Berkeley cette année. C'est trop loin pour que je vous y poursuive & je voyage le moins possible cette année. Mais j'aurais aimé vous souhaiter plus tôt la bienvenue sur ce continent. Passerez-vous par ici à votre retour? & si la date est commode, pourriez-vous vous y arrêter? Je vous lis avec avidité & les *Studi Francesi* avec une admiration toujours aussi vive. Quel beau travail vous y faites!

Et je voulais aussi vous demander conseil pour un domaine qui n'est qu'à demi le vôtre. L'Amérique n'a pas assez de jeunes Italiens distingués qui y viendraient, au moins momentanément, enseigner leur langue. Le printemps dernier, j'ai essayé d'en découvrir en Europe, mais sans grand succès. Si vous saviez trouver quelque jeune homme, sachant un peu d'anglais & ayant quelque expérience, pour l'orienter vers Yale, je vous en serais reconnaissant. Une autre année (il n'est pas libre en 1964–5), nous espérons avoir ici M. Scaglione et nous en réjouissons déjà. Mais il aura besoin d'assistance.

Je suis sûr que vous vous plaisez dans ce magnifique site & cette université si active. Mais Turin (que j'ai enfin visité l'été dernier, lors de l'exposition baroque) ne doit pas aisément se laisser oublier. C'est une ville splendide d'harmonie & de noblesse ordonnée

Croyez à mon très cordial souvenir.
Hri Peyre

## To Frederic Musser:

Jan. 22/64

Dear Mr. Musser:

Thank you for the kindness of your letter. I am glad that your trouble is an "embarras de richesses." I believe that in your place I would—since there has been hesitation—decide to give up the possibility at Wesleyan & accept Goucher or Colgate or other posts which may surely turn up between now & April, & which will be, I believe, even more tempting. You have no need to rush—offers will come to you—& they might provide the stimulant which is at times healthy after several years in the same place. Wayne, incidentally, which will publish you, may not be beautiful (some buildings are) but is a forward looking & very active university, worth your serious consideration. There is a lovely museum in Detroit & very cultured people.

With my best wishes,
Henri Peyre

## À Jean Boorsch:

Le 2 avril 64

Mon cher Jean,

Ce mot vous atteindra peut-être à Taormina. J'ai séjourné à ce même hôtel en 1938; que d'années depuis & d'événements. La Sicile était alors peuplée de touristes allemands & Marguerite s'indignait qu'on la prît pour une Tudesque. Il faisait froid & pluvieux, en avril; mais les jours d'éclaircie la vue était majestueuse. Et nous avions surtout aimé l'Étna et son vin de vignes volcaniques, la lente navigation à Syracuse; dans les eaux où croissent les papyrus et le centre de l'île, Enna. Mais pour vous cette île triangulaire n'est qu'un stade de votre périple: vous êtes infatigable et indécourageable et refusez d'écouter le "Extremum hunc, Arethusa, mihi concede laborem." À votre place, j'aurais eu peur de la Grèce. Prenez garde aux vengeances d'Esculape ou de quelque Turc en furie et tout de même saluez pour moi Epidaure, où j'avais une fois, tout seul, rêvé plusieurs heures.

Ici, temps froid—22–25 Fahrenheit, pour Pâques, mais clair & bleu—et peu d'événements pour nous. Le département respire, soulagé bientôt de ma tyrannie; j'ai quelques remords d'infliger à Brombert ces sottes préoccupations querelleuses de nos Espagnols & aurais bien mieux fait, il y a 6 ans, de ne pas me charger de ça. Mais il y sera peut-être plus habile & plus heureux que moi. Il ne semble pas ravi de ce surcroît de travail, mais vous l'aiderez bientôt—et il est solide. Nous allons avoir 6 ou 7 oraux entre le 15 avril & le 25 mai . . . Cette liste de questions me sort par les yeux & les oreilles, mais ce sera autant de moins pour vous l'an prochain. La Grad. School nous a accordé à peu près tout ce que nous demandions: on s'y montre vraiment gentil pour nous. Le transfert de la bibliothèque du Romance Seminar s'est fort bien effectué & nous n'y perdons pas, somme toute. Quelques conférenciers vont venir—Rousset, Zumthor, Verdier—& ce sera enfin l'été. Lois est impatiente de recouvrer une taille normale et je le suis pour elle. En fin juillet (nous vous aurons revus avant cela), nous déménagerons & je commencerai, avec 40 ans de retard, la vie d'un homme responsable de jardin, ordures, chauffage, éducation d'un bébé. . . .

Nous avons souri de votre indignation devant le prix des huîtres. Mais c'est la fin des mois en "r" et vous passerez ensuite aux crabes &

aux langoustes; je ne suis pas très grand amateur de ces coquillages, mais après la Grèce vous trouverez sûrement, comme je le fis. . . .

Amitiés à Louise & à votre fille.

Bien à vous,<br>H. P.

## To James & Mrs. Osborn:

[postcard: view of Madison Walk, Oxford]<br>May 7 (1964)

Dear Mr. & Mrs. Osborn:

Thank you for your (Jim's) patience with my Shakespearean amateurish disquisitions! A baby was born yesterday to Lois, a big boy, a future Malvolio or Polonius (a son of an old father is sure to be grouchy & cantankerous). Pardon this informal way of letting you know.

Sincerely,<br>Henri Peyre

## À Jean Boorsch:

Le 7 mai /64

Mon cher Jean,

Je suis sûr que vous serez rentrés rafraîchis, égayés, grossis et blondis par la Provence ou la côte d'azur, après vos incursions en Calabre et en Grande Grèce. Et bientôt votre séjour européen va s'achever. Vous nous avez manqué de bien des manières ici; et parce que vos visites matinales, toujours gaies, vos bras chargés de lilas, vos yeux pétillants de mépris pour les démocraties n'étaient plus là; et parce que nos étudiants gradués ont choisi cette saison pour nous accabler de leurs examens & thèses. Sur ces entrefaites, Buffum a été pris d'une grave crise de dépression & j'ai dû me charger de son cours gradué. Et c'est l'objet essentiel de ma lettre: Lois a enfin mûri le fruit de son hymen et, après plusieurs jours de retard & diverses difficultés d'accouchement (qui a duré beaucoup d'heures), elle a eu hier un fils, chevelu, joufflu, aussi laid que moi paraît-il, qu'elle veut appeler "Brice, Henri." C'étaient les noms de mon père & ils sont malheureusement au calendrier chrétien. Elle n'a pas accepté mes prénoms homériques. Elle va bien, malgré deux nuits de "labeur" et envoie à Louise et vous ses amitiés. J'y ajoute les miennes.

La thèse de Miss Walsh est à mon avis remarquable & je vous en félicite—dogmatique certes, irritante, pédante, trop longue & lourde—mais vraiment il y a là de la rigueur, de l'approfondissement, une grande pénétration d'analyse. Ce n'est nullement ma méthode, mais je m'incline devant sa science & sa maturité d'esprit. Cela, raccourci, mérite publication.

Nos bons vœux à tous deux & à votre fille. De votre Yale man, pas de nouvelles. Il semble affirmer son indépendance. . . .

Amitiés,
Henri

## À Konrad et Tamara Bieber:

Le 6 juin 1964

Chers amis,

Je crains d'avoir égaré votre adresse française & je ne sais d'ailleurs combien de temps vous deviez passer en Europe; mais ce mot vous rejoindra peut-être, avec retard. Il ne veut que vous dire combien nous avons été touchés, d'abord de votre si gentille lettre, puis de cet envoi de deux très élégantes chemises d'enfant qui m'ont fait regretter de n'avoir pas rapetissé suffisamment pour porter d'aussi gracieux vêtements et me prélasser dans ce costume au soleil. Cela était infiniment aimable & généreux à vous.

Nous restons ici cet été, un peu par la force des choses, un peu par économie & pour payer la maison (110 Deepwood Drive, Hamden) où nous allons nous transporter au mois d'août—et aussi parce que je promets sans cesse plus de livres que je n'en peux écrire & dois combler mes retards. Comme vous, je me libère de ma position administrative, mais mon âge me vaut encore beaucoup de correspondance & les journées sont plus courtes avec un bébé. Le petit Brice est fort gentil jusqu'ici; ses moments de colère sont brefs, ses larmes sont amères & il ne sait pas encore sourire. Mais cela viendra. Si seulement il devient un jour comme votre fils, le plus souriant & aimable des garçons que j'aie vus à New Haven!

Politiquement & psychologiquement, la France & l'Allemagne doivent être intéressants cette année, mais la littérature semble traîner. J'ai goûté le petit récit d'André Chamson, le roman un peu recherché de LeClézio, deux ou trois autres livres, mais bien peu. Peut-être rapporterez-vous une moisson de nouvelles littéraires d'Europe; vous êtes toujours si bien renseigné.

> Nos vives et reconnaissantes amitiés à tous deux & nos vœux d'agréable été,
> Hri

## To James Lawler:

July 8/64

Dear Mr. Lawler:

I am staying here this summer & the heat is fortunately not excessive. As I may have told you already, after my wife died from cancer two years ago, leaving me rather helpless & totally dispirited, I made the bold move to remarry. My second & young wife has since given me a lovely baby, who engrosses much of my leisure hours. We are moving to a house, 2 or 3 miles away from the campus; &, after 25 years of being a chairman, I have decided to resign from those administrative functions. This is to explain that you are one of the four or five names of persons to whom I have been long meaning to write but have not. I utilized—in a very practical sense, for I borrowed much from you—your Valéry book extensively while giving a course on him last Autumn: & my admiration for it, & for your very fine article in Romanic Review, is very great. You are too kind to my anthology which I did in some hurry, but I hope it may be of service to colleagues. I have since redone my *Classicisme* volume for Nizet & done a collection of studies by Lanson—old but still very important & timely, with a long preface—in part to enable young people to become acquainted with that fine scholar. Percy Mansell Jones "assaulted" him very foolishly, or so I thought, in a recent & flimsy book.

Of course I'll be most pleased to see you on your return trip; just let me know in advance the approximate date of it. If it were after the middle of October, I hope you might give us a lecture here. I'll be here most of the summer, settling, writing (for I have much else promised to publishers).

My very cordial wishes for your summer & very sincerely yours,
Henri Peyre

## À Gita May:

Le 6 août 1964

Chère madame,

Je trouve votre livre au retour d'un voyage & je l'ai aussitôt lu. Vos précédentes publications, vigoureuses, décidées et fort pénétrantes, m'ont assez dit quels sont vos mérites, & j'ai été heureux qu'ils fussent reconnus d'emblée par le Comité Guggenheim. Mais ce sujet-ci était malaisé: beau, tentant, se prêtant dangereusement à la déclamation & au sentiment, mais subtil comme portrait d'une âme, demandant de la mesure & de la justesse, & cependant une sympathie entière. Je l'avais souvent suggéré, mais sans convaincre personne. Je suis content que ce soit vous, & non un novice, qui l'ait traité—et cette manière de le traiter est définitive. Votre livre est très fouillé (un peu sobre sur le mari; mais, c'est le sort des maris mal aimés et trop prêcheurs de vertu), très fin et il constitue enfin un chapitre essentiel de l'immense étude qu'il y aura un jour à entreprendre sur l'influence de Rousseau ou du moins sur les âmes dont il s'est emparé après sa mort. Il y aurait bien des personnages révolutionnaires à faire ainsi revivre; puis Senancour, G. Sand, Nerval, Lamartine, Musset, Stendhal, Balzac & cent autres. Mais nul ou nulle n'a revécu la *Nouvelle Héloïse* comme votre personnage—et vous le montrez bien: c'est un roman très prenant, & qui l'est resté, & Julie est une des femmes les plus féminines de la littérature, malgré, ou même avec, son inclination à moraliser & à épiloguer. Il fallait du talent & du courage pour entreprendre ce sujet, & pour le traiter sans volumineuse lourdeur, & vous aviez cela. La partie la plus énigmatique du siècle, la sensibilité préromantique en reçoit un précieux éclairage. Je suis honoré que vous m'ayez cité parfois, mais ne le méritais point. J'ai souvent voulu m'attaquer au préromantisme, mais, soit hasard de la vie, soit timidité devant un domaine peu défriché, j'ai toujours différé. Avec Fellows & vous et les traditions de vos prédécesseurs, c'est Columbia qui est la pépinière de ces travaux désormais. Une galerie de ce que devinrent sous la Révolution & à travers elle une douzaine de personnages de 1770–1800, y compris Anquetil Duperron pour qui j'ai un faible, serait un bien curieux livre. Sainte-Beuve était celui qui pouvait l'écrire—et qui sait maintenant.

Merci de m'avoir aussitôt permis de lire votre bel ouvrage & croyez, chère madame, à mes sentiments très sincères.

Henri Peyre

## À Franco Simone:

Le 6 août 1964

Cher monsieur & ami,

Je reçois à l'instant l'avis de préparation du volume de Mélanges Siciliano. J'ai trop d'engagements (beaucoup non tenus, hélas!) pour pouvoir promettre un article: voulez-vous m'en excuser? Mais je tenais du moins à vous dire mon admiration pour M. Siciliano, que je place au tout premier rang des critiques italiens de la littérature française. L'immense champ de son activité intellectuelle m'a toujours rempli d'admiration. Et il a pu unir à cela ses fonctions de Recteur.

Je m'efforce moi-même de me libérer de mes besognes administratives, après trop d'années que je les ai remplies, et de me rendre un peu plus dispos d'esprit pour mes écrits. J'ai plusieurs projets en cours, et ai sorti une Anthologie critique de la littérature française contemporaine, que j'ai prié la maison Harper de vous envoyer. Je m'efforcerai de vous faire parvenir quelques autres de mes articles, et cet automne la refonte de mon vieux Classicisme et un livre sur Lanson. Les trois conférences sur le baroque, si agréablement présentées, constituent une lucide mise au point. Je suis de ceux qui pensent que, surtout après ce que vous & Marcel Raymond avez dit d'excellent sur ce sujet, on pourrait laisser le sujet sommeiller quelques années. Votre revue continue à nous émerveiller. Elle est le plus précieux des informateurs pour nous, par la diligence & la vaste variété de ses comptes-rendus. Je la loue souvent & j'espère que vous avez pu recruter aux États-Unis les abonnés que vous devriez avoir. Songez-vous à revenir ici? Je viens de déménager et cela, ainsi que la naissance d'un beau bébé (je m'étais remarié après la mort de ma femme), me retient ici cette année. Croyez à mes très cordiales pensées & à mes bons vœux,

Henri Peyre

## À Arnaldo Pizzorusso:

août 10/64

Cher monsieur,

Le généreux & délicat envoi de votre récent livre m'a comblé. Il m'a rappelé le plaisir que j'ai eu à vous connaître & à vous écouter, & j'en ai été touché. Et la lecture m'en a donné un très vrai plaisir. Vous y mettez tant de connaissances, tant de citations rares et curieuses (heureux pays que l'Italie où on vous permet tant de notes!) que tout le siècle de Fontenelle s'en trouve éclairé. Mais vous n'éludez pas les grands aspects de sa pensée et de sa poétique. Cet aspect de votre livre est très neuf et ni Maigron ni Carré ni d'autres n'avaient ainsi montré l'intérêt des idées littéraires de Fontenelle. Et puis, votre livre est si joliment imprimé et si élégant: le titre en est d'une fine subtilité et la couverture fort curieuse.

Je crois que vous avez vu notre ami Brombert, grand amoureux de Pise & de Florence. Il aimerait comme moi vous voir un jour venir passer quelque temps aux États-Unis. La face que le pays montre en ce moment au monde n'est pas attrayante, mais il y a de belles qualités chez les élèves et dans le public sérieux.

Veuillez croire, cher Monsieur, à mon souvenir le meilleur & à mes remerciements.
Henri Peyre

## To James & Mrs. Osborn:

[postcard: Rubens, *The Flagellation;* postmarked Sept. 7, 1964]

Dear Mrs. Osborn, Dear Jim,

We have moved to a new address (110, Deepwood Drive) in the course of the summer & we shall have friends bring us luck on that occasion on Saturday September nineteenth, from four to five thirty, if they will thus honor us with their presence. We should be pleased if you could come.

Cordially,<br>Lois & Henri Peyre

### To the same:

[postcard: Tintoretto, *Rinvenimento del corpo di S. Marco* (Milan)]
Sept. 24 — 64

Dear Jim,

Your "Malone piece" is most handsome. What luxury expended on that pompous coxcomb, Boswell, by a crowd of modest & highly intelligent men! I fear I cannot go to the Morgan Library on Oct. 7th, though Traherne is someone I need to learn about. I lectured in that very same room just a year ago! My best wishes, however.

Sincerely,<br>Henri Peyre

### To Vera Lee:

110 Deepwood Drive<br>Hamden, Conn.<br>Dec. 20/64

Dear Mrs. Lee,

You made me feel guilty, which, they say, is excellent at this season of remorse, sadistic wishes & masochistic Christmas card wholesale writing. But your second, witty reminder amused Lois no end. You might make a fine career as an entertainer of the brainiest class on TV. I am writing intensively this fall (3 or 4 books to appear soon), plus amusing a baby, boring a young wife & teaching her all her duties to an old Epicure of a husband. And so I just let letters go for a few weeks, until, like cheese & pheasants, they [illegible] *à point*. Pardons mille fois!

*Of course* I like your project on the popular theatre in France—a stiff one, quite a challenge, but also an exciting one—and of course I'll always be glad to recommend you anywhere, for a summer fellowship, to a marital candidate, to a college position. I was at Boston College last June for a day, receiving an hon. degree—not such a bad place, if only they would pay their people well. They are losing fine Yale graduates or colleagues (Langlois, Tumbey) & will lose more.

Your subject, in fact, would require a whole year in France, visits to many a regional center; if you came back with much precise information, it would lead to a book which might sell quite well over here. People are interested in the topic. But much will hang upon the definition of "popular"; many of the shows given at Orange, Arras, Besançon, St. Étienne are not "popular," i.e. inspired by the masses or by populist or socialistic trends directed at the masses. They have done much for decentralization, but to be popular is another affair. Occasionally *Le Cid* or *La Tour de Nesles* has filled a popular audience with enthusiasm, but, as Sartre contended in a striking lecture, the theatre in France has remained very bourgeois. The problem is: should anything "bourgeois" be thus opposed to the popular & indicted as it is by Sartre? Indeed is not the bourgeois theatre the most representative of the new lower classes now ascending? It is hard to know what workmen at Renault or Peugeot like, when & if they go to the theatre. You will need some visits with sociologists, yet not to let yourself be swayed by their fascination with purely quantitative factors.

Joyeux Noël & mes excuses,<br>HP

## To Henry Allen Moe:

    [postcard: A. M. Saint-Paul, *Un coin pittoresque*]
    Jan. 2/65

Dear Henry,

I had seen the announcement & very unworthy & inadequate obituary of a truly great servant of science & of humanistic scholarship. It saddened me deeply. What a marvelous example of conscientious, fair, lucid judgment he gave us all on the Committee! We miss you. I feel a little like a deprived, orphaned man without your occasional kindly smile & the light of your eyes. My own work goes well. I am writing several books, & with the growth of a baby, the thought on the future, my life has been renewed. Is your own health good? Are you & Mrs. Moe traveling, resting, reading? Do both have a happy year 1965 & accept our very best wishes.

Henri

## To James M. Osborn:

Jan. 16/65

Dear Jim,

I am returning that very interesting article by Huxley: it would deserve being reproduced & spread over here. It seemed to agree with, or to strengthen, my own views (though mine are far less scientific) to such a point that I was embarrassed.

I am adding a few casual reprints, which you may discard after you have glanced at them. Please take them, not as any pedantic display on my part, but as a very sincere token of esteem for one in this community, who does much to stimulate others to pursue their research, who generously & tastefully adds much to the artistic & scholarly life of Yale & whose flair may well be envied by every one of your 300 or so colleagues in the Humanities.

I am distressed to see that as I was counting on attending the "Mory" evening where you will reveal something on your finds, we have previously accepted another engagement for that Wednesday. I always regret that those Knights of the Round Table meet on that day of the week, one of the hardest for some of us. I shall miss it & miss learning with enjoyment.

Our best to your wife & to you,<br>Hri

## To Stanley Burnshaw:

Febr. 12/65

Dear Stanley,

The New Churches of Europe is a sumptuous gift, & your generosity in sending it to me is boundless. True, the subject interests me passionately; but I should have heard of the book earlier & ordered it. I am happy & proud to have it. I have already spent long hours going over & through it. I knew the French Churches, & a few in Switzerland, but not those of Germany, Finland, Denmark & I feel urges to travel in search of "sacred architecture" — some day, perhaps. Just now, house, baby, writing commitments detain me & I cannot even find the time to visit friends like you or to invite them here. I long for more leisure & was hoping to have gained it, giving up my administrative responsibilities, but I still have to travel far & wide.

Are you off somewhere this spring? Perhaps to complete your Anthology of Israeli poetry? I hope you are also composing poetry of your own. I read some of the so called "young" poets of America, & I'll say in all frankness that you have more wealth of intellect & of imagination, more dexterity & more mastery of images, words & music than any of them.

My very warm thanks & my very best to Leda.

Yours most cordially,
Henri Peyre

## À Franco Simone:

[carte postale: Carlo Crivelli, *Madonna & Child*]
Le 10 – V – 65

Cher Ami,

Merci de votre très suggestif & très neuf essai sur Pétrarque — il m'a beaucoup révélé sur lui — & merci également de votre belle contribution à l'amitié intellectuelle franco-italienne, où Turin a toujours été à l'avant-garde. Nous reparlerons de cela & de bien des choses lors de votre venue ici. Amitiés.

H. Peyre
(Yale)

## À son frère:

Le 16 juillet 65

Mon cher Jacques,

Je suis touché, plus que je ne puis dire ou écrire et littéralement jusqu'aux larmes, par toute la gentillesse & la délicatesse dans le dévouement avec lesquelles Micheline & toi me soignez, et d'abord nous avez accueillis depuis notre arrivée au Havre cet été. Je bouleverse beaucoup de vos plans, de votre quiétude. Mais je profite sans vergogne de votre aide & je sais bien que, sans les soins délicats de Micheline, sans ta sollicitude fraternelle & tes traitements médicaux, les rendez-vous urgents que nul autre n'aurait pu m'organiser, j'aurais bien moins de chance de me tirer de ce mauvais pas. J'ai horreur de la maladie et n'aime pas non plus m'imposer ainsi à d'autres, même à des parents. Mais pour le moment, ma fierté et mon indépendance souvent un peu ombrageuses sont bel & bien enterrées.

Je suis chagriné aussi pour Lois qui doit se tracasser là-bas & qui avait tant compté sur un été de repos, et pour Brice dont elle est si fière, & pour moi. J'espère du moins lui causer le moins d'ennuis possibles et s'il y a lieu, tu la rassureras.

Mais je te griffonne ce mot un peu grave, mais non point tragique ou découragé, parce qu'il faut tout prévoir. Optimiste, même avec naïveté, je crois que, grâce à vous, je me tirerai de cet accroc. Mais enfin je vais être, comme le Docteur Froment l'a confirmé après toi-même, [à la merci] d'un malheureux hasard. Si quelque chose de fatal se produisait donc dans les semaines qui viennent, voici quelques claires indications.

J'ai fait aux États-Unis mon testament en faveur de Lois. Je n'ai pas de richesses à lui laisser, ou à Brice; et les règles la privent malencontreusement de ma pension de retraite française; mais elle pourrait se tirer d'affaire & élever le bébé, jusqu'à ce qu'elle refasse sa vie. Elle sait là-bas où sont nos papiers. Notre compte en banque est commun, ou "joint." Ici j'ai, pour l'été, des "traveller's cheques" en dollars dont j'ai touché déjà plusieurs à Avignon à la Société Générale, rue de la République. Elle pourrait sans doute les toucher et avoir assez pour arranger son voyage de retour. Sur le France du 12 août, notre passage & celui de l'auto sont payés d'avance. Donc pas de question financière sérieuse.

Mais je voudrais préciser ceci. Si un coup fatal devait m'arriver ici, je tiens formellement à n'avoir rien de chrétien ou de religieux autour de moi et pas d'enterrement ou de cérémonie. Je voudrais être emporté aussitôt, Lois prévenue, vers quelque maison de pompes funèbres et être incinéré, aux moins de frais possible — sans aucun rite d'aucune sorte, & mes cendres dispersées au vent, au jardin du Rayol ou ailleurs. Cela n'a aucune importance pour moi; et je l'écris ainsi, nullement pour jouer au tragique ou pour faire l'original, mais parce que cela a été une longue conviction et une ferme intention chez moi.

Inutile de toucher mot de cela à quiconque, sauf en cas de malheur. Je le répète: mon espoir très ferme est de me rétablir, d'envisager plusieurs années avec Lois qui me rend très heureux et d'amorcer au moins l'éducation de ce gentil petit héritier tardif. Je ne veux ici que regarder en face l'autre hypothèse. Si ce malheur devait m'arriver hors de chez moi, il ne pouvait être mieux adouci que par vos soins ici et les souvenirs de notre père dont cette chambre est pleine et cette maison, qui me rappelle tant de choses & que vous avez si ingénieusement sauvée du déclin.

Je termine ce mot et nous n'en parlerons point. Ce n'était que pour clarifier les choses, lors de la première journée où, enfin, je prends au sérieux et avec lutte confiante, ou la passivité requise, mon état.

            Avec encore mon affectueuse gratitude,
            Henri

## À Michel et Colette Guggenheim:

            Le 26 juillet 1965
            2 rue Chauffard
            Avignon

Chers amis,

Votre visite m'a fait du bien, j'en suis sûr, et plaisir, & j'ai été heureux de voir Mme Guggenheim, ancienne amie et toujours si jeune. Je crois que je me rétablis peu à peu; je me sens du moins fort reposé et nourri de sages & antiques lectures; mais on me répète que temps & patience sont les plus sûrs remèdes.

Je me permets de vous demander si vous pensez qu'en écrivant pour moi à la personne qui dirige cette agence, rue Auber, vous auriez plus de chance que je n'en ai en m'adressant à la Cie Transatlantique, comme je l'ai fait sans succès. La note ci-jointe donne les détails. Mon désir serait de pouvoir changer mon billet, émis aux USA, du "France" départ 12 août pour "France" départ 28 août. Ce dernier départ semble, malheureusement, très chargé. Il n'est pas impossible que mon cœur soit assez raffermi pour qu'on me permette le départ du 12 août, si je me repose à bord & en arrivant; mais mon frère croit que ce serait tout de même imprudent.

Je vous remercie par avance de ce que vous croyez pouvoir faire &, si ce souhait ne peut être exaucé, je n'en serai guère surpris.

Passez une bonne fin de séjour avignonnais et prenez ensuite un bon repos.

Avec mes amitiés,<br>Henri Peyre

## To Sally Cornell:

2 rue Chauffard<br>Avignon (Vaucluse)<br>Aug. 2, 1965

Dear Sally,

At last, I muster my will power, cut off my steady, often tedious, reading, shake off my dreaming lethargy & send you a few lines to supplement my laconic postcard. You are the confidant of the ailing, their conscience, their spiritual ministrant, & you know most delicately how to entertain moods & nurse souls as well as how to restore bodies to some vigor.

Well, I am not really very unhappy; just a little bored & even more vexed in my pride (at being independent, secure from common ills & vulgar woes) that a coronary occlusion should stifle one who indulges few excesses, does not smoke, seldom gets angry, never bends down in prayer & claims to be free from all anguish. But there it is. At any rate, being "at home" with a whole floor all to myself, a library of 2 or 3 thousand books, I have been spared what I dread most since my 1962 memories [illegible]—the nearby presence of other patients, interns, the constant visits of joking, coddling, would be motherly nurses! Lois is in Aix with Brice & comes now and then. I submit gently (!) to pills, advice from my brother, & even begin being proud of that particular ailment which strikes representative men. I have never yet felt any pain. Indeed, I cannot help waxing a little fretful in my seclusion. I tried hard to secure a later passage, but failed, & since airplane just now is not deemed advisable, we shall leave Avignon early on Aug. 10th. My brother will drive us all the way. We should thus board the France on the 12th, as scheduled. I shall lift no luggage, drink moderately, climb few stairs & we should reach N.Y. on the 17th. Lois' brother will meet us & take care of our car, a very tiring affair, on the pier & Lois may have written to Mr. Porter to pick me up. I am not sure. In Aug. and Sept. I shall rest further. I miss Lois & Brice: the latter I haven't seen since July 14th. I hear he walks upright now & mutters a few words—probably in Provençal. He'll be glad to see his foster mother again & Ken's pipe & his Larousse dictionary!

Naturally I have made many promises to myself, which I may not long keep, & Lois ponders, with the heartiest good will, over all she should relieve me of at home. It may be that I'll find this semi-lethargy very pleasant. I was reading, just before this "blow," *The Magic Mountain,* among other dull books I had taken with me for the summer (*Wilhelm Meister, Dr. Jivago, La Vie de Marianne*). Basking or wallowing in disease is not my type. Now I have shifted to poetry: from Shakespeare to the whole of Eliz. B. Browning. (How atrociously bad she can be!)

Simone Weil: she attracts & repulses me. I suppose I am, deep down, envious of mystics & of ascetics, probably because I wish to borrow, or to steal, their strange power & the fascination they hold on people, & utilize those for my crusade of an unbeliever. It may be also that I share with her a secret, almost morbid, desire for independence, a fear of giving myself away in human affection or of being seen through. But my placid & mediocre common sense also revolts against the foolishness of her life, the unconscious selfishness she displayed to her parents, to her pupils, & her silly political vacillations. I liked best, I guess, her essays in La Source grecque, & some of the Pensées which you excerpted from her book, with that uncanny gift you have for going "au fond des êtres & des choses." But every time I reread her, I am thrown back to a healthier mood: to a fierce will to enjoy Pagan life, nature, sunshine, poetry, music (I have a superb musical machine here in my room, with records & the French radio programs, with no publicity whatever). Maybe, insidiously, I also enjoy plumbing the depths of the silliness & illogic to which religious fanatics may sink. I have read or reread here several Fathers of the Church, Ovid, Petronius, etc. I am now fed up with 10 hrs a day of reading, & wish I could run again, swim, climb, "être la matière." My greatest disappointment was rereading *La Tentation de St. Antoine*. God! How tedious, tense & pedantic!

You should write your "pensées & réflexions." It might well be one of the finest & deepest books ever written by a woman.

My best to the Biebers, the Myers & of course to Ken, & all my love.
H

## À Georges May:

[letterhead: *France*]
20 août [1965]

Mon cher Georges,

Je ne suis pas encore réinstallé dans mon bureau et vis dans, ou sur, mes valises—d'où ce papier. Mais je veux vite vous remercier de cette lettre pleine d'affection et de gentillesse. Cela fait bien 25 ans que nous nous connaissons et après ce pauvre DeVane dont la mort m'attriste fort, Boorsch, Cornell et bien peu d'autres, vous êtes ici le plus vieux des amis et certes l'un des plus chers. Une sorte de pudeur, et le désir depuis deux ans de ne pas ajouter à vos fardeaux, m'ont empêché parfois de vous dire toute mon estime et de vous voir à déjeuner ou dans votre bureau. Mais peut-être pourrons-nous nous rencontrer plus souvent. Entre bien d'autres choses, je suis, presque naïvement, fier de l'éclatant succès de votre "règne" de doyen. Vous avez avec simplicité, humour et sagesse, conquis d'emblée l'estime de tous, scientifiques, littéraires, administrateurs, subordonnés et étudiants; et la tâche n'était pas facile. Et cependant vous restez souriant et détendu, jamais pressé ou énervé par nous autres; et vous avez splendidement évité de devenir un homme d'organisation sans opinion à lui, froid et fermé, effrayé de s'exprimer avec franchise sur les hommes. Le Doyen idéal—et il ne tiendra qu'à vous d'aller plus haut....

Je me crois de moins en moins comparatiste, et la relecture de Texte, de Hazard, parfois même du dernier livre d'essais de Wellek, m'agace un peu. Les deux XVIII$^e$ siècles, anglais et français, sont au fond si dissemblables, même dans le roman....

Notre retour s'est bien passé. Lois avait arrangé de me faire prendre au bateau par [médecin et ami José] Delgado et emmener ici, tandis qu'elle se débrouillait avec les bagages et le bébé. Les Porter [Charles Porter, collègue du département, et sa femme Betty, qui avaient occupé la maison de Deepwood Drive pendant l'absence estivale de HP & famille] avaient ici pour nous un repas succulent et la maison plus propre et élégante qu'elle n'avait jamais été. Le bébé est pour 4 jours à Long Island chez sa grand'mère. Je me sens bien, mais j'observe avec assez d'obéissance les instructions qu'on m'a prodiguées: peu ou pas d'escaliers, du repos, et dans quelques mois je devrais me sentir normal — à moins, bien sûr, d'accidents comme celui de Bill [DeVane]. Mais ce repos forcé m'a fait du bien et permis de réfléchir — sans tristesse. Mon tempérament me porte à prendre le dessus et à envisager quelque avenir — avec, je dois l'avouer, des livres à écrire et les lectures à faire ou refaire. Quelque naïveté, peut-être un peu vulgaire, fait croire qu'on a des choses de quelque prix à dire! ...

## To Harry Levin:

[letterhead: *France*]
110 Deepwood Drive
Hamden, Conn.
Aug. 23 — 65

Dear Harry,

How beautifully you write! You are truly a master of the substantial, original, precise but always urbane & elegant essay & I am not sure there are any others writing in America today. I just about landed from Europe &, before even repairing upstairs to my desk & writing paper, I set about reading a dozen or so of the articles or pamphlets accumulated in the hall. Yours gave me genuine pleasure; it is seductive, tersely and firmly expressed, never pedantic. But you do express a number of truths about Oxford. I lectured there two years ago & was saddened by the complacency & often by the mediocrity of our colleagues in Modern Literature & in English — Seznec excepted & even he would perhaps have done greater things if he had stayed at Harvard — & about the conventional idols of today's professors of English. I don't believe I have been contaminated by De Gaulle's Anglophobia, but I confess that the raising of Hardy's poetry to a pinnacle, the deification of Eliot, the exaggerated praise lavished on E. M. Forster & on Durrell, the lack of discernment between the few very great poems of Yeats & the others give me doubts about the acumen of our American colleagues. The so-called "minor" figures of those last sixty or seventy years deserve far more attention than they are granted. Your remarks on literary history & its plight are very far reaching.

I am publishing soon an essay on Lanson & a collection of his finest articles, & a volume for the Humanism series of Princeton on the achievement of American scholars in the field of French, & other volumes or pieces—most of them of too little interest for me to send them to the master of prose & the thinker that you are. Just now, I am spending quiet weeks: I discovered while in France that I must have had a (light) coronary occlusion, & after disregarding it, I agreed to rest for three weeks & read or reread, in my father's home, dozens of Greek & Latin classics. I probably shall live more prudently now, but feel quite well. How is your own health? & your wife's—Our best regard to both of you, & to your daughter.

H. P.

## À Alex Szogyi:

Le 31 août 1965

Mon cher ami,

Je suis profondément touché de la délicatesse & de la fidélité de votre amitié envers Marguerite, qui avait pour vous une grande sympathie, admirait vos talents d'acteur & d'artiste & n'avait jamais douté que vous deviendriez un auteur de talent. Je n'en doutais pas non plus, malgré quelque effroi devant la variété de vos dons & des champs d'intérêt que vous parcouriez & labouriez. Mais c'était parce que, sans avoir votre talent, je me suis toujours blâmé moi-même de quelque excessive versatilité. Elle aurait été reconnaissante de ce témoignage de sympathie & aurait aimé votre livre.

Il est remarquablement bien traduit, avec vigueur, naturel, sans que l'on sente jamais une contrainte dans la souplesse des dialogues, et dans un style dramatique & animé. Les pièces, à part deux ou trois, m'étaient inconnues & le sont, je crois, de beaucoup d'entre nous. Le choix n'en est que plus précieux pour ceux que lasse un peu l'éternelle répétition de la *Cerisaie* & de la *Mouette*. Le comique, dans ces courtes pièces, paraît plus spontané, plus entier aussi. Vos pages d'introduction sont très fines et, sans pédantisme aucun, fort instructives. Et ceci doit être une excellente préparation à ces pièces que vous portez depuis longtemps en vous & écrirez. Votre enseignement vous accorde-t-il quelque loisir?

Nous sommes revenus de France il y a 10 jours, heureux de retrouver une maison commode à mener, une pelouse où peut s'ébattre le vigoureux bébé. Voyager avec un petit énergumène de 15 mois n'est pas de tout repos. Mais nous évoquons déjà les bons souvenirs de cet été: un accroc de santé, une "crise cardiaque" relativement légère, m'a tenu au lit ou au repos trois semaines — mais sans doute avais-je besoin de cet avertissement pour vivre désormais avec un peu plus de prudence, ou de lenteur. Je me sens maintenant fort bien.

Merci encore de votre livre & de votre amitié, & croyez à la mienne.

Henri Peyre

## To Gordon Ray:

110 Deepwood Drive. Hamden<br>[Sept. 8, 1965]

Dear Gordon,

Found on my return from Europe your very courageous & forceful Kenyon address — a model for all of us who wish they could give advice, courage & ideas with such talent — and your equally fine, & richly documented essay on Rare Books. I fear I'll never have room, funds, patience & taste enough to join the ranks of the Collectors. I am content to envy them.

My summer was somewhat marred by the discovery, made by my brother who is a doctor in France, that I had, without pain & without being even aware of it, suffered a coronary trouble with my worn heart. I had to rest for a while & am still taking things lazily for a few weeks but resuming courses & a few trips outside. I feel very well & if the enemy does not strike me again, I suppose I shall enjoy the years to come.

My very best to you & many warm thanks,<br>Henri Peyre

## To the same:

Sept. 9—[1965]

Dear Gordon,

I was too shy when I sent a line yesterday to ask if I could not have one or two more copies of your remarkable *Kenyon* address. I find it one of the truly important pronouncements on our search for leadership, excellence, creativity, etc. in education today—posing the crucial questions—far better, say, than the last number of *Daedalus* on creativity. It should be spread widely & mentioned in our Sunday & daily papers. I'd like to pass it on to others who are concerned. Sorry & cordially,

Henri Peyre

## To John Gassner:

Sept. 20/1965

Dear John,

How generous & thoughtful of you & Mollie to come all the way, offer our boisterous little boy a present which he cherishes more & more, to cheer us up with the sight of your fine condition & full recovery from ordeals worse than mine—& then to leave us the very warmly appreciated gift of your last book. You have been a wonderfully kind & helpful colleague, teeming with ideas, informed on well nigh everything in art & literature, always ready to share your ideas with your colleagues & never assuming the haughty air which a celebrity, almost a living legend like you, might affect! What you have brought to Yale, to the Drama School, to English studies, to foreign literature departments & to your colleagues, who wonder at the richness & suggestiveness of your books, is immense—second to the contribution of no one else in the realm of the Humanities in our time. Thank you, & thank you for the Directions volume, so charmingly inscribed. It is very handsomely printed & illustrated, & it is extraordinarily wise & shrewd, & courageous in your judgments on the moderns, on theatricalism, Formalism, etc. A unity of thought & of penetrating criticism informs the varied essays & carries your reader along with zest.

I hope you'll continue to be well & active & buoyant & that we'll see more of both of you, now that you have decided to become "New Haveners." Much gratitude for your kindness.

> Henri Peyre

## To James M. Osborn:

[postcard: view of La Camargue,
postmarked Dec. 2, 1965]
(For one who once fattened calves & castrated oxen)

Dear Jim,

Your party for the Oxford visitor was as always most cordial & elegant & your postcards mix "utile dulci," the learned lore & humor. I am sure the (at last!) just & laudatory article on Wimsatt in a recent TLS was due to your courteous treatment of the editor last spring & to . . . our uncourteous grilling of him. I hope your wife is well again & your Christmas will not have been preceded by too much fatigue.

> Yours,
> Henri

## To Harry Levin:

Dec. 24, 1965

Dear Harry,

Your presentation of the Poggioli volume is tactful, warm, very faithful to what he was and very vivid. And the volume itself is rich & varied, with very important essays to which we shall often resort. The choice is eclectic, touching on Dante, Pascal, Russia, tragedy, modern French poetry & general problems, & conjures up for his friends that amazing comprehensiveness which was Renato's privilege. For many years, because he was so modest & humorous & unpedantic, we, or I, had imagined that, like many of us Latins, he was at his best in conversation & in scattering brilliant aperçus on politics & literature. But Harvard, your friendship & your example, the beneficent American environment which very often leads foreign born scholars to give their fullest measure over here, were salutary to him. I had warmly praised & admired his Oaten Flute, & the Poets of Russia. This volume of essays, alas posthumous, is one of the best such volumes which could be compiled for any scholar. Looking at his picture on the jacket at the back, recalling his joyfulness, his spontaneous generosity—that kindness & gift of himself rare among us—I felt a whole period of my own past was closed & started reminiscing wistfully. I have never, I fear, told his wife how much his untimely death had saddened me. Will you some day let her know how all of us are grateful to you for erecting this monument?

With my very warm wishes to you & your wife, & of happiness for your daughter,

Hri

## To Stanley Burnshaw:

Jan. 24, 1966

Dear Stanley,

I have allowed weeks & months to elapse & never yet wished you a fruitful & exciting (not dully happy) New Year, never thanked you for the book on the heart attack which amused me & instructed me (& is nicely written), for your ever thoughtful concern for me & many other gestures which show in you the man who has a genius for friendship & fidelity. Yet I have thought of you, envied you occasionally for being away writing, dreaming, living. Do accept our belated wishes now, Leda & her inspired swan.

And I did like your "imaginary" Mallarmé piece. It is highly original in technique, language & metric, a very finished work—a flawless & very acute character & dramatic study. A Browningesque dramatic monologue rejuvenated & rich in insights into the hero of silence. I thought of Baudelaire's sentence that a painting or a poem is the very best form of criticism & truly a creative form too.

I have been well lately & thus far, had no recurrence of any heart weakness. I am prudent, but I teach as usual, write a good deal. (I had a couple of books out, here & in France, & am now redoing old ones, at publishers' insistence.) I travel again to lecture. I refuse to feel like an invalid. My affair of the heart was apparently not so serious as some, such as Gassner's, who has borne it with admirable fortitude.

Have you liked your winter quarters & not missed the literary excitement of N.Y.? Somehow I tried Florida twice & never really enjoyed it. I am always restless during vacations.

I hope you forgive my negligence, and believe as ever, sincerely affectionately yours.

Henri Peyre

## To Robert Penn Warren:

March 15/66

Dear "Red,"

I sent you the small volume by Monique Nathan, though I doubt much can be extracted from it. It was done for a certain, narrowly defined, series. J.-J. Mayoux, Coindreau's preface to *Le Bruit & la Fureur*, of course Sartre's famous essay "À propos de *Le Bruit & la Fureur*" in Situations I, pp. 70–82 are probably the best things in French. Marcel Aymé is no profound critic, but I am enclosing a page by him, & F's interview in the Paris Review & an article, somewhat pedantic, by a brilliant young man who took his Ph.D. with us three years ago, John K. Simon. You'll see if these are usable. There is a good essay in the Cahiers du Sud, April 1935, which I could easily get "Xeroxed" here for you.

As a translator from the French, the best one is Jacqueline Merriam, a 4th year Graduate student in French, former Woodrow Wilson fellow, who has passed all her courses & lives with us. She could consult me in case she is stuck on something. April 15th (with the vacations intervening, & she is then due to be away) is a little close; but she will be willing to do it for a little later. If she could start right now on the first of your essays, before the vacations on March 20th, fine. You can reach her here: 110 Deepwood Drive, Hamden, Tel: 787-4705, before 9 A.M. or in the evening. I asked the German Department & they'll have some one for me by Wednesday & I'll send a note.

Let us say again how much we enjoyed our evening, & liked the company, & your very picturesque & original house. Please convey our grateful regards to your wife & believe me,

> Most cordially yours,
> Henri

## To Gordon Ray:

> Aug. 17—66

Dear Gordon,

I read your last essay, an admirable & a courageous one, on the plane (I finally found one), returning from a symposium on Laughter (my own subject was Rabelais) at the Jesuit University of San Francisco. You pose very basic questions on the present status of publishing & on the future of books. I remain an optimist on the future of scholarly & other books & an admirer of collectors who also read. But we should become aware of the grave issues at stake. The money spent on computers for the humanities seems a waste to me!

We'll rest for two weeks at the Cedars, West Chop, Mass., then start upon the New Year. Are you & Jim well & have you approximately decided on the dates for the 1967 committee meetings? Your essays on this & allied subjects should be collected in an important book. They will impress.

> Cordially yours,
> Henri Peyre

## À Leon Roudiez:

> [letterhead: Sheraton Boston Hotel]
> Le 18 nov. 66

Mon cher Ami,

Je me sens bien vieux quand je pense à Columbia, à mes mois d'enseignement là-bas l'été (avant votre naissance, ou lorsque vous étiez séduit par la musique intérieure du grand sourd bavard!) et à quelques apparitions à cette Graduate Union sous l'égide d'Horatio Smith! Vous avez tant de noms plus jeunes parmi lesquels choisir—et je ne suis guère choquant! Sinon que, assagi, j'écris maintenant contre le nouveau roman et contre la nouvelle critique.

 Mais je ne tiens pas à parler de cela, ou à être contre, nécessairement. Je vais publier ce printemps mon livre, refait et mis à jour, sur le roman, & un autre, refait aussi, & que j'appelle "The Failures of Criticism."

 Je pourrais venir, plutôt vers le 12 avril, où j'aurai peut-être moins de voyages: je reviens de Californie, louer De Gaulle, et dois aller en février mais encore dans l'ouest. Finissez-vous pour 10 heures P.M., par hasard? Parce que, dans ce cas, je me sauverai par le train pour être à mes cours le lendemain matin. Sinon, tant pis.

 Sujets: Je m'intéresse en ce moment à "Renan & la Grèce: Athènes ou Israël," songeant à Horatio Smith, qui lisait & louait Renan; ou à "Baudelaire poète de l'amour," parce que ce sera le centenaire de sa mort; ou à "l'originalité du romantisme français"; ou à "Histoire et littérature aujourd'hui" (sur l'histoire comme littérature); ou enfin (car j'ai été mêlé beaucoup à diverses croisades, aux sujets sur l'éducation, les humanités) "Faut-il sauver les Humanités?"

 Je suis ici, avec une valise de rapports, quelques-uns de moi, pour un comité de l'Académie locale, à essayer de prévoir les problèmes de l'an 2000. Mais cela aurait bien peu à faire avec la littérature & l'érudition.

 Je vous vois bien peu—peut-être à Noël à la MLA? Mais je ne m'y montrerai que le moins possible.

Mes amitiés,<br>Henri Peyre

## À Vera Lee:

   [letterhead: Consulat Général de France à Boston]
   Le 3 déc./66

Dear Mrs Lee,

 J'ai regretté de si peu & si vite vous voir; mais le Consul insistait avec gentillesse pour que nous prenions chez lui un peu de repos avant de sortir à nouveau pour rencontrer d'autres personnes. J'avais bien peu de temps pour voir mes plus anciens amis et n'ai pu que saluer votre visage souriant, votre chevelure flamboyante & vaguement entendre votre projet grec.

Je crois encore que vous devriez réviser le MS, suivre les quelques avis que l'on vous a donnés à ce sujet. Les avis sont souvent bons, même (& surtout) "when they hurt." Et puis vous auriez tout intérêt (financier, & *de carrière*) à le publier ici, en Amérique. Tout livre publié à compte d'auteur & distribué par lui est suspect. Ceux-là mêmes à qui on l'envoie ne l'ouvrent pas. Et une fois un éditeur choisi, votre Collège devrait vous aider à faire les frais.

Bien à vous,<br>
Henri Peyre

## To James Lawler:

Febr. 7/67

Dear Mr. Lawler:

It was indeed a disappointment to hear that you were not able to come here this last fall. I hope the circumstances which forced you to change your plans were not grave ones. Let me, & us, know when you might again come here. You are well known to many of us: indeed no person teaching modern poetry can afford not to study your exegeses. I am not always *fully* in agreement on your interpretations of Valéry, whose bulky (& to me, repetitious) *Cahiers* discourage me. He bayed so unweariedly, & perhaps wearily to us, on some of his favorite tunes: against Pascal, the poverty of philosophy, the inadequacies of criticism! But no other book on Valéry is so objective & so enlightening as yours.

And your reprint on Verlaine's naïveté delighted me! It is superb; it rests on a shrewd accumulation of V's uses of the word dear to him & it goes deep in an enlightening interpretation of "l'espoir luit" & several other poems. Modestly, briefly, it is one of the *important* works on Verlaine.

May I ask you to ask the person concerned to enter my subscription to your review for two years? It is one of the very best I know in our field—

With my very cordial wishes,<br>
Henri Peyre

## À Franco Simone:

Le 7 février 1967

Cher ami,

Votre mot a éveillé en moi des remords de ma négligence. Était-ce négligence pourtant? J'espère que non. J'ai eu, le mois de janvier, beaucoup de voyages pour diverses conférences—au Middle West et ailleurs—puis les dissertations de fin de trimestre d'une lourde classe. J'ai mis quelque temps à lire votre ouvrage, car c'est un véritable ouvrage; un "magnum opus" qui traite de sujets où j'ai médiocre compétence, mais qui me passionnent.

J'aurais dû au moins vous remercier plus tôt de la dédicace, qui m'honore énormément, mes collègues et moi. C'est non seulement un témoignage de votre gentillesse et un souvenir, pour moi, de nos bonnes heures passées ici; mais un tribut de sympathie pour les chercheurs d'Amérique qui nous honore tous, venant de vous. Je vous ai mal, et trop peu, dit quel très vrai plaisir nous avait donné ici votre séjour, et la visite de votre femme, si modeste, mais d'un goût si fin et si lucide—et quelle admirable collaboratrice!

Ce livre, au titre bien trop modeste, est d'une richesse que n'épuisera pas pour moi une relecture. Je le crois l'une des œuvres les plus importantes parues sur de vastes et difficiles sujets: la redéfinition du concept de Moyen Age, le sens de l'antiquité, de l'histoire, du passé entier lors des siècles qui amenèrent la Renaissance, les rapports entre humanisme et Moyen Age et Renaissance, les échanges entre la France & l'Italie. Votre érudition, à travers ces textes si complexes, est vaste et sûre; et vous en portez le poids avec élégance, car tout le livre se lit avec plaisir, y compris les notes. Je voudrais bien en recevoir un second exemplaire, si cela vous est possible, pour le faire connaître autour de moi, car toute la connaissance de ces siècles est renouvelée par vos études. Cette lecture m'a donné le rare plaisir que procure une œuvre achevée, impeccable de documentation, ferme dans son mouvement. Je vous en remercie vivement, et au nom de nous tous ici.

Que devenez-vous, en dehors de ce labeur immense? Allez-vous bien? Votre famille aussi? Je travaille beaucoup et vous enverrai le moment venu quelques produits de mon labeur, dans un domaine plus proche de nous et plus facile. Yale n'a pas changé et l'hiver jusqu'ici a été assez doux. Le bébé devient un petit homme. Vers la fin de l'été, mais guère avant septembre, pour éviter le flot des touristes, nous ferons sans doute une apparition en Europe, car je serai alors en congé. Mais nous aurons de vos nouvelles auparavant.

Merci encore de ce magnifique travail—définitif dans tous les sens. Croyez à ma fidèle amitié et partagez avec votre femme nos vœux amicaux.

Hri Peyre

**Au même:**

Le 6 mars 1967

Cher Ami,

Ces deux exemplaires supplémentaires de votre beau travail sur les origines de nos disciplines historiographiques me sont bien arrivés très promptement & je vous en remercie. J'en ai donné un à la Bibliothèque de Yale & je ferai lire l'autre à divers collègues de ce pays. Il y a une riche substance dans cet écrit, qui est vraiment tout un livre, & la lecture devrait, pour nos jeunes, en être féconde: elle est très suggestive de sentiers nouveaux qu'elle trace.

Depuis m'est survenu aussi le livre de Gabriel Du Bois Hus, présenté par une de vos élèves, Mlle Poli. Quelle conscience, quel fini, et quelle parfaite érudition! Il n'y a qu'en Italie aujourd'hui que l'on exécute un travail aussi impeccable, et qu'en Italie qu'il se trouve une "casa editrice" pour en entreprendre l'impression. Cela a dû coûter des soins & un argent énormes. L'école de vos disciples grossit chaque jour, et je ne sais s'il en existe une autre au monde aujourd'hui où les premiers siècles français soient aussi bien explorés.

Mes amitiés toujours, à vous & aux vôtres,
Hri Peyre

## À Leon Roudiez:

Le 23.IV.67
[carte postale]

Cher ami,

Merci de ce gracieux souvenir de Columbia, fort utile & élégant—mais vous n'aviez nullement à prendre cette peine! J'avais eu plaisir de me trouver parmi vous & le dîner était très cordial.

J'ai suggéré à un jeune, très doué, agrégé ès lettres à 22 ans, chez nous cette année (il a près de 25 ans maintenant) de vous parler. Il doit aller l'an prochain à N.Y.U., mais il est mécontent de la manière dont on a changé les termes convenus là-bas. Il pourrait faire pour la Maison Française (car je ne vois personne autre). Il est un peu changeant, un peu têtu, mais jugez-le vous-même après entrevue. À défaut d'un américain, plus flexible, peut-être?

Bien à vous & merci encore à tous deux & à votre groupe,
H. Peyre

## To James Lawler:

July 8/67

Dear Mr. Lawler:

Once again you & your colleagues have brought out a remarkable number on French contemporary literature—poetry mostly, since the land of sheep & kangaroos has become a haven for poetical students of poetry. Even Sarraute's Golden Apples, which had struck me as the least appetizing of fruits when I tried to read the book, appear almost desirable when baked by your feminine colleague. I enjoyed your essay on Valéry, very new, very revealing and fair, on an aspect of Valéry's career which has remained mysterious. I am more severe myself for the "lost leader's" last years: he became too repetitious and too negative & failed to give younger French poets an orientation which might have been fruitful; but you are more generous. So is Mrs. Robinson, who visited us last winter, and overwhelmed us with her knowledge of all the master's secrets, and of much else "De omni re scibili." I have done a small volume of extracts from Valéry for an American publisher, which invited me to read him over—hence my slight disappointment.

I am staying here this summer, doing two or three other volumes promised when I was rash & a little younger (on criticism—on Sartre—); then I'll be on leave from September through December & expect to spend part of that fall season revisiting a few European museums. I hope that, if you visit this country in the course of next year or later, I shall not be unfortunate enough to miss you. Let me know ahead of time.

Again all my congratulations & good wishes,
Henri Peyre

## To Alex Szogyi:

Oct. 30/67

Dear Alex,

We have just returned from a trip to Europe (I am on leave this term) & found your very kind letter, along with a mass of others. News from you always touches me, arouses old memories most dear to me & conjures up the vision of you as an eager & bright student, cheerful, amused, humorous. You have fulfilled the high hopes we set on you: actor, adapter, producer, soon chairman or (qu'à Dieu ne plaise!) president of a College! Do not however overburden yourself with administrative responsibilities too soon. The most productive years are between 30 & 45; then life gets the better of us.

Naturally I should be glad to lecture at Hunter College for your students sometime. Tell me which days of the week, & which week, might be suitable. I have accepted several trips this year, or this semester, being freer; but one can always squeeze in an afternoon; & to visit you in your institution would be a pleasure.

You do me much honor also in thinking of me for a provisional director of the new doctoral programme in French; but I am too old to consider a move of that sort, too eager after I retire (in 1969) to devote my remaining energy to my writing. I have 3 or 4 books out or in proofs now & I have plans for more. The politics which a position in N.Y. would involve would be too complicated for a mere Frenchman & a tired old man!

But you are kind indeed to think of me; you have always been the most generous of "disciples." I am deeply touched.

> Believe me, very cordially yours,
> Henri Peyre

## À Eléonore Zimmermann:

> Pennsylvania State University
> Le 23—XI—67

Chère amie,

Je vous ai lue en voyageant. J'aime la claustration & le silence dans le bruit des voyages aériens. Votre essai ("Le rôle de Swann et de la société dans l'acte de création proustien," paru dans Studi francesi), difficile parce que très riche, fermement pensé, original, demande quelque concentration. Il est excellent et—ce qui devient difficile quand il est question de Proust sur lequel on écrit tant—exempt de toute banalité, en même temps que de paradoxe trop subtil. Je regrette un peu que vous ne l'ayez pas offert ici, à PMLA ou à MLN ou à une des nouvelles revues (Novel, qui paraît à Brown Univ., s'annonce bien; mais il faudrait là qu'il fût en anglais) . . . Toutes ces revues sont trop lentes & cela est exaspérant. Je perds moi-même tout intérêt à ce que j'ai écrit un an auparavant ou plus & ne puis supporter de le relire ou d'en lire les comptes rendus. Je prie les maisons d'édition de ne jamais m'en envoyer, ce qui amuse les dames qui travaillent là et sont si scrupuleuses. Comme moi & d'autres, vous devez être partagée entre 2 ou 3 pays, & entre écrire pour un public plus large comme celui qu'on atteint parfois en France et le public universitaire d'ici. C'est le sort des "polypatrides." Mais il a ses compensations, nous y gagnons plus de liberté de mouvement & une perspective plus catholique.

Je regretterai pour Rochester si vous partez; sans doute avez-vous besoin de compagnie, d'amitiés stimulantes, et je vous comprends. Mais on ne trouve guère cela après la trentaine et les années d'études en commun . . . Dans mon cas, et comme j'aime m'occuper de politique, d'histoire, de philosophie, je me mêle aux gens de ces disciplines au cours de voyages, de séances de comités au dehors—mais le résultat en est cette "vaporisation du moi" & dispersion que blâme Baudelaire. À mon âge, j'y suis résigné.

Croyez en tous cas à ma sympathie toujours active...

Bien à vous,<br>H. P.

## À Kurt Weinberg:

Le 21.I.68

Cher Ami,

Je vous renverrai demain lundi le MS par la poste. Sa science, son immense érudition, sa subtilité m'ont ébloui et effaré. Je ne sais que dire; ceci est si différent de tout ce que je suis, comme esprit & tempérament. Je suis très mauvais lecteur de symboles, très médiocre en herméneutique, privé de subtilité & de profondeur. Je lis le *Prométhée* pour mon plaisir & j'en ris ou souris. J'y vois un amusement de la part de Gide. Je le rattacherais volontiers à des farces d'étudiants ou de carabins, à Ubu Roi, sans y trouver allégories & allusions. De découvrir que ce petit écrit assez drôle est peut-être aussi tragiquement plein d'allusions à la foi, perdue ou non, de Gide, à la Sainte Cène & à l'Eucharistie, de tensions philosophiques et de science théologique, me gâte mon plaisir. Le critique est dix mille fois plus savant, plus subtil, plus angoissé que ne l'a jamais été l'auteur lui-même.

Avez-vous raison? Je ne sais, ou plutôt la phrase n'a pas de sens. Vous lisez Gide à travers vous-même et vous projetez en lui. Cela est déjà beaucoup que cet écrit se prête à tant de richesses qu'on peut lui attribuer. Gide lui-même aurait souri: il était assez peu philosophe & piètre théologien. Il n'a guère lu, quoi qu'on en dise & qu'il suggère: Leibniz et Dante, et bien peu Goethe, et Virgile—un peu, les Bucoliques, oui, et de travers. Il aurait murmuré la phrase placée en tête du Narcisse, ou est-ce de la Tentative amoureuse "Avant d'expliquer mon livre, j'attends que d'autres me l'expliquent; on dit toujours plus que cela."

Vous savez trop de choses et le montrez peut-être avec intempérance. Les éditeurs, dans ce pays un peu simplet, seront jaloux, ou déconcertés, que l'on puisse à chaque page renvoyer le pauvre lecteur moyen à Philo, Horace, Luther, Ovide, les Goncourt, Baudelaire, Dante, les Pères de l'Eglise. Je suis effaré moi-même de vous voir aussi plongé dans les Évangiles & la symbolique chrétienne: il y a si peu d'athées intelligents, et vous allez finir évangéliste ou pasteur, une fois tout le démoniaque en vous exorcisé par l'admirable sainte (rabelaisienne) qu'est votre femme. J'ai peur qu'un éditeur trouve ceci trop dur à lire et trop foisonnant de références théologiques & de lectures sur divers plans cachés, et redoute que le lecteur (même universitaire) renonce à vous suivre. Le début est dur, et un peu barbare de forme (ou "germanique," si la barbarie commence au Rhin!).

Sérieusement, je me range parmi les simples en esprit à qui le royaume des cieux est promis, et qui le refusent avec véhémence — et je crois que vous compliquez cent fois trop ici, & que ces allusions et sens cachés n'ajoutent pas tellement à ce texte comme œuvre d'art. Mais je suis français, positif, naïf. D'autres lecteurs penseront autrement. De toute manière, publiez cela ici: peut-être comme petit livre à Rochester même; ou à une presse plus aventureuse que la nôtre, qui est devenue très obtuse; ou chez Droz à Genève. Et croyez bien que ma résistance à vous suivre vient de mes propres limitations, mais que mon admiration pour votre savoir et pour votre extraordinaire subtilité en herméneutique gnostique est immense. Dites-moi ce qu'il adviendra de cet écrit.

Bien des choses à Florence & à vous. Beaucoup de travail ici, & pour moi divers voyages. Mais cela va assez bien.

H. P.

## To Henry Hornik:

February 13, 1968

Dear Mr. Hornik:

You are in charge of huge responsibilities indeed, but may I say that I am very glad that you were chosen for that formidable task. I remember our occasional correspondence in the past & several of the articles you wrote, all of unusual vigor & density of thought.

It was good of my former student Szogyi to approach me with that suggestion & I am flattered that you should take it up. I shall still be teaching at Yale next year, but, if the course you have in mind could be arranged at a convenient time. The best for me, if I may say right away, would be on Tuesday afternoon 2–4 for example, or 3–5, I daresay, I could manage it easily. I would naturally arrange to have the students discuss or ask for advice on their work at some convenient time before or after the course which, I imagine, is a two hour affair? Which term?

In the seventeenth century, which you suggest, the title might be: "Pascal and the Moralists" (in French, of course) — or "Le Classicisme" or "Racine" or almost anything you would think most appropriate.

I shall be here on February 20th & it would be a pleasure to see Dean Rees. If she would have lunch with me that day & would drop a line to let me know, I should be pleased. If not at some time at her convenience. The quickest address is Yale Station 2066, phone: area 203, 787-4705, extension 2368. My office is in Timothy Dwight College, room 1552, on Temple Street.

Many thanks & very sincerely yours,<br>Henri Peyre

## To Harry Levin:

[letterhead: Yale Club, New York]<br>Febr. 17/68

Dear Harry,

Your elegant brochure has a tantalizing title, the promises of which it fully & richly holds. You are most generous, en passant, to your friends & especially those of other universities — always the superb but modest aristocrat among us. It takes tact & courage to say, or courteously hint, what you imply of Wellek's magnum opus, which I admire in every one of its chapters & yet find disappointing as a whole. Perhaps the undertaking was too promethean? He betrays a lack of familiarity with the critics of France, & also with the theorists of Spain. But, like Petrarch unable to decipher his Homer, I shall retire (next year) & die unable to read the Slavic writers. And I am always promising writing projects which will not allow me the necessary leisure.

I find myself, insidiously, almost for the first time in my long life, resisting modern trends, disgusted with a good deal of the art I come to NY to look at in the galleries, bored by most of the recent works &

even more by quite a few of the eager & arrogant young critics. That is clearly a sign that I should stop teaching & probably writing. At the same time, our students are so much more gifted & better prepared than thirty years ago that we should leave the field to them with serenity & hope. You are much younger than I; but in spirit, alertness, breadth & incisiveness you are unmatched anywhere.

I'll take the liberty to send you a few productions this spring, since you leave nothing unread. I hear Crane Brinton is quite ill? His last book is touching, fair, kind, but a little pallid.

H. A. Moe would like me to organize a series of four or five short addresses at the Philos. Society in 1969 (probably November). I had repeatedly protested that it is too unfairly hard to elect scholars in modern literature there (& I may ask for your assistance later), while archaeologists, folklorists, anthropologists, ancient historians are *prima facie* deemed respectable—& that, along with law, education, genetics, literature should occasionally provide the subject of symposia. Will you be in America in 1969? & would you consent to speak there? We would easily find topics of interest to that worthy audience: a general movement from several angles? Or the celebration of authors (Wordsworth born 1770, like Hegel & other Germans; Chateaubriand; this year; Napoleon next, etc.).

I shall write you again later, now that I remember (my memory was unclear) that you are at Harvard this spring.

My very warm regards to your wife, wishes of continued happiness to your daughter & very cordially yours.

Henri Peyre

## À Henry Hornik:

Le 1er avril/68

Cher monsieur:

Je suis heureux de vous avoir revu—mal reconnu, mais vous m'en pardonnerez—& laissez-moi vous dire encore mes remerciements pour avoir si bien organisé ces détails pour mon cours l'an prochain. D'ici quelques jours, je vous enverrai une liste des livres essentiels à mettre en réserve. Mais je voulais d'abord vous dire ma confusion à noter que j'ai choisi un jour (vu mes engagements ici), le mardi, qui, comme il se trouve, est celui de Noël, du 1r janvier, et de deux autres fêtes le 24 sept et le 1er octobre dont j'ignorais l'existence. Pour ces deux classes-là, au début même du cours, je tiendrais beaucoup à les remplacer, le mercredi 25 sept., par exemple, et le mercredi 2 octobre à 2 heures. Est-ce faisable, sans gêner d'autres cours?

> Croyez encore à mes très cordiaux sentiments.
> Hri Peyre

## À Wallace Fowlie:

> Le 9 juillet 68

Mon cher Michel,

Votre gentille lettre m'a atteint à Stanford University, Calif. (94305) où je fais un cours d'été cette année. Le seul que j'aie accepté de faire depuis longtemps et sans doute le dernier. Le site est beau—presque trop, trop d'azur, trop de douceur de l'air—mais quelques étudiants sont bons et les quelques collègues que je vois aimables et généreux. Nous avons loué une maison et amené Brice, avec qui je fais des promenades. Mais il me force à jouer au soldat ou au policier, ou à lui redire ou relire des contes de fées (Chaperon rouge, etc.): deux occupations où je suis peu apte! Qu'on est gentil à cet âge: pas encore de révolte, de haine des parents & de la société! Nous allons assez aisément à San Francisco: je continue à beaucoup aimer cette ville. Je vais même y diriger (& y parler) un "symposium" sur Dante à l'Université Catholique de San Francisco. Un P. Jésuite que j'y connais m'y a persuadé. Ce n'est guère mon genre et vous auriez été mieux à ma place. Mais ils n'ont guère d'argent et, puisque je suis là, n'ont pas à me payer de frais de voyage. J'ai été d'ailleurs repris, ou pris, par la *Vita Nuova* & l'admirable *Purgatorio:* les "Dantisti" m'avaient longtemps gâché Dante, avec leurs minuties ridicules et leurs querelles aigres.

Je parlais hier justement de vous avec un jeune poète ici, un surréaliste très doué, Sotère Torregian, qui a bien du mal à publier ses vers et me disait, car il vous admire beaucoup, que vous seriez en Utah. L'idée m'en amusait—mais pourquoi pas? J'ai traversé jadis cet état & l'ai beaucoup aimé. Les habitants y sont droits et francs, et très fraternels. Je crois que vous les aimerez et, sûrement, l'air & le climat. Et je vous félicite de ce récital Rimbaud. Vous êtes, dans mon souvenir, l'un des acteurs les plus originaux que j'ai entendus. Vous réinterprétez les rôles à neuf et vous arrivez à faire passer la rampe à beaucoup de suggestions subtiles et aux secrets que vous dégagez des textes.

Je ne travaille guère ici; mais, à mon retour, je vous enverrai un volume d'essais que j'ai publiés aux Presses de Nebraska (2 ou 3 de ces essais avaient été donnés là en conférence & je devais les y publier). J'ai sorti aussi un petit "Sartre" à Columbia; mais après l'an prochain, qui sera mon dernier d'enseignement, j'espère avoir plus de temps à moi et entreprendre des choses plus neuves.

Les événements de France m'avaient rendu anxieux. Certes, il y a beaucoup à réformer en France & De Gaulle n'y a pas assez pensé. Mais, même dans l'enseignement, il a été plus accompli en dix ans que jamais auparavant dans un même laps de temps. J'aime les jeunes, mais j'ai peur qu'ils ne gâchent leurs revendications les plus légitimes par leur nihilisme, leurs contradictions & leurs divisions. Vous avez dû avoir quelques moments inquiets en France en juin.

Nous n'avons pas de nouvelles de Yale. Ehrmann allait mieux, ou plutôt son mal (une sorte de granulation qui dilapide les reins & d'autres organes) semblait arrêté par des remèdes neufs; mais je crois qu'il a eu une grave rechute en juin et je ne sais s'il s'en tirera. Il va, intellectuellement, vers des abstractions à la mode (Lacan, etc.), mais il en reviendra &, j'espère, écrira avec plus de clarté. La critique & le roman français actuels me paraissent bien secs et froids. Je vieillis beaucoup, sans doute.

Nos très bonnes amitiés et toute mon affection.<br>Henri

Quelle injustice, ce jugement absurde de Bill Coffin! Cela m'a indigné.

## À Franco Simone:

Le 2 sept. 1968

Cher ami,

Ces quatre conférences sur la Critique vous font grand honneur—à votre éclectisme, à votre largeur de point de vue, et aussi à votre flair.

Votre introduction est remarquable: compréhensive, fine, juste; la conférence de Girard est un peu déplaisante de ton & abstruse sans nécessité, mais les autres sont judicieuses et Poulet s'y montre fort modeste. Mes félicitations pour ce petit livre, de très réelle importance: le plus lucide sur ce sujet paru en aucun pays.

Et mes compliments non moins sincères pour la très belle tenue de votre revue: elle reste la première de toutes pour la variété et la sûreté de son information.

Allez-vous bien avec tout cet amas de besognes? Avez-vous quelque temps pour vos vacances en famille, & pour vos travaux?

Croyez à mon très fidèle souvenir, et au nôtre, double, pour vous deux.

Bien cordialement,
Henri Peyre

## To Henry Hornik:

Thursday Sept. 12/68

Dear Mr. Hornik:

I shall duly be there on Tuesday Sept. 17, for the first class & it would give me pleasure if you would give me the advantage of your company for lunch before. I have not seen you really for many, many years & would be interested in hearing your impressions on many things.

Unless I hear from you to the contrary, may I call on you a little before twelve that day? No answer needed.

Sincerely yours,
Hri Peyre

## À Eléonore Zimmermann:

Le 3 oct. 68

Chère amie,

Non, je n'avais pas vu encore ce no. des "Sciences humaines." J'étais en Californie cet été, donnant des cours à Stanford, puis occupé par divers livres depuis longtemps promis, & juste ces jours-ci je me sens enfin libéré de mon passé—hors les cours. C'est ma dernière année et je puis faire quelques projets. Je viens donc de lire votre article ["La Lumière et la voix: étude sur l'unité de Britannicus" avec une dédicace à Henri Peyre]. La dédicace me flatte & me touche plus encore. Vous êtes généreuse envers moi et je suis fier de lire mon nom en tête, car l'article est de tout premier ordre: ingénieux mais pas du tout forcé; modeste, car vous n'imposez pas votre personne au texte et tout ce que vous y lisez s'y trouve en effet; & nul ne l'avait ainsi aperçu. C'est vraiment une profonde analyse de l'unité poétique de la pièce & je ne manquerai pas de m'en servir quand je l'enseignerai, car vous m'ouvrez une perspective neuve. Merci. . . .

Bien cordialement à vous.<br>HP

## To Harry Levin:

October 8/1968

Dear Harry,

I am always a little sad when I have not heard from you for a long time: your prose, even in casual correspondence, is a source of joy, and of nourishment. I hope all has gone well for you & your wife & imagine you are now back from the travels which you were to undertake, in Canada & across the seas. We spent most of last summer in California, at Stanford & San Francisco & missed the "Cultural" Revolution in France (what a strange abuse of that adjective!). I shall retire in another year & am rather impatiently waiting for it.

Meanwhile, very indiscreetly (& if you judge my suggestion inadequate, simply disregard it & do not even reply), I am writing to you to ask if you would be in favor of supporting a proposal of mine to submit the name of Victor Brombert to the Class IV Membership Committee of the Philosophical Society. He is my colleague & successor here as chairman, which embarrasses me not a little; but I do think he is the best scholar-critic in French under 50 or 55 in this country. And the Society always repeats it should appoint brilliant people before they are old (although not many members actually vote for them, unless they are in archeology, epigraphy, Semitic antiquities or Hittite). Literature is sadly underrepresented. But I thought it was worth trying. If you agreed, your name would mean much to our colleagues, I know.

Please accept my very warm wishes & convey them to your wife.

Cordially,
Henri Peyre

Brombert was born in 1923 in Europe; served in the American forces in 1943–45; took his B.A. Yale 1948, Ph.D. in 1953; received a Fulbright to Italy, 1950–51; had a Guggenheim, 1954–55; wrote on "Stendhal & la Voie oblique," 1954

"The Intellectual Hero," 1961
"The Novels of Flaubert," 1966

Has a book out this fall & one next year; wrote a dozen articles, none of them inconsiderable. I believe you know his work well, & him, probably, fairly well.

## To the same:

Oct. 12/68

Dear Harry,

Many thanks for answering so promptly & kindly as you always do — and of course you are right about the injustice & harm to all of us, in having not yet René Wellek on that strange Society. I thought you knew (or perhaps it was just before you were elected) that I had put up René's name for nomination. It reached the members, after passing through the Committee, on which I then sat; then our members failed to vote for him in sufficient numbers. Normally, I believe they consider that the same name, if it failed to rally enough votes, is not put up again for a number of years; but it must be easily 7 or 8 years ago by now, & René is 65 and you perhaps (I should think K. Murdoch would support it) might be willing to send his name for consideration to Kenneth Sutton (now at the Institute for Advanced Studies, New Jersey). After two or three failures of the same kind, I resigned from the Committee on nomination & my recent experience with the Academy in Boston, & on the Emerson-Thoreau prize was likewise frustrating.

>Pardon a hasty note & most cordially yours.
>Henri

## À Konrad Bieber:

>Le 23 oct. 68

Cher Ami,

Vous n'avez rien dit de la santé de votre fils. Ne vous donne-t-elle plus d'inquiétudes? Est-il à peu près guéri, et "rangé"? — pas trop, trop rangé, cependant: cela vient assez tôt.

Vous avez été courageux d'opérer ce changement de résidence, cette cassure avec vos habitudes. Vous avez l'élasticité des sportifs: bien d'autres, la quarantaine approchant, hésiteraient. Il y a un certain confort intellectuel, à rester dans un collège à l'écart et féminin. Mais vous avez eu raison. Il y a, à N.Y., autour de N.Y., avec bien des inconvénients, un ferment spirituel, une volonté de remettre bien des choses en question, qui rajeunit. Je fais, ce trimestre seulement, un cours gradué à la Graduate School des Collèges de la ville—et les étudiants, triés avec soin, que j'ai là sont très doués et vifs. Mais cela fait bien longtemps que j'enseigne, & il me tarde d'avoir quelque loisir enfin.

Votre question sur Thibaudeau m'a fait y songer: je n'ai pas tenu à le rencontrer, & je trouve le roman de lui que j'ai lu froid, sec, mystérieux & finalement dénué d'intérêt humain. La revue *Tel Quel* souvent me tombe des mains. J'ai souvent été un "moderniste" dans mes goûts d'art & de littérature, mais me voilà bien rassis. J'ai trop de préoccupation du politique, du social, des problèmes vivants actuels pour me contenter d'œuvres aussi froidement calculées. Certains romans de Cl. Simon, les derniers surtout, tournent un peu pareillement, & c'est dommage. Sa conférence a paru aux étudiants un peu morte: ils résistent à ce qui est "*lu*," mais il est simple et modeste. Les livres de ces romanciers se vendent si peu en France qu'il leur faut gagner leur vie, & un public, par d'autres moyens.

Votre femme est-elle remise des sérieux ennuis de santé qui vous inquiétaient? A-t-elle pu transférer ses affaires à N.Y. et obtenir la place nécessaire? Elle aussi a montré du courage: elle n'en a d'ailleurs jamais manqué.

Nos amitiés à tous deux,<br>
H. P.

## À Eléonore Zimmermann:

Le 13 déc. [1968]<br>
[postcard]

Chère amie,

    Le bonhomme est fou — ou alors d'une profondeur qui me dépasse & me paraît de l'obscurité perverse. Je ne vois nulle raison à sa dissertation, et il n'a pas compris la lumineuse simplicité de votre article: D'Aubignac, Tintoret, les Romains, Racine en tout cela et un vers de Cinna maladroitement déformé! S'il répond pareillement aux 100 ou 200 articles que, comme moi, il recevra peut-être un jour, je le plains, & je plains ses correspondants.

    S'il en est ainsi, faites-vous une vie en dehors de ce département, avec les gens d'anglais, de musique, de science — soyez assez heureuse. Peut-être un jour devriez-vous aller à Cornell — isolé, mais cordial.

Bien des voeux,<br>
H. P.

## To Lester Crocker:

Dec. 25/68

Dear Lester,

    Your books are irresistible. I opened the *Social Contract* which you generously & very kindly sent me yesterday & could not lay it down until I had finished it, down to the last footnote; & I learned much from the footnotes as well as from the text, & noted down ten titles, such as those by Plamenatz, which I must read. I am retiring next June & hope then to have time & leisure. It is an immensely learned work, & a profound one, tightly argued, passionate, consistent, implacable in its march toward its conclusions. Often, on account of my sentimental attachment to Rousseau, & probably of my diffidence of logical reasoning, I inwardly protested, or regretted admitting that you were probably right. Although you disclaim blaming JJR for what successors had done with his contradictory thought, your chapter on "Influences & analogues" seems harsh. I balked at your implicitly condemning la *Nouvelle Héloïse* & *Émile,* which are to a large extent myths.

Plato would deserve even more having fostered totalitarianism! And the admiration for Sparta was an old cliché even with the Athenians & with all 18th century thinkers, & others down to Barrès. I believe a Hellenist, Ollier, wrote two volumes on that. Deep down, with all my liberalism, to which the recent behavior of our students here & in France has dealt heavy blows, I am not sure I would not agree that the State should educate us so as to make us want what we should want, & that freedom needs to be curbed in several directions. I nurture a secret admiration for Robespierre, and even more for St. Just. You are rigorous, a stern judge; but one to whom I must bow, at least with my reason, for the texts are with you. And I admire you immensely. To be able to write such a deeply thought-out book while writing two others, being Dean, teaching, marrying your children! I hope your health stands it.

Our very affectionate souvenir & wishes to you & your wife —

Thank you,
H. P.

## To Henry Hornik:

Jan. 16/1969

Dear Mr. Hornik:

I am sorry we could only have such a brief talk & I did not get a chance really to express my appreciation of the quality of the work you & the students under you are doing at the City Graduate Center. I seldom have found a graduate course so rewarding & students so responsive; & I have taught graduates, I believe, ever since I first came to Bryn Mawr, in 1925! It was one of their principles, in that feminist college.

After my class yesterday, I saw Miss Kees & I was surprised, & touched, when she told me that you & your colleagues wished to invite me again for next year & perhaps for even more work, since I shall be retired from Yale. I was very honestly surprised & told her I would think a little & consult you before answering.

I have thus far refused several offers to teach next year, even at the most flattering terms: I do not want to leave my house, my notes & the proximity of the Yale library, especially as I plan to be engaged in a rather extensive work on romanticism. But I did tell Miss Kees that I had found teaching your students truly stimulating & that the City Graduate Center is the only place which would indeed tempt me.

But I made the point that I would want first her (or me) to ask you if, very *honestly*, your colleagues who probably wish to teach at the Graduate Center (& there must be many, & gifted ones) would not feel it unfair to them to invite some one from outside the City system & an older (68 years old), hence somewhat well-known man, who might seem to occupy a position or give a course to which they would feel rightfully entitled. I do mean this very sincerely and I believe you might consult your Faculty first, for I have real scruples on that score.

Sometime after next week & once you have had the time to consult others & reflect on this, you would let me know your decision & if your plans for another year developed, we might, when I go to N York some time, talk about details, eventual courses, theses, etc.

It has been, in all truth, a pleasure to work with you.

Most cordially,
Henri Peyre

## À Victor Brombert:

Le 24 février 69

Mon cher Victor,

Laissez-moi vous dire encore combien j'ai été touché de votre attention à mon égard ce jour fatal (que je prends avec une âme fort égale, et même joyeuse) qui est celui de ma 68e année. Votre gentillesse affectueuse pour moi et celle de Beth me touchent profondément. Bien peu d'hommes qui ont parfois occupé trop de place, si tel a été mon cas, ont le bonheur d'avoir des successeurs aussi délicats! Vous avez tous deux autant de cœur que d'intelligence, de délicatesse que d'esprit.

Puis-je ajouter un mot sur la proposition que m'a faite Beth, qui m'a pris à l'improviste & à laquelle j'ai mal répondu. *Très franchement*, voulez-vous lui dire ceci, avant qu'elle n'agisse:

Je suis l'homme le moins fait du monde pour ce genre de portrait-photographie. Je n'ai pour cela ni le physique ni la patience qu'il faut. Si quelqu'un ne m'intéresse pas ou m'ennuie, je prends un visage renfrogné et morne. Un tel portrait ne serait pas *moi*. Et je ne tiens guère à être ainsi commémoré. Il y a des photographies de moi, en grand nombre, prises en général à l'improviste, pendant que je parle quelque part. J'en ai même une, prise sans que je le susse à N.Y., où je suis en habit avec Malraux et St John Perse, avec qui, par hasard, je conversais! N'importe laquelle de ces images conviendrait mieux au bureau du département ou à W.L. Harkness Hall, si c'est cela que vous avez en vue. Ce serait beaucoup mieux *moi-même*. Et je trouve vraiment inutile de faire les frais d'une photographie ambitieuse pour moi.

J'avais dit à G. May que je serais reconnaissant si votre amitié à tous me permettait de prendre ma retraite sans cérémonie, sans discours, presque incognito, et l'avais prié de me le communiquer. Je ne quitte ni la ville, ni vraiment l'université. Je suis encore bien plus engagé dans la profession que je ne le voudrais. J'ai d'autres vanités sans doute, mais pas celle de vouloir m'entendre louer. J'ai recommandé fermement à Holden, il y a 2 ou 3 ans, de réduire à 3 ou 4 lignes ce qu'une notice obituaire dirait de moi, à empêcher rigoureusement tout service religieux ou commémoratif lors de ma fin, & je crois que j'ai donné à Lois une copie de cette lettre. Je n'ai guère d'illusions sur la valeur ou la durée des œuvres d'un critique & ne tiens pas à des éloges funèbres ou de retraite ou à des mentions de mes hâtifs écrits. Si Beth veut bien, je préfèrerais qu'elle ne fît rien, sinon me donner le plaisir de dîner avec vous en fin d'année, quand il y aura moins de visiteurs & moins de besogne. Ceci sans fausse modestie aucune et en entière sincérité.

Imo pectore
Henri

## Au même:

[1969]

Mon cher Victor,

Les deux articles sont *remarquables*. Ne souriez pas de votre univers cellulaire: vous avez deviné là, ou créé de toutes pièces, un thème très riche auquel s'en accrochent bien d'autres, & une clé d'or qui entr'ouvre bien des portes secrètes. Et vous êtes un critique érudit & pénétrant selon mon cœur — parce que, de vous, j'apprends toujours quelque chose. Vous redécouvrez dans Baudelaire des expressions, des formules ("le moi insatiable du non moi") que vous chargez de sens et éclairez à neuf. Et jamais vous ne vous contentez de rien de facile ou de superficiel. Votre article sur Baudelaire, très bien & élégamment écrit entre autres mérites, est l'un des plus pénétrants & des plus *neufs* jamais écrits sur Baudelaire. Et avec la même attention assidue aux secrets des textes, vous dégagez l'originalité de Pétrus Borel, que j'avais lu jadis, trop vite, & peu estimé. Votre conclusion, qui le replace dans un courant si curieux, le grandit en découvreur d'une solitude désirée et redoutée, presque en devancier de divers modernes, est très originale. Vos mille tâches et soucis ne vous empêchent pas de réfléchir avec assiduité, d'aller en profondeur dans des ouvrages mal connus, & de les éclairer pour les autres — et toujours sans forcer les textes, sans viser au paradoxe. Il en est peu aujourd'hui qui satisfassent à ce point les lecteurs comme moi, un peu blasés. Merci.

Henri

## To Henry Hornik:

Febr. 26 — 1969

Dear Mr. Hornik:

Let me thank you again for your very warm words & your respect for ... age & experience. It occurred to me after I left you that the least I might have done would have been to send you a few of my modest & more recent publications, in case you deemed them fit to be placed on the shelves of your office or of the French students' center, if any. I shall do so one of these days.

Keeping the trains' eventual (& often very actual) delays in mind, I think it might be best to arrange for my office hours for students' direction & consultation before the Monday course (3–4 pm, Monday) & after the Tuesday course (4–4.30 P.M.). But there is probably ample time to put down such long range plans on paper.

> Again with my very cordial thanks,
> Henri Peyre

## To Robert G. Cohn:

> March 17/69

Dear Bob,

This is our first day of vacations & I am spending a week of them lecturing in Southern states, but among the letters I wished to answer, yours was foremost. À propos of Malraux & your letter which I sent him, with one of mine, I have to be negative. I have not heard from him. Tant pis! Associations of friends of . . . Gide, Claudel, *et al.* are not much my dish, & Mallarmé's glory will not suffer from the French neglect; the French will, through losing the papers & MSS they might have kept.

But you & your colleagues' statement on the requirements won my approval & yours, my admiration. I was against the ending of requirements here, & sorry that G. May felt he could not withstand the tide. As a department, we have not lost; but that is a minor matter. I believe that some requirements, philosophically, educationally, are very good for the students; & the same is true of grades, of some need for emulation. In truth I am rather glad to retire at the present time. I am not by nature a "laudator temporis acti" & a mourner of the past; but so much of what I had hoped from American youth turns out to be jeopardized by their present behavior. I am against the war & the Defense budget & all that, as vigorously as any one. But I am also for a duty in intelligent people to grow, to mature into some wisdom; & for intellectuals not to be stupidly "pseudo-liberals" & systematically anti-government, De Gaulle, a flexible order—in a word, to be the worst of conformists in their negativism.

Your own wisdom & discernment & courage (much courage is

needed to remain wise) have more than once struck me as one of the best rewards a teacher can have—to be confirmed & fulfilled in what he expected from his former students. Your son likewise is a young man of rare gifts, but modest, kind, shrewd. He came twice to observe our child (for his child psychology course): he is most charming & delicate & has a rare gift for dealing with children. He should be a marvelous father some day.

Lois admires your wife for teaching so far off—she has much to say to others, so why not? But it must break her heart to spend hours on the road instead of in your idyllic garden. Ours, in contrast, is swampy, still half covered with snow, bare, abandoned.

We plan to be away June 13–Aug. 16 or so in France, but here the rest of the time. Do come & see us (& your son) some time—perhaps on your way to Europe.

Our very affectionate feelings,<br>Henri

## To Henry Hornik:

March 29/69

Dear Mr. Hornik:

I believe you mentioned that I might stop in & see you one day; but I have not been to New York much lately, & only to airports. I am not sure when I can have a little free time—perhaps on the 18th of April, a Friday, around 2.30 or 3 P.M. if that is suitable.

I am clearing one of my two offices & may send you two or three more of my earlier "works," if they can be of assistance to students.

For the courses, when you have definitely fixed them, would you wish a list of the few essential books to be purchased, or placed at the disposal of the students? It might save time at the beginning of the course, if the students registered could procure, or even read, some of the works deemed essential.

Does all go fairly well with you?

Most sincerely yours,<br>Henri Peyre

## To Gordon Ray:

[letterhead: Yale University]
May 7, 69

Dear Gordon,

Your learned essay on Maud, charmingly written & bearing its erudition with elegant ease, is a model of method: how to use new material for better literary interpretation. It gave me much pleasure & it recalled to me a time, long past, when, at 19 or 20, I recited Maud to myself, in my broken & faulty English accent, the sections on madness, & on love of course, & even the jingoism on the Crimean war. I likewise adored "The two voices" & "Locksley Hall" &, when I lost a brother very close to me, I would find solace in *in memoriam*. I confess I seldom reopen Tennyson nowadays — and I dare not reread a novel of Meredith, since I know I would never recapture the thrill Clara Middleton & Richard Feverel & Rhoda Fleming once gave me. Perhaps after I retire, which is soon; but after having refused all offers to teach in California & Minnesota & Virginia, I have accepted to give a couple of seminars at the Graduate Center of CUNY, on 42nd St.

We shall leave for two months in France in early June. I imagine you will be in Europe too for a time, forgetting awhile about all the Foundation problems. I trust you, we, are not in danger, in spite of all the foolishness of Congressional Committees & of McGeorge Bundy.

Cordially yours,
Henri Peyre

## To the same:

[letterhead: Yale University]
May 12, 1969

Dear Gordon,

You are kind & generous to suggest a meeting with you in Paris, in the most prestigious of hotels; but, alas! we shall reach Paris by June 16 or so & depart on the 26th, before your arrival. With the child, we shall not be very free there & we think it wiser to depart early for a beach on the Riviera—we don't quite know which, yet. Many thanks & just as many regrets.

Yale seems to have weathered many a potential storm happily: our President has been skillful, flexible & a good diplomat. He is strengthening several aspects of life & organization here &, I must say, making excellent appointments (Donald Taylor, a psychologist, as Dean of the Graduate School; others in the sciences). He is now trying hard to persuade Robert Triffin (economics & finance) to accept a College mastership, assuring him that it will not hamper his research & publication. If Triffin accepts, I imagine he will ask you if he can postpone his Guggenheim—or whether it is preferable for him to reapply in a year or two when he can have a whole year away.

I am glad myself to be through with administration & to retire serenely: I have, after much hesitation, agreed to be professor at the Graduate Center of CUNY on 42nd St., spending thus two days a week in New York at the most; but I hope I still can complete a few writing projects which I have at heart.

Bon voyage & most sincerely yours,
Henri Peyre

## To Henry Hornik:

110 Deepwood Drive
Hamden, Conn. 06517
June 8—69

Dear Henry,

I am very honored & proud of receiving this appointment, & very grateful to the City University & to you for making it most generous. I do hope that I may justify your trust in me & that your New York colleagues will not think I am seizing the courses or the position which would rightfully be theirs. I know I shall enjoy working with them, with the fine students whom you are selecting & attracting to the Graduate Center, & with you.

I shall be away after June 14 until August 16th or so, but the graduate students to whom we are lending our house will forward mail, if there is any important communication which comes for me to the above address.

With very warm thanks & cordial greetings for your own summer,

Sincerely yours,<br>Henri Peyre

## À Kurt Weinberg:

Le 13 — VI — 69

Cher ami,

Vous êtes extraordinaire, & je fais amende honorable: car j'ai pensé plusieurs fois que vous devriez écrire surtout en anglais pour conquérir et attirer le public de ce pays. Mais vous êtes trop fort pour le public d'ici: vous savez trop de choses, et avec quelle précision & quel fini! de Platon aux Latins, à Dante, aux linguistes et philosophes modernes; et vous embrassez trop pour nos faibles esprits empiriques, vous pensez avec trop de rigueur et de finesse pour que nous vous suivions. Votre essai est d'une richesse de réflexion qui fait croire à celui qui vous lit qu'il devient profond aussi. Et il perdrait à être traduit, car votre langue est souple dans sa précision, et d'une vraie beauté littéraire.

Nous partons dans trois jours pour la France — nous ne savons trop où — mais je suis enfin! en retraite à Yale & me sens libéré, et voudrais pendant deux mois vivre, lire, rêver, ne rien écrire. Avec Brice (5 ans), nous ne pourrons sans doute beaucoup voyager, mais nous chercherons quelque lieu ensoleillé.

Florence va-t-elle bien aussi, après son long séjour chez les géants rabelaisiens, ses tâches de professeur et cette énergie et cette inspiration qu'elle vous communique inlassablement? Et vous? Merci de m'avoir si gentiment envoyé ces pages si fécondantes pour moi qui n'ai jamais beaucoup réfléchi à la langue, & croyez nous tous deux, à vous deux, bien fidèlement dévoués.

Henri

## To Gordon Ray:

[letterhead: Yale University]
June 14 — 69

Dear Gordon,

Muscatine is a very admirable scholar & man & an excellent choice. Your kind words touch me. I hope I have been of some service indeed to the Committee, in spite of my occasionally unorthodox views & my propensity to indulge value judgments & even whims. I have always enjoyed the meetings immensely, the work with our colleagues & the cheerful relaxation & conversation over meals & wines. Will you tell Jim Mathias what very deep affection I have felt for him, admiration for his efficiency, his tact & his taste in matters of literature, dance, arts as well as in history. And I admire no less the splendid manner in which you took over an extremely delicate succession and maintained the excellent traditions inherited from a great predecessor, bringing at the same time a new spirit, a wide competence in so many fields and an unerring sense of the real value of men. Having served on that committee for many years, & with you & under you for five or six, is one of the most pleasurable experiences of my career & the one of which I am most proud.

Of course I'll be glad to help with French or any subjects in which I may be judged to have some competence. I had promised myself to rest & write chiefly, but I seem to be inextricably involved in committees & lectures & travel engagements for another year or two at least.

We leave for Paris in two days, & regret that we shall have left Paris already when you reach there.

My cordial regards to Jim, Stephen & to you,

Most sincerely,
Henri Peyre

## À Michel Guggenheim:

[Letterhead: Hotels St. James & d'Albany, Paris]
Le 21 juin 69

Cher ami,

D'une phrase énigmatique (pour moi) dans une lettre de Mario Maurin, j'apprends que vous avez un fils très malade. Je ne savais rien de cela et ma peine, pour vous et Colette, est grande. J'ignore de quoi il s'agit, mais vous rendrai visite en passant à Avignon, où nous irons le 26 pour 4 ou 5 jours. J'espère que vos soins et votre dévouement redonneront la santé à votre enfant. J'ai toujours admiré le calme courage de votre femme et le vôtre. Vous avez triomphé de bien des obstacles en fondant cette session d'Avignon; mais les maladies sont plus décourageantes que tous ces obstacles!

Croyez à ma très profonde et vive sympathie.

Henri Peyre

## To Henry Hornik:

August 19/69

Dear Harry,

We have had a lazy summer in France; but pleasant, very hot & dry, with at the most one or two days of rain per month. The humidity here is trying & we feel pity for those who have had to live through it for weeks. But I am opening & answering mail at a fast rate, devouring periodicals & books. I shall soon start preparing the CUNY courses. I am looking forward to working with those serious & well-prepared students whom you select so carefully & advise. Do not hesitate, naturally, to ask me to direct the work of any who might be doing research in fields where I am competent. I shall enjoy it. One (Mrs. Marie Skalafuris) has written asking me to advise her on her thesis, or direct it, & if you approve, I shall do so. I am going to answer her. Mrs. Aronson impressed me much last year & I shall be interested in her project "La Politique de Rabelais." À propos, I much appreciated your concise, vigorous treatment of Rabelais in the *Studi Francesi*. Unlike others, you do not make a fetish of any secret unity or impeccable structure in the five books, but your view of the progression throughout is illuminating.

I hope you had some rest, after the strenuous task of starting & organizing the French program with such zeal last year, & did not suffer from the heat. I am returning the enclosed. I am not too good on my own bibliography, as I am ashamed, if anything, of writing too much rather than too little, & my additions must be incomplete. I hope to have more time for writing this year.

I shall see you on Monday, Sept. 15th, when classes begin, if not earlier. Again, my thanks, & if ever I can be of any use to your colleagues, please let them know I shall be glad to.

Sincerely yours,<br>Henri Peyre

Beaujour's book is lively & suggestive, even if somewhat insolent & too obsessed by today's critical vogue. I still have to read Bakhtin & put it off, with some suspicion that it will exasperate me.

## To Harry Levin:

110 Deepwood Drive<br>Hamden, Conn.<br>06517<br>Sept. 21/69

Dear Harry,

I am pleased to have a separate offprint of your essay on the Modern Humanities. I had read it in the volume &, I must say without any flattery, been impressed & delighted by it, while the other essays for the most part seemed a little beside the point & rather thin. You bring depth, substance, range of knowledge & life to the subject, as you always do; & it is not easy when "disserting" on the humanities. I had just a few days ago expressed to Stephen Graubard my disappointment at the *Daedalus* issue on the theme of the humanities, which a cantankerous writer in *Encounter* took to task. I have sworn I'll never speak or write again on the topic myself, or take part in any more debate on it. I hope I can keep my word.

I have not in the matter of ceasing teaching after my retirement. After refusing stubbornly to go to several places, most of them too far from my library & notes, I finally agreed to give two seminars at the Graduate Center of New York City University, on one or one & half days a week. The students are few, excellent, responsive, & I almost wish they would contest more; but the undergraduates at Yale at any rate wasted so much time, last year, & talent. I agree with many of their requests on the war & on participating, but they can be exasperating. Yours were even worse, apparently!

I am not too proud of whatever articles I wrote lately, or volumes I put together (chiefly made up of earlier essays); but since you are an omnivorous & much too lenient (to me) reader, I shall take the liberty to send you one or two things. If ever you are to waste a few hours on your way to New York or elsewhere, won't you & your wife stop here for lunch? With no obligation, no lecturing, no honors, just for a chat? I greatly enjoyed talking with your wife when you last were here, last year, & when, modestly & in subdued tones, she mentioned her peregrinations through two continents, years ago, my timid bourgeois eyes gazed at her as at a heroine of Dostoevsky, or Jules Verne.

Give her my regards & accept mine.

Henri Peyre

## To John W. Kneller:

[letterhead: Yale Club, New York]
Sept. 30/69

Dear Mr. Kneller,

I was in Europe this summer, & only lately heard of your election as President of Brooklyn College. I congratulate you very warmly & I have an immense faith in your wisdom & quiet energy & in what you can achieve in a challenging situation. And I am no less happy for Brooklyn College. I have a very special affection for that institution & I had in the past often corresponded with one of your predecessors, Mr. Gideonse, whom I greatly admired. And may I say that as your friend and former teacher I am also very proud?

I have lately retired from Yale & I now teach, two days a week, at the Graduate Center of the City University, on 42nd Street. Perhaps our paths will occasionally cross.

Please give my kind regards to your wife & believe me,

Very devotedly yours,<br>
Henri Peyre<br>
10 Deepwood Drive<br>
Hamden, Conn. 06517

## À Philip Stewart:

Le 6—X—69

Cher ami,

Merci de ce très beau livre, si élégamment présenté, & de l'inscription que vous y avez généreusement mise. Je viens de le parcourir et je vous en félicite. Avoir, ayant commencé le français plus tard que d'autres, possédé aussi à fond et la langue et une littérature parfois obscure ou bien peu explorée est un accomplissement qui vous fait honneur—et un peu aussi à Yale. Votre ouvrage est un des plus solides, des mieux organisés, des plus sérieux avec grâce écrits sur la littérature romanesque du passé; et vous évitez avec finesse tout dogmatisme, toute théorie préconçue imposée au réel.

Peut-être vous verrai-je à Harvard? On m'a prié d'être membre du comité du Board of Overseers qui, le 10 décembre, doit rendre visite à votre département & rédiger sur lui quelque rapport. Je ne veux pas faire de vous un espion ou un "informer" & je ne compte que servir de mon mieux l'intérêt de votre section. Toute suggestion que vous voudrez bien me présenter, d'ici-là, sur les améliorations à offrir, sera la bienvenue.

Les amitiés de Lois & les miennes—et merci.<br>
Henri Peyre

## To Henry Hornik:

October 14/69

Dear Henry,

 I hope this is not hurrying you or Mrs. Kessler. These are the bibliographical lists to be reproduced (in some 20 or 25 copies, I imagine) for the second term courses. The titles are tentative & I suppose you will formulate them as you wish. Not *all* these books should be, or could be, bought by your Library; but quite a number of the students consult books elsewhere also.

 When the schedules for the second term are ready, Mrs. Kessler might leave me one, as I have to calculate in advance some of the absences I may have in the Spring.

 I had a very pleasant talk with H. Block & he agreed that I can best serve as I do now, giving courses in the French section which often are of a "comparative" or broad nature; but that my name may be added to the Comparative section, where I shall be glad to advise & occasionally sit on exam. committees or theses.

Most cordially yours,<br>Henri Peyre

## To James Lawler:

110 Deepwood Drive
Hamden, Conn. 06517
Nov. 20/69

Dear Mr. Lawler,

 Your book arrived, some two weeks ago — & I have by now read it, rereading the chapters which I already knew, with profit, enjoyment &, very truthfully, with more enjoyment than any book on modern poetry which I may have read for 10 or 20 years. It is admirable in the "justesse du ton," the penetration & the wisdom of your criticism, the depth of many suggestive remarks. Unlike many, you support no dogmatic thesis; you do not encumber your interpretation with pretentious abstractions. Every page of it is by a man who feels, lives, loves the poetry. And you are certainly not content with ever repeating what was said earlier. Your "Claudel & Valéry" confrontation is most curious; you are original even, & effortlessly so, on Apollinaire & on the Illuminations, about whom, or which, much had been done lately. You should, with your other colleagues who, since Chisholm have written. . . .

My very grateful & cordial thanks,
H. Peyre

## À René Galand:

[letterhead: Yale Club, New York]
Nov. 25, 69

Cher M. Galand,

Ces échantillons de vos poésies sont jolis; sobres, concis, purgés de toute rhétorique, et durs avec charme et vigueur de conviction & de pitié humaine. Il y a toujours eu un Celte rêveur et poétique en vous, sous le militaire que vous fûtes et le grave érudit.

Nizet est un désordonné de la plus belle eau & je me demande encore comment il arrive à vendre ses livres. Il est vrai qu'il est encore plus vague sur les droits d'auteur qu'il pourrait devoir aux autres! Je n'avais pas vu qu'il eût annoncé votre livre!

Encore mes très bons vœux & amitiés,
Henri Peyre

# the 1970s

## CHAPTER SIX

## À Linda Orr:

> 110 Deepwood Drive, Hamden, Conn. 06517
> Le 8.1.70

Chère madame,

Il est bien difficile de donner des avis, ou même de porter jugement, sur les poésies de quelqu'un de jeune, de doué, d'ardent & dans une certaine mesure, d'inspiré. Vous avez de grands dons: une économie de moyens très frappante; une densité explosive; le courage de fuir le joli, le gracieux, la poésie dite "de jeune fille" & de mettre de l'abstrait dans vos vers & d'y faire entrer ce qui au premier abord semblerait *non* poétique. J'aime le "Mud bath" pour sa force suggestive—pas un mot de trop. Le premier poème me paraît un peu moins heureux, au 4e vers par exemple "yes, only to belkis roll—" & peut-être même l'accent mis sur le mot "momentum," bien qu'il soit, avec un brin de pédantisme, le mot juste pour exprimer ce que vous voulez rendre.

"Sleep" coule mieux, avec plus de vivacité, plus d'esprit. Les images en sont naturelles, mais fraîches en même temps. Vous pourriez l'envoyer à quelque revue. "Clear night" est également heureux, avec ce sens d'une menace tragique, cette cascade un peu surréaliste de notations (fire, laces, caterpillar, door, the night) & la progression, avec un ou deux temps d'arrêt dans les vers plus courts, jusqu'au dernier vers est forte.

"Another room" me saisit moins & je ne suis pas sûr que le "courant passe," que l'on se sente touché. Mais "The Latrine," plus long, en vers d'une richesse de substantifs et de verbes d'action, d'une économie & d'une concentration très habiles, me plaît et joue sur plusieurs plans. C'est à publier—ou à tenter de le publier.

"Dance" est plus ambitieux encore & je crois que vous avez raison de viser haut, de tenter de prolonger l'inspiration, & l'effet sur le lecteur. C'est un vrai drame, entre deux individus, & intérieur aussi, grave et incisif dans son langage, sans rien de joli ou de facile. Vous devriez essayer des poèmes plus longs, incorporant plus de dramatique en eux.

Le dernier n'est ni pastiche ni imitation de Char. C'est un bon maître, car on ne peut pas copier son langage ou son imagerie; mais vous pourriez, comme exercice, traduire quelques poèmes de lui (autres que ceux déjà traduits) & vous faire connaître ainsi.

De toute manière, vous avez du talent et de la modestie, car vous n'essayez pas le brutal, le sexuel, ou l'étalage de l'inconscient. Pas de maniérismes non plus. Vous devriez continuer, essayer de paraître; même si votre amour-propre reçoit quelques heurts, vous les oublierez vite, car vous avez de la vie intérieure, de la sensibilité poétique & une forme déjà assez sûre.

Bien cordialement,<br>HP

## À Buford Norman:

Le 6—III—70

Cher M. Norman,

Je n'ai en vérité pas grand'chose à vous indiquer que vous ne connaissiez déjà. Je crois que votre besoin le plus net en ce moment est de ne plus tarder à écrire—n'importe quel chapitre—de manière toute tentative, de façon à clarifier vos idées pour vous-même, à préciser votre direction.

N'hésitez pas à parler à plusieurs ici—surtout à M. Fabre, qui a écrit de fort bonnes choses sur l'angoisse pascalienne, et à M. Onimus, qui est très au courant de la pensée religieuse moderne. Profitez de leur présence ici.

J'ai rempli & envoyé la recommandation au Bureau du Placement.

Avec mes bons vœux,<br>HP

## To Ben Raeburn:

March 29, 70

Dear Mr. Raeburn:

There is certainly no doubt about it. Stanley Burnshaw's book is a very important one, sensitive, profound, new—one of the great achievements of American criticism, the fruit of years of meditation, of reading, of composing poetry. I believe quite a few of us are serving its diffusion through mentioning it to friends, students, & I have seen it in the hands of several to whom I had recommended it. I shall, indirectly, approach the Saturday Review; but that Review, the N.Y. Times Sunday Book Review & others resent any suggestion by a critic that he do a review for them; & do not accept reviews not requested by them. I have had my differences with them for reasons of that sort. But let us hope, & it is kind & generous of you to make that suggestion, & I feel comforted in my certitude that the book is a great one by the additional testimony of a person like you.

Sincerely yours,<br>Henri Peyre

## À son frère et sa belle-sœur:

Le 26 mai (1970)

... Pour nous, tout va bien—pas la Bourse, bien sûr—mais tout le pays est en désarroi, se dispute, en a soupé de cette guerre, se révolte, a perdu confiance en son avenir et en ses chefs. Si seulement De Gaulle avait vingt ans de moins et pouvait venir aux États-Unis régler nos affaires avec son génie et sa prescience. Hélas! Brice me demande bien parfois pourquoi je ne remplace pas De Gaulle, qu'il révère autant qu'Hercule et Napoléon, ses héros, & même pourquoi je ne suis pas Président du monde! À d'autres ces ambitions. Le repos a du bon. . . .

## À Edward Kaplan:

Aug. 25/70

Cher monsieur,

Je rentre à peine, ou presque, d'Europe & je ne dirai pas que j'ai lu *chaque* ligne de votre MS: j'ai un tel monceau de lettres autour de moi! Mais je l'ai à peu près lu; il m'a intéressé & appris beaucoup de choses. Personne n'a jamais étudié cet aspect de la personnalité, de la psychologie et même de la psychanalyse de Michelet comme vous; et vous avez une connaissance très approfondie de l'homme, mais aussi de la science et de la pensée de son temps, de Hegel à Geoffroy St Hilaire, Lamarck à de plus proches de lui par le temps. Vous avez fourni un *énorme* travail, de plusieurs années sans doute; élucidé avec l'aide de tous les ouvrages d'érudition, de biographie, Larousse du XIXe siècle, etc., tout ce qui entoure Michelet & contribue à l'expliquer. Et vous avez une forte culture philosophique & un esprit de synthèse qui vous permettent de reconstituer tout un système cohérent de pensée chez Michelet. Nul n'a jamais fait ce travail pour tous les livres de Michelet suivant la *Révolution;* et vraisemblablement nul ne le refera de longtemps.

Est-ce publiable? C'est la question que vous posez. Malheureusement, dans son état actuel, & dans l'état présent des choses en Amérique, j'en doute. Idéalement, car ceci est sûrement l'une des thèses dont Columbia doit être le plus fière, votre université devrait vous aider, vous donner un prix ou un subside; mais mes quelques relations avec la Columbia Press me rendent sceptique sur les possibilités de ce côté-là. Ce serait pire encore à la Yale Press, qui a tué notre série *Romanic,* qui n'avait cependant pas perdu d'argent. Je doute que les Presses les plus connues (Harvard, Chicago, Stanford, Rutgers, etc.) le prennent. Peut-être de moins éminentes seraient-elles plus accueillantes & heureuses d'avoir un MS de valeur, même si elles doivent y perdre: Nebraska? (J'y ai publié un livre, où j'y touche au fait à l'histoire & à Michelet, & me suis loué de leur accueil.) Univ. of Mass. at Amherst? Alabama? Texas? Mais vous risquez de passer à cela beaucoup de temps, d'avoir des refus, le conseil de changer beaucoup et d'en être découragé. En fin de compte, Mouton (en Hollande), Minard (Paris), Nizet (Paris) seraient probablement les voies les plus efficaces; mais je serais bien surpris si l'on ne vous demandait pas une contribution aux frais importants. Vous aiderait-on à Columbia pour ces frais? Ou ailleurs, quelque fondation?

Les raisons de ces refus ou résistances que je prévois sont:

1. C'est très "thèse" et on se méfie de cela. Trop de notes; trop de citations (en langue étrangère, ce qui repousse ou rebute les lecteurs américains). Le vocabulaire est parfois abstrus: "empathic understanding of nature's vitality" etc. La terminologie, inévitablement, est spécialisée & abstruse. La lecture est difficile.

2. Beaucoup trop long. C'est construit impeccablement; un chapitre mène à un autre; la progression des idées est claire, mais vous voulez *tout* dire—sur la nature de Michelet, sa philosophie, la science de son temps, etc. On en sort écrasé. Et justement parce que c'est bien enchaîné, il vous sera difficile d'extraire de cela des chapitres pour les publier en forme d'articles & allécher le lecteur éventuel.

3. Le sujet est beau—aux yeux de quelques-uns d'entre nous, qui goûtons cette poésie de la nature, ce panthéisme de Michelet. Mais, à part la *Sorcière* et peut-être la *Bible de l'Humanité,* les livres dont vous traitez ne sont pas lus. Ils n'ont plus été traduits depuis des dizaines d'années. Tout au plus, en France même, connaît-on quelques pages de *l'Oiseau,* de *La Mer.* Qui achètera, qui lira un énorme livre de critique & de psychologie sur des ouvrages aujourd'hui si obscurs—et pour ce qui est de la science, si démodés. Ils valent par ce qu'ils révèlent sur la psychologie secrète de M., sur sa religion, surtout sur sa poésie. Si vous pouviez écrire 2 ou 3 articles (genre Poulet, ou Auerbach) avec une étude stylistique de quelque passage de ces livres, tirer de là vos conclusions sur M. l'homme, le penseur, le biologiste, vous éveilleriez quelque intérêt au sujet.

Je suis décourageant, mais mon expérience sur les perspectives de publication ne rend pas optimiste. Je crois qu'il serait plus courageux de prendre le taureau par les cornes, de couper de moitié au moins, d'éliminer beaucoup de notes & de citations en français, d'altérer ce caractère de thèse exhaustive qu'a votre MS—et alors de voir si, avec un subside considérable, en Amérique, ou peut-être en Europe, ceci serait acceptable pour un éditeur. Dans l'état actuel, en regardant les frais probables, et une vente maxima de 1000 exemplaires sur 5 ans, je crains que toute Presse soit effarée.

Pour ma part, vieux et en retraite, je suis plein d'admiration pour ce que réalisent de jeunes érudits américains: comme substance, force d'intellect, immensité de connaissances, capacité de synthèse & d'organisation, ceci est remarquable—et "gratifying" pour qui a voulu longtemps servir l'enseignement de la littérature & l'érudition aux États-Unis.

Tout ceci ne vous aidera guère, mais parlez-en à Barzun à Columbia, à des historiens, à Rob. Merton, peut-être, et peut-être là vous aidera-t-on.

Croyez à mes bons vœux,<br>Henri Peyre

P.S. Vous donnez l'impression (p. 23) que J.-J. Rousseau a vu les Pyrénées lui-même. Je vous renvoie le MS sous autre pli, assuré.

## À James Lawler:

Le 29 dec. 1970

Cher ami,

Encore un très remarquable article de vous sur Valéry dans le dernier n° de vos Essays in French Literature. Comme toujours, j'apprends beaucoup à vous lire: ce que vous écrivez est si précis, si admirablement documenté et de première main que l'on apprend toujours avec joie car vous donnez le sentiment que ce que vous établissez est définitif. Merci de ce n° qui renferme le bon article sur Char de mon élève Miss Orr et cette excellente étude sur le Surréalisme et le Communisme. Votre revue est sans doute la plus précieuse pour la littérature française de ce siècle. Que lui arrivera-t-il si vous partez?

Les autorités de Californie ont communiqué une fois ou deux par le téléphone avec moi; mais j'ignore le résultat & peut-être n'est-il pas encore clair. Ici, de près, le nombre & la gravité des problèmes de ce pays nous effarent; il y a une désaffection générale, et de l'idéal ou du rêve américain de naguère et à l'égard des universités qui, dit-on, ont mal rempli leur devoir de former la jeunesse. Mais vous ne serez que trop plongé dans ces problèmes si vous venez ici et les gens que je vois d'Angleterre ne sont pas plus optimistes. Ma longue carrière ici me vaut de faire encore partie de plusieurs comités sur ces questions d'éducation, de la défense des humanités & de la littérature, mais j'ai néanmoins quelque loisir pour écrire.

Si vous venez ici, nous nous verrons peut-être un peu plus souvent. Nous irons à Londres, à Paris, dans le Midi de la France en juin–juillet. Peut-être y serez-vous? Je serais heureux enfin de rencontrer Madame Lawler. Les photos de vos deux enfants sont charmantes. Avez-vous réussi à maintenir leur français?

> Acceptez mes vœux fervents & mon fidèle souvenir,
> Henri Peyre

## To Stanley Burnshaw:

> March 18/71

Dear Stanley,

The Spire poem has an extraordinary vigor and a splendid youthfulness. What an admirable old age he had!

Your translations are all good—as far as verse translations can be: the Eluard piece has a shorter, perhaps more staccato rhythm in English, the Spire one a fuller, almost softer one than the original. But such translations have to be transpositions. Thank you for letting me see them.

It was very refreshing to talk with you quietly & as always I admired your courage in organizing your life toward more freedom, more independence, more meditation. Many of us do not reach there, even at an advanced age. You give many of us academics a wonderful example.

I hope Leda will soon be quite, quite well, & able to enjoy the Island. And certainly, if we venture there late this summer, we'll pay you a visit.

> My very cordial wishes,
> Henri

## To the same:

> April 1—71

Dear Stanley,

I have been away for a week in Virginia & rather busy since—hence my delay & I fear you took my very timid suggestions much too seriously. I know of no translator more impeccable & more of a meticulous perfectionist than you.

"Fais une croix": "Mark" is a trifle more specific than "fais," but should go; "make" seems to connote the notion of manufacturing, building, at least to my foreign mind: "faire" of course is vaguer & we say, familiarly, in everyday language, say if someone has lost his purse or a book, "fais une croix là-dessus." "Draw" would have the desired suggestion of assonance [2 illegible words].

"Bonne justice"—keep it in French; "good" is banal—"beneficent" or "fair" would be too precise & too narrow.

"Résonance retrouvée"—yes, "a strain recovered" would be the best. I wish I could think of a longer word & of the slight repetition of sounds "*ré, re,*" but I can't.

I wrote to the President of Wesleyan about [Tebbor?], & then I had a telephone talk with Gourevitch—but when I tried to write so to [Tebbor?], whose address I did not have, I thought he was still at Athens, Ga., & my letter to him was returned, saying "Could not be reached." I hope it works out.

Denoël is a good publishing house & Nadeau a well known critic (author of books on Surrealism, modern novel, etc). Of course, the book should be somewhat adapted to a new public, hardly familiar with poetry in English.

Do convey our heartfelt wishes to Leda & thank you for always writing with such kindness & thoughtfulness.

Yours,
HP

## À son frère:

23 août 1971

... peut-être avions-nous trop entrepris: un séjour moins long en Europe eût été moins coûteux et moins lassant. Mais nous tenions à montrer à Brice bien des paysages et des scènes variés: il comprend vite & observe avec acuité. Et puis l'Europe change vite: trop de gens en vacances, trop de matérialisme avide. Pour moi, le seul de nous trois qui ait de longs souvenirs, et sans que je sois systématiquement ennemi du neuf et du changement, la métamorphose ne me paraît pas toujours heureuse. Derrière la frénésie de jouissance et l'étalage des corps, il est aisé de sentir un mécontentement de toute la civilisation trop complexe d'aujourd'hui. Les crises financière, économique, politique le montrent. Nous ne sommes pas plus maîtres de nos décisions que les gens du Moyen Age ou les petites gens au 18e siècle; et nulle révolution ne changerait grand'chose. . . .

## À son frère et à sa belle-sœur:

Le 6 sept. 1971

. . . Mais, par un réflexe de compensation ou pour satisfaire quelque voracité d'action & de remuement, nous nous sommes occupés beaucoup depuis notre retour. Pour moi, je me suis contenté de dévorer les livres, les revues qui me renseignent ou m'aident à préparer mes cours. Lois a peint les murs (à l'intérieur), nettoyé ce qu'avaient laissé en état un peu négligé les jeunes à qui nous avions confié la maison, & cuisiné. Brice, lui, continue à lire. Mais il est aussi bien content de retrouver quelques garçons de 8 à 10 ans, avec qui il parle un anglais assez vigoureux & même assez vert et joue à toutes sortes de guerres. Il en est à sa phase militariste et rêve d'uniforme. J'essaie bien de lui dire qu'il devrait aussi lire sur les saints, les savants, les poètes, mais cela a moins de prestige. Du moins, sa santé ne nous donne nul ennui. La nôtre est également bonne. Dès lundi prochain (le 13 sept.), je vais reprendre à New York mes cours, lundi & mardi. Cela m'occupe et m'intéresse: Pascal et Balzac. Brice reprend son école le 15 septembre.

Vous êtes tous deux bien trop gentils de parcourir et de louer trop généreusement, mon petit livre. Je ne recherche pas la publicité & il se vendra sans doute. Un article avait déjà paru en juillet, de Claude Mauriac, dans le *Figaro*. Sans doute en effet ai-je toujours gardé en moi pas mal de rêves et d'idéalisations romantiques; et Jacques, derrière son langage expressif et son réalisme de docteur qui n'ignore pas le rôle de la bête derrière, ou dans l'ange, est resté tendre et sentimental, avec un cœur toujours jeune. Ses attentions, & celles de Micheline, à chacun de nos séjours, et lors de ma crise cardiaque naguère, nous touchent profondément. Brice est fier de la petite cloche qui fut son cadeau de départ de son oncle. Je ne suis pas opposé au moderne moi-même, en art et en littérature; mais j'avoue que, depuis 5 ou 6 ans, ce qui se joue et s'écrit en France (à part quelques beaux films) est déplorablement sec, pédant, ennuyeux et même inhumain. Quel malheur que ce grand De Gaulle n'ait pas rencontré autour de lui une ère littéraire comme celle de Louis XIV, ou même celle de 1920–30. Il est vrai que nous étions plus jeunes et plus ouverts alors. . . .

## À Michel Guggenheim:

[letterhead: Yale Club, New York]
Le 18 — X — 71

Cher ami,

Je reconnais à cette belle, émouvante circulaire votre grand cœur & votre humanité. J'ai toujours aimé en vous & en votre femme ce noble courage de n'avoir pas peur du sentiment, des sentiments les plus naturels, les plus généreux, et ce sens que vous avez du tragique de l'existence & de l'insuffisance d'un sec rationalisme. Vous avez tous deux passé par les plus affreuses & torturantes épreuves que deux parents peuvent connaître, et vous avez, à force d'amour & de soins, gagné quelques années de vie et de paix familiale à votre fils. Les mois les plus critiques, je suppose, de sa mutation d'adolescent seront bientôt passés & tout peut-être ira bien ensuite.

J'ai envoyé ma — bien modeste — contribution à l'adresse indiquée. Cela est un de ces moments où je voudrais être riche. Je communiquerai votre lettre à quelques personnes amies. Qui sait, peut-être en sortira-t-il quelques donations?

Je suppose que, pour le reste, cela va bien à Bryn Mawr pour vous, pour les Maurin. Quelles radieuses journées d'automne vous devez avoir là-bas!

Mes très affectueuses pensées,
Henri Peyre

## To James Lawler:

Oct. 25, 1971

Dear Mr. Lawler,

You are most generous to have thus offered me this fine volume. Naturally, going over some of the translated poems, I once again admired the audacity required for such an attempt & balked at a few lines which fail to render, or to convey, the melodious music of the original, or the exact meaning. But Mr. Paul is a bold & a gifted man. The older I get, the more convinced I am that nothing equals the difficulty of translating French into English. Yet it must be attempted, & often. In this country, with the adoption some 25 years ago of the oral method converted into a dogma, we no longer have trained our students to feel & think with precision & rigor. It is a grievous loss.

Your own renderings are impeccable, I must say, & the choice you made is rich, varied, ingenious. The Valéry centenary, thus far & as far as I can see, has not produced anything of vast import, in reviews or books. Perhaps the event at Hopkins where you are to go will result in more substantial publications. No one knows Valéry as well as you, as your terse, pregnant notes to the poems again show. I have only dabbled into the Cahiers, not explored them systematically. Perhaps, when I am really retired (I again teach in New York this year, hence direct many theses), I shall; but I fear I may get impatient with some of Valéry's obsessions & his mordant negativism.

You are obviously already transforming the department & I hope you will be enabled to make the needed changes or additions. California must be too much of a paradise & the very good people who have gone there have, often, not continued being active, in publications at least, very long.

Yes, I do know Rob. Nelson well. I appointed him at Yale some years ago & we have remained close friends. My colleagues, at that time, were less favorably inclined to him than I am, & we let him go. He is a tremendous worker, with ideas, eagerness, vigor & of course intelligence: less subtle than, say, Hugh Davidson (Ohio State), but less moody, more productive, more energetic. Some of his work is hasty, some (his book on Rotrou) tends to be dogmatic; the form (especially in his *Corneille*) is not refined, concise enough. As a man, he is generous, plunges into causes (just now, broadcasting or diffusing French short wave broadcastings on civilization), works incessantly; he is also a little blunt, like a self-made man who has remained a bit rough-hewn, & can rub people the wrong way. He prefers asserting to suggesting. But he has a very kind heart & warmth.

Naturally Judd Hubert, not far from you, especially in seminars & small courses, is superior to him in discernment & refinement. Gaston Hall, in England, has a better critical mind, but is less productive, less energetic &, as a scholar, a bit too dry, too confined to "old fashioned" erudition. Claude Abraham (Florida, I believe), younger, is a man of brilliance & fervor, little known as yet: I believe he works on Malherbe's successors. Wadsworth (Rice) is an impeccable scholar, but a little tired & aging, & lacking in vitality & effectiveness as a lecturer. There is a 17th century society which met last year in Seattle & may meet in the East or the Middle West in 1972. It might be worth your while to go there (around April, I believe).

Pardon all those names. If you come this way or near here, do come & have a visit here. I should be pleased to see you again.

Thank you once more, my regards to your wife, & most sincerely yours.

Henri Peyre

## À Linda Orr:

Le 5 nov. 71

Chère Miss Orr,

Je suis content que l'Iowa ne vous ait pas déçue. Il y a une certaine beauté originale dans les paysages & des gens de premier ordre parmi les professeurs & les écrivains. Qui sait? Peut-être vous y fixerez-vous & ne voudrez-vous plus en partir? Cela est arrivé à d'autres, & ils n'ont pas été malheureux. Vous avez une telle maîtrise du français, de tels dons de critique & de poète que cela m'étonnerait qu'on ne vous garde pas à l'expiration de la 1$^{ere}$ année.

J'ai écrit aux deux Fondations. J'ai tâché de répondre par avance, en les détruisant, aux objections que votre projet risque de soulever: car il est vaste, sans doute trop compréhensif, & ces parallèles (d'un pays à un autre, d'un milieu à un autre, avec classes sociales, traditions, histoire, public si divers) risquent de mettre en valeur surtout des différences; les comités sont sur leurs gardes et ont peur que les candidats ne s'y noient. Mais j'ai dit avec force que vous étiez de taille à dominer le sujet et que cet intérêt, chez vous, vers le milieu historique & politique, supplémentant vos goûts de poète & d'amateur de poésie, était excellent.

Dites mes amitiés aux Aspels. Son livre, à elle, sur Char a-t-il paru? Je ne suis pas ici le mardi, & souvent absent une partie du mercredi;

mais si vous me téléphonez vers 8h du soir le mardi 23, je devrais être rentré.

> Avec mes bons vœux,
> Henri Peyre

## To Gordon Ray:

> [letterhead: Yale University]
> Nov. 13, 1971

Dear Gordon,

Your words on Mrs. Guggenheim in the volume of reports which just reached me are very touching & delicate, & beautifully chosen. And I thank you for your kindness toward my services in the past. I was glad that your decision had been to increase the stipend of fellowships, & perhaps their number, instead of venturing on to other provinces of assistance. My own wish as always is that more so called creative writers & artists might be favored, even at the expense of academic scholars, & that, among the latter, young men might be favored. The really brilliant young men in our fields (30 to 45) are all too few, & it worries some of us.

I trust all is well with you & at the office. After a summer of travel, & of some publishing (I brought out my book on Romanticism, in the hope of exorcizing my inveterate Romantic impulses, & even some writing on Revolutions), I have started teaching at CUNY again, & writing more—"but at length quietness / will cover those wistful eyes" as Robinson Jeffers puts it. Just now I rather enjoy being a septuagenarian.

> Cordially yours & my best to all of you,
> Henri Peyre

## À James Lawler:

> Le 16—11—71

Cher ami,

Avez-vous pris quelque décision pour UCLA? Et les choses s'y sont-elles précisées suffisamment? Je rencontre parfois des Californiens ça &

là, et ils se disent tous mécontents des restrictions budgétaires & de l'esprit conservateur qui règne. Mais nous sommes tous, nous professeurs, un peu gâtés aux États-Unis depuis quelques années. Certes, il y a de la paperasserie, trop d'organisation, et notre temps est rogné par mille besognes médiocres. Mais on peut y être heureux. Je vous avais présenté loyalement le pour et le contre. Mais j'ai vu longuement l'autre jour en Floride Patrick Brady & j'ai été conquis par sa droiture, son sérieux, sa ferveur à débattre d'idées, et sa femme, née grecque, a également de la science & du charme. Mais je vois qu'ils semblent fort heureux ici, et ne regrettent pas l'Australie, qu'ils ont trouvée provinciale, et mal munie d'instruments de travail. Peut-être déchanteront-ils plus tard? Ce que vous avez réalisé là-bas, dans vos livres, et dans les *Essays in French Literature,* m'impressionne fort pour ma part.

Croyez à mon très fidèle & amical souvenir,
Henri Peyre

**To the same:**

110 Deepwood Drive
Hamden, Conn. 06517
Nov. 21—71

Dear James, (will you allow me to call you by your first name—& please reciprocate)

You were thoughtful & generous to send me your article. I wondered at first where it had appeared, but then received the issue of Books Abroad soon after. It is an important article, very sensitive & subtle. You are an expert at deciphering the secret stages of a poem's genesis & at coming to grips courageously with a text & eliciting its profounder meanings. The other essays in the same issue (especially Guillén's reminiscences, & those on Valéry & Spain) were also interesting, if less directly analytical & literary. I must confess I had not known, or I had totally forgotten, the "Comme le temps est calme" of 1930. I was a Valéry fan, I remember, as early as 1922. I was in Cambridge then, & hit upon a copy of *Charmes* & was thunderstruck, & went around the colleges or on the lanes by the Cam River, reciting stanzas to myself. I have since had moments of annoyance at Valéry's repetitious complaints on his mundane & captive life (self-inflicted), at his poetics which never quite elicited the secrets of poetry, at his negative barbs at critics & "romantics" & mystics. I wish he had written more "Poésie et Pensée abstraite" things, & a real analysis of what he found & adored in Mallarmé. But in my present old man's impatience with the recent fiction, poetry & criticism in France, I return to him now & recover my near-ecstasies of old. And I owe much to your first-rate book, to your articles on the *Carnets*. What will happen to the fine group of interpreters of French poetry in Australia now that your leadership is no longer quite so immediately present for them? Will the *Essays in French Literature* survive? I hope so. I often refer students to them.

My best & very cordial wishes,

Sincerely,
H. P.

I suppose you have met Mr. Victor Oswald, German Depart. I have worked closely with him on a committee & admire his judgment. Kindly remember me to him & also to Mr. Pasinetti, once my student here, & a very talented man of letters. Give him my friendly regards also.

## À Michel Fougères:

Le 18 décembre 1971

Cher Monsieur,

Votre livre est vraiment étrange, débordant de talent, plein de folie et de raison, et écrit avec une fougue que les pâles et plats romanciers à la mode, les plus pâles encore critiques, peuvent vous envier. C'est en effet une œuvre surréaliste, mais pas forcée et volontaire comme les leurs l'ont souvent été. Je vous remercie de me l'avoir envoyé et je suivrai certainement ce que vous écrirez désormais. Vous faites surgir tout un monde visionnaire et cauchemardesque, et vous l'imposez.

Croyez à mes vifs remerciements,
Henri Peyre
110 Deepwood Drive
Hamden, Conn. 06517

## To Edith & Henry Allen Moe:

[postcard: Soutine, *La Fille de ferme*]
Dec. 28/71

Dear Edith & Henry,

The "Lady" on the other side hardly seems as cheerful about the New Year! Excuse her! I don't know that I am myself, but my health is good, I continue writing, even teaching in spite of my retirement, advising. But I travel much less—& I miss old friends—none so often, so acutely as I miss Henry's wisdom, lucid & penetrating judgment, wide intellectual curiosity and moral generosity. The virtues which, to me, he embodies are less and less often to be encountered in our profession.

Are you both well? Unafflicted by weariness or ill health, I hope? I have not been able, somehow, to attend the Philosophical Society meetings for a time & I still regret that it displays such favor for archeologists, orientalists, antiquarians & other honorable men, & so little for scholars in the English, American, modern literary fields. I believe it is a lack of boldness, unworthy of Franklin, but that is a minor regret.

Do stay well & active.

Our very warm wishes,
Henri Peyre

## To James Lawler:

Jan. 8, 72

Dear James,

At her request, I am enclosing a brief & more "formal" note on & for Mrs. Hoy. She is a superb teacher. Whether she can conveniently teach now that she has a baby & probably quite a way to drive from her husband's college, I cannot tell, of course.

And again thanks for your letter. You are a brave man, visiting the country in wintry weather &, even more, or worse, affronting that MLA convention & all the more sordid & greedy aspects of our profession displayed there. I was active on the committees of that Association for a long time, & for a time its President, & on several other societies &

academies, & I confess I am glad now to be able to stay away. But one meets fine colleagues also there, & can help promising youngsters—& some of the discussion can be worth while.

I have no lack of work as it is, with some 8 or 10 theses which I direct, & the courses—but I find it rewarding. And I encourage the reading of our little boy, now 7 ½, & a voracious devourer of books on history. His passion is for war, soldiers, cowboys. I believe your children are girls & that may be more restful.

I have no plans for the summer as yet, & we may well move only a little, in the East. Let me know if ever you plan to be near here or in New York. Have you some, any, time left for your own writing, & reading of poetry?

Most cordial wishes,<br>Henri Peyre

## Au même:

Le 7 février 72

Cher ami,

C'est un don précieux que votre article sur Sémiramis, une étude minutieuse comme vous avez le talent de les faire, établie sur les brouillons & les manuscrits, interprétant chaque difficulté avec loyauté, et cependant chaude, communicative, pleine d'amour pour cette poésie. J'admire beaucoup tout ce que vous écrivez et considère que vous êtes au premier rang de nous tous qui avons élu de travailler dans le domaine des lettres françaises modernes. Il se trouve que, ces derniers temps (je donnais à N.Y, un de mes séminaires sur Pascal), je relisais pas mal de Valéry sur Pascal, & hier même, sur Mallarmé, car j'ai promis une conférence à N.Y. Université sur le sujet. Retrouvant dans mes notes plusieurs de vos études, je les ai relues, avec profit, & notamment votre admirable & précis, & juste, long compte rendu dans la Revue d'Histoire littéraire sur les derniers volumes des *Cahiers*. Plus impatient que vous, moins objectif, parfois je me laisse agacer par Valéry: non pas par le poète, mais par ce qu'il y a de négatif, de répétitif aussi dans sa critique de la critique & de la philosophie. Je ne suis pourtant guère pascalien, mais je suis tenté de défendre Pascal contre diverses petitesses de

Valéry — un peu comme a fait Gaède dans son livre si intelligent sur *Nietzsche et Valéry*. Il est presque aussi injuste envers Baudelaire, et envers le romantisme. Mais il provoque, même alors, et on revient à lui, toujours.

J'espère que vos lourdes tâches ne vont pas vous empêcher de poursuivre vos travaux & vos publications. Le métier de diplomate, de conciliateur, de recruteur d'élèves de marque, et de professeur est pourtant absorbant — et l'énormité de L.A. sans doute accapare encore davantage de temps. Pensez-vous néanmoins aller en Europe l'été prochain? Mme Lawler y a sans doute ses parents et divers liens. Si vous passez alors par New York & que je puisse m'y trouver, je vous y verrai volontiers. Nous n'avons encore nul projet nous-mêmes.

L'immensité de ce pays ne vous impressionne sans doute pas autant, Australien, qu'elle le fait pour des Européens. J'ai beaucoup voyagé dans le passé, d'une côte à l'autre — Mais je suis devenu plus casanier. Il y aura bien une réunion, à Minneapolis, de la Société d'Études du XVIIe siècle ce printemps, mais je ne m'y rendrai pas. C'est le domaine, avec la Renaissance, où l'Amérique reste le moins riche en jeunes d'avenir. Hubert, près de chez vous & naguère à UCLA, est un excellent maître, au rayonnement trop limité: il serait de bon conseil. Si Nelson ne vous a pas semblé l'homme idéal (il a très bon cœur et une énergie intellectuelle énorme, mais il manque un peu de finesse, peut-être de justesse d'esprit, & de tact), Tim. Reiss (anglais d'origine, livre sur Alex. Hardy & le théâtre classique), plus jeune, est vivant & a de l'avenir: il a travaillé avec Hubert à Illinois, où je l'avais découvert & fait venir à Yale, où il se plaît d'ailleurs, et plaît. Il est plus jeune: 32 ans peut-être — Il est dommage que Bensimon, très doué, se fasse si peu connaître par des travaux.

Que devient le français, ou l'étude de la poésie française, en Australie — vous parti? Après Lloyd Austin, Davies & d'autres encore. C'est là-bas qu'ont été formés, ou inspirés, les meilleurs — Mrs. Robinson a telle fait rien d'important récemment?

Je termine ce bavardage & vous envoie mes amitiés & vous dis "merci" pour "Sémiramis."

Bien à vous,<br>Henri Peyre

## À Michel Fougères:

Febr. 9—72

Cher monsieur,

Vous êtes très généreux de m'offrir ainsi votre précédent livre sur l'Indochine, et sur vous—que je ne connaissais pas. Quelle tragique, émouvante expérience, rendue avec immédiateté et dans le langage *vécu* et vivant. C'est bien plus difficile que si vous aviez eu recours à un style plus sobrement littéraire & utilisé les procédés de "l'éloignement esthétique," même si cela risque de cesser bien plus vite d'être lisible. Du moins, vous rendez et vous communiquez une tragédie personnelle, & celle d'une guerre, et d'un peuple avec un rare talent.

Je me suis souvenu d'avoir lu votre article des *Temps modernes* & je l'ai relu avec émotion et, hélas, comme Français, sans fierté! Mais c'est plus qu'un document. Vous allez loin, sans faire de la grandiloquence ou de l'analyse, dans la psychologie de ces malheureux "damnés de la guerre."

Merci & avec forte émotion,
Henri Peyre

## À Linda Orr:

Le 25—III.72

Chère Miss Orr,

J'ai mis longtemps à vous remercier, mais j'avais tant à faire ce mois dernier que je me sentais trop prosaïque, & surtout trop paresseux d'esprit, pour jouir avec sincérité de la poésie. Enfin un répit est survenu.

Vous êtes gentille de me tenir au courant de ce que font les jeunes poètes les plus doués. Mark Strand a une maîtrise de sa forme déjà remarquable, et de l'aisance, du naturel, & de la grâce aussi. Et il ne redoute pas d'exprimer des émotions, qui se communiquent au lecteur. Je suis un peu plus étranger à ce que tente Bell; mais son humour a du charme et il manie sa langue en virtuose. Anderson a de la gravité, de la substance; il est un plus académique, mais il a mûri & ciselé sa forme & il doit être jeune encore. Il y versera vite un contenu plus riche. Dubie m'a amusé par sa facilité, la flexibilité de ses vers & ce drôle de dialogue avec Hazlitt. J'ai autrefois beaucoup aimé ce critique impulsif, véhément, perspicace, amoureux de la vie, et si maladroit dans ses amours, si sottement "peuple" parfois. Ces sortes de sonnets sont à la fois chargés d'ironie et de sentiment.

Que devenez-vous? Écrivez-vous beaucoup? Avez-vous repris votre Michelet? L'époque est dure pour les publications des jeunes, pour les postes. Cela attriste beaucoup un vieux comme moi, en fin de carrière: avoir formé des professeurs excellents, les meilleurs que l'Amérique ait eues depuis que j'y enseigne, et ne pas parvenir à les placer décemment. À quoi servons-nous alors? & pendant ce temps la société se détériore de plus en plus, l'argent est roi et le proclame

Enfin—vous êtes du moins parmi des idéalistes.

Heureuse chance, bons vœux & merci,
Henri Peyre

## À Kurt Weinberg:

Le 28.III.72

Cher Ami,

Votre article sur Valéry est un bijou et terriblement habile—y compris dans sa conversion de la prose quelque peu rythmée en vers, dont plusieurs deviennent ainsi fort beaux. Vous êtes le comparatiste idéal, bondissant comme un danseur de Valéry à Lucrèce & à Gide. J'avais cessé de goûter Gide ces dernières années; mais la méchanceté de Valéry (préservez-nous de nos amis!) me ramènerait presque à lui. J'avoue que la lecture des *Cahiers* (je ne l'ai pas faite aussi consciencieuse que vous) me déçoit, & m'agace. Que de pointes perfides! Que d'attaques! De coups de dague d'un escrimeur trop sûr de lui. A-t-on vraiment besoin de s'opposer ainsi à un autre (comme aimait à le faire Spitzer) pour se trouver soi-même, ou se confirmer "in esse suo"? Valéry a gaspillé à cela une intelligence qui aurait pu rester créatrice plus longtemps.

Vous devriez traduire votre article en français. Il aurait pu paraître en anglais dans le no. de Books Abroad. J'ai peur qu'il n'échappe à trop de Valéryens.

Nous allons bien—un peu las d'attendre le printemps—las d'enseigner aussi, pour moi, & de lire des chapitres et des chapitres de thèses. J'ai vu un chapitre du Rabelais dans Mod. Lang. Review. C'est original & fin. Le reste paraît-il?

> Nos bonnes amitiés à tous deux,
> Henri Peyre

## To Gordon Ray:

[letterhead: Yale University]
May 2, 1972

Dear Gordon,

I decidedly am not lucky in the dates of my trips to England or France. I'll be in Paris early in June, but back a few days before you arrive there; it is my loss. I would have liked once to be able to visit booksellers in your company or auctions—although my vice is rather for art than for books; & my grief is that, for the first time in my life (senility?), I have ceased to enjoy contemporary painting, & much of the sculpture.

You make me feel some remorse with your remark about our indulgence in overpublication. I have brought out about a book a year since I retired, & am just finishing one these days—Publishers ask for them &, I imagine, sell them. But I find it hard to keep up with the huge volumes brought out by others....

## À son frère et à sa belle-sœur:

Juin 30, 1972

Chère Micheline, cher Jacques,

Je me suis attardé un peu à Paris. Tout y prend tellement de temps! Mais il faisait beau, y ai vu quelques spectacles. Mon voyage de retour a été sans histoire. Lois & Brice allaient bien, semblaient en bon moral. Brice jouant, apprenant la bicyclette, ravi de ses cadeaux, se bourrant de connaissances sur les guerres. Lois parle peu d'elle-même, se sent honteuse de ne pas avoir toute la vigueur qu'elle pourrait: mais elle ne semble plus obsédée ou tourmentée. Elle s'est mise à inviter des amis à des repas & aujourd'hui elle n'a pas quitté la cuisine. Elle envie Micheline, son travail, la variété de ses intérêts & l'admirable succès qu'a été l'éducation de son fils. Mais elle ne fait pas si mal elle-même. Et j'ai, comme mari, probablement plus de défauts que Jacques. . . .

## À Kurt Weinberg:

Le 13 juillet 72

Mon cher Kurt,

J'ai trouvé à mon retour d'un bref voyage à Paris votre très élégant *Prométhée*. Son ingéniosité de subtil détective, son immense science, la grâce sévère mais insinuante de son style m'ont séduit, sinon toujours convaincu. Pour être juste & par défiance de mon jugement un peu obtus, je m'étais récusé comme rapporteur auprès des Presses de Princeton & avais suggéré Freedman. J'en suis content. Le livre est cher, mais il a une présentation digne du rare contenu.

Mlle Zimmermann va vous manquer. Je l'ai vue à Paris, fatiguée et un peu malade, mais toujours souriante. Sera-t-elle plus heureuse à Stony Brook? Je voudrais en être sûr.

Mes compliments à Florence & nos vœux de vacances. Nous allons nous absenter dans trois jours—fuir, je ne sais trop où, cette chaleur moite.

Bien des vœux amicaux,
Henri

## À Eléonore Zimmermann:

Le 25.VIII.72

Chère amie,

Les deux volumes, magnifiques, si bien présentés, me sont parvenus hier. C'est une folie & vous êtes beaucoup trop généreuse envers moi. Je m'y suis déjà plongé. Mon allemand n'a pas l'aisance que je souhaiterais, loin de là, et récemment c'est l'italien qui m'avait surtout accaparé. Mais je vais savourer beaucoup de ces poèmes, et j'ai jadis énormément aimé en George le traducteur. Sur mes préjugés, vous avez raison. J'avais été beaucoup formé, entre 1918 et 1930, par les choses, les œuvres surtout, de l'Allemagne. Aussi en ai-je voulu férocement à ce qui s'est passé ensuite, à voir de mes amis & de nos collègues, tel Kurt Wais, devenir si atrocement plats et bas. J'ai une fois, il y a longtemps, attaqué Th. Mann dans l'Atlantic Monthly je crois, pour son manque de courage à ne pas rappeler les choses odieuses qu'il avait écrites dans Friedrich und die grosse Koalition. Ses Gedanken in Kriege de 1914, dans Die Neue Rundschau sont révoltantes—et Gundolf alors (Tat und Wort in Krieg, oct. 1914), déclarant: "Attila a plus affaire avec la Kultur que tous les Shaw, Maeterlinck et D'Annunzio fourrés ensemble. L'Europe est finie, sauf l'Allemagne qui, possédant la force de créer, a également le droit de détruire" (Wer stark ist zu schaffen, der darf auch zerstören). Romain Rolland a rappelé cela dans un article attristé de la revue *Europe* en 1931, vol. 26.

Mais Gundolf est mort à temps. Et certes ni George ni Nietzsche ne sont responsables de ceux qui ont mésusé de leurs déclarations. Et puis je suis un vieil attardé et cela est oublié. C'est l'hypocrisie de Nixon ces temps-ci qui m'a empli d'irritation. Merci mille fois. Mais ce qui m'inquiète, c'est votre santé. Qu'est-ce exactement que ce mal si étrange? Avez-vous obtenu un diagnostic plus clair, et encourageant? Rassurez-moi et aussi, un jour dites-moi vos impressions de votre nouveau poste.

Avec beaucoup d'amitié,
Henri Peyre

## À son frère et à sa belle-sœur:

Le 29 septembre 1972

. . . Lois va bien. Son père est mort le 7 septembre, après environ 3 semaines d'hôpital . . . Il est mort stoïquement. Nous sommes allés à l'enterrement. Brice a vu un cercueil et une cérémonie imposante. Grande assistance, car le pasteur Haegert était très aimé dans sa ville—des masses de fleurs. Quelque ecclésiastique luthérien d'un rang élevé a fait un sermon qui m'a exaspéré (résurrection, St Pierre, la foi sauve, et autres âneries). La religion me paraît aussi bête que la foi communiste, ou que l'admiration des badauds ici pour ce Nixon, qu'ils vont sûrement réélire. On n'en revient pas qu'il ait eu le "courage" d'aller en Chine et de tendre la main à Mao. Du coup, tout ce qui est chinois est à la mode et l'acupuncture gagne beaucoup d'adhérents. Comme s'il n'y avait pas déjà assez de piqués en ce pays! Là-bas, vous avez les scandales pour vous distraire et maintenir la santé en suscitant de saines et vertueuses colères. Ici, nous pestons contre les drogués qui se mettent de plus en plus à poignarder des professeurs: deux cette semaine, dont l'un est mort du poignard—après, d'ailleurs, avoir donné son argent! Cela à New York. J'y vais deux, ou même trois, jours par semaine. Mais je m'aventure peu. . . .

## À John Kneller:

Le 2 oct. 1972

Mon cher Président,

Les journées de loisir, de jeu, et les si agréables moments passés avec vous semblent bien loin déjà! Vous avez dû, plus encore que moi, être happé par le travail et vous débattre parmi paperasseries, décisions, réformes, discussions. Mais vous aimez la lutte. Il n'y avait qu'à vous voir à Menemsha—et vous restez serein au milieu des orages. Je vous admire, & je sais assez que je ne suis pas le seul. Vos initiatives à Brooklyn sont unanimement louées. Sans flatterie, je sais, ou on me le dit, que c'est le collège, entre tous ceux de CUNY, où l'enseignement est donné avec le plus d'intelligence & d'efficacité.

J'espère seulement que Madame Kneller n'aura plus à souffrir, par dévouement trop généreux à son mari, des inévitables hostilités que l'on rencontre dès qu'on réalise quelque chose. Elle doit se dire que bientôt on vous élèvera une statue équestre à Brooklyn, avec le Dieu d'Israël vous bénissant.

J'ai moi-même retrouvé les besognes d'administration—sur une plus modeste échelle. Mais nulle part je n'ai, de ma vie, vu autant de bureaucratie! Il y a d'ailleurs d'excellentes choses à ce centre gradué, & les possibilités pour réaliser quelque chose de premier ordre sont immenses.

Voici quelques références sur Nerval. J'espère que vous trouvez quelques moments pour rédiger la suite d'un livre qui, à ce que j'ai pu en juger, est riche de promesses. Si je puis vous être utile en quoi que ce soit (livres, renseignements), dites-le moi. Un jour (mardi ou jeudi sont ceux où je termine à midi à New York), voudriez-vous venir déjeuner au Yale Club & oublier un bref moment vos soucis? Dites-le moi, un peu à l'avance. Cela me ferait plaisir.

Notre mois de septembre, & d'août déjà, a été assombri par la maladie du père de Lois: un cancer grave. Il est mort à l'hôpital à New York le 7 septembre. Brice a eu sa première expérience d'un enterrement, et d'un bien pompeux sermon. Mais il était pasteur.

> Avec mes hommages & les amitiés de Lois à votre femme,
> Henri

## To Buford Norman:

> Oct. 5—72
> 2066 Yale Station

Dear Mr. Norman:

I'll be glad to write, of course! So have the relevant form sent me, or give my name to the person to whom I should write. I remember with genuine pleasure our conversations at Yale & your "flamme janséniste." The scope of your article on "world systems" is enormous—but it is good to see a young 17th century scholar be so audacious. And those baroque poets, whom I am teaching just now, are now & then very rewarding, none of them quite so fresh & gracefully libertine as only a clergyman like Herrick could be.

I take it you like your wheat fields & luscious cattle, & the students (some of them luscious too, perhaps) of Iowa?

> Good wishes,
> H. P.

## À Kurt et Florence Weinberg:

> Le 31 oct. 72

Chers amis,

Vous êtes tous deux trop intelligents & trop subtils pour mon esprit vieillissant, & de tout temps attiré par le positif. Mais j'ai tant lutté pour arracher de moi toute trace de religion que je ne vois pas pourquoi un récit acquiert quelque profondeur spéciale parce qu'on décèle en lui des implications symboliques & chrétiennes. Et n'est-ce pas, comme le font ces hideux "Colloques" qui prolifèrent de tous côtés et où les érudits accomplissent de savantes danses devant le miroir, vouloir réserver la littérature à quelques "more or less happy few" au lieu d'en étendre la jouissance aux naïfs de bonne volonté qui restent en dehors de nos études?

Mais j'admire pour ma part, & je loue à qui veut m'entendre, le livre de Florence—& votre projet, détaillé, réfléchi, profond et riche d'immenses promesses, m'a beaucoup impressionné. Bien sûr, je serais fier d'en dire du bien! Je crois que vous avez là les éléments d'un très grand livre.

J'ai beaucoup de travail cette année, trop pour un homme de mon âge, et rêve d'enfin m'arrêter & lire pour mon seul plaisir. Du moins, je voyage un peu moins, étant souvent retenu à N.Y. Nous allons bien pour le reste et allons faire face à l'hiver.

Mille amitiés,<br>HP

## À John Kneller

November 3, 1972

Dear Jack,

Merci de votre mot de sympathie et d'amitié. Vous n'avez jamais laissé l'efficacité administrative affaiblir en vous la chaleur de la sensibilité. Votre mot sur Hélène Harvitt dans la *French Review* l'a montrée à nouveau. Elle méritait un hommage de nous. Malade depuis si longtemps, elle avait été oubliée et a dû en souffrir.

Il se trouve malheureusement que je dois être à Boston le jeudi 16 novembre. Le 23 est Thanksgiving et vous aurez un peu de repos. Mais si le jeudi 30 vous convenait, je serais heureux si vous pouviez venir au Yale Club à midi 30 par exemple—et comme c'est un peu mon logis, je tiens beaucoup à vous inviter moi-même, peut-être avec une ou deux personnes. Dites-moi d'un mot, ou par un message au Centre Gradué.

Avec notre très fidèle souvenir à votre femme et mes amitiés,
Henri

## À Vera Lee:

Le 13 – XI – 72

Chère amie,

Quel joli essai sur Ionesco, spirituel, désinvolte en apparence, grave et révélateur au fond, vous avez donné à *Drama & Theater!* Je vous en félicite chaudement. Vous avez su rester vive, pétillante d'esprit et... experte à conquérir les grands hommes, & jusqu'à leur femme, & à les faire parler. Merci. C'est un curieux & important document.

Bien à vous — et à votre si gentille fille,
Henri Peyre

## À Jorge Guillén:

110 Deepwood Drive
Hamden, Conn. 06517
30 XI – 1972

Bien cher Ami,

Quel aimable petit livre! Merci cent fois. Je connaissais, par *Books Abroad,* votre amusant souvenir sur Valéry &, d'autrefois, votre traduction du *Cimetière marin,* si belle, et si fidèle — parfois, pour moi, plus belle que l'original. "Gritos entre cosquillas de muchachas." Ou "Bello el embuste y el ardid piadoso." Mais je ne connaissais pas vos "Dormeuses"; une seule belle endormie ne saurait suffire à une homme comme vous. La 3e me plaît le plus — peut-être parce que le sonnet ne me paraît pas une forme poétique vraiment espagnole. Et quelle grâce et quel esprit dans votre "marquise à cinq heures" et dans l'anti-Pascal! Après quelques mouvements d'impatience à son égard (j'en ai eu moi-même envers sa poétique et son acharnement anti-pascalien dans les Carnets ou Cahiers), on revient à Valéry avec ferveur; les critiques, de l'Australie à l'Écosse, le dissèquent; mais il est plus grand que jamais, loin désormais de ces mondanités et simagrées que Mondor a trop scrupuleusement rapportées. Gaède, dans son *Valéry et Nietzsche,* a réussi à écrire un très beau livre sur un sujet qui offrait peu de promesses.

Vous voilà chez votre fille, pour quelque temps. Allez-vous bien? Rappelez-moi à son souvenir, à celui de votre femme, de M. Gilman.

Votre fils impressionne beaucoup la critique; il est un grand professeur, original & profond. Pour moi, je termine, enfin! ma carrière d'enseignement. Elle a été trop longue. J'écris, je lis, et même je rêve un peu. Lois & notre garçon de 8 ans, épris de baseball . . . et d'histoire, vont bien.

Merci de ce très gracieux présent & croyez à ma vieille, toujours chaude, amitié,

Henri Peyre

## À Edward Kaplan:

Le 10 décembre 1972

Cher monsieur,

Vous êtes gentil au possible—je n'avais guère fait que vous lire, y apprendre beaucoup, admirer votre savoir & votre vaste ambition, & dire, ou souffler, à l'occasion, du bien de vous. Parce que, il y a longtemps déjà, j'avais, pas toujours avec succès, préconisé qu'on travaillât davantage sur Michelet en Amérique, j'ai eu comme une vaniteuse confirmation de mon insistance lorsque vous & quelques autres avez écrit sur cette noble figure & cette prodigieuse imagination.

Votre essai sur Bachelard est fort beau: philosophique et profond, compréhensif, et lucidement organisé: à la différence de bien d'autres écrits sur ce philosophe, le vôtre est clair, définit les termes & les groupes d'idées, & indique ou suggère les ressources qu'offre cette philosophie à la critique esthétique & à l'exploration des images. Avec Mrs. Caws, vous êtes le meilleur & le plus sûr, & modeste, interprète de Bachelard de ce côté-ci de l'eau. Il reste peu lu—en traduction, il ne s'est pas vendu du tout. Sans doute lui fallait-il des interprètes pas trop abstrus.

Vous êtes à l'un des endroits les plus agréables de l'Amérique. J'espère que vous y pouvez travailler et que N.Y., dont je goûte trop, à mon gré, cette année, fiévreux et menaçant, ne vous manque pas trop.

Mes bons vœux pour votre femme & votre fils et merci—
Henri Peyre

## À Eléonore Zimmermann:

Le 30—1—73

Chère amie,

Grands Dieux! Que de malheurs! J'étais inquiet d'un mal si étrange, si persistant, quand vous m'en aviez discrètement parlé cet été—et je ne réussis pas encore à comprendre l'origine de tant de douleurs, à votre âge. Au mien, on commence à sentir les doigts raidis, les muscles mal obéissants et j'ai commis assez de péchés pour en trouver, en bon Protestant, les conséquences pénibles presque justifiées. Mais vous! Une injustice de plus de la création, que je porte dans le Grand Livre où j'accumule mes griefs contre Dieu & la Providence. Mais cela ne vous rend pas la robustesse et la joie! Et avec cela opérations, inquiétudes, et ces soucis sur la santé de vos parents, que je sais constants—et la douceur, la vulnérabilité de votre sensibilité qui vous font ressentir ces maux avec plus d'acuité. Que faible est la sympathie en présence de ces constantes et lancinantes peines. Dites-moi du moins, parfois, voulez-vous, comment cela va & si'il y a amélioration?

. . . Comme je termine ma carrière, avec quelque soulagement, je me redis bien souvent que ces querelles intestines dans les départements (de littérature, surtout) sont la plus grave faiblesse de nos institutions—et cela dans un pays où il y a tout de même de la place pour tous les gens un peu doués, et chez des gens qui devraient mettre au-dessus de tout leur amour du beau, de la littérature et leur désir de communiquer aux jeunes leur goût pour la vie de l'esprit!

Qu'on vous dise "réactionnaire" ou autre chose, moquez-vous en! J'ai vu assez de réformes, en 40 ou cinquante ans d'enseignement, pour savoir que les réformes consistent souvent à nous ramener à ce que l'on faisait 15 ans plus tôt. J'ai relu de près, utilisé, fait lire votre Verlaine ce dernier trimestre, car je faisais un cours sur lui et sur Rimbaud. C'est un livre admirable de finesse, de fini aussi, de perspicacité & de goût: l'un des très peu nombreux parmi les livres dans nos domaines qui tiennent, et triomphent de cette dure épreuve qui est leur utilisation par des étudiants à l'esprit critique. Isolez-vous, tant pis! Et travaillez pour vous. Ce groupe des dix-septiémistes (où je n'ai pu aller qu'une fois) est sérieux, sympathique et je crois que vous aimeriez les rencontrer. Tôt ou tard ils devraient avoir leur revue, & un chapitre de votre Racine pourrait y paraître. Une telle revue devrait être meilleure que le médiocre 1$^{er}$ no. de la Nineteenth Century Studies!

Wellesley, il y a un an ou deux, cherchait une dame noire. Envoyez-moi toujours le nom, adresse, âge, etc. de cette personne. Si je puis l'aider, je le ferai.

Mon travail est lourd—& des voyages incessants me fatiguent, dans ces affreux trains. J'ai de très bons étudiants (femmes surtout)—mais les questions de postes à trouver, placement, de relations cordiales à maintenir (avec diplomatie) avec les 12 ou 15 collèges de N.Y. où se donne le MA, et les rivalités des collègues, prennent beaucoup de mon temps. J'ai écrit un petit livre sur Hugo, un autre sur Renan & la Grèce, quelques articles. Mais je n'ai plus le temps ou l'énergie pour les longs projets. Et puis à mon âge, on se dit qu'il y aurait quelque douceur à, gentiment, disparaître.

Mais conservez tout le courage que vous pouvez rassembler. Vous avez beaucoup de choses à dire, et vous savez que ceux qui vous connaissent vraiment vous apprécient avec affection.

Bien des amitiés,
Henri Peyre

## To James Lawler:

Jan. 31, 1973
110 Deepwood Drive
Hamden, Conn. 06517

Dear James, (Please *do* call me by my first name; I should be flattered)

I was sincerely touched hearing your voice on the phone, soon after your return, & I regretted my decision not to attend the MLA meeting: I might have had a few moments' talk with you there. But I have been to those affairs so often in the past that I feel I can now abstain. They are tiring &, I must say, even worse, degrading; they set off the worst side of our profession: ambition, greed, conceit, venality. We entered it out of love for literature & education, & there is not much passion for the life of the mind displayed there. I suppose I am an individualist &, in my work, a solitary person.

I am truly happy that you have decided to return & stay here. You are needed here, & of course you also were in Australia. Much can be accomplished here, with a little vision & a little diplomacy. The very speed & bustle of hectic life often stimulates writing. The young people are good. Still, I understand your quandary. In 1938 (I was then 37), when I was asked to come back & head the Department at Yale, I long hesitated. I was happy & well treated in France & the prospect of traveling easily in Italy, Britain, was appealing. Again some ten years later, I was asked to be a candidate to the Marshall Foch professorship at Oxford & to the Collège de France, & I hesitated. To use pompous language, I felt, however, that the fate of the world might well depend upon the youth now being trained in America & that, since I often lecture & write on education, history, politics, I might be of greater use here. I have missed Europe, but on the whole I have not regretted my decision. I had no children, until I lost my wife & married again, so that the question of children's education was not acute for me. I hope your wife likes America & Los Angeles & will feel fairly happy there. I have visited the Department several times, but I do not know many people there at present. Pasinetti, El Nouty & his French wife, Pucciani (when not too moody & if not too selfish), have charm, & substance.

But I am digressing & inflicting my bad handwriting on you. I put off writing on account of exams, Ph.D. orals, which filled my month of January—but this is the request I would like to make.

You perhaps know a review entitled Review of National Literatures, published at St. John's University in Long Island. It stresses the national character of literatures, with no political bias at all. It is very well directed, intelligent, serious but not pedantic. They have had numbers on Machiavelli, Hegel (I believe), literature of Iran, Black literature—the best lately was vol. III, no. 1, Spring 1972 on "Russia: the Spirit of Nationalism." The editor is a gifted writer (on Sophocles, Hegel, Shakespeare) & novelist, Miss Anne Paolucci.

Her next to one number is to be on Claudel. I have agreed to help her put it together. We may have pieces by Senghor & Barrault on Claudel, one (I hope) by Gadoffre on Claudel & the Japanese soul; perhaps one on Claudel & Israel. I'll do one on Claudel & the French literary tradition. We would like one on "Claudel & Symbolism" (perhaps touching on what Claudel wrote on Rimbaud, Mallarmé, Verlaine, & on the Symbolist "atmosphere" of 1885–95, or on a more limited aspect of the subject). Would you do it? No one is as well qualified. The length is some 15–18 printed pages at the most, the deadline April 10; two copies, typewritten, are requested. There would be a token payment, two dollars a printed page, I believe. It would honor the review, & all your American colleagues, if you would accept & I would be *immensely* pleased.

An Australian colleague of yours, at the suggestion of Mr. Sussex, invited me the other day to a forthcoming convention of modern languages & literatures in Australia. You know how much I admire the scholarly work done in your country: I would have liked to meet more of your colleagues; but I am old, too busy for my own good, & I thought I should refuse—with keen regret, however.

If there were any chance of your coming "East" between now & May, let me know. I am in New York two or three days a week & we could meet there, or nearer to Yale.

With my best wishes for your "vita nuova" & very cordially,
Henri Peyre

## À Eléonore Zimmermann:

Le 18—ii—73

Chère amie,

Cette nouvelle m'emplit de chagrin, d'amertume révoltée contre la destinée. Je trouvais bien étrange, & cela m'avait inquiété, cette fatigue endolorie que vous m'aviez décrite ce matin à la Bibliothèque Nationale—mais je pensais que cela était en partie psychosomatique, une lassitude venant de trop de changements ces dernières années; de quelque irritation à Rochester. Mais s'il s'agit de quelque affection permanente et qui doit ralentir votre énergie, je me sens intérieurement indigné. Vous, si jeune encore, si courageuse, alors que de tels maux devraient plus justement affliger des gens de mon âge. J'ai toujours professé quelque stoïcisme; cela est aisé quand on est en bonne santé—mais je n'ai certes jamais cru aux clichés sur l'approfondissement que peut apporter la douleur ou la beauté morale qui peut provenir de la souffrance physique. J'ai goûté autrefois St Fr. de Sales, & ces autres prosateurs du XVIIe siècle que René Bady a analysés dans un livre trop long mais très neuf. Ils aident à beaucoup mieux comprendre le siècle, tiraillé entre paganisme et foi chrétienne, voulant croire à "la vertu des païens" et chagriné, comme Simone Weil, de devoir les croire condamnés aux limbes. Mais mon appréciation toute littéraire ou intellectuelle, comme celle de Pascal, ne s'étend pas à la moindre participation à leurs vues. Je suppose que je chéris trop mon incroyance, même si, à mon âge, j'ai renoncé à mon vieux, et juvénile, rêve de convertir le monde à la libre pensée et de bannir par là toutes guerres religieuses & idéologiques.

Sans doute le travail aide à oublier, ou distrait de soi; mais la jouissance de l'amitié, de quelques sorties mondaines, de plaisirs raffinés aide aussi à vivre. J'espère que, grâce aux remèdes que l'on découvre souvent ces années-ci, à votre courage, cela ira mieux et que vous ne vous sentirez pas arrêtée dans vos travaux.

Mes récents livres sont peu de chose; je mets davantage dans mon enseignement et c'est peut-être pour cela que je n'y ai pas tout à fait renoncé, me disant avec vanité que je sais beaucoup de choses & peux les communiquer aux autres. Mais la prétentieuse pédanterie des critiques récents que je lis m'irrite et suscite en moi un complexe d'aliénation. Je me sens devenu étranger à mon époque, et assez content de l'être & d'une sorte d'isolement moral.

J'ai, comme il se trouve, pas mal repris Rimbaud, et Mallarmé. Peut-être, avec un peu de loisir, écrirai-je sur le premier. Merci de l'idée.

Je vais à l'occasion—mais il y a peu de ces occasions—mentionner Mlle Brooks, & la recommander ici à Brombert. Le "département" de Yale est encore trop peu féminin. Le sujet qu'elle a traité est difficile, & original. Je me demande si une partie en sera publiée?

Croyez à ma profonde & amicale sympathie.

Henri Peyre

## À son frère et à sa belle-sœur:

Le 25 février 1973

. . . Pour moi, je n'idéalise pas la France trop volontiers et, en vieillissant, je trouve mes compatriotes bien légers et gros parleurs, et, quoi qu'ils en pensent, guère plus intelligents que le reste de l'humanité. Si le gouvernement actuel doit être bousculé, je ne le regretterai pas trop; il a manqué d'audace & de projets marqués au coin de l'imagination. Et puis tôt ou tard—je n'y serai plus—il faudra bien que les communistes arrivent au pouvoir, comme l'ont fait jadis les socialistes, et augmentent encore les impôts. . . .

## To Harold Proshansky:

February 25—1973

Dear President Proshansky:

It is almost two weeks since you called me to your office and kindly asked me to reconsider my decision and to stay on in my present capacity at the Graduate Center for one more year. I should have answered you much sooner, and I am not even sure if I told you how much touched I was by your request and by the students' confidence in me. If I thus hesitated, it is because I am far from certain that you are not taking too much of a risk with a man of my age, and postponing the appointment of a younger person who might prove more receptive to new methods and be perhaps more adventurous. I still believe that the search for such a person might well proceed without delay and that the appointment in the near future of a deputy chairman would be a wise move.

My scruples were very real, and my hesitation altogether free from any maidenly, or half-senile, coyness. There is an abundance of talent and of executive ability among my younger colleagues, and it may not be right not to offer them without delay a chance to prove themselves. Their generosity toward me is most flattering. May I say, then, that I am happy to accept to serve for one more year, and that a strong element in my decision has been the pleasure which I have found in working under your leadership and in cooperation with two very cordial and understanding deans.

Please accept my thanks and believe me,

Very sincerely yours,
Henri Peyre

## À Linda Orr:

Le 8 mars 1973

Chère Miss Orr,

Je vous félicite de cette bonne nouvelle. Il était essentiel pour vous d'avoir cette année de loisir relatif, pour vous mettre en rapport suivi avec les Parisiens et les Micheletistes, et d'autres encore—et peut-être des poètes. J'ai reparlé de vous & de vos éclatants mérites, à Swarthmore, où je crois qu'on vous désire beaucoup, mais vous avez le temps de voir venir. Si c'est possible, avec des coupures & sous une forme plus dégagée, essayez de publier au moins une partie de votre thèse. Cela accélérera le progrès de votre carrière ensuite—mais je n'ai pas peur pour votre avenir. Il est assuré.

J'enseignerai encore une année à N.Y. & puis ce sera fini. J'avais fermement annoncé ma décision de mettre fin à ma carrière, et puis les étudiants ont fait pression sur l'administration & sur moi. Mais ce sera vraiment la fin ensuite. La direction & la lecture de thèses ont leur charme, mais ce charme finit par s'user—et si N.Y. vous donne l'impression qu'on est au centre de tout, la vérité est que je n'ai jamais le temps d'en profiter. Restaurants & cinémas & expositions d'art sont un rêve pour moi, & pour beaucoup de nous, tout autant que pour le poète exilé dans les plaines que vous croyez être.

Bonne chance & bons vœux pour votre année à venir,
Henri Peyre

## À Lester Crocker:

Le 22 IV 73

Cher ami,

Vous nous dépassez tous, & de loin! Quelle énergie, quelle somme de connaissances ordonnée, organisée en un tout harmonieux! Quelle rigueur et unité de ton & de vues! Votre second volume est remarquable, et présenté avec art par MacMillan, et écrit avec sobre et ferme élégance. Bien sûr, vous ne vous laissez pas aller à la sentimentalité ou même à l'indulgence pour ce grand malade. Mais vous ne dissimulez pas la sotte méchanceté de Voltaire; la bêtise de Thérèse, envers qui R. a toujours été généreux & même "gentleman"; les maladresses de ceux que R. irritait. Je crois que vous êtes un juge par trop implacable quand vous accusez Wolmar de duplicité (et R. lui-même, de "double think"); étalez les contradictions du *Contrat social* comme calculées et presque hypocrites. Et vous faites (presque!) de cette aimable Claire une lesbienne et de Julie une sadique, et de JJ un "homosexuel latent." Mais qui de nous, qui s'attache à ses camarades et ressent pour eux de l'affection, à ce compte-là ne le serait pas?

Mais ce ne sont que différences de tempérament. J'aurais été un pâle Girondin et un romantique prêt à tout pardonner; vous avez l'étoffe d'un accusateur jacobin au Comité du Salut public. Mais j'admire votre rigueur et votre minutie à ne rien affirmer qui ne soit appuyé sur des textes. Votre portrait d'ensemble se tient, cohérent, vivant, convaincant—et quand je pense que vous avez réalisé tout cela tout en étant doyen et tiraillé de besognes d'administration! Ces deux volumes constituent une des grandes réalisations des études de français en Amérique.

Sans doute est-ce chez vous le printemps fleuri et presque chaud—et vous nous l'enverrez bientôt. Vous êtes-vous tous deux vite et agréablement réaccoutumés à la Virginie? Je sais que vous y formez un grand & actif département & j'admire votre énergie. La mienne se lasse. J'ai fait pas mal de réformes à ce Centre Gradué à NY: nous y avons des étudiants de doctorat remarquables. Mais cela exige démarches, voyages, et après une année encore que j'ai promise, je me contenterai de vieillir en paix.

Pardonnez ce grossier papier; c'est le jour de Pâques. Deux ou trois camarades de notre fils jouent et crient autour de moi. Mais j'ai passé deux jours à vous lire et à ressentir cette joie que me donne une œuvre scrupuleuse, finie, menée de main de maître. Merci de votre généreux envoi & de m'avoir procuré ce plaisir intellectuel.

À votre femme, nos affectueuses pensées et bien amicalement à vous.

Henri Peyre

## Au même:

> 110 Deepwood Drive
> Hamden, Conn. 06517
> Le 2 mai 1973

Cher ami,

Je plaisantais, bien sûr, en vous comparant à Robespierre—ou à St Just (que j'admire beaucoup)—et voilà que Weightman, que j'estime, mais que je crois ici dans l'erreur, vous trouve trop indulgent! Votre livre est un ouvrage de sérieuse érudition et vous avez voulu tenir la balance égale, & n'aviez pas à prendre parti. Pour ma part, les contradictions de R. m'inquiètent peu; il y en a autant chez Platon ou chez Nietzsche. Et la "fausseté" de certaines de ses vues n'a pas à être dénoncée; il s'agit de mythes, dans l'*Émile* comme dans la *République*. C'est envers les héroïnes de la *Nouvelle Héloïse* et envers l'homme que je vous crois un peu sévère. Mais je ne vous en veux nullement et vous en blâme moins encore. Tout ce que vous écrivez est pensé avec rigueur et emporte mon admiration. Nul dix-huitiémiste aujourd'hui n'est votre égal. Et vous osez ce que Dieckmann ou Fabre n'ont pas osé: faire une vaste synthèse.

Que de voyages en perspective! Je n'ai jamais voulu aller en Australie: cela me fait peur—et l'Asie plus encore—je suis affreusement occidental! Mes bons vœux.

Je vous renvoie l'article, car il est curieux. Merci encore et mille choses à tous les deux.

> Henri

## To Stanley Burnshaw:

> May 13—73

Dear Stanley—

Of course the Quevedo sonnet is practically a translation of one from Du Bellay's *Antiquités de Rome* ("Nouveau venu qui cherches Rome en Rome")—& in this case, Du Bellay is better, I think. But, as you know, everyone borrowed generously in those days; & other sonnets of Du Bellay (a famous "Platonic" one in Olive, "Si notre vie est moins qu'une journée / en l'Éternel . . ." is a translation-adaptation from the

Italian) are borrowed from either neo-latin or Italian poets. So are many of the finest dizains in Scève & very beautiful poems by Ronsard. That creative imitation was an original art in its way.

And *of course,* we do not talk of "feet" in French verse! A few poets, chiefly Baïf in the 16th century, attempted "vers mesurés" and a succession of short & long syllables in French: it did not, could not, work. French verse is *syllabic,* & also accented; but the stress in French is weaker than in any other European language, & more monotonous (always on the last syllable), so that the needed element of recurrence, of unity within the variety, is produced by weak stresses & strengthened by rhymes or assonances. Miss Bishop should have known better!

You arouse my envy with your trip to Iran. Iran & Japan are *the* two countries where I'll never go, but would have liked to visit. Persian miniatures set me dreaming when I was a child, & ever since. But you have more courage than we do.

Are you both well? Is Leda's sight trouble altogether over? We have a good winter & feel well, though I do work hard & spend much time on the train between here & N.Y. I doubt we'll move much this summer; we won't go to Europe & the child will go to a day camp near here. We are not sure we'll go to Martha's Vineyard, in fact. Yet the memory of that mysterious inn, among the tall trees in a fairy-like park, might lure me back. It was a fine evening. You are an admirably, uniquely wise man to rejoice in your carefully tended garden & write poetry unhurried. But some days—when we feel soiled by all the shame in Washington & the puerile behavior of those men, trained in law, all greedy for money & so clumsy in their plots—we also dream of solitude. My old, fond dream of America as a purer, cleaner land than the Old World is sadly shattered.

Trilling's book is indeed pompous, austerely Arnoldian, dull & in the end unoriginal. So was his Washington lecture. Must we all end by preaching so sanctimoniously? The moralist in the attic, in several of us, is a perilous host to harbor.

Most cordially to both of you,
Henri

## To the same:

June 22, 73

Dear Stanley,

Of course! I know your book. I believe I read it years ago, before the war & long before I actually met Spire, & I was very impressed by your discussion on vers libre & your very expert deductions from M. Dondo's views—then the most sensible book on French versification. I simply did not connect it with your later & beautiful, creative achievement in poetry. You know when I look back upon my friends, colleagues & people of my age or thereabout, there are none whose careers I admire as much as I do yours. You have let neither poetics & theory of poetry (sorry, my pen gives in) nor business experience nor family problems interfere with your slow, devoted musical & poetical talent. It dries up, that talent, even in Lowell as was recently cruelly pointed out in the *Times,* by middle age or earlier, in most people. You have had the courage to choose solitude, country life, meditation & to come out with your finest poetical creation at 50 or 55 or whatever your age is. None of the poets of your generation has achieved as much.

I have a little quiet here. We decided not to move much this summer, although we drove quickly to Montreal & Quebec & back last week, & the beauty of those cities, the quiet wisdom of the Canadian people impressed me tremendously. I had always been cool to French Canada before. I need time to reread: just now the whole of Dostoevsky, & Malraux & Balzac. I have published a couple of small books in France this year; but of no great value & I suppose I am too old now to undertake a big one.

I had firmly decided, & announced, that I would not continue teaching, but the students & my colleagues at the Graduate Center made a big fuss & insisted with the President that he persuade me to stay another year. I am condemned to administrative work! I will, & after that, I'll disappear. I am well, but conscious of my age when I fail to respond to modern French novels, to critical structuralism & to the new verbiage.

Our best to Leda & to you & very cordially,
Henri

## À Kurt Weinberg:

Le 26 juin 73

Mon cher Kurt,

Nous passons l'été ici, calmement — aussi casaniers que les Cornell! Mais il ne fait pas mauvais: l'Europe, nous dit-on, est hors de prix; Brice va à un camp d'été où il a de petits amis; & je lis & écris un peu. Vous vous préparez, je crois, si tout va bien, à jouir d'une année en Europe dans le proche avenir, et faites provision d'énergie en attendant. Et sans doute tous deux vous écrivez, et vous pensez.

Je me sens presque étranger à Yale: Cornell, en retraite; Boorsch termine dans un an sa longue carrière; Brombert ira à Princeton en 1975. Je vois peu les nouveaux, et ne vais guère à la ville que pour la bibliothèque, dont je suis, un peu ridiculement, l'esclave. Pour le moment, mes tâches à New York sont allégées. J'ai consenti à les accepter pour une année encore, après m'être beaucoup fait prier, comme une vieille coquette. Mais ensuite ce sera à d'autres à se charger de responsabilités assez lourdes: plus de 90 étudiants de doctorat en français; huit docteurs ce juin-ci.

L'une des meilleures est Mrs. Horowitz. Je vous félicite de l'avoir choisie. Elle est très bon professeur et sa thèse est vraiment de 1er ordre: sobre, claire, sans chichis ou remplissage, dense, bien écrite. Elle mérite d'être publiée sans retard & lui fera honneur. Rochester, qu'on dit très riche, contient-elle des subsides pour aider à la publication? Cela est, à mon avis, bien plus important, et mieux placé, que pour des bourses de recherche d'été. En attendant, je vais lui conseiller de tâter de quelques presses. Cette jeune dame gagnera beaucoup à vos conseils & à votre exemple.

Nos amitiés à tous deux & passez un été agréable.

Bien cordialement,
Henri Peyre

## To the University of Alabama Press:

Yale Station 2066
New Haven, Conn. 06510
July 28—1973

Dear Miss Lynch:

I hope you duly received the strange, unwieldy MS on the violent aesthetics, which I returned on July seventh, with a rather negative report. In case you did not, I am enclosing the receipt from the Post Office for insurance.

A letter from the Presses Universitaires informs me that you were considering translating a small book on Victor Hugo as Philosopher which I published for them a year ago. If I can assist the translator, I trust he will let me know.

I have just completed a small manuscript (it might amount to 70 or 75 printed pages), in English, on "French Literary Imagination and Dostoevsky" (How Gide, Camus & others interpreted the religion, philosophy, Slavic strangeness & art of Dostoevsky between 1910 and 1960). I had meant it for a Comparative periodical, but as it turns out, it would be too long for a Journal. If too short for a full book, I could add 4 or 5 articles, of some 20 pages each, on Comparative topics also ("Gide and literary influences," "Literature and Revolution," "The Absurd in contemporary French literature") which have appeared in little known journals such as "Prose," "Boston University Review," an Australian review. If your editorial board were at all interested, I could send the MS along soon. I thought of your Press since you have shown interest in what I had published in France lately. But do not go out of your way about this, as Southern Illinois Press & another one, where I have done books in English, are often asking me for new MSS.

Very sincerely yours,
Henri Peyre

## To the same:

August 4 — 1973

Dear Miss Lynch:

Thank you for your cordial note of July 30. I am accordingly sending, insured, & submitting my MS on "French Literary Imagination and Dostoevsky," just written, & six other essays in Comparative Literature or in criticism published in the last two years. I hope you will find the whole of some interest.

Sincerely yours,
Henri Peyre

The package is leaving by another mail.

## To Harold Proshansky:

September 10, 1973

Dear President Proshansky:

May I offer my congratulations on your continuing as our respected, & benevolent, despot here — & also my sympathy for the petty messages which some students & graduates of the French Program direct to you periodically? I try to save you — or to save your time — but, as children repeat, "This is a free country." I admire New York immensely, but I had never realized how many citizens in this city believe they are discriminated against. Only the rare French inhabitants don't.

In any case, here is a copy of my reply to Mr. de Robignac.

With apologies & fervent good wishes,
Henri Peyre

## To the University of Alabama Press:

September 28–1973

Henri Peyre
2066, Yale Station
New Haven, Conn. 06510

Dear Miss Lynch:

I am not particularly impatient to hear your plans or your decision concerning my MS which I sent in the first days of August. But if there were any hesitation in your mind or that of any of your advisers, please simply return the MS to me, as I would not be embarrassed to contact other Presses which often ask me to submit some of my writings.

I hope all goes well with you in this new academic year, though people say it may well be a hard one for Presses.

Sincerely yours,
Henri Peyre

## À son frère et à sa belle-sœur:

(Venise) le 16 octobre 73

... La ville garde du charme, même sous ce ciel gris—mais les canaux sont de plus en plus sales, et parfois nauséabonds. C'est la tristesse de vieillir et d'être envahi de trop de souvenirs que ceux-ci deviennent des regrets quand on compare le présent au passé. J'étais plus pauvre lors de mes premiers voyages ici, inconnu, et peu connaisseur en art & en histoire; mais tout paraissait plus radieux et moins encombré—sans ajouter que les moindres consommations, les moindres détails de la vie me paraissent bien chers en Italie, autant qu'en France & peut-être plus qu'en Amérique. Mais je n'ai guère de temps à flâner, sauf le soir: nos réunions durent de 9 heures à 5 ou 6 et ma patience d'auditeur étant à peu près au niveau de celle de Jacques pour les sermons et les conférences, je m'échappe de temps en temps faire un tour dans le cloître & le jardin de San Giorgio Maggiore: le site est merveilleux. C'est la petite île, avec une tour élevée, qui se dresse devant Venise, en allant vers le Lido. Impatient de trop de paroles (en italien, anglais, français & parfois allemand), j'ai même décidé de partir un jour plus tôt, le mercredi, & de changer mon départ d'avion. J'ai essayé de contribuer aux débats sur la crise des Universités une note optimiste, mais je n'ai guère été suivi. Je suis effaré du pessimisme qui règne. Tous ces gens sont des messieurs importants (présidents d'universités ou de centres de recherches; parmi les Français, Jean Frezal, médecin, président de l'Université Descartes, Paris; Pierre Canlorbe, Secrétaire G*al* des enseignants de médecins, tous deux très intéressants; etc.); mais, les Allemands surtout & les Italiens, ils ont été terrifiés par les "événements" de 1968 et par la politisation de l'Université. Ils me semblent fermés aux points de vue des étudiants et redouter la révolte des jeunes au point de voir en eux des ennemis jurés. J'ai tâché de soutenir que nous avons aussi à nous réformer, et à essayer d'attirer à nous les 80% des jeunes qui ne sont pas politisés et attirés par l'extrémisme; mais les professeurs de l'Université de Berlin, de Rome, de Hollande, même d'Australie (et des États-Unis) me semblent terrifiés, démoralisés et ne souhaitent que le retour au passé, à la sécurité, à la recherche poursuivie dans le calme & avec une petite élite d'étudiants sélectionnés. Je soutiens qu'un régime qui ne sait pas gagner la jeunesse à lui et lui proposer un but dynamique est fichu. Comme je ne suis guère suivi, je me tairai le reste des débats. Il paraît d'ailleurs que je parle si vite que les trois traductrices simultanées ont fait grève lors de mes allocutions et les écouteurs sont tombés des oreilles de ces augustes messieurs! Jacques serait mieux à son aise parmi tant de conservateurs!

Mes quelques heures à Avignon ont été bien, & agréablement remplies — de visions du Rocher, du Rhône, de Villeneuve, de souvenirs de tant d'anciennes promenades avec Papa jadis, de conversations avec vous deux; et les vins variés et la cuisine raffinée ont ajouté aux souvenirs que j'en rapporterai. J'ai peut-être trop évoqué, et grossi comme les paroles le font, et mes maux physiques (qu'est-ce qu'un doigt après tout!) et mes soucis personnels. Je ne veux pas passer pour un saint et sous-estimer le désir égoïste que je puis avoir de passer mes dernières années parmi plus de compréhension intellectuelle & amicale que je n'ai trouvé auprès de Lois, depuis qu'une crise et quelque anxiété l'ont fortement marquée. J'aime beaucoup Brice et veux lui laisser des souvenirs heureux, et je m'en veux un peu de l'avoir trop accaparé alors que je suis vieux & que ce n'est pas avec moi qu'il vivra le gros de sa jeunesse. J'ai ce sentiment qu'avoir 75, ou même 72 ans, fait très, très patriarche, même si je ne me sens pas pour le moment tellement usé. Peut-être ai-je eu tort de me remarier à 62 ans, bien que je n'en aie jamais vraiment eu le regret. Mais ces pensées que je vous ai confiées, sont en moi très vagues et incertaines. Je vous en reparlerai plus tard. . . .

## À Eléonore Zimmermann:

Le 23 oct. 73

Chère amie,

Vous avez tout de même pu voyager en Europe &, j'espère, trouvé vos parents en meilleure santé, & point trop inquiets de votre état. Je suis moi-même resté ici cet été, trop appréhensif des foules en vacances en Europe; j'avais à écrire, & ne puis guère le faire sans notes & livres. J'ai fait la semaine dernière, pour un Congrès sur "The University Emergency" un court voyage à Venise, brumeuse, pluvieuse, inondée, mais qui ne comportait guère de repos. Que de déluges de mots, que de problèmes universitaires, moraux, sociaux, et bien peu de résultats.

Votre *Swann* me plaît beaucoup: il est dense et pleine d'acuité. Cet "Amour de Swann" a cessé d'être ma partie préférée dans l'œuvre; vu de près, il n'est pas sans gaucherie, & le rôle dans l'ensemble du roman est trop "obvious." Mais j'avais tant aimé ces volumes lorsque, vers 1922, je me suis pour la 1re fois plongé dans Proust, que j'y retrouve quelque chose de mon ravissement d'alors. Vous êtes un peu sévère envers cet épisode, mais j'admire votre lucidité.

Vous voilà donc Chairman! Bieber devrait remplir ces fonctions. Vous le ferez très bien, et avec cette justice & cette objectivité que nous admirons en vous. Mais ce métier-là absorbe beaucoup d'énergie: lettres, heures de bureau, et (si vous en venez à former des M.A. & des Ph.D.'s) placement: j'ai peur que cela ne vous fatigue. Vous allez mieux, évidemment, & ce travail vous force à vous oublier, mais vous avez aussi beaucoup à dire: chacun de vos articles est substantiel, dense, longuement médité; et vous aurez moins de temps à leur consacrer.

Si mon conseil a quelque prix, ne précipitez pas l'organisation d'un doctorat. Le nombre des étudiants capables de faire une vraie bonne thèse est, tout de même, limité dans le pays. À N.Y., Columbia, NYU, nous en attirons pas mal (90 Ph.D. candidates at our Grad. Center!). Cela demande beaucoup de patience & d'attention, une "faculté" variée, du Moyen Age au moderne, surtout beaucoup de dévouement pour placer ensuite nos "produits," des connaissances çà & là, des services à rendre pour qu'on prenne vos gens. Et finalement les bons undergraduates sont plus excitants à former. Nous n'avons pas de M.A. là où je suis: les divers collèges (Hunter, Queens, City, Brooklyn, *et al.*) donnent le M.A. Nous n'acceptons que les candidats au doctorat, en en renvoyant une portion après un an ou deux (ce n'est pas la partie la plus facile de ma tâche!). Je vous envoie les quelques explications que nous donnons à nos candidats aux divers examens. Quelques bonnes thèses (3 ou 4 publiées déjà) ont été écrites, & j'ai réussi à placer à peu près tous nos gradués—non sans mal—l'an dernier. Quelques-uns pourraient enseigner part-time & nous faisons beaucoup attention à la qualité de leur français & à leur zèle comme enseignants de langue. À l'occasion & en cas de besoin, vous pouvez me téléphoner (212/790-4481) ou m'écrire, ou à notre Placement Office (4th floor, 33 West 42nd St., NY, 10036). Mon bureau est au 10e étage, #1004. Si le voyage n'était pas si long, je vous suggèrerais de venir déjeuner un jour. Mais c'est toute une affaire!

Restez vaillante & confiante. Il me semble que vous avez retrouvé beaucoup de foi et de force, & cela me fait vraiment plaisir—et croyez à ma toujours fidèle amitié.

Henri Peyre

## À son frère et à sa belle-sœur:

Le 24 oct. 73

. . . Ces expéditions enseignent la patience, comme l'enseignent les heures passées à écouter des discussions pédantes et théoriques sur l'avenir de la culture. Je viens de passer lundi toute une journée de pareilles discussions au Séminaire Théologique Juif de New York: il s'y forme des rabbins & théologiens, et, célébrant leur centenaire, ils avaient convié quelques Jésuites et pasteurs, & moi, je suppose, comme incroyant militant. Journée entière de débats entre 40 personnes sur comment formuler une nouvelle morale, remplacer la religion, et incidemment sur l'avenir de l'état d'Israël qui, je l'avoue, me soucie médiocrement. Demain, jeudi, je vais dans le sud, dans l'état de Tennessee, faire un discours à une assemblée de politiciens et d'hommes d'affaires sur un thème non moins abstrait: comment rattacher l'action à la morale! Il faut dire que le pays en a besoin, plongé qu'il est dans le marasme, dégoûté de ses chefs et de la corruption financière de ses gouvernants. Il y a d'une part tant de bonne volonté ici, & même de l'idéalisme qui ne sait trop comment s'affirmer & se traduire en actes; &, à côté de cela, un affreux sentiment d'impuissance devant la criminalité et l'avidité financière. Hier, à mon bureau (car j'enseigne aussi la littérature et, en ce moment, Paul Valéry), une jeune fille qui tape pour moi m'explique son retard: elle a été cambriolée dans son appartement, serrure forcée, argent volé, papiers dispersés; puis arrive un homme qui écrit une thèse sur Stendhal, couvert de blessures: il avait été attaqué dans la rue, battu, volé, par trois noirs, dont deux étaient en liberté provisoire après avoir trempé dans un assassinat—et cela en plein jour dans New York. On finit par accepter cette constante menace en se disant que, tôt ou tard, ce sera son tour. L'Université de la Ville de N. York (où j'enseigne), par le nombre la plus grande du monde (150 000 étudiants), annonce ce matin qu'elle va ouvrir un nouveau collège, uniquement pour les prisonniers: on leur y donnera des cours sur Jean Valjean, *Crime et Châtiment,* Macbeth, et peut-être sur les Évangiles ainsi que sur la sociologie—

Brice & Lois allaient bien à mon retour, & moi-même ai supporté ce voyage sans fatigue. L'amoncellement de lettres à répondre au retour est la punition qui suit ces absences—& un jour prochain, mon malheureux doigt résistera à ces pages & ces pages d'écriture hâtive auxquelles je le contrains depuis si longtemps. J'écrivais hier à un vieil ami français que, l'an prochain, 1974, cela fera un plein demi-siècle que j'enseigne: cela me semble parfois monstrueux. Les patients qu'a soignés & guéris un médecin, du moins, l'oublient, ne serait-ce que pour éviter de le payer—mais les anciens élèves qu'on a eus continuent à vous poursuivre dès qu'ils ont besoin de services, de recommandations, de conseils, & on se sent enchaîné, même dans la retraite. . . .

## To Harold Proshansky:

October 26—73

Dear President Proshansky:

It is very gracious of you to write as you did. I enjoyed my colleagues & my own work on the Humanities Committee; but we seemed to be doing little progress in the end, members were often absent, & I let things go. Still, if you thought it advisable to revive discussions on the subject, I should be at your disposal for new meetings of that or a similar committee in the future. I am flying to Nashville in one hour to try & explain to politicians, businessmen & educators, how to pass from thought to action & from words to deeds. I had occasion to attend last Monday a very abstract series of talks on a similar topic (private morality and public lack of morality) at the Jewish Theological Seminary, where some of us, including a Pagan like me, were supposed to give advice to the new President.

We debated similar & even graver topics last week in Venice at the Conference on the University Emergency. Those are occasions for me to speak warmly of the Graduate Center & of its leaders, past & present.

You smiled at me when I hinted that I would spend time on educating my 9 year old boy. But he is adept at practicing passive resistance & it is he, in fact, who lectures me on the World Series. So I spent the summer instead, having sent him to a day camp, writing books!

Cordially yours,<br>
Henri Peyre

## À Franco Simone:

The Graduate Center, CUNY<br>
33 W. 42nd St.<br>
New York, NY<br>
Nov. 20/73

Cher ami,

Les lignes que vous avez eu la gentillesse d'écrire sur moi, à propos de ce livre que d'anciens étudiants ont préparé en secret, m'ont honoré, & plus encore touché. J'ai toujours eu le sentiment que vous & moi combattions, parallèlement, le même combat, maintenant des valeurs éprouvées & toujours valables et, en même temps, nous ouvrant aux ouvrages nouveaux & accueillant des jeunes. La crise mondiale des universités reste bien grave: mais je crois que c'est à nous, à ceux d'entre nous qui n'ont pas trahi et qu'entoure le respect des autres, de rallier des jeunes. Votre *Dizionario,* vos *Studi francesi,* vos propres livres sur la Renaissance & le XVe siècle & l'humanisme restent et resteront comme un "monumentum aere perennius." Je suis bien plus âgé moi-même: j'ai encore écrit cet été un livre sur le Symbolisme, un autre (en anglais) d'essais critiques, & je dirige encore un département. Mais il est temps de me taire & de laisser d'autres parler. Parmi mes cadets en Europe, vous êtes le plus généreux, le plus accueillant & celui qui a ouvert le plus de voies nouvelles. Je pense à vous avec reconnaissance.

Cela va-t-il bien à Turin? Dites mon souvenir bien respectueux à votre femme & croyez moi, très amicalement vôtre,

Henri Peyre

## To the University of Alabama Press:

[November 1973?]

Dear Miss Lynch:

I know that academic institutions, & their Presses, grind their victims with deliberate lack of speed—but I confess I would like to know what you decide to do with my MS, sent some four, or maybe six, months ago. If you have the least hesitation about publishing it, please let me know: I'll soon collect other essays of another kind (educational, academic politics) for another Press and might present what I sent you to that Press. And my schedule being a busy one, I have to know approximately when to save time for proof-reading. At my age (73 soon) & a few more books to write, I am naturally a little impatient.

Sincerely yours,
Henri Peyre

## À son frère et à sa belle-sœur:

Le 23 nov. 1973

Chère Micheline, cher Jacques,

C'était hier ici la fête traditionnelle, plus honorée que toutes les fêtes dites religieuses, de Thanksgiving, pour laquelle il est de rigueur de manger en famille une énorme dinde, farcie aux marrons, et diverses tartes faites à la maison. C'est un des rares jours où les Américains restent à table plus d'une demi-heure ou d'une heure & se bourrent: le reste du temps, chacun, obéissant aux instructions répétées sans cesse des docteurs & des nutritionnistes, surveille avec méfiance le nombre de calories qu'il ingurgite. Le temps est, cet automne, exceptionnellement doux. Lois est venue ici (à la ville de Westport, où je suis donc le plus souvent cette année et où Brice passe ses 4 jours de vacances) pour ce déjeuner. Elle admire beaucoup cette dame (Mrs. McCormick) chez qui j'habite et que Brice aime énormément. Il insiste pour venir ici chaque fin de semaine & s'y amuse beaucoup avec le garçon, 3 ans plus âgé, et deux aînés. Cette situation paradoxale ne l'est en fait pas tellement. Lois semble presque soulagée de me savoir ailleurs & de savoir Brice content. Elle veut avant tout son bien à lui, et il semble pour le moment très heureux. Bien sûr, je ne suis pas exempt d'inquiétudes pour l'avenir. Pour moi, tout va bien, mais enfin j'avance en âge. Hier et aujourd'hui encore, la page du journal qui est appelée ici celle des "obituaires" consacre deux notices à deux professeurs retraités de mes amis qui disparaissent à 75 et 77 ans. L'annuaire des anciens élèves de l'École Normale célèbre chaque année des anciens de ma promotion qui cassent leur pipe. (Pour éviter ces éloges sentimentaux dont j'ai horreur, j'ai rédigé moi-même il y a quelques années ma notice en la limitant à quelques faits & dates, sans commentaire.) Cela ne me hante pas—mais je voudrais que sa mère puisse alors continuer à élever Brice pour faire de lui un jeune Américain cultivé & peut-être prospère. Quant à en faire un Français, cela paraît hors de question pour le moment, à moins qu'il ne prenne soudain pour la langue française un goût passionné. Pour Lois, elle a des hauts & des bas et parfois des moments difficiles. J'essaie de la persuader de consulter régulièrement un psychiâtre. Comme je ne crois qu'à demi à l'efficacité de ces traitements (nous avons beaucoup de psychiâtres parmi nos amis), je ne me montre sans doute pas très persuasif. Des amies de Lois le lui disent aussi, et son frère (qui lui-même suit un traitement psychanalytique) s'efforce de la convaincre. Sa résistance vient de l'étrange conviction qu'elle a que ces messieurs révèlent les secrets arrachés aux personnes qu'ils traitent et elle a comme une terreur panique de se révéler. Sans doute a-t-elle quelque chose d'origine "chimique" ou physique; mais elle et son frère sont hantés par les souvenirs de querelles entre leurs parents qui les ont impressionnés pour la vie et leur laissent le remords de ne pas aimer assez leurs parents et donc quelque complexe de culpabilité. Dans ses bons jours, Lois a beaucoup de charme. Elle a comme une honte, à d'autres jours, à me laisser voir ses obsessions ou ses craintes irrationnelles & préfère que je ne sois pas là. Je ne suis sans doute pas l'homme le plus patient envers tout ce qui est maladie ou quasi-anormalité. Je pense peu au passé, ou à moi-même, et professe quelque stoïcisme qui ne me rend pas indulgent pour ceux qui préfèrent se plaindre. J'aimerais presque être plus tracassé de complexes. D'une part, je suis farouchement indépendant, & Lois (comme Marguerite autrefois) est frustrée de ne pas faire grand'chose pour moi, qui ne demande rien, et pour ma carrière (qui est achevée). D'autre part, elle a un sentiment de remords, de ce qu'elle ne fait pas grand'chose, justement, pour moi et n'a pas réussi à m'intéresser profondément. Elle admire d'une manière presque embarrassante cette dame (son prénom est Diane), avec qui j'ai beaucoup plus d'affinités intellectuelles et qui est, envers Brice, beaucoup plus patiente qu'elle-même.

Tout ceci est difficile à expliquer de loin, et surtout je m'efforce de ne pas accuser Lois ou de ne pas justifier ma propre conduite, qui n'a rien que d'honorable. Je ne sais ce qui en résultera & si cela vaut la peine à mon âge de divorcer. Il y a Brice à considérer: mais nous sommes tous deux d'accord pour lui épargner tout déchirement. Surtout, il y a que Lois est très seule &, ces temps-ci, insiste pour être, et rester, seule. Je voudrais qu'elle cherche un travail, une occupation régulière, qui la sorte d'elle-même; & peut-être qu'elle se remarie, et trouve ainsi plus d'équilibre. Mais elle ne s'estime pas elle-même assez pour se croire capable d'un travail régulier ou d'apporter quelque chose de valable à d'autres. Il y a tant de ces troubles psychiques et de ces complexes de culpabilité ici autour de nous que ceux qui ne conçoivent même pas la possibilité de traitement psychiatrique, comme c'est mon cas, sont jugés hors de la norme. Pour le moment, elle semble prendre plaisir à rebuter ses amies, celles qui voudraient l'aider, tant elle a peur qu'on parle d'elle ou qu'on ait pitié d'elle. Guérira-t-elle de cela? C'est peu probable. Sur le plan financier, qui inquiétait Jacques, je ferai en sorte que Brice ait le minimum indispensable (assez élevé ici, tant est chère l'éducation) pour que, si sa mère plus tard ne gérait pas bien ce qui lui viendra de moi, il n'en subisse pas les conséquences.

Ce sujet, bien sûr, est triste, & il vous inquiète dans votre affection pour moi, avec raison. Mais j'apprécie beaucoup votre compréhension et la sollicitude de vos lettres, & leur délicate discrétion. Je suis presque gêné de ce que les 7 ou 8 personnes qui me savent absent (le plus souvent) de chez moi & vivant ailleurs, m'approuvent avec chaleur. L'étrange est que, si des personnes disent à Lois leur estime pour elle, elle se refuse à croire qu'elle mérite cette estime et leur en veut. Les troubles mentaux sont étonnamment complexes. Brice s'aperçoit, bien sûr, de l'irritabilité de sa mère, de son apathie; mais il est né avec un caractère stable — si cela est inné.

. . . J'ai été horrifié par la coupure de journal décrivant l'incendie de l'auto du Doyen d'Aix. La stupidité criminelle de certains jeunes est encore plus forte en France qu'ici! Il y a beaucoup trop d'étudiants, et qui ne travaillent pas. Un collègue français de Vincennes m'a rendu visite l'autre jour. Il m'a décrit l'état de cette université neuve en termes crus: graffiti partout, grossièretés, impossibilité de maintenir l'ordre dans certains cours, politisation — Si cela est ainsi, le prestige culturel de la France, pour lequel j'ai travaillé toute ma vie à mon modeste rang, est en sérieux péril. Les collègues français me disent souvent que j'ai été bien avisé de ne pas faire en France ma carrière. Il y a ici des difficultés, mais elles ne m'ont jamais atteint. J'ai seulement eu trop de travail, en partie parce que je le faisais vite et m'en attirais ainsi toujours plus. Mais j'ai aussi, et c'est une récompense, des disciples placés dans tout le pays. . . .

## À Kurt Weinberg:

Le 27 nov./73

Cher ami,

Je trouve votre lettre aujourd'hui — mes compliments. J'en suis heureux comme d'une victoire, car il y a très peu d'élus pour ces bourses et j'avais dit bien haut (par écrit) que vous dépassiez de beaucoup 5 ou 6 autres sur lesquels j'avais écrit, moins chaudement.

Bien sûr, j'écrirai avec plaisir aussi pour Florence. Mais je crois qu'elle diminue beaucoup ses chances si elle se présente comme collaborant au même projet que vous. Un comité (surtout, hélas! un comité de femmes) jugera aussitôt que vous voulez l'employer comme secrétaire et voyager avec elle. Chaque fois que, dans les comités où j'ai siégé, il y a eu des demandes de ce genre, pour un couple, tous les membres ont fait la moue et rejeté la requête. Si j'étais votre femme, j'inventerais un sujet autre, qu'elle n'aurait pas besoin de traiter, ou bien j'offrirais un sujet proche du vôtre, mais sans mentionner le vôtre ou que vous iriez travailler au même endroit. Qu'en pensez-vous?

En tous cas, il y a son livre, qui est remarquable, & que je louerai— et d'autres aussi. Je suis content que Louise Horowitz vous paraisse digne de ce que je vous avais promis d'elle. Elle est vive, spontanée, et droite surtout; et elle a une infinie reconnaissance pour ce que Florence & vous faites pour elle. Votre *génie*—car vous en avez—la fascine. J'espère que leur ménage résistera à cette séparation. Surtout, n'allez pas la rendre amoureuse de vous!

> Bien de l'amitié & vœux cordiaux,
> Henri

## To Harold Proshansky:

> December 5, 1973

Dear President Proshansky:

I apologize humbly to you—I seem to be like an aged courtesan coquettishly fishing for advances from young virile males. Perhaps deep down I enjoy the visits of students who have come to tell me how much they "need" me?

I was deeply touched by your suggestion that I stay on for one more year, with my successor gradually taking over during the second term. I shall be honored to accept. The offer flatters me enormously. It also embarrasses me for many reasons, one of them being that it might become troublesome to you in the future to have allowed such a precedent. But you have skill & vision enough to affront troubles.

Just to show you that I can be nasty & bad tempered & disliked, I am enclosing my most recent article—attacking everybody!

If all right with you, I'll announce this decision to our Executive Council, which meets this Friday, Dec. 7th.

I had meant to have a medical check up before accepting, for I seldom or never call on doctors normally, & it would be only fair to you. But time was short. I trust I am all right.

> With gratitude & regards,
> Henri Peyre

## To the University of Alabama Press:

Henri Peyre
206, Yale Station
New Haven, Conn. 06511
December 7 — 1973

Dear Miss Lynch:

Thank you for your letter of Nov. 28th, just received. I confess I was impatient to hear from you, as other Presses have been asking me for a MS or a collection of essays & I kept them off. I like to feel that things already completed are behind me & I can pass on to others.

If you think you can publish in a fairly near future the Dostoevsky piece & the three essays approved of by your reader, will you go ahead with it? I confess I do not remember what the other essays are, which will be left out, but perhaps you can mail those back to me.

I am engaged in a book in French just now, on Symbolism, & I could not compose other essays to add to the MS in your hands for quite some time. I do, however, have two others, here enclosed: if you wished to add them, I would request permission to reprint. One just appeared in Michigan, as mentioned on the first page. The other is to appear in a Claudel number in the *Review of National Literatures,* in a month or so. If not judged suitable, would you kindly return them?

Please accept my best wishes & believe me sincerely yours,
Henri Peyre

## To the same:

March 6 — 1974

Dear Mrs. De Mellier:

Thank you for the three essays, which I have just received. I am sorry to appear impatient, but, frankly, the delay with which this MS has met has been annoying, the worst in my long career as the author of some 40 books. One other University Press is after me to give them a MS & I would rather you return me the whole package (Dostoevsky & the essays) & I believe it will come out earlier elsewhere.

I would rather *not* evaluate the Stepler MS, since I had at one time directed the thesis which was its earlier version. It would not be quite fair.

Sincerely yours,<br>Henri Peyre

**To the same:**

[letterhead: Graduate School & University Center, City University of New York]
March 25 — 1974

Dear Mr. Walters:

I confess that I have been sadly disappointed by the delay (soon to amount to 6 or 8 months) incurred in reaching a decision on the publication of my MS on "Dostoevsky & French Literary Imagination & other essays." In the course of a long career with more than twenty volumes published by University & commercial Presses in America & about as many in Europe, I had never yet experienced such procrastination. If you firmly believe that work could start on my MS as soon as your committee reaches its final decision, I shall wait one more month. If there is the slightest doubt or hesitation in your mind or that of your advisers, just let me know & return the MS, which would appear probably faster elsewhere. Since I sent you the MS, I have sent one on Symbolism to a French Press where it is already in galley proofs & am completing another one next week in which another Press expressed interest.

I am sorry to appear an impatient author but I am not young enough to feel that I have "world enough and time."

Sincerely yours,<br>Henri Peyre<br>Chairman, French Depart.,<br>Graduate Center

## À Kurt Weinberg:

Le 25 mars 1974

Cher Kurt,

Vous êtes gentil de m'écrire; mais je m'abstiens de donner aucun avis pour le choix de mon successeur, car ces décisions appartiennent au seul Président & il n'appartient guère à celui qui s'en va de désigner son héritier. Surtout cela pose la question des fonds avec lesquels rémunérer le professeur, et les fonds sont rares en ce moment: le plus probable est qu'on désignera quelqu'un de déjà ici, c.a.d. payé par un des collèges de CUNY (Hunter, Brooklyn, Queens) pour raisons budgétaires. Les candidats ne manquent pas, & la principale raison pour laquelle j'ai consenti à durer ici encore une année est que je suis "aimé," ou apprécié, par chacun de mes collègues *contre* quelqu'un d'autre.

Mais j'aime beaucoup Bowman personnellement & j'admire son savoir, très fouillé, très précis & original—et son humour et sa modestie. Il est l'un des plus universellement loués de tous nos anciens de Yale. J'ai plusieurs fois mentionné son nom à mes successeurs de Yale & à des comités de Harvard. Mais je suis vieux, prêt à me retirer de tout & je ne m'attends pas à être écouté.

Allez-vous bien tous deux? Et toujours manipulant de grands projets, et les menant à bout, ce qui n'est pas donné à beaucoup d'entre nous!

Mes amitiés à tous deux,
Henri

## To Edward Kaplan:

April 1—74

Dear Mr. Kaplan:

I congratulate you. Your merits are outstanding, your applications are done with modesty, clarity & they are convincing; the "goods you deliver," to use the coarse cliché, testify to your talent, to your seriousness & to your capacity for intelligent work. I greatly enjoyed your Michelet piece, which I had seen in the very striking number of *Europe:* thank you for the reprint. I am less competent to appreciate "en connaissance de cause" your essay on [Abraham Joshua] Heschel, but I learned from it. The Jewish Theological Seminary did me the honor to invite me to participate in their anniversary celebration last Fall & I was, once again, much impressed by the broad-mindedness, the eagerness to strive for the best in scholarship & in human welfare which animate them. But I was brought up, as a French Calvinist, to be, probably, a rival of the Jews, to also strive for the highest grades at school, & to absorb a lot of the Old Testament; & as I never was favored with any belief, never could even conceive of a First Maker & spent years on studying exegesis (Renan, Feuerbach, the *Golden Bough* which I translated), I make a sort of Hannibal's oath: to bury Christianity and Judaism for ever & restore polytheism as the faith of the West. Naturally, I have failed—hence my estrangement from Jewish theology & a private feud with St. Paul & St. Augustine, my two foes, which I indulged & enjoyed. I am now serene, abjectly defeated, but jealous of the gifts of the Jews which outshine all our meager endeavors. In a year & a half, I'll retire, & then perhaps read some Jewish theology. Meanwhile, I hope you & others whom I envy & admire are not too bitter about present French policy of outrageously selfish expediency, which I am the first to deplore.

Sincerely yours,<br>Henri Peyre

## To David Sices:

April 18—1974

Dear Mr. Sices:

You have very skillfully & successfully managed to renovate the whole subject of Alfred de Musset's theater. Your book is precise & well documented scholarship at its very best; you make ingenious use of the variants and of the changes introduced by Musset, so as to throw light on the manner in which he conceived & composed; but nowhere do you overburden your subject with pedantry. You succeed in writing on plays which you feel intensely & like with precise and terse style and in imparting your feelings to the reader. I was so taken by your serious, but winning manner & by the blending of erudition & of liveliness in your approach that I read your book through as if it were a work of fiction—& of the non-modern kind of fiction which aimed at *interesting* the reader.

My congratulations, & also to your Press [the University Press of New England], which I did not know but which has done a fine job of presentation. Thank you for offering me the book.

Sincerely yours,
Henri Peyre

## À Rosette Lamont:

Le 29 avril 74

Bien chère Rosette,

Cela m'a fait plaisir d'apprendre que, du côté Russe, on avait reconnu et proclamé vos mérites, & l'importance d'un voyage en Russie par un professeur américain éminent et *courageux,* qui n'a pas craint de s'exprimer, avant tous les autres, sur les intellectuels russes persécutés. Il sera curieux et pour moi, pour nous, révélateur de vous entendre & peut-être de vous lire là-dessus. Peut-être tirerez-vous de cette expérience quelques articles? Sur le public théâtral en Russie, l'allure de la foule aux spectacles, sur ce qu'on lit des auteurs français ou américains, et même sur les différences entre la langue entendue & celle que vous aviez apprise, plus affinée et un peu "ancien régime." Bien sûr, dès l'automne, vous arrangerez un "symposium" là-dessus, & peut-être en parlerez-vous, au French Institute ou ailleurs.

Au Centre, il ne s'est rien passé de bouleversant. J'ai insisté pour que, si visite & inspection d'un comité d'évaluation doit avoir lieu, cela soit en automne, tant que je puisse expliquer le sens de ce que nous faisons: j'espère un résultat favorable. Le placement s'avère difficile, et cela nous impose et d'admettre peu de nouveaux étudiants, et de ne pas trop en encourager—même si, comme c'est le cas, nous sommes ainsi réduits à peu de cours. Bettina, comme vous le savez, aura la bourse, comme de juste, et Andronesco va aller, pour une année, au Centre de Recherche de Milwaukee. Vous les avez, avec élan & générosité, soutenu tous deux. Le Symposium de Sonnenfeld a très bien marché: public nombreux, bonnes questions, & il a été discret et efficace. Nous aurons certes Mme Cixous et je lui ai écrit que si je peux servir d'intermédiaire avec Milligan ou Th. Bishop, je le ferai volontiers. Chez nous, Mandelbaum contribuera un peu ($50.00) pour une conférence sur Joyce, qui serait le meilleur sujet. Il a lu ses romans qu'il goûte peu: moi aussi, sauf *Dedans*. Mais elle a un très grand talent & le *Joyce* est un livre de première force. Ce que vous me dites de sa personnalité est convaincant & vous êtes bon juge. Vous avez ce programme du Grad Center à cœur, le soutenez, le critiquez s'il le faut, & il le faut. Merci! Merci aussi de votre amitié. Diane vous dit son affection, & la mienne n'est pas moindre. Mon souvenir à votre mère, & à M. Farmer.

H. P.

## To the University of Alabama Press:

Yale Station 2066
New Haven, Conn. 6511
May 10 — 1974

Dear Mr. Walters:

Many thanks for this contract which I am returning promptly. If there is any hurry about copy editing, then proofs later, or any other communication, after May 20 & permanently thereafter, my best address would be:

290 North Avenue, Westport, Conn. 06880

With thanks & sincerely,
Henri Peyre

## To Florence Weinberg:

May 31 — 74

Dear Florence,

We have not yet had the "Commencement" here &, for the first time in my long career, I have to officiate at it & crown the new doctors. I'll stay around most of the summer, except for 2 or 3 weeks when I'll take Brice to Rome & Athens. Lois has been much depressed these last years, & reluctant to travel, indeed, to venture out of the house. I have been in N. York a good deal & often, on week ends, with Brice at friends in Westport, Conn., where I'll be most of the time in the summer, & taking Brice to the beach there. I keep on teaching & working fairly steadily, & the students & my colleagues apparently insist on my staying on, in spite of my renewed & sincere pleas to retire.

Your grant is modest, but the number of applicants is so huge these days that it is probably wiser to be satisfied with it. I congratulate you on having chosen Des Périers—a fascinating figure & a great writer in my eyes. Neither Febvre nor the young Spitzer has said most of what should be written on him. Valéry's *Faust* is not "mine," I confess, but Kurt will elicit secrets there. He will stimulate us all, as usual.

My best wishes to both of you & most cordially yours,
H. P.

## To the University of Alabama Press:

*Best address* from now on:
Prof. Henri Peyre
290 North Avenue
Westport—Conn. 06880
(Tel: [203] 226-4868)

Dear Mr. Travis:

I received the MS of the translation of my French book on *Romanticism* a few days ago, from its translator, Mrs. Roberts. I am quite pleased with it on the whole & I have written so to the author. It is faithful & accurate, intelligently done & it reads well in English. Still there are a number of corrections which I had to make, sometimes to correct mistakes in typing or in proper names, elsewhere because the meaning had eluded the translator. I am sending you in another package, insured, the corrected copy which is the one which should be used by the copy editor & serve for the printing.

The translator suggests adding footnotes to elucidate allusions: I am not sure those are absolutely necessary or essential, but the decision should be yours.

The translator has dutifully typed the French text, then her English rendering, for the quotations in the text. It seems to me that, except for poetry where the original should appear, the French text (preceding the English version) for the long quotations could be eliminated, & that would save some extra cost.

Inside the chapters, the subsections should follow each other without any blank page, as in the original volume, while the translator has shifted to another page, for clarity's sake.

An important question is that of the title. The original, since it appeared in France, read: *What Is Romanticism?* it being understood that *French* Romanticism is the main theme. If the same title were retained, a subtitle should make it clear that "French literature and art" are the main subject; or else the title might read: *Romanticism in France*. Again the decision should be yours.

I shall be abroad from July 1 to 20, but at the above address most of the summer and subsequently—& would appreciate being notified, roughly, of the approximate date when I would have to read proofs.

With kind regards,<br>Henri Peyre

## À Rosette Lamont:

Le 1er juillet 74

Chère Rosette,

Je trouve votre longue lettre cet après-midi, deux heures avant notre départ par la limousine & l'avion. Votre rapport est magnifique, plein de gratitude pour l'honneur que vous aviez reçu, de tendresse aussi (& malgré tout) pour la Russie artistique & théâtrale &, à sa manière, hospitalière. Les suggestions que vous offrez sont généreuses & adroites: on n'invite pas assez ici d'artistes & de savants de là-bas. Vous étiez, l'autre soir, toute radieuse de votre voyage & de son succès, & ce que vous révéliez est fascinant. Bien sûr, organisez vous-même un colloque là-dessus à l'automne—et peut-être pourriez-vous envoyer une copie de cet intéressant rapport à Dr. G. Ray puisque vous y parlez aimablement de la Fondation Guggenheim.

Pour Prof. Newstead (si seulement les femmes savantes étaient aussi bienveillantes que quelques mâles envers celles en qui elles croient voir des rivales!), tant pis—et vous ferez ce cours, ou celui que vous choisirez, dans le programme français. Nous l'arrangerons à l'automne. Dès le 20 juillet, je serai de retour & irai alors quelquefois au bureau.

Nous devons partir, & les deux petits sont très "excited." Au revoir, et bon été de repos & de travail. J'ai beaucoup goûté, vous l'ai-je dit, la personnalité & la conversation de votre mari: il est remarquable.

Amitiés de Diane & de moi,<br>Henri

## À la même:

Vendredi [12 juillet 1974?]

Chère Rosette,

J'ai trouvé votre lettre alors que je venais de vous écrire. Elle est juste dans sa franchise. L. d'abord a eu tort de retarder, retarder, jusqu'à nous mettre littéralement le couteau sous la gorge. Je n'ai eu son introduction & sa maigre conclusion que mercredi au bureau, des mains de Szogyi—& il me fallait les rendre le jour même. J'avais déjà fait de sérieuses réserves au reste, lorsque vous étiez en Europe, & peut-être vous ai-je envoyé à votre retour la copie de mon rapport provisoire. Je ne sais. Mais je ne blâme pas tant le candidat (un peu superficiel & mince, & surtout atterré par son sujet & par ses juges, & réagissant par une espèce de désinvolture insolente) que nous-même, trop indulgents. Il avait tellement craint pour sa position, ou pour sa promotion à Brooklyn que j'ai consenti à tout hâter pour l'aider. Joint à cela une certaine susceptibilité de son directeur, qui exige que les chapitres lui soient soumis d'*abord* à lui, avant les advisers.

En vérité, nous devrons, à notre 1$^{ère}$ réunion en septembre ou octobre, rétablir & appliquer la règle que le MS doit être soumis aux trois readers au moins *deux* mois avant que la soutenance soit fixée—et nous ne devrions plus permettre ces soutenances d'été (Mrs. Insdorf, Leveau, Miss Serrano) qui sont un gros dérangement pour les professeurs.

L. peut-il opérer les modifications que vous suggérez, même s'il a 3 ou 6 mois de plus? Je ne sais s'il a en lui la force d'esprit & la capacité de travail pour le faire. Il a de bonnes parties, suggérées par Barthes, & de la finesse dans ses analyses, mais peu d'esprit philosophique. S'il était venu vous voir avant 1973–74, & me voir cette année, nous l'aurions guidé autrement. Loy a été beaucoup trop indulgent pour lui.

Il a votre lettre. S'il peut, eu égard à Bklyn. College & à sa position, retarder de trois mois, tant mieux. S'il vient devant notre comité le 1er septembre avec un minimum de changements (suggérés par vous) effectués, nous le passerons sans doute, mais sans éclat. Je suppose que, dès le reçu de votre lettre, il aura pris contact avec son directeur, hors de NY en ce moment, & l'aura consulté. Le charme, l'agrément de style sont des mérites, & il les a; & nous ne tenons pas aux thèses lourdes & sans art, mais tout de même un peu plus d'approfondissement critique était de mise.

Merci—vous avez une perspicacité lucide de jugement que j'admire.

Amitiés,
Henri

## À la même:

290 North Avenue
Westport, Conn. 06880
Le 25 juillet 1974

Chère Rosette,

Notre très rapide, mais fort agréable, expédition à Paris, Rome, Athènes, s'est fort bien passée. Certes, rien d'excitant comme rencontre, rien de très neuf pour moi du moins; mais Brice & Carlo ont été emballés par le musée d'Athènes, l'Acropole, Delphes. L'Italie était plus préoccupée, par la politique & l'économie qui ne vont guère, et, comme la Riviera française, trop encombrée, & trop chère. Mais nous voici rentrés, avec de beaux souvenirs &, pour moi, la perspective de six semaines tout à fait libres de lectures nouvelles. Diane vous envoie ses amitiés: elle est d'une ardeur au travail incroyable. Et vous-même. J'admire que vous sachiez écrire comme vous le faites, loin de toute bibliothèque, avec la mer, le vent (& le brouillard) comme muses. Je vais sans cesse à la bibliothèque de Yale chercher livres & revues. Trop de pédantisme sans doute, & la manie de vouloir se renseigner même sur ce qui n'en vaut pas la peine.

Peu de chose au Graduate Center où j'ai passé une journée cette semaine, sinon de menues corvées. Mais je me demande si vous avez des nouvelles plus précises de Mme Cixous, en particulier sur les jours de la semaine (& de quelles semaines?) où elle penserait pouvoir venir de

Montréal. Je vais écrire à son sujet à Vincent Milligan, à N.Y.U. — mais ils voudront des précisions.

Dominique Leveau a dû vous écrire. Si cela ne viole pas l'indépendance à laquelle votre année de bourse, de recherches (& de privation relative) vous donne droit, il aimerait vous envoyer le MS de sa thèse, dont nous retardons en conséquence la "défense" jusqu'à la seconde semaine de septembre. Il a trop tardé à compléter sa dissertation. Il a du talent & du style, mais pas toujours assez de solidité, de discussion assez précise des termes ("érotisme," "inceste," etc.). Mais c'est un travail qui, avec quelque minceur peut-être, nous fera honneur. Mlle Serrano aura sa soutenance en fin avril: elle aussi a du chic, quelques maniérismes, mais un vrai talent. Tous deux sont placés — Mais tant d'autres de nos "presque docteurs" n'ont pas de poste, ou de perspective de poste.

Peu après la reprise des cours, nous organiserons une date ou deux pour des discussions & colloques, & nous aurons le plaisir de vous entendre sur votre expérience russe, et sur vos travaux. Vous nous avez manqué l'an dernier.

Mes amitiés à votre mari, s'il est avec vous en vacances — son genre de vacances, qui est de bâtir, de décorer, d'inventer — et toute mon affection pour vous.

Henri

## To the University of Alabama Press:

July 31—74
290 North Ave.
Westport, Conn. 06880

Dear Mrs. De Mellier:

Thank you for informing me of the probable schedule of the work to be effected on the Dostoevsky MS & on the Romanticism in translation. I shall be looking forward to working with you.

Sincerely,
Henri Peyre

## À Micheline Levowitz:

290 North Avenue
Westport, Conn. 06880
Le 12 août 1974

Chère amie,

J'ai eu quelque peine à vous imaginer coupant du bois, plantant des clous, soulevant des poutres, ajustant des portes, adressant des prières et des adjurations à de jeunes arbres pour les implorer de vite grandir. . . . Votre mari & vous avez plus de courage que je n'en ai jamais eu! Je ne répugne pas au travail physique, bien que je n'y sois plus guère apte. Mais j'ai comme une répugnance à l'état de propriétaire—peut-être pour avoir, lors de mes vacances de petit enfant, autrefois, trop entendu de discussions rusées ou aigres avec des fermiers et des voisins de village; sans doute aussi, par égoïsme des intellectuels, qui supportent malaisément d'être dérangés de leurs lectures & de leurs gribouillages. J'ai longtemps été affligé de cette étrange maladie, une sorte d'eros livresque ou d'irrésistible désir de lire les livres nouveaux, ou ceux qui étaient à ma portée, simplement pour les dévorer par boulimie, ou peut-être pour me stimuler à écrire moi-même pour les contredire. Mais vieillir, si ce n'est pas toujours mûrir ou acquérir une sérénité qui serait aussi froideur, a cela de bon: qu'on aperçoit la vanité de toute polémique, ou même de critiquer les autres sans les comprendre de l'intérieur. Le temps devenant plus précieux, je m'abstiens de me précipiter vers les livres nouveaux, qui m'emplissent d'ennui. Cela m'a amusé, en regardant à Paris des étalages des libraires, de constater combien peu les nouveautés éveillaient en moi de curiosité. Avoir eu 20 ou 25 ans dans les années 1920–30, quand la NRF & dix autres revues m'emplissaient d'avidité, quand je passais des heures le soir à converser avec quelques amis sur les derniers volumes de Proust qui paraissaient alors, à applaudir (au poulailler) des pièces de Pirandello, de Giraudoux, de Dostoevsky dramatisé! Cela m'a marqué pour la vie, sans doute. Vous ne frémissiez pas à Mauriac—mais je me rappelle le temps, vers 1924 ou 25, où servant dans l'armée, je me précipitais sur les livraisons de la Revue de Paris où paraissait *Le Désert de l'amour,* après avoir découvert avec ravissement *Le Baiser au lépreux.* Plus tard, je copiais de mes mains, dans la salle de réserve de la Bibliothèque Nationale, *Partage de Midi,* découvrais la correspondance Rivière.

Alain Fournier, m'emballais pour *Nadja*—sans doute était-on moins politisé alors, et la littérature ou l'art était tout. L'avènement de Hitler, puis Munich, m'ont ébranlé dans les profondeurs. Ces dernières semaines, devant la tragédie que vivait le pays, le déploiement de ces turpitudes où Nixon et ses acolytes s'étaient vautrés, j'ai retrouvé mon enthousiasme de jeune homme et un dégoût de ces bassesses et de ces tromperies. Je crains maintenant que, l'abcès crevé, les gens ne se croient la conscience pure à bon compte. En fait, les coupables ont été aussi tous ceux qui étaient prêts à offrir des milliers de dollars pour aider Agnew, et Nixon, qui le sont encore probablement; et beaucoup de ceux-là, de la classe dirigeante, sont, pour les vieux professeurs comme moi, de nos anciens élèves. Nous sommes coupables de ne pas leur avoir inculqué assez d'esprit critique, et même d'honnêteté morale. Est-ce notre pédantisme, notre recours aux jargons techniques, notre manque de foi, qui ne nous a pas permis, à nous, éducateurs, de communiquer ce que nous pensions avoir en nous de valable?

Mais je m'égare. Notre rapide voyage en France (j'ai revu les Baux, Saint Rémy & un peu de la Riviera; mais là, sans plaisir). Le voyage à Rome, à Athènes a été riche d'expériences pour mon petit garçon & pour moi. Que de merveilles émouvantes à Delphes, au Musée de l'Acropole—et dans quelques coins de Rome, le Palatin, deux ou trois églises très simples! Puis j'ai lu ici sans penser à rien, ou relu: Jacques le Fataliste entre autres, grâce à vous, mais je n'arrive pas à vibrer à cela; beaucoup de livres sur le 18e siècle & sur la Révolution, je ne sais pourquoi; des épreuves; et des livres de psychologie, dont celui de Miss Mitchell sur le Freudisme & la question féminine, et Becker, "The Denial of Death." Une ou deux visites au Centre Gradué, en somnolence. Je n'y retournerai plus jusqu'au 28 août, où nous aurons la soutenance de la thèse (pleine de talent) de Mlle Serrano—puis la rentrée. Vous serez de retour alors et nous réserverons un jour pour un calme entretien. Vous devriez délimiter avec précision un sujet, assez rapidement faisable, sur Stendhal ou un autre auteur; mais surtout être moins difficile pour vous-même et vous dire qu'il ne s'agit que d'une sorte d'exercice pour vous—le dernier—& que plus tard, si vous obtenez la sécurité d'un poste digne de vous, vous aurez le loisir d'écrire des choses plus méditées. J'admire beaucoup votre très réelle hauteur morale & cette noble ambition de réaliser des écrits dignes de tout ce que vous savez posséder de profondeur & de complexité. Mais à de certains moments & sans se trahir soi-même, il est beau aussi de faire simple.

Le fait que votre *Mauriac* est en français limite les possibilités de publication ici: il y a de nouvelles revues, mais je crois qu'elles n'acceptent que des articles en anglais: *Twentieth Century Lit.* (Hofstra Univ.); *Modernist Studies* (Dept. of English, Univ. of Alberta, Edmonton, Canada) — *Far Western Forum* (20, Poppy Lane, Berkeley, Cal.). Peut-être une revue canadienne serait-elle l'asile le plus propice, & je regarderai un jour prochain à la Bibliothèque de Yale si j'en vois une. La *French Review* est très encombrée &, je crois, demande (comme les Studi Francesi) 2 ou 3 ans avant de faire paraître les articles acceptés. D'ici là! . . .

Mais cet essai sur Mauriac était fort bon, et neuf. Il devra paraître. Il y a peut-être une publication de quelque Société des Amis de Mauriac en France? J'essaierai de me renseigner. Il y a déjà les Amis de Gide — de Proust — de Valéry — de Claudel — de Du Bos — et de Balzac, de Renan, etc. — Jadis j'appartenais à quelques uns de ces groupes, mais je me suis retiré de tout cela, qui ne fait que disperser.

Voici un bien long gribouillage; excusez-le. Rappelez-moi au souvenir de votre mari — et surtout reposez-vous pleinement, au physique & aussi en esprit, avant de retrouver tous vos soucis.

Avec mes bien amicales pensées,<br>Henri Peyre

## To Edward Kaplan:

August 27/74

Dear Mr. Kaplan,

I made haste with your MS, since you are leaving early, & I have to resume my activities in NY in two days. I am flattered that you should consult me, & happy if I can help — but I am not really that much of a specialist on Michelet's works as a naturalist or as a poet of nature, much as I always admired *La Mer, La Montagne* & *L'Oiseau, L'Amour* & *La Femme,* much less, I must say. Perhaps of all the books M. wrote during the Second Empire, I prize *La Bible de l'Humanité* most, which would deserve a monograph.

But I have no hesitation to say that your work, thus revised, is an important one, obviously deserving publication. It reads well, it carries the reader along sweepingly; it is novel in its approach; it is very learned, very well documented on history of science & on the ideological context of 1852–1870, but never heavy & always lucid. I hope you have good luck with the Hopkins Press & perhaps either Amherst College or the ACLS could grant you a subsidy to assist publication. It is important, for your career, for Columbia where you wrote it, for the French 19th century scholarship, that it should appear. There is a strong revival of interest in Michelet just now, & it is likely to continue. You & Linda Orr are the two most prominent young scholars on Michelet in America, but others are following now. I have long urged the young people in this country myself (Oscar Haac, a forthcoming Ph.D. of Yale, Will Morse have taken the advice) to work on M. as the most influential of the French romantics and as the greatest master of French prose. If a Press here hesitates about publishing your translation of the 1869 Preface (as it might), you should try & publish it in a separate little book, along with the curious text "L'Héroïsme de l'esprit" presented by Viallaneix in *L'Arc,* with the powerful Preface to vol. VII on La renaissance, with prefaces or methodological texts by Aug. Thierry, Guizot, Taine (3 vols. of essais de *Critique & d'histoire*), Renan, Fustel, perhaps Albert Sorel, down to Marc Bloch, Lucien Febvre.—Michelet as an historian is far more highly esteemed today than most people suspect, & praised, not only by Febvre, but by Soboul (his first of 2 vols. at Arthaud's, on the preparations for the Revolution, is excellent & relatively impartial), Cobban (The double Identity, or some such title), Cobb, maybe also by Ed. Hallet Carr (What is History?). Speaking of books on & around the subject, I don't believe you mention the two volumes by D. G. Charlton, in England; & you don't seem to make much of Gaulmier, Michelet (devant Dieu), less learned but also less overburdened with inédits & clearer than *La Voie royale.*

I have nothing to suggest as changes or improvements, except tiny details which I marked in pencil on the MS, returned today: p. 108, con*t*inuity, p. 124 & again 205 note 15, Brita*nn*ique; p. 164, Sera*ph*ita is the usual title of the novel; p. 201 note 3, *d*ernier; *ibid.,* en face *de* son œuvre; p. 207, note 34, was Bury J. B.? Or J. M.? p. 216, note 10, dr*o*wns; p. 225 note 8, Bachelard; p. 227 note 26, "quiétude singulière"?

p. 229 note 8, La Mo*th*er? p. 231 note 21, Daed*a*lus; p. 236, line 4, disast*e*rs.

> Also p. 231, note 18, Bruneau's judgment is plain stupid; he never had much sense for style-
>
> p. 114, Th. Gautier has also a little poem on "Des ailes" de Rückert, probably in *Émaux & Camées,* which M. might have remembered.
>
> p. 154, "The future philosopher of positivism" to designate Taine? Aug. Comte, Littré, yes. Taine never was a positivist— If anything, a materialistic pantheist, full of Spinoza, Goethe & Hegel.
>
> You argue subtly that M. was *not* a pantheist. Too bad if he was not, I would say. Sure, God for him is not totally identical with nature; still, he is not transcendent, is not a personal God who created the world, revealed himself to it. Around 1840–70, the orthodox Christians made a lot of fuss to condemn pantheism as a form of atheism. It may well be, but today it is "le divin" which counts, not a personal god—& Teilhard himself, say what he likes, was a pantheist, rejecting creation ex nihilo, revelation, the Son, original sin, & hanging his theology on St Paul, 1st Corinthians XII, 28, Εν πᾶσι πάντα θεός as the omega point.
>
> Much of M's natural history & philosophy anticipates Maeterlinck, & the curious naturalist J. H. Fabre—& Bergson on instinct in *L'Évolution créatrice.* Bergson, incidentally, granted a high place to Ravaisson in a chapter of *La Pensée* & *le Mouvant* (probably the essay you quote—p. 112). A bit too much to assert that M's nature books aimed at "boosting the sagging morale of those hostile to Napoleon III & his régime." That's claiming too much for them.

All these are just tiny crumbs & I had to rush—but I wish you a fine trip & a good year. You are lucky; I never had a full year away from administrative duties for 40 years!

Sincerely,<br>
H. P.

## To Steven Schlesinger:

>Graduate Center CUNY
>33 W. 42nd St. NY

Dear Steve,

I was away when you called, lecturing around Virginia & then too pressed at the office, on my return, to call. I have an old-fashioned reluctance to phone.

Yes, Malaquais is still alive, but no longer a novelist — only Gide once took him for one (& Justin O'Brien for a while). He dabbles in philosophy, took a degree in it, I believe; he has taught as a visitor at 5 or 6 places in America, but never stayed long anywhere. He has a rather prickly personality & apparently has not ingratiated himself much with colleagues & students. I have not seen him for many years.

His wife, however (a French or Swiss lady, from Wellesley, I believe), came to see me last year. She has a substantial grant to work, for 4 or 5 years, on the French & other "refugee" writers, artists & scholars in America during World War II — a huge & loose subject, apparently well subsidized. I fear I failed to note her, or their, address.

I trust all goes well with the Foundation & that it kept its own counsel, as Yale should have done, when McGeorge Bundy urged universities & Foundations to invest aggressively! With the present rate of inflation & the cost of living abroad (I was in Rome & Paris & Athens briefly this summer), you'll have to increase your stipends! The N[ational Endowment for the] Humanities is, in my opinion, squandering funds fruitlessly around & those who apply there lose all "pudeur" & request astronomical sums.

I am probably an old miser wailing in a desert. O tempora! O mores!

>Cordially to everyone in your lofty palace,
>Henri Peyre

## À Rosette Lamont:

>Le 29 août 1974

Ce sont sans doute vos dernières belles journées — si vraiment elles sont là-bas plus radieuses, moins ensevelies dans la brume humide &

collante que les nôtres ici. Je me rappelle jadis mes regrets, ceux de Marguerite surtout, à quitter Martha's Vineyard, lors de la date, ici fatidique, de Labor's Day. J'aime la nature américaine là où elle est grandiose—Rocheuses, Colorado & même N. Hampshire—mais pour quelque raison je ne lui ai jamais été vraiment accordé que dans les sites de cette île. Et Nantucket passe pour plus prenant encore. Ici (à Westport), il y a eu quelques belles & sereines journées & je me suis même retrouvé panthéiste & consentant à coller mon corps sur la plage ensoleillée. Mais je suis loin de comprendre l'attrait des bains de boue, sur lesquels Michelet a écrit des pages mystiquement voluptueuses!

Nous avons eu hier la "soutenance" de Lucienne Serrano. Elle nous a, avec grâce, imposé le déplacement & la date pour que, dès le 1er septembre, sa position à York College soit assurée. Nos candidats sont aussi nos tyrans. Mais sa thèse (très peu "thèse," très personnelle, brillamment écrite) a du talent & nous fait honneur. Les plus traditionalistes parmi nous pourraient froncer les sourcils à tant d'indépendance, parfois désinvolte. Mais je crois que cela vaut mieux que bien des lourdeurs, comme les thèses françaises, plus pesantes que jamais depuis 1968, en sont accablées. Leveau aussi a du talent & de la désinvolture, mais lui aussi a de l'originalité. C'est un anxieux & il n'a pas été facile de lui arracher—enfin—la thèse, puis l'introduction, puis le chapitre un peu mince sur *Athalie* & la conclusion, un peu décevante. Mais lui aussi devait terminer pour conserver son poste. Vous avez été généreuse d'accepter de la lire *in extremis*.

Sheila Endler est aussi venue me voir. C'est, littéralement, une ressuscitée—bien frêle encore. Elle a été 2 ou 3 fois condamnée par les médecins depuis un an, & soumise à d'affreux traitements: douloureux, coûteux. Et elle est sans poste & peut-être incapable, physiquement, de reprendre le sien (dans une école, où elle doit se résigner à enseigner l'histoire). Son courage a été magnifique. Elle aussi devrait terminer sa thèse sur Apollinaire dans les semaines qui viennent, & ce sera un bon travail. Elle ne pourra pas incorporer dans cette thèse tout ce que vous lui aviez suggéré; ses lectures dans les bibliothèques ont été restreintes par sa longue immobilité. Mais elle a tiré ingénieusement parti de vos conseils. Elle redoute la réaction de M. Zéphyr, peut-être moins large d'esprit que vous ou moi devant ces poésies par trop légères. On verra!

Enfin quelques précisions de Mme Cixous. Elle sera à N.Y. University, s'absentant de Montréal, entre le 19 oct. (samedi) & le 23 (mercredi).

Avec l'accord de Tom Bishop, elle pourrait faire un saut chez nous & parler le mardi 22 oct. à 4h15. Elle me dit être une "diurne" & ne pas pouvoir travailler ou discourir après 6 P.M. Je vous demanderai, si vous voulez bien, de la présenter & sans doute voudrez-vous la voir avant ce jour là. Nous aviserons en Septembre & choisirons le sujet de concert. . . .

## To Stanley Burnshaw:

Sept. 6 — 1974

Dear Stanley,

No, we did not venture to Martha's Vineyard this summer. I did take a brief trip to Rome & Athens (& Paris on the way) with my little boy, who is interested in history & art; but for the last two or three years, Lois has not been very well & prefers not to move. She has been depressed & strangely lethargic — not a little, probably, on account of my old age & boring intellectuality; but also on account of grudges against her mother & bad childhood memories. She thus far refuses to see a psychiatrist & distrusts the whole profession. For the last few months, since my work is in New York, I have lived mostly at: "290, North Avenue, Westport, Conn. 06880," with frequent visits to Hamden, & Brice often comes here, to Westport, for vacations & for week ends.

All goes well otherwise. I write & publish a good deal & my duties as chairman in N.Y. (over 90 Ph.D. candidates in our French Program! — where shall we ever place them all?) are heavy.

Of course, I shall be glad to write on, & for, you to the Guggenheim people. I have resigned from that Committee, & from many others, a few years ago. *The Seamless Web,* which I have proclaimed the best book of criticism, or of poetics, of the last few years, has had such an impact that it should be clear to all eyes that your intellectual vitality is that of a forty year old man. Does age play a great part in the Comittee's decisions? Sometimes. As a rule, they (& in the past I did) prefer young men or women, which is natural. But exceptions have been made: for Alfred Kazin for example, for Irving Howe I believe, who must be over fifty or fifty-five. Let us, by all means, try & see. . . .

I envy you your Iranian trip. That's a country where I would gladly visit — but I am through with traveling.

My best wishes to Leda: it is sad to hear she has not been too well all these years—even in that ideal spot on Lambert's Cove.

Cordially yours,<br>
Henri Peyre

## À Rosette Lamont:

Graduate Center<br>
September 9—1974

Chère Rosette,

 Leveau a été assez ébranlé par votre lettre, & il se devait de l'être. Il a du talent, du savoir-faire littéraire & au fond du sérieux, même s'il n'a guère de profondeur. Mais il aurait pu, envers vous, & même envers moi, faire preuve de plus de tact & de "prévenance," en évitant de nous confronter *in extremis* avec un manuscrit imparfait & inachevé. Szogyi a exprimé aussi sa surprise de votre lettre et se sent un peu accusé, sinon coupable. Leveau ne peut sans doute opérer toutes les modifications que vous suggériez, dont certaines auraient exigé une refonte totale; il s'empresse d'en faire quelques-unes. Nous maintenons la date de la soutenance à jeudi 12 à 2 heures, mais vous vous sentirez libre de marquer vos dissidences. Je crois que nous devons, dans ces jugements sur les thèses, être assez francs. Bien sûr, il y a toujours des susceptibilités en jeu. Trois "advisers" ne peuvent être toujours d'accord entre eux, ou avec le "directeur" de la thèse. Ce dernier, s'il a approuvé les chapitres, le plan général, prodigué ses conseils, se sent menacé si les lecteurs font de sérieux reproches à la thèse. Nous avons eu cette légère difficulté, qu'un peu de bonne volonté & d'humour peut résoudre, avec Leroy sur Corneille & Miss Hancock sur Rousseau. Mais c'est le retard cette fois-ci, & l'ultimatum, qui ont rendu la chose plus déplaisante. Je prends sur moi une lourde part du blâme. Leveau, et Szogyi & Loy, louaient bien haut la thèse, tenaient à ce que le candidat soit ou promu ou assuré dans sa position d'enseignant, et nous ont conviés à tout hâter. À l'avenir, & je le proposerai dès notre première réunion, nous devrions appliquer et réaffirmer la règle que la thèse soit présentée aux trois lecteurs deux mois à l'avance, et avant, d'avoir assumé sa forme définitive.

 Vous avez dû être entourée de brume & d'eau cette dernière semaine sur votre île. Brice est au Cap Cod avec des amis & il a sans doute passé plus de temps à la télévision &, j'espère, à la lecture, qu'à la plage. Il reprend demain son école & je donne moi-même mon premier cours ce lundi.

À bientôt donc & nous préciserons alors plans & dates pour Mme Cixous, & pour le Colloque que vous nous avez promis.

Je sais que Diane vous envoie ses amitiés. Et les miennes vous entourent ou vous assiègent.

Bien à vous,<br>Henri

## To Stanley Burnshaw:

September 16—74

Dear Stanley.

Thank you for your words of kind sympathy for Lois' difficulties. You have always been the warmest of friends & I never forgot the most touching visit you paid me, years ago, while I was distressed by my first wife's critical condition. Just now things are quiet, but Lois stubbornly refuses to submit to any treatment. We'll see.

On Friday, October fourth, fine. Please come about 10:30 & we'll have some sort of late breakfast or coffee & talk.

But you should *not* give up like that on the Guggenheim. 68 is not old by my standards & you have achieved enough in the last ten years to prove your youth & intellectual eminence. You tower above 99% of us. Do apply & get 4 or 5 sponsors, me among them. Frame a neat, feasible, challenging project.

Affectionately,<br>Henri Peyre

## À Rosette Lamont:

Mercredi 18 sept. 74

Chère Rosette,

(Ne m'appelez pas "cher Maître"! Il y a longtemps que j'ai cessé de prétendre offrir des modèles et si l'un de nous doit apprendre de l'autre, c'est moi—sur le théâtre, sur la Russie actuelle & bien d'autres choses.)

Votre longue lettre, très belle & écrite avec feu, riche en formules frappées, me dit aussi que vous êtes blessée de diverses choses, et entre autres de maladresses de ma part. Je m'en excuse. Et je vous réponds vite pour éclaircir quelques points.

Pour la thèse de L. vous avez raison. Il y a dans toutes les universités de grosses différences d'une thèse à une autre. 2 ou 3 sont excellentes; d'autres, passables probablement, leur sont très inférieures. Chez nous, celles de Mme X, de Mme Y, de Z, d'autres encore, valaient bien moins que celle de L, peut-être même celle de R. Je crois que celle de L. méritait d'être acceptée, mais il a été très mal conseillé. Loy, tout l'an dernier, ne cessait de dire qu'elle était excellente, rien à y changer. Apparemment il a déchanté après avoir vu vos critiques & peut-être les miennes. Szogyi se sentait personnellement en cause. Notre système étant ce qu'il est, et la cohésion d'un département ayant son prix, je crois que nous avons agi professionnellement en passant la thèse, mais aussi en marquant fortement nos critiques. Et nous allons dès cette semaine réaffirmer des règles plus strictes.

Je persiste à croire que L. a agi bien maladroitement envers moi, mais surtout envers vous. D'abord, il redoutait probablement que vous ne proposiez des refontes importantes, parce que vous réfléchissez avec profondeur, avec l'esprit critique aigu & le point de vue de la scène; & cela était timoré, ou sournois, de ne vous envoyer le MS qu'à la dernière minute. De plus (mais je suis sans doute vieille mode là-dessus), je crois que des égards spéciaux vous étaient dus, parce que vous êtes éminente, parce qu'il empiétait sur votre congé, parce que de tels égards sont dus à une dame. Aussi, car je croyais jusqu'à cette semaine que L. avait 25 ou 26 ans, parce qu'il avait l'air de traiter quelqu'un de plus âgé que lui, et moi beaucoup plus âgé, en camarades et avec fort peu de déférence. Je veux encore croire qu'un Français doit avoir plus de courtoisie que cela.

L'autre question me tient plus à cœur. C'est, comme vous le verrez si l'on vous appelle à prendre ma succession, la plus épineuse de toutes celles qui confrontent un chairman. Jusqu'au 15 août dernier environ, nous avions très peu d'étudiants nouveaux inscrits (maigres débouchés, crise économique). Si bien qu'en avril & mai, j'ai fait faire des feuilles décrivant (avantageusement) notre programme & ses attraits & les ai envoyées à 60 ou 80 collèges. Le Doyen nous a enjoint d'offrir un minimum de cours, 8 au 1er semestre, 7 au second; car le Centre Gradué paie aux divers collèges les professeurs donnant ces cours. Or de ces cours, je dois en donner *un* (j'ai renoncé à en donner deux, comme j'ai refusé des cours à Hall ou à d'autres visiteurs que Brody me recommandait). Un doit être d'Histoire de la Langue (Lipton); un chaque trimestre de littérature médiévale (Sas ou Lonigan). Il faut couvrir le 16e, le 17e siècle: donc un cours tous les deux ou trois semestres à Hornik, Szogyi, Hartle, dorénavant Brody. Restent vous, Brooks, Braun, Micheline Braun, Caws, Charney, Loy, Morris, Louria, Waldinger, Weber, Zéphir. (Encore, non sans perfidie, j'élimine du groupe de professeurs X & Y.) Le semestre de printemps 1975, étaient prévus (en principe) Lonigan, Lipton, moi, Loy, Morris, Hornik, Charney, sept cours. Je pensais que nous pourrions en avoir deux autres, aux frais du programme de litt. comparée: Caws (puisque Mrs. Newstead le lui a demandé directement) & vous. J'ai reposé la question pour le vôtre avant hier. C'est Mrs. Cacciopo qui m'a répondu que sans doute ce ne serait pas possible avant l'automne de 1975. J'ai aussitôt écrit à Mrs. Riese, qui remplace Churchill comme Doyen chargé de ces questions, pour dire que j'établissais un cours en sus des sept, parce qu'il était nécessaire, & justifié parce qu'au dernier moment, fin août, en dépit de la prudence de Mrs. Redish, j'ai accepté 4 ou 5 nouveaux étudiants en plus qui me semblaient qualifiés. Il serait tout de même trop fort que, après toute une année d'absence, vous ne soyez pas représentée dans nos programmes encore une autre année! S'il n'est pas payé par la litt. comparée, il le sera par le programme de français, ou sinon je démissionnerai aussitôt. Zéphir, Mme Louria, Weber veulent aussi un cours—mais ils devront attendre.

Mme Newstead n'est pas très coopérative & refuse les avis—du moins les miens. Je lui parlerai à nouveau, ce vendredi—mais je n'ai guère de moyen de contrainte. Elle n'a pas davantage donné de cours à Loy, Szogyi, qui sont "dans sa faculté." En attendant, pourquoi ne pas donner un cours de caractère "comparatif" (théâtre de l'absurde, ou de la cruauté, ou ce que vous voulez) & le faire connaître, en le décrivant, comme comparatif? Ou sur le sujet plus vaste auquel vous avez travaillé cette année. Nous l'annoncerons, et voilà tout. C'est ce que je voulais dire par "un cours en plus"—en plus de ceux qui étaient prévus lorsque je comptais que vous auriez un cours à cheval sur le programme comparé et le nôtre.

Pour un programme slave, il faudra une décision présidentielle—que je crois lointaine, car il est devenu difficile de placer des slavisants

(Mrs. Beaujour, Mrs. Novins). Mais un Centre Gradué sérieux se doit d'établir un tel programme.

Avec toute mon affection,<br>Henri

## À Edward Kaplan:

Le 15 oct. 1974<br>Graduate Center, CUNY, NY 10026

Cher monsieur,

Vous voilà, sur terre ferme et installé, après votre navigation prolongée, mais le livre de Michelet vous avait accoutumé à méditer sur la mer. J'espère que votre année sera calme, pas trop froide(!), féconde, et je vous envie un peu. Il y a, je crois, 40 ou 45 ans que je n'ai passé à Paris une année entière. Il m'arrive de rêver à la vue du Panthéon telle qu'on l'a de l'Arsenal ou du Pont de la Tournelle; non pas que j'admire particulièrement ce mausolée des grands hommes, mais c'est à son ombre que je suis né, puisque j'ai étudié à l'École Normale. Étrangement, presque toute ma carrière s'est faite loin de Paris; peut-être était-ce nécessaire pour continuer à voir la France en beau?

Je ne sais si vous gagnerez beaucoup à suivre régulièrement des séminaires en France. La critique actuelle me semble bien dogmatique & formelle, & je ne suis pas sûr que les livres de Bachelard continuent à être féconds pour nous, littéraires. Mais allez parfois à la 6e section des Hautes Études & Barthes doit s'intéresser à ce que vous faites; et présentez-vous à l'École Normale (M. Bersani peut-être?) et demandez à assister parfois aux séminaires pour agrégatifs. Cela devrait être possible.

J'ai correspondu avec J. Hopkins Press au sujet de votre MS. Il a été envoyé à un lecteur, je ne sais qui, — mais je l'ai recommandé d'une manière générale. C'est toujours un processus laborieux. Une préface? Je doute que vous en ayez besoin, & ce serait sans doute à M. Riffaterre de patronner votre livre, conçu sous son inspiration. Je suis vieux & mon nom n'a plus grand prestige auprès des jeunes.

Pour la même raison, et bien qu'une telle invitation dût m'honorer, je crois que vous devriez recommander à Amherst de plus jeunes que moi pour l'invitation que vous mentionnez. J'ai beaucoup parlé jadis en Amérique & beaucoup écrit. Je le fais encore ces mois-ci, pour essayer d'expliquer & de défendre les humanités, et pour tâcher de remettre en honneur l'étude des langues là où elle a périclité. J'ai encore quelques livres à l'impression. Mais je ne me sens pas en harmonie avec bien des prétentions de la critique récente, et beaucoup de livres parus ces dix dernières années me tombent des mains d'ennui. Je l'ai crié, avec aigreur, dans un article récent "Is literature dead? Or dying?" du *Michigan Quarterly* & je m'en veux à moi-même de manquer de foi dans les tentatives des jeunes. Je cite parfois les belles phrases de foi en la France qu'a tracées Michelet dans ses derniers volumes de l'*Histoire* du XIXe siècle, si difficiles à se procurer d'ailleurs. J'espère qu'ils seront inclus dans la belle édition de Michelet en cours de publication.

Passez une heureuse année, votre famille & vous et croyez à mes vœux cordiaux.

Henri Peyre

## To Harold Proshansky:

October 18, 1974

Dear President Proshansky:

I have meant, since last Thursday, to congratulate you on your stately inauguration ceremony & particularly on your address. It was densely packed with thought & with far-reaching suggestions. I hope it will be printed; several of us might profit from meditating on its theme & on its reflections. Literature & the arts also have a rich contribution to make to the urban environment of the future, and they reveal much about the past of the cities. Is it rash to hope that the humanities & the arts, and the sense of beauty, be not neglected in the events, colloquia and addresses happening at the Graduate Center?

I am embarrassed at seeming to hesitate or to play the coquettish and coy "old maid," when my colleagues and students, with your approval as I take it, have repeatedly asked me to stay on as the "Officer" for the French Program. My hesitation stems in part from the feeling I have that my staying on is prolonging and delaying a decision to assure a rejuvenated future.

But I shall be glad to state, in this informal, hand-scribbled way, that, if you believe it to be in the interests of the Program and of the Center, it will be a pleasure for me to accept the flattering suggestion & to serve for another year.

Gratefully yours,<br>
Henri Peyre

## To James M. Osborn:

October 30—74

Dear Jim:

My private life has been somewhat disturbed these last months. I have had to take care of my little boy, chiefly on week ends, which has not left me much freedom on Friday afternoons. He is a voracious reader & I had even intended to take him, on October 11th, to see your "exhibition." But "dis aliter visum": it proved impossible for me to free myself that day & I missed your lecture. I regretted it much, for I always enjoy your pleasantly informal and richly informing talks. But I have read your address in the Gazette, & cannot resist telling you my admiring appreciation of it—of your tone, personal yet casual & modest, of the shrewdness & devotion, & vast scholarly range, which putting together such a remarkable collection represents. As one who has long been associated with Yale & who may well have been the most voracious devourer of books in the Sterling Library, may I express my gratitude? You have done more for the university, & for those who care about English literature, than most of us who have taught & "run" departments over the years. If I had my way, a statue would be erected to you somewhere on the campus—or perhaps a marble plate would be placed near the "fosse à ours" of the Beinecke, mentioning your wife's insight and tasteful collaboration also. I remember her with fondness, her devoted cooperation with a demanding husband, as you both briskly walked along St. Ronan St. & joyfully embarked on your spring expeditions to Europe. All Yale scholars are grateful to both of you.

Cordially yours,<br>
Henri Peyre

## À Rosette Lamont:

Le 5—11—74

Chère Rosette,

Un mot d'"affaires." On nous demande d'annoncer avant le 13 février les cours de l'an prochain, premier semestre.

L'heure (tardive, mais plus commode pour nos élèves) de jeudi 7–8.50 vous va-t-elle pour "Literature, written by women"? Voulez-vous répondre d'un mot, ou d'un coup de fil, cette semaine, si cela vous agrée—ou si vous avez quelque objection.

J'ai écrit au Doyen ici pour qu'il fasse appel à vous lorsque Ionesco, dont vous êtes le "standard bearer," participera à un Symposium au Graduate Center, le soir du vendredi 29 mars. Serez-vous là alors?

Amitiés toujours,
Henri

## À Eléonore Zimmermann:

Le 9 nov. 1974

Chère amie—ou chère Eléonore, si vous permettez (et ne m'appelez plus "Monsieur," mais "Henri." Cela fait assez d'années que nous nous sommes sentis liés par bien des affinités & des intérêts partagés.)

Bien sûr, j'ai été heureux de savoir de vos nouvelles, & que vous preniez le temps de m'écrire: je ne crois pas que vous ayez jamais montré de ce que l'anglais appelle de "l'indulgence" envers vos maux. Vous n'avez pas abusé de plaintes, certes. Mais je vous ai vue souffrante et luttant avec un courage peu commun contre des douleurs qui ne vous laissaient que bien peu de répit pour le travail. Sans doute, comme pour beaucoup d'entre vous, les graves soucis que vous causait la santé de votre mère, la relative solitude morale où vous viviez à Rochester, avaient joué quelque rôle dans votre affaiblissement physique. Depuis que je vois Lois se déprimer de manière autrement sérieuse, vulnérable à toute allusion innocente ou se forgeant des chimères de persécution, je comprends mieux combien frêle peut être notre moral et combien j'ai été, toute ma vie, injuste ou insensible en conseillant à d'autres la thérapeutique calviniste (ou stoïcienne) du travail & de la sublimation. Mais *vous*, le travail, vous ne l'avez jamais refusé! Et il était héroïque de votre part d'accepter la direction de ce département. Je vous en admire. Et peut-être cette activité, forcément dispersée, qu'exige ce métier de "chairman" vous a telle forcée à triompher de certains maux. Chez moi, il y a des hauts & des bas, d'étranges obsessions; mais il m'est clair que ce n'est pas un avantage pour une très jeune femme, même si elle l'avait voulu et en partie parce qu'elle n'avait pas trouvé chez son père un vrai père, d'épouser un vieil intellectuel desséché: il eût été mieux pour elle de travailler, d'avoir à aider un mari encore jeune à lutter pour se faire une carrière. Bien sûr, le seul spécialiste qu'elle a consenti à consulter attribue son état parfois instable à quelque dérèglement dans la chimie du cerveau ou du système nerveux (elle avait eu des ennuis analogues étant au Collège); mais là encore, moral et "chimique" me paraissent si liés.

Pour le moment, cela va à peu près. Brice se repose sur moi de beaucoup de choses, travaille bien à son école; mais je suis âgé et l'avenir pour lui m'inquiète. En partie pour avoir la distraction que procure un travail bête mais incessant, beaucoup aussi parce que collègues & étudiants m'ont flatté en multipliant les pétitions aux autorités, je viens d'accepter de rester encore une année à ce Centre. Le travail y "rend," en ce sens que, paradoxalement alors que les positions se font rares, nous attirons apparemment des étudiants de qualité très haute. Cela nous vaudra quelque jalousie de Columbia & NYU; mais rend le travail riche de récompenses — et les professeurs sont doués & coopératifs.

Vous êtes toujours "racinienne" à vos moments de liberté. Quelques-uns le sont autour de moi (Brody, et Doubrovsky, que je vois moins) et mettent là des subtilités psychanalytiques qui me semblent éclairer bien peu l'œuvre elle-même. Il y a trop de critiques, et de critiques d'une intelligence raffinée à l'excès, mais dépourvue d'humilité. Le livre de Knight avait bien des lourdeurs & des longueurs; mais il était honnête, droit dans sa consciencieuse information, et sage. Récemment, j'ai (à part Pascal, que personne autre ne veut enseigner) fait des cours surtout sur soit le XVIe siècle, soit le roman du XIXe & la poésie du Symbolisme. Un jour, je vous enverrai quelques tirages à part, mais la grève postale en France a retardé les épreuves de livres que je devais recevoir. Il y a de pires malheurs!

J'ai gardé un bien bon souvenir de notre rencontre chez les Bieber. Vous avez des collègues pleins de charme & de savoir, et ils vous sont dévoués avec affection. J'entends tellement parler de désunion et d'animosités dans d'autres "départements" que le dévouement à une tâche commune que je crois sentir dans le vôtre me paraît le plus enviable des biens. Je crois trouver le même esprit là où je termine ma carrière.

Dites mes amitiés à Bieber, Petrey, Haac & croyez à mes vœux pleins d'affection.

Henri Peyre

## To the University of Alabama Press:

Nov. 22/74

Dear Mrs. DeMellier:

I lose no time in returning this MS, since you have imposed such a tight schedule on yourself. All your queries are excellent & so are the corrections. The editing has been done with admirable care. I believe I have answered all the questions.

I shall return the "Author's Questionnaire" in another mail, along with the articles, when they reach me.

I have typed two additions to be made to the footnotes 4 & 7. I hope they are clear.

Many thanks for everything. This MS has been so long in the works that I feel quite detached from it!

Sincerely yours,
Henri Peyre

## To the same:

290 North Avenue
Westport, Conn. 06880
Dec. 21—74

Dear Mrs. DeMellier:

I am sorry that my modest essays seem to require such attention & time. I sometimes despair of ever seeing that little book in print in my lifetime! But your corrections are careful & your queries well meant — all of them acceptable to me. I am no stickler for uniformity in print, I confess: an author's mannerisms (my preference for "which" over too many "that," for instance) are an expression of his personality. Baudelaire, W. Whitman & C. G. Jung have all asserted the sacred right for an author to contradict himself. . . .

But editors will have their way!

I keep away from conventions now—after having been too conspicuous in them in the past. I shall not appear at the NY one, but I wish you a good trip there, & some rest after that & happy New Year.

Sincerely yours,
Henri Peyre

## À James Lawler:

Le 21 décembre 1974

Cher ami,

Je ne vous ai pas trop envié de passer ces mois de grisaille dans une France inquiète, privée de communications postales, harassée par ses divisions politiques. Mais l'Amérique ne valait pas beaucoup mieux, comme moral du moins; et le ciel & le soleil & les couleurs de la Californie du Sud ne sont peut-être pas aussi nostalgiquement regrettées par ceux qui ont habité là-bas que par les visiteurs hâtifs comme moi. J'espère que pour votre femme et vous les choses se sont néanmoins bien passées. La vie intellectuelle reste stimulante, au moins parmi critiques et historiens; les romanciers me semblent, eux, ennuyeux & ennuyés, les expositions d'art sont attrayantes. Il y a si longtemps que je n'ai pas passé un automne à Paris. L'éducation de vos enfants ne souffre-t-elle pas de tous ces déménagements? Vous avez l'adaptabilité et l'esprit aventureux de pionniers; je me sens si bourgeois en comparaison.

Mon travail à New York reste lourd, surtout en raison de la rareté des postes et du nombre de "gradués" doués que je voudrais placer; et aussi, forcément, par suite de la paperasserie toujours croissante et des possibilités de dissension dans une faculté composée de gens doués, mais hypersensibles et gratifiés—ou affligés—d'un moi un peu gonflé. Mais je vais bien moi-même et ne vois pas de raison de me plaindre. L'interruption de Noël, puis l'allégement du travail de cours & de routine en janvier vont me permettre de lire davantage.

J'ai lu, avec beaucoup de joie intellectuelle, votre nouvel ouvrage. Même les articles que je connaissais, repris ici, m'ont ravi: j'en ai relu certains deux fois, le texte de "Sinistre" ou de "Semiramis" devant moi.

Sur ce poème, que j'avais toujours traité légèrement, votre chapitre est une révélation: vous avez tout à fait raison de le placer aussi haut. Votre chapitre sur "Valéry & Mallarmé" est riche de textes nouveaux & de réflexions aiguës; vos remarques sur Poe également, à propos d'Eliot, souvent pompeux, distant et en fin de compte mal informé en ce qui concernait Valéry. Par quelque mauvaise humeur, sans doute, d'avoir vu trop de gens louer Valéry après 1925–30, et de ne plus pouvoir me considérer comme l'un des "happy few" qui l'avaient les premiers aimé, je résiste aux poèmes plus tardifs de Valéry, et parfois à sa prose d'officiel. Mais, avec l'aide de vos articles sur les *Cahiers,* de Mrs. Robinson, de la récente édition, je reprendrai un de ces jours les Cahiers, qui m'avaient impatienté dans leur format premier. Je goûte dans votre critique l'absence de ton dogmatique, de tout jargon, de tout sacrifice à la mode; et comment, avec sûreté et goût, vous unissez une rare science (de variantes, chronologie de la composition, métrique) à une admiration personnelle, passionnée et communicative. C'est, curieusement, de Grande Bretagne et d'Australie que nous est venu le meilleur, de beaucoup, sur Valéry. Merci, et de l'envoi si gracieux de votre livre, et d'être le critique & "l'amateur de poèmes" que vous êtes.

    Je serai impatient de vous lire sur Char. Mary Ann Caws avec audace le traduit et l'élucide, sans jamais avoir froissé son ombrageuse susceptibilité. Elle est merveilleuse, elle aussi, de dévouement à la poésie française.

    Peut-être serez-vous plus proche de nous ce printemps. La Nouvelle Écosse, où je n'ai jamais été, est pour moi un pays à demi fabuleux. J'espère que vous vous y plaisez et que l'hiver n'y sera pas trop inclément.

> Croyez à mes vœux pleins d'amitié,
> Henri Peyre

## To Florence & Kurt Weinberg:

Jan. 15—75

Dear Florence & Kurt,

    May this year bring you some peace of mind, plenty of leisure & serene enjoyment of your beautiful art works which impressed me most, many years ago! For me, things go well or fairly well professionally, for the job in NY brings many rewards & I have become quite attached to several very gifted persons there among the students. At home, there are problems; Lois has had moments of depression & leads a very solitary life, away from all her former friends & from her family. She is very kind to Brice who does not suffer too much from that. He needs a change, however, & on weekends & vacations I take him to Westport (290, North Avenue, 06880) where I spend much time with a lady, mother of three sons, one of Brice's age, who is very kind to him & to me. I go to NY often, but after another year, I plan to stop & perhaps to travel abroad more, if my health does not fail me.

I read much, & even write, but I feel more & more out of touch &, what is worse, out of sympathy, with recent criticism & bored by much fiction. It is one of the privileges of age that one may be blunt and unconcerned with fads. I do reread *your* writers (Kafka, Valéry, Gide — & even the Greeks) & teach Pascal. I may even, some day, get to like Rabelais!

Dear Florence. Of course, I shall & should always, be more than glad to write about your achievement & merits. No one has asked me yet. Nor has the Princeton or Rochester Press approached me on the Faust MS. I do not deserve any thanks from Kurt.

> With very heart felt wishes & most cordially,
> Henri

## To Norman & Mrs. McIntosh:

Jan. 26 — 75

Dear friends,

You are admirably faithful to old memories & punctual & that touches me. There you are, ready to retire to the Northwest, after having lived at the two other corners of America, North East & Extreme South: & near a son who will some day be attorney general of US, & a cultured & refined one at that, like his parents. I, so very much older than you, feel like an obstinate die-hard in not having yet withdrawn into silence. I hope to, however, in 1976 & it is with much reluctance that I have accepted to teach & administer one more year at the CUNY Graduate Center. There is so much bureaucracy there, & there are so many fine

& worthwhile Ph.D. candidates, in whose problems (scholarly, career & family) I have to be involved.

The state of the world fills one with gloom; the greed, ambition & corruption everywhere; but, for me, especially in America where I had come, decades ago, hoping to find the new Eden of honesty & purity, are saddening. But it is a comfort to think of the persons like you two who, through the years & living in small, isolated communities, have maintained your love of poetry. I am having 2 or 3 books out these days—my last ones, I trust, & they deal with Symbolism & Verlaine & poetical topics.

You will soon be living in one of the few American states which I do not know, & I doubt I'll ever go there now—I am too old. But, in my dim knowledge of geography & vague dreams, I imagine it as rich with the poetry of forests, leaping rivers & spacious harbors. I hope your years of peace there will be happy ones.

Very cordially yours,<br>
Henri Peyre<br>
2066 Yale Station

## To Robert G. Cohn:

February 6—1975<br>
290 North Avenue<br>
Westport, Conn. 06880

Dear Bob,

Snow, sleet, & the worst face of winter around us—"La saison redoutée du confort" for you, in the Californian Eden! You must be clipping your rose-bushes & taking naps under your banana trees.

This is just a line accompanying a request. Diane McCormick & I would like the MLA to include, for next December convention, a discussion seminar on "The City in French literature." Mrs. McCormick is working on that theme & I, platonically, have been angered & disgusted by the recent program, with its proliferation of groups on the lesbians, the gays, the redskins, the impotents, the masturbators, *et al.* in literature. Those petitions require some ten signatures, & I thought it would be a good thing if they came from varied geographical areas. If you feel like signing the enclosed one & returning it, will you kindly do so? If not, just forget about it.

Affectionately to you and your wife,<br>Henri

## À Rosette Lamont:

Le 17 mars 1975

Chère Rosette,

Quelle chaude & délicieuse atmosphère l'autre soir, quelle grâce hospitalière de vous et de votre mari, qui vous comprend, vous seconde & vous inspire si bien! Ce champagne de marque convenait merveilleusement à la pétillante chinoiserie & faisait oublier la tempête au dehors. Chacun souriait & riait aux délicates plaisanteries des manipulateurs de ces séduisantes marionnettes. La dame au nez pointu couronnée de diamants rappelait quelque directrice du programme de littérature comparée . . . Diane en avait oublié son impatience de mère qui lui fait dix fois par jour soupirer: "Ah! Ces garçons! Quelle plaie! Dans mon autre vie, je ne veux que des filles, comme Rosette & Bettina!" Et vous aviez un choix d'invités éminents et pleins de cordialité affable et simple. Une fois encore, merci d'être une si généreuse et inspirante hôtesse.

Avec notre double amitié,<br>Henri

## À James Lawler:

Graduate Center, CUNY<br>33 W. 42nd St., NY 10036<br>March 20—1975

Cher ami,

J'avais cru que je vous reverrais peut-être à votre passage à N.Y. Mais nous avons dû nous manquer: je ne suis pas là chaque jour, & les voyages depuis votre "Ultima Thulé" (comme je l'imagine) ne doivent pas être aisés. Mais vous savez que j'ai pour vous, non seulement la plus haute estime professionnelle, mais amitié aussi, & chaude appréciation de votre élégance spirituelle, de votre réserve, de ces qualités que je crois anglo-saxonnes & dont un long séjour en Amérique vous déshabitue. J'ai moi-même, peut-être comme séquelle de mon éducation protestante, ou par réaction de défense, quelque pudeur "virile" qui répugne à l'expression des sentiments. Mais il me serait agréable de savoir si ce pays vous plaît, si votre femme s'y est accoutumée sans peine, si vos enfants ne souffrent pas de ces dépaysements répétés, et si les conditions de travail sont tout de même convenables à Dalhousie. Je sais bien peu de chose du Canada, en vérité, & ne me suis jamais aventuré au delà de Québec.

Ces semaines-ci pour moi sont pleines d'"oraux" de Ph.D., & de lecture des thèses de 7 ou 8 docteurs que nous allons lancer sur le marché en juin—sans savoir encore où ils échoueront. La besogne pour le "chairman" est lourde, mais je survis. La santé de Lois semble un peu plus stable, à condition qu'elle se tienne fort isolée et presque séquestrée. Je me suis plongé, à mes heures libres (mais il en faudrait beaucoup), dans la lecture systématique des Cahiers dans La Pléiade—parfois avec irritation, je l'avoue—et je sais que vous & Mrs. Robinson aurez honte de mon philistinisme. Mais que de répétitions, que de rabachages, et pourquoi tant de combats contre philosophie, psychologie & autres moulins à vent! Et quelle étrange obstination à tout vouloir noter, & à le conserver pour la postérité. Cette grande intelligence manquait d'humilité, de charité, parfois même d'humour ou de critique de soi-même. Elle ne dédaignait pas assez la coquetterie—la même qu'il reprochait à la vieille coquette de Gide!

Cela m'a fait goûter davantage encore votre livre, si sobre, si noble de ton, précis en outre, & où vous vous attachez à la poésie et la *sentez* & la faites sentir. Votre essai dans *Critiques* III (publication que je ne connaissais pas) m'a également enchanté. En quelques lignes, sur Degas, Léonard, rapports entre peinture & poésie, vous suggérez beaucoup. D'autres chapitres de ce livre, à côté du vôtre, m'ont déçu. Mais j'ai goûté les deux premiers, de Sitner & de Lynton. Cet échec de notre métier m'a beaucoup hanté, toutes ces années. Nous conceptualisons, intellectualisons tout; mais la critique nous offusque & nous n'enseignons ni à sentir avec intensité & sensualité, ni à imaginer. Peut-être n'est ce pas en notre pouvoir de faire autre chose?

Mais je vous ennuie de ces banales réflexions. Ce mot n'avait d'autre objet que celui de vous remercier du plaisir & du profit que je trouve à tout ce que vous écrivez.

Croyez à mes très bons vœux & à mes très amicaux sentiments.

Henri Peyre

## To Stanley Burnshaw:

April 4—75

Dear Stanley,

The winter has been a good one on the whole for us. Brice is very well, successful at school & apparently undisturbed by his being taken back & forth. Lois seems much more stable in health—in fact, very contented with her rather solitary life & not having to care for me & to feel guilty for not being active as a housewife. She still harbors grievances against her parents & refuses to see her mother who, when she goes through New Haven, has to spend the night at friends. But it seems best not to force Lois, not even to see a psychiatrist. I have given up on that. I am well myself, but very active: I seem to get involved, not only in thesis directing, but in committee work & in reforming things, wherever I go. I shall try & be firm in my decision to quit everything in 1976—even writing. I have had a couple of books out in France (& in French) last month & I'll have one or two over here; but present-day literature, & criticism especially, fail to hold my interest nowadays. I read chiefly in history & politics.

Future plans? I have none. I may go over to Europe this summer, for a few weeks, with the child. I doubt we'll try Martha's Vineyard again: the beaches here at Westport are pleasant & I continue to use the Yale Library even in summer. If I were a poet like you, or a profound thinker & ardent enough a lover of nature, I could meditate in a lonely place, surrounded with trees & flowers. But I am too bookish & too fretful a person for that. I do entertain vague dreams of visiting Iran, but they are only dreams. Some day, in NY, you'll tell me all about your trip.

I'll try to answer your question on quiet places in France: though, in truth, I am no longer informed on prices, quality of cuisine, quietude, etc., in that country, where I am only a tourist when I go now.

The best thing for Blumenthal to do is to consult the admirable Guide Michelin (the big, red one; the 1975 should be out soon). I have only the 1971 here: there (on pp. 58–61) is a list, very special, on "pleasant, very quiet, secluded hotels," marked in red on the maps. Quite a few of them are in the Provence region & on or near the Mediterranean coast. The prices, of course, have changed since 1971—but it is easy to see the *relative* expensiveness of the inns.

I have stayed at "La Colombe d'or" at St. Paul de Vence: artistic, lovely, very busy at lunch, quiet the rest of the time, 3 miles from Vence. I enjoyed it much. There are many restaurants nearby. I have eaten, very pleasantly, at Fayence (Var), 27 kil. from Grasse, Hôtel "France," place de la République—closed, says the guide, from May 15 to June 15. At Èze (Alpes Maritimes), I heard the "Mas Provençal" well spoken of: avenue de Verdun.

I have stayed, at Villeneuve-les-Avignon (Gard), at l'Atelier & liked it immensely: small, picturesque (5, rue de la Foire), no meals except breakfast; very nice people. Close by, meals can be had (expensive) at Le Prieuré & at Hostellerie du Vieux Moulin, also in Villeneuve. During the Avignon festival (July, I guess), those places might be noisier, but I doubt it. Les Baux is expensive & one is a prisoner there; it is too isolated. Roussillon, in the Vaucluse, is very pleasant; hot probably in Summer: Rose d'or & David are the two hotels there. Vence has several hotels (Diana, the most pleasant, I believe), avenue des Poilus, & there are 2 or 3 hotels in Grasse, with many restaurants around: Bellevue, Beau Soleil.

In May, I think your friends might not have to reserve & could try their luck once there, if they have a car—*except* for the Pentecost (Whitsuntide) weekend, always excessively busy. That is by definition 50 days after Easter. They would, I take it, be in Southern France before May 18 (Pentecost). I'll envy them.

      Many cordial regards to you & Leda & best of wishes.
      Henri Peyre

## To the University of Alabama Press:

April 26—1975
290 North Ave.
Westport, Conn. 06880

Dear Mrs. DeMellier:

The proofs were sent you in a Fourth Class package, insured, on April 22. The Index follows herewith. I think it far better not to type it, for it might be a source of mistakes & delay the completion of this long delayed work even further. It seems clear as it stands. If proofs of the Index may be gone over by someone at your office, fine. If not, I'll read them. My address as above will reach me until June 15th. I then plan to be away in Europe for some weeks & to be not easy to reach while moving about.

Thank you for your constant help in all this.

Sincerely yours,
Henri Peyre

## To the same:

290 North Ave.
Westport, Conn. 06880
May 1, 1975

Dear Mrs. DeMellier:

You may by now have received both the proofs & the MS of the Index, & my note in which I was telling you of my probable absence from June 20 to July 20, while I travel in Europe. I forget whether I added, since the question often is asked, that my Social Security number, if needed, is 046-26-4270, & my citizenship, French (for copyright purposes).

Now on the Romanticism book: I agree that the title should remain "What is Romanticism?" as was the case for the Spanish translation.

Also do as you wish about using *only* the chapter titles on the contents page; & I agree that the French text, for *all* but the verse quotations, could well be eliminated. For the quotations in verse, the French alone might suffice in my opinion—or else place the French verse in the notes, as you like.

As to grouping all the notes together at the end of the book, do it if it does save money considerably. But every author & every reader regrets that necessity, since it often means that no one but a few persistent researchers reads the footnotes. Let the policy at your Press prevail, if financial considerations *must* come first.

I am not too anxious to check the edited copy & I would rather trust your own competence & decision there. As to the proofs, if you truly think I should go over them, I'll do it—depending upon *when* they come, for I shall be busy in the Fall & I am at work on another MS in English this Summer. I'll be ready & willing to do what's best for you & the book, of course.

Sincerely yours,<br>Henri Peyre

## To James M. Osborn:

May 16/75

Dear Jim,

Many congratulations on your joining the [American] Academy [of Arts and Letters]. I don't often go there these days, for it is hard of access & I am often too busy elsewhere. But your belonging to it makes me all the more proud to be one of the venerables.

Cordially,<br>Henri Peyre

## À Jorge Guillén:

Henri Peyre<br>290 North Ave.<br>Westport, Conn. 06880<br>Ce 4 juin 1975

Bien cher ami,

Votre mot, que m'a transmis Mme Lida, m'a profondément touché. Que de souvenirs il a fait affluer en moi! De tous les hommes que j'ai rencontrés dans ma longue vie, vous êtes celui que j'ai pu aimer autant que l'admirer. Une certaine pudeur masculine nous empêche trop souvent de dire nos sentiments & nos pensées les plus personnels. Mais cette belle simplicité que vous avez toujours mise dans l'amitié, cette chaleur d'âme dont vous avez le secret, contrastant avec la sobriété évocatrice de votre poésie, sont des dons si rares! Plus je me suis enfoncé dans cette profession (que je m'apprête enfin à quitter), plus je me suis senti chagriné & ulcéré par les petitesses, les querelles, les envies de ces mesquins universitaires. Vous êtes délivré de ces sottises.

Je sais que votre fils s'est acquis une grande réputation de critique & de maître: cela doit vous réjouir. Comment va Gilman, & votre fille? Sans doute vous rendez-vous encore en Europe les étés. Je vais moi-même y aller pour quelques semaines.

Rappelez-moi au souvenir de votre femme, que je n'ai rencontrée que trop rarement, et croyez à ma toujours vive affection.

Henri Peyre

## À Mary Ann Caws:

Le 21—VI—75

Chère Mary Ann,

Je penserai à vous en longeant, dans le train, le Rhône entre Valence, Orange, Avignon. La vue des Alpilles et du Lubéron—chargée de souvenirs d'excursions d'adolescent pour moi, m'émeut toujours. Je parcourais les routes en vélo (non moteur), buvant aux sources, me croyant amoureux, récitant de la poésie (Musset! Hugo!). J'aimais Maillane, Mirabeau, le Mont Ventoux. Ni touristes alors, ni artistes. Nul ne regardait les abbayes romanes—et il n'y avait point de "relais" gastronomique.

La nouvelle de Char malade, effrayé par l'affaiblissement & la mort peut-être, m'attriste. Je m'en veux souvent d'être resté plus fort que beaucoup de mon âge; j'ai pourtant travaillé ferme toute ma vie, & bu du vin chaque jour (sauf pendant les années de prohibition ici). En secret, j'invoquais les dieux du polythéisme païen.

Vous êtes courageuse, de rester gaie, poète & animatrice de nous tous, alors que vous savez votre père se mourant, luttant... Je vous admire, mais ne vous laissez pas abattre & voyagez néanmoins cet été et n'écoutez pas trop ces dentistes toujours prêts à mutiler les "chrysostomes" comme vous; ils m'ont persécuté toute ma vie et voulaient me réduire au mutisme.

 Ne vous inquiétez pas si vous touchez à Villon, Scève et al. Vous le ferez dans un esprit tout autre que X & Z & nul ne vous en voudra. Mais j'inscris votre autre suggestion pour le cours & vous déciderez.

Amitiés,<br>Henri

Nous reviendrons vers le 20 juillet & il y a des documents supplémentaires à fournir à cette "Fleming" commission. Que de menues tracasseries.

 Mille choses aux enfants

## À Eléonore Zimmermann:

290 North Avenue<br>Westport, Conn. 06880<br>Le 20 juillet 75

Bien chère amie,

 Je rentre de France, après un tour rapide dans le Midi, où j'ai encore un frère, un passage à St. Paul de Vence, puis à Florence, Rome, Séville—et je trouve votre lettre parmi bien d'autres. Vite, je veux vous dire la part que je prends à votre chagrin. Je sais que cela n'était pas inattendu; qu'en un sens, après des années d'angoisse, quand l'espoir d'une vraie guérison n'est plus permis, on devrait souhaiter une fin sereine. Mais je sais aussi combien il y a en vous de sensibilité, de capacité d'affection, d'attachement aux vôtres. Il y a bien longtemps, j'avais également perdu ma mère lorsque j'étais en Amérique—pas d'avion alors, pas de possibilité de voyage rapide—et j'avais été tourmenté du remords de m'être expatrié, de regret de la vie plus calmement provinciale que j'aurais pu avoir en France. Et vous avez, bien plus que moi, finesse de sensibilité et peut-être vulnérabilité. Et, seule, malgré le rare don que vous avez d'attirer de profondes amitiés, vous avez dû être travaillée plus encore de ces sentiments de regret, de révolte contre la stupidité de la souffrance qui ne peut aboutir qu'à la mort. Soudain, même au milieu de la vie, on sent qu'on n'a plus personne au devant de soi pour vous protéger, ou à protéger. Peut-être devriez-vous faire venir votre père pour quelque temps. Je ne sais rien de lui, mais il m'a toujours semblé que j'aimerais le rencontrer. Après quelques mois, le souvenir des années d'anxiété s'efface et les souvenirs antérieurs, plus radieux, prennent leur place et consolent. Et, bien sûr, le travail aide: le vôtre, surtout, qui n'a jamais été mécanique ou en surface, dans lequel vous vous mettez avec plénitude. J'espère que votre propre santé a résisté à ces durs moments, à ces voyages.

C'est une merveilleuse nouvelle que vous deviez aller à Berkeley pour un temps. Le décor est le plus beau de l'Amérique; le changement vous distraira. . . .

Qu'y a-t-il donc dans notre profession qui rende ainsi les gens aigris, querelleurs? C'est pourtant l'une des moins accablantes de toutes (sauf pour les "administrateurs"!), et on y côtoie sans cesse le beau et le grand. . . .

## To the University of Alabama Press:

August 10—1975

Dear Mrs. DeMellier:

My congratulations on the birth of your baby. What great news! & in these rather gloomy days, what a splendid act of faith in the future!

I hope that unfortunate volume of mine will appear soon. It must be close to two years since it was first sent to your Press & I confess I never have encountered such an interminable delay before. I have written, & seen through the Press & actually published, two or three other volumes since! I am old & therefore do not feel that the whole future is mine.

As to the *Romanticism* book in translation, I do not need to bother about the proofs unless there are specific questions on which I need to be consulted. Our academic year starts again early in September & I shall be very busy then.

With best wishes & very sincerely then,
Henri Peyre

## To Kurt & Florence Weinberg:

Grad Center, CUNY
33 W. 42nd St. NY 10036
Sept. 19—75

Dear Florence & Dear Kurt,

My congratulations on your return from Europe & on your promotion. I was in Spain for a while with Brice & I enjoyed revisiting & confronting old memories. I had liked Portugal years ago, but felt somewhat embarrassed at enjoying a fascist country & profiting from the poverty of the masses. Perhaps communism would be the solution? After all we read of the CIA & Ford's stupidity & the shameful corruption here, we do not feel too proud. I am winding up my career with some melancholy about the pitiful state of language & humanistic studies. Your university of Rochester is a case in point. It should have one of the best departments in the country, since the place is wealthy & inherited fine traditions. But . . . alas!

Here things are chaotic, with a big increase in the cost for the students & drastic economies to be achieved. Still we have excellent entering students, quite a few of them from Europe, & they are eager, & rash enough to face the prospect, which I make clear to them, of no job when they finish.

Congratulations on the Faust. A close reading of the two volumes of Cahiers exasperated me against Valéry's negativism & his repetitions. Yet there were gems here & there, & even emotion when he wrote on dreams, & on love. I suppose I'll remain an inveterate romantic to the end.

Have a happy academic year,
& most cordially yours,
Henri

## À Hélène et Pierre Pennec:

Le 24 sept. 75

Une partie considérable de ma besogne professionnelle consiste à chercher pour nos candidats de doctorat des sujets de thèse faisables, circonscrits, pas trop ambitieux (car il y a ici une limite de temps de 2 à 3 ans pour écrire une thèse) et pas récemment traité ailleurs. La rentrée est bonne—bonne et attristante à la fois. Il y a des étudiants, et surtout des étudiantes, pleines de promesse, douées, zélées—3 ou 4 sur 12 nouvelles sont françaises. Mais je dois leur dire bien clairement qu'il risque de n'y avoir pas de poste quand leurs études seront finies et que le temps et l'argent passés et commis à cette besogne de longue haleine risquent d'être gaspillés. La Ville de NewYork est en plus graves difficultés que jamais: il ne semble pas possible d'y éviter la faillite. On vient de doubler les frais d'études, ou d'inscription: 2000 dollars par an (c'est 3800 à Yale ou Columbia). Mais ces malheureux jeunes gens, ne trouvant pas d'emploi, ont le courage de vouloir néanmoins prendre des cours et étudier la littérature. Il paraît que tel était le cas aussi lors de la dépression plus grave encore de 1929–39.

. . . (Diane) est aussi pour plus de justice aux Corses, car elle adore les causes idéalistes. Pour moi, j'abandonnerais volontiers la Corse aux Italiens, à l'Algérie, ou même à Israël. L'autonomie régionale a du bon sur le papier. Mais ici où on voit de près la politicaillerie des minorités ethniques, le refus d'un état d'en aider un autre (New York par exemple, qui est dans le marasme), les groupes de telle origine raciale ou religieuse demandant des faveurs spéciales, on est tenté de réfléchir. Les Corses, les Auvergnats, les Bretons, s'ils imitaient l'Amérique, exigeraient un nombre d'étudiants, d'agrégés, d'inspecteurs des finances, etc., proportionnel à leur population. Ici, il n'y a plus que les malheureux Indiens qui ne demandent pas l'accès aux universités en nombre proportionnel à leur population. Mais ça viendra. . . .

## To the University of Alabama Press:

Henri Peyre
290 North Avenue
Westport, Conn. 06880
Sept. 26—1975

Dear Mr. Walters:

Thank you for the clipping you sent me. I'll be looking forward to receiving copies of the volume in the near future. It has been in the works so long that I have almost forgotten its content.

Incidentally, my address has since changed & is as above. Could you kindly pass it on to the person who may be in charge of sending me the author's copies?

Thank you & sincerely,<br>Henri Peyre

## À Rosette Lamont:

Le 3 oct. 75

Ma chère Rosette,

Cette soirée était inoubliable. Votre mère est une admirable personne, qui vous comprend, vous aide, avec une gentillesse comme on devait avoir dans la vieille Russie—avec grâce & courage. On comprend combien elle a dû faire pour votre personnalité, riche & si vivante, pour votre succès & combien elle a mis d'affection dans votre vie. S'il y avait vingt femmes comme elles, & comme vous, au monde, qui hésiterait à être féministe? Et votre mari n'est pas moins compréhensif, lui, si expert constructeur & décorateur, qui consent à emplir nos verres de nectar, sait converser avec chacun, & devine avec un sourire avisé tout ce que nous essayons de dire en français rapide.

Nous avons, Diane & moi, beaucoup aimé vos invités. M. Soudet est un homme de cœur, un idéaliste en politique en même temps qu'un grand homme d'affaires—et l'intellectuel idéal qui *vit* ses idées & n'ignore rien de la "praxis." Nous avons cru comprendre qu'ils ont subi tous les deux un grand malheur—mais ils savent égayer les autres et s'oublier eux-mêmes. J'ai peu parlé avec l'autre monsieur, assez pourtant pour deviner l'acuité de son esprit: sa femme est tout à fait remarquable—d'une intelligence vive, très personnelle et d'un sens littéraire très fin.

Merci d'une soirée—comme on en a rarement ici—dans ce beau décor. Nous en sommes revenus tout exaltés. Voulez-vous dire notre très vraie reconnaissance à votre mère & à Mr. Farmer.

Tout à vous,<br>Henri

## À la même:

Le 6 oct. 75

Chère Rosette,

Deux mots sur la thèse de Mme C. Les paroles de Mrs. Caws vous ont été mal rapportées. Elle n'a nullement insinué qu'elle avait trop peu de temps et trop de projets & que vous en aviez moins! Mais qu'elle n'éprouve guère de sympathie pour le sujet, pour la méthode (ou l'absence de méthode) de la candidate, & qu'elle risquerait de lui demander de tout refaire selon une optique qui ne serait pas celle de Mad C., mais celle de Mrs. Caws—& cela ne serait pas juste.

Mrs. C. vous a eue quand elle était undergraduate à Hunter. Elle pense que vous seriez, non pas moins sévère, mais plus compréhensive à ses efforts. Elle vous serait reconnaissante si vous acceptiez de la guider, et tout le programme le serait. Je ne vois guère que vous, ou Mrs. Knapp, qui aurait pour le sujet quelque sympathie—ou Sidney Braun peut-être? Mrs. C. devait à l'origine faire cette thèse avec G. Mais nous avons laissé G. en dehors de notre faculté désormais.

Quant au reste, ayant lu les deux chapitres que m'a passés Mrs. C., je dois dire qu'ils sont loin d'être au point—et pour la forme (gauche, monotone, répétitive) et pour le contenu. Je n'arrive pas à saisir ce qu'elle veut faire. C'est mal défini, confus. Je dois ajouter que je n'ai jamais admiré Lautréamont, & je manque de sympathie pour ce mauvais romantisme enfantin; et probablement de compréhension de ces secrets freudiens, hystériquement sexuels, "baudelairiens," peut-être, mais fort peu de "mon" Baudelaire.

Mrs. C. vous parlera. Si vous ne désirez pas vous charger de ce fardeau (car c'en sera un), nous verrons à lui trouver un autre "directeur." Peut-être n'aurait-elle jamais dû arriver jusqu'au Ph.D.? Mais elle est déterminée. Vous me conseillerez.

Bien amicalement,
HP

## To the University of Alabama Press:

[No date]

Dear Mr. Walters:

I shall certainly be honored to have a book of mine translated by Mr. Parker, whom I greatly esteem. If I can elucidate any points for him, I shall be glad to assist.

On the *Romanticism* book, I thought I had communicated repeatedly & fully with the translator & told her that, except for her preface, I doubted anything more should be added to an already long book.

I shall look forward to the first copies of the other one when they are finally ready. Many thanks for your kindness,

Very sincerely yours,
Henri Peyre

## To the same:

Nov. 8/75

Dear Miss Nichols:

Your Press, decidedly, has no luck & I do not bring it any! Sorry about the sudden departure of the editor who was laboring over my *Romanticism*. I fear she may have found the book too dull for her. And the delays to the appearance of the Dostoevsky volume seem to be ever more prolonged! Perhaps I shall still see it before I die. I am well, but very old.

Sincerely,
Henri Peyre

## À Vera Lee:

Le 19 — XI — 75

Chère amie,

Quel gracieux, élégant, ingénieux livre; et plein de vivacité, écrit avec joie, ce qui est bien rare dans nos études, jamais facile ou vulgarisé —

primesautier et gai! Je vous en félicite; et votre éditeur, qui doit être une homme de goût & de courage. Je l'ai lu d'un trait, souvent avec un sourire intérieur, & avec le sentiment d'y retrouver la jeune femme connue jadis, et restée jeune.

Que fait votre fille, que je n'ai jamais oubliée? Étudiante? Mariée? Rêvant de ressembler à sa mère, à Mlle de Lespinasse ou à Mme Roland?

Croyez bien à mes remerciements de ce beau cadeau & à mon fidèle souvenir.

Henri Peyre

## To the University of Alabama Press:

Dec. 14/75

Dear Mr. Walters:

Will you forgive me if I ask you to do your best so that my author's copies of the recent "Dostoevsky & other essays" volume be sent to me soon? I would wish to send some to the European reviews which might review the volume, before the summer lull sets in.

If your colleagues wish me to list the six or eight leading reviews in this country (French literature, Comparative Lit) to which review copies should be sent *soon,* I shall be glad to do it. If I need to order extra author's copies, could I be told at what rate?

With thanks & my best wishes,
Henri Peyre

## À Florence et Kurt Weinberg:

Le 20 déc. 1975

Chers amis,

Noël a peut-être du bon, malgré toutes les imprécations que je lance à cette saison de tapageuses réclames & d'achats stupides, puisqu'elle me vaut de vos nouvelles. Florence est l'optimiste de vous deux: elle accroît même le nombre de ses élèves, donc de ses admirateurs. De divers côtés, j'entends dire que le latin reprend, qu'on songe même à restaurer des "requirements." Kurt, lui, est le pessimiste. Comme les gens qui avaient souffert en Europe & espéré en Amérique une vie neuve et un milieu plus généreux (c'est aussi mon cas), il est déçu et amer. Cela est triste en effet, au soir d'une carrière, de voir le beau, l'art, la pensée malmenés, nos études dans ce qu'elles ont de plus humain désertées par la mode; pour moi, de trouver si difficile de caser des étudiants qui comptent parmi les plus doués que j'aie jamais eus.

J'ai persisté cependant à enseigner et à "diriger," parce qu'on m'assure que je maintiens un haut niveau, une atmosphère paisible et que j'évite (ou, simplement, je ne sais pas voir) les dissidences. Nous formons quelques étudiants vraiment de premier ordre. Mais notre "Centre" ne sait s'il aura les fonds nécessaires pour se maintenir, et les politiciens font un sot chantage.

Ne vous découragez pas cependant. Les choses ne vont pas mieux ailleurs dans le monde. Il m'arrive de relire des écrits de Kurt et je suis plein d'admiration pour leur richesse et les ouvertures de vues qu'ils apportent. Sa subtilité même me fascine, parce qu'elle me dépasse. Patientons encore. L'Amérique ira peut-être mieux dans quelques années & vous êtes assez jeunes pour attendre.

Mes vœux vous accompagnent en cette fin d'année.

Henri Peyre

## À G. Mombello:

>Graduate Center
>The City University
>33 W. 42nd St., N. York 10036
>Le 22 déc. 1975

Cher Collègue,

Je serai certainement heureux, flatté et fier de faire partie du Comité de Patronage du volume d'hommages que vous pensez recueillir pour mon ami Franco Simone. Mon admiration pour lui est ancienne & n'a fait que croître au cours des années.

Veuillez bien, à l'occasion, lui dire mon souvenir fidèle & mes vœux.

Henri Peyre

## To Norman & Mrs. McIntosh:

Jan. 3—76

Dear friends,

There you are, near retirement & soon to live near your talented son in that state which has the most imposing scenery in the country. I, at my advanced age (with a little boy of 11), am still teaching, running a big Ph.D. program . . . even writing, but melancholy at the state of language & humanities in America. But I am touched by the fidelity of your message & I think of you, when I recall those post war years of faith & *élan,* as among the kindest of persons, & the most delicately sensitive. Such people restore one's faith in literature & in life.

My very cordial wishes,
Henri Peyre

## À Konrad Bieber:

Début 1976

Cher ami,

Diane est revenue enchantée de San Francisco, & de la "Convention," et émue des paroles aimables et compréhensives que vous y avez, paraît-il, prononcées. Je reconnais là cette gentillesse de collègue généreux et dévoué qui a toujours été la vôtre. Vous et Tamara aviez toujours rendu ces années de Yale où vous étiez là particulièrement agréables et faciles, parce que vous étiez toujours prêts à nous aider.

J'ai eu, & j'ai encore, des difficultés depuis, comme vous savez, et j'atteins à un âge où bien de mes amis meurent: Fabre, Guyon, Maheu, ici Hilles, Pearson, Wimsatt. C'est une hécatombe. Je semble être plein de vigueur et encore d'énergie; mais le sort de Brice, quelque jour forcé de se débrouiller seul, n'est pas sans m'inquiéter. Vous connaissez ces soucis, les ayant aussi subis avec votre fils.

Je continue du moins à enseigner, à écrire, & notre département paraît résister victorieusement aux crises répétées de la ville & de CUNY. Puisse cette année vous apporter santé & repos. Je ne vous suggère pas que nous tentions un voyage à Port Jefferson par la route (je m'y perdrais). Mais quand le "ferry" remarchera, vous viendrez jusqu'ici peut-être.

Toute mon affection & mes très bons vœux,<br>Henri

## À Rosette Lamont:

Le 23 février 76

Chère Rosette,

Que vous étiez belle & pleine de vie & d'allégresse l'autre soir! Les voyages en Europe sont pour vous le plus sûr de stimulants. Vous & votre mari animiez la conversation, unissiez le brillant & la sagesse. Chacun vous admirait. Merci d'être venus, et merci de ces présents: mais ils m'intimident. Je n'ai jamais eu, jamais rêvé d'avoir des cravates aussi somptueuses, & d'un goût aussi fin. Oserai-je jamais les arborer? Elles m'intimident.

Je suis très, très touché de votre affection & de votre exquise gentillesse. Cela a été une expérience de prix pour moi de vous retrouver en venant à CUNY et d'y être accueilli par vous. Je pense souvent à cette fidélité de vous, d'Alex, quand la tâche risque d'être lassante, & je n'ai de vœu plus cher que d'être digne de votre confiance.

Merci à votre mari, si compréhensif &, cela est évident, si heureux avec vous, & à vous.

Henri

## To James Lawler:

290 North Ave.<br>Westport, Conn. 06880<br>March 10—76

Dear James,

I meant to write you *first*—but the whole week after your visit was taken up with students' protests, riots even, pleas for humanities, modern languages—& the usual routine of orals preliminary to the Ph.D.

Our advanced students, pressed by financial worries, try to hurry up their exams.

Your lecture here was beautiful—modest, splendidly delivered, illuminating & truly moving. You read those passages from Char, not only with a perfect, modulated accent, but with emotion. Those quotations were ingeniously & artistically set off by your comments on them. Just after your visit, I received, sent by the poet, *Aromates chasseurs* & I read some pages from it over the week end. My fondest wish just now is to have a full summer to myself, perhaps in Southern France or Italy, & slowly read all of Char's poetry. All I do during the year has to be so hurried.

You are kind to think of having me visit & lecture; but I am old, & not very anxious to travel fast & far. It is with much reluctance that I have continued with this job here. I feel very keenly that, after half a century of my presence in too many fields of educational & scholarly activity in this country, I should make way for younger people—like many aging persons, I am not altogether in sympathy with several of the new trends, & the new books, & do not wish to end up grumbling & mumbling & lamenting that the old days are no more. Some day, I may decide to drive to Gaspé & "Arcane 17," but somehow I end up traveling to Europe instead.

My wife & I are now divorced; but it all occurred without any unpleasantness & we are excellent friends, and both anxious for the welfare of the child. Lois seems to enjoy organizing her life anew; she sold the house in Hamden & took a pleasant apartment in the city. If only she could drive away some threat of depression & self-doubt & work on a regular pursuit, she could be much happier. Responsibilities, sense of guilt, remorse, weighed upon her when we lived together. I seem to meet so many young women in similar moods—quite a few among our best students—& so many couples divorcing around us, that my normal faith in our civilization is badly shattered.

I wish you & your wife happiness, even if Halifax, somehow, appears to me like a place for . . . exiles. It's the silly French prejudice which makes us fear being in the . . . provinces, & in my case a lifelong & truly poisoning obsession with devouring what large libraries have to offer.

Thank you for your visit & talk & very cordially yours,
Henri

## À Kurt Weinberg:

> 290 North Ave
> Westport, Conn. 06880
> March 25—76

Mon cher Kurt,

Vous avez bien fait de reprendre votre ancien article sur Nietzsche & la tragédie classique. Dans cette forme rajeunie, complété, sobrement mais précisément annoté, cela devient l'une de vos productions les plus remarquables. Je vous en remercie, car l'article m'aurait probablement échappé. Certes, Nietzsche force un peu son admiration pour ces Français du XVIIe siècle; il veut à tout prix dénigrer ses compatriotes, brûler ce qu'il a le plus admiré, vilipender son propre romantisme. Pascal, notamment, qu'il a aimé et jalousé, ne lui est connu que très partiellement; mais peu importe. Il a cru trouver là une patrie spirituelle. S'il avait vécu au XVIIe siècle, il aurait été exilé de France ou envoyé à la Bastille; et dans la Grèce du Ve siècle, il aurait partagé le sort de Socrate. Du moins, avec une science impeccable & vaste, vous donnez une synthèse des vues nietzschéennes sur les moralistes & les dramaturges de l'âge de Louis XIV. J'ai plusieurs fois essayé de diriger des étudiants vers une thèse sur "Nietzsche & Pascal"; nul n'a osé le tenter. Avec l'édition récente de N. en traduction, munie d'un index, ce serait à faire. Peut-être quand vous aurez quelque loisir.

J'ai lu que votre Université recevait de gros dons: puissent-ils vous profiter! Chez nous, inquiétude, polémiques, mais on survit & même on croît.

> À Florence & à vous, mes très vives amitiés,
> Henri Peyre

## To Edward Kaplan:

> 290 North Ave.
> Westport, Conn. 06880
> April 21—76

Dear Mr. Kaplan:

I was sorry to hear that your private life had undergone such severe trials lately. At your age & with your generous & highly moral nature, that must be a heart-rending blow indeed. I have no right & no reason to speak, since I do not know your wife & hardly know you; but perhaps both of you were too idealistic from the start, and had too sensitive natures. Have you arranged to share the care of the children, if any? I have seen many, very many divorces among my students, in marriages which had been contracted under my very eyes, often when both members of the couple were studying with me. Very few of them left incurable scars. At your age, & your wife's, a whole existence still stretches in front of you. I can tell from your writings & letters how much nobleness of heart there is in you & what earnest devotion to the life of the mind. Retain your faith in what is best in you & in your own future.

Amherst is an excellent college & I hope, for its sake & yours, you stay there. I don't believe I know any one else on the faculty there, at present, although I know many at the University of Mass. I imagine a more calculating man than you would not have embarked upon such an ambitious philosophical & scientific work as you have done, & would have been content with a smaller volume & a simpler one. Even now, a volume, for instance in the (very uneven) Twayne series on Michelet, would have been easier to publish than your MS.

But I believe a scholar's first work should be ambitious, bulky, even rich & confused—like Renan's *Avenir de la Science* or Chateaubriand's *Essai sur les Révolutions*. Later in life, we are all hurried & do enough hasty works. Few of us have the courage, at 40 or 50, to go back to archives, first hand material & to bring out something new. You have gained a deep knowledge of history of science & history of ideas, & that is invaluable. I personally believe that there is far more in that study than in the very restricted study of poetics & the meticulous—often useless—analysis of language in a very narrowly circumscribed text, such as many favor today.

I have a very good opinion of the U. of Mass Press & if I were you, I should be glad to appear there. The important thing is to have & to buy a few review copies or copies to send to a few key persons, here & abroad. For the rest, you do not expect a book like yours to sell widely; you must be anxious to pass on to other things, maybe even to Michelet the historian or the philosopher of history.

The Toronto report which you sent me is thorough, detailed, well informed and, in some ways, admirable. The author spent attention & time on your MS. He is, clearly, very well informed on Michelet, but too well. And he is over anxious to display his scholarship & to wish for you to have written another sort of book.

On the dates mentioned for Ballanche, Vico, *et al.,* I believe him wrong. Many readers prefer being given them than having to resort to a dictionary. Id. on M & the Orient, M. & India, M. & Greece: all those would be different topics & require other books. Similarly, an article on Michelet & Balzac would be curious, but would not have fallen within the compass of your MS. (Martin Kanes just had a good, severe book on Balzac at the Princeton Press, from the point of view of his ideas on language.)

I differ from your reader, however, on the value of utilizing Barthes & that much overrated (& desiccated) S/Z. I fail to find Barthes' ideas & his dogmatic & conceited theories relevant. His early little book on M. was better, with all its paradoxes; but even so, I much prefer Gaulmier's. I would not redo my MS, in your place, in the light of Barthes. That would be betraying your true nature.

Probably the only useful suggestion was that of linking your consideration of M's ideas as a naturalist to M. the historian. Yet, even there, there are *several* Michelets, & the naturalist in him retains only a few features of the M. of *Le Peuple* & the History of the Renaissance. I personally think less highly of *La Voie royale* than some people do & I do not see at all what Sartre on Flaubert would have brought to your thinking. The reader shows off a bit too much & suggests the writing of another book, which would take you two more years. Too bad for Toronto if it was over-impressed by this report. It will be their loss if it does not publish it.

If & when the U. of Mass. makes up its mind, let me know — & accept my best wishes.

H. P.

## To James M. Osborn:

[postcard: Raphael, *Giuliano de Medici*]<br>May 14 — 76

Dear Jim,

I was very sad to hear from Lois that you had been unwell lately. I cannot imagine you in any way weakened or spiritually depressed: the sturdy walker along St. Ronan St., the former tamer of steers & cows. I am not much around Yale these days, but I know that Yale, Rare Books & scholarship cannot do without you. "Preserve those beams this age's only light." My wishes for a full & fine recovery.

> Cordially,
> Henri Peyre
> 290 North Avenue, Westport 06880

## À Kurt Weinberg:

> 290 North Avenue
> Westport—Conn. 06880
> August 8—1976

Mon cher Kurt,

Votre livre est fort beau—effrayant d'abord par sa couverture, Faustien par son ambition, cartésien par son adresse à "diviser toutes les difficultés" et à faciliter le travail du lecteur par d'habiles subdivisions. Il est remarquablement bien écrit, sans la moindre trace de germanismes—dans une prose digne d'un Heine ou d'un Valéry qui eût écrit en anglais. Et il est remarquablement modeste dans son originalité iconoclastique. Vous y avancez des tas de choses nouvelles, extrêmement ingénieuses—sur Pascal & sur Descartes, notamment, où vos remarques m'ont vivement frappé, & sur Goethe, car j'ai encore tant à apprendre sur lui, & un effort renouvelé incessamment pour arriver à l'aimer sans réserve. Dans sa concision, son élégance, c'est, je crois, un de vos plus beaux livres; et la Presse de Princeton l'a noblement présenté.

Vous êtes un travailleur admirable qui, à 60 ans, savez vous tenir aux textes, les sonder patiemment, les analyser en profondeur et contenez votre énorme savoir (du grec à 4 ou 5 langues modernes, de l'érotisme et du symbolisme de la clé qui "vulvam aperit" au regard froid de Valéry) pour ne pas écraser le lecteur moyen. Il me semble que vous avez tant à dire encore et bien d'autres ouvrages à écrire. Et peut-être la demi-solitude intellectuelle où vous avez vécu à Rochester, jointe à la constante inspiration d'une femme éclairée et compréhensive, a telle été pour vous bienfaisante. L'amitié, la conversation, la société dispersent, comme le répétait Proust.

L'été ici est sans histoire, & souvent sans chaleur & sans soleil. Je lis beaucoup, je m'efforce, sans grande conviction, de trouver quelque sens à Saussure, Benveniste, Kristeva, & quelque phrase artiste dans Derrida. Mais je suis trop vieux pour épouser leur manière ou même les comprendre; béatitude des simples, je t'aime.

Merci de ce précieux don et à tous les deux beaucoup d'amitié,
H. P.

## À Jorge Guillén:

> Henri Peyre
> 290 North Avenue
> Westport, Conn. 06880
> [1976]

Cher ami,

J'avais retardé, puis négligé, de vous féliciter lors de l'honneur que vous avait décerné Books Abroad. J'en avais du remords. Mais la nouvelle de ce prix que vous décerne votre patrie enfin un peu libérée m'a empli de joie, et tous les amis que vous comptez, & les amis de la poésie, se réjouissent. Cet hommage va à l'homme de courage & d'indépendance que vous êtes toujours resté autant qu'au grand poète. Il honore l'Espagne nouvelle autant qu'il vous honore.

Je crois pouvoir me compter au nombre de vos plus anciens admirateurs & de vos amis les plus fervents. Je crois bien que c'était en 1936 — peu avant l'éclatement de la guerre civile — que j'avais été ébloui par la première édition de Cantico. Que cela est loin!

Retiré de Yale depuis 1969, j'enseigne encore (& dirige un très actif département gradué) au Graduate Center de City University, sur la 42e rue. J'écris encore un peu et j'aspire, à 75 ans, à quelque calme repos. Je repense bien des fois à nos rencontres de jadis, à New Haven, à vos enfants alors jeunes (votre fils s'est fait un nom parmi les critiques), à notre chagrin de voir l'Espagne opprimée, à nos espoirs. Quelques-uns de ces espoirs se sont réalisés. Vous & moi survivons, alors que beaucoup de septuagénaires de notre connaissance ont disparu. Je suis content, pour ma part, d'avoir vécu assez pour voir votre grandeur de poète acclamée et la noblesse de votre vie récompensée.

Dites mon amitié aux Gilman, mes sentiments bien respectueux à votre femme & croyez moi,

> Fraternellement vôtre,
> Henri Peyre

## To Harold Proshansky:

> 290 North Ave.
> Westport, Conn. 06880
> June 8—1976
> [203] 226-4868

Dear President Proshansky:

I am hard at work on your paper, learning a lot (also cursing in French & swearing in English) about appropriation of space & the language of psychologists & social scientists. My idea of Hell is to hear & talk their language with St. Peter & the Devil & the Virgin Mary & their first ancestor, Socrates, after I finally consent to leave the Graduate Center & to move to another world. The irony is to be made to think about "appropriation of space" & usurping other people's seats, for a man who owns nothing, no space whatever, except his car & some books.

It is not easy to attempt to turn these phrases into French. "Privacy" simply does not exist as a word. "Appropriation" has very different connotations. It means sometimes "distribution," "repartition," "attribution"; other phrases are likewise untranslatable, at least for a layman.

If there had been time, it would have been necessary to consult similar papers in French on the subject to see what kind of phrases the—supposedly clear—language of Voltaire & of De Gaulle uses to render all those learned words. Perhaps some environmentalist in France could go over my translation & correct it accordingly? As it is, I had to do this in a great hurry. I am today more than half way through, but I expect to have it, in long hand but clear, by Thursday noon & if you would like to have it then sent special delivery to Redding, please tell me. If some one can pick it up in Diana McCormick's house, he might come Thursday late afternoon or Friday. The house is always open, &

the paper would be left in an envelope at the entrance. I doubt a burglar would sneak in & "appropriate" it.

With my wishes for your trip, & hoping that you will forget much about our tribulations & woes at CUNY. Perhaps you might travel to Basel & negotiate a loan there, at the International Bank, to save CUNY—or persuade the Alsatians to ship our cafeteria "foie gras" & Traminer wine to celebrate the reopening of your Center.

Your visit afforded us the pleasure of knowing you & your patient & learned wife (gently "appropriated" by a powerful executive) a little better.

With our regards,<br>
Henri Peyre

## À Rosette Lamont:

290 North Ave.<br>
Westport, Conn. 06880<br>
Le 29 août 1976

Chère Rosette,

Peut-être êtes-vous enveloppés de brume & de bruine dans votre île cimmérienne. Il fait affreusement humide ici; le ciel est bas et écrasant, c'est une fin d'été peu stimulante. Et je me rappelle des journées pareillement alourdies à Martha's Vineyard, quand on attendait un ouragan. Mais vous avez des livres; vous débordez d'idées & de projets; et Fred n'est jamais en peine de bâtir un nouveau pavillon, de décorer une chambre ou, qui sait, un yacht. Mon été sans histoire: morne, monotone, mais reposant. Beaucoup de lecture, & surtout de relecture. Je voudrais pouvoir m'ouvrir davantage à ce qui paraît récemment; mais j'y trouve si peu de joie. Et j'en veux un peu à tant de livres récents d'avoir si aisément oublié les crimes et les infortunes du monde depuis la dernière guerre, les Nazis & les camps russes. Il est trop facile, & lâche, de noyer nos responsabilités collectives dans les laborieuses délectations érotiques ou dans la science-fiction! Il y a tout un passé à exorciser avant de faire face à un avenir que l'on veut déshumanisé. Chaque fin d'été, mes souvenirs reviennent à ces premiers jours de septembre 1939 où je venais, après plusieurs années d'Europe, m'installer aux États-Unis, le cœur lourd de ce que l'on pressentait là-bas. 37 années se sont écoulées depuis. Je les ai remplies de mon mieux, pas toujours selon les rêves chimériques de la jeunesse. Et je me demande parfois comment je ne me sens pas plus vieux que je ne le fais. La sympathie, la sollicitude & la jeunesse d'amis, et surtout d'am*ies* autour de moi (Diane, vous, Bettina) m'ont apporté beaucoup, depuis que j'ai eu le plaisir d'enseigner à New York.

Une autre année s'ouvre — avec bien des incertitudes, sans doute des déceptions à prévoir, & ce constant remords de ne pas trouver de place, dans ce grand pays, pour ces personnes de premier ordre que nous encourageons à penser & à écrire. Vous avez, avec votre habituelle ponctualité, vite lu & renvoyé la thèse de Mrs. Hamish. Merci. Le dernier chapitre (sur L. Labé) n'était pas aussi nourri, aussi fouillé analytiquement, que les précédents; mais c'est une belle thèse, sur un sujet difficile d'accès. À la soutenance, vous nous manquerez. Mais nous n'aurons guère de critiques à présenter & ce ne sera qu'une formalité. Le colloque où vous parlerez ce jour-là est autrement important, & j'espère lire l'ouvrage qui en résultera. Je réserve aussi la date du 22 novembre: ce devrait être un événement significatif, & le titre général est beau. Comment vous y prenez-vous pour obtenir des dons? Alors que le Centre Gradué y est si maladroit. Vous êtes une animatrice & organisatrice hors de pair.

Si, comme il n'est que juste, le congé sabbatique vous est accordé, je crois que vous n'avez pas de plans de voyage lointain & en ce cas nous devrions nous voir un peu à loisir. Amitiés de Diane & les miennes, à vous & à Fred.

Vôtre,<br>Henri

## To Kurt Weinberg:

Henri Peyre<br>290 North Avenue<br>Westport, Conn. 06880.<br>October 1 — 1976

Dear Kurt,

I was stunned to hear that you would be retiring so soon — while you are in full vigor, "producing" even better work than in the past &

having won universal recognition in several countries & ten different areas of research. There should be a Collège de France in this country, to appoint persons like you over 60 and enable young scholars to drink their words. I don't know whether Florence would like such a migration, but if this country is not well enough advised to utilize your services further, perhaps a German University would attract you? Or a Dutch one? I wish I could say "a French one" where Florence might spread her Rabelaisian lore; but the French hardly call upon citizens of other lands.

We have had at the CUNY Graduate Center a dozen Ph.D.'s this year, several just now in the process of publishing their theses—& incidentally the highest rating from the NY State so called "Fleming Commission" which had examined our Graduate Program. Among those who have worked in the XIXth–XXth centuries, two are outstanding; both have had teaching experience, have lived in France, speak the language like natives. They have complete files at our Placement office, at the Center (33 W. 42nd St., NY 10036). They are: Sheila Endler (age 32–4, I'd say?). Thesis, completed & brilliantly defended in 1974 or 5, was on Apollinaire, Poèmes & Lettres à Lou, and Nadine CASTRO (raised in France, I believe an Israeli citizen): thesis on Ghelderode.

I believe the range & variety of their interests, their personality, their broad culture rank them among the top people in their age group (28–32?) in our field. Both, I think, are divorced & therefore more willing to leave N.Y. City than others in our Department, whose wives or husbands have positions in N.Y. as lawyers, doctors, educators, etc.

I now & then hear from Louise Horowitz & from Eléonore Zimmermann: both have been profoundly impressed by your intellectual influence & speak gratefully of you & Florence—as who would not?

Many cordial & warm greetings,
Henri Peyre

## To the University of Alabama Press:

October 10 — 1976

Dear Mr. Walters:

Thank you for sending me the chapter of my Symbolism as translated by Mr. Parker. I feel honored to have a scholar of his stature submit himself to a text of mine. The text is very well rendered. There are only a very few details (typing, spelling of German words, one or two phrases) needing correction.

If it seems safer for the final text of the translation for me to read over the rest of Mr. Parker's version, I shall be glad to do it.

Meanwhile any news about the translation of the Romantisme book? It was due to appear months ago.

I do not have Mr. Parker's address & I am asking you to pass this MS to him, with my thanks.

Very sincerely,
Henri Peyre

## À Konrad Bieber:

290 North Ave.
Westport, Conn. 06880
Nov. 7 — 1976

Cher Konrad,

Nous voilà rentrés dans les premiers froids & la grisaille, & la navigation vers la grande île ne sera plus possible de bien des mois. Mais Diane voudrait réunir, à l'occasion de la MLA de N. York, une douzaine de collègues pour une visite ici & un repas "buffet," le 29 décembre (mercredi) vers 2 heures. Les trains partent de Gd Central à 11.05, 12.05, 1.05 pour arriver ici à 12.11, 1.11, 2.12. Pourriez-vous, & Tamara, y venir? Et si le retour le même jour vous paraissait trop lassant, vous pourriez passer la nuit ici.

J'espère que votre mère se plaira dans sa résidence à N.Y. Je me la rappelle si douce & aimable et raffinée avec naturel & simplicité. Mais quelle inévitable tristesse que de vieillir & voir les amis de son âge disparaître! Je ne m'en aperçois qu'à demi, étant encore actif & même trop pris; mais on sait bien que le déclin est inéluctable; et la mort, coup sur coup, à Yale de Wimsatt, Hilles, Pearson, Reichart, Flint & d'autres amis; en France celle de vieux camarades tels que Guyon & Fabre, m'a attristé. Devant les sottises d'une certaine littérature récente qui se joue à vouloir réhabiliter la collaboration et grandit outrageusement Céline, je me dis parfois que vous devriez écrire une sorte d'autobiographie sur vos origines & vos sentiments envers l'Allemagne, vos années de France (plus héroïques que votre modestie ne veut bien le dire), votre courageuse adaptation à l'Amérique; votre absence de rancœur envers les Français qui ont été "moches," les chagrins secrets, à l'âge le plus frêle, qu'a dû avoir Tamara devant les massacres les plus hideux de l'histoire. Les jeunes ignorent tout de cela, et votre pudeur et sobriété de style vous retiendraient de quelque égocentrisme ou prédication qui ont marqué divers livres sur "l'holocauste."

Mais peut-être préférez-vous ne pas remuer trop de souvenirs? Pour moi, je suis à l'âge où l'on pense beaucoup au passé.

> Dites mon amitié à Tamara & mon souvenir à votre mère, & croyez moi toujours fidèlement vôtre.
> *Henri*

## À Tatiana Greene:

> [postcard]
> Le 7 nov. 76
> Henri Peyre
> 290 North Ave.
> Westport, Conn. 06880

Chère madame:

Merci de votre article, très précis & curieux, avec de très étranges textes. Breton était certes un tyran capricieux et qui aurait, en d'autres temps, fait un bel Inquisiteur! Vous servez la mémoire de ce Jacob que j'ai toujours aimé; et avec Kambler (et une dame qui a, je crois, passé à Columbia sa thèse sur Jacob, & une autre qui est doyenne à Randolph Macon College, & le très Jacobien Oxenhandler à Dartmouth), c'est en

Amérique que vous & eux explorez avec profondeur cette œuvre. Mes compliments & mon amitié.

Henri Peyre

## À la même:

[postcard]
Nov. 16—76

Chère madame,

Bien sûr, vous êtes trop modeste pour vous attendre à des remerciements. Mais votre essai sur Sand est joli et, pour moi, instructif. J'avoue n'avoir jamais lu Rose & blanche, ni Lucrezia, ni d'autres romans, impossibles à trouver. Ce mot ne voudrait que vous dire que vous, & quelques autres "Sandistes," profitant de la mode lancée par le film, le féminisme, par la correspondance Lubin, devriez suggérer avec force en France qu'on réimprime l'œuvre romanesque de G. Sand. Elle en vaut la peine.

Merci & bien à vous,
Henri Peyre

## À Konrad Bieber:

[postcard]
Le 19—11—76
290 North Ave. Westport Conn. 06880

Cher ami,

Pardonnez cette sèche carte. J'aime beaucoup votre essai & je ne renie rien de mon admiration (vieille de 52 ans!) pour Valéry poète & même penseur. Et vous avez raison: on devrait écrire un livre entier sur sa conception de l'histoire & sa pensée politique.

Mais, honoré, choyé par la IIIe république, il s'est toujours méfié de la démocratie, l'a raillée, vilipendée, et sa pensée politique est (comme sa pensée sur la philosophie & la littérature) bien négative. Et tout de même, il a été farouchement anti-Dreyfusard & ne l'a jamais admis avec remords. Il s'était emballé pour Huysmans; & j'ai cité dans un livre d'extraits de lui à Blaisdell-Ginn sa lettre du 22 juin 1890 à P. Louys: "Je n'aime pas les Juifs—car ils n'ont pas d'art"(!). Sans doute faut-il pardonner.

Amitiés à tous deux,<br>H. P.

## À Germaine Brée:

290 North Avenue<br>Westport, Conn. 06880<br>Le 13 déc. 76

Chère Germaine,

Je n'accorde guère à Noël & aux vœux rituels d'attention; mais vous êtes parmi les quelques personnes auxquelles je pense assez souvent & que je regrette de ne pas voir. Vous êtes ma cadette de beaucoup, mais tant de mes amis de mon âge (j'ai 75 ans et plus) ont disparu récemment et d'autres que j'admirais de loin (Queneau, Malraux surtout) qu'il me semble presque héroïque de continuer à être, à parler, à écrire dans un monde où bien des choses vont de travers. Je suis allé une fois (en avril, je pense) à la Philos. Society espérant vous y voir, mais vous étiez retenue ailleurs. Ces réunions sont parfois assez mélancoliques & je ne les fréquente guère; je m'abstiendrai de paraître à la MLA qui est devenue trop foire et fracturée en tant de groupuscules amateurs que je m'y sentirais déplacé. J'espère du moins que votre santé est bonne, votre séjour dans le décor agreste & le climat plus doux des Carolines reposant. Je vis moi-même dans un calme relatif chez cette très bonne amie, Diane McCormick, qui non seulement prend soin de mon fils 3 jours sur 7 & de moi, mais stimule mon intérêt aux choses littéraires. Je la crois un des meilleurs esprits, & des plus sains, ou droits, parmi ceux & celles qui écrivent aujourd'hui sur les lettres. J'aime beaucoup M. A. Caws, vive, brillante, infatigable—et qui ne m'en veut pas trop quand je regimbe devant sa manie—répandue aujourd'hui—de couper les mots français et de lire "ailée" dans tous les "elle est" de Char, et "fête" dans faîte et "homme" et "femme" dans "Hommage et famine." Elle a du moins une capacité de travail peu commune & l'adresse de faire accepter à Char, mon compatriote vauclusien, ces soi-disant ambiguités qui peut-être le flattent. Mais M. Ann, moi & quelques autres menons le bon combat pour essayer de sauver les études de littérature étrangère à ce Centre Gradué où les étudiants comptent parmi les meilleurs du pays. Pauvre ville de N.Y. si mal gouvernée—et pauvre culture si bafouée & malmenée en ce grand pays! Je me crois parfois (quand je lis nos trop subtils critiques, & ces romans d'Ajar, de Guyotat, de Monique Wittig) comme l'un de ces pseudo-classiques qui, vers 1810–15, persistaient à croire au bon sens, à quelque sagesse, au style limpide, alors qu'une rénovation se préparait autour d'eux. Tant pis! Je m'accepte et espère surtout ne pas trop longtemps m'imposer à mes cadets.

Pardon d'un bavardage assez vain—mais acceptez mes vœux pour une année paisible et pour votre bonheur.

Henri Peyre

## To Norman & Mrs. McIntosh:

Dec. 17—76

Dear Mr. & Mrs. McIntosh:

Your note reached me after several delays, for I now live at: 290, North Avenue, Westport, Conn. 06880, closer to my work in N. York. I still go to Yale & use the Library actively, but I have kept out of the French Department, so as to let my successors follow their own policy. It is sad, however, that Guicharnaud is leaving for Harvard, after Brombert's departure for Princeton. The orientation toward linguistics & structuralism does not suit all tastes. What a courageous man you are to tackle l'*Idiot de la Famille*. Brilliant & revealing (on Sartre) as it is in many passages, the book strikes me as much too dogmatic & unfair. But now, little of present day literature moves me: the ransom of old age!

I am sure your son must be pursuing his eminent career & I wish you a pleasant, restful, idyllic New Year.

Sincerely,
Henri Peyre

## To Gordon Ray:

290 North Ave.
Westport, Conn. 06880
Jan. 10—1977

Dear Gordon,

I had meant earlier to thank you for the pleasure your invitation to lunch gave me. I enjoyed, as I always do, talking with you, hearing the news on the Foundation & on the scholarly world—& you & your two brilliant associates are very kind in bearing with my insolent advice giving.

I tried to do this reporting diligently and fast & here it is. You will be judges. As you know, of course, our critical profession (in the French field especially) is now very divided. On the one side, semioticists, structural linguists, calling themselves the vanguard & the new critics of today, scornfully discarding what they consider old fashioned. On the other side, the more traditional critics (historical, philosophical, impressionistic), diffident of the self-styled (& often arrogant) scientific approach to literature. . . .

## To Edward Kaplan:

290 North Ave.
Westport, Conn. 06880
Febr. 3—77

Dear Mr. Kaplan:

I just found your long letter & the enclosures.

First, thanks for the Heschel essay. I learned from it, appreciated its fervor, its style & also, despite the hints of your colleagues, the critical spirit at work there. Mysticism is not my "dish," unless it be some pagan & pantheistic union with nature,—& why, I don't know, I feel remote from Jewish thought & have never quite forgiven Judaism & its offspring for replacing Greek polytheism. But enough on my heresies!

For the rest, I am literally astounded! Of course, I am a devotee of Romanticism myself. I am convinced that criticism should be subjective, warm, with sympathy & empathy for what is being appreciated—especially in a critic's early, young, ardent works. There will be time enough later on, for him to be cut & dried, & cold. I didn't realize, & can hardly believe, that there are still places like Amherst, where, apparently, literary scholars believe in the old fashioned, anti-romantic, "new criticism" of 1940–60, & probably set their standards by T. S. Eliot, Marvell, Pope, etc. I still see my old friends, Cleanth Brooks, Rob. Penn Warren, & Wellek & others, & they have, by now, rallied to the romantic camp, by which Geoffrey Hartman, Harold Bloom & the now fashionable & influential critics swear.

The reports which you let me read are terribly earnest, patient, detailed. Few colleges take such pains about a promotion; yet I seem to sense that they lack fairness, or ingenuity. All that talk about your not adopting a critical, detached position, your not *judging* Michelet's passionate views strikes me as covering up a certain distaste for your manner—not Anglo-Saxon & restrained enough for them.

I do not mean to intervene, or to accuse. I hardly know you personally & I do not know the merits of the case; who else is in the Department; how much room there is at the top; what kind of teaching is most wanted (language, grammar, composition, conversation, civilization, an urbane knowledge of the humanities in a very "humane" sense, leaving out God, the Devil, Jewish prophets, disheveled mystics . . . )

Your case is not, of course, the first one of its kind I have encountered in a long career. My advice, discouraging as it may sound, is: there is not much use fighting, & imposing yourself upon colleagues & Dean in spite of their reluctance. They seldom forgive that. The deeper reasons are of an affective nature. A certain Romantic warmth & religious bent in you is distrusted. In a large university, one man like you is an asset. In a small, complacent, WASP college, with no graduate work, someone safer, more dryly rational may be preferred. Let it be.

I was the one who, as soon as you wrote me of the Committee's probable decision, recommended you to Kent State. If I have a chance, I'll do likewise elsewhere. You might indeed profit from teaching elsewhere, away from NY & the East, alien as such a location may seem at first. In time, write 2 or 3 very dull, cool, pseudo-scientific articles, "detached," on Boileau or Voltaire or any rationalist, & you will pass for "un homme complet."

Meanwhile your private life must be tragically upset. I am full of sympathy.

Sincerely,
Henri Peyre

**To Sherry Kneller:**

290 North Ave. Westport, Conn.
Febr. 14—77

Dear Mrs. Kneller:

You & Jack were ever so kind—to come to Diana's party & to forget your many worries for a little while & then to send me that fascinating book. It arrived a few days ago & I waited until the week end to read it carefully. It is a fascinating demonstration, thoroughly documented & beautifully illustrated. The delicate statues and the tomb pictures recalled to me my years in Egypt; that art was a revelation to me and challenged my preference for Greek sculpture & architecture. You would enjoy going there after you retire or during a sabbatical, & Jack has more of a sense for the mystery & the mystical than I have.

The thesis of the book is provocative. I confess I had never connected the two Thebes. The argumentation is clever and enlightening. Even if it does not carry the conviction fully, there are many details which one finds most revealing. And it is an elegantly written book, one whose author I would like to meet. I'll read more by him.

Meanwhile I am most thankful to you for that enriching present. Give my friendliest thoughts & wishes to Jack for the new semester & believe Diana & me,

Most cordially yours,
Henri Peyre

**À Rosette Lamont:**

Le 18 février 1977

Votre goût est le plus exquis que je connaisse, et toujours original; votre art de faire plaisir à vos amis est savant et votre générosité sans égale. Mais je me sens embarrassé par tant de gentillesse que vous me témoignez en chaque occasion! Je vous dois déjà, & cela est *énorme,* en grande partie d'avoir enseigné ces dernières années à ce Centre Gradué, de vous avoir ainsi mieux connue et appris à connaître—donc à admirer—votre mari, et d'avoir rencontré Diane qui a mis beaucoup de grâce & de réconfort dans ma vieillesse. Vous ajoutez encore des titres à ma reconnaissance & à mon amitié pour vous par de tels dons.

Merci et croyez à ma vive affection. Dites à votre mère mon souvenir toujours plein de sollicitude & mes bons vœux.

Henri

## To Florence et Kurt Weinberg:

March 23—77

Dear friends:

Quels puits de science vous êtes tous deux! Florence a une précision d'érudition, un don d'analyse précise & rigoureuse, une maîtrise du latin inégalée! Elle est polie envers le fils Spitzer, dont l'article m'avait jadis donné grand mal (quand j'étais "editor" à PMLA) & dont les vues sur B des P. avaient fait rejeter son travail à Harvard. Comme certains savants trop savants venus de pays germaniques, il voulait trop prouver & il prouvait trop. Mais l'article est admirable. Ce livre avait été jadis (avec le *Contra Celsum* et quelques dialogues matérialistes de Diderot) ma lecture de chevet—au temps où je croyais encore pouvoir convertir le monde à l'athéisme ou au polythéisme.

Et voilà Kurt qui s'approprie les Protestants et les rend subtils. Il sera bientôt plus universel & impérialiste intellectuel que le grand Spitzer. Ce sonnet (Voulez-vous voir) est d'ailleurs très beau, autant que le trop cité (et volé) "Si notre vie . . ." de l'*Olive,* et tout l'article est un modèle d'étude fouillée. Mes félicitations.

Qu'attend-on, si Kurt vraiment prend une monacale retraite, nouveau Philoctète, ou St Antoine, ou St Siméon, pour nommer Florence prof. distingué de la culture de la Renaissance à Rochester? Nul dans ce domaine ne la vaut en Amérique.

Cela va pour moi. Je cours d'examen de doctorat à examen—12 ou 15 Ph.D.'s cette année et, victoire! Quelques-uns déjà placés!

Amitiés,
Henri

## À Tatiana Greene:

[1977]

Chère madame,

La mort de Bédé m'a plongé dans la tristesse. Je l'avais peu vu ces dernières années, mais nous avions échangé beaucoup de lettres à propos du *Dictionnaire* et d'autres sujets. Le samedi qui suivait le jour où il est mort, il devait venir ici déjeuner, chez Diana McCormick, chez qui j'habite: il s'entretenait avec elle de Balzac, lui téléphonait un jour or deux avant sa fin, pour la tenir au courant de sa santé. Il disait souffrir beaucoup d'un empoisonnement ("Tomaine poisoning") contracté après avoir mangé, à N.Y., du poisson qui n'était pas frais. Le jeudi elle avait essayé de lui téléphoner à plusieurs reprises—en vain. Cela fait tant de disparitions cette année d'amis et de contemporains: Malraux, Queneau, d'autres en France & ici 4 ou 5 vieux amis à moi de Yale. Tristesse de vieillir!

J'ai reçu votre *Desnos* & l'ai lu—& y ai appris. Il est très bien fait, sans doute trop long—ce qui a dû être le cas de bien des articles que Bédé a reçus—du mien notamment, général, sur la littérature de 1900 (j'oublie) à 1970. Il y a des traductions partielles de D., mais sans doute peu importantes. "Desnos. *22 Poems,* translated with an introduction by Michael Benedikt—with prints by Jacqueline Airami. Santa Cruz, Calif., Kayak Books. 1971. Pp. 39—D. The *Voice*. Selected Poems, translated by William Kulik with Carole Frankel. N.Y., Grossman Publications, 1972. XII. 80 pp. Mais je ne connais pas d'ouvrage critique important. Dix fois, j'ai suggéré le sujet à des candidats au Ph.D. Curieusement, nul ne l'a élu.

*Mais,* on a dû conjecturer que je devais m'occuper de ce Dictionnaire. Il n'en est rien. Pour cent raisons: pressenti vaguement par la Col. Press il y a plusieurs années, je m'étais récusé & j'avais même ensuite conseillé à Bédé de refuser. Je suis de quelques années son aîné, & aurai disparu bien avant l'achèvement du Dict. J'enseigne encore, dirige beaucoup de thèses, & ai peu de loisirs. Je suis mal fait pour ce travail précis, minutieux: déteste taper à la machine & n'ai pas l'écriture impériale de Bédé. Enfin je crois que, si l'entreprise continue, elle devrait être guidée par Riffaterre, ou Gavronsky, ou quelqu'un de Columbia même, tout proche de la Presse, & quelqu'un de jeune, qui peut compter sur dix ans devant lui. Pourquoi pas vous? Ou Breunig, libéré de la Présidence. Qu'on ait pu me croire capable de succéder à Bédé me flatte, mais rien ne pouvait le faire croire. Povero Mi!

Avec mes amitiés,<br>Henri Peyre

## À Rosette Lamont:

April 18—77

Chère Rosette,

Pourriez-vous, le 15 avril (lundi) à 6h15, venir prendre un très rapide repas au 18e étage avec Mme Sarraute & quelques collègues, avant la causerie qu'elle doit donner ce même jour à 7h30? Cela lui ferait plaisir, je suis sûr, & à moi. Si cela vous est possible, inutile de répondre. Je vous attendrais alors.

Amitiés,<br>Henri Peyre

## À la même:

Le 9 mai 77

Chère Rosette,

Vous avez, votre mari & vous, apporté beaucoup à cette soirée d'amitié chez Bettina. J'ai, depuis, lu ce n° des Nineteenth Century French Studies & votre article m'a tout particulièrement plu. Il est plein de vie & d'élan, écrit avec talent. Vous vous y révélez stendhalienne—et napoléonienne, et mettez toujours de la vivacité & de la flamme dans ce que vous écrivez. Je suis fier d'être en quelque mesure associé à ce très élégant essai—& de votre si fidèle amitié.

Bien à vous,<br>Henri

## À Micheline Levowitz:

Le 13 juin 1977

Chère amie,

Les scrupules & les doutes m'ont saisi—Car que peut valoir une "préface" de quelqu'un qui ne compte pas parmi les Stendhaliens, qui a souri parfois du fanatisme des Stendhaliens, & qui se sent d'une génération ancienne et vouée déjà à l'oubli. D'autant que vous avez affaire à des gens . . . un peu rapaces . . . et surtout susceptibles. Le directeur de la série pouvait fort bien juger que c'est à lui à présenter, dans quelque avant-propos un peu hautain, les auteurs qu'il a acceptés.

En ce cas, sentez-vous libre & jetez tout bonnement le texte que je viens, hâtivement, de griffonner. Je me trouve pressé par beaucoup d'obligations avant de m'absenter (certaines aussi sottes que d'acheter des souliers, ou des habits pour mon fils, ou de décider quels livres emporter), par des thèses qui surviennent encore, etc., et j'ai écrit bien vite & sans brouillon ces quelques lignes que je ne voulais pas trop pédantes. Maladroit dactylo que je suis, je ne prends même pas la peine de les taper. Et, si vous les croyez utilisables, modifiez-les à votre gré & sans rien m'en dire.

Vous êtes bien trop gentille pour moi & je sais trop bien mes insuffisances & ma médiocrité fondamentale pour ajouter foi aux flatteries. Malgré votre goût du vrai & votre profonde sincérité, vous êtes, je crois, entraînée par trop de gentillesse native. J'ai eu pour seule ambition, en enseignant, en restant en Amérique au lieu d'accepter des chaires dans mon pays, & en me maintenant bien au delà de l'âge normalement jugé "canonique," d'étendre quelque peu le groupe de gens que peut atteindre la littérature. Sans doute aussi suis-je resté patriote à ma manière & ai-je voulu ici présenter la France en beau—et la voir moi-même en beau, alors que, vus de trop près, les Français sont grognons, raisonneurs, sophistes, égocentriques. C'est mon seul point commun avec Stendhal: avoir voulu vivre en dehors de mon pays & préféré les "beautés" étrangères à celles du cru. Ce métier comporte souvent des déceptions, met en contact avec pas mal de jalousie, de mesquinerie, d'ingratitude. Mais parfois survient quelqu'un comme vous, qui sait compenser toutes les menues déceptions avec délicatesse & dévouement, et qui arrive à vous faire croire qu'on a encore quelque chose à apporter à des personnes plus jeunes et riches de tous les dons.

De cela, merci. Passez un été tranquille, économisez beaucoup sur les cigarettes pour payer les frais du livre et entourez votre généreux & compréhensif mari d'affection et de gourmandises.

Bien affectueusement,<br>Henri Peyre

## À Kurt Weinberg:

290 North Avenue<br>Westport, Conn. 06880<br>Aug. 22—77

Cher ami,

Je crois que vous pensiez être en retraite cette année—ou est-ce la prochaine? Et je devine que vous souffrirez de cet isolement relatif, alors que vous avez tant à donner encore, & plus d'activité intellectuelle que jamais. Normalement, un homme qui a écrit en plusieurs langues autant d'œuvres d'une science inégalée et aussi originales aurait eu dix offres de chaires pour quelques années encore; mais la situation semble si funeste dans les universités américaines (& le devient aussi en Europe) que vous vous trouvez, une fois de plus, appartenir à une génération défavorisée. Quelque poste de "senior adviser" s'est-il ouvert pour vous à Rochester même? Y a-t-il pour votre femme une perspective de chaire plus digne d'elle?

Je me prépare moi-même à me retirer de toute activité, & je crois avoir enfin bien gagné ce repos & ce silence. J'ai voyagé un peu en Europe cet été, reprends ces jours-ci les directions de thèses—en me demandant s'il est raisonnable de former tant de docteurs de surplus.

Ce mot est joint à un tout modeste écrit, commémorant un homme que vous admiriez & aimiez. Et il vous apportera mon très amical souvenir à tous deux.

Henri Peyre

## To Florence Weinberg:

> Henri Peyre
> 290 North Avenue
> Westport, Conn. 06880

Dear Florence,

I enjoyed our brief chat, although I could not talk too freely in my office which is always being invaded. I am in N.Y. only two, at the most three, days a week & those are crowded with visitors & committees. My address as above is quicker.

On the question of Hunter, I told Brody that if I had any influence there, I would put it wholeheartedly behind your name. Ever since I first met you, which must be a while now, I was thunderstruck with admiration & thought that Kurt had been richly compensated for all the ordeals of his life. I do not know a single friend of his who did not envy him.

But I distrust those announcements of "vacancies" which *have* to be made for legal reasons & often lead nowhere. Hunter, like NYU, Columbia, *et al.,* is top heavy with tenured professors & I doubt they will really appoint someone from outside. In a few words, what happened was a long standing feud in the Dept. Szogyi is an active, dedicated man, a gifted organizer — in my opinion, a fine "animator." But he stayed too long at the head (what of me!!). He favored younger instructors, who voted for him because he gave them jobs; there are not enough literature courses to go around & the full professors felt vexed, humiliated. Often literature courses were given to younger assistant professors at their expense. A violent, if half concealed, war developed with, against him, Mesdames Caws, Plottel, Charney, Micheline Braun. Ladies can be unforgiving, as you know. Szogyi arranged to be reelected with a majority of one or two. Finally, the President appointed a committee from outside &, on that committee's advice, asked him to step down. The Dean, who came from Pittsburgh, wanted, perhaps still wants, to bring Benj. Bart, from Pittsburgh. What will happen is uncertain. In truth, there are too many tenured people, as in every one of the CUNY colleges, & also NYU, & Stony Brook; no room for the younger members to be promoted; a scramble for the "interesting" courses; & accumulated hatreds & feuds. It is not too different at the Grad. Center, where every one (myself excepted) is at one of the CUNY colleges (City, Queens, Brooklyn, Hunter, etc.), eager to give a graduate course while there is only one course for each professor every third term. I have kept peace & been prevailed upon to stay on year after year because, like the Third Republic in 1873, I was "le régime qui divise le moins." I have, it seems, attracted students & lately, the best I had in my career (Kurt & 2 or 3 others excepted). But I am mortal. Lately, all kinds of committee chairmanships have become my lot; I am 76 after all, vigorous for the present, but I want to rest, too. And one never knows at CUNY whether the budget will be voted.

I believe you would do a great job here. But it would not be easy — with many gifted ladies (mentioned above, plus Bettina Knapp, plus others in Spanish, Italian, ready to harbor suspicions). Brody's name is not too popular. He is a top scholar; but it seems his Don Juanism, his authoritarian bent, have brought him enemies. He is, I believe, judged to be impossible as my successor at the Grad. Center.

Our profession is, in truth, a wretched one these days — with feuds, bitterness, "haines de personnes" & even ideological or methodological quarrels. Poor G. May at Yale feels isolated & "dépassé." Harvard fell back on D. Stone, then Guicharnaud; but they cannot reinvigorate an ailing Dept.

You should be President of your College, or of Bryn Mawr, or of Brown — & Kurt your Prince Consort, publishing a dazzling (paradoxical) essay every six months & lecturing around. By the way, I believe he had an essay on Nietzsche in a book by several hands. If he had a reprint, I'd like to read it.

Now, am I not too old & old fashioned, to be invited to your College — & too well known for a bellicose atheist?

I would gladly come, avoiding Mondays when I teach all day in N.Y.; avoiding March 10–11 when I am to talk elsewhere; & March 30–31, when I am to talk in Nashville, Tenn.

I'll list a few titles on a separate sheet — in English — but they can be easily translated.

With my very warm "amitiés,"<br>Henri

## To the University of Alabama Press:

Sept. 2, 1977

Dear Mrs. Nichols,

I am sorry I was not there when you called. I have Ph.D. exams these days.

In fact, I was going to write the Press in order to congratulate you on the *Romanticism* volume, very handsomely & attractively done.

I had not noticed the mistake on the inside back cover attributing to Mrs. Roberts a translation (of my previous book at your Press) wrongly. I had written it in English & there is no French original for it.

If Mrs. Roberts does not mind, I don't. This Romanticism volume has had enough misfortunes as it is! Let it go—or cross it off, if easier—but do not go to any extra expenses about that.

Sincerely yours,
Henri Peyre

## À Rosette Lamont:

Le mardi 20 sept. 77

Chère Rosette—la "Dame de la Mer,"

Vous voilà revenue de vos grottes marines, prête à affronter avec magnanimité nos mesquineries. Nous avons eu plusieurs soutenances, deux ou trois d'excellents; thèses, & notre début d'année s'annonce prometteur. Pour quelque raison, ou sans raison, un assez bon nombre d'étudiants neufs, plusieurs, semble-t-il, de qualité.

J'ai prié Bettina et, si l'heure vous agrée, je vous adresse la même requête, de venir un moment (à deux heures) lundi prochain le 26 sept dans mon bureau pour parler des projets de publication et des subventions possibles. Il me semblerait avisé de pouvoir sortir deux ou trois livres d'ici 1978–79, où seraient mentionnés les remerciements aux donateurs, dans l'espoir que ces messieurs renouvellent leur don. Il semble bien que chaque ouvrage à paraître, en Amérique ou en France, revienne environ $3000 à l'auteur. Une subvention de $1000, si nous jugeons bon de l'accorder, laisse encore l'auteur fort démuni pour avoir l'honneur de se voir imprimé.

Le même jour à 3h nous aurions la "soutenance" de la thèse proustienne de Catherine Triantaphilidès. Thèse originale & subtile, que Mad. Braun apprécie beaucoup; moi aussi. Mais personne difficile, timide, bourrelée de scrupules & d'hésitations. Cela a été toute une tâche de la décider enfin à achever ce manuscrit. Elle est aussi involuée et susceptible que son auteur. Qu'on voudrait parfois avoir affaire à des gens simples!

J'espère que votre mari aussi est reposé et plein de vaillance pour affronter la rentrée—et la nouvelle administration de la ville de N.Y. Ma vive affection pour vous.

Henri

## À la même:

Wed. Oct. 12th—77

Chère Rosette,

Je ne sais si mon mot, probablement envoyé au bureau, à Queens, vous a rejointe. Cela était pour vous indiquer la date à laquelle nous espérons (enfin!) pouvoir réunir le Comité Exécutif & aussitôt après la Faculté & les étudiants (mardi premier novembre à 2h) et pour vous demander de préciser le titre du cours que vous feriez le semestre prochain (printemps 1978) et de spécifier le jour & l'heure que vous désirez.

Le lundi 17, à 6h15 ou 20, je compte sur votre présence pour dîner, au 18e étage, avec Mme Chedid & 2 ou 3 de nous. Sans doute êtes-vous encore toute riche de la vigueur & de la joie accumulées pendant votre été de Calypso?

Avec toute mon amitié,
Henri

## To John W. Kneller

> 290 North Avenue
> Westport, CT 06880
> Nov. 8, 1977

Dear Jack,

I was deeply touched that you should have taken the time from your multitude of tasks to come and listen to my talks and to introduce me with warmth and kindness. It was just as kind and generous of Sherry to come as she did and I enjoyed her company at lunch. The atmosphere was most cordial. I feel completely "en pays de connaissance" at Brooklyn College and I find the more humanistic and artistic attitude prevailing there (as compared to other CUNY colleges) especially congenial.

I cherish both the posters and the elegant catalogue as souvenirs of my visit, and of my visit to the galleries. Thank you indeed for both.

I am enclosing the number of *Encounter* with the article of the British educator Mr. Rae, which I had found challenging. Perhaps you will have time to read it.

> With very warm regards,
> Henri Peyre

## To Frederick Brown:

> 290 North Avenue
> Westport, Conn. 06880
> Dec. 14—77

Dear Mr. Brown:

I am touched by your kindness in keeping me informed on what you write. Few writings give as much pleasure as yours do—these days especially when the game of criticism has become so narcissistically annoying & so vain.

I suppose this might be part of a future book by you? You are very cleverly sarcastic on le Grand Roi, & I am all with you. I never did like Versailles & its alleys & its pomp & I never return there for a visit without shuddering with indignation.

But, at last (at 76!), last Summer I did visit le Père Lachaise, thanks to your book on it. It surely won't be my own burial place!

Things go fairly well & smoothly, through our ever recurring crises. The quality of the students is the one comforting element: it is surprisingly high. I imagine you have a quiet life, spending only a minimum of time at Stony Brook. I wish I could do likewise, but I probably like administration in the way a convict likes his jail.

Thank you & accept my heartfelt wishes.

Henri Peyre

## To Norman & Mrs. McIntosh:

Dec. 25—1977

Dear Mr. & Mrs. McIntosh:

You are kind to keep me informed of your activity & of your son's prowesses in all fields. "Quo non ascendam?" is his motto.

But please correct my address which, for five or six years, has been: "290 North Ave., Westport, Conn. 06880" as the P. Office has told me it will throw out all letters sent to my old address after Jan. first.

I too traveled a little last summer: England, France; but it is becoming arduous to find room & leisure among the crowds of tourists & at my age. I am nostalgic—in vain—for the more leisurely joys of the old times. I am still active, teaching at CUNY where, mysteriously, there seem to be more candidates for a Ph.D. in French than ever. They refuse to be discouraged. Yale is changing fast, & the Department a little bewildered by the claims of the vociferous new schools, or sets, of critics. Maybe the new President will restore a good morale to the humanists?

My very warm wishes to you both & very kind regards,
Henri Peyre

## To Kurt & Florence Weinberg:

290 North Ave.
Westport, Conn. 06880
Dec. 26/77

Dear Kurt,

I apologize for my confusion about the Nietzsche paper. Of course you had sent it to me & I had read it carefully, & probably told you my warm appreciation of it. I only lately saw it mentioned in TLS, as part of a collective volume & thought it was another piece. I reread it in the copy you sent me & enjoyed it anew. Curious, N's resistance to French (the language) & to France which, except for Nice, he hardly knew; it was so much easier thus to praise Pascal & Fontenelle & others.

It takes me longer to understand & to digest your erudite "mythopoesis." I have read it twice & been dazzled, crushed. So much knowledge, so many allusions or secret puns (phoenix—Feu/Nixe), so many references to Euripides, Apollonius Rhodus, Jamblichus spoil for me the naive enjoyment of the *ix* sonnet, or of the clever but not very great "Salut." Must we really read "en-verre" in "envers" & "en vers" & end or telos in toile, & the weaver's shuttle? Are you not turning Mallarmé into a poet for a half a dozen chosen minds, nearly as subtle as yours (R.G. Cohn, to whom I hope you will send it, Derrida . . . )? Your mastery of all knowledge, from ancient grammarians to Vico & since, is colossal; but poor Mallarmé had none of the leisure we enjoy, nor literary facilities such as ours, no learned, inspiring wife like yours to gently restrain you & occasionally guide you through your subtle explorations. When all is said, is not the *ix* sonnet a rather cold, uninspired, poor piece of poetry?

You are, Kurt—& I mean this—the most learned, the most ingenious, the truest savant of all the men of your generation; but how many of us in this country can follow you? The place for you to be is the Princeton Institute for Advanced Study, where you might continue making those ingenious & provoking discoveries, without having to train the 3 or 4 select students who might make the attempt to follow you.

If I may, I'll keep your paper a little longer to reread it, & then return it, for you should send it to other Mallarmeans. I feel so obtuse, such a Philistine, such a naive Epicurean enjoying literature, when I read you.

I hope the Chicago group which listened to your paper was duly impressed.

Happy New Year.

Henri

Dear Florence,

Thank you for your card & wishes. I hear nothing about the Hunter position & don't know what's being planned, if anything. I remain skeptical that they truly want to appoint someone. The more I sit on committees, the more struck I am by their fundamental hypocrisy; they are *meant* to achieve nothing; and they keep the Faculty busy, fooled & so bored that it eventually ceases to protest.

I'll let you know if I hear anything more. The College has Brody's letter & mine & should at the very least wish more information.

April 4th is a Tuesday, I believe, & would suit me, if I could leave Westport in the morning & reach Rochester in then early afternoon. Let me know when the date gets closer what is decided and accept my very, very warm wishes for the year soon to begin.

Yours,<br>Henri

## À Rosette Lamont:

Le 31–1–78

Bien chère Rosette,

Sans doute êtes-vous sur la voie du retour. Merci de cette jolie carte. Pour Diana, cela devrait bientôt aller mieux. Son fils doit rentrer de l'hôpital dans deux jours, après cinq semaines. Espérons que la science ne découvrira pas d'autres symptômes troublants! Elle a été courageuse et a continué à travailler. Pour elle, nous, moi, ennuis de l'hiver dans une maison entourée de routes glacées, glissantes; autos engourdies par le froid—mais "if winter comes." Espérons.

Vous avez dû voir de belles choses et vous nous en parlerez. Pour la visite d'Ionesco, Roubichou voulait d'abord (pour satisfaire les vœux du visiteur) qu'il donne et présente son film récent: plus d'une heure et demie. Mais le millimétrique requis (36, je crois) n'était pas disponible au Centre—et Ionesco veut partir à six heures pour un autre engagement. Nous avons donc conservé l'entretien. Vous lui poserez des questions, le mettrez en forme. Vous avez l'art de faire parler les étudiants. Souhaitons que rien n'empêche sa venue!

>Vœux affectueux d'agréable retour & toute mon affection,
>Henri

Bien entendu, j'avertis, & invite, Proshansky. Le temps sera si mesuré, de 4 ou 4:15 à 6h que je ne sais s'il sera possible, ou souhaitable, de suggérer aux étudiants de servir vin ou café. Vraisemblablement, l'auditoire sera beaucoup composé de gens du dehors.

## To Florence Weinberg:

>290 North Avenue
>Westport, Conn. 06880
>Febr. 14—1978

Dear Florence,

The people at Hunter are indeed strange! I do not know the chairman of the search committee, though he spoke to me briefly on the phone; but my impression is that he is neither well informed nor very discriminating. I have no idea who is candidate (I doubt there are many; for the state of the Department, with its intestine feuds, is well known) or who is being considered. Often the "search" efforts amount to nothing & the person ultimately designated is from the local staff, anyway.

It would have been pleasant, & stimulating for us, to have you in N.Y., & to talk to Kurt occasionally, or, rather, to listen to him; for his immense range of interest, his vast knowledge & his extreme subtlety intimidate me more & more. You two eclipse Heloise & Abelard (pardon the insult), Mme de Stael & Constant, Julia Kristeva & Lacan, & your forthcoming study of an ambitious topos will, I am sure, dazzle & confound me. Still, at my age (77 next week), I continue to enjoy learning from others.

Once the snow, the ice, the cold finally desert us, I'll plan my trip & let you know what plane I could take which would be the most suitable to you. I probably should come back early (I mean, in the morning) the next day, but if you would like me to meet a group of students of French or politics, on the afternoon of Tuesday, I should be glad to do it.

My warm wishes for . . . a good thaw & a fine spring.

Very cordially,<br>Henri Peyre

## To Edward Kaplan:

290 North Avenue<br>Westport, Conn. 06880<br>Febr. 24—78

Dear Mr. Kaplan:

Your essay is, in my opinion, a remarkable one: done with rigor, insight, showing a reading of the texts in depth & convincing—or at any rate, enriching. The perspective (Kierkegaard-Tillich) opens up original vistas on the two poets. You are a subtle critic, but not one who would insist on displaying his own subtlety at the expense of earlier critics or through straining the meaning of the texts. I would not, perhaps, interpret Rimbaud as quite so anxious, or "para-religious," as you make him out to be—but that may be in my case a lingering reaction against those who, in the past (Claudel himself), overrated Rimbaud's religious "inquiétude." On Baudelaire, the wisest, most impartial book by far is, in my eyes, Pierre Emmanuel's *Baud. devant Dieu*. I agree with you that Bonnefoy, a very fine poet, is also a first rate interpreter of poetry. He was in New Haven last semester & has been in America often. B. Juden & Frank Bowman are learned, have read all kinds of obscure works, but, somehow, I do not get taken by their exegeses. The whole question of the religious quest in the French romantics (once badly mauled by Viatte, Seillière, *et al.*) should be treated again. Perhaps some day you'll do it. Why should not a fervent interest in religion coexist with, & serve, a parallel interest in poetry?

I take it your future is still uncertain. That must be a source of harassing anxiety these days. I have heard nothing from Brandeis. Have you approached Boston Univ.? The Univ. of Mass. in Boston? Smith

College? & why not Harvard? It is childish to hint that, if a man has worked more particularly on Michelet, & on science & literature, he is by definition disqualified to teach poetry! I hope a definite solution or end to that uncertainty occurs soon.

Thank you for letting me read this essay. It is first rate. I'll send it in another mail.

Sincerely yours,<br>
Henri Peyre

## À Florence et Kurt Weinberg:

290 North Avenue<br>
Westport, Conn. 06880<br>
Le 6 avril 78

Chers amis,

Cette visite chez vous & ces moments passés dans la chaude intimité de deux amis, de la fière et mystérieuse chatte, de votre musée hispano-indien m'ont donné une vraie joie. La conversation de Kurt, plus savante et profonde encore qu'autrefois, est un stimulant et, après tant de banalités conventionnelles que l'on entend ailleurs, elle rafraîchit. Et j'ai beaucoup admiré, Florence, votre maîtrise, votre grâce et la cordialité de votre accueil, et chez vous, et à votre Collège. Sans doute est-il dur, et décevant, d'avoir à enseigner tant de cours, parfois élémentaires, à des étudiants que l'éducation cléricale a essayé de borner. Mais j'ai vraiment eu l'impression d'un auditoire réceptif, éveillé, ouvert et d'une très grande bonne volonté. On peut ne pas désespérer des humanités et de la culture américaine avec une jeunesse de pareille bonne volonté. Sans doute il ne se trouve pas beaucoup de gens à Rochester (ou ailleurs) pour saisir les subtilités de l'herméneutique de Kurt ou pour pénétrer avec vous dans la caverne de Platon—ou de Didon & Enée, ou de l'Arioste; mais il n'en irait pas très différemment dans l'Allemagne ou la France d'aujourd'hui. Kurt et moi avons tout de même des raisons d'être reconnaissants à ce pays.

Merci encore de la chaleur réconfortante de votre accueil et croyez à mes vœux pour un printemps serein, actif et reposant.

Henri

## To Robert G. Cohn:

April 26—78

Dear Bob,

A P.S. I just received the Proust Bulletin no. 18 & want to congratulate you. *Of course,* you are right. The recent fashion for seeing bisexuality everywhere & for aspiring to the androgynous state is ridiculous. And it is foolish of some scholars to see hidden or disguised males in Albertine, & Andrée, & other girls. It's not just the curves & the softness of the skin: everything about Albertine, her tastes, her conversation, her behavior, *is* feminine. I have often said &, I believe, printed that Proust is the greatest painter of women in literature.

Flaubert probably never said: "Mad. Bovary, c'est moi." The source of the report is most dubious. A lady from Rouen repeated it to someone who repeated it to Descharmes (I believe). Baudelaire's essay notwithstanding, Emma *is* feminine jusqu'au bout des ongles. How silly can some scholars be!

Yours,
HP

## To Florence Weinberg:

290 North Ave.
Westport, Conn. 06880.
April 28—78

Dear Florence,

The news that you were on your way to Princeton seems to indicate that your "Cave" is being seriously considered there. If so, I rejoice. That is the most pleasant Press in the country to deal with.

We are still moaning here about this endless winter & the refusal of the vernal season to appear; but a few more weeks & we'll be through with the theses. That part of the work saps much of my energy at this time of the year. Half of the finished products, however, are worth while, & that is a more than honorable proportion.

I read, with genuine intellectual pleasure, the MS by Mrs. Baer. It is remarkable—truly an exceptionally sensitive & acute piece of criticism.

I wrote her a hasty note of warm praise, in my enthusiasm; but it deserved a longer critique, which, as far as I was concerned, would not be at all critical. There are "quelques longueurs" at the beginning, before the subject is frontally tackled; but otherwise, it is impeccable; beautifully informed on the criticism of fiction, on narrative technique, & the expression of the self in the novel, & very intelligent & perceptive on Nerval.

I know nothing of the author, her means, her job; but that thesis should by all means be published, even if it entails an initial expense from the author. Rochester Univ. should help finance it: it has not often had such a strikingly good "product" in the realm of literature.

My visit to you has left me with very warm memories & I truly appreciated the audience. Too bad you can't win against your ecclesiastical authorities. At the first good opportunity, you will make a move.

> Most cordially to both,
> Henri

## To Natalie Datlof:

> April 30, 1978

Dear Professor Datlof,

I am very happy to hear that the George Sand Conference went so well. The complete list of events & the picturesque announcement which I received are extremely impressive, and most artistic. Hofstra does things with more taste, and a more eclectic gathering of collaborators, than any State, City or private University in and near New York. My very warm congratulations.

It would be a shame if the proceedings of the 1976 & 1978 conferences were to be delayed for lack of funds. I wish I were a millionaire myself or, next best, I were a friend of wealthy potential donors. How humiliating, at times, to realize one is only a "petit bourgeois" and a humble academic.

I believe it would be worth while presenting the case first, convincingly, to the American Council of Learned Societies. It does, occasionally, assist scholars invited from abroad or American scholars invited abroad. But "scripta manent" while "verba volant": conferences and oral exchanges are fine, but some record should remain of them (ACLS: 345 East 46th St. N.Y.).

Perhaps the Endowment for the Humanities, in Washington, would be responsive? It has not, I fear, assisted publications in the past; but with the new Director, their policy might change. George Sand was no "elitist," but did much for the common man—and woman.

A convinced feminist, or perhaps a group of women voters and champions of women's movements, might be another possibility. I cannot suggest any myself, & I am a little out of touch with such groups & movements, being near retirement. After all, interest on George Sand has been—greatly thanks to you—revived in America.

I am sorry to be of so little concrete help, but good will I have & I am,

Most gratefully yours,<br>Henri Peyre

## À Wallace Fowlie:

290 North Avenue<br>Le 20 mai 78<br>Westport, Conn. 06880

Mon cher Michel,

Votre lettre m'a touché. Je suis, bien sûr, à l'âge où affluent les souvenirs, & vous êtes lié à beaucoup de ceux qui me sont les plus chers. Je passe souvent, chaque fois que je vais voir Lois qui habite à la grande maison d'appartements proche de là, devant la maison (32 High Street) où je vous avais d'abord rendu visite. Un des premiers soirs où vous étiez là, vous aviez convié les Archawski & Mme M (j'oublie), avec ses deux fillettes. Il m'arrive aussi de revoir la route d'où l'on montait chez la chère Mme Lafarge. Mais que de disparus, & je m'étonne parfois d'être encore en vie, assez actif. Vous qui l'êtes encore davantage & n'avez cessé de penser, de sentir et d'écrire, devriez sans peine trouver une position temporaire—un semestre sur deux. Avant, & jusqu'à la récente crise financière & la diminution des étudiants, j'avais pensé, & en parlais avec Szogyi, que l'endroit idéal serait à CUNY. Mais on a brutalement retranché argent et personnel: le français n'est pas florissant

& je pense que le successeur de Szogyi lui-même sera pris dans les rangs des gens d'Espagnol. Je ne reste guère à N.Y. le soir et ne vais à rien—théâtre ou ballet; inertie, sans doute, mais aussi tâches de bureaucrate très lourdes. Je ne continuerai qu'une année encore. Je trouve que les plans d'avenir, qui devraient entraîner une révision totale des traditions et conventions accompagnant le Ph.D., doivent être préparés par de plus jeunes qui ont l'avenir devant eux. Mais, et en dépit du travail parfois monotone et aride, je me suis plu à aider des étudiants—femmes, la plupart, de qualité supérieure.

Je n'irai en France que pour très peu de temps en juin, puis lirai ou flânerai ici. Quand vous aurez une adresse, communiquez-la moi—et soit cet été, soit à New York l'an prochain, nous nous rencontrerons pour déjeuner.

"Votre" livre est beau, très élégant, varié de contenu et bien supérieur à bien des ouvrages de ce genre. L'essai d'Austin Warren est touchant. Tous disent l'amitié, tout autant que l'admiration que tant de gens ont pour vous dans deux pays. L'article de Revault d'Allones m'a rappelé ma première visite rue Chaptal, quand j'étais normalien, pour quelque "sauterie" d'après-midi. Depuis j'ai vu plusieurs fois Mme Siohan. Elle a réussi à réunir, autour du souvenir de Renan, des conférenciers de talent et à publier un excellent bulletin bien plus substantiel que ceux qui sont consacrés à Rivière, à Du Bos, et même à Proust. J'appartiens encore, très nominalement, à plusieurs de ces groupes, "Amis de . . ." Mais je ne me mêle guère aux réunions, fuis les mondains, et d'ailleurs n'ai nulle place pour revues & livres. Je vis un peu en ascète, ou en humaniste à l'antique "contentus sua sorte." Des amis plaisantent sur mon obstination à refuser une autre vie, toute conversion, et la seule pensée du monothéisme; mais l'angoisse ne me visite pas. J'ai beaucoup relu du Kierkegaard, du Kafka, Dostoïevski & j'enseigne parfois Pascal—sans partager leurs conclusions ou leurs anxiétés.

J'imagine que vous êtes en belle santé et encore voyageur—encore musicien aussi peut-être? Ou acteur? Et toujours le même Michel, profond, affectueux, enjoué, débordant d'idées & de talent. Restez-le longtemps encore.

Avec affection,<br>Henri

## À Micheline Levowitz:

Le 9 juillet 1978

Chère amie,

    Oui, ce court voyage s'est terminé avec le dernier jour de juin et, après quelques jours à rattraper le courrier en retard & à se réadapter, je me prépare à jouir d'un été calme et vide. La mer, ici, est proche; la verdure abonde; les arbres sont si gigantesques pour qui revient d'Europe. Il était agréable de marcher dans Paris, même sous la pluie, de découvrir des tas de petits restaurants exotiques (tunisiens, vietnamiens) autour de St Séverin & dans le Marais. Mais j'avoue qu'à mon âge, & quelque secret narcissisme aidant, ce sont mes souvenirs que j'aime à retrouver & je boude souvent le présent. La France est prospère, avide de vacances; les routes sont encombrées d'autos & de Français en vacances. Je m'en réjouis. L'humanité, dans quelques pays de l'Occident, n'a jamais été aussi heureuse qu'aujourd'hui. Elle a cessé de se tracasser du péché, des contraintes morales, même de la pudeur; elle s'efforce de n'avoir plus peur de la mort. Sans doute, les inquiétudes psychologiques d'un autre ordre tourmentent. Mais de charitables docteurs comme votre mari réussissent peu à peu à nous guérir même de cela.

    En vérité, sauf pour la langue et la culture, je me sens au moins autant Américain que Français. C'est avec les Américains que, depuis longtemps, je travaille; j'aime leurs qualités, leur générosité profonde et ce cosmopolitisme qui permet de voir avec impartialité divers pays d'Europe & d'Asie. Mon fils est déjà américain de toutes ses fibres, et cela est tant mieux. Par la faute de gens comme nous, intellectuels qui avons afflué ici depuis 1930, il y a trop de savants et de professeurs ici pour un nombre décroissant de postes, et j'ai scrupule à ajouter à ce nombre de candidats chaque année. Le grand nombre de femmes qui aspirent légitimement à travailler a fait éclater la relative infériorité de beaucoup d'hommes et rendu plus dure la compétition. Nous avons réussi à placer, pour un an en tous cas et loin de New York, plusieurs de nos récents docteurs. Mais c'est chaque fois une lutte.

    J'imagine que, si votre résistance physique, renforcée par un été de repos, le permet, vous continuerez à enseigner à Barnard. Je sais que la tâche y est dure, les déplacements éreintants. Mais il y a traditionnellement eu là quelques-unes des étudiantes les plus douées du pays. Et il n'y a pas tellement d'élèves de premier ordre—pas assez, certes, pour peupler tant de "Graduate Schools" qui se les volent les unes aux autres.

Il m'a semblé, à la lecture des journaux et revues surtout, qu'en politique, le vent souffle en France à l'indifférence, à l'apathie, et certainement à quelque conservatisme. C'est un peu attristant. L'idéalisme semble avoir déserté la gauche après les élections, & déjà avant, en fait. Le parti socialiste, composé surtout de "cadres," d'enseignants, de petits fonctionnaires, de ceux comme moi qui souhaitaient des réformes de structure, est en train de se désintégrer. La flamme ne brille ni n'éclaire dans *L'Express,* le *Nouvel Observateur;* et la littérature courante est vraiment médiocre.

On se console avec le passé. Je relis de vieux auteurs, souvent avec plaisir. Mais je ne connais pas ce Degron. Peut-être pourrez-vous me prêter le livre, car je n'irai guère dans les bibliothèques cet été et j'attendrai l'automne pour lire votre livre. Après tant d'efforts, de soucis, de frais, j'espère qu'il ne vous déçoit pas. Songez maintenant à un autre ouvrage. Vous en avez plusieurs en vous, en puissance.

Je n'écris plus guère moi-même. Diane, plus jeune et ardente, travaille avec obstination, lit des épreuves, et trouve le temps de nourrir trois garçons (souvent leurs "girls" aussi), le mien et moi-même—plus la pelouse à couper, le chien qui requiert attention . . . Vous n'allez pas, apparemment, à votre propriété de campagne cet été? Peut-être est-il plus reposant de rester chez soi en paix.

Bien de l'amitié à votre mari & à vous,
H. P.

## À Claude Vigée:

Henri Peyre
290 North Avenue
Westport, Conn. 06880
Juillet 18—1978

Cher ami,

Que de souvenirs, anciens et pour moi, vieillard, d'autant plus chers, a évoqués le petit livre de vous, et sur vous, que m'a fait parvenir Seghers! J'ai eu plus qu'un plaisir esthétique, une grande & vraie joie spirituelle, à lire & relire vos poèmes. Parmi ceux dont, entre 1948 et 1965, j'avais fait la découverte, y compris ceux d'hommes dont je vous croyais proche (P. J. Jouve, P. Emmanuel, J. Grosjean), je les trouve les plus chargés d'émotion contenue, les plus variés de ton & de facture, et ceux qui survivent le plus triomphalement. Le long essai de l'éditeur m'a paru également discret, informé, agréablement écrit, un peu timide pour marquer votre place, si éminente parmi les poètes de ce demi-siècle. Tout cela m'a remis en mémoire vos premières lettres, il y a bien longtemps, quand vous étiez à Columbus; le choc esthétique de vos premiers vers; puis nos entretiens quand vous étiez à Brandeis. J'admirais déjà alors votre rapidité à avoir, avec aisance, senti et interprété la poésie espagnole et l'anglaise. Plus aisément déraciné que vous, j'étais surpris, & plein de regrets, quand vous m'avez fait comprendre la force de votre attachement à la terre d'Alsace, aux traditions juives et la réaction spirituelle et morale qui était la vôtre aux massacres d'Israélites perpétrés par les Allemands. Un peu égoïstement, car il y avait tant à faire en Amérique pour un professeur français doué, j'avais regretté votre résolution de partir pour Israel. Mais vous avez, je le sais, accompli tout autant et plus là-bas que vous auriez fait ici. J'espère seulement que les épreuves subies par le pays, l'incertitude présente sur son avenir, le chagrin que doit vous causer l'ingrate désaffection exprimée par divers socialistes, "libéraux" français et Gaullistes ne vous ont pas chagriné à l'excès.

Ici, l'atmosphère est trouble; le pays incertain sur son rôle, son avenir; son arrogance d'antan a disparu; les collèges se sont détournés des études de langue & de littérature. Retiré de Yale à 68 ans (j'en ai 77), j'enseigne encore au "Graduate Center" de l'Université de la Ville de New York, y forme d'assez nombreux "docteurs," difficiles à placer; j'écris encore, mais je vais clore bientôt ma carrière d'un demi-siècle d'enseignement ici et me reposer. Par ce mot, je voulais et vous remercier et vous dire mon fidèle et amical souvenir.

Henri Peyre

## À Victor et Beth Brombert:

290 North Avenue
Westport, Conn. 06880
Le 5 août 1978

Chers amis,

J'espère pour vous que vous n'êtes pas encore revenus de ce séjour féériquement oriental pour tomber dans la chaleur moite très éprouvante qui nous afflige depuis plusieurs jours. Votre carte fort pittoresque nous a fait rêver. Je ne sais pourquoi j'ai toujours évité l'Afrique du Nord et assouvi sur la religion islamique ma vaine et sotte rancune d'incroyant qui ne réussissait pas à détacher le monde (& peut-être lui-même) de la religion. Il est trop tard maintenant pour ces "vastes pensées." Je me suis contenté de voir Marrakech à travers vos quelques phrases. Pour Diane & moi, le court séjour en France en juin s'est bien passé—sans les enfants. Carlo, depuis, a été en Pologne, avec un groupe de jeunes musiciens. Brice part demain avec sa mère pour l'Angleterre & l'Écosse, après avoir absorbé voracement du Latin intensif pendant six semaines.

Votre très beau livre m'est parvenu, de Princeton. Je me suis repris à en lire plusieurs chapitres. Mon admiration, depuis que j'avais lu le texte français, n'a fait que croître. Victor écrit admirablement l'anglais. J'envie son style nerveux, pur de toute déformation vers l'éloquence comme en ont tant de nous, professeurs. Et la densité de sa critique est remarquable. J'aime à juger les ouvrages critiques par le plaisir intellectuel qu'ils me procurent: et celui de Victor m'a aussi pleinement satisfait, & exalté, que celui de Joseph Frank et autrefois deux livres de Blackmur (d'essais sur le roman) dont les titres m'échappent. Il y a vraiment une noble tradition de critiques à Princeton.

Ce n'est qu'en refermant le livre que je me suis aperçu que l'auteur m'avait, flatteusement, inclus avec Beth dans sa dédicace. C'est un grand honneur pour moi & j'en suis touché. Léger et impatient comme je le suis, je suis probablement l'homme qui aurait le plus gagné à vivre quelques années en prison. À 12 ou 14 ans, je me récitais—en atroce accent anglais—"The Prisoner of Chillon" et pleurais sur *Picciola* & Silvio Pellico. Plus coriace aujourd'hui, je n'ai même pas pu me prendre au livre récent de Foucault. Mais les prisons plus spirituelles qu'évoque Victor m'ont touché. J'en ai, presque, aimé Huysmans, envers qui j'avais toujours eu une sorte de rancune personnelle, comme envers Léon Bloy & Bernanos. Merci de cet hommage, que je mérite bien peu; et mes compliments admiratifs à l'auteur & à son inspiratrice.

Passez une calme fin d'été et partagez avec les enfants notre amical souvenir,

Henri

## À Philip Kolb:

290 North Avenue<br>Westport, Conn. 06880<br>Aug. 7—1978

Cher ami,

Vous égalez Proust en générosité et en largesse—mais non pas tout de même en louanges hyperboliques et en hautaine indifférence a faits, dates & autres précisions! Merci de ce volume IV, splendidement édité & présenté. Votre préface est dense, lucide & dit tout l'essentiel. Avec magnanimité, vous vous abstenez de juger le rôle d'entremetteuse empressée qu'a joué M. P. entre ce beau noble gandin que devait être Albufera & la demi-mondaine Louisa de Mornand. Vous restez impassible devant ces flagorneries prodiguées à Mme de Noailles et à R. de Montesquiou. Le petit-bourgeois que je suis ne peut s'empêcher de se sentir étouffé et un peu . . . méprisant devant ces mondains et snobs se passant mutuellement la main sur le dos; n'accordant jamais une pensée aux ouvriers, aux paysans, à ceux que voulait, après l'affaire Dreyfus, élever l'Université populaire; aux menaces extérieures de l'Allemagne; à la peinture alors neuve des successeurs de Cézanne et des Fauves. La perspective des "historiens de la culture" que nous croyons être s'avère bien arbitraire & partielle, quand on voit de quoi s'occupaient les gens du gratin. Pauvre Proust à 35 ans détaillant à sa mère (bien peu intéressante elle-même dans ses lettres) ce qu'il absorbait comme médicaments, l'état de ses digestions et ne pensant à son père mort récemment que pour rester chez lui le jour d'anniversaire. De regrets, de chagrin, de souvenirs de ce père qui avait en partie fourni l'argent pour ses loisirs, rien. Certes, entre l'homme vu dans sa vie quotidienne et le créateur, Proust avait raison, il y a un abîme. Mais je ne crois pas qu'il existe un autre cas de correspondance (certes ni Balzac ou Stendhal, ni Berlioz ou Sainte-Beuve lui-même) où l'écrivain ait révélé si peu sur sa pensée et son art. Si encore on pouvait *être sûr* qu'il n'a pas "*meant* what he said, when he laid it on so thick" à Anna de Noailles ou à Montesquiou, aux Daudet, à Antoine Bibesco. Mais hélas! il devait le croire, du moins quand il l'écrivait. Il ne mentait pas perpétuellement & son masque social devait finir par lui coller au visage et être LUI. Il *aimait* leurs vers! Et ceux de Sully-Prudhomme!

Mais ceci pour dire que vos commentaires & ces lettres font rêver. Un Proust tout neuf ressortira de ces 12 ou 18 volumes que vous avez en vos cartons. Grâce à vous, à cette méthode d'infini scrupule, à ces datations ingénieuses de lettres jamais datées, à ces recherches dans journaux, archives, mémoires, faire-parts, etc., à vos notes érudites, nous sommes en possession de toute une tranche de la vie française au début du siècle. Quel dévouement vous avez dépensé! Et cela pour vos collègues & vos successeurs! "Sic vos non vobis . . ." comme le dit un Virgile apocryphe. On dira "le Kolb" comme on dit "le Larousse" ou "le Littré."

Dites mon souvenir à Mme Kolb—à vos savantes (& artistes) filles et croyez à mon amicale reconnaissance.

Henri Peyre

Bien sûr, le "Mirabeau" (dans le Vaucluse, où Maurice Barrès avait vécu & où son fils est mort) ne s'écrit pas comme le Monsieur Mirabaud (page 221) qui avait emmené Proust sur son yacht.

## À Konrad Bieber:

290 North Ave.<br>Westport, Conn. 06880<br>Dec. 20/78

Chers amis,

Les fins d'année sont toujours dures: grisaille, froid, premiers rhumes, lassitude, remords de tout ce qui aurait dû être accompli . . . Je suis un peu las: rhume, etc., mais enfin il va y avoir une pleine semaine de répit & de paresse. Les enfants ici se portent bien, Brice y compris. Sa mère est allée pour quelque temps en Angleterre. Diane lit les épreuves de deux livres, et donne des "papers" en divers lieux. Pour moi, je m'abstiens du MLA & toutes autres réunions. À d'autres la place!

J'espère que la santé de votre mère va se maintenir et que Tamara, elle, est en bonne forme.—Dites aussi, à l'occasion, mon très affectueux souvenir à Eléonore Zimmermann. Ce M. Piquemal a l'air de quelqu'un de très bien. C'est le moment de l'année où il doit venir qui n'est guère favorable. En avril, les maigres fonds sont épuisés, les auditoires possibles hantés par les examens & les thèses. Mais je transmettrai la feuille le concernant à des collègues de sciences politiques. Avez-vous touché le French Institute & le nouvel organisme politico-social à N.Y. University?

Amitiés bien chères et à quelque jour,<br>Henri

## To Edward Kaplan:

290 North Ave.<br>Westport, Conn. 06880<br>Jan. 30—79

Dear Mr. Kaplan,

I had read your fine essay in the *French Review* & I am glad to have this extra copy. It is a serious, in depth analysis of the two poems, stressing their spiritual message, not unfairly, but closely attentive also to the technique & the form. As you gradually gain some distance from some of the ordeals you had to meet these last few years, & feel that you are in a more congenial surrounding, you may temper your seriousness and fondness for anxiety with just a touch of mockery—à la H. Heine or like the author of "L'Ecclésiaste." Your Chairman is a jolly man: I know nothing about his orthodoxy, but he is superbly superorthodox in matters of wine. He would be a fine companion to encounter in Paradise!

I am glad you enjoy Brandeis. The faculty there is one of the most stimulating anywhere & the student body superior. And Boston, libraries, museums are near. I hope you have not too much difficulty taking care of your son. Does he miss his mother, or not having brothers & sisters? There should be good schools in that neighborhood, perhaps even within walking distance.

Accept my thanks & warm wishes.

Henri Peyre

## À Rosette Lamont:

290 North Ave.<br>Westport, Conn. 06880<br>Le mardi 20 mars

Bien chère Rosette,

Je vous ai chagrinée, sans le vouloir, croyez-moi bien, & sans doute avec maladresse. Mais comment pouvez-vous douter de l'affection, plus que paternelle, que je vous porte? Affection qui, plus que toute autre que je ressens, n'a fait que croître depuis que je suis devenu votre collègue, que, beaucoup grâce à votre fidélité, j'ai trouvé comme un rajeunissement à enseigner près de vous à New York.

Ce que j'ai pu vouloir dire, en m'exprimant avec gaucherie, c'est que, dans ces années pour moi lointaines où repartait après la guerre le département gradué de Yale, il y avait quelques étudiants (Cohn, Brombert, Maurin) qui me paraissaient dépasser les autres en maturité, en ambition, en potentiel & dont j'espérais le plus. Maurin m'a un peu déçu, parce que j'ai souvent la faiblesse de croire qu'une activité incessante et une production quantitative sont des marques de succès professionnel. Je n'ai jamais, malgré quelques taquineries et boutades, jugé les femmes en rien inférieures. Mais alors vous n'aviez pas encore toute la fermeté, l'assurance et (si ce méchant mot implique un éloge) la maturité intellectuelle de ces garçons dont deux au moins avaient connu la guerre. Vous les avez vite rattrapés; et, dans le domaine du théâtre notamment et de la littérature moderne, vous êtes devenue beaucoup plus ouverte, plus universellement informée, plus attachée à ce qui vit & vibre dans la production récente de divers pays, qu'aucun de ceux & celles que j'ai jamais eus comme élèves. Je crois avoir exprimé la profonde admiration que j'ai pour vous bien des fois; à nos collègues, aux autorités de New York, à G. May & d'autres à Yale. Intervenant avec quelque force pour la seule fois depuis que j'ai pris ma retraite de Yale, j'ai cet automne déconseillé à May de rappeler Z en lui disant que, pour tout ce qui est littérature dramatique récente, et vivante, vous étiez de cent coudées supérieure à lui. Il n'a pas cru pouvoir changer sa décision & je crois que Yale le regrettera. Mais je m'abstiens désormais de les conseiller.

À Harvard, dans la mesure où j'y ai quelque influence, j'avais écrit dès l'abord, l'an dernier, qu'il serait de leur intérêt de considérer en premier lieu quatre noms: Gita May, Bettina Knapp (en ajoutant que ces deux personnes ne voudraient probablement pas envisager de changement), Rosette Lamont et M. A. Caws. J'ai renvoyé le Doyen qui m'avait consulté (Bowersock) à mes précédentes lettres à Rokovsky vous recommandant. Ils n'ont retenu aucun nom féminin. Ils ont, apparemment, décidé qu'ils devaient d'abord rebâtir leur département dans la période médiévale (en invitant Nykrog) & dans le XVIIe siècle, qui avait jusqu'ici été le domaine de Bénichou (il prend sa retraite cette année) et de Guicharnaud. Si Harvard se décide en faveur de Brody (je suis en dehors de cela désormais), je n'ai pas caché qu'il y aurait des froissements & des difficultés. Mais c'est leur affaire désormais.

Mais, croyez-moi, Rosette, je n'ai jamais trahi l'affection & la fidélité que je vous porte—et si je puis être maladroit, je ne suis pas ingrat à ce point. J'admire ce qu'écrit Brombert, et Cohn; mais, affectivement, c'est de vous, de bien loin, que je me sens proche.

Affectueusement,
Henri

## À Germaine Brée:

> 290 North Avenue
> Westport, Conn. 06880
> Avril 5—79

Chère Germaine,

Je ne saurais vous dire quel très vrai, très grand plaisir cela m'a donné de vous revoir un peu à loisir, de causer librement avec vous, de vous entendre évoquer votre passé, votre famille—et, sur la tâche professionnelle qui nous a permis de nous revoir, de me sentir en accord avec vous. Vous et moi sommes un peu en ce pays des "vaches sacrées," ayant occupé des positions qui impliquaient la confiance en nous de bien des Américains. Nous avons poursuivi des carrières assez parallèles, mais sans nous voir fréquemment. J'ai beaucoup admiré vos livres, et encore votre dernier: tous pénétrants, neufs, suggestifs, dépourvus de toute servitude aux modes du jour. Cela me rassure toujours quand je me trouve d'accord avec vous, et me rassure aussi dans la chaude amitié que je vous porte de vous savoir vaillante, sereine parmi vos fleurs et dans votre maison, et entreprenant de bâtir . . . "Passe encor de bâtir . . ." Votre retraite est active et féconde. La mienne l'est trop & j'en suis parfois irrité—contre moi-même. Que de thèses! Que de manuscrits! Diane McCormick soigne avec dévouement ma vieillesse, me parle de ses écrits & travaux, qui me paraissent très distingués. Elle doit avoir le jugement sûr, car elle goûte et admire fort ce que vous avez fait & faites. Un jour, si quelque cause vous amène par ici (une heure de N. York), vous devriez venir nous voir. Cela lui ferait plaisir, et à moi aussi. Pour l'instant, froid, pluie, désolation des arbres soupirant après le printemps. Pâques peut-être bousculera ce spectre Hiver . . .

Voici mon rapport—bien mal tapé, je crains—mais j'ai dû aller vite, pour passer à d'autres tâches. Je l'envoie par ce même courrier à M. Whitehead. Il me semble que si nous avons des points de divergence, ils seront peu de chose—et cela d'ailleurs est une bonne chose. La visite a été lassante, mais encourageante aussi.

Avec mon amitié et bien affectueusement,
Henri

## To Harvard University Press:

Henri Peyre
290 North Ave.
Westport, Conn. 06880
Tel. (203) 226-4868
Social Sec.: 046-26-4270
April 9, 1979

Dear Ms. [Aida] Donald,

I am sorry, but I seem to have misplaced or lost the title page of the MS; I suppose it can be easily replaced.

I'll be sending the package tomorrow (April 10) by another mail.

I am a poor typist & have no secretary. I trust this is readable.

If you insist on offering me a book, the paperback edition of Keats by Jackson Bate would be welcome. Thank you.

Henri Peyre<br>April 9, 1979

WILKINSON The Intellectual Resistance.

This is a long, a very long MS, the reading of which requires patience, close attention, a good deal of previous information. It is, I shall say at once, highly rewarding and a very fine work, one which not many Presses would have the courage to publish on account of its length and of its scope. It could hardly have been composed anywhere but in this country, where the required impartiality, the "distanciation," the ability to envisage three or more countries in parallel fashion and with equal competence and insight are occasionally found in the best departments of political science. Unhesitatingly, I believe it should be published and it would do credit to Harvard. The material presentation of the MS is unusually good; it should stand in very little need of editing. (1) Although it is not likely that any other work anticipates and rivals it (this must have taken 8 or 10 years of assiduous research), it should appear fairly soon. It has much bearing on topics now timely: the "new philosophers" in France, the trend to "the right" in several European countries, the disaffection from Marxism and leftist ideologies, the more favorable attitude to wartime "collaborators," etc.

The scope is immense: in terms of years, in terms of the multitude of thinkers, writers and politicians discussed, and in its ambitious treatment of three countries. Yet nothing in it is done second hand, or merely from secondary sources. The author has read books, articles, newspapers in the foreign languages. He has talked with several survivors. He is at home in the moods, sensibilities, political reactions of Frenchmen, Germans, Italians—the latter perhaps best of all or with a fuller sympathy. The orientation of the MS demanded going over much ground, touching on many figures, probably too hastily. Some, Malraux for instance, do not receive their due: his evolution between 1935 and *Espoir*, the ideological chapters in that novel around the Spanish civil war, presented in Malraux's imperious and assertive manner, several of the conclusions reached here by the author. (2) But Mr. Wilkinson's design did not allow him space to sketch a few winning or touching individuals, to whom he was drawn: Von Moltke, Meinecke, Parri. As it is, he nowhere produces an impression of undue haste or of superficiality. There was, inevitably, some artificiality in forcing some parallels or hinting at similarities and divergences between very different personalities: Benda and Jaspers, Goebbels and Nizan, Mannheim and Gramsci. The analogies between them, if any, are rather exterior. Still the reader feels enlightened and enriched by such confrontations. Where he considers himself as well informed (in my case, on authors I have known and written on, Sartre, Koestler, Camus), the critical reader will readily pay tribute to the solid documentation, the wisdom and the fairness of judgment, the lucid conclusions of the author.

Long as the MS is, it would be hard to suggest any substantial cuts. A few chapters are slow-moving (e.g. on the Nuremberg trials, pp. 340–65, the account on Vittorini), but they are never tedious and arouse no impatience. The chapter of conclusion could have been more concise and does not altogether eschew repetitiousness. But the work is well organized, logical, balanced. It cannot be read at one sitting. It will be consulted by political thinkers and scientists, cultural historians, literary critics: and I doubt many will find fault either with the rich and wide information or with the author's judgment.

Indeed, his impartiality and his serenity are admirable. There was an incredible amount of sophistry and glibness in many polemical statements by Merleau-Ponty (justifying the Moscow trials ten or twelve years after and contending that "revolutionary justice" is a special and brutally unjust form of justice), by Sartre in many an essay in *Situations* and in his tardiness (& that of S. de Beauvoir) to concede that he never had the masses with him and was unable to communicate with workmen. There was plain, outright cowardice in many German intellectuals, and their passivity in the face of the persecution of the Jews is not adequately brought out in this work. Mr. Wilkinson likewise understates the very wide, almost unanimous acceptance of Fascism by the Italian intelligentsia, at least until 1936–38, and those writers (Malaparte, the Futurists, even Pirandello) who acclaimed Fascism. As an American, he proves amazingly lenient to those intellectuals in France who passionately argued for a position equally opposed to both Russia and America, while they well know that, without the American military (subsequently nuclear) umbrella, they would not even have been able to think freely.

Naturally, a work of this kind focuses the attention on the writings (often abstruse, involved, pedantic) of authors and thinkers, and cannot evaluate the scant influence of those authors (in Italy especially, or in France of Mounier and the *Esprit* group) in their country. The process through which ideas become disseminated and influential and dynamic remains a mystery, which Stuart Hughes and a few others have tried to elucidate. Those "Uninfluentials" of the Resistance, like those of World War I in the trenches, had enjoyed for a time the communion with "the people," knowing all along that it never could survive the emotional circumstances of the war and of the Occupation. None of those prophets of 1941–45 had the stuff of a statesman, the knack for organization and efficiency. Mr. Wilkinson's conclusions are melancholy, but justified. Another era was bound to dawn, in which the illusions and delusions of the Resistance are derided. The "philosophers" of today look upon the prophets and heroes of 1940–45 as the young men of 1820–30 did upon the veterans of Napoleon's armies in France. Even internationalism is tepid and sounds unexciting among those who are, painfully, half-heartedly, consenting to the birth of a European assembly.

This is truly a significant, thought-provoking and well written work.

Henri Peyre

A book by Victor Brombert, *The Intellectual Hero,* Lippincott & Co., 1961, might have deserved a mention.

(1) Page 407 does not exist, it seems.—p. 408, was not the Marshall speech at Harvard delivered in 1947, not 1946?—p. 437, middle. "boisterous" is misspelt.—p. 446, lines 8–9, "was" is repeated.—p. 544, "Hollywood" is misspelt.—p. 675, note 32, "Fubini," not "Fu*r*bini."—Pp. 418, 429, 436, "autarchy" should be "autarcy." "Autarchy," from the Greek "archon," which gave "archont," means to rule by oneself. The x is rendered by "ch." "Autarcy," sufficient in, or unto, itself, is spelt with a "k": "autarkes" gave Latin "arcere," to confine, to enclose, and should not be spelt with an "h." It means, of course, "self-sufficiency."

(2) The Harvard Press published, about twelve years ago, a volume on Malraux's political attitudes by Mr. Wilkinson. I imagine it was another author with that name.

## To the University of Alabama Press:

Henri Peyre
290 North Avenue
Westport—06880
May 13, 1979

Dear Mr. Squibb,

I am returning the Xerox copy of Mrs. Roberts' translation of my Hugo volume, with answers to your sheet of queries and a few corrections in pencil here & there.

The Translator's Preface is fine, interesting & poses, or answers, a number of questions connected with the difficulty of translating verse. I knew of Mrs. Roberts being appointed at Ottawa, as I wrote to recommend her there, at Ottawa's request.

I would not entitle the book: "HUGO. His Life and Works," as it is not that. The approach throughout is to Hugo as a philosopher in his poetry. "Life & Works" is both too wide, & rather conventional. Please avoid it.

I cannot answer the queries on "Atheneum Society" and on "Chesterfield Society" for the William Shakespeare book. I cannot find those titles in libraries here. Mrs. Roberts might have the information. I doubt any copyright & permission to reproduce is involved.

A few remarks:

1) It is totally useless, and needlessly adding to the printing cost, to add the first, or Christian, names before the names of very well known authors, such as Michelet (Jules), Baudelaire (Charles), Zola (Émile) and others where the "de" would be needed:

E.g. François-René de Chateaubriand,
Alphonse de Lamartine,
Alfred de Vigny

2) It is the common practice, at the beginning of any bibliography of books dealing with anything French, to have a note stating: "Wherever the place of publication for books in French is not mentioned, Paris is to be understood." It avoids repeating Paris every time—

Here only in a very few cases another city is mentioned: Lyon, Besançon, Montreal.

3) I do not see any necessity to quote the French original, poetry or prose, in footnotes, and again at the end, for all the brief quotations translated in the text. It only distracts the reader's attention. Since the longer poetry extracts are NOT quoted in the original French, & should not be, why quote those small fragments in French, at the bottom of the page *and* as "Notes" at the end?

I hope this answers your questions & I am

Very sincerely yours,<br>
Henri Peyre

## À Micheline Levowitz:

290 North Avenue<br>
Westport, Conn. 06880<br>
20 mai 79

Chère et . . . lointaine amie,

Une année de plus terminée, ou presque. À mon âge, on est surpris de se trouver encore vivant, à peu près actif, un peu las et secrètement flatté et honteux à la fois de se croire essentiel—presque indispensable. Il y a quelque séduction morbide (mais, trop normal; j'ai besoin de me trouver un tout petit peu de morbidité) à vivre, lors des moments d'insomnie, avec la pensée de la mort. Il m'arrive même de croire l'humanité si bête, superstitieuse, volontairement aveuglée, que l'on se laisse aller à souhaiter sa fin dans quelque gigantesque explosion. Est-ce jalousie secrète de ceux qui viendront après nous, jouiront des fleurs, des fruits du printemps, de l'amour, des livres?

En tous cas, voici quelques semaines de paresse devant nous. L'année au bureau a été compliquée par de sottes et inutiles lenteurs administratives. Je finis par croire que la bureaucratie est la plaie du monde civilisé, et cela tue, ou presque, l'ancienne foi que j'avais au socialisme—lequel tourne invinciblement à bureaucratie et étatisme. Il est triste de craindre, au soir de la vie, de n'avoir plus d'espoir en une société plus juste. J'avais perdu, avant beaucoup d'autres, étant né plus tôt, mes illusions sur la

Russie de Staline. Je m'étais réfugié dans l'admiration de Trotsky et je suis ému en lisant sa biographie et quelques-uns de ses essais. Mais je ne crois plus guère à une gauche non-communiste—et je suis plus loin encore de ces arrivistes que sont les "nouveaux philosophes." Reste la fierté de l'isolement et de l'indépendance. Je crois que je n'irai même pas en France cet été. Je préfère, de loin, croire que mes compatriotes valent tout de même mieux que leur politique intérieure et que leur récente littérature, si naïvement scatologique.

Allez-vous vous reposer un peu vous-même—à la campagne? Votre sujet de cours est beau, stimulant. Il me tenterait si j'étais plus jeune et pouvais refaire toutes les lectures qu'il comporte. Mais il vous faudra choisir: 1ère grande guerre et ses suites en littérature? Problèmes sociaux de 1930–38? Occupation, résistance et son contraire? (La récente surestimation de Drieu la Rochelle, même de Céline, m'indigne.) Existentialisme; Valéry et sa "repensée" de l'histoire; courants religieux. Il vous faudra choisir quelques œuvres seulement. Mais on dit les étudiantes de Barnard les meilleures du pays et ce doit être vrai. (Le sort s'acharne tragiquement sur elles ces temps-ci!)

Le Diderot? Laissez-moi un jour le relire, bien que je n'aie guère de compétence spéciale et sois même devenu assez froid envers la pensée, sinon l'art, de Diderot. Pourrait-il paraître dans les Studies on Voltaire, moins "clique" que les Diderot Studies; inégales sans doute. Mais l'important serait des tirages à part à envoyer à 10 ou 20 personnes. J'aimerais aussi relire votre Mauriac. Était-il assez technique, de ton et d'allure? J'oublie. Beaucoup d'études à caractère psychanalytique font peur aux revues littéraires et ne sont pas assez "professionnelles" pour les psychologues. Je croirais, pour moi, que vous aviez pénétré assez lucidement Mauriac, avec originalité et pénétration, pour écrire 2 ou 3 autres études sur lui (art de l'autobiographie—peinture de l'adolescent—poésie dans le roman) qui feraient un mince volume. Pourquoi pas? J'apprécie fort la vitalité de Mrs. Wehde, mais elle a dix autres préoccupations et je doute qu'elle ait un "livre" sur Mauriac avant . . . cinq ans. Pour l'instant, on écrit peu sur lui en France.

Mes vœux à votre mari—et ma fidèle et chaleureuse amitié,
Henri Peyre

Je ne sais plus si Kim Ruan m'a dit une date précise pour son mariage? Que de courage elle a, parmi ses malheurs!

## To the University of Alabama Press:

May 30—79

Dear Miss Davis:

I am returning the MS of the Symbolism translation. There were a number of mistakes, in the translation & in the typing. I trust I have caught most of them.

Two important remarks:

Since most French books (99%) are published in Paris, it is useless & wasteful to insert "Paris" every time. Usually, there is a footnote somewhere, or at the beginning of the bibliography, stating: "Unless otherwise specified, the place of publication for all books in French is understood to be Paris."

Adding the first names of authors is equally useless and wasteful. It is not usually done, & it does not have to be, for well known names (e.g. Hugo, Valéry, Verlaine, Baudelaire) — & it is a source of confusion if the first name is inserted by the copy editor (e.g. La Tour, for there were several La Tours; Renoir, the painter's name was "Auguste").

If the man's last name was preceded by a "de," the "de" should be inserted if the first, or Christian name, is also used: e.g. not "de Vigny," "de Gobineau," "de Lamartine," but: "Alfred de Vigny," "Arthur Gobineau," "Alphonse de Lamartine."

The only exception is when the last, or family, name has but *one* syllable: then one may use "De" without the first or Christian name: e.g. "De Gaulle," "De Thou," "De Man."

Some people — that is the rule in Great Britain — use two initials (e.g. J. D. Guigniaut, here — or in England: A. J. P. Taylor, E. M. Forster), but not the first, or Christian, name.

It seems ridiculous to add "Jean" before "Racine," "William" before Shakespeare, "Thomas" before Carlyle, or even "Algernon" before Swinburne. Most Presses I have dealt with have agreed to discontinue that insertion of first names before French & other continental writers: Goethe, Petrarch, Leopardi, Lenau, Guillén.

In any case I have complied with your request & added the first names.

Thank you for your very careful & painstaking editing &

Sincerely yours,
Henri Peyre

## À Micheline Levowitz:

Dimanche 10 juin — (1979)

Chère amie,

Vite un mot qui peut-être vous saisira avant votre départ de vacances. Cela vous reposera de quitter New York dès le début de l'été et, si je n'avais encore tant de papiers accumulés à trier, chapitres de thèses, lettres en souffrance, je m'absenterais volontiers aussi pour tout oublier. L'année n'a pas été mauvaise: pas d'accroc de santé, pas plus d'affaiblissement pour moi que celui, graduel, de l'âge; et celui-là est compensé par un peu plus de sagesse et de souriante résignation. Pas trop de disputes & de jalousie parmi nos collègues. Quelques-unes des thèses ont soulevé des dissentiments chez certains collègues, qui ne peuvent tolérer qu'on ne suive pas à la lettre chacune de leurs suggestions et qui couvent leurs candidats comme des enfants spirituels. Tout s'est réglé en fin de compte. Certes, nous ne produisons pas que des chefs d'œuvre: ce serait bien encombrant si tel était le cas. J'ai toujours pensé que le 2me ou le 3e livre après la thèse est celui où l'on peut plus librement se trouver & se prouver. On verra. Dans votre cas, le 1er était une œuvre de maître — sans flatterie. Les trois auteurs de dissertations stendhaliennes que nous avons couronnés le 7 juin (Mlle Park, M. Zephyrin, Mad. Ruthman) vous ont lue, admirée, mais non égalée. Le second de ces récents docteurs seul était juste, juste "dignus intrare." Mais il a pris sa retraite, a eu 2 ou 3 attaques de cœur, a failli périr sur son ms. stendhalien. La 3e a produit un gros bébé, mâle, le jour même du Commencement, auquel elle a failli cependant assister. J'aurais dû "délivrer" (drôle de terme — de quoi? de quels complexes?) le bébé aussitôt après lui avoir passé le capuchon d'hermine autour du cou — & je n'ai pas de mains de chirurgien. Malgré bien des moments d'impatience, car il faut sans cesse lutter avec administration, "registrar," doyenne, comités, je me suis attaché à ce Centre Gradué—moins snob, moins sottement content de soi que les institutions où j'avais précédemment enseigné. Mais je suis convaincu qu'une plus jeune orientation, tournée vers l'avenir, est désormais nécessaire. Je m'étonne moi-même de me surprendre tellement intéressé à l'avenir (politique française, énergie, remplacement éventuel d'un socialisme usé et suranné par une autre forme de démocratie) alors que cet avenir ne sera certes pas le mien. Ce n'est même pas faiblesse de père vieilli, reportant sur son fils ses rêves non réalisés, car mon grand garçon de 15 ans est fort indépendant, très différent de moi et américain 95%. Pourquoi pas? Surtout, il est normal, bien adapté (comme un vrai Philistin), et aussi peu averti sur ses complexes, pulsions, refoulements secrets que moi-même.

C'est peut-être un peu—subconsciemment—pour ne pas entendre les Français exposer leurs âneries & leurs mesquins préjugés sur la politique & l'économie que je m'abstiens d'aller en Europe cet été. Il est plus facile de les aimer, et même de les comprendre, de loin. Dès ma toute première année en Amérique (1925–26!), fermé à bien d'autres aspects du pays & alors à son conservatisme capitaliste, j'avais goûté surtout la largeur d'information & de vues qui permet qu'on s'intéresse à 4 ou 5 pays d'Europe à la fois & même à l'Asie. Paris, soudain, où j'étais né, qui me manquait, me semblait provincial. Si j'étais resté en France, j'aurais assez vite été happé par la politique—mon plus vif intérêt—& j'y aurais été maladroit et malheureux.

Dites-moi ce que vous apprendrez de votre *Diderot*. En attendant, j'aurais plaisir à relire votre *Mauriac* & peut-être à vous conseiller de le reprendre, ou de tenter 2 ou 3 études, dans le même esprit, sur d'autres romanciers de ce siècle et à les réunir en volume. Je suis convaincu que, toute préoccupation de carrière mise à part, ce que vous avez à dire, & dites fort bien, est valable et important.

Votre sujet de cours est énorme mais beau. Il demande un esprit d'engagement, et en même temps d'impartialité: vertu que je n'ai guère eue moi-même quand tout en moi s'est révolté contre Maurras, Brasillach, Céline, Drieu (sottement surfait aujourd'hui) et contre d'anciens élèves à moi (curieusement, des juifs; e.g. Rima Drell Reck), invinciblement attirés par cette "pensée" de droite—et par ceux-là mêmes qui les couvraient d'insultes. Si jamais je puis vous aider, dites-le moi. L'ouvrage anglais, trop long, de Zeltin sur la France, est remarquable et la traduction en impressionne les Français.

Voilà donc Kim Ruan fiancée? Je croyais que cela était déjà fait. Ses soucis de santé m'avaient inquiété, et l'inachèvement de son travail—peut-être sur un thème trop vaste & vague. Quant à sa famille au Viet Nam, cela est bien triste; mais je crois qu'à partir de 20 ou 25 ans, il convient d'oublier un peu ceux qui vous ont élevés. C'est le plus sûr moyen de ne pas être ensuite forcé de les haïr. Vous et votre mari êtes magnifiques d'amitié et de compréhension envers elle. Je ne sais plus rien de Mme Vastro et suis déçu que son livre, patronné par Mme Knapp, n'ait pas encore paru. Vous avez dû recevoir ce rapport que j'ai rédigé sur nos résultats & activités (il a été envoyé à 2 ou 300 personnes ou chefs de département, etc.); je crois que les "accomplissements," comme dit l'anglais, de nos anciens y font très respectable figure. À d'autres maintenant à prendre la relève.

Jouissez sans arrière-pensée de votre repos. Mes amitiés à votre mari—et affectueusement à vous.

H. P.

## À Eléonore Zimmermann:

290 North Avenue
Westport, Conn. 06880
18 juin 79

Chère Eléonore, (Que ce nom m'intimide toujours! C'est l'un des plus nobles prénoms que je connaisse.)

Votre belle lettre, écrite à la veille de votre départ, était restée sans réponse, comme vous vous y attendiez. Je vous ai enviée, car cela fait des siècles que je n'ai pas passé de printemps en Europe—et je ne pense même pas m'y rendre cet été. C'est une des mélancolies de l'âge avancé que l'on ne compte plus guère d'amis, et je n'en ai plus ou presque plus en France. Et peut-être y a-t-il derrière cela un manque de goût pour les évocations du passé; je n'ai aucun goût pour me rappeler les années de lycée ou d'École Normale, les naïvetés d'autrefois. À mes yeux, il faut attendre d'avoir 35 ou 40 ans pour devenir vraiment celui que l'on veut être. Mais alors on est menacé de quelque sclérose. Je supporte aisément les jeux des enfants, & ici, avec les 3 fils de Diane & le mien, cela me rajeunit de les observer ou de discuter avec eux. Mais quelque agacement me saisit devant les adultes (nouveaux philosophes, politiciens arrivistes comme Servan-Schreiber, Bernard H. Lévy, Revel, se tournant vers le conservatisme, suiveurs de Roland Barthes sans peine) s'attardant à des tours de virtuose bien futiles. La vie littéraire et universitaire française ne m'attirerait pas; il me manque davantage de ne pas voir quelques expositions, comme celles de l'expressionnisme allemand, puis du constructivisme russe qui ont eu lieu au Centre Pompidou. Je serai curieux, à l'automne, de savoir quelles auront été là-bas vos impressions.

Ici, année terminée (au Graduate Center de CUNY, du moins): sans anicroche; plusieurs thèses assez remarquables—toutes par des femmes. C'est elles décidément qui, dans nos études, ont l'originalité, l'audace et la persistance. Je resterai une année encore, puisqu'on remet toujours de me remplacer; mais je m'avoue content d'avoir passé mes dernières années d'enseignement parmi des étudiantes (bien peu ont moins de 28 ou 30 ans) douées, sérieuses, "eager," dénuées de ce qu'il y avait parfois à Yale de snobisme et de contentement de soi.

[Sans signature]

## To Florence and Kurt Weinberg:

> 290 North Avenue
> Westport, Conn. 06880
> July 22—79

Dear Florence & Kurt,

At last, in the midst of a gloomy spring, beset with dire predictions on all sides, some good news! Congratulations to Florence on the fellowship! She is as learned as she is beautiful, & amid so many sarcastic, disgruntled, envious people in our profession, her smile always radiates kindliness. I admire her, among other things, for finding such depth & meaning in Rabelais, one of my pet "allergies." And now Fischart, whom I don't know, & Chess as an archetype! She should be at the Institute for Advanced Studies at Princeton, or at Wisconsin, & not at Rochester. But she escaped Hunter College, anyway, where things will be uncertain & disturbed for another twenty years—until the present professors at last resign. She is meanwhile winning the battle at St. John Fisher—against all odds—& that is, I hope, a sign of a new trend in our profession: administrators can be made to listen to a determined faculty!

I trust your year will be pleasant & restful. On dit que le lac de Constance est une très belle région. J'ai dû y passer, et à Innsbruck, puis dans la Bavière du Sud, peu avant la guerre, quand Hitler sévissait, menaçait, aboyait, & le souvenir que j'en ai gardé est un cauchemar. La communication que va donner Kurt sur la traduction est profonde et abstruse, presque trop courte pour les questions variées que cela pose. Mais cela devrait ouvrir un débat animé.

Le Mallarmé est bien plus qu'une exégèse d'un sonnet que je n'avais jamais cru trop énigmatique, ou très beau—mais une étude *très* considérable sur Mallarmé: l'une des plus suggestives que j'aie lues. Elle réinterprète "Ses purs ongles," sonde les secrets (involontaires, peut-être) mis par Mall. dans ses *Mots anglais*. Cela étend & approfondit le très frappant article que j'avais déjà lu dans le *Forum;* en vérité, ce devrait paraître comme brochure séparée, ou peut-être partie du livre sur Mall. que Kurt doit écrire, & porte en lui. Mon esprit obtus résiste sans doute à entendre "mainte à l'en verre" dans "l'envers" ou à déchiffrer une césure dans la "coupe" de champagne—mais cela "is my loss." Que de science chez vous deux, qui avez au bout de vos doigts Pindare, Euripide, Iamblique, Porphyre, sans parler des deux Testaments et des modernes en 4 ou 5 langues! Je suis ébloui, éberlué, même lorsque je reste sceptique et philistin. J'en suis au stade, ou à l'âge, où j'aime la poésie pour me la réciter en marchant au bord de la mer, ou en conduisant, mais loin de toute herméneutique. Si toutefois il en faut une, celle de Kurt me paraît autrement solide que les gnoses de Harold Bloom ou même celles de Geoffrey Hartman.

Je vois que l'exemplaire reçu porte au crayon les corrections d'épreuve. Dois-je vous le renvoyer? Si oui, dites-le moi d'une simple carte. Sinon je relirai ce texte plus tard dans l'été.

Merci très chaleureusement et beaucoup d'amitié,
Henri

## À Frederic Saint Aubyn:

> 290 North Ave
> Westport, Conn. 06880
> Aug. 30 — 79

Cher Monsieur Saint Aubyn,

    Je ne connaissais pas cette revue, & très peu Simon Fraser University. Mais il y a dans ces numéros bien des choses d'intérêt & je garde précieusement votre bibliographie. Elle est riche, techniquement impeccable & sera utile. Bien sûr, comme toutes les bibliographies, elle s'enrichira chaque année de nouveaux titres. Vous êtes courageux et homme d'avenir de ne pas avoir été arrêté par cela. J'imagine que vous réunirez ces quatre articles en un court volume, pour qu'il soit catalogué, accessible dans les bibliothèques. C'est en France qu'un tel petit volume devrait paraître; et je crois que vous devriez le faire précéder d'un essai de vous sur Butor, au moins sur ses œuvres récentes, que peu de gens ont eu le flair ou la hardiesse de goûter. Votre récent article dans la revue australienne est, à cet égard, original et très utile.

    La situation littéraire est triste en France; au lieu de déchiffrer, comme vous avez l'originalité de le faire, les auteurs d'aujourd'hui, on semble se complaire à une attitude nostalgique & réactionnaire. Que de bruit fait autour de Drieu la Rochelle! Un gros volume de Grover et Andreu sur lui chez Hachette! Du drôle dans Le Roi Salomon d'Émile Ajar, mais enfin, des ficelles comiques bien usées. Tournier ressasse ses premiers livres, et cela manque de fraîcheur. Probablement suis-je atteint par la mauvaise humeur des vieux qui voudraient la jeune génération plus brillante que la leur!

    Merci, en tous cas, de m'avoir permis de feuilleter ces pages, qui me serviront — et croyez à mes sentiments toujours fidèles.

Henri Peyre

Je n'ai pas sous la main le livre récent de Diane McCormick: The City as Catalyst., Associated Univ. Presses. Rutherford, New Jersey. Mais je sais qu'elle y a un chapitre sur L'Emploi du Temps.

    Vous avez su la mort soudaine de K. Cornell, qui souvent parlait de vous—

## À Eléonore Zimmermann:

> 290 North Avenue
> Westport, Conn. 06880
> Le 24 Sept. 1979

Chère Eléonore,

    Que vous êtes gentille, bienveillante! Je suis très, très touché de la sympathie que vous ressentez pour cet absurde accident arrivé à mon fils, et vous remercie de ces avis & "recettes." J'ai noté et copié ce que vous disiez de certaines vitamines et potages—et nous mettons à profit ces sages conseils. Soit scepticisme de vieux qui a survécu à son passé, soit simple sottise de ma part, je n'ai jamais su grand'chose sur les vitamines & les pilules & m'en suis toujours abstenu. Mais il ne s'agit pas de moi dans le cas présent. Sa mère est beaucoup plus prévoyante & elle le soigne avec sollicitude. Diane, rentrée d'une brève équipée au Mexique, fait de même quand il vient à Westport deux jours par semaine. Peut-être que dans un mois cette cruelle expérience sera, sinon oubliée, au moins dépassée.

    J'ai souvent rêvé d'aller en Norvège. À 18 ans, j'avais été passionné d'Ibsen, & surtout de romans norvégiens. Le hasard a fait que je n'ai réussi à visiter que le Danemark, & la Suède que je n'ai guère aimée. La mer baltique m'avait enchanté, un été, & même les côtes septentrionales allemandes. Les plages du Midi de l'Europe sont si encombrées & enlaidies que je ne les hanterai plus jamais. Vous êtes fortunée d'avoir eu, au pays de Selma Lagerlof—et de Séraphita—un introducteur expert, affectueux et patient. C'est un pays, j'imagine, qui ne se livre pas facilement au visiteur non initié.

    Pour moi, cet été a été calme et monotone. Cela avait son charme. J'avais entrepris de relire les auteurs que, vers 1945–70, j'avais le plus goûtés. C'est une expérience curieuse, que de se regarder réagissant autrement. Gide m'a semblé vieilli; Sartre, exaspérant parfois par sa dialectique; Simone de Beauvoir, plus dure et sèche que je ne me la rappelais. Envers Camus, par contre, je fais amende honorable. À relire Merleau-Ponty et autres de ses contradicteurs de 1950–60, je trouve que Camus avait plus de modestie, de noblesse, et de bon sens aussi. Les sinuosités dialectiques des Hégéliens & Marxistes français (celles de Goldmann, par exemple, sur le tragique et les prétendues bases économiques de la littérature janséniste; celles de récents structuralistes) me paraissent artificielles souvent, teintes de vanité, et inutilement pédantes. G. Hartman lui-même, que j'aime personnellement beaucoup, Harold Bloom & d'autres à Yale ne sont pas exempts de dogmatisme. Et ils se plaignent maintenant de l'éloignement des études littéraires chez les étudiants que nous avons formés. Nous sommes en partie responsables. Je lutte encore pour nos études & dans quelque mesure nous réussissons même à placer nos docteurs. Mais il y faut de l'obstination!

[Sans signature]

## To John W. Kneller

290 North Avenue<br>
Westport, CT 06880<br>
September 29, 1979

Dear Jack,

I was very much touched by your kind concern for my son, and so was Brice, to whom I reported it. It turned out that he needed a second and then a third operation on his broken jaws. He is still on a tedious and insipid, liquid diet; but his morale is good; he has resumed his studies at school and he is not too bitter about the world and its cruelty.

Work has been going on now for two weeks at CUNY. I hope you are enjoying the respite from your hectic activities of the last few years. I believe a meeting of a committee (on languages?) has been called for the morning of Thursday, October fourth. Will you stop by the French office (#1040, I believe) that you will share with two colleagues (they do not come to the Center every day) and, after the committee, we might have lunch together upstairs and talk for a while. If you do not reply (and there is no need for you to), I shall look forward to seeing you then.

With very cordial greetings to your wife and my wishes to you for a quiet year.

Henri

## To John W. Kneller:

290 North Avenue  
Westport, Conn. 06880  
Tuesday Oct. 9, 79

Dear Jack,

Just a line on the subjects of eventual, or future, courses. It is a very touchy subject with our colleagues and I believe it would be wiser & more diplomatic to have you offer a graduate course next Fall (1980), after you have been with us some time as a colleague, have perhaps advised some of our graduate students, attended the few meetings of faculty & students we have in the course of the year. As you may guess, every member of the Graduate Faculty (21 of us) asks to give a graduate course as often as possible, in part because it relieves him or her of a course at the college. I have to say "no" two out of three times, since we are allowed (mine, Central Appointment, excluded) only five courses per semester. We are left with ten courses per year & do not have enough students to fill out more courses than that. When I had the Executive Committee of our Program, & then the Faculty, vote on your joining us, I stated that you would actually start working with us after 1979–80, when you were supposed to be on leave. Unless we had a large influx of students, & were justified in creating more courses, it would at present cause some discontent to cancel a course by a colleague to make room for one by you.

Meanwhile would you think of two, or three, possible titles of courses which you would like to offer eventually? Our colleagues have done that, & reserve the right to change & offer new fields, & the Executive Officer chooses the courses according to the needs of the students & the general balance of fields & themes.

I have—once again—asked to retire after this year, but it would still be my responsibility to prepare (in Jan. or Febr. next) the list of courses for the first semester of 1980–81.

I have written a couple of pages on the charge # 5 assigned to us by Ms. Grandjouan—very *un*original, & shall send you a copy within a few days.

Cordially & again, welcome among us.

Yours,  
Henri

## To the same:

October 25, 1979

Dear Jack,

If you would like to, you might take part on this second (oral) exam on Wednesday, November 21. The candidate talks for 7 or 8 minutes on each question, then answers our own questions, clarifies some points. About 12 to 15 minutes for each of the six topics and another ten for the exploration of one poem, given her and the members of her committee 3 or 4 days before.

Mrs. Knapp and I would be the regular examiners with you, if you accept.

We have no vita, no information whatever on you in our office files. Would you provide us with some? Or should we ask the Central Office for it?

I shall have to be absent this coming Monday.

Don't be too severe on the MS thesis. We have to keep students encouraged—and attract others.

Cordially,
Henri

## À Eléonore Zimmermann:

290 North Avenue
Westport, Conn. 06880.
Le 8 novembre 1979

Chère Eléonore,

Cela me fera plaisir de vous revoir lors de ma visite et je me sens très honoré de cette invitation à parler à votre Université. J'y compte bien des amis—trop indulgents pour moi—car quelqu'un de plus jeune, de plus vigoureux et peut-être de plus sympathique à certains mouvements récents dans la littérature critique aurait été mieux indiqué pour parler chez vous.

Je ne veux pas jouer au modeste, mais je n'ai vraiment nul document sur moi et je ne crois pas que vous deviez dire autre chose sur moi que quelques brèves phrases irrévérencieuses. Je suis né à Paris en 1901; j'ai enseigné plus d'un demi siècle à Bryn Mawr, Yale, New York, en France et en Egypte. J'ai beaucoup écrit—trop sans doute, et souvent avec hâte journalistique. J'ai surtout enseigné, avec zèle et parfois passion, et c'est cela dont je suis fier seulement. Très tôt, j'ai pensé que ma vocation était d'élargir le public qui pouvait aimer la littérature & les arts. D'où mon peu de goût pour divers aspects de la critique, et l'"arrogance" avec laquelle je le dis. J'ai eu bien des récompenses: décorations, honneurs académiques, et publié, m'a-t-on dit l'autre jour, plus de quarante livres. Mais ma vraie récompense a toujours été l'attachement de mes anciens élèves.

Je serais touché et ému si vous deviez me dédier votre prochain livre, Eléonore—et je n'ai pas besoin d'avoir lu votre manuscrit pour cela. Je le lirai si je puis vous être utile et si vous me croyez compétent en littérature racinienne; mais il me semble que, d'abord, vous devriez faire hommage de votre ouvrage à votre père, à qui vous devez certainement beaucoup.

Diane va bien et elle regrette d'être prise à Brooklyn le jeudi—elle travaille beaucoup & dit parfois que vous êtes parmi les deux ou trois modèles qu'elle se propose. Brice, enfin, est remis, ou à peu près. Je ne pense pas qu'il reste, moralement, blessé de ce regrettable accident. Vos sages conseils m'ont aidé à le nourrir lorsqu'il ne pouvait mâcher.

Merci encore, du fond du cœur, et toute mon amitié,
Henri

## To Buford Norman:

November 9, 1979

Dear Mr. Norman:

I remember you clearly, of course, as that bright, spiritual young man who was unusual in being an expert in theological & religious matters & read Pascal intelligently. This semester, for the last time in my long career, I am giving a seminar on Pascal: since most of the students here are Jewish, & "mature" people, 30 to 40 years old as an average, we have had very lively discussions on Pascal & the Old Testament, Pascal as the forefather of French anti-Semitism(!), etc. I have occasionally read an article or two by you, but I'd be glad to read more of what you have written.

The publisher of the 17th century anthology has decided not to retain it on his list. So a new anthology of the prose of that age would seem to be in order—with fresh views & new texts: more extracts, perhaps, from the memorialists and from the religious writers (St François de Sales, Bossuet, *et al.*).

It is hard to give advice from such long distance. As you know, positions are scarce these days; if I were you, I certainly would not give up a tenure one unless & until I had a firm offer elsewhere (Iowa State? Kansas? Oklahoma?). I believe you come from the South, & you might start discreet inquiries in Texas, Florida, North Carolina. I am an old man (78 ½) & trying annually to retire. My contacts with the profession are few nowadays & I avoid going to conventions. But I would be glad to have a curriculum vitae on you & to read some of your writings. I may add that the recent trend of some Pascal studies (Hugh Davidson, Morot-Sir, Marin), reducing the tragic thinker to a man obsessed with language problems & desiccating him, has struck me as barren.

I am well. My recent work has been in other periods than the XVIIth century, but I keep up with it & still attack God now & then.

> Cordially yours,
> Henri Peyre

## À Rosette Lamont:

> Nov. 13, 1979

Chère Rosette,

Vous avez le goût le plus exquis, et vos attentions à me décorer doublement, d'une couleur choisie pour s'harmoniser avec mon "mérite," me touchent. Vous pensez toujours aux autres et à leur faire plaisir. Mon plaisir est vrai & grand, mais je rougis d'être ainsi gâté. Merci, très affectueusement.

Je mets ces deux lettres dans votre boîte. Si elles vous conviennent, fermez-les et envoyez-les. Pour Mme Marchessault, mieux vaut ne rien faire et réserver nos efforts, & notre auditoire, pour Mme Delbo.

> Avec beaucoup d'amitié,
> Henri

Je dois aller parler à Stony Brook jeudi & ne vous apercevrai sans doute pas.

## To John W. Kneller:

Nov. 29, 1979

Dear Jack,

I am distressed to hear that you have to be hospitalized for a while. Twice, but a long time ago, I had myself to be operated on for a hernia & I do not relish the imprisonment in hospitals. I thought it particularly outrageous that such a "complaint" should afflict someone who never practiced any sport & never strained himself. You, at least, run, swim strenuously and jump on your horse. I hope all will be well very soon & you'll have a restful Christmas with Sherry & your daughter.

Your report on the exam is admirable & I am grateful to you. Most of us write only a few perfunctory lines, since no one sees those reports, except the student (if she so chooses) & the Chairman. Mrs. Guers-Martynuk is indeed an able & serious person. The same afternoon, she found a job as the person in charge of the Language Lab. in one of the CUNY community colleges.

You'll be glad to learn that Diana received notice from your successor of her promotion to a full professorship. Her immediate reaction was to say she will always be grateful for your faith in her. She has justified it those last two years with tangible & impressive results in the form of articles & books.

She sends you & Sherry, as I do, the very warmest wishes & regards.

Henri

## À Eléonore Zimmermann:

Le 7 déc. 79

Chère Eléonore,

Vous ai-je vraiment donné l'impression que je "résistais" quelque peu à votre MS? Ce n'est pas du tout le cas. J'ai voulu dire que l'intention du livre, l'originalité très réelle de son angle d'approche, l'ingéniosité — jamais excessive — de vos remarques et votre indépendance de jugement gagneraient à être soulignées dès le début. Votre modestie et votre réserve, si rares ces temps-ci, vous ont retenu de tenter la moindre "réclame" pour ce que vous apportez, qui a de la force en même temps que de la finesse. Je suis honoré & touché de votre intention de me dédier l'ouvrage, mais j'ai bien peu fait pour vous aider. Je me rappelle vos débuts à Yale, quand vous arriviez déjà "formée" & très savante de Swarthmore. J'étais ravi de votre largeur d'intérêts & de connaissances, comme venaient dans nos brèves conversations les noms de . . . Verlaine, certes, ou Rimbaud — et aussi de Meredith (que je continue à lire), de Stifter, de St George peut-être ou de Gottfried Keller. Mon allemand s'est bien rouillé depuis!

J'ai encore quelque remords d'avoir paru "attaquer" des collègues dont l'âge, les vues ne sont pas les miens. Bien sûr, je suis trop vieux et, comme disait Lamartine, "J'ai trop vu, trop senti . . . dans ma vie" (non pas, cependant, trop aimé). Cela m'amuse de constater les renversements de tendances. Il y a 30 ou 40 ans, vers 1940–45, je revenais à Yale; j'avais publié en Europe un gros livre sur Shelley, plein d'amour passionné pour lui. Le Doyen, tous les professeurs d'anglais, alors acquis au "New Criticism," férus de T. S. Eliot, me disaient: "Il est heureux que vous soyez full professor. Car aujourd'hui, on rejetterait quelqu'un qui dit admirer 'Alastor,' 'Epipsychidion,' 'The Witch of Atlas,' 'The Triumph of Life.' "

L'autre jour, j'achète à la COOP un livre, Deconstruction, par Geoffrey Hartman, De Man, Harold Bloom, Derrida. C'est un volume délirant d'admiration (en langage barbare) pour Shelley et "The Triumph of Time." Auprès de lui, Yeats et un peu Ashbery, Pope, Dryden, Boswell, les demi-dieux de 1940–60, sont bien mal traités. En France, Lacan, dit-on, n'a plus un seul élève à ses cours de l'École Normale. Derrida, fort peu. Sic transit gloria mundi, comme aimait à citer De Gaulle.

Mais je m'égare — & je dois courir à un autre comité pour "sauver" les langues.

Passez d'agréables fêtes, portez-vous bien et au revoir — bientôt "Dans un mois, dans un an."

Toute mon amitié,<br>Henri

## To John W. Kneller:

Dec. 28, 1979

Dear Jack,

Do not take those variations in ladies' moods too seriously. I encouraged Ms. Leadley, obviously a sensitive & touchy person, to go ahead & aim at completing an acceptable thesis by April or so. She is grateful to you, who have been far more devoted & conscientious than either Mrs. Charney or myself. Some of those not-so-young scholars feel that correcting their writing is a "violation" of their personality! Forget about it for the present. Let her write more & submit it to us in a few weeks, & I am sure she will be full of gratitude for your patient assistance.

Meanwhile, my wishes, & Diana's, for your vacations & the New Year — & Sherry's.

Yours, en vive amitié,
H. P.

## To Buford Norman:

Dec. 29 — 79

Dear Mr. Norman:

I sent at once a letter to the Yale Placement Office. I admired your modesty, but I think it is misplaced. Why should you not be a full professor now, on the strength of what you have achieved, which is substantial, & of the qualities of intellect & of character that your letters reveal? If a really good position (with tenure) offers itself at an Assoc. prof. rank, you will always be free to accept it & "de voir venir." Let me know some time if anything promising appeared at San Francisco. I have ceased, a few years ago, attending those conventions; they are a sorry sight & the indifference, at times almost sadistic, of the older & tenured people, keeping young applicants at bay or tantalizing them, is revolting. Besides, I am too old to submit to the fatigue; & where I am, except for my own position of chairman which I am trying hard to relinquish, there are no vacancies. The full professors from the senior CUNY undergraduate colleges provide our staff of some 20 full professors.

I shall not discuss your very interesting remarks on Pascal & on *Phèdre:* they are illuminating, even if paradoxical. Why don't you, without waiting much further, undertake a small book on some aspect of Pascal? or of Fénelon, a fascinating personality & one little discussed in this country? Lately, the few & far between XVIIth century scholars in this country have been in demand: Brody (who did good articles on La Bruyère, St. Simon) left CUNY for Harvard; Rountree (once at Yale) is at Univ. of Mass. & being promoted; he is bringing out a book on Barthélémy D'Argonne; Albanese has not been well treated at Ann Arbor, but he is now at Nebraska; an older Yale graduate, Eléonore Zimmermann, is completing a book on Racine & is a full prof. at Stony Brook. Emory, now a rich place, might be a fine place for you to move to, if you like the South. Iowa is not devoid of charm, in my memory, at least; & Iowa City has had, at times, very fine poets, & scholars: Wellek, Hartman, & others; but I imagine that Ames is an isolated place. At least, being somewhat remote, geographically, you have been spared the late epidemics of pedantic jargon & of pretentious & pseudo-terrorist thinking which some of your contemporaries at Yale have fallen for at Cornell & J. Hopkins. The last French Studies (Oxford) calls J. Mehlman's pretentious & murky book on "Revolution, 18 Brumaire, Hugo," etc., a pompous, "impish & specious bit of nonsense." I am afraid I agree.

I'll return to thesis chapters on my desk & to dozens of letters to answer. I never can take the time to type them & impose my poor hand upon all my correspondents. They do not seem to resent it.

With my cordial wishes,
Henri Peyre

## À Jean Boorsch:

290 North Avenue
Westport, Conn. 06880
Le 31 déc. 79

Mon cher Jean,

Je ne suis guère l'homme des examens de conscience, ou même des regards en arrière, mais je me dis tout de même que je vous ai bien peu vu cette année qui meurt, & sais bien peu de vous — alors que bien rares se font les vieux amis & les presque contemporains. Mais je suis encore beaucoup à N. York; je voyage entre Westport & New Haven; m'occupe un peu de Brice & de Lois; griffonne encore quelques méchants articles, parfois avec colère, ou sarcasme. Et je crois que vous voyagez beaucoup.

Comment va Louise? Ses malaises se sont-ils dissipés? On dit que la venue de descendants rajeunit, & occupe, les grands-parents. Est-ce le cas? Votre fille est-elle en belle santé, & heureuse? J'avais été content de revoir le peintre & sa très gentille femme, le jour où on m'a lié d'un collier appelé cravate. Dites-lui mes pensées, & aux autres enfants, que je me rappelle si jeunes, riches d'avenir.

Si je réussis à le faire, & me trouve un successeur, je compte enfin terminer mes longues années d'enseignements — à 79 ans! Peut-être serai-je encore assez vaillant pour revoir Paris — Venise — Rome. Ce qu'on me dit des prix m'effare & N. York est déjà assez ruineux. Un jour, redites-moi le nom, l'adresse de la très agréable & claire "Résidence" où vous étiez, Boulevard Raspail.

J'imagine que vous allez hiverner en quelque autre hémisphère & vous admire, & Louise — sans vraiment vous envier — enfoncé que je suis dans quelque "morne incuriosité," mère de l'ennui.

Croyez du moins, tous deux, à mes vœux de vieil & fidèle ami.
Henri

# the 1980s
## Chapter Seven

## À Rosette Lamont:

> 290 North Ave.
> Westport, Conn. 06880
> Febr. 22 — 80

Chère Rosette,

Quelle gracieuse & ingénieuse carte — et fidèle image d'un arroseur au gros nez, versant son aimable poison, comme je l'ai fait tant d'années. Quelques modestes fleurs sont devenues de puissants arbres; vos branches, à leur tour, dispensent à d'autres "le mystique aliment qui fera leur vigueur." Merci — et de ce champagne, particulièrement délicieux. Diane & moi l'avons bu hier soir — seuls désormais, tous les enfants partis — c'est un avant-goût de la retraite pour moi & je ne déteste pas cette venue de "l'automne des idées." Vous avez rendu agréable & aimablement enivrant ce passage à l'octogénariat.

> Amitiés à votre mari et toute ma plus fidèle affection.
> [Sans signature]

## To Mark Smith:

>290 North Avenue
>Westport, Conn. 06880
>Tel. (203) 226-4868
>March 27/80

Dear Mr. Smith:

I found your letter & the MS at the Graduate Center on Monday (the above address is quicker & perhaps safer). I may have spoken with you that day at Stony Brook, but I confess I forget now. I wish I could have retained a more vivid memory of my former students at Yale. I may since have read things by you—but your last name is, to me, confusing. Its French equivalent, at least, could assume several forms: Fabre, Favre, Febvre, Lefèvre *et al.*

I am *deeply* touched by your idea, your courage, & the speed with which you have at once acted upon this project. I am embarrassed also, I confess.

Let me say this first: certainly, if this old book of mine is worth translating at all, I am sure you *should*, & would, be the person to do it. The sample you sent me is excellent indeed; I'll go over it with more care next weekend & return it to you.

The questions I have are these:

1) One can never be sure that a Press will accept such a MS & publish it. In this case, the book in French (first done in 1933, almost half a century ago; republished during World War II by Droz in Switzerland, without my knowing it; then in N.Y., under a slightly different title; then by Nizet in Paris in 1965) must have sold relatively widely. I was never told how many copies were printed, nor did I ever receive any royalties—that is common for "les livres d'érudition," ou dits tels.

>[No signature]

## To the same:

Henri Peyre
290 North Avenue
Westport, Conn. 06880
April 5, 1980

Dear Mr. Smith:

I went over your MS again & let me say again that I like it very much. It is an excellent translation. Still, I cannot help, on this second reading, thinking that the text of my original volume is very dated. What was "recent" or fashionable in 1935 or 1955 has been superseded. It all has to be "repensé" & rewritten. *It is best to leave this project in abeyance until I stop teaching — maybe this Summer — & can work on the text further.*

Meanwhile, impressed as I am by your rendering, I hope I may have an opportunity to put your name forward with some Presses, praising your skill.

[No signature]

## À Konrad Bieber:

290 North Avenue
Westport, Conn. 06880
April 5, 1980

Cher Konrad,

Cette réunion à North Dartmouth était déplorablement organisée, lugubre malgré la relative originalité de l'architecture, sans rien de chaleureux ou de vivant. Je vous ai aperçu, écouté avec intérêt (comme toujours, vous étiez modeste, discret, et direct), mais n'ai pas eu l'occasion de vous féliciter ou de vous parler. Je voulais vous dire plus longuement les raisons de mon hésitation devant l'offre flatteuse de M. Smith de traduire mon vieux Classicisme.

Je l'ai écrit à M. Smith. Le livre a vieilli; après tout, il datait pour l'essentiel de 1933! Des tas de points de vue nouveaux ont été mis en avant depuis lors (baroque, maniérisme, histoire du XVIIe siècle renouvelée, renouvellement de nos vues sur le cartésianisme, Pascal, les moralistes; sur Poussin & les arts). Mon livre s'adressait à des Français ou à des spécialistes de français. S'il devait avoir en vue un public de langue anglaise, je devrais le réorienter et en récrire divers chapitres. Ce que M. Smith m'a soumis est fort bien traduit & si je récris le livre en français, je ne souhaiterais certes nul autre traducteur que lui. Mais je veux d'abord réfléchir, lire ou relire nombre de livres ou d'articles parus sur le classicisme depuis 1950. Il me faudra pour cela le loisir de l'été, & celui auquel j'aspire après janvier 1981 (si je suis encore en vie et lucide), lorsque j'ai résolu & annoncé ma retraite de CUNY.

Je vous suis reconnaissant d'avoir encouragé M. Smith & de l'aider dans cette tâche délicate, où vous êtes un expert hautement estimé: la traduction. Merci, et mes vœux—trop tardifs pour Pâques—mais du moins pour un calme printemps et pour votre été. J'irai sans doute en France en juin, avec Diane & Brice—mais un peu effrayé par les prix.

> À Tamara & vous, notre affection,
> Henri

## À Jean Boorsch:

> 290 North Ave.
> Westport, Conn. 06880
> Le 6 avril 80

Mon cher Jean,

J'imagine que vous voilà tous deux revenus de votre île "amoureuse"—ou cela veut-il dire "rouge" comme les mûres—ensoleillés, Louise libérée des maux qui vous inquiétaient, prêts à tailler vos lilas et à choyer votre petite fille (j'ai oublié si c'est une fille ou un garçon). Votre longue lettre, ivre de ces souvenirs de pérégrinations en plusieurs continents, riche de tant de regards jetés sur le passé, était fascinante. Quelle précision dans vos précises évocations du nombre de milles parcourus, de tonnes d'essence consommées, de ces villes dévorées! Quelle fierté de ce passé de pérégrinations, sans jamais un accident. Jusqu'à ces dernières années, je ne me penchais guère sur mon passé—sotte passion pour une activité affairée & brouillonne, peut-être, chez moi; vague peur de "regarder en arrière / le cadavre de mes jours," les rêves de jeunesse non réalisés? Puis, las des livres récents, de l'art de ces dernières années, désabusé de ces travaux critiques dont je m'impose la lecture (bien en vain, car je ne comprends toujours ni Derrida, ni même Hartman, ni le dernier French Studies de Yale dédié à Ehrmann, ni les prétentieuses élucubrations de Mehlman) et de trop de chapitres de thèse, je me suis dernièrement replongé dans ce que j'aimais à 18 ans: les Grecs, les romantiques anglais, Nietzsche, les élégiaques latins. Mes beaux projets d'apprendre le russe une fois en retraite se sont évanouis. Je vais, enfin en janvier prochain au plus tard (j'attends encore la nomination d'un successeur), cesser d'enseigner. après quelque 55 ans. Je pense que je resterai bonnement oisif, tranquille, vaguement ennuyé. . . .

## À Eléonore Zimmermann:

> 290 North Avenue
> Westport, Conn. 06880
> Le 13 mai 1980

Chère Eléonore, (je ne cesse d'être rêveur devant ce nom de reine)

Votre lettre & l'envoi me font plaisir; et j'avais été touché déjà de votre carte, si gentille, lorsque vous aviez appris que j'avais eu un anniversaire. Je n'ai ni honte ni regret de vieillir; mais après la mort de plusieurs autres que j'admirais (Malraux, Sartre, Queneau, Caillois) & d'amis qui étaient mes cadets (Bédé), je me sens gêné de survivre, presque humilié dans ma vanité, comme si les Parques m'oubliaient. Je vais bien cependant et devrais m'estimer heureux de ne pas, comme vous devez le faire, avoir recours aux médecins. J'ai finalement fait accepter ma décision de me retirer le 31 janvier prochain & j'espère que d'ici-là mon successeur sera enfin nommé. Notre "Programme" est en bon état: mais le recrutement de nouveaux étudiants de valeur est difficile, tant que les perspectives de positions sont si médiocres.

Reposez-vous cet été et, si vous pouvez vous libérer quelque peu des soins médicaux, jouissez du très grand charme de ce lac & de ce pays. Souffrez-vous de quelque affliction précise? et douloureuse? Je fais des vœux (je ne sais à quel Esculape les adresser) pour votre santé. Je ne serai guère absent en Europe que 3 ou 4 semaines, & de retour vers le 10 juillet.

> Très affectueusement à vous,
> Henri

## À Micheline Levowitz:

> 290 North Ave.
> Westport, Conn. 06880
> Tel. (203) 226-4868
> Le 16 mai 80
> (je n'y suis pas souvent!)

Chère amie,

Cela fait bien de l'écriture en effet. Mais je suis toujours si pressé que je m'explique mal, sans doute. Alors juste quelques précisions.

C'est le 31 janvier 1981 que se termine, sur ma demande, ma carrière New Yorkaise. Il en est bien temps. Le mois suivant, j'aurai 80 ans. Jamais je n'avais cru devoir ou pouvoir vivre jusque là et cependant je trouve encore à la vie beaucoup de saveur. Mais si quelques années me sont encore accordées (pas trop pourtant — c'est mon vœu sincère), je les voudrais reposées, entrecoupées de lectures. J'ai aimé travailler à NY. J'y ai connu une dizaine de personnes, comme vous & Diane, d'une noble et profonde personnalité, riches de grandes possibilités; je les ai peut-être aidées à se trouver elles-mêmes. Le milieu était moins snob, moins juvénile et parfois arrogant, que celui que j'avais connu dans mes longues années antérieures d'université privée. Je m'étais plu jadis à enseigner en France, à préparer les agrégatifs à leur concours. Mais ils étaient défiants, intimidés, affreusement compétitifs; si peu d'élus dans ces concours. Et la préparation de ces épreuves comportait trop de bachottage. Un ouvrage comme le vôtre, si le professeur peut y revendiquer quelque part modeste, est pour lui une vraie satisfaction.

Je pensais qu'on aurait consulté les alumnae les plus éminentes comme vous sur qui pourrait me succéder. On aurait dû le faire. Je ne m'en suis pas mêlé moi-même. La situation sera difficile, car les étudiants nouveaux sont peu nombreux, & je tiendrais surtout à ce que règnent paix & bonne entente. Il ne manque pas de petits esprits dans notre profession.

Ce M. Séailles me paraît être l'un d'eux. Vous pouvez certes lui écrire. Je doute qu'il vous réponde. Après 3 mois ou plus, je lui avais écrit que nous aimerions une réponse, ou pouvoir placer nos articles ailleurs. D'un mot rapide, que j'ai dû jeter, il m'avait — enfin! — répondu que le no. envisagé ne pouvait comporter d'article sur un personnage, ou un seul roman, mauriacien; mais seulement marquer l'anniversaire de la mort du romancier (Est-ce le dixième?). Il m'avait très spécifiquement prié d'écrire sur "Mauriac s'éloigne-t-il?" Je l'ai fait, & suppose qu'il a gardé mon article, dont je n'ai pas d'exemplaire ici. J'ai très, très peu de place et ne garde ni lettres ni rapports ni mes notes—& fort peu de livres. Ce dépouillement, d'ailleurs, me plaît.

Si j'étais vous, je me ferais invulnérable. Vous êtes très au-dessus de ces petitesses. Publier compte sans doute quand on n'est pas encore établi dans la profession et assis, ou rassis; mais cela prouve bien peu! Le vrai test est l'audience que l'on trouve auprès des étudiants. Je connais peu le département de Barnard aujourd'hui; mais je serais surpris si, et vos élèves et vos collègues ou doyens, ne vous rangeaient pas, dans leur estime, très haut, à l'égal des deux ou trois sommités.

Cela n'empêche pas que vous avez en vous un livre entier à écrire sur Mauriac—peut-être fait d'essais, dont quelques uns seulement pourraient être d'herméneutique psychanalytique. Pourquoi ne pas vous y mettre cet été? Négligez les sottes railleries de vieux parmi nous qui ne veulent pas voir ou admettre la richesse des bonnes interprétations freudiennes de la littérature. Chez certains (c'est mon cas pour Lacan), c'est de la paresse, un attachement au style "d'honnête homme"—et aussi lassitude de vieux. Je ne lis plus de critique, si je puis m'en abstenir, et relis les très grands: des Grecs, pour le moment; quelques Allemands. Encore ne retrouvé-je pas, relisant Nietzsche ces jours-ci, mon enthousiasme de la 18e année.

Ayez en vous une foi solide. Le témoignage des "editorial boards" ne doit pas vous faire douter de vos dons—ce Séailles, que je sache, n'a rien écrit lui-même. En tous cas, je n'ai jamais rencontré son nom au bas d'un article. Vous avez l'affection & l'estime intellectuelle de votre mari, que je devine être un homme profond & remarquable. Vous avez sûrement l'estime de quelques collègues à Barnard—peut-être même à Columbia? Voyez-vous parfois Riffaterre? Et vous devriez rester proche des 4 ou 5 amies intelligentes que vous deviez avoir au Centre, ou de 2 ou 3 professeurs qui devraient suivre l'une de nos brillantes anciennes.

Vous m'avez amusé à évoquer Botrel—et trois de mes haines les plus vigoureuses: Bernstein, Léautaud, Guitry. Un certain côté "parisien," qui irritait jadis le jeune homme idéaliste et péremptoire que j'étais, est sans doute cause que j'ai choisi de faire ma carrière hors de France—pour mieux aimer, de loin, mon pays natal & mes compatriotes.

Au fait, je connaissais bien Gougenheim; nous étions de la même promotion à Normale. Les 3 volumes sur les mots français sont drôles, & instructifs.

Sur le Symbolisme, mon livre en français sur le sujet est épuisé, mais doit paraître en traduction américaine cette année. Je vous l'enverrai alors. Sur les générations en général, & leur utilisation en histoire littéraire, j'avais jadis écrit un livre, très juvénile & ambitieux. Les Espagnols et Sud américains, que ce concept fascine, l'ont traduit; les Russes m'ont attaqué. Mais je n'en ai plus un seul exemplaire & ne veux pas le refaire. Ce sujet est loin de moi. Si vous vouliez des "conseils" plus précis, récrivez-moi.

Ces deux ou trois semaines ("Registration," dernières soutenances de thèse) vont être bousculées. Vers le 12 juin, j'irai en Europe pour 3 ou 4 semaines—puis resterai à Westport le reste de l'été, avec de rares déplacements à NY, si le Centre requiert ma présence. Restez-vous vous-même à votre adresse agreste? Ou allez-vous à votre "Résidence secondaire"?

     Mon souvenir à votre mari et mes souhaits
     très fervents de repos annuel.
     Henri

## To Harold Proshansky:

     Henri Peyre
     290 North Avenue
     Westport, Conn. 06880
     June 3—1980

Dear President Proshansky:

The pressing administrative and financial issues which your office, those of the Deans and the monthly meetings of Executive Officers constantly have to confront, do not allow much of an opportunity to envisage long range questions. Some of those questions, however, will have to be faced in the near future. May I here point to some which concern more particularly the language departments?

It seems clear that the recruitment of new students in French,

German, perhaps also in other foreign literatures and in Comparative Literature, has lately been difficult. Some of those Programs are faced with extinction unless new students enter them in 1981–82. Cutting down the number of courses so as to have less to pay to the Colleges is not a solution. Ph D. candidates in French, for instance, have to be trained in a literature which ranges through nine hundred years. No graduate school worthy of the name, and worthy of the quality of our students at CUNY, can afford not to offer courses in, say, the medieval era, or the Renaissance, or the 18th century, every second or third term.

Obviously the difficulty of finding teaching positions has deterred potential applicants lately. It has affected us, even though we have, comparatively to other graduate schools, done rather well in placing our graduates. Should we bow to the trend away from languages and humanities and do away with programs in French, German, Russian?

If we decided to do so for financial motives, the prestige of the Graduate School would be gravely jeopardized. It seems inconceivable to many who have the future of educational institutions at heart, that we would not resist the trend and fight for a continued study of languages in City Colleges, at the very time when a Presidential Commission on Foreign Languages, appointed two years ago by President Carter, has declared such a study to be vital in the national interest. A Task Force, appointed by the Chancellor and ably presided over by Professor Grandjouan of Hunter, submitted early last Fall (1979) a carefully thought out and highly constructive report. We are very disappointed that no action has, as yet, been taken on it. Time, however, is of the essence. The variety of ethnic backgrounds of New Yorkers, the manifest destiny of the city as a cosmopolitan cultural center, the growing need for industrial, commercial, financial administrators having to deal with foreign corporations or with the United Nations and the UNESCO, should, it seems, favor the study of foreign cultures. Secretaries, translators, diplomatic personnel, teachers likely to be sent to African, Asiatic, South American countries, specialists in teaching English to foreigners as a second language, all stand in need of advanced language training. Only last Sunday (June first), the Business section of the New York Times ran a substantial article on the growing number of foreign-born executives taking over the highest positions in a variety of American corporations. Other thoughtful articles in The Wall Street Journal and elsewhere have outlined the growing role of foreign born diplomats, economists, political thinkers, international lawyers, university presidents, whose advantage (among others) lay in a mastery of foreign tongues and in the ability to deal competently with other nations. There are cogent reasons why the City University should, far from neglecting the study of languages, move ahead to interest business people and Federal and State organizations in founding here in New York a center for the study of languages.

Some plans had been tentatively submitted:

1) the possibility for the French Program at the Graduate Center of offering an M.A., as is done in German, Classics, Comparative Literature. That raises delicate problems; but they might be discussed with the senior colleges now offering the M.A.

2) The possibility of organizing a translation program, in an institution which counts a number of eminent translators (Profs. Brooks, Lamont, Mandelbaum, Allen McCormick, Rabassa, Waldinger, and many others). Professor Waldinger has drafted a report on this subject, which was submitted to Dean Rees.

3) The establishment of courses on urban issues as presented in foreign (and American) literatures.

Such a reorientation of the language programs (toward the "culture" and "civilization" of foreign countries, stressing historical, social and present day political issues) should, I believe, be discussed constructively by a group of departments which are no less vitally concerned with the continuation of language programs as ours is: English, History, linguistics, art, theatre, et al. The one gap which has struck me in our Graduate Center is the lack of contacts among departments which (in other universities with a campus, Faculty Clubs, professors living closer to the classrooms and to the Library) are often grouped into a "division." Far from me to suggest that we should increase the amount of administration and bureaucracy that we have at present! Still, some vital problems involving the future should occasionally be discussed cooperatively and not in the condition of isolation (and umbrageous independence of each Program) now prevailing.

If there is any validity in the above remarks, they might perhaps prove conducive to a useful reorientation of foreign language programs, now seriously threatened.

Sincerely yours,<br>Henri Peyre

## À Gita May:

Le 13 juin 80

Chère Madame:

Je crois vous connaître de si longue date. Il y a en effet longtemps que je suis vos écrits avec grande estime & profit, mais il me semble que je n'ai guère eu l'occasion de vous rencontrer. Cela m'a fait plaisir de vous entrevoir jeudi dernier. J'avais lu récemment votre Stendhal et l'avais aimé. Vous attribuez aux femmes et aux amours plus de place dans sa vie que, vieux, froid & désabusé moi-même, je ne ferais; rêver à elles et, en vérité, les tenir un peu à l'écart était sa tactique et celle de bien des hommes; mais vous le faites revivre avec sympathie et conviction.

Merci de cet essai sur G. Sand et sur l'énorme action de Rousseau sur sa personnalité; c'est très finement senti et rendu. Quel riche volume d'études il y aurait à faire, ou à refaire, sur la manière dont ces romantiques de 1830–48 ont revécu Rousseau, senti à travers lui: Stendhal, Balzac, Lamartine, Sand, Nerval, Musset et autres! Vos quelques pages sont très suggestives.

Croyez à mes sentiments de grande estime et de vive amitié intellectuelle.

Henri Peyre

## To Harvard University Press:

> Henri Peyre
> 290 North Ave.
> Westport, Conn. 06880
> June 15/80

Dear Ms. Donald:

I do not mind being quoted & I'd leave it to you to decide what sentence & what phrasing suit your purpose best. I am leaving tomorrow for Europe & happen to be a bit hurried. I expect to be back around July 14th, as I told yesterday on the phone another person from your Press.

> Sincerely yours,
> Henri Peyre

## À Wallace Fowlie:

> 290 North Ave.
> Westport, Conn. 06880
> Le 14 juillet 80

Bien cher Michel,

Je suis rentré d'Europe il y a deux jours, avec Diane (qui m'a facilité bien des choses en conduisant la plupart du temps, dans le trafic de Paris, d'Amsterdam, de Dijon, Grenoble, Nice) et mon grand fils de 16 ans, Brice, robuste et affectueux compagnon. Mais que de foules de touristes partout, à Rome & Pompéi! Et que de cherté de vie, de prix exorbitants des hôtels; et pourtant je ne suis guère gastronome. Parmi un monceau de lettres, je trouve la vôtre. Elle me rassure un peu: car je m'étais beaucoup soucié de votre santé, et de la solitude dans laquelle risquait de vous laisser l'interruption de ce besoin de généreuse communication qui est le vôtre et que satisfaisait l'enseignement. Mais votre lettre semble dire que vous ne conservez nulle trace de ces opérations pour des maux mystérieux, où le traumatisme psychique de la transition à la retraite a dû jouer son rôle. Cela est rassurant pour vos amis.

Je crois avoir été une fois à cette Université où me hantaient des souvenirs de lecture de Faulkner. Je relisais en voyage *As I Lay Dying*: quelle puissance de langue! On parle moins de lui en Europe, après sa grande vogue; un tri, forcément, sera fait parmi ses livres. Cleanth Brooks était chagriné, ces dernières années, du peu d'audience qu'avaient rencontré ses ouvrages critiques, mais la mode en critique est encore plus volage qu'ailleurs. Je connais aussi Scott Bates, depuis longtemps; il est curieusement très féru du langage érotico-obscène d'Apollinaire; il a eu la patience de s'adapter au Sud. J'enseignais Apollinaire ce semestre dernier. Je donnerai un dernier cours cet automne à N. York, puis je prendrai définitivement ma retraite. J'ai insisté pour le faire. À 80 ans, il convient de céder la place. Mon regret est qu'il est, récemment, devenu difficile de recruter de très bons étudiants gradués. La pénurie des postes a fini par décourager les meilleurs. Nous avons eu pourtant une série de thèses remarquables, mais c'est aux undergraduates qu'il vaut mieux ces temps-ci nous adresser, et reformer une série nouvelle de curieux de littérature. Je crois que vous serez content des auditeurs que vous trouverez à Exeter et aussi à Holy Cross, que je connais moins.

Je vous admire d'écrire avec toujours autant d'ardeur, de persistance—et de talent. Je ne pense plus entreprendre de livre moi-même; tout au plus quelques articles que j'avais promis. Un livre de vous sur Dante devrait être passionnant, et utile. Les Italiens et les "Dantistes" d'ici se sont tellement concentrés sur des études de détail, minutieuses, pédantes, qu'ils ont éloigné de Dante bien des lecteurs potentiels—du *Paradiso,* très beau par endroits, des Canzone & de la Vita Nuova. Gillet avait fait un bon livre de vulgarisation; Gilson et Auerbach des ouvrages originaux et aisément lisibles. Les traductions ne sont guère de mon goût: ni Singleton, ni Binyon (affreux) ni Bergin, trop familier et antipoétique. Sans doute retraduirez-vous ce que vous voudrez citer & faire aimer.

Linda Orr est digne de vous, son premier maître. Elle aime la poésie et la pratique. Un séjour à Paris l'avait un peu trop marquée de l'influence de Lacan, Derrida, gens que je goûte peu; la mode des mots d'esprit ("puns") et des jeux de mots avec des barres obliques m'horripile, mais elle en est revenue. Bien des gens avaient été envisagés pour votre succession; elle était difficile. Lawler m'avait paru le meilleur; c'est un critique de premier ordre, modeste, clair, fin. Mais il n'avait pas, je crois, emballé son auditoire; & il se plaît à Chicago. À Yale, la situation n'est pas brillante: trop de dogmatisme chez Hartman, De Man, Bloom, peu de critique vraie; la plus douée, Shoshana Felman, s'égare dans les subtilités. Mais je m'abstiens de conseiller et de juger. Chaque génération doit se trouver elle-même.

Je serai impatient de lire votre prochain volume de souvenirs. Quelques articles sur Henry Miller (un très bon, de juin, dans le Monde) m'ont paru très bons, et m'ont rappelé nos années de Yale. Il reste un grand prosateur. Je suis moins séduit par Anaïs Nin, et par Djuna Barnes, qu'on republie. Peut-être résisté-je trop à certaine littérature féminine?

Passez un été agréable & à l'automne, à New York ou ici. Peut-être pourrons-nous nous revoir?

Avec ma vive affection,<br>Henri

## À Germaine Brée:

Le 2 août 80

Chère Germaine,

Diane me dit qu'elle vous écrit un mot pour vous dire combien elle a apprécié votre efficace & généreuse recommandation. La Fondation Guggenheim vient de lui annoncer qu'une bourse lui sera accordée. Elle en est ravie. Elle a travaillé d'arrache pied ces dix dernières années, publié sans arrêt. Elle donne beaucoup d'elle-même à son enseignement; & cela sans négliger les soucis que causent trois grands fils, et le vieux bonhomme grognon que je suis. Enfin elle aura une année de libre! Merci.

Je suis émerveillé de votre énergie inlassable: vous allez enseigner à NYU cet été, entre le soin de votre maison en Caroline et de votre résidence "secondaire" en Michigan. Ne vous fatiguez pas trop cependant! Vous donnez beaucoup de vous-même à vos disciples et à vos livres. Vous ai-je dit combien j'admire la virtuosité & l'élégance sobre avec lesquelles vous avez embrassé cette littérature récente et contemporaine—sans une seule banalité? Cela a dû exiger un lourd travail de condensation.

J'imagine qu'en juin & une partie de juillet nous serons en France— mais ensuite, si vous êtes encore à N. York & vouliez venir jusqu'ici

(1h15 de NY) chercher un peu de campagne, de mer ou de soleil, vous nous feriez plaisir à nous rendre visite.

Passez une bonne fin d'année scolaire, & croyez à ma vive affection.

Henri Peyre

## À Florence et Kurt Weinberg:

290 North Ave.
Westport, Conn. 06880
Le 10 août 1980

Chers Florence & Kurt,

Votre double lettre, et les riches documents qui les accompagnaient, m'ont donné une vraie & grande joie. La seule vraie tristesse de vieillir est de voir décroître le petit nombre d'amis auxquels on tenait; et les souvenirs des autres deviennent plus chers. Et parmi ces anciens étudiants devenus des maîtres autrement savants et profonds que leurs professeurs de jadis, nul n'a continué à penser, à interpréter des textes difficiles, à écrire avec une érudition formidable, et pourtant avec grâce et élan, comme Kurt Weinberg. Je ne lis plus guère d'allemand, sinon parfois de la poésie; & je n'ai jamais bien possédé la langue. Mais, dictionnaire en mains, j'ai déchiffré le long et important article sur "Une Charogne." Timoré par nature sans doute, défiant de la subtilité que je ne possède pas et des gloses que je crois restes de l'âge théologique (comme l'appelle A. Comte), j'ai abordé l'essai avec un peu de défiance. Je ne suis pas l'herméneute dans le fouillis de ses sentiers et je ne suis qu'à moitié convaincu: mais les rapprochements et les analyses m'ont séduit. Une lecture aussi détaillée et pénétrante enrichit le lecteur le plus traditionnel et permet de jouir plus voluptueusement du poème; je me récitais la "Charogne" à 16 ans, quand Baudelaire est entré dans le domaine public et qu'on l'achetait pour cinq sous en 1917, et, si Olympio me lasse, "Le Lac" reste pour moi un admirable poème.

L'article sur Mallarmé en "yx," après bien d'autres exégètes de cet énigmatique sonnet, apporte du neuf et, à travers Vico, *Les Mots anglais* et d'autres rapprochements, illumine les vers du maître et les fait aimer davantage. Je résiste à lire "nier" dans "Rien" et "scies reines" dans "sirènes." *Pace* Lacan et même Freud, les jeux de mots et les ambiguïtés aussi calculées ne m'émeuvent pas. Je voudrais que Mallarmé n'y ait trébuché que sans le savoir: Le "Faune," le "Toast funèbre," "Quand l'ombre menaça," plus directs, plus graves, me touchent davantage. Mais en vérité je suis mal à l'aise dans la critique, et si j'attends avec impatience et plaisir ma retraite prochaine, c'est pour retrouver une naïveté presque bête à, simplement, lire et relire. Si ma mémoire n'est pas trop défaillante, je voudrais réapprendre de l'Eschyle, du Lenau, même du Swinburne et mon cher Shelley, et me les réciter devant la nature, comme il y a 60 ans. Ne plus lire de thèse, ne plus ouvrir de critique, et même de philosophe: quelle sereine perspective.

Florence est une merveilleuse savante. Quelle prodigieuse érudition, depuis Platon et Porphyre, les Pères de l'Eglise et les scolastiques, et, bien sûr, les diverses Renaissances, elle a accumulée! Je connaissais jadis un peu Folengo. Mais nullement Fr. Colonna; et j'ai toujours été piètre au jeu d'échecs, que les fils McCormick pratiquent autour de moi avec passion. Elle n'est nullement à sa place à ce Collège où elle doit lutter pour, simplement, aider les humanités à survivre. Ne pourriez-vous, elle et vous, demander à l'Institute for Advanced Studies de Princeton, ou à celui de Cornell, de vous inviter—au moins pour un an? Je sais que Jauss est accueillant, ouvert à tout, chaleureux; mais c'est en Amérique que vous avez été d'abord appréciés, et, avec tout son charme, Konstanz n'est pas un grand foyer d'érudits. Avez-vous pu rendre visite à Freiburg? À Heidelberg? À Bonn? Je ne suis plus au courant de la "Romanistique" allemande, ou de celle de Vienne. Et les polémiques, les bavardages et les poses prétentieuses des philosophes parisiens, "nouveaux" ou non, m'exaspèrent.

Mais en vérité je me sens détaché de notre profession et de l'érudition. J'ai voyagé 2 ou 3 semaines en Europe, d'Amsterdam à Rome, dans le froid & sous la pluie, et je m'en voulais de ne pas retrouver les délices des voyages de jeune homme, quand routes et plages étaient presque désertes et je regrettais plus encore les prix d'autrefois! Pauvres retraités! La ruine nous menace.

Je pense que Mary Ann Caws me succédera au Centre Gradué de CUNY. Elle est d'une activité effarante; et il y aura à faire pour maintenir la paix, et pour attirer des étudiants nouveaux en assez grand nombre. Nous avons jusqu'ici eu de la chance et assez bien placé nos "docteurs." Mais tout se rétrécit désormais. Louise Horowitz semble heureuse, mais son mari n'est pas bien traité et elle en est chagrinée. Elle vous est, à tous deux, très attachée comme l'est Sally Cornell, qui, souvent, parle de vous. Elle à part, je ne vois à peu près plus personne à New Haven & à Yale.

Merci de ces dons et de prêter à d'autres un peu de votre science, et merci tout autant de la fidélité de vos sentiments.

Avec grande affection,<br>Henri

## To Frederick Brown:

290 North Ave.<br>Westport, Conn. 06880<br>Sept. 15, 1980

Dear Mr. Brown:

I do not think you should be anxious, or nervous, about your recent book. It is excellent, & it shall be pronounced so by any critics who are not sectarians & the slaves of fads. It is a source of regret for me that Yale has lately become a refuge, or a chapel, for such people.

Your Zola project is well presented & convincing. I am writing warmly in support of it. Let me know what eventually happens both at the ACLS & at the SUNY office.

Your review of the Hermaphrodite book (which I have not read) is very ably done & makes one want to buy the volume. It is more than can be said for most reviews!

Cordially yours,<br>Henri Peyre

## To Robert G. Cohn:

290 North Avenue<br>Westport, Conn. 06880<br>Oct. 19—80

Dear Bob,

I always enjoy hearing from you & I am grateful for your "communications." You & I & some others pursue the fight for more attention to the "Humanities" in American higher education & more ardent love for literature & the arts. I shall preach that doctrine & try to spread the contagion of my life-long faith in two or three more colleges this fall—& then take refuge in silence. There is much that is not heartening in the present trends & I am sad to watch many of my past efforts come to naught or too little. Still I refuse to despair. We have had a number of truly good theses in New York lately. The problem now is the difficulty of recruiting new students. Strangely, it stems in part from our own success in finding positions for the students enrolled, or who might be enrolled. We have placed rather easily those (bachelors, divorced, or simply adventurous) who were willing to go to remote states. Others manage to locate two or three part-time jobs in some of the many colleges of New York, or in the UN & banks as translators or in agencies of many kinds and interrupt their studies. I have enjoyed those last 8 or 10 years of teaching in CUNY after my retirement from Yale; and it now saddens me not to be able to leave things in rosier conditions. I have accepted to carry on until January 31, 1981. I shall then be close to 80! There was much fear of feuds & rivalries over my succession as "chairman." X, whom you probably remember, was anxious to take over; but she is not too warmly admired. Mary Ann Caws was chosen in preference to her, & is more widely known as a scholar. She should do well. But the job entails so many tiresome details, so much bureaucracy, that it risks cutting down her "production" & her leisure for enjoying poetry. As I see, you yourself have kept away from those "executive" positions & you have a new Chairman, not personally known to me. You have been wise.

I profoundly admire your fidelity to Mallarmé & I shall look forward to reading your *Igitur*, & perhaps your recent *Hérodiade* piece. I have read & reread your *Toward the Poems of Mall,* & found it always ingenious, illuminating & convincing. Your Rimbaud continues to impress, & to inspire, scholars & students. You will leave a lasting mark upon studies of poetry here & abroad. I doubt there are more than three or four other scholars in French, among those who started their studies in the aftermath of World War II, of whom that could be said.

I remember those years, 1945–55, rather fondly. We entertained such lofty hopes then—expecting so much of the Left in France, of Soviet Russia, of American leadership. The French Communists have behaved sheepishly, perfidiously, & made any Left government impossible. The Nouveaux Philosophes & the crypto Fascists of the Right are certainly no better. The French are disgustingly cynical just now. I am afraid Begin is not much better. My hostility to all religions, Moslem being the worst & the others just a little less objectionable, has stayed with me. But my foolish hope of some return to Paganism is, by now, disabused. I am glad I don't vote in this country, or anywhere, for Reagan fails to win my confidence. He has too superficial a mind, & he is manipulated by the "Puissances d'argent." My visceral reaction, ineradicable, is to distrust all the rich. I have never owned a stock or a bond & I have stripped myself of all possessions, except for a VW car & a few books, & spurned what I could have inherited in France after my father's death. At times, like last July when I traveled to Amsterdam, Burgundy, Rome, Naples with my son, I felt a bit squeezed, & aghast at the astronomic prices. But I am probably all the better for avoiding gourmet meals. I have much enjoyed the exceptionally colorful autumn we had & are having here & I sit in the garden, rereading Mallarmé at times, also Homer (with a dictionary) & my dear English & German romantics.

Have a serene year & keep up the fight for the causes dear to us. My regards to your wife & much paternal & brotherly affection to you.

Henri

## À Renée Wehrmann:

Le dimanche 30 nov. — 80

Chère amie,

Vous ne m'en voulez pas, j'en suis sûr, de vous avoir grondée un peu au téléphone. Je sais combien d'obstacles vous avez rencontrés depuis 4 ou 5 ans. J'admire fort le courage dont vous avez fait preuve après votre veuvage, et les épreuves que la chance d'avoir un enfant très doué, mais difficile, impose à une mère seule. Vous avez tenu à continuer à enseigner, et cela vous a aidée à surmonter ces obstacles; et vous devez être, il est aisé de le voir, un professeur vivant, ardent, consciencieux & attentif. Et enfin, vous avez presque terminé une thèse. La principale condition pour accomplir ce genre de travail est la concentration: et vous vous intéressez à trop de choses qui vous distraient, vous avez des obligations de famille, vous n'aviez pas maintenu, ces dernières années ou décennies, l'habitude d'écrire, de polir votre style. Parce que vous êtes douée, et une amie, et que je vous sais capable de faire un travail distingué, je me laisse aller, peut-être, à exiger beaucoup de vous.

Si vous terminez pour, disons, le milieu de janvier, pour soutenance le 24 ou le 29 au plus tard, fort bien. Sinon, tout ira également bien pour vous après mon absence. Je ne me suis jamais cru irremplaçable.

En attendant, de la part de Diane & de la mienne: nous serions *très* ravis si, le samedi treize décembre, vous veniez vers une heure de l'après-midi, déjeuner, avec votre frère et votre belle-sœur. Je ne sais pas leur adresse, & je n'ai pas noté leur nom (en sanscrit). Mais ils sont tous deux vivants, élégants, artistes, débordants d'idées, enthousiastes de l'Amérique. Lui moud les grains de blé, les pois chiches, les épis de maïs et en tire de la matière mentale grise, et il la répand autour de lui comme le semeur de V. Hugo ou du dictionnaire Larousse. Son épouse l'écoute, sourit, l'admire, le contredit parfois (j'espère), et, gentiment, fait croire à leurs amis qu'ils sont dignes de sa vivacité intellectuelle.

Si cela leur convient & à vous, inutile de téléphoner (concentration!); une carte suffira. L'adresse & le chemin vous sont connus.

Amitiés,
H. P.

## À Konrad et Tamara Bieber:

> 290 North Ave.
> Westport, Conn. 06880
> Jan. 9, 81

Chers amis,

C'est une grande date dans la vie que de devenir grands-parents. C'est un peu ce que je me suis senti quand un fils est né à ce vieil homme que j'étais; et, avec quelques soucis, cela m'a apporté aussi un rajeunissement. Vous avez tant de jeunesse tous deux, tant d'élasticité & de générosité que, j'en suis sûr, votre nouvel état vous apportera bien des joies et rapprochera votre fils de parents qui ont tant fait pour lui. Diane et moi vous félicitons et vous offrons beaucoup de vœux pour l'année qui vient de naître.

Elle est, cette année, bien glaçante ces jours-ci. Nous survivons, avec quelques ennuis d'auto et de chauffage; ce sont, pour moi, mes dernières semaines d'enseignement. 6 ou 7 thèses que je dirigeais sont complétées et seront "défendues" la dernière semaine de janvier; après quoi, je lirai librement, rêverai, voyagerai peut-être. L'état de la profession, que j'avais beaucoup voulu servir, m'attriste; mais j'ai trouvé chez ces étudiants à N. York beaucoup de dons et un très touchant attachement.

Je vous remercie de m'avoir remis en contact avec les Deguise. J'ai beaucoup d'amitié pour eux. Le souvenir de quelques visites à New London de votre temps et du leur est un des plus vivaces de ma longue carrière. Il semble que là aussi la cordialité amicale & confiante de jadis n'ait pas survécu. Je repense fréquemment à ces années-là, et elles me revenaient en mémoire récemment avec la nouvelle de la mort de R. Gary. C'est à vous que je devais de l'avoir connu, et mieux estimé. J'ai moins goûté certains de ses derniers livres; mais je crois que je me détache des romans français, de ceux de ces années-ci, du moins.

<blockquote>
Diane joint aux miens ses vœux pleins d'affection.<br>
Félicitez votre fils de ma part.<br>
Henri
</blockquote>

## À Edward Kaplan:

<blockquote>
290 North Ave.<br>
Westport, Conn. 06880<br>
Jan. 15/81
</blockquote>

Cher monsieur:

Je suis heureux que vous vous sentiez plus assuré de l'avenir à Brandeis, où je sais que vous êtes fort estimé. Il y a là un groupe de professeurs ouverts, intelligents, d'esprit original et des étudiants de haute qualité. Vous avez assez de raisons d'avoir foi en vous pour ne pas hésiter, le moment venu, à reconstruire votre vie privée.

J'aime beaucoup votre article. Il est abondamment et impeccablement informé, scrupuleux, et en même temps très personnel. Votre exégèse, littérale et littéraire, mais aussi morale, est, je crois, la plus juste & la plus féconde pour élucider Baudelaire. Je n'ai pour ma part que médiocrement goûté les essais, souvent prétentieux et entortillés de Klein ou Mehlman (mes anciens élèves) et de P. de Nab, bon ami. Mettre en jeu Hölderlin, Blake *et al.* pour discuter quelque allégorie baudelairienne n'illumine pas grand'chose. C'est un des périls du "Comparatisme" qui, je l'avoue, m'en a détaché.

Croyez à mes très bons vœux. À la fin de ce mois, approchant de 80 ans, je me retire—enfin!—de tout enseignement. J'ai dirigé des centaines de thèses et il est temps que d'autres prennent la relève. Je serai heureux de lire, de rêver, d'écrire un peu, et de voyager à l'occasion.

Cordialement,<br>Henri Peyre

## À Jean Boorsch:

Le 10 février 81

Bien cher Jean,

J'ai pris en effet ma retraite définitive le 31 janvier après 7 ou 8 ultimes soutenances de thèses que je dirigeais & que leurs auteurs voulaient terminer. J'ai eu quelque mal à me retirer (jalousies, cabales), mais Mary Ann Caws, mon successeur, est intelligente, éminente, sur-active. J'étais devenu très attaché à cette besogne à N.Y. Etudiants (du sexe féminin en majorité) doués, dévoués à leur travail, intéressants; beaucoup avec des "problèmes" personnels dont je n'avais pas idée à Yale. Mais j'ai tenu à tout briser, à refuser tout cours désormais, toute conférence. Ma carrière a été assez interminable comme cela. J'ai encore des lettres en retard, pour deux semaines, un article ou deux. Puis je lirai à loisir, rêverai peut-être. Je me retourne vers les choses d'autrefois: quelques pages d'Homère de temps en temps, élégiaques latins. Les Français de ces dernières années m'ennuient, quand ils ne m'exaspèrent pas. Je vais souvent à Yale, lis tout de même les ouvrages récents, vois Brice qui en a encore pour un an et demi à Hopkins et hésite où se présenter pour le Collège. Ma santé est fort bonne—malgré l'hiver rigoureux, l'âge, quelques trous de mémoire, ma faiblesse chronique à reconnaître les gens. Diane dit que c'est parce que je ne m'intéresse pas à eux. Il y a du vrai, sans doute.

Vous aimez donc obstinément cette Floride. J'imagine que ce climat est bon pour Louise: va-t-elle vraiment bien? Ses enfants ne lui manquent pas? . . .

## To John W. Kneller:

March 5—81

Dear Jack,

You were a splendid leader, or "conductor" of that finely orchestrated ceremony on Febr. 20, & your words touched me deeply, as did your flattering reply to that request of Georges May. I knew nothing about it & he handed me those heavy, & elegant, boxes of letters. I am embarrassed by those kind words & take them with some skepticism: few of them dare mock an octogenarian! Still they bear testimony to the lasting value of literature in the formation of bankers, lawyers, surgeons, pastors, who happened to have been impressed by their undergraduate reading of French works 20 or 35 years ago.

The tributes arranged at the Graduate Center were, to me, equally moving. I have enjoyed my work there & found some excellent friends among the students & my colleagues. It happens that I am leaving the Program just as it is in the throes of serious difficulties; but a new leadership & new initiatives may perhaps reverse the trend. Mary Ann Caws is a remarkable person, prodigiously active; & I know that she is happy to have your assistance & counts heavily on you.

I knew nothing of the drive for scholarship funds that M. A. Caws had organized. I saw, only by chance, a list of generous donors—among them you & your brother. It is very generous of you—one more evidence of the fidelity of your affection for a former teacher. I am proud to have, early in your career, enjoyed the confidence & friendship of persons like you & your wife.

Diane & I are leaving today for Egypt. Diane very much wanted to go there &, after resisting a lot, I finally agreed to go also. She would not leave me alone here. We'll be back before the end of March, & spring may by then transfigure Westport. I have reread the book by Velikovsky that Sherry once offered me. The thesis is perhaps frail, but the book is intelligent & artistic & conjured up old memories in me.

Have a fine spring yourselves & à bientôt—
Henri

## To Philip Stewart:

290 North Avenue
Westport, Conn. 06880
May 31—81

Dear Mr. Stewart,

It was thoughtful & kind of Mr. Haig to invite you to that pleasant & picturesque gathering on his terrace. I was dazzled by the profusion of flowers, the gigantic trees, the youthfulness of the faculty present. Your wife was radiant in her white elegance, both coy and pure like Bernardin's Virginie, and more like Laclos' Cécile when a knowing and blasé gleam flashed in her eyes. I hope that officiating as a chairman's wife, with her traveling and her impeccable writing, will not impose too much effort on her. I forgot to congratulate you on your courage in assuming that unrewarding task. You have been already generous & courageous in doing so much for the AATF.

I found your circular letter on my return. It is foolish, blind & ungenerous of many proud professors not to help the *Review* more, not to attend our conventions; a campaign might be attempted through personal letters to some 100 or more chairmen, asking them to bring to the attention of their staff (junior *and* older members) their interest in belonging to the AATF & of *writing* for the F. Review. MLA, L'Esprit créateur, Stanford French Review have done that. Could not well known professors be persuaded to offer papers or to lead a discussion group at the annual convention, as is done by the XIXth century studies group, the XVIIth century group & others? Shattuck, Brombert, Lawler, Girard, Doubrovsky, some ladies too. I expressed myself candidly to Mr. Haig on my dislike of the facile & uncritical interviews recorded mechanically and displaying the naively inflated egos of my compatriots & my regret that not more critically constructive reviews by recognized authorities appear in the columns of the F.R. I believe that many members (especially those who teach in the schools) would be glad to be kept informed, every other year, by review articles on the state of the drama, the cinema, the novel, the poetry; on educational reforms in France; on what the historical studies, especially active & original in France (history of mentalities, of sensibility, reinterpretations of the Revolution, etc.), bring to literature. Articles might be courteously solicited reassessing Gide or Claudel or Camus, or Sartre, Barthes, two, ten, twenty years after their deaths. Aragon, Simone de Beauvoir, Char will be the next ones to disappear. Could they not be appraised, & hastened to their graves, in advance? Centenaries of Apollinaire, Larbaud, Martin du Gard, Dostœvsky & his impact on France, fall this year or fell recently: would not your readers like to read an appraisal of those authors? What about a competent article examining three or four recent French dictionaries? Or encyclopedias (Encyclopedia Universalis, Columbia Dictionary of Modern Literature, 1980; *et al.*). Of course you do not pay your authors & should not. But is our profession that mercenary? I doubt you will gain many members at the present time (our Placement office being probably only moderately successful) unless you publish more outstanding articles, & not just chapters of dissertations and those conversations in which interviewer and interviewed never utter a single memorable remark. It should be possible just now, in our field, to do better than PMLA! Even than Novel or French Forum, & certainly than Mod. Language Notes & Mod. Language Quarterly.

But it is easy also to give advice—on the top of my nearly 60 years of teaching & of my grandfatherly "gâtisme." I'll stop & read the Sunday paper.

Warm regards to those Duke colleagues of yours who remember me & to your wife.

Cordially,<br>Henri Peyre

## À Mary Ann Caws:

June 1, 81

Chère Mary Ann,

Vous faites mille fois trop pour moi; il est temps, & même urgent, que je sois oublié! Je recevrai l'ultime honneur de cette médaille, comme un vieux soldat. Après cela, que l'on renie, critique et oublie ce que j'ai été ou fait.

Pour ces essais proposés pour le volume de la "University Press of New England," il ne m'appartient pas de donner un avis, ou de prononcer des exclusives. Certains des MSS seront moins bons que d'autres.

Il n'y aura nulle unité de ton: du très grave, ou des spéculations se prenant très au sérieux (Cohn), du très factuel & détaillé & historique (Hartle) au plaisant et spirituel (Martin), et de l'excellente méditation critique (M. Braun, E. Kern). Si la Presse de N. England n'impose pas de limitation et consent à faire les frais, fort bien. Si vous devez faire un choix, mettez tout sur le dos de quelque comité aux décisions sans appel. La seule conception d'un tel livre à moi dédié est un immense honneur, immérité à mes yeux.

À cet hommage qui me touche si profondément, vous en joignez un autre en offrant de me dédier ce riche, savant et très original livre, Metapoetics of the Passage. Vous y êtes subtile, ingénieuse mais jamais avec artifice ou recherche précieuse. Vous avez un angle d'approche à ces poèmes très divers, et cependant reliés l'un à l'autre par des affinités que vous découvrez et illuminez—qui est fécond; et vous savez, avec tact, discrétion critique, dominer ces textes par votre personnalité, artiste et philosophique à la fois. Éclairer Desnos par Scève, Crane par Valéry, peut au premier abord sembler paradoxal et de la virtuosité d'esprit. Virtuose—certes vous l'êtes. Vous ouvrez des points de vue neufs en confrontant Paz, Merrill (que je ne connais pas du tout) et des surréalistes français. Vous respectez chaque fois l'individualité de Garelli, ou Dupin, ou Deguy, en les interprétant selon *leur* vision; en même temps, et sans les classer de force dans quelque tiroir, vous faites ressortir ce qu'ils ont en commun. Dans toutes vos remarques, on sent une vibration d'amour pour la poésie, et en même temps une vue philosophique de la littérature. Vous n'abdiquez rien de votre ingéniosité et jouez spirituellement avec les mots-clés (passage, et al.); mais vous ne cherchez jamais à faire s'écrier au lecteur: "Ce qu'elle est maligne!" C'est un très beau livre, moderne dans son ton, le choix des textes, mais très mûr et classique.

(Page 120, le premier vers du dizain CCXV est incorrect: c'est je m'*en* absente.)

Si ma mémoire doit survivre aux limbes de l'oubli, ce sera grâce à ce livre où mon nom est inscrit et au recueil d'essais que vous avez avec dévouement quasi amoureux préparé.

Merci,<br>H

Je joins une autre lettre avec l'autre manuscrit—le colossal.

## To Mr. and Mrs. Robert Penn Warren:

> Henri Peyre
> 290 North Avenue
> Westport, Conn. 06880
> June 17—81

Chers amis,

It was a most lovely evening at your house. The company, the meal, the stimulating conversation, the elegant charm of the house enchanted us. I especially enjoyed our conversation on the present & woeful state of literature & criticism in France. I am taking the liberty to enclose a few pages in which I had lately deplored the sterilizing criticism perpetrated by the French snobs. And I am returning the Alastair Reid volume; I read it at once, copied several of the pieces which moved me deeply ("My Father, Dying," "A lesson for beautiful Women," "The Figures on the Frieze," "New Hampshire"). Those, & others, count, in my opinion, among the finest (technically) & the most unassuming, the freshest & the deepest poems of this age—not unworthy of being set beside RPW's works. I am grateful to you for pointing Reid out to me. I am often suspicious of *The New Yorker*.

Diane joins me in expressing our very affectionate thanks & wishes. Have a serene & restful summer.

> Yours,
> Henri

## À Mary Ann Caws:

> 290 North Ave. Westport, Conn. 06880
> Le 5 juillet 81

Chère Mary Ann,

Vous voilà retournée parmi les anges—dans le pays des berlingots, du Chateauneuf, des scorpions, des poètes et penseurs. Jamais, lorsque, lycéen à Avignon, je ne rêvais que d'évasion, de renier le soleil, l'ail, les mouches, je ne me serais douté que le Vaucluse pût devenir un pays de poètes et de penseurs comme vous deux, et vos deux enfants! Hölderlin,

Lenau, Shelley, Swinburne étaient mes idoles, et Nietzsche—et ils me paraissaient étrangers au monde de joueurs de boules où je me croyais emprisonné. Cézanne, Vasarely, Char, Bonnefoy et vous deux, penseurs et poètes, avez changé tout cela—vous êtes vraiment l'architecte, ou la grande prêtresse, d'un siècle éclaté.

Peut-être du moins, après vos errances, avez-vous trouvé le soleil et les parfums de lavande? Ici, depuis 4 jours, pluie, affreuse humidité—un 4 juillet arrosé et raté. La pelouse est d'un vert insultant. Cela fracasse toute velléité d'énergie et d'optimisme—et ça s'ajoute au marasme qu'entretient ce Président, admirateur de Coolidge, complice d'une majorité qui se prétend "morale" et convaincu que Dieu a créé le monde en six jours—et le regrette depuis. Diane travaille, écrit. La seule vue de votre colossal manuscrit l'avait un moment intimidée: elle a vite compris que vous êtes inimitable. Je médite un peu, très peu, moi-même; je rêvasse. J'ai essayé de lire *Glas* (sur lequel Hartman a déjà écrit un livre): c'est trop indigeste pour mon estomac—et puis ce constant recours à Genet, ces réductions de Hegel à aigle (comme, paraît-il, le prononce le français moyen) et cette obsession phallique et d'un homo (sapiens) semper erectus n'est guère faite pour amuser, ou emplir d'envie, un patriarche comme moi. Doubrovsky a fait un livre ingénieux, souvent profond, "parcours critique." Mais il voit partout l'obsession de la mère, celle de Proust et derrière Junie, Agrippine convoitée par Néron, et enfin tuée par lui. Quel dommage que nous ne puissions pas tous être orphelins! soupirait Poil de Carotte. Le jour où les hommes feront tout seuls les enfants que deviendra la critique psychanalytique? Carlo, le seul des 3 fils ici cet été, se gorge de musique—ou de bruit. Brice, à New Haven, travaille dans un restaurant de plage; j'espère qu'il en sortira à jamais dégoûté des oignons frits et des pommes frites.

Ce mot ne voulait que vous remercier de votre message—de tout ce que vous . . . avez fait pour mon embarrassement depuis mon 80e anniversaire—et de votre admirable succès au Centre Gradué. Vous aviez redouté cette direction—à tort. Vous avez injecté là un nouveau moral, attiré des disciples, pacifié les hostilités latentes. Vous avez le droit de vous reposer enfin.

Nos vœux pleins d'amitié & d'affection,<br>H & D

# To Robert Penn Warren:

290 North Avenue
Westport, Conn. 06880
Sept. 6—81

Dear Mr. Warren:

Generosity is a very rare attribute of great men of letters. With this latest book of poems, there should be no doubt in the minds of impartial readers that you tower above all other living poets in English. Your generosity to Diana & myself has no limits; we treasure these two volumes which gave us so much pleasure—as did that most pleasant evening at your house, when Eleanor, with admirable simplicity, presided over the company, the dinner and a "jardin de délices." I am particularly grateful to those volumes of poetry, for we read them over what, without them, would have been a weekend of gloom. To hear or read an inept, fumbling President, and a multitude of commentators, discourse on MX missiles, silos, tridents and the annihilation of all that makes life worth living, & no voice arising to preserve beauty and poetry! For an 80 year old man who had chosen, once, to come to America as to the home of hope, idealism, fraternity, & to find, after McCarthy and Nixon and Kissinger, that present team of "King's Men" in charge!

I deeply enjoyed all your poems in Rumor verified—the meditative ones, which, totally devoid of pretentiousness and of affectation of depth, make the aged reader that I am share in the gravity of stone & the ecstasy of the wind, & a shallow & prosaic unbeliever suddenly "stumble upon a momentary eternity," and no less the evocations of nature in Vermont, in the West, the cycle of seasons, the prodigality of "white petals of apple blossoms" and of dogwood berries, "jewels flamed to the sun's flame." The inveterate romantic that I am, who first heard you when you lectured on Coleridge at Yale and was reassured that the "New Critics" responded as he brashly did to Wordsworth's nature poetry (and would some day be reconciled to Shelley's), confided to his memory a number of majestic, noble, moving lines: on "the last human dream that a moment can compose infinity" or on being "absorbed in the innocent solipsism of the sea." But there is none of the inflated diction of some romantics in your verse: an extraordinary sparseness of language, a concrete grasp of the real and an intense enjoyment of colors; & also a sense of irony & of humor: the bear "like a fat banker in his club window leaning." The "stirrings of your heart" long ago and the "true love" of the ten year old boy for the beautiful woman later crushed by a mortgage in the "Four Versions" of love, in the elegant & kindly inscribed volume, are a delight to read: the novelist in you survives in the poet. Your mastery of your instrument, as the French call it, is superb; but mere technique never takes over & becomes display of virtuosité. Simply, at seventy-five, with all your creative force intact, you allow yourself not a single impurity, "pas une seule défaillance" and the sensibility is youthful & warm, as in no other poet, English or French, that I know today.

Your wife must be proud of her share in fostering & developing your creative inspiration, while she maintained intact her own rare talent. Please convey to her our regards & our thanks & accept my enthusiastic admiration — & Diana's.

Henri Peyre

## À Micheline Levowitz:

> 290 North Ave.
> Westport, Conn. 06880
> Le 28 sept. 81

Chère amie,

J'avais lu que vous aviez été invitée à Cerisy et je m'étais réjoui que la qualité de votre livre, l'authenticité de votre beylisme, et l'originalité de votre approche psychologique, analytique, mais toujours sensitive, vibrante et littéraire dans son expression, soient reconnues en Europe. Nos compatriotes, vous le savez (je crois que Del Litto est devenu français, compensant l'italianité "milanese" de Beyle), sont affreusement égocentriques, jaloux de leur province ou de leur canton, aboyant en chiens de garde dès que quelqu'un, surtout du Nouveau Monde et, dit-on, riche en dollars et en loisirs (quelle ironie!), semble les menacer. Vous avez un beau sujet, et on dit Cerisy un lieu de rencontres cordiales. M. A. Caws y a été, je crois. J'ai toujours refusé moi-même, isolé et un peu ours que je suis. Mais j'avais connu la fondatrice, et même jadis son père (Desjardins) et son ex-mari, Heurgon, normalien peu après moi. Je suis atteint d'une maladie que j'ai toujours regrettée: l'impatience, qui me rend peu apte à écouter les autres. Mes rares mauvais souvenirs d'enfance sont ceux des sermons que je devais écouter, à 10 ou 12 ans. J'y ai pris en horreur le décalogue, Jacob, Jonas et autres et ne pouvais m'empêcher de regretter que Saint Paul n'ait pas été lapidé avec Étienne, ou livré aux lions à Rome! Je suis devenu plus tolérant depuis — mais par principe et pour éviter de bailler trop ouvertement, je ne vais jamais à enterrements ou mariages (ma seule exception depuis 15 ans a été celui de votre amie indochinoise et angoissée, ou camusienne). Un de mes cauchemars récurrents est que je suis sur la "couche" d'un psychanalyste et dois remonter dans mon passé enfoui; et je suis "dumb-struck" — saisi de silence maladif — me sentant châtré, mutilé, eunuque, parce que sans inconscient, structuré ou non.

Je vis dans le plus grand calme et pour l'instant beaucoup dans la nature, lisant pendant des heures sur quelque chaise longue parmi la verdure, regardant les nuages. Bien des lectures m'impatientent, y compris, je l'avoue, celle, très consciencieusement refaite, des journaux intimes de Stendhal. Que de place accordée à des amours puériles, à du mauvais théâtre et à l'opéra. J'ai finalement, une fois dans ma vie, à Stockholm, entendu du Cimarosa, mais je dois vous paraître coupable d'hérésie! Le grand Stendhal est ailleurs. Je relis beaucoup des Russes, des Allemands, des Grecs anciens. Les Français récents, même Modiano, Gary-Ajar, Tournier (qui écrit superbement), ne me charment guère. Avez-vous lu, en anglais, *Sophie's Choice,* et *The White Hotel* (de Thomas), profanation du Freudisme, à mes yeux.

Je ne bouge guère et trouve du charme à mon calme et à ma quasi solitude. Diane enseigne, écrit activement, et nous discutons peu. Mon fils vient souvent; mais il est très indépendant, a ses amis de son âge; un abîme de 62 ans entre nous crée des intérêts très divers. Je n'essaie pas de me mettre à la musique "Rock," à cet évasionnisme des récits & films de guerre des astres ou planètes de singes.

Vous vous donnez sans doute trop généreusement à votre enseignement, et il vous fatigue plus que de raison; peut-être vos voyages, le soin de votre maison pèsent-ils trop lourdement sur vous. Ménagez-vous davantage — et réservez un peu de votre énergie intellectuelle pour écrire. Vous méritez d'être lue — et le serez en 1990, comme Stendhal, ou en 2020, sinon aussitôt. Permettez-moi de compter parmi vos premiers lecteurs.

Vos impressions et réflexions sur Mitterrand m'ont ému. Elles ont remué en moi le souvenir de très vieux enthousiasmes: victoire en 1924 du bloc des gauches; transfert au Panthéon des cendres de Jaurès (ce fut grandiose), puis 1936 et front populaire. Mais alors je redoutais l'aveuglement de la France et de la gauche, car j'avais vu les Nazis monter en Allemagne. Les divisions françaises lors de la guerre d'Espagne, les hésitations de Blum (et des Anglais), la sottise des anarchistes espagnols et des Catalans, refusant d'aider Madrid, m'avaient ulcéré — puis Munich. C'est ce qui m'a déterminé à accepter de poursuivre ma carrière en Amérique.

Heureusement Mitterrand est courageux, pratique dans son idéalisme. J'espère beaucoup; mais que d'obstacles à l'horizon — financiers, économiques, et aliénation de techniciens français précieux qu'attire déjà l'émigration. L'idéalisme, très sincère, de Cheysson & autres devra, très vite, s'accompagner de réalisme: vente d'armes aux Arabes, développement de l'énergie atomique. Le chômage va être très, très dur à résorber. Il y a un peu trop de professeurs dans le cabinet et l'idéalisme dans les buts doit s'accompagner de lucidité réaliste dans les moyens. En tous cas, c'est autrement mieux que sous ce vaniteux de Giscard.

Mon fidèle souvenir au Docteur et mes vœux pour une année *presque* reposante.

Avec ma grande & vraie affection,
Henri Peyre

## To Robert Penn Warren:

[Undated; postmarked Oct. 5, 1981]

Dear "Red,"

It was very generous & thoughtful of you to send me the Mark Strand book. I barely knew his name. At once, I read all the poems in the book & I was deeply impressed. "From a library" & "Elegy for my father" moved me. I also admired "Seven Days," a virtuoso piece; & the humor of "White," & the graver last poem "Leopardi." There are extremely skillful ones also in the early volumes. The whole book brought me a sort of revelation & I intend to read more by him. Thank you.

Henri Peyre

## À Eléonore Zimmermann:

3 nov. 1981

Chère Eléonore,

Que vous êtes généreuse & gentille de partager avec moi cette belle lettre! J'en ai été très touché. Il faisait un beau soleil lumineux hier, quand elle m'est arrivée, qui rappelait la lumière méditerranéenne. La veille, dimanche, j'avais relu (m'étant remis au grec depuis ma retraite) quelques idylles de Théocrite. J'avais repensé à la Sicile, justement, où j'ai été deux fois dans ma vie. J'avais adoré ce pays alors. Le connaissez-vous vous-même? Les temples et les paysages de Sélinonte & de Ségeste; ceux, plus discrets, plus élégants, d'Agrigente où je me sentais prêt à adresser des prières aux dieux antiques; le centre, plus sauvage, d'Enna; les édifices byzantins de Monreale & Cefalu; Syracuse, à bien des égards surpassant les théâtres & les temples de la Grèce; et la rivière Anapo, près du port de Syracuse, où croissent les seuls papyrus que l'on trouve en Europe. Moi aussi, romantique invétéré, j'aime que les ruines soient des ruines où l'on puisse rêver au passé en le transfigurant à sa guise. Lors de mon second voyage en Sicile—c'était en 1937, je crois, sous le Fascisme et alors que les Allemands, alliés aux Italiens, envahissaient autobus et hôtels, comme des pays conquis, ou à conquérir—la modernisation brutale, la presse des touristes arrogants, la banalisation des menus d'hôtel, m'avaient attristé. J'ai songé depuis à retourner vers ces paysages. J'ai hésité, enfin reculé. Je sais trop que mes souvenirs d'un éblouissement ancien avaient été transfigurés par le passage du temps et l'imagination. J'ai été déçu, presque personnellement blessé, à revoir l'Egypte, affreusement vulgarisée depuis quarante ans, où la saleté & la misère mêmes sont plus grossières. Je finis par préférer le narcissisme voluptueux de l'évocation solitaire, plus reposante, de souvenirs d'autrefois. La très belle lettre de votre père m'a fait songer à nouveau à tout cela. S'il en a le temps, dites-lui qu'il aurait peut-être plaisir à lire des pages vieilles d'un siècle ou plus, mais dont le ton vieillot, ravi, m'avait jadis séduit: "Vingt Jours en Sicile" (1875) d'Ernest Renan, dans *Mélanges d'Histoire & de Voyage* (tome ii des *Œuvres Complètes*). Ce doit être un homme admirable et adorable que votre père: le ton dont il vous écrit, la poésie de ses évocations et de sa prose, l'intimité de vos rapports affectueux avec discrétion et noblesse, révèlent un homme attachant et *vivant* sa culture. Vient-il parfois vous rendre visite en Amérique? Comme il doit être fier de vous, qui avez hérité de lui une personnalité sensitive, artiste, ferme derrière sa douceur! Bien peu d'entre nous ont avec leur père de tels rapports.

Mon allemand est bien rouillé, mais j'ai goûté cette prose, riche dans sa simplicité. Jadis (à 16, 18, 20 ans), j'avais lu avec ravissement Nietzsche, Goethe (je n'ai plus retrouvé mes émotions d'autrefois en relisant récemment *Dichtung und Wahrheit* & *W. Meister,* & je n'arrive pas à mettre les mains sur le *Voyage en Italie*), Lenau que je me récitais en parcourant les montagnes, Hölderlin dont je tiens en partie ma nostalgie de la Grèce; j'avais rêvé d'un suicide à deux à la Kleist, mais devant un plus beau site. Puis les années 1936 et 38, où j'ai voyagé à nouveau en Allemagne, m'ont traumatisé: les discours de Hitler à Nuremberg, les jeunes fanatiques Nazis entrevus à Munich, la lâcheté d'intellectuels convertis à la bassesse et à la flagornerie devant Goebbels, comme Kurt Weill. Ces souvenirs se sont enfouis dans mon subconscient. Je suis retourné en Allemagne 3 ou 4 fois depuis la guerre, à Baden-Baden, à Freiburg, à Wiesbaden, à Ulm; mais je ne puis m'empêcher de voir, dans ces gens rutilants de santé, dans les paysans, d'anciens fanatiques du Nazisme. Je me suis dépris de ce qui m'avait séduit dans l'Allemagne romantique. Je me suis d'ailleurs dépris tout autant de mes compatriotes, avec leur réhabilitation des collaborateurs de 1940–44, leurs "nouveaux philosophes" experts en publicité, leur glorification de Drieu la Rochelle et aujourd'hui de Tournier: beau prosateur sans doute, mais incurablement pédéraste et, dans son *Roi des Aulnes* et ailleurs, si indulgent pour Goering. Peut-être pour cela j'évite même Paris et les milieux littéraires et leurs modes. Il y a quelque mélancolie à sentir derrière soi un trop long passé.

Merci encore de m'avoir, grâce à ces très belles pages, fait rouvrir mon dictionnaire allemand, et ramené à des souvenirs siciliens depuis longtemps enfouis....

Assez vous imposer mon écriture et ma prose.

Toute mon amitié,
Henri

## À Micheline Levowitz:

Le 9 janvier 82

Chère amie,

Quel papier! Vraiment mallarméen, "le vide papier que sa blancheur défend"! J'ai une sainte horreur des cadeaux, dont je ne sais que faire, ayant peu de besoins et étant guéri des désirs. Quelque jeune "admirateur" a décidé pourtant que j'aurais toujours besoin de papier à lettres. Mais je ne suis plus à l'âge des longues lettres. J'en ai trop reçu, lorsque j'étais directeur de conscience de pas mal de jeunes: une, inoubliable, de 85 pages, d'une jeune femme, juive, révolutionnaire, plusieurs fois emprisonnée, que j'ai finalement fait envoyer en France, où elle fut accueillie par Simone de Beauvoir, mentionnée dans ses livres. Puis, à 50 ans, elle est devenue "lawyer" et soutien de l'ordre. Une autre de 68 pages d'un jeune homme, israélite aussi, pour expliquer & glorifier son homosexualité. Il n'a jamais terminé ses études, est parti pour Israël où il est devenu, m'a-t-il plus tard annoncé, père de cinq enfants. Tout arrive. Vieilli & retraité, j'ai enfin cédé à l'amollis—semant sentimental—& envoyé une dizaine de courts billets ou cartes de Noël. Et je ne suis plus confronté que par ces grandes feuilles, dont la vue m'a du moins rappelé "Brise marine," que je récitais avec élan à 16 ans. Je m'imaginais déjà alors triste dans ma chair et futur lecteur de tous les livres. Cela m'a amusé récemment, lisant beaucoup de, & sur, Bernard Berenson, de trouver, décuplé, cet enthousiasme pour dévorer tous les livres. Mais lui—juif lithuanien: j'ai toujours eu envers les juifs un cuisant complexe d'infériorité—dès ses années de Harvard, savait l'arabe, l'araméen, le russe et avait résolu de lire une page d'un auteur grec chaque jour de sa vie. C'est la seule règle que je m'impose dans mes vieux jours; encore n'est-ce pas aisé. J'avais oublié combien est déroutante la conjugaison de ces verbes avec tant de modes et d'étranges formes dialectales.

Enfin je vous souhaite, & à votre mari, une année un peu plus reposante—sans angoisse de santé, sans trop d'irruptions de l'inconscient non-structuré, avec des nouvelles favorables de la politique française & un séjour spirituellement reposant à Cerisy. Cette Mme Heurgon-Desjardins, morte, je crois, était la fille d'un autre Desjardins—un professeur de lycée que Proust, qui l'avait eu comme maître, mentionne quelque part dans son roman. Il devait être une sorte de Protestant; il est vrai que je soutiens que tous les Français, race sévère, préoccupée de morale et d'éducation spirituelle, le sont, sans le savoir. Il avait fondé "l'Union pour la Vérité," que hantaient Gide, Martin du Gard, et préconisé "l'action morale." Belle époque de foi!

Je conserve ma foi politique—ou du moins mon espoir—que la France est sur la bonne voie, s'attire le respect des autres nations et peut réussir cet ambitieux changement de société. Ce ne sera pas aisé, certes, et le chômage ne va pas se résorber là-bas mieux qu'ici. Mais—Léon Blum aimait à le répéter—une société qui n'arrive pas à faire place à ses jeunes et à utiliser leur élan, se condamne elle-même. Le malheur est que la tentation a été forte de rallier les jeunes en les militarisant & les envoyant se faire tuer. Je crois que cela est fini. Mais c'était pour moi, sur la fin de ma carrière, une source de chagrin, d'avoir tant de mal à placer nos jeunes, dans notre profession; et les lettres que je reçois de ceux-là mêmes (de Yale ou du Centre Gradué) pour qui nous avions déniché des postes au diable (Minnesota, Nebraska, Tennessee) les dépeignent isolés, perdus, pleins de nostalgie de New York.

Comment vont les choses à Barnard? Le Collège est-il menacé? S'y convertit-on à la sémiotique? Votre programme est-il très chargé? Je crois encore que vous avez beaucoup à dire & seriez contente de vous exprimer—par écrit. Je le fais moi-même par moments, sans avoir grand'chose à dire et sans me soucier même de publier. Je ne me tiens pas au courant des développements présents en psychanalyse; mais il doit y avoir des possibilités pour des essais neufs en matière de psychanalyse appliquée à la littérature. Ce que je puis connaître de la critique Jungienne m'a déçu et rebuté; & je ne vois pas qu'on ait, en critique littéraire, tenté d'appliquer les vues d'Adler, qui me séduiraient davantage. Voyez-vous ceux d'entre vos "condisciples" (Mme Castro? Belmonas?) qui se sont dirigés vers quelque application de la psychanalyse? Y font-ils une carrière qui les satisfait?

Je ne vais jamais à New York, ou ailleurs, & me complais à quelque indolence. Je sais que je ne puis plus rien pour changer la vie—en général ou celle de quiconque. Je vous souhaite une année neuve aussi placide que j'espère la mienne.

Bien amicalement,<br>Henri Peyre

## À Eléonore Zimmermann

Le 16 février 82

Chère Eléonore,

Nous avons le droit d'être fiers de ce que font nos collègues d'Amérique. Le délicat & précieux envoi de l'Italienische Reise m'a beaucoup touché. C'est une très élégante édition, et qui va faire revivre mon allemand. J'avais lu ce livre il y a des vingtaines d'années, lors de mon premier voyage en Italie, m'identifiant, mais moins païennement, avec le voyageur des Élégies romaines et résolu à me libérer de l'idéalisation de quelque Frau von Stein. Qu'il faut d'années pour mûrir! Quel âge a votre père? Vient-il jamais vous rendre visite en Amérique? Il doit être le plus intéressant & le plus affectueux des pères. Merci de ce cadeau que je chérirai et de votre si délicate attention — & de la jolie carte. . . .

Henri

## À Micheline Levowitz:

290 North Ave.
Westport, Ct. 06880
Le 1er mars 82

Chère amie,

Ma 1ère lettre du mois de mars. Le ciel, hier, était plus clair; des oiseaux semblaient être revenus de leur envol vers les chauds climats et, enfin! osaient rivaliser avec les méchants appels gutturaux des corbeaux. En Europe, autrefois, on récitait de gentils poèmes de Th. Gautier ou de Wordsworth sur "le premier sourire du printemps" ou "This is the first fine day of March." Je souris souvent, quand des bribes de Musset, voire de Heredia, me reviennent en mémoire, tandis que je me rase et aperçois une lumière printanière par la fenêtre. Je n'idéalise certes pas ma jeunesse, ou l'enseignement qu'on nous dispensait alors dans les lycées français. Personne alors n'avait entendu parler de psychanalyse. En classe de philosophie, on discutait Hume, William James, Bergson. Aussi avec quelle avidité plus tard, arrivant à Paris, nous découvrions (en 1920–

23, j'étais alors normalien) Proust, Valéry, Giraudoux, Cocteau. Mon meilleur ami alors (Juif parisien comme il se trouve, avec qui j'ai aussi servi dans l'armée; il a été tué à la guerre en 1940) était féru de Stendhal et prenait quelquefois la classe d'Arbelet dans un lycée; il était enthousiaste de ce maître et de Stendhal que nul alors ne lisait. Les poètes d'aujourd'hui (Bonnefoy, Deguy, Dupin—Ashbery ici) sont plus graves, plus profonds, mais j'ai bien plus de peine à les retenir par cœur ou à les intégrer à ma vie intérieure. La mémoire est la première faculté qui faiblit avec l'âge. J'ai eu 81 ans l'autre jour. Comment peut-on vivre si vieux?

J'étais à Columbia jeudi dernier, parlant à un congrès à l'Institute on Western Europe, 118th Street. Mon message, auquel je m'adonne un peu comme à un ultime testament, est la nécessité de dépasser le nationalisme—en partie grâce à l'enseignement et à la diffusion de l'étude de la littérature. Cela prendra deux siècles mais on devrait sans retard s'y adonner. Nous avons 10 ou 12 millions d'élèves dans les collèges et universités d'Amérique—a "captive audience"—et nous en touchons quelques-uns, tout de même. Quel crime contre la jeunesse, de consentir à ce qu'elle grandisse en ignorant tout de Balzac, Goethe, Tolstoï, Zola! Que nos illusions étaient radieuses, quand nous pouvions croire à un monde meilleur, plus juste, plus droit. J. Reed était sans doute un naïf; Victor Serge (je l'ai beaucoup admiré) parfois un maladroit. Mais que d'espoirs ont été anéantis par l'inhumanité de Staline ensuite, la bêtise de Marchais aujourd'hui. Il y avait de nobles âmes parmi ceux qui devinrent les transfuges du Communisme: Malraux, Silone, Koestler, Edgar Morin . . . L'Amérique de Reagan est lamentable, comparée à celle de 1930–38.

Assez de regrets du passé! Non, je ne crois pas aller en France cet été, & j'ai cessé de paraître aux Congrès. Je ne suis jamais allé à Cerisy, en fait. Mais on dit que l'atmosphère y est cordiale. M. A. Caws, Rosette Lamont y ont été & peuvent vous en parler. J'ai aimé ce que j'ai lu d'Orlando, sur *Phèdre;* moins le lourd Stendhal de Robert André. L'homme est très gentil et chaleureux: il a enseigné en Amérique, à Wesleyan (Conn.) où je l'ai un peu connu. C'est un très bon, et courageux, romancier. Si c'est le même R. André, donnez-lui mon fidèle souvenir.

Surtout n'ayez crainte. Vous serez très appréciée là-bas. Sans vanité, je crois que les meilleurs d'entre nous, Américains ou Français d'Amérique, soutiennent aisément la comparaison avec les professeurs de France. Et les Français en sont venus à le reconnaître.

J'espère que l'avenir de Barnard reste assuré. C'est un des meilleurs collèges d'Amérique, & qui mérite de survivre. Est-il menacé?

                Henri
                Mes amitiés à votre mari et à vous.

## À Mary Ann Caws:

                Le lundi 3 mai 82

Chère Mary Ann,

Je ne réponds pas toujours à vos communications qui, toujours, me flattent et m'intéressent, mais avec l'approche de la fin de l'année scolaire, il convient tout de même que je vous dise combien je suis heureux & fier du succès que remporte, sous votre direction, le Programme de français. Les études ont acquis une nouvelle jeunesse sous votre inspiration et vous avez l'art de faire participer tout le monde & de permettre à chacun de donner ce qu'il peut offrir de mieux comme contribution à une tâche collective. Voulez-vous, si l'occasion s'en présente, le dire de ma part lors de la cérémonie qui honorera J. Kneller vendredi. (Je dois être à New Haven ce jour-là & l'explique à Jack.) Et je suis très, très heureux que l'Institut d'été de Renée Waldinger soit enfin reconnu comme il le mérite, et aidé. Elle a monté cela avec détermination, courage & talent, à un moment où on recevait peu d'encouragement. Elle est une organisatrice de premier ordre.

Je regrette personnellement que votre fille choisisse Harvard, mais cela se comprend. J'aurais pu, à Yale, la voir parfois; peut-être l'aider en cas de difficulté et voir ses parents retournant aux lieux où ils se sont connus. "Tristesse d'Olympio!"

Pour moi, mon absence de New York ne signifie certes pas que je boude dans quelque solitude aigrie. Je passe beaucoup de temps à rêvasser, lire & relire, et je reviens de la bibliothèque de Yale chargé d'ouvrages que, depuis des années, je voulais lire, ou relire. J'ai bien regretté de ne pas revoir & écouter Yves Bonnefoy. Je reste naïvement fier de l'avoir un peu "découvert" lors de ses tout premiers poèmes. Il est devenu aussi un critique de grande originalité. Ses interventions, dans des colloques organisés par Gadoffre à Vendôme (je crois), sont toujours lucides et profondes. J'ai été content que le Collège de France l'ait préféré à Genette, dont les récents écrits me paraissent pédants et, en fin de compte, minces.

Je ne voudrais pas jouer le jeu de fausse modestie; mais j'ai le sentiment qu'il est un peu déplacé d'un homme âgé, qui a longtemps enseigné et parlé, qui ne se sent pas très en sympathie avec bien des théories & des critiques récents, de rester trop en vue. C'est la raison pour laquelle j'ai préféré ne pas voir paraître à Princeton de mes anciens articles. C'est aussi pourquoi il me semble que je ne devrais pas me produire trop vaniteusement dans des entretiens ou débats. Je crois que j'ai, au cours de cinquante-cinq ans d'enseignement, dit le meilleur de ce que je pouvais avoir à dire. Il faut aussi savoir se faire oublier et souhaiter que nos disciples nous contredisent et nous combattent.

Allez-vous en France cet été? Vous devez avoir besoin de vous reposer, de lire & d'écrire en paix . . . Mes vœux de bonnes vacances à vos enfants aussi.

Affectueusement,
*Henri*

## À Micheline Levowitz:

Le 17 mai 82

Chère amie,

Je me trouve bêtement pressé par le temps, comme, bien sûr, un retraité n'a plus le droit de l'être. Mais je passe bien des heures à flâner et la campagne, ces derniers jours, est splendide, insultante presque dans le déploiement de ses couleurs, embaumée de lilas & de rhododendrons. Tout mon romantisme de jeunesse, refoulé pas très profondément, remonte en moi. Je ne vais pas jusqu'à me réciter Musset ou Hugo, ou Chateaubriand, &, à l'encontre de la mode actuelle; je ne me sens pas pris par George Sand, ou même par "la Faute de l'abbé Mouret." Mais je lis des romantiques allemands ou anglais; le voile de la langue étrangère les fait paraître plus pudiques & mystérieux. Dans mes moments de dégoût devant l'avidité et la rapacité des politiciens, je rouvre les vieux historiens: Suétone, Tacite surtout sur les monstruosités de Caligula & de Néron. Leurs crimes éclipsent de loin les attentats de New York & même les horreurs perpétrées par Staline, sinon par Hitler. Que la lucidité est rare en politique! Bien entendu, je me l'attribue! À lire ou relire les déclarations de Sartre dans ses dernières années, je suis saisi d'étonnement devant son étroitesse et son obstination. Je l'avais beaucoup aimé autrefois & avais dès 1945 rallié des auditoires autour de son existentialisme, alors tout jeune. Il en avait été touché. Quelle étrange fatalité force de bons esprits à se renier eux-mêmes. J'avoue éprouver la même déception en relisant bien des pages de Freud, ou en rouvrant des livres comme ceux de Norman O. Brown, Life against Death, qui m'avaient jadis impressionné. Je suis excédé, et un peu dégoûté moralement, par ces interminables ressassements sur le rôle de la masturbation, de la coprophilie, de la "penis envy" dans les premières années de la vie. Vive la sublimation, quoi qu'on en dise! Le livre, *The White Hotel,* de D. Thomas fait beaucoup parler de lui, même en France, et une ennuyeuse vie de prostituée imaginaire, The Flute Player, je crois. Je plains votre mari de devoir écouter tant de confessions et opérer tant de "transferts." Il y a beau temps qu'un tel métier m'aurait rendu misogyne.

Je voulais seulement vous souhaiter un bon été, un séjour agréable & fructueux à Cerisy & vous signaler (si on ne vous l'a déjà dit) que vous êtes citée, parmi les grands beylistes, dans l'article de Peter Brooks, dans le récent (May 82) PMLA. Les étrangers ne cessent de nous envier la guillotine.

Bien des vœux pour votre mari & vous. Je pense rester à peu près immobile ici.

Amicalement,<br>Henri Peyre

## To E. M. Halliday:

July 30—82

Dear Hal,

Your all too brief visits always fill us with new ideas, fresh perspectives; impress us with the rash magnitude of your projects for exploration of the West, your dreams of conquest—perhaps merely symbolical—

of more female hearts & your secret sadness of a new Alexander, sighing because there are few worlds left for you to invade.

Last time, you left me with a present which I enjoyed. I have finished reading the book (Poets in their youth). Eileen Simpson is, naturally, anecdotic, light, overimpressed with that circle of literary figures; but shrewd, incredibly patient. What a melancholy picture emerges of those poets, moody, inordinately narcissistic, drinking to recapture the inspiration & the writing facility which have eluded them & yielding finally to their obsession with suicide. "Poètes maudits" they were & expert at making their women suffer. I only, & remotely and diffidently, approached, or happened to meet, a few of those men of letters (Ed. Wilson, Philip Rahv, in his old age, Richard Blackmur) & felt repelled by their monstrous egocentrism & sorry for their women companions. Your son, thank God! has humor, modesty, generosity as well as talent.

I hope Diana will find time to read this book, & turn away temporarily from her writing on the deterioration caused by old age & sexual obsessions of males over sixty. That's her present subject of research, *re* old Hulot in Balzac's *Cousin Bette*—a rather horrible book.

Cordially & thankfully yours,<br>
Henri

Our best to Jenny (I still can't write her name).

## À Lester Crocker:

290 North Avenue<br>
Westport, Conn. 06880<br>
Le samedi 14 août [1982]

Cher Lester,

J'ai été saisi d'un grand élan d'approbation admirative de votre très bel article, et vous l'ai dit au téléphone, mais gauchement; très vieille mode que je suis, je me sers mal de cet instrument. Mais dès la première fois, dans quelque classe d'anglais au Lycée, où l'on m'avait fait lire cette pièce de Shakespeare, elle m'avait rebuté: cette Portia, la sottise des coffrets, le rôle prêté à Shylock & même les tirades sur "the quality of mercy" me semblaient fades, et le traitement de l'usurier ou du prêteur juif, barbare. Vous analysez les diverses attitudes avec une précision lumineuse et avec une totale impartialité; je n'y retrouve même pas ce brin de colère que vous inspirait parfois Rousseau. Ce que Shakespeare pouvait penser au fond de lui, nous ne le savons pas. Mais il a certes partagé et absorbé tous les préjugés médiévaux de son époque, & cela nous chagrine. Comme me chagrine Balzac, quand il s'acharne contre, et sur, ses banquiers alsaciens juifs et ses prostituées, qui toutes s'appellent "Sarah" ou "Esther." Pour moi, mon admiration est souvent allée à des aînés ou à des amis de mon âge, comme Raymond Aron, qui se trouvaient être nés dans une famille israélite et étaient de plus sûrs rationalistes—des esprits plus ouverts, et autrement équilibrés et "occidentalisés" et hellénisés—qu'à Sartre vieilli, qui a proféré tant d'énormes bêtises. De mon père, fervent Dreyfusard, j'avais hérité une susceptibilité très vive à tout racisme. Cela ne m'a pas rendu admirateur sans réserves d'Israël aujourd'hui et de Begin; mais je crois avoir le droit de penser avec indépendance.

J'espère que votre année new-yorkaise s'est bien passée et que vous avez pu jouir des joies intellectuelles qu'offre la grande ville. Je n'y vais presque jamais moi-même; et cet été, renonçant à tout voyage, je suis resté à la campagne à lire & relire, parfois à écrire, et surtout à rêvasser. La maison de Diane a un grand jardin et je retrouve là mon goût "rousseauiste" de la paix des champs.

Tous deux, nous serions très heureux si, le dimanche 29 août, vous pouviez venir pour le repas du milieu du jour et quelque repos et conversation paisible. Le train qui part de Grand Central à midi 05, le dimanche, arrive à Westport à une heure 05. Si vous deviez venir en auto, je vous enverrais une carte. Dites-moi d'un mot si vous pouvez tous deux venir. Cela nous ferait plaisir.

Vives amitiés,<br>Henri

## To Buford Norman:

Sept. 17—82

Dear Mr. Norman:

Thirteen years after my retirement from Yale, I still hang around the Library and W. L. Harkness Hall, though I refrain from advising my successors. My son, age 18, has just entered the University as a freshman! I read a good deal in the Library, mostly on contemporary French politics & on history, on which I occasionally write. Recent novels & much of today's criticism bore me or irritate me; so I keep at safe distance from it. I enjoy having much free time & should feel Pascalian, "sachant rester en repos dans une chambre." I must own that my leisure has in no way brought me closer to religion & that my feeble meditations seldom center on death, & even more seldom on another life. This one is long enough!

I *never* keep any copy of my earlier letters; it's my way of feeling free from my past. So I'll write a new & fresh letter when I am asked to report on you. I suppose I'll receive also a page on what you have accomplished (age, writings), so as to refresh my memory on you, & recall to me the special slant, or angle, from which you are treating Pascal. In my last seminar on him at CUNY, some female students (Jewish in majority) insisted that Pascal was the forerunner, or the culprit, for anti-Semitism in France & the massacre of the rue Copernic. They even suspected me of some anti-Semitism, since I have an inferiority complex to many Jews who are terribly gifted & apparently not revolted by the Old Testament (as I am) & by Begin's imperialism. It's fun at 80 or 81 to be still deemed "dangerous."

My good wishes for the Novel conference in March. It should be a success. I doubt I will attend. I do not go to colloquia anymore. I am too impatient of critical jargon.

With cordial greetings,<br>Henri Peyre

## À Frederick Brown:

Le 5 oct. 82

Cher ami,

J'ai écrit aussitôt & espérons, car c'est un beau & grand projet. Ici, pour moi, tout va bien. Je ne bouge guère et lis assidûment. Il est agréable de jouir des lectures sans avoir à songer à critiquer, à enseigner et disséquer.

Bon courage pour votre Camus. Etrange, la hargne avec laquelle ce

McCarthy (très bien informé d'ailleurs, bon esprit critique) met en relief toutes les insuffisances philosophiques de Camus et les faiblesses sexuelles ou autres de sa vie privée. Après avoir autrefois été dur pour la "pensée" de Camus, j'ai essayé une réévaluation de ses vues politiques, dans un article de la revue Laurel, que je n'ai pas conservé. Il avait raison souvent, contre les admirateurs obstinés de Staline et les arguties de Sartre.

Bien des vœux,<br>H. P.

## To Robert G. Cohn:

290 North Avenue<br>Westport, Conn. 06880<br>October 18—1982

Dear Bob,

Your letter of some two weeks ago was most welcome. I always enjoy hearing from you. In my retirement and welcome quietude, as my reveries often take me back to my past, I find you associated with those years after World War II. I have, rashly, accepted to give a lecture at Bryn Mawr, where my American career began over half a century ago; &, in a talk which will probably be the last one I'll give, I offered as a title "Sartre s'éloigne-t-il?" I have thus been rereading his early plays, including "Les Mains sales," the short stories & the novels, & recalled the years when he visited Yale & when you started the Yale French Studies. I still admire those early works immensely. But I wonder if it is not my own past which I fondly want to relive. I suppose I shall have to say candidly how disappointed & irritated I have been with Sartre's political aberrations since 1968, with the last five or six volumes of *Situations* & even with the *Flaubert*. The "aveuglement" of my compatriots—many of them old Normaliens (Leroy-Ladurie in Montpellier-Paris, Althusser's disciples, Sartre himself) where "le fantôme de Staline" & the cult of "le Père du Peuple" & of Thorez was concerned—fills me, retrospectively, with dismay. I hate to turn conservative in my dying days & to be driven to the right, as those ex-Stalinists are all doing. My son warns me every weekend on the "generation gap" between us. But I confess the rejection of culture & of thinking by the present generation of college students is a calamity in my eyes. The little I see of my successors at Yale is not encouraging. I had wanted to believe that wisdom had flown west & to Stanford in particular. Your reports, these last few years, & the inability of students there to realize how uniquely valuable is what you have to say on Mallarmé (& Rimbaud & Proust & art & poetics) have killed my illusions. In the New York colleges, in Brooklyn (where Diana teaches &, personally, seems to be very successful & to have quite a following), the recent classes of students are deserting the humanities & the arts. I almost feel that all my efforts, these fifty years, have borne little fruit.

I fervently hope your *Ways of Art,* continued, will appear soon. I found your first volume difficult, to be sure, but the most rewarding I had read for a long, long time. How is René Girard doing? Has he quite a following at Stanford? Has he drawn students to literature?

Diane was going over her MS, accepted in principle, with the suggestion that she shorten it. I believe she has now done so, & excised some fifty pages. As she was going over it, in the next room, I heard her remarks of loud gratitude for the extraordinary care with which it had been read. When your letter came, I thought it would not be indiscreet to tell her that *you* had been the reader. She is immensely grateful. She hopes to receive—or rather to ask for—a modest financial assistance from the Guggenheim to help pay for the publication, & a copy of the report, or reports, will probably have to be sent to the Committee. I trust that will be available.

I am touched by the efforts of M. A. Caws to honor me with a volume to which you would contribute; but also embarrassed by all the pains she takes. I *know* very well that I never was a great man or an original thinker. I loved literature & felt much affection for my students—& the enjoyment of poetry has remained my greatest satisfaction.

I do not travel much these days but I hope that, when you come east, or perhaps on your way to Italy next year, you & your wife will stop here. We would truly *love* to see you again.

Warm regards to Valentina & much affection to you,
Henri

## To Frederick Brown:

>290 North Avenue
>Westport. Ct. 06880
>Nov. 2—82

Dear Fred,

My congratulations on your beautifully written article on "La Cérémonie des Adieux" in the *New Criterion*. It is a gloomy book & it saddened me, reminding me of a remark of Nietzsche about the sorry & moving sight of great & tragic personalities crumbling down. You restrain your own pity masterfully & also your secret anger. I had admired Sartre so much in the years 1938–1955, when I brought him to Yale to lecture, & we devoted some early *Yale French Studies* to him. Were you already at Yale then? I forget. Then, with "Les Communistes & la paix," "le Fantôme de Staline," his blind advocacy of "la révolte" per se, his childish anarchism & the *Flaubert*, which I find unbearably boring & a masterpiece of "mauvaise foi," I turned against him. His nasty repudiation of all his male friends (Camus, Merleau-Ponty, Aron), his silly pride at being turned by Victor into an honorary Jew & his rabâchage against the bourgeoisie have belittled him. The Underground man was perhaps right when he remarked that no one should live beyond the age of forty.

At close to 82, I realize how selfish & foolish I must have been myself at clinging to teaching & writing & that I am now turning conservative. At least, I have never been, like so many other former Normaliens, a devotee of "Le Père du Peuple," "le grand génie," Stalin! And I trust I have not stifled the independence & the talent of my former students. I feel naïvely proud when I read your balanced, discriminating & expertly written articles.

>Cordially yours,
>Henri Peyre

## To Mary Ann Caws:

>Henri Peyre
>290 North Avenue
>Westport, Ct. 06880
>November 17—82

Dear Mary Ann,

I have probably been remiss, or slow, in replying to several kind messages from you—in part because, occasionally breaking my vow of a Trappist's silence, I have been away & lectured at one or two places; also because your last (& most touching & flattering) letter & the MSS it enclosed must have been delayed in the mails & reached me only yesterday. The grateful, deeply felt thanks I owe you are thus piling up into a Mont Ventoux. Let me, in the old Cartesian way of dividing up the difficulties, express them serially.

First, many thanks for the New Directions book on Perse. Your introduction is concise, suggestive, modest, informing & remarkably "juste de ton." The selection is ingenious, fair, comprehensive. Some of his admirers may miss the "Poème à l'Etrangère," which we recited to each other (Thornton Wilder and one or two of us) in 1941. During the war years, I saw much of Léger when he often visited M. de la Grange (married to a Sloan lady, furniture fortune) in Guilford, near New Haven. He was, along with Malraux, the most fascinating conversationalist I have known—& the most consistently egocentric. Then I met him at Mrs. Mina Curtis (sister of Lincoln Kirstein), where he was staying, & bored, for he needed an audience; like most men, that's why he married. He accepted an honorary degree at Yale; I saw him then, & again in Washington after he finally married. I have avoided writing on him, I confess, because I have reservations on his greatness as a poet & there is no point in expressing them now. I campaigned actively for his Nobel Prize & gave to the Rare Book Library at Yale letters & dedications in which he calls me "son grand électeur." I have refrained from writing or speaking on the men of letters I have known (St. Exupéry, Gide, Malraux, Sartre, Perse), mindful of their vanity, or pride, and reluctant to seem to exalt my puny self through my acquaintance with them.

Then thank you for the copies of Georges May's kind & humorous preface & of Oxenhandler's ingenious & thoughtful essay on Dante &

Beckett. I do have scruples & very sincere embarrassment at being made so much of. You, who have so many tasks already (with your unceasing writing & publishing activity, outdoing even Mrs. Knapp & Mr. Matthews), your brilliantly effective chairmanship, your MLA presidency, your family, etc., devote far too much time & energy to honoring me, half-posthumously. I do not deserve any such tributes. I have been a conscientious teacher & that's about all. I refuse to have any of my books reprinted &, very candidly, I do not think any funds should be squandered away on a volume "honoring" me. That Stanford Press, Eléonore Zimmermann told me, is very expensive. Could I contribute to the expense, at least? Do let me know, in confidence & in all sincerity.

The success of the French program, under your ardent, inspiring leadership & Renée Waldinger's discreet & efficient organization, is remarkable. I am, vicariously & half-posthumously, as it were, very proud of it. My years of teaching there have left nothing but very pleasant memories & I rejoice at the éclat you have given to its program, at your diplomat's skill in establishing a community of purpose. You, your colleagues & the administration have honored me lavishly at my retirement & since. I think my name should now be dropped & everyone's vision be centered on the future.

A word about my inability to free myself on December 3rd, a Friday. It just happens that the new director of the Humanities at the Rockefeller Foundation has asked me to participate in a meeting (on restoring foreign languages & other sad perennial issues) on Dec. 2–3, & again on Dec. 9th. I hardly go anywhere else these days, preferring to stay quietly home & meditate. I hope to be present at the party on Monday, December 13th, & greet friends & students. I am sorry I have to miss Mrs. Braun's & I'll explain it to her.

It does seem to me that visitors from France, other colleagues in America, scholars more inclined to interpret recent critical trends, should, in the Program's interest, be preferred as lecturers to one whom his age & tastes direct toward the past. It is hard, for an old person, not to "regarder en arrière / le cadavre de ses jours" and, in a half disguised fashion, not to talk about himself. My interests, lately, have gone towards politics & recent history: "Malentendus franco-américains," "L'Amérique devant les intellectuels français," "French predictions of American-Russian antagonism." I did lecture at Bryn Mawr on "Sartre s'éloigne-t-il?" &, almost in spite of myself, must have been severe on the older Sartre, especially in the political field, which, to me, renders his philosophy & would-be ethics questionable ... Somehow, I have felt that "Justice pour Camus" might be opportune, after the "éloignement" in which several people relinquished him between 1970 & 1980. Some day, the man who started his career in feminist Bryn Mawr in 1925–8 and ended it in the woman-dominated atmosphere of CUNY (often impatient at one of our colleagues' insistent vindication of Simone de Beauvoir) will summon up his courage & treat of "Woman's absence in the 20th century novel" (Montherlant, Green, St. Exupéry, Sartre, Malraux, Camus, Marguerite Yourcenar *et al.*); a touchy subject, naturally, I much deplore that absence.

I seem to be imposing an unduly long letter upon you, & I apologize. I receive news occasionally of former students & I'll pass them on some time for your newsletter. Some are proving nobly creative & awaiting progeny: e.g. Esther Stern (Bloom is her married name), now at 307, Pine Street, Philadelphia, 19106, teaching somewhere there, spreading the view of Pascal's responsibility for French "anti-Semitism" & lecturing on Pascal's tragic vision. She also lectures at the Univ. of Pennsylvania on a similar Pascalian theme. I regret that I am not one to keep letters; but I am touched by those former students' messages.

Warm congratulations on your being *intronisée* among "Los Angeles" next month. I shall applaud from afar ...

With much affection,<br>Henri

## À Wallace Fowlie:

290 North Ave.<br>Westport, Conn. 06880<br>Le 20 déc. 82

Cher Michel,

Je vous ai vu, écouté avec émotion, lors du service en mémoire de Catherine Coffin. Puis vous avez disparu & je n'ai pas réussi à vous parler. Je ne me suis pas attardé ensuite. J'étais profondément ému et triste. C'est toute une partie de mon passé, embellie et aussi attristée par le souvenir, qui disparaît avec elle. À ce passé, vous êtes étroitement associé: par des soucis partagés, des admirations & amitiés communes, nos conversations, les jeunes étudiants que vous aviez le don d'inspirer, d'assembler, de rendre proches de l'aîné un peu officiel que j'étais. J'atteindrai bientôt 82 ans & m'étonne de ma résistance à tant de lectures (je ne fais presque rien d'autre), de survivre à tant d'amis. Je me déplace peu, trouve les réunions professionnelles sèches et lugubres, bien des critiques vains et pédants. Il est difficile, sans doute, de ne pas devenir bougon et grognon avec les années. Je m'en veux d'avoir trop peu revu Catherine ces dernières années. Ses fils me disent que sa mort, sans déclin aucun, est celle qu'elle souhaitait. C'est aussi celle que j'envie.

J'ai égaré votre adresse "cléricale," mais peut-être retournez-vous à Duke pour le répit de Noël & j'y adresse ce mot.

Avec mes souhaits de ferme santé et ma profonde amitié,
*Henri*

Quel courage a Ralph Kirkpatrick, quelle noblesse en lui. C'est un des 5 ou 6 hommes, avec Focillon, Malraux, vous, que je suis le plus heureux d'avoir connus.

## À Micheline Levowitz:

Le 15 janvier 1983

Chère amie,

Mes vœux sont tardifs; et c'est par paresse, car je devrais avoir plus de temps que jamais je n'en ai eu. Mais la correspondance absorbe beaucoup de mon loisir. J'ai ce pointilleux scrupule de répondre à toutes les lettres, & j'en reçois beaucoup, à ce moment de l'année, d'anciens étudiants. Cette fidélité me touche et j'apprends souvent beaucoup, par leurs lettres, sur leurs lectures, leurs goûts (ma plume est rebelle—effet de la neige au dehors, peut-être), leur famille. Il y a parmi ceux qui ont choisi la carrière d'enseignants, et aussi parmi d'autres, des personnes de premier ordre, de caractère noble et droit, pour moi, ce que l'Amérique offre de mieux. Quelle tristesse que si peu de ces gens-là arrivent à la politique! J'ai parfois correspondu avec certains hommes arrivés à la direction des affaires, Acheson, George Ball, George Kennan à propos d'articles que j'avais écrits sur la politique et sur (récemment) les prophéties françaises de la rivalité éventuelle américano-russe. Ils sont informés, lucides, généreux et largement les meilleurs des hommes d'état et des diplomates d'aujourd'hui. Eugène Rostow, que Reagan vient de congédier, avait été de mes élèves et est resté un bon ami. (Sa femme est psychanalyste.) Mais tous semblent en ce moment en "désarroi": c'est le mot à la mode. Nul ne sait où se tourner et comment obtenir les sacrifices requis. Cette course aux armements est une monstrueuse et criminelle stupidité; je suppose que je devrais me tourner davantage vers mon maigre moi et vers ceux dont je devrais m'occuper. J'ai prêché beaucoup ces dernières années contre la nationalisme et tâché d'indiquer, en partie par la littérature, quelques moyens de le "transcender." Mais je renonce. On devient égoïste et découragé avec les années. La triste chose est que les natures les plus douées, celles de Sartre par exemple, ne résistent pas au vieillissement et au rabâchage dogmatique. Relire les écrits de Sartre après 1965–68 est attristant. Il a voulu à toute force croire à la grandeur de Staline et à la sainteté de la révolte pour la révolte. Je l'avais bien connu, beaucoup admiré, et me suis détaché de lui depuis, retournant à Camus, plus droit et plus lucide en fin de compte que Sartre et que les *Mandarins* avaient tant vilipendé. Je retourne de plus en plus vers la poésie, qui avait toujours été ma vraie passion.

Je ne vais pour ainsi dire jamais à New York, car je me fatigue vite et ma curiosité s'émousse. Il semble que les choses aillent bien au Centre Gradué et j'admire l'activité de Mary Ann Caws. Je crois pourtant qu'elle devrait davantage rassembler les anciens étudiants et les mêler à ses conseils. Il y en a beaucoup, ou au moins quelques-unes, comme vous, qui nous font grand honneur, et auraient des suggestions utiles à offrir. Votre Stendhal est un livre de réelle valeur et sera estimé de plus en plus; et vous avez bien davantage à dire, & à écrire, sur Stendhal ou sur d'autres. Il a paru un livre de Michel Guérin, La Politique de Stendhal, aux Presses Universitaires, préfacé avec force éloges par Régis Debray. L'auteur écrit élégamment, prétentieusement, avec luxe d'allusions; il touche aux trois grands romans, a de fines suggestions. Mais quel manque de simplicité! Que de tarabiscotage! Nous gagnons beaucoup à enseigner en Amérique, où on attend de nous des attitudes plus droites et que nous servions les jeunes avec dévouement, et avec joie. Barnard est un collège de premier ordre et un cours comme celui que vous donnez, qui exige beaucoup du professeur, doit être aussi un plaisir et offrir en lui sa récompense.

Donnez-moi un jour prochain des nouvelles de votre santé, physique et morale. Vous avez une chance rare d'avoir un mari compréhensif, intelligent et qui sait vous laisser pleine liberté de décision. Le fameux rapport hégélien "maître-esclave," insidieusement, se glisse dans tant de mariages! Et n'hésitez pas à m'envoyer votre travail sur Stendhal et la langue anglaise. Avez-vous laissé le texte de votre communication de Cerisy pour une éventuelle publication des divers essais?

Que l'année vous soit clémente et acceptez, pour vous & votre mari, mes vœux chargés d'amicale sollicitude.

Henri Peyre

## À Tatiana Greene:

Le 22 février 1983

Chère amie,

Vous êtes d'une très grande générosité, qui me touche profondément. Je ne connaissais pas ces lettres. Il y a longtemps, par un jeune ami qui avait été l'élève du P. Blanchet (l'auteur de "La Littérature et le spirituel"), j'avais appris combien la correspondance de Max Jacob était goûtée de ceux qui la connaissaient. Puis je n'avais que peu à peu appris à admirer le poète; peut-être par préjugé contre les convertis, aussi par éloignement de certaines puérilités affectées ou cultivées. J'ai changé depuis & quelque hasard a fait que, moi-même d'un tout autre bord et fermé à tout mysticisme, j'ai souvent loué des écrivains catholiques et en ai approché plusieurs (Claudel, Mauriac, Maritain, Teilhard). En tous cas, ces lettres (celle sur Rimbaud du 19 février 35, sur Apollinaire, les très fines remarques sur le Surréalisme & la défiance d'Aragon, dont on veut faire un grand romancier ces jours-ci et qui a trahi bien des causes et des amis) témoignent d'un esprit digne et sage. Votre évocation de Mlle Mespoulet est émouvante. Je me rappelle maintenant avoir été invité à la rencontrer, rue de Chevreuse, un soir; ce devait être l'été, dans la cour ou le jardin, et probablement en 1925. J'hésitais alors à quitter Paris et à accepter un poste à Bryn Mawr; je répugnais à cette carrière universitaire. Le feu de cette dame, son animation, ou son "anima" claudélienne et si peu professeur, m'avait impressionné et conquis. Je l'envie d'avoir durablement frappé et orienté une personne de vos dons poétiques et de votre piété quasi filiale.

Je conserve ces pages et peut-être vous les renverrai plus tard, pour que vous puissiez les communiquer à quelqu'un d'autre. J'ai à peu près l'âge de J. Hytier et j'ai passé le stade de l'accumulation de livres & de papiers.

Avec mes remerciements,<br>Henri Peyre

## To Robert G. Cohn:

290 North Ave. Westport.<br>Febr. 28 / 83

Dear Bob,

I relished & treasured your last letter. Your letters always make me nostalgic for an earlier era, when Yale welcomed the bright generations of conquerors of Nazism, critical feuds were not yet bitter. I often ponder over my debt to you & to a few other students who helped open myself up to different tastes & fresh views. Among my pleasant & lasting memories of California, that of a visit to your garden stands out. I understand that your winter months have been rainy and foggy there; we here have lived through a colossal accumulation of snow. I have to subdue my instinct of an active fighter against the visitation of natural calamities, & to refrain from shoveling the heaped up Mallarmean purity outside. I was 82 a few days ago & even though I am not in too bad a shape, I am reminded of my soon having to cross, or rather drown in, "le peu profond ruisseau." It comforts me to think that you have reached a state of happiness in your home life & that your original ideas meet with approval from readers of your MSS & more & more from students & fellow humanists. I hope to live long enough to read your *Ways of Art*. You are probably more in sympathy with the present state of letters & arts in France than I am just now.

I have not written out my recent lecture on Camus, but I may send you an article on him of a few years ago. I, too, found the McCarthy book well informed, but insensitive, grossly unfair & hasty. More & more, I found Camus courageous & modest, more lucid & much wiser on the Russian camps, on Stalinism, than either Merleau-Ponty or Sartre. It is not in politics alone that the aging Sartre erred. He ceased, ever since 1965 or 68, to live up to the ideal of "bonne foi." Rereading on the revolting trials (& confessions of the accused) of Bukharin & Zinoviev filled me with indignation. But I am proud of not having turned, in reaction, to the condemnation of socialism & of all hope for a generous regime in my native land. The forthcoming elections should not disown Mitterrand too bitterly; his mistakes may still be corrected.

I believe you will be in France & Italy next fall. I shall envy you. I probably shall not feel up to traveling abroad this coming summer; but if you have leisure enough when you leave for Europe, do make the détour to come here—or maybe I'll go to New York to have lunch with you. Diana would be happy to meet your wife—& you, of course. You have been the link between her & the Stanford series. Incidentally, you & your colleagues do a fine job of the Stanford French Review: the last number I received is *very* good, & beautifully edited.

> With my very warm wishes for a pleasant spring,
> Henri

## To Bettina Knapp:

Febr. 28/83

Dear Bettina,

The present of that volume of letters is one I treasure. I opened the book yesterday & could not lay it aside. I was entranced by it. There are many names there reminding me of my early years in this country, of my voracious reading of the periodicals in the twenties & thirties, of my youthful enthusiasm for Lewis Mumford, a hallowed name for me then & now, of Edmund Wilson, Stark Young, Waldo Frank (also one of my admired men of letters then) & others. But it is not *me* that I was rediscovering in the exchange of letters. The thrill for me was to enjoy the greed for ideas, the deep concern for literary and social values, the seriousness of the criticisms in those letters & the rich & warm personality of David Liebowitz. His epistles are even more thoughtful, more humane, more searchingly sincere than those of Lewis Mumford. Your succinct & modest introduction, your even more succinct footnotes, your editing are a splendid tribute to a man who had genuine greatness. I do not know his creative works & some day, if time is granted me, I hope to read some of them. But he surely has a very eminent place among the finest letter writers of America. Several of his letters would deserve a place among the most informing, the wisest and the *kindest* written in this century: the one defining his philosophical and political view of Communist Russia (August 17, 1944) pp. 50 & ff; the next one (pp. 54 ff.) judging Katherine Ann Porter & Van Wyck Brooks (hard on the latter, but just, I believe); his clear sighted evaluation of Dos Passos (p. 60). He quietly demolishes one of my former idols, Santayana, & I expect he is right. I lately took up again *The Last Puritan* & *The Sense of Beauty*, & failed to recapture my relish of old; his prose is affected & he was in love with his own ego. D. L. must have been the ideal friend, worthy of all that Montaigne praised in friendship, a delicate & frail art work, even rarer than love: his revelation, restrained & discreet, of himself (p. 114 for example), his concern about his correspondent's health, his political views of Kennedy (pp. 126 ff), his candid reservations or strictures on some of his friend's books, tactfully phrased, are models of courage tinged with affection. I personally share his dislike of Jung the man, who colors (to me) the ambitious attempts of Jung the "thinker" & the moralist; he is harsh on T. S. Eliot, probably to an excess, and ferocious on Mary McCarthy. But then he probably could not help comparing women writers to his superior & tactful wife & to his gifted daughter, and he found the pretentiousness of those women writers wanting. He is harsh also on academics, & probably with good reason. How many of us teachers can match that poise, that serene critical discrimination, that lucid & unpretentious style? The later years were colored with failing health and with the changes in taste & in publishers' policies which caused those two great minds & fine writers to feel no longer wanted. Yet Mumford is still widely read & very much present among us. Mumford's *The Brown Decade* deserves a better treatment than his friend gives it. What beautiful integrity in those two men! & D. L.'s feeling for nature and gardening and the wisdom of country living (as well as his lucidity and nobleness) have been fully "inherited" by (or transmitted to) his son in law.

You may well be proud of having had such parents, and of being fully worthy of them. Only in your letter writing, with your epistolary "imperatoria brevitas," have you evinced a determination not to rival your father. But this publication is not solely a filial tribute. It is a generous gift to posterity. Thank you for letting me share it.

Cordially,
Henri

## À Jean-Jacques Demorest:

> 290 North Ave.
> Westport, Ct. 06880
> April 8—83

Cher—et lointain—ami,

En retraite, enfin (après plus d'un demi-siècle d'enseignement), vivant dans le calme et parmi des lectures et relectures, il m'arrive de repenser à ceux que j'ai connus—trop peu et le plus estimés. Et je me demande comment vous allez, si la situation s'est stabilisée ou améliorée autour de vous, si votre santé physique & morale se trouve bien de cet air que l'on dit salubre et sec, et quelles sont vos réflexions & pensées. Je lis assidûment sur la politique française, présente ou passée. Elle est parfois attristante. Comme bien des vieux, je suis attristé de voir se réaliser les prédictions que j'avais émises sur le socialisme trop utopique et maladroit. Il y a une figure qui grandit derrière tout cela & que Mitterrand, de plus en plus, imite et réincarne: c'est celle de De Gaulle. Il reste le plus lucide des grands hommes de ce siècle, & peu de ses cadets l'ont senti & dit comme vous. Un jour, vous devriez écrire vos souvenirs d'avant 1941, puis de guerre, & même d'après-guerre. En avez-vous le loisir?

Je n'ai pas l'espoir de vous rencontrer de bientôt. Je voyage peu, m'enterre dans ce coin paisible et y attends la venue tardive du printemps. Mais croyez à la fidélité de mes amicales pensées.

> Henri Peyre

## À Gérard Defaux:

> Le 11 avril 83

Cher ami,

Excusez ce papier de jadis, inépuisable. Les secrétaires plaisantaient sur le volume de ma correspondance et y pourvoyaient.

Ce n'est pas pour vous souhaiter un printemps digne des poètes du XVIe siècle! Il ne cesse de pleuvoir & on dit le sud plus mal loti encore que nous. Mais c'est pour vous féliciter du numéro—du volume, plutôt—Montaigne des Y.F. Studies. Il est en tous points remarquable: solide, sérieux, sans compromis avec la moindre facilité; mais d'agréable lecture; jamais lourd, pas du tout ennuyeux. Il compte nombre d'articles qui vont rester importants pour les études de, & sur, Montaigne. Il mêle des jeunes encore étudiants avec des critiques chevronnés. C'était notre dessein en lançant, il y a bien des années, les Y. Fr. Studies. Et, avec sa pénétration analytique, la richesse de sa pensée, il conserve quelque nonchalance et des sourires. Votre article m'a beaucoup plu, et votre introduction, ironique mais ferme, instruite des dernières modes critiques et de la prétentieuse promotion du lecteur, marque avec finesse ses distances. Ce numéro est, et restera, un volume qui comptera dans les études "montanistes." Il a dû vous coûter bien du temps & des soins.

Diane et moi espérons que tout va bien pour vous deux & que votre direction n'est pas lourde à l'excès. Acceptez notre bien fidèle souvenir.

Henri Peyre

## To Enid Peschol:

290 North Avenue
Westport, Ct. 06880
May 27 / 83

Dear Enid,

You were very kind to send us the fine &, when all is said, courageous & almost cheerful, consoling essay, due to the collaboration of two exceptional talents, & a marriage of the two cultures. The intern's experience, as graphically described, is moving. I have long been familiar with the tunnel (in the New Haven hospital) & it has left me with some gloomy memories. I visited several of my students & colleagues when they were terminally ill there, & my first wife when she died from cancer. Now at 82 & more, I am familiar with the prospect of dying. I face it with some cheerfulness, even. My sole anxiety is that the Yale–N. Haven hospital may not be willing to accept my dead body—though I tried to explain to them that some of the interns or doctors might have studied with me, read my writings & perhaps would be curious to explore how a professor's brain works & how functioned the heart of a dry, cynical compatriot of Voltaire.

The literary section of your article is lively, poetical, intelligently informative like all you write. Again, it produces an impression of near-cheerfulness. You have an amazing courage. You always did & faced the disappointments in our profession, the polemics & controversies, with fortitude. You challenged the most difficult & complex French poets & you rendered them in English more skillfully than any other translator.

Colette must be a lively companion by now. Soon enough, you will be surprised to see her enter Yale or Harvard, as I am myself with Brice just completing his Freshman year at Yale & preparing to leave for France to gain the practice of French which I lazily failed to give him. We shall remain here, partly because, if it ever stops raining, it should be lovely & quiet, also because the expense of a child in college has become ruinous. Diana is well. She should soon receive from Stanford the proofs of the Proustian volume which you generously helped her improve. She sends you her wishes & appreciation of your fine essay of victory over Death.

> With much affection & our compliments to your husband,
> Henri Peyre

## À Gita May:

> 290 North Avenue
> Westport, Ct. 06880
> July 11—83

Chère madame,

L'envoi de votre essai, qui m'aurait échappé, m'a touché et la lecture, par un jour d'été clair et digne du ciel Provençal, m'a fort intéressé. Quel roman, en effet, que la vie de JJ, revécu et transfiguré dans ses Confessions! Et vous éclairez le livre d'un jour neuf en le rapprochant de *Gil Blas*. Il y a beaucoup de Lesage chez Smollet, Sterne et même Diderot & Sade, et un art d'inventer des mensonges qui deviennent vrais, c.a.d. le vrai, chez ce champion de la sincérité. Fabrice del Dongo, plus tard, avec plus d'inclination à la rêverie et plus de sentiment de classe, aura encore, à travers Rousseau, quelque chose du Gil Blas. Vos pages sont denses et très suggestives.

    Je crois que vous avez accepté d'assumer, à Columbia, une difficile succession. Je vous en félicite, même s'il vous y faudra sacrifier un peu de votre temps et exercer votre patience. Passez, en attendant, un été reposant.

Henri Peyre

## À Jean-Jacques Demorest:

290 North Avenue<br>Westport, Ct. 06880<br>Le 17 août 1983

Cher ami,

    Sans doute vous apprêtez-vous à repartir pour votre désert occidental: la sécheresse d'un long et dur été aura fait place à une douceur automnale quand vous y arriverez. J'imagine que votre femme et vos filles auront trouvé agréables le climat et l'atmosphère intellectuelle et humaine, dans ce pays que je connais peu—seulement, il y a des années, pour y avoir passé quelques jours, immobilisé par un accident survenu à mon auto. Je suis trop âgé pour voyager vers l'ouest; je vais seulement, à la fin de ce mois, revoir l'Andalousie et Madrid.

    Ce mot ne voudrait que vous remercier de votre lettre, si cordiale et écrite d'une plume experte & alerte. Vous êtes un remarquable épistolier et je vous ai envié d'avoir, avec sage prévision, choisi un domicile breton aussi poétique de nom et sans doute aussi pittoresque. Vos impressions de la France, mélancoliques avec humour et tolérance, m'ont amusé. Je suis attristé par les sottises de mes compatriotes, l'aveuglement de tant d'intellectuels, et l'affreuse langue—soit pédante et germanique avec maladroite lourdeur, soit effarante de grossièreté—qui est celle des successeurs de Pascal & de Voltaire et de De Gaulle. Ce devrait être une consolation, pour ceux qui ont vu clair et pensé avec noblesse comme vous, de se dire que Mitterrand réincarne De Gaulle, dans ses manières extérieures sinon dans sa fermeté d'âme et la vigueur de son style. Mais le pays se vide de sa substance et, rageur et vexé, s'en prend aux autres—Amérique surtout—au lieu de rectifier son orientation. J'ai été amené à parler des perspectives présentes pour la France, ça et là, mais avec tristesse, puisqu'il faut bien déplorer tant de maladresse..

> Mes vœux pour une année active mais sereine et mon très fidèle souvenir.
> Henri Peyre

## À Eléonore Zimmermann:

Le 24 août 83

Chère Eléonore,

Quelle bonne, confiante, affectueuse lettre, qui m'a rassuré sur votre santé, votre moral et—étrangement—ressuscité en moi quelque goût de "Wanderlust." À la fin d'un été serein et paisible, très chaud, monotone aussi, j'ai accepté la suggestion de Diane de secouer un peu mon consentement à la paresse, et nous partons pour passer les dix derniers jours de vacances en Espagne du Sud. S'il y fait chaud aussi, ce sera plus sec qu'ici, et plus pittoresque. Diane reprend ses cours vers le 7 ou 8 septembre; mon fils est revenu rayonnant de son séjour en France, même un peu provençalisé après 6 jours dans le Midi, et va se réinstaller à Yale. Pour moi, je retrouverai mes lectures et relectures. Je dois être devenu bien rétif aux nouveautés, car le roman monacal et trop policier et pédant à mon goût d'Umberto Eco m'a empli d'ennui. Nos contemporains sont d'étranges gens; ils se plairaient, pourvu que ce fût à la mode, à dévorer *L'Astrée* ou quelque interminable roman de Gomberville, ou *La Pucelle,* comme certains font des traités de sémiotique ou le *S/Z* de Barthes, acclamé comme une révélation critique. Il est probable que la capacité d'endurance à l'ennui diminue avec les années . . . Je suis content que vous ayez vu la Normandie sous un beau jour ensoleillé. Méridional par quelques-unes de mes racines, j'ai toujours aimé les arbres de la Normandie, les dunes, la brume matinale, même le cire. Il n'y a que les fromages et les crèmes dont je ne suis pas amateur. Les dîners trop subtils de Ribevelle n'auraient pas été pour moi! Cabourg m'avait jadis un peu déçu; et j'ai regretté plus tard d'avoir, sur les instances de Diane, visité Illiers—dans le réel, laidement et banalement prosaïques. Ma première lecture, éblouie, des J. Filles remonte à 1920 ou 21; et j'en veux un peu à ceux aujourd'hui à qui sa lecture ne coûte nul effort, & qui savent tout sur sa vie et ses vices. Un article du dernier *Express* conte qu'un inédit récemment découvert montre qu'Odette, pour 20 francs, avait "accordé ses faveurs" (vénales) à Cottard. Tant mieux pour Cottard, que cela n'avait guère affiné. Croisset est, vous avez raison, bien attristant; et aussi le centre de Rouen. Hérésie de ma part: j'avais, à Copenhague, trouvé le musée des Vikings bien ennuyeux. Je manque d'esprit d'aventure. Pour me faire pardonner, je vous enverrai un numéro de revue consacré à la littérature norvégienne. J'ai eu jadis une vraie passion pour Ibsen, l'ai même enseigné, et pour Selma Lagerlof & quelques autres; puis les Russes m'ont séduit.

Dites bien des choses amicales aux Bieber de nous deux. Acceptez mes vœux pour la santé de votre père; peut-être un séjour ici le remettrait-il en état? Et mes plus affectueuses pensées.

Henri

## À Konrad Bieber:

Le 20.IX.83

Cher Konrad,

Votre femme va mieux, je crois, et ses inquiétudes sont quelque peu apaisées. Elle a toujours été animée d'un courage plus qu'humain et elle triomphera encore. Et vous êtes d'une famille dont la longévité tient du prodige! J'ai été content de lire la notice sur Hugo Bieber, qui serait centenaire aujourd'hui. Doctorat en 1911! Secrétaire de Dilthey. C'était une époque de géants, cette décennie 1905–15. Mon allemand est trop rouillé pour que je tente de le lire sur Heine. Ce poète est le seul qui m'ait jadis fait pleurer; j'avais 15 ou 16 ans et je me récitais "Nordsee," ses poèmes d'amour; plus tard, ses derniers vers torturés par la souffrance physique. Et je l'aimais d'avoir aimé Napoléon. Puis je suis passée à la poésie anglaise. Peu curieux de musique, de cinéma, j'ai vécu beaucoup pour la poésie & d'elle, sans être capable d'en écrire.

Oui, j'aurais dû rester en relation avec Denise Alexandre & ses filles. J'avais été très proche d'elles autrefois. Marianne était une enfant de génie; et j'aimais aussi sa sœur Brigitte, moins primesautière, peut-être plus heureuse dans sa vie. Denise habite-t-elle en France aujourd'hui? Un jour, donnez-moi son adresse. Il me semble avoir derrière moi un si long passé, qui perce parfois dans ma mémoire lors des heures d'insomnie. On devient si "égoïste," ou "self-centered" avec les années, à contempler ce qu'Apollinaire appelait "le cadavre de ses jours."

Passez une année sans tristesse et féconde—et merci, toujours, de vos gentilles pensées & attentions.

Henri

## À son frère et à sa belle-sœur:

Le 5 octobre 1983

Chère Micheline & cher frère,

J'ai un peu tardé à vous dire combien m'avait touché votre lettre, écrite peu après le séjour de Brice à Avignon & sa soirée avec vous à Nice. Les généreuses paroles de Micheline à son égard m'ont, naturellement, fait plaisir; car, sans vouloir l'influencer trop, j'ai eu grande part à son éducation, à la formation de son esprit et peut-être de son caractère. Je ne lui ai pas légué mon sens un peu maniaque de l'ordre ponctuel, ou mon goût pour la poésie, ou même cette suffisance qui me fait, à un très "grand âge," me contenter de la solitude et répondre avec impatience aux coups de téléphone—si souvent superflus. Mais il est naturel qu'il ait besoin de camarades, de discussion avec eux et je ne tiens pas à ce qu'il soit trop attaché à un vieux père qui peut lui manquer d'un jour à l'autre . . .

Il y a 8 jours, Mitterrand était à New York & j'avais été invité, avec quelques 50 "notables" français et américains, gens décorés, à le rencontrer, à lui serrer la main & prendre avec lui une collation au champagne. Il sentait bien que la majorité d'entre nous n'était pas favorable à sa politique. Il a parlé avec modération et quelque tristesse—en termes qu'aurait approuvés De Gaulle, mais sans l'assurance de celui-ci. Je lui ai glissé quelques mots critiques sur Mauroy et le pleurnichage peu adroit sur l'absence de soutien des "intellectuels de gauche." Il semble que les choses aillent un peu mieux en France & que le gouvernement se rende compte qu'il y a une limite aux impôts sur les "riches"—et, j'espère, sur les retraites des non-riches comme moi—et que les industriels sont ceux, presque seuls, qui peuvent, par l'embauche, réduire le chômage. Je dois donner le 1$^{rer}$ novembre une conférence sur la situation en France, & ne sais encore ce que je dirai. Il ne convient pas, à l'étranger, de se montrer trop décourageant envers son pays. On n'a jamais entièrement raison contre lui. Il est pénible de le voir traiter avec apitoiement par les journaux américains. Et puis, un être trop attaché à quelque sagesse raisonnable (dans ses idées, sinon dans sa vie) échoue à sentir ce qu'il y a de dynamique dans son pays. Je me le disais en lisant divers articles sur les mémoires de Raymond Aron, mon cadet de 4 ans à Normale, que j'ai beaucoup admiré. Il a toujours vu clair, mais il a aussi toujours été trop sage. Par contre (je crois vous l'avoir dit déjà) je me suis vivement détourné de Sartre et de ses attitudes politiques dans ses dernières années. Il a prodigué les âneries. Des centaines de Français, intellectuels et intelligents, mais dénués de sens pratique, ont proféré d'énormes sottises entre 1938 et 50, ou 56, quand ils étaient fanatiquement attachés au communisme stalinien—Edgar Morin, par exemple, dont l'"Autocritique" mérite la lecture. Encore ont-ils reconnu leur égarement, sur le tard, dû à la quête d'une foi. Le besoin de religion est à la source de bien des maux. . . .

## Aux mêmes:

Le 18 octobre 1983

Chère Micheline, cher frère,

Votre lettre, datée du 25 septembre, ne m'est parvenue que le quinze octobre! Près d'un mois! Cela est apparemment dû à une grève des postes. Mais c'est tout de même intolérable! Le régime de la Gauche est d'une veulerie insigne et tout mon effort pour rester impartial et détaché cède à l'indignation. Je ne vais pas jusqu'à souhaiter au pouvoir en France un Pinochet, comme le fait Jacques dans ses paradoxes courroucés. Mais les stupidités de ce régime Mauroy Defferre Mitterrand finiront par amener une droite semi fasciste au pouvoir, comme ce fut le cas en Europe pendant les années 1930–38 d'assez sinistre mémoire. L'élection de Dreux, les indignations contre l'immigration clandestine, bientôt les protestations actives des cadres et des classes moyennes contre une fiscalité chaque année plus dévoratrice sont des signes menaçants. Je n'ai, pour ma part, pas une seule action et reste indifférent aux cours de la Bourse, de Paris ou de New York. Mais, non content de diminuer ma pension de moitié par l'effet du change, le gouvernement impose maintenant une taxe sur ce qui en reste, et déduit un paiement pour la Sécurité Sociale (française), alors que je n'ai, de la France, ni sécurité sociale ni assurance maladie. Ma seule compensation, toute symbolique, est d'être décoré: et je n'arbore jamais de décoration. . . .

## À Micheline Levowitz:

290 North Ave.
Westport, Ct. 06880
Le 22 octobre 1983

Chère Micheline,

Le gracieux don de votre dernier-né nous touche beaucoup, Diane & moi. Malraux nous est également cher: Diane va l'enseigner à Brooklyn cette semaine & le relit; je rouvre fréquemment ses livres moi-même, m'impatiente parfois devant ses formules péremptoires, mais ne ressens jamais avec lui cette déception que m'ont causée d'autres de mes admirations de jeunesse: Sartre, Picasso, même Gide. Votre très beau livre, modeste, compréhensif, renvoie aux ouvrages de Malraux, et c'est un de ses mérites. Qui plus est, sa prose, ardente, vibrante, nerveuse, est souvent l'égale de celle du maître. En quelques lignes, vous faites surgir les plus provocantes méditations malruciennes: celles de ce texte, "D'une jeunesse européenne" que j'avais jadis recopié de ma main; les pages sur la Grèce et celles que Malraux prononça sur l'Acropole; les dialogues d'Alvear, les monologues de Kassner dans ce livre fiévreux qui vaut beaucoup mieux que son auteur lui-même ne l'a dit, et les entretiens des *Noyers*. Votre essai court et vole, il frappe de lapidaires formules, il plonge dans des "entonnoirs" pascaliens et opère des raccourcis d'abîme. Plus qu'aucun de nous, et certes que nul des férus de sémiotique, vous avez le don du style et savez apprécier les affirmations lyriques — de Malraux, de Merleau-Ponty parfois et de cet Elie Faure, qui m'a beaucoup et longtemps séduit dans le passé. J'avoue que j'hésite à rouvrir l'*Esprit des Formes*. Quand j'ai mentionné ce titre et deux ou trois livres de Focillon que je plaçais également très haut à Malraux, il a paru distrait ou absent. Il avait raison — comme lorsqu'on insinuait qu'il avait parmi ses prédécesseurs ou intercesseurs W. Worringer; il ne l'avait certainement jamais lu.

Nous avons goûté la fraîcheur toute juvénile de ces pages — je suis un peu éberlué par le titre et par la photographie qui vieillit et éteint le Malraux, celui d'avant *Lazare* en tous cas. Mais quel élan dans ces 150 pages! Quelle vigueur! Nous tous, et certes la N. Sarraute d'Enfance, sommes des vieux décatis à côté de vous. Ne faites pas trop vite la paix avec vos erreurs passées (s'il y en eut) et avec la soif de l'éternel ou du transcendant! Vous avez encore trop à dire, & le dites trop splendidement.

Nos compliments à Lev qui vous inspire et brûle devant vous l'encens de ses cigarettes—et merci de nous avoir permis d'être des premiers à lire ce livre incomparable sans rien de monstrueux, ou de prétentieux.

Avec profonde affection,<br>Henri

La célèbre phrase de Tchen dit: "s'il n'y a ni Dieu ni Christ"—sauveur ou salut, plutôt que "divinité."

## À Wallace Fowlie:

290 North Avenue<br>Westport, Ct. 06880<br>Le 12 nov. 83

Cher Michel,

Quel livre plein de grâce, de modestie, écrit avec talent et cette si rare qualité quand on parle de soi, le naturel! C'est également un livre courageux. Il fallait pour l'écrire avoir atteint l'âge de l'expérience; pouvoir regarder en arrière une longue carrière de professeur, dont le succès et l'influence ont été égaux à nul autre en ce pays; quelque nostalgie, mais aussi du détachement de soi; et une simplicité non calculée. Vous avez été musicien, acteur, conférencier, un peu moine et une manière de saint, le plus adorable des amis mais avant tout professeur; et vous ne le dissimulez pas. C'est encore le plus beau des métiers, celui qui laisse le plus de liberté spirituelle, qui nous permet de nous renouveler souvent si nous savons écouter et comprendre les jeunes qui s'attachent à nous; et les meilleurs d'entre eux, pour nous contredire ou nous dépasser. La périlleuse tentation des professeurs qui ont rédigé leurs souvenirs est d'enfler ridiculement leur moi, de se prendre naïvement au sérieux, et de se laisser aller à de mesquines remarques sur la politique universitaire, leurs collègues, les autorités. Vous avez avec virtuosité & galamment évité tous ces pièges. Votre titre, si ingénieusement trouvé, votre ton enjoué et franc, l'apparence de discontinu et de nonchalance laissée à vos chapitres, le ton d'un entretien souriant avec des élèves ou des amis: tout cela évite à ces récits et réflexions tout soupçon de lourdeur. Vous ne vous montrez certes jamais indiscret; vous oubliez généreusement ceux qui ont pu vous nuire, vous critiquer, ou les laideurs de caractère qu'il nous est à tous arrivé de rencontrer. Vous n'étalez certes pas votre moi—mais le peu que vous dites de votre mère, de votre tante, de votre père surtout, dont je ne me souviens pas de vous avoir jamais entendu parler, m'a intéressé et ému. Sur un point seulement—votre religion, ce qu'elle a signifié pour vous, quelle action a pu avoir sur vous Maritain (ou, plus littérairement, Claudel, ou Bernanos, ou Mauriac, ou Gr. Greene peut-être, ou tel autre de ces convertis anglais qui m'ont agacé comme Evelyn Waugh), quels combats intellectuels a peut-être soutenus votre foi—je vous ai trouvé réticent. Peut-être écrirez-vous cela ailleurs? (Ecclésia, à propos, ne veut pas dire, en grec ou en latin, "appel," mais "assemblée.") Il est vrai que, totalement, farouchement étranger au christianisme comme je l'ai été depuis, qu'à douze ans, j'ai commencé à pleurer la mort des anciens dieux et à déplorer l'escroquerie intellectuelle commise par les premiers théologiens, puis Constantin, je n'ai cessé d'étudier des âmes, ou des esprits, fervents de religion.

Ce livre devrait séduire, charmer, distraire et faire penser; il sert la profession qui a été la nôtre et la montre dans sa noblesse et ses joies.

Merci de m'avoir permis aussitôt de le lire et merci de Diane, qui est un remarquable professeur.

Allez-vous bientôt clore votre "période militaire"? Je vous vois mal là-bas trop longtemps. Pour moi, je savoure, je l'avoue, mon inactivité. À part de rares conférences (et plutôt politiques) et quelques articles amateurs, je me plais à lire toute sorte de choses au hasard.

Après votre retour vers ces régions, nous espérons enfin vous voir un peu à loisir.

Affectueusement,
Henri

## À Micheline Levowitz:

Nov. 19—83

Chère amie,

J'aime recevoir de vos nouvelles, mais vous avez, je le sais, bien d'autres soucis et tâches que d'écrire. Il me suffit de savoir parfois que vous conservez un bon moral, avez l'énergie d'accomplir votre métier de professeur et vous savez estimée et recherchée par les connaisseurs et spécialistes des auteurs sur lesquels vous avez dit des choses originales et durables. De mon côté, à part de rares conférences, que je n'accepte qu'avec hésitation, je me répands peu, ne voyage plus et écris un minimum de lettres. J'ai suffisamment donné de conseils dans ma vie, trop parlé et écrit; et, sans me sentir nullement vexé ou aigri de cela, j'en viens à juger que je dois laisser à d'autres la place. Cela m'agace que l'on me dise que "je ne porte pas mon âge" et semble vigoureux. Je ne déteste pas d'être vieux et de le paraître. Pourquoi s'illusionner? Après 80 ans, on ne peut ignorer que les mois de vie sont comme un sursis et que la seule incertitude est sur la manière dont on disparaîtra. Les amis de notre âge alors tombent l'un après l'autre, et on les envie presque. Diane m'entoure de soins affectueux, et cela maintient le goût à quelques plaisirs de la vie. Mon fils est affectueux et travaille avec sérieux. Cela m'a, sur le tard (puisque je n'avais pas eu d'enfant avant 63 ans), passionné de le voir se développer, trouver sa voie. Sa mère a décidé d'aller habiter à Londres, où il lui a rendu visite cet été. Il se trouvera très seul à ma disparition, et je préfère qu'il ne tienne pas trop à moi. Mais il a de la vigueur et du sérieux et, ce qui me plaît le plus, il ne semble pas avoir de complexe d'avoir grandi avec une mère parfois étrange, un père entouré de livres. Je pense qu'il ne sera, pas plus que moi, porté à se révéler aux psychanalystes, ou à d'autres confesseurs. Cela facilite la vie quotidienne de n'avoir, ou de croire n'avoir, ni "Id" ni "surmoi."

Quoi qu'on dise, et même si cela n'est pas une surprise, c'est un énorme morceau de soi qui disparaît avec la mort d'un père. Vous vous y attendiez, sans doute; vous respectez sa mémoire, ses croyances, sa si belle dignité morale et vous pouvez encore encourager et soutenir votre mère. Mais regardez en avant aussi. Ayez foi, fermement, en votre riche arsenal de possibilités. On se moque gentiment de ma manie de citer trop souvent le Christ (athée ou antichrétien que je suis) ou St. Paul (que j'ai en horreur). Mais ce n'est pas dans le Nouveau Testament, c'est dans les dernières pages de "La Condition humaine" que Malraux fait dire à Gisors: "Il faut aimer les vivants, et non les morts." J'ai, depuis ma 1ère lecture de ce roman, il doit y avoir 50 ans, toujours aimé et Gisors et May, et Malraux est la plus fascinante créature humaine que j'ai rencontrée. Il m'avait dit son admiration inégalée (sauf pour Tolstoï peut-être) pour Stendhal. À propos, j'ai refusé de traiter (en conférences ou par écrit) le thème de "la peur de l'amour chez Stendhal," auquel j'avais songé. Il est indiscret et d'un goût douteux de prétendre sonder ces secrets dans les êtres et d'exploiter leurs révélations—si souvent mensongères—pour se mettre soi-même en valeur. J'ai laissé beaucoup s'affaiblir mon goût pour la critique littéraire. La politique, et rien moins que l'avenir du monde, le fol espoir de vouloir influencer la politique américaine et d'indiquer à la France comment redresser ses erreurs des deux dernières années, sont devenues mon dada! Je vous envoie le livre de Sh. Felman. Elle est brillante parfois; mais vous avez raison, elle donne dans un jargon prétentieux et elle est devenue trop sûre d'elle-même. L'Amérique gâte vite les gens de talent qu'elle accueille, très généreusement, d'Europe. Sa "thèse" sur la folie est trop répétitive et repose sur un jeu de mots sur le terme "folie." Trop sage moi-même, je suis très attiré en littérature par la *vraie* folie. Je relisais ces derniers temps Lenz de Büchner, les poésies de Lenau (que je me récitais à 20 ans en voyageant en Autriche), un de mes poètes anglais favoris, Th. Lowell Beddoes, et *Aurélia*. Mais si les fous *en littérature* me fascinent, je les fuis dans la vie réelle. Je n'ai ni patience ni vraie charité. Merci, par avance, du catalogue d'Abravanel. Je n'achète guère, ou pas, de livres moi-même, n'ayant ni argent ni place. Je vis ici dans une seule pièce, avec, surtout, arbres, oiseaux et, hélas! amas de feuilles mortes au dehors. Mais j'en recommande aux bibliothèques.

Conservez votre vigueur physique et le moral stoïque et confiant dont votre lettre apporte la preuve. Je vous souhaite de merveilleux résultats de vos cours. Barnard passe pour avoir les étudiantes les plus stimulantes de ce pays.

Diane me demande souvent de vos nouvelles et vous admire, en vous connaissant trop peu. Elle avait souhaité vous rencontrer à ce colloque à N.Y. en octobre, mais il y régnait pas mal de confusion.

Bien des amitiés,
Henri Peyre

## To Robert G. Cohn:

290 North Avenue
Westport, Ct. 06880
Dec. 16 — 1983

Dear Bob, (Will you insist on addressing me as "Mr." to my dying day?)

Any letter from you brings up old, & to me very dear, memories of our steady friendship, of your coming to New Haven as a returning warrior, eager, brilliant, prompt to discern flaws in our teaching, stimulating — slightly feared by some, admired by all — & generously communicating to some of us your enthusiasm for Mallarmé, for poetry, for the most challenging aesthetic values & for moral honesty. I remember those years with pleasure, & how I & others benefited from your fruitful initiatives (Y. Fr. Studies, among others) & how we have remained in your debt. You will now be drawing near retirement, & are fully ready for another reinterpretation of Mallarmé. I still walk around here — at a slow pace, for my heart is weaker — reciting to myself some of the poems I know by heart. For mnemotechnical purposes, I value more & more the rhymes in Mallarmé's verse, in Verlaine's, in Baudelaire's, in Valéry's. Some of the most entrancing "trouvailles" in the poets were due to rhymes. We cannot go back to them, I realize; yet how difficult it is to entrust to one's memory & to one's inner life, the poetry of Bonnefoy, Deguy, Roubaud, even Char. A truly searching study of Mall.'s poems in prose by you will bring out the originality of Mall. with that medium. I was somewhat disappointed (& she knows it) with M. A. Caws' volume on the Poem in Prose. Why always harp on Baudelaire's *Spleen de Paris,* when the pieces in *Divagations,* or in *Connaissance de l'Est,* & of course Rimbaud, are so much better? I hope to live to read your projected work on *Divagations.* I remember my élan of joy, almost of rapture, when, young, I bought a copy of *Divagations* & devoured it in Paris. I never forgave Mondor's Pléiade for not respecting the integrity of that volume. My fond dream was, long, that Gallimard might ask you to do a new Pléiade volume of Mallarmé; critical edition, index, etc. I suppose it is too much to hope for & I have no power to persuade any one in France, anyway.

Your piece on language, computers, et al. is sharp, profound & vigorous. I fully agree & admire. I insist upon staying away from computers, mechanization of any kind, & much that is in vogue. There is some relief in returning to what I truly enjoy, in art, Greek, Lucretius, antichristian literature, romantic & other poetry; I only wish I had also other passions, such as yours for gardening & flowers & for music. I survive almost exclusively on ever avid reading & some conversations on sundry topics with Diana, who takes sedulous care of me. My son is immersed in ambitious historical & political studies at Yale. He will be here next week, as will Diana's 3 sons: one from Japan, married to Japanese; one from Florida; the youngest in N. York, organizing exhibitions of very modern (post 1980) paintings.

Remember me to your wife & accept my very warm feelings & wishes.

I hope your request will be readily granted. A copy of my letter is enclosed.

Yours,
Henri

## À Renée Wehrmann:

Dec. 22/83

Chère amie,

Pardonnez à ce vilain & vulgaire papier; je n'en ai pas de luxueux avec nom, adresse (et couronne ducale) comme les cocottes de jadis et ces grands ducs russes dont vous descendez. Votre frère, qui nous avait traités avec tant d'élégance lors de notre obtention du doctorat et qui collectionne avec goût des œuvres d'art, aurait honte du plébéien que je suis! Mais j'ai une étrange allergie à tout ce qui est magasins, achats, luxes et empaquetage sous papier colorié et cordons rutilants.

Je ne vous en souhaite pas moins un Noël agréable, à vous et votre fils, et une année prospère, et intellectuellement riche; vous travaillez sur l'inceste; Diane sur le vieillissement, qui est pire encore. Moi, je rêvasse, revis mes péchés de jadis et imagine ceux que j'aurais dû commettre. Vous avez, ces 4 ou 5 dernières années, réalisé des miracles—survécu à un deuil affreux, triomphé d'un fils hypercritique, établi M. du Gard à son rang, et cultivé vos amitiés.

Ici, il va y avoir du monde, des jeux, des joutes verbales. Le Japonais semble heureux, et de son mariage (heureusement agrémenté, en ce pays raffiné, par la diversion de quelques geishas) et du Japon en général. Il a admiré vos mallarméennes verreries. Les autres fils semblent contents de leur succès et se montrent (presque) dociles et reconnaissants. On aura tout vu.

Ce mot était, en vérité, pour vous confirmer que, après recherches assez attentives, je ne trouve pas *une seule* traduction courante et "available" de *Manon Lescaut*. Vous avez raison. C'est incompréhensible et c'est dommage. J'ai toujours goûté ce livre. En 1937, en mission française en Louisiane, j'avais osé en parler en public. On m'avait dénoncé à l'archevêque de New Orleans (car on n'en parle jamais dans ce pays-là) et il avait été question de demander mon excommunication. Comme je ne suis pas catholique, cette punition resterait sans effet. L'auteur avait vu, et fait, bien pire.

Ayez un peu de repos. Dites mes pensées à votre fils, à votre frère & belle-sœur et croyez-moi,

Bien fidèlement et semi-paternellement vôtre,
Henri Peyre

## To John W. Kneller:

Febr. 5, 84

Dear Jack,

I am fascinated by your brother's book. He is a man of immense knowledge, able to embrace the most abstruse contemporary or recent movements of philosophy, linguistics, psychology of education. Inevitably, his presentation of the thought of Husserl, Chomsky, Sartre, Gadamer, Ricœur, *et al.* simplifies extremely complex systems of thought; it owes something to previous commentators; he simplifies through his attempts at clarifying & at utilizing ambitious and very abstract views for the benefit of teachers. But his bibliography is most impressive. He is widely read in several languages; he discriminates among a huge mass of treatises; he lucidly underlines what is most valuable & *utilizable* in the works of ambitious thinkers and, with lucid orderliness & a gently severe critical appraisal, he points to the weaknesses of those grave thinkers & brings out what may best enrich the training of educators. Your brother must be endowed with an uncanny plasticity and a tremendous capacity for work. He never submits slavishly to anyone else's thought; he retains his full independence and asserts it. I learned a great deal from reading this book attentively; he revealed to me thinkers such as Apple, Goodman, Kohl, Oakeshott, who were mere names to me, & helped me assess in a relative & discriminating spirit others like Kirk, Kozol, Nozick, whom I had encountered but did not know where to place. I do not hesitate to say that I admire your brother immensely and that he ranks very high among the serious educators of educators. A solid, serious, pleasantly readable work of "haute vulgarisation," threading its way among the mazes of modern theoretical thinkers, is a masterpiece in its fashion.

And, from what you say, your brother is also a practical man & a shrewd investor! You may be proud of him! I had not learned so much, with avidity & gratitude, from *any* book, for a number of years.

Thank you for your visit. I'll return the book by mail soon.

Yours,
H. P.

## À Eléonore Zimmermann:

Le 14 — III — 84

Chère Eléonore,

Toute parole est vaine et je n'en chercherai pas. Simplement, je prends part à votre immense peine et souhaite que, peu à peu, la douceur de souvenirs tendrement chers adoucisse votre chagrin. J'aurais aimé connaître votre père. J'aurais partagé avec lui un amour pour la littérature, pour la poésie surtout, qui semble avoir été la ligne de force de son existence, & qui l'a été de la mienne. À mon âge avancé, je me nourris encore de souvenirs de quelques voyages et paysages de l'Europe, et de poèmes que je me récite en songeant aux années où ma mémoire, plus exercée, se les récitait par cœur.

Que votre solitude soit distraite par des souvenirs de bonheur partagé et la fierté d'avoir jusqu'au bout maintenu avec votre père une communion intellectuelle aussi bien que sentimentale.

Avec ma très vive sympathie,<br>
Henri Peyre

## To George Margolis:

290 North Ave.<br>
Westport, Conn. 06880<br>
April 7, 84

Dear George,

Your wife allowed me to read the letter from Dr. Rufsvold, most impressive in its conciseness, your truly moving autobiographical piece, "Why not me?" & the humorous, moving, highly sincere piece by your son on a memorable dinner "with Donald." Josh has real talent and may well become an effective story teller while remaining what, as I understand, he is: a successful man of action. Please congratulate him on my part some time. Your own essay touched me deeply. Somehow—shyness, maybe; excessive modesty; desire to let your wife exercise her eloquence & display her ebullience—you do not reveal yourself fully in conversation. Your piece in the Dartmouth Magazine on Dr. Rufsvold had made a strong impression on me. Your "Why not me?" struck me even more. It reveals, in a restrained, discreet but effective manner, much of your personality, of the events & circumstances which molded you & enabled you to become what you are. It made me proud to have been granted the gift of your friendship. A certain Gallic irony, correcting my early Protestant training, long made me diffident of persons who "do good" and take their social responsibility seriously. As I grew old, gravely concerned about the survival of what in our civilization deserves to be saved, anguished by all the evil instincts at play around us, I have come to understand and respect a person like you: utterly devoid of selfishness, generously devoting his time & his years of what might have been quiet retirement to helping his fellow beings. A few hundred persons like you & our world perhaps would indeed survive, and deserve to survive.

May I add that traveling with you in Brazil, getting to know your son there, & his companion, not only inspired me with gratitude for the kindness which both of them lavished on us, cumbersome intruders; it also provided an example, a model even, of deep & intelligent affection, of full confidence between a father & his children. Not many families ever succeed in striking that felicitous balance between affection and duty, dispensing and receiving advice & retaining freedom of decision. As Diana often remarked, you & your wife have indeed proved that happy families do exist, even if, as wrote the author of Anna Karenina, they do not make history.

I'll retain the documents if you do not need them. Our warm wishes for the explosion of a radiant spring, after so many relapses of winter.

Cordially,<br>
Henri

## To Stanley Burnshaw:

290 North Avenue<br>
(Tel. 203-226-4868)<br>
April 14—84

Dear Stanley,

I forget when you are due to leave your warm Florida retreat, some time this month, probably. Although we still have cool, even cold evenings & mornings, a few timid snowdrops are appearing & a few green buds. Soon it will be time to clear the grass, here, of fallen branches & sticks. I am too old to do much. Diana is busy with her teaching at Brooklyn College. Her 3 sons are all away, one in Florida, one in Japan. My own is too busy with his courses at Yale, & lazy. So we let things go. I rather like wildness & disorder anyway, in nature. And sometimes although I am totally retired & try to avoid all demands upon my time, I seem to be busy with book reviews of scholarly works (often of 500 or 600 pages!) & with reading. I do not have the energy to write long, full, interesting letters as you do.

I am sorry you seem disappointed by the sluggish sales of the Refusers. To us, academics, any sale over 1000 or 1500 copies is rewarding! Your book is *first*-rate. It engrossed & retained my admiring attention. I would remain proud of it if I were you. I do not know of a tribute to one's father so moving as yours, & in such discreet, restrained taste.

If I could entertain any belief in the possibility of God's existence, & if I did not harbor such a childish hatred of the Old & New Testaments, your book might have brought about my conversion to Judaism. At the age of 8 or 10, looking at pictures of Arcadia, the Vale of Tempe, the Gulf of Salamin, Cape Sunium, I fell in love with Aphrodite, Poseidon, & the Greek language, & decided I was, & would for ever be, a pagan polytheist.

I have nothing to say of any worth on Frost & leave the great man to you. The Prévost essay in USONIE did include translations of some lines & gave an intelligent, & admiring account of the poet. Jean Prévost was the author of first rate books on Stendhal & on Baudelaire, & of novels. He was killed by the Germans in 1942 or 44. I had seen much of him in the early twenties.

Now on my whereabouts. I usually hardly go anywhere & choose to stay here & rest. My telephone is at the top of this letter & I could get you at the Westport station if you chose to come for a visit. As it happens, I have had to accept several visits to New York, as follows.

> Mon. May 14th—I'll have to attend a reception in my honor, to mark the "event" of a volume of essays done by colleagues or friends in my honor.
> Sat. May 12th, I'll take part in a Symposium at N.Y.U.
> Sat. May 19 & Sun. May 20th, I'll attend a commencement at Stony Brook, where I *had* to accept a hon. degree (I have collected some 14 or 15 already, years ago, & swore I would never accept another one. I hate that medieval pomp; but I *had* to). I am likely to be here, quietly, the rest of that week: May 23 or 25 or later; I'll let you know if I have to alter my plans. I'll rush this, in case you are to absent yourself for Easter.

Most cordially,
Henri

## À Eléonore Zimmermann

Le 30 avril 84

Chère Eléonore,

Avez-vous recouvré quelque paix spirituelle après l'acuité de votre immense douleur et trouvé dans des souvenirs chers quelque adoucissement à la peine de cette grande absence? Je me le suis demandé plusieurs fois ces derniers temps. Voici que le renouveau de la nature, si longtemps espéré cette année, remet de l'espoir et quelque impatience à revivre, même dans l'organisme las qui est le mien.

J'ai reçu avant hier un exemplaire du volume collectif qui m'honore. Il est présenté avec élégance et ce que j'ai pu jusqu'ici feuilleter du contenu m'a impressionné par la qualité de sérieux, de finesse et de l'écriture dénuée de prétention & de jargon. Votre essai, que j'ai lu un des premiers, m'a beaucoup frappé. Mallarmé, il est vrai, a méconnu le "passant considérable" Rimbaud; sans doute l'a-t-il peu compris. Cela arrive entre créateurs: Monet et Cézanne, Renoir et Seurat. Mais, à leur insu et à l'insu de Mallarmé surtout, ils avaient en effet beaucoup en commun; ou, en tous cas, des traits parallèles qu'on avait trop peu remarqués avant ce très fin et très juste article. Je vous remercie d'avoir ainsi contribué à cet ouvrage qui m'honore grandement, et me touche par l'affection que me portent tant de fidèles "anciens."

Avec mon amitié et mes voeux de printemps serein,
Henri Peyre

## To John W. Kneller:

290 North Ave. Westport. Conn.
April 28/84

Dear Jack,

Diana brought me *the* Book. I opened it at once & read several chapters of it last night, yours included which I very much like: it illuminates for me one of the most mysterious sonnets of Nerval. The level of the contributions is very high. I am going to read them with close attention & shall write to several of the authors who thus honored me.

But my most heartfelt & grateful thanks go to you. I realize, despite your discreet modesty, how generous you have been all along in the creation of "my" Institute, in convincing your brother & other persons of good will to contribute financially to the publication of this handsome volume. Ever since your Yale years, throughout your Oberlin career, at your Brooklyn inauguration & since, you have been the kindest, & overgrateful, friend to your old professor. Your fidelity touches me immensely. And your wife, with her constant & delicate modesty, has been just as generous & kind to me.

The task of gathering those essays, of reading & rereading them, & the proofs, of seeing the volume through the Press, must have been a heavy one. I am sure that you bore most of the burden. As you have in preparing the forthcoming reception at the Cultural Counselor's Office. I am touched by all you & Mary Ann have done.

Thank you for the list of guests. It seems perfect. I would only suggest including Konrad Bieber & his wife, Tamara. Box 208, Port Jefferson, L.I. NY 11777 (Stony Brook). He has always been a faithful & grateful friend. You probably knew him at Yale. Perhaps also some one from Columbia: Gita May (Chairman) or Tatiana Greene or Roudiez. I have always had excellent relations with the French Department there & at Barnard. I'll offer the same suggestion in a note to M. A. Caws.

Most cordially,
Henri

## À Germaine Brée:

Le 14 mai 1984

Chère Germaine,

Votre lettre, si gentille et même touchante, nous a émus tous deux. Certes, vous avez raison de trouver pénible l'atmosphère de hâte, de compétition, de multiplication d'articulets pressés & souvent de bien mince contenu, qui est celle que l'on respire à trop de nos réunions. Je n'y participe plus guère, quant à moi, & jouis de ma tranquillité présente, puisque enfin le printemps nous est venu. Mais je crois que cette fièvre, cette trop grande promptitude de nos jeunes collègues à se mettre en avant & à se faire remarquer, nuisent à la qualité de nos publications en Amérique. Il y a, en fin de compte, très peu de "scholars" dont les livres marquent, apportent des réflexions & des aperçus un peu mûrs. L'exemple de ceux qui ont su attendre, réfléchir, composer un ouvrage organisé (Auerbach, Hazard, Hytier, vous-même) et ainsi marquer en profondeur nos études, est pourtant là.

Mais la nouvelle, annoncée avec une désinvolture stoïque, que vous allez être opérée de la cataracte, m'a profondément secoué. Je ne savais pas que vous souffriez de quelque faiblesse de la vue. Cette opération, dit-on, est délicate & demande une infinie patience. Acceptez nos vœux pour que tout se passe pour le mieux et prenez ensuite un long & total repos. Lorsque tout ira bien, envoyez-moi un mot pour me rassurer. "Till her eyes shine, I live in darkest night," dit Philip Sidney à la fin d'un sonnet inclus dans son *Arcadia*. Ma santé n'est pas sans fragilité, à 83 ans; mais ma vue me permet encore d'incessantes lectures. Je me sens fortuné.

Avec notre amitié à tous deux,<br>
Henri Peyre

## À Florence et Kurt Weinberg:

290 North Ave.<br>
Westport, Ct. 06880<br>
Le 23.V.84

Bien chers amis,

Quelle belle, cordiale, rassurante lettre! Votre jeunesse et votre courage me font envie! Kurt, qui a traversé dans ses jeunes années tant d'épreuves, a donc triomphé de maux divers, de divers chevaux trop fougueux, et ne souffre que de quelque léthargie. Un peu de somnolence n'est pas sans charme. À mon âge (10 ou 12 ans de plus que lui), je m'y laisse aller volontiers. Cela permet d'oublier les colères politiques que provoque la lecture du journal. Les choses semblent aller un peu mieux en France; mais, ici, les âneries de Reagan & de sa clique m'emplissent de mépris courroucé.

Certes, la critique présente m'irrite & m'emplit d'amertume. Je suis attristé par les récents écrits d'anciens de Yale que j'avais admirés & aidés.

Aussi cela est une joie pour moi de savourer cette ingénieuse, délicate, et même tendre "explication" de l'Autre Eventail. Je sais le poème par cœur et me le récite souvent dans mes moments d'insomnie. Mais Kurt m'en a révélé divers secrets. Sa critique, fine, ingénieuse, toujours soumise au texte, en fait ressortir plusieurs détails que le lecteur moins perspicace (c.à.d. moi) n'avait pas aperçus. Merci.

L'article de Florence m'a ébloui! Quelle érudition! Quelle puissance d'analyse, des termes (c'est si essentiel pour Pascal), des idées! Elle a *tout* lu sur les deux penseurs & leurs rapports; elle n'ignore rien de leur milieu, de l'héritage antique, augustinien, scolastique peut-être. Le diagramme est trop géométrique pour l'antigéomètre que je suis, dérouté toujours par le mot "âme." Mais dans ces quelques pages, Florence a mis les plus fines en même temps que les plus savantes définitions de termes pascaliens (et cartésiens) que j'aie jamais lues. Elle est au premier rang des exégètes et penseurs dans notre profession. Ardents compliments!

Je vais passer quelques jours en France, à la fin de ce mois — pour revoir mon frère & mes neveux — mais reviendrai vite ici. Je n'ai plus le goût ou la force d'affronter les fatigues de longs voyages & les foules. Je me nourris beaucoup de souvenirs d'amitiés anciennes & toujours vivaces, dont la vôtre.

À tous deux, merci et bien cordialement,<br>Henri

## To Edward Kaplan:

290 North Ave.<br>Westport, Ct. 06880<br>June 17—84

Dear Mr. Kaplan:

Back from a short European trip, I found in my mail your book & I am touched by the handsome & generous gift. Thank you. The U. of Mass. Press has done a very handsome job of it: striking cover, elegant printing, & a presentation (your own text, the translated Journals, the footnotes, the epigraphs) that is harmonious, learned, not over erudite, and appealing to the reader. My warm congratulations.

You certainly have served the memory & the work of Michelet with persistence, fidelity & remarkable intelligence. Your remarks (on M's sexual life, ancillary loves, imprudence & foolishness, weird passion) remain discreet throughout. There is room for more Freudian explorations, & for different ones from Barthes', in Michelet's life. But, shrewdly, you relate M's cult of history both to his sexual complexes & to his worship of death. At times, I felt almost sorry for you, a young, enthusiastic, deeply religious person, for having to live with that cult of death so intensely. At my advanced age, I confess I have banished that obsession from my concerns. I'll accept dying in a pagan way, I hope, & never give any thought to the decay of my flesh. I shall either be dissected by medics or be cremated, & my coffin will not tempt curious, or sickly, observers. But then, I have no genius, no obsession, no complex. I am dismally, hopelessly normal!

I trust your own private life is proceeding happily, though I am not sure you really want happiness; & your career at Brandeis provides you with professional satisfaction. If you have a chance, convey my very warm souvenir to Mr. Gendzier & Mr. Sachs & believe me,

Very cordially yours,<br>
Henri Peyre

## To John W. Kneller:

June 24—84

Dear Jack,

I enjoyed your brother's lecture *immensely*. It is written with clarity, ease & charm; he has a wonderfully organized mind, with a fondness for dividing ideas & analyzing concepts (first, second, third) which I also tried to have—except that I usually forgot my point # 3 or # 4, & students smiled at me. I believe I may say that, among humanists & critics, I am one of those who always kept a stubborn faith in education ("paideia") as the surest means of eventually changing man. I have always enjoyed lecturing to fellow-teachers & not so much on methods (of which I know little) as on the philosophy underlying our profession; from Plato to Bergson, Whitehead &, as your brother hints, D. H. Lawrence. You may be proud of him—& of your own career & achievement as an educator of courage and ever full of new ideas.

We took a brief trip to France, mostly to visit what family I still have over there. It was a pleasant change, after the steady rains of May, & before the invasion of mosquitœs now to be endured. That absence delayed my writing to you, as I meant to do formally, to thank you again for all you & Sherry have done for the "Institute," the fellowship honoring me & the volume: a truly handsome book, full of serious & deep essays & impeccably edited. I am immensely grateful.

Our best to you & your wife. We'll probably stay here quietly most of the summer, now & then go to the beach. We hope to see a little of you then.

With affection & gratitude,<br>Henri

## À Michel Guggenheim:

Le 1r juillet 1984

Cher Michel,

J'ai passé très peu de jours, au début de juin, à Avignon, avant que votre Institut n'ouvrît, & j'ai regretté de vous manquer. Bien des souvenirs m'envahissent quand je revois cette bonne ville, où j'avais passé, impatient, quelques années de mon adolescence. Mon frère, sa femme étaient en bonne santé. Lui, docteur, a insisté pour me faire visiter les centres médicaux dans la banlieue Sud—fort impressionnants, en effet. Diane, ma compagne, et moi séjournions à l'Hôtel d'Europe, place Crillon—élégant et même luxueux. Je n'ai pu obtenir, des quelques vieux, très vieux (comme moi) amis que j'ai revus, d'information sur le Centre Bryn Mawr–Avignon. Cela doit faire plus de vingt ans qu'avec une foi et une intuition remarquables vous avez fondé cet Institut. Sans doute continue-t-il à prospérer? Je regrette, personnellement, le départ de la précédente municipalité (& celle de Grenoble) et suis attristé par la tendance actuelle: bien trop sévère pour Mitterrand et jouant dangereusement avec le racisme & le réactionnarisme. Mais, exilé volontaire, je n'ai nulle influence ni avis à donner.

J'aurais aimé savoir de vos nouvelles, de celles de votre femme et de votre fils. Nous devons, vous et moi, être parmi les peu nombreux survivants des années de guerre ou de l'immédiat après-guerre. J'ai toujours goûté votre amitié, votre largeur de cœur et d'esprit, votre sens de la fraternité humaine; mais je vous revois trop rarement. Un jour peut-être passez nous rendre visite dans le Connecticut. Maurin y est venu un jour. Diane (dont le nom complet est Festa-McCormick, sous lequel ont paru ses livres, le dernier sur Proust tout récent) a beaucoup entendu parler de vous & aimerait vous connaître. Si un jour vous désiriez un professeur de talent, pour le français, langue & littérature, je crois que vous ne regretteriez pas de songer à elle. Pour moi, je jouis de ma paresseuse retraite. Je lis beaucoup, écris un peu, voyage rarement, nourris quelque tristesse de l'état de la France & du monde, maudis ce sorcier ignare de Reagan qui a obstinément le sort pour lui. Je me rappelle que vous vous intéressez à la politique—un de mes intérêts aussi, peut-être en raison de mes origines méridionales.

À l'occasion, dites-moi des nouvelles de votre fils & de votre Institut et croyez tous deux à mes fidèles & amicales pensées.

Henri Peyre

## À son frère et à sa belle-sœur:

Le 24 juillet 84

Chère Micheline & bien cher & toujours juvénile frère,

Il y aura demain huit décennies que tu apparaissais en ce monde. De ce jour-là, ou presque, datent mes premiers souvenirs d'enfance & ceux de ma première chute dans un panier de prunes. Felix casus! comme aurait pu dire St. Augustin, puisqu'elle trahissait déjà mon embarras d'avoir un rival dont le savoir médical, la compréhension des âmes à travers les enveloppes corporelles, la chaleur d'affection fraternelle et l'attentive générosité devaient m'accompagner toute mon existence. Nos vœux affectueux, alors que tu franchis ce seuil intimidant de 80 ans. À travers des mers & des océans (je dois avoir passé deux ans de ma longue existence en Angleterre, quatre en Egypte, 53 dans le Nouveau Monde), parmi bien des diversités d'intérêts, de goûts, d'attitudes politiques et autres, nous sommes restés très proches; la chaleur de votre accueil en juin dernier, les fraternelles & toujours délicates attentions de Micheline—la plus compréhensive & indulgente des belles-sœurs—nous l'ont prouvé une fois de plus. . . .

## À Victor Brombert:

Le 20 août 1984

Cher Victor,

Votre livre est très beau—esthétiquement et par son contenu et l'élégance, sobre, très peu hugolienne, de votre style. Les Presses de Harvard ont accompli une tâche admirable; la couverture est digne du contenu et les pages d'illustration, ingénieusement choisies, fort bien reproduites, illuminent vos remarques.

J'ai lu le livre avec appétit et enthousiasme, sans lassitude aucune, même lorsque je reconnaissais certains développements pour les avoir lus en articles. Les derniers chapitres—sur l'Homme qui rit et 93 et la conclusion—sont pour moi les plus forts et pas un seul moment l'intérêt ne faiblit. Comme il est sans doute naturel pour le vieillard que je suis, qui, selon une formule usée, "se souvient surtout de lui-même," je revivais les heures de ma jeunesse où je découvrais ces deux romans, alors relativement peu lus. À chaque page ou presque, avec une pénétration aiguë dans les arcanes du texte, avec une minutie qui ne lasse jamais, vous découvrez et révélez des choses neuves. Et votre ton reste celui d'un chercheur érudit; attentif à citer ses prédécesseurs ou des interprètes d'aujourd'hui; modeste, mais jamais dogmatique ou pédant. Pour quelque raison, probablement tenant à de très vieilles réactions de ma part, je frémis moins aisément à la lecture de ce qui concerne N[otre] D[ame] de Paris et Les Misérables. Je n'arrive pas à me délivrer de quelque snobisme prétentieux en présence de ces livres, et des drames de VH, que je lisais à douze ans dans des éditions illustrées. Mais la faute est en moi. Je n'ai pas la place ici pour acheter toute l'édition de J. Massin, mais je vais racheter ND de Paris et l'apprécier mieux grâce à vous; et j'ai vaincu mon ancien préjugé à l'encontre des *Misérables*. Quelque vestige de puritanisme en moi, et ma guerre obstinée contre la croyance en Dieu (*pace* votre fille!) me retiennent de goûter et la foi hugolienne (il pense parfois à lui quand il dit être plus sûr de l'existence de Dieu que de la sienne propre) et les naïfs développements sur "le dernier mot." Je m'en veux secrètement de proférer instinctivement le mot de cinq lettres dès que je me coupe en me rasant, casse un verre ou—plus fréquemment encore—prends à un carrefour la mauvaise route. Mais les jurons empruntés à d'autres langues (aux corbeaux! en grec: "per Bacco" ou "damn it") semblent littéraires sur mes lèvres et me soulagent, ou me châtient, moins. C'est très ingénieux de votre part d'avoir groupé vos chapitres sous le titre de "visionary novel." Baudelaire, puis Rimbaud, sans peut-être le vouloir consciemment, nous ont amenés à mieux goûter le visionnaire Hugo, et j'ai le souvenir de mes derniers entretiens avec Focillon, en 1941–43, qui tournaient toujours autour des visionnaires en art, sur lesquels il écrivait dans ses dernières années. Je l'ai littéralement vu mourir et reçu son ultime râle, alors que vous vous prépariez à débarquer en Normandie.

Un très beau livre: sobre, extrêmement savant, impeccablement informé et qui, sans trémolos, communique la passion du critique au lecteur. Merci de nous l'avoir envoyé. Diane le lira avec plus d'attention encore que moi dès qu'elle aura terminé les 2 ou 3 chapitres qu'elle s'est imposée d'écrire cet été, pour un prochain ouvrage.

Où en est le roman de Beth? Nous comptons un de ces jours vous voir. Votre fille doit sans doute arriver à la fin de ses études à Yale? Le fils, lui, va regagner son collège. Brice a pris trois cours d'été très savants (présocratiques, philosophie politique, etc.). Malgré mes mises en garde, il insiste à dévorer des philosophes, des romans qui me tombent des mains d'ennui (Pynchon) et les divers ouvrages d'Harold Bloom. Je le voudrais plus tourné vers la "praxis," comme on dit, et même vers des gains matériels.

> À vous deux nos bien affectueuses pensées,
> Henri

J'avoue ne pas connaître du tout "La Révolution." Je le reproduirai sur l'édition de Massin, un de ces jours, à Yale. Quelqu'un (je l'écrivais récemment, je crois, à Gaudon) devrait réunir en un volume bon marché et commode Promontorium Somnii, PS de ma vie, la préface philosophique des Misérables, quelques textes du Reliquat de Will. Shakespeare et peut-être cette "Révolution."

## À Gita May:

>290 North Avenue
>Westport, Ct. 06880
>Le 26 août 1984

Chère amie,

Cela m'a fait plaisir de recevoir, & de lire, votre essai sur Diderot critique d'art. J'ai, comme bien d'autres, été longtemps plutôt froid envers les Salons. M'occupant à Yale d'une thèse sur Greuze (l'auteur est, je crois, "curator" de la Collection Frick aujourd'hui, E. Munhall) m'avait aidé à renoncer en partie à mes préjugés. J'avais encore essayé de détourner Seznec de consacrer tout ce temps, & cette érudition, aux Salons. Puis, les relisant, me découvrant ardent admirateur de Chardin (et de Watteau, que je viens de voir à Washington), j'ai peu à peu changé d'avis. Votre jugement, si modéré et nuancé, me paraît très juste; il est exprimé avec élégance et fermeté. Merci de me l'avoir communiqué.

Je n'écris plus guère que des articles, ne me sentant pas le courage d'affronter l'avenir et d'insulter quelque jalouse Némésis, en entreprenant de gros livres. Si j'en trouve un ou deux touchant à l'art, je vous les enverrai. Croyez en attendant à mes remerciements et à mes vœux pour votre lourde tâche.

>Bien cordialement,
>Henri Peyre

## À Konrad Bieber:

>September 9 — 84

Cher Konrad,

Je vous félicite de votre belle initiative. J'admire la fidélité de vos admirations, le dévouement dont vous avez toujours fait preuve pour les natures droites & généreuses. L'âge de Vercors, qui doit être proche du mien, sera peut-être contre lui; et aussi sa modestie, car il n'a pas, comme d'autres (Claude Simon, Robbe-Grillet & même Borges), recherché la publicité & cultivé paradoxes ou subtiles techniques. Mais il est bon d'essayer. Si par miracle le prix lui était décerné, ce serait grâce à vous.

D'ordinaire, chaque automne (en novembre d'habitude, je crois) l'Académie suédoise envoie à certains d'entre nous une lettre, nous priant de suggérer nos candidats. Je pense qu'elle le fera cette année. Préférez-vous que j'écrive alors, directement, comme je l'ai fait par le passé? Parfois je me suis trouvé avec les gagnants: Mauriac, St. J. Perse, Pasternak. D'autres fois, pour Graham Greene, Malraux et J. Guillén, j'ai échoué, & senti chez les Académiciens un mur infranchissable. Si vous préférez que je vous écrive à vous, je le ferai; mais je crois moins efficace que vous ayez l'air d'organiser une campagne concertée. Vous me direz ce que vous croyez le mieux.

Je vais lire en attendant quelques derniers Vercors; avoue l'avoir un peu négligé ces derniers dix ans. Mais les autres (Robbe-Grillet, Tournier, Vonnegut, Pynchon, Mailer, même Updike) m'ennuient de plus en plus.

J'espère que vous allez assez bien, et Tamara surtout, dont le courage m'emplit toujours d'admiration. Transmettez-lui nos vœux — et aussi à Eléonore à l'occasion, qui a dû rentrer d'Europe.

Bien chaudes amitiés,
Henri

## À Michel Guggenheim:

Le 10 sept. 84

Cher Michel,

Diana m'a montré votre aimable & généreuse lettre. Elle serait très heureuse de participer à cette session à Avignon, dont j'ai gardé un très chaleureux souvenir moi-même. L'action culturelle que vous avez exercée sur cette vieille ville rachète, pour moi, tout le mal que m'en dit mon frère, excédé par le brouhaha du festival, l'invasion de la pègre, les vols & les assassinats. Il ne peut croire qu'ici nous ne fermons jamais à clé les portes!

Si cela se fait, pour Diane & le théâtre, et, bien sûr, si je survis à un autre hiver, cela me ferait plaisir de l'accompagner & de vous revoir. Mais il serait bien agréable pour moi de vous revoir auparavant. J'ai bien des fois, dans mes heures solitaires et mes retours sur le passé, pensé à vous tel que vous étiez, étudiant plein de hardiesse; à votre femme, dont l'idéalisme & la générosité politique m'avaient touché (et sont plus que jamais nécessaires, en ces jours de politique cléricale et ultra conservatrice); et à votre fils. Je crois qu'on m'a dit, en réponse aux questions que je pose sur sa santé, qu'il peut travailler à quelque besogne et ne va pas trop mal. Votre courage & celui de sa mère ont été surhumains. Il m'arrive d'y repenser, comme mon fils à moi (20 ans) a surmonté ses handicaps (mon âge avancé, deux "muggings" à New Haven, éloignement de sa mère) & entre en Junior year à Yale; et s'affaire comme "chairman" du parti libéral!

Si un jour vous vous sentiez de pousser jusqu'ici en auto, tous deux ou tous trois, cela me ferait plaisir.

Bien des pensées fidèles à votre femme (bêtement, j'ai oublié son prénom) et ma vieille amitié.

Henri Peyre

## À Bettina Knapp:

290 North Ave., Westport, Ct. 06880<br>Jeudi 20 sept. / 84

Chère Bettina,

(Excusez cet antique papier—signe chez moi d'un "regressus ad uterum" ou du moins "ad tempus actum.") Vous êtes la générosité même, de permettre à un vieil ami (who, like Iago, is "nothing if not critical"), qui vous admire depuis longtemps, de vous lire—et de s'instruire à cette lecture. Merci, une fois encore. Ce livre rouge est beau, esthétiquement présenté, et courageux: car il ne sacrifie en rien à la facilité. Il puise avec prodigalité dans les formules latines, la mythologie grecque, les traditions hébraïques, cabalistiques, finlandaises, l'anthropologie et d'autres sciences encore. Vous maîtrisez tout cela et vous réinterprétez des œuvres archiconnues (Montaigne, Corneille, Goethe), grâce aux ectypes et archétypes découvrez en elles des perspectives neuves. Vous êtes envers le lecteur peu renseigné et médiocrement Jungien (c'est mon cas) pleine d'indulgence. Vous résumez consciencieusement les œuvres, comme dans un cours où il convient de guider l'auditoire. Vous ne forcez pas la note et nulle part vous n'imposez vos interprétations. Vous êtes pleine de tact et de délicatesse: cette vulgaire et charnelle Christiane Vulpius devient, pour vous, "an earth principle." Les mensonges si masculins, ou mâles, de Goethe, de Novalis, de Montaigne lui-même, leur sont pardonnés et vous ne témoignez nulle colère féministe. Dans le fond, vous savez très bien que le principe féminin, ou femme, finit toujours par gagner. Victoire éternelle de "vagina dentata"! Les chapitres sur Nachman, la Kalevala et Attar étaient, pour moi, des révélations: car je ne savais RIEN sur eux; et je n'ai jamais affronté l'étrange drame de Yeats. J'ai plus d'"animus" que d'"anima," et le regrette. Et j'avoue que je ne suis pas hanté par le passé, les ancêtres connus et inconnus, directs ou lointains. Ni Jung ni Freud ne m'ont jamais obsédé. Même à mon âge avancé, l'avenir seul m'intéresse et l'avenir de l'homme—négligeant, oubliant, "brushing aside" les souvenirs archétypaux et les complexes œdipiens. J'ai toujours voulu croire au progrès; cela demande une foi robuste et aveugle en l'avenir, en cette période de cléricalisme reaganien; de prechi-precha d'un pape voyageur et bavard et démuni de charité—donc condamné par St. Paul lui-même à faire résonner de creuses cymbales. Mais si votre démonstration patiente, habilement didactique, ne peut me convertir, elle m'intéresse, et je salue plus que jamais en vous une énergie phénoménale et une universelle curiosité. Comment avec ce gigantesque labeur trouvez-vous encore le temps de séduire votre mari; de soigner avec amour vos fils; de fréquenter théâtre et cinéma; de parcourir la Chine, le Japon, l'Irlande et autres pays; et peut-être même de pratiquer en secret la danse du ventre et d'acheter des robes?

L'hommage à votre mère est noble et le nom de votre père m'est cher depuis que j'ai lu ses très touchantes lettres. Leurs âmes s'en réjouissent peut-être dans quelque purgatoire.

Bien sûr, vos épreuves n'ont pas été impeccablement corrigées—ecstasy page 5 est une fois avec un "c"—Apollo p. 12 devient Apolo—solitude p. 78 devient solidute. Frazer devient Fraser—Histoire (bibliographie) historie. Mauvais dactylographe que je suis, je me rassure quand je vois une femme supérieure parfois aussi taper "the wrong letter."

Merci de ce livre & de ce don. Diane le lira à son tour, une fois libérée de ses tâches et de ses maux.

Avec grande affection,<br>Henri

## À Eléonore Zimmermann:

Le 7 octobre 1984

Chère Eléonore,

    Vous m'avez procuré un très vif plaisir, d'autant plus vif qu'il était inattendu, en m'envoyant cet élégant petit livre, encore revêtu du souvenir de votre père; l'un des hommes que je regrette le plus vivement de n'avoir pas connu. Je savais qui était Carl Burckhardt, Bâlois respecté dans le monde des livres. Les premières pages m'ont vite séduit, amusé (comme le fait toujours pour moi, homme aux raides cheveux, le mot allemand "Friseur"), vite conquis. Rilke, en 1924, parcourait les rues de Paris qui me sont familières. Deux ans après, il mourait. J'étais alors à Bryn Mawr, frais émoulu de Paris; j'avais par hasard annoncé sa mort à une dame viennoise, Beryl Ernst, et elle avait failli s'évanouir dans mes bras. Peu de gens alors connaissaient ses Elégies. Dans mon mauvais allemand, je déclamais l'ouverture de la Première, sans souhaiter moi-même être entendu de quelque membre de la hiérarchie des anges. Je poursuivais la lecture de votre opuscule & croyais reconnaître la librairie du Quartier latin. J'avais possédé l'édition bien dépassée de Ronsard de Blanchemain. Le vieux bibliothécaire, attablé devant le repas presque rituel et fort alléchant, Lucien Herr, m'était bien connu. J'étais alors dans ma dernière année d'École Normale. Herr m'avait pris en amitié. Je causais souvent avec lui—de politique, de poésie, et même de Hegel. Peu après, je partais pour l'armée, puis pour l'Amérique, & ne l'avais plus retrouvé à mon retour. C'est une des personnes qui m'ont le plus marqué. Ces pages de Burckhardt sont finement écrites, romancées avec simplicité & grâce. Elles mériteraient de paraître en traduction ici, si ce n'est déjà fait. Merci de ce don, pour moi très touchant.

    Je vais aussi bien que possible et ne m'ennuie même pas trop. Je vis dans le présent, lis bien des livres nouveaux, sans élan. Que la littérature était riche, en comparaison, dans ces années 1920–40, et pas en France seulement! Je m'enflammais pour Rilke, les deux Mann, Hofmannsthal, D. H. Lawrence, V. Woolf, Proust bien sûr, les premiers Malraux et Cocteau. Quelle morne moisson ces derniers temps. Vieillir, c'est aussi, hélas! se plaindre, se souvenir, regretter. Olympio déclame trop, mais il n'est pas si ridicule. "C'est toi qui dors dans l'ombre, ô sacré souvenir!" Je vous plains certes d'avoir dû trier tant de restes encore vibrants, mais il y a quelque douceur aussi à cela. Vous paraissez mélancolique . . . Pour nous, l'enseignement n'est, après tout, qu'une partie de notre vie profonde. Je jouis beaucoup de lire au hasard, de relire et de n'être plus tenté d'assister à des congrès savants ou pédants. Le sérieux, plein d'un contentement de soi que je trouvais peu digne de Lévi-Strauss et de Jacobson (deux bons amis des années de guerre) avec lequel ils s'extasiaient sur leur lecture des "Chats" me faisait sourire. Se pâmer devant ce médiocre sonnet; se demander longuement quel sens lire dans "L'Erèbe les eût pris pour ses coursiers funèbres" qui ne me paraît nullement ambigu, me semblait risible. Il y a tant de bien plus grands morceaux chez Baud: L'Irrémédiable, le Rêve parisien, Une Martyre, et al.! Jacobson est devenu grand homme, prenant au sérieux ses très contestables théories. J'ai revu parfois Lévi-Strauss à Paris. Comme nous tous, il a vieilli, est devenu un peu "académicien." Rien ne gâte nos grands hommes de France comme d'être idolâtrés ici. Cela a nui à Barthes et à Foucault. Auerbach avait su rester simple, Hugo Friedrich aussi (que je n'ai jamais rencontré) et J. Pierre Richard a eu le bon esprit de se renouveler à temps. . . .

## À Konrad Bieber:

Oct. 29—1984

Cher Konrad,

J'espère que vous supportez allègrement cette extraordinaire saison d'automne. La douceur de l'air, les brumes matinales, les feuilles de chêne et d'érable se détachant à regret des branchages me rappellent ma romantique jeunesse, lorsqu'en Angleterre ou dans les environs de Paris, je m'identifiais à ces mélancoliques personnages, plus poètes que moi qui, vainement, aurais voulu être leur émule. À 83 ans passés, je me complais sottement à ces rêveries narcissistes. Je voudrais oublier la tristesse que me font ressentir les débats, discussions, hypocrites prêchages politico-religieux. Nous avons formé tant de jeunes à l'esprit libre, informés sur le monde, libres de préjugés, semblait-il; ceux qui devraient aujourd'hui remplacer Acheson, Kennan, George Ball. Que sont-ils devenus? Avons-nous prêché dans un désert.

Mes colères silencieuses sont peut-être le signe que j'ai encore quelque vitalité, et quelques illusions. Ma santé paraît bonne. Je me laisse aller à les exprimer, parce que votre femme et vous avez toujours été, à mes yeux, les êtres les plus fidèles à un idéal qui est aussi le mien. Tamara reste-t-elle vaillante? Vous aussi?

Voici la copie de ma lettre à l'Académie suédoise. Je ne fais guère de progrès en dactylographie et les machines à la mode ne sont pas pour le maladroit que je suis. Je mets une naïve coquetterie à rester maladroit.

Mes bien affectueuses pensées,<br>Henri

## À l'Académie suédoise:

290 North Avenue, Westport, Conn. U.S.A.<br>Novembre 1 — 1984

À Monsieur le Secrétaire de l'Académie suédoise, Svenska Akademien, Stockholm Monsieur le Secrétaire:

Je prends la liberté de suggérer et de recommander au choix de l'Académie suédoise, pour le prix Nobel de littérature de l'année 1985, l'écrivain français François Vercors (Jean Bruller).

Ma grande estime pour le talent et la personnalité de cet écrivain date des années de guerre (1943–45), lorsque son courage moral, son indépendance d'esprit, l'originalité de son inspiration et la force de son style sobre et puissamment évocateur nous furent révélés par *Le Silence de la Mer*. D'autres écrits, tel *La Marche à l'Etoile,* suivirent, en tous points dignes de ce chef d'œuvre. Vercors, par la suite, fit paraître plusieurs ouvrages de fiction, des récits de voyage et d'analyse psychologique des peuples, qui montrèrent que son inspiration n'avait été ni tarie par l'accès à l'âge mûr ni gâtée par le succès. Jamais il ne s'est répété. Il a toujours fui la publicité. Il ne s'est allié à aucun groupe ou à aucune école. Il n'a lancé, et encore moins suivi, aucune mode littéraire. Son long et puissant ouvrage, *Moi, Aristide Briand,* fait revivre avec force la personnalité d'un grand homme politique européen. L'ouvrage évoque la vie profonde d'un homme, que reconstruisent l'imagination et la pénétrante compréhension d'un romancier historien. Il évoque également "les occasions perdues" par l'Europe dans les douze années qui suivirent la première guerre mondiale. Ces ouvrages ont témoigné de la vitalité du talent de Vercors et sa foi, jamais diminuée, en une cause qui mérite de rallier aujourd'hui les personnes de bonne volonté et de foi en l'avenir du monde, à une époque que nous sommes nombreux à juger affligeante. Le choix d'un tel homme ferait honneur à l'Académie suédoise et à la littérature.

Veuillez croire, Monsieur le Secrétaire, à l'expression de mes respectueux sentiments.

Henri Peyre

(Professeur "émérite," ancien Président de la Modern Language Association of America)

## À Michel et Colette Guggenheim:

[letterhead: Yale University]
290 North Avenue
Westport, Ct. 06880
Le 21—XI—84

Chers amis,

Votre visite nous a apporté un très vrai & grand plaisir. Diane a beaucoup aimé converser avec vous deux et, mère (relativement) heureuse de trois grands garçons, ayant eu de graves soucis pour la survie de l'un d'eux, né avec un cœur fragile, ou pire, elle a été émue de sympathie & admiration en écoutant les propos, si sobres & discrets, de Colette. Les épreuves que vous avez tous deux traversées et surmontées, en conservant beaucoup de jeunesse et un indomptable courage, auraient totalement démoli bien d'autres. Vous avez conservé une jeunesse d'esprit, une jouissance de l'art (& des vieilles pierres) et une lucidité sage dans vos jugements sur notre profession, qui réconfortent l'ancien, et vieux, maître que je suis. En pleine sincérité, puis-je vous redire ce que Diane m'a fait mieux comprendre, aussitôt après votre départ, que votre profonde humanité l'avait rassurée sur notre profession qui, lors de plusieurs congrès auxquels elle a assisté, lui a souvent paru pédante et bouffie de vanité. Merci à tous deux d'être ainsi restés *vous*.

J'espère que nous reverrons Colette & peut-être votre fils—ici ou lors de quelque voyage à Philadelphie—et ce sera un plaisir de trouver Michel dans son "Palais," pour moi, chargé de souvenirs. Que de fois, sur ma bicyclette encore primitive, j'ai gravi les côtes de Bellevue & de Tavel! Si je vois ces lieux en 1985, à mon âge avancé, il me semble que ce sera un adieu final.

Je joins quelques écrits au hasard—un ou deux sur l'art, pour votre fils peut-être.

Dites bien mes vœux de *calme* bonheur à Mario, et, de nous deux, chaudes amitiés.

Henri

## À Gita May:

Nov. 30—1984

Chère madame & amie,

C'est un véritable chef d'œuvre mineur que ce long essai sur Diderot. Tout y est, écrit avec sobriété et une rare élégance de style. Vous faites revivre sobrement avec délicatesse & tact l'homme. Vous ne cachez rien, du rôle de la sexualité, de son regrettable mariage. On sent un vaste savoir, minutieux et précis, mais dominé par un esprit ferme, filtré par un goût sélectif. Je l'ai lu, dévoré aussitôt, retrouvant ce que je croyais savoir déjà et le comprenant mieux. Je ne connaissais pas cette série d'ouvrages de chez Scribner's. Si d'autres chapitres sont à la hauteur du vôtre, ce doit être une remarquable série. J'espère que vous republierez ces 50 pages en un volume séparé. Il est littéralement parfait.

Avec mes compliments & remerciements,<br>Henri Peyre

## À Micheline Levowitz:

Le 21 déc. 84

Chère amie,

Je ne suis guère l'homme des cartes d'anniversaire & de circonstance & j'avoue que tout ce qui touche à cette réclame publicitaire de fin d'année m'irrite. Mais j'ai de mon côté survécu à l'usure des ans et, non sans quelque faiblesse de jambes et de mémoire et dessèchement du cœur, continué à lire, à écrire un peu, à penser vaguement et, en défiance têtue de toute confession psychanalytique, à oublier mes péchés passés. Mais votre carte très sobre ne dit pas comment vous allez, ce qu'est votre santé physique et morale, si l'enseignement continue à vous satisfaire sans vous épuiser à l'excès, comment vont votre mari et vos parents. On a parlé et écrit sur Stendhal, puisque l'anniversaire de sa naissance en offrait l'occasion, & je l'ai un peu relu, comme tout le monde—parfois avec impatience, souvent avec allégresse renouvelée. Je me retourne fréquemment vers mes lectures de jadis, en diverses langues anciennes ou modernes: sorte de narcissisme, à se retrouver soi-même dans ce que l'on a aimé. Mes colères se tournent vers, c'est-à-dire contre, les tendances politiques d'aujourd'hui et je me sens plus que jamais mal à l'aise dans l'Amérique de Reagan et ses acolytes, et inquiet sur les réactions déçues et étroites des Français. Diane travaille, écrit, maintient mon intérêt dans diverses œuvres littéraires et veille sur mon déclin. Pour le reste, peu de nouvelles et nulles trop affligeantes. Dites-moi à l'occasion des vôtres et croyez à ma lointaine, mais fidèle amitié.

Henri

## À son frère et à sa belle-sœur:

Le 23 décembre 1984

... Le récit de cette explosion m'a fait frémir! Je ne savais même pas que Mme Thatcher avait rendu visite à Avignon! Vos vitres en éclats! Encore beau que murs & toiture aient résisté! Je ne le montre guère quand on vous rend visite, car je ne suis pas très démonstratif; mais je sais par mes rêves, ou rêveries demi-conscientes, et fréquentes associations d'idées, combien en réalité mon paysage intérieur et ma vie intellectuelle & sentimentale ont été formés par ce no. 2, Rue Dorée. Je me rappelle souvent notre emménagement là; puis la maladie & la mort d'Émile; nos études surveillées, jusqu'à nos jeux de bille sur les tapis et le labeur maternel à cirer, polir, épousseter. Micheline a donné à ces vieilles pièces une allure tout autre. A-t-elle conservé et transporté de son magasin quelques pièces rares? ...

## To Robert Penn Warren:

[postcard; no date]

Your poem in the Atlantic is the most moving I have read these last five years: melancholy, profound, admirable in its directness and its diction. My own heart is full of recollection of more than eighty years ago &, at close to 84, I await "that last communal trance." It is a comfort & a source of deep inner joy for me to have read this before I disappear.

Gratefully,
Henri Peyre

## À Konrad Bieber:

Le 18 janvier 85

Cher Konrad,

Mes félicitations pour votre prompte et pleine victoire sur ce mal qui semble nous atteindre, nous, pauvres mâles. Pour moi, vous restez et resterez toujours le jeune homme athlétique que j'avais rencontré pour la première fois à New York—je ne sais plus en quelle année—et le noble et courageux interprète de la France résistante. Tant d'autres ont préféré montrer le côté égoïste, mesquin, raciste des Français—lequel existe, bien sûr. On se précipite maintenant pour écrire sur Camus: Lottman, McCarthy, mais avec une absence de sympathie & de chaleur qui le déshumanise. Votre livre reste une des œuvres les plus pénétrantes sur ces courants de pensée & de sensibilité des années cruciales.

Le Jean-Paul Aron, *Les Modernes,* est souvent drôle, rempli de petits potins, combatif, mais adroit à dégonfler les prétentions & l'histrionisme des milieux littéraires parisiens. Dans ma paisible retraite, souvent absorbée par des lectures graves, je me distrais de temps à autre avec des livres plus drôles: certains de Kundera, éloquents dans leur dénonciation du communisme stalinien mais trop adonnés au libertinage. Le récent Doubrovsky, *La Vie L'Instant,* est plein de talent & de verve; mais quelle furie à dépeindre ses exploits amoureux et à parler éternellement de soi. L'un de mes cauchemars est de rêver que je suis chez un psychanalyste et ne sais que dire ou que faire surgir de mon inconscient.

Un jour, si vous en avez le temps, & le goût, vous devriez écrire avec votre discrétion modeste coutumière vos souvenirs de résistant en France, d'émigré ensuite; votre attitude envers plusieurs cultures et héritages religieux ou autres, et quelques souvenirs sur des écrivains que vous avez connus et compris—Gary, par exemple, dont la fin de vie reste pour moi une énigme,—Béguin, Chadourne. . . .

Bien des vœux de Diane & moi pour la santé de Tamara, la vôtre—et le bonheur de votre fils & belle fille.

Amitiés,<br>Henri

## To John W. Kneller

290 North Ave.<br>Westport, CT 06880<br>January 18, 85

Dear Jack,

I am deeply touched by your generous and kind devotion to the crumbling old teacher that I am and must seem to you, the ever robust and imaginative organizer. I very much doubt I deserve being preserved for the future ages! Above all, any questioners or interviewers should treat me as a friend to be teased and criticized, not as an old fogy not to be contradicted.

When the dates for the Fridays are final, just drop me a card, so that I am clear about reserving them. March 22nd and May 10th, is it?

I enclose a recent review on one of the fields of interest which you have always cultivated: poetry. And my warm wishes for Sherry's health—and yours.

With affection,<br>Henri

## To the same:

February 1, 1985

Dear Jack,

Once again, I am profoundly touched by your kindness and grateful for all the trouble you take in arranging these two conversations: the dates set are convenient and I have noted them. And many thanks for arranging to have Diana and me dine and converse with you and your wife on the evening of February 28th. It is not false (or authentic) modesty which prompts me to add that I am not, at 84, and never was a "sacred cow" or bull whose every bellowing should be recorded! Je me sens humble ou petit, auprès de vous, espert organisateur, de Mary Ann Caws, magicienne de l'ubiquité, de son mari, penseur austère.

Non! Je n'ai pas trouvé trace de "L'Amie commune." À propos de quoi exactement ce titre est-il mentionné?

Bien des vœux affectueux pour vous deux.
Henri

## To Sherry Kneller:

[postcard: Rembrandt, *Equestrian Portrait*]
Febr. 15, 1985

Dear Sherry,

What a dreary & trying winter! With, now & then, heart warming glimpses of glittering snowy landscapes! You probably stay indoors a good deal, as I do, nursing my wearied bones. I'll be 84 when I have the audacity to inflict a bitter & angry lecture on you & other friends, on February 28th. Your generous invitation to the dinner at the Century, later, will pacify my anti-Sartrian wrath. Thank you from both of us.

Henri

The horse is as I imagined Jack's steed to have been. The hat would be marvelous on his head.

## À Alex Szogyi:

Le 18 février 85

Bien cher Alex—le plus généreux et affectueux des amis,

Vous ne voulez pas oublier que cette semaine va ajouter une année encore à mes 84 hivers. Pourquoi, comment vit-on si vieux, quand on n'est plus guère utile, que le froid & la glace vous font grelotter, qu'on se ferme au neuf? Je rassemblerai mon énergie un jour prochain pour aller voir l'exposition de Caravaggio. Ce peintre, que j'aime, est, dans ma pensée, lié à vous. Vous parliez si bien de lui, une fois.

J'espère que ce dur hiver ne vous a pas été trop rigoureux; vous qui parcourez la grande ville en tous sens, toujours actif; et trouvez encore le moyen de rire & de faire rire avec l'âcre G. Dandin. Le samedi deux mars ne serait pas commode pour moi. Je tâche de me réserver les samedis pour le repos & la visite occasionnelle de mon fils. Mais, si je comprends bien, "votre" pièce est jouée aussi la veille, le vendredi premier mars? Pourrions-nous venir ce soir-là? Je dois, je crois, être à N. York la veille, le 28 février & nous pourrions ainsi rester la nuit. À tout hasard, j'inclus une demande pour deux places & vous la confie.

Chaudes amitiés,
Henri

## To Sherry and John Kneller:

March 3, 85

Dear Sherry and Dear Jack,

You had organized a truly delicious and an unusually pleasant dinner at the Century, on the occasion of my lecture. Diana and I were deeply touched by your generosity and by the cordiality showed by all the guests. It was a memorable occasion. I especially enjoyed talking with my neighbors at table, especially Mrs. Luke—about her travels abroad, gardens she had visited, species of flowers. She is a very artistic person, and I found Mr. Wilson, who was seated at her left, especially interesting in his evocation of foreign lands. He plans to visit Turkey this spring, while the aged and weary man I am can hardly do more than relive old exotic adventures.

I hope your throat is improving, with a silent, relatively warm and beautifully sunny weekend. I took a walk by the beach on Saturday and the water was as blue as the Mediterranean. Rest well and accept very, very warm and grateful thanks for that dinner so expertly planned by Sherry and you, and for devotion and zeal to the Institute which honors me — and you.

Most cordially,<br>Henri Peyre

## À Germaine Brée:

Le 7 mars 85

Bien chère Germaine,

J'ai été profondément touché de tant de gentillesse & de générosité. Vous avez assisté, patiemment, à cette célébration de mon entrée dans cette imposante, effrayante, 85e année, que Diana, avec son dévouement inlassable, a tenu à marquer — un peu à mon corps défendant. Cela m'a permis de causer un peu avec vous. Je n'ai plus guère de compagnons ou d'interlocuteurs partageant les souvenirs qui sont les miens, ou mes goûts et parfois mes dégoûts, mes colères (rares, mais exaspérées) contre écrivains à mes yeux trop loués (Céline et autres). Dès vos premiers articles et livres, sur Racine, Proust, Gide, j'avais trouvé en vous, vous connaissant personnellement assez peu alors, un esprit que j'admirais sans réserve, une sensibilité littéraire ardente et lucide à la fois, une compréhension jamais partisane ou étroite des mouvements d'idées & de sensibilité. J'ai non moins admiré votre don de professeur, qui vous a fait former beaucoup de jeunes esprits qui vous sont restés dévoués et que vous avez contribué à ouvrir et à mûrir. Nos carrières ont été souvent parallèles: nous avons, l'un et l'autre, dépensé pas mal de notre énergie à aider des associations professionnelles, à aider et juger des "departments" français, à encourager ceux qui un jour nous succèderaient. Jamais mon admiration pour votre talent, votre courage intellectuel, votre respect, jamais pharisien ou conventionnel, des valeurs morales, n'a faibli. Vous êtes la première, et le premier, de nous tous, Français d'Amérique. La France le reconnaît & le proclame aujourd'hui. Si l'on songe au discret mépris dans lequel, il y a cinquante ans, on tenait en Europe ceux qui avaient choisi de faire en Amérique leur carrière, et au respect qui nous entoure aujourd'hui, le contraste est grand et le mérite vous en revient en grande partie. C'est avec appréhension et chagrin presque personnel que Diane, qui vous est profondément attachée, & moi, avions appris les maux survenus à vos yeux. Vous semblez avoir, avec héroïsme, dépassé cela. Vous étiez, ici, en excellente forme & nos convives vous ont trouvée jeune, ferme, lucide et admirablement courtoise. Ce sera un plaisir de vous revoir lors de cette "fête" du 13 avril; je vous redirai alors le plaisir que me donne votre livre.

Merci de cet envoi. L'ouvrage est splendidement présenté. J'avoue m'être aussitôt précipité sur les photographies, puis sur plusieurs chapitres, vite dévorés. Bien sûr, avec l'inévitable narcissisme des vieux, j'ai retrouvé beaucoup de mon passé dans ces pages. J'avais approché plusieurs de ces écrivains; lu beaucoup de revues d'avant-garde; découvert Proust, à l'École Normale, en 1922–23, avec voracité; puis Malraux, Giono, les Surréalistes. Vous savez avec science & avec art relier, sans déterminisme ou lourdeur, les écrivains à leur milieu. En vous feuilletant, j'ai revécu mes angoisses des années lourdes de menaces, entre 1936 et 39, que je passais alors en France; mon effondrement lors de la défaite de 1940 et mes efforts, ensuite, pour éveiller les auditoires américains, si lents à comprendre que leur intérêt & leur générosité profonde les forceraient à sauver l'Europe. Je crois que nous pouvons dire, vous & moi (avec quelques autres, disparus, dont Focillon, que j'ai beaucoup aimé), que nous avons été entendus ici de pas mal d'Américains et avons eu quelque part à leur meilleure compréhension de la France. La fidélité de vos disciples et amis est touchante. Ce gros, savant et beau livre va longtemps contribuer à former ici, sans nul dogmatisme et nul jargon, les opinions et les goûts en matière de littérature française. Je suis presque embarrassé à me sentir constamment en accord avec vous.

Merci de ce beau don—et de celui du Douanier Rousseau, à qui je résiste parfois, je l'avoue, peut-être par quelque difficulté en moi à "retrouver mon enfance à volonté." À bientôt et, à l'occasion, revenez nous accorder un peu de votre présence—à Westport ou à New York.

Merci du fond du cœur,<br>Henri

Je vois que le nom de Morot-Sir n'a pas été retenu dans la liste finale du Philosophical Society. Je ne sais pourquoi c'est là un groupe difficile à influencer. J'y avais jadis combattu pour diverses personnalités littéraires, car on y préfère des archéologues, spécialistes d'études bibliques, et des gens de Princeton & de Philadelphie. Je n'ai plus guère assisté aux réunions ces dernières années et je me tiens à l'écart de tout comité. Place aux jeunes!

## To John W. Kneller:

Sunday, March 31, 85

Dear Jack,

We all seemed hurried after the impressive and picturesque theatrical "séance" last Thursday and I was whisked away by Diana and her dinner guests. We missed you, incidentally, and Sherry—the most discreet, the most refined of all the faculty wives I have ever met, the only one who *feels* art and beauty and does not theorize and pedantically talk about it all.

Anyway, I never thanked you properly. Generously, you put me "en avant," make me talk for a probably uncaring posterity, before my voice resigns itself to eternal silence. But you are the one who provided the funds, the outrageously expensive machinery, bought the three or four operators, supervised the whole show from above and I am immensely grateful to you. It all seemed to proceed smoothly, since you had settled every detail impeccably.

Spend restful and, I hope, cheerful vacations and convey my wishes for a total recovery to your brother.

Diana's and Henri's affectionate wishes for Sherry and you.

Henri

## À Germaine Brée:

> 290 North Avenue
> Westport, Ct. 06880
> April 2, 1985

Chère Germaine,

C'est le deuxième jour d'avril—mais bien froid encore, & incertain, dans ces parages. Forsythias, magnolias, ne nous égaient pas encore. Peut-être en apercevrons-nous chez vous à la fin de la semaine prochaine. Voici Pâques, fête mémorable jadis en France. Les seuls souvenirs encore vivaces que j'ai conservés de mon enfance, nominalement protestante, sont ceux du sermon sur la résurrection que l'on nous conviait à entendre ce jour-là. Je plaignais intérieurement le malheureux pasteur, distingué, disert, paraissant convaincu, qui, chaque année, évoquait pour ces railleurs insolents que mes frères et moi étions les détails sur le tombeau vide et ce Joseph d'Arimathie qui me rendait rêveur. Quel interminable passé il me semble avoir derrière moi! J'ai passé il y a près de deux mois le cap de la 84e année. Il y aura en septembre prochain exactement soixante ans que, tout guilleret et incroyablement naïf dans ma sophistication affectée, je débarquais à Bryn Mawr et me sentais surveillé, avec bienveillance d'ailleurs, par ces dames, alors habitant Low Buildings. Ce collège, auquel je suis resté attaché, m'a en partie formé.

Vous êtes pour moi une cadette, courageuse, indomptable, avec une carrière militaire et d'aventureux voyages au Canada, en Australie, en Egypte, et la méditation & composition des 5 ou 6 livres que je considère comme les plus forts de tous ceux que Français d'Amérique (et même en France) ont écrits. Vous êtes restée si modeste & si admirable de simplicité que je crains de vous embarrasser en parlant un peu—sur vous, ou autour de vous, le 13 avril. Mais je me sens honoré d'avoir été invité à le faire. À Hartford, samedi dernier, je vous ai remplacée, à la prière insistante de Susan Dunn. J'ai essayé de traiter, bien hâtivement, le sujet que vous aviez à l'origine proposé, avec son titre un peu énigmatique. J'ai été, dès 1920, l'un des premiers lecteurs de Proust, et j'ai été plongé dans une grande tristesse le jour de Novembre 1922 où j'ai lu, dans un journal anglais, la nouvelle de sa mort.

Je suis heureux, et Diane aussi, de ces nouvelles de votre voyage à la Nouvelle Orléans. Votre vision est donc restaurée à merveille, et votre vigueur est intacte. Je suis, pour ma part, très peu porté vers l'autobiographie, et j'avoue que ceux qui ont, ces dernières dizaines d'années, prodigué des ouvrages sur leur vie ("L'âge d'homme" & autres livres de Leiris; "le Pacte autobiographique") me lassent. Fowlie écrit avec quelque charme & j'aime beaucoup l'homme en lui; mais il n'a jamais osé se livrer vraiment. Doubrovsky, lui, ne le fait que trop et ne sait pas oublier son personnage. À vos heures de loisir, ne songeriez-vous pas à retracer vos souvenirs? Enfance protestante, îles "hugoliennes," Oran, Amérique, entourage de Camus, disciples; vous avez occupé, et continuez à occuper, dans les rapports franco-américains et dans la critique littéraire, une place unique. Les ouvrages français et anglais sur la littérature (et l'arrière-plan social et historique) du 20e siècle, que vous avec hardiment accepté d'écrire, dépassent de loin tout ce que Français de France, Suisses et franco-américains ont écrit.

J'ai lu Gusdorf assidûment, naguère, mais ne l'ai jamais rencontré. Ce qu'il a écrit est parfois hâtif, trop abondant sans doute, insuffisamment creusé, mais nous a tous servis & aidés. Ces congrès sont sans doute critiquables et lassants, donnent asile à bien des communications superficielles; mais ils ont, depuis la deuxième guerre surtout, resserré les rapports intellectuels franco-américains. Votre rôle y a été le plus efficace.

Diane attend son fils Carlo, moi sans doute le mien, pour Pâques—et plusieurs de leurs amis. Elle est admirable de dévouement et experte à mener de front écrits, cuisine et jardinage. Je cultive égoïstement mon manque de sens pratique. Savez-vous que, et Brice, et Carlo de son côté, disent que, de toutes les personnes rencontrées ici (ils sont d'ordinaire sévères pour ceux dont le "generation gap" semble les séparer), c'est par vous qu'ils sont le plus impressionnés. Vos neveux et nièces doivent penser de même.

Bonne Pâques et chaleureuses amitiés de Diane & moi. Nous devons prendre un avion très tôt, le matin du 13, pour ne pas risquer de retard.

Henri

## À Michel Guggenheim:

Le 2 avril 85

Cher Michel,

Ce n'est pas encore le printemps ici: quelques très timides fleurs, mais toujours le froid humide et l'attente impatiente de ce soudain éclat qu'est en Amérique l'intrusion du printemps. Cette approche de Pâques éveille, dans le vieux demi-solitaire que je suis, les souvenirs de jadis: longues vacances alors en France, voyages à la campagne, gaieté familiale. Je pense assez souvent à vous deux, & à votre fils—que vous avez, miraculeusement, préservé, aidé à vivre presque normalement, avec tant de bonté & de dévouement. Je ne suis pas, dans le fond, aussi rationaliste que vous me croyez. Il m'arrive même de guider ma vie selon des rêves, et de croire au "hasard objectif" des surréalistes. Mais l'utilisation de la foi religieuse à des fins politiques, que pratiquent Reagan & ses conseillers, me répugne.

Ce mot était pour vous souhaiter, à tous deux & à votre fils, des congés et fêtes de quelque agrément; et aussi dû à la nouvelle que m'apporte le journal de ce matin. La mort de Spanel, à qui j'avais écrit, il y a 3 ou 4 jours, pour solliciter son intérêt pour le programme Bryn Mawr–Avignon. Ce sera donc en vain.

Je l'avais connu un peu, avions tous deux pensé, et dit, du bien de De Gaulle et le voyais ouvert & généreux. J'ai écrit assez longuement, en lui envoyant une copie de vos "reports," à J. M. Guéhenno, dont j'avais assez bien connu le père, et que je vois parfois. Je n'ai pas de réponse; mais j'ai essayé d'insinuer que, tout comme le programme de N.Y. University (sur la France sociale et politique) que les services culturels français ont largement subventionné, le vôtre mérite l'appui officiel.

Il faudrait pouvoir toucher des riches veuves? Anciennes de Bryn Mawr? Financiers comme Istel (qui aide N.Y.U.); gens d'affaires. J'avoue n'y être pas très apte. J'ai toujours préféré quelque médiocrité financière, soi-disant "dorée," et mon égoïste liberté. Je ne pense pas que Claude de Messières nage dans la prospérité, mais j'essaierai d'avoir son adresse: il y a longtemps qu'il n'a plus donné signe de vie.

À Avignon, où nous devrions arriver dès le 13 juin, nous logerons, en fin de compte, chez mon frère: 2, rue Dorée—laissant Diane libre de voir ses collègues et élèves. J'ai souvent goûté la conversation de Domenach, celle de Charpier jadis, et d'autres de votre "faculté."

> Bien des choses à tous deux & à votre fils.
> Henri

## To Robert Penn Warren:

April 3, 1985

Dear & warmly admired Poet,

The arrival of your green-red-grey book was the best surprise & the most gratifying event for us, in this hesitant, fumbling cruel spring. Diana & I are deeply touched, as we have been these last few years, by your ever warm & generous friendship. As intellectual snobs & would be art amateurs, we always felt a bit out of place in this Westport uncommonly cool & aloof community. Your presence, the radiating & vivacious warmth of Eleanor, occasionally the meeting of your gifted children and of friends of yours like the Blums, your wife's expert artistry at preparing meals neither Breton nor Roman à la Tivoli, have made us feel less estranged among these labyrinthine paths than we would have been otherwise. You enabled us to experience "the possibility of joy in the world's tangled & hieroglyphic beauty." And now this generous gift allows us to share much of your past, of your love for natural beauty, of Red's childhood & even of the touching memories of his father, of his fortitude in having conquered the Saharan desert, kept the Touareg at bay, in triumphing over sickness & surgery. As he writes, after a dinner party conjured up in evocative verse, he shows to us "what is left to say when the last logs sag & wink" & as "all begins again. And you are you."

We have read, & even reread most of these poems over the last three days. The volume, in its range over more than sixty years, is certainly among the most varied, the richest and the *deepest* to have appeared in our half-century. I had missed most of the early poems, whose artistry and "length of breath," as the French put it, are astonishing. "Reading late at night" on Tiberius, an emperor maligned, they say, by historians, meditating on universal vanity at Anacapri, where I remember dreaming in my younger days. The belated romantic that I have remained, despite the once "new" criticism & Eleanor's dislike of Shelleyan effusiveness, relished your nature poetry: of the West, the South, Vermont, and those haughty birds & wild animals which I only enjoy through their transfiguration thanks to poetic language. And, even if it is not fashionable these days perhaps, to me there is an added resonance to poetry which is laden with a deeper and ethical content, like some gnomic verse or French maxims, yet never indulges didacticism and pomp. "History is not truth. Truth is in the telling" and elsewhere "history is the other name for death." At my advanced age, in this symbolic sunset of a long life, I respond to the poet who faces up to "the time when you must speak / to your naked self." If my memory is not yet too weak, I hope to recite several of your lines to myself, while driving or walking or dreaming.

Thank you, & your wife & muse, for a unique joy.

Henri &—more coyly, Diana

## À Germaine Brée:

Lundi 16 avril 1985

Bien chère Germaine,

Que je vous dise, l'esprit au repos et parmi ce calme de la campagne, sonore des maladroits pépiements d'oiseaux, combien ces heures auprès de vous nous ont émus, Diane & moi, et vos autres amis. Nous ne vous avons pas téléphoné hier matin dimanche. Il se trouve que ce luxueux logis de Reynoldia House, vrai musée historique, était aussi une prison: pas de téléphone, pas de clé, si bien que le soir du samedi, à onze heures, le très aimable & admirable ancien président qui nous ramenait avait trouvé toutes les grilles & les portes fermées, et cela a été toute une aventure de trouver le Cerbère qui possédait les clés. Le matin, il était prudent de ne pas s'aventurer au dehors, parmi les tulipes et les arbres fleuris; nous n'aurions pu nous "réintroduire dans notre histoire," pour paraphraser le méchant Mallarmé. Mais Tom Mullen nous a emmenés, avec Susan Dunn, à un "breakfast" élégant au Stouffers, puis à l'aéroport.

En tous cas, les heures de la soirée, à table, sont pour nous inoubliables. J'ai assisté à diverses reprises à des dîners et cérémonies de félicitations & de célébration: JAMAIS je n'avais rencontré la chaleur d'affection, la simplicité émouvante et élégante de manières, de paroles, l'évidente sincérité dans les hommages qui abondaient à Wake Forest. Les personnes à qui j'ai un peu parlé m'ont frappé par leurs qualités d'esprit & de cœur. Le "Provost" est un homme admirable, un grand organisateur et un fervent de poésie. Mullen et sa femme sont délicieux de dévouement empressé, de gentillesse, et aussi de savoir. Il m'a parlé de ses recherches historiques aux Archives à Paris et à Londres, à la B.N.; elle, des romantiques allemands qui ont accompagné toutes mes années et mes lectures de poésie depuis ma découverte de l'Allemagne, à 18 ans. Nous nous sommes aussitôt sentis leurs amis. L'ancien Président (dont le nom précis m'échappe) et sa femme sont des personnes remarquables de profonde humanité. Nous avons été, vous & moi, formés dans le respect de l'intellectualité, et de l'intelligence, et avons été des érudits à notre manière. Je sais que j'ai le défaut de trop citer, peut-être de trop savoir, & que j'ai trop parlé de moi dans mon allocution. "Mon cœur fait de l'esprit, le sot, pour se leurrer," dit un vers de Tristan Corbière; c'était pour déguiser un peu mon émotion, car je me sentais pris d'émotion fraternelle en évoquant votre carrière. Une certaine pudeur ne m'a pas permis, dans le passé, de vous dire l'admiration et l'affection que je vous porte. De voir votre maison, votre salle de travail et son fouillis de livres, de rencontrer, à ce très touchant et délicieux repas, plusieurs membres de votre famille, si pleins de reconnaissance & de tendresse pour vous, nous a, tous deux, émus. Ces heures étaient inoubliables, et dignes en tous points, sans nulle pompe, de ce que vous avez accompli pour l'Amérique et la présence française ici, depuis bien des années.

Et, au sein de cette apothéose, vous restiez simple, directe, émue avec naïveté, souriante. J'espère que les journées d'explosion printanière qui viennent vous laisseront quelque repos. Nous devons être en France (pour moi, sans doute, l'ultime voyage) du début de juin au milieu de juillet. Mais avant, ou ensuite, rendez-nous visite si vous le pouvez; ou quand vous serez proche, à Northampton. Diane aime votre compagnie et la simplicité directe de cette savante dont elle a admiré les livres. Pour elle, pour bien d'autres, vous êtes le modèle—inégalé mais inspirant.

De tant d'amitié prodiguée, & de gentillesse, nous allons garder un souvenir ému.

Encore merci,<br>Henri

## À Charles Mackey:

April 16/85

Dear Mr. Mackey:

C'était un plaisir d'avoir de vos nouvelles. Il m'arrive de penser à vous, grand, modeste, toujours plein d'indulgence pour vos anciens maîtres. Je ne vais plus guère à Boston, et d'ailleurs reconnais mal les figures des "anciens," mais je vous félicite d'avoir accepté cette tâche professionnelle. Mon sérieux semi-puritain & mon absence d'humour ne me rapprochent que peu de Prévert—mon aîné d'un an. Mais j'essaierai d'être juste envers lui & vous enverrai un texte le mois prochain. Je dois beaucoup m'absenter en avril.

      Croyez à mon fidèle & cordial souvenir.
      Henri Peyre

## Au même:

Le 6 mai 85

Cher Charles Mackey:

Vous êtes généreux & aimable d'avoir accepté cette lourde responsabilité à la French Review. Comme membre depuis presque toujours et ancien président de l'AATF, je vous en remercie. Et je me rappelle toujours avec plaisir votre séjour à Yale & parfois nos rencontres à Boston.

Mais je suis un dactylographe d'une maladresse qui va croissante, et j'ai renoncé à écrire & à publier à cause de cela. Ceci est déplorable. Mais je sais que je ne ferais pas mieux si je le retapais. Je suis l'ennemi des machines plus modernes, que je ne sais pas manier. Si ceci est par trop mal présenté, ne le publiez pas et je passerai le livre à quelqu'un de plus adroit.

      Mes plates excuses et toute mon amitié.
      H. P.

## À Michel Guggenheim:

Le vendredi 10 mai

Cher Ami,

Guéhenno, entrevu hier un moment, me dit qu'il a pu vous trouver quelque aide pour des bourses. Je lui ai répété que nul programme ne le méritait autant que celui de Bryn Mawr–Avignon—deux de mes patries intellectuelles et sentimentales.

Pour moi, ce sera un plaisir de vous entrevoir là-bas. Le décor ici est en ce moment plus coloré et même féerique; chez vous aussi sans doute. Mais en ressuscitant mes très jeunes années, je trouverai peut-être quelque charme aux terrasses des cafés de la Place Clemenceau.

Bien affectueuses pensées à votre femme et à votre fils.

Bien à vous,<br>Henri

## Au même:

Le samedi, 18 mai 85

Cher Michel,

Dernières semaines d'une longue année scolaire—paresseuse pour moi, retraité—mais qui m'a récemment fait voyager en Oklahoma, Carolines, et hier encore à N.Y., où Victor Brombert m'interviewait sur vidéo-tape pour la postérité—comme si je devais passer à la postérité! Mais il a été indulgent. L'affection de tant d'anciens élèves me touche.

Bien sûr, si vous ne croyez pas ma présence à une "Table Ronde" trop encombrante, ou encombrée de souvenirs, je serai heureux d'officier à une telle séance dans ma ville presque natale. Un thème plus limité serait peut-être préférable, et axé sur le présent: "L'Amérique d'aujourd'hui vue par les intellectuels français" ou bien "La littérature française contemporaine vue d'Amérique"—comme vous déciderez.

Nous pensons partir le huit juin, nous arrêter à Paris 4 jours et prendre pour Avignon le train le 13 juin, vendredi. Diane serait ainsi prête pour l'ouverture de votre session. Nous repartirions aussitôt ses cours terminés, le samedi six juillet, pour Nice, puis Florence, où mon fils doit se trouver, prenant des cours d'italien.

Que de vieilles connaissances seront là pour moi! Charpier, Domenach, Ahearn! Votre femme seule nous manquera. Dites-lui nos très amicales pensées.

À bientôt,<br>Henri

## À Philip Kolb:

290 North Avenue. Westport. Conn. 06880.
Le 6 juin 1985

Cher ami,

Ces deux volumes (XI–XII) sont un don précieux. Ils m'ont procuré un très vif plaisir. J'y ai retrouvé le souvenir de mes colères & de mon indignation, contre ceux qui, en 1911–13, rejetaient l'œuvre proustienne, contre cet épais Souday, ce froid et hautain Copeau. L'incompréhension des contemporains pour les grands hommes parmi eux est un thème auquel je suis revenu avec acharnement. Un de vos disciples, par contre, devrait écrire sur Louis de Robert. Si j'étais plus jeune, j'aimerais le tenter. Les belles lettres à Mme Strauss consolent de la sottise d'autres correspondants. Vos notices sont remarquables en tous points: elles constituent de véritables et pénétrantes analyses de la personnalité de Proust; et elles sont écrites d'une plume libre, alerte, parfois ironique. Quant à vos notes, leur science est éblouissante. Quel travail représentent ces datations, éclaircissements, identification de citations. Vous êtes un modèle de chercheur, pour moi, retraité, qui parfois écris encore, mais ne pourrait émuler votre dévouement à une seule tâche.

Je pars pour quelques semaines en France, puis reviendrai ici, près de la mer & dans la verdure, pour la fin juillet & août.

Rappelez-moi, à l'occasion, au souvenir de votre fille, la "musicienne du silence" si discrète. A-t-elle jamais écrit quelque chose sur Berlioz?

Toute ma reconnaissante amitié,<br>Henri Peyre

## À Michel Guggenheim:

Le 4 juillet 85

Bien cher Michel,

La visite à votre Chartreuse, si frappante dans son pittoresque et artistement préservée, puis ce dîner vraiment féerique au Bercail vont longtemps rester dans notre souvenir. Je crois bien n'avoir jamais vu Avignon aussi splendide que lors de ce lever de lune sur le Rocher, d'une rive du Rhône tellement plus mystérieuse que je me rappelais cette île, si souvent jadis le lieu de mes promenades d'adolescent rêvant de quelque "ailleurs." Vous aviez réuni une compagnie cordiale, stimulante, ni pédante ni prétentieuse. Il est clair que chacun de vos professeurs, et sans doute la plupart de vos étudiants, ont pour votre ferme et souple direction une affectueuse admiration. Moi qui, à l'origine, avais sous-estimé les possibilités culturelles de cette vieille ville, peux vous dire combien je suis frappé par la réalisation qui vous est due. Vous avez accompli cette très belle et lourde tâche avec bien peu d'aide, et de Bryn Mawr et d'Avignon; vous vous êtes montré, sans rouerie ou calcul, un adroit politique. Bien peu de Franco-américains sont, au même degré que vous, fidèles aux deux patries culturelles. Votre spiritualité, le courage de l'âme qui vous a permis de surmonter les plus dures épreuves, votre talent d'animateur font mon admiration. Vous voulez bien dire que vous m'avez gardé quelque reconnaissance, et comme Français et comme universitaire américain qui a longtemps travaillé à mieux rapprocher les deux pays; je suis moi-même reconnaissant à ce glorieux cadet que vous êtes. Diane a senti très vite, comme moi, combien de chaleur, de générosité, de persévérance rayonnent de vous. Elle a aimé travailler pour un "chairman" qu'elle estime et a, d'emblée, aimé.

Je viendrai vous serrer la main pour vous dire au revoir. Nous repartirons de Rome le 12 juillet & serons à Westport pour le reste de l'été, et ensuite. Colette aura passé par de bien dures épreuves cet été & les paroles d'encouragement sont trop creuses devant de telles menaces. Mais dites-lui bien notre affection et, bientôt, venez avec elle & Jean-Pierre nous rendre visite. J'aimerais le revoir.

Heureuse fin de session et merci encore & mille vœux.

Henri

# À Armand Hoog:

290 North Ave., Westport, Ct. 06880
Le 18 juillet 85

Cher Armand,

Nous avons passé quelques semaines en Europe: à mon âge plus qu'avancé, je trouve, à revoir Paris, un frisson de surprise et me voir défiant le destin, avec la mélancolie de songer à mes contemporains disparus & l'égoïste satisfaction de me dire que j'ai survécu. Que de disparitions récentes parmi mes contemporains, & même mes cadets, de l'École Normale, mes collègues de Yale! Et puis, combien est morne la littérature de ces vingt dernières années, tant critique que narrative ou se voulant imaginative! Les derniers Duras, ridiculement surfaits, les Robbe-Grillet, les romans de cet obsédé et ce monstre de vanité qu'est Tournier, m'irritent et m'ennuient. À mon retour d'Italie (où mon fils de 21 ans suit des cours d'été à Florence), j'ai trouvé, parmi l'accumulation de courrier, votre roman.

Merci, de songer encore à ce vieil aîné que je suis et de votre souvenir. Je ne sais que peu de chose de vous dans votre retraite, par quelques rencontres avec votre fille que Diane McCormick (avec qui j'habite) et moi aimons beaucoup; et me suis souvent demandé ce qu'il est advenu de votre autre fille & de votre fils. Est-ce à lui que votre roman est dédié? Je lis parfois et avec admiration pour son savoir et l'intérêt qu'elle porte au passé franco-américain, ce qu'écrit votre femme. Et votre roman m'a ravi. Il est alerte, immensément drôle, désinvolte d'allure, amusant d'ironie, et d'une jeunesse étincelante. Vous savez rire et sourire, & faire rire avec quelques grains de pitié, de ces jeunes gens hantés par leurs notes universitaires, des utopistes si gauches dans leur quête de l'harmonie, et des pédants de l'Université, avec un rare talent. On est très vite conquis, comme on l'est à la lecture de Stendhal, par votre Gilles et ses amours, vos amusantes évocations de naïves "topless girls" ou épouses de l'économe-triste; et vous êtes, dans vos randonnées en corbillard, vos tragiques peintures d'acrobates suicidaires, et les entretiens silencieux avec la mère du jeune échappé d'Europe, à la fois maître d'un humour jamais forcé et plein de tendresse. Vous avez, j'imagine, passé la soixantaine; mais vous êtes le plus jeune, et le plus compréhensif de la jeunesse, de tous les auteurs que j'ai pu lire depuis ma retraite. Et votre maîtrise du franglais canadien est immensément drôle, & celle d'un expert linguiste. J'espère qu'assez de Canadiens seront amusés par votre talent de caricaturiste et de styliste. Votre prose alerte et agile est la plus divertissante et la plus vivante que j'ai lue depuis longtemps. Que vous ayez préservé intact votre talent de prosateur et votre sens du concret & du vivant, parmi des années de vie universitaire, fait mon envie. Nous sommes, auprès de vous, de vieux desséchés et des lourdauds empêtrés dans leur prose universitaire. Votre roman devrait divertir nos compatriotes, sevrés de récits lisibles et drôles depuis si longtemps. Il m'a donné un vrai & grand plaisir. Merci!

Dites à votre femme mon fidèle & amical souvenir et croyez à ma très affectueuse, & admirative amitié.

Henri Peyre

## To John W. Kneller:

September 26, 1985

Dear Jack,

I much enjoyed your kind visit and our talk. And once again I admired your vigor and your wisdom. And I envy your memory—names often elude me when I want to display my pedantry.

The book I meant is: Le Style indirect libre by Marguerite Lips, Payot, 1926. I believe Victor Brombert used it in his excellent volume in English on Flaubert . . . I find Naomi Shor more and more involved and pretentious; but she had a highly technical article on Flaubert's style in the journal *Littérature* . . . I cannot find John Lapp's article on "Mémoire." I must have sent it to St. Aubyn for his gift of Rimbaud items to his Missouri old college . . .

I forgot if you said you had the volume (Twayne) by St. Aubyn on Mallarmé. I remember it as modest, clear and helpful. I have it somewhere and can mail it to you, if you want to borrow it.

Many cordial greetings to your wife and my wishes for that lointain ami inconnu, your brother.

Cordially,
Henri

## À Philip Kolb:

290 North Avenue<br>
Westport, Ct. 06880<br>
Le 26 octobre 1985

Cher Philip, (si vous permettez cette familiarité; il y a assez longtemps que je vous admire et vous lis)

Encore une fois merci. Vous êtes bien trop généreux & je devrais moi-même me procurer ces volumes. Je suis sans doute l'un des très rares survivants parmi ceux qui ont lu Proust dès 1919, juste avant mon entrée à l'École Normale, et que sa mort en 1922 a attristés. J'ai vite dévoré ce volume XIII et votre émouvante introduction. Les moindres billets sont curieux, et vos notes, impeccables de savoir, résultat d'infinies recherches, constituent une toile de fond à la vie littéraire d'alors. Les lettres sur Agostinelli sont émouvantes et jettent un jour révélateur sur Albertine. Offrir un avion et une auto à un ami-amant, quelle folie! Et, en 1914, quel danger courir! Ces gens-là aimaient mieux qu'aucun d'entre nous, banals maris et pères de famille — et leurs occasions de souffrir sont cent fois plus fréquentes.

Vous devez être splendidement organisé pour pouvoir ainsi multiplier, régulièrement, les parutions des volumes. J'imagine que vous avez dû accumuler les annotations utiles pour le reste des huit années à paraître. Ce monument que vous avez élevé avec énergie et intelligence surpasse de beaucoup tout ce que les pauvres critiques accumulent, avec pédantisme et souvent en déformant tout.

Rappelez-moi au souvenir de Mme Kolb et de vos filles et croyez moi fidèlement et en admiration,

Vôtre<br>
Henri Peyre

## À John W. Kneller:

Le 9 oct. 1985

Cher Jack,

Excusez ce vieux et inépuisable papier à lettres et mille fois merci de me communiquer votre impressionnante bibliographie. Elle est riche, variée et mentionne tous les ouvrages récents de quelque importance. J'imagine que tous ou presque tous se trouvent à la bibliothèque du Graduate Center. J'y commandais ou recommandais pas mal de livres lorsque j'enseignais là. Ici nos rayons débordent et je n'achète plus rien; tant que ma santé me permet d'aller à Yale et le hasard de m'y garer, je poursuis mes lectures. Je n'ai pas d'autre intérêt "créateur" et je vous envie d'être musicien, sportif, artiste en ordinateurs—et sans doute jardinier et réparateur de maison et d'arbres. L'ouragan ici nous a rendu la vie difficile pendant 5 ou 6 jours: ni lumière, ni eau, ni cuisine, ni bain. Mais les nombreuses branches tombées n'ont du moins pas démoli le toit! On revit ces jours-ci et balaie! Les ouragans sont si beaux en peinture ("Maine Coast in fury") et en poésie: "Car c'est l'ouragan qui gouverne / Toute cette étrange caverne / que nous nommons création," dit Hugo dans "Les Mages." Mais je préfère de beaucoup "Éclaircie" dans le même volume des *Contemplations!*

Nos affectueuses salutations à Sherry. Je suis si content qu'elle et vous ayez eu un agréable séjour à Paris.

J'inclus un récent compte-rendu, touchant à un critique et maître (Auerbach) que vous avez dû connaître.

Bien des amitiés,<br>Henri

## À Konrad Bieber:

[postcard]<br>Le 31—X—85

Cher Konrad,

Nous avons perdu—mais la très belle lettre de Vercors vous récompense & me touche. Elle apporte la preuve qu'il y a tout de même quelques hommes de lettres qui restent modestes! Simon, rencontré une fois ou deux, est un très brave homme et dans ses premiers livres, avait du talent. Depuis il est devenu illisible. C'est un prix qui tombe droit dans l'eau. Personne ne va même essayer de lire ses romans. Tant pis!

Cela va bien pour moi—j'accomplis bien peu. Mais je me sens pour le moment en ferme santé. Je vous admire tous deux de résister aux maux de l'âge et de savoir maintenir votre mère en forme. Le nouveau petit-fils doit la réjouir. Mes vœux à Tom & à sa femme et à vous deux.

Henri

## À Gita May:

Nov. 7, 1985

Chère amie,

    Vous n'attendez sans doute pas de réponse; mais je ne puis m'empêcher de vous dire quel plaisir intellectuel c'est de lire un exposé aussi complet, aussi lucide, harmonieusement organisé que votre essai sur G. Sand. Vous savez lui rendre justice avec "fairness" et tact. Nul romantique n'a senti comme elle la musique. *Spiridion* est un étrange et saisissant roman "religieux," et les lettres d'amour à Bourges sont parmi les plus vraies écrites par des auteurs du siècle dernier. Merci de m'avoir communiqué ce très bel essai.

Mon amitié,<br>Henri Peyre

## To Robert Hirschfield:

Henri Peyre<br>290 North Avenue<br>Westport, Conn. 06880<br>Nov. 26—1985

Dear Dean Hirschfield:

    I gather that some delay has occurred, and difficulties may have arisen before the *Apostrophes* project could start. It may be that doubts have also come up about the advisability of undertaking an ambitious program of twenty or more presentations, of over one hour each, in a foreign language and that there is some uncertainty as to the kind of audience or of viewers the emissions would reach and how they might be received. May I say that I confess to entertaining some doubts myself;

and, for what they are worth, I am taking the liberty of submitting them to you and to the very competent persons assisting you on this project.

The unexpected and remarkable success of Pivot's *Apostrophes* in France is due in part to certain features of French life which may not be duplicated here. One is the very large share allotted in France to literature and to literary controversies and debates. Those are granted far more time on television than is customary in this country, where political news, crimes, accidents, and certainly publicity, are stressed on TV. A number of the men of letters who appear on *Apostrophes* or whose works are discussed there are known to the French audiences, through articles which they contribute to dailies and weeklies; those articles (often casual remarks and "chronicles" on almost any topic of current interest) are often featured prominently on the first page of newspapers. If similar essays are printed at all in the American press, they are relegated to a modest and obscure place on page 30 or 40. Teachers and writers make up two thirds of the cabinets or ministers of the present government. Prime ministers and Presidents of the French Republic (De Gaulle, Pompidou, Giscard d'Estaing, Mitterrand), Mitterrand's ministers and close advisers such as Attali, Debray, Lang, have all written books, even volumes of verse or, like a predecessor of Mitterrand, Edgar Faure, detective stories. Neither F.D.R. nor Reagan was expected to have written books (unless it be, some day, their memoirs, with the help of "ghosts") or to have read much Shakespeare, Jane Austen, Melville, Tolstoy or the Bible.

The books discussed on *Apostrophes* are in majority recent volumes, of passing interest, which viewers of the program may be tempted to purchase or to borrow from libraries. Very few of them would be available in New York, Chicago, Dallas or Seattle. Even fewer could be found for sale in American bookshops, for a number of reasons. One of those reasons is that such French books are markedly more expensive over here, in part because the unsold copies cannot be returned readily or easily to the publishing house in France. Most of the books discussed are too recent to have been translated.

It also happens that a number of authors presented or discussed on *Apostrophes* are by foreign, i.e. non French authors (Kafka, Kundera, Styron, Scott Fitzgerald, Fred. Prokosch, Thomas Buchanan, Gordon Liddy, Jane Fonda) or they treat non-French authors (Byron, for example, or Oscar Wilde) or figures once well known (Beau Brummell) on whom French biographers happen to have written lately. Those may not appear so interesting or novel to audiences in this country as they do in Europe.

Two kinds of subjects are granted much space in *Apostrophes*. One is education in France, which happens to be in a critical and much debated state just now; e.g. No. 22, "De l'école à l'université" and No. 8: "des fabriques de cancres," that is, schools producing uncultured misfits. There are problems galore in American education, but, for a number of reasons (multiracial and multilingual society, autonomy of each state in educational matters, the pragmatic and technological orientation of society), they are very different from the French ones.

The other subject is women; "le Corps," chiefly the female body, No. 3; women's literature ("romans d'amour," No. 1); seducers (in the feminine, "séductrices"), No. 10; Women in the couple, No. 14; women with strong personalities (femmes de caractère, No.17); feminist movements, Lesbianism are granted much attention which is natural enough. But the result is that several of the programs may appear here as a more fitting subject for "ladies'" magazines than for high-brow, or even low-brow, female graduates of Hunter, Vassar, Wellesley, who might over here be the ones most familiar with French and interested in intellectual developments abroad.

This is in no way meant to be negative. But I wonder about the wisdom of undertaking such a large number of apostrophic emissions without as yet any inkling on how they will be received or without sorting out the most appropriate. My advanced years may make me too prudent. But I would feel reassured if Ms. Brysac, Ms. Childes, perhaps Prof. Jack Kneller reflected on the possible difficulties to be encountered.

Yours very sincerely,
Henri Peyre

## À son frère et à sa belle-sœur:

Le 10 décembre 85

... Je n'ai rien dit sur la santé—c'est qu'il n'y a rien à dire de neuf, et tant mieux. Les yeux de Diane lui donnent quelque souci—possibilité (*lointaine*) de cataracte—mais deux amies ont passé par là, et il semble qu'on opère et corrige cela en quelques heures. Le mot m'a toujours fait peur. Étonnamment, car je lis toute la journée, mes yeux à moi ne me donnent pas d'ennui. Que ferais-je sans cela? Je ne suis guère méditatif, pas du tout mélomane, et peu amateur de conversations, téléphoniques ou orales. On verra? Quant à mes organes situés plus bas, cœur, poumon, ils fonctionnent; je ne les force pas. Je suis vite à bout de souffle, ne prends guère de risque. Il est clair que mon organisme est usé; on le serait à moins, à 85 ans passés. Ma hernie ne semble pas empirer. Je vis au jour le jour. Si tout va bien, en février, je franchirai le cap des 85 ans — ce que je ne croyais certes pas pouvoir espérer, en juillet dernier. Cela m'intimide. . . .

## To John W. Kneller:

290 North Avenue<br>
Westport, CT 06880<br>
226-4868<br>
Tuesday, Dec. 10, 85

Dear Jack,

I hope the advent of real winter has found you and your wife in fine health and in good spirits. I have not stopped on the tenth floor and I am sparing of my efforts. My health is frail and I feel fortunate that I am still surviving at close to 85.

My *Apostrophes* talk proved a much more burdensome work than I had imagined when I imprudently accepted it. It requires much reading, hunting for recent books which the Yale Library does not as yet own, cutting down the introductions to one minute and 25 seconds. It would be far easier to write four pages than three-quarters of one! To be quite candid with you, I had doubts and scruples about offering one hour and a quarter in French to an audience probably not well used to oral French. The program is for French audiences in France and not for the highbrow or the well-informed at that. I passed on my scruples and hesitations to Dean Hirschfield: an intelligent and vigorous man, eager to feed his cable TV programs, whom I enjoyed meeting. His assistant, Claire Childes, is a well-informed, cultured lady, very helpful. Hirschfield is convinced that the whole operation is worthwhile. So I continue doing introductions or opening remarks and will have them on a screen, somewhere in Brooklyn, if I understand right. For your information a copy of my letter stating my hesitations (and probably my regrets for having undertaken that mission) is enclosed.

I hope your brother is by now in perfect health. My—and Diana's— warm wishes for the New Year.

Cordially,<br>Henri

## À Mary Ann Caws:

Le 3 janvier 1986

Chère Mary Ann,

Ce chiffre de 1986 m'impressionne! Je vais toucher à ma 85e année! Et cela fera plus de soixante ans que, jeune insolent croyant tout savoir ou presque, j'ouvrais à Bryn Mawr ma carrière américaine, me croyant invulnérable—mais secrètement intimidé par tant de présence féminine et l'œil soupçonneux des féministes couronnées. Depuis, et de loin, mon respect pour ce College et ses anciennes comme vous n'a fait que croître.

J'ai quelque remords d'avoir par mégarde et sans doute indiscrètement conservé ces feuilles d'un caractère autobiographique que vous aviez jointes à votre projet "Guggenheim." J'ai, bien sûr, écrit il y a déjà pas mal de temps. Merci de m'avoir laissé lire ceci—qui m'a impressionné.

Une carte de vous suggérait que je parle au Centre en février. J'ai négligé d'y répondre. En vérité, je n'y connais plus personne, sauf quelques collègues déjà âgés, et je me sens bien ancien pour me mettre en avant ou me faire écouter. Très franchement, je crois que des voix neuves seraient mieux qualifiées. Je me suis accoutumé à une existence de paresse et de relecture de vieux livres, depuis ma retraite définitive—et je dois avouer que mes parutions "apostrophiques," sous l'égide du Doyen de l'audiovisuel et de la charmante organisatrice, Claire Childes, m'embarrassent et m'exaspèrent un peu. Il y faut surveiller la couleur de sa cravate, les plis de sa veste (et les rides de son visage), le ton de sa voix, les particularités de son accent. Quelqu'un de plus bouillant et dynamique eût été un meilleur choix—vous sûrement, ou Peter. Nous verrons si je tiendrai jusqu'au bout!

La raison majeure de mon hésitation est d'ailleurs que, lassé et rebuté par les livres récents que j'essaie de lire et, je l'avoue, par la manière sautillante de Barthes, celle plus lourde et appuyée de Foucault (pour ne dire du mal que des morts), je me suis récemment tourné vers le passé. Sans doute est-on las de Victor Hugo, dont j'aurais été tenté d'esquisser une démolition. J'ai relu pas mal de Claudel et, selon le genre d'auditoire, "Claudel and woman" ou "Claudel & the eternal feminine" ou, dans un autre ordre, "Claudel & English Literature" pourrait être une possibilité. Ou "Raymond Aron & French American relations": je l'ai beaucoup relu car à Paris on s'est mis, depuis ses *Mémoires* et sa mort (et par opposition à Sartre), à beaucoup parler de lui. J'ai enfin rédigé un essai sur "Protestantism & French Literature," pour me libérer, peut-être, du soupçon d'être condamné à ennuyer, qui poursuit les anciens Protestants, même devenus des athées militants. Mais un tel titre est peu attrayant. À vrai dire, je ne sais plus trop à quoi s'intéressent surtout les jeunes.

Diane est à ses examens à Brooklyn & vous enverrait ses amitiés—et à vos deux grands enfants. Je vous adresse les miennes, et nos vœux, et espère que la santé de votre mère ne vous a pas récemment trop inquiétée. Si vous devez passer plusieurs mois, en 1986, en Europe, nos pensées, un peu jalouses (car je ne voyage plus guère), vous accompagneront.

Bien des choses à tous deux,
Henri

## To John W. Kneller:

January 13, 1986

Dear Jack,

Somehow I had hoped I would see you during this season of turmoil and festivities. But Brice, one or two sons of Diana, friends visited here, and the cold weather does not encourage me to venture outside much. I feared, having had no news from you, that perhaps you were unwell—or your wife. I hope it is not the case. I cannot think of you as submitting to disease.

You are one of the very best connoisseurs and lovers of poetry. Have this essay which I send you as a modest tribute. I still write a little now and then but won't undertake any long project. My "accident" last summer has been a warning and the nearness of my 85th anniversary impresses me.

I shall not blame you for having suggested your old teacher, whom you always overesteemed, for the Apostrophes undertaking. I must confess that I find it trying to my health and to my patience. A much younger person should have been chosen. The repetitious rehearsals, the exacting and fussy attention to details of speech, of physical appearance, to gestures teach me how incredibly patient actors and politicians must be when submitting to audiovisual ordeals.

Our best to Sherry and yourself,<br>Henri

## À son frère et à sa belle-sœur:

Le 22 janvier 86

Chère Micheline, cher Jacques,

Journée sereine ici, qui tranche sur le froid très dur qui a sévi vers le milieu du mois. Je viens de faire une promenade au soleil, le long d'un fleuve qui n'a pas l'impétuosité du Rhône, n'est bordé que de maisons vulgaires. Rien de ces fenêtres qui reflétaient le soleil, de ces échappées vers la Tour Philippe le Bel & le Palais, que nous nous arrêtions, Papa & moi, pour contempler, lors de nos promenades. Bien souvent, ces souvenirs très chers me reviennent; et, incliné à la réserve comme je l'étais, craignant peut-être d'être trop influencé, je regrette amèrement d'avoir trop peu questionné Papa sur son passé, de m'être trop peu confié moi-même. Je m'écartais sottement de ce qui était méridional, histoire locale et . . . jardinage, qui n'a jamais été mon fort. Paris, l'Angleterre m'attiraient, par contraste. Les souvenirs qui affluent à ma mémoire de vieux, et d'oisif, sont mêlés de regrets. Du moins, surtout après ces inoubliables semaines passées chez vous en 1985, je me sens très proche du couple que vous êtes—aimant, affectueux, généreux et stimulant pour nos esprits d'émigrés. . . .

## To Robert G. Cohn:

290 North Avenue, Westport, Ct. 06880
Jan. 28 / 86

Dear Bob,

    I like every word of your letter very much & I applaud your courageous & obstinate fight for the Humanities & for the intelligent teaching of literature. You may go against the grain, as I do & have been doing for some time, but I cannot believe that our protests will have been in vain. The reactions of former students of mine, of others who traveled in Russia lately and were struck by the paramount interest taken by Russians (Marx-trained probably) in their great writers, & the protests here of Defaux (Johns Hopkins) & others against the merging of literature, & of French, into social, inter-disciplinary programs, "genres" and categories supposedly "comparative," are similar to yours. Literary studies at Yale were gravely hurt by well-meaning persons, like the late Paul de Man & Geoffrey Hartman. Montaigne, Racine, Baudelaire, Mallarmé hardly count for them. Their sacred texts are an obscure essay of Rousseau on language, Hoelderlin, Nietzsche. Well & good! But literary values should not be lightly sacrificed by the very persons to whom they have been entrusted. Your letter to Juilland is cogent & impressive. I hope he & you can reverse a trend which is not in the interest of the future generations that we are supposed to prepare for some sort of leadership.

    At 85, I am too old to put up fights and my advice would be disregarded. I talk, when I have a chance, along the lines which you indicate: but the state of our studies fills me with sadness. Out of old, fond souvenirs which we share, I'll send you a couple of admonitions or of amateurish articles, such as I indulge in now & then. Sometime, give me news of your wife, who made a strong impression on me, & of your son. I take it you are still far from retirement yourself.

My very warm wishes,
Henri

I shall be deeply touched by your gift of new & revised books. The *one* & only thing I am proud of is the continued "attachement" shown by a few generous & very gifted former students. I had some trouble (heart) last August, but, somehow, survived it & am frail, but in good spirits.

## À Kurt et Florence Weinberg:

> 290 North Avenue
> Westport, Ct. 06880
> Le 28.1.86

Chers Kurt et amie des grottes,

J'apprends que Kurt a été éprouvé par une maladie redoutable, et que ma vieillesse redoute fort. Qu'en est-il? Comment supporte-t-il cette épreuve, et comment va son moral? J'imagine qu'il subit, sur le tard, les contrecoups de la dure existence qui lui avait été imposée par les années de Nazisme & de guerre. Lit-il? Écrit-il?

Je repense souvent aux cavernes (plus poétiquement appelées "antres") que vous explorez—d'Homère et Porphyre, à quelques romans récents et médiocres, placés dans les grottes du Périgord. Où en est ce grandiose ouvrage?

Ma santé m'a donné de sérieux ennuis. Finis les longs espoirs et les publications de longue haleine. Après tout, j'atteins, à près de 85 ans, l'âge de la résignation au silence! Je survis—placidement.

> Acceptez, sur ce gauche papier, les vœux affectueux d'un très ancien & fidèle ami.
> Henri Peyre

## À Mary Ann Caws:

> Samedi 8 février 1986

Chère Mary Ann,

J'ai été désolé d'ajouter à vos soucis et tâches en cette difficile période, en décommandant ma venue à N. York hier. Mais la neige ici s'accumulait: j'aurais eu de la peine à arriver jusqu'à la gare; et l'auditoire aurait été fort clairsemé de toute manière, par cet après-midi de neige et de boue.

S'il est vraiment désirable que j'apparaisse au "Centre," avec ma lassitude de 85 hivers et mon sujet rébarbatif, arrangez un autre jour. Je ne suis pris ici que le lundi, par des soucis "domestiques"—libre les autres jours. Je me déplace rarement, et suis heureux que mes simagrées devant le groupe de techniciens que j'apostrophe (& qui corrigent ma diction, mon apparence vestimentaire, & le reste) soient terminées. C'était une plus grande fatigue que je n'aurais cru et cela m'a confirmé dans ma conviction que le rôle d'acteur n'était certes pas le mien.

Si vous *deviez* annoncer à nouveau un titre, voulez-vous le modifier en "Protestantism in *French* Literature" ou même "Is There a French Protestant Literature?" Il paraît difficile de ne pas répandre de l'ennui avec la promesse d'un tel sermon—par un incroyant déterminé.

Votre annonce officielle de votre libération (de vos fonctions exécutives) inspirera bien des regrets; mais vous avez assez de soucis, et d'ailleurs d'engagements oratoires & de projets d'écrits, pour avoir droit à un peu de loisir. Un jour prochain, vous nous direz si nous pouvons en quelque mesure, Diane & moi, amicalement vous aider—et vous nous parlerez aussi de votre fille si supérieurement douée et de ses plans.

Bien des amitiés de nous deux, enneigés ici et maugréant contre ce triste hiver,

Henri

## À Alex Szogyi:

Febr. 4/86

Cher Alex,

Je vous renvoie ce très flatteur, & hautement mérité, témoignage. Conservez-le—et je vous dis merci pour cette carte tigrée. Vous vous croyez parfois le veau dévoré par quelque tigresse; mais vous n'avez rien de cet animal trop mésestimé & dont, quand je vivais en France, je dégustais avec plaisir les escalopes. Vous êtes un combatif—mais sans furie.

Je sais mal, ou je ne sais rien, de ce qui se passe au Centre, dont je me tiens à l'écart, car je ne vais guère à N.Y. & ne veux en rien gêner mes successeurs. Mais, bien imprudemment, j'avais accepté la requête du Doyen de l'Audiovisuel, Dean Robert Hirschfield, d'écrire de brèves introductions à 24 Apostrophes. Écrire, & faire court, était déjà un gros labeur. Mais il m'a fallu, par matinées gelées d'hiver, aller au centre d'enregistrement de 195 Chambers St. (un Community College, fort bien équipé) & là me soumettre à des répétitions sans nombre, par "teleprompter": corrections de ma cravate, mon gilet, mes cheveux, mes poses; parfois accidents mécaniques. J'ai appris que je n'aurais jamais pu ou voulu être acteur; encore moins, "star." Je n'ai aucun don pour cela — et comme nous n'avons pas ici de videocassette ou de câble, je ne me verrai pas dans mes maladroites poses histrioniques.

Enfin c'est terminé & je retrouve mon calme de vieux retraité. Diane prend de moi le soin le plus affectueux, car je suis souvent grognon. Pour m'améliorer, j'essaie de lire des comiques: Feydeau! Shepard! Et même Shaw, mais je reste un obstiné agélaste. Je vous admire de sentir le théâtre & d'y jouer avec talent.

Mille bonnes choses,<br>Henri

## À son frère et à sa belle-sœur:

9 février 86

... La médecine est loin, ici, d'être gratuite! Aussi y a-t-il une révolte contre les docteurs, riches et parfois bien pressés ou maladroits. On les accuse beaucoup de tuer, ou de mutiler, les malades. Article inclus que Micheline peu traduire. Nous en avons eu plusieurs cas: d'adolescentes restées handicapées à vie par des traitements trop brutaux ("tests," pilules, expérimentation imprudente) par des psychiatres. Les modes sévissent en ces matières. J'en ai été la victime quand, il y a 30 ans, le dentiste m'a privé de beaucoup de mes dents pour les remplacer par des dentiers qui, usés ces temps-ci ou par suite de contraction de mes gencives, tiennent mal en place. Quand je rencontre mon ancien dentiste (retiré, car il est riche, et s'exerçant à la littérature pour distraire ses loisirs) me dit avec le sourire: "Les techniques se sont améliorées depuis. Aujourd'hui, on ne vous arracherait plus vos dents aussi vite." Seulement, elles ne repoussent pas. Il est vrai que nul ne prévoyait (car je menais alors une vie très intense, pressée qui eût dû m'user) que je vivrais jusqu'à 85 ans. Ce même dentiste, artiste amateur, avait moulé mon visage et fait de moi un masque, comme celui de Pascal mort dans les éditions des *Pensées*. Je l'avais avec mépris fourré à la cave dans un débarras, où Brice l'a retrouvé. Diane s'en est saisie et l'a suspendu dans son appartement new-yorkais, à côté de 2 ou 3 masques primitifs du Congo ou du Bénin....

## À Kurt et Florence Weinberg:

290 North Ave.
Westport, Ct. 06880
Le 18 février 86

Chers amis,

Merci de votre double lettre. Elle m'a beaucoup touché—et profondément attristé aussi. Moi non plus, je ne parle pas volontiers de maladies, et ma chance (si c'en est une) est que, malgré 2 ou 3 atteintes assez sérieuses à mon cœur, j'atteins ces jours-ci à ma 85e année. Je survis, à condition de ne me remuer que le moins possible.

Mais il m'arrive souvent de me demander si cet effort pour vivre en vaut la peine. Que ce monde est affligeant! Bêtises et perfidies des hommes politiques; corruption; tromperie universelle. J'aurais tant voulu conserver la foi que j'avais en l'Amérique dans mes années d'adolescence. Cette foi vacille plus que jamais.

Mais assez de ma morosité. Il pleut sur la neige, il pleut jusque dans la maison ici. Je me demande ce qu'il en est à Rochester & j'imagine Kurt galopant parmi la neige, méditant quelque interprétation hardie de Mallarmé ou de Kafka.

Ce mot voudrait surtout dire à Florence que, si je puis en rien aider à faire paraître un de ses livres, je le ferai volontiers—dans la mesure où mon nom de "rétro" (comme nous appellent les jeunes en France) a quelque poids. Mon souvenir de son *Rabelais* est bien vague; mais si vous avez, Florence, une lettre de moi sur ce sujet, utilisez-la et communiquez-la à Lang. Sinon, je devrai jeter un coup d'œil au MS.

Pour l'"Antre," je me rappelle avoir écrit (à Guggenheim Foundation, je crois) la lettre la plus chaude jamais. Mon échec m'a attristé, & vexé. Il faut bien le dire: il y a comme une hiérarchie, et bien de l'inégalité, dans les rangs que nous assignent les comités de sélection. Il est difficile de pousser un professeur d'une institution peu connue au-dessus de quelqu'un qui est à Stanford, Chicago, Harvard. Ma compétence n'est certes pas universelle. Mais si je puis vous aider en quelque chose, Florence, dites-le moi sans vous gêner.

Excusez ce mot hâtif mais qui se veut, plus que jamais, d'amitié & de sympathie.
Henri

## À Paul Archambault:

Le 20 février 1986

Cher Monsieur Archambault:

Votre présent m'arrive, avec quelque retard (car mon adresse, depuis 1981, est ci-dessus: celle d'un retraité), mais juste avant la clôture de ma 85e année. Il me touche fort. Je connaissais assez bien Les *Angoisses* . . . et avais dirigé à Yale une thèse de Secor sur ce livre; mais je n'avais jamais lu ces Épîtres, & ce que vous dites avec franchise du style, m'inspire peu de regrets. Mais il y a là des lettres assez fortes, comme la Xe, et la IVe des "Invectives"—et une forte personnalité. Vous étiez l'homme désigné pour interpréter & traduire ces épîtres; et votre femme, au sourire fin et intelligent, doit vous avoir inspiré & aidé. Vous avez pour vous une riche connaissance des Anciens (Cicéron, Ovide, Diogène Laerce), des Provençaux et du Moyen Age. Et votre méthode de travail et d'interprétation est sérieuse, libre des modes et de toute prétention. Le livre se lit fort bien, et enrichit & nuance notre idée de la Renaissance et des femmes alors. J'avais plusieurs fois suggéré à des jeunes de songer à une anthologie des lettres (imaginaires le plus souvent) de la femme abandonnée: Hérodiades, Héloïse, Helisenne, peut-être Louise Labbé, la soi-disant religieuse portugaise, Mlle de Lespinasse, Juliette Drouet, "La Voix humaine" de Cocteau, la femme trahie dans L'*Échange* de Claudel, etc. Mais les féministes n'aimeraient guère cela et un mâle serait accusé de "chauvinisme porcin."

Que devenez-vous par ailleurs? J'ai parfois des nouvelles de J. H. Matthews, mais il est si susceptible que l'on préfère ne pas trop s'approcher de lui. À mon grand âge, je voyage d'ailleurs très peu et Syracuse est pour moi un beau nom et un souvenir d'autrefois. Vos Presses ont présenté ce livre avec élégance. Mes compliments.

Mes remerciements aussi à votre femme et mon très amical souvenir.

Henri Peyre

## À Germaine Brée:

290 North Avenue, Westport, Ct. 06880
Febr. 28/86 (226–4868)

Chère Germaine

Je suis heureux, & Diane l'est également, de vous savoir vaillante, voyageuse, échangeant un décor pour un autre et résistant à cet hiver que je trouve éprouvant. Il est vrai que j'ai franchi l'autre jour le cap de la 85e année: j'en suis intimidé, ébranlé et ressens comme une injustice, en ma faveur, cette survie alors que tant d'autres ont disparu. La sollicitude que me prodigue Diane seule m'a permis de subsister ainsi.

Peut-être, en avril, voudrez-vous, de Northampton, venir nous rendre visite? Il se trouve qu'en mars un neveu à moi (45 ans environ), sa femme et leurs deux fillettes (2 & 6 ans) vont, de France, venir aux Etats-Unis—lui, pour affaires; eux, par curiosité. Ils occuperont l'appartement de N. York une partie du mois & nous serons pas mal pris avec eux. Puis le second fils de Diane, Marco, renonçant au Japon, arrivera vers Pâques et sans doute logera à N.Y. et prendra des cours (de sociologie) au Graduate Center. Son retour nous réjouira.

Je n'irai pas au Colloque "Duras"; mais peut-être vous lirai-je, si vous écrivez votre communication. Je me déplace le moins possible. Diane goûte fort *Moderato Cantabile* &, je crois, doit l'enseigner. Moi aussi, & j'ai aimé plusieurs de ses films. Je suis tiède envers ses romans récents, *La Douleur* surtout; et je ne lui pardonne pas l'ennui dont m'a accablé l'interminable *Marin de Gibraltar* et la déception causée par les *Petits Chevaux de Tarquinia*, au titre alléchant. J'admire votre compréhension, plus généreuse que ma méchante humeur.

Nous allons assez bien, entourés de neige & de boue. La vision de Winston Salem en fleurs, au printemps dernier, et le souvenir de tant de gentillesse là-bas illuminent notre maussade humeur.

Profonde affection,
Henri

## To Robert Penn Warren:

March 1—1986

Dear Red,

Congratulations, I know, sound vain. Yet accept a very simple & heart-felt note. Diana & I truly love you & Eleanor, admire you, & cherish your friendship, & we are naively but profoundly proud to know you. You have made Westport (which I, at first, took to be a swarm of Philistines) synonymous with poetry & a thing of beauty. The evening last year of celebration under the tent with a feast worthy of sovereigns at the "camp du drap d'or," harmoniously orchestrated by Eleanor remains unforgettable in our memories. I was flattered that you generously attended the dinner marking my 85th year, & my son is immensely proud to have spoken with you. "We must not count years. For happiness has no measurable pace." I often read, & reread, your poetry. Even if you were to compose invectives at the "Empire of evil," funeral dirges for Reagan, joyful odes to departing tyrants, palinodes cursing our allies of yesterday in Manila, Hawaii & Chile, they would be great poetry.

Your children must be proud of their father, & of a mother who has ceaselessly understood & inspired you. Happy April 24 & our deep affection,

Henry & Diana

## To Florence Weinberg:

290 North Ave.
Westport, Ct. 06880
March 12/86

Dear Florence,

I had known for many years that you were a remarkably learned person, as well as a person of delicate taste, an artist in your life & the ONE companion who could love, understand, inspire that exceptional man, Kurt. But you wear your immense knowledge with such grace, you organize your demonstrations with such mastery & lure your reader to share them with such gentle tact that I had not fully realized that, with your rare modesty, you are one of the érudits beyond compare today. Your place is not at St. John Fisher but at the Princeton Institute for Advanced Study. You, of all persons, should be freed from the drudgery of reading papers & correcting exams. I read your book at once, understood or assimilated only a portion of it, but I enjoyed it greatly because I learned so much from it: I, who never reread Rabelais & professed to remain an obdurate "agélaste" when I confront him, found Fischart almost attractive—& your analyses of the quotes from his version or recreation are refined and subtly convincing. You truly seem to have been, & stubbornly remained, joyful, elated, "bacchic" if un-Christian, when diving into the literature of heraldry & necrophilia. Yet what a task it must have been to order your sources & references, check all the proper names & learned languages in your proofs, reread & revised the MS. A staggering enterprise. And the book, discreetly illustrated, closely printed, is artistic!

It is good to hear that Kurt remains courageous, patient, impetuous on his mare &, I know, appreciative of your devotion. I do not have his mettle & my wearied limbs could not guide a horse. At best, I walk, very little &, luckily, can still drive. Being over 85 is impressive. I almost feel heroic.

Many thanks & warm congratulations to both of you.

Henri

## To Haskell Block:

March 17

Dear Haskell,

I am touched that you should remember to offer me reprints of your fine articles. They bring me some welcome break in my very monotonous life. I enjoyed every one of them; your very ingenious reflections on silence in modern poetry. It's a rich & relatively new theme which I hope you may pursue some day. Your range of acquaintance with modern poetry in several languages is broad & you have an unmatched skill for rapprochements. On the value of poetical revelations of poetry, I resist more than you do if I happen to know the foreign language intimately; but I admire those who attempt it. Deep down, I regret that both Baudelaire & Mallarmé wasted their time & their ingeniousness on Poe, when they could have tried with other English poets, Shakespeare & Keats included. But I happen to be in a minority among the French. Even as a teenager I failed to be moved by Poe's stories & later I thought Valéry either lacked discrimination or indulged preposterous paradoxes when he made so much of Poe—far more than ever Baudelaire himself had done. If I find an article or two I once wrote on that subject, I'll send them off to you, as the wisest & coolest expert in that province of comparative studies.

I trust all is well with you. I lead a quiet, over-prolonged life myself & enjoy my retirement—after half a century or more of reading theses & advising the young. Diana takes good care of me & is admirably & tirelessly active herself.

> With my very cordial thanks & wishes,
> Henri Peyre

## To Robert G. Cohn:

April 14—86

Dear Bob,

Your second, wrathful, indignant letter reached me just before the weekend. It filled me with sadness, because I am deeply attached to you, also deeply appreciative of your rare qualities as a sensitive human being & a passionate & generous soul; and you are hurt, wounded by what is happening in our profession, & ruining the humanities at Stanford. Your protest is beautifully phrased, witty, indignant & should lead several of your colleagues to pause. I am embarrassed to see my name mentioned; for I have the awareness of being a "has been" & wish only to yield to those like you, more gifted & more combative than myself. But I subscribe to every line of your beautiful manifesto. That drowning, stifling of literary values into a potpourri of pseudo-sciences is nothing less than an assault against not just tradition, but intelligence & honesty. One wonders what students trained in that manner will turn into. I like & esteem Serres, & some of Girard's books: both are very gifted persons; but also outrageously partial & dogmatic. There should be room in a department for other approaches than theirs & for sheer enjoyment of beauty. Do not allow yourself to become bitter and to indulge polemics if it turns into self-destructiveness. What you say, represent & write is far too valuable for that, & it will outlive the obscurist & verbose theories of those who at present disagree with us. Go to your semester in Touraine with a free & forgiving mind; enjoy your stay there; let the students profit by your example of a lover of poetry & of an interpreter of aesthetic & ethical values who has known how to resort wisely to the help which anthropology, psychoanalysis, & other more or less "scientific" disciplines can afford. As you look back, you may tell yourself that you have revealed & shared with others, in Mallarmé, Rimbaud, & innumerable others, "things which have been kept secret," if not "from the foundation of the world," at least to many duller & more cowardly minds.

Adding a few words re: your previous letters, I, too, regret the change for the worse which has come over Jean P. Richard. His first & his second volumes offered such promises! What is there in the Paris atmosphere which corrupts & waylays people like him—& even Genette? As to Barbara Johnson, she utters the most preposterous statements (on Baudelaire's poems in prose among others) & is not contradicted or criticized! Mallarmé always retained a sense of humor &, more precious still, a gentle irony, even if he accepted the rhyme "Hamlet-lait" & was enraptured by the sounds in "Ulalume." Too bad we do not have a recording of his recitation of his own "Tel qu'en lui-même"—& of the English version of it which he sent to the lady of Baltimore. We do have recordings, I am told, of Valéry's own poetry, with every other line being made "a vers faux" by the poet's southern accent.

Maintain your own, original & creative "divagations" & your own sense of moderation in the face of dissent, error, foolishness & your admirable honesty & "purity," even if there are quagmires close to you!

Congratulations & love to your wife & inspirer.<br>Henri

## À Eléonore Zimmermann:

[postcard]<br>Le 20 avril 86

Chère Eléonore,

Merci de votre souvenir parisien. J'espère que l'installation ne vous a pas donné trop de peine: je déteste déménager et réorganiser mes maigres possessions. Je vous imagine entre Voltaire et les Filles du Calvaire: ce nom m'avait toujours fait rêver. Et, lors de mes années de "chairman," je me comparais volontiers à St. Sébastien, "la plaie et le couteau." J'ai tout de même survécu, paré les coups au cœur comme un démon de Goya, et passé mon 85e anniversaire. Long, froid hiver ici: divers ennuis. Mais nous allons assez bien.

Agréable été et fidèles pensées,<br>Henri

## À Victor Brombert:

Le 23 mai 86

Bien cher Victor,

Intimidé, embarrassé, je sors, pour une fois, mon seul convenable papier à lettres. Jamais je n'avais pensé que vous prendriez au sérieux ma sotte taquinerie sur la rareté de vos épîtres! Jamais je ne me suis senti loin de vous; encore moins, "estranged," négligé. Beth est sans doute la femme que j'admire le plus au monde, dont la conversation me provoque, me stimule, m'instruit—en les domaines les plus variés, de la musique, l'art, les papes de la Renaissance, aux experts en amours mâles. Votre fille a une chaleur de cœur, une vivacité d'esprit, une profondeur dans le regard qui nous vont au cœur, à Diane & à moi. Et elle stimule, s'il en était besoin, mon opposition à toute foi. Et vous, Victor, vous êtes un tendre en même temps qu'un fort. Si j'ai pu jadis faire quelque impression sur votre formation intellectuelle, les rôles sont bien renversés. Je suis le premier à dire votre supériorité intellectuelle. Vous nous dépassez tous, Levin, moi, *et al.*, car jamais vous ne consentez à une seule banalité ou à écrire rien de facile ou de déjà-dit. Je ne vous ferais pas rougir en vous disant cela lors de votre prochaine visite, mais le papier ne rougit pas. Ne vous fatiguez pas à l'excès; répudiez les tâches trop accaparantes et les discussions vaines. Ce que vous découvrez dans chacun de vos articles, en sondant les mots, les images, déchiffrant les symboles, reconstituant les personnages, fait mon admiration & mon envie.

Votre lettre m'a touché—et je venais de lire votre essai sur les trains. Il est trop riche, trop précis dans ses allusions, trop suggestif pour rester sous cette forme. Faites en un petit livre, abondamment illustré. Cela frapperait, et se vendrait. Je suis de ceux, nombreux sans doute, dont les plus chers souvenirs de rêverie, de mélancoliques départs, de rendez-vous donnés à quelque personne chère aux gares parisiennes et à d'autres, sont liés à des salles d'attente, à des buffets de gare, même à de grossiers chants de soldats partant pour les manœuvres, à la Gare de l'Est, et criaillant "Il est cocu, le chef de gare."

Je venais de relire votre essai, *très* original, sur Natalie et *Le Lys* balzacien. J'en avais perdu le texte jadis et le livre, en l'honneur de Poulet, trop divers, trop inégal, m'avait peu impressionné. Votre contribution y était de loin la meilleure; comme dans le volume "Flaubert" (mal) arrangé par N. Schor; comme d'autres essais balzaciens de vous (votre très dense et profonde introduction à la Peau de Chagrin). J'ai passé par des phases de colère contre Le Lys, la mauvaise foi, à mes yeux méprisable, de Félix et de son Henriette, contre la sentimentalité. C'est un de mes dadas que Balzac a beaucoup nui à ses romans avec son retour des personnages et l'intrusion de 5 ou 6 noms de ses créations là où elles n'ont que faire. Pourquoi nous souvenir que, et Félix et Natalie, dans d'autres romans, se conduisent comme des salauds? Pourquoi rendre incroyable une aussi longue et fastidieuse lettre-roman que Natalie n'aurait jamais eu la patience de parcourir? J'essaie de persuader Diane, qui doit parler (en 20 minutes) de la femme balzacienne à une réunion à Bryn Mawr les 6 et 7 juin, de louer les courtisanes balzaciennes et d'immoler les dames du *Lys,* d'*Honorine,* de *Béatrix* et leurs ennuyeuses épîtres. Elle me croit un vieillard lubrique! Il est vrai que votre collègue, qui interprète les romans libertins ou de périlleuses liaisons à travers les forteresses de Vauban, ou son mari plus hardi mais moins convaincant encore, n'ont pas été très inspirés en traitant de ces touchantes femmes dont on doit rêver dans le repaire agreste de Princeton.

Mais je me laisse aller à ma méchanceté souterraine et à ma prolixité incorrigible. Au plaisir de vous accueillir le neuf. Laissez-nous savoir l'heure. Diane, au retour de Bryn Mawr, s'arrête à N.Y. pour un ballet le dimanche 8. Votre fils doit terminer heureusement ses années de collège, comme fait Brice ces jours prochains. C'est une libération pour vous, parents.

Chaude affection,<br>
Henri

## To Florence Weinberg:

290 North Avenue, Westport, Ct. 06880
June 3, 1986

Dear Florence,

Kindly excuse this old, old paper, to which I have for years not had any claim or any right. The secretaries, in years past, were convinced that, at my rate of ten letters a day, I could never exhaust the supplies they put aside for me.

I have reread your impressive MS. It is an arduous, demanding reading. It is also a rewarding one. Leaving all compliments aside (a person like you deserves better than flattery & compliments), I do not hesitate to say that it is one of the most learned volumes I have ever read; along with its extraordinarily vast erudition, it has clarity of style, a very harmonious organization; it carries the reader along, so that he never once is tempted to lay the MS aside. There are very few, if any, scholars alive today who could match your range of penetrating reading, your insight into familiar texts rejuvenated by your interpretation & their relatedness to the myth of the cave before & after, Plato, Virgil, Porphyry. You illuminate works on which one thought all had been said: Ulysses & Calypso, Aeschylus, Prometheus, Philoctetes, Vergil's Silenus, an enchanting Horatian poem; &, with perfect naturalness, you pass on to Gottfried, Gawain & Ariosto. Your work is nowhere burdened or shackled by your tremendous erudition: the extensive Greek passages may baffle some readers, but they are no display of pedantry. You embrace anthropology, history of myths, hermeneutics, and throughout, one feels you enjoyed gathering that mass of information and reflecting upon it. I had dabbled in anthropology in my youth (translating Frazer, associating with Malinowski, Evans, Pritchard, Cumont, later Eliade), was once much impressed by Michel Bréal (on Hercules & Cacus), even hailed Proclus as a great philosophical poet. But I had never encountered that sweep of knowledge and that thrill of epiphany which your work communicated, almost effortlessly. You *are* one of the *great* scholars of our time. It is shockingly unjust that, teaching in a small college, you were not selected for grants by Foundations or invited by the Princeton Institute for Advanced Studies, where you belong. Do you have to contribute, yourself, to the expense of publish-

so little news to impart, or to exchange — see no friends, since I have almost none left & accept my boredom resignedly. Brice is taking intensive German language courses at Yale & works some evenings (telephoning people to persuade them to give money to hospitals, their former schools & colleges). I see little, almost nothing of him &, while the Yale Library is being cleaned, the books & catalogues reclassified & displaced, I do not drive to New Haven. Diana is in New York a good deal: her son, back from Japan, stays in her apartment. I do not feel up to visiting there, running for trains, climbing stairs. I choose to sit in the green garden & to read at my leisure. I reopen books which I once had tried (in vain) to like (novels by Jane Austen, Thackeray, Hardy), but I am not attuned to those dull Victorians. Somehow England (where, I think, you & Kenneth were never much inclined to travel) has faded out of my intellectual landscape. I still recite to myself English poetry as a sedative, or to relive, in a Narcissistic & complacent way, the thrills of my first discovery of London & the English countryside. I was 19 then, & naively filled with a sense of wonder at what I thought was exotic & more appealing than my provincial & Protestant French background. Naturally, the persons I knew then are all dead by now. Some nights, in my dreams, I imagine I am myself. Kenneth's disappearance that March weekend was a shock to me, almost a personal blow. We confided very seldom & very little to each other. But he was, like you, in a reserved manner, so understanding & his wide range of intellectual interests stimulated my own curiosity. I had, somehow, partly on account of talks with you, intended to visit Iran before I died. In Cairo, I once had the late Shah attend, smiling & aloof, a lecture of mine in French — in 1938, probably — and I loved to visit Iranian antique dealers & haggle over the price of miniatures. I did not find in any library the book by his widow, which you mentioned; it is probably wiser to let one's dreams of old be quietly buried. I have lately tried to reread the "Thousand and one Nights," the first illustrated book which I cherished at the age of five. I failed to recover my old enthusiasm. I am left even colder by the Old & the New Testaments, when I happen to reopen them. Somehow, the Greek world of myths & of tragedies remains my spiritual climate. The present seems unreal in comparison. I give a nonchalant glance at the N.Y. Times over my cup of coffee in the morning. How prosaic is all the news, Reagan's contradictions, the greed of drug dealers & of politicians, the petty scandals! When the weather permits, or seems inviting, I give up the paper & arrive to the beach & walk for 8 or 10 minutes—my limit—after which I get tired.

Next week, or perhaps early in July, I'll drive to New Haven & trust I'll find you in good spirits. This was just petty talk in lieu of the visit which I would have liked to pay you.

With love.<br>Henri

## To Florence Weinberg:

290 North Ave.<br>Westport, Ct. 06880<br>Aug. 26/86

Dear Florence,

You are an admirable letter writer! If I had been more alert, I would have, much earlier, expressed my appreciation of your beautifully written, touching epistle of late July. But I was constantly complaining of the humid heat, chatting with my brother & his wife (who came from France on their *first* visit ever to America, once I told them I felt too old & frail to travel myself) & probably feeling secretly envious of your immense erudition, which humbles my naive male conceit as it probably does your husband's incredible range of "savoir." His, unlike my limited one, includes the Jewish world, of which I have remained ignorant, Hebrew perhaps, even Arabic, & the deciphering of half-mystical secrets in Kafka, Mallarmé & others. I lately resolved only to reread a few old books & to *un*learn—so as to rid myself of the silly, paralyzing thought that I should no longer accumulate knowledge which I would not transmit to anyone. My envy of you is not only of your erudition; it is also of your flowing, graceful style & of the simplicity with which you describe your Catskills retreat, the pure, clear lake, & your wanderings in the byways near Rochester. I take it that Kurt is in good health & good spirits & that you continue to make his life spiritually rich & rewarding. You are a miracle worker, since you succeeded in helping your mother REPLACE a knee. I never knew that that delicate joint or arrangement of boxes could be replaced! My congratulations to you & Kurt, & my wishes for years of fair health & peace for your mother.

All is well, or appears to be, for me. Diana takes sedulous & comforting care of me, & I have thus far only minor ailments & can afford to disregard them. I vituperate against Reagan & the subservient Senate, worthy successor to Nero's Senate, instead of attacking a non-existent God, as I used to do in my younger days. A cool breeze is blowing just now & will herald a better season. "Adieu! Vive clarté de nos étés trop courts."

Warm wishes for you & Kurt,<br>Henri

## À Tatiana Greene:

Ce 7 sept. 86

Chère amie,

J'apprécie fort l'envoi aimable que vous me faites de ce très intéressant essai, comme j'ai goûté de précédents envois de vous, sur Max Jacob, entre autres. Incroyant obstiné, parfois intransigeant que je suis, je porte un grand intérêt aux questions religieuses et je me suis parfois complu à me plonger dans l'histoire des hérésies—un peu comme le personnage central du récent roman de Updike, *Roger's Version*. Mais, à mon âge, je n'y mêle pas l'érotisme vulgaire que lui prête son créateur.

L'attitude—ou les diverses attitudes—de G. Sand envers le christianisme est un beau & riche sujet. Vous le reprendrez peut-être, ou y conduirez un ou une de vos disciples. Depuis la renaissance des études sandistes—et même avant, avec Jean Pommier—on a accordé enfin à *Spiridion* plus d'attention; et on traite Pierre Leroux moins cavalièrement que le faisaient Maurois et d'autres Français, sottement & exclusivement épris de clarté dite classique. Mais G. Sand a tant écrit, & on la lit si vite, que bien peu ont sondé comme vous le faites *Mlle de la Quintinie* et *Jean Zyska*—que je n'ai jamais lu et que vous me révélez. Vos remarques savantes et fines, et les textes que vous citez p. 147, ouvrent la porte à bien des réflexions. Si j'étais plus jeune, ou si j'enseignais encore, je dirigerais volontiers mon attention & celle d'autrui vers divers aspects de la pensée religieuse de G. Sand. Ses relations avec Renan mériteraient un essai séparé. Je doute fort que la lettre que vous citez page 148 ait été adressée à Renan, qui a toujours soutenu que l'immortalité de l'âme était cent fois plus incroyable que la croyance en Dieu—du moins à ce dieu semi-hégélien qui n'est pas, mais qui sera. Il y a dans la Correspondance de Renan (Œuvres Complètes, C. Lévy, vol. X, pages 380–2) le texte d'une longue lettre de Renan à G. Sand, datée d'août 1863— pleine de considération pour G. Sand. Renan la plaçait très haut, bien avant sa mort, & depuis la lecture de *Spiridion* dans sa jeunesse. Il la met au 1er rang des écrivains français dont la France est fière, dans une lettre du 17 mars 1871 à l'historien allemand Mommsen.

Autre détail pédant, p. 147. G. S. a-t-elle mis au féminin (comme le français le faisait jadis) le mot Évangile—qui est devenu masculin? "L'Évangile éternel" de Joachim de Flore (XIIe siècle) avait été loué par Michelet dans son très beau volume de la Renaissance comme la 1ère apparition de la Renaissance après le sombre Moyen Age.

Encore merci de votre envoi. Je compte lire tout le livre un jour prochain. Merci aussi de votre autre article sur "Le Diable aux Champs" & mon très amical souvenir.

Henri Peyre

## À son frère et à sa belle-sœur:

Le onze sept. 1986

Chère Micheline, cher Jacques,

Journée de chaleur revenue, après quelques bouffées de vent. Il fait même humide et lourd. J'étais dehors, sur la terrasse, sur une des vieilles chaises longues où Micheline lisait parfois, tandis que Jacques égrenait son chapelet de souvenirs et, parfois, d'indignation. Il a conservé une étonnante jeunesse, à dénoncer les injustices politiques, fiscales et sociales. Plus désabusé que lui, je m'en accommode et ne nourris nul espoir de les voir jamais corrigées. Quelque lapin bondissait sur l'herbe récemment fauchée. Hier, c'était une famille de faisans, craintifs et sveltes. Par égard pour mon frère, et pour essayer, faiblement, de le remplacer auprès de Laura (tout en prenant bien garde de ne pas la toucher), j'observe avec plus d'attention cette chienne vieillissante. Elle me paraît si triste— de cette tristesse morne, hébétée, qui est celle d'autres animaux: chevaux, ânes tels que je les ai retrouvés en Egypte, éléphant auquel je rendais souvent visite à Lyon où j'habitais près du parc, et chameaux plus encore. Il semble qu'il n'y ait que les oiseaux pour refléter un peu de joie dans leurs regards—et peut-être, mais j'en doute, le Minou sacré de la rue Dorée—qui m'avait plutôt paru avide et ne répondant aux paroles caressantes que par ses griffures. . . .

## À Eléonore Zimmermann:

Le 2 octobre 1986

Chère Eléonore,

Votre longue, très belle et chaleureuse lettre me comble! J'avais totalement oublié la mienne, et les suggestions ou corrections de pédagogue que j'avais dû y offrir, en vieux et chatouilleux lecteur de manuscrits ou en retraité qui croit avoir des loisirs. Pardonnez ce que j'ai pu dire. J'apprends beaucoup, comme je l'ai toujours fait, à vous lire. Vous avez la maîtrise de trois langues au moins, et d'autant de littératures. Cela est donné à peu d'entre nous. Mon allemand, qui fut la 1ère langue étrangère (à 7 ans), est aujourd'hui bien rouillé. Diane se moque de ma prononciation de l'italien. Et mon grec ancien, longtemps pour moi la plus belle des langues, souffre de la faiblesse croissante de ma mémoire.

Mais assez sur mon "moi" encombrant. J'ai été heureux d'avoir de vos nouvelles, et rassuré. Vous occupez une grande place dans mes affections, et j'avais redouté pour vous le grand vide que laisserait la disparition de votre père. La présence stimulante et compréhensive de Svere a dû vous aider à passer du sentiment de vide affreux à la relative douceur des souvenirs. Et l'établissement à Paris vous a sans doute occupée et procuré le sens d'un nouveau départ. Vous êtes plus que généreuse—imprudente peut-être—à suggérer que vous prêterez éventuellement une partie de ce logis à des amis en visite à Paris. Diane en est, comme moi, touchée. Mais pour le moment je ne songe guère à faire des plans de voyage en Europe, ou ailleurs. Je sens, dans mes jambes vite lasses, dans mon cœur qui s'essouffle, et probablement dans ma pauvre cervelle, le poids de mes 85 ans. Je me déplace le moins possible et ne déteste pas le calme solitaire de cette maison entourée de grands arbres. C'est imprudemment, il y a quelque temps, que j'avais accepté d'aller à cette réunion "George Sand" à Hofstra. Sans avoir une admiration aveugle pour beaucoup de ses livres, j'ai toujours pensé qu'elle était sous-estimée comme romancière. Elle était loin d'être une féministe acharnée: en fait, on l'a parfois traitée de misogyne, et elle a eu bien peu d'amitiés féminines. Cela n'a que peu d'importance à mes yeux. Sa correspondance est d'une richesse inégalée; bien supérieure à celle, trop louée, de Flaubert si fermé et étroit dans les lettres qu'il a échangées avec elle à la fin de sa vie. Taine, Renan, Walt Whitman, Henry James; en Angleterre les sœurs Bronte, George Eliot, Browning & sa femme, et d'autres dont Ruskin, ont loué Sand avec plus d'effusion que les Français, souvent mesquins envers toute littérature féminine. La lutte que devaient, entre 1815 et 1950, mener les femmes les plus douées pour se faire accorder quelque minimum de droits, était dure, épuisante. George Sand a lutté pour le droit au divorce, à l'amour; elle a eu l'audace d'affronter de grands hommes (de Mérimée et Musset à Chopin & à d'autres) et de tenter d'élargir le cadre du roman: *Spiridion* reste pour moi un beau roman philosophico-religieux. Sa correspondance de femme cruellement traitée par tel amant égoïste, marié d'ailleurs (Michel de Bourges), est à vous arracher des larmes. Dans mes vieux projets abandonnés, j'avais l'esquisse d'un livre sur les femmes abandonnées et leurs colères et leurs plaintes (et leur vengeance) de Médée à Marguerite Yourcenar et à un film bref de Cocteau dont le titre m'échappe. Ovide l'avait fait jadis, dans ses *Héroïdes*. Et j'avais songé à un autre livre, plus pathétique encore, sur les amants d'homosexuels abandonnés, dont Proust, Gide, Cocteau lui-même, E. M. Forster. Puis j'ai préféré lire et relire les belles poésies d'amoureux; enfin, j'ai laissé derrière moi tout ce qui touche à l'amour. Sans l'avoir cherché (puisque je ne me suis trouvé père qu'à 63 ans), j'ai, naïvement, découvert que la paternité est quelque chose de plus fort encore que la sexualité, juvénile ou attardée. J'ai du moins persisté à lutter (en paroles et par lettres de recommandation, ou d'indignation) pour les femmes raillées bêtement par les hommes, dont Enid Starkie, dont vous parlez. Elle était lesbienne et buvait un peu trop. Quelle femme, à Oxford, n'eût fait de même?

Merci du poème d'Antony Deschamps; c'était un poète de grande promesse, à l'esprit ouvert. Et bon courage pour vos lectures autour de Baudelaire: Levavasseur, Prarond, Asselineau (sur lequel on ne sait presque rien), Nadar lui-même, Philoxène Boyer. La question toujours obsédante est: en quoi et pourquoi les poèmes de Baudelaire (dont un bon quart sont banals) sont-ils pour nous supérieurs à d'autres, émanant du même cercle? Pierre Seghers a publié une anthologie des *Poètes maudits d'aujourd'hui* (1946–70). Ils ont eu bien des prédécesseurs en 1830–60. . . .

## À son frère et à sa belle-sœur:

Dimanche 12 octobre (1986)

. . . J'ai peine à me rappeler ce que je savais, ou lisais, à six ans: quelques images accompagnant les Mille et une Nuits ou les fables de La Fontaine, que je ne goûtais guère: ces animaux qui parlent et discutent, ces laboureurs qui invoquent Dieu ou ces savetiers qui se disent heureux de chanter. Curieusement, les paraboles enseignées à l'école du dimanche, Lazare ressuscité, les pêches miraculeuses, St. Paul ébloui sur son chemin de Damas, m'ont laissé un souvenir de puérilités sottes. Sans doute étais-je déjà alors porté vers le rationalisme? Ou plutôt vers le polythéisme, Neptune et Vénus et même ce lourdaud d'Hercule et Protée dans sa caverne sous-marine me semblaient plus vrais. Ces jours-ci sont ceux des fêtes juives (Yom Kippur?), observées au Collège de Diane, ce qui lui accordera répit à ses voyages. Nos amis, en grande majorité juifs, observent ces rites. S'imaginer qu'un Dieu a choisi un certain peuple pour lui confier son culte me semble d'une rare outrecuidance. Marilyn & son mari, les plus raffinés & modestes des amis, n'osent pas, évidemment, abandonner ces superstitions. Diane, toujours compréhensive, les avait à déjeuner samedi dernier pour la Nouvelle Année juive et avait préparé des pommes trempées dans le miel, un autre dessert dont l'origine doit remonter à Moïse et quelque poisson plus ou moins rituel (Dieu merci! pas des anguilles, dont j'ai horreur). . . .

## À Renée Wehrmann:

Le 13 octobre 1986

Chère Renée,

Vous m'écrivez avec bien trop de modestie, et trop d'amabilité envers moi: je ne crois pas mériter votre générosité, mais elle me touche beaucoup. Vous êtes l'une des trois ou quatre personnes avec lesquelles, ces dernières années, j'ai eu le plus de *vrai* plaisir à travailler. Vous avez toujours réfléchi avec personnalité et longuement au beau sujet que vous avez choisi de traiter. Vous avez élagué les aspects faciles: biographie, analyse de l'œuvre, et même caractérisation, pour vous attacher surtout à la technique romanesque et au style. Vous aviez raison. Votre livre, sobre, bref, se lit avec aisance. Il n'use pas de coquetterie pour déguiser son origine universitaire. Vous analysez avec finesse quelques scènes-clés et on sent, à travers votre objectivité de critique, qu'elles vous ont émue. Votre analyse, technique sans lourdeur pédantesque, explique et communique cette émotion. Vos chapitres m'ont paru neufs et frais, et voici que j'ai envie, à la première occasion, de relire *Les Thibault.* Vous êtes trop discrète & trop modeste en jugeant l'auteur, avec sobriété & sans le grandir. En vérité, dans cinq ou six des volumes de l'original, le livre *reste* un roman habile, honnête et sans ficelles et émouvant. Il survit aisément aux tentatives, naguère trop acclamées, de Simon, Sarraute, Pinget et Robbe-Grillet—et, je crois, même aux *Faux-Monnayeurs,* trop truqués.

Le livre est agréablement présenté et relié. S'il y a quelque justice dans notre profession, il devrait servir votre carrière. La dédicace au souvenir de votre mari est noble et touchante. Votre fils en sera ému.

Je ne vais plus guère à New York—ou nulle part. Je me fatigue vite, et lis, relis, vaguement médite. Je me rappelle avec plaisir les années où j'ai enseigné au Centre de New York et nos entretiens. Dites à l'occasion mon souvenir à M. Gainas.

Bien des choses de Diane comme de moi et chaleureuse amitié.

Henri

## To Natalie Datlof:

October 23, 1986

Dear Natalie,

Will you bear once again with one of my hand scribbled notes?

It is now a week after the G. Sand conference. I look back upon it with immense gratitude & with inner joy. I have attended many, in my long career: but, literally, *never* a single one so cordial, so friendly, so smoothly run and organized with thoughtfulness & an unfailing attention to every detail. M. Lubin, other prestigious guests, & I myself were treated regally, with every detail of meals, transportation, impeccably attended to. The papers were serious, prepared with utmost care, delivered without any infringement of time, and with a modesty, an absence of conceit & of egotism which contrasted with professional exhibitionism displayed elsewhere. Mr. Ugrinsky was present everywhere, admirably efficient & in contagious joyful mood, assisting us all. You have an excellent talent—genius, I should call it—for organization: with none of the impersonality and stern manner of officials in administrative positions: but ever human, gentle, smiling, with never a sign of impatience at our questions. I especially admired the gentle & devoted ways in which your young colleagues & assistants helped the guests, guided them, answered their queries. The spirit which prevails at Hofstra is uniquely cordial & cooperative. A conference like the George Sand one, and the previous ones which I attended, on Malraux & on Dostoevsky, run with imagination & an admirable breadth of mind, attentive to the visitors' unspoken wishes, place Hofstra in the forefront of American institutions in the educational, scholarly and diplomatic fields.

Very heartfelt thanks to you, Mr. Ugrinsky, & to your Dean—one of the most charming of men.

With devotion,<br>
Henri Peyre

## To Enid Peschol:

290 North Avenue<br>
Westport, Ct. 06880<br>
Thursday Oct. 30 / 86

Dear Enid,

It is good of you to let us read your essays: we admire that intellectual cooperation of husband & wife; of a scientific mind & of an artistic sensibility. You are a model of a young wife who, while raising a daughter to become an energetic & opinionated & erudite young lady, while inspiring a busy husband & affording him "le repos du guerrier," thinks, reads, writes & enlightens others.

This latest article of yours is beautifully learned (even in the technique of shaving, puncturing abscesses, cutting off organs) & entertainingly discovers fresh meanings in Beaumarchais & Rossini. It is written with graceful skill & it instructed Diane (who occasionally teaches the play) & myself who had not reread it for years. Many thanks to you & Dick.

We have been busy of late. I had to display more energy than I really have in traveling to address a George Sand conference at Hofstra (Hempstead, L.I.), another one on Paris at Brooklyn College. I now propose to enjoy some quietude & the last lovely days of the expiring Summer.

Many thanks to both of you & to the young operatic fan.

Henri

**To the same:**

290 North Ave.
Westport, Ct. 06880
October 31, 1986

Dear Enid,

Your book arrived two days ago & I devoured it at once. It fascinated me. You & Dick have done a very difficult job with apparent ease, modesty, simplicity and rare skill. It is notoriously difficult to have a husband and a wife collaborate on a book & marry two different types of mind & of talent. You two have made it successfully. The reports by Dick on his experiences are candid, extraordinarily devoid of boastfulness & of conceit, candid about the ambivalence of pity & anger, devotion & hate in a surgeon. They made me experience vicariously a surge of sympathy for interns, doctors, surgeons, the harassment of wife & child entailed by that profession. I felt selfish having lived a life of placid teaching & writing & relative leisure. And Diana felt, as I did, much sympathy for the ordeals which the medical profession imposes upon a wife.

You are to be admired, though, & not pitied. Instead of escaping into social & mundane activities, you have, courageously & ingeniously, chosen the hard, but rewarding solution: to put to use your training as a literary scholar, translator & poet. It took much knowledge of several literary traditions to discover those literary parallels. You present them skillfully, not concealing that they remain parallels & at times not very close ones, but that they throw light both on the relation of literature to real life & on the humanistic, humane & human implications of medicine. The introduction is a warm, *lived* & convincing plea for enlarging the vistas (& the sensibilities) of doctors. You & Dick are probably, in your modest & engaging way, steering the medical profession towards a new orientation. It is a splendid achievement.

Congratulations & grateful thanks,
Henri

## À son frère et à sa belle-sœur:

Premier jour de novembre 1986

... Pour le moment, je vis comme je l'ai fait depuis dix ou douze ans, sans tracas de santé. Je me plains de mes trous de mémoire; de ne pouvoir marcher beaucoup ou monter des escaliers trop raides. Je le fais donc le moins possible, ne vais guère à New York quand je peux l'éviter. Hier, nous ne sommes pas allés rencontrer le ministre Léotard (culture) en visite aux États-Unis. Les réceptions officielles n'ont guère d'attrait. Il s'est trouvé que j'avais en effet plusieurs engagements promis, auxquels je me suis rendu. Le congrès George Sand (programme ci-inclus), 3 jours, avec force discours, certains pédants. Le mouvement féministe a contribué à la replacer parmi les romanciers du XIXe siècle qui comptent. On exagère sans doute. Elle a combattu pour le droit de la femme au divorce, à des amours libres, à gagner sa vie et à gérer ses biens; et grâce à elle en partie, ce progrès a été réalisé, ou accéléré. Les romans pour adultes qu'elle a écrits (*Lélia, Jacques, Consuelo*) valent ceux de Victor Hugo; et même ses romans champêtres renferment des pages assez fortes, parmi d'autres trop douceureuses. Ma tâche plus difficile était de questionner et faire parler cinq romanciers français qui ont eu, en 1985, les prix littéraires à Paris: Queffelec (Goncourt), Baudreau, Besson, Mlle Billetdoux. J'inclus la feuille avec les titres de leurs livres et leur visage. Ça s'est bien passé. Mais il est délicat de grouper des auteurs, dont chacun se croit unique, original, et n'aime pas qu'on soupçonne chez lui des influences ou des affinités (pas même celles de Balzac ou de Dostoïevski). L'idée, bien sûr, était de montrer aux Américains qu'il y a un roman français vivace, après Proust, Mauriac, Bernanos, Sartre, Camus,

Tournier; et d'amener les éditeurs américains à les faire traduire et paraître ici. Peut-être Micheline voudra-t-elle lire un ou deux de ces romans? Certains, je dois dire, sont bien longs; et les scènes d'amour dit "physique" (Colette disait: "Les plaisirs, qu'on appelle, à la légère, physiques"), souvent incestueux, parfois "bisexuel" y abondent. Mlle Billetdoux n'est pas la moins hardie. Jacques préfère ne pas gaspiller son temps à ces légèretés d'aujourd'hui, peut-être les classiques de demain. Je dois dire que je préfère souvent les œuvres antérieures, dont on est sûr qu'elles ont survécu. . . .

## À Mary Ann Caws:

290 North Avenue
Westport, Ct. 06880
Samedi 15 novembre 1986

Chère Mary Ann,

Je vous remercie de votre mot si cordial, qui me touche fort. Je regrette ces menaces plus précises à quelques muscles de mon cœur qui me retiennent de me rendre à New York & de participer, en observateur et donneur de conseils, aux activités de ce Graduate Center, auquel je reste très attaché. Mais il faut bien que je me rende enfin à l'inévitable affaiblissement d'un organisme usé.

J'avais oublié que vous deviez vous absenter pour plusieurs mois. Je vous félicite de cet honneur, amplement mérité, qu'est une invitation à Cambridge. Cette ville m'est restée chère: j'y avais, normalien, fait mes débuts dans l'enseignement en 1922–23; et je suis resté ébloui dans mes souvenirs par la rivière, les "backs" des collèges, la poésie de Grantchester. Les Presses de Cambridge sont aujourd'hui les plus intelligemment actives de toutes celles du Royaume Uni. Je suis heureux pour vous que vous puissiez envisager un repos relatif, ou un ralentissement de votre fiévreuse activité. Ménagez-vous un peu. Vous avez dû passer par des épreuves pénibles ces dernières années. J'ai bien souvent pensé à vous, à vos enfants. Mon vieil âge me permet de vous dire quel attachement sentimental m'a dès longtemps lié à vous; quelle fierté, sans doute naïve, j'ai sentie à avoir toujours cru en vous. J'admire cette capacité d'enthousiasme que vous avez conservée et qui vous fait accueillir bien des innovations qui déroutent les gens plus prudents, dont je suis.

Conservez cette flamme juvénile. Vous représentez, dans l'enseignement des littératures aux États-Unis, quelque chose d'unique et d'ouvert. Vous m'avez souvent fait penser à la phrase de Keats, dans l'une de ses lettres, qu'à 20 ans j'avais voulu prendre pour devise: "Better be imprudent moveables than prudent fixtures." À CUNY, je souhaite heureuse chance à vos successeurs, car vous n'êtes pas facilement remplaçable. Croyez à l'ardente sincérité de mes vœux pour vous et les vôtres. Diane, j'en suis sûr, les forme également.

Affectueusement à vous,<br>Henri

## À Vincent Giroud:

December 6, 1986

Cher ami,

Le gracieux envoi de votre livre m'a touché, et le livre m'a amusé et plu. Il est en effet dans le Style Bourget (en mieux), Abel Hermant plus encore—avec de la virtuosité, du snobisme un peu sot, mais des promesses de vrai talent. Je vous trouve même sévère. Cela vaut mieux que ce que Proust, Gide, Giraudoux lui-même, faisaient, ou promettaient, à 22 ou 25 ans. En vérité, vous avez une plume alerte, beaucoup de finesse, de l'ironie aussi et de l'humour: pourquoi ne feriez-vous pas un livre sur P. Morand? Les gens de mon âge, s'il en survit, aiment à se rappeler le grand plaisir, nuancé d'irrespect, et la découverte d'un ton neuf, que leur donna vers 1922–24, *Ouvert la Nuit* et le recueil suivant. Jean Prévost & 4 ou 5 autres, à l'École, trépignaient de joie. Et le *Londres,* plus tard, a fait comprendre & aimer cette ville à toute une génération de Français, ravie d'enlever à Maurois son monopole des choses d'Outre Manche. Et le talent de P. M. ne s'est pas éteint avec son riche mariage, son officialité et sa maladresse pendant la 2e guerre.

Je crois comprendre, d'après l'annuaire de l'École, que vous êtes à J. Hopkins? Je vous en félicite. Si vous songez à faire carrière américaine, c'est le point de départ idéal. Et il devrait là y avoir de la place pour une personne d'avenir.

Croyez à mon très cordial souvenir,<br>Henri Peyre

Bien sûr, le futur auteur de *Bouddha vivant* a pu, en 1908–10, avoir dans l'esprit le nom d'Anquetil-Duperron — *très* grand orientaliste et homme de courage, mort sous le 1er Empire. Lyme Regis est une très jolie ville de bord de mer en Dorsetshire, tout près du Devonshire. Joseph Texte était un grand nom pour les comparatistes — mort trop jeune.

## À Wallace Fowlie:

Le 21 déc. 1986

Bien cher Michel,

*Sites* m'a enchanté — vous réussissez avec élégance, talent et humour à parler de vous et de quelques autres, et du "genius loci" de deux ou trois pays, sans aucune lourdeur, sans nulle indiscrétion, sans obsession de votre moi. Sur quelques points sans doute, le vieil ami que je suis voudrait savoir davantage: votre père, l'influence sur vous de votre mère ou votre révolte contre sa religion; ce que vous avez trouvé dans le catholicisme, et peut-être ce qui vous a parfois impatienté chez ses fidèles et ses officiants; ce que vous reprochez à votre éducation américaine et surtout à la France envers laquelle vous êtes trop indulgent. Je suis bien déçu par la littérature de ces dix ou vingt dernières années, je l'avoue; & je me demande si jamais il est possible de s'emballer pour des écrivains et artistes de 20 ou 40 ans plus jeunes. J'y renonce.

Mais sur Proust, sur Rimbaud, sur Mallarmé, je vous lis avec émotion, retrouvant mes émotions de jeunesse. Vos pages sur vos rencontres à Chicago, à Haïti sont dramatiques et pittoresques. Vos souvenirs sur Catherine Coffin, Mabel Lafarge ont fait surgir en moi tout un passé très cher. Je n'ai jamais oublié mes premières rencontres, à votre logis de High St., avec les Archawski, Mme Mercier — et combien profondément j'ai été chagriné, vexé, humilié, lorsque quelques sots à Yale n'ont pas su reconnaître vos dons *hors de pair* de professeur. Yale a bien changé! Alors on y redoutait les catholiques et leur influence sur les jeunes élevés en Anglo-Saxons protestants! Incroyant, ou me proclamant tel, j'ai toujours honni Voltaire, Anatole France et tous les puritains. Il n'y a que sur votre ferveur dantesque que je me sépare de vous: immense poète, certes, même pour un médiocre italianisant comme moi. Mais je ne puis épouser, ou transférer sur le plan esthétique, ses féroces haines — Br[unetto] Latini et autres. À le lire, je deviens un partisan farouche des papes. Peut-être aurais-je dû être un saint? Mais l'assurance de Th. Merton & de certains convertis m'a irrité plus que de raison. Je ne pense pas survivre au delà de 86 ans (février 1987) & ne le désire certes pas. Dans mes heures d'insomnie, j'évoque souvent mon passé, dont vous êtes une part très chère et, blasphème à vos yeux, je me rendors à force de me réciter les sonnets de Mallarmé. Mallarmé comme soporifique? Non — mais cela m'intrigue de retrouver ses rimes, ses adjectifs. Le malheur de ma vieillesse est que ma mémoire n'est plus du tout rétentive. Elle trébuche devant "l'Ouverture ancienne" et "Quand l'ombre menaça de sa fatale loi," et je n'arrive pas à me rappeler les vers non rimés, de Bonnefoy par exemple, ou de Char.

Diane vous remercie de l'inclure dans votre don. Elle vous lira dès qu'elle aura un peu de répit, de ses cours, & des préparatifs culinaires de ces fêtes. Ma pensée vous accompagnera en fin décembre et ensuite dans votre nouveau poste d'enseignement.

Affectueusement,<br>Henri

## À Konrad Bieber:

Dec. 22/86

Cher Konrad,

Je sais que nulle réponse n'est nécessaire; mais vous et Tamara êtes de si chers et de si fidèles amis, depuis ces lointaines années où vous logiez à Wall Street, N. Haven, et êtes restés si proches et toujours généreux, que je tiens à vous dire les vœux que je forme pour votre santé et votre paix spirituelle. Tamara a supporté stoïquement de dures épreuves toutes ces années, toujours avec grâce et énergie. Vous avez terminé une belle carrière, et votre fils et sa progéniture vous apportent aujourd'hui la consolation d'un avenir serein.

Je vais à peu près bien, avec un cœur fragile, des jambes faibles et un cerveau qui s'étonne de ma survie obstinée, alors que tant d'autres sont enlevés — avant-hier Herbert Dieckmann. Diane va connaître un peu de répit, après ses voyages harassants de Westport à Brooklyn. Mais la visite de ses 3 fils, et de Brice, va faire d'elle pour quelques jours une pâtissière et une cuisinière. Injustice du sort, qui maintient les mâles dans la maladresse manuelle; et je n'en ai même pas de remords! Nos vœux pleins d'affection à vous deux, et à votre fils—et aux amis de Stony Brook ou de Port Jefferson, Eléonore notamment.

Heureuse année,<br>Henri

## À Eléonore Zimmermann:

Le 27 déc. 1986

Chère Eléonore,

Autre mélancolique fin d'année! Je ne crois pas être l'homme des regrets, des remords moins encore—mais des souvenirs embellis par la rêverie, oui—et combien de souvenirs accumule une existence de 85 ans et plus! Le temps présent, la maladresse des gouvernants en France, les scandales répugnants ici, le culte de l'argent partout et la corruption ouverte m'emplissent de mépris de notre époque. Mais, lisant dans mes longues heures d'oisiveté beaucoup d'histoire & les souvenirs et révélations sur les années 1930–45 en France (antisémitisme, aveuglement des dirigeants et de peuple), je me console presque. La présence des jeunes (3 fils de Diane venus ici pour Noël, le mien de Yale où il est étudiant gradué en histoire) m'emplit de pitié pour eux qui auront à subsister dans ce monde, mais tout de même redonne espoir. Ils sont insouciants et vivent dans le présent. C'est l'avantage, inégalé, de notre profession qu'elle nous maintient longtemps en familiarité avec les illusions, les rêves et les ardeurs des jeunes, découvrant la vie et l'art. . . .

Vous touchez à quelques questions qui mériteraient ample discussion. Vous le faites avec, je crois, un sens très sûr des limitations de Baudelaire l'artiste et une saine indépendance de la critique baudelairienne courante, qui a tendu à établir un culte autour de lui et de lui. J'ai beaucoup regretté que les lettres à sa mère aient faussé les perspectives d'une étude impartiale. Elles sont émouvantes, tragiques, exaspérantes aussi—mais ne touchent guère, ou pas du tout, à l'*art* baudelairien. Quel dommage qu'il n'ait pas laissé de lettres (à Gautier, à Nerval, à Soulary, à une dizaine d'autres experts du sonnet, ou du pantoum, ou de la répétition de rimes ou de vers) qui nous révéleraient comment il méditait ses poèmes. Voyait-il (ou écoutait-il ses amis, s'ils lui en faisaient la remarque) les curieuses faiblesses de beaucoup des tercets de ses sonnets:

y compris "Correspondances," "Ma jeunesse ne fut qu'un ténébreux orage," "Bientôt nous plongerons dans les froides ténèbres," les *Chats* (si ridiculement surfaits), "Sois sage, ô ma douleur," *et al*. Valéry y a touché, parfois avec méchanceté, et je crois avoir commis quelque part un petit article là-dessus; je verrai si je le retrouve. Mais le problème est réel. A-t-il *voulu, calculé* ces soudains prosaïsmes, ces gaucheries? Sont-elles essentielles à sa poétique? Les livres les plus lucides sur Baudelaire, comme celui de Judd Hubert, se sont trop souciés de suivre *une* piste (pour Hubert, celle des ambiguïtés); mais trop peu de montrer en quoi il est proche et en quoi différent des 4 ou 5 poètes de la même génération, écrivant en 1842–57; ou alors, comme dans les notes trop savantes et "out of place" de l'édition Crépet et Blin, ils se sont fourvoyés dans la chasse aux soi-disant "sources." N'hésitez pas à écrire ce que vous avez découvert, et pensé, sur Baudelaire, y compris sur ce pseudo-problème de l'architecture du recueil; laquelle est factice, imaginée après coup, et soulignée par le poète parce qu'il *voulait* qu'on y croie, tout comme Proust sur la soi-disant structure infaillible de son roman. C'est d'esprits libres et de sensibilités fraîches comme la vôtre qu'on a besoin en critique. Et les magies (musicales, aussi) de Baudelaire ont échappé à trop de commentateurs.

Vous savez cela, et le sentez, bien mieux que moi, mais il vous aurait fallu un milieu stimulant dans lequel essayer vos idées et les confronter. Il n'est pas trop tard.

Me voilà, de mon fauteuil de sénile dispenseur de conseils, vous traitant en disciple, alors que je me suis souvent incliné devant votre finesse. Je rouvre parfois votre Verlaine et l'admire plus que jamais.

Mon fidèle souvenir à Svere — et, de Diane et moi, chaudes pensées d'amitié en ce début d'ère nouvelle.

Henri

## À Norman & Louise MacIntosh:

Dec. 30 — 1986

Chers amis,

Quelle exemplaire fidélité est la vôtre! Je suis touché d'apprendre de vos nouvelles et de retourner en pensée aux lointaines années où vous arriviez à New Haven — déjà fidèles Baudelairiens! Je relis souvent ce poète, me récite parfois des pièces des *Fleurs du Mal,* de Mallarmé, de Rimbaud. Mais, à bientôt 86 ans(!), ma mémoire fléchit. Je survis à tant de mes contemporains et amis, déjà disparus, que cela me paraît presque une injustice—du moins, une anomalie.

J'ai eu de sérieuses difficultés au cœur: valve usée, comme votre femme—mais ai refusé de tenter une opération. Pour le moment, en prenant quelques précautions, je survis et jouis de ce qui me reste de vigueur. Le fils que j'ai eu de mon tardif mariage est "graduate student" à Yale. Après avoir songé à faire du droit, il se spécialise en histoire européenne et diplomatique. Comme d'autres jeunes, il préfère se tenir à l'écart de l'avidité et de la corruption qui souillent la vie américaine—et probablement européenne aussi.

Mes vœux pour le rétablissement total de Louise. Je conserve d'elle un souvenir plein d'affection et d'estime pour son intelligence, sa douceur et sa compréhension de son mari. Mes compliments pour la carrière, et le bonheur, de votre fils et belle fille.

Très fidèlement,
Henri Peyre

## À Stirling Haig:

Jan. 10/87

Cher Stirling,

Elégant, solide, profond cadeau, très bien présenté et dans lequel j'ai appris *énormément:* plus, je crois bien, que dans tout autre livre sur Flaubert. Vous êtes, avec courage, allé *droit* au plus difficile: le dialogue, la narration rapportée, l'emploi des temps, le fameux "style indirect libre." Sur chaque aspect, vous êtes précis, analytique avec finesse, jamais pédant ou usant d'un langage rebutant. Pas une faille dans vos raisonnements serrés. C'est une étude de premier ordre, et qui témoigne chez vous de grands dons pour la stylistique la plus sophistiquée.

Diane, qui travaille justement sur l'*Éducation* l'a commencé & va le lire de près. Elle est frappée d'admiration comme moi.

Merci. Bon souvenir à votre femme.

H. P.

## To Florence Weinberg:

290 North Ave.
Westport, Ct. 06880
Jan. 12/87

Dear Florence,

It's a rare treat to receive a letter like yours—with news, intelligent remarks, all couched in a beautiful style & no affectation whatever. You know how much I respect your scholarship & your ability to explore & illuminate the darkest grottoes of myth & letters. I admire you just as much as a woman & for all that you have done, with understanding & deep feeling, for Kurt. I think of him often (without quite succeeding in picturing him to myself riding a mare) & of the afflictions which, thanks to you, he seems to bear almost lightly. I have been thus far (at 87 soon! or 86, rather) been relatively spared by disease & handicaps; but my much weakened heart would not allow me to leap over dale & brook or to force myself to swim. And he is, you announce, planning a book on a tantalizing but enormous subject. Few men, since Spitzer, have the combination of precise knowledge of words, their origins & connotations, & of the concepts associated with words, that Kurt possesses. Do accept my ardent wishes for both of you for the year just starting.

I do not write myself & do not travel either. I have without too much regret settled down to a sedentary existence, with leisurely reading & a smooth resignation to passivity. Diana, my "compagne" & savior, has one or two of her three grown up sons visit occasionally; none lives here any longer. Brice comes seldom, taken up as he is with the enormous amount of reading required by the study of history. Once in a great while, I visit New Haven, or rather Hamden to chat with Sally Cornell or with Louise Boorsch, immobilized in a wheelchair after a bad stroke. Her courageous patience, her refusal ever to utter a word of complaint, are admirable. Most of the persons Kurt & I once knew are gone by now. The young, so far as I can tell from my son's roommates, are hardly interested in politics & the current, hideous spectacle of real corruption & deceit. You two would share my indignation, but I won't inflict it upon you in my bad writing. At present, any one who calls himself a "liberal"—as the inhabitants of this house do—is crushed by the complacent majority & reduced to silence. We have failed to train generations endowed with critical spirit & with courage.

It is to the North Carolina Humanities Center that you would like to go? It is well spoken of &, I would think, peaceful, & the spring there should be radiant. Would Kurt bear well a trip there & an eventual change to California? Think twice before such a move & leaving your house which I remember as furnished with original taste and full of treasures. Let me know what happens & how Kurt fares.

Very affectionate pensées,<br>Henri

## À Vincent Giroud:

290 North Ave.<br>Westport, Ct. 06880<br>Le 14 janvier 1987

Cher ami, (Ne m'appelez pas "Monsieur le Professeur"—entre archicubes! Vous m'intimidez!)

Merci de ces amples nouvelles. Vous êtes un errant et vous avez bien raison de l'être. On ne se fixe que trop tôt. Pour le moment, explorez le monde et ne vous éloignez néanmoins pas trop de Paris. Quitte à ressentir quelque impatience en ce moment, c'est là que se fera votre carrière littéraire. Avec votre don de style, votre ouverture d'esprit, votre liberté aussi, vous devriez être écrivain plus que simple universitaire et peut-être critique ou courriériste littéraire dans la presse. Tôt ou tard, vous écrirez sur l'Amérique et, bien sûr, vous y reviendrez en professeur d'échange. Je regrette que J. Hopkins ne vous ait pas bien traité, ou compris. Il y a eu parfois là un milieu ouvert, cosmopolite, savant. Je ne sais ce qu'il en est ces temps-ci. Les livres publiés là paraissent être surtout des traités de théorie et de critique abstruse, genre que je ne lis plus. Paresseusement, je préfère revenir vers l'ère plus inspirée, plus aventureuse et ironique de Morand, Giraudoux et Malraux.

Je vais peu à Yale; mon âge outrageusement avancé me conseille la prudence. J'y ai de très heureux souvenirs et, sans doute embellissant le passé, je me dis que nous étions jadis moins gonflés de nous-mêmes qu'Harold Bloom, Peter Gay et quelques autres. Cela fait des années que je n'ai pas été en Angleterre, Londres excepté. Le Londres de Morand, de Valéry Larbaud me reste cher. J'avais, normalien échappé à la routine sorbonnarde, beaucoup aimé Cambridge, moins connu des Français qu'Oxford. Mais je n'ai jamais été à Strawberry Hill, et l'ennuyeuse correspondance d'Horace Walpole, comme celle de Boswell (aux noms honorés à Yale), m'écartent de ce lieu. À Oxford, je croyais retrouver Shelley, Swinburne, Pater, longtemps mes demi-dieux, un peu aussi, mais plus tièdement Ruskin, que vous retrouverez si vous enseignez à Amiens. Je vous souhaite un poste de ce genre, semi parisien, au moins pour l'instant, et une année agréable.

Croyez à mon bien cordial souvenir,
Henri Peyre

## À Vera Lee:

Jan. 15/87

Mon adresse est, depuis longtemps, 290 North Avenue Westport Ct. 06880 — car je suis, enfin, *pleinement* en retraite.
Chère Vera Lee,

Que c'est gentil de vous souvenir de moi et de me distraire par ce livre divertissant, désinvolte et agréablement sautillant en apparence, écrit avec verve, et fort solide et sérieux en vérité! Quelle érudite bibliographie! Que de savoir accumulé, et porté avec grâce et esprit. C'est un fort bon livre et qui sait n'en rien alourdir des œuvres qui doivent rester des fontaines de plaisir malin, discrètement pervers. Vous allez amener ma retraite sénile à lire ou à relire *Faublas,* "Point de lendemain," le Sopha, peut-être même Laclos auquel je n'ai jamais autrefois pris plaisir. Adroitement, vous offrez les aspects séduisants de ces romans, qui savaient aussi être ennuyeux. Et vous composiez cet ouvrage quelque peu libertin, illustré avec goût, alors que vous trôniez parmi des gens d'église et sans doute des abbés galants. Aujourd'hui, dit-on, ces abbés se marient. Votre fille en a-t-elle épousé un? Je n'ose pas dire "séduit," car je me la rappelle sensée, fine autant que jolie, justement fière de sa savante mère. Que fait-elle? Vous a-t-elle accompagnée en France? Je crois qu'il y a ces jours-ci une exposition Boucher, à Londres ou à Paris. Allez-vous voir le vaste Musée d'Orsay? Trop vieux moi-même et trop fragile pour voyager, je me contente de regretter l'ancien musée des Impressionnistes et, durant mes longues heures vides, de résister à la "difficulté d'être" que ressentait Fontenelle. Je n'ai pas encore tout à fait atteint son âge.

Merci de m'avoir donné ce plaisir de l'esprit—et de votre joli et courageux article sur le crime chez les Puritains. Vieil incroyant que je suis resté, j'avais craint que vous ne deveniez une maussade convertie, une sœur de charité peut-être. Directrice d'une bibliothèque, cela est plus rassurant. Je ne crois pas connaître cette bibliothèque, à Boston.

Je suis, vous aussi, bien loin de Yale & n'y connais presque plus personne: May, cependant, et Brooks que vous citez. J'y ai mon fils (22 ans), étudiant gradué et j'entrepose mes livres à un bureau au "basement" de W. L. Harkness. Vous y régniez jadis sous les combles et en souriant.

Merci et mon très fidèle souvenir,<br>Henri Peyre

## À Eléonore Zimmermann:

Le vendredi 17 janvier (87)

Chère Eléonore,

Merci de me donner de vos nouvelles & je suis heureux qu'elles semblent bonnes. Peut-être que l'aurore d'une année fraîche encore vous donne une nouvelle provision de courage? Il m'en faut pour vivre à peu près normalement alors que j'entre dans ma 86e année—avec bien, bien peu de survivants d'un tel âge. Je croyais pourtant mériter une fin plus hâtée, n'ayant jamais beaucoup ménagé mes efforts. Mais en ces domaines aussi, il n'y a pas de justice.

Le désordre sur ma table et autour de moi est indescriptible. Je ne trouve même plus de papier vierge; et après quelques nouvelles tentatives sur une machine à écrire prétendue plus pratique, i.e. électrique, je m'aperçois que je multiplie les fautes plus que jamais. Je renonce à rien écrire qui doive être tapé. Le monde ne s'en portera pas plus mal.

*Re:* Baudelaire. Il y a certes un livre à faire sur le sonnet chez lui, et sans doute bien des détails curieux à mettre en valeur. Il y en a un aussi, ou une brève étude, sur la femme, ou le corps féminin dans sa poésie:

la fixation qu'il semble avoir eue sur les fortes épaules ou les bras dignes d'Hercule de la femme admirée; et, mais cela est plus répandu, les pieds de la femme (parfois tenus dans ses mains, pour les réchauffer) et ses genoux, caressés comme par un suppliant antique. Surtout on pourrait recueillir les nombreuses allusions aux yeux de la femme. La Concordance dit que le mot "yeux" est celui qui revient le plus fréquemment dans les *Fleurs,* plus même que le mot "cœur." Parfois les adjectifs sont abstraits & banals: ardents, clairvoyants, sereins, profonds et vastes, mystérieux—et, hélas! "charmants." D'autres fois, ils sont comparés à des puits ou des citernes: surtout ils sont "polis" comme des pierres précieuses, sans expressions, vides, métalliques. Le sonnet en question, "Avec ses vêtements" est énigmatique et intriguant. Peut-on y déceler une logique interne? Vous le pensez, plus que je ne le fais moi-même. Je me pose peu de questions devant un poème ou un tableau que j'aime. Le sonnet est étrange & déroutant, d'abord par l'abondance des comparaisons (trois "comme") plus lentes, plus majestueuses que des métaphores—d'abord, évocation d'un mouvement de serpent, à qui la femme qui marche fait penser le poète, et la suggestion d'un Orient lointain et sacré, celui des jongleurs de l'Inde. Puis (v. 5–8), la femme devient paysage (comme ailleurs dans les Fleurs: e.g. "À celle qui est trop gaie"), elle devient comme la nature, indifférente: la houle des mers, que Baud. aime à évoquer ("La Vie antérieure"), est un peu banale, mais le verbe "elle se développe" est original et empreint de majesté.

Cette "nature étrange et symbolique" est probablement une de ces ambiguïtés qu'avait signalées Hubert (je n'ai pas ici son livre). La femme devient paysage, "nature," "symbolique" (l'adjectif ne revient qu'une seule autre fois dans les Fleurs), c.à.d. à double sens: et femme et tableau de nature; et "ange" pur, éthéré et sphinx (égyptien), énorme animal accroupi. Elle est déshumanisée, pareille à quelque astre refroidi dans le ciel, et imposante dans sa froideur de statue, refusant de s'abaisser à l'une des prétendues fonctions féminines, la maternité ou la fécondité. Baud. mêle curieusement les clichés, qu'il répète, et de grands vers, amples, splendides dans leur noblesse.

Sur ce sonnet, et bien d'autres thèmes, je suis bien loin d'avoir le secret des énigmes. Ma "nature" est d'accepter, avec jouissance ou volupté, mais non de transformer ma volupté en connaissance. Je préférais, quand j'enseignais, communiquer et partager mon plaisir.

Je retrouve ce vieil et probablement insignifiant article, écrit pour célébrer une dame à Penn State dont j'oublie le nom.

Pardon de mon écriture & chaudes amitiés—aussi à Svere.

H.

Il vaudrait la peine de voir ce que fait de ce sonnet la traduction des Fleurs de Richard Howard, dont on m'a dit du bien. Je ne l'ai pas.

## À Hélène et Pierre Pennec:

Ce 5 février 1987

Chère Hélène et cher Pierre,

Cette date m'intimide. Cela va faire mon 86e début de printemps! Je ne puis me plaindre de ma santé, même si les marches de plus d'un kilomètre ou deux ou les efforts un peu pénibles me sont interdits. Je ne souffre de rien de sérieux et mes longues heures vides, ou passées à la lecture ou à la rêverie, ne me pèsent pas trop. J'ai bien quelque scrupule à me trouver ainsi bêtement satisfait de moi, comme un petit marquis de Molière. Mais je balaie vite ces scrupules—et comme un remords de menacer de vivre peut-être plus longtemps que n'avait fait mon père, et certainement plus vieux que bien de mes amis. Diane m'entoure de sollicitude et de gentillesses. Brice partage de temps à autre avec moi l'intérêt qu'il trouve à ses lectures, ou l'impatience qu'il ressent de suivre tant de cours pas toujours scintillants. Et parmi les plus vrais plaisirs que j'ai il y a celui de recevoir de temps à autre de vos lettres.

Ce mois dernier, nous avons été touchés (Diane, trop prise par ses déplacements forcés, les devoirs à corriger, ses quelques écrits, me charge souvent de vous dire ses remerciements et d'excuser la rareté de ses lettres) par l'affection de vos lettres. Hélène nous a écrit en termes chargés de sensibilité et de tendresse, et pour partager les réflexions toujours pénétrantes qu'elle fait sur ses lectures; elle a une riche et profonde sensibilité, une âme "naturaliter christiana," une piété que je partage envers les souvenirs de sa mère ou de mon père. Je ne crois pas aux bienfaits des épreuves de santé ou à la valeur de la souffrance & trouve cela aussi vain chez Musset que dans les sermons chrétiens. Dès l'âge de 13 ou 14 ans où j'ai résolu d'arracher en moi toute influence religieuse, je m'étais voulu païen et polythéiste; mais je dois bien reconnaître que les longues épreuves que, tous deux, vous avez endurées ont développé en vous la vie intérieure, la compréhension des autres et aussi une bonté rare. Je ne crois pas avoir jamais entendu Pierre dire rien de mesquin ou de méchant. Il n'en veut même pas aux plus sots des politiciens, aux inquisiteurs du fisc comme le fait ou le dit Jacques, aux grévistes qui gênent vos voyages, aux erreurs ou aux négligences des médecins qui vous ont jadis mal soignés. Je ne suis pas très coléreux moi-même; mais j'ai besoin de temps à autre de me révolter contre les scolastiques d'aujourd'hui (déconstructeurs critiques, philosophes épris de mots); contre les pédants d'autrefois qu'il m'arrive de relire, par masochisme, sans doute: Plotin; théologiens juifs; pères de l'Eglise; Origène, qui s'est refusé à comprendre Celse (ô honte) et les pires de tous, un peu vos compatriotes d'Afrique du Nord—Tertullien et St. Augustin. Le pauvre Brice a dû, pour l'un de ses cours, absorber "La Cité de Dieu," lui que j'ai refusé de faire baptiser et qui, à dix ou douze ans, comme je l'emmenais à l'hôpital pour panser une blessure à la suite d'une chute, répondant à l'admission au questionnaire rituel, "Religion?" répondait à la secrétaire, une calme noire, "atheist." Embarrassée, elle avait transcrit: N.R. (no religion). En toute honnêteté, je dois avouer que les quelques fois où, pour maintenir un reste de mon ancienne (et très affaiblie) connaissance des langues anciennes, il m'arrive de rouvrir Hérodote ou Plutarque ou Tite-Live, leur foi puérile aux oracles et aux "lectures" des entrailles des animaux me les fait vite refermer. Jacques parle de son Minou avec tendresse, et Louise tenait à avoir plusieurs chats. Quand il a passé quelques jours ici, il se disait indigné que je n'adresse jamais la parole au vieux chien de la maison. Je lui donne à manger avec un geste de mépris condescendant, puisque je suis souvent seul ici, mais lui en veux de sa stupide présence et d'aboyer à cinq heures du matin quand le livreur du lourd New York Times dépose le journal à la porte.

Mais assez de ces petitesses personnelles et assez parlé de ma santé, puisqu'elle résiste pour le moment à diverses faiblesses que l'on a trouvées à mon cœur.[ . . .] Être propriétaire est une source de soucis. Ici, Diane a tous les quelques mois à faire réparer les toitures, les gouttières, les serrures, à faire couper les branches d'arbres bien vieux. Je regrette alors d'avoir passé bien du temps à lire des poètes anglais plutôt qu'à m'exercer à des travaux de réparation et de mécanique. Ma vieille machine à écrire vient de se détraquer et se moque de mes doigts maladroits et aujourd'hui un peu arthritiques. Tout le monde (Diane y passe des heures) manipule des ordinateurs avec disquettes et modes d'emploi savants. Il n'est question que de cela et de diverses "compatibilités" les quelques fois où nous avons ici un visiteur. Je me réfugie dans un silence boudeur. Tout au plus suis-je capable de faire marcher la télévision; mais pas encore de mettre les "cassettes" de films que l'on emprunte ici à la bibliothèque et qui remplacent pour nous le cinéma, auquel nous n'allons plus guère. Affronter le froid, la neige et la boue, démarrer les autos refroidies (il n'y a pas ici de garage), s'efforcer de tenir les yeux ouverts devant un film qui m'ennuie: c'est trop pour moi. Le privilège du grand âge est qu'on peut grogner librement et être traité avec une inattention gentiment indulgente.

Il a fait, et fait encore, bien froid cet hiver—au-dessous de zéro depuis plusieurs semaines, neige sur les arbres et les buissons, glace durcie et glissante. Jusqu'ici pourtant, pas de rhume ou de grippe, mais le printemps ne survient guère ici avant le milieu d'avril, bien que New York soit à la latitude de Rome ou de Naples. Les croyants disent que cela est dû au Gulf Stream qui réchauffe les côtes de la Bretagne et non celles de la Nouvelle Angleterre. Mais ce Gulf Stream m'a toujours paru être un mythe, comme la résurrection ou la virginité de Marie (mère de 3 ou 4 frères et sœurs de Jésus) ou Lourdes et Thérèse de Lisieux. Cette dernière a les honneurs d'un film qu'on dit bon mais que mes principes m'ont retenu de voir.

Pierre a eu la gentillesse de nous écrire longuement, et avec sa lucidité coutumière, sur la situation politique en France, les fluctuations de l'opinion et le caractère singulier de ces grèves, parties de la base et spontanées et échappant aux directives des syndicats. Je lui suis reconnaissant de la peine qu'il prend ainsi et de nous faire part de ses réflexions. Je lis quelques revues françaises et souvent *The Economist* et le *Manchester Guardian* hebdomadaire; mais il est rare de rencontrer une pénétration et une sûreté de jugement comparables à celles de Pierre. De loin, bien des querelles et débats paraissent infimes et grossis par l'esprit de parti. Le Carrefour du développement par exemple, ou la Nouvelle Calédonie (que nous aurions dû abandonner il y a 50 ans) ou les bouderies, minauderies et valse-hésitation de Barre, Giscard (ambitionnant de présider à l'Europe), de Mitterrand lui-même, paraissant prendre Chirac en pitié après avoir semé divers obstacles ou pièges sur son chemin. Je persiste à croire que la droite a été peu habile à paraître favoriser les thésauriseurs qui avaient placé leurs fonds en Suisse, les nuées d'actionnaires se précipitant sur Paribas et autres privatisations et les riches en général. Le gouvernement a été plus mal inspiré encore, dans un pays qui idolâtre l'égalitarisme, à tenter ces réformes d'universités sans y préparer l'opinion et à offrir comme règle ou norme les augmentations de salaire au choix ou au mérite, c.a.d. au gré des faveurs des chefs. Cela se fait ici, où le capitalisme est plus sauvage. Mais aux Etats-Unis, malgré les apparences, le mythe de l'égalité est moins vénéré. Tous les jours, les entreprises renvoient de leurs salariés et ils espèrent se placer ailleurs. Cela entraîne de graves misères individuelles. Ces jours-ci, avec les grands froids, on feint de se préoccuper davantage des "homeless" qui dorment par terre dans les gares ou sur le pas des portes des riches. Il y a une vraie générosité individuelle mais aussi une outrecuidance des riches. Le pire du scandale autour des ventes d'armes à l'Iran et du détournement de fonds aux mercenaires contre le Nicaragua est que Reagan et sa clique ont accepté, et sollicité, l'intrusion de millionnaires dans la politique étrangère. Les ultra-riches, en général conservateurs et cléricaux ("moral majority"), en viennent à décider eux-mêmes de la politique et à prêcher l'anticommunisme. Le moral dans le pays et dans la presse est au plus bas. Tout respect pour le Président, convaincu de mensonge et surtout d'incompréhension totale des questions les plus graves, a disparu. Mais dès l'origine (comme d'ailleurs Wilson en 1912 et d'autres), il avait été choisi et imposé par un petit groupe de puissants millionnaires, industriels et banquiers. L'embarras sera de trouver un successeur. Bush, vice-président, que j'ai un peu connu, fait triste figure et s'est trop attaché aux basques de Reagan. Hart (aussi alumnus de Yale) ne saisit pas l'opinion. Cuomo non plus, pour le moment.

D'autres soucis sont dans l'air: le dollar, la rivalité commerciale avec le Japon, qui se fait détester autant qu'envier ici — une peur, vague encore mais qui croît, des "Asiatiques" que l'on juge supérieurs intellectuellement (surtout aux noirs et aux hispaniques). Si Yale, Harvard, Berkeley admettaient vraiment leurs étudiants sur leur mérite et leurs résultats aux concours (surtout en math, biologie, chimie biologique, "computer science"), leurs universités compteraient 75% d'Asiatiques. Les plus forts sont les Coréens et, plus encore, les VietNamiens. Cela va devenir un problème aigu, avec la vexation et la jalousie des noirs, qui ne réussissent qu'aux sports. Je serais curieux de savoir ce que Pierre a pensé vraiment des Ethiopiens qu'il a aidé à former, des Africains; il jouit, évidemment parmi eux d'un très grand respect, intellectuel, moral et largement humain. C'est là la récompense la plus vraie pour un professeur. J'aurais, plus jeune de 50 ans, souhaité être son élève.

Merci aussi à Pierre de ses très utiles réflexions sur les historiens, que je transmets à Brice. J'ai lu, et il a parcouru, Le Goff, sur le Purgatoire, qui m'a un peu déçu, & son autre gros livre sur la civilisation médiévale. Brice a lu aussi Furet, sur "repenser la Révolution," traduit en anglais. Il a enseigné parfois ici, au Michigan, où j'avais conseillé à Brice d'aller. Furet est très estimé ici. Je ne savais pas que vous l'aviez connu. St. Hilaire a dû être, à plusieurs égards, une véritable École Normale Sup., une pépinière d'esprits fervents, méditatifs, mûris par la maladie et se stimulant les uns les autres.

Je ne lis guère de livres nouveaux français et les romans m'ont déçu, comme, je crois, ils vous déçoivent aussi. Je préfère donc relire, ou lire de l'histoire. Il y a à Westport une assez bonne bibliothèque municipale, où je vais parcourir les revues et emprunter des livres, évitant ainsi le voyage jusqu'à Yale, par ces chemins glacés où, à pied, je risque une chute. Il y a un bon choix de biographies: de Goethe, de Russes et d'Anglais. Cela ne fait pas toujours estimer ou admirer ces grands hommes, que de lire en détail les récits de leurs admirateurs. Je cite beaucoup Goethe, comme tout le monde, et Nietzsche, mais ne professe pas leur culte. J'avais connu Vlad. Nabokov, que j'avais voulu faire engager à Yale. Il avait mis tout le comité contre lui en déblatérant sottement contre Dostoïevski & Balzac, alors que (c'était vers 1946 ou 47) j'essayais de faire fonder une chaire de littérature russe. Je l'ai revu plus tard; mais quel monstre de vanité, de contemplation de soi et d'acrimonie contre les autres, surtout les Russes exilés qui se ralliaient à la Russie victorieuse après Stalingrad. Je n'ai jamais trouvé le moindre intérêt humain à *Ada* ou à *Lolita*. Il est vrai que je me dis "agélaste" et que je n'ai en effet guère le sens du comique, qui me paraît souvent à base de méchanceté.

Assez parlé de moi. Je n'écrirai plus que de brèves lettres, car vous avez mieux à faire que de m'écouter. Je vous embrasse tous deux — et au nom de Diane et Brice, et Carlo qui ne vous a pas oubliés.

Henri

Si j'envoie quelques vieux nos de revues, pour exercer l'anglais de Pierre, ne vous dérangez pas pour remercier. Cela n'en vaut pas la peine.

## À Paul Archambault:

Le 20 février 1987

Cher M. Archambault:

Non, je ne savais rien de ce tragique événement. Et cela me cause une véritable & profonde douleur. J'avais vu bien rarement, trop rarement J. H. Matthews. Mais nous nous écrivions fréquemment; il m'envoyait régulièrement ses livres. Je les plaçais très haut dans mon estime. Sur le Surréalisme sous toutes ses incarnations (et auparavant sur Zola), il laisse une œuvre de premier ordre: d'une information vaste et sûre, d'un goût éclairé, et surtout d'une indépendance d'esprit parfois farouche, sourcilleuse, dédaigneuse des modes auxquelles se plient des érudits plus timorés. Il a accompli, à *Symposium,* une tâche immense, avec générosité et tact, avec discrimination aussi. Il aurait dû occuper l'une des positions les plus en vue dans ce pays, avec de nombreux étudiants avancés; mais peut-être redoutait-on son jugement parfois impatient, sa franchise à dégonfler les prétentions et les vanités. Pour tous dans la profession, dans la critique et l'appréciation de la littérature moderne, c'est une énorme perte.

Merci de m'avoir annoncé cette pénible nouvelle. J'écrirai un mot à sa veuve. Je suis très âgé, vis très seul. Je lis beaucoup, et relis-consulte souvent les livres de J. H., les vôtres aussi. Récemment, pour un long essai, non encore paru, sur la littérature critique concernant Camus, je relisais et citais votre très importante étude sur l'ouvrage scolaire (dans le sens le moins noble du mot) du jeune Camus sur la philosophie du début de l'ère chrétienne. Vous avez été le premier, et le plus solidement informé, à en révéler les faiblesses, avec netteté et avec tact. Je vous imagine très jeune et vigoureux encore, et préparant d'autres travaux de marque, grâce à cette double familiarité que vous avez avec la littérature chrétienne (ou païenne) et l'ère médiévale. Dites bien à vos collègues le chagrin que j'éprouve à cette perte qui nous appauvrit tous.

Avec mes vœux bien cordiaux,
Henri Peyre

## To Sherry and John W. Kneller:

Feb. 24—87

Dear Sherry and Jack,

I was deeply touched by your presence here on the intimidating evening when I was entering what must be my 87th year. I have known you and felt affectionately drawn to you for longer than any other friends. I have admired the wisdom, the taste, the courage of Jack and the patient understanding of his wife for as long as I can remember. You have been extraordinarily generous in gathering friends and donors to honor my name and my modest achievement. You have made the Graduate Center another home for me, after my long years at Yale. I am grateful to you for the generosity and fidelity of your friendship.

The news of Jack's brother's endangered health saddened me. Kindly convey my wishes to him, my appreciation of his kindness and my great esteem for his career as a thinker and educator.

Yours most cordially,
Henri

## À Rosette Lamont:

Ce jeudi 12 mars 1987

Bien chère Rosette,

Votre élégant cadeau, enveloppé avec soin et accompagné de cette très belle carte, printanière à l'avance, m'a énormément touché. Vous avez toujours été envers moi d'une fidélité dans l'amitié qui m'a soutenu parmi ces années de vieillissement progressif. Je songe souvent au passé, ayant atteint l'âge où une activité amoindrie et une paresse progressive amènent bien des moments d'insomnie et de retour vers le passé. Et de ce passé vous faites étroitement partie depuis vos débuts à Yale, puis nos rencontres à New York et les calmes et touchants entretiens avec votre mère—un modèle pour moi de finesse de sensibilité et d'intelligente compréhension des êtres. Vous avez réussi cette très rare combinaison d'une vie extérieure intense, parmi étudiants, représentations théâtrales, voyages en Europe, et en même temps d'une existence mariée paisible et stimulante. Votre mari est un homme remarquable de discrète et pénétrante compréhension. Je viens en effet de passer ce cap difficile et effrayant de 86 années; et vous êtes parmi les quelques personnes dont la délicatesse dans la fidélité m'a le plus ému et encouragé. Cette cravate, d'un goût sobre et raffiné, me donne un rare plaisir, esthétique et émouvant parce qu'il vient d'une amie aussi dévouée et compréhensive. Vos récents articles sur le théâtre en France sont tout vibrants d'amour, lucide et critique, de l'art dramatique parisien et d'un rare bonheur de style. Bien peu d'entre nous, universitaires, peuvent écrire avec un tel bonheur d'expression dans un grand journal, sans abdiquer leur jugement critique. C'est une nouvelle heureuse, et qui fera honneur à CUNY, que le séjour prochain à New York de Jean Milly. Je le connais un peu par ses travaux proustiens, mais je suppose qu'il a acquis également une haute réputation dans divers domaines de la littérature française de ce siècle.

Je ne vais plus—ou très, très peu—à New York. Mon corps usé redoute le froid, les foules, les escaliers. Mais un jour prochain, la saison plus clémente revenue, j'espère vous voir et vous remercier de vive voix. Diane vous dit son amitié et son admiration.

Mille bons vœux et merci,
Henri

## À Konrad Bieber:

Le 17 mars 87

Cher Konrad,

Merci de votre savant et élégant article. Vous avez toujours été généreux pour les auteurs français et fidèle à votre souhait de voir France et Allemagne se comprendre amicalement. Cela est aujourd'hui une réalité et les choses de l'Allemagne de l'Ouest sont mieux comprises et senties par les Français que celles des Etats-Unis et de l'Angleterre. C'est pour moi un extraordinaire phénomène que les Allemands aient accepté—jusqu'ici sans beaucoup protester—la séparation des deux Allemagnes. Un de mes amis allemands me disait en souriant que la phrase entendue à Bonn, reprenant l'ancienne devise française sur l'Alsace-Lorraine, est "Parlons-en toujours! N'y pensons jamais!"

Je serais, si j'écrivais là-dessus, *très* sévère pour le nationalisme bête et béat de Barrès, écrivain que je ne puis supporter. Mais je vous approuve de parler avec sympathie de Romain Rolland, que j'ai beaucoup aimé jadis, surtout dans ses lettres, et contre qui les Français s'étaient tournés vers 1925–40, après avoir trop loué *Jean Christophe* avant 1914.

Votre retraite est active et, j'espère, calme et heureuse, si la santé de Tamara se maintient. Pour nous ici, la vie continue et nous attendons impatiemment la fonte définitive de la neige et les premiers vols d'oiseaux printaniers. J'ai franchi, il y a quelques semaines, le cap, effrayant, des 86 ans et je m'étonne d'être encore vivant, bien qu'un peu frêle et vite las.

Merci de l'article. Affectueux souvenirs à Tamara et, à l'occasion, à Eléonore.

Henri


## À Vincent Giroud:

>290 North Avenue, Westport, Ct. 06880 (Tel. 276-4868)
>Le 25 mars 1987

Cher Ami,

Merci de vouloir bien éviter les formalités respectueuses — et de votre aimable lettre, d'un style vif & jeune qui me rajeunit. L'adresse de Strawberry Hill a ravivé en moi de vieux regrets. J'étais si bêtement épris de poésie romantique lorsque, jadis, j'étais en Angleterre que je n'ai jamais voulu aller à Twickenham, ni reconnaître l'originalité de Pope (Maynard Mack m'a enfin converti). Je me contentais de me réciter un poème de Donne, "Twickenham Gardens."

Vous avez un beau sujet avec Oxford, vu (ou entrevu, dans le cas de Mallarmé) ou rêvé par les Français. Le hasard de la vie m'avait fait préférer Cambridge, chargé de souvenirs pour moi. Mais un jour (ne tardez pas trop) revenez à P. Morand et, pourquoi pas, écrivez sur lui une thèse — de "Tendres Stocks" à des nouvelles amusantes, un peu trop appuyées et exagérées, comme "La Présidente," il mérite une étude critique originale et, pourquoi pas, désinvolte. La Sorbonne en a vu d'autres! Y a-t-il d'autres inédits de lui en Amérique? Au Texas, peut-être?

Je me sens bien âgé et fragile, et vais peu à New Haven; mais laissez-moi savoir quand vous y serez. Ou bien, venez jusqu'à Westport un jour; le printemps va enfin venir. Il neigeait encore il y a deux jours.

Bien cordialement,<br>Henri Peyre

## À Philip Kolb:

290 North Avenue<br>Westport, Ct. 06880<br>Le 25 mars 87

Cher ami,

Vous ne sauriez imaginer la joie que j'ai eue à reconnaître votre écriture et à ouvrir, avant hier soir, votre lettre. Si mon âge avancé me permettait de sauter, j'aurais bondi jusqu'au plafond. Un c[omte] rendu de Murray dans la dernière *French Review,* mars 1987, vous avait donné pour "mort et irremplaçable." Irremplaçable, certes, vous l'êtes; et c'est pourquoi nous prions (pour moi, le dieu des athées ou des païens) de vous laisser en vie et de boucler les ultimes volumes de la *Correspondance*. Mes félicitations, et à Madame Kolb de vous maintenir en pleine forme, et à vos filles—les plus douées et les plus fines qui soient jamais venues étudier à Yale.

Mes compliments et écrivez à Jack Murray que, comme dans *Le Menteur* (et Alarcon), "Les morts que vous tuez se portent assez bien."

Mille chaudes pensées,<br>Henri Peyre

## To John W. Kneller:

Wed. March 25/87

Dear Jack,

I hope the arrival of spring will bring you relief from the woes you and your wife suffered this winter. Perhaps your brother's health may even improve. He is one of the persons whom I most earnestly wish I had met.

But I am not likely, at 86 plus, to travel to California, or to Europe, or indeed to New York, where I almost never go. The atmosphere at the Graduate Center, to which I felt deeply attached, has changed—inevitably. You are most kind to want to keep the "Peyre Institute" alive. Is it wise, though? I truly feel very, very ancient and rather tactless in offering another lecture there. Please think twice before arranging one. Would it not be better to have another member of the present faculty address the group? And why not yourself? You have always been far too modest and you have far too seldom allowed others to share your exceptional "sense" for poetry and for music.

I responded rather coolly to your suggestion of Victor Hugo as a topic. We made much of him just two years ago, on the 100th anniversary of his death and I personally am not much of an admirer of his novels. I shall not make the effort to see *Les Misérables* as now transfigured.

My own bent would be to attempt a timely and challenging subject, which has concerned me and even worried me much lately, such as "Anti-Americanism in Western Europe Today." Or else: "The Present State of Franco-American Relations." Another possibility would be: "Raymond Aron, the Tocqueville of the Twentieth Century." He has been made far too little of by Americans when and since he died in 1983.

If a subject on a literary man were deemed preferable and omitting those whom I must have lectured on already at the Center (Camus, Sartre), my own preference just now would go to either Paul Claudel or André Malraux, whom I reread with warm admiration.

I have stubbornly refused ever to write my memoirs. But, inevitably, I often reminisce, as old persons will, and if it did not smack of conceit too much, I might talk on "Encounters with Eminent Writers (Claudel, Gide, Breton, Saint-Exupéry, Malraux, Sartre)".

As to a date, you would have to see about a room (not too large, I hope) and Diana's schedule. She teaches at Brooklyn on Mon., Wed., Friday.

Excuse my informality. My typing is worse than ever.

Affectionately to Sherry and you,<br>Henri

## À Michel, Colette, et Jean-Pierre Guggenheim:

Ce 7 avril 87

Chère Colette, Cher Michel et Cher Jean-Pierre,

Votre visite nous a donné une vraie et grande joie. Vous apportiez, non pas précisément le grand soleil de votre Midi (tout relatif), mais la camaraderie la plus chaleureuse, l'amitié confiante, les libres débats d'idées et la tendresse sentimentale qui vous unit tous trois, et vous unit aussi à vos amis. Vous paraissiez en bonne forme, et aviez pour quelques heures relégué vos soucis. Nos entretiens avec Jean-Pierre nous ont permis de mieux apprécier la finesse et l'intensité de son esprit et la chaleur de son cœur. Ses deux parents n'ont rien perdu de leur foi idéaliste dans un monde qui crie son besoin de plus de droiture et de bonté. Colette est une admirable femme, que bien des épreuves, y compris la récente disparition de ses parents, ont rendue profonde sans jamais saper son courage. Michel, homme d'action en même temps qu'impeccable professeur, sait joindre à une rare pénétration d'esprit une perception intuitive des secrets des êtres. Il déchiffre les secrets des coïncidences que la masse des mortels n'aperçoit pas et interprète des signes du destin qui nous échappent. Il ne s'est pas trompé souvent et quand les obstacles s'accumulaient, il a triomphé d'eux. Sa création de Bryn Mawr–Avignon demandait un acte de foi peu commun. Et il a toujours conservé une modestie, un oubli de soi qu'ont rarement ceux qui ont le privilège d'interpréter les secrets des dieux. Diane s'est sentie comme moi stimulée et affectivement réchauffée par votre présence.

Le retour s'est, j'espère, bien passé. Vous reviendrez; et, lorsque enfin nous aurons dépassé ces épreuves d'orage et de vent furibond, nous espérons avoir la visite de Mario et de sa femme. Je ne la connaissais qu'à peine: mais les moments passés à Avignon en sa compagnie nous ont enchantés. Eux, et vous, avez noué pour moi de nouveaux liens, et plus forts, avec cette ville que je prétendais traiter avec quelque hauteur d'exilé volontaire se voulant cosmopolite.

J'écrirai sur une autre feuille quelques impressions sur le manuscrit que m'a laissé Michel. Il a sans doute quelques-uns des inconvénients du genre: diversité hétéroclite, inégalité—cela était inévitable. Mais le tout est de qualité. Il est digne de la commémoration d'une courageuse entreprise. Et que d'efforts la réunion de pages si diverses, probablement encore à "éditer," représente-t-elle!

Bien affectueusement<br>Henri

## To Florence Weinberg:

May 4—87

Dear Florence,

I have read much of your book in its definitive format & I am even more convinced that it is one of the most erudite, broadest, pleasantest (for it does mix "utile dulci" expertly & gracefully) and most courageous volumes I have seen in a long time. It takes the force of conviction and, literally, the courage of a native of New Mexico to quote Greek profusely, and Spanish and Italian, Pindar, the Argonautica, to emend mistaken readings of the ode to Pyrrha, and to emerge young and fresh—just a little poorer—from a 5 or 10 year stay in a grotto, transfigured into locus amœnus. Thank you for the generous gift of this volume. It will be, and it is, dear to me because it comes from one of the women whom I silently admire most and to whom I feel inwardly most grateful for all that she has brought to her husband and what she does now to keep him in cheerful spirit and a proud rider. You & he would have brought much to the Center in the Triangle and it was stupid and blind of the authorities not to have realized it. The volume is pleasant; as far as I can tell, free from misprints, and not outrageously expensive as the prices of books go. I trust libraries will order it & you may recoup some of your investment, in due time. It will long be quoted & appreciated.

I continue to be fairly well, though weak, and to curse the chilly weather which refuses to depart. I neither ride nor swim, and have time for reading. Your book will inspire me to reread or read Dodds, Zielinski, perhaps even Silius Italicus, and some Plutarch. Lately, I reopened *Daphnis & Chloe,* which must have been my earliest erotic reading at 11 or 12. I was disappointed, but it's the grotto there which led me to inquire on your opus.

> With warm appreciation to both,
> H. P.

## À Marcel Gutwirth:

> Le dimanche 28 juin (1987)

Cher M. Gutwirth:

Votre très beau livre m'arrive—retransmis par le Graduate Center. Mon adresse, depuis pas mal d'années, et ma retraite, est: 290, North Avenue, Westport, Conn. 06880. Je me rends très rarement à New York: escaliers, métros, fatiguent mes très vieux os. Je reste ici, dans un décor presque champêtre, et lis assidûment.

Puis-je vous dire que, me tenant à l'écart des délibérations et décisions de mes anciens collègues de CUNY, je ne vous ai pas écrit, mais j'ai été vraiment très heureux que vous ayez accepté de présider aux destinées du "programme" de français. J'ai pour vos livres, pour votre personnalité, pour la sagesse, la finesse, l'originalité modeste et profonde de vos écrits, une très grande estime. Mon âge, sans doute aussi quelque prudence native, et un goût de la clarté que je crois partager avec vous, m'ont, ces dernières années, rendu méfiant d'une certaine critique prétentieuse et courant après les modes de Paris, qui a fait du mal à mon ancien département de Yale. J'ai vraiment aimé les dix ou douze années que j'ai passées à CUNY. La maturité, l'indépendance, souvent l'originalité des bons étudiants m'ont enchanté. Je vous souhaite un séjour paisible—pas trop cependant—et je sais que vous n'aurez pas de peine à améliorer l'enseignement avancé.

Votre livre m'a donné une vraie joie intellectuelle et spirituelle. Il est d'une érudition discrètement dissimulée, modeste, mais extraordinairement vaste: de Babrius et Romulus anglicus, Roman de Renart, Marie de France à tous les modernes qui, en allemand, italien, et en langues plus familières à la plupart d'entre nous ont traité de La Fontaine. *Rien* ne vous échappe, mais vous ne faites nullement parade de ce savoir. Vous revenez aux textes, les illuminez par des remarques d'une rare finesse; votre commentaire ne cherche jamais à impressionner; il est plein d'humour, de délicatesse, de jouissance esthétique. Ce n'était pas peu de chose que d'oser, après Mad. de Mourgues, Mad. Kohn, Lapp, Spitzer, et surtout Valéry, Giraudoux et autres, dire des choses *senties,* fraîches, pénétrantes sur La Fontaine. J'ai toujours jugé les *Fables* l'un des livres les plus difficiles à présenter avec simplicité et naturel. Vous y réussissez avec adresse, et sans jamais recourir à l'artillerie lourde des classifications pédantesques et du jargon critique. J'ai lu votre livre d'affilée, pendant ces journées de chaleur, et y ai trouvé un souffle printanier rajeunissant. Merci de m'avoir permis de le lire sans retard et de votre inscription, qui m'a touché.

> Croyez-moi votre très cordialement dévoué,
> Henri Peyre

## À Wallace Fowlie:

Le 8 juillet 87

Mon cher Michel,

Je pensais à vous ces jours-ci: cela m'arrive souvent, comme je revis diverses phases de mon long passé et évoque ceux qui me sont restés chers. Je suis, relativement, en assez bonne santé moi-même; mais je craignais pour la vôtre. Vous avez plus de sensibilité, plus de tourments intérieurs, que le vieux racorni que je suis. Je me plais à cette indolence, coupée de beaucoup de lectures et de relectures, qu'apporte la retraite, et Diane (et mon fils parfois) me tiennent compagnie. Enseignez-vous encore? Votre vie matérielle quotidienne s'organise-t-elle sans trop d'obstacles? Le triste de mon grand âge (vous n'en êtes pas là!) est la solitude morale où nous laissent tant de contemporains qui disparaissent.

Ces pages sur Maritain sont parmi les plus vives, les mieux enlevées et les plus alertes, les plus révélatrices aussi que vous ayez écrites. Elles m'ont enchanté. J'avais beaucoup aimé l'homme en Maritain, souvent rencontré dans les années de guerre à l'École Libre des Hautes Etudes à New York et à Yale. J'aurais dû conserver certaines de ses lettres, et quelques billets de Raïssa, dont j'avais loué la poésie. J'aimais moins "Art et Scolastique" (qui doit avoir été le sujet du premier compte rendu critique que j'ai écrit en anglais) et ce qu'il a écrit sur Bergson et sur Péguy. J'ai été attristé par "le Paysan de la Garonne" et quelque ressentiment bien humain, qu'il avait à la fin de sa vie contre Teilhard de Chardin et l'influence de Simone Weil.

Mais j'admire vos récits ou souvenirs sur lui, sur T. S. Eliot, sur la maison d'Henriette Psichari. Cela est évoqué avec poésie et avec humour, ainsi que la pesanteur rabâcheuse d'Irving Babbitt et le lansonisme attardé de Morize. Pourquoi ne poursuivriez-vous pas vos livres de souvenirs: de vos années de Harvard, de Yale, de Duke, de votre *unique* compréhension de la poésie française et de Dante? Vous avez fait sentir et aimer Rimbaud et Mallarmé mieux qu'aucun d'entre nous en Amérique. Si vous jouissez de loisirs, vous devriez écrire à nouveau sur la poésie dont vous avez imprégné tant de jeunes. À ce propos, merci de ce que vous dites sur Hart Crane. Je continue à le relire et à l'aimer et me le récite parfois la nuit, quand le sommeil se dérobe.

Je ne sais si vous allez encore en Europe. Je me sens trop âgé et trop fragile pour les voyages. La lecture de pages comme les vôtres me rajeunit.

En profonde amitié,<br>Henri

## À Pierre Petitmengin:

31 août 87

Cher camarade & fidèle collègue,

Vous êtes bien trop aimable de vouloir bien accuser réception des quelques envois de livres "américains" qu'il m'arrive de faire à l'École. Ne prenez pas cette peine. Il y a bien, bien longtemps, peu après mon arrivée à l'École en 1920, j'avais été accueilli très cordialement par le légendaire Lucien Herr à la Bibliothèque et n'avais jamais oublié le sentiment de "possession" de tant de livres qui m'avait envahi alors. Vous êtes le digne successeur de ce grand homme. Merci en votre nom à tous.

J'ai mis à la poste deux ou trois livres ces derniers jours.

Cordialement,<br>Henri Peyre

## À Hélène et Pierre Pennec:

Lundi 14 sept. 87

Chère Hélène, cher Pierre,

Nous sortons, péniblement (car le ciel reste menaçant et l'humidité est oppressive) de deux journées de pluie battante qui ont gonflé les rivières & inondé les routes. Les pires catastrophes sont en général réservées aux états de l'ouest & du centre; dans nos régions, la nature se conduit & nous traite avec plus de mesure. Mais dans cette vieille maison on redoute toujours accidents à la toiture, bois pourri des planchers se trouant, énormes branches d'arbres centenaires se détachant. Pour moi qui avais longtemps vécu en appartement, évitant ce genre de soucis, c'est une constante alerte. Et, bien sûr, ma lourde charge d'années ne me permet guère d'aider; sinon de mes conseils. Diane pare à tout avec vigueur, les jours où ses cours ne la requièrent pas à N. York ou plutôt à Brooklyn. Mais que de menus tracas.[ . . .]

Pour le moment, l'économie américaine est prospère, au moins dans tout ce qui est "tertiaire" (services, technologie, banque, assurances), et on s'y insère sans trop de difficulté. Le chômage est proportionnellement bien moins élevé qu'en France ou qu'en Angleterre. Mais il y a pas mal d'inquiétude souterraine, en raison du déficit énorme et de la concurrence des régions qui bordent le Pacifique. On redoute une crise; et l'arrogance de naguère, quand le pays était fermement assuré d'être le numéro UN, a fait place à un sentiment d'inquiétude, sinon d'infériorité. J'enverrai ces jours prochains, pour Pierre qui se meut avec aisance dans ces questions économico-sociologiques, un numéro de la revue *Daedalus*. Un long article de Daniel Bell, spéculant sur les conditions qui prévaudront dans vingt ans, m'a beaucoup impressionné. L'auteur est très intelligent, aussi très sûr de lui, emporté par son dogmatisme; mais il a le courage de se risquer à offrir des pronostics. J'avais siégé avec lui autrefois, dans un comité censé prédire et préparer l'avenir, et l'an 2000. L'audace de Daniel Bell avait effaré le prudent petit-bourgeois que je suis, qui ose parfois traiter de questions d'économie et d'avenir sans avoir jamais touché directement aux affaires. Amené à prononcer parfois des allocutions devant des groupes de Rotariens ou d'alumni de Yale et d'ailleurs, je me fiais hardiment à mes intuitions et brandissais quelques chiffres pris à l'*Economist*. En fin de compte, je ne me trompais pas tellement plus que les prophètes attitrés. Mais la prudence m'est venue avec l'âge, et d'ailleurs je ne parais plus en public. Je crains mes trous de mémoire, le soudain oubli des noms propres ou des chiffres, sans parler de la fatigue. Et puis c'est aux jeunes qui verront le début du siècle prochain, à le préparer et à prévoir. Il est reposant de revenir à son passé et aux rêves de jadis. Mais, et ceci n'est en rien une flatterie, nulle part je n'aperçois de lucide analyse de la situation politique aussi fine et juste que dans les commentaires de Pierre Pennec. Seulement, j'ai scrupule à lui imposer ces longues lettres très réfléchies alors qu'il a droit à son loisir et peut-être à surveiller sa santé.

Entre parenthèses, cela m'intéresserait de savoir ce que vous avez fait, vu, en Bretagne. Pierre a-t-il encore là des parents? J'ai conservé un souvenir assez net des Côtes du Nord et aussi du Morbihan. La région de Brest et de Quimper m'avait paru trop dure, et peut-être que je l'envisageais à travers les évocations de Michelet. Pour quelque raison (c'était bien avant la 2e guerre et l'occupation allemande), je n'avais pas été conquis par St. Malo. Trop de souvenirs littéraires encombrent l'esprit d'un livresque comme moi, Renan, Chateaubriand, et autres, et un curieux américain, de l'illustre famille des Adams, Henry Adams, dont le livre "Saint Michel et Chartres" est ici un classique — comme l'est son autobiographie, sévère pour son pays et pour l'éducation américaine au siècle dernier. Jadis (vers 1940–50), je voyais souvent la nièce d'Henry Adams, Mme Mabel Lafarge. Convertie au catholicisme, elle était obsédée par les questions de religion. Je lui amenais Maritain (qui n'avait pas d'auto), entre autres, et le peintre Chagall, que Maritain voulait convertir et que j'ai failli tuer, un jour d'hiver et de neige, dans un violent dérapement. Mon admiration d'alors pour Claudel étonnait et amusait mes amis. J'ai toujours eu un faible pour les convertis et les gens religieux, qui croient avec force au péché originel, à un Dieu créateur et même à un autre monde. Mes amis se moquaient toujours du nombre de religieuses qui choisissaient de préparer leur thèse avec moi. Une, qui a 85 ans, me bombarde encore de lettres et a tricoté pour moi une couverture aux couleurs vives dont s'enveloppe Brice quand il préfère dormir devant la télévision plutôt que dans sa chambre. Hardiment, cette sœur m'avait défendu dans une revue catholique d'alors (vers 1950 ou 60), où mon athéisme avait été dénoncé, en affirmant que j'avais une "âme" religieuse. Son évêque, quelque part dans l'ouest, l'avait réprimandée et menacée. Cela est bien loin et je suis plus qu'assagi. Ma suggestion (en grande partie taquine) de réunir cinquante millions d'agnostiques américains dans une ligue préparant un avenir plus sage, n'a jamais été prise au sérieux. Ces jours-ci, le Pape s'efforce d'attirer à la foi les millions d'"Hispaniques," qui seront la moitié du pays dans un quart de siècle; et dans le Sud triomphe un Protestantisme ignare et attardé, et riche, qui vise au pouvoir politique. Le pape voyageur de commerce m'agace; mais Diane, née dans la religion catholique à demi païenne, comme elle est en Italie, est autrement violente. Elle répète qu'elle voudrait le voir assassiné! Son autre sujet de colère ces temps-ci est la nomination probable de Bork, ancien professeur de droit à Yale, à la Cour Suprême. Ce juge, apparemment très compétent, est un ancien "radical" (c'est-à-dire homme de gauche) devenu conservateur. Il est vrai que ces neuf grands Juges disposent, de par la Constitution américaine, d'un très grand pouvoir. Les féministes surtout ont peur qu'il n'ajoute sa voix à ceux qui s'en prennent à l'avortement, permis et même aidé par des subventions. Je ne fais pas autorité en la matière et j'évite de heurter les dames féministes qui ne pardonnent pas. Mais en même temps, il est clair que les pays d'Amérique Centrale, ceux d'Asie et même l'Afrique du Nord ne peuvent prospérer que s'ils pratiquent un contrôle serré des naissances.

Nos débats doivent vous paraître bien lointains, et même désuets; l'intervention des religions dans la vie politique n'inquiète plus les Français. Pourtant la grande levée contre la restriction de l'école libre a secoué les Français, comme l'a fait la tentative de sélection plus sévère à l'entrée des facultés qui est pratiquée ici par l'énormité des frais dans les universités de choix. Le mot célèbre et raillé de Guizot, "Enrichissez-vous!" est partout mot d'ordre ici. Seuls quelques intellectuels peuvent vivre en dehors de la poursuite de l'or (auri sacra fames) comme le fait Carlo. Critique dans des revues d'art d'avant-garde, interprète de quelques artistes expérimentaux, il refuse de monnayer les tableaux que lui donnent ses amis peintres. Il refuse également d'avoir un compte en banque et, au grand chagrin de sa mère, d'obtenir une assurance maladie et quelque sécurité sociale. Il le regrettera un jour. Il a 26 ans et la vie de bohème devrait bientôt prendre fin. Sa jeune femme, anglaise et plutôt sévère, l'aide en travaillant comme "barmaid" et rêve de faire des scénarios de films d'avant-garde. Nous les voyons rarement d'ailleurs.

Diane est absente, pour ses cours. Elle va bien et a supporté sans fatigue excessive son travail de l'été—en partie, amis divers qui devaient passer ici quelque temps, attirés par la plage autant que par sa compagnie. Son travail sur *L'Éducation sentimentale* est achevé. Ce n'est qu'un long article, ou un chapitre d'un livre à venir, sur la peinture du vieillissement dans quelques romans. La Cousine Bette, je crois, les Mémoires d'Hadrien, un de Maupassant (Fort comme la mort), un de Zola, & d'autres. C'est une tâche à lointaine échéance. Comme vous deux, et comme moi, elle s'est beaucoup détachée des romans de Sartre, de ceux de S. de Beauvoir plus encore, et ne lit guère les œuvres récentes. On fait trop d'éloges des moindres livres de Marguerite Duras, pour les deux tiers bien ennuyeux. Sans doute est-elle mieux faite pour le cinéma. Hélène Cixous, Modiano sont peu attirants. Pinget, très sympathique, répand l'ennui à hautes doses. Apostrophes vous ont-elles révélé des romanciers neufs et saisissants? Hélène lit-elle quelques uns des poètes? J'ai connu un peu René Char, Yves Bonnefoy davantage, car il est souvent venu chez nous, André du Bouchet aussi. Mais je n'ai plus la capacité ou la souplesse qu'il faudrait pour ouvrir les plus jeunes. Les revues françaises que je parcours sont bien vides. Les Temps modernes, surtout, comme l'a dit Pierre. Et j'ai renoncé il y a quelques années à Esprit, qui me semblait un peu chapelle, content de soi et manquant de "virilité." J'ai sans doute eu tort. Du moins, il y a là des gens honnêtes, sérieux, loyaux. Diverses publications de droite, partisanes, amères, trouvent des fonds et tâchent de susciter des polémiques partisanes, comme il y en avait en abondance vers 1935–40. J'ai gardé de ces années un mauvais souvenir. Rarement, en dehors de l'affaire Dreyfus, Paris ne m'avait paru si divisé, haineux, partisan—et vénal.

Voyez-vous des étrangers à Nice? Anglo-saxons, africains ou anciens élèves de Pierre? Tunisiens peut-être? Si vous vous déplacez, ce qui est aisé par autobus dans cette région, vous irez sans doute à Antibes—le musée Grimaldi et les Picasso nous avaient beaucoup frappés—et nous étions, avec Carlo et Brice, fervents visiteurs de la Galerie Maeght, au-dessus de St Paul de Vence. Vous y êtes sans doute allés souvent de Menton.[ . . .]

J'arrête ici mes gribouillages. *Surtout,* ne vous croyez pas obligé de me répondre. La longue lettre de Pierre sur la situation politique n'a renseigné, et comblé, pour longtemps. Mitterrand paraît à Jacques machiavélique et partisan. Il est certes très adroit, et pousse probablement un peu Le Pen pour embarrasser et diviser la droite. Mais il fait figure d'homme d'état et mon ancienne estime pour ses rivaux s'est bien refroidie. Vous entendez sans doute parler de Léotard, votre voisin. Il me paraît que Giscard est bien fini, et n'a pas grandi de stature depuis sa défaite.

Finissez heureusement l'été et reposez-vous de vos pérégrinations. Pensez-vous passer à Nice les mois d'hiver? Le mistral sévit-il à Nice? Encore merci très profondément de votre don, qui me touche beaucoup—Affection de Brice & Diane.

Henri

## À Vincent Giroud:

Le 29 sept. 87

Cher ami,

Mes chaleureuses félicitations pour votre nomination. Cela fait bien des années que j'apprécie l'amicale confiance de Miss Wynne, une autre de mes collègues et amies se retire! Je ne vais plus guère à Yale moi-même et sens de plus en plus le poids de mes ans accumulés. Je n'ai jamais eu grande compétence en matière de livres rares et de manuscrits, et n'ai fréquenté que par intermittences la bibliothèque Beinecke—le regrettant d'ailleurs. Je vous envie cette position-clé où vous pourrez déployer beaucoup d'imagination et d'ingéniosité. Si je puis être en quelque chose utile au repérage de bibliothèques disponibles et de livres rares, faites-le moi savoir. Un jour prochain, je rassemblerai mon énergie et essaierai de vous rendre visite. Je vous préviendrai, au numéro de téléphone que vous avez aimablement indiqué: 432-2872.

À bientôt et très cordialement,
Henri Peyre

## À son frère et à sa belle-sœur:

Le 12 octobre 1987

. . . Guggenheim a sondé Diane pour lui demander si elle enseignerait volontiers, pendant les trois premières semaines, à Avignon, dans le programme Bryn Mawr–Avignon. Je lui conseille vivement d'accepter. Je ne veux surtout pas qu'elle sacrifie sa carrière professionnelle à mes faiblesses de presque nonagénaire et à mes incertitudes. Il me paraît presque téméraire, présomptueux et marque d' "hubris" de croire que je serai encore de ce monde en juin ou juillet 1988 — et capable de voyager. Quoi qu'il arrive, j'aime à penser que Diane, qui vous aime tendrement tous deux, vous reverra alors. Ses trois enfants n'ont plus étroitement besoin d'elle. Depuis septembre, elle loge ici et soigne Brice; lequel va bien, vit paresseusement et ne s'oriente guère vers une fructueuse carrière. Cela nous tracasse, bien sûr; car il devrait gagner sa vie, se choisir fermement une carrière et travailler, tandis qu'il passe beaucoup de temps à lire sur la politique et à regarder cette maudite télévision. Il a beaucoup de dons intellectuels, mais ne les utilise pas. Est-ce faiblesse héréditaire de volonté? Ou dû à mon indulgence excessive de vieux parent qui l'a trop gâté? Lui fallait-il une vie plus dure? Une aide psychologique, pour raffermir sa volonté, lui rendrait-elle service? Il est de compagnie agréable, parle intelligemment, est estimé de ses amis de Yale; mais nous sommes bien forcés de lui asséner des prêchages et des avertissements. Je lui ai dit qu'il ne peut pas avoir beaucoup de mois à m'avoir comme pilier (frêle) de secours. . . .

## To Stanley Burnshaw:

290 North Avenue, Westport, Ct. 06880
Monday, Oct. 26/87

Dear Stanley,

These last weeks must indeed have been hard on the warmhearted, devoted, sensitive man that you are — confronting a long & happy married life with a gifted & understanding partner. I thought of you repeatedly &, in my many hours of solitude & often of sleeplessness at night, I often relive my memories of the blessed island of West Chop, where I spent several summers, & of my visit to your beautiful house in Vineyard Haven. Some day, when painful memories take on a poetical charm, you may feel like writing memoirs of your past or even poems, in which your wife & what she meant for you would be portrayed. It is another phase of your fruitful & rich literary career which may open up with your move to New York, with, perhaps, closer contacts with your literary friends.

I stay here, almost never moving, as my legs are easily tired & my heart is frail; I do not feel up to facing crowds, busy streets, subways. I stay home, admire the red & yellow splendor of the fall or read—& mostly reread, for I seem to derive scant pleasure from the new books. I am not literally depressed; but inevitably, at nearly 87, saddened by the realization of my powerlessness to recover the enjoyment of things of beauty & original thoughts.

If ever you come here, let me know & we might have a pleasant hour of talk . . .

Cheer up & affectionate thoughts,<br>Henri Peyre

## À Vincent Giroud:

[Sans date]

Cher ami,

(En attendant de pouvoir vous rendre visite) bon article de Renée Winegarten sur Paul Morand dans le récent *New Criterion* (Nov. 1987) — pour le cas où vous reveniez un jour à ce sujet.

Cordialement,<br>H P

## À Lester Crocker:

Le 7 déc. 1987

Cher Lester,

Votre mot m'a touché — non tant par les éloges que vous décernez à un bien modeste article et qui sont dûs à votre généreuse amitié, mais par les réserves que vous formulez et qui m'ont poussé à réfléchir. Je n'ai, en fait, jamais connu Aron personnellement, mais j'admire bien des aspects de sa personnalité et beaucoup de ses livres. L'attitude odieuse qu'a adoptée Sartre vieilli envers son ami de jadis a beaucoup fait pour m'éloigner de Sartre. Si j'avais rencontré Aron, pendant et après les années de guerre, je crois que je lui aurais posé des questions proches de celles que vous formulez. Je n'ai de leçon de patriotisme, ou de cosmopolitisme, à donner à personne; mais n'y a-t-il pas quelque raideur, dissimulant quelque embarras secret, chez une personne d'origine juive à ne pas avoir dénoncé plus haut le Nazisme? Lévi-Strauss, dont j'étais très proche à N. York en 1942–45, était plus rigide encore sur ce point, et quelques amis normaliens, juifs parisiens (Schuhl, Friedmann), que j'estimais très haut. Peut-être pour se différencier d'autres israélites moins cultivés, moins fortunés aussi, immigrés en France bien après leurs familles, ces Juifs parisiens, presque tous élèves du Lycée Condorcet dans le VIIIe & le IXe, se voulaient absolument français et rien d'autre.

Je me permettais alors de trouver cela étrange, peut-être hypocrite. Dans un domaine voisin, je me suis toujours refusé moi-même (étant athée presque de naissance, incapable de relire les Évangiles, miracles, résurrection, etc., sans répugnance) d'être parfois considéré comme protestant plutôt que comme Français sans foi sinon un rationalisme humanitaire. Puérilement sans doute, je ne puis croire que des hommes intelligents croient au peuple élu, ou à la résurrection, ou au paradis et à l'immortalité. 2 ou 3 fois j'ai tenté de créer une société d'agnostiques américains. Je n'ai rencontré que des prudents ou des sceptiques. À diverses reprises, dans des conférences ou des débats, j'ai avec ferveur soutenu que *tous* nous devions assumer notre responsabilité pour n'avoir pas empêché l'holocauste, fait la guerre lors de Munich, ou même plus tôt encore en 1938, lors de l'Anschluss. Bien peu m'ont suivi. Je sais pertinemment que j'ai surpris et irrité pas mal de mes amis d'origine juive en me disant surpris qu'ils persistent dans leurs coutumes différentes, fêtes spéciales, superstitions, alors qu'ils sont tous aussi incroyants que moi. Plusieurs n'ont pas ressenti l'holocauste plus durement que je ne l'ai fait, moralement et intellectuellement. Jeune encore (et avant de vous lire avec admiration sur ce sujet) j'avais été révolté par *The Merchant of Venice*. Je n'ai jamais pu tolérer les ironies cruelles de Voltaire contre les Juifs. J'ai parfois reproché à Brombert, May, Rosette Lamont, de ne pas être plus acharnés contre l'antisémitisme. J'avais flairé quelque chose de louche dans la carrière de Paul de Man et m'étais abstenu de le pousser à Yale, alors que Brombert, Hartman, Bloom s'emballaient pour lui. J'ai manqué, non pas (je crois) de charité, mais d'imagination en ayant de la peine à comprendre que d'autres croient à la Vierge, aux fêtes de l'Assomption et à l'Ascension, aux diverses fêtes juives. Je m'en veux à moi-même. Dans le fond, malgré mes 50 ou 60 ans d'Amérique, je suis resté affreusement français et convaincu que tout le monde devrait être agnostique, rationaliste et humaniste à la manière française.

Ceci dit, et pardonnez ce long discours, puis-je ajouter que je vous considère, vous et votre femme, comme parmi les 5 ou 6 personnes dont je me sens le plus proche et que je tiens en très haute estime et affection. Parfois seulement je vous ai souhaité un peu plus rousseauiste!

> En grande amitié, et vœux de bon voyage de nous deux,
> Henri

## À Frederick Brown:

> Le 21 décembre 1987

Cher ami,

J'ai tardé à vous écrire. J'ai bien des excuses: la presse du mois chargé qui va de Thanksgiving à Noël, ma santé qui a exigé diverses visites au cardiologue (j'ai tout de même près de 87 ans et survis, à ma grande surprise). Mais après le premier jour de la nouvelle année, tout devrait être plus calme. Voulez-vous alors envoyer un mot ou téléphoner et vous viendriez nous rendre visite un jour; je suis à peu près toujours libre, vieux retraité oisif. Mais Diane enseigne, participe à d'inévitables comités à New York, fait la cuisine et, en ce moment, des paquets enveloppés de papier rutilant et ficelés de cordons dorés. Quelle sotte, diabolique saison de l'année!

> À bientôt et vœux chargés d'amicaux souvenirs,
> Henri Peyre

## À Jean Boorsch:

Mercredi 22 déc. 87

Cher Jean,

 Vous m'avez devancé, avec cette très délicate carte de Rubens, et j'en suis touché — un peu confus, aussi — je projetais de passer vous voir et saluer Louise un de ces derniers jours. Mais je me déplace beaucoup moins — très peu, en fait. Le poids des ans accumulés se fait sentir chez moi; il en est temps. J'hésite davantage à conduire. Ma mémoire des lieux et des routes, qui n'a jamais été très bonne, défaille. J'absorbe moins de livres nouveaux et vais, en conséquence, plus rarement à la bibliothèque de Yale.

 Mais mon amitié et mon affection pour vous deux ne sont en rien affaiblies. Dites bien à Louise mes pensées, mes vœux et, une fois de plus, mon admiration pour son courage et sa patience. Va-t-elle assez bien? J'imagine que vous attendez plusieurs de vos enfants pour ces fêtes; et, si c'est sur vous que retombe le travail culinaire, je vous admire. Je suis de plus en plus rebelle à ces travaux — "œuvre de choix qui veut beaucoup d'amour," disait, je crois, Verlaine, dans des vers qu'on donnait jadis aux jeunes filles à commenter. Ici, les quatre garçons (le mien habite plus ou moins ici) doivent amener des camarades, et leur femme ou amie, et je plains la pauvre Diane, qui a enseigné à N.Y. jusqu'à mardi soir. Achats, repas, lits à improviser, courses à la gare. Vous avez eu la bonne fortune d'avoir des filles dans votre progéniture!

 Si je vous rends visite un jour prochain, vous me direz comment est votre santé et vos projets de voyage d'hiver. Pour moi, j'ai renoncé aux voyages. Je n'aime pas devoir écouter mon corps et ses plaintes, mais le cardiologue m'a imposé des pilules; j'en avale parfois, moi qui n'ai encore jamais pris de ma vie vitamine et aspirine. Aveu de défaite!

 Je n'avais pu me rendre à la séance qui célébrait le lancement de la méthode dite "Capretz"; par fatigue, je crois; aussi, par un sentiment de gêne à voir votre nom moins honoré qu'il n'aurait dû l'être. Tout de même, à l'époque héroïque de la guerre, des cours intensifs, de résistance aux empiètements des linguistes accapareurs, c'était vous qui ouvriez la voie et luttiez. Mais "sic vos non nobis" — est-ce Virgile qui dit cela des abeilles? Vous êtes parmi les sages.

Mon souvenir à vos enfants—Très chaude amitié à Louise (de Diane aussi) et à vous. Bon 1988.

Henri

## À Vincent Giroud:

Le 5 janvier 1988

Cher Ami,

Ce mot sera bref—pour vous remercier du vôtre—et vous dire que je dois renoncer—au moins pour le moment—à vous rendre visite et même à aller en auto à New Haven. J'ai eu pendant mon sommeil, il y a quelques jours, une attaque cérébrale qui me prive de la vue de mon œil gauche et ferait de moi sur la route un danger public. À plus tard peut-être, si cela s'améliore?

Cordialement,<br>Henri Peyre

## To Stirling Haig [letter sealed and stamped but not sent]:

Jan. 11—88

Dear Stirling Haig:

What a welcome New Year's present—elegant in presentation, engrossing & stimulating to read & providing much food for reflection. It is kind & generous of you to offer it to the two of us at this time. Diana is only just completing her first semester's course at the Graduate Center & will probably take a little time before reading you. She is just now revising for publication a MS essay of hers on l'*Éducation Sentimentale* & will appreciate your "Coffret." I have more leisure & I enjoyed every one of your chapters. The "Chimaera" introduction is ingenious & alluring; your afterword modestly refrains from overstressing the links between the various chapters. The unity is in your elegant presentation & in your fine, smooth, unpedantic & unpretentious style. Your variations on the "blue" & "bleuâtre" are entertaining & provoking, as are your amused & gently humorous lines on Starkie-Barnes controversies. The rapprochement, more or less planned, between *Indiana* & Vigny's récits, Stendhal and Hugo bring out curious features of those novelists. You even succeed in making *Bel Ami* & *Fromont jeune,* two novels for which I always sustained a feeling of ennui, alluring, or almost so. It is, truly, one of the most stimulating volumes on French fiction of the XIXth century, impeccably informed & opening all kinds of new vistas.

Here, the blues have invaded our souls; snow & more snow, cold, melancholy & relative solitude after the departure of Diana's sons, who spent a very cordial four days for Christmas. I was visited, a few nights ago, by a stroke which greatly impaired my eyesight & caused this erratic & irregular handwriting, which I trust you will forgive. Our regards & warm wishes to your wife, happy New Year to your family and a thousand thanks.

Henri Peyre

## À Georges May:

12 janv. 1988

Cher Georges,

Je n'ai pas eu le plaisir de vous apercevoir dans votre bureau cette année toute neuve encore. Le fait est, comme vous l'avez peut-être appris, que ma santé a été fortement ébranlée: dans la nuit du 28 déc. dans mon sommeil j'ai été victime d'une "attaque" cérébrale, ou stroke; probablement pas très grave, puisque j'ai jusqu'ici survécu; mais perte de vision, au moins latérale, de mon œil gauche; incapacité de conduire; difficulté à lire, bien que je m'y obstine; que puis-je, que sais-je faire d'autre? Examens neurologiques, cardiologiques. Vague espoir que le temps remette quelque ordre dans ma pauvre tête. À près de 87 ans, je ne me fais pas d'illusions. Diane me soigne merveilleusement, me distrait, me conduit. Brice également. Je n'ai parlé de cet accident qu'à très peu de personnes et je préfère n'être pas dérangé sans objet. Mais je tenais à vous faire savoir mon état. C'est le cas de mettre en pratique mon orgueilleux et très théorique stoïcisme!

Amitiés et vœux à Martha et à vous,
Henri

## À Mary Ann Caws:

> 290 North Ave.—Westport, Ct. 06880
> Ce 15 janvier 88

Chère Mary Ann,

Merci de vos affectueuses paroles et de vos vœux. Cela nous manque également de ne pas vous voir; nous aimerions suivre en pensée vos deux enfants, si doués et si aimables. Vous êtes férocement prise par tant d'activités diverses et vos écrits. Reposez-vous parfois tout de même. Peut-être songez-vous à de grands voyages?

Diane va bien. Elle avait tous ses fils, et Brice, et de leurs amis pour Noël; & cela était gai et fatigant, mais dans une atmosphère familiale pleine de douceur.

Puis le 28, en dormant, j'ai eu une attaque cérébrale—sans doute pas trop grave, puisque j'y ai survécu. Mais ma vue, du moins d'un œil, est affectée. Je ne puis plus conduire, ne peux guère marcher et je lis encore—je ne sais rien faire d'autre—mais avec difficulté et mon écriture dit ma faiblesse.

Très chaleureux vœux pour vous et les vôtres, et pour vos trois départements et vos écrits.

> Affectueusement,
> Henri

## To Florence Weinberg:

> January 20/88

Dear Florence,

I had just answered the enclosed, apologizing for my faulty writing, when your very kind letter arrived here. I'll answer it briefly, with warm thanks. Let's hope, as you say encouragingly, that I may recover in part my eyesight. I depend upon it so much, alas! Meanwhile Diana is a wonderful help & Brice, as it happens staying here until he decides upon his career, is also a great comfort.

I have to make this brief. I apologize & offer my thanks.

> Henri

## À Vincent Giroud:

Le 20.1.88

Cher Ami,

Le coup assez dur que j'ai eu ne me rend pas, pour l'instant, très présentable. Merci de votre mot. Je vous ferai dire si cela va mieux.

Cordialement,
Henri Peyre
290 North Ave.
Westport, Ct. 06880

## To Edward Kaplan:

Jan. 25/88

Dear Mr. Kaplan:

I fear I cannot answer you adequately: I cannot even write straight. Some two weeks ago, a stroke gravely affected my vision. I still manage to read, but I cannot drive. My morale remains good, but whatever scant prospects I still could have (at 87) are shattered.

I congratulate you on your intelligent enjoyment of life & on your loving understanding of Russia—and on the fine moral convictions which I have always sensed in you, & which I share.

The De Man revelations (they were not altogether a surprise for me) are indeed shattering. Two weeks ago, an article in the weekly *The Nation* made them even more disturbing. Personally, I had always been very reserved on his theories of criticism & a little annoyed by the cultist climate which he allowed his students to spread around them. I for one never swerved from my belief that literature *has* a content (aesthetic, psychological, philosophical, social, and *also moral* or ethical). And any racism has been my bête noire. The French Right & the former collaborators in the past attacked me ferociously on that score.

But just now I feel sorry for his widow & retrospectively sorry for him who concealed those very grave "errors" all his life & duped his friends—at Yale, mostly Jews (Derrida, Bloom, Hartman, Brombert).

Best wishes,
Henri Peyre

## À Édouard Morot-Sir:

> 290 North Avenue
> Westport, Ct. 06880
> Le 13 février 88

Cher ami,

Je suis touché de l'aimable pensée que vous avez eue de me faire parvenir ces trois essais si substantiels, si denses de réflexion approfondie et si fermement écrits. Celui sur le langage & la Critique de la Raison dialectique m'impressionne mais me dépasse; je ne me sens pas très propre à fournir un effort intellectuel rigoureux. J'ai eu, les tout derniers jours de décembre, une attaque qui a beaucoup affaibli ma vue et me rend la lecture difficile. Cela est pour moi, lecteur acharné et assidu, peu propre aux autres distractions (musique, télévision), un coup assez dur. Sans doute à près de 87 ans devais-je m'y attendre. Sur "le Songe" et ce que vous appelez avec ingéniosité "l'imagination ironique" de Perse, avec qui j'avais autrefois souvent parlé, je vous ai trouvé original et neuf et très juste. Votre science en matière d'histoire de la chimie dépasse mes médiocres connaissances et m'instruit. J'admire votre rigueur intellectuelle et la diversité de vos connaissances. Ni l'Amérique ni votre rôle de diplomate surmené ne vous ont jamais convié à céder à la facilité ou à la hâte. C'est une belle leçon pour vos cadets.

Je ne veux pas vous imposer plus longtemps mon écriture désordonnée. Mais vous m'avez manqué (à moi & à beaucoup d'autres) ces dernières années et j'envie Germaine Brée qui, plus proche de votre région, doit parfois s'entretenir avec vous. Sans doute, comme elle (et moi, votre aîné à tous), serez-vous bientôt à la retraite. Vous préférerez, j'imagine, rester en ce pays, près des vôtres. La politique américaine m'irrite, avec ce péril d'un cléricalisme étroit et arrogant. Si j'avais trente ans, sans doute ne resterais-je pas ici. L'ironie est que mon fils (23 ans) est passionné de politique, suit avec passion les élections et les "caucuses" et rêve d'une carrière dans ce domaine. Mes ironiques remarques d'un vieux "croulant" ne réussissent pas à le dissuader. Dites mes pensées respectueusement affectueuses à votre femme et croyez à mes remerciements.

Henri Peyre

## À son frère et à sa belle-sœur:

Le 18 février 1988

...Parlant de fiançailles (pardon de mon orthographe plus qu'incertaine!), il y a quelque six mois, sur l'insistance de Diane, elle et moi nous sommes rendus chez un fonctionnaire municipal et nous sommes régulièrement, ou légalement, mariés. Nous avons diffusé la nouvelle le moins possible. Je ne puis m'empêcher de trouver un peu ridicule et affreusement égoïste d'imposer officiellement mon grand âge de croulant à une personne aussi jeune, généreuse, pleine d'ardeur à vivre. Il se trouve que, il y a deux ans, je crois, quand, à la suite d'un afflux d'eau dans mes poumons et de sérieux "ennuis" cardiaques, Diane m'avait, d'urgence, conduit à l'hôpital de Norwalk. On lui avait fait des difficultés. Je ne voulais à aucun prix rester à l'hôpital, soumis à des tests incessants et au voisinage d'autres malades. On avait répondu à Diane qu'elle n'avait, n'étant que ma compagne, pas l'autorité de s'opposer aux avis médicaux. Elle avait argumenté, indignée, et avait gagné. Depuis elle pensait qu'une légalisation de nos rapports était opportune; j'hésitais beaucoup, jugeant cela un peu ridicule. Mais c'est chose faite. Cela ne change rien à son nom, qui reste celui de son ancien mari, qu'elle ne voit jamais. (Il a eu 3 ou 4 femmes légitimes depuis.) La cérémonie, qui ne mérite pas ce nom, était la plus prosaïque des formalités: trois minutes, deux signatures. Nous n'en avons même pas noté la date. Pas même de vœux de fidélité ou de bonheur. J'ai fait taire mes scrupules. À 86 ans, qu'avais-je à apporter? À la maison, je m'occupe deux matinées par semaine de rassembler les ordures et parfois je lave la vaisselle. Encore suis-je grondé pour ne pas utiliser la machine à laver! Et je donne à manger à Laura, sans jamais condescendre à la toucher ou à lui adresser la parole. Le monde animal m'est étranger—sauf peut-être celui des ânes. J'aimais les ânes du Caire, que l'on enfourchait pour aller jusqu'aux Pyramides; et Jacques se rappelle notre affection enfantine pour l'âne de Mérindol. Ici, quand la neige enfin fondra, si je suis encore de ce monde, je saluerai les premiers rouges-gorges et les daims....

## À Pierre et Hélène Pennec:

> 290 North Avenue. Westport, Ct. 06880
> Le 26 février 88

Chère Hélène, cher Pierre,

Quel beau cadeau que votre belle et longue lettre, arrivée ici le 19 février et apportant vos réflexions, toujours intéressantes et stimulantes pour moi. Il nous semble ainsi rester très proches de vous, parfois même plus qu'on ne se sent en présence réelle. Oui, j'ai donc franchi ce cap redouté des 87 ans il y a trois jours. Cela impressionne. Je me rappelle que peu avant sa mort, ayant atteint un âge presque aussi avancé, Papa m'écrivait: "Comment peut-on être aussi vieux?" La durée de la vie s'est allongée depuis 30 ans; est-ce dû à une meilleure hygiène? Aux pilules que nous avalons? Vitamines pour Diane? Pilules pour le cœur dans mon cas depuis un an, et maintenant aspirines auxquelles on découvre des propriétés rares? Il y a derrière cela beaucoup de publicité pharmaceutique, qui m'exaspère et me gâche la télévision et qui enrichit les grandes firmes suisses et américaines. Dans nos cas, le vôtre et le mien, il y a, je crois, et surtout la sagesse de savoir se plier à des régimes modérés et l'affection mutuelle. La terreur des gens âgés est celle de la solitude. Et l'angoisse des très vieux comme moi n'est pas de disparaître, mais de laisser un vide et de bouleverser l'existence de ceux qui se consacraient à vous. Vous faites tous deux un couple rare et pour moi admirable, surtout parce que vous avez subi les mêmes épreuves, gagné un combat difficile à force de courage et que vous partagez des goûts analogues et une longue file de souvenirs communs. C'est une rare bonne fortune que vous ayez retrouvé à Nice de vieux amis, avec qui vous pouvez revoir les environs, peut-être même vous aventurer en Italie ou en Espagne. Je n'avais guère aimé les fresques de Cocteau à Villefranche; mais si vous le pouvez, allez voir la chapelle de Matisse à Vence, les tableaux de la galerie Maeght à St. Paul de Vence. J'avais jadis séjourné à l'hôtel de St. Paul de Vence (est-ce la Goutte d'Or? ou la Colombe?) et y avais rencontré quelques peintres, alors à la mode. C'est probablement devenu à la mode depuis lors, et envahi.

Pardon de mon écriture ... fantaisiste et de ma répugnance pour la ligne droite et pour la partie gauche de la page. Ma vue latérale de ce côté-là reste très incertaine et à mon âge, je n'ai guère l'espoir que cela se remette. Mais je lis sans trop d'effort, je médite peut-être un peu plus que par le passé. Je dois renoncer à ce mot d'ordre, "Vite! Vite!" que Brice me reprochait. Peut-être même, encouragé par Diane qui craint que mon moral ne se détériore, vais-je essayer de conduire, au moins en plein jour et par les chemins que je connais; mais je redoute l'éventualité d'un accident. Il y a de l'arrogance à se vouloir indépendant et vous-mêmes n'avez pas trop souffert de ne pas avoir d'auto à votre disposition, parmi les montagnes de l'Isère. Sans doute disposez-vous, à Nice, d'abondantes facilités de circulation, autobus et train. Je me rappelle quelle épreuve cela était, simplement de traverser la promenade des Anglais! Avez-vous quelque goût pour les casinos et le jeu? Je n'ai jamais été beaucoup tenté moi-même; et je n'avais pas assez de ressources pour les risquer. Jacques dit y avoir gagné gros jadis; mais il est porté plus que moi à l'exagération et il a aussi plus de goût pour la spéculation financière. Mes souvenirs de Nice sont radieux: le pittoresque du vieux Nice, l'émerveillement devant les couleurs de la mer en arrivant par l'aéroport. Avez-vous de votre appartement une vue qui vous inspire? Une fois tout à fait installés, envoyez-nous une photo de votre intérieur et nous penserons à vous dans votre décor.

Le soir du 21 février, nous avons pensé à vous. Nous avons ouvert l'une des boîtes de pâté de foie gras que vous nous aviez envoyées et Diane portait un châle que lui avait donné Hélène. Nous avons bu à votre santé, les trois fils de Diane, de 25 (Carlo) à 34 ans étaient venus, un couple d'amis aussi et Brice. Mon appétit n'est pas très ardent et j'ai pas mal maigri cette dernière année mais je n'ai pas perdu goût à la vie et mon moral reste ferme, même si je me répands plus que de raison en plaintes sur l'horreur de la vieillesse et prédis ma fin prochaine. Je la prédis depuis si longtemps qu'on sourit de me voir encore de ce monde. Mes loisirs sont amples, mais je les emplis de souvenirs, de quelque relecture de poésies jadis beaucoup aimées et parfois de films, ou de "vidéocassettes" à la télévision. Je ne vais guère au cinéma et n'ai pas vu le Joyce-Huston, les Morts, dont Brice & Diane m'ont dit beaucoup de bien, comme vous; et j'ai obstinément refusé de me déranger pour les films de Pagnol, Jean de Fleurette, qu'on a beaucoup loués ici. Je ne suis guère sensible à cet humour méridional ou qui prétend l'être: peut-être réaction anti-provençale du Provençal que je suis, qui avait toujours regretté de n'être pas Breton ou même Écossais. Hélène parle de sa lecture de romans américains. Je les ai goûtés jadis, mais m'en suis bien dépris:

Fitzgerald, Lewis et autres. Faulkner demande trop d'effort et il est, pour moi, trop cantonné dans le Sud du pays. Depuis la mode ici est passée aux romans féministes, qui ne m'emballent pas non plus. Le trop fameux "Deuxième Sexe" est bien démodé et affreusement pédant et je me range maintenant à l'avis de Pierre, qui a toujours été très réservé sur le mérite durable des romans sartriens. Je ne regrette pas de l'avoir goûté en son temps: puis l'énorme pavé d'ours qu'est son travail sur Flaubert, venant après le non moins lourdaud et massif *Genet,* m'a éloigné de Sartre. Il a fini en homme haineux et assoiffé de popularité politique, abdiquant tout bon sens et toute sérénité. J'imagine que même les jeunes ne le lisent plus guère, sauf peut-être ses premières pièces et ses nouvelles. Vers 1938–45, j'étais emballé par tout cela et je préfère, sans relecture, conserver jalousement le souvenir de mes enthousiasmes. Dans le même esprit, je me refuse à relire Giraudoux et même Mauriac. J'avais encouragé (par lettre) mon frère à aller assister dans la Cour du Palais des Papes au *Soulier de Satin* de Claudel, jadis aussi un de mes enthousiasmes. Mais je n'y serais sans doute pas allé moi-même. Mieux vaut préserver intacts nos souvenirs.

Si Hélène lit l'anglais sans trop d'effort, j'aimerais lui envoyer quelques romans américains de ces dernières décennies. Qu'elle me le dise. Et peut-être vos amis s'intéressent-ils à ce qui paraît ici: économie? Ou politique, élections, art? Pierre également. Dites-moi *sans gêne* aucune quels livres ou magazines je pourrais lui envoyer. Cela me ferait plaisir. Ces temps-ci, la mode est de critiquer, très durement, la civilisation américaine, le très lent progrès de l'antiracisme, l'éducation et ses criantes insuffisances. Je suis moins sévère pour ma part. Rien ne me paraît plus épuisant que d'enseigner, dans les établissements correspondant en France aux écoles primaires ou supérieures des grandes villes. Les querelles et combats sont journaliers entre blancs et noirs, Portoricains et Cubains. Les élèves viennent avec des revolvers & des poignards, violent les maîtresses dans les lavabos ou les couloirs. Le métier est méprisé, mal payé. Il ne devient supportable qu'au niveau de ce qui s'appelle ici le "college": 15–20 ans. Diane a de la chance à Brooklyn d'avoir surtout des classes avancées et ceux qui prennent des cours de langue sont une élite. Surtout, Brooklyn est une ville juive—la plus nombreuse du monde—et les Juifs sont davantage attirés vers les choses de l'esprit et veulent réussir financièrement et socialement. Nous-mêmes ici n'avons pas un seul couple, parmi nos amis, qui ne soit juif. Récemment, leur sens de supériorité est ébranlé: 6, 7 pour dix des premières places (bourses données au concours, doctorats) vont aux rivaux: les "Asiatiques": Taiwan, Singapour, Coréens, Chinois surtout. Quand j'enseignais à New York au "Graduate Center," je m'étais naïvement étonné, lors des cérémonies de "commencement," de voir que huit sur huit des lauréats en microbiologie, en chimie spécialisée, même en physiologie et pathologie, étaient des "Asiatiques." Jamais un seul noir. Ils sont, bien sûr, fortement "motivés," comme on dit ici. Ils n'ont jamais passé de temps à la télévision. Ils sont déjà, en tant qu'immigrants (comme naguère les Juifs polonais et russes), une minorité décidée à réussir. Les Japonais donnent généreusement et orgueilleusement des leçons aux Américains. Ils achètent des maisons croulantes à N. York, les reconstruisent et les revendent. Le pays est inquiet et se sent joué. Dans les universités comme Yale, Princeton, Harvard, on n'ose pas remettre des "quotas" contre lesquels les Juifs avaient protesté il y a 50 ans. On essaie d'arrêter les "Asiatiques" en augmentant les coefficients des épreuves de lettres, d'histoire américaine, de sciences dites sociales, où les Jaunes sont défavorisés en raison de leur maîtrise moindre de la langue. Mais cela ne pourra pas durer. Le fameux "melting pot" qui devait américaniser les émigrants d'Europe, jadis, ne peut plus rien "melt" ou fondre. La France a des problèmes analogues et la Russie en a de pires. J'avais un jour écrit, en souriant, que De Gaulle pouvait se retirer de la vie active et écrire un livre, "À quoi tient l'infériorité des Anglo-Saxons." Cela est devenu une réalité. Nul, d'ailleurs, ne parle plus des "Anglo-Saxons." Le centre du monde de demain est désormais localisé autour du Pacifique.

Les très perspicaces réflexions politiques de Pierre, dans votre récente lettre, m'ont fait penser. J'admire la sûreté de ses vues et l'indépendance de ses jugements. Les coupures sur Gorbatchev sont curieuses, et justes. Ici, il y a eu un emballement un peu sot pour lui. On a honte de Reagan, habile mais si peu instruit et maladroit en paroles. Le malheur est que personne de vraiment supérieur n'apparaît pour lui succéder. Diane souhaiterait Cuomo, qui refuse d'être candidat. Brice est passé de son allégeance à Dukakis à Gore—mais ils font piètre figure. Bien sûr, on disait cela de Roosevelt en 1930–32; puis de Nixon. L'exercice du pouvoir révèle les hommes. Les exigences financières et oratoires de la télévision exigeraient des surhommes. Où les trouver? Il semble qu'en France on se soit un peu dépris de Barre et il est vrai que Chirac a manqué d'adresse et de présence. Réélire Mitterrand ne servira qu'à retarder une solution d'avenir. Si Mitterrand amène avec lui un socialisme rajeuni et constructif, cela peut donner une sorte de centrisme orienté quelque peu à gauche qui assurerait quelque stabilité. Observez-vous autour de vous, dans le Midi, une vraie montée Le Pen, ou est-il en perte de vitesse? L'économie semble aller assez bien: c'est le cas ici également. Mais ni l'Europe de l'Ouest ni les Etats-Unis ne paraissent pouvoir préparer l'avenir, contre la concurrence japonaise et devant une éventuelle poussée soviétique en Allemagne dénucléarisée. Ici, périodiquement, le sujet revient sur le tapis d'une diminution marquée des forces américaines en Europe. Un jour cela se fera. L'espoir, ici et ailleurs, est que nul, pas même la Russie, n'osera se lancer dans la folie d'une guerre destructrice de toute civilisation. Mais l'exemple de Napoléon s'engageant dans la campagne de Russie, celui d'Hitler un siècle et quart plus tard, sont assez pour ébranler toute confiance dans la sagesse des dirigeants et des peuples. J'ai jadis appartenu à des groupes de soi-disant sages qui essayaient de prédire, et de préparer, l'avenir. Nul de nous avant 1940 n'aurait jamais osé imaginer qu'il y aurait deux Allemagnes et que l'Europe s'en accommoderait. "Parlons-en toujours, n'y pensons jamais," dit un de mes amis allemands, sur la réunion éventuelle des deux moitiés de l'Allemagne. Apparemment, on y est résigné; comme l'est l'Autriche à rester un pays mineur. On a fait campagne ici contre Waldheim et son passé bien louche. Mais personne n'a jamais rien dit quand il était Secrétaire Général des Nations-Unies. Ici, à Yale surtout et ailleurs dans le pays, il y a eu récemment un scandale suivant la révélation que Paul de Man (aujourd'hui disparu) avait, en Belgique occupée, en 1943–45, écrit de virulents articles pro-Nazis et antisémites. Il ne l'a jamais révélé ensuite et a lancé de savantes et pédantes théories critiques: "déconstructionnisme," notamment. J'avais flairé en lui quelque embarras lorsque je lui demandais s'il avait subi l'influence de oncle, Henri De Man, socialiste devenu, non seulement Flamingant farouche, mais pro Hitlérien. Mais je m'étais abstenu de déclarer mes doutes ou mes soupçons. Il était d'ailleurs malade et est mort d'un cancer au foie. Pour moi, l'énigme était d'essayer de comprendre pourquoi et comment des socialistes (dont j'ai bien connu certains: Marcel Déat, Max Bonnafous, à l'École Normale) étaient soudain devenus des partisans enthousiastes de l'"Ordre nouveau" hitlérien. Certains, qui avaient fait la première Guerre dans les tranchées, ont été ébranlés par la défaite rapide de 1940 et en ont voulu à leurs cadets qui avaient si vite abandonné le combat. L'atmosphère en

France, vers 1936–39, était, je dois le dire, odieuse. C'est une des raisons pour lesquelles, en 1939, j'ai quitté sans regret la France des Croix de Feu, de *Candide, Gringoire, Je suis Partout:* la haine sévissait partout. J'avais personnellement été attaqué, comme "universitaire de gauche," par Claude Roy et autres; alors que, dans le fond, comme je le dis à Brice qui ne voit cela que du dehors, mon gauchisme, qu'on appelle ici "libéralisme" est surtout intellectuel et raisonné. Dans le fond, mon tempérament est celui d'un homme d'ordre et d'un timoré, éloigné de tout fanatisme et de toute violence.

[ . . .]

Brice essaie d'écrire un peu; il a publié un article ou deux, sur des sujets politiques. Mais je reste inquiet pour son avenir et je lui en veux de se montrer si peu épistolier—notamment envers vous qui l'avez aidé et qu'il admire et aime. Pour le moment, il m'aide beaucoup, puisque je m'avoue affaibli et dépendant des autres. Il va bien d'ailleurs. Diane vous embrasse et souhaite une visite de vous ce printemps—mais elle n'ose pas y compter. D'elle, de Brice et de moi, beaucoup de tendre affection—et pardon encore de mon écriture.

Henri

## À Konrad Bieber:

Le 26 février 88

Cher Konrad,

Cet envoi de fleurs, particulièrement bien choisies et si délicates, a réjoui ma journée d'implacable vieillissement. Je vous en remercie et cette pensée fidèle m'a beaucoup touché. Il me semble avoir à Stony Brook une seconde famille et un noyau de fidèles amis experts à oblitérer le passage des années. Je ne vous vois guère—et mon récent accident de santé ne me laisse pas espérer que je puisse entreprendre des voyages. Ma coordination est affaiblie; mon écriture doit le trahir. Et j'ai perdu toute mobilité physique. Mais je lis encore, avec plus d'effort; et j'ai un passé assez long et assez lourd pour que je puisse, avec narcissisme, évoquer d'anciens souvenirs.

L'exemple que je voudrais pouvoir suivre est le vôtre—celui de Tamara. J'admire immensément sa belle fermeté et son courage devant les maux qui l'ont assaillie. Et cela après les cruelles épreuves que lui avaient, à elle et à vous, infligées le Nazisme, puis la guerre. Je repense souvent à vous, à l'art avec lequel, à New Haven, à New London, et dans votre charmante maison de Port Jefferson, construit une vie neuve. J'espère que les nouvelles de votre fils vous satisfont. L'avenir du mien m'inquiète parfois. Il est passionné de politique et essaie du journalisme, ce qui déroute ma stabilité de vieil universitaire. Mais il est intelligent et a reçu une bonne éducation. Qu'il fasse sa carrière. Les trois fils de Diane ont, chacun de son côté, arrangé à leur guise leur existence. Ils étaient là le 21 février pour me souhaiter quelque joie encore, et une heureuse fin de vie.

Merci, chère Tamara et cher Konrad, avec toute notre affection à tous deux.

Henri

## To George Margolis:

March 18/88

Dear George,

Your kind visit, our conversation & the reading of your letter to the Dartmouth President & the piece "Why not me?" have brought to Diana & me much needed encouragement in the gloomy week we are living. I am personally not only full of affection for you & your wife, grateful for all that you have done through the years for Diana, but profoundly happy to have encountered a man with the idealism, the intense, intelligent devotion to the most important cause of our time. The task you have set yourself is second to none today in importance if some civilization & some faith in the future of mankind are to be preserved. Your devotion is admirable, as is your revolt against the gross inequalities and the revolting greed of our civilization. "Why you?" You are an exceptional person. I have met well known writers, artists, politicians in my life, but few whom I esteem as deeply as I do you. Your retirement could have been a lazy & selfish one like mine; you might easily have let the world have its selfish way & basked in the realization that you had raised a uniquely happy family of gifted children and encouraged a devoted wife to pursue her artistic vocation. But you have, unselfishly, achieved more than that & fought for a better society. If there were a thousand people like you, the world would be more livable. Thank you for being yourself.

With affection,
Henri

## To Florence Weinberg:

March 21/88

Dear Florence,

I am grateful for the kindness of your letter, full of sensitiveness & generosity. The news on Ted Morris makes me very sad; he embodied youth, vigor, dash & élan for me. And Kurt's courage in the face of more trouble is amazing. He & you are superhuman beings—and you are back with Hesiod, of all poets, & to the seventeenth century! I hope the Tennessee position goes to the one, the only one, in my eyes, who is fully worthy of it. If I am consulted by Washington University, I shall consider it an honor to sing your praise. I stand second to none in my sincere admiration for your immense & discriminating knowledge.

Spring is still remote here. Snow, cold & much gloom with my impaired eyesight & Diana (who feeds me, upholds my courage, keeps me alive) had a bad fall in the New York subway & broke her knee: operation; inability to bend the repaired knee cap; months of patient waiting for the bones to be repaired. How sad is old age with its retinue of woes & complaints! Sally Cornell, in Hamden, broke her back. Dostoevsky was right. No one should live beyond sixty.

With profound sympathy,
Henri

## À son frère et à sa belle-sœur:

Le 31 mars 1988

... Ma conviction est que George Bush, fidèle à Reagan, l'emportera et ce sera une présidence terne, dénuée de vision imaginative et de chaleur. Ici et en France, ce que la majorité souhaite est une vie calme, prosaïque, chargée d'ennui, sans aventures; et nul ne souffre de l'absence d'intellect ou de vision chez les dirigeants. En France du moins, on a la prétention de croire que les candidats ont des idées à eux, et du style—ils écrivent des livres. Peut-être ont-ils tort, comme Barre, qui semble être en perte de vitesse et ne réaliserait jamais ses promesses ou n'atteindrait pas ses objectifs. Il paraît que Giscard a publié un livre, assez amusant même; l'avez-vous vu? C'est un cynique. Mais Chirac au fond ne l'est pas moins et il est capable de faire des avances à Le Pen pour profiter de ses votes. On dit que Le Pen aurait aisément de 10 à 12% de l'électorat et constituerait une vraie force. Je le trouve répugnant et dangereux. Mais si je vivais en France, et parmi les escroqueries et cambriolages par des Nord-Africains, ou même devais les observer chaque jour à mendier et gambader place de l'horloge, peut-être rabattrais-je de mes nobles principes? Ici, et même à New York, nous prenons bien garde de ne pas nous mêler aux noirs et hispaniques. Mais les divisions raciales dans le pays sont un très grave problème pour l'avenir. On pense qu'un jour, au 21e siècle, l'espagnol sera devenu la langue la plus courante et on tente de restreindre l'immigration. C'est une peur dissimulée ou refoulée, mais profonde. Cela explique en partie le mouvement qui pousse bien des gens, surtout dans le Sud (protestant), vers des sectes étranges et surtout vers des prédicateurs qui évoquent Satan et les peines de l'enfer. Certains de ces pasteurs ont été convaincus d'escroqueries, de coucher avec des prostituées ou de séduire des petits garçons; mais tout leur est pardonné. Il n'y a plus que les vieux moralistes classiques comme moi pour s'indigner.

Merci, cher frère, de ces articles du *Monde,* sur Proust et autres. Cela amuse Diane et Marilyn qui travaille sur Proust. Un jour je le relirai en entier, peut-être. En attendant, je n'ai nullement le fétichisme de sa personne, des cravates qu'il a pu porter, des meubles de son appartement, de ses écrits et de son bureau. Je n'ai, il est vrai, rien du collectionneur et ne conserve aucune lettre. J'en ai reçu jadis de gens célèbres: Valéry, Malraux, Breton, Char et les ai ou jetées, ou données aux bibliothèques. ...

## To Sally Cornell:

April 28/88

Dear Sally,

    The month of May is close. It should usher in a radiant blossoming of the two or three magnolias around here; there are already daffodils along the houses of neighbors &, in the garden next to ours, apple trees are fragrant. I had never realized how much my morale is conditioned by the weather & the rebirth of nature, probably because I always lived in the midst of cities before: Avignon, in the dark, medieval center of the town, five minutes from the massive "Popes" palace; then Paris, only resplendent in early March when the chestnut trees shaded the café terraces; London & Cambridge, where I lived in the early twenties. In truth, I never found pleasure in gardening & preferred to declaim poetry, hymns to flowers & paeans to trees in my bookish way, while my father put me to shame by digging, clipping, growing vegetables, watering. What an intellectual snob I was! In my young years, every spring we used to spend 8 or 10 days at my grandmother's in an ancient Protestant village, half destroyed by the Catholics in the sixteenth century. I enjoyed playing with my brothers & the village urchins, watching the masons build walls & the blacksmith make horseshoes. For 2 or 3 years, I even took my Protestant religion seriously, arranging fights against the half of the village which was Catholic. I attended the Easter sermon, incredulous and bored. I have never forgiven pastors for making us believe in childish stories of miracles and of the resurrection. When my brother died in 1918, at 16 years of age, I revolted against the lip service paid to belief in another life and rejected all my would-be religious education. Even to this day, I read & reread histories of religion & experience recurrences of my stubborn antichristian conviction. My favorite reference book is by a great Jewish French scholar, long dead: Orpheus. Yet my friends (Georges May among them) have always teased me for being a hater of faith and yet secretly drawn to religious writers, Renan, Claudel, Mauriac, Green. I suppose I am a crusader (for atheism) at heart, but a person for whom the religious issues count much. Many believers are in truth bored by them. My one remaining cult is pantheism & I love nature more ardently now than when I ran & swam & raced with the wind, like Shelley in his famous ode which I still recite to myself.

To come down to earth & daily routine: here things are a little better with Diana, somewhat more robust & able to bend her knee a little — even to drive very slowly. For a time, with my sight extremely weak on sunless days & both of us stuck with cars we could not manipulate, daily life was really difficult. Now & then a young colleague of Diana came & helped us a little, but at 4 miles from any grocery, it was a tough existence. Brice was here off & on; but he now has a job in New York & commutes every day. He enjoys the work & feels proud making a little money on his own. He still hopes eventually to resume his studies, in some Law School, perhaps in the West. I am feeble myself, devoid of appetite & of zest for living, & truly ready to bid farewell to this world. I do not count on surviving much beyond this summer; I even dread the prospect of visiting my brother in late June when Diana gives courses to the Bryn Mawr–Avignon Summer School. All I could do, I suppose, is to fly directly from New York to Nice, rest there a day or two, & go to Avignon. A warm welcome would greet us there; but I fear I would wax impatient at my brother's stories & feel estranged from him & from my childhood memories, after my long American stay.

How are you yourself, & how about your back ache? It is sad that, after seventy (& in my own case, way beyond eighty), we inevitably fall back upon enumerating & lamenting our woes. You remain admirable, never complaining, never cursing & finding a renewed youth in flowers & birds & the company of cats. You cheerfully keep up with the news of your friends. Some of the reports I hear, through Brice, are distressing: Wellek in a nursing home; Boorsch struck by some internal intestinal hemorrhage. I cannot attempt to visit them. I had, vaguely, hoped that my half blindness would slowly surrender to a clearer vision; but my foolish hopes have been frustrated. One does not get better after 85 & that's it.

My thoughts go to you & my memories often take me back to the talks Kenneth & I had when Brice was a little boy & then an adolescent. I seem to know no one any more at Yale & it is better so: I probably would not be very sympathetic to some of the methods of interpretation which have since flourished. There was a scandal around the revelations on Paul de Man's past. I kept out of that, feeling pity & regret for his widow.

Very affectionate wishes.<br>
Henri

## À son frère et à sa belle-sœur:

Le 1er mai 1988

... Il me semble toujours présomptueux de formuler des plans à l'avance et de paraître compter ainsi sur une victoire de la vieillesse contre le destin. Que de disparus autour de nous, Jacques et moi! et quel scepticisme on acquiert, après quelques décennies, sur les changements politiques, quand on se rappelle les fureurs à propos de la guerre civile espagnole, des congés payés, de la droite toujours aveugle et sotte se tournant contre Blum, Doriot et le pétainisme! Comment ce Le Pen peut-il faire croire aux Français que leurs maux présents seraient guéris si l'on renvoyait les immigrés! On nous attribuait jadis de l'esprit critique. Mais nous sommes aussi bêtes que les Allemands et les Autrichiens que j'avais vus, en 1936, se jeter dans les bras d'Hitler. ...

## À Mario et Penny Maurin:

Lundi 23 mai 88

Chers amis,

Notre dimanche a été attristé par votre absence et la nouvelle que Penny s'était trouvée indisposée. Cela va-t-il mieux? N'était-ce qu'un incident relativement léger? A-t-elle, pour le reste, eu un début de printemps tolérable? Tout semble être allé mal ces mois derniers pour plusieurs de nos amis ou connaissances et mon vieux scepticisme est presque tenté de questionner les astres. Mais comment agir sur eux, alors que nous n'avons jamais réussi à guider ou à transformer nos enfants? Naïfs, ou vaniteux professeurs que nous sommes, nous nous disons que nos étudiants et disciples seuls nous accordent quelque rôle dans leur formation. Il eût été bien agréable de nous entretenir avec Penny (son nom officiel est-il celui de l'épouse d'Ulysse?) que nous voudrions beaucoup mieux connaître, et je suis pour ma part attristé d'avoir depuis le temps héroïque où il nous avait à Yale, éblouis par son savoir et son originalité eu si rarement l'occasion de parler à loisir avec Mario. Votre visite ne sera que remise et peut-être nous verrons-nous à Avignon, si vous y venez tous deux au début de l'été? Ou à Westport en fin juillet ou août. Pour le moment, le jardin est radieux de couleurs variées d'arbres en fleurs et jamais l'herbe n'a été aussi insolemment verte. Mais cette humidité obstinée nous fait rêver d'une brusque bouffée de mistral purifiant. Cela n'améliorerait sans doute pas ma vue affaiblie; mais Diane, fille de l'Adriatique, soupire après un chaud soleil. Après sa chute et son genou, encore endolori, elle a subi de mystérieuses douleurs internes qui ont tenu les médecins perplexes. On pense maintenant qu'il s'agit d'un "Lyme disease," identifié à Lyme, Conn., résultant de la piqûre d'un tique qui serait transporté par les daims ("deer"). Il y en a en effet parfois qui viennent se repaître de l'herbe nouvellement fauchée et qui gambadent çà et là. J'espère que votre jardin ne tente pas leurs pareils à Rosemont.

Rassurez-nous d'un mot sur la santé de Penny; acceptez nos regrets et nos vœux; et à bientôt peut-être.

Henri

## À Mario Maurin:

Le 3 juin 88

Merci, cher Mario, de votre mot et de ce texte *très réussi* et très drôle. Vous avez tous les talents, dont celui de parodiste et de poète. J'avais, en prévision de votre passage, pris sur mes rayons et passé à Diane votre livre sur Leopardi. Je me suis pris à le relire. À 18 ans, j'avais été fanatique de ce poète; je cultivais alors le plus noir pessimisme, maudissais la vie avant de l'avoir vécue et j'avais récité "La Ginestra" lors de mon premier voyage à Naples. J'ai relu votre livre. il est *remarquable* en tous points— d'érudition vaste mais discrète, de justesse de ton, de finesse psychologique, de courage critique qui loue mais souligne aussi les faiblesses. Ce devrait être traduit et servir dans les classes d'introduction à Léopardi. Puis-je sans flatterie vous dire que vous écrivez une prose ferme, souple, sobre—l'une des meilleures de toutes les œuvres critiques de ces dernières dizaines d'années. Et je vous imagine également maître de votre style en italien, en espagnol, en catalan. Vous a-t-on dit que vous avez un rare et précieux talent d'écrivain? Heureuse Penny de vivre avec un tel homme!

Ici cela va mieux—un peu bousculé par la convalescence de Diane, notre prochain départ.

> À bientôt. Mille bonnes choses à tous deux,
> Henri
> 290 North Avenue
> Westport, Ct. 06880

## À Philip Kolb:

> Le 8 juin 88

Cher ami,

Encore une fois, que je vous dise toute mon admiration. Jamais le moindre signe de fléchissement; nulle perte de cette acuité de vues, de ces ingénieuses enquêtes, de cette originalité d'interprétation qui sont votre marque. Enfin vous apercevez la sortie de cet interminable tunnel. Votre monument est le plus généreux, le plus minutieusement assidu qu'on ait consacré à un grand écrivain français. Et chez vous pas une minute d'impatience ou d'agacement! Avec tout mon amour pour Proust, que je lis depuis 1920, parfois j'aimerais qu'il invite ses duchesses ailleurs qu'au Crillon, au Ritz ou chez Larue, qu'il hante des restaurants d'étudiants, traverse la Seine, interroge des prostituées, rencontre des pauvres... Mais je suis à demi gâteux et las des mondains. Après d'assez durs accrocs de santé, je m'arrange pour survivre tout de même, et, secrètement, je vous prends comme mon modèle.

Mes remerciements. À l'occasion, mon souvenir à votre fille et ma chaude amitié.

> Henri Peyre

## À Georges May:

> 15 juillet 1988

Cher Georges,

Oui, c'était une aventureuse, sotte, téméraire décision que de faire, à 87 ans, ce voyage, avec un cœur très atteint, une immense faiblesse générale, mon incapacité à marcher droit et vingt autres faiblesses. Diane avait accepté de donner un cours (qui a eu un grand succès) au centre Bryn Mawr–Avignon. Mon frère, qui m'est profondément attaché et que j'aime, avec ses traits amusants et exaspérants de méridional et sa femme avaient arrangé pour nous un appartement dans la vieille maison familiale. Nous avons été entourés de soins et d'affection. Tout s'est bien passé et nous sommes revenus le onze juillet. Mais ma fatigue est extrême. Je suis à vrai dire tout près de ma fin; le voyage de retour était dur. Il est fou de voyager ainsi, malade et décrépit. Bien sûr, je parle plus que jamais de ma mort prochaine et j'en attriste Brice et Diane—et les fils de Diane à l'occasion. Ce séjour à l'ombre des Papes ne m'a pas rapproché de la foi et, quand vous apprendrez cette fin si souvent annoncée (et désirée), vous n'aurez qu'à en informer qui à Yale se souvient de moi. Vous avez été et vous restez à travers les années l'ami dont je me sens le plus proche, le plus sûr et le plus discret. Vous avez beaucoup compté dans ma carrière et dans ma vie.

J'y vois trop mal et écris trop étrangement pour vous infliger de plus longs adieux. Peut-être, si Brice ou Diane me conduit, tenterai-je une visite à Yale. J'ai dû déserter cette bibliothèque qui m'est si chère. Le long souvenir de notre amitié et de notre collaboration m'accompagne, les longs moments où, dormant mal, je repense au passé. Dites bien à votre femme quelle grande part j'ai eu à son existence, depuis la naissance de votre aînée et combien j'ai estimé ce qu'elle a fait pour vous. Croyez à mes vœux pour vos deux filles. Et acceptez que je vous serre dans mes faibles bras, à l'espagnole.

Bien à vous.<br>Henri

Vous ai-je dit que, il y a un an ou deux, mon mariage avec Diane a été "régularisé"; on lui refusait sans cela de m'éviter le séjour à l'hôpital, dont j'ai une maladive horreur. D'ailleurs, n'ai-je pas toujours été un affreux bourgeois, et content de l'être?

## Au même:

22 juillet 1988

Bien cher Georges,

Votre visite, si affectueuse et cordiale, m'a vivement touché et a fait plaisir également à Diane, que votre souriant humour a reposé de mes lamentations trop monotones sur le chagrin que je vais lui causer et que je n'ai fait qu'empirer en le prédisant trop indiscrètement. Sans doute ai-je en secret un goût du dramatique plus marqué que je ne l'avais cru! Ces examens médicaux répétés, ces soumissions à des machines imposantes et humiliantes pour mon orgueil de mâle, cette efficace surhumanité me font davantage apprécier le prix de cette simplicité que vous mettez dans l'amitié. Votre dévouement m'a toujours beaucoup touché. Et je me rappelle avec émotion mes entretiens avec votre père, votre frère et la compréhension dévouée que leur manifestait Martha. J'ai toujours regretté de trop mal la connaître.

À ce propos, j'ai négligé de vous remercier du double et généreux présent que vous avez apporté: la boîte de biscuits français et le livre ovidien [dans un numéro de la revue *Corps Écrit*]. Vous êtes curieusement resté le plus français et le plus parisien des franco-américains, jusque dans votre langage, et en même temps le mieux adapté à ce pays. Nul autre parmi nous n'aurait pu fonctionner avec une telle aisance comme Doyen et "Provost," puis revenir à votre charrue de Cincinnatus. Merci de ce présent délicat et du livre. La variété des essais sur les métamorphoses m'a instruit et diverti également. Les essais sont savants, précis et écrits avec variété et charme. Vous avez eu du goût et un sage discernement à rester fidèle à cette publication.

Je sais que je ne devrais pas vous infliger plus longtemps mes lignes courbes, pas même pour formuler les remerciements que j'avais négligé d'exprimer. Acceptez mes excuses. Mais le fidèle attachement que vous m'avez témoigné, en cette semaine—probablement la plus éprouvante de ma longue vie—m'a beaucoup touché, et a touché Diane. Merci à vous et à votre femme, et nos vœux très chers pour sa santé et cette de vos filles.

Bien à vous et merci.
Henri

## To Florence and Kurt Weinberg:

Aug. 4—88

Dear Florence & Kurt,

Will you pardon a very few lines, badly scribbled. Your very kind letter this summer, from Missouri, touched me much. I have always remained very attached to you. But I can hardly write. I had a stroke in July, on returning from a rash trip to Europe, & I have been hardly able to see, or to move, since. This clearly is at age 87 my long delayed end. The thought of Kurt's ordeals & of his superhuman patience is to me an example. I am very well taken care of; all is as well as can be in these circumstances.

A very affectionate farewell,
Henri

## À Georges May:

18 août 1988

Cher Georges,

Cette nouvelle, ou cet [auto] accident, me chagrine—presque d'une manière personnelle et j'en veux au sort, ou à votre écraseur. C'est porter un coup au "dimidium animae meae." Encore le mériterais-je si c'est moi qui avais été frappé, mais vous, si modéré et placide conducteur! Je me demande où cela vous est survenu, et en quelles parties de votre voiture, et par la faute de qui? Un jour vous me le direz au téléphone. Soignez bien vos blessures en attendant et dites à Martha ma tristesse et mon indignation. Hélas! enchaîné moi-même par mes diverses faiblesses, je ne peux rien pour vous aider. Tenez-moi au courant de votre récupération.

Enfin cet affreux temps oppressif paraît s'atténuer.

Souhaits à vous deux,
H—

vous atteindra même si vous avez quitté le Michigan pour votre "royale" résidence. Qu'il vous apporte nos vœux affectueux.

Henri

## To Robert G. Cohn:

290 North Avenue<br>Westport, Ct. 06880<br>October 6—88

Dear Bob,

    I write very few letters nowadays & my handwriting, since I had a stroke or two this last year, is probably worse than ever. But I cannot resist telling you how much I enjoyed your free, ingenious, incisive remarks on several themes treated by Baudelaire; & your original and entertaining "Mallarmean" treatment of Derrida. Of course *you* are right on "hymen," though at my advanced stage in life I do not presume to be competent to discuss that delicate membrane. I am glad, & somewhat relieved that you have remained yourself, artistic & poetical amid those fierce feminists demolishing the "canon" at Stanford! What strange rage fills the hearts of those scions of the well-off classes in your university!

Cordial wishes,<br>Henri

## À Georges May:

26 nov. 1988

Cher Georges,

    Merci de votre affectueux message. Tout ce qui vient de vous me touche et me relie à mon passé de Yale et à ce département rajeuni et prospère auquel je reste attaché. Je continue à trouver paradoxal et presque ridicule que je survive à tant d'autres; j'en ai eu quelquefois presque honte et me dis que j'aurais dû commettre plus d'excès. Mais il est bien tard pour que je mette à fumer la pipe! Et ces repas de Thanksgiving, axés sur l'abondance et imposant 48 heures d'épuisants efforts à la cuisinière, me semblent des survivances d'un autre âge. Tout s'est d'ailleurs bien passé ici; jeunes et leurs amis, dinde, farce et tout le rituel. Diane a enfin surmonté ses divers maux: genoux, "Lyme disease" transmises par les daims qui viennent gambader sur la pelouse, et je suis moi-même en bien meilleure forme qu'il y a six mois. J'espère que vous avez eu une réunion de famille pleine de chaleur.

Il m'arrive de me faire conduire à Yale pour renouveler mon stock de livres, mais j'aurais mauvaise grâce à aller gaspiller le temps d'un ami actif et je professe n'avoir pas de goût pour les bavardages et les potins. Du moins vous restez très présent à mes pensées.

Vœux de Noël sinon de Thanksgiving à Martha et à vos filles — et petits enfants nés ou à naître.

Toujours bien vôtre,<br>Henri

J'ai également été très attristé par la mort de Brewster. Je l'avais connu undergraduate, isolationniste, puis l'avais souvent vu à Martha's Vineyard. Je l'estimais beaucoup.

## À Lester et Billie Crocker:

Dimanche 4 déc. — 88

Chers amis,

Votre aimable et généreuse visite hier nous a donné une vraie joie. Vous êtes tous deux parmi le très petit nombre d'amis dont la présence et la conversation nous réjouissent. Vous n'hésitez pas à prendre la peine de venir par le train, d'interrompre votre loisir de "weekend" et vous arrivez chargés de dons et de bienfaits. Billy flatte notre gourmandise et cet alléchant gâteau va régaler les amis de Carlo qui viennent ici aujourd'hui. Le Talbot est une rareté que nous garderons pour une occasion toute spéciale. Les handicaps inévitables de mon grand âge m'invitent à me rattraper sur des gourmandises raffinées et sur les vins de choix que Lester est expert à sélectionner. Nous et nos invités et mon neveu avons été ravis de votre présence et séduits par votre conversation. Si je survis jusque là, je serai impatient d'apprendre comment se seront passées ces séances sur les Droits de l'Homme et la transfiguration en révolutionnaire (ou presque) du sage et pondéré Lester. Cette invitation académique honore, en sa personne, le beau travail accompli par l'érudition et la critique américaines. Personnellement, le souvenir de mes visites, jadis, à Cleveland, de nos rencontres à Londres et à Paris, de nos entretiens toujours amicaux, de la générosité de Billy, splendide hôtesse, me sont parmi les plus chers de ma longue carrière franco-américaine.

Je ne me sens pas le droit de vous imposer trop longtemps ma maladroite écriture. Même par une journée ensoleillée comme celle-ci, ma vision est défaillante. Votre visite, vos présents de choix nous ont beaucoup touchés, Diane et moi. Passez de bonnes et surtout de reposantes semaines en cette fin de 1988 et dites nos vœux à nos enfants.

Avec affection,<br>Henri

## To Stanley Burnshaw:

290 North Ave.<br>Westport, Ct. 06880<br>December 7—1988

Dear Stanley,

You are the most affectionate, the most generous of friends, and the most impeccable man of affairs. I confess I am embarrassed by such lavish payment for a very modest & by now forgotten contribution to a volume which was solely *your* creation, *your* idea. We, the contributors, were amply rewarded by being allowed to fill in the niches you had prepared for us. Please consider yourself from now on as the *sole* author. The marked success of the book is a tribute to your imagination & to your gift for converting friends to your creative ideas. None of us should receive any more payment.

I am glad for you that you are able to go to Florida & that you will teach there. You have all the gifts of a thoughtful and effective teacher. I always thought you would have been a remarkable university president. You chose another career. You have provided us teachers with valuable tools & far reaching suggestions.

I am well—relatively—still immobilized, since I cannot drive or travel, & with an impaired vision. I take my enforced quietude with patience. I do not feel any pain. I merely stay quiet, read, reread, & somehow meditate. I never was a devotee of conversations by phone, so that people do not disturb me. Diana takes excellent care of me, & keeps me up with the news of the academic world. She teaches three days a week in Brooklyn & at the CUNY Graduate Center. Her sons, and mine, were here for Thanksgiving & will return for Christmas. They are all lively and truly devoted. I eat little and drink even less. A dull and monotonous life. At 87 I have learned to adapt to near solitude. I still recite poetry to myself, but my memory is no longer able to learn new ones. I have reread some of your works lately and admired your seminal aesthetic ideas.

Pardon my poor writing. Enjoy Florida. You will be much in my thoughts.

Henri

## À Jean Boorsch:

Le 9 déc. 88

Chère Louise, cher Jean,

Je n'ai jamais été très adonné aux jolies cartes de Noël et je préfère, ces temps-ci, ne pas imposer mon écriture déformée à mes amis. Mais en cette fin d'année, il m'arrive souvent de penser à vous, à la splendide patience de Louise, à votre dévouement de mari et de père, et à votre longue et solide amitié. Sans doute prenez-vous quelque vacance en Floride peut-être. Reposez-vous et restez joyeux si possible.

Je ne puis m'aventurer en auto depuis ces accidents qui ont très affaibli ma vision et je n'ai personne pour me conduire à Yale. Diane est trop prise par ses cours et de fréquentes visites de ses fils, d'amis de ses fils, de neveux à moi venant de France. Elle veille avec une admirable sollicitude sur ma santé défaillante. Hier encore, j'ai failli être emporté par une faiblesse soudaine: hôpital, tests à n'en plus finir, lutte féroce pour refuser de rester à l'hôpital. Ma solide constitution de paysan (parvenu) a résisté. À 87 ans, je sais bien que ce n'est pas pour longtemps. Mais je jouis encore de quelques joies et je lis avec assiduité.

Diane vous envoie ses vœux pour vous et votre famille. J'y joins les miens. Je n'ose plus "regarder en face le cadavre de mes jours" et calculer depuis combien d'années je vous connais tous deux—qu'importe d'ailleurs! Aucun nuage n'a jamais terni notre amitié.

Partagez avec vos enfants nos bien affectueuses pensées et croyez à nos vœux pour l'année à venir.

Henri

# A Brief Biography of Henri Peyre

Henri Maurice Peyre was born to Brice Henri and Marie Tuvien Peyre in Paris on February 21, 1901. An excellent student at the École Normale Supérieure and then at the Sorbonne, he received his *licence* in 1922, and passed his *agrégation* in 1924, before spending two years in the French army. At some point in his studies, Peyre had met Daniel Mornet, a professor at Columbia (and subsequently at the British Institute in Paris), and Albert Feuillerat of Yale. Both had been sufficiently encouraging about their teaching positions in America to persuade him to do likewise—so Henri Peyre came across the ocean, to teach first at Bryn Mawr College, in Pennsylvania, from 1924 to 1927. There he met and married Marguerite Vanuxem in 1927. When Feuillerat invited him to Yale, on a five-year appointment, he accepted.

He received his *doctorat d'état* from the Sorbonne in 1932, with his study of Louis Ménard (1822–1901) and a *Bibliographie critique de l'hellénisme en France* (1843–1870); both works were published by Yale University Press in the same year. The French ministry assigned him to a three-year post at the University of Cairo, from 1933 to 1936, and then at the University of Lyon, where he began teaching in 1937.

But Henri Peyre had enjoyed America on his first visit, and he returned to Yale after just one year in Lyon, in 1938. He became the chair of the French department the next year, a post he held until his retirement from Yale, where he had been a Sterling Professor, thirty years later. In 1969 he came to the Graduate School of the City University of

New York, to become chair or executive officer of the Ph.D. Program in French, a post he held until 1980. At his retirement from the Graduate Center, the Henri Peyre Institute was created in his honor.

Besides writing a massive number of books, articles, and essays, he was active in the profession, serving as the president of the American Association of Teachers of French and of the Modern Language Association, as well as on the boards of the National Endowment for the Humanities, the Guggenheim Foundation, the American Council of Learned Societies, the American Philosophical Society, and the American Academy of Arts and Sciences. He was awarded the Légion d'Honneur by the French government.

On the personal side, soon after the death of Marguerite in November 1962, Henri Peyre married Lois Haegert of New Haven; they had a son, Brice. After their divorce he married Diana Festa, with whom he shared a home in Westport, Connecticut, and an apartment in New York, until his death on December 9, 1988, at eighty-seven.

M. A. C.

# Index

Abraham, Claude, 700
Adams, Donald, 566
Adams, L. Wayne, 122
Alden, Douglas, 284–85
Aldington, Richard, 568–69
Allison, John, 127, 153, 162
Alonso, Amado, 302
Alonso, Damaso, 350
Althusser, Louis, 909
American Association of Teachers of French, 480
American Philosophical Society, 407, 598, 613, 665, 669–71
Amis, Kingsley, 544
Andersson, Mrs., 205
Andersson, Theodore: appointment of, 217–18; departmental policy issues and, 249–50, 328, 339; Junior Year in France program, 259–60, 275–76; MAT program and, 509–10; miscellaneous correspondence, 290, 302; promotion of, 340–41, 469–70, 488–89
*André Malraux Review*, xi
Andrews, Wayne, 599–600, 603
Angell, James Rowland, 93
Anouilh, Jean, 512
antiwar movement, Peyre's comments on, 684–85

*Apostrophes* project, 981–85
Aragon, Louis, 211
Archambault, Paul: death of J. H. Matthews, 1032–33; Peyre's comments on book by, 993
Arnaud (French exchange student), 465
Aron, Jean-Paul, 960
Aron, Raymond, 1037
Arrom, José (Professor), 529
Artinian, Artine, 432–33
Ashburn, Frank, 299
atheism, Peyre's discussion of, 745, 808–9, 883, 940, 945, 1004–6, 1068–69
*Atlantic Monthly*, 189–90, 193–94
*Atys et Osiris*, Peyre's translation of, 14–15
Aubyn, Frederic Saint, Peyre's comments on revue, 853
Auden, W. H., 544
Auerbach, Erich: appointment of, 302, 316, 321, 327, 348, 495; death of, 520; graduate studies duties of, 497–98, 517; research assistance request for, 359; retirement of, 514–15, 519; salary discussions concerning, 443, 478
Austin, Lloyd, 621
*Avenir de la Science*, 795

Bachelard, Gaston, 716
Baer, Mrs. (graduate student), 827–28
Bakhtin, Mikhail, 684
Baldensperger, Fernand, 146, 162, 577
Baltimore Symposium, 255
Balzac, Honoré de, 287, 294–95, 588, 906
*Band of Angels*, 460–61
Bard College, 407–8, 429, 455
Barker, Joseph E.: Junior Year in France program and, 247–50, 259–61, 264–68, 274–76, 284–86; retirement of, 500–501, 511
Barret, Jean-Pierre, 486
Bart, Benjamin, 816
Barthélémy (French graduate student), 411
Barthes, Roland, 796
Barthold, Allen J., 90, 92, 95, 109, 134–35
Bartholomew, Marshall, 406
Bataillard, Jean, 486
Bate, Jackson, 841
Bates, R. C.: Feuillerat retirement and, 163, 178; French Department issues, discussion of, 91, 154–55, 172, 175; tenure issue and, 115
Baudelaire, Charles: *Baudelaire devant Dieu*, discussion of, 825; Caws discussion of, 934; CUNY lectures on, 676; Peyre's comments on, 391, 566, 988, 996–98; works discussed by Peyre's colleagues, 353, 453, 652, 879, 1078; Zimmermann's discussion of, 1019–20, 1025–26
*Baudelaire devant Dieu*, 825
Baudet, P., 122
Beaujour, Michel, 684
Beaumarchais, Pierre Augustin Caron de, 1012

Beauvoir, Simone de, 278, 842, 914
Bédard, Pierre: conference arrangements correspondence, 257–58, 317–18; conference speaker references, 243–44; conference topics discussion with, 107–8, 110–11; French-German war, role in, 159–60; French literature and the war effort, 167; invitation to Peyre to speak at institute, 143; literary jury proposal, 156–57; meetings with Peyre, correspondence about, 87, 127–28, 185–86, 233, 378; Merleau-Ponty discussed with, 266; miscellaneous correspondence, 130–31; occupied France conference correspondence, 185–86; Peyre's comments on reports of, 150–51; presentation planning, 195–96; Saint-Exupéry conference correspondence with, 177–78; thank you notes from Peyre, 46–47, 194–95
Bédé, Jean-Albert, 229, 812
Bégué, Armand, 501
Béguin, Albert, 323
Beinecke Library, Peyre correspondence in, xv
Bell, Daniel, 1043–44
Bénichou, Paul, 315, 536
Bergin, Thomas, 530–31
*Betrachtungen eines Unpolitischen*, 189–90, 194
Beyer, Charles Jacques, 261
Bieber, Konrad: aging, discussions with Peyre on, 803–4; comments on meeting, 867–68; Didier death, correspondence about, 390; family matters and news in correspondence with, 836–37, 884–85, 1018–19, 1064–65; literature discussed with, 671–72, 791–92, 960–61; miscellaneous correspondence, 633–34, 926–27, 955–

56, 980–81; Peyre's comments on essay by, 805–6; Romance series correspondence, 409; speaking engagement, correspondence about, 539; summer of *1961* in New Haven, 577–78; Swiss Academy candidates, correspondence about, 950–51; tribute to Peyre and, 942; writing of, Peyre's comments on, 538–40, 1034–35
Blackmur, Richard P., 522, 906
Block, Haskell, 996–97
Bloom, Harold, 809
Bluhm, Heinz, 560
Bonnefoy, Yves, 825
Bonno, Claude Dominique, 319
Book of the Month Club, 197–98
Boorsch, Jean: appointments to French Department and, 95–96; birth of Peyre's son Brice, 632–33; "Contes Modernes" account, 523–24; curriculum issues and, 208; departmental issues and, 179, 348, 515, 517; exchange of news with Peyre, 615–16, 863–64, 868–69, 886, 1052, 1081–82; Feuillerat retirement and, 154, 163, 200; illness of, 1069; miscellaneous references, 270; Peyre's assessment of, 328; Peyre's reply to sympathy letters, 601; Peyre's trip to Italy, 631–32; sabbatical leave correspondence about, 465; sympathies on wife's death, 604; tenure issues discussion, 91, 115–16, 121–22; *Yale French Studies* contributions, 278
Borgerhoff, E. B. O., 261
Borglum, George P., 284–85
Botsford, Keith: bursary student positions, 215–16; career advice to, 219–20, 233–34, 428–29, 454–55; exchange of news with Peyre, 436–37, 506–7; French Depart-

ment news discussed with, 245–46; graduate school application at Yale, 309–11; graduate studies of, 346–47; invitation to Peyre for tea, 210; in Iowa, 292–93; miscellaneous correspondence, 256–57, 309, 402; Peyre on poets and critics, 231–32; Peyre's comments on article by, 349; Peyre's comments on book by, 312–13; Peyre's illness and, 237–38; recommendation request for Bard College, 407–8
Bowman, Frank P., 437, 744, 825
Brady, Leslie, 249
Braun, Micheline, 816
Brée, Germaine: Baudelaire, correspondence on, 879; exchange of news with Peyre, 806–7, 878–79, 968, 971–72, 1077–78; invitation to visit, 994; MLA discussed with, 575; Peyre's comments on work by, 621, 964–66; Reid Hall summer program and, 296; similarities with Peyre, 839–40; tribute to Peyre, 942–43
Breton, André, x, 192, 224
Brinton, Crane, 429, 665
Brody, Jules, 816–17, 823, 863
Brombert, Victor, xvii; American Philosophical Society correspondence, 669–70; Didier death, correspondence about, 393; French Department, correspondence about, 515–16; literature discussed with, 843, 978; Peyre's comments on writing of, 676, 834–35, 948–49, 999–1000; on Peyre's retirement, 674–75
Brooke, Tucker, 153, 162
Brooks, Cleanth, 809
Brooks, Nelson, 506–10, 521–22
Brooks, Van Wyck, 920
Brown, E. K., 192

Brown, Frederick: comments on writing of, 820–21, 911; exchange of news with Peyre, 908–9; miscellaneous correspondence, 881, 1051
*Brown Decade, The,* 920
Browning, Elizabeth Barrett, 645
*Bruit & la Fureur, Le,* 653
Bruller, Jean, 956
Bryn Mawr College: Flexner lectures, Peyre's participation in, 155, 288, 431–32, 457; Peyre offered post at, 17–18; Peyre's assistant-professorship at, 40; Peyre's lecture at, 909–10, 913–14; publication rights discussion with, 431–32; Reid Hall summer program and, 296–97
Buck, Norman S.: Andersson appointment correspondence, 217–18; curriculum reforms, correspondence on, 103; faculty appointments correspondence, 514–17; merger of French and Spanish-Italian departments, 529–31; student criticism of French department, correspondence on, 362–64
Bucknell University, 504
Buffum, Imbrie, 329, 445–46, 495, 517
Bukharin, Nikolai, 918–19
Bundy, McGeorge, 679, 758
Burnshaw, Stanley: authors discussed with, 569; Bompiani project, 578; death of Marguerite Peyre, correspondence about, 605; Institute of Book Publishing and, 535; literary criticism by, 582, 601; Marguerite's illness, correspondence about, 596–97, 601; miscellaneous correspondence with, 1048–49; Peyre's heart problems, correspondence on, 652–53; Peyre's reviews of books by, 691; Peyre's writing, correspondence about, 468–69, 559–60, 563–64, 576, 585–90, 1080–81; poetry, correspondence on, 618–19, 725–27; publications of, 641, 939–40; request for Peyre's recommendation for Guggenheim, 760–62; translations by, 695–96
Burnshaw, Valérie, 566
Bush, Geoffrey, 490
Byron, George Gordon Noel (Lord), 282

*Cahiers,* 656, 699, 784
Caillois, Roger, 455–56
Camus, Albert, 544, 557–58, 908–9, 911, 918–19
Capretz, Pierre, 475, 495, 516
*Carnets,* 703
Carr, Ed. Hallet, 756
Castro, Nadine, 802
Caws, Mary Ann, xiii–xiv, xvii, 806, exchange of news with Peyre, 781–82, 891–92, 903–4; at Hunter College, 816; miscellaneous correspondence, 1015–16, 1055; Peyre on receiving a medal, 889–90; response to request for a speaking engagement, 985–86; snowy trip to New York, 989–90; teaching at CUNY, 887, 910; tribute to Peyre and, 942; writing of, 912–14, 934–35
Champenois, Madame Petit-Dutaillis, 17
Champfleury (Jules François Félix Husson), 391, 453
Champigny, Robert, 368
Char, René, xi
Charlton, D. G., 756
Charney, Hannah, 816
Chateaubriand, François René, 282, 795
Childes, Claire, 981–85

*Chimera, The,* 191–93, 195
Choquet (French exchange student), 411, 458
*Cimetière marin,* 715
City University of New York (CUNY) Graduate Center: curriculum at, correspondence about, 1037–38; graduate theses published from, 802, 882; Kneller's graduate courses at, 856–57, 862; language programs, correspondence concerning, 872–75; negotiations for Peyre's appointment at, 673–74, 676–78; Peyre as professor at, 722, 727, 773–74; Peyre offered post at, 680–81, 683–85; Peyre's reappointment at, 741, 767; Proshansky's inauguration at, 766; tenure issues at, 817; tribute to Peyre at, 887
Clark, Ruth, 192
Claudel, Paul, xi; MLA conference discussion of, 719–20; Peyre's comments on, 28–29, 825, 1068; on Shelley, 51–53; *Yale French Studies* discussion of, 278
Clough, Arthur Hugh, 587
Cobban, Alfred, 756
Cocteau, Jean, 191–92, 513
Coffin, Mrs. William Sloane, 223
Cohen, Gustave: appointment to Yale, correspondence on, 144–47, 149–50, 157–58; Feuillerat retirement, correspondence on, 154, 163, 178; French Department issues, correspondence on, 151, 173, 175
Cohn, Robert Greer: career as teacher, 677–78; humanities discussed with, 988–89, 997–98; illness of, correspondence on, 350–52; miscellaneous references to, 822; MLA seminars correspondence, 774–75; Peyre's criticism of work by, 270–71; writing by, correspondence concerning, 331–

32, 827, 881–83, 909–10, 918–19, 1078; as Yale student, 221
Coleridge, Samuel Taylor, 893
"College Plan" at Yale, 72
Collignon, Jean, 260–61, 264, 279, 341, 363
Columbia Summer School, Peyre's lectures at, 74
Columbia University, offer of professorship to Peyre, 223–25, 227–32
communism, Peyre's discussion of, 333, 919–20. *See also* fascism; Stalin, Josef
Comparative Literature project, 225–26
*Contemplations,* 67–68
*Contemporary Novel,* 586
Cornell, Kenneth: budget and salary issues and, 173–74; draft notice issues and, 163, 167–68, 178; Feuillerat retirement and, 154, 163, 200; foreign exchange program and, 264; French Department issues, 158–59; graduate school duties of, 310, 519; military service of, 209–10; publication activity of, 328; tenure issues, 135–36
Cornell, Sally, 609–11, 644–46, 1003–5, 1066, 1068–69
*Coup de Dés, Un,* 270–71
*Cousin Bette,* 906
Crocker, Lester, 625–27, 672–73; Peyre's comments on books by, 622–23, 723–25; thank you note from Peyre, 1079–80; writing of, Peyre's comments on, 481–82, 622–23, 723–25, 906–7
Cronmiller, Bruce, 363
cummings, e. e., 198, 374–75, 544
Curtiss, Mina, 481, 912

*Daedalus,* 684
d'Ancona, Levi, 276

*Daphnis & Chloe,* 1040
Darzins, John, 559
Datlof, Natalie, 828–29, 1011–12
d'Aumale, Vicomte, 142
Davidson, Eugene, 458–59, 586
Davidson, Hugh, 699, 859
Davis, Robert Gorham, 543–44
Defaux, Gérard, Peyre's comments on numéro, 921–22
de Gaulle, Charles, 924
Delattre, André, 319
De Man, Paul, 988, 1056, 1069
DeMellier (UAP editor), 742–43, 752, 770–71, 778–79, 783
De Messières, René, 250, 384–85
Demorest, Jean-Jacques: exchange of news with Peyre, 921; Peyre's comments on books by, 491, 513–14; thank you note from Peyre, 924–25
Derrida, Jacques, 822, 1078
De Schweinitz, Margaret, 261
Des Périers, Bonaventure, 748
Desroches, Richard, 483
DeVane, William C.: budget and salary correspondence with, 201–3, 372, 475, 514–17; curriculum reform correspondence, 103, 136–39, 206–8; faculty appointments correspondence, 440, 445–46, 458, 488, 495–98, 514–17; French department policies, correspondence on, 211, 248, 327–29; MAT program discussions and, 507–10; Reid Hall summer program correspondence, 296–97; Richardson retirement correspondence, 496–98
Diderot, Denis, 626, 846
Didier, Pierre, 365, 386–87, 389–93, 405
Dieckmann, Herbert, 368, 401, 417–18
*Divagations,* 934

Donaldson, Norman V., 169–71
Donne, John, 587
Dos Passos, John, 920
Doubrovsky, Serge, 960
Douglas, Kenneth: budget and salary issues and, 173, 198–203, 442–43, 482, 519; departmental policies and, 179, 185, 515; on leave, 341; miscellaneous references, 270; promotion to Associate Professor, 372; scholarship of, 328–29; *Yale French Studies* work, 557–58
*Dr. Zhivago,* 645
draft notices, correspondence about, 163–65, 167–68, 178–79
Du Bois, Charles: invitation to visit the University of Egypt, 59–61; on Shelley, 47–48
Dupuis, Marc, 486, 516
Duras, Marguerite, 994
Durrell, Lawrence, 648
Dwight, Timothy, 239

Edelman, Nathan, 261
Edsall, Lynn, 91, 154, 179, 200
Egypt, Peyre's appointment in, 72–73, 75
Eliot, T. S., 544, 569, 647, 809, 861, 920
El Nouty, Pucciani, 719
Éluard, Paul, 211
*Émile,* 673
Emmanuel, Pierre, 319, 544, 825
*Encounter,* 684, 820
Endler, Sheila, 802
*Esprit* group, 843
*Essai sur les Révolutions,* 795
"Essays and Studies in Honor of Albert Feuillerat," 153–54, 162–63, 165–66, 169–71, 180–81
*Essays in French Literature,* 703
Experimental Program proposal, 206–8

Ezban (Yale instructor), 163, 173, 179

Fackenthal (President), 228, 230
family correspondence of Peyre, xix
fascism, Peyre's discussion of, 842–43
Faulkner, William, 544
Favreau (Yale instructor), 91, 149
Febvre, Lucien, 400, 748, 756
Feineman, Miss (Dean's assistant, Yale), 376, 411
Fénelon, Franz, 863
Fernand-Laurent (French deputy), 183–84
Fesler, James, 428
Feuillerat, Albert (Professor): France-Amérique organization and, 240; French Department policies and, 85–86, 92–94, 108–9, 131–32; Graduate Studies program and, 96, 98–99; Ham's dismissal and, 115–16, 121–22; memorial volume for, 153–54, 162–63, 165–66, 169–71, 180–81; Peyre's appointment to Yale and, 70–71, 74; retirement of, 176, 178, 199, 321, 514
Firkins, O. W., 198
Fischart, Johann, 996
Flaubert, Gustave, 827
Focillon, Henri, 149–50, 152–53, 163, 165
Foreign Area program, 174–75, 182–83
*Form & Idea in Modern Theatre*, 596–97
Forster, E. M., 544, 648
Fougères, Michel, 703, 707
Foulet, M. L., 17
Fowlie, Wallace, xiv; academic situation, 829–30; death of Catherine Fowlie, 914–15; departmental policy issues and, 183, 191–92; exchange of news with Peyre, 666, 876–78; Feuillerat retirement and, 154, 163, 178–79, 199–200; forthcoming meeting, 580–81; Guggenheim fellowship of, 239; miscellaneous correspondence, 408; Peyre's assessment of, 368; Peyre's comments on books by, 930–31, 1017–18; Peyre's comments on writings by, 1041–42; promotion to Associate-Professor, 212; salary issues and, 186–88, 203; tenure issues and, 135
Frame, Donald, 261, 284
France, Peyre's observations concerning, xx, 778, 882–83, 919, 982–83
France-Amérique organization, 239–40, 276–77
Francis, Marie-Cécile, 486
Frank, Waldo, 919
Frazer, Sir James, 14–16, 18–20
Frazer, Lady, 4–5, 14–15, 18–20
Freeman, Bryant, 460–61, 466, 495
French Center at Yale: expenditures for, 364–65; Peyre's proposal for, 106–10, 123–24
French Department (Yale University): academic reforms in, 103–7; budget discussions, *1930s*, 90–94; budget discussions, *1940s*, 134–36, 153, 173–74, 181–84, 186–87, 198–204; budget discussions, *1950s*, 363–64, 514–17; "Contes Modernes" account, 523–24; course requirements, correspondence on, 86–87, 89–92, 677–78; curriculum reforms in, 206–8; departmental assessment, 359–62; establishment of, xvi; faculty appointments, *1930s*, 90–99; faculty appointments, *1940s*, 105–6, 111–17, 134–36, 198–201, 212, 217–18;

French Department (Yale University) (*continued*)
faculty appointments, *1950s*, 319, 338–39; French exchange program, 1940s, 221–23, 247–50, 259–61, 264–65, 274–76, 284–85; French exchange program, *1950s*, 334–35, 368–69, 438, 500–501; Graduate Studies program, 94–99, 219, 560–62; MAT program at, 488–89, 505–10, 517, 521–22; merger with Spanish-Italian department proposal, 529–31; PhD salary differential, correspondence on, 524–25; progress report on, 327–29, 341; requirements for majors and, 136–39; student criticism of, 174–76, 221, 362–64; tenure issues at, 115–17, 120–22, 135–36; undergraduate program reforms, 362–64; visiting-professor position, 111–17, 126–27, 133; wartime difficulties in, 171–74

*French Literary Imagination and Dostoevsky*, 729–31, 737, 742–43, 752, 770–71, 778–79, 783, 789

French theatre, Peyre's discussion of, 639

Freud, Sigmund, 588

Friedman, Gabrielle, 501

Friedman, Melvin, 471

*Friedrich un die grosse Koalition,* 190

Frohock, W. M., 229, 284, 492, 494, 559

Frost, Robert, 544, 566, 940

Frye, Northrop, 575

Fulbright program, Peyre's comments on, 281–82

Furniss, Edgar: Andersson leave of absence request, 469–70; Atelier room proposal, 154–55; Auerbach retirement correspondence, 519; budget and salary correspondence, *1940s*, 133–36, 153, 171–74, 181–84, 186–88, 203–5; budget and salary correspondence, *1950s*, 314–15, 321–22, 324–25, 365–66, 382–83, 429–30, 442–43, 466–68, 474–75, 485–86, 514–17; Cohen appointment correspondence, 144–47, 149–50, 157–59; course and curriculum policies and, 103–10, 462–63; criticism of French Department and, 174–76; departmental chairmanship discussed with, 325–27; Didier's death, correspondence concerning, 386–87, 389–393; faculty appointments correspondence, *1940s*, 208; faculty appointments correspondence, *1950s*, 333–34, 338–42, 437–39, 459, 462–63, 468, 482–83, 514–17; foreign exchange program correspondence, 333–34, 366–67, 368–69; French Department policies, *1930s*, 84–87, 94–99; French Department policies, *1940s*, 131–32, 134–36, 171, 178–79, 348; French Department policies, *1950s*, 324–26, 348; funding requests to, 458–59; Hill's illness, correspondence concerning, 419–20; library budget discussions, 376–77; Marx appointment correspondence, 316; MAT program discussions, 488–89; May's administrative duties, correspondence concerning, 415–16; Morehouse, correspondence on death of, 404–5; Peyre's sabbatical announcement, 449–50; PhD salary differential, correspondence on, 524–25; promotion policies correspondence, 373; Richardson retirement correspondence, 496–98, 503; Romance series correspondence, 409; sabbatical policies correspondence, 465–66; Sterling Professorship correspondence, 478–79; tenure policies and, 120–22, 129–30

Galand, René, 341, 363, 688
Gallimard. *See* Librairie Gallimard
Garey, Howard, 324, 424, 497–98, 515–16
Gassner, John, 512–13, 553–54, 596, 650–51; death of Marguerite Peyre, 607, 612
Gassner, Mollie, 607, 612
*Gates of Horn*, 595
Gaulmier, Antoni-Eugène, 756, 796
*Gedaken im Kriege*, 193
*Générations*, 237
Germany, Peyre's view of, 213–14, 265
Geuthner publishers, Peyre's work for, 15–16, 19
Giamatti, A. Bartlett, xiii–xiv
Gide, André: Caws' criticism of, 912; departmental curriculum including, 191–92, 463–64; literary criticism of, 708; Peyre's criticism concerning, 588, 758, 773; questions to author, 76–79
Gilman, Margaret, 192, 453
Gilmore (Yale instructor, 1939), 91, 110
Ginter, Harry, 376
Girard, René, ix, 910, 997
Giraud, Mrs. Raymond D., 523
Giraud, Raymond D., 458–59
Giraudoux, Jean, 512, 553–54
Giroud, Vincent: congratulations on nomination, 1047; encouragement on finding a position, 1023–24; miscellaneous correspondence, 1049, 1053; Peyre, memories of Strawberry Hill, 1035–36; Peyre's comments on book by, 1016

Glass, Meta, 250
Goetz, Professor, 348
Goetz, Thomas, 1002–3
Goll, Yvan, 192
Goodman, Paul, 454
Grandjouan, Clairève, 873
Graubard, Stephen, 684
Green, J., 588, 1068
Green, Otis, 575
Greene, Tatiana, 942; death of Bédé, 812–13; Peyre, on receiving a set of letters, 917–18; Peyre, on religion, 1006–7; Peyre's comments on article by, 804–5
Griswold, Whitney: Andersson promotion correspondence and, 488; Auerbach appointment correspondence, 316; Didier death matters and, 389–90; foreign exchange programs, correspondence on, 560–62; French Department policies and appointments, 352–53, 439–40; Humanities revival correspondence, 427–28; MAT program discussions, 505–6; merger with Spanish-Italian department proposal, 531; Morehouse death and, 405–6; Morot-Sir meeting, 573–74; Peyre's television appearances, correspondence on, 548–49; Reid Hall summer program correspondence, 573–74; Rostow Légion d'Honneur award, 570–71
Guérin, Maurice de, 283, 353
Guers-Martynuk, Simone, 860
Guggenheim, Michel, 409; exchange of news with Peyre, 946–47, 970; family matters, 698; miscellaneous correspondence, 951–52, 974–75; Peyre, on close friendship with, 1038–39; reflections on cultural accomplishments, 976; request for assis-

Guggenheim, Michel (*continued*) tance, 643–44; sympathies on son's illness, 683; thank you note from Peyre, 957–58

Guggenheim Fellowship: Peyre's application for, 39–46, 62–63; Peyre's committee work with, 283–85, 299, 592, 597–98, 760–62

Guicharnaud, Jacques, 338, 515, 586, 807, 817

Guillén, Jorge: accommodations at Yale, 226–27; best wishes from Peyre, 254; congratulations on award, 798–99; family matters, correspondence on, 307, 358–59; lecture invitations, correspondence on, 216–17, 499; manuscript review, request to Peyre for, 234–35; miscellaneous correspondence, 213, 236–37, 479–80, 627, 780–81; MLA committee appointments and, 544; reading suggestions, 381–82; references request by, 528–29; Salinas article, Peyre's comments concerning, 378–79; teaching positions for Spanish, 196–97; thank you note from Peyre, 442; writing by, Peyre's comments on, 343–44, 349–50, 422–23, 444–45, 581–82, 715–16

Guilloto, Vincent, 193

Gusdorf, Georges, 968

Gutwirth, Marcel: advice on Guggenheim bursary, 383; bursaries, 250; Peyre's comments on book by, 1040–41; university positions available, 235

Haac, Oscar, 756

Haegert, Lois. *See* Peyre, Lois Haegert

Haig, Stirling, 888–89, 1021, 1053–54

Hall, Gaston, 526, 699–700

Halliday, E. M., 905–6

Ham, E. B., 91–93, 113–17, 120–22, 134–35

Hanotaux (Minister of Foreign Affairs), 240

Hardy, Thomas, 647

Hartman, Geoffrey, 409, 471, 809, 988

Harvard University: Chapman scholarship offered to Peyre, 17; French Department faculty, discussion of, 367–68, 371–72, 470, 492–94; Peyre's comments on, 289–90, 302, 308–9

Harvard University Press, 840–43, 876

Harvitt, Hélène, 714

Hazard, Paul, 111, 129, 133

Hemingway, Ernest, 544

Hendel, Charles, 127

Henri Peyre French Institute, formation of, x, xiv

Herbert, Marie-Louise (sister): on life in London, 2; Peyre's comments on chapters by, 273–74, 291–92; spring at Bryn Mawr, 30–33

*Hérodiade,* 882

Heschel, Abraham Joshua, 745

Hesse, Hermann, 544

Hill, Raymond T.: curriculum issues and, 86–87; departmental budget issues, 173–74, 324; Feuillerat memorial volume and, 163, 165, 199–200; French department policies, 327–28, 348; graduate studies program's duties, 96, 497; library budget discussions, 376; miscellaneous correspondence, 202; retirement of, 348, 514; tenure issues discussion, 115, 121

Hirschfield, Robert, 981–85

Hofstra University, 1012

Hölderlin, Friedrich, 988
Hoog, Armand, 340, 371–72; exchange of news with Peyre, 977
Hornik, Henry: course arrangements, 665–66; Peyre's CUNY Graduate Center professorship and, 673–74, 676–78, 680–81, 683–84, 687; Peyre's Hunter College lectures and, 663–64, 668
Horowitz, Louise, 802
Howes, Barbara, 191–93, 195
Hoy, Mrs. Jocelyn B., 704
Hubert, Judd, 699–700; academic news, 373–74; administrative appointments, discussion of, 369; career assistance for, 353, 357–58, 498; Peyre's comments on essay by, 397; publishing of, encouragement in, 366; sympathies on wife's death, 604–5; about upcoming issues of journals, 511
Hubert, Sister Marie-Louise, 289, 306–7, 322–23
Hudon, Louis, 130–32
Hughes, Stuart, 843
Hugo, Victor, 278, 282, 980, 1037
Hunter College: Peyre's assessment of, 816–17, 823–25; Peyre's lectures at, 660–64, 673–74, 676–78
Huss, Gabriel Du Bois, 658
Hytier, Jean, 492–94

*Idiot de la Famille*, 807
Idoine, Mlle., 501
*Igitur*, 882
Institute of Book Publishing, 535
*Intellectual Hero, The*, 843
*Invitée*, 449
*Irresponsibles, The*, 188

Jackson, Joseph, 90, 92, 95, 134–35, 153, 192
James, Henry, 23
Jaray, Gabriel Louis, 240
Jasinski, René, 401, 417, 470, 493, 536
Jeffers, Robinson, 544, 610
Jewish Theological Seminary, 736, 745
Johnson, Alvin, 145–47
Johnson, Barbara, 998
Jolas, Maria, 562–63
Jones, Frank, 192
Jones, H. M., 564
Jones, Percy Mansell, 634
Joyce, James, 315
Judaism, Peyre's comments on, 745, 808–9, 908, 940, 1005, 1010
Juden, B., 825
Julian the Apostate, xi
Jung, Carl, 920

Kafka, Franz, 587–88, 773
Kanes, Martin, 796
Kaplan, Edward: career advice for, 794–96, 808–10, 825–26; exchange of news with Peyre, 765–66; literature discussed with, 1056; Peyre's comments on article by, 885–86; Peyre's comments on essay by, 716; Peyre's comments on manuscript by, 692–94; publications of, 744–45, 755–57, 837–38, 944–45
Kennedy, John F., 920
Kent State University, 809
Kerr, Chester, 586
Kerr, Edith, 548–49
Kierkegaard, Søren, 825
Kirstein, Lincoln, 912
Knapp, Bettina, 817, 919–20, 952–53
Kneller, John, xi, xvii; *Apostrophes* project correspondence, 984–87; brother's work, Peyre's comments on, 936–37, 945–46; career advice to, 290–91; comments on studies by, 261–64; exchange of

Kneller, John (*continued*)
news with Peyre, 712–13; graduate course at CUNY center of, 856–57, 862; illness of, 860; literature discussed with, 978; meeting arrangements, 714; payment to, 565–66; Peyre's 86th birthday celebration, 1033; Peyre's comments on bibliography by, 979–80; Peyre's son Brice, correspondence concerning, 855; as president of Brooklyn College, 685–86, 820; tribute to Peyre, correspondence about, 887, 961–64, 966; writing of, 302–3, 810, 941–42; *Yale French Studies* correspondence, 277–83
Kneller, Sherry, 810, 820, 962–64, 1033
Kolb, Philip, 446–47; miscellaneous correspondence, 1072; Peyre's comments on article by, 487; Peyre's comments on books by, 422, 490–91, 835–36; Peyre's comments on two volumes, 975; Peyre's comments on writings by, 1036

La Fontaine, Jean de, 298, 300
Lafuma, Louis, 323
Lagarde, Jean de, miscellaneous correspondence, 387
Lahor, Jean, 509
Lamartine, Alphonse de, 282
Lamennais, Félicité Robert de, 282
Lamont, Rosette: Diana's health, correspondence on, 823–24; miscellaneous correspondence, 751–52, 775, 792, 813; Peyre on their relationship, 838–39; publication plans, discussion of, 818–19; students' theses evaluations, 761–62; student's work discussed with, 750–51; summer vacation, 758–60; thank you notes from Peyre, 786–87, 810–11, 859–60, 865, 1033–34; university affairs, discussion of, 762–65, 768; voyage to Russia, 746–47; war years discussed with, 800–801; writing by, Peyre's comments on, 420–21, 749–50
Lancaster, Henry Carrington, 577
Lang, B. R., 192
Lang, Mrs. Cecil, 466–67, 495
Lang, Peter, 1002
Lange, Victor, 543–44
Lapp, John, 978
*Last Puritan, The*, 920
Law, Jean, 607
Lawler, James, 620–21, 634–35, 656; exchange of news with Peyre, 775–77; lectures by, 792–93; MLA, correspondence concerning, 704–5, 718–20; Peyre's comments on articles by, 694–95, 705–6; Peyre's comments on work by, 771–72; Peyre's views on academic environment, 701–3; publications by, 687–88, 702–3; return to United States, 718–20; Valéry centennial publications correspondence, 698–700
*Learning Another Language*, 510
Leblon, Jean M., 390
Leconte de Lisle, Charles Marie, 610
Lecuyer, Maurice A. F., 363
Lee, Vera, 313–14, 619–20, 638–39; inquiry about future plans, 265; Peyre's comments on books by, 656, 788–89, 1024–25; Peyre's comments on essay by, 715
Leet, Dorothy, 296, 574
Léger, Alexis, 223, 481, 912; sympathies on wife's death, 605–6
Leopardi (Italian poet), 610
Leroy, Maxime, 283

Leroy-Ladurie, Emmanuel, 909
Levin, Harry (Professor): book discussions with, 454, 512; book on Joyce by, 315, 317–18; Brombert nomination to American Philosophical Society, 669–71; Comparative Literature project and, 225–26; Dieckmann appointment discussion with, 489–90, 492; discussions on France with Peyre, 399–402, 417–18; faculty appointments correspondence, 302, 308–9, 339–40; French literature, correspondence on, 594; Harvard discussed with, 289–90, 367–68, 371–72, 470, 492–94, 583–84; humanities, correspondence on, 684–85; literary criticism by, 570, 576–77, 611–12, 619, 664–65; Marguerite's illness, correspondence about, 595; miscellaneous correspondence, 333, 443, 534–36; MLA Committee appointments, 543–45, 557–58; Oxford University, correspondence concerning, 647–48; personal life in correspondence with, 617–18; Peyre's second marriage, correspondence about, 611–13; Poggioli memorial volume of, 651–52; work on Balzac, 287; *Yale French Studies* contribution, 241
Lévi-Strauss, Claude: book request, 455–56; Peyre's comments on book by, 477–78
Levowitz, Micheline: aging discussed with, 753–55, 932–33; career discussed with, 845–46; exchange of news with Peyre, 899–900, 901–5, 915–17, 958–59; Peyre on life abroad, 814; trip to Paris, 831–32; writing by, Peyre's comments on, 848–50, 870–72, 894–96, 929–30

*Liaisons Dangereuses, Les,* 594
Librairie Gallimard, 559–60
Liebowitz, David, 919–20
Lipari, Angelo, 86–87, 96, 98, 162, 165
Lips, Marguerite, 978
*Literature & Sincerity,* 599–601
Lohmann, Mr., 109, 219
Lowell, James Russell, 587, 727
Lubin, 1011–12
Lucas, Martha, 250
Lucrèce (Titus Lucretius Carus), 550
Luquiens, Frederick Bliss, 86, 96, 98
Lynch (UAP), 729–31, 737, 742

MacIntosh, Norman, exchange of news with Peyre, 1020–21
Mack, Maynard, 193
Mackey, Charles, accepting responsibility for the *French Review,* 973
MacLeish, Archibald, 188–89
*Magic Mountain, The,* 645
Magny, Mme. Claude-Edmonde, 522
Malaparte, Curzio, 842
Malaquais, Jean, 758
Mallarmé, Stéphane: Caws' discussion of, 934; Cohn's work on, 270–71, 822, 910, 988; Peyre's comments on, 652, 996–98; student theses on, 882
Malraux, André, 211, 912
*Mandarins,* 449
Mankin, Paul, 516
Mann, H., 544
Mann, Thomas, 189–90, 193–94
Marcel, Gabriel, 278
March, Harold, 312
Margolis, George, 938–39, 1065–66
Marin, Louis, 859

Maritain, Jacques, 126–27; Peyre's availability to attend a conference, 204–5; Peyre's comments on book by, 410; sympathies on illness, 434–35; sympathies on Mme. Maritain's illness, 572
Marvell, Andrew, 809
Marx, Jean, 259, 316
Masui, Jacques, 564
Matheson, W. H., 437, 516
Mathias, James F., 283–85, 682
Matthews, J. H., 1032–33
Maupassant, Guy de, 432–33
Mauriac, François, 755, 846, 1068
Maurin, Jeanne, Peyre's advice on university arrangements, 320
Maurin, Mario, xiii–xiv; academic opportunities, advice on, 268–69, 370–71, 402–3; arrangements for meeting with Peyre, 447, 472; exchange of news with Peyre, 377, 457, 531–32, 1070–71; request for article, 517–18; thesis critiqued by Peyre, 298–301, 307, 345–46; university affairs discussed with, 541–42; writing by, Peyre's comments on, 330, 335–38, 354, 1071–72
Maurois, A., 112, 544
Mauron, Charles, 270
Mauzi, Robert, 626
May, Georges, xix, xvii; budget and salary issues and, 393, 482, 517; career opportunities at Yale, discussion about, 279–80; "Contes Modernes" account, 523–24; as department head, 817; exchange of news with Peyre, 549–50, 551–53, 554–55, 646–47, 1078–79; Focillon discussed with, 161; French departmental matters, correspondence on, 330–31, 334–35, 341, 435, 817; future plans discussed with Peyre, 187; Junior Year in France appointment, 438–39; memories of London, 339; military duty of, 180; miscellaneous correspondence, 207, 342, 567–68, 1068; Peyre illness, correspondence concerning, 1072–73; Peyre's European trips, discussion of, 280–81, 311; Peyre's stroke, correspondence concerning, 1054; promotions of, 328, 445–46; speech by, Peyre's comments on, 168; teaching career of, 161–62, 341; thank you note from Peyre, 1074; Undergraduate Studies duties, 415–16, 424, 495, 677–78; University of Illinois position, correspondence concerning, 214–15; writing by, Peyre's comments on, 912–13, 950, 981
May, Gita, 942; Peyre's comments on book by, 635–36; Peyre's comments on essays by, 875, 923–24, 958; Peyre's comments on work by, 555–56
Mayoux, J.-J., 534–35, 557–58, 653
McAfee, Helen, 211
McBride, Katharine, 288, 431–32, 457
McCarthy, Mary, 918, 920
McCarthyism, comments on, 401
McCormick, Diane(a?), 774–75, 799–800
McIntosh, Malcolm: books about the nineteenth-century novel, 542–43; career advice, correspondence about, 453, 467, 500; exchange of news with Peyre, 534; literary criticism, discussions on, 453–54; marriage to Lois announced to, 628; miscellaneous correspondence with, 807, 821; Peyre's comments on Alabama to, 477; Peyre's comments on books by,

390–91, 558–59; Peyre's comments on essay by, 294–96; retirement of, 773–74, 791
McIntosh, Mrs. Malcolm, 425–26, 628, 773–74, 791, 807, 821
Mead, Katherine Harper, 382–83
Medieval Academy, 158
Meeks (Dean), 142, 240
Mehlman, J., 863
*Mélanges d'Histoire et de Voyage*, 898
Melville, Herman, ix
Mendenhall, Thomas C., 488
Meredith, George, 679
Merleau-Ponty, Maurice, 842, 911, 918
Merriam, Jacqueline, 653
Michelet, Jules, 692, 755–56, 795–96, 809, 825, 944–45
Miller, Arthur, 544
Ministre de l'instruction, 62–63
*Mistral*, 568–69
Mitterrand, François, 919
Mitterrand, Mauroy Defferre, 896
*Modernes, Les,* 960
Modern Language Association (MLA): Committee appointments, 543–44, 557–58; Peyre's activities with, 575, 704–5, 718–20, 774–75
Modern Language Association of America, 545
Moe, Edith, 704
Moe, Henry Allen, 283–84, 299; American Philosophical Society and, 665; death of Marguerite Peyre, correspondence about, 601–2; Guggenheim Fellowship committee correspondence, 283–84, 299, 592, 597–98; miscellaneous correspondence with, 639–40, 704; Peyre's Guggenheim Fellowship application and, 40–41, 44–46, 62–63; Peyre's second marriage, correspondence about,

608–9; retirement from Guggenheim Foundation, 612–13
Mohrt, Michel, 244
Mombello, G., 790
Montaigne, Michel de, 920, 988
Moraud, M., 500
Moravia, Alberto, 544
Morehouse Andrew: budget and salary issues and, 186–88; death of, 404–6, 446, 514; departmental appointments and, 96; departmental policy discussions, 183, 249; Feuillerat retirement and, 154, 163, 200; graduate school duties of, 310; Peyre's assessment of, 328; tenure issues and, 115, 121
Morely, Christopher, 197–98
Morize, André, 133, 162, 192, 493
Morot-Sir, Édouard, 571, 573, 859; Peyre, on suffering a stroke, 1057
Morris, Ted, 257, 494, 1066
Morse, William, 756
Moulton, William G., 575
Mounier, Emmanuel, 843
Mumford, Lewis, 919–20
Murdoch, K., 670
Murry, Middleton, 569
Muscatine, Charles, 682
Musser, Frederic, 487–88, 504, 624–25, 630; assistance in finding a position, 502, 504–5
Musset, Alfred de, 745–46

Nathan, Monique, 653
Nelson, Robert, 459, 475, 516, 699
Nerval, Gérard de, 278, 280, 302–3, 588
*New Criterion,* 911
New School for Social Research, French Institute proposal, 152–53
*New York Times,* Peyre's letter to, 213–14
Nietzsche, Friedrich, 794, 822, 911

Nordmeyer, Henry W., 203
Norman, Buford, 713, 858–59, 862–63, 907–8; academic advice, 690–91
*Nouvelle Héloïse,* 673
Noyes, Edward S., 521–22
Nyman, Carl, 310–11

O'Brien, Justin, 229, 758
*Order of the Day,* 193–94
Orpheus, 1068
Orr, Linda, 756; assistance with project, 700–701; exchange of news with Peyre, 723; Peyre's comments on poetry by, 689–90, 707–8
Osborn, James: American Academy of Arts and Letters, election to, 780; birth of Pyere's son Brice, correspondence about, 632; faculty appointments discussed with, 439, 584; French Department issues and, 139–41, 311; illness of, 796–97; literary criticism, correspondence about, 621–22, 628, 640; Marguerite Peyre's illness and death discussed with, 595, 597; miscellaneous correspondence with, 436, 567, 572–73, 637–38; Peyre's heart ailment, correspondence on, 650–51; retirement discussed with, 767; writing discussed with, 563
Oswald, Victor, 703
Oxenhandler, Neal, 912–13
Oxford University Press, Peyre's publications with, 431–32, 457, 586

Pamplume (Monsieur), 244
Pardé, Hélène, 17–18
Park, Marion E., 17–18, 155
Pascal, Blaise: literary criticism of, 858–59, 863, 908, 914; Peyre's discussion of, 291, 322–23, 705–6, 794
Pasinetti, Pier, 429, 703, 719
*Paul et Virginie,* 594
Peckham, Lawton P. G., 229
Pegram, George B., 229–30
Pei, Mario, 229
Pennec, Hélène: difficulties facing doctoral students, 784–85; exchange of news with Peyre, 1027–32, 1043–47, 1059–64
*Pensées,* 353
Perse, Saint-John: lunch invitation, 547; Modern Language Association of America, 544–46; request for a reading, 480–81; thank you note and copyright request from Peyre, 551; thank you note from Peyre, 566; writing by, Peyre's comments on, 272, 484–85, 912
Perse School, 15
Peschol, Enid, 922–23, 1012–14
Petitmengin, Pierre, 1042
Peyre, Brice (son of Henri), xix; accident of, 855; as adult, 1069; birth of, 632; childhood of, 644–46; Henri's stroke and, 1055; miscellaneous references to, 705, 767, 986–87; mother's illness, discussion of, 747–48, 760, 773, 777; Weinberg correspondence concerning, 784; as Yale student, 908, 923, 935, 939, 1004, 1022
Peyre, Brice and Marie Tuvien (parents): first year teaching, 20–27; lecture preparation, 28–30; on life as a student, 2–7, 8–9; missing Paris in the spring, 33–34; preparing for Yale, 35–36; university application, 12–14; visit to Penn State College, 37–39; visit to Princeton, 36–37
Peyre, Brice Henri (father): family news, 412–14; military training,

53–55; news from Peyre in America, 385–86; role in French-German war, 81–85, 88–89, 117–20, 124–26; visit to Lyon, 66–69; visit to Salzburg, 63–66

Peyre, Diana, xvii–xviii; children of, 935, 1081; fall and injury of, 1066, 1069; Henri's stroke and, 1055; miscellaneous references to, 810, 891, 894, 919, 939; promotion to full professor at Brooklyn, 860; teaching career of, 939, 1004, 1013, 1053, 1081; travels with Peyre, 887; writing of, 906, 910, 923

Peyre, Henri: birth of son Brice, 632; correspondence of, ix; divorce from Lois, 793; draft notice of, 163–65; heart problems of, 644–46, 648–50, 987–88; illness and death of wife Marguerite, 595–603, 610, 617–18; illness of, 237–38; memorial service for, xiii; PhD program at CUNY and, x; publications of, 44–46; retirement from Yale, 683–86; second marriage of, 608–11; stroke and vision problems of, 1055–56; teaching skills of, xvi–xvii; Yale French Program headed by, ix–x

Peyre, Jacques (brother), 987; birthday correspondence with, 947; books discussed with, 1–2; Diana's health, 983–84; Diana's teaching position at Avignon, discussion of, 1048; difficult times, 48–51; family news, 394–96, 425, 642–43, 697–98, 709–10, 711–12; French and American politics discussed with, 1067; French-German war, discussion of, 99–102, 147–48; French politics discussed with, 691–92, 721–22, 927–29; George Sand discussed with, 1014–15; Judaism discussed with, 1010; life in Egypt, 55–59, 61–62; life in Lyon, 69–70; marriage to Diana discussed with, 1058; memories of family, correspondence on, 987; miscellaneous correspondence, 959, 1007–8, 1070; Mitterrand discussed with, 927–29; modern medicine discussed with, 991; retirement discussed with, 731–33; student life discussed with, 7–8, 9–12; travel plans, correspondence on, 527–28, 532–33, 696–97; trip to New York, 734–35

Peyre, Lois Haegert, xvii, 611, 637–38; birth of son Brice, 632; depression and mental illness of, 747–48, 760–61, 773, 777; divorce from Henri, 793; marriage to Henri Peyre, 608–12, 622

Peyre, Marguerite Vanuxem, xvii–xviii; death of, 601–3, 610, 617–18; illness of, 595–98, 600–601

Pierre-Quint, Léon, Peyre's comments on book by, 450

Pirandello, Luigi, 842

Pivot, Bernard, 982

Pizzorusso, Arnaldo: arrangements to meet with Peyre, 616–17; Peyre's comments on book by, 637

Plamenatz, John, 672

Plato, 673

Plottel, Jeannine, 816

Poe, Edgar Allan, 997

"Poème à l'Etrangère," 912

*Poem Itself, The*, 564–65

Poggioli, Renato, 303, 319, 368, 566, 651–52

Poirion, Daniel, 520

Pope, Alexander, 809

Porter, Katherine Anne, 920

Poulet, Georges, 319, 340, 492
*Power of Blackness,* 583–84
Prévost, Jean, 940
Princeton Institute of Advanced Study, 822, 996
*Prométhée,* 662, 710
Proshansky, Harold: appointment of Peyre at CUNY, 722; CUNY language programs discussed with, 872–75; Humanities Committee correspondence with, 735–36; inauguration at CUNY Graduate Center, 766; Peyre's editing of writing by, 799–800; Peyre's reappointment at CUNY, correspondence concerning, 741, 767; student criticism at CUNY and, 730
Proulx, Alfred, 438, 495
Proust, Marcel, 303, 490–91, 626, 827, 835–36, 899, 910

*Quinzaine Littéraire, La,* xix

Rabelais, François, 278, 683–84, 773, 996
Racine, Jean, 988
Raeburn, Ben, 691
Rahv, Philip, 906
Ramsey, Warren, 368
Ray, Gordon: Guggenheim Foundation correspondence, 613–14, 654, 679–80, 682, 701, 808; illness and death of Peyre's wife and, 596; Peyre's heart ailment correspondence, 649–50; Peyre's publications, correspondence about, 709
Read, Herbert, 569
Reagan, Ronald, 883, 959
Reid, Alastair, 891
Reid Hall summer program, 296–97, 573–74
religion, Peyre's discussion of, 745,
808–9, 883, 940, 945, 1004–6, 1068–69
Renan, Ernest, 795, 1068
Renou (Yale exchange professor), 393
Reverdy, Paul, 211
Review of National Literatures, 719
Rhodes, S. A., 332
Rice University (formerly Rice Institute), 17, 598
Richard, Jean P., 998
Richardson, Henry B.: appointments to department and, 84, 96, 216–17; curator appointment of, 420; departmental policy issues, 183, 328; Feuillerat memorial volume and, 200; replacement for, 496–98, 503; retirement of, 514–15; salary issues and, 173–74, 443, 519; tenure issues, 115, 121; as Undergraduate Studies director, 340, 363, 415–16, 424
Rideout, Blanchard, 264–65
Rimbaud, Arthur, 825, 882, 910, 934, 998
Ritchie, Francis, 429
Rivière, Jacques, 587
Robbins, Marcus, 383–84, 523–24
Roberts, William, 411–12
Roberts, Mrs., 818, 844
Robespierre, Maximilien, 673
Rockefeller Foundation, 913
Rolland, R., 338
Rose, R. Selden, 96, 162
Rossini, Gioacchino, 1012
Rostow, Eugene, 570–71
Roudiez, Leon: exchange of news with Peyre, 441, 461–62, 654–55; Peyre's Paris visit, 533; sympathies on wife's death, 602; thank you note from Peyre, 659; tribute to Peyre and, 942; university affairs, 449; writing by, Peyre's comments on, 460, 594, 599

Rountree, Benjamin C., 863
Rousseau, Jean-Jacques, 278–80, 303, 672–73, 988
Rudich, 339–40
Rudin, Gabriel, 428
Rudolph, Paul, 549
Russier, Jean, 322

Sainte-Beuve, Charles-Augustin, 278, 280, 570
St. Aubyn, Frederic, 978
St. Exupéry, Antoine de, 211, 9912
Salacrou, Armand, 278
Saleil, Jeanne, 573
Salinas, Pedro: Peyre's trip to France and Italy, 286–87; sympathies on illness, 355; thank you note from Peyre, 307–8
Salvan, Albert, 261
Sand, George, 282, 1006–7
*Sang des autre,* 449
Santayana, George, 920
Sarraute, Nathalie, 562–63, 659
Sartre, Jean-Paul: Camus and, 909; Cohn's criticism of, 918–19; curriculum at CUNY including, 660; on fascism, 842; inclusion in department curriculum, 211; Peyre's criticism of, 807, 911–14
Schenck, E. M., 18, 192
Schlesinger, Steven, 758
Schopenhauer, Arthur, 588
Schorer, Mark, 543–44
Scruggs, K. M., 192
*Seamless Web, The,* 760
Secor, Walter, 501
*Sense of Beauty, The,* 920
Seronde, Joseph: faculty appointments correspondence, 90, 93, 514; Feuillerat retirement and, 199–200, 321; Peyre's appointment to Yale and, 70–71, 74; tenure issues correspondence, 113, 115, 117
Serres, Michel, 997

Seymour, Charles: appointments to French Department and, 94–95, 243; Columbia appointment offer to Peyre, correspondence concerning, 223–25, 230–32; d'Aumale visit announcement, 142; Feuillerat memorial volume and, 153–54, 162–63, 165–66, 180–81; France-Amérique organization discussion, 239–40, 276–77; French Department policies and, 103–7, 122–23, 126–27; French Graduate studies program and, 219; French Institute activities and, 152–53; French visiting professor proposal and, 122, 133; Ham's dismissal, 115–17; Marx visit to Yale, 259; miscellaneous correspondence with, 246; Peyre's appointment as Yale professor, 70–71, 73–76; Peyre's request for deferral of post, 72–73; Peyre's wartime status, 80–81, 163–65; recall of Cornell from military and, 209–10; Reid Hall summer program correspondence, 296–97, 573; retirement age policy discussed with, 244–45; student foreign exchange program correspondence, 221–23
Seznec, Jean, 192, 289, 308, 315, 319–20, 647
Shapiro, Harvey, 257
Shattuck, Roger, 315, 494
Shaw, Pricilla Washburn, 541
Shelley, Percy Bysshe, 52–53, 893, 1066
Shore, Naomi, 978
Sices, David, 745–46
Sidney, Philip, 587
Simmons, Ernest, 229
Simone, Franco: academic advice to, 352; article request to Peyre, response to, 636–37; career advice to, 355–57; conferences dis-

Simone, Franco (*continued*) cussed with, 667–68; Italian professor, assistance on search for, 629–30; miscellaneous correspondence with, 406, 434, 525–26; retirement discussion with, 736–40; subscription renewal, 623; thank you notes from Peyre, 301, 317, 641; writing by, Peyre's comments on, 568, 591, 657–58
Simpson, Eileen, 906
Simpson, Hartley, 411–12; budget and salary correspondence with, 514–17, 520–21; faculty appointments correspondence, 514–17
Singleton, Charles S., 401
"Situation of Surrealism between the Two Wars, The," x
*Situations*, 842, 909
Smith, Horatio, 192–93, 224, 229
Smith, Mark, 866–68
Soboul, Albert, 756
*Social Contract, The*, 672–73
social contract theory, 342
Sorbonne, Peyre on faculty of, 70–72
Southern Illinois Press, 729
Spender, Steven, 544
Spire, André, 727
Spitzer, Leo, 492, 577, 748
Squibb (UAP editor), 844–45
Stalin, Josef, Peyre's comments about, 909–11, 918–19
Stanford University, 910, 997–98, 1078
St. Aubyn, Frederic, 978; Peyre's comments on revue, 853
Stephens, James, 424
Stern, Eleanor, 914
Stewart, Philip, 686, 888–89
St. Exupéry, Antoine de, 211, 9912
Stone, D., 817
Strand, Mark, 896
*Stream of Consciousness, The*, 471
Sturm (instructor), 91, 135, 149–50
Swedish Academy, suggested candidate for Nobel prize in literature, 957
Sweetbriar College, 247–50, 267–68, 275–76, 438, 501
symbolism, 433
Szogyi, Alex: exchange of news with Peyre, 963; at Hunter College, 660–61, 663, 816–17; introductions to 24 Apostrophes, 990–91; Peyre's comments on book by, 649; thank you note from Peyre, 381

taboo, in literature, 14–16, 19
Tafoya, Francis, 463
Tate, Allen, 255, 471–72
Taylor, Donald, 680
Tenney, 173, 178–79, 185
Tennyson, Alfred, 679
*Tentation de St. Antoine, La*, 646
tenure issues, Peyre's discussion of, 115–17, 120–22, 135–36, 816–17
Thibaudeau, Albert, 671
Thomas, Ruth, 589, 606
Thorp, Willard, 575
*Three Essays*, 193–94
*Thunder on the Left*, 197–98
Tillich, Paul, 825
*Times Literary Supplement*, 190
Tinnin, Alvis, 439–40, 483
Torrey, Norman L., 193, 227–29, 243, 249
*Toward the Poems of Mall*, 882k
Toynbee, Arnold, 598
Travis (UAP editor), 748–49
Triffin, Robert, 680
Trilling, Lionel, 726
*Tristes Tropiques*, 477–78

Ugrinsky, Alexej, 1012
*Un Coup de Dés*, 270–71
*Unheroic Bourgeois Hero, The*, 458–59

University of Alabama Press: additions to manuscript for, 742; contract correspondence with, 747; delays by, Peyre's complaints about, 731, 737, 742–43, 783, 785–86; editing correspondence with, 770–71, 779–80; Peyre's publications with, 729–30, 752, 785–86; production schedule correspondence, 752, 788; review copies correspondence, 789; translation correspondence with, 788, 803, 844–45, 847–48; *What Is Romanticism?* manuscript correspondence, 748–49, 818
University of Lyons (France), Peyre as Comparative Literature professor at, 63
University of Michigan, 17
*Unmediated Vision, The*, 471

Valéry, Paul: centennial celebration of, 698–700; Cohn's discussion of, 997–98; Lawler's work on, 620, 656, 702–3, 705–6, 772; literary criticism of, 659–60, 708; Weinberg's work on, 773, 784, 997–98
Varney, Jeanne M., 229
Vercors, François, 956
Verlaine, Paul, 656
*Vie de Marianne, La*, 645
*Vie L'Instant, La*, 960
Vietnam War, Peyre's opposition to, xi–xii
Vigée, Claude: arrangements to meet with Peyre, 444; Guggenheim Foundation correspondence, 379–80, 448; meeting plan, 452–53; move to Israel by, 582–83; Peyre's request for an article, 344–45; poetry discussed with, 403–4, 546–47, 579–80; thank you notes from Peyre, 234, 336–37, 437, 440–41; writing by, Peyre's comments on, 252–54, 256, 272–73, 398–99, 450–51, 471, 832–33
Vigny, Alfred de, 279, 282–83
*Vocabulary of Jacques de Henricourt, The*, 202
Voltaire (François-Marie Arouet), 278
*Voyage de Bougainville*, 490

Wade, Ira, 261, 339
Wadsworth, Philip A., 149–50, 494, 700
Wahl, Jean, 160, 319
Waldinger, René, 913
Walters (UAP editor), 743, 747, 785–86, 788–89, 803
Warren, Robert Penn: congratulatory correspondence with, 995; dedication of book to Peyre, 460–61; Fowlie recommendation request, 212; miscellaneous references to, 809; poetry, discussion concerning, 893–94, 960, 970–71; translation correspondence with, 653–54; writers discussed with, 891, 896
*Ways of Art*, 910
Wehrmann, Renée: lunch invitation, 883–84; miscellaneous correspondence, 935–36; Peyre's comments on book by, 1010–11
Weil, Simone, 645–46
Weinberg, Florence: career of, 827–28, 851–52, 996, 1022–23; family matters discussed with, 747–48, 772–73, 784, 1005–6, 1022–23, 1066; Hunter College, correspondence on, 816–17, 823–25; husband Kurt's retirement, correspondence on, 802; Peyre's stroke, correspondence concern-

Weinberg, Florence (*continued*) ing, 1055, 1075; writing of, Peyre's comments on, 1001–2, 1039–40

Weinberg, Kurt: assistance with publication, 992; career of, discussions concerning, 423–24, 584–85, 590–91, 789–90; family matters discussed with, 416–17, 728, 740–41, 772–73, 784; illness of, Peyre's correspondence concerning, 989; literary criticism by, correspondence on, 463–65, 536–38, 540, 708–9, 943–44; miscellaneous correspondence with, 629; miscellaneous references to, 429, 476, 811; Nietzsche discussed with, 794; Peyre's retirement, correspondence on, 815, 879–81; Peyre's stroke, correspondence concerning, 1075; post-retirement plans of, 822–23; religion discussed with, 713–14; retirement of, 801–2, 817; Romance series correspondence, 409; successor to Peyre, discussion of, 744; visit with Peyre, 826; writing by, Peyre's comments on, 414–15, 473, 662–63, 681, 710, 797–98

Weiss, Ted, 408

Wellek, René, 664, 670–71, 809, 1069

Wesleyan University, 624–25

*What Is Romanticism?*, 748–49, 779–80, 783, 788, 818

Wilder, Thornton, 544, 912

*Wilhelm Meister*, 645

Wilkinson, James D., 841–43

Will, Samuel, 284–85

Wilson, Edmund, 906, 919

Wordsworth, William, 893

Work in Progress, correspondence on, 139–41

World War II, Peyre's immigration difficulties and, 80–81

Wright, E. H., 229

*Writers and Critics,* 193

Yale Corporation, Peyre's appointment as professor, 75

*Yale French Studies,* xi, 241, 277–83, 327, 515, 517, 557–58, 911

Yale University: French Department established at, xvi; Peyre's assistant-professorship at, 40; tenure policies at, 91–92. *See also* French Department (Yale University)

Yale University Press: Peyre's correspondence with, 169–70; Peyre's publications with, 586, 588–90

Yeats, W. B., 648

Young, Karl, 145, 147, 153, 162

Young, Stark, 919

Zay, Jean, 72

Zimmermann, Eléonore, 802; academic advice to, 418–19; Baudelaire discussed with, 1019–20, 1025–27; dissertation by, Peyre's comments on, 672; exchange of news with Peyre, 782–83, 850–52, 854–55, 869, 901; miscellaneous correspondence, 857–58, 897–98, 925–26, 998–99, 1008–10; on Peyre's retirement, 717–18, 733–34; Peyre's wife Lois, correspondence concerning, 768–70; publications by, 863; Stanford Press and, 913; sympathy correspondence from Peyre, 720–21, 937–38; thesis by, Peyre's comments on, 802, 860–63; writing by, Peyre's comments on, 394, 661–62, 668–69, 711, 941, 954–55

Zinoviev, Gregory, 918–19